DINOSAURS
THE ENCYCLOPEDIA
Supplement 3

2

DINOSAURS
THE ENCYCLOPEDIA
Supplement 3

by Donald F. Glut

Foreword by LUIS M. CHIAPPE, PH.D.

Volume 2
(Part III entries Iguanodon–Zuniceratops; Part IV;
Appendix; Glossary; Bibliography; Index)

McFarland & Company, Inc., Publishers
Jefferson, North Carolina, and London

To Howell W. Thomas
and all the other colorful denizens at the
Department of Vertebrate Paleontology,
Natural History Museum of Los Angeles County

Front cover art: *Archaeoceratops oshimai* (Michael W. Skrepnick).

Volume 2

LIBRARY OF CONGRESS CATALOGUING-IN-PUBLICATION DATA

Glut, Donald F.
Dinosaurs: the encyclopedia : supplement three / by Donald F. Glut :
foreword by Luis M. Chiappe.
p.   cm.
Includes bibliographical references and index.

ISBN 978-1-4766-8902-9 (softcover : acid free paper) ♾

1. Dinosaurs — Encyclopedia.   I. Title.
QE862.D5G652   2021
567.9'1'03 — dc20   95-47668

British Library cataloguing data are available

Manufactured in the United States of America

*McFarland & Company, Inc., Publishers
Box 611, Jefferson, North Carolina 28640
www.mcfarlandpub.com*

Table of Contents

• Volume 1 •

Acknowledgments		v
Foreword, by Luis M. Chiappe, PhD		vi
Preface		ix
I	Introduction	1
	The Mesozoic Era	11
	New Discoveries, Ideas and Studies	16
	No Consensus Yet—Ectothermy versus Endothermy	114
	Dinosaurs and Birds	117
	Dinosaur Extinctions	138
II	Dinosaurian Systematics	145
III	Dinosaurian Genera *(Abrictosaurus–Hypsilophodon)*	205

....

• Volume 2 •

III	Dinosaurian Genera *(Iguanodon–Zuniceratops)*	363
IV	*Nomina Nuda*	599
V	Excluded Genera	605
A List of Abbreviations		609
Appendix: Dinosaur Tracks and Eggs		613
Glossary		653
Bibliography		665
Index		709

†IGUANODON

Ornithischia: Genasauria: Cerapoda: Ornithopoda: Iguanodontia: Euiguanodontia: Dryomorpha: Ankylopollexia: Iguanodontoidea: "Iguanodontidae."

Diagnosis of genus (as for type species): Iguanodontoid of Barremian/early Aptian age, reaching maximum body length of 11 meters; two free supraorbitals roofing upper margin of orbit; vertical maxillary tooth rows reaching maximum of 29, dentary 25; no more than two teeth in each vertical tooth row; oval foramen in zygomatic arch located between quadratojugal and quadrate; nasal bones neither thickened nor strongly flexed dorsally; sacrum comprising fused vertebrae; scapular blade little expanded distally; intersternal ossification; forelimb long (70 percent length of hindlimb), stoutly constructed; carpals co-ossified, bound by ossified ligaments; phalangeal count of manus 2,3,3,2,4; first phalanx of digit I of manus a flat disk, ungual relatively enormous conical spine; manus very large (in proportion to forelimb length), stoutly constructed; ilium with broad brevis shelf caudally, caudal end tapering to rounded point, main body deep, laterally flattened, with straight, slightly everted dorsal margin that is thickened above ischial tuber; rostral process of ilium triangular in cross section, slightly downturned, with distally expanded tip; rostral ramus of pubis laterally compressed, parallel-sided, distally expanded; three distal tarsals; metatarsal I reduced to obliquely oriented, transversely flattened splint lying against medial surface of metatarsal II (Norman and Sues 2000).

Comments: In a paper published in 1999, Éric Buffetaut stated that, after Gideon Mantell (1825) originally described the genus *Iguanodon*, "Cuvier did not think it necessary to modify the passage about the peculiar teeth from Tilgate Forest in the third edition of *Recherches sur les ossemens fossiles*, published in 1825," and also, "as a result, the name *Iguanodon* never appeared in Cuvier's major palaeontological work" (see *S2*). In subsequent research on Cuvier's work, however, Buffetaut (2000) found the latter remark to be incorrect.

According to Buffetaut (2000), Cuvier did not, as previously stated, use the name in his discussion of the "extraordinary" Tilgate Forest reptile in the

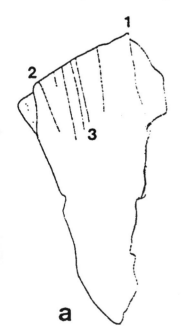

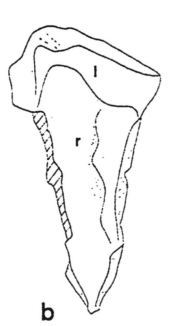

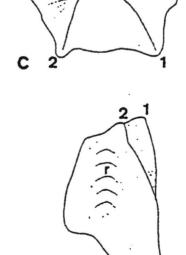

Mandibular tooth from the La Cantalera locality of Spain, referred to *Iguanodon* sp., in a. lingual, b. labial, c. occlusal, and d. mesial views. Scale = 10 mm. (After Ruiz-Omeñaca, Canuda and Cuenca-Bescós 2001.)

second edition of *Recherches sur les ossemens fossiles*, published in 1824. However, Cuvier did, in fact, use *Iguanodon* as early as 1825 in his third edition of *Discours sur les révolutions de la surface du globe*. Among his remarks in that volume about Mantell's finds, Cuvier stated:

"C'est à M. Mantell, de Lewes en Sussex, que l'on doit la de'couverte de ce dernier animal, ainsi que des autres grands reptiles de ces sables inférieurs à la craie. Il l'a nommé *Iguanodon*."

Ruiz-Omeñaca, Canuda and Cuenca-Bescós (2001) reported for the first time a newly discovered European Mesozoic vertebrate locality containing remains referred to *Iguanodon* sp. Named La Cantalera, the locality consists of the gray clays of the Lower Cretaceous (lower Barremian) Blesa Formation, in the Cuberta de Oliete, north of the province of Teruel, Spain. *Iguanodon* sp. is represented by left (MPZ 97/469) and right (MPZ 97/470 and MPZ 97/471) mandibular teeth, and a left maxillary tooth (MPZ 97/472). (Other indeterminate dinosaur fossils reported by Ruiz-Omeñaca *et al.* from this site include remains belonging to "iguanodontids" [MPZ 97/473-97/476, 97/485-97/490-97/502, 97/503], hypsilophodontids [MPZ 97/491-97/501], ornithopods [MPZ 97/477-97/484, 97/504-97/518], camarasaurid sauropods [MPZ/464-97/465], and theropods [MPZ 97/466-97/468]; also remains of various kinds of crocodiles, turtles, and invertebrates, and fragments of theropod, crocodilian, and chelonian eggs.) Most common of all teeth found at this site are those of *Iguanodon* and other ornithopods. They are all worn and resorbed, and had been shed while feeding. Sedimentological information and paleobiological data gleaned from invertebrates identified this site as having been formed in a nonpermanent water marshy area. The presence of abundant plant remains and herbivorous coprolites, the latter belonging to two different forms of ornithopods (iguanodontoids and hypsilophodontids), further suggested to the authors that these dinosaurs had consumed algae as well as other kinds of plants.

During the late nineteenth century, L. F. De Pauw, the chief museum preparator of the Musée Royal d'Histoire Naturelle in Brussels, mounted the first of numerous skeletons from Bernissart, referred to the (now) type species *Iguanodon bernissartensis* (see *S2*), in a bipedal posture, based upon a drawing by Dollo published in 1883. Approximately a century later, Norman (1980), following Galton's (1970) proposal that the backbones of most ornithischians were horizontally oriented, argued that this species was primarily a quadrupedal animal, this assessment based mostly on the robust morphology of the forelimb, the hyper-extendable digits of the manus, and the rela-tively long forelimb as compared to those of other ornithischians (see *D:TE*).

Recently, however, Norman's reconstruction was challenged by Steeman (2001), based upon a cast of the paratype (IRScNB-R52) of *I. bernissartensis* mounted at the Musée Royal d'Histoire Naturelle, in the Norman-proposed quadrupedal, slow-walking position (see Bultynck 1992). Steeman criticized this mount, observing that the forelimb bones — each manus with palms facing caudally to caudo-medially — are no longer in full articulation, and that the elbow and shoulder joints are dislocated.

According to Steeman, the morphology of the forelimb of *I. bernissartensis* does not allow for the orientation as reflected by the quadrupedally mounted cast. Rather, as originally mounted under Louis Dollo's direction, the forelimbs of the Bernissart *Iguanodon* specimens are observed to be in perfect articulation, palms of the manus facing medially. In this orientation, that author noted, and with the forelimb correctly articulated and fully flexed, the humeral head is properly in the glenoid and the olecranon process can slide in the olecranon fossa as the limb extends. In life, Steeman asserted, the forelimb would have been oriented with the palm of manus facing medially, this orientation making unlikely the idea that the front "limb was used for locomotion and support of mass only when walking slowly across difficult terrain and for stability, for example during feeding and drinking." Further evidence supporting this orientation includes trackways attributed to *Iguanodon* (see Charig and Newman 1962; Thulborn 1984), showing medially facing palms, and also the original preserved positions of the Bernissart skeletons, in which all the mani are also preserved with medially facing palms (Casier 1960).

Milner, Embery, Hall, Milan, Waddington and Langley (2003), in a published abstract, reported briefly on the discovery and isolation of bone-associated, noncallagenous proteins from *Iguanodon* from the silty clay sandstone beds (Barremian) in Smokejack's Pit, Surrey, England. As Milner *et al.* reported, proteinaceous products have been recovered from *Iguanodon* bone samples, these representing the first evidence of proteoglycans — *i.e.*, structural proteins that control hydroxyapatite crystal growth in bone — in fossil material. These proteins, the authors explained, "demonstrate the role of mineralized tissues in the protection of these proteins from degradation over long periods of time."

Notes: The species *Iguanodon suessi* Bunzel 1871 and also *Mochlodon robustus* Nopcsa 1900 were founded upon remains from the Upper Cretaceous of Transylvania, these species later being referred to the genus *Rhabdodon*. According to Norman (2000), restudy of the original specimens, plus newly collected material from additional Romanian sites, indicate that these species represent two morphs of a new and as yet unnamed ornithopod genus.

In a review of the ornithischian dinosaurs from the Lower Cretaceous (Berriasian) of England, Norman and Barrett (2002) referred the species *Iguanodon hoggii* Owen 1874 to the genus *Camptosaurus* (see entry).

Key references: Buffetaut (1999, 2000); Bunzel (1871); Casier (1960); Charig and Newman (1962); Cuvier (1924, 1825); Dollo (1883); Mantell (1825); Milner, Embery, Hall, Milan, Waddington and Langley (2003); Nopcsa (1900); Norman (1980, 2000); Norman and Barrett (2002); Norman and Sues (2000); Owen (1874); Ruiz-Omeñaca, Canuda and Cuenca-Bescós (2001); Steeman (2001); Thulborn (1984).

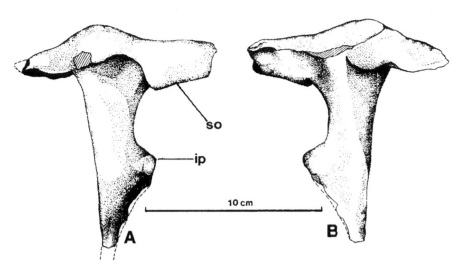

Ilokelesia aguadagranensis, PVPH-35, holotype right postorbital in A. lateral and B. medial views. (After Coria and Salgado 2000.)

ILOKELESIA   Coria and Salgado 2000

Saurischia: Eusaurischia: Theropoda: Neotheropoda: Neoceratosauria: Abelisauroidea.

Name derivation: Mapuche *ilo* = "flesh" plus *kelesio* = "lizard."

Type species: *I. aguadagranensis* Coria and Salgado 2000.

Other species: [None.]

Occurrence: Río Limay Formation, Neuquén Province, Argentina.

Age: Middle Cretaceous (Cenomanian to early Turonian).

Known material/holotype: PVPH-35, right postorbital, right quadrate, occipital condyle, vertebrae (partial ?third cervical, ?fourth cervical, caudal dorsal, five articulated midcaudals), three fragmentary cervical ribs, eight proximal hemal arches, eight pedal pre-ungual phalanges, two pedal ungual phalanges.

Diagnosis of genus (as for type species): Medium-sized theropod, distinguished by the following autapomorphies: quadrate having very reduced lateral condyle and border of articular surface formed entirely from medial condyle; cervical vertebrae having poorly-defined diapo-postzygapophysial laminae; caudal dorsal vertebrae with infraparapophysial laminae concave ventrally, parapophysis oriented ventrally; caudal dorsal vertebrae lacking pleurocoels; caudal vertebrae in central third of tail with distally expanded transverse processes bearing cranially and distally projecting processes; distal edge of caudal transverse processes slightly concave in midpart (Coria and Salgado 2000).

Comments: The new type species *Ilokelesia aguadagranensis* was founded upon an incomplete skeleton (PVPH-35) (first reported by Coria, Salgado

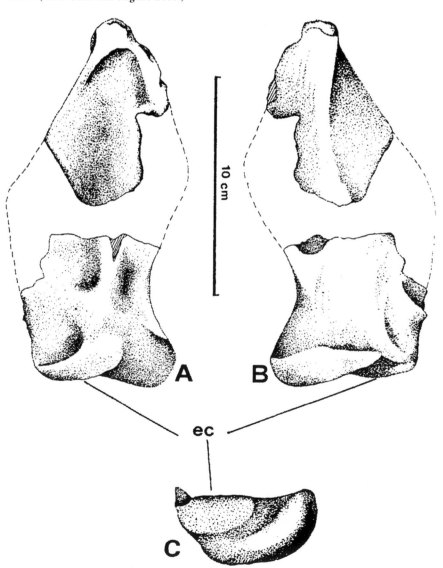

Ilokelesia aguadagranensis, PVPH-35, holotype right quadrate, in A. cranial, B. caudal, and C. ventral views. (After Coria and Salgado 2000.)

Ilokelesia aguadagranensis, PVPH-35, holotype possible fourth cervical vertebra, in A. dorsal, B. lateral, c. cranial, and D. caudal views. (After Coria and Salgado 2000.)

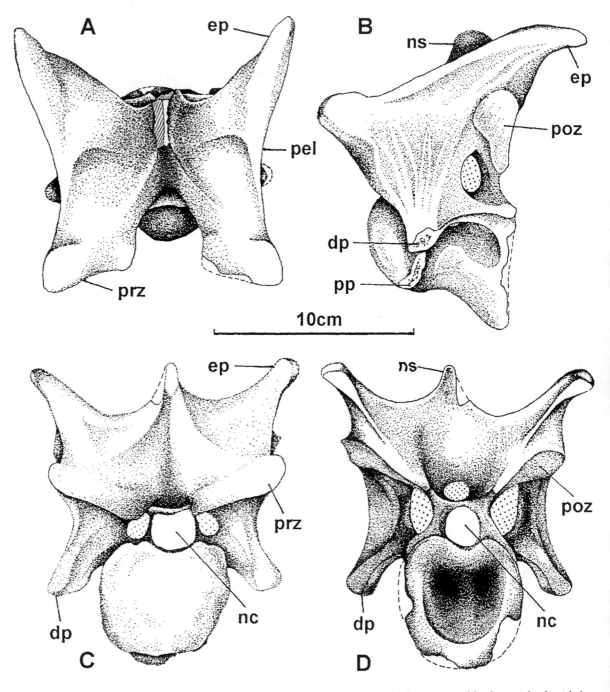

and Calvo 1991 as the sister group to Abelisauridae and Noasauridae) from the Huincul Member of the Río Limay Formation (Cenomanian to early Turonian; see Leanza and Hugo 2001), Neuquén Group (Cenomanian to early Campanian, with a 24 million-year duration; Leanza and Hugo), Aguada Grande, near Plaza Huincul, Neuquén Province, Argentina (Coria and Salgado 2000).

Coria and Salgado followed Novas (1992*a*) in recognizing Abelisauria as the sister group to the "Ceratosauria" (see "Systematics" chapter). The authors compared *Ilokelesia* with all other known abelisaurs from South America, and also with the neocer-

atosaurian *Dilophosaurus* and higher coelophysids because of their close relationships with abelisaurs. A phylogenetic analysis performed by Coria and Salgado revealed *Ilokelesia* to be the sister group of Abelisauroidea, sharing with it the following apomorphies: Postorbital having intraorbital projection; quadrate having reduced lateral condyle; dorsal surface of neural arches of cervical vertebrae clearly delimited from lateral side of diapophyses by highly developed prezygapophysial lamina; cervical ribs with wide, strongly flattened caudal branches; caudal vertebra having transverse process bearing antero-caudally expanded distal ends.

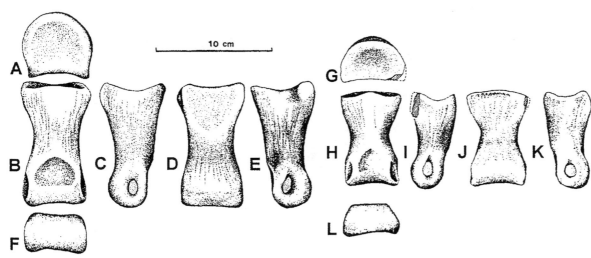

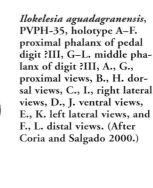

Ilokelesia aguadagranensis, PVPH-35, holotype A–F. proximal phalanx of pedal digit ?III, G–L. middle phalanx of digit ?III, A., G., proximal views, B., H. dorsal views, C., I., right lateral views, D., J. ventral views, E., K. left lateral views, and F., L. distal views. (After Coria and Salgado 2000.)

As Coria and Salgado, noted, *Ilokelesia* shares with *Dilophosaurus* plus higher Coelophysidae a lack of pleurocoelic foramina in the dorsal vertebrae, this character interpreted as homplastic. Also, *Ilokelesia* is plesiomorphic relative to Abelisauroidea in the following features: 1. Jugal process of postorbital perpendicular to horizontal branch; 2. cervical vertebrae having well-developed neural spines; and 3. epipophyses of cervical vertebrae without cranial projection.

Key references: Coria and Salgado (2000); Coria, Salgado and Calvo (1991); Leanza and Hugo (2001); Novas (1992*a*).

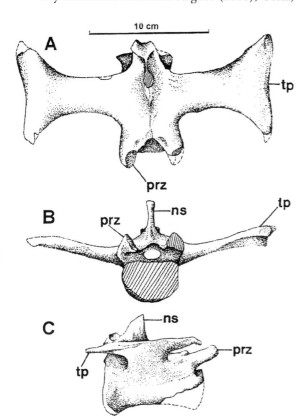

Ilokelesia aguadagranensis, PVPH-35, holotype caudal vertebra, in A. dorsal, B. proximal, and C. lateral views. (After Coria and Salgado 2000.)

INCISIVOSAURUS Xu, Cheng, Wang and Chang 2002

Saurischia: Eusaurischia: Theropoda: Neotheropoda: Tetanurae: Avetheropoda: Coelurosauria: Maniraptoriformes: Maniraptora: ?Metornithes: Oviraptorosauria.

Name derivation: Latin *incisus* = "cutting" + Greek *sauros* = "lizard."

Type species: *I. gauthieri* Xu, Cheng, Wang and Chang 2002.

Other species: [None.]

Occurrence: Yixian Formation, Liaoning Province, China.

Age: ?Early to ?Middle Cretaceous (?Barremian–?Aptian).

Known material/holotype: IVPP V13326, almost complete skull, partial cervical vertebra.

Diagnosis of genus (as for type species): Oviraptorosaur display the following derived characters: upper dentition highly heterodont (large incisiform first premaxillary tooth, much smaller, subconical second to fourth premaxillary teeth, very small lanceolate maxillary teeth); mesial margins of teeth having large, high-angled wear facets; longitudinal crest on ventral surface of basisphenoid; contact between accessory ventral flanges of pterygoids; subsidiary ectopterygoid fenestra; triradiate palatine with very short maxillary process (Xu, Cheng, Wang and Chang 2002).

Comments: The oldest and most basal known definitive member of Oviraptorosauria, the genus *Incisivosaurus* was based on a nearly complete skull and an incomplete cervical vertebra (IVPP V13326) collected from the lowest part of the Yixian Formation at Lijiatun, Shangyuan, Beipiao City, Lioning

Incisivosaurus

Incisivosaurus gauthieri, holotype (IVPP V13326) skull in a. lateral, b. occipital, and c. ventral views, mandible in d. lateral, and e. medial views. Scale = 4 cm. (After Xu, Cheng, Wang and Chang 2002.)

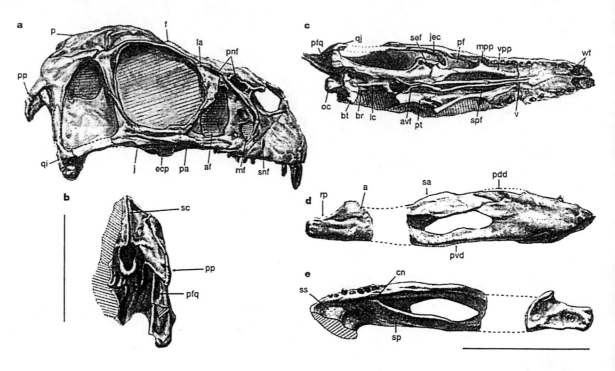

Province, China (Xu, Cheng, Wang and Chang 2002).

Xu *et al.* referred *Incisivosaurus* to the Oviraptorosauria based upon the following derived features: Skull having short preorbital region; main body of premaxilla large; external naris dorsally positioned; pendant paroccipital process; ectopterygoid vertically oriented; dentary symphysis fused; posteroventral process of dentary long, shallow; splenial straplike; mandibular fenestra large; retroarticular process long.

In describing the type species *Incisivosaurus gauthieri*, Xu *et al.* observed characters of the holotype closer to more typical theropods and also characters previously unknown among all Theropoda. The skull (basal length about 100 millimeters) is relatively low and long (the length of the snout constituting 48 percent of basal skull length), as opposed to shallow and short as in other oviraptorosaurs. The jaws are toothed, thereby lacking some of the specializations found in Oviraptorosauridae or other, more inclusive oviraptorosaurian clades. Consequently, the authors stated, *Incisivosaurus* shows a cranial morphology intermediate between typical coelurosaurians and oviraptorosaurids, thereby narrowing the morphological gap between the Oviraptorosauria and other theropods.

Xu *et al.* utilized *Incisivosaurus* to challenge a number of recent suggestions by various authors that oviraptorosaurs are more closely related to birds (or are in fact secondarily flightless birds) than to nonavian coeluerosaurs (see "Introduction," section on controversies regarding the relationships of dinosaurs to birds). As pointed out by these authors, *Incisivosaurus*

lacks the features used to support this hypothesized relationship—*e.g.*, toothless jaws, short nasals, long parietals, quadrate with lateral cotyle for quadratojugal, rodlike jugal bar, long maxillary process of palatine, absence of subsidiary palatine fenestra, ectopterygoid articulating primarily with lacrimal and maxilla laterally, absence of jugal hook on ectopterygoid. Therefore, these birdlike features seem to have evolved independently—the results of convergence—both in derived oviraptorosaurians and avialians.

The authors found particularly interesting in this genus the paired first premaxillary teeth, noting their similarity to the incisor teeth—utilized in gnawing—known in certain specialized mammalian lineages including rodents, multituberculates, and some primatomorphans. Additionally, the peglike premaxillary teeth suggest those seen in some herbivorous sauropods, while the lanceolate cheek teeth resemble those of therizinosauroids (offering more supporting evidence for a close Oviraptorosauria-Therizinosauroidea relationship). No other known theropod displays so high a degree of tooth differentiation as that observed in *Incisivosaurus*. Furthermore, the large wear facets on the teeth are indicative of tooth-to-tooth occlusion. All of these dental features suggest that *Incisivosaurus* was an herbivorous animal.

As Xu *et al.* noted, the discovery of this new genus offers an example of convergent evolution, demonstrating that nonavian theropod dinosaurs were considerably more ecologically diverse that previously suspected.

Note: In an article published in *National Geographic* magazine (see Sloan 2003), a painting by artist

Portia Sloan depicted *Incisivosaurus guatheri* as a turkey-sized, feathered animal with large eyes and beaver-like incisors.

Key references: Sloan (2003); Xu, Cheng, Wang and Chang (2002).

†INGENIA

Saurischia: Eusaurischia: Theropoda: Neotheropoda: Tetanurae: Avetheropoda: Coelurosauria: Maniraptoriformes: Maniraptora: ?Metornithes: Oviraptorosauria: Oviraptoridae: Ingeniinae

Comments: In 1996, the Mongol Highland International Dinosaur Project collected new material, referred to the small theropod *Ignenia* sp., including a skull, sacrum, and pelvis (PC 100\2112), from the Upper Cretaceous (middle Maastrichtian) Nemegt Formation of southwestern Mongolia. Lü, Dong, Azuma, Barsbold and Tomida (2002) described this material, comparing it with both nonavian theropod dinosaurs and birds.

As observed by Lü *et al.*, based upon this recently collected material, *Ingenia* shares the following nine characters with birds, some of these being similar to the primitive birds *Archaeopteryx* and *Confuciusornis*, others to modern birds:

1. Premaxillae completely fused, frontal process of premaxilla long, extending caudally to level of lacrimal (character occurring in *Oviraptor philoceratops* [see Barsbold, Maryańska and Osmólska 1990],

also in the avian clades Enantiornithes, Ichthyornithoformes, and Neornithes [see Chiappe 1996; Chiappe, Norell and Clark 1996], but not in dromaeosaurids and *Archaeopteryx* [see Chiappe]; 2. lacrimal curved, open posteriorly (found in all oviraptorosaurs where observable (Barsbold *et al.*], outline similar in outline to *Confuciusornis sanctus* [Martin, Zhou, Hou and Feduccia 1998], but more robust); 3. jugal bar slender, rodlike, anterior part platelike (as in *Confuciusornis* and ornithurine birds [Elźanowski 1999], unlike *Archaeopteryx* and known nonavian theropods where jugal bar is stout and platelike; 4. articulation between quadrate and quadratojugal mobile (fused in all known nonavian theropods, mobile condition more similar to birds); 5. more than eight sacral vertebrae (less than eight in all known nonavian theropods, at least 14 in all known birds except primitive forms, *e.g.* *Archaeopteryx* and *Confuciusornis*); 6. ilia lying close together dorsally (fused dorsally in modern birds, widely spaced in *Archaeopteryx* and *Confuciusornis*); 7. 13 cervical vertebrae (more than in any other known small nonavian dinosaurs, eight in *Archaeopteryx* and nine in *Confuciusornis* (Martin *et al.*), generally more than 12 but less than 25 in modern birds); 8. cervical ribs fused to vertebral centra; 9. impression of insertion of M. brachialis anticus on humerus (condition similar to modern birds, not present in primitive birds like *Confuciusornis* (Chiappe, Ji, Ji and Norell 1999), not reported in nonavian theropods).

Skull (PC 100/2112) referred to *Ingenia* sp., right lateral view. Scale = 3 cm. (After Lü, Dong, Azuma, Barsbold and Tomida 2002.)

Sacrum and pelvis (PC
100/2112) referred to *Ingenia* sp., right lateral view.
Scale = 5 cm. (After Lü,
Dong, Azuma, Barsbold
and Tomida 2002.)

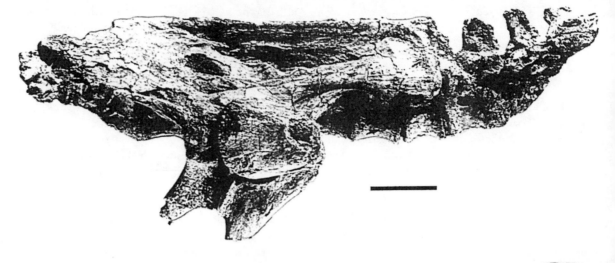

Courtesy North American Museum of
Ancient Life.

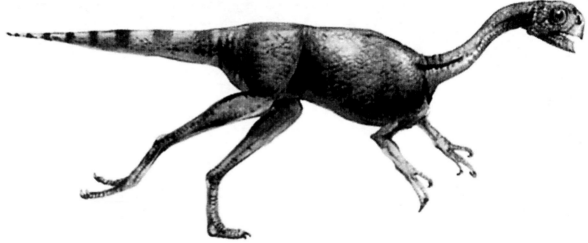

Life restoration of *Ingenia
yanshini* painted by Kelly
Pugh.

Lü *et al.* were in agreement with some recently published workers that oviraptorosaurs are birds rather than nonavian theropods, an issue currently under debate (see "Introduction," section on birds, for details).

Note: Qiu and Huang (2001) reported that, since 1996, 2,038 fossil eggs in 182 nests (including 176 nests of round eggs and six of long eggs) have been found in Upper Cretaceous rocks of Heyuan Basin, on the banks of the Dongjiang River, to the north, south, and east of Heyuan City, in Guangdong Province, China. In 1996, additional bone fossils of *Ingenia*, a member of the oviraptorosaurian clade Ingeniinae [=Ingeniidae of their usage], were found at that same locality, which constitutes the second locality yielding remains of this dinosaur besides Inner Mongolia. According to Qiu and Huang, the eggs have been positively identified as those of the oviraptorosaur.

Key references: Barsbold, Maryańska and Osmólska (1990); Chiappe (1996); Chiappe, Norell and Clark (1996); Elźanowski (1999); Lü, Dong, Azuma, Barsbold and Tomida (2002); Martin, Zhou, Hou and Feduccia (1998); Qiu and Huang (2001).

†IRRITATOR—(=*Angaturama*; =?*Spinosaurus*)
Saurischia: Eusaurischia: Theropoda: Neotheropoda:
    Tetanurae: Avetheropoda: Spinosauroidea: Spinosauridae: Spinosaurinae.
Age: Early Cretaceous (?Albian).
Known material/holotype: SMNS 58022, almost complete skull, missing rostral portion of snout, preserved in large calcareous concretion with bones from both mandibular rami.

Diagnosis of genus (as for type species): Nasals having prominent median bony crest terminating caudally in knoblike, somewhat dorsoventrally flattened projection; dorsal surface of parietals facing posterodorsally, vertical axis of braincase inclined anteroventrally; caudal surface of basisphenoid having deep, dorsoventrally oval median recess; surangular with broad lateral shelf (Sues, Frey, Martill and Scott 2002).

Comments: *Irritator challengeri*, an enigmatic dinosaur from the Romualdo Member of the Lower Cretaceous Santana Formation, is distinguished as the only spinosaurid for which a substantially complete skull (SMNS 58022) is known. The type species, first

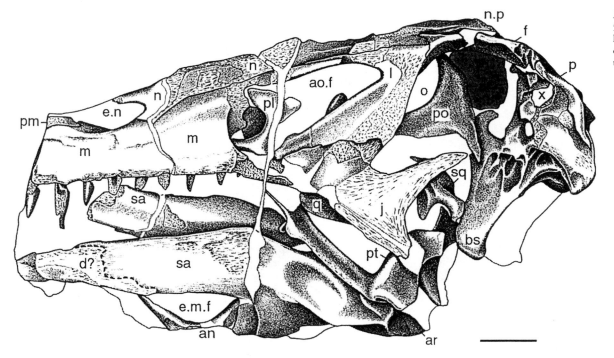

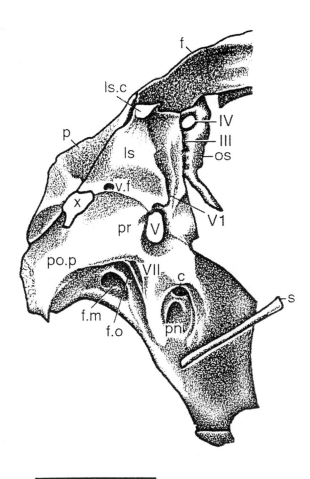

Irritator challengeri, SMNS 58022, holotype braincase in right lateral view. Scale = 5 cm. (After Sues, Frey, Martill and Scott 2002.)

identified belonging to a large pterosaur, was first described as a theropod dinosaur in 1996 by Martill, Cruickshank, Frey, Small and Clarke before the holotype had been fully prepared. Martill *et al.* referred this specimen to the theropod group Maniraptora (see *D:TE* for details). Subsequently, Kellner (1996), finding no evidence supporting referral of this genus to the Maniraptora, referred *Irritator* to the Spinosauridae (see *SI*), an assignment embraced widely by other authors (*e.g.*, Charig and Milner 1997; Sereno, Beck, Dutheil, Gado, Larsson, Lyon, Marcot, Rauhut, Sadleir, Sidor, Varricchio, Wilson and Wilson 1998; Taquet and Russell 1998; Sues, Frey, Martill and Scott 2002).

In the years following the description by Martill *et al.*, the holotype of *I. challengeri*, as recounted by Sues *et al.*, has been fully prepared by David M. Martill. The newly prepared skull has, consequently, invalidated some of the originally reported observations by Martill *et al.*. It has also provided much new information regarding both the skull structure of this dinosaur and the origins of the type specimen.

As pointed out by Sues *et al.*, the matrix enclosing the skull corresponds closely to that of concretions from the Romualdo Member of the Santana Formation. That the *I. challengeri* holotype was derived from this provenance was further confirmed by the presence in the matrix of the ostracod crustaceans *Pattersoncyperis* and also isolated scales of the ichthyodectid fish *Cladocyclus*, both of which are commonly found in Romualdo Member concretions. A dealer in fossils, who had worked as a collector, recently identified for Martill the unprepared specimen from

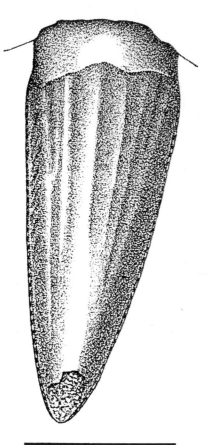

Irritator challengeri, SMNS 58022, holotype right eighth maxillary tooth, labial view. Scale = 1 cm. (After Sues, Frey, Martill and Scott 2002.)

a photograph, confirming that it had been found near Buxexé, a small farming community and a site near Santana do Cariri. Furthermore, the nature of the concretion and also its texture and color are consistent with concretions from this region. Sues *et al.* found it feasible that SMNS 58022 was recovered from one of several localities in the valley of the Caririacu River; however, Sues *et al.* were unable to determine the provenance of this specimen more accurately "than to confirm its derivation from the Romualdo Member of the Santana Formation," this member, the authors suggested, probably of Albian age (based primarily on the presence of various fish taxa; see Maisey 2000), but possibly Cenomanian.

Sues *et al.* fully described SMNS 58022 and proposed a new diagnosis for *I. challengeri*, noting that, as adequate skull material is not known among other spinosaurids, it was "not clear at what taxonomic level the individual features listed above are diagnostic."

Among the Spinosauridae, Sues *et al.* noted, *I. challengeri* most closely resembles what is known of the skull of *Spinosaurus aegyptiacus* (see Stromer 1915), sharing with that species the following apomorphies in the dentition: Maxillary tooth crowns straight or slightly

recurved and conical, rather than labiolingually compressed; carinae of tooth crowns distinct, lacking serrations; enamel thin, having several ridges ("fluting") on labial and lingual surface of crown (*e.g.,* Stromer; Sereno *et al.*). Therefore, the authors suggested that *Irritator* could eventually prove to be congeneric with *Spinosaurus*. For the present, however, a detailed comparison between these taxa is not possible, given the minimal cranial material known for the latter genus. Sues *et al.* did, however, accept the suggestion Charig and Milner that *Irritator* is congeneric with *Angaturama* (see SI).

As Sues *et al.* noted, *Irritator* and *Baryonyx* ("and the probably congeneric *Suchomimus*"; see *Baryonyx* entry) share the following derived character states of the skull and teeth that are not found in any other known theropod dinosaurs: 1. Skull remarkably narrow throughout entire length, especially in snout region; 2. external nares long, low, situated far back on sides of elongated snout rather than near rostral end of snout; 3. maxillae broadly contacting each other medially, forming extensive secondary bony palate; 4. maxillae forming greatly elongated subnarial ramus, separating premaxilla and nasal below external naris, longer cranio-caudally than deep dorsoventrally; 5. maxillary teeth with straight or slightly recurved crowns, round to subcircular in transverse section rather than labiolingually flattened; 6. (if holotype of "*Angaturama limai*" represents rostral end of snout of *I. challengeri*) apomorphic presence of seven premaxillary teeth; 7. fused caudal portions of nasals terminating

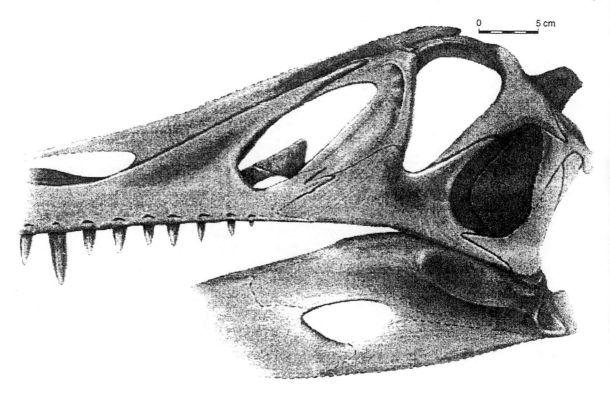

Irritator challengeri, partially reconstructed skull and mandible, based on holotype SMNS 58022, in left lateral view, supralabial foramina on lateral surface of maxilla based on *Baryonyx tenerensis*. Scale = 5 cm. (After Sues, Frey, Martill and Scott 2002.)

in knoblike median projection caudally; 8. narrow (postnasal) fenestra (see Charig and Milner) apparently between frontal, caudal end of conjoined nasals, and prefrontal on either side of skull roof; 9. more acute angle (about 35 to 40 degrees) than in other theropods (about 75 to 90 degrees); 10. braincase short cranio-caudally, deep dorsoventrally, extending ventrally far below occipital condyle; 11. basipterygoid processes of basisphenoid elongate, diverging only slightly ventrolaterally. These features, Sues *at al.* stated, support recognizing the family Spinosauridae Stromer 1915, as defined and diagnosed by Sereno *et al.*

Sues *et al.* observed that the skull of *I. challengeri*—with its deeply implanted, vertically oriented teeth, having conical, straight, or at best slightly recurved crowns—so different in structure from the skulls of such other large theropods as *Allosaurus* and *Tyrannosaurus*, does not seem to be well adapted to catching and processing large, resistant prey. This, the authors noted, seems to reflect different modes of feeding. As Sues *et al.* envisioned, spinosaurids probably "rapidly and forcefully seized smaller prey, which was then processed by dorsoventral motion of the head facilitated by the powerful neck musculature." However, as fish seem to have formed at least part of the diet of *Baryonyx*, there is no evidence suggesting that spinosaurids were entirely or even predominantly piscivorous.

Key references: Charig and Milner (1997); Kellner (1996); Martill, Cruickshank, Frey, Small and Clarke (1996); Sereno, Beck, Dutheil, Gado, Larsson, Lyon, Marcot, Rauhut, Sadleir, Sidor, Varricchio, Wilson and Wilson (1998); Stromer (1915); Sues, Frey, Martill and Scott (2002); Taquet and Russell (1998).

†JAINOSAURUS

Saurischia: Eusaurischia: Sauropodomorpha: Sauropoda: Eusauropoda: Neosauropoda: Macronaria: Camarasauromorpha: Titanosauriformes: Somphospondyli: Titanosauria: "Titanosauridae."

Diagnosis of genus (as for type species): Caudal vertebrae procoelous, laterally compressed, with high centrum; two cranial hemophosial facets large, widely apart from each other; caudals very similar to *Titanosaurus indicus*, both having flat sides, the latter having more pointed cup (Mohabey 2001).

Comment: Mohabey (2001), in a review of dinosaur eggs known from India, also rediagnosed the type species *Jainosaurus septentrionalis* [*Jainosaurus septentrionalis* of his usage] (see above).

Key reference: Mohabey (2001).

JENGHIZKHAN—(See *Tarbosaurus*.)

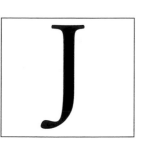

JIANGSHANOSAURUS Tang, Kang, Jin, Wei and Wu 2001

Saurischia: Eusaurischia: Sauropodomorpha: Sauropoda: Eusauropoda: Neosauropoda: Macronaria: Camarasauromorpha: Titanosauriformes: Somphospondyli: Titanosauria: "Titanosauridae."

Name derivation: *Jiangshan* [County] + Greek *sauros* = "lizard."

Type species: *J. lixianensis* Tang, Kang, Jin, Wei and Wu 2001.

Other species: [None.]

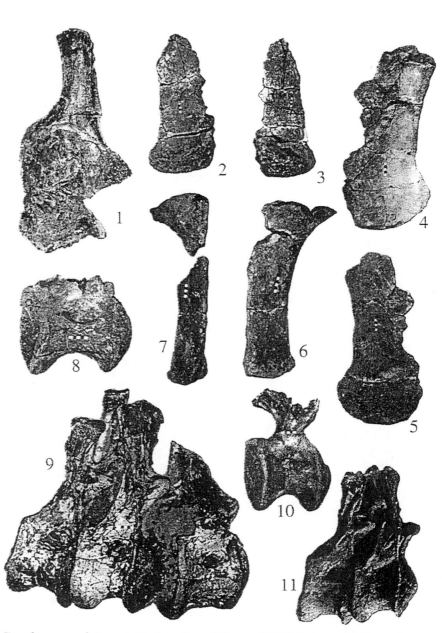

Jiangshanosaurus lixianensis, Zhejiang Natural Museum M1322, holotype 1. left scapulocoracoid, 2–3. left pubis, lateral and medial views, 4–5. right pubis, lateral and medial views, 6–7. left and right ischia, medial view, 8. seventh dorsal vertebra, right lateral view, 9. ninth through 11th dorsal vertebrae, lateral view, 10. ninth dorsal vertebra, lateral view, and 11. 10th and 11th dorsal vertebrae, lateral view. Scale = 5 cm. (After Tang, Kang, Jin, Wei and Wu 2001.)

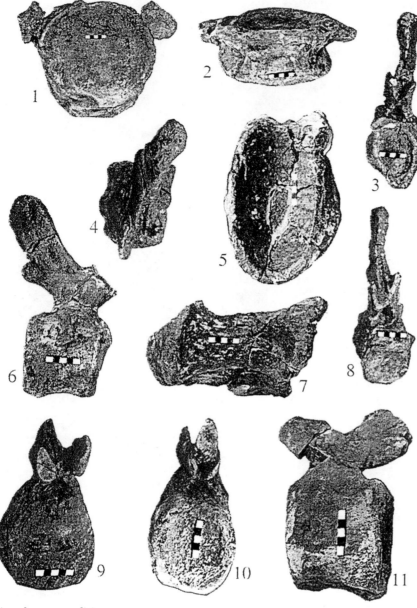

Jiangshanosaurus lixianensis, Zhejiang Natural Museum M1322, holotype 1–2. first caudal vertebra, proximal and ventral views; 3., 4., 6., 8. 13th or 14th caudal vertebra, proximal, distal, lateral, and dorsal views; 5., 7. seventh dorsal vertebra, cranial and ventral views, and 9–11., 16th or 17th caudal vertebra, distal, proximal, and lateral views. Scale = 5 cm. (After Tang, Kang, Jin, Wei and Wu 2001.)

Occurrence: Jinhua Formation, Jiangshan, Zhejiang, China.

Age: Middle Cretaceous (Albian).

Known material/holotype: Zhejiang Natural Museum M1322, relatively complete left scapulocoracoid, five caudal dorsal and middorsal vertebrae, three caudal vertebrae, portions of both sides of pubis and ischium, portions of left femoral shaft.

Diagnosis of genus (as for type species): Dorsal neural spines with developed concavity and lamina, margin of lamina thin; cranial convexity on articular surface of dorsal centra strongly developed, articula "ball" nearly hemispherical, ventral surface almost concave; (preserved) dorsal ribs apparently distinctly pneumaticized; acromial process of scapula having large proximal expansion, width approximately 150 percent of minimum blade width; scapular glenoid facing medially, coracoid glenoid laterally; scapular glenoid opening with right angle; supracoracoideus fossa large, flat, oval shaped; coracoid foramen located almost at center of coracoid, far from suture connecting scapula; articulations between proximal caudal centra distinctly procoelous, (preserved) middle caudal centra mildly procoelous; caudal neural arches located on proximal half of centrum; absence of pleurocoels in caudal centra (Tang, Kang, Jin, Wei and Wu 2001.)

Comments: Sauropod taxa from the Early to Middle Cretaceous of China have been rare, known from only a few genera with relatively few species. A new Middle Cretaceous type species, *Jiangshanosaurus lixianensis*, different from all of those taxa previously described and offering new data regarding the evolution and distribution of "titanosaurid" sauropods in China, was founded upon a partial postcranial skeleton (Zhejiang Natural Museum M1322) recovered by Wei Feng, Wu Wei-Tang, and Kang Xi-Min presumably from the lower part of the Jinhua Formation (Albian; 105 million years ago), in Lizian Village, Jiangshan County, Zhejiang Province (Tang, Kang, Jin, Wei and Wu 2001).

As observed by Tang *et al.*, the middle and caudal vertebrae of *J. lixianensis* compare with those of diplodocoids and "titanosaurids," characterized, for example, by a developed concavity and lamina on the neural arch, a deep pleurocoel on both sides of the dorsal centrum, and being strongly convex on the cranial side of the centrum. The pneumatic dorsal rib of the new taxon is similar to that of titanosaurs. The diagnosis of the vertebrae and scapulocoracoid of *J. lixianensis* are closest in both size and form to the "titanosaurid" *Alamosaurus* (see Gilmore 1922, 1946) and were, therefore, referred by Tang *et al.* to the "Titanosauridae" [the present writer's quotation marks].

Key references: Gilmore (1922, 1946); Tang, Kang, Jin, Wei and Wu (2001).

JINZHOUSAURUS Wang and Xu 2001

Ornithischia: Genasauria: Cerapoda: Ornithopoda: Iguanodontia: Euiguanodontia: Dryomorpha: Ankylopollexia: Iguanodontoidea: "Iguanodontidae."

Name derivation: "Jinzhou [geographic area including type locality] + Greek *sauros* = "lizard."

Type species: *J. yangi* Wang and Xu 2001.

Other species: [None.]

Occurrence: Yixian Formation, Liaoning Province, China.

Age: ?Early to ?Middle Cretaceous (?Barremian–?Aptian).

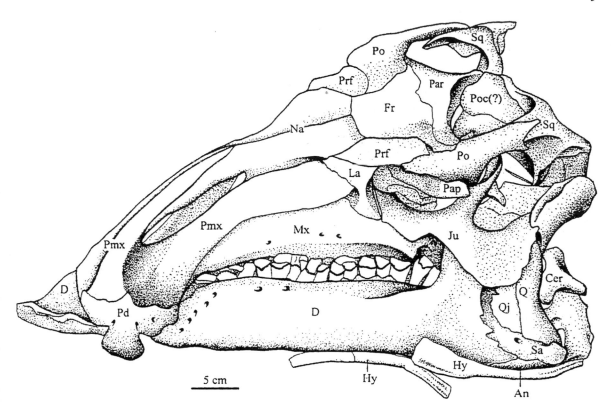

Jinzhousaurus yangi, IVPP V12691, holotype skull in left lateral view. (After Wang and Xu 2001*b*.)

Known material/holotype: IVPP V12691, almost complete skeleton including complete skull.

Diagnosis of genus (as for type species): Large "iguanodontid" [see "Systematics" chapter] (approximately 7 meters in length); skull about 500 millimeters long, 280 millimeters high; antorbital portion long, 64 percent of skull length; maxilla triangular in lateral view, with long, narrow rostral extension; absence of antorbital fenestra; frontals fused into single element; frontals extending rostrally, near rostral border of orbit, not contributing to formation of orbit; quadrate having curved shaft; outside of supratemporal foramen pointed forward; quadratojugal large; ventral process of predentary very weakly bifurcated; dorsal and ventral margins of dentary straight; more than 16 dentary teeth, teeth becoming larger distally (Wang and Xu 2001*b*).

Comments: The genus *Jinzhousaurus* was founded upon a nearly complete skeleton (IVPP V12691) recently collected from the lacustrine deposits of the Dakangpu Member of the middle part of the Yixian Formation (recently dated by Jiang, Chen and Cao 2000 as very Late Jurassic, near the Jurassic–Cretaceous boundary, an assessment based on the evidence of various invertebrate faunas; dated as possibly 120 to 125 million years old by Smith, Harris, Omar, Dodson and You 2001, based on radiometric data; as middle Early Cretaceous by Swisher, Wang, Zhou, Wang, Jin, Zhang, Xu, Zhang and Wang 2002, based on ^{40}Ar/^{39}Ar dating of the Yixian and Tuchengzi for-

mations), at Baicaigou, Toutai, Yixian County, in western Liaoning, China. The genus and species *Jinzhousaurus yangi*—"Yang's Jinzhou dragon"—were first published in a preliminary announcement by Wang and Xu (2001*a*), after which Wang and Xu (2001*b*) described the skull, a detailed description of the postcrania pending full preparation of the specimen.

Wang and Xu (2001*b*) identified *J. yangi* as an "iguanodontid" based upon its cranial and dental morphology, differing from other members of the "Iguanodontidae" based upon both plesiomorphic (*e.g.*, relatively small number of dentary teeth, very weakly bifurcated ventral process of predentary [more like uni-lobed]) and apomorphic (*e.g.*, rostrally extended frontal [near rostral margin of orbit], frontal not participating in border of orbit, absence of antorbital fenestra, these conditions similar to those in hadrosaurs) characters. As the authors pointed out, this unusual combination of characters offers important information for assessing the morphological transition towards the Hadrosauridae.

Comparing *J. yangi* with other advanced ornithopods, Wang and Xu (2001*b*) observed the following: *J. yangi* shares various features with *Iguanodon* (*e.g.*, long, tall snout, preorbital portion half length of skull, triangular maxilla with long, shallow rostral process, entirely fused frontals, palpebral contacting prefrontal). It differs from that genus in having a dentary with a straight ventral margin and a laterorostrally directed supratemporal fenestra. Also, *J. yangi* bears various striking similarities to *Probactrosaurus* (*e.g.*, squamosals contacting each other, well-developed primary ridge on lateral surface of maxillary tooth crown). *J. yangi* differs from that genus in the morphology of the quadrate and dentary, the dental morphology of *Probactrosaurus* being more similar to that of hadrosaurs. *J. yangi* also shares with *Camptosaurus* and *Ouranosaurus* various features (*e.g.*, straight ventral margin of dentary, recurved quadrate shaft, oval supratemporal fenestra with anterolaterally directed long axis). These taxa differ, however, in general cranial morphology. The above comparisons, the authors stated, suggest that *J. yangi* differs from all other known "iguanodontids" and represents a new taxon.

As noted by Wang and Xu (2001*b*), the discovery of *J. yangi* represents the first large-sized dinosaur known from the Jehol Group fauna of Liaoning, increasing the diversity of the biota of that area. Also, the holotype of this dinosaur remains to date the most complete "iguanodontid" specimen yet reported from Asia.

Key references: Jiang, Chen and Cao (2000); Smith, Harris, Omar, Dodson and You (2001); Swisher, Wang, Zhou, Wang, Jin, Zhang, Xu, Zhang and Wang (2002); Wang and Xu (2001*a*, 2001*b*).

†JOBARIA

Saurischia: Eusaurischia: Sauropodomorpha: Sauropoda: Eusauropoda.

Comment: Wilson (2001), in an abstract, briefly discussed the anatomy of the African type species *Jobaria tiguidensis*, thus far (represented by a number of partial articulated skeletons) the most completely known Cretaceous sauropod (see *S2*). As Wilson noted, previous phylogenetic assessment of *Jobaria* resolved it to be the sister taxon of Neosauropoda. The author found it surprising that the genus "acquired relatively few autapomorphies in the interval between its predicted Late Jurassic divergence from Neosauropoda and its actual appearance in Early Cretaceous aged sediments, making it an ideal outgroup."

Note: Wilson's analysis (see "Systematics" chapter),

Skull (cast) of *Jobaria tiguidensis* on exhibit at Dinofest (2000–2001), Navy Pier, in Chicago.

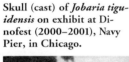

Skeletal casts of two dinosaur *Jobaria tiguidensis*
individuals displayed at
Dinofest (2000–2001), Navy
Pier, in Chicago.

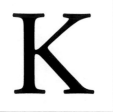

incorporating 221 characters scored for *Jobaria* and 17 neosauropod genera, identified both well-supported nodes and areas of poorer resolution, his results including the following: Neosauropoda a monophyletic clade including Diplodocoidea and Macronaria (as suggested by earlier analyses); Diplodocoidea including Rebbachisauridae, Dicraeosauridae, and Diplodocidae, its monophyly and interrelationships supported mostly by cranial and vertebral synapomorphies; the arrangement of basal macronarian taxa, primarily those within Titanosauria, based on a preponderance of appendicular synapomorphies, these differences unaccounted for due to missing data. Results of Wilson's analysis suggested that Macronaria and Diplodocoidea, while having similar diversity, lineage duration, body size range, and missing data, had divergence and subsequent diversification shaped by innovations that were focused in different parts of the skeleton. In each case, Late Cretaceous survivors of both clades represent the morphological extremes—"diplodocoids survive in the form of shovel-snouted, slender-backed rebbachisaurids, found in Africa and South America; macronarians persist as stocky, wide-gauged titanosaurs, which were present on most continental landmasses."

Key reference: Wilson (2001).

KHAAN   Clark, Norell and Barsbold 2001

Saurischia: Eusaurischia: Theropoda: Neotheropoda: Tetanurae: Avetheropoda: Coelurosauria: Maniraptoriformes: Maniraptora: ?Metornithies: Oviraptorosauria: Oviraptoridae: ?Oviraptorinae.

Name derivation: Mongolian *khaan* = "ruler."

Type species: *K. mckennae* Clark, Norell and Barsbold (2001).

Other species: [None.]

Occurrence: Djadokhta Formation, Omnogov Aimak, Mongolia.

Age: Late Cretaceous (Campanian–Maastrichtian).

Known material: Three nearly complete skeletons.

Holotype: IGM 100/1127, almost complete skeleton, nearly entirely articulated.

Diagnosis of genus (as for type species): Oviraptorid differing from all other known oviraptorids in that metacarpal III is not expanded proximally and does not contact distal carpals; differs from *Oviraptor* in lacking parietal crest; differs from *Ingenia* in that metacarpal I is not extremely broad; from *Conchoraptor* in that long axis of oval narial opening is more horizontally oriented, nasals are fused; from *Citipati* in that dorsal process of premaxilla projects posterodorsally (rather than vertically), occiput is vertical (rather than facing posterodorsally), fused nasals are not as deep caudally with less extensive pneuma-

tization rostrally, jugal extends further caudally but not as far rostrally, posteroventral part of dentary underlies angular ventrally (rather than overlapping it laterally), coronoid process of mandible is not as deep; differs from *Nomingia* in that distal caudal vertebrae are not fused and ischium is less strongly concave caudally (Clark, Norell and Barsbold 2001).

Comments: The genus *Khaan* was founded upon a nearly entire skeleton (IGM 100/1127), disarticulated only slightly in the thorax area, recovered from the Mark's Second Egg locality in the Djadokhta Formation, Ukhaa Tolgod, Gurvan Tes Somon, Omnogov Aimak, south-central Mongolia. Specimens referred to the type species *K. mckennae* consist of an almost complete skeleton (IGM 100/973) from Granger's Hill, Ukhaa Tolgod, and an almost complete skeleton (IGM 100/1002) missing the distal half of its tail, found near the holotype at Mark's Second Egg (Clark, Norell and Barsbold 2001).

This taxon was previously identified tentatively as *Ingenia* in nontechnical writings (see Dingus, Gaffney, Norell and Sampson 1995; Webster 1996). Subsequent preparation of the skeleton, however, revealed that this taxon lacks features distinctive to that genus (mostly characters of the manus). Consequently, Clark *et al.* referred it to the new genus and species *Khaan mckennae*.

As Clark *et al.* observed, the skull of *K. mckennae* lacks the cranial specializations of another newly described oviraptorid genus, *Citipati* (see entry), and also the dorsal crest of the species of *Oviraptor*. *Khaan* most closely resembles *Conchoraptor*, differing from that genus mainly in features of the narial region. Except for the distinctive autapomorphy of the proximally reduced third metacarpal, the postcranial skeleton of this new genus is unspecialized.

Note: *Khaan* currently ties with *Minmi* in having the shortest generic name for a dinosaur.

Key references: Clark, Norell and Barsbold (2001); Dingus, Gaffney, Norell and Sampson (1995); Webster (1996).

KOTASAURUS

Saurischia: Eusaurischia: Sauropodomorpha: Sauropoda *incertae sedis*.

Diagnosis: Differing from all known sauropods in the following features: dorsal vertebrae with simple neural spines (without spinal laminae); lack of pneumatocoel on base of neural arch that opens into neural canal; iliac blade low; scapula having narrow proximal surface; limb bones relatively slender, femur retaining lesser trochanter; chevrons "v" shaped, with well-developed articular facets on dorsolateral corners (Yadagiri 2001).

Comments: In 1988, P. Yadagiri named and described the new type species *Kotasaurus yamanpalliensis*, one of the earliest and most primitive of all known sauropods, founded upon an ilium (21/SR/PAL) from the Lower Jurassic Kota Formation of India (see *D:TE*). Following Yadagiri's preliminary description, as well as the collection, sorting, and preparation of additional specimens, Yadagiri (2001) published an osteology of this dinosaur, at the same time revising his original diagnosis of the genus and species.

Yadagiri (2001) recounted that the Kota Formation has, to date, yielded numerous individuals of *Kotasaurus*. Excavated near Yamanpalli village, this collection, housed at the Geological Survey of India in Hyderabad, presently includes 31 distal cervical vertebrae, 65 dorsal vertebrae, 19 sacral vertebrae (one with three fused centra, two with two fused centra, a sacral rib, sacricostal yoke and isolated sacral centra), 192 caudal vertebrae (99 proximal and 93 distal caudals), three ilia, five fragmentary iliac plates, 14 pubic peduncles, seven ischiadic peduncles, four pubes (two restored and two proximal parts), 17 humeri (seven complete, three distal parts, and seven proximal parts), 21 tibia (six complete, eight distal parts, and seven proximal parts), eight fibular (six complete and two incomplete), and 23 femora (nine complete, 14 incomplete) (see Yadagiri 2001 for complete list of specimen numbers).

Yadagiri (2001) noted size variation in all the recovered skeletal elements, the largest femur measuring 1,390 millimeters in length, the smallest 1,130 millimeters, the largest humerus 850 millimeters in length and the smallest 680 millimeters. However, as the osteological characters of the various individuals are similar, that author regarded all of the above remains as belonging to the same species.

From some of the above material, Yadagiri recently mounted a composite skeleton at the B. M. Birla Science Center in Hyderabad, India.

As Yadagiri (2001) observed, *Kotasaurus* exhibits a number of the sauropod synapomorphies established by Wilson and Sereno (1998), these including the following: Sacrum having four coossified vertebrae; ilium with abbreviated ischiadic peduncle and extensive cranial process; pubis lacking transverse "apron"; ischium having symphyseal contact restricted to rostral portion; femur having straight, slender shaft, elliptical in cross section, long axis of ellipse oriented medio-laterally, fourth trochanter with acuminate, slightly declined tip; shape of distal end of tibia for

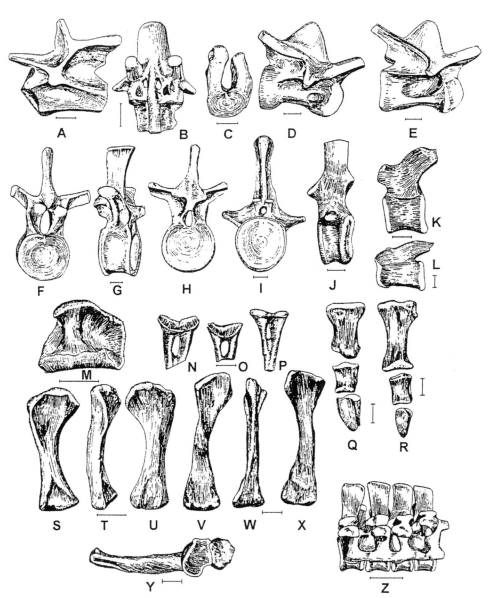

reception of astragalus; also, many features of cervical and dorsal vertebrae.

However, Yadagiri (2001) pointed out, the following characters also indicate a prosauropod condition: Humerus less expanded proximally and distally, both ends slightly twisted, lacking craniocaudal expansion in dorsal end; femur retaining lesser trochanter (symplesiomorphy shared with prosauropod ancestor); astragalus with astragalar peg and prominent boss in dorsolateral corner (indicating prosauropod condition).

Based upon sauropod features found in the pelvic girdle, vertebrae, and tarsal elements, Yadagiri (1988, 2001) classified *Kotasaurus* as a sauropod with some "prosauropod-like" features. The autapomorphies of this genus, recognized by Yadagiri (2001), include a low iliac blade and simple dorsal vertebrae. *Kotasaurus* can be differentiated from *Barapasaurus*, another

Kotasaurus yamanpalliensis, A. lateral and B. cranial view of axis; C. axis (cranial view); D.–E., cervical vertebrae (lateral views); F., G., H. dorsal vertebra (cranial, lateral, and rostral views); I.–J. proximal caudal vertebrae (proximal and lateral views); K.–L. distal caudal vertebrae (lateral views); M. astragalus (cranial view); N.–P. chevrons (proximal views); Q.–R. metatarsals and phalanges (cranial view); S.–U. humerus (cranial, lateral and posterior views); V.–X. ulna (lateral, cranial, and rostral views); Y. scapulocoracoid (lateral view); and Z. sacrum (lateral view). Scale = 20 cm (S–U, Y, and Z); 10 cm (V–X); others, 5 cm. (After Yadagiri 2001.)

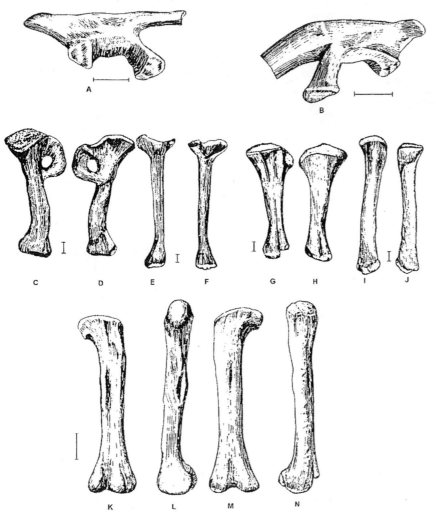

Kotasaurus yamanpalliensis, A.–B. ilium (lateral and medial views); C.–D. pubis (medial and lateral views); E.–F. ischium (cranial and rostral views); G.–H. tibia (rostral and cranial views); I.–J. fibula (medial and lateral views); K.–N. femur (rostral, medial, lateral, and cranial views). Scale = 20 cm. (A., B., K.–N.); others, 10 cm. (After Yadagiri 2001.)

primitive sauropod from the Kota Formation, by such characters as the following: Simple dorsal vertebrae, lacking laminae on neural spines (present in *Barapasaurus*); low iliac blade; femur retaining lesser trochanter; neural canal "normal" (*i.e.*, essentially tubular feature running almost entire length of neural arch); absence of pneumatocoel on base of neural arch, opening into neural canal; and upwardly (rather than downwardly) directed transverse process of dorsal vertebrae.

The phylogenetic analysis of the sauropoda by Wilson and Sereno had placed the primitive sauropod genera *Vulcanodon*, *Shunosaurus*, *Barapasaurus*, and *Omeisaurus* as a sequence of sister taxa leading to a clade of advanced sauropods. According to Yadagiri (2001), the character analysis of *Kotasaurus* shows that, in addition to those four taxa, *Kotasaurus* is also a basal and primitive sauropod taxon.

Key references: Wilson and Sereno (1998); Yadagiri (1988, 2001).

†KRITOSAURUS

Ornithischia: Genasauria: Cerapoda: Ornithopoda: Iguanodontia: Euiguanodontia: Dryomorpha: Ankylopollexia: Iguanodonoidea: Hadrosauridae: Euhadrosauria: Lambeosaurinae.

Occurrence of new species: Aguja Formation, Texas, United States.

Age of new species: Late Cretaceous (Campanian).

Holotype/known material of new species: TMM 4252-1, skull (including nasals, maxilla, part of both dentaries, jugal, quadratojugal, other skull elements), nearly complete manus.

Comments: Wagner and Lehman (2001), in a brief preliminary report published as an abstract, announced a new species of the genus *Kritosaurus*, based upon a skull and manus (TMM 4252-1) collected from the Aguja Formation (see below) of Big Bend National Park, Texas. The skull, the most complete duckbilled dinosaur skull yet found in the Park, at last positively identifies the Big Bend hadrosaurian taxon.

The authors referred TMM 4252-1 to *Kritosaurus* on the basis of the following features: Recurved narial crest; prefrontal and premaxillary articulations not contacting on lateral surface of nasal; and penetration of nasals between frontals on skull roof. The dentary symphysis is unusual, Wagner and Lehman observed, being formed by the rostrodorsally directed processes of each dentary, this resulting in a W-shaped union of the mandibles (as restored) in rostral aspect. The skull and mandibles are transversely wider than in other species of this genus. According to Wagner and Lehman, the restructured rostrum could be functionally similar to the structure of the rostral dentaries in *Anantotitan copei*, recognition of the unique structure of the rostral mandibles in both species possibly constituting "the first documentation of an unequivocal trophic specialization within Hadrosauridae."

As pointed out by Wagner and Lehman, the lower shale member of the Aguja Formation is stratigraphically older than the upper shale member, the latter being the main fossiliferous horizon of that unit. As there is no evidence of such upper-shale member taxa as *Chasmosaurus mariscalensis* in the lower shale, possibly the latter, when extensively prospected, will therefore reveal a unique (possibly earliest middle Campanian) dinosaurian fauna.

Westgate, Pittman, Brown and Cope (2002), in an abstract, reported on continuing prospecting in the Aguja Formation at Canon de Santa Elena National Area of Protection in Chihuana, Mexico. The authors noted that recent collecting has focused upon a disarticulated skeleton referred to *Kritosaurus* sp., including portions of the skull, the vertebral column, and most of the large limb elements. Taphonomic

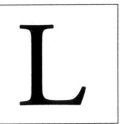

evidence indicated the occurrence of a preferential post-mortem orientation of the long bones of this specimen prior to burial in anoxic mud.

As reported by Westgate *et al.*, other dinosaurian taxa found at this site include maniraptoran, tyrannosaurid, and ceratopsian (referred to *Chasmosaurus mariscalensis*), represented by teeth and limb elements, with hadrosaurid elements dominating the assemblage. Other material reported these authors from the fluvial sands lateral to the *Kritosaurus* skeleton include associated flora (*e.g.*, conifer [Araucariaceae] and palm [*Sabalites* sp.]), and skeletal remains of fishes (*e.g.*, gar and bowfin), turtles, and goniopholid crocodiles.

Note: See also Westgate, Brown, Cope and Pittman (2002), an abstract for a poster, in which the authors present a preliminary report on a Late Cretaceous fossil site in the San Carlos Formation near Ojinaga, Mexico, which has already yielded various hadrosaurid, tyrannosaurid, and ceratopsian remains, in addition to vertebrates including gar fish, soft-shelled chelonians, and goniopholid crocodiles.

Key references: Wagner and Lehman (2001); Westgate, Brown, Cope and Pittman (2002); Westgate, Pittman, Brown and Cope (2002).

†LEPTOCERATOPS

Ornithischia: Genasauria: Cerapoda: Marginocephalia: Ceratopsia: Neoceratopsia: Leptoceratopsidae.
Geographic range: Scollard Formation, Dinosaur Park Formation, Alberta, Canada; Lance Formation, Wyoming, Two Medicine Formation, Hell Creek Formation, Montana, United States.

Comments: In an abstract, Ott and Buckley (2001) briefly reported on a partial skull of the primitive ceratopsian *Leptoceratops* (cf. *gracilis*) recovered in 1992 from the Hell Creek Formation (Upper Cretaceous; Maastrichtian) of Carter County, Montana, west of Camp Cook, South Dakota. Ott and Buckley identified this specimen as belonging to *Leptoceratops* based on the following features: 1. Basioccipital excluded by exoccipitals from border of foramen magnum; 2. postorbital hornless; 3. solid parietal frill having dorsal sagittal ridge; and 4. supraoccipital included in border of foramen magnum. The partially articulated specimen was identified as belonging to a juvenile individual based upon the unfused sutures.

Ott and Buckley pointed out that this specimen is significant in extending the range of *Leptoceratops* approximately 250 miles east of any previously published occurrence, at the same time establishing the presence of this genus in Montana. Furthermore, the Hell Creek Formation, generally regarded as a meandering fluvial, coastal plain deposit, is dominated faunally by *Edmontosaurus* and *Triceratops*, while upland

environments from western Wyoming to south-central Alberta have yielded specimens of *Leptoceratops*. Finding *Leptoceratops* in Montana, along with two specimens from coastal plain deposits in Alberta's Dinosaur Park Formation, "indicate that the biogeography of *Leptoceratop* may need to be reevaluated."

Lambert, Godefroit, Li, Shang and Dong (2001), in describing a new species of *Protoceratops* (see entry), *P. hellenikorhinus*, performed a cladistic analysis which found *Leptoceratops* and more advanced neoceratopsians to form their own clade; that at least one character ("vertical-notch shear tooth occlusion pattern") was acquired convergently in *Leptoceratops* and the more advanced *Montanoceratops*; and that there were apparently two migrations of neoceratopsians between North America and Asia, the latter scenario suggesting that the common ancestor for *Leptoceratops* and more advanced neoceratopsians originated in North America.

Makovicky (2001), in performing his own phylogenetic analysis incorporating new information gleaned from specimens of *Montanoceratops* (see entry), referred *Leptoceratops*, *Montanoceratops*, and *Udanoceratops* to their own family, which he named Leptoceratopsidae (see "Systematics" chapter for details).

Key references: Lambert, Godefroit, Li, Shang and Dong (2001); Makovicky (2001); Ott and Buckley (2001).

†LESOTHOSAURUS

Ornithischia: Fabrosauridae.

Comments: New specimens of the primitive ornithischian genus *Lesothosaurus* (see *D:TE*) were described in 2002.

Knoll (2002*a*) described in detail a subadult skull (MNHN LES 17) of *Lesothosaurus* collected during a 1963 expedition comprising F. Ellenberger, P. Ellenberger, J. Fabre, L. Ginsburg, and C. Mendrez, from the Upper Elliot Formation (Upper Triassic: upper Carnian or lower Norian; see Hancox 2000) at Masitise (or Masitisi), between Alwynskop and Moyeni (Quithing), Lesotho. The skull is articulated, uncrushed, and almost complete, including the lower jaws; it is missing the rostral end of the snout (inclusive of predentary and premaxillae), the bony bar separating the infratemporal and supratemporal fenestrae (possibly due to preparation in 1967), and both orbits are incomplete. Although not yet catalogued, this skull had been referred by Sereno (1991) to the type species *Lesothosaurus diagnosticus*.

As Knoll (2002*a*) could not determine the species to which this skull belongs, that author suggested referring to it as *Lesothosaurus* sp. indet.

Lesothosaurus

Subadult skull (MNHN LES 17) referred to as *Lesothosaurus* sp. indet. in A. left lateral and B. caudal views. Scale = 1 cm. (After Knoll 2002*a*.)

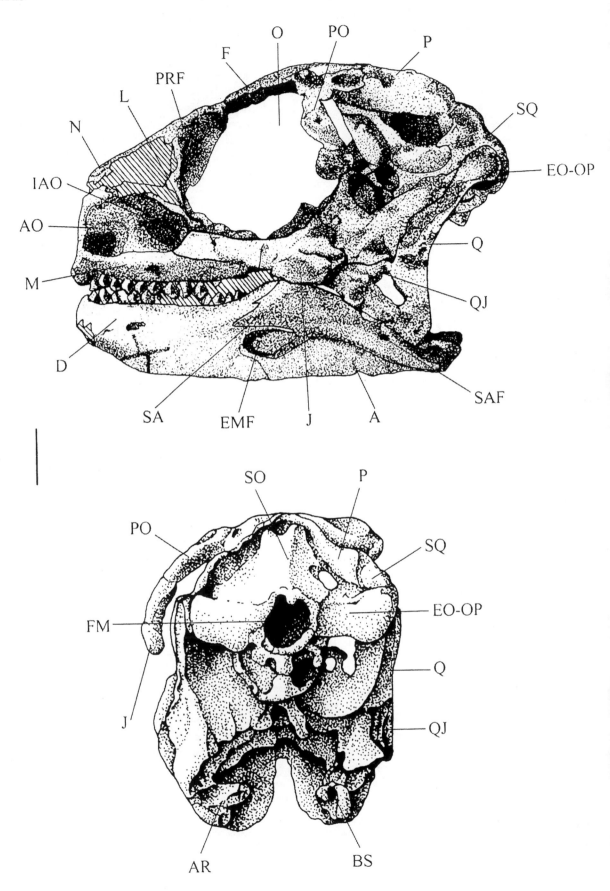

Knoll stated that MNHN LES 17 offers new information about the cranial morphology of *Lesothosaurus*, particularly concerning the occipital region. As that author observed, the paroccipital processes of this skull are roughly horizontal. Consequently, they are different from the curved, dorsally directed paroccipital processes that Sereno described in the type species *Lesothosaurus diagnosticus*; however, they are similar to the conditions seen in the syntype specimen BMNH RU B 23 and also the referred skull BMNH R 8501 (see *D:TE*).

Although Sereno had referred MNHN LES 17 to *L. diagnosticus*, and while acknowledging that this skull exhibits many features in common with the syntype specimens of that species, Knoll noted various ways in which they differ: Orbit of MNHN LES 17 approximately 1.3 times larger in absolute size and larger still proportionally to skull size than in BMNH RU B 23; orbit of MNHN LES 17 more angular, that of BMNH RU B 23 "egg-shaped" in outline; in MNHN LES 17, straighter ventral branch of postorbital than in BMNH RU B 23; retro-articular process of mandible more prominent and coronoid eminence not as high in BMNH RU B 23 as in MNHN LES 17; no equivalent large gap between supraoccipital and parietal in MNHN LES 17 (probable juvenile condition); supraoccipital of BMNH RU B 23 flatter than in MNHN LES 17; parietal in MNHN LES 17 possibly paired (?juvenile feature); angle formed by paroccipital processes in BMNH RU B 23 and MNHN LES 17 different, extremities of paroccipital processes apparently wider in the latter specimen; supratemporal fenestrae approximately 1.3 times longer in MNHN LES 17 than in BMNH RU B 23, wherein all contours of these openings are delimited by an unobtrusive crest.

As Knoll observed, MNHN LES 17 most likely had a short snout, the orbits are proportionally large, and the braincase is rounded, having no sagittal crest on the skull roof, all of these being classic juvenile features among dinosaurs. Furthermore, the dentaries of this specimen have the same dimensions as the specimen MNHN LES 9, referred to by Gow (1981) as representing an individual of "intermediate" age.

As pointed out by Knoll, a possible large fabrosaurid — known from three specimens — from the Upper Elliot Formation of South Africa, has been discussed by various authors (*e.g.*, Attridge and Charig 1967); Sereno (1986, 1991; Gow and Latimer 1999). One specimen from Lesotho, including a vertebra, neural arch, scapulocoracoid, ilium, ischium, incomplete femur, incomplete tibia, and a fibula, is housed in The Natural History Museum, London. Another specimen from South Africa, a partially articulated skeleton, is housed at the Museum of Comparative

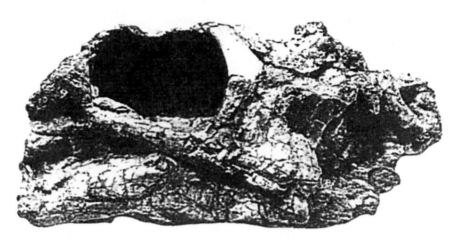

Incomplete skull (MNHN LES 18) provisionally referred to *Lesothosaurus* sp. Scale = 2 cm. (After Knoll 2002*b*.)

Zoology, Harvard University. The third specimen (NM QR 3076), an incomplete articulated skeleton, is on exhibit at the National Museum (Bloemfontein).

Preliminary studies of NM QR 3076 by Fabien Knoll and J. Welman have revealed that, while very large, this specimen is extremely close to the small species *L. diagnosticus*. Knoll noted that, of the six autapomorphies listed by Sereno (1991) to diagnose this species, the following are present in this specimen: Slot in maxilla for lacrimal; rostral premaxillary foramen; lateral exposure of brevis surface on postacetabular process (plesiomorphic for all ornithischians); and reduced pedal digit I (also seen in stegosaurs and some basal ornithopods). Knoll noted that the short forelimb (also seen in some basal ornithopods) can be seen in the specimen at Harvard and the ischium of the specimen at London bears a shallow dorsal groove. Sereno (1986) had already noted the presence of an obturator process on the ischium of the "large fabrosaurid" (this feature not clear in BMNH RU B17, one of the syntypes of *L. diagnosticus*) the presence of this feature having been discussed (*e.g.*, Sereno 1986, 1991; Thulborn 1992).

Knoll accepted the Fabrosauridae as a valid clade of primitive ornithischians comprising two congeneric species that seem to occur in the Upper Elliot Formation of southern Africa. (although these forms could someday prove to be conspecific, with the smaller *L. diagnosticus* being represented by juvenile individuals of the "large fabrosaurid"). Indeed, "MNHMN LES 17 may be a young of the 'large fabrosaurid', because it is, at one and the same time, much larger than some specimens referred to *Lesothosaurus diagnosticus* by Sereno (1991), such as BMNH R 11956, and a probably juvenile individual."

Subsequently, Knoll (2002*b*) described another skull (MNHN LES 18) of *Lesothosaurus*, this one also from the Upper Elliot Formation of southern Africa.

As chronicled by Knoll (2002*b*), this specimen — a partial skull (missing most of the snout, the premaxillae, naries, nasals, squamosals, and predentary) with some associated cervical vertebrae — had recently been found, regrettably lacking an identifying label, in the collections of the Muséum National d'Historie Naturelle in Paris. As observed by Knoll (2002*b*), the specimen has suffered somewhat from vertical compression (*i.e.*, lithostatic pressure), yet only slightly from transverse or oblique forces, the mandible and hyoid bones, for example, still in their natural relative positions.

As Knoll (2002*b*) noted, Paul Ellenberger (1970), in his report on Stormberg ichnites, had cited the existence of a few dinosaur skulls, although such material could not be found in the collection of the Laboratoire de Paléontologie of the Muséum National (personal observation by Knoll). More likely, according to L. Ginsburg (personal communication to Knoll, 1999), MNHN LES 18 was found during one of Ellenberger's field expeditions while prospecting in Lesotho, between Alwynskop and Moyeni (Quthing district), near Masitise (or Masitisi). Knoll (2002*b*) found this to be fairly probable because many of the Lesotho finds were near Ellenberger's three missions of Likhoele (Mafeteng district) and Masitise (see Ambrose 1991), and because the larger MNHN LES 17 (see above) was also found the Upper Elliot Formation at Masitise.

In describing the specimen and comparing it material (BMNH RU B 17, BMNH RU B 23, BMNH R 8501, and BMNH R 11956) belonging to *Lesothosaurus diagnosticus*, Knoll (2002*b*) noted that, owing to the incompleteness of MNHN LES 18, it could not be decided if this specimen has a slot in the maxilla for the lacrimal or a rostral premaxillary foramen, both of these characters constituting cranial autapomorphies for *L. diagnosticus* (see Sereno 1991). The mandibles of both MNHN LES 18 and BMNH RU B 23 offer a similar "finger-like" retro-articular process, a problematic character considered by Galton (1978) to be diagnostic and by Peng (1997*b*) as a synapomorphy for the Fabrosauridae.

Knoll (2002*b*) found differences between MNHN LES 18 and BMNH RU B 23 explainable by individual variation, incompleteness of the material, fractures, and deformations (*e.g.*, orbit square, supratemporal fenestra oval, and much smaller mandibular fenestra in MNHN LES 18; orbit more circular, supratemporal fenestra more reniform, and mandibular fenestra larger in BMNH RU B 23). Furthermore, the comparatively greater cranial roof at the parietal yet small orbit in MNHN LES 18 can probably be attributed to ontogenetic causes.

Based upon size alone, Knoll (2002*b*), MNHN

LES 18 appears to be closer to the "large fabrosaur" specimens (see above) rather than to such specimens as BMNH RU B 17, BMNH RU B 23, BMNH R 8501, and BMNH R 11956. Therefore, pending a more adequate understanding of the range of morphological and size variation of the south African fabrosaurid(s), Knoll (2002*b*) provisionally referred to MNHN LES 18 as *Lesothosaurus* sp.

Key references: Ambrose (1991); Attridge and Charig (1967); Crompton and Attridge (1986); Ellenberger (1970); Galton (1978); Gow (1981); Gow and Latimer (1999); Knoll (2002*a*, 2002*b*); Peng (1997*b*); Sereno (1986, 1991); Thulborn (1992).

LIAOCERATOPS Xu, Makovicky, Wang, Norell and You 2002
Ornithischia: Genasauria: Cerapoda: Marginocephalia: Ceratopsia: Neoceratopsia.
Name derivation: "Liaong" (province in China) + *ceratops* (suffix commonly used for horned dinosaur names, from Greek *keratos* = "horn" + Greek *ops* = "face").
Type species: *L. yanzigouensis* Xu, Makovicky, Wang, Norell and You 2002.
Other species: [None.]
Occurrence: Yixian Formation, Shangyuan, Liaoning, China.
Age: ?Early or ?Middle Cretaceous (?Barremian or ?Aptian).
Known material: Two skulls, subadult and juvenile.
Holotype: IVPP V12738, almost complete skull, adult.

Diagnosis of genus (as for type species): Neoceratopsian characterized by sutures between premaxilla, maxilla, nasal, and prefrontal, intersecting at common point high on side of snout; several tubercles on ventral margin of angular; foramen on caudal face of quadrate, near articulation with quadratojugal; small tubercle on dorsal border of foramen magnum; parietal frill having thick caudal border (Xu, Makovicky, Wang, Norell and You 2002).

Comments: The oldest and most basal of known neocerapsian dinosaurs, the genus *Liaoceratops* was established upon a nearly complete skull (IVPP V12738) from the lacustrine lower part of the Yixian Formation (recently dated by Jiang, Chen and Cao 2000 as very Late Jurassic, near the Jurassic–Cretaceous boundary, an assessment based on the evidence of various invertebrate faunas; dated as possibly 120 to 125 million years old by Smith, Harris, Omar, Dodson and You 2001, based on radiometric data; as middle Early Cretaceous by Swisher, Wang, Zhou, Wang, Jin, Zhang, Xu, Zhang and Wang 2002, based on $^{40}Ar/^{39}Ar$ dating of the Yixian and Tuchengzi formations), Yanzigou and Lujiatun, Shangyuan, western Liaoning Province, China. A second skull (IVPP V12633), recovered from the same locality, represents a juvenile individual of the type species *L. yanzigouensis* (Xu, Makovicky, Wang, Norell and You 2002).

As described by Xu *et al.* the holotype skull compares in size to those of other basal ceratopsians (*e.g.*, *Psittacosaurus* and *Chaoyangsaurus*); however, incomplete sutural closures between cranial elements suggest that this specimen belongs to a subadult animal.

In describing the referred skull, Xu *et al.* noted that it measures about half the length of the holotype and displays a number of juvenile characteristics, these including the possession of fewer teeth, vaulted frontals, a weaker jugal horn, and proportionately shorter and narrower frill (ontogenetic features also seen in *Psittacosaurus* and *Protoceratops*; see Coombs 1982 and Brown and Schlaikjer 1940, respectively). Comparing both *L. yanzigouensis* skulls, Xu *et al.* observed that the contribution of the squamosal to the margin of the frill increases allometrically during growth, the squamosals forming half this margin in the adult (the squamosal contribution to the frill decreasing proportionately during ontogeny in *Protoceratops*).

In performing a cladistic analysis, Xu *et al.* found *Liaoceratops* to be the most basal member of Neoceratopsia, sharing with other members of this clade the following derived characters: Lateral process of rostral; expanded frill having participation of squamosal; spherical occipital condyle; deep temporal bar; triangular postorbital; laterally convex surangular. However, *Liaoceratops* also possesses some primitive characters that place it in an intermediate position between the parrot-like psittacosaurids and higher neoceratopsian. Primitive ceratopsian characters retained in this genus include the following: Quadratojugal flat, not transversely expanded; rostral unkeeled; absence of epijugal; maxillary teeth with weakly developed primary ridges and oblique angles of occlusion. This combined suite of both primitive and derived characters, the authors pointed out, establishes *Liaoceratops* as a significant taxon in "documenting an incremental evolution for certain neoceratopsian diagnostic characters."

Xu *et al.* noted that *Liaoceratops* also displays certain characters that have traditionally been used to diagnose either the Psittacosauridae or more exclusive neoceratopsian assemblages. For example, the new genus has a weak ventral flange on the dentary and a ventrally wider infratemporal fenestra (as in some but not all species of *Psittacosaurus*; see Sereno 1990*a*). The mosaic distribution of characters in *Liaoceratops*, therefore, "introduces homoplasy to the data, which strips away some traditional psittacosaurid synapo-

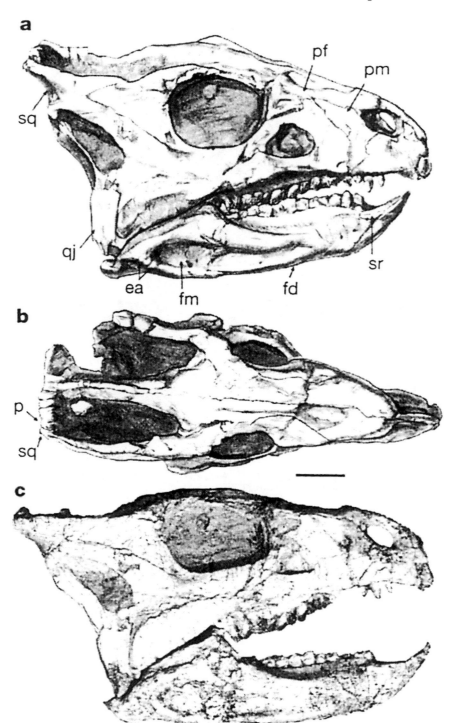

Liaoceratops yanzigouensis, IVPP V12738, holotype immature skull in a.–b. right lateral, c. dorsal, and d. ventral views. Scale = 4.5 cm. (After Xu, Makovicky, Wang, Norell and You 2002.)

morphies, and repolarizes certain characters within Neoceratopsia, causing a reversal in the phylogenetic order between *Asiaceratops* and *Archaeoceratops*.

As pointed out by Xu *et al.*, *Liaoceratops* co-occurs with specimens of *Psittacosaurus* in the lowest part of the (probably Lower Cretaceous) Yixian Formation, while *Chaoyangsaurus* occurs in the underlying (probably Late Jurassic) Tuchengzi Formation. Thus, the Ceratopsia split between Psittacosauridae and Neoceratopsia no later than the very earliest

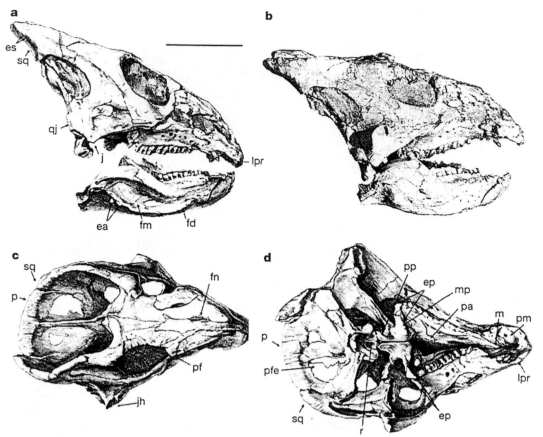

a

es
sq
qj
j
lpr
ea   fm   fd

b

c

sq
p
fn
pf
jh

d

pp
ep
mp
pa
m   pm
p
pfe
lpr
sq
r
ep

Liaoceratops yanzigouensis, IVPP V12633, referred juvenile skull in a.–c. right lateral, and b. dorsal views. Scale = 1 cm. (After Xu, Makovicky, Wang, Norell and You 2002.)

Known material/holotype: IVPP V12560, almost complete skeleton, juvenile.

Diagnosis of genus (as for type species): Ankylosaurian unique among known forms in having shell-like ventral armor, trapezoidal sternum with slendor, distally pointed posterolateral process and short medial articular margin, and pes more than twice length of manus (Xu, Wang and You 2001).

Comments: To date the smallest reported ankylosaur specimen (measuring only 34 centimeters or less than 13 inches long) and the first complete apparent nodosaurid found in Asia, the new type species *Liaoningosaurus paradoxus* was founded on a nearly complete, very well-preserved skeleton (IVPP V12560) collected from the Yixian Formation (recently dated by Jiang, Chen and Cao 2000 as very Late Jurassic, near the Jurassic–Cretaceous boundary, an assessment based on the evidence of various invertebrate faunas; dated as possibly 120 to 125 million years old by Smith, Harris, Omar, Dodson and You 2001, based on radiometric data; as middle Early Cretaceous by Swisher, Wang, Zhou, Wang, Jin, Zhang, Xu, Zhang and Wang 2002, based on ^{40}Ar/^{39}Ar dating of the Yixian and Tuchengzi formations).

In describing this specimen, As Xu *et al.* observed that it seems to represent a juvenile individual, as evidenced by the unfused vertebral centra and neural arches. Also, in contrast to all other known ankylosaurs except *Gargoyleosaurus* (Coombs and Maryańska 1990; K. Carpenter, personal communication to Xu *et al.*), the proximal caudal centra are about as long as they are wide.

Performing a phylogenetic analysis of *Liaoningosaurus*, the authors found this genus to place with the Nodosauridae, although this result was not strongly supported. Indeed, *Liaoningosaurus* was found to exhibit an unusual combination of characters, suggesting that it could represent yet another lineage within Anklosauria. *Lianoningosaurus* exhibits various juvenile features including the following: Fewer large-sized maxillary teeth compared to the number in adult ankylosaurs, postacetabular process of ilium facing rather laterally, olecranon process moderately developed, pubic peduncle, distinct finger-like lesser trochanter, tibia and femur about equal in length, all manual and pedal unguals claw-shaped. As these

Cretaceous, with both lineages apparently having acquired at least some of their diagnostic features rapidly during the latest Jurassic and perhaps earliest Cretaceous. "The combination of these temporal constraints with the previously unsuspected mosaic evolution introduced by *Liaoceratops*," the authors stated, "indicates a more rapid rate of character evolution at the base of Ceratopsia and its major subclades than was hitherto recognized."

Key references: Coombs (1982); Brown and Schlaikjer (1940); Jiang, Chen and Cao (2000); Sereno (1990*a*); Smith, Harris, Omar, Dodson and You (2001); Swisher, Wang, Zhou, Wang, Jin, Zhang, Xu, Zhang and Wang (2002); Xu, Makovicky, Wang, Norell and You (2002).

LIAONINGOSAURUS   Xu, Wang and You 2001

Ornithischia: Genasaura: Thyreophora: Eurypoda: Ankylosauromorpha: Ankylosauria: ?Nodosauridae.

Name derivation: "Liaong" (province in China) + Greek *sauros* = "lizard."

Type species: *L. paradoxus* Xu, Wang and You 2001.

Other species: [None.]

Occurrence: Yixian Formation, Liaoning Province, China.

Age: ?Early or ?Middle Cretaceous (?Barremian or ?Aptian).

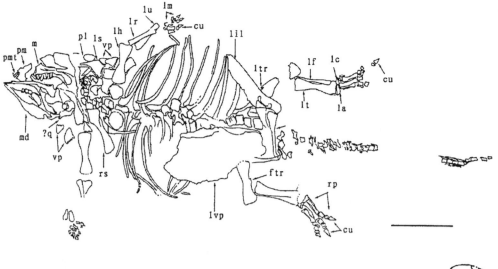

Liaoningosaurus paradoxus,
IVPP Vl2560, holotype in-
complete skeleton (juve-
nile). Scale = 4 cm. (After
Xu, Wang and You 2001.)

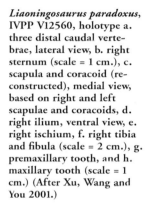

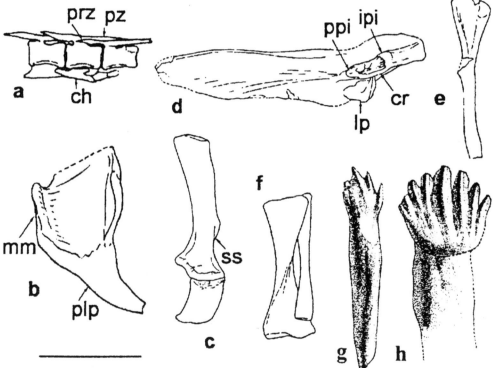

Liaoningosaurus paradoxus,
IVPP Vl2560, holotype a.
three distal caudal vertebrae, lateral view, b. right
sternum (scale = 1 cm.), c.
scapula and coracoid (re-
constructed), medial view,
based on right and left
scapulae and coracoids, d.
right ilium, ventral view, e.
right ischium, f. right tibia
and fibula (scale = 2 cm.), g.
premaxillary tooth, and h.
maxillary tooth (scale = 1
cm.) (After Xu, Wang and
You 2001.)

features are also distributed among basal thyreophorans and other juvenile and adult ankylosaurs, the authors suggested that ontogenetic shifts in developmental timing may have played a significant role in the
evolution of the Ankylosauria.

Key references: Coombs and Maryańska (1990);
Jiang, Chen and Cao (2000); Smith, Harris, Omar,
Dodson and You (2001); Swisher, Wang, Zhou,
Wang, Jin, Zhang, Xu, Zhang and Wang (2002); Xu,
Wang and You (2001).

†LILIENSTERNUS

Saurischia: Eusaurischia: Theropoda: Neotheropoda:
Coelophysoidea.

Type species: *L. liliensterni* (Huene 1934),
Other species: *?L. airelensis* Cuny and Galton 1993.
Syntypes: HMN BM.R.2175, partial skeletons, sub-
adult.

Comments: In a review of the Triassic theropods
of Europe, Rauhut and Hungerbühler (2000) commented upon *Liliensternus* (Welles 1984; see *D:TE*),
"the best represented Triassic theropod from Europe,"
this genus based upon the associated but disarticulated
remains of at least two individuals (HMN BM.R.
2175) from the Knollenmergel (upper Norian; see
Bachman, Beutler, Hagdorn, and Hauschke 1999;
Beutler 1998a, 1999b) of Thüingen, Germany. As it
is almost impossible to separate these remains, Rauhut

and Hungerbühler suggested that they be retained collectively as syntypes of the type species *Liliensternus liliensterni*, with the comparatively larger elements regarded as belonging to the lectotype.

Rauhut and Hungerbühler agreed with Rowe and Gauthier (1990) that the type species *Liliensternus liliensterni* belongs in the "Ceratosauria" (see "Systematics" chapter) as a sister taxon to the Coelophysoidea, this assessment based upon the well-developed horizontal ridge on the maxilla.

Regarding the species *L. airelensis* Cuny and Galton 1993, based on a fragmentary associated vertebral column and parts of the pelvis (Caen University collection) from the Upper Triassic–Lower Jurassic of Couches d'Airel, Normandy, France, Rauhut and Hungerbühler commented that this material could represent a distinct and diagnosable species. However, its referral to *Liliensternus* can only be tentative, based upon various differences in the cervical vertebrae (*e.g.*, two pairs of pleurocoels as opposed to the one in the type species). The authors added that the importance of these differences for distinguishing genera depend upon the collection of more complete material of this species. Because of its similarity to *L. liliensterni*, Rauhut and Hungerbühler referred ?*L. airelensis* to the Coelophysoidea with some certainty."

Notes: Rauhut and Hungerbühler addressed a single caudal vertebra (SMNS 4385) from the Upper Triassic (Norian) Middle Stubensandstein of Stuttgart-Heslach, Baden-Württemberg, Germany, originally described by Huene (1907–08) as *Tanystrophaeus posthumus*, and subsequently maintained in the collections of the Staatliches Museum für Naturkunde Stuttgart, informally labeled as "*Nicrosaurus*" sp.

As described by Rauhut and Hungerbühler, the specimen is a relatively stout caudal vertebra having strongly elongated prezygapophyses. The neural spine is quite low and no transverse processes are present. The elongated prezygapophyes identify the specimen as belonging to the Theropoda. As in *Liliensternus*, the caudal exhibits a rather broad ventral groove. Otherwise, Rauhut and Hungerbühler found the specimen to be indeterminable, both generically and specifically, and regarded "*T. posthumus*" as a *nomen dubium*.

These authors also considered the species "*Megalosaurus*" *cambrensis*, based upon a natural mold (see *S2* for photograph) in a slab of sandstone recovered from the Uppermost Triassic of southern Wales, and originally described by Newton (1899) as *Zanclodon cambrensis*. As Rauhut and Hungerbühler noted, all determinable characters (*e.g.*, very low and broad interdental plates) of this specimen agree very well with both *Liliensternus liliensterni* or *Dilophosaurus wetherilli*; however, although this specimen might represent a distinct taxon, it exhibits no derived characters allowing for a formal diagnosis, this taxon therefore regarded as a *nomen dubium*.

Key references: Cuny and Galton (1993); Huene (1907–08, 1934); Rauhut and Hungerbühler (2000); Rowe and Gauthier (1990); Welles (1984).

LOSILLASAURUS Casanovas, Santafe and Sanz 2001

Saurischia: Eusaurischia: Sauropodomorpha: Sauropoda: Eusauropoda: Neosauropoda: Diplodocoidea *incertae sedis*.

Name derivation: "Losilla [village in the district of Los Serranos, Valencia, Spain]" + Greek *sauros* = "lizard."

Type species: *L. giganteus* Casanovas, Santafe and Sanz 2001.

Other species: [None.]

Occurrence: Collado Formation, Valencia, Spain.

Age: Late Jurassic to Early Cretaceous.

Known material: Partial postcranial skeleton (mostly vertebrae), cranial fragment.

Holotype: Lo-5, proximal caudal vertebra with centrum.

Diagnosis of genus (as for type species): Autapomorphies including: neural spine of cranial caudal vertebrae having lateral enarded outline (cutlass-like shape) in dorsal view; ratio of approximately 0.5 of cranio-caudal dimension of neuroapophyseal base to height; singular combination of synapomorphies [see below] including: centra of middorsal and caudal vertebrae opisthocoelous; median keel of cervical centra reduced or absent; cavity in dorsal surface of every cervical parapophysis; lateral surface of cervical centra greatly excavated but with oblique accessory lamina; infraprezygapophyseal lamina in middle cervical and caudal vertebrae, bifurcaded; dorsal vertebral centra pleurocoelous; index of extension (length of vertebral centrum/width of caudal) of caudal dorsals greated than 1; transverse processes of caudal dorsal vertebrae strong dorsolaterally; transverse processes of caudal dorsals situated vertically above parapophyses; centro-parapophyseal lamina; accessory lamina in infrapostzygapophyseal cavity of middle and caudal dorsal vertebrae; neural spines of dorsal vertebrae with prominent suprapostzygapophyseal lamina; dorsal neural spines with triangular process; dorsal neural spines, in cranial view, with lateral margins that diverge strongly toward extremity; proximal caudal centra moderately procoelous; length of proximal caudal centra greater, length to height ratio approximately 0.5 to 0.6; "dorsalization" of neural spines of proximal caudal vertebrae; neuroapophysis transversely compressed, in form of cutlass; back of proximal caudal vertebrae winglike; middle and distal portions of

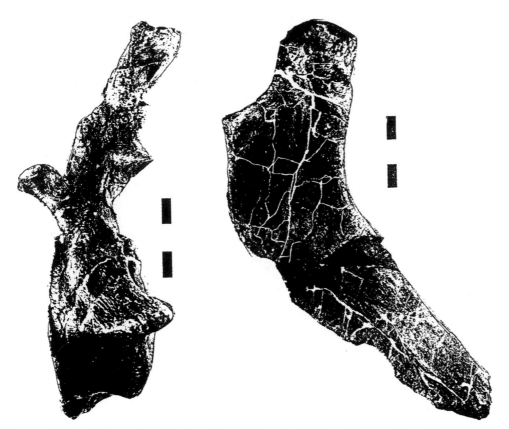

Left: Losillasaurus giganteus, Lo-12, referred distal middle caudal vertebra, left lateral view. *Right: Losillasaurus giganteus*, Lo-20, referred left ischium. (After Casanovas, Santafe and Sanz 2001.)

pubis located approximately in the same extremely proximal levels (Casanovas, Santafe and Sanz (2001).

Comments: The type species *Losillasaurus giganteus* was founded upon a proximal caudal vertebra (Lo-1) collected from the La Caqada site, in the Collado Formation (previously regarded as Lower Cretaceous "Weald facies;" reassigned to the Jurassic–Cretaceous boundary "Purbeck facies"), Barranco de Escaiz, village of Losilla, municipality of Aras de Alpuente, Valencia, Spain. A paratype specimen (Lo-10) consists of another proximal caudal vertebra. Additional referred material from the same locality includes (Lo-1 to Lo-4) fragments of cranial cervical vertebrae, (Lo-11) a middorsal vertebra, (Lo-17a-c, Lo-18a-b) portions of caudal dorsal vertebrae, (Lo-24) a dorsosacral vertebral centrum, (Lo-15 and Lo-25) sacra, (Lo-6, Lo-12, and Lo-13) proximal caudal vertebrae, (Lo-23) a partial proximal caudal, (Lo-7) an almost complete left humerus, (Lo-8) a distal fragment of a left ulna, (Lo-9) a distal fragment of a left radius, (Lo-14 and Lo-22) almost complete right and left sternal plates, respectively, (Lo-22) an almost complete left sternal plate, (Lo-19) a fragment of a left pubis, (Lo-20a-b) fragments of a left ischium, (Lo-21a-c) fragments of a left ilium, (Lo-16) a proximal fragment of a right metacarpal II, and (Lo-26a-b) proximal cranial fragments (Casanovas, Santafe and Sanz 2001).

According to a cladistic analysis performed by Casanovas *et al.*, *Losillasaurus* is related to the clade formed by (*Barosaurus* plus *Diplodocus*) + *Dicraeosaurus*.

Key reference: Casanovas, Santafe and Sanz (2001).

Note: Other dinosaurian remains described from the Collado Formation include two spatulated, indeterminate sauropod teeth, the tooth of an indeterminate theropod, and postcranial remains belonging to the stegosaur *Dacentrurus armatus*.

Key reference: Casanovas, Santafe and Sanz (2001).

†LOURINHANOSAURUS

Saurischia: Eusaurischia: Theropoda: Neotheropoda: Tetanurae: Avetheropoda: Spinosauroidea: Megalosauridae *incertae sedis*.

Comments: Ricqlès, Mateus, Antunes and Taquet (2001) reported on a number of excellently preserved embryos, tentatively referred to *Lourinhanosaurus*, preserved as tiny isolated skeletal elements *in ovo*, found in Paimogo, near the city of Lourinhã, Portugal. As the authors pointed out, this discovery, for at least two reasons, "is an event of unprecedented interest for the study of early ontogeny of dinosaurs": 1. Being of Late Jurassic (late Kimmeridgian–Tithonian) age, the material extends the temporal range of

dinosaurian embryology back almost 80 million years; 2. it belongs to the Theropoda, a clade widely linked to the ancestry of birds.

Noting the vast amount of minute information arising from their histological study of this material, Ricqlès *et al.* included "only the most salient aspects" in their published paper. Ricqlès *et al.* observed the following:

Endochondral ossification in the ends of both short and long bones involves extensive, well-developed pads of hypertrophied calcified cartilage permeated by marrow buds. This cartilage contains numerous longitudinally oriented pipes or tubules, opening either in the marrow cavity or at the surface of the cartilaginous "epiphysis," some of these spaces originating from the marrow cavity probably working as erosion bays that carved into the cartilage towards the epiphysis. Within the cartilage are tubules that may be genuine cartilage canals, ontogenetically independent from the erosion bay as seen in birds. Furthermore, some metaphyseal regions exhibit a large central "well" filled by matrix, lined by thin, bony trabeculae and occasionally containing small islands of calcified cartilage, this suggesting an avian type "cartilaginous medullary cone" mostly formed by uncalcified cartilage (not fossilized). This suggests a close relationship with the avian condition of long bone histogenesis. Patterns of periosteal ossification suggest high initial growth rates modulated by precise, locally specific changes in rates of new bone deposition, and possibly also of extremely active growth in length.

As Ricqlès *et al.* observed, bone-specific details and their differentiation, although at a much reduced scale, already show in these embryonic specimens. Although the histological construction of such details fundamentally differs between embryos and adults, "the stability of such morphological characters along the extended Theropod 'ontogenetic' trajectory is striking," this suggesting "that the (genetic) control on shape is at the same time precocious, powerful and permanent."

Noting that the vertebral centra of the embryonic specimens have similar proportions to those of the contemporaneous theropod *Lourinhanosaurus*, while their proportions differ from those of *Allosaurus*, a theropod for which a growth series is available, Ricqlès *et al.* tentatively referred these embryos to the theropod from Portugal.

In an abstract for a poster, published as a preliminary report for a forthcoming revision of the Megalosauridae, Allain (2002*b*) found *Lourinhanosaurus* to be a member of the Megalosauridae.

Key references: Allain (2002*b*); Ricqlès, Mateus, Antunes and Taquet (2001).

†MAIASAURA

Ornithischia: Genasauria: Cerapoda: Ornithopoda: Iguanodontia: Euiguanodontia: Dryomorpha: Ankylopollexia: Iguanodontoidea: Hadrosauroidea: Hadrosauridae: Hadrosaurinae.

Comments: Past interpretations of the relatively small forelimb of duckbilled dinosaurs have included its serving as a paddle for swimming (as per earlier ideas of hadrosaurs being mostly aquatic animals; see, for example, Osborn 1912*b*), or being able to support just a fraction of the animal's weight when on land (Ostrom 1964). Quadrupedality has, therefore, generally been excluded from the various theories proposed, although quadrupedal trackways attributed to hadrosaurs have been reported (Currie, Nadon and Lockley 1991).

Recently, Dilkes (2001) investigated ontogenetic growth in the limbs of *Maiasaura peeblesorum*, a hadrosaurine from the Upper Cretaceous (Campanian–Maastrichtian) Two Medicine Formation of Montana. Dilkes' study tested "the hypothesis that there is an ontogenetic shift in stance for the hadrosaur *M. peeblesorum* by investigating the morphometric and biomechanic aspects of growth of the forelimb and hindlimb from nestling to adult." Included in Dilkes' study were nestlings from the 1978 nest (YPM-PU 22440; formerly Princeton University collection), also excavations from Camposaur (MOR-005), both sites being located in Teton County.

Dilkes' study supported "a hypothesis of age-dependent selection of stance" with the following scenario proposed: *Maiasaura* juveniles were basically bipedal animals. During ontogeny, the individual's stance shifted to quadrupedality. Furthermore, the patterns of allometric growth differed between forelimb and hindlimb. Regarding the forelimb, morphometric results revealed a probable allometric enlargement of the postural muscles, allometric increase in the lever arms of the protractor muscles, and increased robustness of the humerus to enhance the resistance of this bone to bending stresses. The hindlimb, by contrast, was found to be characterized by a comparative decrease in the resistance of the femur and tibia to the same kind of stresses. Furthermore, this study showed an allometric enlargement of the fourth trochanter of the femur and positive allometry of the lengths of the third and fourth metatarsals.

Dilkes found the most probable explanation for these differing growth patterns to be stresses — the result of gravity and the muscular forces necessary for moving the body — that the limb bones experienced during growth. As that author noted, bone can adjust to such stresses in three ways (*i.e.*, changing mechanical properties of bone material, changing angulation of vector of ground-reaction forces, and changes in

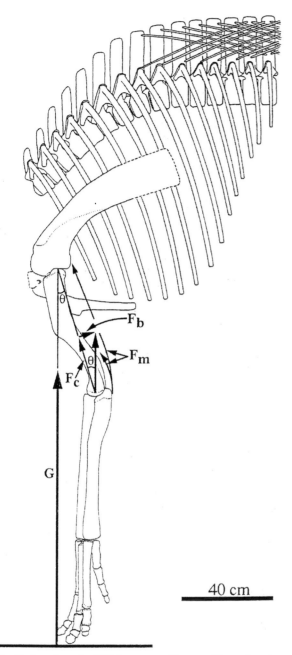

Forelimb and trunk of *Maiasaura peeblesorum* illustrating the pattern of major forces acting on the humerus. F_c = compressive force; F_b = bending force; F_m = force of muscles attached to olecranon process; G = ground-reaction force. (After Dilkes 2001).

skeletal allometry), any combination of the changes maintaining a similar safety margin (failure stress: functional stress) throughout a size range.

In the case of *Maiasaura*, Dilkes found that the relatively larger "hindlimb was sufficiently robust at a young age to accommodate increased postural and lomomotory stresses through largely isometric growth, whereas a behavioral shift to quadrupedality in older individuals necessitated an allometric response in the forelimb."

Earlier studies have suggested that the manus of hadrosaurs, lacking a complex of ossified carpals that would virtually lock the manus and antebrachium to the carpus, would be at continual risk of failure during locomotion, restricting the use of the forelimb to a quadrupedal stance. However, Dilkes noted the following osteological weight-bearing adaptations in the manus: Flexor muscles attached to the caudal surface of metacarpals III and IV which probably reinforced the reduced carpus; metacarpals II through IV firmly united, articulating in an arc configuration more resistant to bending than if the metacarpals were aligned in a transverse row; possible hyperextension at the metacarpal-phalangeal joints; phalanges bound together by skin, probably also by ligaments; and manus having a broad contact with the ground.

Note: Tanke and Brett-Surman (2001) reviewed the occurrences of dinosaur eggshell material and described some bones (RTMP collections) of nestling-sized hadrosaurs, recovered in 1992 from the Late Cretaceous (Campanian) of Dinosaur Provincial Park, in southern Alberta, Canada. As these authors noted, eggshell fragments are rare and have been found in this area at only in two microfossil sites dominated by invertebrate shells. The skeletal material comprises 43 specimens mostly consisting of edentulous dentary fragments, limb bones in various stages of completion, pedal elements, vertebral centra, and also various other remains.

Describing these fragmentary eggshells, Tanke and Brett-Surman observed that they have a pebbled surface texture and are similar to those of *Maiasaura* and also to eggshell from the Devil's Coulee hadrosaur nesting site (see Currie 1988). Many of the skeletal elements, the authors pointed out, show little or no stream abrasian, suggesting that they originated from places near Dinosaur Provincial Park or from the Park itself.

In the past, it was generally believed that duck-billed dinosaurs nested only in upland environments (*e.g.*, see Sternberg 1955; Horner 1982, 1984*a*). This new material, however, supports more recent opinions (*e.g.*, Fiorillo 1987, 1989) that hadrosaurs also nested in lowland environments. It has not yet been established, however, if a certain genus nested in one of these types of environment or both.

Key references: Currie (1988); Currie, Nadon and Lockley (1991); Dilkes (2001); Fiorillo (1987, 1989); Horner (1982, 1984*a*); Osborn (1912*b*); Ostrom (1964); Sternberg (1955); Tanke and Brett-Surman (2001).

†**MAJUNGATHOLUS**

Saurischia: Eusaurischia: Theropoda: Neotheropoda: Neoceratosauria: Abelisauria: Abelisauroidea: Abelisauridae.

Comments: In an abstract for a poster, Rogers and Miller (2002) briefly discussed the paleonenvironmental and taphonomic perspectives on the Late Cretaceous ecosystem in which the domed, relatively large-bodied theropod *Majungatholus atopus*— known from the Maevarano Formation of northwestern Madagascar — occupied a prominent niche.

M. atopus, the authors noted, seems to have shared its world with relatively few dinosaurs, these including the abelisauroid theropod *Masiakasaurus knopfleri* and two titanosaurs (*Rapetosaurus krausei* and an as yet unnamed form referred to as "Malagasy Taxon B"). Recently discovered, very well-preserved skeletal remains, as well as continuing analyses of the sedimentology and taphonomy of the formation and associated units, have afforded an excellent opportunity to reconstruct *Majungatholus'* world.

While acknowledging that *Majungatholus* was arguably well adapted for life on the expansive floodplains of the Mahajanga Basin, Rogers and Miller speculated that this dinosaur may have frequented the broad, sandy channel belts draining Madagascar's central highlands. There, the authors presumed, this dinosaur hunted or scavenged.

Numbering among the various aquatic vertebrates populating these shallow rivers, Rogers and Miller noted, were fish, frogs, turtles, and numerous small and large crocodilians. All of these taxa seem to have been adapted for seasonal fluctuations in the availability of water, "because the fluvial sediments that entomb their remains indicate a variable and flood-prone discharge regime, and associated paleosols suggest that the ambient climate was semiarid." These sediments also offer clues suggesting localized and maybe seasonal mortality pulses.

According to Rogers and Miller, *Majungatholus* may have taken advantage of the hardships of other taxa, including its own kind, during periods of environmental distress, supplementing its diet by preying upon weakened animals. The authors noted that one subadult *M. atopus* specimen exhibits conspecific tooth marks, indicating that *Majungatholus* was sometimes a cannibal, feeding "with considerable rabidity upon the well-muscled axial skeleton in a fashion similar to that of many modern carnivores."

Key reference: Rogers and Miller (2002).

MALEEVOSAURUS—(See *Tarbosaurus*.)

†MAMENCHISAURUS—(=*Zigongosaurus*)
Saurischia: Eusaurischia: Sauropodomorpha: Sauropoda: Eusauropoda: Neosauropoda: Macronaria:

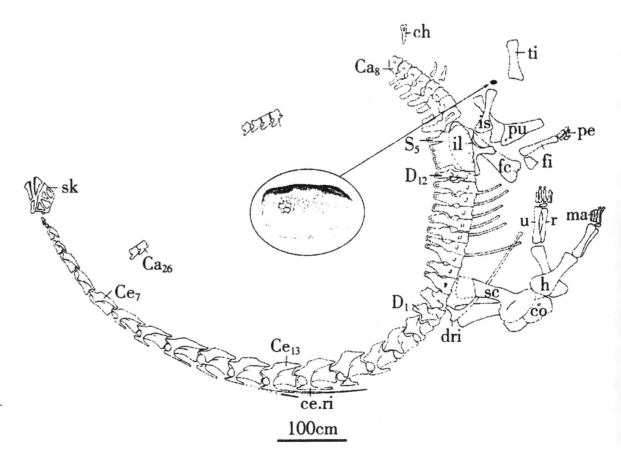

Mamenchisaurus youngi, ZDM0083, holotype skeleton as found. Drawing by Yu Young. (After Ouyang and Ye 2002.)

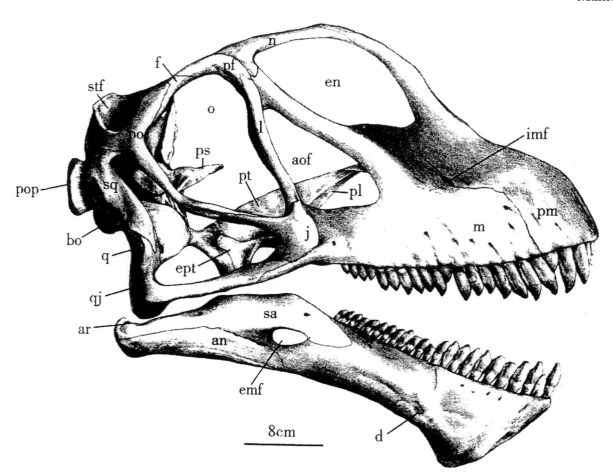

Mamenchisaurus youngi, ZDM0083, holotype skull (restored slightly on right side. Drawn by Yu Young. (After Ouyang and Ye.)

8cm

Camarasauromorpha: Titanosauriformes: Somphospondyli: Euhelopodidae: Euhelopodinae.

Diagnosis of genus: Large size, skull extremely small; skull of general *Camarasaurus* type, but longer, narrower; occipital crest well developed; mandible slender, with high symphyseal region; external mandibular foramen; teeth closely arranged; teeth having prominent wear facets, denticles on distal carinae degenerate; 18 to 19 cervical, 12 dorsal, four to 5 sacral, and more than 50 caudal vertebrae; presacral vertebrae opisthocoelous, having cancellous structure in varying degrees; caudal cervical and caudal dorsal spines bifurcated; cervical vertebrae elongated, with long ribs; proximal caudal vertebrae procoelous, middle to distal caudals amphiplatyan, distal caudals fused, expanded; middle region of tail with typically diplodocid forked chevrons; scapula longer than femur, distal blade expanded; sternum small, subcircular; ratio of length of forelimb to hindlimb about 3/4 to 4/5; small manus and pes (Ouyang and Ye 2002).

Diagnosis of *M. youngi*: Medium-size mamenchisaurid, about 16 meters in total length; (cranial) all most external openings large, resulting in extremely lightly structured skull; snout well developed, V-shaped in dorsal aspect; external naris in dorsolateral/middle region of skull; orbit pear shaped, antor-bital triangular in outline; length and height of lateral temporal fenestra equal; crainal roof backwardly inclined, quadrate slightly forward; large maxillary and premaxillary forming relatively broad facial region; thin parietal, frontal, and nasal; slender lacrimal, postorbital, and quadrate; well-developed occipital ridge of supraoccipital; dentary very long, having marked "droopy" anterior end; external mandibular foramen in posteromedial part of mandible; long dental battery (including many teeth); four premaxillary, 18 maxillary, and 23 to 24 dentary teeth; teeth spatulate, crowns somewhat slender; teeth showing prominent wear facets; well-developed denticles on anterior edge of unworn teeth; (postcranial) 18 cervical, 12 dorsal, five sacral, and over 50 caudal vertebrae; presacral vertebrae opisthocoelous, centra with cancellous structure; lamina structure simple; caudal cervical and cranial dorsal neural spines slightly bifurcated; cervical vertebrae moderately elongated, longest one 3.2 times as long as average dorsal vertebrae length; pleurocoels in cervical vertebrae not well developed; cervical ribs extremely slender, forking anterior end in middle cervicals; slightly developed pleurocoels in dorsal vertebrae; all sacral centra coossified, neural spines of first four sacrals coossified; anterior caudal vertebrae strongly procoelous, distal caudals amphiplatyan; scapula large,

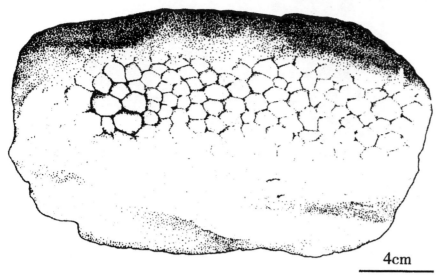

Mamenchisaurus youngi, ZD0083, fossil skin impression. Drawn by Yu Young. (After Ouyang and Ye 2002.)

In 2001, Ye Yong, Ouyang Hui, and Fu Qian-Ming described a new specimen (ZDM0126) of *Mamenchisaurus hochuanensis*, collected from the Upper Jurassic of Zigong, Sichuan, China. The nearly complete skeleton includes distal caudal vertebrae, the pectoral girdle, forelimb, and, most importantly, the skull and teeth, all of which were absent in the holotype of this referred species (see *D:TE*).

Ye *et al.* described the skull of *M. hochuanensis* as follows: Basically similar to that of the referred species *M. youngi* (see below), being lightly constructed and resembling the skull of *Camarasaurus*; occipital condyle hemispherical; basioccipital process well developed; paraoccipital process well developed, triangular in dorsal view; basipterygoid process of basisphenoid slender; middle part of parietal very narrow, only 46 millimeters wide; no pineal foramen; frontal thin, wide; premaxillary relatively short and thin, nasal process well developed; maxillary relatively long and large; dentary long, thin, with relatively "droopy" anterior end; teeth small, spatulate, crowns relatively high and narrow; well-developed medial ridges in internal surface of crown; denticles well developed on anterior edge of crowns of unworn teeth.

The authors described the distal caudal vertebrae as fused with each other, centra not expanded, neural arch remarkably expanded, size of neural canal and height of neural spines increased; distal caudals "cockscomb-shaped" in side view.

Furthermore, Ye *et al.* noted the following: Scapula long, large, with slender shaft; sternum small,

long; sternum small; humerus short, about 72 percent length of femur, proximal end of humerus remarkably expanded, head strikingly inclined inward; ulna longer than radius, 69 percent length of humerus; metacarpal I and V short, II through IV slender; phalangeal formula of manus 2-2-?1-?1; ilium long, low, anterior process and pubic peducle developed; pubis and ischium of equal length, pubis stouter than ischium; femur slender; tibia 57 percent length of femur; fibula slender; metatarsal I stout; phalangeal formula of pes 2-3-?3-?2-?1 (Ouyang and Ye 2002, slightly revised after Pi, Ouyang and Ye 1996).

Comments: More specimens of the extremely long-necked sauropod *Mamenchisaurus* continue to be found and described.

Mamenchisaurus youngi, ZDM0083, holotype skeleton mounted at the Zigong Dinosaur Museum. Scale = 100 cm. (After Ouyang and Ye 2002.)

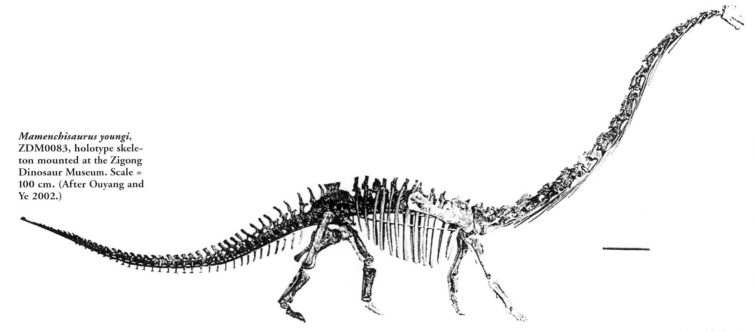

Photograph by Yu Gang.

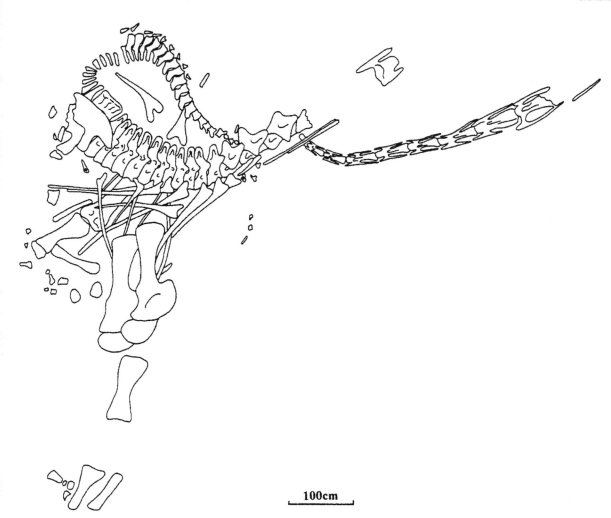

100cm

oval-shaped; clavicle short, having two processes in proximal end; humerus short, nearly 70 percent length of femur; proximal and distal ends of humerus remarkably expanded, deltoid crest not well developed; ulna longer than radius, 70 percent length of humerus; proximal end of ulna relatively expanded, having prominent radiale-fossa; radius straight, flat; femur long, flat, with remarkably expanded ends.

As pointed out by the authors, all the vertebrae are well preserved in the known species of *Mamenchisaurus* save for the distal caudals, the features of which, consequently, are unknown. Based upon the materials included in ZDM0126, Ye *et al.* observed that the distal caudal vertebrae are fused with one another, expanded, and "cockscomb-shaped." These caudals, the authors suggested, may have served as a defensive weapon or an acute sense organ.

Zhang and Li (2001) described new materials, including a seventh caudal vertebra, right pectoral girdle, right ilium, and right forelimb belonging to the species *Mamenchisaurus jingyanensis*, collected from the early Late Jurassic of the Sichuan Basin, China.

At the same time, these authors referred *Mamenchisaurus* to the "Bothrosauropoidea," a clade that has not yet been generally adopted, based on its high skull and spatulate teeth.

One of the most important *Mamenchisaurus* specimens yet collected, the holotype (ZDM0083) of

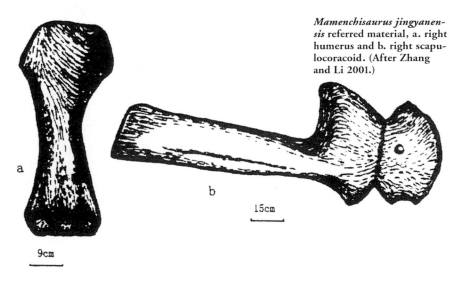

Mamenchisaurus jingyanensis referred material, a. right humerus and b. right scapulocoracoid. (After Zhang and Li 2001.)

a

b

15cm

9cm

Mamenchisaurus

Mamenchisaurus jingyanensis referred material, a. right ilium and b. seventh caudal vertebra. (After Zhang and Li 2001.)

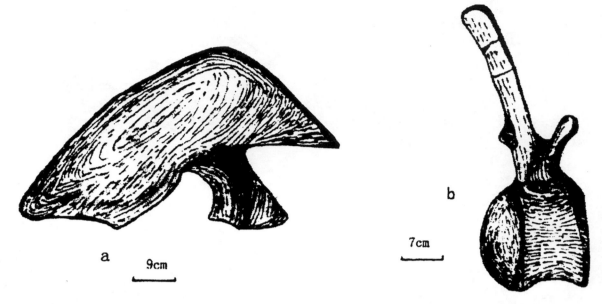

a   9cm

b   7cm

M. youngi (see *S1*), has finally been fully described by Ouyang and Ye (2002). As these authors related, the specimen is virtually complete, including an almost perfect skull and teeth, lacking only the distal caudal vertebrae. It was excavated in 1989 from the Shangshaximiao Formation in Xinming, Zigong, Schuan, China. A preliminary report on this specimen was first published by Pi, Ouyang and Ye (1996). (As Ouyang *et al.* pointed out, due to limited space, the editor of Pi *et al.*'s Chinese-language report deleated the detailed description of the skull, the English-language summary, and the plates illustrating the holotype material.)

Ouyang rediagnosed the genus *Mamenchisaurus* (see above); also, the authors rediagnosed the family "Mamenchisauridae" (*Mamenchisaurus* now usually regarded as a member of the euhelopodid subfamily Euhelopodinae, the latter currently a senior synonym of Mamenchisauridae; see "Systematics" chapter).

In describing *M. youngi*, Ouyang and Ye reported that a block of skin fossil impression (preserved skin impressions being quite rare among sauropods) was found in rock near the distal end of the left ischium, this demonstrating that the animal was covered with scaly skin differing from the smooth skin of elephants. As described by these authors, scales projected from the epidermis. These scales are polygonal in shape, measuring from six to 15 millimeters in diameter, and are closely arranged in a mosaic pattern.

Comparing *M. youngi* to the other species of *Mamenchisaurus*, Ouyang and Ye noted the following differences (refer to diagnosis of *M. youngi*, above): *M. constructus* (short cervical ribs, anterior ends grooveshaped; tibia shorter than fibula; distal end of tibia relatively expanded, almost equal in width to proximal end; *M. hochuanensis* (cervical vertebrae extremely elongated, neck alost half total length of axial skeleton; 31 presacral and 4 sacral vertebrae; dorsal vertebrae with poorly developed pleurocoels); *M. sinocanadorum* (larger than *M. youngi*; fewer mandibular teeth; greater ratio of length of third cervical vertebrae to axis); *M. anyuensis* (over 23 meters in length; dorsal vertebrae with lower neural spines, well-developed pleurocoels; and *M. jingyanensis* (larger than *M. hochuanensis*, with vcry similar skull; pleurocoel of cervical vertebrae more well developed.

Regarding *Zigongosaurus fuxiensis* (see *D:TE, S1,* and *S2*), Ouyang and Ye cited citing its possession of such basal *Mamenchisaurus* features as bifurcated neural spines of caudal cervical and cranial dorsal vertebrae bifurcated and procoelous proximal caudal vertebrae. Also, the authors pointed out that this species displays a few primitive characters similar to those found in *Omeisaurus*, while its horizon is lower than that of any of the species of *Mamenchisaurus*. Consequently, Ouyang and Ye suggested that *Z. fuxuensis* be referred, at least for the present, to "*Mamenchisaurus* sp. indet."

In comparing the known *Mamenchisaurus* species, that author proposed the following evolutionary trends in this genus: 1. Small (14 meters) to medium (20 meters) to large (over 26 meters); 2. increase in ratio of skull length to total length; 3. denticles on margins of crowns from developed to poorly developed; 4. increase in neck length; 5. caudal cervical and cranial dorsal neural spines from slightly to obviously forked; 6. anterior caudal vertebrae from slightly to obviously procoelous; 7. cancellous structure of presacrals from slightly to well developed; 8. pleurocoels in cervical vertebrae from not developed to developed; and 9. limbs in cross section from slender and circular to "brawny" and elliptical.

(Revised) from *Predatory Dinosaurs of the World* (1988), copyright © Gregory S. Paul.

One of a group of predacious *Yangchuanosaurus shangyouensis* diverts a *Mamenchisaurus hochuanensis* from its herd, as pterosaurs fly by, in this illustration by Gregory S. Paul.

Ouyang and Ye noted that, because of their basic type, their extremely long necks, and their occurrence in the Sichuan Basin, *Mamenchisaurus* and *Omeisaurus* are often thought of as being closely related. However, the authors pointed out, there are numerous differences between these two sauropod genera, these including the following: (*Omeisaurus*) greater ratio of neck to total length; cervical vertebrae extremely elongated, neural arch low; distal end of scapula not expanded; humerus long, approximately 80 percent femoral length; skull large, heavy, external naris smaller than orbit, teeth large, sturdy. Because

• 397 •

of the similarities between *Mamenchisaurus* and *Omeisaurus*, however, Ouyang and Ye suggested that they could have a similar ancestry.

In discussing the skull of *M. youngi*, Ouyang and Ye noted the very small brain (relative to body size) yet very large orbit with well-developed sclerotic rings, this to the authors an animal of low intelligence yet with good vision. Possessing such a long neck and apparently good eyesight, Ouyang and Ye speculated, allowed this dinosaur to analyze rapidly the food conditions and presence of enemies within a large area. Features of the teeth, including the prominent wear facets, indicated to the authors that the food of *Mamenchisaurus* included both tender and rough plant matter.

Ouyang and Ye also pointed out that the caudal vertebrae of *M. youngi* possess high and stout neural spines, suggesting a very stout tail. Furthermore, the tail is long, with distal caudals having an expanded appearance. Therefore, the authors speculated, the tail of *Mamenchisaurus* was not only adapted for balancing the body, but could also have functioned as a defensive weapon.

Features of the limbs, the authors observed (*e.g.*, well-developed crest and fossa, humeral head well developed and strikingly inclined, femoral head well developed and forming right angle with shaft of femur, almost 90-degree angle between metacarpals and axial line of phalanges), show that *Mamenchisaurus* was a terrestrial animal.

Note: Hengst (2002), in an abstract, briefly reported on sauropod material referred to *Mamenchisaurus* collected in 1999 near the Village of Lao Chang Qing in the Lower Jurassic Lufeng Formation, east and south of Lufeng, Yunnan Province, China. The material, indicating several individuals, was discovered as part of an assemblage including numerous turtles, plus a single, unidentified theropod. To date of this writing, 239 sauropod bones had been uncovered (also five theropod bones and five turtles), the sauropod remains including an intact sacrum, pubes, ilia, ischia, many articulated vertebral elements, five scapulae, some limb bones, and a manus. The site is distinguished as the most southern occurrence known for this genus. As Hengst reported, local authorities have decided to leave these fossils partially exposed *in situ* similar to the display at Dinosaur National Monument, with an educational facility to be built at the site at some later date.

Key references: Hengst (2002); Ouyang and Ye (2002); Pi, Ouyang and Ye (1996); Ye, Ouyang and Fu (2001); Zhang and Li (2001).

†MANDSCHUROSAURUS (=?*Charonosaurus*)

Ornithischia: Genasauria: Cerapoda: Ornithopoda: Iguanodontia: Euiguanodontia: Dryomorpha: Ankylopollexia: Iguanodontoidea: Hadrosauroidea: Hadrosauridae: Euhadrosauria *incertae sedis*.

Known material: Incomplete skull, postcranial elements representing more than a dozen individuals.

Diagnosis of genus (as for type species): Number of vertical tooth rows relatively low (35) (Norman and Sues 2000).

Comments: In 1925, Anatoly Nikolaenvice N. Riabinin named and briefly described a new species of giant hadrosaur, *Trachodon amurense*.

As related by Godefroit, Zan and Jin (2000, 2001), this taxon was founded on a partial skeleton (IVP AS collection) excavated under the supervision of fossil preparator N. P. Stepanov during the summers of 1916 and 1917, from the Upper Cretaceous of Jiayin County, Heilongiang Province, Manchuria. Between 1918 and 1923 this skeleton was prepared by Stepanov, then mounted in 1924 under Riabinin's supervision at the Central Geological Museum in St. Petersburg (then Leningrad) (see *D:TE* for photograph). Riabinbin (1930) later described this material in greater detail, referring it to a new genus and species, *Mandschurosaurus amurensis* (see *D:TE*). In the same paper he acknowledged that the mounted skeleton most likely comprised the remains of several individuals. Later, Yang (1958), in a report on dinosaur remains from Laiyang, stated that this skeleton has been so much reconstructed that its real characters are difficult to observe.

Hadrosaur specialist Michael K. Brett-Surman (1979), in a revision of the Hadrosauridae, found none of the elements referred to *Mandschurosaurus amurensis* to exhibit "one single landmark or major morphological feature," and, consequently, designated this taxon to be a *nomen dubium*, an opinion later followed by Maryańska and Osmólska (1981) and then Weishampel and Horner (1990).

However, during the summer of 1977, the Heilongjiang Provincial Geologic Survey conducted reconnaissance along the south bank of the Heilongjiang River, near the town of Yulaingzi, in Jianyin County. As reported by Yang, Wei and Li (1986), in a paper until recently available only in Chinese (translation by Will Downs of the Department of Geology, Northern Arizona University, published in 2002), a joint expedition was subsequently formed by members of the Heilongiang Provincial Museum, the Geologic Survey, the Provincial Office of Culture and Education, and the Cultural Center, to conduct large-scale systematic paleontological digs in Heilongjian Province during the summers of 1978 and 1979. These excavations included two localities from three distinct stratigraphic levels more than one kilometer away from the type locality from which Riabinin collected the remains of *M. amurensis*.

As Yang *et al.* reported, more than 1,400 dinosaur bones, weighing over 10 tons, were collected by the team during those two years, most of them hadrosaurian (although tyrannosaurid, ornithomimid, ornithischian, and turtle remains were also recovered from this locality), which these authors referred to *M. amurensis* based on their close resemblances to the type material of that taxon.

Most common among the recovered elements arc tibiae, nine right and nine left, reflecting the presence of at least nine individuals. Three skeletons were eventually mounted at the Heilongiang Provincial Museum from the collected bones, including a very large mount (6.48 meters or almost 24 feet high, and 11.24 meters or almost 38 feet long) comprising about 80 percent genuine bone, including 12 cervical vertebrae, 20 dorsals, nine sacrals, and 88 caudals; and a small mount (4.17 meters or about 14 feet high, and 9.32 meters or more than 30 feet long), including a maxilla, dentary, angular, 12 cervical vertebrae, 20 dorsals, nine sacrals, 65 caudals, a pair of sternal plates, humeri, ulnae, radii, ischia, tibiae, fibulae, and most carpals and tarsals.

Based on both the type and more recently collected material, and with the assistance of paleontologists Zhao Xijin and Zhimin Dong, Yang *et al.* proposed the following appended diagnosis for *M. amurensis*: Quadrate straight; maxilla almost triangular, apex at its midpoint, 30.0 centimeters long, tooth count 25 to 44; mandible 44.1 centimeter in length, tooth count of 44 to 45; teeth prismatic with marginal denticles, replacement overlapping, crown higher laterally than medially, lateral side smooth; scapula thick, straight, with expansive terminus; ischium terminus expanded; nine sacral vertebrae, caudalmost having faint ventral groove; femur large, robust, medially constricted, fourth trochanter well developed, distal end of femur flat and broad, condyles spherical, foramen circular; rather large species.

As Yang *et al.* pointed out, the hadrosaur specimens from the Jiayin region of Heilongjiang Province are not taxononomically significant, although they are important for three reasons: 1. They supplement characters previously unknown on the holotype of this species; 2. they comprise the only mounted hadrosaur skeletons in Northeast China; and 3. "they represent a leading role among the exhibits in the Heilongjiang Provincial Museum for the propagation of science and the dispelling of superstitious beliefs."

In 2000, Godefroit *et al.* (2000) erected the new lambeosaurine genus *Charonosaurus* (see entry) to embrace more recently recovered material, Godefroit *et al.* (2000, 2001) implying that specimens previously referred to *Mandschurosaurus amurensis* might belong to the new genus. The authors also followed Brett-Surman, Maryańska and Osmólska, and Weishampel and Horner in regarding that type species as a *nomen dubium*. However, Yang *et al.*'s report, in which they revised *Mandschurosaurus* as a valid genus, was not available in English at the time those authors offered their opinions. As noted by Godefroit *et al.* (2001) senior author Pascal Godefroit was not granted permission by the Heilongjiang Provincial Museum to include its material in their study. Also, *Charonosaurus* is a lambeosaurine, while none of the previously described remains referred to *Mandschurosaurus* can be assigned positively to any hadrosaurid subfamily. Therefore, as Godefroit *et al.* (2000) based their diagnosis of *Charonosaurus* primarily upon materials described subsequent to Yang *et al.*'s publication, this document — tentatively at least, for the present — has retained both *Mandschurosaurus* and *Charonosaurus* as separate taxa.

More than a decade and a half following the original publication of Yang *et al.*'s paper, Norman and Sues (2001), in a review of various ornithopods from Kazakhstan, Mongolia, and Siberia, stated that *M. amurensis*, founded upon very poorly preserved type material, is distinguished only by its comparatively low tooth count plus generalized hadrosaurid anatomical features.

Key references: Brett-Surman (1979); Godefroit, Zan and Jin (2000, 2001); Maryańska and Osmólska (1981); Norman and Sues (2000); Riabinin (1925, 1930); Weishampel and Horner (1990); Yang (1958); Yang, Wei and Li (1986).

MASIAKASAURUS Sampson, Carrano and Forster 20001
Saurischia: Eusaurischia: Theropoda: Neotheropoda: Neocertosauria: Abelisauroidea: Noasauridae.
Name derivation: Malagasy *masiaka* = "vicious" + Greek *sauros* = "lizard."
Type species: *M. knopfleri* Sampson, Carrano and Forster 2001.
Other species: [None.]
Occurrence: Maevarano Formation, Madagascar.
Age: Late Cretaceous (Maastrichtian).
Known material: Miscellaneous skull and postcranial remains representing approximately 40 percent of the skeleton.
Holotype: UA 8680, almost complete right dentary with several teeth.

Diagnosis of genus (as for type species): Abelisauroid having mesial four dentary teeth procumbent, first inclined at 10 degrees above horizontal, lying in alveolus slung below ventral margin of dentary;

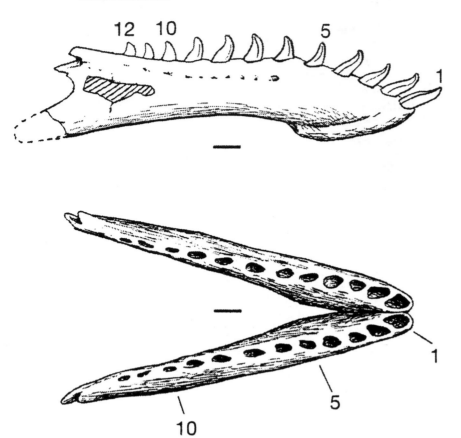

Masiakasaurus knopfleri, (top) dentary and lower dentition reconstructed with full compliment of teeth, based on holotype UA 8680, right lateral view, and (bottom) reconstructed dentary, dorsal view, illustrating relative sizes and orientations of alveoli. Scale = 10 mm. (After Sampson, Carrano and Forster 2001.)

first alveolus large, ventrally expanded lateral to mesio-distally long dentary symphysis; lower dentition markedly heterodont; first four teeth weakly spatulate, elongate, terminating in distally hooked, pointed apex; mesial dentary teeth bearing two weakly serrated distal carinae, have faint distal ridges; more distal teeth transversely compressed, recurved, distal carinae serrated (Carrano, Sampson and Forster 2002).

Comments: A bizarre genus and species of predatory dinosaur with remarkably derived jaws, and the first new dinosaur to be named and described in the year 2001, *Masiakasaurus knopfleri* was founded upon a well-preserved right dentary (UA 8680) colleted by a research team led by University of Utah paleontologist Scott D. Sampson from the Anembalemba Member of the Maevarano Formation in Mahajanga Basin, near the village of Berivortra, in northwestern Madagascar.

Referred material from the same locality, most of it recovered as isolated elements, and listed by Carrano, Sampson and Forster (2002) in a subsequent and more detailed report, include the following: (FMNH PR 2177–79, 2222; UA 8682) dentaries; (FMNH PR 2124, splenial; FMNH PR 2166) ?angular; (FMNH PR 2183) maxilla; (FMNH PR 2165, 2180, 2226) premaxillar/anterior dentary teeth; (FMNH PR 2164, 2170, 2181–82, 2198–2201, 2220–21, 2228) distal maxillary/dentary teeth; (FMNH PR 2139–41) cervical, (FMNH PR 2111, 2113–14, 2137–38, 2144–45, 2171, 2207, 2229; UA 8701) dorsal, and (FMNII PR 2142), sacral vertebrae; (FMNH PR 2133, 2204, 2230) proximal, (FMNH PR 2110, 2125–26; UA 8688, 8692) medial, and (FMNH PR 2127–28, 2156–57, 2162–63, 2168, 2202–03; UA 8689–91, 8695–96, 8702–03) distal caudal vertebrae; (FMNH PR 2143; UA 8693–94) humeri; (FMNH PR 2132, 2205, 2224–25, 2227) manual phalanges and (FMNH PR 2136, 2169) unguals; (FMNH PR 2108–09) pubes; (FMNH PR 2115, 2117, 2120, 2123, 2148–50, 2153, 2208, 2215; UA 8681, 8684, 8712), femora; (FMNH PR 2112, 2118–19, 2121, 2152, 2214; UA 8685, 8687, 8710–11), tibiae; (FMNH PR 2116, 2122), tibia with partial fibula and astragalocalcaneum; (FMNH PR 2235), calcaneum; (FMNH PR 2147, 2151, 2154, 2175, 2206; UA 8683), metatarsals II, (FMNH PR 2146, 2155) III, and (FMNH PR 2214, 2234) IV; FMNH PR 2129–31, 2136, 2158–61, 2167, 2172–74, 2176, 2216–19, 2223; UA 8686, 8700, 8713–14) pedal phalanges; and (FMNH PR 2134–35, 2236) unguals.

Carrano *et al.* noted that, despite these remains being isolated materials, the following factors suggested to the authors that they belong to a single taxon: 1. Several elements (*e.g.*, dentary, femur, tibia, metatarsal II, and pedal phalanges) are known from multiple specimens spanning a considerable range of size, the maximum size attained by each element being consistent with a single adult individual approximately 1.8 to 2.0 meters (about 6.2 to 6.8 feet) in length; 2. these elements exhibit no conflicting phylogenetic data to suggest the presence of a possible second distinct and small-bodied taxon; and 3. low dinosaurian diversity seems to be a genuine characteristic of the fauna of the Maevarano Formation.

Prior to the formal naming and describing of *M. knopfleri,* the discovery was announced in various newspapers and popular magazines, these stories capitalizing on the fact that the dinosaur's specific name was erected in honor of rock music star Mark Knopfler of the group Dire Straits, whose recordings were played while the field team dug out the "German shepherd-sized" dinosaur (about 1.8 meters or over 6 feet, including the tail, according to Sampson *et al.*).

Sampson *et al.* initially diagnosed the type species *M. knopfleri* as follows: Differing from all other known theropods in that most rostral dentary teeth are procumbent, first tooth set in large, ventrally expanded alveolus that is almost horizontally oriented; also in that lower dentition is strongly heterodont; first four teeth elongate, weakly serrated, carinae positioned labiolingually; each of these teeth terminating in pointed apex that hooks caudally; teeth becoming increasingly recurved and transversely

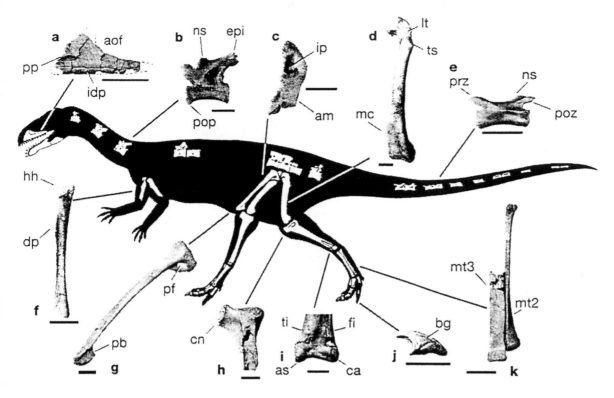

Masiakasaurus knopfleri, composite skeletal anatomy based upon various isolated specimens, including a. (FMNH PR2183) partial right maxilla, medial view, b. (FMNH PR2139) caudal cervical vertebra, left lateral view, c. (FMNH PR2108) left pubis, dorsal view, d. (FMNH PR2117) left femur, cranial view, e. (FMNH PR2126) medial caudal vertebra, left lateral view, f. (FMNH PR2143) partial right humerus, medial view, g. (FMNH PR2108) left pubis, lateral view, h. (FMNH PR2118) proximal left tibia, lateral view, i. (FMNH PR2112) left tibia/fibula/astragalocalcaneum, cranial view (dashed lines emphasizing contacts between elements), j. (FMNH PR2155) pedal ungual, lateral view, and k. (FMNH PR2129) right metatarsal II, cranial view. Scale = 1 cm. (After Sampson, Carrano and Forster 2001.)

compressed with increasing caudal position in jaw, possessing more standard, mediodistally positioned carinae.

As noted by Sampson *et al.* in that first technical report, *Masiakasaurus* is most notable for the unusual and unique derived morphology of the lower-jaw teeth. The number of dentary-tooth positions varies in the collected material from 10 to 12, with the slightly enlarged first alveolus almost horizontally oriented so that the first dentary tooth is forwardly directed. The first four dentary teeth are radially arrayed, these becoming progressively more vertical and parasagittal more distally. The overall effect of this orientation of the lower teeth is that of an underbite, this condition not known in any other carnivorous dinosaur.

Performing a cladistic analysis of *Masiakasaurus*, the authors found that the genus possesses a suite of abelisauroid synapomorphies including the following: Specialized caudal dentary margin having enlarged intramandibular fenestra; humerus with straight shaft, head enlarged and bulbous; ilium and pubis with peg-and-socket articulation; mediodistal crest of femur hypertrophied, forming thin lamina; cnemial crest of tibia large, laterally curved, dorsally elevated; grooves on pedal unguals triangularly arranged.

As Sampson *et al.* pointed out in the first report, all known abelisaurid members of the Abelosauroidea are relatively large-bodied theropods, known only from the Late Cretaceous of India, Madagascar, and Argentina, distinguished by a suite of derived features,

while noasaurid members of that clade are represented by small-bodied forms (all of them fragmentary) restricted to the Late Cretaceous of Argentina. As *Masiakasaurus* shares some derived features (*e.g.*, cranially positioned neural spines, reduced metatarsal II) with the noasaurid *Noasaurus*, the authors found it reasonable to suggest that this new genus could represent "a geographical extension of the Noasauridae outside of Argentina." However, the scarcity of material belonging to *Noasaurus* made its relationship with the form from Madagascar (as well as with other fragmentary taxa) obscure.

Subsequently, Carrano *et al.* described in detail the osteology of *Masiakasaurus knopfleri*, at the same time offering an emended diagnosis based solely on the holotype.

In that follow up publication, in which they performed a more extensive cladistic analysis, Carrano *et al.* noted that the vertebrae of *M. knopfleri* are similar to those of abelisaurids in having a reduced neural spine, in lacking pleurocoelous fossae on the centrum, and in having an extensively pneumaticized neural arch. The skeletal structure of the limbs is relatively gracile, bearing numerous abelisauroid synapomorphies (see above).

Based upon a cladistic analysis incorporating 158 characters and 23 theropod taxa, Carrano *et al.* again found *Masiakasaurus* to have a close relationship with the Argentine *Noasaurus* and Indian *Laevisuchus*, suggesting that these three genera form a clade (Noasauridae) within Abelisauroidea. *Masiakasaurus* and *Noa-*

Life restoration of *Masiakasaurus knopfleri* by Berislav Krzic.

saurus, the authors noted, share a number of synapomorphies including the following: Cervical neural spine on anterior half of centrum; metatarsal II having reduced shaft; simple maxillary palatal process; and antorbital fossa with prominent rim. In turn, *Laevisuchus* shares with abelisauroids (see Novas and Bandyopadhyay 1999) and noasaurids the following synapomorphies: Cervical neural spines anteriorly placed; and cervical epipophyses small caudally (see also "Systematics" chapter).

Two distinct morphs—"gracile" and "robust"—were observed by Carrano *et al.* among the collected samplings of *Maskiakasaurus*. The "robust" morphs, the authors noted, are distinguished by pronounced muscular and ligamentous attachments; in "gracile" specimens, these sites are less distinct. Also, the "robust" tibiae show fusion—this lacking in "gracile" specimens—with the tarsal elements. Among the recovered remains, six femora (FMNH PR 2117, 2123, 2149, 2208, and UA 8684 and 8712) and four tibiae (FMNH PR 2116, 2119, and 2122) demonstrate the "robust" morphology; seven femora (FMNH PR 2115, 2120, 2215, 2148, 2150, 2153, and UA 8681) and eight tibiae (FMNH PR 2112, 2118, 2121, 2152, 2214, and UA 8687 and 7819–11) the "gracile." As the authors

pointed out, no other elements had been sufficiently well sampled to distinguish these morphs; nor were the sample sizes sufficient to demonstrate statistically significant differences for several measured parameters, even though consistent trends were observed. Also, lacking articulated specimens, Carrano *et al.* could not empirically show that "robust" femora correspond to "robust" tibiae. The authors cautiously commented upon the significance of the two morphs, not attributing to them any sexual importance, especially given the lack of any primary or secondary sexual features in these specimens. While citing the unlikelihood of two closely related taxa living in such proximity, Carrano *et al.* stressed that their description of these morphs was "as *individual* variations" possibly representing sexual dimorphism.

Carrano *et al.* stated that "The most striking characteristics of *Masiakasaurus* are the unusually heterodont, procumbent dentition and associated anterior jaw morphology," the special morphologies of the anterior dentary teeth presently unknown among other theropod dinosaurs. However, somewhat analogous anterior tooth morphologies can be seen in certain mammals, including carpolestid primates. Given that most of the skull of *Masiakasaurus* is unknown,

Head of the theropod *Masiakasaurus knopfleri* as restored by artist Berislav Krzic.

the authors found its tooth morphology difficult to interpret. Nevertheless, "the orientation and morphology of the anterior dentary teeth suggest use in prehension — grasping small, whole prey items (such as invertebrates, small vertebrates, or even fruits) — rather than tearing or clipping parts of larger prey." The authors further noted that the distally positioned carinae on the anterior teeth "are better positioned for grasping than tearing," while "the rounded apex argues against its use in incising."

Puzzling to Carrano *et al.* was their observance that the distal dentary teeth of *Masiakasaurus* retain the more generalized morphology — *i.e.*, recurved, laterally compressed, and finely serrated — found in most other theropods. Additionally, the serrated carinae are both mesially and distally positioned, suggesting that the teeth were employed in holding, cutting, or slicing. Although the authors could not explain this combination of tooth morphology, they speculated that *Masiakasaurus* could have been "insectivorous or piscivorous using its anterior teeth for acquiring small, whole prey items and its posterior teeth for maceration."

As Carrano *et al.* pointed out, the presence of this new taxon in the Maevarano Formation is significant for three reasons: 1. It establishes the presence in this area of small-bodied, nonavian dinosaurs although of low diversity; 2. remains representing most regions of the skeleton indicate that this is a new taxon (Sampson *et al.*); and 3. this taxon apparently belongs to the Abelisauroidea, significantly expanding the morphological diversity of this group and, consequently, further strengthing the faunal connections

between the Late Cretaceous faunas of Madagascar, South America, and India. Furthermore, Sampson *et al.* noted that the Late Cretaceous radiation of North American coelurosaurs into both small-bodied forms (*e.g.*, ornithomimids, dromaeosaurids, and troodontids) and large-bodied forms (*e.g.*, tyrannosaurids) parallel that of abelisauroids in Gondwana.

Key references: Carrano, Sampson and Forster (2002); Novas and Bandyopadhyay (1999); Sampson, Carrano and Forster 2001.

†MASSOSPONDYLUS

Saurischia: Eusaurischia: Sauropodomorpha: Prosauropoda: Massospondylidae.

Diagnosis of genus (as for type species): Autapomorphies comprising the following: skull at least 10 percent wider than high; anterior base of cultriform process of parabasisphenoid process at least 20 percent of its length; only anterior surangular foramen present (Hinic 2002).

Comments: Hinic (2002), in an abstract for a poster, redescribed the skull of *Massospondylus carinatus*, noting that a revision of the cranial anatomy of this type species "is an essential prerequisite for determining which anatomical features are diagnostic for the species."

According to Hinic, the description of the skull and mandible of this taxon emphasizes the importance of the following characters: Nasal overhanging antorbital cavity; maxilla contributing to palatine in ventral aspect of skull; triangular fossa of lacrimal; number of surangular foramina; relative width of skull; relative width of base of cultriform process of parabasisphenoid.

Based on a redescription of the cranial anatomy of *Massospondylus*, Hinic found new data useful in testing the monophyly of the Prosauropoda, and also independently to evaluate previous hypotheses on the evolutionary relationships within the Prosauropoda and Sauropoda (see "Systematics" chapter).

Key reference: Hinic (2002).

†MEGALOSAURUS [*nomen dubium*]

Saurischia: Eusaurischia: Theropoda: Neotheropoda: Tetanurae: Avetheropoda: Spinosauroidea: Megalosauridae: Megalosaurinae.

Comment: In their paper on *Poekilopleuron* (see entry), Allain and Chure (2002) briefly reviewed the genus *Megalosaurus*, at the same time stressing the need for a thorough revision of this taxon, which was "beyond the scope" of their present study.

As these authors pointed out, numerous fossil bones have, over the years, been referred to the type species, *Megalosaurus bucklandii* (see *D:TE*), although all of these elements are of uncertain relationship to the lectotype (see, for example, Molnar, Kurzanov and Dong 1990) rostral portion of a lower right jaw with teeth (OUM-J13506) (see, for example, Buckland 1824 [the first formal description of *Megalosaurus*]; Cuvier 1824; Owen 1846). Moreover, Allain

and Chure pointed out that different kinds of large theropods have been found within a single quarry, the authors citing such medium-sized to gigantic sympatric Upper Jurassic Morrison Formation forms as *Allosaurus*, *Ceratosaurus*, *Elaphrosaurus*, *Marshosaurus*, *Stokesosaurus*, and *Torvosaurus*.

Examination by Allain and Chure of OUM-J13506 found no diagnostic features (see Molnar, Kurzanov and Dong; Benton and Spencer 1995; Rauhut 2000*b*). Therefore, these authors considered "the genoholotypic specimen of *Megalosaurus bucklandii* a *nomen dubium* and [recommended] that the name *Megalosaurus* be restricted to the dentary (OUMJ13506), pending thorough taxonomic revision in progress by L. Canning, P. M. Barett and P. Powell."

Notes: From an historical perspective, Delair and Sarjeant (2002) recounted in detail the early discoveries and namings of English dinosaurs, their report focusing upon bones now believed to belong to *Megalosaurus*, yet found long before this genus was formally named and described by William Buckland in 1824.

As Delair and Sarjeant related, the first authenticated discovery of a dinosaur bone comprised the distal articular condyle and partial shaft of a femur probably belonging to *Megalosaurus*. This specimen, collected no later than 1677 from a quarry in the parish of Cornwell and probably of Middle Jurassic

Megalosaurus bucklandii, cast of lectotype partial right dentary.

Photograph by the author, courtesy The Academy of Natural Sciences of Philadelphia.

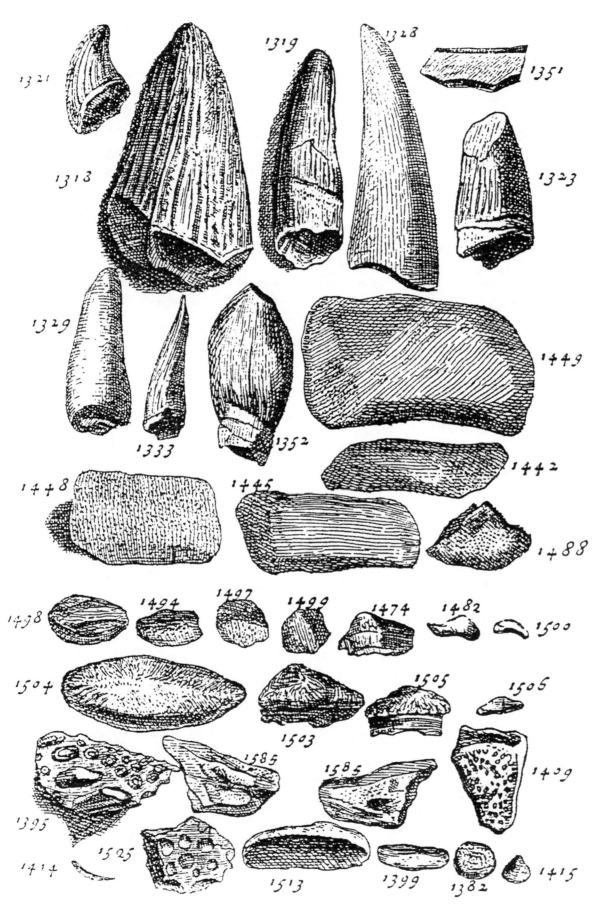

Megalosaurus

Fossils described during the late 17th century by Edward Lhuyd as "Imitations of Fish Teeth." Specimen number 1328 may belong to *Megalosaurus* and number 1352 is that of a sauropod named *Rutellum implicatum*.

(late Bajocian–Bathonian) age, came into the possession of Sir Thomas Pennyston, most likely the owner of the quarry or land.

Pennyston subsequently presented the specimen to Robert Plot, the first keeper of the Ashmolean Museum at Oxford University, Plot describing and illustrating it in his *Natural History of Oxfordshire* (1677). Naturalist Richard Brookes reillustrated the bone in 1750, naming it, because of its shape, *Scrotum humanum* (see *D:TE*), which, postdating the establishment of Linnaean nomenclature, "could be claimed as the earliest validly published generic and specific name for a dinosaur" (see Halstead 1970), thereby potentially constituting a senior synonym of *Megalosaurus*. Consequently, L. Beverly Halstead and William A. S. Sarjeant formally requested the International Zoological Commission for Zoological Nomenclature to suppress that older name as a *nomen oblitum*.

However, the ICZN had, by then, deleted the *nomen oblitum* clause from the International Code of Zoological Nomenclature. Furthermore, the ICZN responded that, as it could not be demonstrated unequivocally that this specimen belonged to *Megalosaurus* and because Brookes' name was probably intended to be merely descriptive, the name *Scrotum humanum* was simply a *nomen dubium* not requiring such action (see Halstead and Sarjeant 1993).

(Note: Numerous other *nomina dubia*—e.g., *Megalosaurus*, *Antrodemus*, *Astrodon*, etc.—have been given their own entries in this series of volumes and, for that reason, the present writer considered awarding *Scrotum* that status in this book. However, given that *S. humanum* "could be claimed" for the earliest published dinosaur taxon, that this taxon was probably published only for "descriptive" purposes, and that the name appeared almost a century before the concept of a dinosaur was understood, the author has opted not to give the name its own entry.)

As Halstead and Sarjeant recounted, Brookes' appelation for the specimen was taken literally by Jean-Baptiste Robinet, the French philosopher who had proposed "a bizarre early theory of the transmutation of species," interpreting the fossil bone as the petrified scrotum of a giant human being.

Delair and Sarjeant went on to discuss other seventeenth and eighteenth century dinosaur finds. These included a tooth (specimen number 1328) figured by Welsh naturalist Edward Lhuyd (1699) that could relate to *Megalosaurus*, the latter illustrating a probable *Megalosaurus* tooth as well as other fossils (see below) interpreted by him as "Imitations of fish Teeth."

Of special note among this early recovered material is the broken shank of a dinosaur limb bone (specimen A1), collected at Stonesfield, in Oxfordshire, England. The specimen was one of many included by John Woodward of Gresham College, London, in his catalogue of British fossils published shortly after Woodward's death in 1728. As Delair and Sarjeant noted, this specimen, if complete, would have closely resembled the hind limb bone of a theropod like *Megalosaurus*. Housed in the Woodwardian Collection in the Sedgwick Museum, Cambridge University, this specimen is distinguished as "the earliest-discovered dinosaur bone that can still be identified with confidence" (see Delair and Sarjeant 1975; see Delair and Sarjeant 2002 for more detailed information on these early discoveries).

In conclusion, Delair and Sarjeant (2002) noted that *Megalosaurus* is almost certainly the earliest dinosaur to be discovered and that William Buckland was the first scientist to name and describe a dinosaur properly. Moreover, the majority of these early discoveries, from the tooth illustrated by Lhuyd and beyond, predating Buckland's description of *Megalosaurus* in 1824, were made at Stonesfield (probably from the Stonesfield Slate, Bathonian) with virtually all of these finds representing megalosaurs of about the same size. Furthermore, the larger assemblages of bones acquired by Buckland in or earlier than 1818 suggest a comparably-sized animal. The authors further pointed out that all of these bones were discovered "during the extraction of stone from closely spaced adits" rather than from an open pit. Finding improbable (though not impossible) the occurrence at a single locality of bones representing a number of similar-sized megalosaurs, Delair and Sarjeant (2002) suggested that most or all of this material "were the scattered remains of a single individual, coming to light sporadically over a period of several decades."

Among the teeth illustrated by Lhuyd was a specimen which he named *Rutellum implicatum*. As observed by Delair and Sarjeant, this "more laterally and blunter" specimen (number 1352) is surely that of a cetiosaur, thereby representing "the earliest record of any part of a sauropod skeleton." As noted by Gunther (1945), this specimen was collected from Caswell, near Whitney, in Oxfordshire.

Erratum: In 1832, Meyer introduced *Megalosaurus bucklandi* (with one "i") into the literature, a misspelling that has been perpetuated by myriad subsequent authors. Indeed, that misspelling also appeared in *D:TE* and *SI*.

Key references: Allain and Chure (2002); Benton and Spencer (1995); Buckland (1824); Cuvier (1824); Delair and Sarjeant (1975, 2002); Gunther (1945); Halstead (1970); Halstead and Sarjeant (1993); Lhuyd (1699); Meyer (1832); Molnar (1990); Molnar, Kurzanov and Dong (1990); Owen (1846); Rauhut (2000*b*).

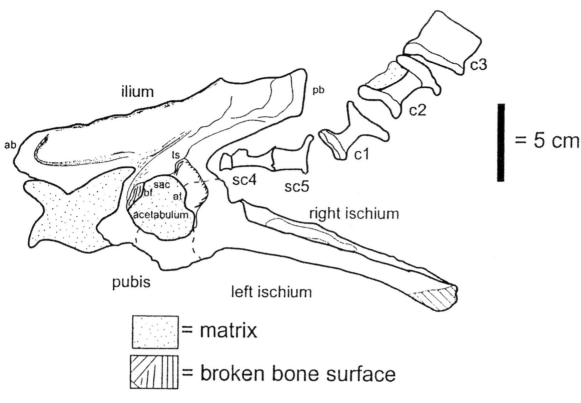

MNA V2588, pelvic region from the Moenave Formation referred to *Megapnosaurus* (=*Syntarsus* of their usage) sp. (After Lucas and Heckert 2001.)

= matrix

= broken bone surface

†MEGAPNOSAURUS—(=*Syntarsus* Raath 1969; =?*Coelophysis*)

Saurischia: Eusaurischia: Theropoda: Neotheropoda: Coelophysoidea: Coelophysidae.

Name derivation: Greek *megas* = "large" + Greek *apnoos* = "dead" + Greek *sauros* = "lizard."

Type species: *M. rhodesiensis* (Raath 1969).

Other species: *M. kayentakatae* (Rowe 1989).

Comments: In 2001, entomologists Ivie, Slipinski and Wegrzynowicz pointed out that the name *Syntarsus* is preoccupied by a beetle, *Syntarsus* Fairmaire 1869 (Coleoptera: Zopheridae Colydiinae). The authors mused that the new name was chosen because "at the scale of an entomologist, it looks like a big dead lizard," and that it may be "the first name for a dinosaur ever proposed in an entomological journal."

Lucas and Heckert (2001) described two incomplete pelvic regions (MNA V2588 and V1968; specimens previously discussed in an abstract by Morales 1994) collected from the Thybony site on Ward Terrace, in the Dinosaur Canyon Member of the Moenave Formation (stratigraphically the lowest unit in the Glen Canyon Group), near Cameron, Arizona. The better preserved specimen, MNA V2588, comprises a left ilium, incomplete left pubis, almost complete ischia, and five incomplete caudal centra; MNA V1968 consists of an almost complete right ilium, the proximal portion of a right pubis, the proximal end of a right femur, an incomplete, distorted right ischium, a fragment of the probable distal ends of both ischia, and several ribs or gastralia.

Lucas and Heckert referred these specimens to the "Ceratosauria" (see "Systematics" chapter) based upon a single synapomorphy (see Gauthier 1986), a relatively wide brevis shelf of the ilium. The lack of a large ischial boot in these specimens eliminate them from the "ceratosaurian" group Neoceratosauria (*e.g.*, Novas 1991). Because these pelves conformed to descriptions of *Megapnosaurus* [=*Syntarsus* of their usage] *rhodesiensis* (Raath 1977) and *S. kayentakatae* (Tykoski 1998), the authors referred them to *Megapnosaurus* ["*Syntarsus*"] sp.

Close to the Triassic–Jurassic boundary, the Moenave Formation had been dated in the past as

MNA V1968, pelvic region from the Moenave Formation referred to *Megapnosaurus* (=*Syntarsus* of their usage) sp. (After Lucas and Heckert 2001.)

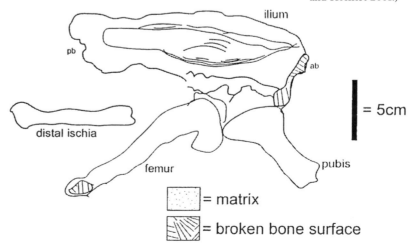

= matrix

= broken bone surface

either of Late Triassic or Early Jurassic age. However, based upon the presence of various Early Jurassic palynoflora, fossil dinosaur and crocodylomorph footprints, fishes, and mostly tetrapods, especially the crocodylomorph *Protosuchus*, Lucas and Heckert dated this formation as entirely of Early Jurassic (Hettangian) age.

Key references: Gauthier (1986); Ivie, Slipinski and Wegrzynowicz (2001); Lucas and Heckert (2001); Morales (1994); Novas (1991); Raath (1969, 1977); Rowe (1989); Tykoski (1998).

†**MICROCERATOPS**   Bohlin 1953 [*nomen dubium*]
Ornithischia: Genasauria: Cerapoda: Marginocephalia: Ceratopsia: Neoceratopsia.
Type species: *M. gobiensis* Bohlin 1953 [*nomen dubium*].
Other species: *M. sulcidens* Bohlin 1953 [*nomen dubium*].

Diagnosis of genus: [No modern diagnosis published.]

Comments: As chronicled by Paul C. Sereno (2000) in a detailed review of the marginocephalians of Asia, Birger Bohlin, in 1953, erected the new genus and species *Microceratop gobiensis* based on fragmentary remains collected from two localities in different horizons on uncertain ages (see Dong and Azuma 1997) in Gansu Province, China (see *D:TE*). (According to Dong Zhi-Ming, personal communication to Sereno, the holotype dentary of *M. gobiensis* does not possess any complete crowns and seems to be lost.) At the same time, Birger referred a second species to the genus, *M. sulcidens*, founded upon two isolated teeth, some vertebrae, and elements of the manus and pes representing a relatively small individual. Dodson and Currie (1990), in their review of the Neoceratopsia, regarded this species as a junior synonym of *M. gobiensis* but, Sereno pointed out, without giving reasons to support this synonymy. As the holotypes of these species exhibit no diagnostic features, Sereno regarded both of them as *nomina dubia*.

In a recent reassessment of the Neoceratopsia, Makovicky (2001) found *Microceratops* to be the sister taxon to Coronosauria, these two taxa forming a clade diagnosed by three characters — fenestrated frill, divergent temporal bars, and squamosal with postquadratic process (see "Systematics" chapter).

Note: The skeleton referred by Maryańska and Osmólska (1975) to *Microceratops gobiensis* was referred by Sereno to the new genus *Graciliceratops* (see entries, *S2* and this volume).

Key references: Bohlin (1953); Dong and Azuma (1997); Makovicky (2001); Maryańska and Osmólska (1975); Sereno (2000).

†**MICROPACHYCEPHALOSAURUS**   Dong 1978 [*nomen dubium*]
Ornithischia: Genasauria: Cerapoda: Marginocephalia: ?Pachycephalosauria *incertae sedis*.
Type species: *P. hongtuyanensis* Dong 1978 [*nomen dubium*].

Comment: As recounted by Sereno (2000), Dong Zhiming (1978) erected the new genus and species *Micropachycephalosaurus hongtuyanensis* upon "fragmentary postcrania of discordant size." Dong referred this taxon to the Pachycephalosauria (see *D:TE*), an assessment later accepted by Maryańska (1990) in her review of that group. As pointed out by Sereno, however, the material exhibits no pachycephalosaurian features or autapomorphies, and this taxon should be regarded as a *nomen dubium*.

Key references: Dong (1978); Maryańska (1990); Sereno (2000).

†**MICRORAPTOR**
Saurischia: Eusaurischia: Theropoda: Neotheropoda: Tetanurae: Avetheropoda: Coelurosauria: Maniraptoriformes: Maniraptora: Metornithes: Paraves: Deinonychosauria: Dromaeosauridae *incertae sedis*.
New species: *M. gui* Xu, Zhou, Wang, Kuwang, Zhang and Du 2003.
Occurrence of *M. gui*: Jiufotang Formation, Dapingfang, Liaoning Province, China.
Age of *M. gui*: Early Cretaceous.
Known material of *M. gui*: Three incomplete skeletons with feather impressions.
Holotype of *M. gui*: IVPP V13352, almost complete skeleton with feather impressions.

Diagnosis of *M. gui*: Differing from *M. zhaoianus* in having prominent biceps tuberocity on radius, much shorter manual digit I, strongly curved pubis, bowed tibia (Xu, Zhou, Wang, Kuwang, Zhang and Du 2003).

Comments: Two new specimens of the Chinese type species *Microraptor zhaoianus*— distinguished as both an important taxon regarding insights into the origins of birds (see below) and also the smallest known nonavian theropod (see *D:TE*)—have been described by Hwang, Norell, Qiang and Gao (2002), these specimens exhibiting details not preserved in the holotype (IVPP V12330).

As reported by Hwang *et al.*, these new specimens (CAGS 20-7-004 and CAGS 20-8-001) were collected by farmers from Qianyang, a village southwest of the city of Yixian in Liaoning Province.

CAGS 20-7-004, the authors stated, is preserved on a single slab with several counterpart pieces also preserved. The specimen is partially articulated, although some elements (*e.g.*, the lower jaws) lay close to the

Microraptor zhaoianus, referred skeleton (CAGS 20-7-004), view of entire mounted slab. (After Hwang, Norell, Qiang and Gao 2002.)

edge of the slab. Regrettably, this specimen had been "poorly prepared and covered with low grade shellac" prior to its acquisition by the Chinese Academy of Geological Sciences, where this material was subsequently housed.

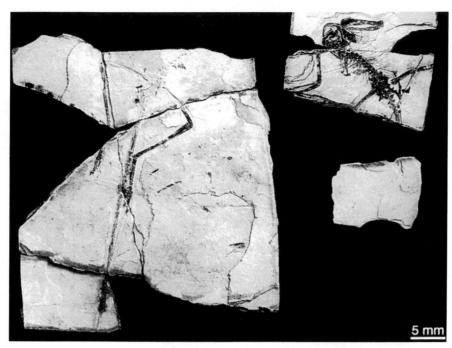

Microraptor zhaoianus, referred skeleton (CAGS 20-8-001), view of all slabs and counterpart elements. (After Hwang, Norell, Qiang and Gao 2002.)

CAGS 20-8-001, while a better preserved specimen than CAGS 20-7-004 and one that is almost completely articulated, is missing much of the skeleton. The specimen consists of seven slabs. As not all of these slabs have been split along the same planes, the dorsal surfaces of the pectoral girdle, forelimbs, trunk, pelvis, proximal femora, and proximal caudal vertebrae are exposed, as are the ventral surfaces of the distal femora, tibiae, fibulae, pes, and distal caudal vertebrae. The counterslab only reveals the midsection of the body.

Hwang *et al.* referred with confidence these specimens to *M. zhaoianus* based upon the following diagnostic characters: Teeth serrated only on distal carinae, consticted between crown and root; midcaudal vertebrae long, three to four times length of proximodorsal vertebrae (see Xu, Zhou and Wang 2000); CAGS 20-7-004 also having large, strongly recurved pedal unguals with large tubercles (this feature, considered diagnostic of *M. zhaoianus* by Xu *et al.*, also found in all dromaeosaurs where such features are adequately preserved); CAGS 20-8-001 exhibiting cranial accessory crest just distal to lesser trochanter on femur; both new specimens having long midcaudal vertebrae (see Xu *et al.*).

Xu *et al.*, in their original description of *Microraptor*, had cited a number of significant morphological details suggesting the avian affinities of this dinosaur, these including the following: Teeth waisted, with loss of serrations; ischium platelike, with caudal process and distal obturator process; and enlarged sacral vertebrae. As Hwang *et al.* also noted, a number of morphological details preserved in CAGS 20-

Microraptor gui, IVPP V13352, holotype skeleton. Scale = 5 cm. (After Xu, Zhou, Wang, Kuwang, Zhang and Du 2003.)

7-004 and CAGS 20-8-001 but not the holotype further indicate such affinities, these including the following: Sharply bent scapulocoracoid; laterally facing glenoid; humerus longer than scapula; sternum articulating with coracoid cranially; free uncinate processes; and reduced antiliac shelf.

According to Hwang *et al.*, the newly described *Microraptor* specimens confirm some of the troodontid affinities previously noted by Xu *et al.* (*e.g.*, waisted posterior teeth having serration only on posterior carinae; robust metatarsal IV; laterally compressed metatarsal II). The genus is particularly similar morphologically to *Sinovenator*, the most basal known troodontid, both taxa displaying the following features: Maxillary and dentary teeth entirely unserrated (see Xu, Norell, Wang, Makovicky and Wu 2002); teeth slightly inset medially; denticles relatively the same size; no pneumatic foramina on dorsal centra; scapulocoracoids L-shaped, glenoids facing laterally; pelves opisthopubic; ischia with distally located obturator and caudal processes; and partially arctometatarsalian feet. As Hwang *et al.* noted, the above similarities corroborate the conclusion of Xu *et al.* that *Microraptor* is the most basal of all known dromaeosaurids, the large number of similarities between this genus and *Sinovenator*, therefore, not being surprising. Furthermore, as both *Microraptor* and *Sinovenator* occupy the most basal positions of their respective clades, these taxa are most likely quite close to the basal split of the Deinonychosauria, thereby retaining many plesiomorphic characters.

Comparing *Microraptor* with other members of the Dromaeosauridae, Hwang *et al.* noted that this genus differs from other members of that family in vertebral features, the presacral vertebrae being quite unusual. To date, the carotid processes present on a cervical vertebra are unique among dromaeosaurids. The elongated dorsal centra resemble more closely those of the birds *Archaeopteryx* and *Rahonavis* than the "blocky" centra seen in other dromaeosaurids. Another unusual feature of *Microraptor* is that the dorsal vertebrae lack pneumatic formina (most tetanurans having such foramina on the centra of the axis, cervical and most proximal dorsal vertebrae).

Phylogenetic analyses by Hwang *et al.* resulted in the following conclusions: 1. *Microraptor* is the sister taxon to other dromaeosaurs; 2. Deinonychosauria is a monophyletic taxon and the sister group to Avialae (see Gauthier 1986); 3. small size is plesiomorphic at the node of Deinonychosauria plus Avialae (Paraves); and 4. including "*Microraptor* in the Theropod Working Group Matrix results in the loss of a pes with a slender, laterally compressed metatarsal II and a robust metatarsal IV as a troodontid apomorphy."

A second species of *Microraptor* has recently been described. This new species, *Microraptor gui*, was founded upon two nearly complete skeletons, the holotype IVPP V13352 and a referred specimen IVPP V13320, collected from the Early Cretaceous Jiufotang Formation, Jehol Group, of Dapingfang, Chaoyang County, southwest of Chaoyang City, in western Liaoning Province, China. The specimens were recovered by the Liaoxi team of the Institute of Vertebrate Paleontology and Paleoanthropology during field seasons of 2002 and 2002 (Xu, Zhou, Wang, Kuwang, Zhang and Du 2003).

To test the authenticity of the holotype, in lieu of recent forgeries involving feathered specimens, Xu *et al.* (2003) carefully examined both IVPP V13352 and V13320 under the microscope, utilizing high-resolution X-ray computerized tomography (CT).

In describing this species, Xu *et al.* (2003) noted that *M. gui* is a small theropod, the holotype measuring about 77 centimeters long. The trunk is relatively short (as in the basal troodontid *Sinovenator* and the basal oviraptorosaur *Caudipteryx*), being from 44 to 50 percent the length of the hindlimb. Although long, the tail has comparatively few vertebrae (approximately 26). The middle and distal caudal vertebrae are elongate, as in other basal dromaeosaurids, basal troodontids, and in the bird *Archaeopteryx*. The sternum differs from that of other known dromaeosaurids, where two unfused sternal plates are present, in being a single, flat, large bone. The fused scapula and coracoid resemble those of *Microraptor zhaoianus*, the type species, and of *Sinornithosaurus* in various features (scapula shorter than humerus; glenoid fossal facing laterally; angle between scapula and

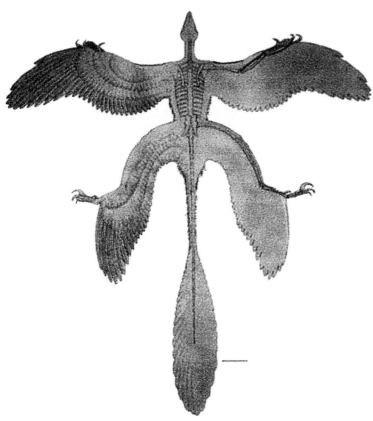

Life restoration of *Microraptor gui* showing the morphology and distribution of feathers. Scale = 6 cm. (After Xu, Zhou, Wang, Kuwang, Zhang and Du 2003.)

coracoid less than 90 degrees; coracoid with large supracoracoid). The pelvis exhibits several derived features as found in *M. zhaoianus*, *Sinornithosaurus*, *Sinovenator*, and basal birds (tapered postacetabular process of ilium; retroverted pubis; ischium short, with distally located obturator process and two dorsal processes). The pes resembles that of the type species in displaying the sub-arctometatarsalian condition of slender, strongly curved claws.

Xu *et al.* (2003) identified *M. gui* as a dromaeosaurid based upon the following derived characters: Prezygapophyses and chevrons extremely elongate; manual phalanges III-1 significantly longer than III-2; pedal digit II specialized; and metatarsal V long.

The authors referred this species to *Microraptor* based on the following features: Metacarpal III subequal in length to II; manual phalanx III-2 extremely short, less than one-quarter length of manual III-1; manual III-3 extremely slender, shorter in length than III-1; and small distal articulation of manual digit III-3 skewed ventrally.

As noted by Xu *et al.* (2003), the preserved integument exhibits two types — plumulaceous and pennaceous feathers. In their complete description of these structures, the authors observed that plumulaceous feathers, measuring from 25 to 30 millimeters in length, cover the body, those attached to the skull

roof being up to 40 millimeters long (in IVPP V13352). Some feathers on the head show well-organized pennaceous vanes, these feathers probably having a functional relationship to display, as in some modern birds. Large pennaceous feather are preserved attached to the distal part of the tail, the forelimb, and hindlimb. Remiges are preserved in a pattern resembling that found in modern birds.

Noteworthy, the authors pointed out, are the few relatively small feathers preserved attached to the manual digits of IVPP V13352, these displaying well-organized pennaceous vanes, possibly representing the precursor to the alula, a spurious wing associated with flight control in most birds excluding *Archaeopteryx* and *Confuciusornis*.

Unusual, however, are the remexlike feathers preserved along the hindlimbs, these feathers being arranged in a pattern similar to the arm feathers. At least 14 large pennaceous feathers are attached to the metatarsus, these differing from the primary feathers in being more or less perpendicular to the metatarsus. Pennaceous feathers are found on the tibia, these apparently shorter than those on the metatarsus. Feathers are also present beginning with the 15th to 18th caudal vertebra, continuing to the end of the tail.

According to Xu *et al.* (2003), the most unusual feature of these specimens is the attachment of pennaceous feathers to the entire length of the metatarsus. As this feature was observed by the authors in both recovered specimens of *M gui*, and also in four other specimens (TNP00996, IVPP V13351, and IVPP V13476, all identified as *Microraptor* sp., and IVPP V13477, an inderminate dromaeosaurid genus and species), they exluded the possibility that they might, in fact, be artifacts of preservation. Pennaceous feathers are also associated with the femur and tibia, with asymmetrical vanes. The leg feathers in this species, the authors noted, are generally "arranged in a pattern similar to wing feathers in modern birds, suggesting the presence of a hindlimb wing," this interpretation concordant with various early hypotheses (*e.g.*, Heilmann 1926) suggesting a tetrateryx, or four-wing stage in the evolution of birds.

The discovery of *Microraptor gui* reveals salient, previously unknown features about dromaeosaurs — *i.e.*, asymmetrical forelimb, hindlimb, and tail feathers, asymmetrical pennaceous feathers having been suggested to possess the aerodynamic function required for flight. "The forelimb and the leg feathers would make a perfect aerofoil together, analogous to the patagium in bats or gliding animals," these features collectively suggesting to Xu *et al.* (2003) "that basal dromaeosaurids probably could glide, representing an intermediate stage between the flightless nonavian theropods and the volant avialans." Consequently, some nonavian theropods seem to have evolved large, highly specialized pennaceous leg feathers for aerodynamic function, these features being later reduced and lost in birds that depend entirely on their forewings to fly.

According to Xu *et al.* (2003), the metatarsus feathers of *M gui* are consistent with hypotheses that basal dromaeosaurs were cursorial animals and that flight evolved from the ground up (see "Introduction," section on birds and dinosaurs). As the authors pointed out, such long feathers attached to the feet would prove a hindrance for a small, cursorial animal. Based in part upon the new information from the preserved integument, Xu *et al.* (2003) concluded "that basal dromaeosaurs were arboreal animals, and that the ancestor of birds first learned to fly by taking advantage of gravity before flapping flight was acquired in birds" (*e.g.*, Chattergee 1997).

Interestingly, the discovery of *Microraptor gui* conforms to early speculations of a "proavis" (see, for example, Heilmann) a feathered gliding animal intermediate between reptiles and birds.

Key references: Chattergee (1997); Gauthier (1986); Heilmann (1926); Hwang, Norell, Qiang and Gao (2002); Xu, Norell, Wang, Makovicky and Wu (2002); Xu, Zhou and Wang (2000); Xu, Zhou, Wang, Kuwang, Zhang and Du (2003).

†MINMI

Ornithischia: Genasaura: Thyreophora: Eurypoda: Ankylosauromorpha: Ankylosauria.

Known material: Three specimens.

Holotype: QM F10329, partial postcranial skeleton with armor.

Comments: Relatively few members of the Ankylosauria are represented by skeletons preserving armor *in situ* as it was arranged in the living animals, among these being *Minmi*, a small ankylosaur from the Early Cretaceous of Australia, named and described by Ralph E. Molnar in 1980 (see *D:TE*). In 1996, Molnar briefly described an almost complete, largely articulated specimen (QM F10329; see *SI*; also see *D:TE* for photograph) of *Minmi* collected by the Queensland Museum from marine rocks of the Allaru Mudstone (Albian), south of the Flanders River in north-central Queensland. Molnar (1996) referred this specimen to *Minmi* sp. (see *D:TE, SI*).

More recently, Molnar (2001c) reported that another specimen (QM F33286)—partly disarticulated and to date undescribed—had been collected from the Allaru Formation of north-central Queensland, this one showing patches of ossicles of what seems to be undisturbed belly armor. This new specimen and also the holotype (QM F10329), that author noted, also contribute to what is now known of the disposition of armor in *Minmi*.

In describing in detail the armor of this genus, Molnar (2001c) divided it into three kinds of elements—"ossicles, small eliptical keeled scutes (trunk), large elliptical keeled scutes (neck, shoulders, and possibly tail), large keeled scutes bearing a sharp apex or spike (hips), rhomboid keeled scutes, elongate ridged scutes, and (probably) triangular plates (all three on the tail)."

As observed by Molnar (2001b), the armor on *Minmi* is distributed as follows: Comparatively large scutes arranged on neck (possibly forming incomplete ring) behind head, and at base of neck and shoulders; small scutes of trunk, at least medially, arranged in parasaittal rows, intervening regions being occupied by pavement of small, probably closely fitting together (like tiles) ossicles; strongly keeled scutes, each with caudally directed spike, making up short row posterolateral to back portion of ilium; ossicles on limbs; modest-sized scutes on proximal (stylopodium) and middle (zuegopodium) segments; caudal armor arrangement unclear, no evidence for tail club; also, no large cranial armor plates coalescing with cranial bones (as in other ankylosaurs).

Carpenter (2001b), in performing a cladistic analysis of the Ankylosauria, found *Minmi* to be more derived than the ankylosauromorph *Scelidosaurus* and the closest sister taxon to the ankylosaurian family Nodosauridae. This genus, Carpenter stated, "represents a primitive ankylosaur or an ankylosaur that has secondarily lost numerous more derived ankylosaur characters."

In 2000, Molnar and Clifford originally described in detail a cololite—consisting of plant material, such as fragments of fibrous or vascular tissues—found in QM F18101. The authors followed that original report with another, published in 2001. According the Molnar and Clifford (2001), this discovery confirms that ankylosaurs were herbivorous animals.

Molnar and Clifford (2001) stated that the presence in these gut contents "of several fruiting bodies suggests that they were consumed deliberately and thus implies that *Minmi* may have played a role in dispersal of their parent plant." As no gastroliths were found with the specimen, breaks in the plants do not seem to have been torn by the grinding of such stones. Furthermore, the breaks of the fibrous pieces indicate that the fragments were cut from the plants, presumably by this dinosaur's teeth or beak. As some ankylosaurian specimens show tooth wear suggesting that tooth-to-tooth contact took place during the cutting of the pieces, pulverizing the food may have occurred in the mouth, the food retained there by cheeks.

Comparing this cololite with the gut contents of living tetrapods, including various lizards (*e.g.*, agamids) and birds (*e.g.*, geese and emus), Molnar and Clifford (2001) found that the comminution of vegetable matter "is significantly greater in *Minmi* than in at least some modern lizards," demonstrating that ankylosaurs processed their food in a fashion more like modern birds; moreover, "ankylosaurs effectively and uniformly reduced the plant material taken in to a degree that has not been surpassed among the modern birds here examined."

Key references: Carpenter (2001*c*); Molnar (1980, 1996, 2001*c*); Molnar and Clifford (2000, 2001).

†MONGOLOSAURUS [*nomen dubium*]

Saurischia: Eusaurischia: Sauropodomorpha: Sauropoda: Eusauropoda: Neosauropoda *incertae sedis*.
Age: Early to Middle Cretaceous (Barremian–Albian).

Comments: In a report describing new titanosauriform material from Japan (see "Introduction," section on sauropods), Barrett, Hasegawa, Manabe, Isaji and Matsuoka (2002) reassessed the Mongolian genus *Mongolosaurus* [*nomen dubium*], which was founded on teeth and very incomplete postcranial remains (see *D:TE*).

According to Barrett *et al.*, the presence of peg-like teeth in the type specimen of the type species *Mongolosaurus haplodon* supports the referral of this taxon to the Neosauropoda, as do various characters of the cervical vertebrae (*e.g.*, caudodorsally inclined neural spine, large pleurocoel subdivided by accessory oblique lamina). Lacking any apparent unambiguous autapomorphic features, Barrett *et al.* considered *M. haplodon* to be a *nomen dubium*, "Neosauropoda indeterminate."

Key reference: Barrett, Hasegawa, Manabe, Isaji and Matsuoka (2002).

†MONOCLONIUS

Ornithischia: Genasauria: Cerapoda: Marginocephalia: Ceratopsia: Neoceratopsia: Coronosauria: Ceratopsoidea: Ceratopsidae: Centrosaurinae.

Comment: The genus *Monoclonius* was regarded by Sampson, Ryan and Tanke (1997) as a *nomen dubium* (see also Ryan, Russell, Eberth and Currie 2001), interpreted by these authors as an indeterminate immature taxon (see *Centrosaurus* entry; see also Dodson and Tumarkin 1998 for a contrary assessment).

Note: In the forthcoming revised edition of *The Dinosauria*, Dodson, Forster and Sampson will list *Monoclonius* as a provisionally valid genus (P. Dodson, personal communication 2003).

Key references: Dodson and Tumarkin (1998); Ryan, Russell, Eberth and Currie (2001); Sampson, Ryan and Tanke (1997).

†MONTANOCERATOPS

Ornithischia: Genasauria: Cerapoda: Marginocephalia: Ceratopsia: Neoceratopsia: Leptoceratopsidae.

Comments: Makovicky (2001) described in detail an isolated, well-preserved but partial braincase (AMNH 5244) collected in 1910 by the American Museum of Natural History from the Horseshoe Canyon Formation, on the east bank of the Red Deer River, in southern Alberta, Canada. The specimen, Makovicky noted, preserves the supraoccipital, both opisthotic-exoccipitals, the basioccipital, basisphenoid, both laterosphenoids, and parts of the fused parietals.

Makovicky observed that AMNH 5244 lacks such ceratopsid synapomorphies as the following: Reduction of number of hypoglossal exits from three to two; fusion of laterosphenoids dorsal to brain cavity; and very deep paroccipital processes. It shares, however, a number of braincase characters—*e.g.*, vertical supraoccipital, deep notch between base of each basipterygoid and body of basisphenoid, caudally everted basioccipital tubera (a unique feature among ceratopsians)—with two other North American non-ceratopsid neoceratopsians, *Montanoceratops cerorhynchus* and *Leptoceratops gracilis*. However, other characters—*e.g.*, midline depression on supraoccipital, narrow notch rather than tab separating basioccipital tubera—separate AMNH 5244 from *L. gracilis*, permitting its referral to *M. cerorhynchus*.

Incorporating AMNH 5244 and new information based upon Makovicky's reidentification of parts of the holotype (AMNH 5464) skeleton of *M. cerorhynchus*, that author performed a preliminary phylogenetic analysis of basal neoceratopsian relationships. Contrary to recent phylogenetic analyses that have placed *Montanoceratops cerorhynchus* and *Leptoceratops gracilis* at very different positions within Ceratopsia, with *Montanoceratops* a sister taxon to the Ceratopsidae, Makovicky's analysis positioned *M. cerorhynchus* as the sister taxon to a *L. gracilis-Udanoceratops tschizhovi*, this new clade given the family name of Leptoceratopsidae (see "Systematics" chapter).

The Horseshoe Canyon Formation, Makovicky noted, is temporally equivalent to the St. Mary River Formation of southernmost Alberta (Eberth 1997*a*) and northern Montana (Ryan and Currie 1998), the latter area having yielded the holotype and referred specimens of *M. cerorhynchus*. AMNH 5244, therefore, extends the paleogeographic range of this species.

Key reference: Makovicky (2001).

NEIMONGOSAURUS Zhang, Xu, Zhao, Sereno, Kuang and Tan 2001

Saurischia: Eusaurischia: Theropoda: Neotheropoda: Tetanurae: Avetheropoda: Coelurosauria: Maniraptoriformes: Maniraptora: Metornithes: Therizinosauroidea.

Name derivation: "Nei Mongol [general location of discovery site]" + Greek *sauros* = "lizard."

Type species: *N. yangi* Zhang, Xu, Zhao, Sereno, Kuang and Tan 2001.

Other species: [None.]

Occurrence: Iren Dabasu Formation, Nei Mongol, China.

Age: Late Cretaceous.

Known material: Incomplete skeleton, sacrum, two individuals.

Holotype: LH V0001, partial skeleton including partial braincase, rostral end of right dentary, most of axial column excluding atlas, some mid- and caudal dorsal vertebrae, and distalmost caudal vertebrae, pectoral girdle, forelimb elements including left and partial right scapulocoracoids, furcula, humeri, and left radius, pelvic girdle including partial ilia, hindlimb elements including femora, tibiae, left distal tarsals 3 and 4, most of left pes.

Diagnosis of genus (as for type species): Basal therizinosauroid reaching from 2 to 3 meters in body length, differing from other therizinosauroids by proximal caudal vertebrae having fossa under transverse process, radius with prominent biceps tuberosity, proximal phalanges of pes having well-developed heels, tibia having extremely long fibular crest (much longer than half length of tibia), lateral surface of preacetabular process twisted to face dorsally; caudal vertebrae characterized by widely divergent prezygapophyses (distribution poorly known in other therizinosauroids) (Zhang, Xu, Zhao, Sereno, Kuang and Tan 2001).

Comments: *Neimongosaurus* is the first taxon belonging to the unusual and poorly known theropod group Therizinosauroidea to preserve most of the axial vertebral column and almost all of the long bones of a single individual. The long-necked genus was established upon an incomplete skeleton (LH V0001), with its axial column and left pes found in articulation collected in fluvial sandstones of the Upper Cretaceous Iren Dabasu Formation (estimated to be of late Turonian–Conacian or late Turonian age; see Archibald, Sues, Averianov, Danilov, Rezvyi, Ward, King and Morris 1999; Averianov 2002) at Sanhangobi, Sunitezuooqi, Nei Mongol Autonomous Region (southwest of the city of Erlian), Inner Mongolia, China. The type specimen was found by a team from the Department of Land and Resources, Hohhot, in 1999. Referred to the type species, *N. yangi*, was a sacrum (LH V0008) comprising six coosified vertebrae articulated with both ilia, collected from the same locality (Zhang, Xu, Zhao, Sereno, Kuang and Tan 2001).

Zhang *et al.* assigned *Neimongosaurus* to the Therizinosauroidea based upon the following characters (some also found in ornithomimosaurs and oviraptorsaurians): U-shaped mandibular symphyseal region; downturned mandibular symphysis; edentulous anterior dentary; tooth having basal constriction, subcircular tooth root, lanceolate crown; cranial cervical neural spines low, moderately long; caudal cervical vertebrae "X"-shaped in dorsal aspect; proximal end of humerus angular; humerus with caudal trochanter; cranially located ball-like ulnar and radial condyles separated by narrow groove; long, slender pubic peduncle, short ischial peduncle; metatarsus short.

As the authors noted, *Neimongosaurus* seems to be more derived than the basal therizinosauroid *Beipiaosaurus*, yet less so than therizinosaurids. In *Neimon-*

Neimongosaurus yangi, LH V0001, holotype right dentary in A. lateral, B. medial, and C. dorsal views, fifth cervical vertebra in D. lateral, E. ventral, and F. caudal views, G. cranial dorsal vertebrae (presacrals 15–16), lateral view. Scale = (A–C) 1 cm. (D–G) = 4 cm. (After Zhang, Xu, Zhao, Sereno, Kuang and Tan 2001).

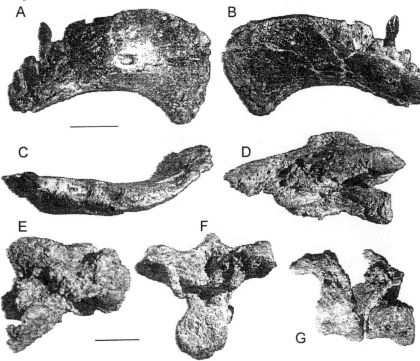

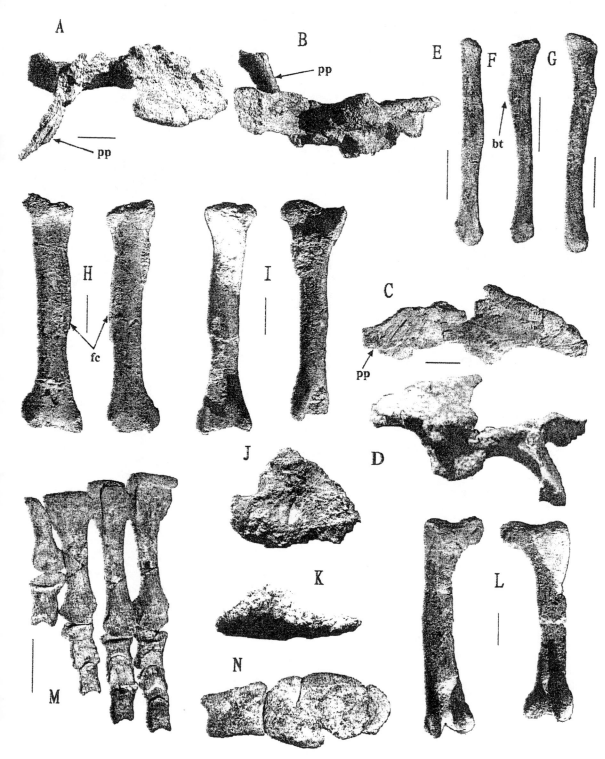

Neimongosaurus yangi, LH V0001, holotype left ilium, A. dorsomedial, B. ventral, C. lateral, and D. medial views, left radius, E. cranial, F. lateral, and G. medial views, left and right tibia, H. caudal, I. cranial, J. proximal, and K. distal views, L. right and left femora, caudal view, left pes, M. dorsal and N. cranial views. Scale = 4 cm. (After Zhang, Xu, Zhao, Sereno, Kuang and Tan 2001.)

gosaurus, unlike the condition in *Beipiaosaurus* (wherein the tibia is shorter than the femur; see Xu, Tang and Wang 1999), the tibia is shorter (85 to 90 percent) than the femur; also, the metatarsus is shorter relative to the tibia (metatarsus III to tibia ratio 39 percent in *Beipiaosaurus*, 34 percent in *Neimongosaurus*). Furthermore, the strongly beveled base of the first metatarsal and its participation in the artic-

ulation with the tarsus in the new genus seem more derived than in *Beipiaosaurus*. However, *Neimongosaurus*, Zhang *et al.* pointed out, is plainly less derived than members of the Therizinosauridae (as redefined; see "Note" below), in which the ilium is very deep and laterally flared, and the pedal unguals are extremely narrow and blade-shaped. According to Zhang *et al.*, "*Neimongosaurus* provides important

Neimongosaurus yangi, LH V0001, holotype A. complete caudal series, lateral view, B. mid-dorsal vertebrae (presacrals 17–22), lateral view, furvula, C. cranial and D. caudal views, left scapulocoracoid, E. ventral and G. lateral views, F. left coracoid, lateral view. Scale = 4 cm. (After Zhang, Xu, Zhao, Sereno, Kuang and Tan 2001.)

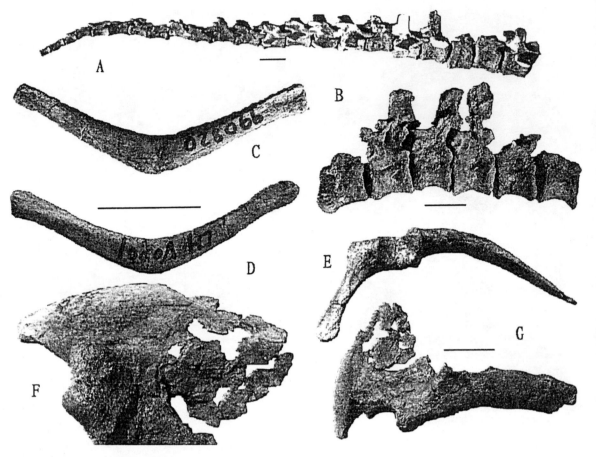

information regarding diversity within Therizinosauroidea and also important comparative data for determining the phylogenetic relationships of this derived subgroup within Coelurosauria." The long neck (seemingly 14 cervical vertebrae in *Neimongosaurus*) and relatively short tail (25 to 30 caudals in this genus), especially, suggest a close relationship between therizinosauroids and oviraptorosaurs. However, a more thorough phylogenetic analysis would require more detailed comparisons between the groups and the recovery of more complete remains.

Note: As pointed out by Zhang *et al.*, the current widespread use of the term Therizinosauroidea should be given a phylogenetic definition recognizing its current uncertain status within Coelurosauria, while also clearly uniting all taxa more closely related to *Therizinosaurus* than to other coelurosaurian outgroups. As defined by these authors, Therizinosauroidea includes "All coelurosaurs closer to *Therizinosaurus* than to either *Ornithomimus*, *Oviraptor*, *Velociraptor* or Neornithes." However, Therizinosauridae was more usefully restricted by Zhang *et al.* "to derived members of the clade than as formerly defined by Sereno (1998:65) to encompass the entire group," the family redefined as "*Segnosaurus, Nanshiungosaurus, Therizinosaurus*, their common ancestor and all descendants."

Key references: Sereno (1998); Xu, Tang and Wang (1999); Zhang, Xu, Zhao, Sereno, Kuang and Tan (2001).

†NEMEGTOSAURUS

Saurischia: Eusaurischia: Sauropodomorpha: Sauropoda: Eusauropoda: Neosauropoda: Macronaria: Camarasauromorpha: Titanosauriformes: Somphospondyli: Titanosauria: Nemegtosauridae.

Comments: Since it was named and first described by Alecksander Nowiński in 1971, *Nemegtosaurus* has been an enigmatic genus with a checkered phylogenetic history. Based on an incomplete, elongated and lightly constructed, diplodocid-like skull (ZPAL MgD-I/9) recovered from the Nemegt Formation of Omnogov, Mongolian People's Republic, the type species *Nemegtosaurus mongoliensis* was regarded by Nowiński as a "dicraeosaurine" diplodocid, seemingly intermediate, in some features, between *Dicraeosaurus* and *Diplodocus* (see *D:TE*).

McIntosh (1990), in his review of the Sauropoda, observed that the holotype of *Nemegtosaurus* closely resembles the skull of *Dicraeosaurus*, but also pointed out the possibility that the affinities of the Asian genus could be with the titanosaurs. Nevertheless, *Nemegtosaurus* has, until only relatively recently, been classified

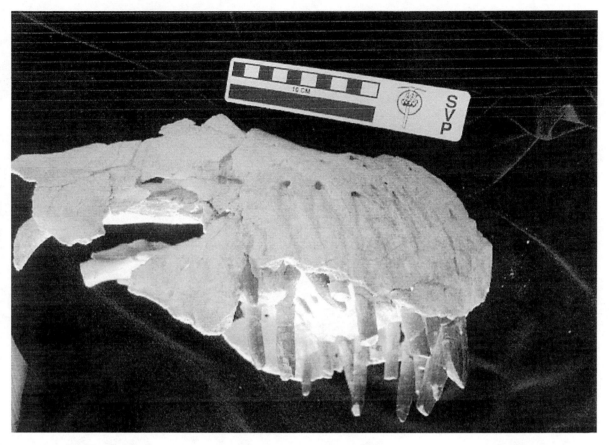

Nemegtosaurus mongoliensis, ZPAL MgD-I/9, holotype rostral part of skull (unrestored; for reconstruction, in which left mandible has been restored as the "right" (R. M. Sullivan, personal communication, 2003), see photograph, *D:TE*), left lateral view.

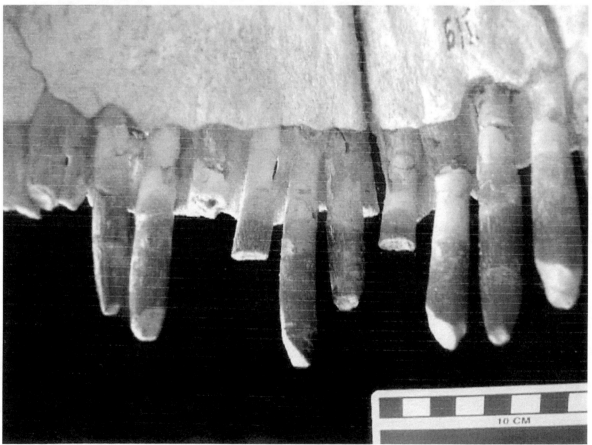

Nemegtosaurus mongoliensis, ZPAL MgD-I/9, detail of holotype maxillary teeth.

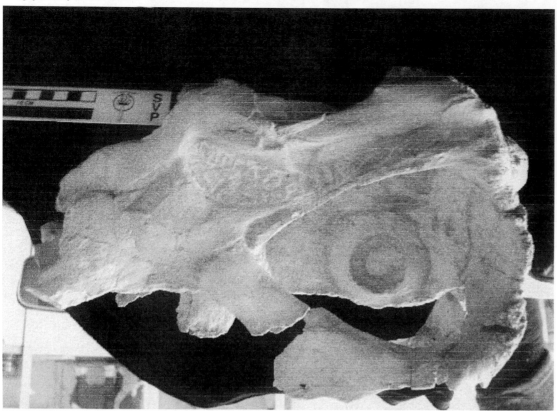

Nemegtosaurus mongoliensis, ZPAL MgD-I/9, holotype caudal part of skull.

tanosauroid," found it most parsimonious to regard the Nemegtosauridae as a diplodocoid closely related to the Diplodocidae and Dicraeosauridae (see *S2*).

More recently, Curry Rogers and Forster (2001), in a paper describing the confirmed titanosaur *Rapetosaurus* (see entry), noted that this new taxon provides the best opportunity yet to resolve the phylogenetic position of *Nemegtosaurus* and also *Quaesitosaurus*. Concerning these Mongolian genera, Curry Rogers and Forster noted that "*Rapetosaurus* is particularly illuminating because its elongated skull with retracted nares exhibits a general similarity to diplodocoids, whereas its skeleton shows striking commonalities with brachiosaurids and titanosaurs."

Performing a phylogenetic analysis, Curry Rogers and Forster found *Rapetosaurus* to form a clade including *Malawisaurus*, *Nemegtosaurus*, and *Quaesitosaurus*, these taxa united by four ambiguous cranial synapomorphies: (frontals having fused midline contact; parietal not contributing to post-temporal fenestra; occipital region cranio-caudally deep, with paroccipital processes posterolaterally oriented [reversal]; basipterygoid process being at least four times that of basal diameter). All of these characters were found to be shared by at least one diplodocoid. *Nemegtosaurus*, *Quaesitosaurus*, and *Rapetosaurus* were also found to be united by 11 synapmorphies, two of them (posterodorsal process of splenial; about 90-degree angle

by most workers as either a Dicraeosaurid or a "dicraeosaurine" diplodocid.

Later studies by other workers (*e.g.*, Calvo 1994*a*, 1994*b*; Salgado and Calvo 1997; Wilson 1997) suggested that the affinities of both *Nemegtosaurus* and the closely related Mongolian genus *Quaesitosaurus* (see entry) were not with diplodocids or dicraeosaurids, but rather with the Titanosauria (see *S1*).

Upchurch (1994, 1995) had referred *Nemegtosaurus* to its own family, the Nemegtosauridae, which he assessed to be allied with the Diplodocoidea. Subsequently, Upchurch (1999), while acknowledging the possibility that *Nemegtosaurus* could be a "ti-

Nemegtosaurus mongoliensis, ZPAL MgD-I/9, holotype left mandible.

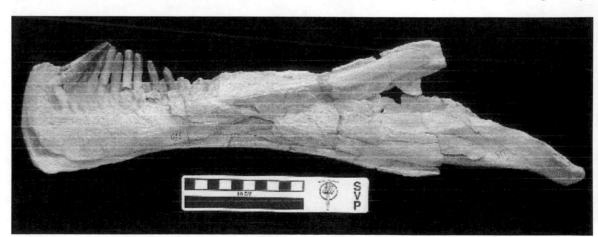

between long axis of mandibular symphysis and that of mandible) unambiguous. Furthermore, *Nemegtosaurus* and *Rapetosaurus* are united by seven ambiguous cranial characters, five of these also occurring in at least one diplodocoid (external nares retracted to position between eyes; anterior prefrontal process; frontal contributing to supratemporal fenestra; external nares facing dorsally or rostrodorsally; "stepped" snout profile absent; ectopterygoid process of pterygoid lying ventral or caudal to lacrimal; slenderness indices for teeth more than 5.0). While not ruling out a possible closer relationship with diplodocoids, Curry Rogers and Forster found it most parsimonious to regard *Nemegtosaurus* and allied genera as titanosaurians.

Key references: Calvo (1994*a*, 1994*b*); McIntosh (1990); Nowiński (1971); Curry Rogers and Forster (2001); Salgado and Calvo (1997); Upchurch (1994, 1995, 1999); Wilson (1997).

†NEOVENATOR

Saurischia: Eusaurischia: Theropoda: Neotheropoda: Tetanurae: Avetheropoda: Carnosauria: Allosauroidea.

Comments: In a report in the magazine *Dino-Press* on the latest discoveries of dinosaurs on the Isle of Wight, England, Darren Naish (2002*b*) related Stephen Hutt's recent discovery that the skull of the genus *Neovenator* (see *SI*) possessed twin, curving crests on the nasal bones, these features thereby rendering inaccurate all previously published life restorations of this theropod.

Naish further stated that front-limb materials including fragmentary metatarsals, plus other elements, have been recovered from the Isle of Wight, some of them now in private collections. Some or all of these specimens may pertain to *Neovenator*. Unfortunately, the holotype of the type species *Neovenator salerii* does not possess a forelimb for comparison.

In an abstract for a poster, published as a preliminary report for a forthcoming revision of the Megalosauridae, Allain (2002*b*) found *Neovenator* to be a basal member of the Allosauroidea.

Note: Naish (2003), in an abstract, briefly reported on various pathological dinosaurian specimens recently recovered from the Wessex Formation (Lower Cretaceous: Barremian) of the Isle of Wight. Among these, remains of *Neovenator salerii* exhibit a lesion on the left tibia, a damaged pedal ungual, osteoarthritis on pedal phalanges, diffuse idiopathic skeletal hyperostosis(DISH) on the caudal vertebrae, and multiple fractures on ribs and gastralia. Remains of *Iguanodon atherfieldensis* include a broken prepubic process and ribs, the presence of spondylitus deformans, neural

spines displaying loop-shaped osteophytes, other neural spines having been partially tilted or rotated prior to healing, and fusion of ribs to their transverse processes (the latter suggesting a very old individual). As interpreted by Naish (2003), these pathologies could have been the consequences of "accidental fall, intraspecific combat or from interaction with prey."

Key references: Allain (2002*b*); Naish (2002*b*, 2003).

†NIGERSAURUS

Saurischia: Eusaurischia: Sauropodomorpha: Sauropoda: Eusauropoda: Diplodocoidea: Diplodocidae.

Comments: In an abstract, Sereno and Wilson

Photograph by the author, courtesy Dinosaur Museum.

Skeletal cast (based on holotype MIWG 6348, a mostly complete skeleton, and also *Allosaurus fragilis*) of the basal allosauroid theropod *Neovenator salerii* on display during the mid–1980s at the Dinosaur Museum, Dorchester, England. Recently this dinosaur was found to possess a pair of cranial crests.

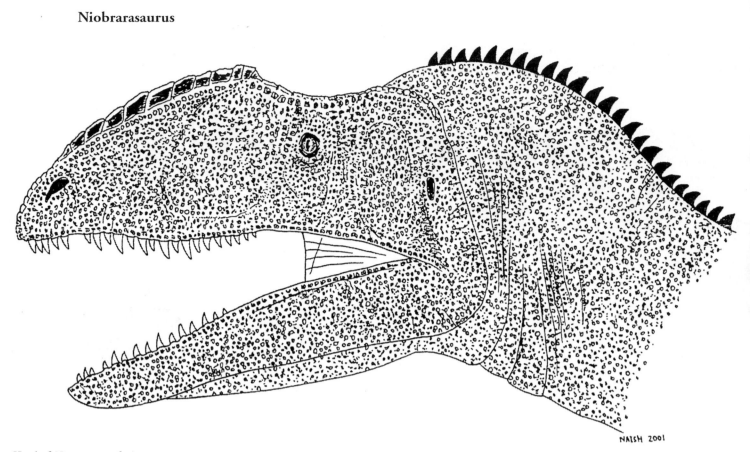

NAISH 2001

Head of *Neovenator saleri* restored by paleontologist Darren Naish as possessing a raised crest surmounting each nasal bone. (After Naish 2002*b*.)

(2001) briefly described the tooth batteries in the Cretaceous diplodocid, *Nigersaurus taqueti* (previously referred by Wilson 1999 to the Rebbachisauridae; see *S2*). As observed by Sereno and Wilson, the batteries "are characterized by enhanced tooth replacement, increase in the number of tooth positions, absence of discrete alveoli, size differential between upper and lower crowns, and markedly asymmetrical enamel thickness." Additional features noted by the authors include "the extreme transverse width of the lower jaws, which extend lateral to the side of the skull, and the transverse orientation of the entire dentary tooth row."

Sereno and Wilson pointed out that the skull of this genus is quite lightly constructed for a sauropod, especially one having a fully developed tooth battery. This advanced condition is presaged in other diplodocoids, thereby permitting "a general reconstruction of the timing and stepwise evolution of this advanced condition among diplodocoids." This timing, the authors noted, is comparable "to the timing of floral replacement by angiosperms on land."

Key references: Sereno and Wilson (2001); Wilson (1999).

†NIOBRARASAURUS
Ornithischia: Genasaura: Thyreophora: Eurypoda: Ankylosauromorpha: Ankylosauria: Nodosauridae.

Comments: The first evidence of a nodosaurid in the Upper Cretaceous (early Campanian) Smoky Hill Chalk Member of the Niobrara Chalk (well known for its excellently preserved fish, marine reptiles, *Pteranodon*, and tooth birds) was reported in an abstract by Hamm and Everhart (2001). The specimen, consisting of an isolated radius and ulna (found within the biostratigraphic zone of *Clioscaphites vermiformis* and *C. choteauensis*), was recovered from the Smoky Hill Chalk Member in Lane County, Kansas. Bite marks and the partially digested look of the proximal and distal ends of these elements suggested to that author that the material had been scavenged by the shark *Cretoxyrhina mantelli*.

As briefly described by Hamm and Everhart, the lengths of the radius and ulna are approximately half that of the comparable holotype elements (MU 650 VP) of *Niobrarasaurus coleii* (see *D:TE*), indicating a juvenile individual measuring approximately 3 meters (slightly over 10 feet) in length. Comparing this specimen with remains of the only two nodosaurids documented from the chalk, *N. coeleii* and *Hierosaurus sternbergii*, the authors found it to most closely resemble the former, and therefore tentatively referred it to that species.

Key reference: Hamm and Everhart (2001).

NOTHRONYCHUS Kirkland and Wolfe 2001
Saurischia: Eusaurischia: Theropoda: Neotheropoda:

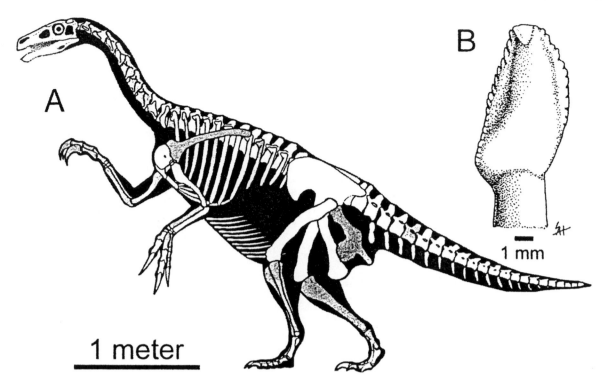

Nothronychus mckinleyi, A. skeletal reconstruction including holotype MSM P-2117 (shaded), based on *Alxasaurus*, B. holotype tooth in labial view. (After Kirkland and Wolfe 2001.)

A

B

1 mm

1 meter

Tetanurae: Avetheropoda: Coelurosauria: Maniraptoriformes: Maniraptora: Metornithes: Therizinosauroidea: Therizinosauridae.

Name derivation: Greek *nothros* = "slothful" + Greek *onyx* = "claw."

Type species: *N. mckinleyi* Kirkland and Wolfe 2001.

Other species: [None.]

Occurrence: Moreno Hill Formation, New Mexico, United States.

Age: Late Cretaceous (middle Turonian).

Known material/holotype: MSM P-2117, partial disarticulated skeleton including isolated teeth, fragmentary skull elements (including caudal part of skull), several cervical vertebrae, ?first dorsal vertebra, anterior caudal vertebra, ribs, fused gastralia, scapula, right humerus, complete right and partial left ulna, metacarpals, manual phalanges, two manual unguals, ischia, tibiae, right fibula, partial metatarsals, pedal phalanges, two pedal unguals.

Diagnosis of genus (as for type species): Teeth having serrations extending close to constriction with circular root; anterior dorsal vertebrae having long pedicle and large pleurocoel encasing multiple separate pneumatic foramina; scapula slender with laterally facing glenoid; humerus slender, straight, with short deltopectoral crest, lacking spur on humeral shaft; manual unguals with flexor tubercle not extending below proximal articulation, lacking dorsoproximal lip; ischium thin, almost excluded from acetabulum, with large, rectangular, medially located obturator process; fibula with M. iliofibularis at about midshaft; pedal unguals thick (Kirkland and Wolfe 2001a).

Comments: The first undisputed North American therizinosaurid, the type species *Nothronychus mckinleyi* was founded upon a partial associated skeleton (MSM P-2117) collected from the Haystack Butte locality, in the Lower member of the Moreno Hill Formation (probably *Collignoniceras woollgari* Zone; see Wolfe and Kirkland 1998), southern Zuni Basin, Catron County, New Mexico. In addition to this new taxon, the Moreno Hill faunal assemblage also contains the ceratopsian *Zunceratops christopheri*, and skeletons of a unnamed nodosaurids, hadrosaurids, and a basal coelurosaur (Kirkland and Wolfe 2001a).

Subsequently, in an abstract, Kirkland and Wolfe (2001b) reported the more recently recovered caudal portion of the skull which they added to the holotype.

In their original description of *N. mckinleyi*, Kirkland and Wolfe (2001a) observed the following: The teeth are unlike those of any other known North American dinosaur, having a distinctive tall, subsymmetrical crown and constricted root. The serrations of the anterior carina are larger than those on the distal carina, as in the therizinosaurid *Segnosaurus* (see Perle 1979), although the serrations extend most of tooth crown length unlike the condition in other known therizinosaurids. The cervical vertebrae resembles those of most other known therizinosaurids, being large, having slightly platycoelous to amphiplatyan centra, and having a reduced neural spine (*e.g.*, Perle; Russell and Dong 1993; Xu, Tang and Wang 1999). The anterior dorsal vertebra is quite similar to that of *Alxasaurus*, the capitular facet being low on the centrum and the latter having a large pleurocoel and hyposphene (Russell and Dong); it is unlike *Nanshiungosaurus* in having a high pedicle (Dong 1979). The scapula is of lighter construction than in other therizinosaurids save *Alxasaurus*, although the glenoid extends onto the lateral surface as in therizinosaurids other than that genus (Barsbold 1976; Perle; also H. Osmólska, personal communication to Kirkland and Wolfe, 2000). The proximal end of the manual unguals do not show the posterodorsal lip characteristic of therizinosaurs and oviraptorosaurs (Sues 1997). The ischium (the right ischium originally misidentified by Wolfe and Kirkland as a squamosal of *Z. christopheri*), in side view, are "remarkably similar to those of *Segnosaurus* (Perle, 1979)." The pedal unguals are thicker than in most known therizinosaurids excluding *Chilantaisaurus zheziangensis* (see Dong).

Later, Kirkland and Wolfe (2001b) briefly described the skull of this dinosaur as small (typical of therizinosaurids, just 80 millimeters high and 79 millimeters across the parrocciptal process) for an animal having a tibia measuring 614 millimeters in length. The braincase is entirely coossified, this specimen preserving the basisphenoid, basioccipital, supraoccipital, plus most of the paroccipital processes. The authors observed that it is similar to that of the Mongolian *Erlikosaurus andrewsi*, the only other therizinosaurid for which a braincase is known, this similarity being "most apparent in the great ventral expansion of the extensively pneumaticized basisphenoid, which is likewise subdivided into a large medial space and lateral areas for middle ear cavities."

Kirkland and Wolfe (2001b) further described this braincase as follows: Basipterygoid processes and basitubera indistinct; hollow paroccipital processes, separated from foramen magnum by deep depression, flattened caudally, inclined backwardly at 10 to 15 degrees, shorter than in *Erlikosaurus* (indicating more narrowly constructed skull); occipital condyle only 12.4 millimeters high by 15.2 millimeters; foramen magnum almost circular, 18.5 millimeters wide; (unlike *Erlikosaurus*) supraoccipital above foramen magnum oriented almost horizontally, lacking nuchal arch; (as in *Erlikosaurus*) pneumatic portion of braincase not extending over midline of foramen magnum.

Although a phylogenetic analysis of *Nothronychus* was currently in preparation by Kirkland and Wolfe (2001a), the authors noted that this genus shares with the Early Cretaceous *Beipiaosaurus* and *Alxasaurus*, the most primitive known therizinosaurids, various features including a slender scapula and forelimb. However, *Nothronychus* also displays derived characters (*e.g.*, laterally facing glenoid on scapula, extensive contact for pubis on obturator process) shared with other Late Cretaceous members of the Therizinosauridae. This, Kirkland and Wolfe (2001a) speculated, may reflect an intermediate phylogenetic position. Subsequently, Kirkland and Wolfe (2001b) also noted that, based upon the teeth and the skeleton's postcranial elements (*e.g.*, vertebrae, scapula, and ischia), *Nothronychus* seems to be closest to *Segnosaurus* and *Erlikosaurus*, this possibly helping to "resolve the age of the Baynshirenian of central Asia as closer to Turonian than Campanian [in age]."

Zhao and Xu (1998) had reported therizinosauroids in Asia during the Early Jurassic, although this identification may not be confirmed (M. Lamanna, personal communication to Kirkland and Wolfe, 2000; [see also, however, Xu, Zhao and Clark 2001 and *Eshanosaurus* entry]). Excluding a possible Lower Jurassic theizinosauroid, Kirkland and Wolfe (2001a) noted that the discovery of *Nothronychus* supports the hypothesis "that the North American-Asian connection established in the early Cenomanian (Cifelli *et al.*, 1997; Kirkland *et al.*, 1997, 1998, 1999) was also a factor in the middle Turonian." Furthermore, this "strengthens the documented paleogeographic ties between western North America and Asia throughout the Late Cretaceous."

Notes: The generic name of this dinosaur first appeared in an anonymously written article published in the *New York Times* on June 19, 2001. A subsequent report by John Stanley giving the specific name appeared in the *Arizona Republic* that same month.

Although *Nothronychus* is distinguished as the first therizinosaurid known from North America, it is not the only one. In an abstract, Gillette, Albright, Titus and Graffam (2001) briefly reported on the discovery of the rear half of a therizinosaurid skeleton found in the marine Tropic Shale (Upper Cretaceous: late early Turonian in the upper *Watinoceras coloradoense*-lower *Mammites nodosaoides* biozone interval, based on the occurrence of these ammonoids species) of southern Utah. Excavation of the slightly disarticulated specimen began in 2000, prompted by the discovery of a dinosaurian phalanx, with more digging probably in 2001. Material collected to date of Gillette *et al.* report includes caudal ribs, several dorsal vertebrae, the sacrum, caudal vertebrae, chevrons, ilia, pubes, ischia, femora, tibiae, astragali, six metatarsals, and phalanges.

As taphonomically interpreted by Gillette *et al.*, the carcass of this as yet unnamed dinosaur sank into soft mud, the flesh subsequently disintegrating, the bones then slightly shifting as they settled. Later, but prior to burial, the surfaces of these bones were colonized by invertebrates, the decaying carcass then "forming both a substrate and nutrient basis for a small bioherm-like structure of ammonite and bivalve shells."

Gillette *et al.* identified this specimen as that of

a therizinosaurid based upon the opisthopubic pelvis and tetradactyl pes, although the authors noted that further assessment must await the excavation and preparation of the remainder of the skeleton. As Gillette *et al.* pointed out, the recognition of therizinosaurs in North America greatly expands the clade's known global distribution, the early late Turonian occurrence of this group on that continent postdating their earliest (Albian) Asian record, this "implying origin in Asia in the Early Cretaceous with subsequent diversification and dispersal in early Late Cretaceous time at least as far as the eastern shore of the Western Interior Seaway."

Key references: Barsbold (1976); Cifelli, Kirkland, Weil, Deinos, and Kowallis (1997); Dong (1979); Gillette, Albright, Titus and Graffam (2001); Kirkland, Britt, Burge, Carpenter, Cifelli, DeCourten, Eaton, Hasiotis and Lawton (1997); Kirkland, Cifelli, Britt, Burge, DeCourten, Eaton and Parrish (1999); Kirkland, Lucas and Estep (1998); Kirkland and Wolfe (2001a, 2001b); Osmólska (2000); Perle (1979); Russell and Dong (1993); Sues (1997); Wolfe and Kirkland (1998); Zhao and Xu (1998).

†NUTHETES

Saurischia: Eusaurischia: Theropoda: Neotheropoda: Tetanurae: Avetheropoda: Coelurosauria: Maniraptoriformes: Maniraptora: Metornithes: Paraves: Deinonychosauria: Dromaeosauridae.

Occurrence: Lulworth Formation, Isle of Purbeck, England.

Known material: Dentary fragments with teeth, isolated teeth.

Holotype: DORCM G 913, partial left dentary.

Diagnosis of genus (as for type species): Small dromaeosaur, tooth denticle size difference index ranging from 1.14 tp 1.55, denticles perpendicular to tooth margin (Milner 2002).

Comments: Fossil remains assigned to the theropod type species *Nuthetes destructor* were recently reassessed by Milner (2002).

Remains of *N. destructor* redescribed by Milner include the holotype (DORCM G 913), a partial left dentary from the Cherry Freshwater Member (see Clements 1999) of the Lower Cretaceous (Berriasian) Lulworth Formation, Middle Purbeck, Purbeck Limestone Group, Isle of Purbeck, England (described by Owen 1854); also the following referred specimens: BMNH 48207, a split slab with dentary fragments containing teeth (figured by Owen 1878); BMNH 48208, numerous isolated teeth (figured by Owen 1878); BMNH 15870–76, isolated teeth; BMNH R 15870, isolated teeth (figured by Owen 1879) collected by R. Coran; and CAMSM J13951, an isolated tooth,

previously identified as lacertilian, from the Mammal Bed.

In describing the holotype tooth, Milner noted that it is the anterior fragment of the dentary with nine teeth (Owen's original 1854 description counting seven teeth, his accompanying figures showing six), is compressed, and measures 37.5 millimeters in length. According to Milner, the very small jaws and teeth probably represents a juvenile animal within the approximate size range of 1.8 meters in length.

Variation in denticle size, while useful in measuring variation and growth, does not facilitate comparison between different sized teeth (see Farlow, Brinkman, Abler and Currie 1991). Rauhut and Werner (1995), however, proposed a denticle size difference index (or DSDI) — the ratio of the number of denticles per unit length on the mesial and distal carinae of a tooth — and showed that this index is independent of tooth size and, therefore, has taxonomic value. Comparing the mean DSDI value for the above listed Purbeck teeth with a range of other theropods, Milner found that data gleaned from the Purbeck specimens compare most favorably with the velociraptorine dromaeosaurids *Deinonychus* and *Saurornithoides*. Based on these data, Milner referred *Nuthetes* to the Dromaeosauridae.

Nuthetes represents the first dromaeosaur known in Great Britain, thereby filling a gap in the stratigraphical occurrence of the Dromaeosauridae in Europe between the Kimmeridgian (Portugal) and Barremian (Spain). As Milner pointed out, the presence of a dromaeosaur in the Purbeck Limestone "is consistent with the palaeobiogeographic distribution of the family as currently understood."

Notes: In 1879, Richard Owen referred to his *Nuthetes*, described by him in 1854, a number of phosphatic "granicones" collected from the Purbeck Limestone Formation of Dorset, in southern England. Owen (1879) believed these objects to be dermal bones or armor not unlike the scutes of some modern lizards (see S2). Puzzling for more than 130 years, they were recently reinterpreted by Barrett, Clarke, Brinkman, Chapman and Ensom (2002), — based on anatomical, histological, and geological evidence — as limb osteoderms of turtles, possibly of the species *Helochelydra anglica* or "*Tretosternon*" *bakewelli* (see Barrett *et al.* for details).

Milner also reported on other theropod teeth included in the Purbeck fauna. These include a large isolated tooth crown (BMNH 44806, originally referred by Dames 1884 to *Megalosaurus dunkeri;*) from an unknown locality, comparing closely with teeth of *Allosaurus*; the distal half of an isolated right metatarsal III (BMNH R 6908), the only element representing a large theropod yet found on the Isle of

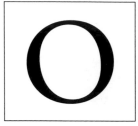

Purbeck (as preserved, measuring 254 militers long, 44.4 millimeters wide across the distal articulation, with a shaft circumference of 82 millimeters just below the broken end), almost certainly pertaining to a "eumaniraptoran"; and a small phalanx (CAMSM J 13956), exposed on a small matrix block from the Mammal Bed at Durlston Bay, Swanage (measuring 24 millimeters in length, 13.5 millimeters wide across the proximal end, and 10 millimeters across the distal articulation), corresponding in general morphology with the pedal phalanx III-1 of *Allosaurus*.

Key references: Barrett, Clarke, Brinkman, Chapman and Ensom (2002); Clements (1999); Dames (1884); Farlow, Brinkman, Abler and Currie (1991); Milner (2002); Owen (1854, 1878, 1879).; Rauhut and Werner (1995).

†OMEISAURUS

Saurischia: Sauropodomorpha: Sauropoda: Eusauropoda: Neosauropoda: Macronaria: Camarasauromorpha: Titanosauriformes: Somphospondyli: Euhelopodidae: Euhelopodinae.

New species: *O. maoianus* Tang, Jin, Kang and Zhang 2001.

Known material/holotype of *O. maoianus*: ZNM N8510, skeleton including nearly complete cranium, vertebrae (three cervicals, four dorsals, and 22 caudals), pubes, ischia, left ilium, humeri, radii, ulnae, right femur, tibiae, right fibula, right astragalus, metacarpals, right metatarsus, left metatarsal, some digits.

Occurrence: Shang-Sha-Xi-Miao Formation, Jingyan, Sichuan Province, China.

Age: Early Late Jurassic.

Diagnosis of *O. maoianus*: Mid-cervical vertebrae having very low neural arches on very elongate centra; long axis of supratemporal fossa oriented transversely (rather than cranio-caudally); cranial margin of supratemporal fossa formed entirely by postorbital and parietal; pleurocoels of cervical vertebrae subdivided by bony septum extending caudoventrally; tooth crown denticles best developed on convex mesial crown margin, fewer in number on concave distal margin; at least 23 dentary tooth; larger external mandibular fenestra than in other *Omeisaurus* species and *Mamenchisaurus*; minimum shaft diameters of metatarsals III and IV approaching that of II; ectopterygoid articulating laterally with jugal; muzzle-like region of snout (Tang, Jin, Kang and Zhang 2001).

Comments: Another species of *Omeisaurus*, an extremely long-necked Chinese sauropod genus, was named in 2001 by Tang, Jin, Kang and Zhang. This new species, *Omeisaurus maoianus*, was based upon a partial skeleton with skull (ZNM N8510) recovered by Jin Xingsheng and Zhang Guojun from the lower part of the Shang-Sha-Xi-Miao Formation (early Late Jurassic) in the vicinity of Jingyan, in the western Sichuan Basin of China. The skeleton was subsequently prepared under the direction of Zhang Yi-hong and mounted at the Zhejiang Natural Museum. Sufficient data suggests that the specimen was yielded from the same Upper Jurassic Shang-Sha-Xi-Miao Formation horizon in which the type species *O. jungh-siensis* has been found, thereby making this new species geologically younger than *O. tiafuensis* from the Lower Shaximiao Formation (Tang, Jin, Kang and Zhang 2001).

In comparing *O. maoianus* with the relatively complete species *O. tianfuensis* (and also with other sauropods; see paper for details), Tang *et al.* observed a number of differences, including the following: Regarding the femur, the external form of the bone, the position of the fourth trochanter, and its outline in distal aspect are relatively similar in both taxa (see He, Li and Cai 1988). In the femur of *O. maoianus*, the outer condyle of the distal end is somewhat wider than the inner condyle, the postexternal side is deeply concave, and the fourth trochanter is elongated to 19 percent of shaft length (only 12 percent in *O. tianfuensis*). The tibia of *O. maoianus* is comparatively more slender (length to minimum width of the tibial shaft

Omeisaurus maoianus, ZNM N8510, holotype skull and mandible in left lateral view. (After Tang, Jin, Kang and Zhang 2001.)

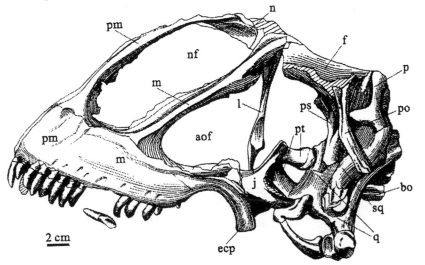

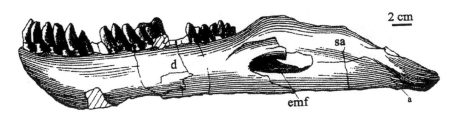

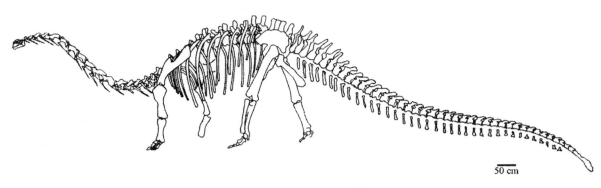

Drawing of the skeleton of *Omeisaurus maoianus* as mounted at the Zhejiang Natural Museum. (After Tang, Jin, Kang and Zhang 2001.)

50 cm

about 8.7:1) than that of *O. tianfuensis* (ratio of 5.8:1), suggesting that *O. maoianus* was a relatively larger animal than the other species. The ratio of shaft lengths of tibia to femur is 0.52 in *O. maoianus* and 0.62 in *O. tianfuensis*. It was the observation of Tang *et al.* that these two species differ mostly in details of the tibia; comparisons with *O. junghsiensis* could not be made, as the tibia is not known in that species.

Tang *et al.* noted that the third metatarsal of *O. maoianus* is approximately 38 percent of the tibial length, proportionately distinctly larger than in *O. tianfuensis* (27 percent). The ratio of length of metatarsals V to IV is about 0.90, similar to that of *O. tianfuensis* (0.89). The humeri in both *Omeisaurus* species are very similar, the degree of expansion of their proximal ends about the same, although in *O. maoianus* the humerus is somewhat smaller. In *O. maoianus*, the deltoid crest is lower than in *O. tianfuensis*. Also, the humerus of *O. tianfuensis* measures more than four-fifths the length of the femur; that of *O. maoianus* is comparatively short, measuring 68 percent of the femoral length. The authors noted that both species differ in the form of their radii and ulnae. In *O. maorianus*, these bones are somewhat short and stout, the proximal end of the ulna expanding prominently (1.7 ratio of maximum width of proximal end to that of distal end); in *O. tianfuensis*, the degree of expansion is less (1.9).

Comparing the pelvic girdles, Tang *et al.* noted that in *O. maorianus* the ilium is distinctly high, the ratio of height of the acetabulum to maximum length of the ilium being about 0.48; the average ratio for *O. tianfuensis* is 0.38. The dorsal and anterior margins of the ilia of both species are similar; however, in *O. maoianus* the lower margin of the anterior process intersects the anterior margin of the pubic peduncle with an acute angle, in *O. tianfuensis* with an almost right angle. Additionally, the proximal end of the pubis expands slightly more prominently in *O. maoianus* than in *O. tianfuensis*.

Tang listed the following 91 anatomical characters pertaining to *O. maoianus*: Rostral end of snout broad and rounded in dorsal view; caudal rim of external naris caudal to rostral margin of antorbital fenestra; rostral rim of external naris anterior to rostral margin of antorbital fenestra; external nares facing laterally; subnarial foramen small, subcircular; subnarial foramen outside fossa of external naris; muzzle-like region on snout; ascending process or premaxilla caudolaterally directed; premaxilla formed from heavy main body and distinct ascending process; caudolateral process of premaxilla; maxilla-lacrimal contact near caudal margin of antorbital fenestra; flangelike structure attached to base of maxillary ascending process; absence of additional antorbital fenestra; absence of sheet of bone partially backing rostral portion of antorbital fenestra; jugal contribution to caudolateral margin of antorbital small or nonexistent; rostral process of quadratojugal two to three times length of dorsal process; absence of maxilla-quadratojugal contact; rostral process of quadratojugal expanding dorsoventrally at rostral tip; rostral process of quadratojugal straight or curving gently upwards towards rostral tip; angle between rostral and dorsal rami of quadratojugal 90 degrees or less; rostral margin of infratemporal fenestra below midpoint of orbit or further anteriorly; rostral margin of infratemporal fenestra below midpoint of orbit or more caudally; caudal end of prefrontal in dorsal aspect acute, subtriangular, inset into rostrolateral corner of frontal; rostrocaudal length of frontals less than their combined transverse width; supratemporal fenestra facing dorsally or dorsolaterally; absence of postparietal fenestra; squamosal-quadratojugal contact; proximal end of quadrate concealed in lateral view by squamosal; dorsal margin of supratemporal fenestra formed by parietal, postorbital and squamosal; ectopterygoid process of pterygoid below lacrimal or more caudally; ectopterygoid process of pterygoid below rostral rim of orbit or more rostrally; ectopterygoid process of pterygoid robust, projecting below level of jaw margin; excavation in caudal surface of quadrate; long axis of quadrate shaft oriented approximately perpendicular to long axis of dentary margin (in transverse portion leading to symphysis), is stout, rounded rostrocaudally, does not project far below rest of dentary; mandible in dorsal aspect broadly rounded, U-shaped; angle between long axis of mandibular symphysis and that of mandible about 45 degrees; external mandibular fenestra open; long diameter of external mandibular fenestra 10 to 15 percent length of mandible; jaw articulation below mandibular tooth row; premaxillary tooth crowns longest in upper jaw; denticles (serrations) on tooth crowns; lingual surface of tooth crown concave; prominent grooves near mesial and distal margins of labial surface of each tooth crown; tooth crowns spatulate; long axis of tooth crown procumbent; position of most mesial tooth in tooth row just below antorbital fenestra; opisthocoelous articulations between cervical vertebral centra; opisthocoelous between middle and caudal dorsal centra; prominent midline keels on ventral surfaces of cervical centra, ventral surface of each cervical centrum transversely concave and bounded on either side by prominent ventrolateral ridges; height to width ratio of cranial cervical centra about 1.25; lateral surfaces of cervical centra with deep excavation divided into cranial and caudal portions by oblique accessory lamina; "single" infraprezygapophyseal laminae on middle and caudal cervicals; flat articular surfaces of middle and caudal cervical prezygapophyses; cervical neural spines low (height of vertebra generally not exceeding length of centrum); absence of bifurcation of presacral neural spines; pleurocoels in dorsal centra moderately deep, with rounded caudal margins; height of dorsal neural arches higher than that of dorsal centra; dorsal transverse processes directed laterally or slightly upwards; transverse processes of caudal dorsal vertebrae caudal or caudodorsal to parapophysis; 55 or fewer caudal vertebrae; articulations between proximal caudal centra — first centrum almost amphicoelous, second to seventh mildly procoelous; articulations between middle and distal caudal centra amphicoelous/amphiplatyan; centrum length divided by centrum height (in most proximal caudals) approximately 0.5 to 0.6; distal end of tail comprising relatively short caudal centra; absence of pleurocoels in proximal caudal centra, ventral surfaces of proximal caudal centra transversely rounded; centra of middle caudals with subcircular or laterally compressed transverse cross section; neural arches of middle caudals over middle of centrum; absence of "dorsalization" of neural spines of proximal caudals (spines simple laterally compressed plates lacking laminae); first caudal rib linked to lateral surface of neural arch and prezygapophysis by fanlike stout ridge; ventral blades of middle and distal chevrons with proximally directed process; absence of prominent process on ventral portion of proximal end of humerus (proximal end transversely convex in cranial aspect); craniomedial process of proximal end of ulna with strongly concave proximal surface; radius slender (maximum width of proximal end 25 percent or less radius length); metacarpal I shorter than II or III; length of longest metacarpal divided by length of radius = more than 0.45; metacarpal V reduced to bone splint; semicircular arrangement of metacarpals; absence of brevis fossa on caudal process of iliac blade; lateral profile of dorsal margin of ilium strongly convex; ischiadic peduncle of ilium greatly reduced; ratio of ischium to pubis length about 1.3; middle and distal portion of pubis approximately in same plane as proximal end; length of ischiadic articular surface of pubis divided by pubis length at least 0.45; width across ischiadic shaft (at midlength) divided by length of ischium less than 0.10 to 0.15; distal end of ischium just slightly expanded relative to rest of shaft; femoral shaft straight; femur without lesser trochanter, fourth trochanter low crest-shaped, on caudomedial margin of shaft; femoral shaft elliptical or subrectangular in horizontal cross section; tibia to femur length ratio less than 0.56; metatarsal I robust, maximum length divided by transverse proximal width 1.72; laterodistal process on metatarsal I.

Performing histological studies of the teeth of *Omeisaurus*, Tang *et al.* noted that the enamel microstructure pattern comprises a curved columnar pattern lacking enamel prism. Also, the dentine exhibits unique structural features such as dentinal tubule and an enamel-dentine junction differing from those features observed in the sauropod *Shunosaurus*. Consequently, the authors suggested, features observed via histological studies might have phylogenetic significance in the classification of sauropod dinosaurs. Furthermore, elemental analysis on the thin cross section of *Omeisaurus* teeth could play an important role in the partitioning of food sources correlating with the environments in which these animals lived. Comparing the teeth of *Omeisaurus* with those of other sauropods, Tang *et al.* concluded that this genus, exhibiting a more derived type of enamel, may represent a higher phylogenetic clade than *Shunosaurus* (see entry), even though both genera are from the same locality.

Key references: He, Li and Cai (1988); Tang, Jin, Kang and Zhang (2001).

†OTHNIELIA

Comments: Brill and Carpenter (2001) described a baby ornithopod discovered by Mike Williams, during field work by the Denver Museum of Natural History in the early to middle 1990s, in five maroon sandstone blocks, preserved in part and counterpart slabs, in the Upper Jurassic Morrison Formation of Garden Park, Colorado. Nicknamed "Mike's Baby," the skeleton (DMNH 21716) includes a femur, humerus, partial tibia and fibula, (articulated) five caudal cervical,

Photograph by the author, courtesy North American Museum of Ancient Life.

at least five anterior dorsal, and four sacral vertebrae, caudal vertebrae, two phalanges, several ribs, and paired frontals with a postorbital. This specimen seems to represent a single individual, based upon the proximity, orientation, and sizes of the preserved elements. The very small bones distinguish DMNH 21716 as "one of the youngest articulated Morrison ornithopods found to date."

Brill and Carpenter identified DMNH 21716 as probably a juvenile based on the following features: Small bones, heads of femur and humerus small, bladelike; transverse processes apparently incompletely fused to centra of cervical vertebrae, neural arches not fused to centra in all vertebrae; ends of long bones appearing very spongy, incompletely formed; femur length (approximately 78.5 millimeters) about one-third that of adult; straight humeral shaft, sutures and pronounced emargiation of frontal above orbit (differing from that of adult).

Although the scarcity of diagnostic characters prevented a positive identification of this specimen, Brill and Carpenter found it reasonable to refer DMNH 21716 to the hypsilophodontid *Othnielia rex*,

based on the ratio of the lengths of the tibia and femur, absence of a pit close to the fourth trochanter of the femur, and the sloped shape of the proximal end of the humerus (see Galton 1983).

Comparing this specimen with an adult *O. rex* specimen (YPM 1882), and based upon the respective lengths of their femora and caudal cervical vertebrae, Brill and Carpenter deduced that DMNH 21716 was about one-third the length of the fully grown individual, or about 750 millimeters. As no eggs or

Mounted skeletons (casts) of *Othnielia rex*.

Life restoration of *Othnielia rex* painted by Kelly Pugh. The frill is conjectural.

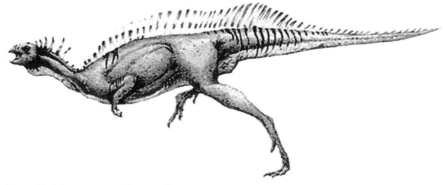

Courtesy North American Museum of Ancient Life.

P

hatchlings for this taxon have yet been found, the authors could not determine its age.

Key references: Brill and Carpenter (2001); Galton (1983).

Erratum: In *S2*, "Systematics" chapter, *Othnielia* was listed twice, under Hypsilophodontidae and also incorrectly under Ornithopoda *incertae sedis*.

†OVIRAPTOR

Saurischia: Eusaurischia: Theropoda: Neotheropoda: Tetanurae: Avetheropoda: Coelurosauria: Maniraptoriformes: Maniraptora: Metornithes: Oviraptorosauria: Oviraptoridae: ?Oviraptorinae.

Type species: *O. philoceratops* Osborn 1924.

Other species: [None.]

Comments: The holotype skull (AMNH 6517; see *D:TE* for photograph) of the type species *Oviraptor philoceratops* is poorly preserved, being mediolaterally crushed, abraided and, when first described by Henry Fairfield Osborn in 1924, only partially prepared. The skull was later described in greater detail by Smith (1993), who also attempted a reconstruction and an interpretation of its functional morphology.

Recently, Clark, Norell and Rowe (2002), in a paper describing the cranial anatomy of the oviraptorid *Citipati osmolskae* (see *Citipati* entry), redescribed in AMNH 6517. As noted by these authors, comparison between *C. osmolskae* and AMNH 6517 elucidates a number of features that were previously unclear regarding *O. philoceratops*. Among these many features, the following contradict Smith's description: Ectopterygoid and rostral end of palatine in typical oviraporid position, *i.e.*, facing laterally rather than ventrally (see Osmólska 1976; Elźanowski 1999); bone identified as ectopterygoid is actually quadrate; occiput facing caudally, in line with rest of skull, and not rotated (albeit slightly compressed mediolaterally); unclear if skull is amphikinetic, "mesokinetic hinge between the frontal and parietal bones" [Smith] not apparent, contact between frontal and prietal having not been preserved; portion of right frontal adhering to right postorbital; one of "knob-like paroccipital processes" [Smith] corresponding to occipital condyle; slender bone splint (lost since Smith's description) probably representing part of nasals; large accessory antorbital fenestra in rostral part of antorbital fenestra; surangular extensive, but probably not forming ventral edge of caudal part of mandibular ramus or extending rostrally beneath mandibular fenestra; articular surface of quadrate probably not as elongate as in *Citipati*.

According to Clark *et al.*, IGM 100/42, a specimen previously referred to *Oviraptor philoceratops* is more similar to *Citipati osmolskae* than to *O. mongoliensis* "in the shape of its narial region and in the presence of an accessory opening on the lateral surface of the ascending process of the premaxilla." Consequently, these authors referred this specimen to *Citipati*. The authors further pointed out that, in the past, the better preservation of this specimen has warranted its being relied upon for anatomical details of *O. philoceratops*. Consequently, caution should be exercised concerning referring to previous characterizations of *O. philoceratops*.

Note: Clark *et al.* also addressed the status of *Oviraptor mongoliensis*, a second species that had been referred to the genus by Barsbold (1986), founded upon a crested skull (GI 100/32) from the Nemegt Formation of Mongolia (see *D:TE*). According to these authors, "there is little evidence to place it in this genus." While this species shares with *O. philoceratops* a parietal crest, although one much larger, it "differs from it in having a maxilla and dentary as short as those of all other oviraptorids except *O. philoceratops*. The name "*Rinchenia*" was informally given to this potentially new genus by Barsbold in 1997.

Key references: Barsbold (1986, 1997); Clark, Norell and Rowe (2002); Elźanowski (1999); Osborn (1924); Osmólska (1976); Smith (1993).

PARALITITAN   Smith, Lamanna, Lacovara, Dodson, Smith, Poole, Giegengack and Attia 2001

Saurischia: Eusaurischia: Sauropodomorpha: Sauropoda: Eusauropoda: Neosauropoda: Macronaria: Camarasauromorpha: Titanosauriformes: Somphospondyli: Titanosauria: "Titanosauridae."

Name derivation: Greek *paralos* = "near the sea (paralic referring to tidal environments)" + Greek *Titan* (offspring of Uranus and Gaea, symbolic of brute strength and large size)."

Type species: *P. stromeri* Smith, Lamanna, Lacovara, Dodson, Smith, Poole, Giegengack and Attia 2001.

Other species: [None.]

Occurrence: Bahariya Formation, Bahariya Oasis, Sahara, Egypt.

Age: Upper Cretaceous (Cenomanian).

Known material: Partial skeleton, ?dorsal vertebra.

Holotype: CGM 81119, two fused caudal sacral vertebrae, proximal caudal vertebra, dorsal and sacral ribs, incomplete scapulae, complete right and incomplete left humeri, distal metacarpal, several other elements.

Diagnosis of genus (as for type species): Very large "titanosaurid" characterized by proximal caudal centra more wide than tall; prominent tabular process on caudal margin of scapula distal to proximal

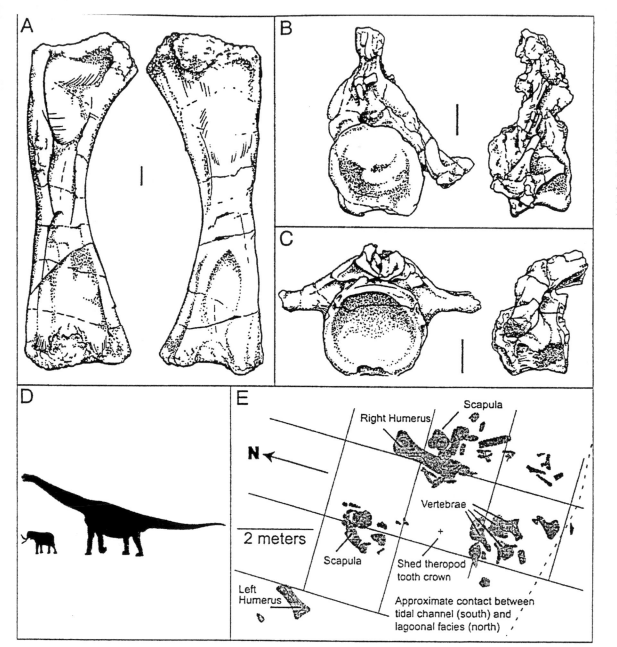

Paralititan

Paralititan stromeri, CGM 81119, holotype A. right humerus in cranial and caudal views, B. first caudal vertebra in distal and right lateral views, C. proximal caudal vertebra in proximal and right lateral views (scale bars = 10 cm.), D. size comparison between this species and an African elephant, and E. quarry map showing the type specimen as found. (After Smith, Lamanna, Lacovara, Dodson, Smith, Poole, Giegengack and Attia 2001.)

expansion; humerus having medial ridge on proximocaudal face and rectangular radial condyle (Smith, Lamanna, Lacovara, Dodson, Smith, Poole, Giegengack and Attia 2001).

Comments: An extremely large sauropod (seemingly the second largest known to date), *Paralititan stromeri* is distinguished as the first tetrapod reported from the Bahariya Oasis in the Sahara desert of Egypt since 1935. The holotype (CGM 81119) of this new taxon, a partial postcranial skeleton, was discovered in 1999 by a field team led by Joshua B. Smith (intrigued by sites first worked in the early twentieth century by Ernst Stromer von Reichenbach; see Stokstad 2001*b* for details), a graduate student at the University of Pennsylvania, Philadelphia, in the Bahariya Forma-

tion (see Lacovara, Lamanna, Smith, Grandstaff and Smith 2002 for a recent brief report on the concentration and preservation potential of vertebrate fossils in this formation), Baharija Oasis, southwest of Cairo, near Gebel Fagga. The specimen was found in low-energy paralic sediments that represent vegetated tidal flats and tidal channels, rich in plant remains including leaf compressions and (for the first time associated with a sauropod) stems of the mangrove tree fern *Weichsella reticulata* (Smith, Lamanna, Lacovara, Dodson, Smith, Poole, Giegengack and Attia 2001).

Smith *et al.* suggested that possibly referrable to this new genus and species, *Paralititan stromeri*, is a large cranial dorsal vertebra (1912VIII64; destroyed) described by Stromer in 1932, a specimen that was opisthocoelous, pleurocoelous, and wider caudally than tall.

Paralititan was identified by Smith *et al.* as a "titanosaurid" based upon the following shared characters: Caudal sacral vertebrae lacking pleurocoels; proximal caudal vertebrae having strongly concave proximal articular surface, well-developed distal articular condyle, ventral excavation, and postspinal lamina; humerus with proximolateral process and strong supracondylar ridges; manual phalanges reduced or absent.

Smith observed in *P. stromeri* a number of differences that precluded its referral to *Aegyptosaurus* (holotype 1912VIII61, destroyed), the only other described Bahariya sauropod, these including the following: *Aegyptosaurus* substantially smaller (length of humerus about 59 percent that of *Paralititan*); possibly possessed pleurocoelous proximal caudal vertebrae; had weakly medially convex scapula with no dorsomedial prominence; humerus with weak proximomedial expansion and more medially located dectoral crest restricted to proximal third of element; and lacked autapomorphies of *Paralititan*.

As Smith *et al.* observed, the closely associated bones of the holotype of *P. stromeri* could not have been transported to the burial site as clasts. Also, the shallow, vegetated tidal flat precludes the floating of such a large carcass to this location. Therefore, the authors deduced that this dinosaur walked to the site of burial, traversing tidal flats and along tidal channels, apparently spending time among the mangroves, before dying. Evidence also indicated that the carcass was then scavenged by some kind of carnivorous dinosaur.

Estimating the body size of *Paralititan* (the humerus measuring 1.69 meters long) and comparing this genus with the gigantic *Argentinosaurus* (humerus unknown, but estimated by Smith *et al.*, based on more completely know titanosauriforms, to be about 7.5 percent longer than that of *Paralititan*), the authors deduced that the Egyptian genus is probably not as large as that South American genus. Nevertheless, *Paralititan* "represents one of the heaviest terrestrial vertebrates yet discovered."

Notes: Prior to the publication of Smith *et al.*'s paper describing *Paralititan*, newspaper accounts stated that this dinosaur was approximately 100 feet (or almost 30 meters) in length and weighed about 75 tons (nearly 62 metric tonnes).

In an abstract, Lacovara, Smith, Smith, Lamanna, Johnson, Dodson and Nichola (2001), stated that many of the embayments and elongated seaways, created during the marine waters transgressions of the Cretaceous period, should have known conditions favoring the "development of halophytic plants in mangrove and salt marsh environments." As these authors pointed out, vegetated tidal flats in today's world are second in importance only to rain forests in biomass productivity per area. Indeed, during the Cretaceous, such coastal environments may also have been extremely important habitats for large vertebrates such as dinosaurs.

Lacovara *et al.* briefly reported that "mangroves and marshes may have been among the most productive habitats available to Cretaceous fauna," recent discoveries by these authors implying "very high levels of productivity from a mangrove environment contemporaneously occupied by three large theropod and two large sauropod dinosaurs." Along with similar deposits of the same age in western North America, the North African findings "have begun to shed light on the ecological importance of coastal biomes during the Cretaceous."

Key references: Lacovara, Lamanna, Smith, Grandstaff and Smith (2002); Lacovara, Smith, Smith, Lamanna, Johnson, Dodson and Nichola (2001); Smith, Lamanna, Lacovara, Dodson, Smith, Poole, Giegengack and Attia (2001); Stokstad (2001*b*); Stromer (1932).

†PARARHABDODON

Ornithischia: Genasauria: Cerapoda: Ornithopoda: Iguanodontia: Euiguanodontia: Dryomorpha: Ankylopollexia: Iguanodontoidea: Hadrosauroidea: Hadrosauridae: Euhadrosauria.

Comments: The type species *Pararhabdodon isonensis*, from the Late Cretaceous (Maastrichtian) of Spain, was first described by Casanovas, Santafé-Llopis and Isidoro-Llorens (1993) as a basal iguanodontian (see *D:TE*), and later by Laurent, Le Loeuff and Buffetaut (1997) as a lambeosaurine (see *SI*). Subsequently, Casanovas, Pereda Suberbiola, Santafé and Weishampel (1999*a*) found *Pararhabdodon* to be a basal member of the Lambeosaurinae.

More recently, however, Head (2001), in reassessing the iguanodontian *Eolambia* (see entry), also reconsidered the phylogenetic placement of *Pararhabodon*. As recounted by Head, Casanovas *et al.* (1999*a*) had referred *Pararhabdodon* to the Lambeosaurinae based upon its "possession of a medial maxillary shelf, rounded jugal contact, and angular deltopectoral crest of the humerus." However, Head pointed out, a truncated or rounded maxillary-jugal contact is not an established synapomorphy of lambeosaurines; furthermore, the jugal is not known in *Pararhabdodon*. As an angular deltopectoral crest is present primitively in the humeri of iguanodontians (see Norman 1998), and because the number of maxillary and dentary tooth positions is lower (about 35 in each) than seen in either hadrosaurid subfamily (see Forster 1997*a*), Head found it more likely that *Pararhabdodon* could be basal with respect to both Hadrosauridae and Lambeosauridae.

Key references: Casanovas, Santafé-Llopis and Isidoro-Llorens (1993); Casanovas, Pereda Suberbiola, Santafé and Weishampel (1999*a*); Forster (1997*a*); Head (2001); Laurent, Le Loeuff and Buffetaut (1997); Norman (1998).

†PARASAUROLOPHUS

Ornithischia: Genasauria: Cerapoda: Ornithopoda: Iguanodontia: Euiguanodontia: Dryomorpha: Ankylopollexia: Iguanodontoidea: Hadrosauroidea: Hadrosauridae: Euhadrosauria: Lambeosaurinae.

Comments: Titus, Gillette and Albright (2001), in an abstract, briefly reported on an articulated partial (about 25 to 30 percent complete) lambeosaurine skeleton recovered from the late Campanian Kaiparowits Formation, within the Grand Staircase-Escalante National Monument, Utah. The discovery is significant as representing "the most complete Campanian dinosaur yet found in southwestern Utah."

To date of their writing, during which excavation of the specimen was ongoing, identified recovered material includes 33 caudal vertebrae (with all chevrons and processes), a deeply weathered sacrum, a deeply eroded ?ischium, and several pedal elements (including a moderately well-preserved metatarsal and astragalus). The *in situ* good preservation of numerous ossified tendons suggested to Titus *et al.* minimal taphonomic loss. The overall preservation and such features as the ossified tendons supported the authors' speculation that the specimen was relatively complete when it was buried, only to be found following significant erosion, this idea further supported by the many unidentifiable bone fragments found down slope from the site.

Titus *et al.* assigned this specimen to the Lambeosaurinae based upon its overall morphology, and also on the height of its vertebral neural spines. To date, only the rare, long-crested genus *Parasaurolophus* has been reported from the Kaiparowits Formation. However, although all known features of this new specimen compare favorably with that genus, the authors preferred referring generic identification pending the possible recovery and preparation of additional elements. "This specimen, along with others that await excavation," Titus *et al.* stated, "indicate that facies favorable for the preservation of articulated macrovertebrates may be more widely developed in the Kaiparowits than previously thought."

Key reference: Titus, Gillette and Albright (2001).

†PARONYCHODON — (See *Richardoestesia*.)

†PHUWIANGOSAURUS

Saurischia: Eusaurischia: Sauropodomorpha: Sauropoda: Eusauropoda: Neosauropoda: Macronaria: Camarasauromorpha: Titanosauriformes: Somphospondyli: Titanosauria: Nemegtosauridae.

Comment: In a continuing study of *Phuwiangosaurus* (see *D:TE, S2*), a sauropod from the Upper Cretaceous of Thailand, Éric Buffetaut and Varavudh Suteethorn (2003), in a brief report published as an abstract, again addressed the question regarding its affinities within Sauropoda. These authors also discussed the affinities of the Nemegtosauridae, the family to which this genus had been tentatively assigned, as well as those of the related genera *Nemegtosaurus* and *Quaesitosaurus*.

According to Buffetaut and Suteethorn's report, new evidence concerning the type species *Phuwiangosaurus strindhornae* "shows that it clearly is a nemegtosaurid and that the family Nemegtosauridae should be placed among the Titanosauroidea."

As Buffetaut and Suteethorn pointed out, this taxon was first described based only on postcranial remains, which made difficult comparisons with members of the Nemegtosauridae. However, recently collected specimens, including an almost complete skeleton with a partial skull have helped to clarify the relationships of this species. The authors noted that the teeth, upper jaw, and braincase, preserved in this specimen, closely resemble those of the nemegtosaurids *Nemegtosaurus* and *Quaesitosaurus*. Therefore, *Phuwiangosaurus* should be referred to the Nemegtosauridae as the earliest known member of that family.

"What we now know of the skull of *Phuwiangosaurus sirindhornae* thus shows," Buffetaut and Suteethorn concluded, "that the Nemegtosauridae should be placed among the Titanosauroidea, not the Diplocoidea."

Key reference: Buffetaut and Suteethorn (2003).

†PHYLLODON

Ornithischia: Genasauria: Cerapoda: Ornithopoda: Hypsilophodontidae: Hypsilophodontinae.

Diagnosis (tentative) of genus (as for type species): Small hypsilophodontid having unusually high and symmetrical maxillary tooth crowns, showing higher labial than lingual side; apex especially pronounced, small and often denticulate cingulum on distal part of lingual side; dentary crowns high triangular to leaf-shaped, without cingulum; apex in maxillary and dentary crowns often subdivided into two

Phyllodon

Teeth (IPFUB collection) from Guimarota, Portugal referred *Phyllodon henkeli*: A. Outline of complete premaxillary tooth; B. premaxillary tooth with denticulate mesial carina, lingual view; C. premaxillary tooth with non-denticulate carina, labial view; D. outline of complete, slightly worn maxillary tooth, lingual view; maxillary tooth, (E) labial and (F) lingual views; maxillary tooth, (G) lingual and (H) mesial views; dentary tooth, (I) labial and (J) mesial views; K. outline of complete, worn dentary tooth; and L. very small dentary tooth, ?lingual view. Scale = 1 mm. (After Rauhut 2001*b*.)

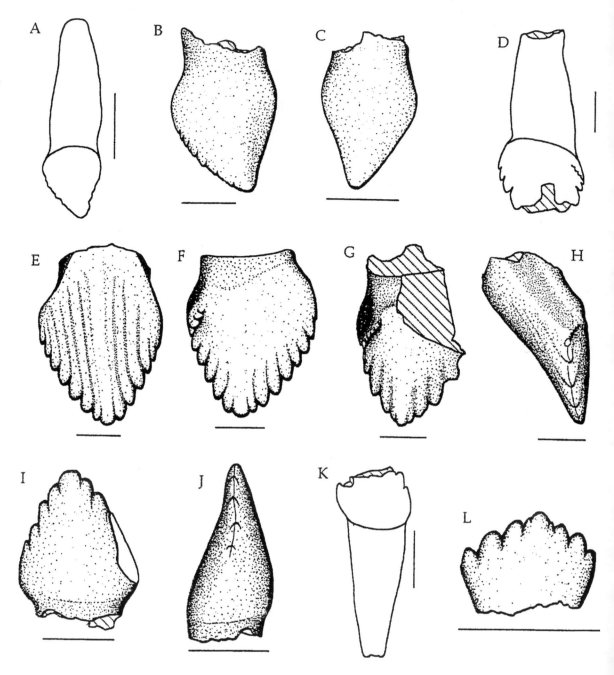

to three small denticles; (when present) denticles in premaxillary teeth better developed on mesial than on distal carina (Rauhut 2001*b*).

Comments: In a report on herbivorous dinosaurs recovered between 1972 and 1982 (see Krebs 1991) from the lignite coal mine locality in the vertebrate-bearing layers of the Late Jurassic (Kimmeridgian, based on ostracods; see Helmdach 1971; Schudack 1993, 2000) Alcobaca Formation (see Helmdach) of Guimarota, near the city of Leiria, in central Portugal, Rauhut (2001*b*) described material that that author referred to *Phyllodon henkeli*. Included in these remains are approximately 124 teeth (IPFUB Gui Or 7-50; including premaxillary, cheek, maxillary, and

dentary teeth) and (tentatively referred) four fragmentary dentaries (IPFUB Gui Or1-4).

Rauhut identified the teeth as ornithischian based upon their shape (asymmetrically subconical, often slightly recurved, displacing the apex of the crown caudally and slightly medially) and the presence of large marginal denticles. The author referred them to *P. henkeli* because they correspond quite closely with those originally described by Thulborn (1973) as a new genus and species, *Phyllodon henkeli*, and because they come from the same locality that yielded the holotype of Thulborn's taxon.

These very small teeth (*e.g.*, fore to aft basal length of the dentary teeth varying between only 0.5

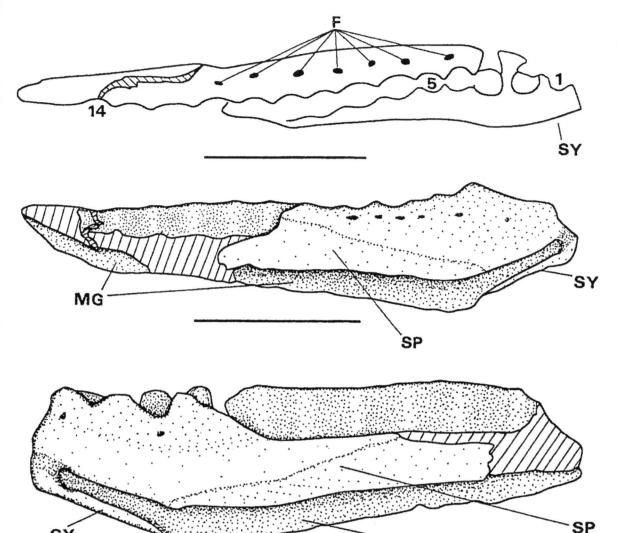

Phyllodon

Dentaries possibly belonging to *Phyllodon henkeli* from Guimarota, Portugal: Left dentary (IPFUB Or 1) in (top) occlusal and (middle) views; (bottom) right dentary (IPFUB Or 2) in medial view. Scale = 5 mm. (After Rauhut 2001*b*.)

and 3 millimeters) from the Guimarota beds were interpreted by Rauhut as belonging to quite young individuals. This further suggested that at least the presumably most distal dentary teeth were comparatively more broad in juvenile individuals than adults.

As Rauhut observed, the teeth of *Phyllodon* differ from those of other known hypsilophodontids in the following characters: Denticles in premaxillary teeth better developed on medial than on distal side; maxillary tooth crowns almost symmetrical, significantly higher than long; apical denticle on maxillary and dentary teeth subdivided into two to three smaller denticles.

Rauhut acknowledged that using tooth characters to diagnose dinosaurian taxa can be of only questionable validity. However, the differences distinguishing *Phyllodon* from other hypsilophodontids suggest that this may be a valid genus, although confirmation of this assessment is dependent upon the

recovery of additional material. Based on tooth characters, that author proposed a new although tentative diagnosis of *P. henkeli* (see above).

According to Rauhut, the dentaries, while not preserving teeth *in situ*, most likely belong to the same taxon as the teeth, as the only other ornithischians known from the Guimarota locality are iguanodontians. In the latter, that author pointed out, the dentary is different in regards various features (*e.g.*, contact to splenial and homodonty within dentary) from the dentaries from Guimarota (heterodonty, as indicated by size of alveoli).

Comparing the teeth of *Phyllodon* to those of other known members of the Hypsilophodontidae, Rauhut observed the strongest similarities to be in the Late Jurassic North American genus *Drinker*. In both forms, the maxillary teeth have a denticulate cingulum on the distal part of the lingual side; also, all *Drinker* teeth exhibit subdivided denticles as in the apical denticles of *Phyllodon*. These shared derived characters, that author stated, indicate a close relationship between these two genera.

Note: From the same site, Rauhut also described three teeth (IPFUB Gui Or-5-6 and Gui Or 51) of an iguanodontian and five teeth (IPFUB Gui Sd 1— Gui Sd 5) belonging to a possibly brachiosaurid sauropod. More common at this locality, however, are theropods, also known from teeth, this material having already been described by previous authors (see Rauhut for references).

Key references: Krebs (1991); Rauhut (2001*b*); Thulborn (1973).

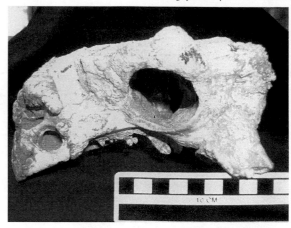

Pinacosaurus grangeri, AMNH 6523, holotype skull in left lateral view.

†PINACOSAURUS

Ornithischia: Genasaura: Thyreophora: Eurypoda: Ankylosauromorpha: Ankylosauria: Ankylosauridae.

Comments: In an abstract, Hill, Witmer and

Norell (2001) reported the occurrence of the first diagnostic ankylosaur specimen, a juvenile of the type species *Pinacosaurus grangeri*, from Ukhaa Tolgod (an Upper Cretaceous locality well known for its excellently preserved theropod, squamate, and mammals specimens), in southern Mongolia. This newly recovered specimen comprises an almost complete skull with associated mandible and osteoderms exhibiting such ankylosaurid synapomorphies as these: Two pairs of "horns" projecting from jugals and squamosals; skull relatively wide; absence of premaxillary teeth.

Hill *et al.* referred this specimen to *P. grangeri* based upon the following features: Nasal region with three pairs of openings; premaxillary sinus large; quadrate not coossified with paroccipital process. The authors identified the specimen as a juvenile on the basis of its small size, and also the incomplete fusion of the secondary dermal ossifications to the skull roof, exposing sutural boundaries. As Hill *et al.* pointed out, juvenile ankylosaur skulls are both "rare but crucial for understanding the basic anatomy of the highly fused and apomorphic adult skull." Morphological information will be added to previously published phylogentic analyses of the Ankylosauria, thereby identifying "diagnostic characters that improve genus-level resolution of ankylosaur relationships."

The authors also noted that this new specimen offers data regarding the ontogenetic sequence of secondary dermal ossification, including the following: Dermal ossifications covering only narial region, jugals, and squamosals, supporting the hypothesis that these appear in these areas during early ontogeny; two well-developed osteoderms found in close apposition but unfused to ventrolateral edges of mandible (fused to underlying bones in all known adult specimens), suggesting early appearance but fusion only during later ontogeny.

Key reference: Hill, Witmer and Norell (2001).

Pinacosaurus mephisto-cephalus, IMM 96BM3/1, holotype skeleton mounted at the third Dinofest event (the "World's Fair of Dinosaurs") held in Philadelphia, Pennsylvania (1998).

PLANICOXA DiCroce and Carpenter 2001
Ornithischia: Genasauria: Cerapoda: Ornithopoda:
 Iguanodontia: Euiguanodontia: Dryomorpha: An-
 kylopollexia: Iguanodontoidea: "Iguanodontidae."
Name derivation: Latin *plani* = "fat/level" + Latin *coxa*
 = "hip."
Type species: *P. venenica* DiCroce and Carpenter 2001.
Other species: [None.]
Occurrence: Cedar Mountain Formation, Utah,
 United States.

Age: Early Cretaceous (?Barremian).
Known material: Miscellaneous postcranial elements.
Holotype: DMNH 42504, left ilium.

 Diagnosis of genus (as for type species): Caudal
vertebrae having paired ventral ridges connecting
proximal and distal chevron facets; head of humerus
extending onto caudal surface; postacetabular blade of
ilium short, horizontal (DiCrose and Carpenter 2001).

 Comments: *Planicoxa* is distinguished as the first
iguanodontian genus known from the Lower Cretaceous

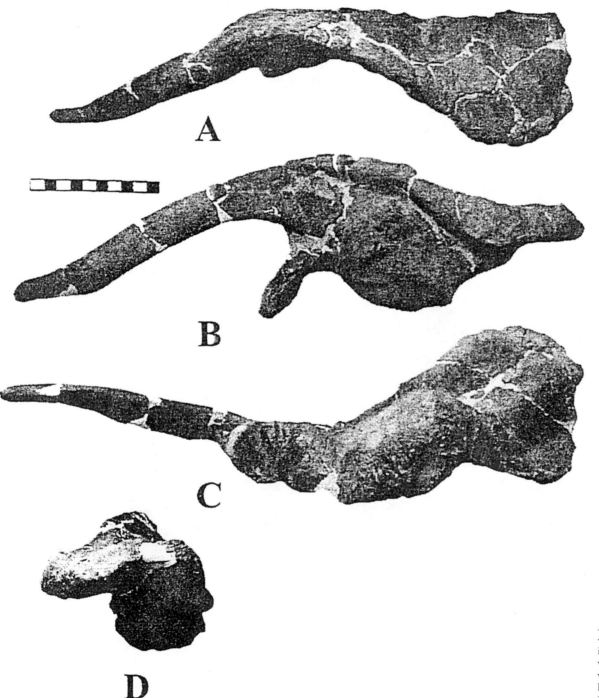

Planicoxa venecia, DMNH
42504, holotype left ilium
in A. dorsal, B. lateral, C.
ventral, and D. caudal
views. Scale = 10 cm. (After
DiCroce and Carpenter
2001.)

Planicoxa

Planicoxa venenica, reconstructed partial skeleton including holotype ilium DMNH 42504 and referred specimens.

Poison Strip Sandstone Member (?Barremian; Kirkland, Cifelli, Britt, Burge, DeCourten, Eaton and Parrish 1997; or more generalized ?"Neocomian"; B. B. Britt, personal communication to Tidwell, Carpenter and Meyer 2001) of the Cedar Mountain Formation, near Arches National Park, in eastern Utah. The genus was established on a well-preserved ilium (DMNH 41504) found by a Denver Museum of Science and Nature volunteer team in spring, 1998, from fine- to medium-grained sandstone suspended with gray,

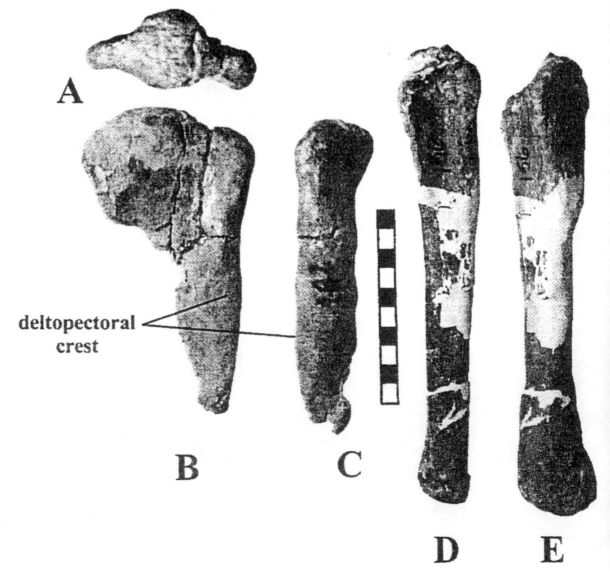

deltopectoral crest

Planicoxa venecia, DMNH 42508, referred left humerus in A. proxima, B. cranial, and C. medial views; DMNH 42507, referred left ulna in D. cranial and E. medial views. Scale = 10 cm. (After DiCroce and Carpenter 2001.)

black, and white chert pebbles, at a site named Tony's Bone Bed (DiCrose and Carpenter 2001).

As DiCrose and Carpenter reported, paratype specimens from the same quarry include the following: DMNH 42511, neural arch of cervical vertebra; DMNH 42516, 42518 to 42522, 42524, seven dorsal vertebral arches; DMNH 42513, 42515, and 42525, three dorsal centra; DMNH 42523, 42526, and 42527, three dorsal rib fragments; DMNH 42510, sacral vertebra; DMNH 42514 and 42517, two caudal centra; DMNH 42508, proximal end of left humerus; DMNH 42507, left ulna; DMNH 42505, left femur; DMNH 40917, right femur; DMNH 40914 and 40918, two right tibiae; DMNH 42506, distal end of left tibia; DMNH 42506, distal end of left tibia; DMNH 42509, left metatarsal II; and DMNH 42512, pedal phalanx.

Associated fauna from the same quarry includes an unidentified ornithopod, both adult and juvenile specimens of the new sauropod *Venenosaurus* (Tidwell *et al.*), and a theropod (?*Utahraptor ostrommaysorum*).

DiCroce and Carpenter described *Planicoxa* as a medium-sized form, its right (and larger) femur (DMNH 40917) measuring 52 centimeters in length.

The authors identified *Planicoxa* as a "euornithopod" [see "Systematics" chapter] based upon the absence of a neural spine on the cervical arch (see Sereno 1998, 1999*b*), and also observed the following: Unlike other known members of the "Euornithopoda," the postacetabular process of the ilium is cranio-caudally short and horizontal. This feature — showing an expanded scar for the M. ilio-femoralis internus and functioning as an antitrochanter — constitutes an autapomorphy heretofore not reported in this clade. The origin of the M. ilio-tibialis lateralis is along the dorsal rim of the ilium. Ventrally, the overhanging postacetabular blade of the ilium is separated into two areas, the most anterolateral site corresponding to the origin of the M. ilio-fibularis (identified by Galton 1969 in *Hypsilophodon*), the more posteromedial area the ventral aspect of the brevis shelf, the latter traditionally regarded as the site for the M. caudi-femoralis brevis (see, for example, Romer 1927; Galton), after the crocodile (Romer 1923*a*); based on bird anatomy (*e.g.*, Drushel and Caplan 1991), however, these origins may constitute, respectively, the M. ilio-fibularis pars cranialis for the anterolateral muscle scar and the M. ilio-fibularis et caudalis for the posteromedial muscle scar.

DiCrose and Carpenter further referred *Planicoxa* to the Iguanodontia as a possible "iguanodontid," but did not offer a cladistic analysis of this new genus demonstrating this referral.

Key references: Carpenter and Meyer (2001); DiCroce and Carpenter (2001); Drushel and Caplan (1991); Galton (1969); Kirkland, Cifelli, Britt, Burge, DeCourten, Eaton and Parrish (1997); Romer (1923*a*, 1927); Sereno (1998, 1999*b*); Tidwell, Carpenter and Meyer (2001).

†PLATEOSAURUS

Saurischia: Eusaurischia: Sauropodomorpha: Prosauropoda: Plateosauridae.

Type species: *P. engelhardti* Meyer 1837.

Other species: *P. ajax* (Huene 1907–08) [*nomen dubium*], *P. bavaricus* (Fraas *see in* Sandberger 1894) [*nomen dubium*]; *P. erlenbergiensis* Huene 1907–08 [*nomen dubium*], *P. giganteus* (Huene 1932) [*nomen dubium*], *P. longiceps* Jaekel 1913–14, *P. magnus* (Huene 1907–08) [*nomen dubium*], *P. plieningeri* (Huene 1907–07) [*nomen dubium*], *P. quenstedti* Huene 1905 [*nomen nudum*], *P. reinigeri* Huene 1905 [*nomen dubium*], *P. robustus* (Huene 1907–08) [*nomen dubium*], *P. torgeri* (Jaekel 1911) [*nomen dubium*], *P. wetzelianus* (Huene 1932) [*nomen dubium*].

Diagnosis of *P. engelhardti*: First and second sacral ribs originating from complete length of first centrum and from caudal 75 percent of second centrum; third to seventh caudal centra having ventrally converging articular surfaces (forming 12- to 20-degree angle); pelvic girdle and hindlimb massive; pubis having open obturator foramen; distal portion of femur straight in craniocaudal views [additional characters awaiting detailed description of all Ellingen specimens by M. Moser] (Galton 2001*e*).

Diagnosis of *P. longiceps*: Ventral medially directed, peglike process on middle of palatine; transverse sub-vertical sheet of bone between superior half of basipterygoid processes [fuller diagnosis awaiting completion of more detailed cladistic analysis of Prosauropoda (Upchurch and Galton, in press) (Galton 2001*e*).

Comments: *Plateosaurus* is a very large prosauropod dinosaur definitely known from the Upper Triassic of Europe and Greenland, and represented by numerous specimens. Over the years, many species have been referred to this genus, most of them from Germany. However, it has only been relatively recently that this genus, the material assigned to it, and its various referred species have been subject to critical review and cladistic analysis. Prosauropod specialist Peter M. Galton (2001*b*, 2001*e*), in a continuing series of highly detailed articles on the prosauropod dinosaurs of Late Triassic Germany, further discussed this well-known genus (see *D:TE, S2, S2*).

The syntypes (UEN 550, 552, 554–6, 559, 561–3) of the rare type species *Plateosaurus engelhadti* consist of just a few vertebrae (two dorsals, an incomplete sacrum, and two caudals), three dorsal rib

Material belonging to *Plateosaurus*: A–D, proximal caudal vertebrae and chevrons referred to *P. longiceps*, A. SMNS 13200b, B. left lateral view, C. first caudal vertebra with vestigial chevron, ventral view, D. GPIT IV, part of holotype of *Pachysaurus wetzelianus*, left lateral view; E. skeleton (GPIT I) as preserved, mostly right lateral view; F. *P. engelhardti*, UE 556, syntype distal part of left femur, caudal view with proximal cross section of shaft; G–H, ilia and sacra, dorsal view, G. *P. longicep*, part of holotype of *P. fraasianus*, H. postcrania referred to "*Sinosaurus*," dorsal view. Scale = 5 cm (A–D, F–H) and 50 cm. (E). (After Galton 2001*b*: B–D, from Huene 1932, E from Huene 1928, F. after Meyer 1837, H. from Yang [Young] 1948.)

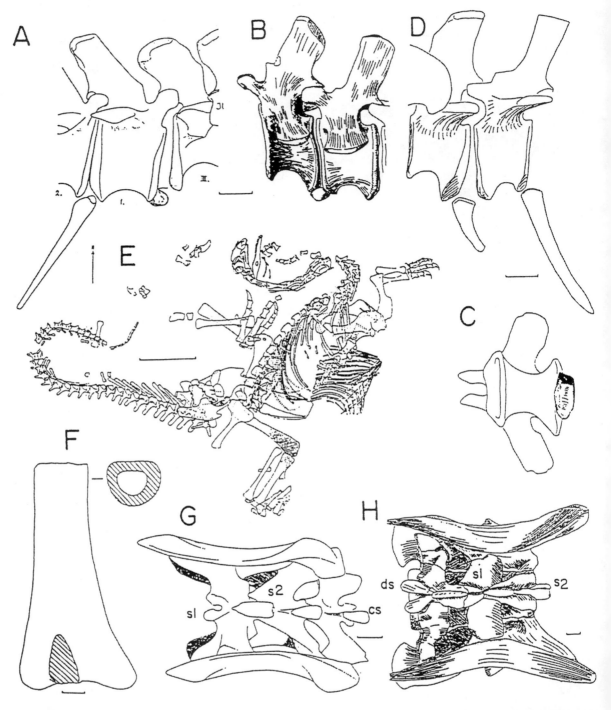

pieces, the distal half of a left femur, and a left tibia. As observed by Galton (2001*b*, 2001*e*), these specimens exhibit three autapomorphies: First sacral rib originating from complete length of first centrum; second sacral rib originating from caudal 75 percent of second centrum (Galton, 2000, 2001*e*); and distal portion of femur apparently originally distally straight in craniocaudal aspects. Galton (2001*b*, 2001*e*) noted that these features contrast with the plesiomorphic condition (from the anterior 50 to 75 percent and anterior 75 percent of the sacrum for the first and sec-

ond sacral ribs) found in the numerous referred *Plateosaurus* specimens from Trossingen (upper Norian; see Bachman, Beutler, Hagdorn, and Hauschke 1999; Beutler 1998*a*, 1999*b*), Germany, in the other species of this genus (where this condition can be determined), and in other prosauropods (Galton 1999; 2000). Furthermore, the femur is distally curved in craniocaudal aspect in most other known *Plateosaurus* species where this condition can be determined (Galton, 2000, 2001*e*, 2001*e*) and most other known prosauropods (Galton and Upchurch, in press).

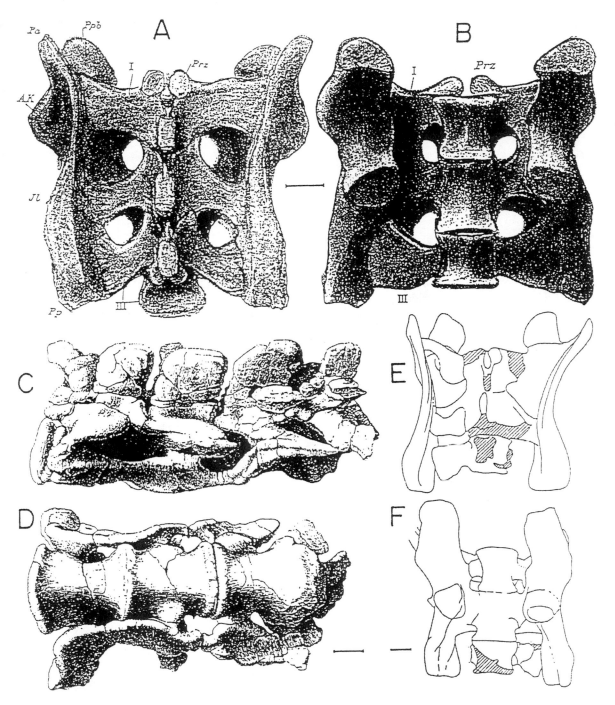

Sacra of *Plateosaurus*: A–B, *Plateosaurus longiceps*, part of HMN XXV, sacrum and ilia in A. dorsal and B. ventral views; C–F, sacrum and incomplete first caudal vertebra, part of holotype (SMNS 80664) of *P. plieningeri*, in C. left lateral and D. ventral views; E–F, sacrum with ilia, part of holotype (SMNS 53537) of *P. reiningeri*, in E. dorsal and F. ventral views. Scale = approx. 5 cm. (After Galton 2001*b*: A–B from Jaekel 1913–14, C–D from Plieninger 1857, E–F drawn from photographs, not corrected for distortion or parallax, from Galton in press *a*.)

Addressing the issue of *Plateosaurus* skulls, Galton (2001*b*, 2001*e*) noted that a number of skulls have been referred to this genus, including four complete skulls referred by Huene (1932) to as many separate species (*P. erlenbergiensis*, *P. fraasianus*, *P. plieningeri*, and *P. quenstedti* [see below]), a complete skull from Halberstadt, the holotype of *P. longiceps* (see Galton 1985*b*; Huene 1907–08), and a partial skull belonging to the holotype of *P. erlenbergiensis* found near Stuttgart (Galton 1985*b*; Huene 1907–08). Huene (1932) found the differences between these skulls (but not the skeletons) to be minimal, making specific sep-

aration based on them to be hardly possible. Galton (1985*b*, 2001*b*, 2001*e*) further stated that the observable differences between these skulls can best be attributed to individual variation and differences in preservation, that author also finding it unlikely that two such large herbivores would be sympatric, six of the species recognized by Huene (1932) occurring in the same horizon and locality.

In reviewing in detail the other European species that have been referred to *Plateosaurus*, Galton (2001*b*, 2001*e*) stated the following:

The species *Plateosaurus* (*Zanclodon*) *bavaricus*

Fraas *see in* Sandberger 1894 (see also Huene 1907–08), based upon fragments of the seventh and a middle caudal vertebra and the distal end of a tibia (UW collection; specimen not seen by Galton), from the Upper Keuper of Altenstein near Marolsweisach near Würzburg, Lower Frankonia, Bavaria, previously regarded by Galton (2000; see *S2*) as a *nomen nudum*, was designated "a *nomen dubium* because the material is generically indeterminate."

Plateosaurus longiceps Jaekel 1913 was based on three of the 50 or so specimens collected from the Knollenmergel (upper Norian; see Bachman, Beutler, Hagdorn, and Hauschke 1999; Beutler 1998*a*, 1999*b*) of the Baerecke-Limpricht clay pit in Halberstadt, Sachsen-Anhalt, Germany. The holotype is a complete skull (MB R.1937 [the formerly published HMN XXIV is a field number; Huene 1932 mentioned seeing other remains, including the first five cervical and 13 other vertebrae, the sacrum with ilia, the ischium, scapula, femur, tibia, and fibula in the block containing the skull, these elements having been either mislaid, destroyed, or lost; Heinrich, personal communication to Galton 2001*b*). Other remains referred to this species include the neural arches of the sacral vertebrae, the first to thirty-fourth caudal ver-

tebrae, the left pelvic girdle, and a complete right hindlimb with a sigmoid femur (MB HMN I); and a partial skull (MB HMN XXV; see Galton 1985*b*) with a reasonably complete skeleton lacking most of the tail (Jaekel 1913–14), with a sigmoid femur, and sacrum of the Trossingen type. (These latter two specimens, formerly regarded as syntypes, are not, Galton 2001*b*, 2001*e* pointed out, as they were described by Jaekel in the second part [1914] of his 1913–14 publication.) *P. longiceps* Jaekel 1913 is the valid name for specimens possessing the Trossingen-type sacrum, having priority over *P. trossingensis* Fraas 1913 (published respectively in June and November; M. Moser, personal communication to Galton 2001*b*).

Plateosaurus trossingensis Fraas 1913–14 was founded on an almost complete skeleton (SMNS 13200), lacking the left forelimb and several vertebrae beyond the 25th caudal, from the lower bed (Upper Stubensandstein) at the Obere Müle, Trossingen (first described by Huene in 1926). Galton (1985*b*, 1990, 1992) formerly referred this species to *P. engelhardti*. According to Galton's (2001*b*, 2001*e*) more recent assessments, however, this species is valid, differing from the type species in the form of the sacrum — the first and second ribs originating from the cranial 50 to 75

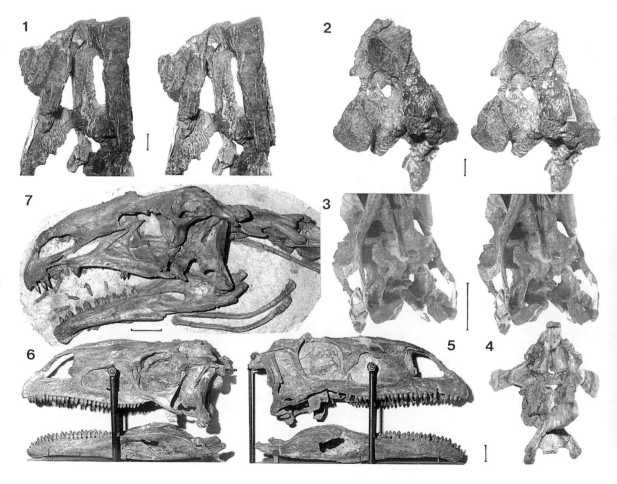

Plateosaurus cranial material: 1. SMNS 6014, holotype of *Plateosaurus erlenbergiensis* from Erlenberg, caudal part of horizontally sectioned palate and jaws, stereo ventral view (from Galton 1985*c*); 2. SMNS 6014, right sidewall and floor of braincase, with piece of right quadrate, stereo posterolateral view (from Galton 1985*c*); 3. *P. longiceps*, SMNS 13200, holotype of *P. trossingensis* from Trossingen, caudal part of skull, stereo ventral view; 4. *P. longiceps*, AMNH 6810 from Trossingen, braincase, rostral view; 5.–6., *P. longiceps*, MB R.1937 (=MB HMN XXIV) from Halberstadt, complete skull, right and left lateral views, respectively (from Galton 1985*c*); 7. *P. longiceps*, MB HMN.1927.19.1 from Halberstadt, complete skull with ceratobranchials and first three cervical vertebrae. Scale = 1 cm. (1, 2, 4) and 5 cm. (3., 5–7). (After Galton 2001*e*.)

percent and 75 percent of their respective centra (as opposed to 100 percent and the caudal 75 percent in *P. engelhardti*), and the sigmoid femur with the distal part curved (as opposed to straight) in craniocaudal aspect.

According to Galton (2001*a*, 2001*e*), *Plateosaurus intiger* Fraas 1915 *see in* Huene 1915 [*nomen vanum*] and *Plateosaurus fraasianus* Huene 1932 [*nomen vanum*], both founded upon the skeleton (SMNS 13200) from the lower bonebed at the Obere Mühle at Trossingen (see Galton 2001*e* for the nomenclatural entanglements regarding these names), are also subjective junior synonyms of *P. longiceps*.

Plateosaurus erlenbergiensis Huene 1905 (not 1907–08, Galton 2001*b*, 2001*e* noted, as previously erroneously reported) was established on a specimen (SMNS 6014) comprising a partial skull (see Galton 1985*b*), including the maxillae, the palate, most of the braincase, and the caudal part of the lower jaw, and postcranial skeleton including the caudoventral portion of the third sacral centrum, portions of bones of the pectoral girdle and forelimb, a complete ilium, ischium, most of the hindlimb elements including a sigmoid femur, and a complete pes, from the Knollenmergel of Erlenberg, between Stuttgart and Vaihingen, Württemberg (see *S2* for more details). Two cranial autapomorphies were recognized by Galton and Upchurch (in press) in their detailed cladistic analysis of the Prosauropoda; nevertheless, this species was considered by Galton (2000, 2001*b*, 2001*e*) to be a *nomen dubium*, its type material insufficiently complete to diagnose it as a valid species.

Plateosaurus ingens (Rütimeyer 1856), type species of the genus *Gresslyosaurus*, is known from the following syntypes: Postcranial remains including an incomplete sacrum (NMB NB1584 and 1585), four caudal vertebrae (NMB NB1572–1574 and 1577), a left metacarpal II (NMB NB1578), the distal end of left metatarsal V (NMB NB 1576), the proximal end of the left tibia (NMB NB1582), and two pedal phalanges (NMB NB53 and 1591) (see Huene 1907–08l; cast of ungual phalanx of pedal digit IV (Huene 1907–08) located by Galton 1968*a*), from the Upper "*Zanclodon*" Knollenmergel (Middle Keuper, Upper Norian) of Niederschönthal, near Füllinsdorf, near Liestal, Kanton Baselland, Switzerland (for an historical report on early Swiss research on dinosaurs, including material referred to *Gresslyosaurus ingens*, see Benz and Haller-Brem 1997). Galton (2001*b*) first noted that, although the preserved parts of the second sacral vertebra and rib are of the Trossingen type (see Huene 1907–08), the incompleteness of the type specimen, lacking both skull and femur, relegates this species to *nomen dubium* status. Subsequently, Galton (2001*e*) found the similarity of *P. ingens* to the material from Trossingen to refer this species to *P. longiceps*.

Plateosaurus poligniensis (Pidancet and Chopard 1862), the type species of *Dimodosaurus*, is known from the following specimens: Syntypes including the neural arch of an anterior dorsal vertebra (POL 1), an incomplete right scapula (POL collection), a compressed right femur (POL 75), fibulae (the right lacking distal end) (POL 37), and three pedal phalanges, collected from a bonebed in the Marnes irisées supérieures (Knollenmergel equivalent) of the Boise de Cassagne, between Poligny and St. Lothain, Départment du Jura, in southeastern France; lectotype (POL; lectotype specimens one through four as cataloged by Chopard 1883, fifth specimen a right ilium from another individual), including eight articulated vertebrae (dorsals 11 to 15 and first three sacrals with articulated left ilium; see Huene 1907–08); and paralectotypes, comprising the remaining elements figured in Chopard's reconstruction, including the distal end of the left tibia with articulated astragalus and displaced calcaneum, and the complete right fibula (the complete anterior left dorsal rib figured by Chopard could not be located by Galton 2001*b*). Although the sigmoid femur compares favorably with the femur from Trossingen, and the (lost) sacrum appears to have been of the Trossingen type, further comparisons were not possible and there is no skull; hence, Galton (2001*b*) regarded this species as a *nomen dubium*. Subsequently, Galton (2001*e*) found this species to be a probable junior synonym of *P. longiceps*, based upon the sigmoid form of its femur and its Trossingen-type sacrum (although one individual — "*Gresslyosaurus* cf. *plieningeri*" [see Huene 1907–08] — possessing a distally straight femur, as well as *Thecodontosaurus*-like teeth from Villette near Arbois [see, for example, Gaudry 1890; Galton 1998], may be referrable to *P. engelhardti*).

"*Plateosaurus*" *plieningeri* (Fraas 1896), previously *Zanclodon plieningeri* Fraas 1896 (originally *Smilodon laevis* Plieninger 1846*a*, the latter subsequently made the type species of the genus *Zanclodon* Plieninger 1846*b*), was founded on an incomplete left maxilla (SMNS 6045) from the Lettenkohle (Lower Lettenkeuper, Middle Triassic) of Gaildorf, near Schwäbisch Hall, Würtemberg, Germany. The specimen belongs to an archosaurian taxon of uncertain affinities, having tapering, recurved, and unserrated teeth that do not resemble the teeth of any prosauropod (see Galton 2001*b*, 2001*e*). Furthermore, they may be too old to be even dinosaurian, as prosauropods are only known from unequivocal skeletal remains dating to Upper Triassic rocks (see also *Ruehleia* entry). Over the years, other material had been referred to *Z. laevis*, including a partial skeleton collected by Albert

Reiniger from the upper Middle Keuper Knollen-mergel or Trossingen Formation (Upper Triassic), of Degerloch in Stuttgart (this and another specimen subsequently referred by Plieninger 1857 to *Belodon plieningeri*, a species now known to be phytosaurian), such referrals leading to the widespread yet incorrect use of *Z. laevis* for all subsequent prosauropod discoveries from the Middle Keuper of Württemberg (see Galton 2001*e* for more details).

Plateosaurus quenstedti Huene 1905, originally *Zanclodon quenstedti* by Koken (1900) [*nomen dubium*], was based on one of non-*Zanclodon* prosauropod specimens (GPIT A), first referred to *Zanclodon laevis*. This specimen includes portions of most of the cervical vertebrae, the dorsal vertebral series (with ribs) as far as dorsal number eight, an articulated sacrum, the complete pelvis, and most of the fore- and hindlimbs (see Quenstedt 1867–68, although the correct date for this publication has been questioned). It was recovered from the Knollenmergel (middle Upper Keuper, later Norian) of "Jächklinge" (Brand-klinge), Tübingen-Pfrondorf, Württemberg. As revealed by Galton (2001*b*), Koken's species is a *nomen nudum* for reasons including that "the undated reference to Quenstedt was not specific enough"; therefore, according to the rules of the International Code of Zoological Nomenclature (1999), the correct name for this taxon is *Plateosaurus quenstedti* Huene 1905. Galton (2001*b*, 2001*e*) noted that the femur of this species is distally curved, but the specimen lacks a skull, the sacrum is incomplete and, as illustrated by Huene (1907–08), is indeterminate.

Plateosaurus reiningeri Huene 1905, founded upon an incomplete postcranial skeleton (SMNS 53537), including some cervical vertebrae, the tail, portions of the scapula, forearm, manus, and pes (see Plieninger 1857), from Knollenmergel, near Degerloch near Stuttgart, Germany. Although the sacrum is of the Trossingen type (Galton, 2001*e*, in press *a*), Galton (2001*b*, 2001*e*) noted that this species is not a junior synonym of *P. engelhardti*, as suggested by Wellnhofer (1993); furthermore, there are no autapomorphies for this species, due to the lack of a skull and the poor preservation of the femur (see Huene 1907–08; Galton, in press *a*), *P. reiningeri*, therefore, considered to be a *nomen dubium*.

Plateosaurus plieningeri (Huene 1907–08), originally referred to the genus *Gresslyosaurus* as *G. plieningeri* Huene 1907–08, was founded on postcranial remains (SMNS 80664) originally comprising 17 vertebrae (including the complete sacrum), ribs, an ilium, pubis, the distal ends of the femur and ?fibula, metatarsal V, and the ends of other metatarsals (see Plieninger 1857), from the Knollenmergel of Degerloch, Stuttgart. As observed by Galton (2000, 2001*e*;

see papers for details), the first two sacral ribs originate from about the anterior 50 to 75 percent and anterior 75 percent of their centra, as in sacra from Trossingen; consequently, it is not a junior synonym (*contra* Wellnhofer) of *P. engelhardti*. Lacking the skull and most of the limb bones, this species was regarded by Galton (2001*b*) as a *nomen dubium*.

Plateosaurus robustus (Huene 1907–08), originally referred to *Gresslyosaurus* as the species *G. robustus* Huene 1907–08, was based on a type specimen (GPIT B) originally including several vertebrae (mostly centra) from all regions, and parts of the manus, pelvic girdle, and hindlimb. Because of the incompleteness of this specimen (only two Trossingen-type sacral vertebrae, lost femur perhaps incorrectly reconstructed as straight), Galton (2001*b*, 2001*e*) regarded this species as a *nomen dubium*.

Plateosaurus ajax (Huene 1907–08), type species of the genera *Pachysaurus* Huene 1907–08, *Pachysauriscus* Kuhn 1962, and *Pachysaurops* Huene 1961 (not 1959; Huene got his publisher to predate this paper to establish priority over Kuhn 1959; M. Moser, personal communication to Galton), was based on a holotype (GPIT C) originally comprising mostly incomplete vertebrae from the caudal part of the neck, most dorsal vertebrae, pectoral girdles, parts of the manus, pieces of the distal end of the femur, and pieces of the tibia and fibula. This species also, due to the unsatisfactory nature of its holotype, was regarded by Galton (2001*b*) as a *nomen dubium* and subsequently by Galton (2001*e*) as a *nomen nudum*.

Plateosaurus magnus (Huene 1907–08), originally *Pachysaurus magnus* Huene 1907–08, was founded on a holotype (GPIT D) originally consisting of the third sacral vertebra, ribs, the pectoral girdles, humeri, parts of the radius, the left metacarpus, and a fragment of an ilium and a tibia, recovered in the late 1870s from the Knollenberg (Trossingen Formation, upper Middle Keuper, late Norian) of Brandklinge, near Tübingen-Pfrondorf, Germany. Formerly regarded by Galton (1985*b*, 1990*a*, 1992) as a junior synonym of *P. engelhardti*, this very incomplete species was more recently considered by Galton (2001*b*, 2001*e*) to be a *nomen dubium*.

Plateosaurus torgeri (Jaekel 1911), another *nomen dubium* (Galton 2001*b*), was founded on a fairly complete postcranial skeleton (MHN III; specimen lost) from the Knollenmergel of the Baerecke-Limpricht brick-clay pit, south of Halberstadt, Sachen-Anhalt, Germany. This species had also formerly been listed by Galton (1985*b*, 1990, 1992) as a junior synonym of *P. engelhardti*.

Plateosaurus wetzelianus (Huene 1932) was based on the poorly preserved holotype (GPIT V) of *Pachysaurus wetzelianus* Huene 1932, consisting of eight dorsal vertebrae, an incomplete third sacral vertebra with a partial second sacrum attached, the adjacent 13 caudal vertebrae, the distal two-thirds of the left humerus, the ventral half of the left ilium, ischia, pubes, an almost complete left hindlimb including a sigmoid femur of the Trossingen type, and a pes. Originally thought by Galton (1985b, 1990, 1992) to be a junior synonym of P. engelhardti, this species was reinterpreted by Galton (2001b, 2001e) as a *nomen dubium*.

Plateosaurus giganteus (Huene 1932) was based on the poorly preserved holotype (GPIT E) of *Pachysaurus giganteus* Huene 1932, comprising three very long metatarsals (II through IV), with associated phalanx (identified also as three fibulae, one with an attached calcaneum; D. B. Weishampel, personal communication to Galton 2001b), from the upper bonebed (Upper Stubensandstein) at the Obere Mühle, Trossingen. This species, once regarded by Galton (1985b, 1990, 1992) as a junior synonym of P. engelhardti, was reassessed by Galton (2001b, 2001e) to be a *nomen dubium*.

Non-European prosauropod material has also been referred to *Plateosaurus*, and these specimens were also addressed by Galton:

Several specimens (MCZ collection), including a nearly complete adult skeleton, a skull, and two partial juvenile skeletons, from the Fleming Fjord Formation (Upper Triassic: Norian) of Jameson Land, East Greenland (see Clemmensen, Kent and Jenkins 1998) were referred by Jenkins, Shubin, Amaral, Gatesy, Schaff, Clemmensen, Downs, Davidson, Bonde and Osbraek (1994) to *Plateosaurus engelhardti*. Galton (2001e), however, found this material to be "probably referable to P. longiceps."

Galton (2001b, 2001e) noted that the species *Plateosaurus cullingworthi* Haughton 1924, based on two partial skeletons (SAM 3341, 3345, 3347, 3350, 3351, 3603, and 3607) from the Lower Elliot Formation (Upper Triassic: upper Carnian or lower Norian; see Hancox 2000), South Africa, is a junior synonym of *Euskelosaurus browni*.

Plateosaurus stormbergensis Broom 1915 was based upon a right femur, metacarpal I, and fragments of vertebrae and a pubis from the Lower Elliot Formation of South Africa. Identified by Heerden (1979) as "cf. *Euskelosaurus*, sp. indet.," this species was regarded by Galton (2001b) as another *nomen dubium*.

Casamiquela (1980) briefly described as *Plateosaurus* sp. a partial skull and three partial skeletons (approximately 3 meters in length) recovered from the Upper Triassic (Norian) El Tranquilo Formation of southern Argentina. However, as Galton (2001e) pointed out, a series of intermediate-sized skeletons link these larger individuals to the extremely small

(length approximately 25 to 30 centimeters) and almost complete holotype skeleton of *Mussaurus patagonicus* (see *D:TE*) from the same site (see Bonaparte in Galton 1990). *M. patagonicus* cannot be referred to *Plateosaurus* as the third sacral vertebra in the larger skeletons is a dorsosacral (F. E. Novas, personal communication to Galton), not a caudosacral (as in *Plateosaurus*).

Addressing Wellnhofer's observation that the femur of *Camelotia borealis*, described by Galton (1985d) as a melanorosaurid, may be congeneric with *Plateosaurus* (as the species P. *borealis*) or even conspecific with P. *engelhardti*, Galton (2001b) emphasized that "A cladistic analysis of the Prosauropoda shows that *Camelotia* groups with *Melanorosaurus* and *Riojasaurus* as the Melanorosauridae, the sister taxon to the Anchisauridae (*Ammosaurus*+*Anchisaurus*, so it is well removed from the Plateosauria, Plateosauridae and *Plateosaurus* (Galton & Upchurch, in prep.)."

Again, Galton (2001b) addressed in detail the question of whether *Plateosaurus* was bipedal or quadrupedal, this dinosaur having been portrayed in both postures by various authors and artists over the past almost eight decades (see Galton 2000, 2001b, and *D:TE*, *S2* for details). As he had in his 2000 paper, Galton (2001b) concluded that the more massive Ellingen specimen (BSP 1962 XLVI; see *S2* for illustration of reconstructed skeleton) of P. *engelhardti* described by Wellnhofer was an "obligatory quadruped," while the Trossingen individuals "were probably more facultatively bipedal than the Ellingen specimen."

Notes: Galton (2001b) additionally discussed the long abandoned notion that *Plateosaurus* and other prosauropods were carnivorous animals, this idea having originated when loose shed teeth of predatory or scavenging theropods were intermixed with prosauropod remains. Galton (1984a) had already offered evidence supporting the hypothesis that prosauropods were herbivores (see *Plateosaurus* entry, *D:TE*). More recently, however, Barrett (1996, 2000) briefly reported that "herbivorous iguanines," once believed to be strict vegetarians, sometimes display severe growth disorders when meat is excluded from their diets. Furthermore, the teeth of these lizards are adapted for at least a partially carnivorous diet. The more rostral area of the tooth row is suited to capturing small prey, the teeth being sub-conical in cross section, with fine serrations on the distal edges, recurved, and terminating in a sharp point. Therefore, the serrated tooth morphology of the remaining teeth is an adaptation to herbivory while remaining omnivorous or carnivorous, rather than an *a priori* adaptation to herbivory.

As Galton (2001b) pointed out, the similarities

between the teeth of prosauropods and those of these lizards is striking, "suggesting that prosauropods were also opportunistic or facultative omnivores who supplemented their mostly herbivorous diet with small prey carrion (see also Barrett). Galton (2001*b*) further recalled that a badly worn partial maxilla belonging to the sphenodontid *Clevosaurus* was found directly associated with numerous worn gastroliths inside the ribcage of a specimen referred to the Early Jurassic prosauropod *Ammosaurus* (see Shubin, Olsen and Sues 1994); also, Galton (2001*b*) suggested that the huge ungual phalanx of the prosauropod manus might have, in addition to defense, been utilized in ripping open carrion.

Key references: Barrett (1996, 2000); Benz and Haller-Brem (1997); Broom (1915); Casamiquela (1980); Clemmensen, Kent and Jenkins (1998); Fraas (1913); Galton (1984*a*, 1985*b*, 1985*d*, 1986*a*, 1985*d*, 1990*a*, 1998, 1992, 2000, 2001*b*, 2001*e*); Galton and Upchurch (in press); Gaudry (1890); Haughton (1924); Heerden (1979); Huene (1905, 1907–08, 1915, 1926, 1932, 1959, 1961); Jaekel (1911, 1913–14); Jenkins, Shubin, Amaral, Gatesy, Schaff, Clemmensen, Downs, Davidson, Bonde and Osbraek (1994); Koken (1900); Kuhn (1959); Pidancet and Chopard (1862); Plieninger (1846*a*, 1846*b*, 1857); Quenstedt (1867–68); Rütimeyer (1856); Sandberger (1894); Shubin, Olsen and Sues (1994); Wellnhofer (1993).

†PLEUROPELTUS   Seeley 1881 [*nomen dubium*]— (See *Struthiosaurus*.)

Type species: *P. suessii* Seeley 1881 [*nomen dubium*].

†POEKILOPLEURON

Saurischia: Eusaurischia: Theropoda: Neotheropoda: Tetanurae: Avetheropoda: ?Spinosauroidea *incertae sedis*.

New species: *P.? valesdunensis* Allain 2002.

Occurrence of *P. bucklandii*: Carrière de la Maladrerie, Caen, Normandy, France; occurrence of *P.? valesdunensis*: Calcaire de Caen Formation, Calvados, France.

Age of *P.? valesdunensis*: Middle Jurassic (middle Bathonian).

Known material/holotype of *P.? valesdunensis*: MNHN 1998–13, almost complete skull, associated partial postcranial skeleton.

Diagnosis of genus (as for type species): Large theropod having elongate midcaudal neural spines as long as length of their corresponding centrum; deltopectoral crest extending down to midlength of humerus; ulna lacking olecranon process; distal end of radius as wide as proximal end; strong ulnar process at midlength of caudomedial edge of radius; convex lateral margin of ascending process of astragalus (Allain and Chure 2002).

Diagnosis of *P.? valesdunensis*: Tetanuran characterized by very low skull, at least three times longer than high; parietals not visible in lateral view; upper temporal fenestra having straight medial margin; jugal ramus of ectopterygoid with well-developed ventral process; deeply grooved caudal margin of ectopterygoid ahead of subtemporal fenestra; double curvature of anterodorsal margin of maxillary nasal ramus; postorbital ventral process U-shaped in cross section; absence of quadrate-quadrojugal fenestra; large external mandibular fenestra; mylohhyoid foramen largely opened anteroventrally (Allain 2002*a*).

Comments: As noted by Allain and Chure (2002), *Poekilopleuron bucklandii* is historically significant as one of the earliest discovered dinosaurs, having been first described in 1838 by J. A. Eudes-Deslongchamps. Also, this taxon represents, although incomplete, one of the best preserved Middle Jurassic European theropods. Its holotype and only known specimen, an uncatalogued partial skeleton once housed in the Musée nde la Faculté des Sciences de Caen, included 21 caudal vertebrae, several chevrons, gastralia, ribs, a humerus, radius, ulna, metacarpal I, manual phalanges, a femur, tibia, astragalus, metatarsal III, and pedal phalanges. This specimen was unfortunately destroyed during World War II (Bigot 1945; see also *D:TE*).

Fortunately, as Allain and Chure reported, casts (MNHN 1897-2) of the holotype gastral basket,

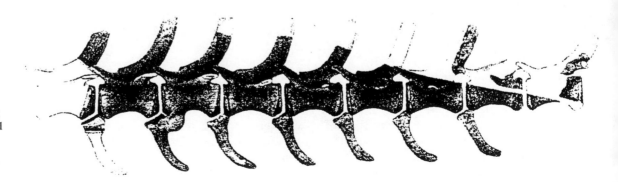

Poekilopleuron bucklandii, holotype articulated caudal vertebrae in lateral view. (After Allain and Chure 2002, based on Eudes-Deschamps 1838.)

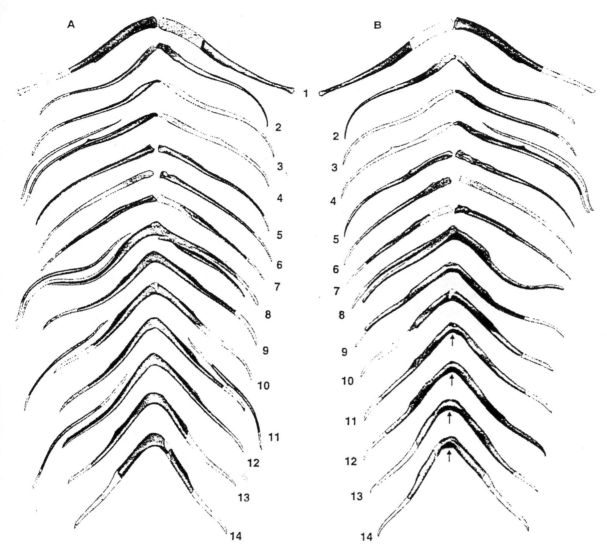

Poekilopleuron bucklandii,
new reconstruction of holotype gastral basket, in A.
ventral and B. dorsal views.
(After Allain and Chure
2002, based on Eudes-De-
schamps 1838.)

humerus, radius, ulna, metacarpal I, and pedal phalanges, given in 1897 to the Muséum National d'Histoire Naturelle in Paris by A. Bigot, are still therein
preserved (with casts of the humerus, radius, ulna,
and pedal phalanges also housed at the Yale Peabody
Museum of Natural History, catalogued as YPM
4938). Allain and Chure redescribed this cast material and also the best preserved bones (*i.e.,* caudal vertebrae, tibia, and astragalus) that Eudes-Deslongchamps (1838) had figured.

As Allain and Chure pointed out, the limited
and fragmentary nature of the only known specimen
of *P. bucklandii,* coupled with its destruction which
prevents examination, complicates making a phylogenetic analysis of this species. Following Holtz
(2000), this taxon seems to be a tetanuran theropod,
based upon a number of features (*e.g.,* well-expanded
humeral ends, humeral torsion, distal end of tibia expanded to back calcaneum, fibular distal end less than
twice craniocaudal width at midshaft, mediolaterally
reduced and craniocaudally wide astragalar ascending

process, extensive contact between metacarpals I and
II, and metacarpal I about as broad as long). However,
this species does not exhibit the derived features seen
in more advanced Neotetanurae (*e.g.,* medial process
on caudal margin of articulating surface of astragalus,
as in all allosauroids for which the astragalus is known;
dramatic bend in L-shaped middle chevrons seen in
Acrocanthosaurus, Allosaurus, and *Neovenator*).

As Molnar, Agriman and Gasparini (1996) had
observed, *P. bucklandii* shares two features — medial
buttress and truncate medial malleolus — with the
basal tetanurans *Acrosanthosaurus atokensis, Allosaurus
fragilis, Erectopus superbus, Megalosaurus bucklandii,*
and *Piatnitzkysaurus floresi.* While assignment of *Poekilopleuron* to the Spinosauroidea is but weakly supported, Allain and Chure tentatively referred the genus
to that clade, pending a more detailed phylogenetic
analysis of the megalosaurids of Europe (or any per-
mutation on the name Megalosauridae) currently in
progress (Allain 2002c).

Addressing the possibility that *Poekilopleuron*

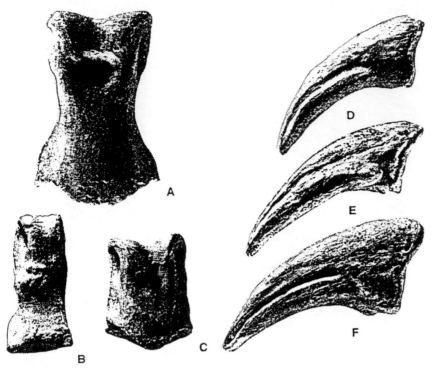

Poekilopleuron bucklandii, MNHN 1897-2, A. plaster cast of holotype second phalanx of third right pedal digit, dorsal view; B. plaster cast of first phalanx of first left pedal digit, dorsal view; C. plaster cast of third phalanx of fourth left pedal digit, dorsal view, D. ungual phalanx of fourth ?left digit, E. ungual phalanx of third ?right digit, and F. ungual phalanx of second left digit. (After Allain and Chure 2002.)

the progracilis zone, Pierre de Caen (an homogeneous, fine-grained biomicrite) of the Calcaire de Caen Formation, Conteville, Calvados, France. This discovery prompted a field team from the Muséum National d'Historie Naturelle to carry on excavations at the locality, finding an excellently preserved, nearly complete megalosaurid skull with partial skeleton (MNHN 1998-13), the skull being the most complete one yet recovered belonging to a megalosaurid (Allain 2002*a*).

Allain tentatively identified MNHN 1998-13 belonging to the genus *Poekilopleuron* (see *D:TE*). As Allain pointed out, except for a few caudal vertebrae and two gastralia, there is currently no comparable material between the type species *P. bucklandii* and the new species. Although the affinity between *P. bucklandii* and the new megalosaurid were uncertain, that authur, pointing out that both taxa are sympatric, tentatively referred MNHN 1998-13 to that genus as the holotype of the new species *Poekilopleuron? valedunensis*.

As Allain observed, the new taxon is distinguished from the type species in having a well-developed spur, anterior to the neural spine of the neural arches of two middle caudal vertebrae.

(For Allain's phylogenetic analysis of Theropoda, see "Systematics" chapter.)

Key references: Allain (2002*a*); Allain and Chure (2002); Bigot (1945); Eudes-Deslongchamps (1838); Holtz (2000); Molnar, Angriman and Gasparini (1996); Paul (1988*c*).

might be congeneric with *Megalosaurus* (see entry), as suggested by some authors (*e.g.*, Paul 1988*c*), Allain and Chure noted that, since there is no dentary material of *P. bucklandii* for comparison, such a synonymy cannot be determined.

In 1994, A. Dubreuil found numerous fossil bone fragments near the village of Conteville, located in

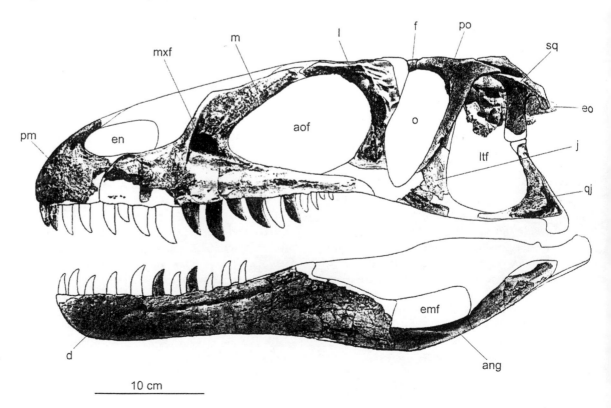

Poekilopleuron? valesdunensis, HMNH 1998-13, holotype skull, left lateral view. (After Allain 2002*a*.)

10 cm

†POLACANTHUS

Ornithischia: Genasaura: Thyreophora: Eurypoda:
  Ankylosauromorpha: Ankylosauria: Polacanthidae.
Type species: *P. foxii* Owen 1865.
Other species: *P. rudgwickensis* Blows 1996.
Known material/holotype of *P. rudgwickensis*:
  HORSM 1988.1546, fragmentary skeleton includ-
  ing almost complete dorsal vertebra, dorsal cen-
  trum, proximal caudal centrum with fragments of
  others, proximal end of left scapula with fragment
  of fused coracoid, distal end of humerus, almost
  complete right tibia, rib fragments, two dermal
  ossifications, numerous indeterminate fragments.
Occurrence of *P. rudgwickensis*: Wealden Marls, West
  Sussex, England.
Age of *P. rudgwickensis*: Early Cretaceous (Barremian).

   Diagnosis of genus (as for type species): Moder-
ate- to large-sized nodosaurid with average adult body
length of five meters; atlas and axis separate (fused in
advanced nodosaurids, *e.g.*, *Panoplosaurus* and most
ankylosaurids); dorsal surface of centra of presacral
vertebrae deeply V-shaped, excavated by neural canal;
synsacrum comprising five dorsosacral, four sacral,
and one or two sacrocaudal vertebrae; transverse
processes of caudal vertebrae present as far as distal
third of tail; chevrons not fused to caudal centra; coracoid coossified to scapula (not fused in *Hylaeosaurus*);
absence of supraspinous fossa (present in most nodosaurs, *e.g.*, *Sauropelta*); humerus having large deltopectoral crest extending to midlength of shaft (condition closer to ankylosaurids, *e.g.*, *Euoplocephalus*,
crest ending more proximally in most nodosaurs, *e.g.*,
Sauropelta; Coombs 1978a); preacetabular process of
ilium short, scarcely divergent (widely divergent in
other nodosaurs, *e.g.*, *Sauropelta*, and ankylosaurids,
e.g., *Euoplocephalus*; see Coombs); femur having distinct lesser trochanter and fourth trochanter at midlength of shaft; tibia 37 percent shorter than femur;
bilateral rows of dorsolaterally located conical spines
along trunk (unknown in *Hylaeosaurus*), tallest over
pectoral area; tall, laterally flattened, triangular, laterally located cervico-pectoral spines on solid, curved
bases (smaller than *Hylaeosaurus*); large flat, rectangular dermal shield covering ilia and synsacrum, ornamented dorsally, with large oval, ridged bosses laterally, low round bosses medially, separated with
tubercles (unknown in *Hylaeosaurus*); large tall-
spined, flattened plates possibly extending laterally
from edges of sacral shield (unknown in *Hylaeosaurus*);
bilateral rows of laterally flattened, hollow-based caudal plates; distal tail ending in bone mass composed
of oval dermal bones overlying fused vertebral core
and ventral ossified tendons (unknown in *Hylaeosaurus*) (Blows 1996, modified after Pereda-Suberbiola 1994).

   Diagnosis of *P. rudgwickensis*: Significantly (approximately 30 percent) larger than *P. foxii*; dorsal vertebrae large, robust, having wide, round centrum faces

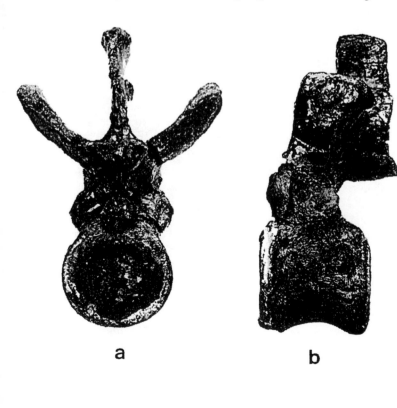

a   b   c

60 mm

Polacanthus rudgwickensis,
HORSM 1988.1546, holo-
type cranial dorsal vertebra
in a. caudal and b. left lateral views, c. caudal dorsal
vertebra in right lateral
view. (After Blows 1996.)

Polacanthus

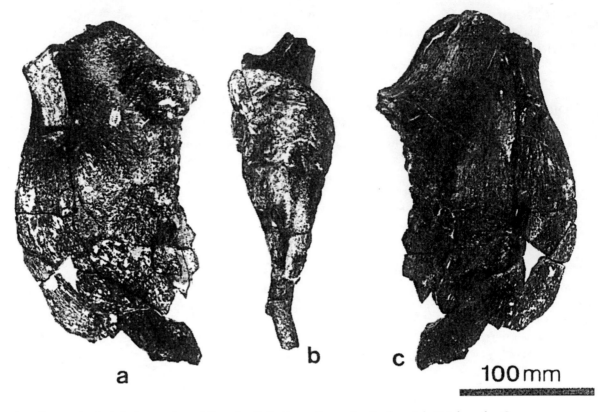

a   b   c   100mm

(smaller, with slightly heart-shaped faces in *P. foxii*); proximal caudal vertebrae having tall, round articular faces (slightly heart-shaped in *P. foxii*); lateral processes with two inferior ridges merging into margins of centrum, forming depression between them (not present in *P. foxii*), one superior ridge occupying almost entire length of centrum, forming tall neural arch (less well developed in *P. foxii*); scapular spine close to dorsal border (displaced more ventrally in *Hoplitosaurus* [=*Polacanthus* of Blows usage] *marshi*, condition unknown in *P. foxii*); caudal ribs large, deep (smaller and shallow in *P. foxii*); tibia long (shorter in *P. foxii*); massive presacral dermal spines, bases rounded, solid over caudal end (smaller, oval, ventrally hollowed in *P. foxii*); scutes ventrally hollowed, very thin, rounded, roof-shaped, with tall dorsal keel (unknown in *P. foxii*) (Blows 1996).

Comments: *Polacanthus* is historically significant as one of the first armored dinosaurs to be described (see *D:TE*), named in an anonymously published article by Richard Owen (1865), who informally introduced this genus to the readership of *The Illustrated London News* as "A new Wealden dragon."

In 1995, William T. Blows discovered a specimen of *Polacathus*—the first belonging to this genus from the mainland Barremian of southeast England—that had been in the collection of the Horsham Museum in Sussex, England, for about a decade (see anonymous 1995). The specimen (HORSM 1988.1546) consists of a partial postcranial skeleton recovered in 1985 from the Rudgewick Brickworks Company quarry, near Rudgwick, N.G.R.TQ 085 343, West Sussex. Observing differences between this somewhat larger specimen and material referred to *P. foxii* (see diagnosis, above), Blows (1996) subsequently described HORSM 1988.1546 as the holotype of a new species, *Polacanthus rudgwickensis.*

As Blows pointed out, the occurrence of a substantially larger species of *Polacanthus* in beds equivalent in age to those on the Isle of Wight, which have yielded remains of the type species, is significant for several reasons: 1. This widens the geographical range of *Polacanthus* to the mainland Weald (this being expected, as most other dinosaurian groups—*e.g.,* theropods, sauropods, and ornithopods—found on the Isle of Wight are also known from this horizon on the mainland; 2. the new species could offer additional support for the presence of two Wealden biozones (see, for example, Norman 1987); although the absence of *P. rudgwickensis* in equivalent-age rocks on the Isle of Wight may be a collection anomaly, it may rather suggest that the newly described specimen could be separated as a distinct species on geographical grounds, occupying a separate niche.

The first mention of *Polacanthus* from the Iberian Peninsula, Spain, appeared in a report by Pereda-Suberbiola, Meijide, Torcida, Welle, Fuentes, Izquierdo, Montero, Pérez and Urién (1999). Pereda-Suberbiola *et al.* described in detail various ankylosaurian dermal armor elements (PS-FES), which

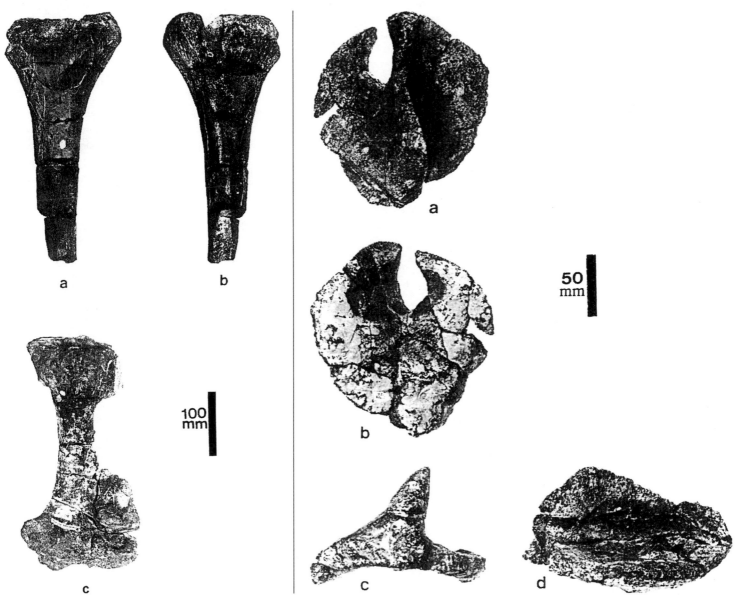

Left: Polacanthus rudgwickensis, HORSM 1988.1546, holotype incomplete tibia in a. caudal and b. cranial views, compared with c. BMNH R1107, holotype left tibia of *Polacanthus foxii* in cranial view. (After Blows 1996.) *Right: Polacanthus rudgwickensis*, HORSM 1988.1546, holotype presacral spine in a. dorsal, b. ventral, c. caudal, and d. lateral views. (After Blows 1996.)

these authors referred to *Polacanthus* sp., collected from red clays of the Fuente Espudia locality, Urbion Group, belonging to "Weald facies" of the western Cameros Basin (Lower Cretaceous: Barremian–Aptian), near Salas de los Infantes (Burgos Province). The material — including two caudal spines, several very small osteoderms, and various fragments apparently belonging to a single individual — was referred to *Polacanthus* based upon the form of the caudal spines.

Pereda-Suberbiola *et al.* further noted that previous finds (*e.g.*, Santafé, Casanovas, Sanz and Calzada 1982; Sanz 1983; Sanz, Buscalion, Pérez Moreno, Moratalla and Jiménez 1990) in the same area may also be referable to *Polacanthus*.

Note: For a survey review of thyreophoran remains from the Iberian Peninsula, including details on specimens referred to *Polacanthus, Dacentrurus, Dracopelta, Taveirosaurus,* and other taxa, see Pereda Suberbiola and Galton (1999).

Key references: [Anonymous] (1995); Blows (1996); Coombs (1978*a*); Norman (1987); Owen (1865); Pereda-Suberbiola (1994); Pereda Suberbiola and Galton (1999); Pereda-Suberbiola, Meijide, Torcida, Welle, Fuentes, Izquierdo, Montero, Pérez and Urién (1999); Santafé, Casanovas, Sanz and Calzada (1982); Sanz 1983; Sanz, Buscalion, Pérez Moreno, Moratalla and Jiménez (1990).

†PROBACTROSAURUS

Ornithischia: Genasauria: Cerapoda: Ornithopoda: Iguanodontia: Euiguanodontia: Dryomorpha: Ankylopollexia: Iguanodontoidea.

Type species: *P. gobiensis* Rozhdeskvensky 1966.

Other species: [None.]

Age: Early to Middle Cretaceous (Barremian–Albian).

Diagnosis of genus (as for type species): Ornithopod reaching probable maximum body length of 4–6 meters; premaxillary beak margin ventrally deflected; small, vertical ectopterygoid sutural facet on jugal; jugal slender; maxillary teeth narrow, with prominent primary ridge, no subsidiary ridges; dentary teeth narrow, diamond-shaped, with low, distally offset primary ridge, shorter and low subsidiary ridges mesially and distally; tall, interlocking teeth forming high, caudally inclined battery; two replacement crowns beneath functional teeth in dental battery, marginal denticles mammillate; prominent "acromial" process on anterior edge of scapula; scapular blade straight, little expanded distally; deltopectoral crest low, rounded; radius and ulna elongate; small, conical pollex spine; elongate and bunched metacarpals II–IV; six fused sacral vertebrae; elongate horizontal anterior process to ilium; prepubic blade deep, distally expanded; ischium stout, curved, "booted," with large triangular, proximally positioned obturator process; curved distal femoral shaft; distally expanded condyles on femur; anterior intercondylar groove partially enclosed (Norman 2002).

Comments: In 1966, Anatoly Konstantinovich Rozhdestvensky described a new ornithopod dinosaur that he named *Probactrosaurus*, founded upon an abundance of fossil material collected from in the region of Neimongol (Inner Mongolia). At the time, Rozhdestvensky referred two species to this genus, the type, *Probactrosaurus gobiensis*, and *P. alashanicus* (see *D:TE*). Later, Dong (1997) referred yet a third species, *P. mazongshanensis* to *Probactrosaurus* (see *SI*).

More recently, David B. Norman (2002) published the first major review of the genus since the original work by Rozhdestvensky. Norman's paper was "intended to improve knowledge of the type species of *Probactrosaurus* and discusses the wider issue of iguanodontian ornithopod systematics and hadrosaur origins" (to be discussed further by Norman and Weishampel, in press). Norman chronicled in detail the history of the original discoveries of material referred to *Probactrosaurus*, that author also reassessing the genus and considering the validity of its three species.

Norman's study was based upon his restudy of all of the currently available fossil material of *P. gobiensis* and *P. alashanicus* collected during the early Sino-Soviet expeditions to Inner Mongolia in 1959 to 1960 (see Chow and Rozhdestvensky 1961) currently housed at the Palaeontological Institute Nauk, in Moscow (missing material including the holotype caudal skull roof of *P. alashanicus*).

Among these specimens referred to *P. gobiensis* are the following: PIN 2232/1 (holotype) — mounted partial skeleton including partial skull roof, right premaxilla (2232/1-2), left jugal (2232/1-1a), right surrangular (2232/1-4), seven poorly preserved cervical vertebrae, six dorsals, four sacrals, 22 caudals, scapulae, left coracoid, right and partial left humeri, ulnae, radii, metacarpals ?II, ?III, IV, and ?V, left femur, left tibia, fibulae, and left metatarsals II–IV; 2232/2-1 — neurocranial fragment; 2232/2-2, partial left dentary; 2232/2-5 — coracoid; 2232/2-8 — humerus; 2232/2-9 — metacarpal; 2232/3-1 — metacarpal; 2232/9-2 — partial left maxilla; PIN2232/10 — mounted partial and restored skeleton including right dentary, partial skull roof, maxilla (2232/10-2), six cervical, 18 dorsal, seven sacral, and 24 caudal vertebrae, coracoids, left sternal plate, humeri, radii, mani, ilia, ischia, pubis (acetabular fragments), femora, tibiae, fibulae, right metatarsals II–IV, left pedal phalanges (II-i, II-iii, IV-i-iv), right pedal phalanges (I-i-iii, III-i-iv, IV-i-v), manual phalanx ?V-ii or Viii (2232/10-69); 2232/11-2 — manual phalanx III-iii; 2232/11-4 — pollex ungual; 2232/11-5 — ungual manus II; 2232/17-1 — skull roof; 2232/18-1 — partial left dentary; 2232/18-5 — metacarpal III; 2232/18-6 — metacarpal; 2232/18-8 — phalanx manus II-i; 2232/18-9 — right femur; 2232/19-1 — left ilium; 2232/21-1 — humerus; 2232/23-1 — predentary; 2232/23-2 — two isolated dentary teeth with roots; 2232/23-3, quadrate; 2232/23-56 — pubis; 2232/24-1 — worn dentary tooth; 2232/27-3 — scapula; 2232/29-2 — right ischium; 2232/32-1 — left tibia; 2232/32-1 — left tibia; 36-1 — skull roof; 2232/

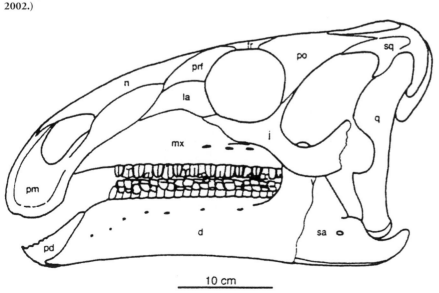

Tentative reconstruction of the skull of *Probactrosaurus gobiensis*, based upon dissociated elements in the collections (PIN 2232/) of the Palaeontological Institute Nauk. (After Norman 2002.)

10 cm

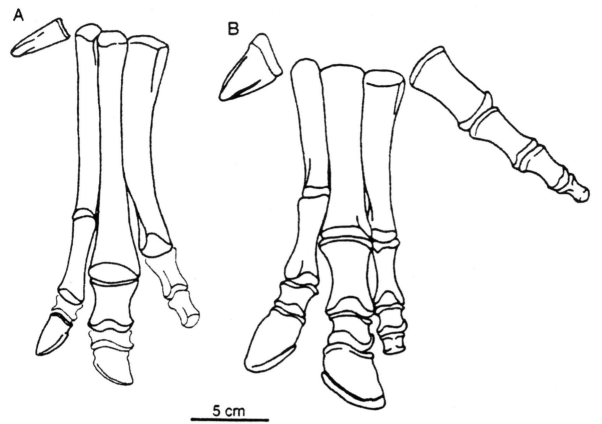

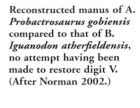

5 cm

36-2 and 36-3 — dentaries; 2232/37-7 —?ilium (labeled *P. alashanicus*); 2232/39-1— left femur; 2232/3 — left dentary with teeth; 2232/2; field number 12017), metacarpals, left ilium; and (field number 12068) metacarpal II; the following specimens referred to *P. alashanicus*, PIN 2232/40-3 — caudal vertebra; 2232/40-5 and 40-6 — left metatarsal block II, III; 2232/41-1— dentary; PIN 2232/41-2 and 41/3 — scapulae; 2232/41-4 — incomplete left humerus; and 2232/42-1— right dentary.

Norman described *Probactrosaurus* as "a very generalized ornithopod in terms of what is currently known of its cranial and postcranial anatomy." The skull, Norman noted, displays no sign of nasal or dorsal cranial region expansion or elaboration. The maxillary teeth are narrow, resembling those of "nonhadrosaurian" iguanodontians. The dentary teeth are in a state of transformation regarding crown shape, being smaller, more lanceolate, and more nearly symmetrical than those in more basal ornithopods and iguanodontians (*e.g.*, *Camptosaurus*, *Iguanodon*, *Ouranosaurus*, and *Altirhinus*). The dentition is rather like that of hadrosaurids, having closely packed crowns, roots showing well-defined vertical facets for adjacent replacement teeth, an occlusal surface that becomes high and backwardly tilted as well as broaded buccolingually by the addition of another crown, and alveoli forming parallel-sided slots; unlike in hadro-

saurids, however, the edges of the tooth crowns bear mammaillate denticles.

Norman noted that the shoulder girdle and humerus of *Probactrosaurus* are quite similar to those of nonhadrosaurid iguanodontians. Distally, the forearm is notable for its relative elongation, the retention of a small, conical pollex spine, and the marked slenderness of metacarpals II through IV. In general, the rest of the postcranial skeleton, as now known, is similar to that of other iguanodontians (*e.g.*, *Iguanodon atherfieldensis*; see Norman 1986), although the femur seems to lack the specializations found in hadrosaurids.

Norman (2002) compared the two species of *Probactrosaurus* as erected by Rozhdestvensky, *P. gobiensis* having been distinguished by a skull slightly wider across the orbits than across the occiput (among other features), and *P. alashanicus* having a skull not broader across the orbits than the occiput (among other features). Rozhdestvensky had noted that both species resembled one another in general appearance and dimensions. As Norman (2002) observed, the differences in skull structure — *e.g.*, overall width, height, shape of supratemporal fenestrae, presence or absence of sagittal crest — all seem to be (as Rozhdestvensky had acknowledged) the result of distortion and are, therefore, subjective. Norman (2002) found no significant differences in the dental morphology of

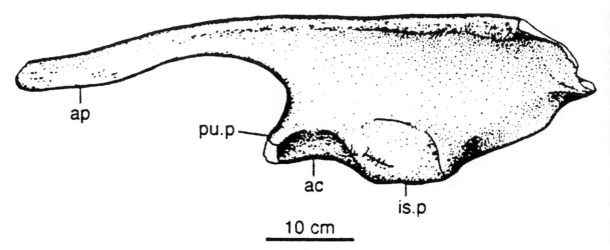

Left ilium (PIN 2232/19-1), missing small part of acetabular margin and caudal blade, of *Probactrosaurus gobiensis*, left lateral view. (After Norman 2002.)

10 cm

specimens assigned to the two species, whereas elements referred to either species vary depending on preservational condition, or are either very similar to or even indistinguishable from each other. Consequently, Norman (2002) considered *P. alashanicus* to be a junior synonym of the type species.

Regarding *"Probactrosaurus" mazongshanensis*, a taxon based on fragmentary remains, Norman (2002)

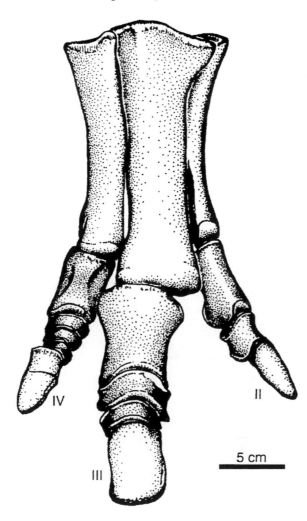

Right pes (PIN 2232/10) of *Probactrosaurus gobiensis* in articulation, drawing based upon mounted skeleton. (After Norman 2002.)

5 cm

noted that the dentary crowns of this species a not very similar to those of *P. gobiensis*, but instead bear a closer resemblance to those of *Altirhinus*. Therefore, Norman (2002) removed this species from the genus *Probactrosaurus*.

In performing a phylogenetic analysis (see "Systematics" chapter), Norman (2002) found *Probactrosaurus* to be the basal sister taxon of the Hadrosauridae, thereby "belatedly confirming the views originally promulgated by A. K. Rozhdestvensky."

Note: The continental dinosaur-bearing strata that yielded *Probactrosaurus gobiensis* in the Dashuiguo area of Inner Mongolia, China, were again redated by Van Itterbeeck, Bultynck, Li and Vandenberghe (2001) as of "upper Lower Cretaceous [=Early to Middle Cretaceous] (Barremian–Albian)" age (see also Rozhdestvensky 1966), based upon fossil charophyte floral evidence. Based on the type of soil, the fossil fauna and flora, and the presence of satin spar veins and evaporitic crystals, Van Itterbeeck *et al.* deduced the paleoclimate of this area to have been subhumid, with seasonal dry periods.

According to Norman (2002), the above estimation, in general terms, "correlates with expectations based solely on anatomy and phylogeny," although "for this to be of value palaeobiogeographically, improved stratigraphic resolution is required."

Key references: Chow and Rozhdestvensky (1961); Dong (1997); Norman (1986, 2002); Norman and Weishampel (in press); Rozhdestvensky (1966); Van Itterbeeck, Bultynck, Li and Vandenberghe (2001).

†PROCOMPSOGNATHUS

Saurischia: Eusaurischia: Theropoda: Neotheropoda: Coelophysoidea *incertae sedis*.

Comments: Rauhut and Hungerbühler (2000), in their review of the Triassic theropods of Europe, reassessed the type species *Procompsognathus triassicus*,

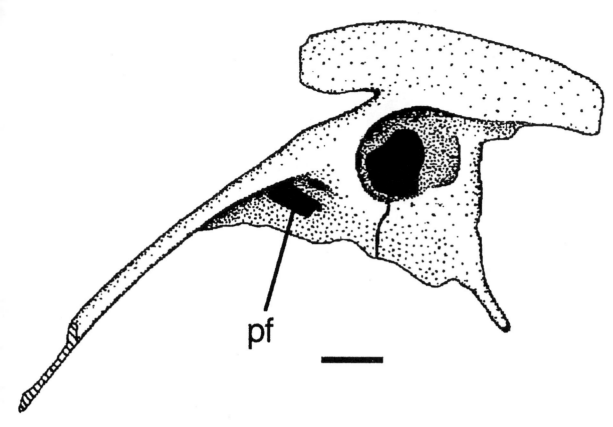

pf

based on an incomplete skeleton (SMNS 12591) from the Middle Stubensandstein of Pfaffenhofen, Württemberg, Germany (see *D:TE, S1*).

Earlier, Sereno and Wild (1992) noted the presence in *P. triassicus* of a sigmoid trochanteric shelf identical to that in such neoceratosaurians as *Coelophysis* and "*Syntarsus*" [=*Megapnosaurus*], after which Novas (1996*a*) found this character to be a synapomorphy of Dinosauriformes. According to Rauhut and Hungerbühler, however, the precise shape of this structure in *P. triassicus* could be interpreted as an indication of a "ceratosaurian" relationship for this species. Also, the presence of elongate dorsal vertebrae and rather triangular dorsal transverse processes could be criteria for referring *Procompsognathus* to the "Ceratosauria," perhaps even in the Coelophysoidea. More material must be recovered, however, before a more positive systematic referral can be made.

Rauhut and Hungerbühler regarded *P. triassicus* as provisionally valid, characters perhaps distinguishing it from other Triassic theropods including an elongate hindlimb (tibia/femur ratio about 1.2; metatarsal III/femur ratio about 0.74).

Note: Rauhut and Hungerbühler also reconsidered an articulated left pelvic girdle (BMNH PV RU P77/1) including parts of the sacrum, the caudalmost dorsal vertebrae, and an associated left femur lacking its distal end, collected from the Upper Triassic (?Norian) Pant-y-ffunnon locality in southern Wales, and

referred by Warrener (1983) to ?:*Syntarsus*" [=*Megapnosaurus*] sp. Rauhut and Hungerbühler described the specimen as follows: Vertebrae long, somewhat low, having low but long neural spines; sacral vertebrae fused, sutures between vertebrae visible only as slight swellings; pubis and ischium fused to ilium, not to each other; ilium measuring 52 millimeters in length, dolichoiliacic, preacetabular part significantly shorter than postacetabular part, showing well-developed brevis shelf and strong lateral expansion of dorsal rim of acetabulum; preserved part of pubis showing slightly bowed shaft, small, dorsomedially opening obturator foramen and much larger pubic foramen beneath it; fused pubes in anterior view forming rather broad apron; obturator process of ischium not offset from pubic peduncle, small notch distally between process and ischial shaft; femoral head downturned, trochanteric shelf well developed; fourth trochanter represented by long, low, proximally located flange.

As observed by Rauhut and Hungerbühler, all of the above characters are very similar to the African and North American coelophysid *Megapnosaurus* [previously named *Syntarsus*] (see Raath 1969; Rowe and Gauthier 1990), which is why they were referred to ?"*Syntarsus*" [=*Megapnosaurus*]. However, in all of the above characters that are comparable (*e.g.*, shape of dorsal vertebral centra, width of pubes in anterior view, development of trochangteric shelf), the Welsh specimen is also very similar to *Procompsognathus*. According to Rauhut and Hungerbühler, future discoveries of additional materials may demonstrate that the taxon from Wales may be referrable to *Procompsognathus*.

Key references: Novas (1996*a*); Raath (1969); Rauhut and Hungerbühler (2000); Rowe and Gauthier (1990); Sereno and Wild (1992); Warrener (1983).

†PROSAUROLOPHUS

Ornithischia: Genasauria: Cerapoda: Ornithopoda: Iguanodontia: Euiguanodontia: Dryomorpha: Ankylopollexia: Iguanodontoidea: Hadrosauroidea: Hadrosauridae: Euhadrosauria: Hadrosaurinae.

Comments: The first known record of juvenile specimens of *Prosaurolophus* was reported by Pierce (2002) in a published abstract for a poster. Two excellently preserved skeletons belonging to this genus were collected from marine sediments of the Upper Cretaceous (Campanian) Bearpaw Formation of southern Alberta, Canada.

Found near Mayberries, the first of these specimens consists of a semiarticulated partial skull and postcranium; the second, found in the St. Mary's River Valley near Welling, is articulated and preserves the skull, vertebral column and ribs cranial to the sacrum, the forelimbs, some disarticulated elements including the ilium and a partial femur, a skin impression in the abdominal region, and numerous ossified tendons running down the vertebral column. As Pierce noted, both specimens, because of their anatomy and geographic location, have been referred to *Prosaurolophus* cf. *maximus*.

Pierce commented that, these specimens having been found in marine deposits, it would be intriguing to speculate that these were marine animals. However, as that author pointed out, such a claim is not supported by the evidence. Moreover, a number of factors (*e.g.*, the isolated occurrence, completeness of the specimens, and distance from the paleoshoreline, the latter at the time being positioned west of the Rocky Mountains foothills) suggest "a unique, instantaneous, taphonomic event rather than paleobiology." The author deduced that these duck-billed dinosaurs, after getting caught in the undertow of a near shore, rapidly flowing river, were probably swept out to sea. Still, this scenario does suggest that these dinosaurs lived in a terrestrial environment near the sea.

Key reference: Pierce (2002).

PROTOCERATOPS

Ornithischia: Genasauria: Cerapoda: Marginocephalia: Ceratopsia: Neoceratopsia: Coronosauria: Protoceratopsidae.

New species: *P. hellenikorhinus* Lambert, Godefroit, Li, Shang and Dong 2001.

Occurrence of *P. hellenikorhinus*: Bayan Mandahu Formation, Inner Mongolia, China.

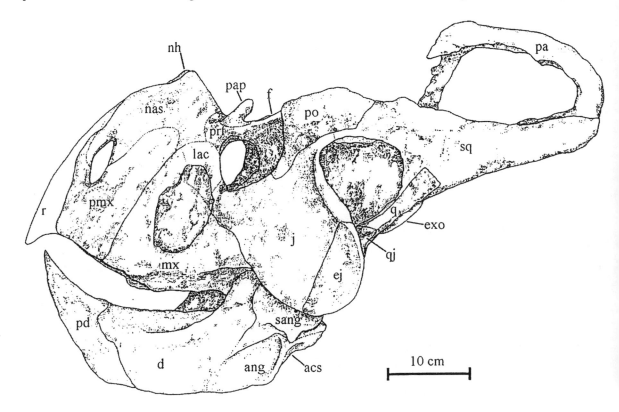

Protoceratops hellenikorhinus, IMM 95BM1/1, holotype skull in left lateral view. (After Lambert, Godefroit, Li, Shang and Dong 2001.)

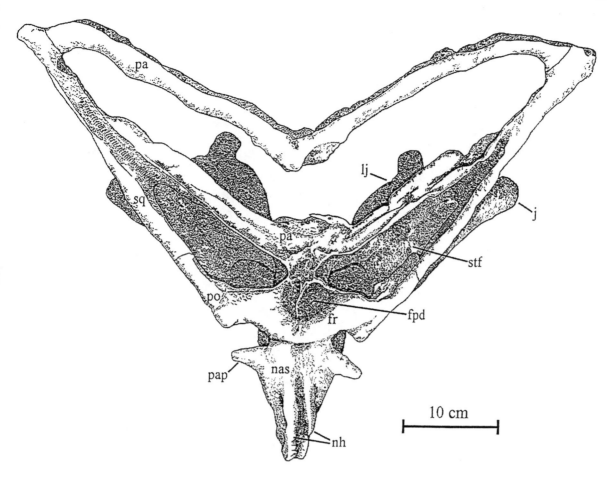

Protoceratops hellenikorhinus, IMM 95BM1/1, holotype skull in dorsal view. (After Lambert, Godefroit, Li, Shang and Dong 2001.)

Age of *P. hellenikorhinus*: Late Cretaceous (Campanian).

Known material of *P. hellenikorhinus*: Nine incomplete skulls, postcranial remains, subadult to adult, male and female.

Holotype of *P. hellenikorhinus*: IMM 95BM1/1, nearly complete skull (male).

Diagnosis of genus: Protoceratopsid having the following apomorphies: predentary tip reaching or standing higher than level of dorsal edge of coronoid process; double nasal horn; the following characters — either plesiomorphic or their polarity uncertain, based on current data — differentiating the genus from sister-taxon *Bagaceratops*: frill inclined in caudodorsal direction; parietal fenestrae better developed; squamosal-jugal suture visible laterally on rostrodorsal edge of infratemporal fenestra; absence of additional antorbital fenestra; higher mandible (Lambert, Godefroit, Li, Shang and Dong 2001).

Diagnosis of *P. hellenikorhinus*: Ventral edge of dentary straight; caudal edge of angular formed by caudally facing triangular surface; long projection of squamosal contacting quadratojugal; straight, strongly reduced longitudinal ridge on maxilla (Lambert, Godefroit, Li, Shang and Dong 2001).

Comments: The most emblematic dinosaur from Mongolia's Gobi Desert is probably the primitive neoceratopsian *Protoceratops*, the type species of which, *P. andrewsi*, was originally described by Walter Granger and William King Gregory in 1923.

A new species of this genus, and one thus far unique in possessing two parallel nasal horns, *Protoceratops hellenikorhinus*, was founded upon an isolated well-preserved complete skull (IMM 95BM1/1) collected by the Sino-Belgian Expeditions of 1995 and 1996, from the Bayan Mandahu Formation (possibly correlated with the Djadokhta Formation), at Bayan Mandahu, Bayan Nor League, Inner Mongolia. The skull is missing only the rostral bone (and rostralmost portion of the premaxillae), the caudal portion of the basioccipital, and the longitudinal median ridge of the frill formed by the parietals. The specimen was found with it snout pointing upwards, a common pose for *Protoceratops* skulls in both the Bayan Mandahu and Djadokhta formations (see Jerzykiewicz, Currie, Eberth, Johnston, Koster and Zheng 1993). A referred almost complete skull (IMM 96VM1/4) from the same locality has been designated the paratype. Other recovered material pertaining to this species include various partial skulls (IMM 96BM5/5, 96BM1/1, 96BN1/7, 96BM5/2, 96MB5/3, 96BM6/4, and 96BM2/1), one skull (IMM 96BM6/4) being associated

Protoceratops hellenikorhinus, IMM 95BM1/1, holotype skull in rostral view. (After Lambert, Godefroit, Li, Shang and Dong 2001.)

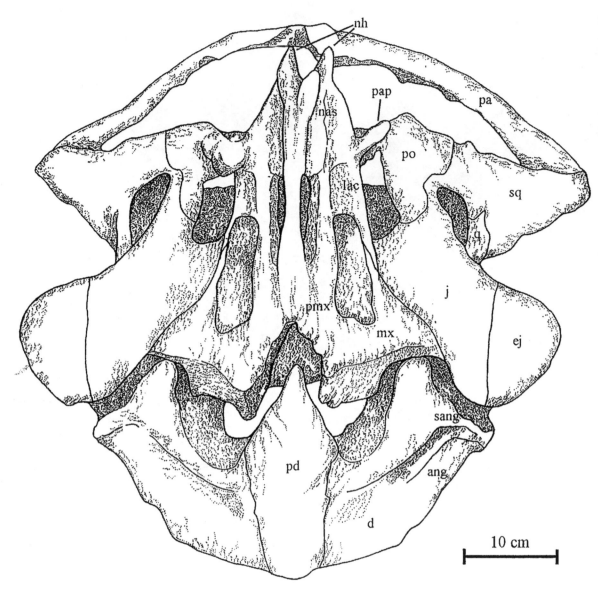

with a series of caudal vertebrae and a right hindlimb (Lambert, Godefroit, Li, Shang and Dong 2001).

Lambert *et al.* described *P. hellenikorhinus* as a relatively large species of *Protoceratops*, the basal length of the holotype skull being 430 millimeters, the total length 720 millimeters. The cranial autapomorphies of this species (see diagnosis, above) can apparently be linked, the authors noted, to the development of the mandibular adductor musculature.

As observed by Lambert *et al.*, a pattern of variation can be seen in the specimens of *P. hellenikorhinus* indicative of sexual dimorphism. The larger holotype and skulls IMM 96BM5/5 and IMM 96BM1/1 — grouped together because they share a number of characters (*e.g.*, very high nasals with pair of individualized horns, relatively short antorbital length, external nares having long axis relatively close to vertical) — were interpreted by the authors as representing male morphs. The paratype and IMM 96BM1/7 —

sharing various different characters (*e.g.*, low nasals devoid of well-marked horn, relatively long antorbital length, external nares having more oblique axis) — were interpreted as female specimens. As Lambert *et al.* pointed out, the Bayan Mandahu specimens are not well enough preserved to employ Dodson's (1976) method for sexually scoring *Protoceratops* skulls.

Lambert *et al.* further attempted to establish a discriminant function separating male and female specimens and combining both the species *P. hellenikorhinus* and *P. andrewsi*, based upon measurements taken on the rostral area of the skull. This analysis included a sampling of 19 *P. andrewsi* skulls housed at the American Museum of Natural History, identified by Dodson as adult males, adult females, and juveniles. The results of this analysis were then employed in Lambert *et al.* consideration of ontogeny in the Bayan Mandahu specimens.

Although incomplete, IMM 96BM5/3, the

Protoceratops

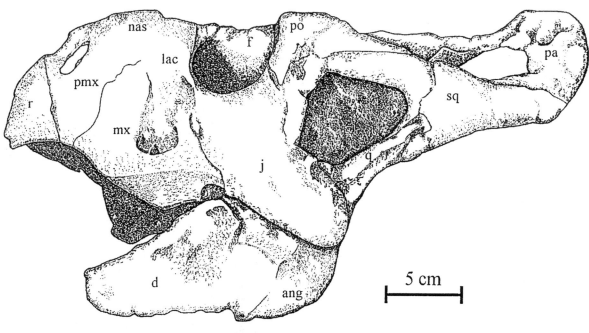

Protoceratops hellenikorhinus, IMM 95BM2/1, referred skull of subadult male, left lateral view. (After Lambert, Godefroit, Li, Shang and Dong 2001.)

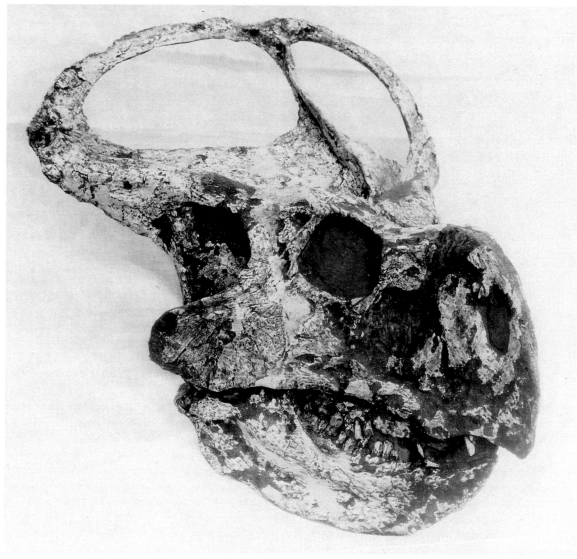

Skull (FMNH P14045; formerly AMNH collection) of the protoceratopsid ceratopsian *Protoceratops andrewsi,* collected in Mongolia.

Protoceratops

Skeleton (cast) of adult and hatchling *Protoceratops andrewsi* on display at the Mesa Southwest Museum. The actual specimens were originally part of The Great Russian Dinosaurs Exhibition, that first showed at this museum in 1996.

smallest of the Bayan Mandahu skulls (estimated total length of 120 millimeters, more than one sixth the length of the largest male adult, IMM 96BM5/5), exhibits the autapomophy of this species of a contact between the squamosal and the quadratojugal on the caudoventral corner of the infratemporal fenestra. IMM 96BM2/1 is the second smallest of these skulls (total length of 389 millimeters). Earlier, Dodson had suggested that sexual maturity in *P. andrewsi* may be recognized when males can be distinguished from females, based upon various morphometric characters. Consequently, Lambert *et al.* stated, IMM 96BM2/1, which already shows a relatively significant nasal height and a sub-vertical long axis of the external nares, can be regarded as belonging to an adult male. However, the nasal horns in this skull are not individualized; therefore, their development is delayed relative to the appearance of sexual discriminant characters as observed for this species. Consequently, IMM

96BM2/1 was interpreted by the authors to be a subadult (the term used by Sampson, Ryan and Tanke 1997 for centrosaurine individuals displaying sexual maturity but lacking several adult features).

Lambert *et al.* pointed out that several tiny *Protoceratops* skulls collected at Bayan Mandahu by the Sino-Canadian Dinosaur Project of 1988 and 1990, were identified by Dong and Currie (1993) as embryos of *P. andrewsi*. As Lambert *et al.* observed, however, these specimens cannot be identified at the specific level from the published descriptions and figures, diagnostic characters either not being preserved or being very hard to distinguish in such young individuals. Therefore, based upon current information, the authors, finding the presence of *P. andrewsi* at Bayan Mandahu very unlikely, designated these specimens *Protoceratops* sp.

As Lambert *et al.* observed, a number of other features, explainable by neither sexual dimorphism

Life restoration of *Protocer-atops andrewsi* painted by Kelly Pugh.

nor ontogeny, can be found among the *P. hellenikorhinus* skull. Among these, the level of the ventral margin of the orbit, relative to the rostral and caudal parts of the skull, varies (*e.g.*, dorsal margin of antorbital fossa lower, relative to ventral margin of orbit, lower in IMM 96BM5/5 than in holotype). In the holotype, the longitudinal ridge on the maxilla is much reduced, but even moreso in IMM 96BM1/7 and 96BM2/1. Only some of these skull exhibit the character "contact between squamosal and quadratojugal on the caudoventral corner of the infratemporal fenestra" (this possibly explained as a preservational artifact, due to the slenderness of the distal end of the ventral projection of the squamosal, which can easily be lost).

Furthermore, the fragmentary specimen IMM 96BM6/4, which includes caudal postcranial remains, is difficult to identify at the generic level. The shape of the caudodorsal projection of the jugal rather suggests that the skull belongs to *Protoceratops*. However, the skull's maxilla lacks the longitudinal well-marked ridge characteristic of *P. andrewsi*, while the caudal neural spines project distally, in contrast to the almost perfectly vertical spines in *P. andrewsi* (see Brown and Schleikjer 1940). Lambert *et al.* referred this specimen to their new species, while pointing out that no current criteria differentiate IMM 96BM6/4 from *Bagaceratops rozhdestvenskkyi* (see Maryańska and Osmólska 1975), a taxon also known from the Bayan Mandahu Formation (see Dong and Currie). However, while *Bagaceratops* differs primarily from *Protoceratops* in the possession of various cranial features (*e.g.*, supplementary antorbital fenestra, shorter, almost horizontal frill probably lacking parietal fenestrae, "odd" nose horn), these diagnostic skull parts have not been preserved in IMM 96BM6/4.

In comparing the new species to the type species, Lambert *et al.* noted that adult males of *P. hellenikorhinus* are larger than those of *P. andrewsi*, the latter, as studied by Dodson, not exceeding 491 millimeters. The two species also differ in the following ways: Longitudinal ridge on maxilla well marked and more dorsal in medial part than in rostral and caudal parts, ridge continuous with ventral margin of jugal in *P. andrewsi*, ridge strongly reduced, rectilinear, discontinuous with ventral limit of jugal in *P. hellenikorhinus*; nasal horns not well developed, only incipient, dorsal margin of nasals forming horn regularly convex in *P. andrewsi*, rostral border of nasal horns distinctly concave, appearing more individualized in *P. hellenikorhinus*; contact between ventral process of squamosal and quadratojugal, on caudoventral corner of infratemporal fenestra, diagnostic for *P. hellenikorhinus*, not observed in *P. andrewsi*; exoccipital proportionally much shorter in holotype (not preserved in other specimens) of *P. hellenikorhinus* than in *P. andrewsi*; rostral margin of predentary straighter in *P. hellenikorhinus* (closer to juveniles of *P. andrewsi*) than in *P. andrewsi*, wherein rostral and ventral margins of predentary are not distinct, forming continuous curve; ventral border of dentary straight in *P. hellenikorhinus*, straight in juveniles of *P. andrewsi*; caudal triangular surface of angular with more lateral orientation in *P. andrewsi*; fronto-parietal depression not extending rostrally beyond level of caudal margin of orbit in *P. andrewsi*, extending rostrally up to middle of orbit in *P. hellenikorhinus*; and splenials not contacting in holotype of *P. hellenikorhinus*, contacting in *P. andrewsi*.

A cladistic analysis by Lambert *et al.* concerning the phylogenetic relationships of *Protoceratops* resulted in a single most parsimonious tree (see "Systematics" chapter) in which the family Protoceratopsidae was found to be monophyletic, including the sister taxa *Protoceratops* and *Bagaceratops*.

Key references: Brown and Schleikjer (1940); Dodson (1976); Granger and Gregory (1923); Dong and Currie (1993); Jerzykiewicz, Currie, Eberth,

Johnston, Koster and Zheng (1993); Lambert, Godefroit, Li, Shang and Dong (2001); Maryańska and Osmólska (1975); Sampson, Ryan and Tanke (1997).

†PSITTACOSAURUS—(*Protiguanodon*; =?*Luanpingosaurus*)

Type species: *P. mongoliensis* Osborn 1923.

Other species: *P. mazongshanensis* Xu 1997, *P. meileyingensis* Sereno, Zhao, Cheng and Rao 1988, *P. neimongoliensis* Russell and Zhao 1996, *P. ordosensis* Russell and Zhao 1996, *P. sinensis* Yang [Young] 1958, *P. xinjiangensis* Sereno and Chao [Zhao] 1988.

Diagnosis of *P. mongoliensis*: Antorbital fossa triangular; lateral margin of prefrontal upturned; jugal horn posteroventrally extended; obtuse angle between two planes of lateral surface of jugal; posterodorsal margin of orbit formed by frontal; horizontal frill; caudal margin of shaft of quadrate slightly excavated; dorsal end of quadrate separated from parocciptal process by squamosal (Xu and Zhao 1999).

Diagnosis of *P. sinensis*: Skull broadly proportioned; lower adult tooth count; sutural contact between premaxilla and jugal; small jugal-postorbital horn core; jugal horn laterally expanded; anterior surface of lateral aspect of jugal noticeably larger than caudal surface; acute angle between two planes of lateral aspect of jugal; mandible laterally convex; absence of external mandibular fenestra; tooth rows laterally convex (Xu and Zhao 1999).

Diagnosis of *P. xinjiangensis*: Jugal horn anteriorly flattened; rostral surface of lateral aspect of jugal much larger than caudal surface; maxillary crowns having denticulate margin that curves caudomedially onto side near crown; iliac postacetabular process proportionately elongate; distal extension of ossified epaxial tendons onto proximal half of tail (Xu and Zhao 1999).

Diagnosis of *P. meileyingensis*: Skull proportionally tall; snout very short; orbit sub-triangular; raised rugosity on quadratojugal; quadrate shaft having strong caudal emargination; quadrate shaft angled anterolaterally; prominent ventral dentary flange (Xu and Zhao 1999).

Diagnosis of *P. neimongoliensis*: Frontal narrow; ischium distinctly longer than femur, distal end of ischium not horizontally flattened; rostral ramus from squamosal not reaching rostral wall of supratemporal fenestra (Xu and Zhao 1999).

Diagnosis of *P. ordosensis*: Two pits on maxilla; jugal horns prominent, groove on ventral surface of jugal; eminence on caudal frontal; posterodorsal corner of skull depressed, squamosal therefore being positioned below level of central body of postorbital;

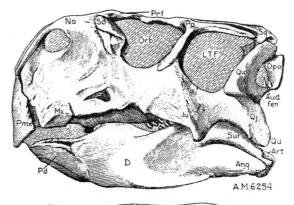

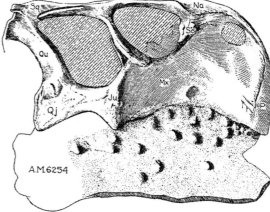

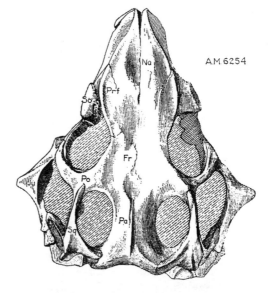

Psittacosaurus mongoliensis, AMNH 6254, holotype skull in (top) left lateral, (middle) right lateral, and (bottom) dorsal views. (After Osborn 1923.)

acute angle between two planes of lateral aspect of jugal, former much smaller than latter (Xu and Zhao 1999).

Diagnosis of *P. mazongshanensis*: Snout rather long; outer surface of maxilla presenting planes; maxillary protuberance strongly developed laterally and ventrally, with right angle between two planes of lateral surface of jugal; middle lobe pronounced;

Skeletons (casts) of *Psittacosaurus* mounted at the North American Museum of Ancient Life.

secondary ridges on tooth crowns long, slim (Xu and Zhao 1999).

Comments: To date, two genera and 13 species have been referred to the Psittacosauridae, the most primitive family belonging to the Ceratopsia (see *Psittacosaurus* entries, *D:TE, S1*). As noted by Xu and Zhao (1999), most these taxa are now considered to be invalid, exhibiting no distinguishing characters that can be used to diagnose them. Xu and Zhao accepted only seven psittacosaurid species, all referrable to a single genus *Psittacosaurus*. For each of these species, the authors also offered a new diagnosis.

As noted by Xu and Zhao, fossils of *Psittacosaurus* are distributed through the Lower Cretaceous basins of northern China, associated fauna including other reptiles, amphibians, birds, and mammals. Furthermore, the *Psittacosaurus* fauna can be divided into two subfauna — an early sub-fauna of probable Early Cretaceous age, including psittacosaurs, basal therizinosauroids, basal dromaeosaurs, and primitive pterosaurs, and a late sub-fauna of probably early Late Cretaceous age, including derived psittacosaurs and also dromaeosaurs comparable to North American and Mongolian forms from Middle and Upper Cretaceous beds.

Brinkman, Eberth, Ryan and Chen (2001) reported on a new specimen belonging to one of the valid *Psittacosaurus* species, *P. xinjiangensis*, a partial adult skeleton (UGM XG94Kh201) recovered during sedimental studies from a massive, flat-based, silty-to-fine-grained sandstone sheet in the middle of the Lower Cretaceous Tugulu Group (Bureau of Geology and Mineral Resources of Xinjiang Uygur Autonomous Region 1986), in the Urho area (south of Urho), Junggar Basin, Xinjiang, China. The specimen comprises isolated skull pieces (including partial jugal preserving base of jugal horn; articulated fragments of occipital, quadrate, and squamosal portions of left maxilla; basioccipital portion of braincase; and portion of left jugal) and lower jaw fragments, the atlas, a centrum, much of the presacral vertebral column, the complete sacrum, partial right forelimb, and complete right hindlimb. As the authors noted, this specimen is important as the first documentation of the adult morphology of *P. xinjiangensis*, while also providing additional evidence regarding individual variation in this species.

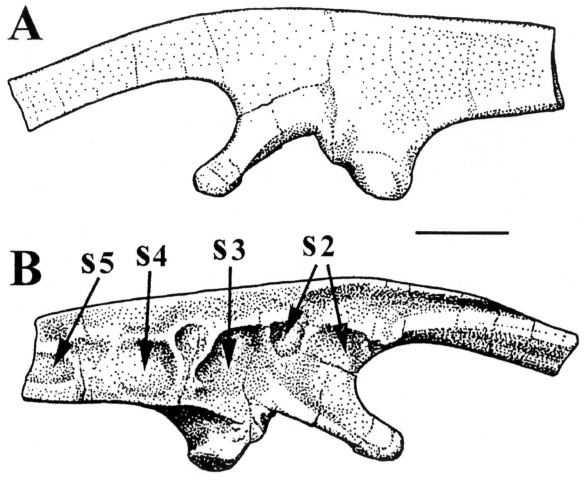

Brinkman *et al.* referred UGM XG94Kh201 to *P. xinjiangensis* based upon the following features: Jugal horn anteriorly flattened; increased number of denticles in dentary teeth over other *Psittacosaurus* species; and elongate postacetabular process of ilium. It differs from the holotype (IVPP V7704) of *P. xinjiangensis* in having dentary teeth with fewer denticles (a maximum of 18 instead of 21) and with the denticles apparently variable along the tooth row. Brinkman *et al.* interpreted these differences as representing intraspecific variation; furthermore, as the smaller type specimen possesses a higher denticle count, this may indicate that a decrease in the number of denticles has ontogenetic significance. However, the denticle count increases during from juveniles to adults in the species *P. mongoliensis* (see Sereno 1990*b*). Therefore, Brinkman *et al.* noted, additional specimens belonging to this species are required to determine if the lower number of denticles in UGM XG94Kh201 reflects ontogenetic change or adult intraspecific variation.

Regarding the ontogenetic stage of UGM XG94Kh201, Brinkman *et al.* pointed out other features of this specimen in addition to its being larger (approximately the size of AMNH 6254, holotype of the type species *P. mongoliensis*; see Osborn 1924*a*) than the holotype of *P. xinjiangensis*. Brinkman *et al.* cited Sampson, Ryan and Tanke (1997), who observed that, in ceratopsid dinosaurs, the presence of striations on skull bones is a juvenile feature that was lost as the animal matured. Consequently, the presence of such striations in IVPP V7704 and their absence in UGM XG94Kh201 suggest a similar pattern of ontogenetic development in psittacosaurs.

Brinkman *et al.* observed that a striking feature of UGM G94Kh201 is the posture, as preserved, of the hindlimb — folded in a squatting position — which is frequently seen in specimens of both *Psittacosaurus* and basal ceratopsids such as *Protoceratops*. Although this posture has generally been assumed to be artificial, its frequency among specimens suggests that it might be a normal resting posture, perhaps "exaggerated by the compression of the elements resulting from the loss of soft tissue." As interpreted by Brinkman *et al.*, the so-common crouched position of the Urho specimen could be "a natural position that would have reduced their body profiles during inclement weather and might have been a natural position for other activities such as feeding or nest incubation."

This first discovery of *P. xinjiangensis* at Urho is

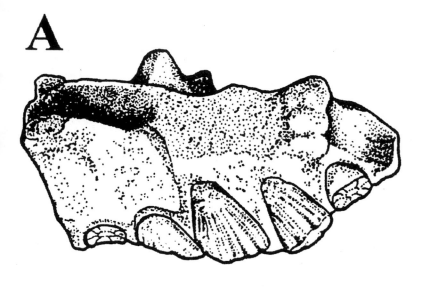

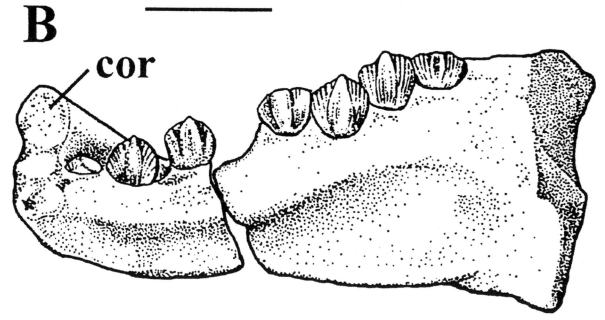

Psittacosaurus xinjiangensis, UGM XG94Kh201, A. right maxilla and B. left dentary, medial views, showing broken base of coronoid process (C.). Scale = 1 cm. (After Brinkman, Eberth, Ryan and Chen 2001.)

significant in documenting the presence of this species at this locality of an ornithischian other than the stegosaur *Wuerhosaurus*, an occurrence not surprising considering the general similarities between the Urho and Delanshan localities (*e.g.*, Dong 1973).

Anton (2001), in an abstract, reported briefly on a unique study postulating that gastroliths, in addition to aiding in digestion (as in extant crocodilians and birds), may also have served a thermodynamic function in small to medium-sized dinosaurs such as *Psittacosaurus*. Anton's hypothesis was "based on the substantially greater thermal conductivity that clasts exhibit compared to water (the chief constituent of taxa), which would therefore increase the rate of conductive heat transfer from the substratum to a static system (*i.e.*, a resting individual)."

The author employed a thermodynamic model to assess how such stones enhanced the flow of heat from the ground to a basking *Psittacosaurus mongoliensis*, the results of this modeling indicating that the transfer of heat increased from two to three times for this species when gastroliths were present. Thus, utilizing gastroliths as thermoregulators permitted these small to moderate-sized dinosaurs to spend less time basking in the sun and more in pursuing other activities, such as foraging. Additional benefits, Anton noted, would include a less exposure both to the sun and to potential predators, as well as a more efficient means of utilizing available heat during times of limited insulation. Finally, "energy absorbed by gastroliths may have extended activity levels in *P. mongoliensis* as heat was transferred from the clasts into the ceratopsian between basking episodes."

The type species *Luanpingosaurus jingshanensis*

Psittacosaurus

Psittacosaurus xinjiangensis, UGM XG94Kh201, right hindlimb folded in squatting position, in A. ventral and B. dorsal views. Scale = 2 cm. (After Brinkman, Eberth, Ryan and Chen 2001.)

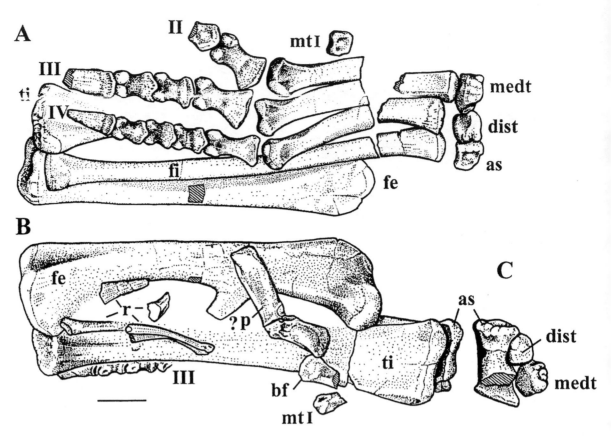

Life restoration of *Psittacosaurus* painted by Kelly Pugh.

Cheng *see in* Chen 1996, a *nomen nudum*, was listed by Wang *et al.* (2000) as a synonym of *Psittacosaurus*, although it originates from Upper Jurassic rocks (see "Nomina Nuda" chapter).

Key references: Anton (2001); Brinkman, Eberth, Ryan and Chen (1996, 2001); Dong (1973); Osborn (1923, 1924*a*); Russell and Zhao (1996); Sampson, Ryan and Tanke (1997); Sereno (1990*b*); Sereno and Chao [Zhao] 1988; Sereno, Zhao, Cheng and Rao (1988); Xu (1997); Xu and Zhao (1999); Wang *et al.* (2000); Yang [Young] (1958).

†PTEROSPONDYLUS
Saurischia: Eusaurischia: Theropoda: Neotheropoda: Coelophysoidea; Coelophysidae.

Comments: In their review of European Triassic theropods, Rauhut and Hungerbühler (2000) reassessed *Pterospondylus trielbae* (see *D:TE*), a taxon established upon an isolated dorsal vertebra collected from the Baerecke quarry, in the Knollenmergel of Halberstadt, Sachsen-Anhalt, Germany.

As originally described by Huene (1921, 1932), the vertebra has an elongate centrum resembling the condition found in *Procompsognathus* (see entry). However, Rauhut and Hungerbühler observed that the transverse processes in both *Pterospondylus* and *Procompsognathus* are triangular and strongly back-turned, a condition seen also in *Megapnosaurus* ("*Syntarsus*") (see Raath 1969) and regarded by Rowe and Gauthier (1990) as a synapomorphy of "Ceratosauria" (see "Systematics" chapter). As the transverse processes in *Dilophosaurus* and *Liliensternus* are less strongly back-turned and less significantly triangular as in *P. trielbae* and *Megapnopsaurus*, this character could represent a synapomorphy of a more restricted "ceratosaurian" clade. Therefore, Rauhut and Hungerbühler concluded that, although *P. trielbae* cannot be formally diagnosed and remains a *nomen dubium*, this species is probably referrable to the Coelophysidae.

Key references: Huene (1921, 1932); Raath (1969); Rauhut and Hungerbühler (2000); Rowe and Gauthier (1990).

PUKYONGOSAURUS Dong, Paik and Kim 2001
Saurischia: Eusaurischia: Sauropodomorpha: Sauropoda: Eusauropoda: Neosauropoda: Macronaria: Camarasauromorpha: Titanosauriformes: Somphospondyli: Euhelopodidae.
Name derivation: "Pukyong [National University]" + Greek *sauros* = "lizard."
Type species: *P. millenniumi* Dong, Paik and Kim 2001.
Other species: [None.]
Occurrence: Hasandong Formation, Galsari, Hadong-gun, South Korea.
Age: Early Cretaceous (?Hauterivian or early ?Aptian).
Known material/holotype: PKNU-G.102-109, fragmentary skeleton including seven incomplete cervical vertebrae, almost complete dorsal centrum, cervical rib, incomplete dorsal rib, complete chevron, partial ?clavicle, isolated bones.

Diagnosis of genus (as for type species): Medium-sized sauropod having somphospondylous vertebrae; neural spine of cervical vertebrae tall, proximally directed; parapophyses on lateroventral edge of centrum, just distal to articular condyle (as in *Euhelopus* and *Camarasaurus*); ventral side of cervical centrum bent, with keel, flat (as in *Euhelopus*); hemal canal of chevron open, not bridged over dorsally (Dong, Paik and Kim 2001.)

Comments: The type species *Pukyongosaurus millenniumi* was based upon a fragmentary postcranial remains (PKNU-G.102-109) collected from the same level of the same quarry (implying a single individual) in the Hasandong Formation (in the middle of the Sindong Group; possible Hauterivian, based on charophyte, spore, and pollen study [Seo 1985] or early Aptian, based on paleomagnetism [Doh, Hwang and Kim 1994; also, see "Note" below], Gyeongsang Supergoup, in Gyeongsang Basin, Gyeongsangnam-do, Hadong-gun, Galsari, South Korea. The material, to

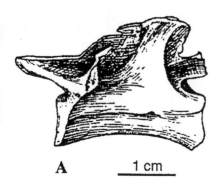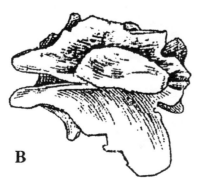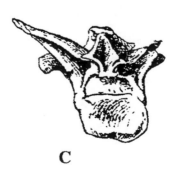

A   1 cm   B   C

Pterospondylus trielbae, holotype dorsal vertebra in A. left lateral, B. dorsal, and C. caudal views. (After Rauhut and Hungerbühler 2000, modified after Huene 1921.)

Pukyongosaurus

Pukyongosaurus millenniumi, a. PKNU-G.102, holotype incomplete cervical vertebra, b. PKNU-G.106, holotype dorsal vertebra, lateral views. Scale = 5 cm. (After Dong, Paik and Kim 2001.)

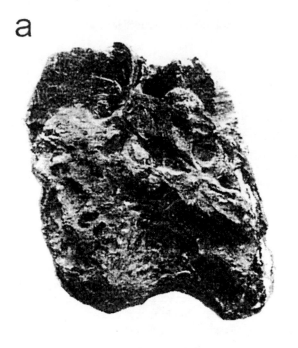

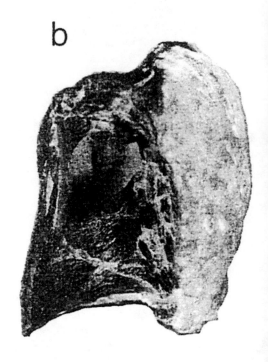

date of this writing not entirely prepared, was collected in 1998 by a field team from Pukyong National University. It represents the first dinosaur named from the Hasandong Formation and the most yet collected in Korea (Dong, Paik and Kim 2001).

As *P. millenniumi* is mostly represented by vertebrae, and because specializations on sauropod vertebrae are more readily recognizable than those on limbs or girdles, Dong *et al.* compared the vertebrae of this new form with those of both Jurassic and

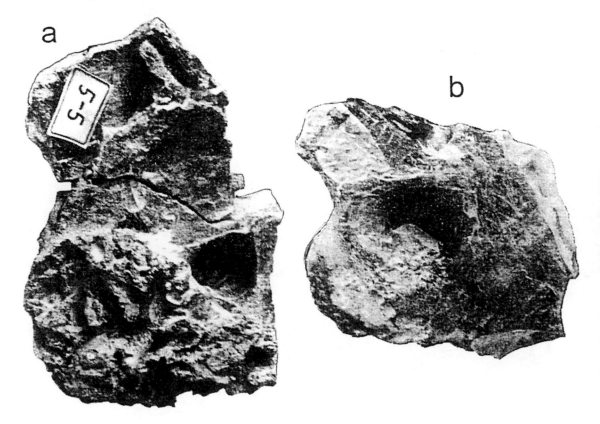

Pukyongosaurus millenniumi, a. holotype neural spine and neural arch of cervical vertebra and b. fragment of cervical vertebra. Scale = 5 cm. (After Dong, Paik and Kim 2001.)

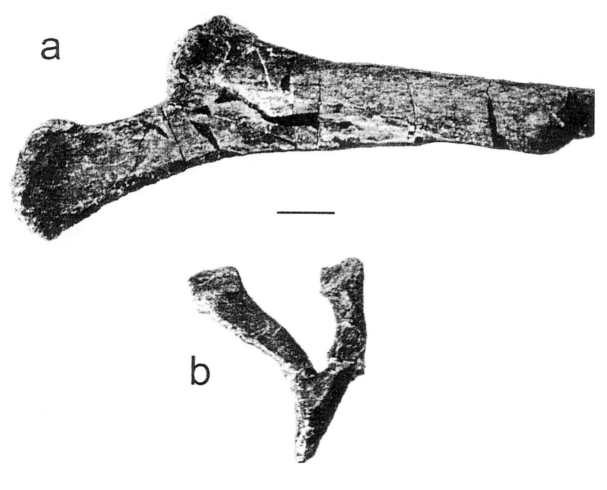

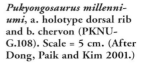

Cretaceous sauropods. Especially important regarding *P. millenniumi* are the cervical vertebrae, being elongate, located well cranially, and possessing extremely high neural spines. Furthermore, the hemal canal of the chevron of the preserved caudal vertebra is not bridged over dorsally, separating it from the Diplodocidae, *Mamenchisaurus* (=Mamenchisauridae of their usage, although *Mamenchisaurus* is generally regarded as a member of the Euhelopodidae), and Shunosaurinae (=Shunosauridae of their usage), in which the dorsal portion of the hemal canal is bridged and the chevrons are distally forked.

Dong *et al.* observed that the morphologies of the cervical and middorsal vertebrae of *Pukyongosaurus* most closely resemble those of members the family Euhelopodidae. The cervical vertebrae of *Pukyongosaurus* are of typical of those belonging to the Somphospondyli. Moreover, the authors suggested that *Pukyongosaurus* and *Euhelopus* share a sister-taxon relationship within Somphospondyli.

According to Dong *et al.*, a more satisfactory diagnosis of this new sauropod depends upon the finding of additional material. Its discovery has salient ge-

ographical and stratigraphical implications in eastern Asia, supporting the view that the Hasandong Formation is of Early Cretaceous age. Furthermore, the discovery of *Pukyongosaurus* constitutes evidence suggesting that dinosaurs of Early Cretaceous Korea are similar to those from Shandong Province, China.

Note: In a detailed paper discussing the paleoenvironments and taphonic preservation of dinosaur bone-bearing deposits in the Hasandong Formation, Paik, Kim, Park, Song, Lee, Hwang and Huh (2001) reported on the sauropod specimens deposited on the Hasandong floodplain. Paik *et al.* noted that these dinosaurs lived in dry woodlands having oxidized soils, an association comparable to the habitats in the Upper Jurassic Morrison Formation of the Western Interior of the United States (see, for example, Dodson, Behrensmeyer, Bakker and McIntosh 1980) and in Upper Cretaceous deposits of Utah (*e.g.*, Fouch, Lawton, Nichols, Cashion and Cobban 1983), Mongolia (Jerzykiewicz and Russell 1991), and India (*e.g.*, Sahni, Tandon, Jolly, Baipai, Sood and Srinivasan 1994). According to the authors, these carcasses, lying on floodplains, were severely weathered and had been scavenged

prior to burial by both carnivorous animals and dermestid beetles. Volcanic activity close to the basin may have resulted in rapid burial of the unweathered bones. Bone preservations of the Hasandong dinosaurs was facilitated by calcareous pedogenesis acting upon the deposits.

Key references: Dong, Paik and Kim (2001); Paik, Kim, Park, Song, Lee, Hwang and Huh (2001).

†QUAESITOSAURUS

Saurischia: Eusaurischia: Sauropodomorpha: Sauropoda: Eusauropoda: Neosauropoda: Macronaria: Camarasauromorpha: Titanosauriformes: Somphospondyli: Titanosauria: Nemegtosauridae.

Comments: In recent years, the generic validity of *Quaesitosaurus*— known only from a nearly complete skull (PIN 3906/2) from the Barungoyotskaya Svita (Barun Goyot Formation), Omnogove, Mongolian People's Republic (see *D:TE*)— has come into question. Wilson (1997), in an abstract, suggested that the type species *Q. orientalis* could be conspecific with another Mongolian form, *Nemegtosaurus mongoliensis*, an assessment that was not accepted by all workers (*e.g.*, J. S. McIntosh, personal communication, 1998) (see *SI*).

In a recent paper by Curry Rogers and Forster (2001), in which these authors described the new titanosaur *Rapetosaurus* (see entry), these accepted *Quaesitosaurus* as a valid genus. Performing a phylogenetic analysis, Curry Rogers and Forster found *Quaesitosaurus* to share a sister-taxon relationship with the titanosaur *Malawisaurus* supported by 10 ambiguous characters including four postcranial features shared by at least one diplodocid. *Quaesitosaurus*, *Nemegtosaurus*, and *Rapetosaurus* were found to be united by 11 shared characters, two of these (posterodorsal of splenial; approximate 90-degree angle between long axis of mandibular symphysis and that of mandible) being unambiguous. *Rapetosaurus* and *Nemegtosaurus* were found to be united further by various other characters (see entries and "Systematics" chapters).

Key references: Curry Rogers and Forster (2001); Wilson (1997).

QUILMESAURUS   Coria 2001

Saurischia: Eusaurischia: Theropoda: Neotheropoda: Tetanurae *incertae sedis*.

Name derivation: "Quilmes" [city in Argentina] + Greek *sauros* = "lizard."

Type species: *Q. currieri* Coria 2001.

Other species: [None.]

Occurrence: Allen Formation, Río Negro Province, Argentina.

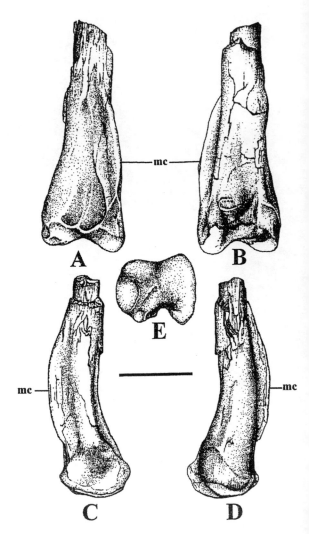

Quilmesaurus curriei, MPCA-PV-100, holotype distal right femur in A. cranial, B. caudal, C. medial, D. lateral, and E. distal views. Scale = 10 cm. Illustrations by Aldo Berosia. (After Coria 2001.)

Age: Late Cretaceous (Campanian–Maastrichtian).

Known material/holotype: MPCA-PV-100, partial right femur, complete right tibia.

Diagnosis of genus (as for type species): Medium-size; femur having strong, well-developed mediodistal crest; tibia having hook-shaped cnemial crest, lateral maleolus twice size of medial, distal end asymmetrical (Coria 2001).

Comments: *Quilmesaurus*, a "very peculiar" theropod genus, was founded on the distal portion of a right femur and a right tibia (MPCA-PV-100), collected during the late 1980s by a field crew led by Jaime E. Powell for the Universidad Nacional de Tucumán, from the fluvial sandstones at the Salitral Ojo de Agua locality, in the lower part of the Allen Formation of Río Negro Province, Patagonia, Argentina. The new type species *Quilmesaurus currei* is included in a skeletal assemblage of dinosaurs including titanosaurian sauropods (Salgado and Coria 1993,

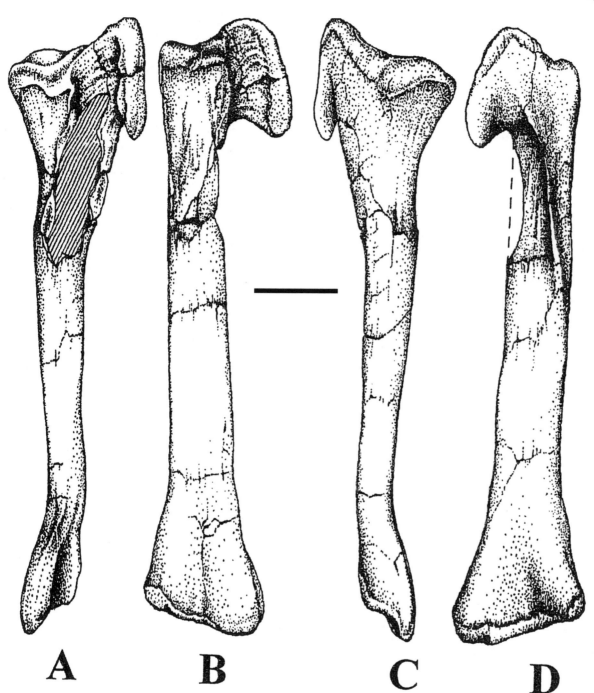

Quilmesaurus

Quilmesaurus curriei, MPCA-PV-100, holotype right tibia in A. lateral, B. caudal, C. medial, and D. cranial views. Scale = 10 cm. Illustrations by Aldo Berosia. (After Coria 2001.)

A   B   C   D

lambeosaurine hadrosaurs (Powell 1987), and ?nodosaurid ankylosaurs (Coria and Salgado 2001; see paper for a survey report on all ankylosaur material from this locality, including more recently collected specimens), also dinosaur (?titanosaurian) eggs. It is significant as the first theropod recorded from the Allen Formation of Argentina (Coria 2001).

Coria identified *Quilmesaurus* as a theropod based upon the features including the following: Bone shafts highly pneumatized; femur with expanded mediodistal crest; distal end of tibia expanded for triangular ascending process of astragalus. Although this genus is not a "ceratosaur" (showing no evidence of fused proximal tarsals; see Rowe and Gauthier 1990; see also "Systematics" chapter), it shares one feature (tibia having very well developed cnemial crest, this condition possibly primitive among theropods) with the neoceratosaurians *Ceratosaurus* and *Xenotarsosaurus* (Martínez, Gimènez, Rodriguez and Bochatey 1986). Furthermore, Coria noted, this genus shares with the allosauroids *Giganotosaurus* (Coria and Salgado 1995) and *Sinraptor* (Currie and Zhao 1993) a notch present on the distal articular surface of the tibia.

R

As Coria pointed out, the association of *Quilmesaurus* with the sauropods, hadrosaurs, and ankylosaurs also known from the Allen Formation involves the coexistence of both South American and North American forms. However, *Quilmesaurus* "does not show any unquestionable feature related with Laurasian forms, which would be expected since it was found at the same levels where North American related fauna is common" (including ankylosaurs and hadrosaurs). Rather, *Quilmesaurus* has numerous plesiomorphic characters (*e.g.*, femur without well-developed anterior intercondylar groove, facet for ascending process of astragalus less than 20 percent of tibia shaft length) more similar to typical South American forms (*e.g.*, *Giganotosaurus*, *Piatnitzkysaurus*, and a few undescribed forms (see Coria and Currie 1997; Calvo, Rubilar and Moreno, in press).

Key references: Calvo, Rubilar and Moreno (in press); Coria (2001); Coria and Currie (1997); Coria and Salgado (1995); Currie and Zhao (1993); Martínez, Gimènez, Rodriguez and Bochatey (1986); Powell (1987); Rowe and Gauthier (1990).

RAPETOSAURUS Curry Rogers and Forster 2001
Saurischia: Eusaurischia: Sauropodomorpha: Sauropoda: Eusauropoda: Neosauropoda: Macronaria: Camarasauromorpha: Titanosauriformes: Somphospondyli: Titanosauria: Nemegtosauridae.
Name derivation: Malagasy *Rapeto* [mischievous giant of Malagasy folklore] + Greek *sauros* = "lizard."
Type species: *R. krausei* Curry Rogers and Forster 2001.

Other species: [None.]
Occurrence: Maevarano Formation, Mahajanga basin, Madagascar.
Age: Late Cretaceous (Maastrichtian).
Known material: Adult skull material, skull material representing at least two juvenile individuals, associated juvenile postcranial remains.
Holotype: UA 8698, disarticulated skull including right maxilla with eight teeth, left maxilla, right lacrimal, left jugal, nasals, right quadrate, pterygoids, partial basiocciptal, right paroccipital process, left dentary with 11 teeth, angulars, right surangular, five associated teeth.

Diagnosis of genus (as for type species): Characterized by the following autapomorphies: expanded antorbital fenestra extending over tooth row; preantorbital fenestra position caudal to antorbital fenestra; subnarial foramen positioned anteriorly dorsoventrally elongate; jugal process of maxilla posterodorsally elongate and narrow; frontals having median dome; quadrate having V-shaped quadratojugal articulation; supraoccipital having two anteriorly directed median parietal processes; pterygoid with extremely shallow basipterygoid articulation, dorsoventrally expanded anterior process; basipterygoid processes diverging at distal extremes only; dentary having 11 alveoli extending two-thirds length of dentary's length; teeth gracile, cylindrical, with high-angle planar wear facets; 16 cervical vertebrae having constricted neural canals and continuous pre- and postspinal coels devoid of pre- or postspinal laminae; 11 dorsal vertebrae having deep lateral pleurocoels; neural spines of dorsal

Composite skeletal reconstruction by Mark Hallett of *Rapetosaurus krausei*, based on holotype UA 8698 (juvenile skull and postcrania), paratype MAD 96102 (isolated adult skull), and referred specimen MAD 952248 (juvenile frontals, dentary, and teeth), in (top) dorsal, left (split cranial/caudal), and (below) left lateral views. Scale = 1 m. (After Hallett and Curry Rogers 2000).

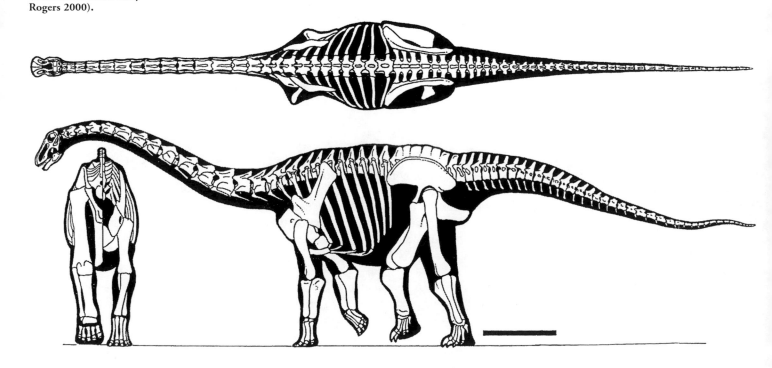

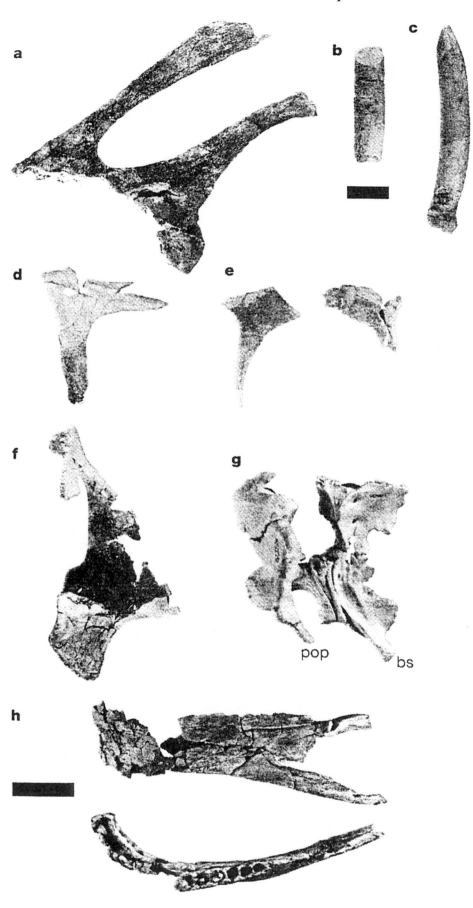

vertebrae with strong pre- and postspinal laminae in deeply excavated cranial and caudal pleurocoels; dorsal vertebrae with median interpre- and interpostzygapophyseal laminae; middle and caudal dorsal vertebrae having divided spinodiapophyseal lamina; six sacral centra with deep lateral pleurocoels; all centra of caudal vertebrae procoelous, with convex ventral margin lacking excavation; proximal caudal centra transversely broad, proximocaudally compressed; middle to distal caudal centra with constant length to width ratio; proximal to middle caudal neural spines having spinoprezygapophyseal, prespinal, and postspinal lamina on rectangular and proximally positioned neural arches; chevrons present throughout 80 percent of tail; iliac peduncle of ischium comprising one-quarter of acetabulum; ischial peduncle of ilium low, poorly developed; pubis more than twice length of ischium; scapula and coracoid having equal glenoid contribution; scapular blade not distally expanded; humerus to femur length quotient 0.80; radius and ulna having oblique interosseus ridges (Curry Rogers and Forster 2001).

Comments: The most complete titanosaur yet discovered (formerly known informally as "Malagasy Taxon A (MTA); see Curry Rogers 2001a, 2001b)," offering a view of titanosaur anatomy from head to tail, the genus *Rapetosaurus* was founded upon a disarticulated skull (UA 8698) collected from the Anembalemba Member of the Maevarano Formation, in the Mahajanga basin of northwestern Madagascar. Juvenile remains from the same locality referred to the type species, *Rapetosaurus krausei*, includes (FMNH PR 2184–2192, 2194, 2196, 2197, 2209 [about 75 percent complete], and 2210) a right exoccipital, opisthotic, laterosphenoid, supraoccipital, associated right and left frontals, two right prefrontals, a left surangular, a right parietal, left squamosal, right quadrate, right pterygoid, right angular, six associated teeth, a fused basioccipital, basisphenoid, parasphenoid, an associated juvenile skeleton including a midcaudal vertebral centrum, and (UCB 92829) another midcaudal centrum (Curry Rogers and Forster 2001).

Rapetosaurus krausei, cranial elements, UA 8698 (holotype) a. left maxilla, lateral view, b. worn maxillary tooth, lingual view, c. unworn maxillary tooth, mesial/distal view, d. right lacrimal, lateral view, e. right and left nasals, dorsal view, f. right quadrate, rostral view; g. FMNH PR 2184 and 2197 (referred), articulated supraoccipital, exoccipital/opisthotic, basioccipital, basipterygoid, basisphenoid, and laterosphenoid, right lateral view, h. UA 8698, dentary, left lateral (top) and dorsal views. Scale = 5 cm. (a, d–h) and 1 cm. (b, c). (After Curry Rogers and Forster 2001).

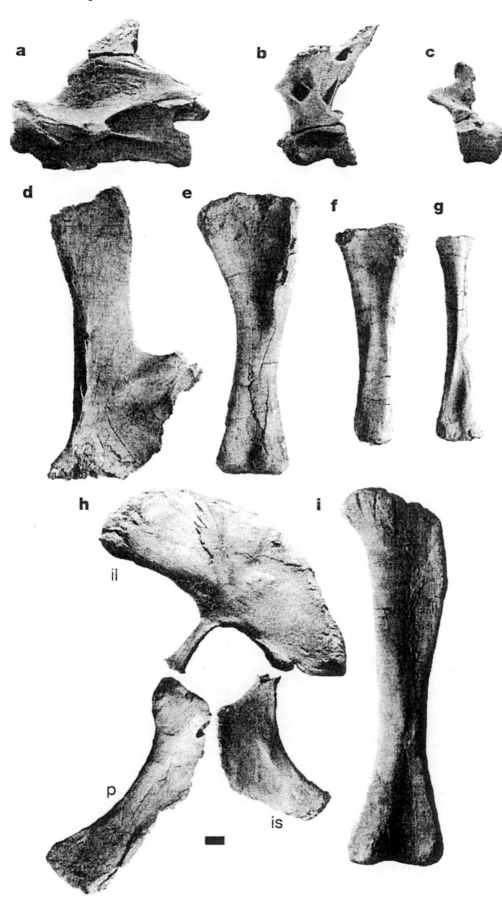

In describing this new genus, Curry Rogers and Forster noted that the skull of *Rapetosaurus* is unique among all known sauropods in that the enlarged antorbital fenestra "extends anteriorly over the tooth row and is bound ventrally by an elongate, narrow jugal process." The straight maxillary profile and cylindrical teeth resemble skulls of diplodocids more than to the "stepped" snout of brachiosaurids. Unlike diplodocids, the teeth in *Rapetosaurus* occupy the rostral two-thirds of the maxilla. The external nares, as in diplodocids, "are retracted to the level of the orbit and incompletely divided by medial nasal processes," thereby confirming, the authors affirmed, "that the nostrils were located on the top of the skull" (see Witmer 2001 for a contrasting opinion). The basipterygoid processes are comparatively longer than in other known titanosaurs, fitting into shallow facets on platelike pterygoids (as in *Nemegtosaurus*). As in *Antarctosaurus*, *Saltasaurus*, and *Malawisaurus*, *Rapetosaurus* possesses elongate, recurved paroccipital processes. From the associated bones of the lower jaw, Curry Rogers and Forster estimated the length of the skull of an adult *Rapetosaurus* to be approximately 40 centimeters (about 15.5 inches).

Comparing *Rapetosaurus* to other titanosaurs, Curry Rogers and Forster observed that the dorsal neural spines are craniocaudally compressed and broad, tapering at their distal extremes only (as in *Alamosaurus* and *Titanosaurus colberti*). Unlike other known titanosaurs, the dorsal and sacral vertebrae of this new genus have deep pleurocoels, and the proximal caudal neural spines possess a strongly developed spinoprezygapophyseal lamina.

Conducting a phylogenetic analysis, Curry Rogers and Forster found

Raptetosaurus krausei, postcranial elements from referred juvenile skeleton FMNH PR 2209, a. cervical vertebra 10, left lateral view, b. dorsal vertebra 4, left lateral view, c. proximal caudal vertebra, left lateral view, d. left scapula, lateral view, e. left humerus, cranial view, f. left ulna, cranial view, g. left radius, caudal view, h. left pubis, ischium, and ilium, lateral view, and i. left femur, cranial view. Scale = 3 cm. (After Curry Rogers and Forster 2001.)

Reconstructed skull and life restoration by Mark Hallett of *Rapetosaurus krausei*. (After Hallett and Curry Rogers 2000).

Rapetosaurus to be a member of the Titanosauria, exhibiting a suite of titanosaurian features (see Salgado, Coria and Calvo 1997; Salgado and Calvo 1997; Wilson and Sereno 1998; Upchurch 1998), and closely allied with *Nemegtosaurus* (see "Systematics" chapter).

The revised phylogeny proposed by Curry Rogers and Forster of the globally distributed Titanosauria provides an opportunity to explore vicariance during the Cretaceous. This analysis suggests, the authors noted, that the biogeographic history of *Rapetosaurus* could be linked to Africa, Asia, and India, contrasting with that proposed earlier (Krause,

Curry Rogers, Forster, Hartman, Buckley and Sampson 1999) for the Maevarano Formation fauna suggesting extensive faunal interchange between South America, India, and Madagascar. However, Curry Rogers and Forster pointed out, the significance of these biogeographic possibilities, "must be tested in the context of a more global analysis of titanosaur phylogeny and, we hope, with the addition of more cranial and postcranial data."

Unlike other titanosaurs, which coexisted with large-bodied ornithischians (mostly ankylosaurs, hadrosaurs, and ceratopsians), *Rapetosaurus* shared its environment only with other titanosaurs, this suggesting "a different herbivore community dynamic on Madagascar that is seen elsewhere in the Cretaceous."

Key references: Curry Rogers (2001*a*, 2001*b*); Curry Rogers and Forster (2001); Krause, Curry Rogers, Forster, Hartman, Buckley and Sampson (1999); Salgado, Coria and Calvo (1997); Salgado and Calvo (1997); Wilson and Sereno (1998); Upchurch (1998); Witmer (2001).

†REVUELTOSAURUS
Ornithischia *incertae sedis*.

Comments: In 1989, Adrian P. Hunt described the new genus and species *Revueltosaurus callenderi*, founded upon a single tooth (NMMNH P4957) from the Bull Canyon Formation (Chinle Group) of New Mexico. At that time, Hunt classified *Revueltosaurus* as a possible ornithischian or perhaps a sister taxon to the Ornithischia. Since the original discovery, numerous other teeth have been referred to this taxon (see *D:TE*).

In a later abstract, Hunt (1989), while pointing out the global extreme rarity of Triassic body fossils, briefly discussed this "most common Upper Triassic ornithischian dinosaur." As noted by Hunt, since the discovery of *R. callenderi*, all large (over one centimeter) and numerous small ornithischian dinosaur teeth from the Chinle Group have been referred to this species.

A more recent reexamination by Heckert (2002*a*) of the holotype and referred specimens of *R. callenderi*, however, have revealed the following: 1. *Revueltosaurus callenderi* is a valid type species, despite conflicting cladistic arguments; 2. numerous teeth referred to this species, especially those from the *Placerias* quarry southwest of St. Johns, Arizona, rather represent more basal ornithischians; and 3. teeth assigned to *R. callenderi*, from the Blue Hills, north of St. Johns and Lamy, New Mexico, are referrable to a new (and as yet unnamed; see "Note" below) species.

While not providing details, Heckert stated that this new species is more derived than the type species and constitutes one of the most derived of all Triassic ornithischians. It is also older ("Adamanian": *i.e.,* latest Carnian) than *R. callenderi* ("Revueltian": *i.e.,* early to middle Norian). Both species, according to Hunt, "have great potential as index taxa of their respective faunochrons and support existing biochronologies based on other tetrapods, megafossil plants, palynostratigraphy, and lithostratigraphy."

Note: Andrew B. Heckert, in his 2001 PhD dissertation on the microvertebrate record of the Upper Triassic lower Chinle Group of the southwestern United States and the early evolution of dinosaurs

(University of New Mexico, made available in 2002 from University Microfilms International, document AAT 3041086), introduced the new above mentioned species "*Revueltosaurus hunti*" (from Arizona), "*Crosbysaurus harrisae*" (Texas, Arizona, and New Mexico), and "*Protecovasaurus lucasi*" (see "Nomina Nuda" chapter). Based upon teeth, all three of these new ornithischian taxa will presumably be formally named and described at some future date.

Key references: Heckert (2002*a*, 2002*b*); Hunt (1989).

†RHADINOSAURUS Seeley 1881 [in part, *nomen dubium*]—(See *Struthiosaurus*.)
Type species: *R. alcimus* Seeley 1881 [in part, *nomen dubium*.

†RICHARDOESTESIA—(=*Paronychodon*; =?*Euronychodon*)
Saurischia: Eusaurischia: Theropoda: Neotheropoda: Tetanurae: Avetheropoda: Coelurosauria: Maniraptoriformes: Maniraptora: ?Metornithes: Oviraptorosauria: Caenagnathidae.
New species: *R. isosceles* Sankey 2001.
Occurrence of *R. isosceles*: Aguja Formation, Big Bend National Park, Texas, Milk River Formation, Oldman Formation, Dinosaur Park Formation, Horseshoe Canyon Formation, Saskatchewan, Lance Formation, Wyoming (Currie, Rigby and Sloan 1990; Baszio 1997), Hell Creek Formation (personal

LSUMG 489: 8238, *Richardoestesia isosceles*, holotype tooth, (left) lateral and (right) caudal views. Scale = 1 m. (After Sankey 2001.)

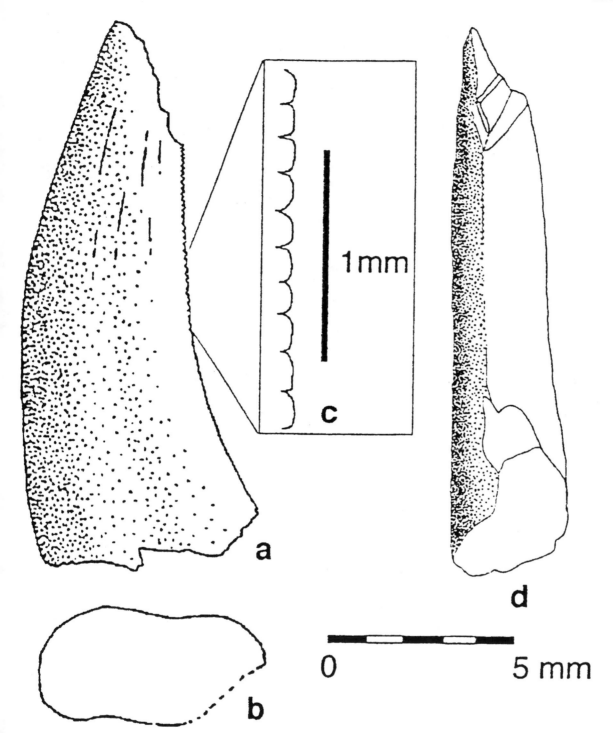

IPS 18 372, *Richardoestesia*-like theropod tooth from the Aren Sandstone Formation of Spain, in a. lateral, b. ventral, and d. distal views; c. detail of denticles (After Prieto-Márquez, Gaete, Galobart and Ardévol 2000.)

1mm

0   5 mm

observation of Sankey), North Dakota, South Dakota, United States.

Age of *R. isosceles*: Late Cretaceous (late Campanian to early Maastrichtian).

Known material of *R. isosceles*: Teeth.

Holotype of *R. isosceles*: LSUMG 489:6238, tooth.

Diagnosis of *R. isosceles*: Teeth straight; narrow; shaped like isosceles triangle in lateral view (see Currie *et al.* 1990; Baszio 1997*b*); tooth shape labio-lingually flattened oval in basal cross section; denticles minute (0.1 millimeters in height and mesiodistal width); square; size uniform from base of tooth to tip; length of carinae extended; if present, mesial denticles often much smaller than distal denticles; interdenticle spaces usually minute, barely visible; denticles spaced closely; denticle tips straight or faintly rounded, not pointed; seven to 11 denticles per millimeter (Sankey 2001, modified from Currie *et al.* and Baszio).

Comments: A poorly known, small theropod

A

B
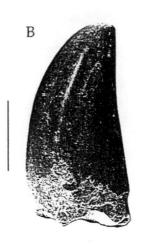

C

D

based mostly on teeth, *Richardoestesia* was established upon a pair of dentaries (CMN [formerly NMC] 343), the left lower jaw being almost complete, collected from what is now the Dinosaur Park Formation in Alberta, Canada. Charles Whitney Gilmore (1924) originally referred this specimen to the species *Chirostenotes pergracilis*. Almost 70 years later, Currie, Rigby and Sloan (1990) referred these jaws to the new genus and species *Ricardoestesia* [note spelling; see "Notes" below] *gilmorei*. Although the generic name was inadvertently misspelled *Richardoestesia* in all but one instance in the paper by Currie *et al.* (R. E. Sloan, personal communication to G. Olshevsky 1992), it is the latter spelling that has been adopted into usage (see *D:TE* for more details and also a photograph of the holotype).

In their 1990 publication, Currie *et al.* identified various theropod teeth from the (lower Campanian) Milk River Formation (see Russell 1935), and also the Scollard Formation of Alberta, the Frenchman Formation of Saskatchewan, the Hell Creek Formation of Montana, and the Lance Formation of Wyoming (Estes 1964; Carpenter 1982) as referrable to the genus *Richardoestesia*. However, many of the teeth differ from those of the holotype of *R. gilmorei* in showing no evident curvature in lateral view and in resembling elongate isosceles triangles. Consequently, Currie *et al.* suggested that the teeth originating in Maastrichtian-age formations could represent a species of *Richardoestesia* other than the type species, the authors noting that these specimens would be described at some later date. Subsequently, Baszio (1976*b*) and Peng (1997*a*), each working on dinosaur teeth from Late Cretaceous rocks in Alberta, recognized more such straight *Richardoestesia* teeth, both authors referring these specimens to *Richardoestesia* sp.

More recently, Sankey (2001*a*), in a review of dinosaurs from the late Campanian Aguja Formation, Talley Mountain Area, Big Bend National Park, Texas, recognized the above straight and triangular teeth as

a new species of this genus, which she named *Richardoestesia isosceles*, selecting as the holotype LSUMGS 489:6238, a fragment of a small tooth (about 2 millimeters in length) from the Aguja Formation, Big Bend National Park, Texas. Sankey referred to this new species various other teeth including LSUMG 489:6233, 6234, 6235, 492: 6264, AMNH 8133 (figure number 69*b* in Estes), and RTMP 91.1709.

As Sankey observed, the two species of *Richardoestesia* have different relative abundances that reflect their different paleoecologies. *R. isosceles* is abundant in the Milk River, Scollard (personal observation by Sankey), Lance, and Hell Creek formations. However, this species is more rare in the Oldman, Dinosaur Park, and Horseshoe Canyon formations, units that represent more closed and wet habitats (see Baszio 1979*a*). Sankey noted that finding this species in the Talley Mountain supports interpreting the Aguja Formation as having dry, open habitats. It was Baszio's (1979*b*) suggestion that the small, straight, and pointed teeth in this species were mainly used in fish eating; according to Sankey, this species may also have specialized in eating insects.

Sankey pointed out that this is the first reported occurrence of *R. isosceles* in the Aguja Formation, its presence there demonstrating that this was a widely occurring taxon within the Western interior. Furthermore, that author noted, this species may also be present among the small, birdlike theropod teeth found among the Terlingua fauna (see Rowe, Cifelli, Lehman and Weil 1992).

In a subsequently published abstract, Sankey (2002) regarded the "common, but enigmatic Maastrichtian theropod" *Paronychodon* (see *D:TE*), a genus known only from teeth, as a morphotype of *R. isosceles*, this assessment based upon both morphology (teeth straight to slightly recurved) and relative abundance of specimens.

Rauhut (2002) described a number of dinosaur teeth collected from the vertebrate-bearing layer of the Uña Formation (Lower Cretaceous: Barremian; date based on palynomorphs, see Mohr 1987, and charophytes, see Schudack 1989), Uña, Province of Cuenca, northeast of the city of Cuenca, in east-central Spain. Fossil material collected from this locality include fishes, anurans, squamates, crocodilians, mammals, and dinosaurs (briefly described in an abstract by Rauhut and Zinke 1995, who noted the striking similarity of this fauna to those of Late Cretaceous North America), including an indeterminate sauropod (one tooth, IPFUB Uña Sd 1), a probably new basal euornithopod (14 teeth, IPFUB Uña Ir 1-10), and various theropods (*e.g.*, velociraptorine [67 teeth, IPFUB Uña Th 36, 38, 40–47, 50–52, 63, 65, 66, and 70] and dromaeosaurine [37 teeth, IPFUB Uña Th 37, 39, 48, 48, 67, 71–80] dromaeosaurids) represented by teeth. Also included in this dinosaurian fauna are teeth resembling those of *Richardoestesia* "*Paranthodon*" (=*Richardoestesia*; see above).

A total of 47 teeth (collectively catalogued as IPFUB Uña Th 1–20, 64, 68, and 81), characterized by strongly elongate and just slightly recurved shape, because of their close resemblance to teeth of *Richardoestesia* (particularly specimens from the North American Dinosaur Park Formation and Aguja Formation), were referred by Rauhut to cf. *Richardoestesia* sp. An additional 14 teeth (IPFUB Uña Th 53, Th 55–61, and Th 69), moderately curved but slightly compressed laterally, were referred by that author to cf. "*Paronychodon*" (=*Richardoestesia*) sp., because of their resemblance to teeth from North America described as *Paronychodon lacustris* and a tooth from Portugal, virtually indistinguishable from *P. lacustris*, described as *Euronychodon portucalensis*.

The discovery of these remains, Rauhut noted, demonstrates the striking similarity between faunas of the Early Cretaceous of Europe and Late Cretaceous of North America. However, as more basal theropods have also been reported from various Early Cretaceous European localities, the latter seems to have been an age of transition between the typical Late Jurassic and Late Cretaceous theropod faunas known from the Northern Hemisphere.

Notes: Prieto-Márquez, Gaete, Galobart and Ardèvol (2000) described, in a preliminary report, a theropod tooth (IPS 18.372) closely resembling teeth of *Richardoestesia*. The specimen was associated with a dinosaur nesting site, called L'Abeller, in deltaic deposits of the Upper Cretaceous (Campanian; *e.g.*, X. Orue-Etxeberria, personal communication to Prieto-Márquez *et al.*, 1998) Aren Sandstone Formation in the northern part of the Tremp syncline, south-central Pyrenees, in northeastern Spain.

In describing IPS 18 372, Prieto-Márquez *et al.* noted that the tooth is bladelike, with a distally re-

curved, laterally compressed crown having a concave distal keel and convex mesial keel. The length of the tooth is 5.8 millimeters and the width at the base 3.1 millimeters. In its overall morphology (subrectangular basal cross section) and minute and rectangular to square-shaped denticles the specimen resembles quite closely teeth of *Richardoestesia gilmorei* (see Currie *et al.* 1990), moreso than to any other known theropod taxon.

This tooth, noted Prieto-Márquez *et al.*, is significant as the first theropod tooth known from the southern Pyrenees and "the first Coelurosauria reported from the Late Cretaceous foredeep of the south-central Pyrenees." While the L'Abeller specimen displays close affinities with *Richardoestesia*, the scarcity of the former's material plus the uncertain status of *R. gilmorei* preclude assigning IPS 18 372 to any clade below the level of Maniraptora. However, the authors pointed out that "the presence of a *Richardoestesia*-like theropod in the Late Cretaceous of the Pyrenees would extend 50 millions of years the fossil record of this form in Spain."

Sankey, Brinkman, Guenther and Currie (2002) reported that more than 1,700 small theropod teeth (also some small, indeterminate bird teeth) had been recovered by the Royal Tyrrell Museum of Palaeontology, following 15 years of screening, from microvertebrate sites in the Judith River Group (Campanian) of southern Alberta. This collection, the authors noted, allows for the refining of our understanding of the diversity and variation of small theropod dinosaurs included in this assemblage.

In addition to previously known taxa, this sampling resulted a series of morphologically distinct groups recognized by Sankey *et al.* as possibly representing some new taxa. Teeth displaying such *Paronychodon*-like as a flat surface with longitudinal ridges on the side were resolved into discrete morphotypes, two referred to *Paronychodon lacustris* and two postulated as representing distinct taxa, presently designated "?*Dromaeosaurus* morphotype A and Genus and species indet." The teeth of *P. lacustris* and ?*Dromaeosaurus* morphotype A both exhibit distinctive wear patterns suggesting that "tooth functioning involved contact between the flat surfaces of opposing teeth." Both species of *Richardoestesia*, *R. gilmorei* and *G. isosceles*, were found in this assemblage.

Study of this material furthermore resulted in the recognition that *Saurornitholestes* (see entry) constitutes a valid genus.

Sankey, in her review of the Aguja Formation dinosaurs, also noted the following: Earlier reports of the theropod *Troodon* sp., based exclusively on a complete tooth crown (LSUMG 140:6117) from the Talley Mountain and Terlingua microsites in this formation, are specious. The tooth closely resembles in size and shape pachycephalosaurid teeth in the collections of the Royal Tyrrell Museum of Paleontology (see Baszio 1979*b*; Sues and Galton 1987) and therefore belongs to the Pachycephalosauridae, consequently excluding *Troodon* from the Ajuga Formation fauna.

Sankey also reported large fragments of large, robust, and recurved teeth (LSUMG 488:5483 and 489:6239) belonging to an undetermined theropod unlike any previously described and, therefore, possibly representing a new taxon. The teeth have a fore to aft basal length of 9.0 and 5.5 millimeters, respectively. They are most similar to teeth of *Dromaeosaurus* in the RTMP collections and in Currie *et al.* and Baszio (1979*b*), however the mesial carinae in these specimens do not twist lingually as in the dromaeosaurid *Dromaeosaurus*. Teeth of the dromaeosaurid *Saurornitholestes* are smaller than these, more sharply recurved, more labio-lingually flattened, and have more sharply pointed denticles. The shape and size of the denticle are not tyrannosaurid-like, thereby ruling out their belonging to young tyrannosaurids (see also the abstract by Sankey 2001*b*).

George Olshevsky, in a 2002 email communication, explained in detail the problem between the two spellings, *Richardoestesia* and *Ricardoestesia*: As related to Olshevsky by Robert Sloan, the intended spelling for this generic name was *Ricardoestesia*— without an "h"— when it was introduced into the paleontological literature by Philip J. Currie, J. Keith Rigby, Jr., and Sloan in the book *Dinosaur Systematics: Approaches and Perspectives* (1990). However, someone on the editorial staff of the book's publisher, Cambridge University Press, subsequent to proofreading by the authors, altered the spelling to *Richardoestesia*. Apparently the Cambridge editor had changed the spelling throughout some (but not all) of the text, seemingly wanting the spelling to emulate the well-known "generic names honoring contemporary paleontologists employed by South American paleontologist Florentino Ameghino, who had specifically used the combining form richardo-." Olshevsky (1991), noting that the *Richardoestesia* spelling appeared first in Currie *et al.*'s article, used that spelling in his checklist published in the first *Mesozoic Meanderings*.

In the second *Mesozoic Meanderings* list (1992), in deference to Sloan and his co-authors, Olshevsky attempted to "do what I, in my small way, could do to get the h-less spelling established." Thus, Olshevsky (1992) "deliberately chose to ignore my nomenclatural act in the first MM #2 printing and reversed it in the second." Acknowledging that the two different spellings in the original paper exposed the typographical error, Olshevsky (1992) proposed that *Ri-cardoestesia* be accepted as the correct spelling of the genus. Olshevsky (1992) reasoned that enough workers used the spelling without the "h," and also "if nobody noticed what I had done in the first printing, in time the h-less spelling would preponderate. Then, even if someone did turn up my original revision, a good case could be made to retain the h-less spelling, which is the way the authors originally wanted it," preponderant usage carrying considerable weight in issues of zoological nomenclature.

Although for the next ten years Olshevsky tried to ensure that the spelling lacking the "h" was used in any dinosaur-related document, mentioning that genus, for which he had dealings, the incorrect spelling *Richardoestesia* predominated in the literature. As Olshevsky pointed out in his email, both spellings are correct in terms of being equally valid Latinizations, albeit the spelling without the "h" is that preferred by the authors of the genus. While the spelling with the "h" is currently the correct one, according to the ICZN rules, Olshevsky strongly recommended that future users of the name become proactive and utilize the name *Ricardoestesia* in favor of *Richardoestesia* in any published works citing the genus." I will continue to do so myself, of course," Olshevsky stated, "and if it requires petitioning the ICZN to resolve the matter, I'll try that, too. BUT: If I hear from the original authors … that they no longer care which spelling becomes accepted, I will abandon this effort."

Key references: Baszio (1997*a*, 1997*b*); Carpenter (1982); Currie, Rigby and Sloan (1990); Estes (1964); Gilmore (1924); Peng (1997*a*); Prieto-Márquez, Gaete, Galobart and Ardèvol (2000); Rowe, Cifelli, Lehman and Weil (1992); Olshevsky (1991, 1992); Rauhut (2002); Rauhut and Zinke (1995); Russell (1935); Sankey (2001*a*, 2001*b*, 2002); Sankey, Brinkman, Guenther and Currie (2002).

RUEHLEIA   Galton 2001
Saurischia: Eusaurischia: Sauropodomorpha: Prosauropoda: Plateosauridae.
Name derivation: Latinized reference to ["Hugo] Rühle [von Lilienstern" of Bedheim].
Type species: *R. bedheimensis* Galton 2001.
Other species: [None.]
Occurrence: Trossingen Formation, South Thuringia, Germany.
Age: Late Triassic (upper Norian).
Known material: Two skeletons, one complete.
Holotype: MB (Rühle von Lilienstern Collection, no number), incomplete skeleton presently including vertebrae (cervicals 3–10 and dorsals 1–15 (three more cervicals were found in summer 2002, MB collection, P. M. Galton, personal communication

Photograph of a 1930s post card supplied by R. Werneburg.

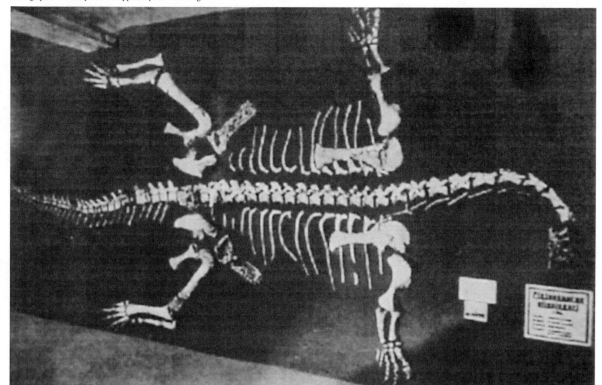

Ruehleia bedheimensis, MB (unnumbered, Rühle von Lilienstern Collection), composite holotype (formerly referred to *Plateosaurus plieningeri*) comprising two individuals, as originally mounted by Hugo Rühle Von Lilienstern in 1934 (as a "Schmuckstück" or ornamental piece) on a wall at the Paläontologisches Heimatmuseum Bedheim, in the Schloss Bedheim, Thuringia, Germany, this skeleton measuring about 8 meters in length. (After Galton 2001*b*.)

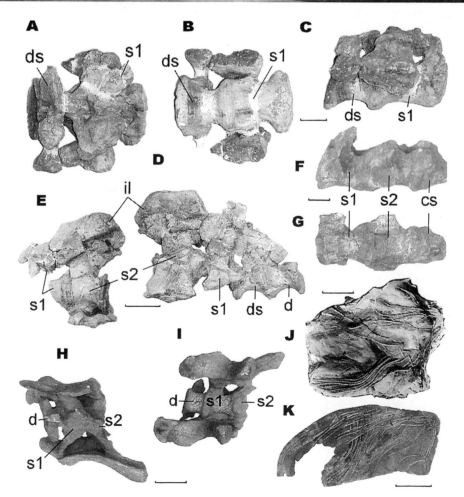

Ruehleia bedheimensis specimens from Grosser Gleichberg, Römhild, originally referred to *Plateosaurus plieningeri*: A.–C. MB RvL 1, holotype dorsosacral vertebra, sacral vertebrae 1 and 2 (cranial portion of centrum), in A. dorsal, B. ventral, and C. left lateral views; D.–E. MB RvL 2, D. incomplete last sacral vertebra, dorsosacral, sacrals 1 and 2, and left ilium, dorsal view, E. sacral vertebra 2, part of centrum of sacral 1, and part of left ilium, ventral view; F.–G., *Plateosaurus* sp., SMNS 6058, from Erlenberg, incomplete sacrum, F. left lateral and G. ventral views; H.–I., *P. quenstedti*, AMNH 24384, cast of holotype GPIT A, last dorsal vertebra, first sacral, cranial part of second sacral, and ilia (right incomplete caudally), H. dorsal and I. ventral views; J.–K., *P. longiceps*, partial set of gastralia from Trossingen, J. AMNH 6810 (in plaster jacket), K. SMNS 12949. Scale = approx. 5 cm. (After Galton 2001*e*.)

Ruehleia

Ruehleia bedheimensis, MB Rvl. 1, holotype elements: A. incomplete right scapulocoracoid, lateral view; B.–C., right humerus in B. medial and C. cranial views; D. right radius, lateral view; E. right ulna, lateral view; F. right manus, dorsal view, unguals in lateral view; G. caudally incomplete right ilium, medial view; H. left ilium, lateral view; I.–K., right pubis in I. dorsal and J.–K. lateral views, K. with detail of proximal end; L. ischia, right lateral view; M.–O. right femur (fourth trochanter restored from left) in M. medial, N. caudal, and O. cranial views; P. right tibia, lateral view; and Q. left tibia, medial view. Scale = 10 cm. (A, G–J, L–Q) and 5 cm. (B–F, K). (After Galton 2001*e*.)

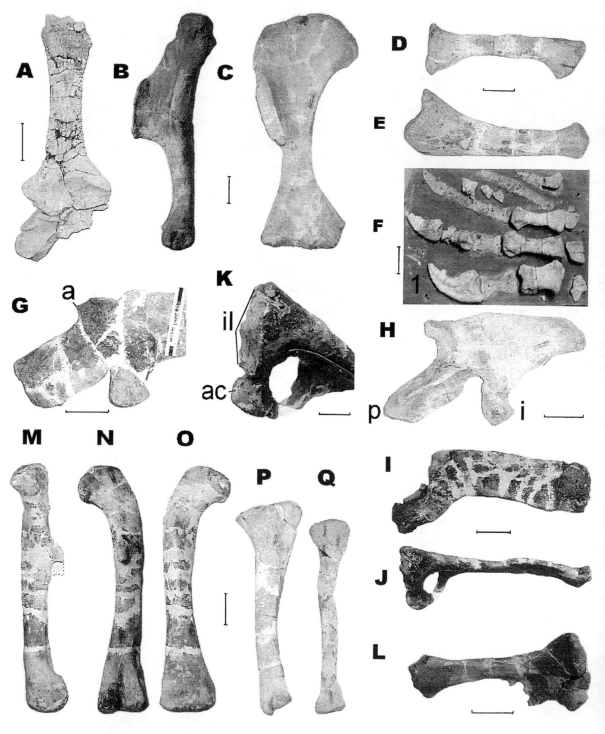

2002), partial sacrum, and approximately 20 caudals), right scapulocoracoid, humeri, right radius and ulna, incomplete right and left manus, pelvic girdles, femora, tibiae, right astragalus.

Diagnosis of genus (as for type species): Sacrum with three vertebrae, including dorsosacral; ilium having very large pubic peduncle and extremely short cranial process; proximal end of pubis with length of articular surface for ilium much longer than wide, acetabular portion very short (equaling half width of iliac surface); manus having three large carpals with complicated proximal articular surfaces (Galton 2001*b*).

Comments: The history of the genus now known as *Ruehleia* has its origins approximately one half century ago.

As recounted by Peter M. Galton (2001*b*), Hugo Rühle von Lilienstern, M. Lang and Friedrich von Huene, in 1952, described two skeletons referred to *Plateosaurus plieningeri*, collected from the Knollembergel (Trossingen Formation; of upper Norian age, see Bachman, Beutler, Hagdorn, and Hauschke 1999; Beutler 1998*a*, 1999*b*), near Schleusingen, southwest of Hildburghausen, South Thuringia, Germany. The larger of these specimens (MB, correct abbreviation; Heinrich, personal communication to Galton 2001*b*), a reasonably complete skeleton, was originally exhibited as a slab mount (*e.g.*, Rühle von Lilienstern 1935*b*) on a wall of Paläontologisches Heimatmuseum Bedheim, Schloss Bedheim, Thuringia. The second specimen is a smaller and incomplete skeleton (Rühle 1936). Recognizing this material as representing a new genus and species, Galton (2001*b*) renamed it *Ruehleia bedheimensis*.

This type species was identified by Galton (2001*b*) as "a plateosaur" (*sensu* Galton and Upchurch, in press). The holotype and referred material will later be described in detail by Galton (*e.g.*, Galton 2001*e*).

Key references: Galton (2001*b*, 2001*e*); Galton and Upchurch (in preparation); Rüle von Lilienstern (1935*a*, 1935*b*, 1936); Rüle von Lilienstern, Lang and Huene (1952).

†SAUROPELTA

Ornithischia: Genasaura: Thyreophora: Eurypoda: Ankylosauromorpha: Ankylosauria: Nodosauridae.

Comments: In a preliminary report, presented as an abstract for a poster, Parsons and Parsons (2001) described the cranial phylogenetic characters of a recently collected skull (MOR 1073, this specimen including associated postcranial remains) of *Sauropelta* cf. *S. edwardsi* from the basal portion of Unit VII of the Cloverly Formation (Lower Cretaceous; Aptian), in the Middle Dome region of central Montana. As the holotype (AMNH 3032) of *Sauropelta edwardsi* does not include a skull, and because most of the cranial remains referred to the type species has been fragmentary, MOR 1073 contributes substantially to understanding the skull anatomy of this armored dinosaur. The authors noted that the skull of MOR 1073 compares favorably with AMNH 3035, a caudal cranial fragment of *S. edwardsi*. MOR 1073 is to be described and figured in detail in a subsequent publication by Parsons and Parsons.

As Parsons and Parsons noted, "some of the characters of this new skull, especially in its anterior portion, may raise questions as to the accepted understanding of what cranial features help to discriminate between the Nodosauridae and the Ankylosauridae families of the suborder Ankylosauria."

Key reference: Parsons and Parsons (2001).

†SAUROPOSEIDON

Saurischia: Eusaurischia: Sauropodomorpha: Sauropoda: Eusauropoda: Neosauropoda: Macronaria: Camarasauromorpha: Titanosauriformes: Brachiosauridae.

Diagnosis of genus (as for type species): Centra of cervical vertebrac extremely elongate; EI (redefined from Upchurch 1998 by Wedel, Cifelli and Sanders 2000*b* as craniocaudal length of centrum divided by midline height of cotyle) midcervicals greater than 5; differing from all other known sauropods in possessing

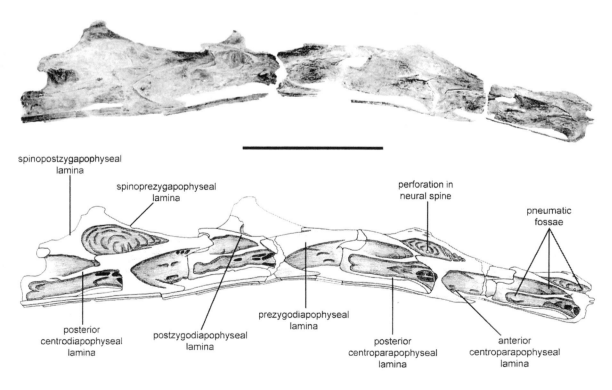

spinopostzygapophyseal lamina

spinoprezygapophyseal lamina

perforation in neural spine

pneumatic fossae

posterior centrodiapophyseal lamina

postzygodiapophyseal lamina

prezygodiapophyseal lamina

posterior centroparapophyseal lamina

anterior centroparapophyseal lamina

Sauroposeidon proteles, OMNH 53062, holotype articulated cervical vertebrae 5 to 8, right lateral view, the interpretive drawing (below) emphasizing the laminae and pneumatic fossae. Scale = 1 m. After Wedel, Cifelli and Sanders 2000*b*, redrawn from Wedel *et al.* 2000*a*.)

Sauroposeidon proteles, OMNH 53062, holotype cervical vertebrae in right lateral view, A. C6, pneumatic bone unshaded, B. hypothetical appearance of air sac system reconstructed based on that of the ostrich (*Struthio camelus*). (After Wedel, Cifelli and Sanders 2000*b*.)

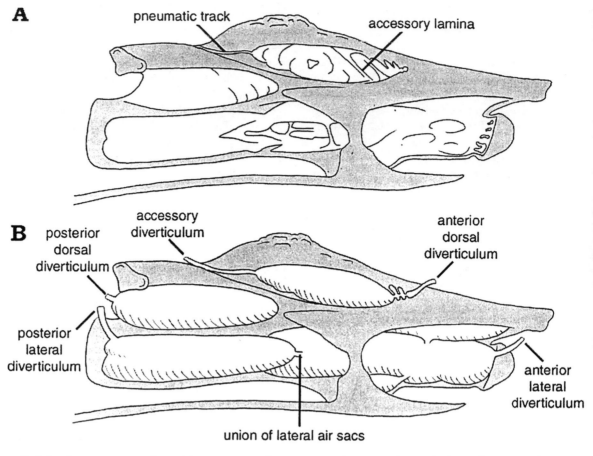

well-defined centroparapophyseal laminae extending to caudal ends of centra, diapophyses located approximately one third length of centrum behind cranial condyles, deeply excavated neural spines that are perforate in cranial cervicals, and hypertrophied central pneumatic fossae extending caudally to cotyles; internal structure entirely composed of pneumatic camellae separated by bony septa ranging in thickness from less than one to approximately three millimeters; total length of cervical rib equal to or exceeding length of three centra (Wedel, Cifelli and Sanders 2000).

Comments: The gigantic sauropod *Sauroposeidon proteles* was first described in a preliminary report by Wedel, Cifelli and Sanders (2000*a*), this genus known only from the Antlers Formation of Oklahoma (see *S2*). Subsequent to that report, the authors published a detailed study concerning the osteology, paleobiology, and relationships of this taxon, at the same time offering a revised diagnosis of the genus and species, and also more fully describing and illustrating the type material.

As noted by Wedel *et al.* (2000*b*), the holotype (OMNH 53062), four articulated cervical vertebrae with their cervical ribs preserved in place, was found lying on its right side, the preservation of the ribs in their natural positions with no postmortem distortion suggesting that the specimen was buried with the

musculature in place. The loss of such ribs from centra cranial to the specimen and retention of those belonging to the specimen indicate that the neck was pulled apart by parallel to its long axis by forces unknown. The authors further noted that the animal's size and the delicate state of the specimen's preservation seemingly preclude significant fluvial transport of the recovered vertebrae or the rest of the animal.

In describing the holotype, Wedel *et al.* (2000*b*) estimated the total centrum length of the longest preserved cervical vertebra (C8) to be approximately 1,250 millimeters, and a length from the cotyle to the right prezygapophysis of 1,400 millimeters. The vertebrae are extensively pneumaticized, the lateral faces of their centra and neural spines being occupied by large pneumatic fossae that penetrate to a narrow median septum, these fossae being larger, deeper, and more elaborate than those found in basal sauropods. The authors speculated that, if *Sauroposeiden* was descended from an ancestor similar to *Brachiosaurus*, "these fossae were probably derived by reducing the exterior walls of the lateral cemerae to externalize the lateral air sacs."

Wedel *et al.* referred *Sauroposeidon* to the Brachiosauridae as that genus and *Brachiosaurus* share a number of synapomorphies, these including the following: Elongate cervical centra and long cervical ribs

Courtesy Matthew J. Wedel.

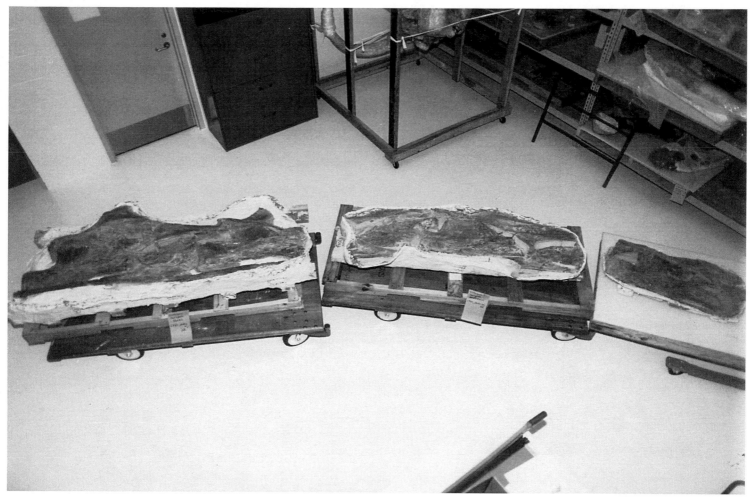

Sauroposeidon proteles, OMNH 53062, holotype cervical vertebrae 5 to 8.

(present in other sauropod lineages, but apparently independently evolved in brachiosaurids); midcervical vertebrae with marked transition in neural spine height; neural spines set forward on centra, prezygapophyses consequently substantially overhanging condyles; and trends toward elongation and pneumatization of cervical vertebrae (these conditions taken to extremes in the 30–40 million years younger *Sauroposeiden*). The authors noted that the pneumatic camellae seen in vertebrae of *Brachiosaurus* have expanded to fill the entire internal volume in *Sauroposeidon*; but as such camellae are also found in Titanosauriformes, this feature should be regarded as a "symplesiomorphy" of *Brachiosaurus* and *Sauroposeidon* (*contra* Weidel *et al.* 2000*a*).

Comparing the known material of *Sauroposeiden* with more complete materials belonging to other sauropods, particularly *Brachiosaurus*, Wedel *et al.* inferred that *Sauroposeidon* could have been slightly larger than the mounted composite skeleton of *Brachiosaurus brancaii* (HMN SII) mounted at the Museum für Naturkunde der Humboldt-Universität zu Berlin; see *D:TE* for photograph), or that, more un-

likely, if the neck (11.25 to 12 meters in length) of *Sauroposeidon* is atypically long (as in *Mamenchisaurus*), it was about the same size or smaller than the Berlin mount. Assuming that *Sauroposeidon* had a shape similar to that of *Brachiosaurus*, the authors estimated the mass of the former as possibly between 50 and 60 metric tons (about 56 to almost 64 tons), noting also that the comparatively more gracile neck could imply a more slender and lighter-weight body (see below).

Addressing the issues of neck posture and biomechanics in sauropod dinosaurs, Wedel *et al.* cited the somewhat traditional notion (*e.g.*, Janensech 1950; Paul 1987*b*, 1988*a*) that the necks of brachisaurids were held in almost a vertical position and utilized in permitting these animals to feed upon vegetation beyond the reach of shorter taxa. Wedel *et al.* pointed out that the neck of the approximately 8-meter (about 21-foot) tall *Sauroposeidon* is significantly longer than that of *Brachiosaurus*, while the next tallest herbivore in the Antlers fauna is *Tenontosaurus*, an ornithopod having a maximum height of about 3 meters (slightly more than 10 feet). Consequently, the authors found

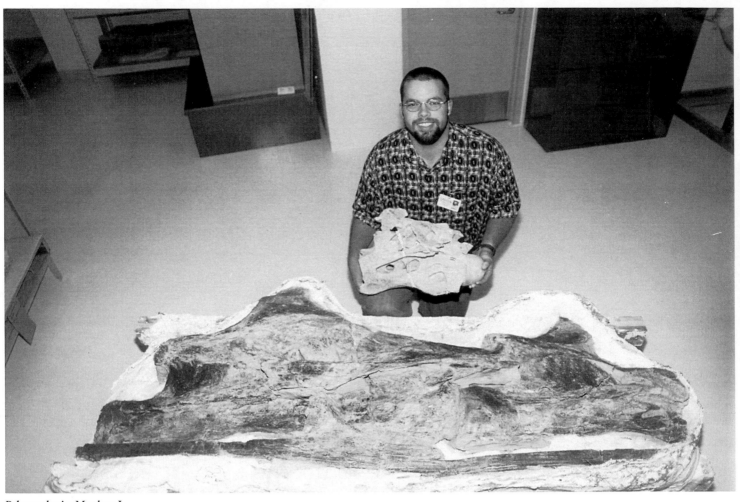

Paleontologist Matthew J. Wedel holding for comparison a cervical vertebra (probably number 6) of *Apatosaurus* with a holotype cervical vertebra (OMNH 53062) of *Sauroposeidon proteles*.

it unlikely that these two plant-eating forms competed for available vegetation in any meaningful way. However, the authors also noted, the added two- to three-meter neck length of *Sauroposeidon* would have doubled the volume of the feeding envelope of that of *Brachiosaurus*; and, while simple locomotion could have extended that envelope, "a long, mobile neck may have evolved in part to overcome the mobility limitations imposed by large body size."

In comparing the air sac system of *Sauroposeidon* and other sauropods with that of birds, Wedel *et al.* found it likely that sauropods may also have possessed similar systems (though not as complex as in birds) in the thorax and abdomen, although the nature and extent of such systems could not be determined. However, the authors noted, even a limited air sac system in sauropods would double or even triple the volume of air contained within the animal's body cavity, considerably lightening its mass. (Earlier comparing sauropods with mammals, Alexander 1985, 1989 calculated that the lungs of these dinosaurs occupied between eight and 10 percent of the internal volume.) As no current mass estimates for sauropods factor in this

postulated air sac system, they may, the authors calculated, be too heavy by at least 20 percent. Furthermore, as "mass affects both food intake (Weaver 1983) and respiratory requirements (Paladino, Spotila and Dodson 1997), the presence of air sacs in sauropods would change most of what has been proposed regarding sauropod metabolism."

In the past, the demise of sauropods has been linked to the rise of angiosperms during the Middle Cretaceous period (*e.g.*, Bakker 1986). *Sauroposeidon* was among the last of the North American Middle Cretaceous sauropods, this dinosaurian group seemingly having become extinct by early Cenomanian times (the beginning of the so-called "sauropod hiatus," after which, during late Maastrichtian times, titanosaurian sauropods were reintroduced to the North American continent; see Lucas and Hunt 1989). The extinction of *Sauroposeidon* and other sauropods of its time predates, however, the significant Middle Cretaceous (Cenomanian) radiations of angiosperms. Therefore, Wedel *et al.* deduced that the extinction of these giant dinosaurs cannot be related to changes in flora.

Notes: Utilizing computed tomography (CT) of the pneumatic internal structures in the cervical vertebrae of sauropod dinosaurs, these produced by the elaboration of air sacs during sauropod evolution, Wedel *et al.* proposed a new classification system for these structure types. The authors, in order to provide a more accurate, empirically-based nomenclature for describing these structures in the presacral vertebrae of all eusauropod dinosaurs, proposed the terms "acamerate," "camellate," "camerate," "polycamerate," "procamerate," "semicamellate," and "somphocamellate" (see "Glossary" for definitions by these authors).

Naish (2003), in a published abstract, briefly reported that a sauropod cervical vertebra, measuring 1060 millimeters, has been found in the Wessex Formation on the Isle of Wight, England. The largest such vertebra yet reported from Europe, it compares favorably in size with those of *Brachiosaurus* and *Sauroposeidon*. Moreover, the vertebra shares some derived characters (*e.g.*, extensive lateral fossae, well-developed distal centroparapophyseal laminae) with the latter genus.

Key references: Bakker (1986); Janensch (1950); Lucas and Hunt (1989); Naish (2003); Paladino, Spotila and Dodson (1997); Paul (1987*b*, 1988*a*); Upchurch (1998); Weaver (1983); Wedel, Cifelli and Sanders (2000*a*, 2000*b*).

†SAURORNITHOIDES

Saurischia: Eusaurischia: Theropoda: Neotheropoda: Tetanurae: Avetheropoda: Coelurosauria: Maniraptoriformes: Maniraptora: Metornithes: Paraves: Deinonychosauria: Troodontidae.

Comments: During the 1920s, the American Museum of Natural History's third Central Asiatic Expedition collected various troodontid remains from Upper Cretaceous exposures of Mongolia in what is now part of the China. From 1987 to 1990, the Sino-Canadian Dinosaur Project collected additional troodontid specimens from the Early to Late Cretaceous of China.

These specimens include IVPP V10599, comprising sacral and caudal vertebrae, and a pelvis, belonging to the type species *Saurornithoides mongoliensis*, recovered in 1988 from (Late Cretaceous: ?Campanian) Djadokhta-equivalent exposures at Bayan Mandahu; IVPP 230790-16, a metatarsal representing an unknown troodontid species, collected in 1990 from the Upper Cretaceous Iren Dabasu Formation (estimated to be of late Turonian–Conacian or late Turonian age; see Archibald, Sues, Averianov, Danilov, Rezvyi, Ward, King and Morris 1999; Averianov 2002), near Erenhot; AMNH 21751, the distal ends of left and right third metatarsals, and AMNH 21772, a metatarsal, both specimens belonging to unknown troodontid species and collected during the 1920s from the Iren Dabasu Formation near Erenhot; and IVPP V9612, the holotype of *Sinornithoides youngi*, collected in 1988 from the Lower Cretaceous Ejinhoro Formation of the Ordos Basin (see *Sinornithoides* entry).

In 2001, all of the above material was described in detail in a joint paper co-authored by Philip J. Currie and Dong Zhiming (2001*b*). Of the isolated bones from Iren Dabasu, these authors noted that the fauna includes a troodontid equivalent in size to *S. mongoliensis*. The lack of comparable material, however, prevented the authors from further identifying the Iren Dabasu form; although, based on certain features—*e.g.*, the tonguelike caudal extension of the distal articular surface for phalanx III-1, plainly seen in both third metatarsal fragments of AMNH 21751, being characteristic of advanced troodontids (see Wilson and Currie 1985)—it seemingly represents an advanced member of the Troodontidae.

As noted by Currie and Dong, the above specimens, plus other recently described material from North America, permit a better understanding of the phylogenetic position of the Troodontidae, especially regarding the systematic relationships of this clade to ornithomimids, dromaeosaurids, other theropods, and birds. Although most workers (*e.g.*, Holtz 2000) regard dromaeosaurids as closer to birds than troodontids, the latter "are nevertheless one of the closest avian outgroups within the Theropoda."

Addressing the proposal of Holtz, Brinkman and Chandler (2000) that troodontids, because the size of their tooth serrations scale with herbivorous rather than other carnivorous dinosaurs, could have been plant eaters, Currie and Dong pointed out that troodontids have anatomy consistent with that of carnivorous rather than herbivorous habits; that the structure of individual denticles (*i.e.* distally curved toward the tooth tip, sharply pointed, with razor-sharp enamel ridges between denticles, and blood grooves at the base) does not differ significantly from that of other theropods (see Currie 1987; Currie, Rigby and Sloan 1990); and that the discovery of troodontid teeth with a juvenile hadrosaur (see Ryan, Currie, Gardner, Vickaryous and Lavigne 2000) imply a predator-prey association.

Key references: Currie (1987); Currie and Dong (2001*b*); Currie, Rigby and Sloan (1990); Holtz (2000); Holtz, Brinkman and Chandler (2000); Ryan, Currie, Gardner, Vickaryous and Lavigne (2000); Wilson and Currie (1985).

†SAURORNITHOLESTES

Saurischia: Eusaurischia: Theropoda: Neotheropoda:

Tetanurae: Avetheropoda: Coelurosauria: Maniraptoriformes: Maniraptora: Metornithes: Paraves: Deinonychosauria: Dromaeosauridae *incertae sedis*.

Comments: The validity of the type species *Saurornitholestes langstoni* was confirmed by Sankey, Brinkman, Guenther and Currie (2002) following a study of myriad theropod teeth collected by the Royal Tyrrell Museum of Palaeontology from the Late Cretaceous (Campanian) Judith River Group of southern Alberta, Canada, the theropod assemblage of this area also including teeth of referred to *Dromaeosaurus*, "*Paronychodon*" [=*Richardoestesia*], and *Richardoetesia* (see *Richardoestesia* entry, "Notes").

As Sankey *et al.* observed, the teeth of *Saurornitholestes* (*S. langstoni* being the most common small theropod tooth known from the Judith River Group; see Baszio 1997*a*) differ from those of *Richardestesia gilmorei* in being more recurved with larger, longer, and sharper denticles. They also differ from *Richardoestesia isosceles* in having smaller denticles at the base and tip of the teeth (denticles of more uniform size in *R. isosceles*). They differ from the teeth of *Dromaeosaurus albertensis* in being flatter and more gracile, the denticles having pointed tips, and with mesial carina following the mesial edge of the tooth (twisting lingually in *Dromaeosaurus*).

Sankey *et al.* noted that wear on the *Saurornitholestes* teeth is typically on the side of the teeth near the tip, this, as well as the narrow bladelike shape of the teeth, suggesting to the authors that the teeth mainly functioned in cutting and slicing.

Saurornitholestes may have been a prey animal as well as a predator. Tooth-marked dinosaur bones, most of the reported specimens having pertained to herbivorous dinosaur, offer insights into theropod feeding behaviors and biting strategies. Jacobsen (2001), a specialist in such bones, described a tooth-marked dentary belonging to a partial skeleton (TMP88.121.39) of *Saurornitholestes*, recovered in 1988 from the Upper Cretaceous (Campanian) Dinosaur Park Formation, along the Milk River, in southern Alberta. The specimen, currently under study by Philip J. Currie and David J. Varricchio (in preparation), includes several skull elements (including a left dentary), the right scapula, right coracoid, right humerus, several ribs, gastralia, the right femur, right tibia, fibula, right metatarsus, pedal phalanges, a few unguals, and the articulated distal tail section.

As described by Jacobsen, the dentary is very well preserved and measures approximately 12 centimeters in length. There are 15 tooth positions, 10 teeth being visible, five fully erupted, and three partially erupted. Two additional broken teeth show wear facets, revealing that they were nevertheless functional. The lingual side of the dentary shows three tooth marks, two bearing serration marks as parallel grooves or striae and having a similar morphology, one mark on the bone, the other on the crown of the seventh tooth.

In attempting to deduce what kind of theropod was responsible for these bite marks, Jacobsen excluded another *Saurornitholestes*, noting that the shape and size of serration in these marks are not like those of this genus. Comparing these marks with the teeth of other theropods of comparable size, that author found them to be most consistent with the teeth of a small and possibly juvenile tyrannosaurid, genus unknown. Jacobsen observed that the placement and perpendicular orientation of these marks, relative to the upper dentition, indicates that they were not produced by occluding teeth. Furthermore, the marks seem to have been made by the same animal, as evidenced by the absence of any other type of serration pattern on the specimen.

As Jacobsen pointed out, bite marks in recovered theropod bones are rare, especially in small taxa (*e.g.*, *Saurornitholestes*) having small, thin, and hollow bones that are highly susceptible to carcass consumption and preservational biases.

This find is significant, that author noted, in showing that tyrannosaurids fed not only on herbivorous dinosaurs, but also on carnivorous forms.

Key references: Baszio (1997*a*); Jacobsen (2001): Sankey, Brinkman, Guenther and Currie (2002).

SCANSORIOPTERYX Czerkas and Yuan 2002 — (=*Epidendrosaurus*).

Saurischia: Eusaurischia: Theropoda: Neotheropoda: Tetanurae: Avetheropoda: Coelurosauria: Maniraptoriformes: ?Maniraptora *incertae sedis*:

Name derivation: Latin *scandere* = "climb" + Greek *pteryx* = "feather, wing."

Type species: *S. heilmanni* Czerkas and Yuan 2002.

Other species: [None.]

Occurrence: Yixian Formation, Liaoning, China.

Age: ?Early to ?Middle Cretaceous (?Barremian–?Aptian).

Known material/holotype: CAGS02-IG-gausa-1/DM 607, almost complete, mostly articulated skeleton including lower half of skull, preserved as natural mold in slab and counterslab, feather impressions, ?skin impressions, juvenile.

Diagnosis of genus (as for type species): Manual digit III elongated, almost twice length of II; metacarpals II and III short, approximately 30 percent length of humerus; second phalanx of manual digit II long, almost 170 percent length of first (Zhang, Zhou, Xu and Wang).

Comments: A controversial taxon, the type species *Scansoriopteryx heilmanni* was founded upon

Scansoriopteryx heilmanni, CAGS02-IG-gausa-1/DM 607, holotype (juvenile) skeleton as preserved in the main slab. After Czerkas and Yuan (2002).

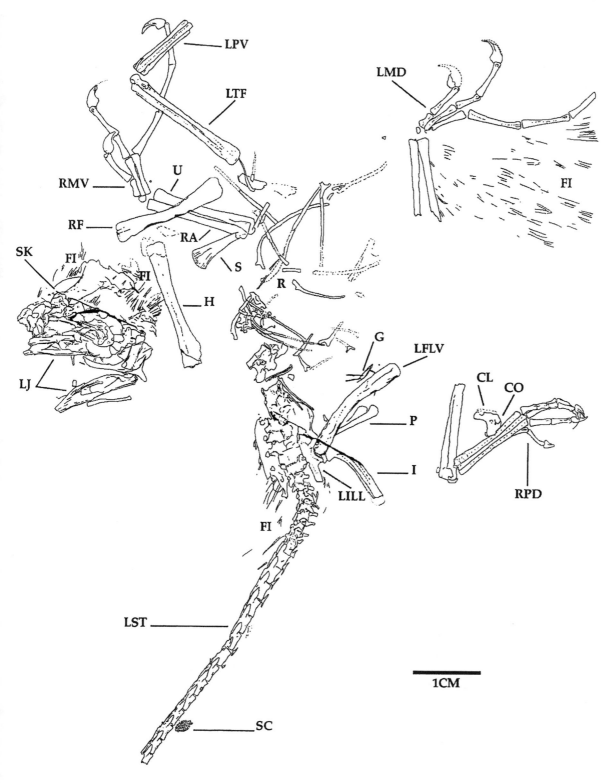

the well-preserved small, partial skeleton (CAGS02-IG-gausa-1/DM 607) "of a juvenile [apparently a nestling with an estimated age of approximately three weeks] saurischian resembling a theropod" from the Dawangzhansi fossil site in the basal part of the Yixian Formation, in Lingyaun City, western Liaoning, China. Preserved in two slabs, the specimen is missing the cervical vertebral series, cranial dorsal vertebrae, a humerus, pedal phalanges, the shoulder girdle save for the caudal end of a scapula, the second coracoid, and clavicle (Czerkas and Yuan 2002).

Stephen A. Czerkas and Chongxi Yuan published their paper naming and describing this new theropod

Holotype (juvenile) skeleton (IVPP V12653) of *Epidendrosaurus ningchengensis*, apparently a junior synonym of *Scansoriopteryx heilmanni*, a. photograph of main-slab, b. composite drawing based on main slab and counter-slab. (After Zhang, Zhou, Xu and Wang 2002.)

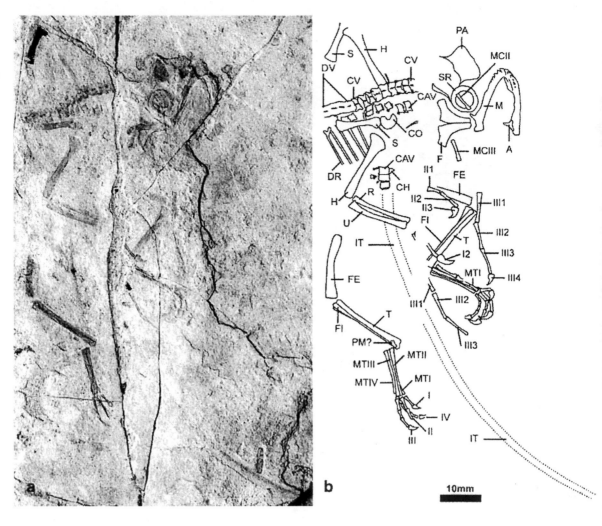

as a chapter, illustrated with color photographs of the holotype material, in the book *Feathered Dinosaurs and the Origin of Flight*, edited by Sylvia J. Czerkas (2002), the publication date as printed in the book being August 1, 2002 (see below).

Czerkas and Yuan diagnosed *S. heilmanni* as follows: Unique among known Saurischia in having digit III of manus elongated to almost twice length of digit II; closely resembles *Archaeopteryx*, differing from that genus in the following: definite contact between elongate ventral process of postorbital and ascending process of jugal; lower jaw having large fenestra; tail with greater development in articulation of zygapophyses; pelvis similar to that of *Archaeopteryx* in having same number of sacral vertebrae and in general shape of ilia, differing in having small, unexpanded pubic peduncle; pubis significantly short, not retroverted; longer ischia; acetabulum not entirely perforated.

The authors reported that preserved in the specimen are wispy, downlike feather impressions around parts of the body, including the caudal part of the skull, the pelvis, the proximal part of the tail, the trunk region, and most significantly, "emanating from the lateral edge of the ulna and manus where these impressions are more elongate." Microscopic inspection revealed these impressions to comprise V-shaped patterns with filaments branching from the base, these filaments representing individual barbs. According to Czerkas and Yuan, the minute size, morphology and pattern of distribution of these structures "are consistent with representing downlike feathers, or perhaps even more specifically, natal-down." Also, a patch of nonimbricating tubercles, located near the 19th caudal vertebra, offset from the tail and extending for a one-centimeter distance, was tentatively interpreted by the authors as scaly skin.

The total skull length was estimated by the authors to be as much as 20 millimeters, about half again as large as that of *Archaeopteryx*.

In describing this specimen, Czerkas and Yuan noted that its most astounding feature is the length of the third digit of the manus, comparatively longer, the authors observed, than that of any known saurischian. It is also unique, Czerkas and Yuan stated, in not having its penultimate phalanx longer than its proximal phalanges, this pattern of progressive reduction being consistent with the ancestral condition found in Pseudosuchia (see Gauthier 1986). Also indicative of a primitive stage, Czerkas and Yuan stated, are the great robustness and length of the third metacarpal. Gastralia — slender rods having delicate tapering ends — rare in collected theropod specimens, were preserved in front of the right femur. These, the authors noted, resemble those of nonavian theropods, *Archaeopteryx*, *Protarchaeopteryx*, *Caudipteryx*, and other early birds.

This genus, based upon Czerkas and Yuan's description and interpretation, is controversial for more than one reason, one of these regarding the generally accepted theories regarding the evolution of theropods and birds and also the evolution of flight (see "Introduction," sections on dinosaurs and birds). As recounted by Czerkas and Yuan, the holotype was originally unveiled in April, 2000, at the Florida Symposium on Dinosaur/Bird Evolution presented by the Graves Museum of Archaeology and Natural History, as an "arboreal theropod," with its unusual and unique manus adapted for climbing. However, the authors claimed that terminology seems to be contradictory, "as according to definition, 'theropods' do not climb" (although R. E. Molnar, personal communication 2002, pointed out never having "seen any definition of theropods in which 'not climbing' was a feature"). Furthermore, one of the synapomorphies of the Theropoda (*sensu* Gauthier) is the second digit being the longest in the manus. As the third digit of *Scansoriopteryx* is considerably longer than digit II, "it must represent a highly derived specialization from that of typical theropods, or must represent a pre-theropod status." (As noted by Molnar, personal correspondence, "Surprisingly, no one has seemed to see the analogy of this elongate digit with that of *Daubentonia* [the aye-aye]. This analogy would suggest that this elongate digit is an autapomorphy related to scansoriality and thus not relevant for determining systematic position.")

Czerkas and Yuan titled their paper naming and describing *S. heilmanni* "An arboreal maniraptoran from northeast China," thus identifying this taxon as a very specific kind of coelurosaurian theropod, as Maniraptora is currently defined. In their paper, the authors offered two separate possible interpretations for the systematic placement of *Scansoriopteryx* — either as having derived reversals that secondarily resemble primitive conditions (with this genus derived from a theropod lineage) or as truly plesiomorphic conditions (descending from a pre-theropod saurischian ancestor). Weighing both scenarios, the authors found the combination of manual digit III possessing a more elongate and robust third metacarpal, plus

phalanges that become progressively shorter distally, as well as various primitive characteristics observed throughout the body as a whole to be the more parsimonious of the two interpretations, which in effect would exclude *Scansoriopteryx* from Maniraptora. Furthermore, Czerkas and Yuan referred this genus to its own family, Scansoriopterydidae, but did not diagnose this new higher taxon; nor did they present a phylogenetic analysis of the genus.

According to Czerkas and Yuan, *Scansoriopteryx* is, in many ways (*e.g.*, saurischian-style pelvis with remarkably long pubes, elongate and robust ischia, relatively small pubic peduncles), more primitive than *Archaeopteryx*, a genus it closely resembles in many ways (*e.g.*, number of caudal vertebrae, basic tail structure, sacral vertebrae, shape of ilia, length of forelimb, and general skull morphology). These primitive features also suggest that the almost closed acetabulum is a true plesiomorphic condition and not a reversal. (As noted by Molnar, personal communication, "If this specimen represents a hatchling, these features may not be admissable; as Gauthier [among others] emphasized that one must use adult character states. After all, if one uses the 'hatchling' states of a frog, it would be classified as a fish, not an anuran.")

Furthermore, the authors stated that while *Scansoriopteryx* was clearly incapable of flight, its pes is that of an animal that could perch, consequently suggesting "that perching in an avian manner appeared before *Archaeopteryx* and not as a result after the development of more advanced flight abilities occurred." As already suggested by Olshevsky (1992), the hind foot of *Scansoriopteryx* tends to support the postulation that all true theropods descended from arboreal ancestors. Therefore, interpreting *Scansoriopteryx* as an arboreal precursor of *Archaeopteryx* also identifies it as a "proto-maniraptoran," thereby suggesting "that dromaeosaurs and other maniraptorans are derived from arboreal ancestors which had already achieved the ability to glide or possibly fly at least to some extent." Consequently, the authors speculated, "the primitive semilunate wrist articulation evolved in concert with the gliding, incipient stages of becoming volant and need not be treated as being either inexplicable or due to evolutionary influences unassociated directly with flight" (this following, according to Molnar, personal communication, only if the way these features are associated with gliding or flight are specified).

Czerkas and Yuan posited that, as shown by the fossil record and also by studies of extant birds (*e.g.*, Olson 1973), there exists within Aves a strong tendency of becoming secondarily flightless. Paul (1988*b*) had previously suggested some theropod dinosaurs were secondarily flightless; furthermore, according to

Czerkas and Yuan, this tendency towards becoming more terrestrial may have occurred over time among arboreal ancestors like *Scansoriopteryx* and basal birds (see Olshevsky; Paul 2002*a*). This, the authors stated, would explain the primitive avian characters seen in birdlike dinosaurs (*e.g.*, maniraptorans) more parsimoniously than either the cursorial or "ground up" theory of the origin of flight or recent phylogenetic analyses (*e.g.*, Padian, Hutchinson and Holtz 1999).

According to Czerkas and Yuan, the discovery of *Scansoriopteryx*, therefore, supports more strongly the "trees down" concept of the evolution of birds than the cursorial or "ground up" idea [these scenarios usually applying to the evolution of flight rather than that of birds *per se*], although the relationships between dinosaurs and birds do not fit the claims of either camp. As stated by Czerkas and Yuan, all theropods — based on the cursorial theory — were strictly terrestrial. (However, as pointed out by Molnar, personal communication, "only those theropods ancestral to birds need have been strictly terrestrial. It does not prohibit some other group from being both arboreal and irrelevant to the evolution of birds.") Interpreting *Scansoriopteryx* as ancestral to Maniraptora, however, suggests that members of this group became cursorial relatively late and independently of "true theropods." Therefore, while some theropods may have become cursorial from tree-climbing ancestors before the arrival of Maniraptora, "the maniraptorans became cursorial much later after having achieved some degree of gliding or actual flight capabilities." Czerkas and Yuan consequently posited that, while the "trees down" advocates were correct in linking arboreality to the origin of birds, they were wrong in regarding maniraptorans as nonavian theropods resembling birds by independent convergence.

Considering *Scansoriopteryx* to be the most primitive known ancestor to birds, Czerkas and Yuan suggested that the reduction of digit III in *Archaeopteryx* and other maniraptorans occurred independently of theropods, following the achievement of gliding. Therefore, contrary to both scenarios, this assessment would in effect remove Maniraptora from the clade of true Theropoda, positioning them as direct descendants of arboreal, nontheropod, avian ancestors, "true theropods" having lost the elongated digit III upon becoming cursorial.

Czerkas and Yuan concluded that *Scansoriopteryx* is the lone known representative of the avian lineage stemming from a basal stock of arboreal saurischians (Saurischia, by definition, one of the two main subdivisions of Dinosauria), their dinosaurian status depending on the definition of Dinosauria. (As pointed out by Molnar, personal communication, by definition all saurischians are dinosaurs; therefore, *Scanso-*

riopteryx must be dinosaurian.) "However," Czerkas and Yuan stated, "while birds did not necessarily evolve from dinosaurs as widely believed from cursorial theropods, dinosaurs may be related to the avian lineage in being derived from a common ancestor within the earliest stages of saurischian archosaurs" (see also *Cryptovolans* entry).

Another controversy over this new taxon arose 21 days after the stated publication date of Czerkas and Yuan's paper. On August 21, another paper, coauthored by Chinese paleontologists Zhang, Zhou, Xu and Wang (2002) and issued "online" by the journal *Naturwissenschaften* (published by German company Springer Verlag), named and described *Epidendrosaurus ninchengensis* as a new juvenile and apparently arboreal coelurosaurian theropod from China.

Subsequently, one of the authors of the second paper, Fucheng Zhang, sent a mass emailing (dated October 4) to numerous members of the paleontological community (including the present writer) attempting to explain the situation. Zhang stated in his email that, while having a different name and based upon another holotype specimen, *Epidendrosaurus ninchengensis* and *Scansoriopteryx heilammi* represent the same genus and species of dinosaur. Also, Zhang's missive essentially argued two points:

1. The paper by Zhang *et al.* was published online on 21 August 2002. According to the editor of *Naturwissenschaften* and other scientific journals, the online version constitutes a valid publication and not a pre-release, with Springer Verlag being one of the few publishers having real online citable and searchable publications. When a print version follows the electronic version, then the latter's first claim is valid. Consequently, *Epidendrosaurus ningchengensis* should be accepted as a valid name.

2. One of the authors of the first paper (Czerkas) had "worked on a smuggled fossil from China" which is the same species as *E. ninchengensis*. Czerkas, Zhang stated, after seeing the online publication, wrote a letter to its authors arguing that he had published his name for the species at the earlier date of August 1. However, according to Zhang *et al.*, the Czerkas book was still in press on August 1. Zhang further stated that some copies of the first paper faxed to him and his coauthors from August 26 to 29 lacked fixed page numbers, suggesting to them that the book's "publication date is not true."

To date of this writing, the August 1, 2002 date, as printed in the book *Feathered Dinosaurs and the Origin of Flight*, must be regarded as the earlier of the two publications, at least until it is otherwise demonstrated that the paper by Zhang *et al.* indeed predates that of Czerkas and Yuan. Therefore, for purposes of the present volume, the name *Scansoriopteryx heil-manni* is accepted as having priority over "*Epidendrosaurus ningchengensis*."

As reported by Zhang *et al.*, their type species "*Epidendrosaurus ningchengensis*" was established upon a skeleton (IVPP V12653) preserved as a slab and counterslab, collected from Daohugou, a new locality in east Nei Mongol, in Ningcheng County, Liaoning Province, in northeastern China. (This locality, the authors noted, has also yielded numerous fossils of salamanders, insects, and plants, and also an anurognathid rhamphorhynchoid pterosaur preserving a covering of hair.)

According to Zhang *et al.*, numerous features of this genus (*e.g.*, structures of foot and hand, frontal with deep cerebral fossa) clearly identify it as a member of the Coelurosauria. Other features (*e.g.*, forelimb long relative to hindlimb, caudally bowed ulna, pedal digit IV longer than II, closer in length to III) indicates that the genus probably belongs to the Maniraptora. Although phylogenetic analysis by Zhang *et al.* placed "*Epidendrosaurus*" very near the transition to birds, the incomplete preservation of a juvenile specimen precluded the authors from giving the genus a more definite phylogenetic position. (Based upon proportions of the postcranial skeletal elements, Zhang *et al.* identified IVPP V12653 as representing a juvenile individual.)

Unlike Czerkas and Yuan, Zhang *et al.* noted that this genus is distinguished from all other known coelurosaurs (rather than all saurischians) in its extremely long third manual digits. The forelimb (unlike that of other nonavian theropods) is slightly longer than the hindlimbs, and the humerus is longer than the femur. Also, the penultimate pedal phalanges of digits III and IV are markedly longer than the neighboring proximal phalanges, while in digit II the second phalanx is just slightly longer than the first. Collectively, these features, especially the elongated second phalanx manual digit II and the forelimb, suggested to Zhang *et al.* also that this dinosaur possessed the probable capability to grasp and grab and was, therefore, an arboreal animal.

Zhang *et al.* further pointed out that the pes of "*Epidendrosaurus*" is unique among nonavian theropods in having metatarsal I articulated with II at such a low position that the trocheae of metatarsals I through IV are nearly on the same level, similar to the condition in perching birds.

Zhang *et al.* observed that the relatively long manus of "*Epidendrosaurus*" is better adapted to grasping and grabbing than it is to flapping flight. Also, this dinosaur is more similar to advanced birds than *Archaeopteryx* in some arboreal features. Hence, the ability to climb trees must have been acquired before birds

(*Archaeopteryx* plus other advanced birds), and while arboreal habits were critical in the immediate ancestors of birds in the evolution of flight, "the initial appearance of tree-adaptation in theropods was probably not directly related to flight but to other functions, such as seeking food or escaping from predators."

Note: In his online missive to colleagues, Zhang stated that the specimen described by him and colleagues and also the one described by Czerkas and Yuan belonged to the "same species." However, according to Molnar (personal communication), *Epidendrosaurus* is represented by a much less complete specimen than *Scansoriopteryx* and, based upon the published illustrations, cannot be synonymized with confidence. Molnar further suspects that these specimens could represent two distinct and valid taxa. If these type species are, in fact, distinct, their separation has yet to be demonstrated in the paleontological literature.

Key references: Czerkas (2002); Czerkas and Yuan (2002); Gauthier (1986); Olshevsky (1992); Olson (1973); Padian, Hutchinson and Holts (1999); Paul (1988*b*, 2002*a*); Zhang, Zhou, Xu and Wang (2002).

†SCELIDOSAURUS

Ornithischia: Genasaura: Thyreophora: Eurypoda: Ankylosauromorpha: Scelidosauridae.

Comments: The type species *Scelidosaurus harrisonii* (see *D:TE, S1*) is distinguished in paleontological history as the earliest virtually complete dinosaur to be discovered (in Dorset, England, in 1850) and scientifically described (see Norman 2001*b* for the first detailed account of the work on *S. harrisonii* by Richard Owen, who named and described this dinosaur in 1861).

In an abstract, Norman (2001*a*) reported that, following long-term acid preparation of previously collected material, and also the more recent recovery of important supplementary material, it is now "possible to describe the anatomy of this early (Sinemurian) orninithischian and reconsider its systematic position." In briefly describing *S. harrisonii*, Norman (2001*a*) observed the following: (Cranially) possession of adherent dermal ossicles, prominent supraorbital "horns," much-reduced external antorbital fenestra and fossa; caudal portion of palate unusual for dinosaur in retaining ossified, articulated epipterygoid; (postcranially) neck protected dorsally by partial rings of coossified dermal ossicles, dermal scutes farther caudally forming parallel rows along back, flanks, and around tail; shoulder girdle including sternal elements; ilium with long, dorsoventrally compressed preacetabular process, entire blade tilted

Scelidosaurus

Photograph by Kenneth Carpenter, courtesy The Natural History Museum (London).

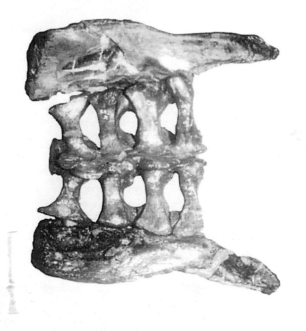 

Pelvis (part of holotype BMNH R1111) of *Scelidosaurus harrisonii* in (left) dorsal and (right) right lateral views, the horizontally wide ilium identifying it as an ankylosauromorph.

laterally; acetabulum very deep, with well-developed inner apron effectively occluding "normal" fenestra; pubis with short, curved cranial process; acetabular region robust, having important role in articulation of head of femur; pubic rod elongate, lying beneath and parallel to ischium; prominent pendant fourth trochanter at about midshaft of femur, prominent proximal cranial trochanter, greater trochanter enlarged but confluent with femoral head; femoral head expanded medially, slightly ventrally, neither strongly offset nor globular; ankle conventionally mesotarsal (contrary to previous descriptions), pes with four well-developed digits, pes probably functionally tridactyl.

Although *Scelidosaurus* has previously been classified as a basal thyreophoran (see *D:TE, 1,* and *S2*), Norman (2001*a*), although not stating any reasons, noted that "much evidence suggests that this dinosaur is the most basal member of the clade Ankylosauria, this being consistent with Dong's (2001) recent referral of both *Scelidosaurus* and *Bienosaurus* (see entry) to the Scelidosauridae, regarded by Dong as a clade of primitive ankylosaurs.

Carpenter (2001*c*) identified a number of apomorphies in *Scelidosaurus* that have traditionally been regarded as diagnostic of the Ankylosauria, these including the following: Skull having cortical remodeling, resulting in ornamentation on jugal, maxilla, postorbital, and posterolateral corner of mandible; horizontal expansion of ilium; massive body of pubis; body armor composed of multiple transverse or parasagittal rows of keeled scutes and plates; and two rows of cervical armor. However, as Carpenter pointed out, *Scelidosaurus* also lacks numerous other ankylosaurian synapomorphies (*e.g.*, skull wider than tall).

Therefore, to accommodate *Scelidosaurus*, Carpenter proposed that the new taxon Ankylosauromorpha be erected to embrace both *Scelidosaurus* and Ankylosauria.

Barrett (2001), a specialist in dinosaurian feeding mechanisms, published a detailed study on tooth wear and the possible jaw action of *S. harrisonii*. The author stressed that the feeding mechanisms in thyreophorans is poorly understood, this mainly due to a lack of specimens possessing well-preserved tooth rows.

Barrett's analysis was based upon two specimens for which skull material has been preserved — the lectotype, BMNH R1111 and main source of this study, including a nearly complete, three-dimensional skull, this specimen prior to preparation with the skull and lower jaws in complete articulation (see Owen 1861); and BRSMG Ce1785 (juvenile), including a partial, mediolaterally crushed skull, missing most of its left side, median skull roof elements, braincase, and left mandible, and preserving both premaxillae, maxillae, right lacrimal, right jugal, right quadratojugal, right postorbital, right quadrate, some crushed palatal elements, a partial right dentary, and right surangular.

In generally describing the *Scelidosaurus* skull, Barrett observed the following: Skull long and shallow in lateral aspect; snout sloping anteroventrally from point dorsal to orbits; skull narrowing rostrally in dorsal aspect, snout narrow, pointed (see Owen); premaxillae (of BRSNG Ce12785) meeting in midline, forming small premaxillary secondary palate; mandible extremely robust, lacking external mandibular fenestra, coronoid process of moderate height; maxillary and dentary tooth rows bowed medially (as in ankylosaurs; see Coombs 1978a); maxillary and dentary tooth rows deeply inset, large buccal emargination; jaw joint slightly offset ventrally relative to tooth row. Barrett also pointed out that the skull is essentially akinetic, streptostyly having been prevented by extensive overlapping contacts between the quadrate, squamosal, quadratojugal, and pterygoid.

Identifying opposing teeth in the upper and lower tooth rows, Barrett observed correspondence between tooth wear on the upper teeth and that on the opposing lower teeth (although in almost every instance the upper- and lower-teeth wear facets have different morphologies — maxillary teeth with small apical wear facets, dentary teeth with large bowl-shaped wear facets). Also, while one tooth of an opposing pair can be completely unworn, the corresponding tooth in the other row can be heavily worn. This suggests, given the limited evidence available, that occlusal contact of the upper and lower teeth was present in *Scelidosaurus*. Barrett noted that the tooth crowns in this genus are apparently aligned, meeting in almost direct opposition to each other, the lingual surfaces of the upper teeth occluding against the labial surfaces of the lower teeth. This arrangement, according to Barrett, explains in part the distribution of wear along the tooth rows, some of this wear having been formed by tooth-to-tooth contact during occlusion.

Regarding the extent of wear between the upper and lower tooth rows, Barrett postulated that this could be answered in part by the contrasting morphologies of the maxillary and dentary teeth. During occlusion, that author stated, "the maxillary teeth would, in effect, fit into a basin walled lingually and ventrally by the labial surface of a dentary tooth crown," this arrangement, therefore, providing "an effective puncture and crushing mechanism, with the dentary teeth acting as a row or mortars and the maxillary teeth representing a series of pestles." Such a mechanism could explain the differences in wear between the tooth rows — the lower teeth continually undergoing stresses pertaining to crushing food, the upper ones pushing food down into these basins, with the presence of pits on the crown surfaces being consistent with this kind of jaw action.

Note: Barrett also reviewed feeding mechanisms in other thyreophoran dinosaurs for which adequate skull material is known, resulting in the following speculations: A precise occlusion was apparently not present in the primitive thyreophorans *Scuttelosaurus* and *Emausaurus*, and in the stegosaur *Huayangosaurus* (and possibly other stegosaurians). Most ankylosaurs (including *Priodontognathus*), on the other hand, seem to have had — as did *Scelidosaurus* — precise occlusion, with "an efficient puncture-crushing mechanism that

would result in the production of tooth-tooth wear on the labial and lingual surfaces of the opposing tooth crowns.

Key references: Barrett (2001); Carpenter (2001c); Coombs (1978a); Dong (2001); Norman (2001a, 2001b); Owen (1861).

†SCIPIONYX

Saurischia: Eusaurischia: Theropoda: Neotheropoda: Tetanurae: Avetheropoda: Coelurosauria.

Comment: In 1999, Ruben, Dal Sasso, Geist, Hillenius, Jones and Signore reconstructed the intestinal tract of the genus *Scipionyx* as an analogy to extant crocodilians, this interpretation suggesting this dinosaur and others lacked dorsal avian-style air sacs. Subsequently, this assessment has come under criticism (*e.g.*, Martill, Frey, Sues and Cruikshank 1999), who opined that, as the original material of *Scipionyx* has been crushed flat, it is not reliable in preserving the viscera's original three-dimensional configuration.

More recently, Van Leer, Harwell, Ruben and Jones (2002), in an abstract, attempted to clarify this situation, via abdominal radiology of barium-fed experimental animals, by surveying gastrointestinal anatomy in lizards, crocodilians, and birds. Results of Van Leer *et al.*'s experiments showed "a surprisingly tight correlation between overall visceral anatomy in *Scipionyx* and crocodilians." These authors again concluded, therefore, "that soft tissues preserved in *Scipionyx* were likely to have been preserved *in situ* and that presumptions that theropods possessed abdominal air-sacs should be viewed with skepticism."

Key references: Martill, Frey, Sues and Cruikshank (1999); Ruben, Dal Sasso, Geist, Hillenius, Jones and Signore (1999); Van Leer, Harwell, Ruben and Jones (2002).

†SEGISAURUS

Saurischia: Eusaurischia: Theropoda: Neotheropoda: Coelophysoidea.

Comments: In 1936, Charles L. Camp described a new, small theropod type species, *Segisaurus halli*, based entirely upon an incomplete postcranial skeleton (UCMP 32101) from the Lower Jurassic Navajo Sandstone of Arizona (see *D:TE*).

As reported in an abstract by Senter and Hutchinson (2001), recent additional preparation of the holotype skeleton has revealed new information about this dinosaur. Senter and Hutchinson observed the following in UCMP 32101: Clavicles (previously incorrectly identified as a single clavicle) fused at the midline, forming a furcula, preserved in the specimen articulated with the coracoids; post-cervical vertebrae lacking pneumatopores; femur with a small lesser trochanter, a large fourth trochanter, and a trochanteric shelf; tibia exhibiting a fibular crest; long bones thin-walled (as in other theropods). An obvious autapomorphy is the ischial foramen in the proximal ischial apron.

According to Senter and Hutchinson, various lines of evidence, including sutural fusion and bone histology, indicate that UCMP 32101 represents at least a subadult (see Rowe and Gauthier 1990), possibly a full adult, animal. Consequently, the lack of fusion in the pelvis and other areas of the skeleton do not reflect juvenile status, but rather seem to have phylogenetic importance. The authors' preliminary phylogenetic analysis supports referral of *Segisaurus* to the Coelophysoidea, although the genus is certainly basal to the Coelophysidae.

Key references: Camp (1936); Rowe and Gauthier (1990); Senter and Hutchinson (2001).

†SELLOSAURUS

Saurischia: Eusaurischia: Sauropodomorpha: Prosauropoda: Plateosauridae.

Type species: *S. gracilis* Huene 1907–08.

Other species: *S. fraasi* Huene 1907–08 [*nomen dubium*], *S. minor* (Huene 1907–08) [*nomen dubium*], *S. trossingensis* (Huene 1907–08) [*nomen dubium*].

Comments: In one of a continuing series of papers on Late Triassic German prosauropod dinosaurs, prosauropod specialist Peter M. Galton (2001*b*) discussed the various species that have been referred to *Sellosaurus* (see *D:TE, S2*), and also variations in the sacra of this genus. In brief:

Sellosaurus gracilis, the type species of this genus, was founded upon an incomplete postcranial skeleton (SMNS 5717)—including two dorsal vertebrae, sacrum with right ilium, nearly complete tail (to 44th caudal vertebra, partly with attached hemal arches), left scapula, pelvis, left femur, proximal end of fibula, and phalanges; Huene 1907–08)—from the Lower Stubensandstein of Heslach, Stuttgart. Huene (1926), after comparing the tibia of this species with that of the holotype of *Plateosaurus engelhardti*, referred *S. gracilis* to that genus as the new species *P. gracilis*. Later, Galton (1984*b*, 1985*a*) recognized *Sellosaurus* as a valid genus, Galton (1984*b*, 1985*b*, 1990*a*) referring to the type species all prosauropod remains from the Lower and Middle Stubensandstein of Württemberg.

Subsequently, Galton (2001*b*) tentatively accepted *Sellosaurus gracilis* "as the valid name for the prosauropod material from the Lower and Middle Stubensandstein of Württemberg. This species, Galton (2001*b*) noted, is plainly distinct from *Plateo-*

saurus, yet for the present only seems to exhibit shared derived characters (Galton and Upchurch, in press). Galton (2001*b*) further stated that "a detailed comparison is needed between the holotype and the referred material to establish the correctness of the referrals and the validity of the species" (Galton, in preparation).

Two species of *Sellosaurus* were regarded by Galton (2001*b*) as junior synonyms of *S. gracilis*—*S.* (?*Thecodontosaurus*) *hermannianus* (Huene 1907–08), based on an isolated right maxilla (SMNS 4388) from the Lower Stubensandstein of Heslach; and *S.* (?*Palaeosaurus*) *diagnosticus* (Huene 1932), based on a partial disarticulated skull and partial postcrania, lacking ischia, most of the pes, and most of the tail, from near Pfaffenhofen.

The following *Sellosaurus* species were considered by Galton (2001*b*) to be *nomina dubia*: *S.* (*Teratosaurus*) *trossingensis* (Huene 1907–08), based on an articulated tail and pieces of the hindlimb, including most of the right pes (GPIT 18064), from the Middle Stubensandstein of the Untere Müle, near Trossingen, Württemberg; *S.* (?*Teratosaurus*) *minor* (Huene 1907–08), based on three dorsal vertebrae, the second sacral vertebra, pubes, and the right hindlimb (SMNS 11838), from the Middle Stubensandstein, Weisser Steinbruch quarry, in the Stromberg region, near Pfaffenhofen, southwest of Brackenheim, Württemberg; and *S. fraasi* Huene 1907–08, based on a caudal dorsal vertebra, the second sacral vertebra, five caudal vertebrae, some ribs, ilia, ischia, pubis, and a femur (SMNS 12038), collected near Pfaffenhofen.

Galton (2001*b*) published in greater detail on his work involving the number of sacral vertebrae in specimens of *Sellosaurus* (see Galton 1999, *S2*), noting that the following specimens possess sacra with three vertebrae: GPIT collection, belonging to a large individual, including a reasonably complete caudosacral vertebra, collected from Aixheim, in Rottweil; SMNS 5715, the holotype of *S. gracilis*; SMNS 12217, consisting of an isolated caudosacral vertebra from the Middle Stubensandstein, Stromberg region, Weisser Steinbach quarry (see above); and SMNS 12669 (see Galton 1999; Huene 1932), including an almost complete sacrum from the Middle Stubensandstein of Pfaffenhofen, Stromberg. In some specimens (*e.g.*, SMNS 12684), Galton (2001*b*) noted, the third vertebra is a dorsosacral, while in others (*e.g.*, SMNS 12669) it is a caudosacral.

Specimens listed by Galton (2001*b*) with sacra having two reptilian vertebrae plus a dorsosacral include SMNH 17928, a sacrum (originally described by Galton 1984*b* a caudosacral "based on the mistaken assumption that the sacrum was displaced caudally

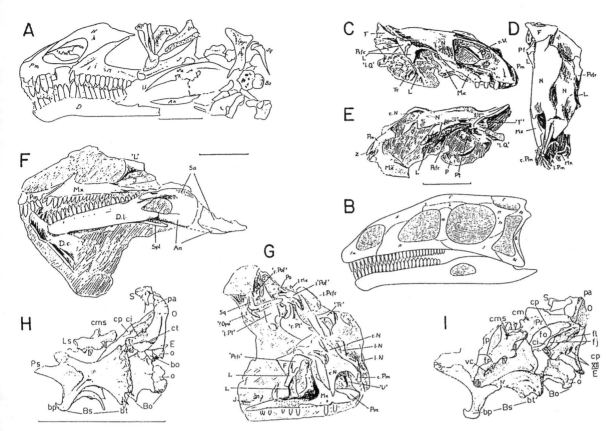

Sellosaurus

Partial skulls of *Sellosaurus gracilis*: A–B, from Trössingen, GPIT 1831a in left lateral view, A. as preserved and B. reconstructed; C–I, from Pfaffenhofen, C–E, SMNS 12216, cranial part in C. right and D. left lateral and E. dorsal views; F–G, SMNS 12684, partial skull block, mostly F. left and G. right lateral views; H–I, SMNS 12667 (syntype of *Efraasia diagnostica*), braincase in H. ventral and I. left lateroventral views. Scale = 5 cm. (After Galton 2001*b*: A–B from Huene 1915, C–G from Huene 1932, H–I from Bakker and Galton 1985.)

relative to the ilium during preservation") from the Lower Stubensandstein, Ochsenbach, Stromberg region, Nordwürttemberg; SMNS 14881, also from the Lower Stubensandstein, Ochsenbach, including sacral vertebrae and ribs; SMNS 12667 (juvenile), the holotype of *Palaeosaurus diagnosticus* Huene 1932 and the type species of the genus *Efraasia* (see *Sellosaurus* entry, *D:TE*); SMNS 12685, including the first two sacral vertebrae (misidentified by Huene 1932 as the second and third); and GPIT 18 392, from the Middle Stubensandstein, Trossingen (upper Norian; see Bachman, Beutler, Hagdorn, and Hauschke 1999; Beutler 1998*a*, 1999*b*) (second sacral having been misidentified by Huene 1932 as the third).

Considering the options in explaining the dichotomy between these two morphs, Galton (2001*b*) speculated that this might be regarded as a generic or a specific difference. However, Galton (2001*b*) pointed out, aside from having either a dorsosacral or a caudosacral vertebra, the rest of the skeletons of these two morphs "appears to be very similar and typically prosauropod," with the main difference — *i.e.* "the size and form of the distal sutural surface for the ilium on the end of the third sacral rib" — attributed to individual variation. The ratio of sacra having two sacral vertebrae to those having three is currently 5:4, which Galton (2001*b*) acknowledged to be a somewhat small sample; nevertheless, this ratio suggested

to that author that the different sacral types most likely represent sexual dimorphism.

Notes: Galton (2001*b*) pointed out that, in *Sellosaurus gracilis*, the form of the first and second sacral vertebrae of sacra with a caudosacral is similar to that of *Plateosaurus*, this condition corresponding to that of more primitive archosaurs having only two sacrals. In *Plateosaurus* (and other prosauropods, including *Ammosaurus*, *Euskelosaurus*, *Melanorosaurus*, *Saturnalia*, and *Thecodontosaurus*), that author noted, the sacral vertebrae are usually identified as reptilian sacrals numbers one and two plus a caudosacral.

Sereno and Novas (1992) misinterpreted at least one *Plateosaurus* specimen (SMNS 13200), as the sacrum comprises a dorsosacral vertebra plus reptilian sacrals one and two. However, this condition, as pointed out by Galton (2001*b*), can be seen in the prosauropods *Lufengosaurus*, "*Gyposaurus sinensis*" (=*Lufengosaurus hueni*; see Galton 1976*a*), *Jingshanosaurus*, *Massospondylus*, *Riojasaurus*, *Yunnanosaurus*, and prosauropod postcrania that had been incorrectly referred to the theropod *Sinosaurus* (see entry, *D:TE*). Therefore, Galton (2001*b*) determined that "it is incorrect to try to characterize prosauropods by the addition of a third vertebra into the sacrum, either as a dorsosacral … or as a caudosacral." Examining the sacral-count conditions in other dinosaurs (see Galton 1999 for details and references), Galton

(2001*b*) "concluded that the reptilian sacral count of two vertebrae is retained in the Dinosauria (so a plesiomorphic character) and that the addition of a third sacral vertebra, a dorsal, is not a synapomorphy for the group." Moreover, Galton (1999) noted that in *Sellosaurus gracilis*, males retain the reptilian count of two sacral vertebrae, while females add a caudosacral, the form of the latter displaying an individual-variation range agreeing with its recent incorporation into the sacrum (see also Galton, in press).

Yates (2003), in a preliminary report, briefly addressed the taxonomy of the sauropodomorph dinosaurs from Germany's Löwenstein Formation. As Yates pointed out, the current hypodigm of *Sellosaurus gracilis* contains substantial variation (*e.g.*, differences in dentition, skull structure, sacrum composition, structure of caudal vertebrae and pelvis).

In examining this variation via a specimen-based parsimony analysis of the Löwenstein Formation sauropodomorphs, Yates found two discrete taxa to comprise the current hypodigm of *Sellosaurus*. "The more common of these two is a plesiomorphic form for which the correct name is *Efraasia minor* comb. nov.," Yates posited. "The less common form (which includes the holotype of *Sellosaurus gracilis*) is found to share a number of synapomorphies with *Plateosaurus engelhardti* and is placed in this genus as *Plateosaurus gracilis*." Yates did not, at that time, provide additional data supporting the above hypotheses. For that reason, and also because Yates' proposal appeared as an abstract pending the presumed future publication of a longer and detailed paper, *Sellosaurus* retains its status — in the present document, at least — as a valid genus including two species.

Key references: Galton (1976*a*, 1984*b*, 1985*a*, 1985*b*, 1990*a*, 1999, 2001*b*, in press); Huene (1908, 1926, 1932); Sereno and Novas (1992); Yates (2003).

†**SHANSHANOSAURUS**—(=?*Tarbosaurus*)
Saurischia: Eusaurischia: Theropoda: Neotheropoda:
Tetanurae: Avetheropoda: Coelurosauria: Mani-

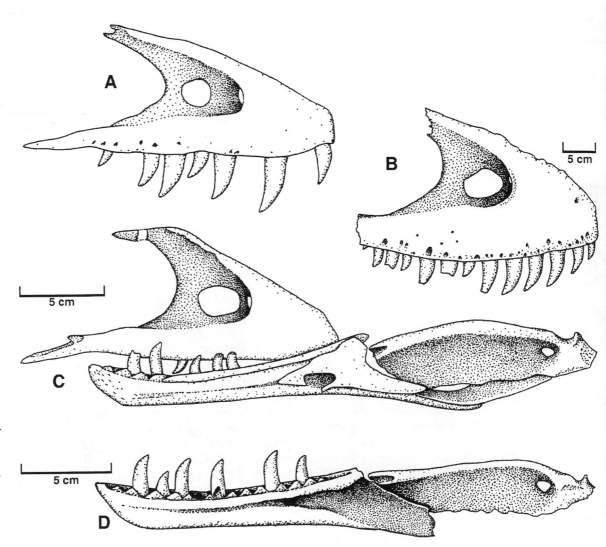

For comparison, A–B., maxillae (GIN 100/177) of young *Tarbosaurus bataar*, C. skull elements (IVPP V4878) of *Shanshanosaurus huoyanshanensis*, and D. mandible (RTMP 94.12. 155) of young *Gorgosaurus*. (After Currie and Dong 2001*a*.)

raptoriformes: Arctometatarsalia: Tyrannosauroidea: Tyrannosauridae: Tyrannosaurinae.

Comments: In 1977, Dong Zhiming named and described the new theropod type species *Shanshanosaurus huoyanshanensis*, represented by a single specimen (IVPP V4878)—a partial skull, most presacral vertebrae, ribs, gastralia, right scapulocoracoid, right humerus, a pubic boot, and portions of both tibiae—recovered from the Upper Cretaceous Subashi Formation at Lianmuqin, Shanshan County, in the Turpan Basin of Xinjiang, in northwestern China. Dong, believing that the sutures of the skull were fused, originally described this material as pertaining to a mature yet small theropod dinosaur. Later, Paul (1987*a*, 1988*b*) identified *Shanshanosaurus* as a tyrannosaurid belonging to the questionable subfamily "Aublysodontinae" (see *D:TE*).

Subsequent additional preparation of the holotype demonstrated that many of the sutures were not fused, this leading to the suggestion that the specimen might actually represent a juvenile of a large tyrannosaurid. As noted by Currie (2000*c*), two other Mongolian tyrannosaurids, *Tarbosaurus bataar* and *Alioramus*, are known from equivalent-age beds. While good skeletons of these dinosaurs have been found in sites nearly 1000 kilometers to the east, Currie pointed out, "no known physical barriers separated these regions in Late Cretaceous times."

In a joint paper, Currie and Dong (2001*a*) redescribed IVPP V4878 in detail, their study being part of a more extensive reexamination of tyrannosaurid systematics. As observed by Currie and Dong, *Shanshanosaurus* possesses such uniquely tyrannosaurid characters as the following: Large mylohoid fenestra in splenial; small external mandibular fenestra; large caudal surangular fenestra; presacral centra pleurocoelous; scapula with well-developed acromial process; pubic boot relatively larger than in other theropod families; limb bones lacking specialization of other coelurosaurian families (except for Ornithomimidae).

However, the authors noted, while all of the diagnostic features of *Shanshanosaurus* identify it as a member of the Tyrannosauridae, the proportions of the bones resemble more closely those of much smaller theropods, these including cervical vertebrae with very low neural spines (similar to those of other coelurosaurs). The neck of this dinosaur seems to have been strongly flexed, but not to the degree seen in adult *T. bataar* specimens (see Maleev 1974), this suggesting that the degree of neck curvature could have been determined by ontogenetic factors.

In their new description of IVPP V4878, Currie and Dong noted the large maxillary fenestra, as also found in *T. bataar*, *Daspletosaurus*, and *Tyrannosaurus*

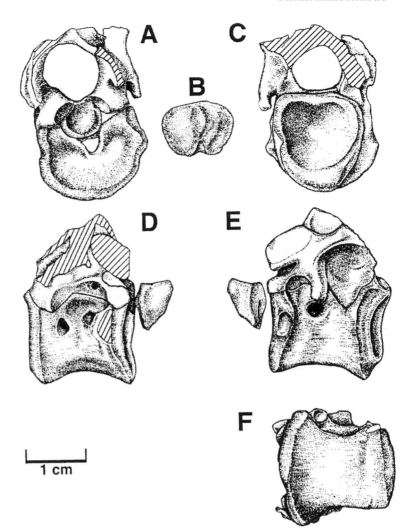

Shanshanosaurus huoyanshanensis, IVPP V4878, holotype axis and odontid, A–B. cranial, C. caudal, D. right lateral, E. left lateral, and F. ventral views. (After Currie and Dong 2001*a*.)

rex. The authors suggested that, given the geographic proximity of *T. bataar* to *Shanshanosaurus*, the latter could be a juvenile of that better known form, the large size of the maxillary fenestra being consistent with that idea. However, given that *Shanshanosaurus* is known from but one juvenile specimen, and because other Mongolian tyrannosaurids (*e.g.*, *Alioramus*) have been identified (which, in their early ontogeny would have been quite similar to one another), an unequivocal synonym could not be proposed. As Currie and Dong pointed out, *Alioramus* differs from *T. bataar* and other tyrannosaurids in various ways, including the presence of two distinct rows of labial foramina in the maxilla (see Kurzanov 1976). *Shanshanosaurus* more closely resembles *T. bataar* in having more widely distributed foramina across the external surface of the maxilla. Nevertheless, the authors cautioned, lacking more diagnostic adult *T. bataar* remains from Shanshan, "it is probably best to maintain *Shanshanosaurus* as a distinct genus."

Identifying *Shanshanosaurus* as a juvenile tyrannosaurid offers salient clues regarding the ontogeny of

Shanshanosaurus huoyan-shanensis, IVPP V4878, holotype presacral vertebrae in A–O, left lateral views (lower part of L. in caudal view). (After Currie and Dong 2001*a*.)

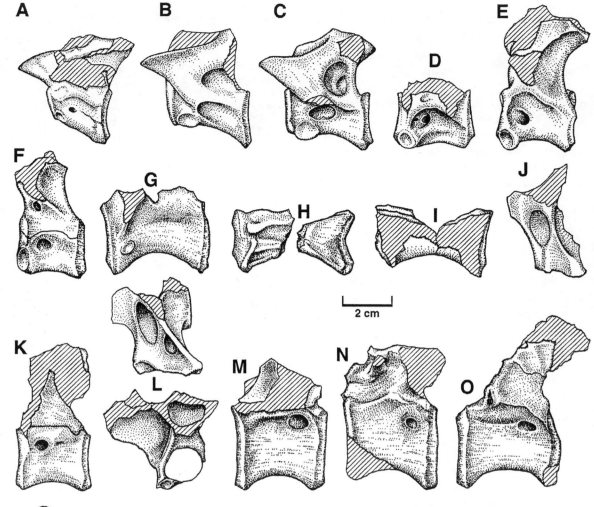

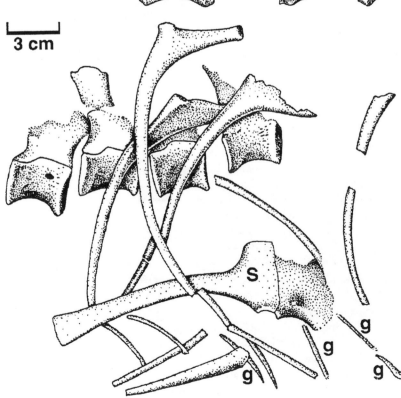

tyrannosaurids. As Currie and Dong stated, the holotype of this theropod — except for various isolated teeth and bones — "represents the smallest (youngest) specimen known of a tyrannosaurid" (approximately 2.3 meters or less than 8 feet in length). Despite its small size, the authors noted, *Shanshanosaurus* possesses an enlarged pubic boot, and the femur and tibia exhibit conspicuous processes and muscle scars, features consistent with the Tyrannosauridae. The snout and mandible, being long and of low proportions, are characteristic of small tyrannosaurs (see Carr 1999); these features, however, do not identify IVPP V4878 as a juvenile. The ontogentic stage of *Shanshanosaurus* "is better determined by the lack of fusion between the odontid and the axis and the fact that the neural arches and centra are not coossified."

Furthermore, Currie and Dong observed that the humerus of *Shanshanosaurus* resembles a slender version of that seen in other known (adult)

Shanshanosaurus huoyanshanensis, unprepared slab of bones (holotype IVPP V4878) showing four presacral vertebrae, four dorsal ribs, gastralia, and scapulocoracoid. (After Currie and Dong 2001*a*.)

Shanshanosaurus huoyanshanensis, IVPP V4878, holotype right humerus in A. medial, B. caudal, and C. lateral views. (After Currie and Dong 2001*a*.)

3 cm

5 cm

Shanshanosaurus huoyanshanensis, IVPP V4878, holotype right femur in A. cranial, B. medial, C. lateral, D. caudal, H. proximal, and I. distal views, right tibia in E. proximal and F. cranial views, G. left tibia in caudo-lateral view, and J. distal end of pubis, right lateral view. (After Currie and Dong 2001*a*.)

tyrannosaurids (see Lambe 1917; Maleev); therefore, evidence suggesting that young tyrannosaurids possessed relatively longer forelimbs is not supported by this genus.

Although some workers (*e.g.*, Paul 1988*b*) interpreted *Shanshanosaurus* as a member of the "Aublysodontinae," Holtz (2001), in performing a cladistic analysis of the Tyrannosauridae (see "Systematics" chapter), noted that, as the premaxillary teeth are unknown in this genus, all remaining similarities with that subfamily are symplesiomorphic. Contrarily, Holtz's analysis found *Shanshanosaurus* to be a tyrannosaurine more advanced than *Alioramus*, in possessing a reduced maxillary (eight) and dentary (12) tooth count. However, *Shanshanosaurus*, if this identification is correct, is distinguished as the only known tyrannosaurid having a retroarticular process and somewhat procoelous cervical vertebrae.

Key references: Carr (1999); Currie (2000*c*); Currie and Dong (2001*a*); Dong (1977); Holtz (2001); Kurzanov (1976); Lambe (1917); Maleev (1974); Paul (1987*a*, 1988*b*).

†SHANTUNGOSAURUS

Ornithischia: Genasauria: Cerapoda: Ornithopoda: Iguanodontia: Euiguanodontia: Dryomorpha: Ankylopollexia: Iguanodontoidea: Hadrosauroidea: Hadrosauridae: Euhadrosauria: Hadrosaurinae.

Occurrence: Xingezhuang Formation, Wangshi Group, Shandong Province, China.

Comments: In 1973, Hu Chengzhi described the new type species of giant hadrosaurian dinosaur *Shantungosaurus giganteus*, founded upon numerous fossil remains representing a number of individuals collected from the "lower part of the Upper Cretaceous" Xingezhuang Formation (comprising gray-green siltstones, mudstones, calcerous concretions, and marl modules) in the Lower Member of the Wangshi (Wanngshih) Group, near Xingezhuang Village, Zhucheng County, Shandong Province, China. A mounted composite skeleton of this species was displayed from 1972 to 1982 at

the Palaeontological Hall of the Beijing (Peking) Museum of Natural History (see *D:TE* for information and a photograph of this skeleton).

Recently, Hu, Cheng, Pang and Fang (2001) reported more fully on *S. gianteus*. As noted by these authors, the composite skeleton (NGMC V 1780) is presently mounted at the National Geological Museum of China with the missing cranial and postcranial parts restored in plaster.

For the first time, Hu *et al.* described this specimen in detail. The incomplete type skull (measuring 1,630 millimeters in length) is "rather long, low, and narrow in front but high and broad posteriorly." The caudal area of the cranium "is tolerably preserved from the plane of the exoccipital to anterior end of the frontals." Similarities were noted between *Shantungosaurus* and *Edmontosaurus regalis* (*e.g.*, rather straight

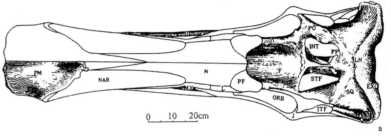

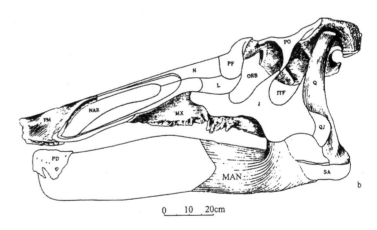

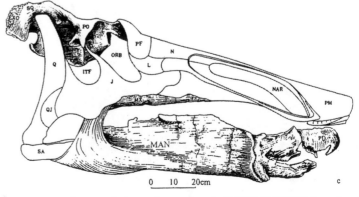

Shantungosaurus giganteus, holotype incomplete skull (NGMC V 1780) in a. dorsal, b. left lateral, and c. right lateral views. (After Hu, Cheng, Pang and Fang 2001.)

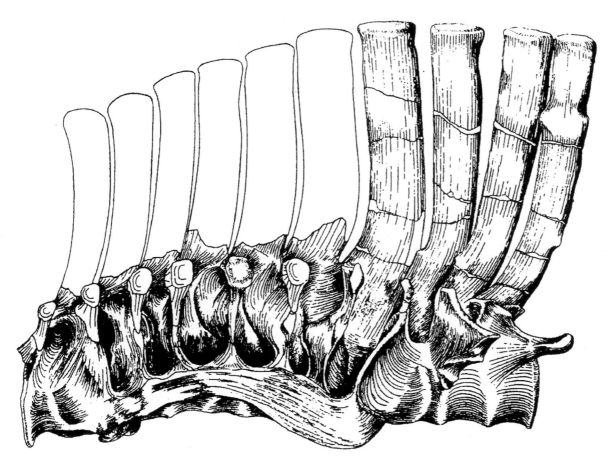

quadrate, structure of dentary tooth grooves), but the Chinese form is much larger.

Among the collected remains referred to *S. giganteus*, Hu *et al.* reported, are the following elements: Frontal; left quadrate; five right and five left maxillae; left premaxilla; a right and two left dentaries; partial right predentary; over 200 isolated teeth; vertebrae (17 cervicals [cranial rib nearly vertical, rather than oblique as in *Tanius* "chinkankouensis" [=*T. sinensis*] and *E. regalis*], 30 dorsals with [higher neural spines than in *Mandschruosaurus* and *Edmontosaurus*], four sacra [more slender than in *Kritosaurus*], and over 100 caudals); seven scapulae (caudal border in parallel position, closely resembling that of *Tanius sinensis*); one right and three left ilia; one left and three right ischia; and three left and four right femora.

Note: Hu *et al.* reported that associated with the above remains were a crocodilian tooth, a small chelonian fragment, and numerous theropod fossils including remains referred to a new species of *Tyrannosaurus*, ?*T. zhuchengensis* (see *Tyrannosaurus* entry).

Key references: Hu (1973); Hu, Cheng, Pang and Fang (2001).

SHENZHOURAPTOR   Wang 2002
Saurischia: Eusaurischia: Theropoda: ?

Name derivation: "Shenzhou [Chinese spacecraft]" + Latin *raptor* = "thief."
Type species: *S. sinensis* Wang 2002.
Occurrence: Liaoning Province, China.
Age: ?Early to ?Middle Cretaceous (?Barremian–?Aptian).

Comments: The genus *Shenzhouraptor* has not yet been formally described. The type species *Shenzhouraptor sinensis* was informally described as a "flying dinosaur," offering additional supporting evidence for a dinosaur-bird relationship.

†SHUNOSAURUS
Saurischia: Eusaurischia: Sauropodomorpha: Sauropoda: Eusauropoda: Neosauropoda: Macronaria: Camarasauromorpha: Titanosauriformes: Somphospondyli: Euhelopodidae: Shunosaurinae.

Diagnosis of genus (as for type species): Cranial features unique among Sauropoda including the following: Tooth morphology combination of cylindrical and spatulate form; pterygoid extremely small and slender small; pterygoid with fossa on dorsal aspect; forked quadrate ramus of pterygoid; external nares at level of orbit; emargination of ventral margin of maxilla/jugal bar behind tooth row; vomers not participating in formation of choanae; quadratojugal

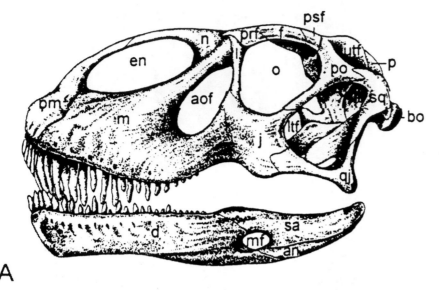

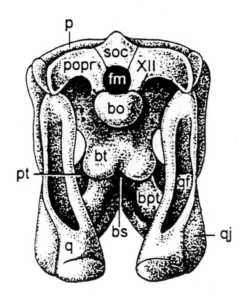

A

B

5 cm

Shunosaurus lii, referred skull (ZG65430) in A. left lateral and B. occipital views. (After Chatterjee and Zheng 2002.)

participating in jaws articulation; extremely deep basisphenoid recess; trochlear (IV) nerve having exits; basipterygoid process not wrapped by caudal process of pterygoid; postorbital containing lateral pit; occlusal level of maxillary tooth row downwardly convex, that of dentary upwardly concave ("like a pair of garden shears"); replacing tooth invading on labial side of functional tooth; dentary tooth count at least 25 (Chatterjee and Zheng 2002; for diagnosis based on postcrania, see Zhang 1988).

Comments: Arguably the best known basal sauropod is *Shunosaurus*, a medium-sized (11 meters in length), relatively short-necked, club-tailed form

represented by several complete skeletons collected from the Middle Jurassic of Zigong, China (see *D:TE, S1*).

In 2002, Sankar Chatterjee and Zhong Zheng described in detail a well-preserved, nearly complete and somewhat disarticulated skull (ZG65430) from the collections of the Zigong Dinosaur Museum of Sichuan Province, China. The skull, which offered to Chatterjee and Zheng "a wealth of three-dimensional anatomical formation" concerning the type species *Shunosaurus lii*, was collected from the Dashanpu quarry at the museum. Most of the gross preparation of this specimen was executed at the Institute of Vertebrate Paleontology and Paleoanthropology in Beijing; preparation of the braincase was done at the Museum of Texas Tech University. When reconstructed, the authors noted, the skull measures 495 millimeters in length, 170 millimeters in width, 218 millimeters in height, and has a tapering snout.

In the past, Zhang (1988) described and figured several skulls referred to *Shunosaurus*, two of which are relatively complete, one of these (T5401) ascribed to a juvenile individual and the other (T5403) to an adult, both differing considerably from one another in the shape of the snout. Chatterjee and Zheng pointed out that the smaller juvenile skull has a narrow and pointed snout, seemingly an autapomorphic feature, while the snout of the adult is rounded and blunt, resembling that of other sauropods. As these authors further noted, ZG65430 most closely resembles the juvenile specimen; furthermore, the disarticulated nature of many of the cranial elements and also the loss of interdental plates indicate that the animal to which this skull belonged was not completely mature at its time of death.

Chatterjee and Zheng referred ZG65430 to *Shunosaurus* based on the following characters: Tooth morphology heterodont, exhibiting both cylindrical and spatulate teeth; occlusal level of maxillary tooth row downwardly convex, that of dentary upwardly concave; emargination of ventral margin of maxilla/jugal bar behind tooth row; dentary tooth count at least 26.

As Chatterjee and Zheng pointed out, ZG65430 allowed for an endocast to be made reconstructing the brain morphology, the cranial nerves, arteries, and veins. Furthermore, the shape of the dental arcade, the morphology and wear of the teeth, the nature of the articulation of the jaw, and the posture of the neck shed new light on this dinosaur's feeding strategy (see below).

The authors observed the following details regarding ZG65430: Skull akinetic and monimostylic; brain relatively small, narrow, primitively designed; teeth spatulate, stout, showing well-developed wear facets indicative of coarser vegetation.

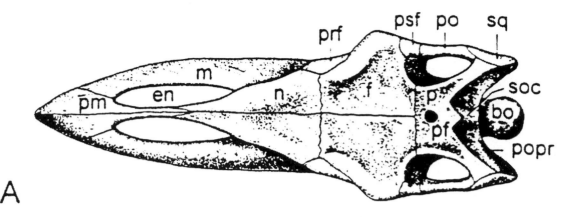

Shunosaurus lii, referred skull (ZG65430) in A. dorsal and B. ventral views. (After Chatterjee and Zheng 2002.)

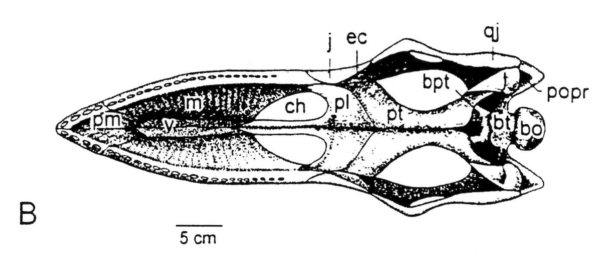

5 cm

Regarding tooth replacement in *Shunosaurus*, Chatterjee and Zheng inferred the following sequence: 1. The new tooth erupted on the distal-lingual side of the tooth row; 2. a "window" was present on the base of the lingual side of the functional tooth; 3. the replacement tooth tunneled through this window, appearing at the labial side; 4. the base of the functional or "old" tooth, being worn out, was left in a precarious condition; and 5. the replacement tooth than took the position of the old tooth and grew.

Chatterjee and Zheng recognized replacement teeth in *Shunosaurus* based on their small size, their location at the base of an old tooth, and their lack of wear facets. Five stages of functional teeth (F) and three of replacement teeth (R) were recognized in the order of their increasing age: R1— small incipient tooth showing tip of crown; R2— crown fully erupted; R3 — crown reaching labial margin of maxilla (similarly for functional teeth); F1— fully developed, crown intact, root with no signs of wear; F2 — crown tip beginning to wear; F3— small wear facet in mesial and distal side; F4— wear facet expanded; and F5 — occlusal facet reduced, rostral and caudal facets dominant, extending to crown base.

The authors concluded the following regarding tooth replacement in *Shunosaurus*:

1. The odd and even replacement series are from back to front, the direction of wave replacement being independent of tooth number and morphology, relying rather on Z-spacing (*i.e.*, "Zahnreihen" spacing, referring to "each member of a set of equally spaced caudally sloping parallel lines that intersected a tooth at every tooth position" (see Chatterjee and Zheng for details).

2. The total life of a tooth is comparatively long, the time replacing it relatively short, the proportion of the replacement period being 20 percent of the total tooth development.

3. Average Z-spacing is 2.66, the individual or entire Zahnreihen being highly organized, the slope between them showing slight variation.

4. Jaw motion is entirely orthal, the pattern of wear facets suggesting that the upper tooth row sheared past the labial side of the lower series, the teeth occluding in alternate fashion.

Based upon the architecture of the skull, morphology of the teeth, and posture of the neck, the authors concluded that *Shunosaurus* was adapted to low browsing or ground feeding.

Shunosaurus

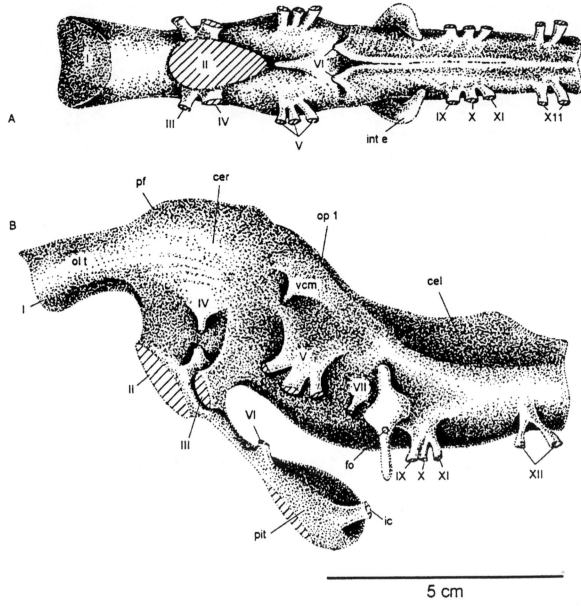

5 cm

Chatterjee and Zhang offered a new diagnosis of *Shunosaurus lii* based exclusively on autapomorphic cranial features. Consequently, this diagnosis (see above) would supplement and emend Zhang's earlier diagnosis, presumably retaining the data pertaining to the postcranial skeleton (see *D:TE*).

Due to the lack of substantial skull material, the encompassing group Sauropoda cannot yet be defined based on cranial characters (see Upchurch 1998; Wilson and Sereno 1998). However, Chatterjee and Zheng pointed out, *Shunosaurus*, being the earliest sauropod for which skull remains are known, occupies an important phylogenetic position, both offering the critical morphology of basal Sauropoda and, consequently, offering important insights regarding the modification of sauropod cranial morphology from the more primitive prosauropod condition.

The authors further noted that, with Prosauropoda considered to be the sister taxon to Sauropoda (see Galton 1990*a*), *Shunosaurus* shares the following 27 synapomorphies with the Eusauropoda (Upchurch 1995): Premaxilla, stepped rostral margin (Wilson and Sereno); long maxillary border of external naris (Gauthier 1986); external naris retracted upward, backward (McIntosh 1990); antorbital fenestra smaller than external naris; absence of antorbital fossa (Wilson and Sereno); quadratojugal, rostral process expanded dorsoventrally at its tip, longer than dorsal process (Gauthier); quadrate, caudal fossa (Wilson and Sereno); external mandibular fenestra much reduced (Russell and Zheng 1993); dentary, rostral end increasing in depth towards symphysis (Upchurch 1998); tooth crown lacking ridges; tooth enamel with wrinkled texture (Wilson and Sereno); tooth crown ending below antorbital fenestra (Gauthier); precise crown to crown occlusion (Wilson and Sereno); rostral end of snout broadly rounded in dorsal view (Upchurch 1998); ventral border of external naris lying higher than that of orbit (McIntosh); lacrimal head sloping backward relative to base; length of jugal reduced, antorbital and lateral temporal fenestra thereby crowded and approaching each other (Upchurch 1995); quadratojugal, ascending process failing to reach descending process of squamosal (Gauthier); frontal excluded from supratemporal (Wilson and Sereno); supratemporal fenestra, long axis oriented transversely (Wilson and Sereno); prominent supraoccipital platform; premaxillary dental count of four; less than 20 maxillary teeth (Gauthier); tooth row terminating rostral to antorbital fenestra (Gauthier); teeth procumbent, forwardly sloping (Gauthier); constriction between tooth crown and root; palatine, lateral ramus narrow (Wilson and Sereno).

In their recent description of the sauropod *Omeisaurus maoianus* (see *Omeisaurus* entry), Tang, Jin, Kang and Zhang (2001) made a detailed comparison, based upon histological studies of the teeth of that species and those of *Shunosaurus lii*, these authors proposing that certain observed differences could have phylogenetic significance. Among the conclusions reached by Tang *et al.*, based upon the more derived enamel type observed in the teeth of *O. maoianus* (despite both taxa originating from the same locality), was that *Omeisaurus* could represent a higher phylogentic clade than *Shunosaurus*.

Tang *et al.*'s study suggested that the teeth of *Shunosaurus* are, in some ways, intermediate between those of the prosauropod *Anchisaurus* and the sauropod *Omeisaurus*, with the disparity in enamel appar-

Reconstruction of the skeleton of *Shunosaurus lii*. (After Chatterjee and Zheng 2002, modified from Wilson and Sereno 1998).

ently successive among these three sauropodomorphs. In *Anchisaurus*, the roughly parallel crystallites of the enamel represents the prosauropod type, the slightly bifid crystallites in *Shunosaurus* the "basal" sauropod type, and the curved crystallites in *Omeisaurus* the more derived sauropod type. Also, the diameters of dentine tubules become progressively larger from *Anchisaurus* to *Shunosaurus* to *Omeisaurus*. As noted by Tang *et al.*, further studies on the dental microstructure of other neosauropods could offer information that will help to clarify further the relationships of these dinosaurs.

Key references: Chatterjee and Zheng (2002); Galton (1990a); Gauthier (1986); McIntosh (1990); Russell and Zheng (1993); Tang, Jin, Kang and Zhang (2001); Upchurch (1995, 1998); Wilson and Sereno (1998); Zhang (1988).

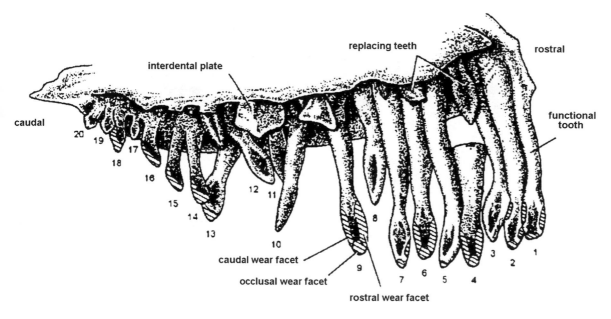

Left maxilla (lingual view) of referred skull (ZG65430) of *Shunosaurus lii*, showing tooth wear facets, replacing teeth, interdental plates (after Chatterjee and Zheng 2002).

†SHUVOSAURUS

Saurischia: Eusaurischia: Theropoda *incertae sedis*.

Comments: In 1993, Sankar Chatterjee described the new genus and species *Shuvosaurus inexpectatus*, founded upon specimens representing at least three individuals collected from the Upper Triassic (Norian) Dockum Formation of Texas. Chatterjee interpreted this taxon possibly to be a primitive and toothless ornithomimosaur, which he referred to a new family, Shuvosauridae, although the Ornithomimosauria was only unequivocally known from the Cretaceous period (see *D:TE*).

Subsequently, Long and Murry (1995; see also Murry and Long 1997), although these authors had not studied in detail the holotype specimen (TTU P 9280), reinterpreted *Shuvosaurus* as a possible toothless rausuchian (see "Excluded Genera," *S1*).

More recently, Rauhut (1997), in a brief report, redescribed and again reinterpreted the holotype skull of *S. inexpectatus*. As noted by that author, the skull exhibits numerous apomorphic characters that justify Chatteree's referral of it to a new genus and probably also to a new family.

However, Rauhut found that, *contra* Long and Murry, *Shuvosaurus* differs from rausuchians (and also other basal crurotarsan reptiles) in various features — loss of postfrontal; paroccipital process ventrolaterally directed; lacrimal dorsoventrally elongated, inverted L-shaped, exposed on skull roof; deep basisphenoid recess; ectopterygoid having expanded medial part and deep ventral fossa. As Rauhut pointed

out, all of these features are found in theropods, the latter three possibly constituting synapomorphies for Theropoda (Gauthier 1986).

Although Rauhut referred *Shuvosaurus* back to the Theropoda, he was not able to refer it to any specific clade within that group. According to that author, *Shuvosaurus* lacks several ornithomimosaurian synapomorphies (*e.g.*, expanded parasphenoid capsule, short and broad basipterygoid processes; see, for example, Barsbold and Osmólska 1990). *Shuvosaurus* differs from coelurosaurs in general in various features (*e.g.*, relatively small brain cavity, lack of two accessory antorbital openings in maxillary, presence of ventral groove rather than deep ventral pocket; see, for example, Barsbold and Osmólska; Currie 1995). *Shuvosaurus* also differs from all known tetanurans in having a prefrontal that is mostly exposed on the rostral orbital rim (displaced caudally and frequently medially in Tetanurae). As Rauhut noted, the preceding characters show *Shuvosaurus* to be a basal theropod, although its precise phylogenetic position cannot now be determined.

As Rauhut concluded, "*Shuvosaurus*, with its highly derived skull morphology, is a good example for a significant early differentiation within theropods," while also showing how little is presently known about the early evolution of the Theropoda.

Key references: Barsbold and Osmólska (1990); Chatterjee (1993); Currie (1995); Gauthier (1986); Long and Murry (1995); Murry and Long (1997); Rauhut (1997).

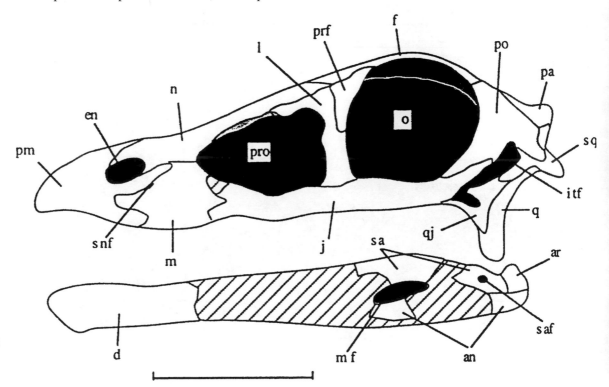

Shuvosaurus inexpectatus, TTU P 9280, holotype skull (reconstructed), left lateral view. Scale = 5 cm. (After Rauhut 1997.)

†SHUVUUIA

Saurischia: Eusaurischia: Theropoda: Neotheropoda: Tetanurae: Avetheropoda: Coelurosauria: Maniraptoriformes: Maniraptora: Metornithes: ?Paraves: Alvarezsauridae: Mononykinae.

Diagnosis of genus (as for type species): Autapomorphic characters including articulation between quadrate and postorbital, elongated basipterygoid processes, hypertrophied prefrontal/ectethmoid, and presence of sharp ridge on medial margin of distal tibiotarsus (Chiappe, Norell and Clark 1998); differentiated from closely related mononykine *Mononykus olecranus* in having less compressed cervical centra bearing large pneumatic foramina, humeral head continuous with deltopectoral crest, pubis subcircular in cross section, femoral and tibiotarsal shafts bowed lateromedially, and less excavated medial margin of ascending process of astragalus (Chiappe *et al.*); pes with much longer proximal phalanx of hallux than in *M. olecranus*, intermediate phalanx of digit II subequal in length to its ungual phalanx (much shorter in *M. olecranus*), and longer, more slender intermediate phalanges of digit IV; differs from mononykine *Parvicursor remotus* in that pedal digit IV is longer than half length of metatarsal IV (in *P. remotus*, digit IV less than half of metatarsal IV), and this digit being shorter than digit II (without counting ungual phalanges); lacks ventral keel in most rostrally located synsacral vertebra, and less coossification between proximal tarsals and tibia (Chiappe *et al.*) (Suzuki, Chiappe, Dyke, Watabe, Barsbold and Tsogtbaatar 2002).

Comments: Suzuki, Chiappe, Dyke, Watabe, Barsbold and Tsogtbaatar (2002) described a new specimen (MPD 100/120) of the very birdlike theropod *Shuvuuia deserti* (see *Shuvuuia* entry, S2), consisting of a partial skeleton found by an expedition of the Hayashibara Museum of Natural Sciences-Mongolian Paleontological Center in the Late Cretaceous (Campanian) Tögrögiin Shiree locality, South Gobi Aimak, in southern Mongolia. The specimen preserves part of the skull including almost complete mandibular rami, most of the cervical, dorsal, and caudal vertebrae, postions of scapula, corocoid, and ilium, fragments of forelimb elements, a complete manus, distal ends of femora, and most of the hindlimb bones. As calculated by the authors, this new specimen is about 60 percent as large as the holotype (MGI 100/975) of *S. deserti*.

Suzuki *et al.* identified MPD 100/120 as a mononykine based on such derived characters as the following: Medial border of tibiotarsus strongly projected proximally; fibula greatly reduced, not reaching proximal tarsals; and reduced proximal end of metatarsal III (*i.e.*, arctometatarsial condition; see Holtz 1994*b*).

The authors noted that, within the Mononykinae, this specimen shares a number of derived characters with the holotype and referred material of *S. deserti*, these including the following: Centra of cervical vertebrae laterally compressed, with large pneumatic foramina, lateromedially bowed tibiotarsal shaft, less excavated medial margin of ascending process of astragalus, and crest on mediocranial edge of distal end of tibia. Moreover, in respect to all overlapping elements, MPD 100/120 cannot be distinguished from the holotype and referred specimens of *S. deserti*. The lesser degree of coossification of the tibiotarsus and carpometacarpus in *S. deserti*, previously identified by Chiappe *et al.* as a derived feature relative to other mononykines, Suzuki *et al.* regarded this as possibly due to immaturity.

As noted by Suzuki *et al.*, this specimen presents

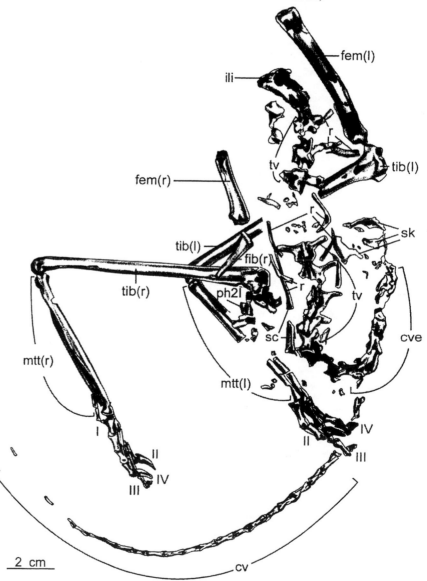

Shuvuuia deserti, referred partial skeleton (MPD 100/120). (After Suzuki, Chiappe, Dyke, Watabe, Barsbold and Tsogtbaatar 2002.)

2 cm

a number of features — primarily in the manus, pes, and caudal vertebrae — previously unknown either in *S. deserti* or in any other alvarezsaurids. The well-preserved and articulated right manus, for example, confirms the presence of manual digits II and III among members of the Alvarezsauridae. As previously predicted based on the size of the distal articulations of the carpometacarpus (see Perle, Chiappe, Barsbold, Clark and Norell 1994; Chiappe *et al.*), these digits are considerably smaller than the first digit. The tail of this specimen, being almost complete, reveals that previous calculations for the number of caudal vertebrae (*i.e.*, 25 or 26; see Chiappe, Norell and Clark 1996) in mononykines underestimated that count by at least 10 vertebrae. The most informative aspect of the tail, Suzuki *et al.* pointed out, is its distal half, where the caudal vertebrae are exposed in both dorsal and side views. This reveals a gradual shortening of the individual vertebrae towards the end of the tail. The complete and articulated hallux likewise offered more morphological data, showing that the hallux, though quite similar, differs from that of *M. olecranus* in the relative length of its proximal phalanx.

Alvarezsaurids have been regarded either as birds or nonavian theropods. Suzuki *et al.* evaluated the hypothesis proposed by Sereno (1999*b*, 2001), which placed the Alvarezsauridae within Theropoda close to Ornithomimoidea, concluding that this assessment is only weakly supported (see "Systematics" chapter). Furthermore, the newly discovered details of MPD 100/120 allowed Suzuki *et al.* to propose an emended diagnosis of *S. deserti*, including that information.

More recently, in an abstract for a poster, Dufeau (2002) briefly reported on his study, with the aid of X-ray tomography, of two very well-preserved skulls of *S. deserti*, a juvenile and a larger and more completely ossified probable adult, collected from the Djadokhta Formation at Ukhaa Tolgod, Mongolia, by a joint expedition of the American Museum of Natural History and the Mongolian Academy of Sciences (see *S2*). Although no salient observations were cited in this preliminary report, Dufeau stated that this study will yield "some of the morphological novelties and other pertinent cranial characteristics as seen in the skulls of *Shuvuuia deserti*". Also, in addition to offering "ontogenetic markers for alvarezsaurids, these two specimens add data to test current hypotheses of the phylogenetic position of alvarezsaurids among coelurosaurs."

Key references: Chiappe, Norell and Clark (1996, 1998); Dufeau (2002); Holtz (1994); Perle, Chiappe, Barsbold, Clark and Norell (1994); Sereno (1999*b*, 2001); Suzuki, Chiappe, Dyke, Watabe, Barsbold and Tsogtbaatar (2002).

†SIAMOTYRANNUS

Saurischia: Eusaurischia: Theropoda: Neotheropoda: Tetanurae: Avetheropoda: Coelurosauria: Maniraptoriformes: Arctometatarsalia: Tyrannosauroidea.

Comments: In 1996, Éric Buffetaut, Varavudh Suteethorn and Haiyan Tong described the type species *Siamotyrannus isanensis*, a theropod based on a fragmentary postcranial specimen from the Lower Cretaceous (Barremian) Sao Khua Formation of northeastern Thailand (see Buffetaut and Suteethorn 1999 for a recent short review of the dinosaurs of Thailand, including *Siamotyrannus*). The authors considered this taxon to be a primitive member of the Tyrannosauridae (see *D:TE*).

More recently, however, Holtz (2001), in performing a phylogenetic analysis of the Tyrannosauridae (see "Systematics" chapter), reached the conclusion that *Siamotyrannus* lies outside of this family, but shares with it the following synapomorphies: Horizontal medial shelf from preacetabular blade to sacral ribs; broad, ventral hooklike projection from preacetabular blade of ilium; dorsal surfaces of iliac blades converging closely along midline; ilium with pronounced midline crest; and pronounced semicircular scar on caudolateral surface of ischium, just ventral to iliac process.

While sharing these characters with the Tyrannosauridae, *Siamotyrannus* has a pair of midline crests on the ilium, rather than the single crest found in tyrannosaurids. This suggested to Holtz that *Siamotyrannus* could be an ancestral member of the tyrannosaur lineage; lacking the skull and other additional material, however, its position at present remains uncertain.

Key references: Buffetaut and Suteethorn (1999); Buffetaut, Suteethorn and Tong (1996); Holtz (2001).

†SINORNITHOIDES

Saurischia: Eusaurischia: Theropoda: Neotheropoda: Tetanurae: Avetheropoda: Coelurosauria: Maniraptoriformes: Maniraptora: Metornithes: Paraves: Deinonychosauria: Troodontidae.

Comments: Between 1987 and 1990, the Sino-Canadian Dinosaur Project collected from three localities in the China a number of troodontid specimens, some of these belonging to the Lower Cretaceous species *Sinornithoides youngi* (see *D:TE*).

Currie and Dong (2001*b*) later described in detail the holotype (IVPP V9612) of this species, the best and most complete skeleton of a troodontid yet found, lacking only the skull roof and most of the cervical and dorsal vertebrae, collected in 1988 from the Lower Cretaceous Ejinhoro Formation of the Ordos

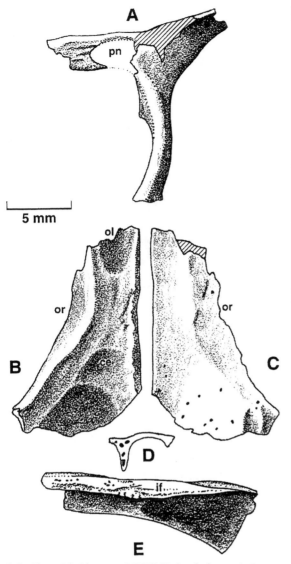

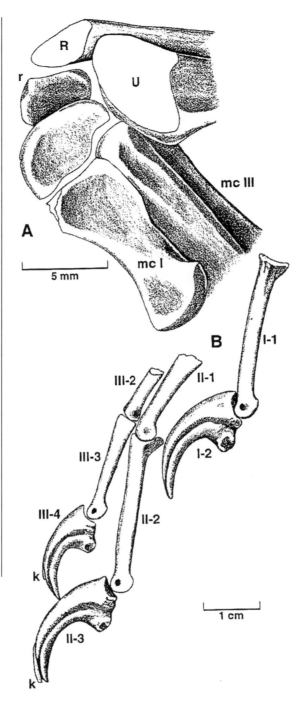

Left: Sinornithoides youngi, IVPP V9612, holotype (sub-adult) A. left lacrimal in ventrolateral view; right frontal in B. ventral, C. dorsal, D. rostral, and E. medial views. (After Currie and Dong 2001*b*.) *Right: Sinornithoides youngi*, IVPP V9612, holotype forelimb, A. radius, ulna, and metacarpals, B. manual digits. (After Currie and Dong 2001*b*.)

Basin, in exposures near the village of Muhuaxiao (Russell and Dong 1993; see *D:TE*).

In their description of this skeleton, Currie and Dong noted its immaturity, evidenced by the following features: Long bones showing surfaces (characteristic of immature individuals); cervical ribs not fused to corresponding ribs; scapula and coracoid not fused; ilium, pubis, and ischium separate; and ends of paired pubes not fused. Moreover, as the neural arches are indistinguishably fused to their centra in the middle and distal areas of the tail, and the astragalus and calcaneum are indistinguishably fused, the type specimen seems to represent an animal approaching maturity, with an adult size possibly comparable to that of *Troodon* or *Saurornitholestes*.

As Currie and Dong pointed out, *Sinornithoides* possesses all of the autapomorphies expected of a troodontid, although some of these features are more fully developed in Late Cretaceous members of the Troodontidae —*e.g.*, tooth serrations enlarged compared to those of other theropods, but not to the degree as in *Troodon* and *Saurornithoides* (see entry).

As Currie and Dong stated, the Troodontidae can be defined by numerous characters suggesting a long independent history for the group dating prior to the Early Cretaceous, these including the following:

Sinornithoides youngi, IVPP V9612, holotype (subadult) dentition from left side of skull (denticles not visible in this view), A. premaxillary teeth, B. mesial teeth, C. maxillary tooth, D. dentary tooth (fourth alveolar position), and E. rostral part of dentary illustrating first seven tooth positions. (After Currie and Dong 2001*b*.)

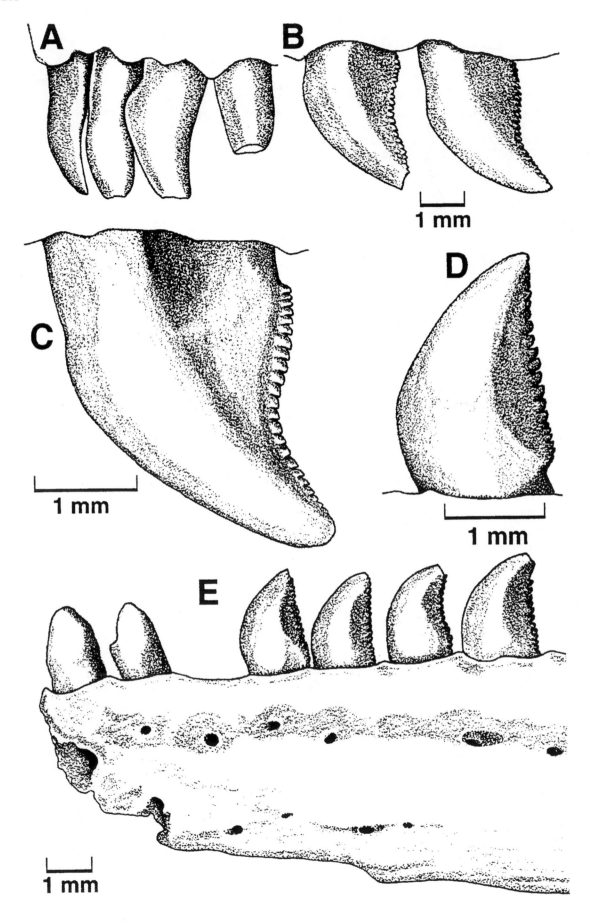

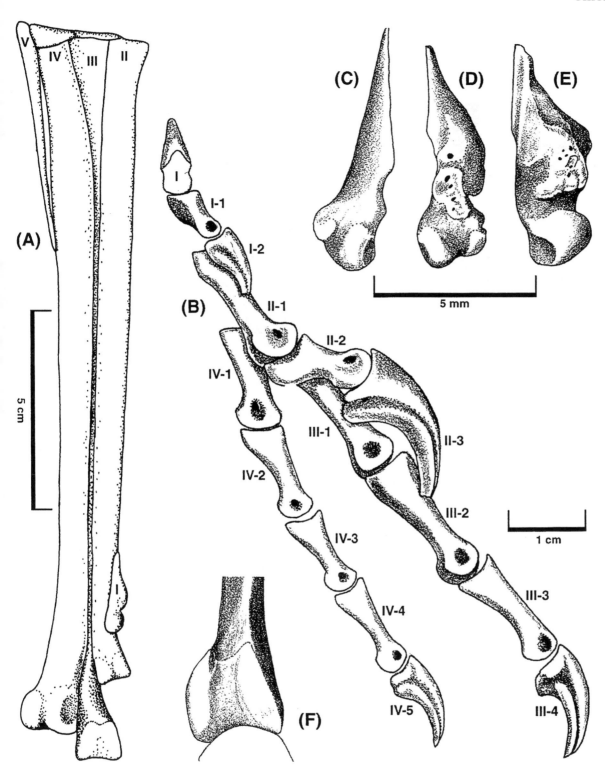

Sinornithoides youngi, IVPP V9612, holotype (subadult) A. left metatarsus in caudal view; B. left pedal digits, medial view; right metatarsal I in C. ventral view; left metatarsal I in D. ventral and E. medial view; and F. distal end of left metatarsal III, caudal view. (After Currie and Dong 2001*b.*)

Distinctive teeth having large serrations and constrictions between crown and root; loss of interdental plates in dentary; distal dentary teeth implanted in paradental groove instead of sockets; femur with trochanteric crest; fusion of astragalus and calcaneum; metatarsal II with relatively short, mediolaterally compressed shaft; and tonguelike extension of distal articular surface of metatarsal III.

Key references: Currie and Dong (2001*b*); Russell and Dong (1993).

†SINORNITHOSAURUS

Saurischia: Eusaurischia: Theropoda: Neotheropoda: Tetanurae: Avetheropoda: Coelurosauria: Maniraptoriformes: Maniraptora: Metornithes: Paraves: Deinonychosauria: Dromaeosauridae *incertae sedis.*

Sinornithosaurus

Sinornithosaurus millenii, reconstruction of holotype (IVPP V 12811) skull in A. left lateral and B. dorsal views. Scale = 50 mm. (After Xu and Wu 2001.)

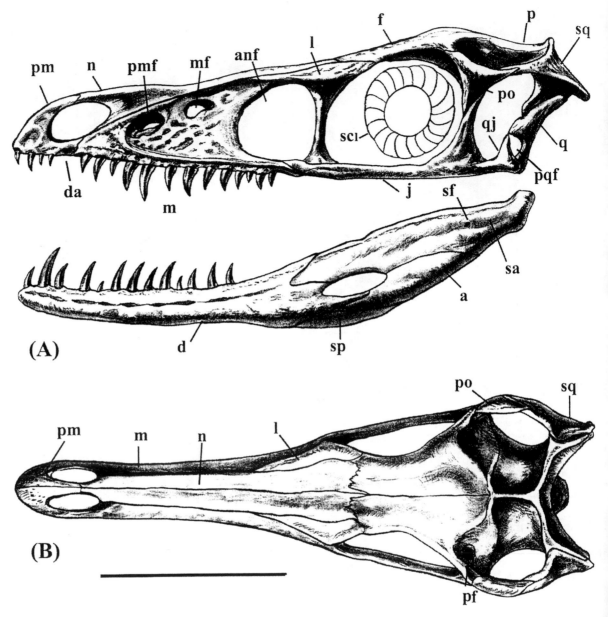

Diagnosis (as for type species): Distinguished by the following autapomorphies: deep excavation on postventral margin of premaxilla; diastema between premaxillary and maxillary teeth; semicircular maxillary fenestra having straight ventral margin; large promaxillary fenestra; number of pits and ridges on anterolateral surface of antorbital fossa; posterolateral process of parietal long, sharply caudally directed; column-like margin of pterygoid process of quadrate; large excavation on posterolateral surface of parasphenoid process; bifurcated distal margin of dentary; distinctive groove distal to mesial carina on lingual surface of premaxillary tooth crowns (Xu and Wu 2001).

Comments: In 1999, Xing Xu, Xiao-Lin Wang and Xiao-Chun Wu described *Sinornithosaurus milleni*, a new genus and species of basal dromaeosaurid theropod from the Yixian Formation of Liaoning Province (possibly 120 to 125 million years old; see Smith, Harris, Omar, Dodson and You 2001, based on radiometric data), China. The holotype and only specimen (IVPP V12811) consists of a disarticulated skeleton with the skull, plus integumentary filaments that were originally interpreted as possibly plesiomorphic feathers (see *S2*).

More recently, Xu and Wu (2001) fully described the skull of this dinosaur, at the same time offering a revised diagnosis of the type species based upon cranial features, and also discussing similarities to the skulls of other dromaeosaurid theropods and to those of *Archaeopteryx* and other early birds, the latter, possibly having phylogenetic implications, as follows:

1. Mandible relatively short compared to skull length: The mandible of *Sinornithosaurus* is about 135

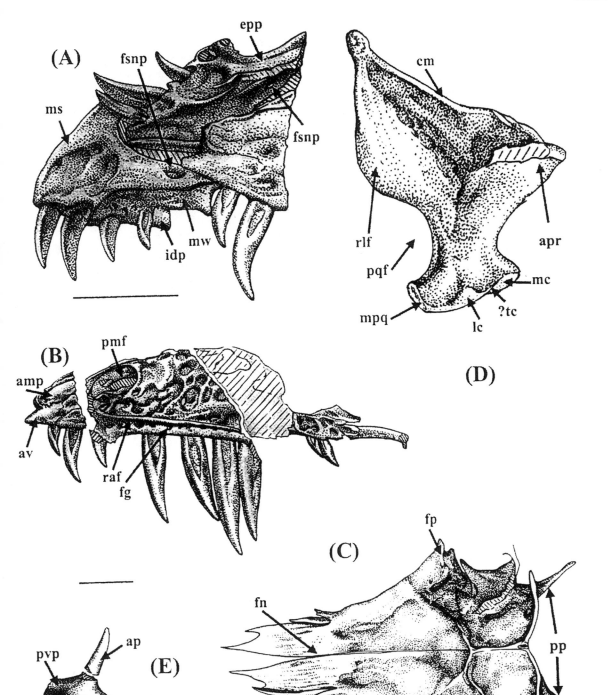

Sinornithosaurus millenii, IVPP V 12811, holotype right and left premaxillae in A. medial view, B. left maxilla, lateral view, C. left prefrontal, frontals, and parietals, dorsal view, D. right quadrate, rostral view, and E. right quadratojugal, lateral view. Scale = 10 cm. (After Xu and Wu 2001.)

millimeters and the length of the skull about 152 millimeters, the mandible to skull length ratio being less than 0.89 (ratio more than 0.90 in most nonavian theropods; 0.91 in *Velociraptor*, 0.97 in *Bambiraptor* and *Deinonychus*, and 0.96 in *Sinornithoides*; 0.87 in seventh specimen of *Archaeopteryx*; see Elźanowski and Wellnhofer 1996).

2. Main body of premaxilla long and shallow:

The main body of the premaxilla of *Sinornithosaurus* is especially long and shallow below the narial opening (in *Archaeopteryx*, main body of premaxilla, except for long ramus rostral to external naris, is identical to that of *Sinornithosaurus*; see Wellnhofer 1992; main body much deeper in troodontids and other dromaeosaurids; main body also long and shallow in some less closely related theropods, including some

Reconstruction of filamental integumental appendage of *Sinornithosaurus milleni* from the dorsal surface of the snout. Scale = 5 mm. (After Xu, Zhou and Prum 2001.)

ornithomimids and *Compsognathus*; see Ostrom 1978).

3. Premaxillary angle sharp: In *Sinornithosaurus*, this angle is about 45 degrees (much smaller in other theropods, including other dromaeosaurids and troodontids; see Kirkland, Burge and Gaston 1993; angle sharp in birds, some ornithomimids, and *Compsognathus*; see Ostrom).

4. Position of ventral margin of narial opening: In *Sinornithosaurus*, this border is nearly at the same level as the ventral margin of the antorbital fossa (comparable to condition in Avialae and *Compsognathus*; see Ostrom; in most theropods, including other dromaeosaurids and troodontids, ventral border of narial opening apparently dorsal to ventral margin of antorbital fossa; narial opening more dorsally situated in oviraptorosaurians, *e.g.*, *Caudipteryx*; see Sereno 1999*b*).

5. Narial opening relatively large: In *Sinornithosaurus* (and in *Bambiraptor* [Burnham, Derstler, Currie, Bakker, Zhou and Ostrom 2000], and in some troodontids), this opening is large relative to the antorbital (opening even larger in Aviale and some oviraptorosaurian, *e.g.*, *Caudipteryx*; smaller narial opening in most other nonavian theropods).

6. Diastema between premaxillary and maxillary teeth: In *Sinornithosaurus*, the premaxillary and maxillary teeth seem to have been separated by a diastema, this inference based upon the morphology of the caudal end of the premaxilla and the rostral end of the maxilla (this feature atypical of theropods, reported in "ceratosaurians"; see Rowe and Gauthier 1990; see also "Systematics" chapter; also present in *Compsognathus* and *Archaeopteryx*; see Wellnhofer, Ostrom, respectively).

7. Excavated posteroventral margin of premaxilla: In *Sinornithosaurus*, the lateral surface of the caudal premaxilla is deeply excavated (London specimen of *Archaeopteryx* apparently sharing this feature; see Wellnhofer).

8. Parietal wide: In *Sinornithosaurus* (also in *Bambiraptor* and *Archaeopteryx*; see Burnham *et al.*, Elźanowski and Wellnhofer, respectively), the parietal is wider than the interorbital portion of the frontals (slightly narrower parietal in troodontids, although wider than in most other known nonavian theropods), the wider parietal indicating an enlarged braincase.

9. Posteroventral process of quadratojugal short, blunt: *Sinornithosaurus* and other dromaeosaurids share a diagnostic reversed T-shaped quadratojugal (see Paul 1988*c*) because of the development of the posteroventral process, this character being also found in *Archaeopteryx* (Elźanowski and Wellnhofer).

Reconstruction of filamental integumental appendages of *Sinornithosaurus milleni*, disassociated from the integument, preserved overlying one another in matrix near the skull. Scale = 5 mm. (After Xu, Zhou and Prum 2001.)

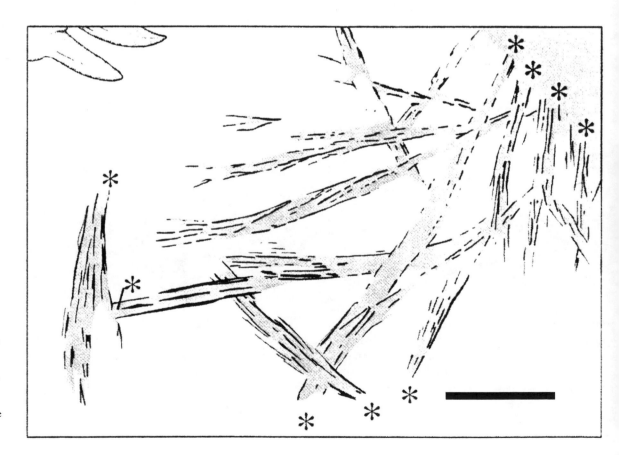

Sinornithosaurus is similar to *Archaeopteryx* in this character, in that the posteroventral process is quite short and blunt (long and slender in other dromaeosaurids; quadratojugal L-shaped in most other nonavian theropods, lacking distinctive quadratojugal-squamosal process).

10. Quadratojugal reduced: In *Sinornithosaurus*, the quadratojugal is much smaller than in most nonavian theropods, the ascending process being especially short, this suggesting the absence of a contact between the quadratojugal and the squamosal (the absence of this contact regarded as an autapomorphy of birds including *Archaeopteryx*; see Ji, Currie, Norell and Ji 1998).

11. Pterygoid process of quadrate triangular, with ventrally situated apex: The pterygoid process of the quadrate in *Sinornithosaurus* is plainly triangular with a ventrally located apex, this feature shared with *Archaeopteryx* (see Walker 1985) (apex more dorsally located in other nonavian theropods—*e.g.*, *Bambiraptor*, *Dromaeosaurus*, and *Velociraptor*—possessing this structure).

12. Quadrate ramus of pterygoid bifurcated: In *Sinornithosaurus* and apparently *Archaeopteryx* (Elźanowski and Wellnhofer), this ramus is bifurcated (also in *Tyrannosaurus rex*; see Molnar 1991; however, not observed in most other theropods).

13. Dentary very shallow: In *Sinornithosaurus*, the length the ratio of length to depth of the dentary is approximately 13, close to that (14) in *Archaeopteryx* (less than 10 in most nonavian theropods, including dromaeosaurids).

14. Caudal margin of dentary bifurcated: This feature is seen in *Sinornithosaurus* and the basal bird *Confuciusornis* (see Chiappe, Ji, Ji and Norell 1999) (also in oviraptorosaurians, *e.g.*, *Caudipteryx*; see Ji *et al.*; and in various primitive theropods).

As Xu and Wu pointed out, these characters shared by *Sinornithosaurus*, *Archaeopteryx*, and other early birds offer additional data supporting a close relationship between dromaeosaurids and avians. Furthermore, the presence of numerous similarities between *Sinornithosaurus* and other maniraptoran groups "suggest that the diversification of Maniraptora may have occurred quite rapidly."

The proposed nonavian theropod status of two feathered genera from the Liaoning beds, *Caudipteryx* (see S1, S2) and *Protarchaeopteryx* (see S1), has been questioned by some workers, mostly those specializing in fossil birds. Indeed, a number of workers (*e.g.*, Feduccia 1999; Jones, Farlow, Ruben, Henderson and Hillenius 2000; Martin and Czerkas 2000) have suggested that these taxa are not dinosaurs but, in fact, flightless birds. Also disputed *e.g.*, Gibbons 1997; Dalton 2000) has been the earlier interpretations of fila-

mentous structures in *Sinornithosaurus* and also *Sinosauropteryx* (see S1) as primitive feathers or "protofeathers."

Noting that the evolutionary origin of feathers is obscured by the lack of morphological antecedents to the earliest structurally modern feathers in the Late Jurassic bird *Archaeopteryx*, Xu, Zhou and Prum (2001) searched for evidence that would confirm a theropod origin of feathers by documenting "unambiguously feather-like structures in a clearly nonavian theropod," *S. milleni*.

Additional preparation of the holotype of *S. milleni* revealed to Xu *et al.* (2001) new details regarding the morphology of its filamenous integumental appendages. As noted by the authors, these structures are preserved around the specimen as carbonized filaments. Generally the appendages measure from 30 to 45 millimeters in length and one to three millimeters in width, many of them remaining closely associated with the integument of the skull, neck, forelimbs, legs, and tail, others disassociated from the skeleton and preserved in the surrounding matrix.

Xu *et al.* dismissed the likelihood that these filamentous appendages might be collagenous dermal or musculoskeletal structures, pointing out that they are preserved as integumental structures, and "are too numerous and broadly distributed to be partially ossified tendons."

Addressing the possibility that these integumentary appendages might have been hairlike structures, Xu *et al.* (2001) pointed out that the preservation of so many randomly arranged, compound structures overlying one another indicates that these appendages were disassociated from the skin and from each other prior to preservation. However, some of the component filaments have remained in association within each appendage. The authors found it unlikely that single, unbranched, independent, hairlike filaments from independent integumentary structures would have been preserved in groups of overlying filaments of about the same size. Furthermore, "Multiple hairlike filaments from independent integumental structures might remain associated if they were attached to a single piece of skin that sloughed off the body during decomposition," an interpretation Xu *et al.* found improbable given the varying orientation of the disassociated, overlying appendages in IVPP V12811.

As Xu *et al.* noted, the feathers of birds "are characterized by a complex, branched structure of keratinaceous filaments that grow by a unique mechanism from cylindrical feather follicles" (*e.g.*, Lucas and Stettenheim 1972), this structure being the most distinctive morphological feature of feathers. The appendages observed by Xu *et al.* (2001) in *Sinornithosaurus* exhibit — especially notable in appendages disassociated

Life restoration of *Sinornithosaurus milleni* by Berislav Krzic.

to evolving structures required for flight.

Notes: Ji, Norell, Gao, Ji and Dong (2001) described a specimen (NGMC 91) of a feathered theropod dinosaur from the Fanzhangzi quarry in the Yixian Formation, southwest of Lingyuan City. Preserved on a slab (91-A) and counterslab (91-B), the specimen consists of a complete articulated skeleton, the specimen being sprawled out with the head directed toward the right side of its body. Preserved near the left foot of the specimen was the small fish *Lycoptera*.

Ji *et al.* noted that the integrity of the specimen "is assured because both slabs match up exactly and the integumentary articulated covering lies below flakes of rock in several places: it is therefore not painted, scratched into the matrix or otherwise enhanced." The authors noted that, although the bones are very well ossified, the rather large size of the head relative to the body indicates that the specimen probably represents a subadult individual.

Ji *et al.* referred NGMC 91 to the Maniraptora primarily due to the specimen's possession of a large semilunate carpal in the wrist. The presence of elongate bifurcating prezygapophyses and chevrons spanning several vertebrae indicate that the specimen belongs within or is closely related to the Dromeosauridae (see Ostrom 1990).

Comparing NGMC 91 with other taxa, Ji *et al.* found it to be similar to the dromaeosaurid *Sinornithosaurus*, both forms having similar teeth and sharing several characters with the Dromaeosauridae. However, both of these forms, with *Microraptor*, exhibit various features (*e.g.*, nonginglymoid distal articular surfaces of metatarsals, arctometatarsalian metatarsals) that are uncharacteristic of dromaeosaurids. Inevitably, the authors noted, some characters (*e.g.*, the unusual bowed metacarpal) of NGMC 91 may prove to be diagnostic, although they might rather have been affected by ontogeny. Incorporating measurements of NGMC 91 and *Sinornithosaurus* into an allometric model created for *Archaeopteryx* (see paper for details), Ji *et al.* determined that the hindlimbs of the former taxa were substantially longer than the hindlimb of *Archaeopteryx*.

In describing NGMC 91, Ji *et al.* noted that the skull is long and triangular, more so than in any other known dromaeosaurid. The teeth are typically dromaeosaurid, being heavily recurved and strongly serrated, with large blunt denticles distally. The cervical vertebrae are short and amphicoelous, the thoracics

from the body during preservation and deposited around it — two kinds of compound structures comprising multiple filaments, and with two kinds of branching structures that are unique to the feathers of birds: 1. Filaments joined in a basal tuft, and 2. those joined at their bases in series along a central filament. Significantly, the authors found these structures to be indistinguishable from the contour feathers of the holotypes of *Confuciousornis sanctus*, *Eoenantiornis buhler*, and *Changchengornis hengdaoziensis*, unequivocal birds also present at Lioning.

It was the conclusion of Xu *et al.* that the compound filamentous structures and two kinds of feather-like branching in the integumental appendages of *Sinornithosaurus*—a basal member of the Dromaeosauridae, a theropod lineage (with or without Troodontidae) largely regarded as the most closely related to birds)—are most likely homologous with avian feathers. This assessment, the authors noted, was strengthened when combined with the body of existing independent phylogenetic evidence supporting a theropod ancestry of birds (see *D:TE*, *S2*, *S2*). Furthermore, Xu *et al.* (2001) stated, the plesiomorphic feathers of this genus "support the hypothesis that feathers evolved and initially diversified in terrestrial theropod dinosaurs before the origin of birds and flight": also, "feathers evolved filamentous structure, basal branching, and a rachis with barbs" prior

platycoelous. The tail is unusual in that its distal two thirds shows no individual vertebral segments, thus possibly constituting a single rodlike structure or being an artifact of preservation. The furcula is boomerang-shaped and, although smaller, resembles that of *Sinornithosaurus*. The humerus, radius, and ulna are of subequal length, the hand approximately one-third longer than these bones, the forelimb proportions relative to the femur being consistent with other described dromaeosaurids. Quill knobs are not present on the ulna. As subsequently observed by Norell, Ji, Gao, Yuan, Zhao and Wang (2002), NGMC 91 is probably referrable to *Sinornithosaurus*.

According to Ji *et al.*, the discovery of NGMC 91—a theropod possessing feathers but lying outside the Avialae—constitutes "important evidence that the origin of feathers is unrelated to the origin of flight in Avialae."

Key references: Burnham, Derstler, Currie, Bakker, Zhou and Ostrom (2000); Chiappe, Ji, Ji and Norell (1999); Dalton (2000); Elźnowski and Wellnhofer (1996); Feduccia (1999); Gibbons (1997); Ji, Currie, Norell and Ji (1998); Ji, Norell, Gao, Ji and Dong (2001); Jian, Chen and Cao (2000); Jones, Farlow, Ruben, Henderson and Hillenius (2000); Kirkland, Burge and Gaston (1993); Lucas and Stettenheim (1972); Martin and Czerkas (2000); Molnar (1991); Ostrom (1978); Paul (1988c); Rowe and Gauthier (1990); Sereno (1999b); Smith, Harris, Omar, Dodson and You (2001); Walker (1985); Wellnhofer (1992); Xu, Wang and Wu (1999); Xu and Wu (2001); Xu, Zhou and Prum (2001).

†SINOSAUROPTERYX

Saurischia: Eusaurischia: Theropoda: Neotheropoda: Tetanurae: Avetheropoda: ?Coelurosauria: ?Maniraptoriformes.

Diagnosis of genus (as for type species): Small theropod (largest specimen 1.2 meters in length); coelurosaur (defining characters from Holtz 2000 including amphiplatyan cervical centra, boat-shaped distal chevrons, boat-shaped pubic boot, fibula having proximal end 75 percent width of proximal end of tibia, cranio-caudally thin but tall ascending process) having short, powerful front limbs, first digit of manus longer than humerus or radius; powerful proximomedial flange on first metacarpal; differing from *Compsognathus* in having front limb relatively smaller compared to hindlimb (lengths of humerus plus radius divided by sum of femur and tibia lengths about 30 percent, in *Compsognathus longipes* 43 percent) (Currie and Chen 2001).

Comments: The tiny Chinese dinosaur *Sinosauropteryx prima*, usually classified as a compsog-

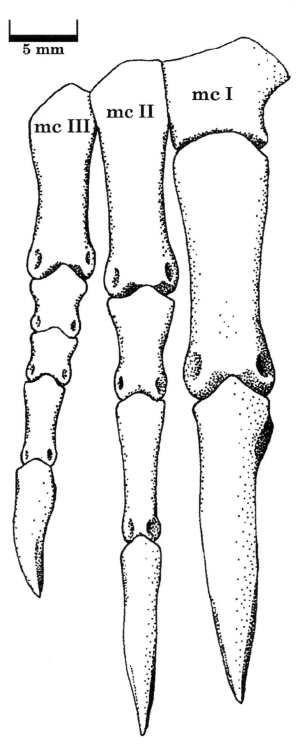

Reconstructed manus of *Sinosauropteryx prima* (juvenile) showing elongated first finger. (After Currie and Chen 2001.)

5 mm

mc III   mc II   mc I

nathid (see below) and currently known from three juvenile specimens—the complete holotype part and counterpart (NGMC 2123 and NIGP 127586) and the nearly complete referred specimens (NIGP 127587 and NGMC 2124; see "Notes" below); (see *S1* for photographs of NIGP 127586 and 127587, *S2* for photographs of NIGP 127586 and 12587)—was fully described by Currie and Chen (2001), who also proposed a revised diagnosis of the genus and species.

Sinosauropteryx

Sinosauropteryx prima (juvenile specimens), a. counterpart of holotype (NIGP 127586) and b. referred (NIGP 127587) specimens. Note: In the latter, the right coracoid has been moved one centimeter closer to the body than preserved in the specimen. (After Currie and Chen 2001.)

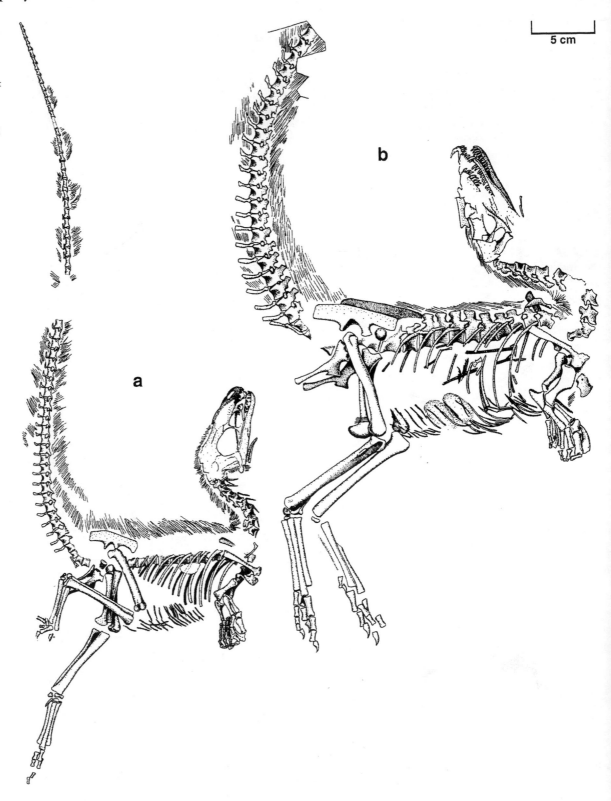

Currie and Chen suggested that differences in preservation might explain the differences between *Sinosauropterx* and the European *Compsognathus*, a very similar genus for which feather-like structures are not known. The Chinese genus, the authors noted, is mainly different in its possession of shorter cervical ribs and a shorter but more robust arm. Another supposed difference is the lack in *Sinosauropteryx* of opisthocoelic cervical centra and caudal transverse processes. As Currie and Chen pointed out, coelurosaurs normally do not possess opisthocoelic cervical vertebrae, but do have caudal transverse processes, this suggesting that better preserved specimens of the European form may display amphiplatyan cervical centra and caudal transverse processes. As to the apparent lack of feather-like structures preserved with *Compsognathus* specimens, they pointed out that the interpretations of possible integumentary structures reported with both *Compsognathus* specimens (see Huene 1901; Bidar, Demay and Thomel 1972) have been questioned (Ostrom 1978). Furthermore, Ostrom's conclusions that *Compsognathus* was not feathered (see *D:TE*, *Compsognathus* entry) was founded upon negative evidence which cannot eliminate the possibility that that genus was also feathered.

Additionally, Currie and Chen pointed out that the reduction or loss of the ischial boot, and the possession of more than 15 caudal vertebrae with transverse processes, have been regarded as synapomorphies of Coelurosauria. However, as both *Sinosauropteryx* and *Compsognathus* have weak expansions at the distal ends of their ischia, and because the former genus has over 15 caudal vertebrae with transverse processes, Currie and Chen proposed that these characters should be transferred from the Coelurosauria to the more restrictive clade Maniraptoriformes (implying that *Sinosauropteryx* and *Compsognathus* are maniraptoriforms). Various other characters used to diagnose Coelurosauria, according to Currie and Chen—*e.g.*, reduction of ischium to 70 percent or less of pubis length, expanded circular orbit—are at least partially size-related.

In a published abstract for a poster, Longrich (2002) submitted a revised systematic study of Theropoda focusing upon the relationships of *Sinosauropteryx*. Longrich's analysis found the Compsognathidae to be a polyphyletic group, with *Compsognathus* identified as a derived coelurosaurian. *Sinosauropteryx* was apparently "found to be an allosaur-grade theropod (*e.g.* quadrangular obturator process, >50 caudals, >15 caudal transverse processes, bifurcate neural spines), perhaps allosaurid or basalmost Coelurosauria." However, apparently not included in this analysis was the small theropod *Aristosuchus* (see entry), regarded by Naish (2002) as a compsognathid.

Regarding *Sinosauropteryx* as the most primitive known theropod possessing feathers, while pointing out that more basal dinosaurs (*e.g.*, *Carnotaurus*, *Ceratosaurus*, sauropods, and ornithischians) bore scales, Longrich suggested that insulatory feathers were apparently a novelty of the Tetanurae. Considering the similarity to *Sinosauropteryx*, Longrich speculated that allosaurids were probably also feathered, while more primitive taxa (*e.g.*, *Torvosaurus*, spinosaurids, and "Yangchuanosauria" [see *Yangchuanosaurus* entry) could have borne either scales or filaments.

Longrich further stated that the dark stains on the tail of *Sinosauropteryx* are too regular to represent an artifact, seemingly corresponding to integumentary pigments (or striping camouflage). This interpretation, according to the author, "supports their identification as insulatory fibers," with stains present dorsally (but not ventrally) "corresponding to countershading camouflage rather than fiber distribution."

All of the collected *Sinosauropteryx* specimens are covered with integumentary structures that have been referred to in the popular press as both "feathers" and "protofeathers" (see *S1* for pro and con interpretations), these structures extending along the caudal half of the skull, then neck, back, hips, and both sides of the tail. These structures, Longrich suggested, probably covered most of the body, as indicated "by the density of the covering dorsal to the body and by the few random patches of integumentary structures that can be seen in other regions of the existing fossils."

Although it had been suggested that feathers originally appeared as display structures (*e.g.*, Mayr 1960), Currie and Chen pointed out that the density, distribution, and relatively short lengths of these structures in *Sinosauropteryx* suggest that they were not used for display. Rather, as both NIGP 127586 and 127587 could represent females, male individuals may have possessed more elaborate integumentary structures for display, and these structures may have been colored for display purposes. Consequently, "the existing *Sinosauropteryx* specimens do not support the hypothesis that feathers evolved primarily for display, but do not disprove it either."

Also, Currie and Chen pointed out, the integumentary structures in *Sinosauropteryx* plainly have no apparent aerodynamic characteristics and, if representing the covering of the ancestors of birds, indicate that feathers evolved for a reason other than flight (*contra*, for example, Parkes 1966). Addressing Feduccia's (1996) argument that feathers are too complex to have developed for reasons other than flight, Currie and Chen explained "that feathers would have been preceded by less complex structures." Indeed, the relatively simple, multibranched structures in *Sinosauropteryx* "are suitable for modification into the more complex structures required for flight."

In considering the hypothesis that *Sinosauropteryx* and other small theropods were endothermic and that feathers in these dinosaurs may have evolved primarily for the retention of body heat, Currie and Chen pointed out that the integumentary structures in the Chinese "compsognathids," therizinosaurids, and dromaeosaurids—while less complex than down feathers and the "hair-like" feathers of secondarily flightless birds—were apparently more complex than mammalian hair; thus, "Their simplicity would not have made them ineffective for insulation when wet,

Sinosauropteryx prima (juvenile specimen), cranial bones: a. right side of rostral part of skull (NIGP 127586), right lateral view; b. right squamosal (NIGP 127586); c. orbital region (NIGP 127587); d. dorsal surface of right nasal (NIGP 127587); f. right quadrate (NIGP 127587); e. scale for c., d., and f. (After Currie and Chen 2001.)

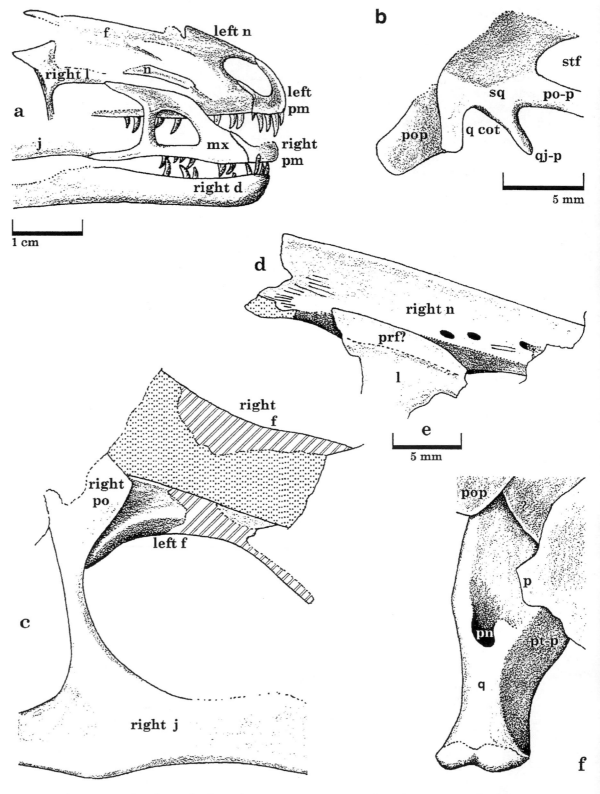

any more than mammalian hair is." The authors concluded that the "the aerodynamic capabilities of bird feathers are not compromised by the previous evolution of less complex protofeathers that had some other function, such as insulation" (see also Padian, Ji and Ji 2001; "Introduction," section on birds; also see below).

Regarding the suggestion by Ruben, Dal Sasso, Geist, Hillenius, Jones and Signore (1999) that liver tissue had been preserved in NIGP 127586 and NGMC 2123 (see *SI*), Currie and Chen pointed out that their paper was published before these authors had seen the specimens and that "the only evidence they had for the presence of a liver was the position and shape of the dark stain that could be seen in the photographs." As demonstrated by Currie and Chen in their description of these specimens, however, the front margin of this stain is actually an artifact. Furthermore, even if the stain represented a real edge, it was unlikely (though conceivable, yet impossible to show) "that the liver would have maintained its position and shape as the specimen decomposed and collapsed into two dimensions."

Indeed, almost since Professor Chen Pei-Ji of the Nanjiung Institute of Geology and Paleontology revealed photographs of the holotype of *Sinosauropteryx prima* at the 1996 meeting of the Society of Vertebrate Paleontology in New York, the integumentary structures preserved on the fossil became a source of interest and controversy, a minority of the scientists investigating it doubting that these structures represented anything having to do with feathers (see S2). Padian *et al.*, in a paper on feathered dinosaurs and the origin of flight, commented on this debate, citing particularly the opinion of Geist, Jones and Ruben (1997), who, based solely on photographs of the holotype specimen, interpreted these structures as frayed collagenous fibers of the midline that had become disturbed after the animal's death.

Padian *et al.* pointed out the following concerning these integumentary structures: First, these structures do not, *contra* Geist *et al.*, occur only on the midline, as this specimen is not seen in perfect lateral view, the dorsal midline of the skull not being contiguous with the specimen's profile. Second, taphonomic factors in the Liaoning, China, deposits have favored, regardless of local anatomy, the preservation of soft-tissue structures along the perimeter of the specimens. However, these structures in the holotype do not occur only along the perimeter, but also in other areas (*e.g.*, side of skull, behind right humerus, in front of right ulna; see Chen, Dong and Zhen 1998). Consequently, Padian *et al.* posited that the interpretation of these integumentary structures as "collagenous fibers from the body midline is simply indefensible."

Comparing the integumentary structures of *Sinosauropteryx* with true feathers, Padian *et al.* noted that the main differences are that 1. "the filaments of *Sinosauropteryx* are finer and denser by almost an order of magnitude," and 2. "there is no central shaft around which the filaments are organized (they do not appear to branch), nor any obvious secondary structures such as barbules." Consequently, these authors brought up the question of why these structures might be identified as the relatively new (and ill-defined) term "protofeathers."

The authors responded by first pointing out that these are integumentary and, therefore, ostensibly epidermal structures—topologically sharing the same position on the body as true feathers, morphologically sharing the same filamentous features, and compositionally appearing to have similar keratinous structure, thereby passing "the tests of similarity that have been operational since Richard Owen synthesized the concept of homology in the 1840s." Additionally, as these structures covered the body, "either feathers evolved from them, or they evolved from similar antecedent structures, or they are completely different and homologous only at a more remote epigenic level." Because feathers are now recognized in other coelurosaurian nonavian lineages, Padian *et al.* accepted the structures in *Sinosauropteryx* as passing "the test of phylogenetic congruence."

Favoring the homology of these integumentary with true feathers, Padian *et al.* enumerated the known facts that 1. these structures are found in *Sinosauropteryx* in the same place as feathers; 2. they have at least some features of feathers (*e.g.*, based on thin, nonbranching, filamentous, high aspect ratio structures); 3. they must have served at least some functions of feathers (*e.g.*, *de facto* insulation, colors providing camouflage, species recognition, *etc.*); and 4. they fit the general expectation of what a simple precursor structure to a feather could have been like. The authors found it unimportant whether or not the integumentary structures of *Sinosauropteryx* are the same as the feathers of extant birds, there being few structures existing with which feathers and these filaments can be compared.

A recent dissenting note regarding the interpretation of the integumentary structures as having to do with feathers was published as an abstract for a poster by Jones, Ruben, Havner and Geist (2002). As these authors stated, the fossilization of feathers "generally involves autolithification of bacteria associated with the decaying feather," the lithified bacteria forming a mold that is subsequently infilled after the feather decays. According to Jones *et al.*, while previous identification of fossil feathers and reputed feather precursors have frequently been based solely on morphology, the presence of fossilized bacteria could allow for a more precise identification of such structures.

Jones *et al.* analyzed, via scanning electron microscopy, integumentary samples from various ornithodiran fossils (including *Sinosauropteryx*, the therizinosauroid *Beipiaosaurus*, and the bird *Confuciusornis*) from the Yixian Formation of Liaoning, to determine the presence or lack thereof of fossilized bacteria. Results of this study, according to Jones *et al.*, were "inconsistent with some previous interpretations of feather precursors in a number or Yixian specimens."

Camera lucida drawings of integumentary structures of *Sinosauropteryx prima* (interpreted by some workers as "protofeathers") holotype counterpart NIGP 127586: a. back of skull at jaw articulation; b. along margin of top of skull; d. over first six caudal vertebrae; e. at base of neck and front of thoracic region; f. above scapula; and g. over distal caudal vertebrae; c. scale for b., d., and e. Cross-hatching indicates broken bone. (After Currie and Chen 2001.)

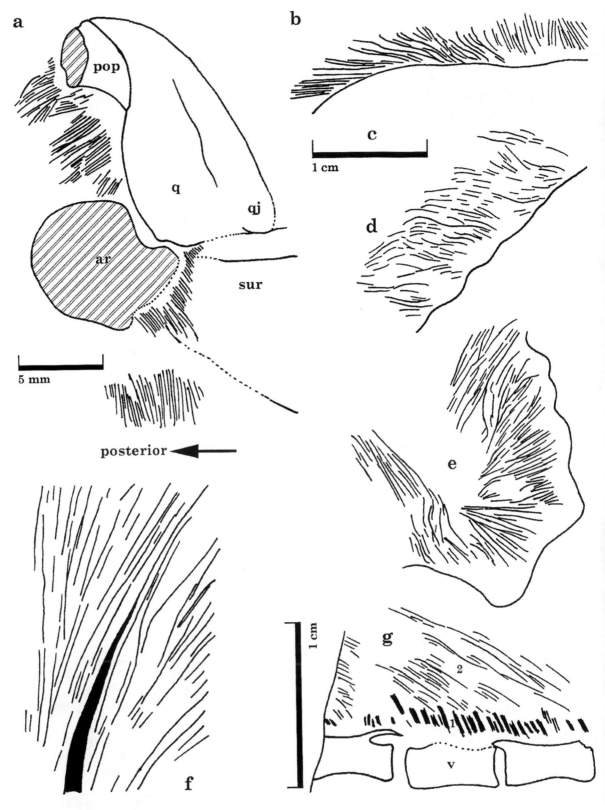

Notes: Ruben *et al.* also claimed to have identified preserved liver tissue in *Scipionyx* (see *S1*), a small theropod from Italy, as well as "diaphragmatic muscles." However, according to Currie and Chen, while the skeleton of *Scipionyx* does preserve evidence of some soft tissues, the vague shape of the alleged "liver" can only be seen via ultraviolet light, and the skeleton had collapsed into two dimensions following decomposition, the preservation of any soft structures retaining their original shapes being unlikely. Furthermore, the alleged "diaphragmatic muscles" are represented by a series of faint stractches "that could be explained in many other ways."

Hwang, Norell and Gao (2002), in an abstract for a poster, briefly reported on a new unusually large, primitive coelurosaur from the Yixian Formation (Jehol Group) at Sihetun, northeastern China, an area from which the known theropods are otherwise quite small. As the authors reported, the specimen, except for part of the missing tail (only the first 25 caudal vertebrae are preserved), is nearly complete and well preserved. Hwang *et al.*'s conservative estimate was that the animal's total length would be approximately 1.6 meters (over 5.6 feet), distinguishing it as second only in size to *Beipiaosaurus* among all known Jehol Group theropods.

From a preliminary study of the specimen, Hwang *et al.* observed the following coelurosaurian characteristics: Manus elongate; chevrons on caudal vertebrae flattened; teeth unserrated on mesial carinae. Most of the theropods from Liaoning are maniraptorans, the authors pointed out; however, this new specimen lacks various typically maniraptoran features.

Hwang *et al.* further also noted the following: Manus elongate, but forelimb just 49 percent length of hindlimb; small semilunate carpal, subequal in size to lateral distal carpal; centra of caudal vertebrae homogeneous in shape, chevrons elongated; distal portion of hindlimb not particularly elongated relative to femur; general proportions very similar to *Sinosauropteryx*, both taxa having long tails, short forelimbs, and relatively short distal hindlimb portions; also sharing with *Sinosauropteryx* dorsal vertebrae having fan-shaped neural spines, limited cranial expansion of pubic foot, robust digit I wider than radius, elongate chevrons along most of tail, and nonossified sternal plates, suggesting a close relationship between these two taxa.

Longrich, in his preliminary report on the systematics of *Sinosauropteryx*, found the specimen NGMC 2124 not to represent that genus, but rather a new coelurosaurian theropod differing from *Sinosauropteryx* in a number of characters, including the following: Neural spines of caudal vertebrae short, simple, chevrons short, expanded, changing shape after caudal 12; caudal centra longer, ?fewer; dorsal vertebrae elongate; tibia and metatarsus elongate; manus gracile, penultimate phalanges elongate, ungual of pollex not enlarged; ilium having strongly arched dorsal margin, large cranial hook, broad pubic peduncle.

In Lonrich's opinion, the affinities of NGMC 2124 seemingly lie with advanced coelurosaurs, possibly basal maniraptorans, perhaps related to *Ornitholestes*, *Coelurus*, or *Compsognathus*.

Key references: Bidar, Demay and Thomel (1972); Chen, Dong and Zhen (1998); Currie and Chen (2001); Feduccia (1996); Geist, Jones and Ruben (1997); Holtz (2000); Huene (1901); Hwang, Norell and Gao (2002); Jones, Ruben, Havner and Geist (2002); Longrich (2002); Mayr (1960); Naish (2002); Ostrom (1978); Padian, Ji and Ji (2001); Parkes (1966); Ruben, Dal Sasso, Geist, Hillenius, Jones and Signore (1999).

SINOVENATOR Xu, Norell, Wang, Makovicky and Wu 2002

Saurischia: Eusaurischia: Theropoda: Neotheropoda: Tetanurae: Avetheropoda: Coelurosauria: Maniraptoriformes: Maniraptora: Metornithes: Paraves: Deinonychosauria: Troodontidae.

Name derivation: Greek *Sinai* = China + Latin *venator* = "hunter."

Type species: *S. changiae* Xu, Norell, Wang, Makovicky and Wu 2002.

Other species: [None.]

Occurrence: Yixian Formation, Liaoning, China.

Age: ?Early to ?Middle Cretaceous (?Barremian or ?Aptian).

Known material; Two partial skeletons.

Holotype: IVPP V12615, partial skull and skeleton.

Diagnosis of genus (as for type species): Troodontid having the following derived characters: straight, vertical rostral margin of antorbital fenestra; frontal having vertical lamina bordering lacrimal; surangular T-shaped in cross section; prominent cnemial crest continuous with fibular crest (Xu, Norell, Wang, Makovicky and Wu 2002).

Comments: Thus far the oldest known theropod genus that can be referred with confidence to the family Troodontidae, *Sinovenator* was founded on a disarticulated partial skeleton recovered from fluvial deposits of the lowest part of the Yixian Formation (recently dated by Jiang, Chen, Cao and Komatsu 2000 as very Late Jurassic, near the Jurassic–Cretaceous boundary, an assessment based on the evidence of various invertebrate faunas; dated as possibly 120 to 125 million years old by Smith, Harris, Omar, Dodson and You 2001, based on radiometric data; as middle Early Cretaceous by Swisher, Wang, Zhou, Wang, Jin, Zhang, Xu, Zhang and Wang 2002, based on $^{40}Ar/^{39}Ar$ dating of the Yixian and Tuchengzi formations), based on radiometric data), at Lujiatun and Yanzigou, Shanyuan, western Liaoning, China. Referred to the type species, *Sinovenator changiae* (see "Note" below), from the same locality, was an incomplete articulated skeleton (IVVP V12583). Found associated with this new dinosaur were the remains of the ceratopsian *Psittacosaurus*, the ornithopod *Jeho-*

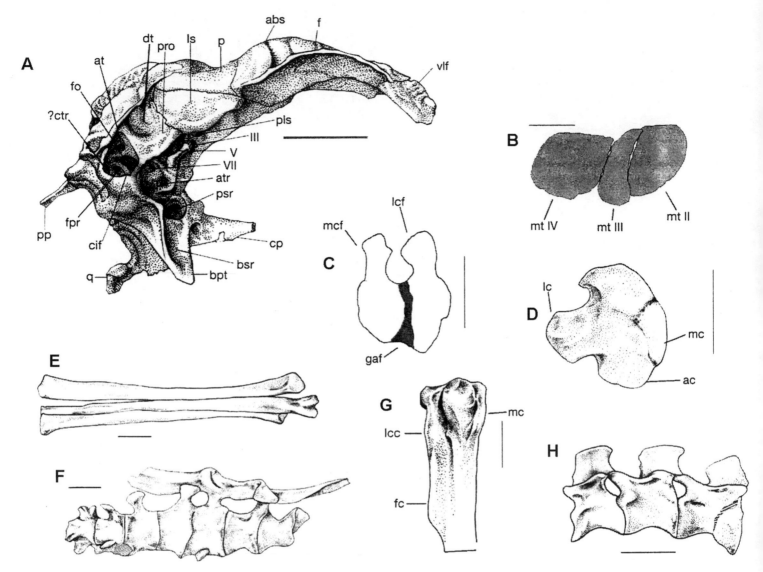

Sinovenator changiae, IVPP 12615, holotype, A. braincase in right lateral view; B. and E., left metatarsus, proximal (B) and (E) cranial views; C. right femur, distal view; D. and G., right tibia, (D) proximal and (G) cranial views; F. sacrum, ventral view; and H. cranial dorsal vertebrae, lateral view. Scale = 1 cm. (After Xu, Norell, Wang, Makovicky and Wu 2002.)

losaurus, and the mammal *Repenomamus* (Xu, Norell, Wang, Makovicky and Wu 2002).

In describing *Sinovenator*, Xu *et al.* noted that this is a small theropod, its length estimated to have been less than one meter (about 3.4 feet). The skull is triangular in side view, the snout shallow, the postorbital region deep and dorsally convex. The supratemporal fenestra is reduced in top view, and the exposed endocast resembles one reconstructed for the bird *Archaeopteryx* (see Chatterjee 1997). Unlike other troodontids, there are five rather than six sacral vertebrae, and the pubis is caudally oriented.

As Xu *et al.* pointed out, the Yixian Formation deposits that yielded the two *Sinovenator* specimens do not preserve soft tissues. Nevertheless, these specimens predate other known coelurosaurs (*e.g.*, *Beipiaosaurus*, *Caudipteryx*, *Protarchaeopteryx*, and *Sinosauropteryx*) that have been preserved with feather-like integumentary structures from beds occurring higher within the same formation.

According to Xu *et al.*, numerous skull features identify *Sinovenator* as a troodontid, these including the following: Naris significantly larger than premaxilla; braincase with oval, taller than wide foramen magnum, shallow "V"-shaped incisure between basal tubera, absence of basisphenoid recess, pit on ventral surface of laterosphenoid; row of foramina located in groove caudally on subtriangular labial surface of dentary.

Other skull and also postcranial features of *Sinovenator*, however, do not appear in more derived troodontids, and more resemble those in dromaeosaurids and avialans: Long, slender caudal process of premaxilla, excluding maxilla from external naris (as in dromaeosaurids and most other theropods, but not other troodontids); jugal with long, slender, caudally oriented postorbital process (as in dromaeosaurids); large fossa adjacent to base of cultriform process (parasphenoid recess) (as in the basal dromaeosaurid *Sinornithosaurus*); denticles apparently absent on mesial

Courtesy Peter J. Makovicky.

teeth, small on maxillary teeth (as in dromaeosaurids); middle sacral vertebrae wider than cranial and caudal sacral vertebrae (as in the basal dromaeosaurid *Microraptor*); glenoid fossa facing laterally, scapula and coracoid forming less than 90-degree angle in side view (similar to dromaeosaurids and other derived maniraptorans); ilium small, less than 60 percent femora length (as in *Archaeopteryx* and *Sinornithosaurus*); pubic peduncle deep, wide, slightly caudally oriented (as in *Archaeopteryx* and some dromaeosaurids); ischium small, obturator process distally positioned, posterodorsal and posteroventral processes present (as in some advanced maniraptorans and basal birds); metatarsus very similar to *Sinor-* *nithosaurus* and *Microraptor* (although metatarsal II is markedly short and slender, as in troodontids); foot more closely resembling subarctometatarsalian condition found in *Sinornithosaurus* than nonarctometatarsalian condition.

Via phylogenetic analysis, Xu *et al.* found *Sinovenator*— a theropod presenting both the above-mentioned troodontid and nontroodontid features — to be the most basal known member of the Troodontidae, while Troodontidae and Dromaeosauridae are sister taxa within the monophyletic clade Deinonychosauria, which, in turn, is the sister taxon of Avialae (as shown in some earlier analyses). As the authors pointed out, *Sinovenator* is significant as the most primitive member of Troodontidae, resetting character polarities at the base of this clade. Also, the discovery of *S. changiae* enriches what is known of the transition of various osteological characters to the conditions in birds, most importantly the laterally projected glenoid of the scapulocoracoid and the opisthopubic pelvis, the former now regarded as diagnostic of Paraves, the latter diagnostic of the more inclusive clade Metornithes (see "Systematics" chapter).

Note: The type species was named *Sinovenator changii* by Xu *et al.*; however, as independently pointed out by David Marjanovic and Ben Creisler (personal communication to G. Olshevsky, 2002), the specific name, as it honors a woman (Meeman Chang of the Institute of Vertebrate Paleontology and Paleoanthropology, Academia Sinica), must be revised to *S. changiae*.

Key references: Chatterjee (1997); Smith, Harris, Omar, Dodson and You (2001); Xu, Norell, Wang, Makovicky and Wu (2002).

SPHAEROTHOLUS Williamson and Carr 2003
Ornithischia: Genasauria: Cerapoda: Marginocephalia: Pachycepalosauria: Pachycephalosauridae.
Name derivation: Greek *spaira* = "ball" + Greek *tholos* = "dome."
Type species: *S. goodwini* Williamson and Carr 2003.
Other species: *S. buchholtzae* (Brown and Schlaikjer 1943).
Occurrence: Kirtland Formation, New Mexico, Hell Creek Formation, Montana, United States.
Age: Late Cretaceous (Campanian).
Known material: Two or three partial skulls.
Holotype: NMMNH P-27403, partial skull lacking facial and palatal bones, including almost complete frontoparietal, right supraorbital 2 (posterior supraorbital *sensu* Sereno 2000), right postorbital, right squamosal, much of basicranium.

Diagnosis of genus: Differs from all other known pachycephalosaurids in possession of parietosquamosal bar that decreases in depth laterally (in caudal aspect), bordered by single row of nodes and one lateroventral corner node (Williamson and Carr 2003).

Diagnosis of *S. goodwini*: Parietosquamosal bar (in caudal aspect) reducing in depth laterally, to lesser extent than in *S. buchholtzae*, parietal reduce to thin slip between squamosals (Williamson and Carr 2003).

Diagnosis of *S. buchholtzae*: Parietal (in caudal aspect) widely exposed between squamosals, wide enough to bear parietosquamosal nodes, caudal margin of parietosquamosal shelf shallowing to greater degree than in *S. goodwini*, lateral corner node reduced in size relative to *S. goodwini* and located above ventral margin of parietosquamosal bar, nodes in lateral margin of parietosquamosal shelf reduced on squamosal and coalesce into ridge on postorbital (Williamson and Carr 2003).

Comments: The new genus and species *Sphaerotholus goodwini* was founded upon a partial skull (NMMNH P-27403) collected from the De-na-zin Member of the Kirtland Formation, within the Bisti/De-na-zin Wilderness Area, San Juan County, San Juan Basin, New Mexico.

Williamson and Carr tentatively referred to the type species, as cf. *Sphaerotholus goodwini*, a nearly complete dentary, a squamosal fragment, and an additional skull fragment (NMMNH P-30068) from the Farmington Member of the Kirtland Formation, at Pinabete Arroyo, in San Juan County, on lands of the Navajo Nation, San Juan Basin, New Mexico. This specimen, the authors stated, had been collected illegally by persons unknown (see Archer and Babiarz 1992), found in association with a partial skeleton of the theropod *Daspletosaurus* (Carr and Williamson 1999). Considering the rarity of pachycephalosaurian material from the Kirtland Formation and the close association of the elements, Williamson and Carr assumed that they belong to a single individual.

The authors tentatively referred NMMNH P-30068 to the type species "based on the presence of a single row of discrete and subconical nodes on the lateral margins of the parietosquamosal shelf preserved on the squamosal fragment." They cautioned, however, that although *S. goodwini* is the only North American pachycephalosaurian possessing a single row of nodes at that location, this character could be plesiomorphic for domed pachycephalosaurians.

Williamson and Carr also described a second species of *Sphaerotholus*, *S. buchholtzae*, based upon a partial skull (RTMP 87.113.3) collected by Emily A. Giffin (now Buchholtz) from the upper part of the Hell Creek Formation, in western Carter County, Montana.

This specimen was originally assigned by Giffin (1989) to a referred species of *Stegoceras*, *S. edmontonense* (Brown and Schlaikjer 1943), after which Sullivan (2000*a*) referred *S. edmontonese*, including RTMP 87.113.3, to a newly erected species of the Mongolian genus *Prenocephale*, which Sullivan named *Prenocephale edmontonensis* (see *Prenocephale* entry, S2).

However, as Williamson and Carr pointed out, many of the characters used by Sullivan to diagnose *P. edmontonensis* came not from the holotype material (CMN [formerly GSC and NMC] 8830) but rather from RTMP 87.113.3. The holotype, originally referred by Brown and Schlaikjer to *Troödon edmontonensis*, and also the paratypes (CMN 8831 and 8832), consist of complete frontoparietal domes lacking the prominent frontonasal boss bordered by

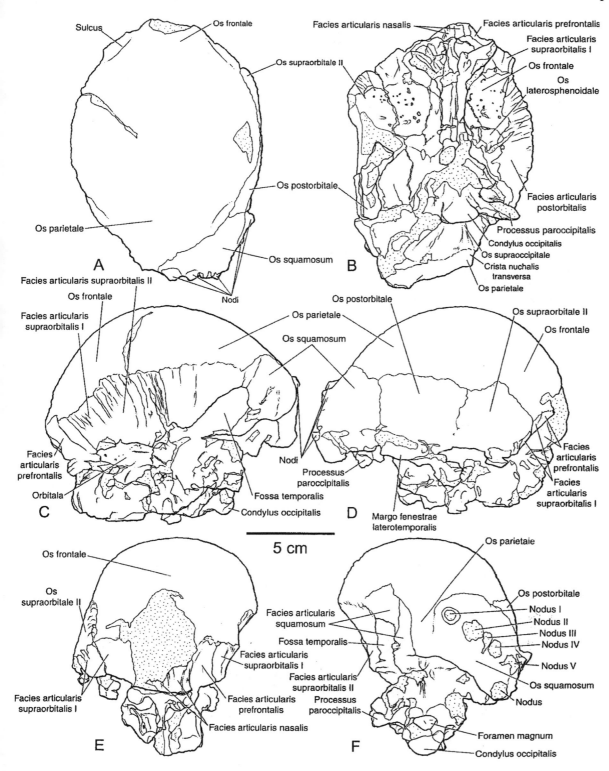

Sphaerotholus goodwini, NMMNH P-27403, holotype partial skull in A. dorsal, B. ventral, C. left lateral, D. right lateral, E. rostral, and F. caudal views. (After Williamson and Carr 2003.)

grooves, an autapomorphy for *Stegoceras* (see entry), a low frontoparietal boss being plesiomorphic for pachycephalosaurids. Furthermore, both CMN 8830 and 8831 exhibit various features (*e.g.*, caudodorsally inclined temporal chambers, relatively smooth transition caudally between dome and parietosquamosal shelf, relatively small paired nodes near parietosquamosal contacts at caudal margin of parietosquamosal shelf) shared among such pachycephalosaurines as *Prenocephale*, *Tylocephale*, and *Sphaerotholus buchholtzae*. As these specimens do not include characters allowing for their confident referral to any of those taxa, Williamson and Carr regarded *E. edmontonense* as a *nomen dubium*. Moreover, they tentatively referred this material to cf. *Sphaerotholus* sp., regarding "it much more likely that they represent a North

American taxon that is in close temporal and geographic proximity rather than an Asian pachycephalosaur" (*contra* Sullivan).

Williamson and Carr tentatively referred to *Sphaerotholus* sp. a frontoparietal (LACM 64000) from the Hell Creek Formation of Montana, this specimen having been referred by Sullivan to *P. edmontonensis*. As observed by Williamson and Carr, this specimen closely resembles frontoparietals previously referred to *Stegoceras edmontonense* and also that of *S. buchholtzae*. The authors noted that an additional Hell Creek specimen (LACM 15345), lacking any generically diagnostic characters, represents an indeterminate pachycephalosaurid.

Performing a phylogenetic analysis, Williamson and Carr found *Stegoceras* to be the sister taxon to all other domed pachycephalosaurians, with derived pachycephalosaurids comprising two principal clades — *Stygimoloch*, *Pachycephalosaurus*, and *Sphaerotholus*, and a lineage including the Asian forms *Tylocephale* and *Prenocephale*.

Note: Williamson and Carr also described a nearly complete pachycephalosaurian frontoparietal dome (NMMNH P-30067), collected in 1999 by Paul Sealey from Hunter Wash, Hunter Wash Member of the Kirtland Formation, in the Bisti/De-na-zin Wilderness Area, San Juan County, New Mexico. Not complete enough for generic identification, the authors referred this specimen to Pachycephalosauridae

incertae sedis. The presence of an open dorsotemporal fenestra suggested to Williamson and Carr that NMMNH O-30067 represents a subadult individual, this opening in domed pachycephalosaurs closing during ontogeny (see *Stegoceras* entry).

Key references: Archer and Babiarz (1992); Brown and Schlaikjer (1943); Carr and Williamson (1999); Giffin (1989); Sereno (2000); Sullivan (2000*a*); Williamson and Carr (2003).

†SPINOSAURUS — (=?*Irritator*)

Saurischia: Eusaurischia: Theropoda: Neotheropoda: Tetanurae: Avetheropoda: Spinosauroidea: Spinosauridae: Spinosaurinae.

Comments: A new specimen of the rare dinosaur *Spinosaurus* was described by Buffetaut and Ouaja (2002). The fragmentary specimen, found largely encrusted in limonitic limestone, consists of an incomplete dentary (paleontological collection of the Office National des Mines, Tunis, number BM231) recovered as a surface find from the summit of the Jebel Miteur hill (part of the Dahar escarpment; the top of Jebel Miteur formed by a bonebed corresponding to the lower part of the Chenini Sandstones, the lower member of the Ain el Guettar Formation; see Barale, Philippe, Tayech-Mannai and Zarbout 1997), in the Middle Cretaceous (early Albian) of Tataouine Governorate, in southern Tunisia. Other vertebrate

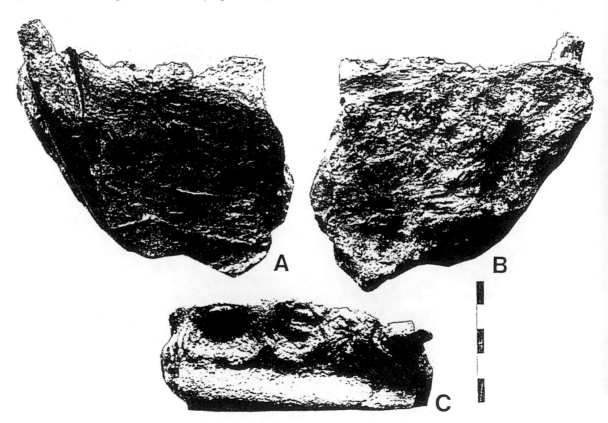

Jaw fragment (paleontological collection of the Office National des Mines, Tunis, number BM231) referred to *Spinosaurus* cf. *aegyptiacus*. Scale = 50 millimeters. (After Buffetaut and Ouaja 2002.)

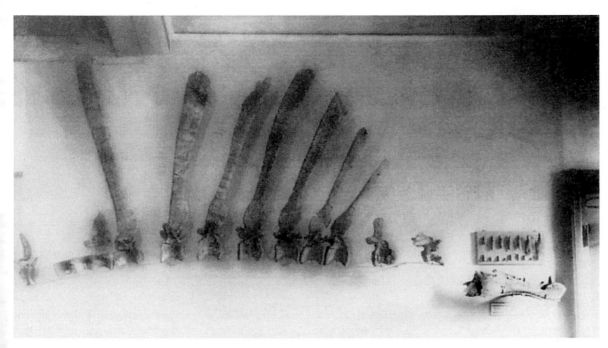

Photograph courtesy Helmut Mayr, Paläontologische Museum, Bayerisch Staatssammlung für Paläontologie und Geologie, Munich, Germany. Photograph restoration by Pete Von Sholly.

Holotype partial skeleton of *Spinosaurus aegypticacus* as mounted by paleontologist Ernst Stromer at the Alte Akademie, home of the Bavarian State Collection of Paleontology and Historical Geology, Munich, a building destroyed during World War II (April 1944) by Allied bombers. For information on Stromer and his collection, see *The Lost Dinosaurs of Egypt*, by William Nothdurft (2002), with Josh Smith, Matt Lamanna, Ken Lacovara, Jason Poole, and Jen Smith.

material found at this bonebed include teeth referred to the theropods *Carcharodontosaurus* and *Spinosaurus*, sauropod bones, shark teeth, lungfish toothplates, *Lepidotes*-like teeth and scales, and crocodilian teeth.

The specimen, as described by Buffetaut and Ouaja, consists of the rostral portion of a left dentary, measures 155 millimeters in length, and contains four alveoli as preserved.

In comparing this specimen with other spinosaurids (*e.g.*, the Egyptian *Spinosaurus aegyptiacus* and the British *Baryonyyx walkeri*), Buffetaut and Ouaja found it to compare most favorably with the former, not differing from that species in any significant way at least as far as the mandible is concerned; but it is clearly different from the latter. Thus, agreeing with Sereno, Beck, Dutheil, Gado, Larsson, Lyon, Marcot, Rauhut, Sadleir, Sidor, Varricchio, Wilson and Wilson (1998) that there is but one valid species of *Spinosaurus*, Buffetaut and Ouaja referred the jaw to *Spinosaurus* cf. *aegyptiacus*. However, the authors noted, the Tunesian specimen seems to represent a smaller individual than the holotype of *S. aegyptiacus*, possibly having a tooth row length of about 460 millimeters (520 millimeters in the Egyptian specimen).

This recent find is significant, Buffetaut and Ouaja pointed out, in confirming the presence of the genus *Spinosaurus* in the Albian of Tunisia. In reviewing the known spinosaurids of Africa, and accepting the two subfamilies Baryonychinae and Spinosaurinae as valid, the authors noted that baryonychines are known only from rocks of Aptian age, while spinosaurines are known only from those of Albian and Cenomanian age. This could suggest the replacement of the Baryonychinae by the Spinosaurinae during the

Aptian–Albian transition, perhaps as part of a more general faunal change occurring at the same time. Because spinosaurines seem to be more derived than baryonychines, the authors suggested, "an ancestor-descendant relationship between *Spinosaurus* and an earlier baryonychine cannot be excluded," while alternatives to Sereno *et al.*'s proposed vicariance scenario may be suggested.

Key references: Buffetaut and Ouaja (2002); Sereno, Beck, Dutheil, Gado, Larsson, Lyon, Marcot, Rauhut, Sadleir, Sidor, Varricchio, Wilson and Wilson (1998)

†STAURIKOSAURUS

Saurischia: Eusaurischia: Herrerasauridae: ?Theropoda.

Comments: *Staurikosaurus* is a very primitive bipedal dinosaur from the upper part of the Santa Maria Formation (Middle–Upper Triassic) of Brazil (see *D:TE*). Galton (2001a), addressing the question of whether or not the primitive type species *Staurikosaurus pricei* can be distinguished as the earliest saurischian, noted the following:

Previous workers (*e.g.*, Novas 1992a, 1996a) have demonstrated that *S. pricei* belongs in the family Herrerasauridae, a group that is regarded by most (but not all) workers as dinosaurian and probably belonging to the saurischian clade Theropoda. As Galton pointed out, *Staurikosaurus* retains a number of primitive characters (*e.g.*, subcircular distal end of tibia, proximally located deltopectoral crest on humerus [if that element is correctly identified], axially unshortened neural spine to first sacral vertebra, scapular spine [not present in *Herrerasaurus*] not strongly reduced distally [if distal end is correctly identified]). The femur, however, is more derived than in *Herrerasaurus* in various features (*e.g.*, loss of trochanteric shelf, reduction of lesser trochanter), thereby being more similar to the femora of many prosauropods. The possession by *Staurikosaurus* of two sacral vertebrae is a plesiomorphic character for Dinosauria, also known in other herrerasaurids, in some primitive prosauropods (*e.g.*, *Sellosaurus gracilis*, *Saturnalia*, and *Riojasaurus*) and in *Eoraptor*.

Bonaparte (1982) considered the Rhynchocephalian Assemblage of the Santa Maria Formation to be older, probably, than the Ischigualasto Formation of Argentina, from which *Herrerasaurus* is known. Therefore, Galton stated, if Herrerasauridae is correctly referred to the Dinosauria (see, for example, Sereno and Novas 1993; Novas 1994, 1996*a*; Hunt 1996), then *Staurikosaurus*, as well as other dinosaurs from the same assemblage, including *Guabisaurus* and very early prosauropods (*Saturnalia*; also an unnamed prosauropod having a *Massospondylus*-like skull, see Kellner, Azevedo, Rosa, Boelter and Leal 1999), then these probably constitute the earliest dinosaurs (?early late Carnian) yet described from the Americas.

Recently, Flynn, Parrish, Rakotosamimanana, Simpson, Whatley and Wyss (1999) described prosauropod jaw specimens from the early Carnian (Upper Triassic) of Madagascar, these remains heralded as the earliest records for dinosaurs, the animals having coexisted with dicynodonts and rhynchosaurs (see *S2*). As pointed out by Galton, however, dicynodonts and rhynchosaurs are also found in the Santa Maria Formation. Furthermore, a partial prosauropod femur collected from the equivalent of the Molteno Formation (?lower Carnian; see Anderson and Anderson 1984) in Zimbabwe coexists with the rhynchosaur *Hyperodapedon* and, consequently, could be the same age. As the Molteno Formation underlies the Elliot Formation (Upper Triassic: upper Carnian or lower Norian; see Hancox 2000) in South Africa, Galton noted that the femur from Zimbabwe — as well as the dinosaurs from the upper part of the Santa Maria Formation of Brazil, the Ischigualasto Formation of Argentina, and the Upper Triassic of Madagascar — predate the dinosaurian fauna (*Blikanasaurus*, *Euskelosaurus*, and *Melanorosaurus*) from the Lower Elliot Formation (Upper Triassic: upper Carnian or lower Norian; see Hancox 2000) of South Africa (see Galton and van Heerden 1998).

Note: In another study, Heckert and Lucas (2000), while noting the great antiquity of *Staurikosaurus*, *Herrerasaurus*, and *Eoraptor*, noted that probably theropods of early late Carnian (Otischalkian) age, including fragmentary remains published by Hunt and Lucas (1994) and Lucas (1994), from the Chinle Group of New Mexico, and perhaps *Alwalkeria* from the Maleri Formation of India, are older, based on the occurrence of the phytosaur *Paleorhinus*.

Key references: Bonaparte (1982); Flynn, Parrish, Rakotosamimanana, Simpson, Whatley and Wyss (1999); Galton (2001*a*); Galton and Van Heerden (1998); Heckert and Lucas (2000); Hunt and Lucas (1994); Hunt (1994, 1996); Novas (1992*a*, 1994, 1996); Sereno and Novas (1993).

†STEGOCERAS — (=*Gravitholus*)

Type species: *S. validum* Lambe 1902.
Other species: *S. breve* Lambe 1918.

Comments: *Stegoceras* remains the best of all known "dome-headed" taxa, thanks to the number of specimens that have been referred to this genus.

Recently, pachycephalosaur specialist Robert M. Sullivan (2000*a*) referred the Canadian type species *Ornatotholus browni* to the type species *Stegoceras validum*, suggesting that the differences between the former "flat-headed" and latter "dome headed" forms might be sexually dimorphic. This synonymy had already been suggested by Goodwin, Buchholtz and Johnson (1998); later, Willaimson and Carr (2003) also suggested but could not demonstrate that the holotype (AMNH 5450) of *O. browni* could represent a juvenile of *S. validum* (see below).

Sullivan (2000*b*) later referred two species of the North American genus *Stegoceras*—*S. edmontonense* and *S. breve*— to the Asian genus *Prenocephale* as two new species, *Prenocephale edmontonensis* and *P. brevis* (see *S2*; also, see below).

In their paper describing the new pachycephalosaurian genus *Sphaerolothus* (see entry), Williamson and Carr (2003) discussed two taxa having bearing on the genus *Stegoceras*:

Stegoceras breve was originally described by Lambe (1918); as stated above, Sullivan (2000*b*) referred this species to *Prenocephale brevis*. Williamson and Carr, however, found this species — known only from a few frontoparietal specimens from the Judith River Group of southern Alberta — to be the most basal member of the genus *Stegoceras*, based upon their common possession of grooves in the frontal above the orbit. Comparatively small (frontoparietal lengths ranging from 57 to 72 millimeters; see Sullivan 2000*a*), showing distinct sutural contacts between the frontal and parietal, and also distinct sutural contacts between the parietals. These specimens, as Williamson and Carr noted, seem to represent subadults.

Also reevaluated by Williamson and Carr was the genus *Gravitholus* and its two species, *G. albertae* (the type species) and *G. sternbergi*. Sullivan (2000*b*) believed that *Stegoceras sternbergi*, described by Brown and Schlaikjer (1943) based on a frontoparietal from the Judith River Group of southern Alberta, and *Gravitholus albertae*, described by Wall and Galton (1979) based on a partial skull from the Judith River group of southern Alberta, were conspecific (see *D:TE*). As observed by Williamson and Carr, *Gravitholus* and *Stegoceras* share the unambiguous common possession of grooves in the frontal. They also share the ambiguous possession, under ACCTRAN, of various features (*e.g.*, parietals widely exposed between squamosals in caudal view, laterally deep parietosquamosal bar, postorbital extending far dorsal to second supraorbital, and under DELTRAN, another (horizontal adductor chamber ceiling). Furthermore, the two genera share the unambiguous possession of various other features (*e.g.*, dome pear-shaped in dorsal view, high, strongly convex nasofrontal boss, caudal margin of dome perpendicular to parietosmosal shelf). As the relationship of *Gravitholus* and *Stegoceras validum* did not receive character support under either optimization, Williamson and Carr regarded *G. albertae* as a *nomen dubium* referable to *Stegoceras* sp.

Williamson and Carr noted that the species *Gravitholus albertae* was diagnosed by Wall and Galton by its very wide dome. However, as Williamson and Carr pointed out, this width is due in part to the incorporation of the postorbital bar into the dome of the only two known specimens, a state apparently not recognized by Wall and Galton (see Sullivan 2000*a*). This species was also referred by Williamson and Carr to *Stegoceras* sp.

Williamson and Carr also identified as *Stegoceras* UCMP 130051, a partial skull (found to be indeterminate by Goodwin 1990) from the Judith River Formation, on the south bank of the Milk River, Super Coulee, in Hill County, Montana. As these authors noted, this specimen unambiguously shares with *Stegoceras* the feature of grooves on the frontal. Ambiguously, it shares with *Stegoceras*, under ACCTRAN, parietals widely separated between the squamosals in caudal view and absence of rostral nodes, and, under DELTRAN, a horizontal ceiling of the adductor chamber. Furthermore, UCMP 130051 and *Stegoceras* are united based upon a number of features (*e.g.*, pear-shaped boss, postorbital extending far dorsal to second supraorbital, caudal margin of dome blending with parietosquamosal shelf along curve).

Williamson and Carr considered three other related specimens, all of which they regarded as Pachycephalosauridae *incertae sedis*:

Those authors identified as Pachycephalosauridae *incertae sedis* CMN 8830 the holotype of *Stegoceras edmontonensis*, a frontoparietal recovered from the Horseshoe Canyon Formation, Red Deer River, Alberta. Cladistic analysis by the authors failed to resolve the identity of this specimen, but found Sullivan's (2000*a*) referral of it to *Prenocephale* to be unwarranted. Furthermore, Williamson and Carr found CMN 8830 to be undiagnostic, its distinctive features being plesiomorphic, the taxon a *nomen dubium*.

Next considered was AMNH 5450, the holotype of *Ornatotholus browni*, a frontoparietal from the "Belly River Formation" [=Oldman Formation], Red Deer River, Alberta. Cladistic analysis by Williamson and Carr found this specimen to be positioned as the sister taxon of Pachyephalosauridae, a result consistent with their interpretation of the specimen representing an indeterminate juvenile pachycephalosaur.

Finally, SMP VP-1084, a partial skull from the Den-na-zin Member of the Kirtland Formation, San Juan Basin, Mew Mexico, was discussed by Williamson and Carr. Sullivan's (2000*a*) referral of this specimen to *Prenocephale* was not supported by Williamson and Carr's character analysis, their only conclusion being that SMP VP-1084 did not enter the clades of *Stygimoloch* plus *Pachycephalosaurus* and *Stegoceras*.

Williamson and Carr postulated that, "under DELTRAN optimization, the most recent common ancestor of the Pachycephalosaurias "occurs in Eurasia and the evolution of the group is marked by the dispersal of the recent common ancestor of *Stegoceras* and that of the clade of *Stygimoloch* + *Pachycephalosaurus*, and *Sphaerotholus* into western North America prior to the late Campanian." Under ACCTRAN, however, "the most recent common ancestor of Pachycephalosauridae dispersed into North America, followed by dispersal of the *Tylocephale* + *Prenocephale* clade into Asia by the late Campanian," this scenario indicating diversification of pachycephalosaurids in North America prior to the late Campanian.

Under both DELTRAN and ACCTRAN optimizations, the authors stated, diversal events had taken place by late Campanian times. As noted earlier by Williamson and Carr (2001) in an abstract, the first appearance in North America of the Pachycephalosauria during late Albian times suggests that the initial dispersal (presumably across Beingia) took place during low-seasonal stands before the Cenomanian global rise in sea level. Also, with *Ornatotholus* regarded as a juvenile pachycephalosaurid, the authors saw no evidence of North American "flat-headed" forms.

Williamson and Carr (2003) pointed out that, as the majority of pachycephalosaurian specimens consist only of isolated frontoparietals, most taxa have been established just on that part of the skull, usually distinguished by differences in dome shape, the degree of closure of the dorsotemporal fenestra, and differences in ornamentation, particularly that on the parietosquamosal shelf. Hence, recognizing diagnostic and phylogenetically useful characters in this group of dinosaurs mostly involves understanding dome variability and cranial ornamentation. From a hypothetical growth series of *Stegoceras validum*, Williamson and Carr (2003) proposed "that dome development, closure of the dorsotemporal fenestrae, and modified cranial ornamentation are congruent ontogenetic phenomena." The authors offered the following possible allometric scenario:

1. The skull roof of the "juvenile" *Stegoceras* was hypothesized by Williamson and Carr (2003) as "characterized by a flat or slightly thickened frontoparietal roof, open and large dorsotemporal fenestrae, and unreduced parietosquamosal shelf" (see Sereno 2000), this hypothetical growth stage possibly represented by the holotype of "*Ornatotholus*" *browni* (=*Stegoceras validum*). The authors observed that the dorsal skull roof of this specimen "is studded with closely-spaced, tubercular ornamentation." These low and rounded tubercles have swollen heads that "sometimes tend to be weakly elongated or coalesced with adjoining nodes," forming linear ridges. The tubercles cover the dorsal surface of both the frontoparietal and marginal roofing bones. The frontoparietal suture, lying within a deeper transverse groove, is open.

2. The domes of "subadult" individuals "are mound-like and incorporate the frontals and rostral portion of the parietals." The caudal portion of both the parietal and marginal skull-roofing bones is flat, retaining a prominent parietosquamosal shelf. Although open, the dorsotemporal fenestrae can show asymmetry in their size. Closure of the frontoparietal suture varies at this stage. Williamson and Carr (2003) postulated that as the dome expands during ontogeny, the nodes are "stretched" over the dorsal surface of the dome and are almost obliterated. The authors suggested that, in *Stegoceras* and other pachycephalosaurian dinosaurs, the nodes at the margin of the parietosquamosal shelf are actually hypertrophied tubercular nodes. The caudal and lateral margins of subadult and adult skulls are ornamented by comparatively unmodified tubercles. Before becoming more fully incorporated into the enlarging dome, each marginal roofing bone — particularly the lacrimals, prefrontals, supraoccipitals, and squamosals — becomes swollen, their expansion resulting in deep pits at the junctures between these bones and the frontoparietals.

3. The "adult" development stage "is grossly expanded into a broad convex dome that incorporates most of the parietosquamosal shelf," the latter having been reduced to a thick lip overhanging the occiput, the dorsotemporal fenestrae being closed. *Contra* Sullivan (2000*a*), Williamson and Carr (2003) found that suture closure between the frontoparietal and marginal roofing bones is apparently variable in subadults and adults, thereby not being reliable as a growth stage criterion.

From this ontogenetic series, Williamson and Carr (2003) concluded "that dome development, state of the dorsotemporal fenestrae, size of parietosquamosal shelf, and state of the frontoparietal suture are not phylogenetically or taxonomically informative among derived pachycephalosaurians." Consequently, a well-developed squamosal shelf and open dorsotemporal fenestra should not be used as criteria in diagnosing *Stegoceras*, as these features are not found in adults of this genus. However, various other skull roof features — *e.g.*, shape of dome and frontal boss, details of ornamentation, slope of parietosquamosal shelf in caudal aspect, length of nasal process of frontal, others — are phylogenetically informative.

Key references: Brown and Schlaikjer (1943); Goodwin (1990); Goodwin, Buchholtz and Johnson (1998); Lambe (1902, 1918); Sereno (2000); Sullivan (2000*a*, 2000*b*); Wall and Galton (1979); Williamson and Carr (2001, 2003).

†**STEGOSAURUS**

Ornithischia: Genasaura: Thyreophora: Eurypoda: Stegosauria: Stegosauridae.

Type species: *S. armatus* Marsh 1877.

Other species: *S. ungulatus* Marsh 1879, ?*S. affinis* Marsh 1887 [*nomen dubium*], *S. stenops* Marsh 1887, *S. longispinus* Gilmore 1914.

Comments: In 1877, North American paleontologist Othniel Charles Marsh named and described the genus *Stegosaurus*, a dinosaur well known today for its two alternating rows of dermal plates surmounting its neck, back, and the proximal part of the tail, and the paired tail spikes. The holotype of the type species *Stegosaurus armatus* was a partial skeleton (YPM 1850) that, to date, has not yet been fully prepared or described (see *D:TE*).

After more than one and a quarter a century, however, progress is finally being made in getting this elusive specimen available for study. In a detailed paper including a reconstructed chronology of late 19th to early twentieth century discoveries, recoveries, and interpretations of *Stegosaurus* specimens, Carpenter and Galton (2001) related how the type specimen of *S. armatus* is, at last, undergoing full preparation at the Morrison Museum of Natural History in Morrison, Colorado. As reported by these authors (who published the first photographs of YPM 1850), the specimen seems to comprise only the caudal portion of the skeleton. Although not enough of the

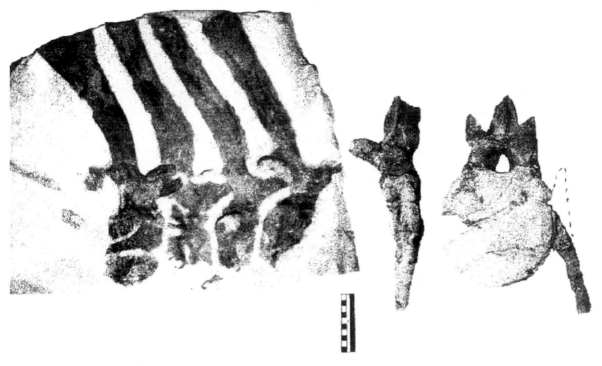

Stegosaurus armatus, YPM 1850, holotype proximal caudal vertebrae in right lateral view, preserved in sandstone, and proximal caudal vertebra in (left) left lateral and (right) proximal views. Scale = 10 cm. (After Carpenter and Galton 2001).

Stegosaurus armatus, YPM 1850, holotype (left) neural spines of proximal caudal vertebrae in right lateral view, preserved in sandstone, (right) proximal middle caudal centra, preserved with chevrons in two blocks, and (bottom) distal middle caudal vertebrae as preserved. Scale = 10 cm. (After Carpenter and Galton 2001.)

specimen, to date of their writing, has been prepared to allow a full diagnosis, enough have been noted to confirm its generic identify (*e.g.*, tall neural spines with laterally expanded summits on proximal caudals; dorsoventrally expanded caudal ribs on cranial caudals; proximodistally short cranial caudal centra; and very large dermal plate).

However, the main focus of Carpenter and Galton's study was the referred species *Stegosaurus ungulatus*, which Marsh named and described in 1879. Tra-

ditionally, one of the diagnostic features of *U. ungulatus* has been its presumed possession of four spikes, as opposed to the standard two of other species. Indeed, Marsh's (1891) first published skeletal reconstruction of *Stegosaurus* (the species *S. ungulatus*) depicts its skeleton, the authors noted, as "a large, elephantine animal with a paired row of plates along its back, a single row on its tail, and four pairs of spikes on the end of its tail." In 1910, the skeleton of *S. ungulatus* was mounted at the Peabody Museum of

Photograph by Kenneth Carpenter.

Photograph by Kenneth Carpenter.

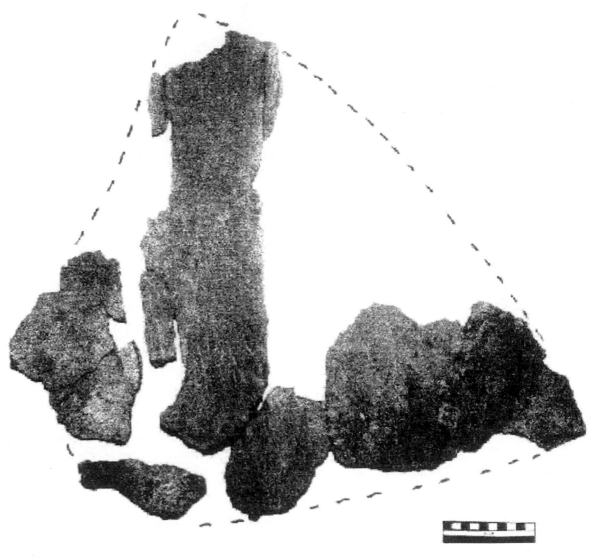

Stegosaurus armatus, YPM 1850, holotype fragments of a large dermal plate (based on other *Stegosaurus* specimens and its size, possibly from the pelvic region). Scale = 10 cm. (After Carpenter and Galton 2001.)

Natural History (see Carpenter and Galton for additional recently published photographs). The original mount, a composite of supposedly the holotype and referred material, showed an animal with disproportionately long legs, a rather short tail, two rows of paired plates, and four pairs of tail spikes.

For almost a century, this skeletal mount has been a source of interest and mystery, as has been the eight spikes surmounting its tail. However, there has never been any compelling evidence in the paleontological literature demonstrating the presence of eight spikes in any *Stegosaurus* specimen. Carpenter and Galton set out to clear up this mystery, determining if Marsh's skeletal reconstruction and the skeleton at Yale's museum were, in fact, based on any actual fossil evidence.

Utilizing archival letters of Marsh's fossil collectors (Arthur Lakes, William H. "Bill" Reed, and Marshal P. Felch), quarry maps made by collectors as required by Marsh, Carpenter and Galton attempted "to recreate Marsh's thinking in making the first skeletal reconstruction of *Stegosaurus*."

Among Carpenter and Galton's findings were the following:

Between his first description of *Stegosaurus* in 1977 and his skeletal reconstruction of *S. ungulatus* of 1891, Marsh's ideas concerning this dinosaur were slowly yet continually evolving, sometimes drastically so (his original conception of *Stegosaurus*, for example, being a giant aquatic turtle). Such changing ideas included Marsh's opinion regarding the number of tail spikes this dinosaur possessed. Moreover, by the time of his 1891 skeletal reconstruction, Marsh had a wealth of specimens at his disposal, some of them including distal tails with associated spikes. None of these specimens, according to the records of Marsh's collectors and the published description of the material, possessed more than the standard two pairs of spikes; furthermore, several (not just the supposed two) different specimens collected from different quarries contributed to the mount displayed at the Peabody Museum.

Carpenter and Galton concluded, therefore, that

Composite skeleton of *Stegosaurus ungulatus*, sporting an eight-spiked tail, mounted at the Yale University's Peabody Museum of Natural History.

the notion of an eight-spiked tail, as a diagnostic feature of *S. ungulatus*, is based on an erroneous assumption by Marsh as well as other workers; that attributing eight tail spikes to this species was founded upon weak evidence that has not been supported by subsequent discoveries; and that the genus *Stegosaurus* appears to be "characterized by four distal caudal spikes, which is not variable among the different species."

A number of recent studies have focused upon specific parts of the body of *Stegosaurus*. Peter M. Galton (2001*d*), a specialist in stegosaurian dinosaurs, described in detail the endocranial cast—which approximately represents the form of the brain (see Hopson 1979)—of *Stegosaurus*, based upon four specimens:

1. A complete endocranial cast from an undistorted braincase (CM 106; first figured by Huene 1914) referred to *Stegosaurus ungulatus*; collected in 1900 by O. A. Peterson and Charles Whitney Gilmore from a quarry at Sheep Creek, Albany County, Wyoming, this specimen includes the right prefrontal and supraorbitals, both frontals, postorbitals, squamosals, braincase, right quadrate, the caudal part of both nasals, the rostral part of the right dentary, and various other skull and mandible pieces (Galton, in preparation); 2. USNM 4934, the holotype of *Stegosaurus stenops*, an almost complete skeleton collected by Felch in 1886 at Garden Park, Fremont County, Colorado, including a complete three-dimensional skull (see *D:TE*); 3. USNM 4936, a partial skeleton collected by Felch at Garden Park, including the caudalmost part of a distorted skull with frontals, postorbitals, squamosals, and the braincase (endocast first figured by Gilmore 1914); and 4. YPM 1853, the holotype of *S. ungulatus*, a partial skeleton, including the caudal part of the skull with partial postorbitals, squamosals, quadrates, parts of ?supraorbitals, and the right ?lacrimal (see Carpenter and Galton), collected by Arthur Lakes at Como Bluff (see Connely 2002 for a recent brief report on the paleoecology of the Morrison Formation at that locality), Carbon County, Wyoming (endocranial cast first figured by Marsh 1880).

Galton's study led to following conclusions:

USNM 4936 was referred by Marsh (in Gilmore) to the type species, *Stegosaurus armatus*, Gilmore to *S. stenops*, Huene to *Stegosaurus* sp., and Ostrom and

Stegosaurus

Photograph by Clifford A. Miles, courtesy North American Museum of Ancient Life.

Below: Skeleton (cast) of *Stegosaurus stenops* with the correct number of four tail spikes, mounted by Western Paleontological Laboratories, Inc., with the spikes projecting laterally off the tail. The specimen was recovered from Bone Cabin Quarry West in Albany County, Wyoming, and is mounted at the National Museum of Natural History, Tokyo, Japan.

Above: Tail spikes (cast) of *Stegosaurus* as correctly mounted by Western Paleontological Laboratories, Inc., based upon research by Kenneth Carpenter.

Photograph by Clifford A. Miles, courtesy Western Paleontological Laboratories and National Museum of Natural History.

Stegosaurus dorsal dermal plate. According to a 2002 study by Frank Sanders, Kenneth Carpenter, and Lorrie McWhinney, the plates restricted the movement of the tail in this genus.

McIntosh (1966) back to *S. armatus*. As Galton pointed out, however, the rib of the first dorsosacral vertebra seems to form a slender, sheetlike additional rib (see Gilmore; Ostrom and McIntosh), a condition found in the holotype of *S. stenops*. In USNM 4936, the top of the neural spine of the first caudal vertebra is convex, rather than forked as in the more distal caudals, as in *S. stenops*, and rather than concave, as in the last sacral vertebra (and presumably first caudal vertebra) of *S. ungulatus*. Primarily for these reasons, Galton identified USNM 4936 as belonging to *S. stenops*.

Also, the endocast of CM 106, which includes most of the inner ear, is similar to that of *Kentrosaurus*, a stegosaur from the Upper Jurassic of Tanzania. Endocasts of YPM 1853 and USNM 4936 were figured accurately by Marsh and Gilmore, respectively; but the endocast of YPM 1853 is incomplete, the original lateral view figured my Marsh not indicating the reconstructed parts. Marsh (in Gilmore) correctly identified the pituitary fossa on the complete adult endocast of USNM 4936; therefore, Galton concluded, Hopson's later reidentification of this fossa as a cartilage-filled space between the bones of a subadult is not correct.

McWhinney, Rothschild and Carpenter (2001) subjected both to visual examination and computed tomography (CT scanning) several *Stegosaurus* aberrant tail spikes — left and right cranial spikes belonging to *S. stenops* specimen DMNH 2818, a nearly articulated and somewhat smaller adult skeleton found by Bryan Small in 1992 at Garden Park, Colorado; and an isolated right spike (USNM 6646) of *S. ungulatus* (described by Gilmore), recovered east of Como Bluff, Wyoming. Also, the authors compared these spikes with the "normal" spikes belonging to another specimen of *S. stenops* (DMNH 2818).

McWhinney *et al.* deduced from their analysis that the right proximal dermal spike of DMNH 2818 and also USNM 6646 suffered from posttraumatic chronic osteomyletis, a bone disease, this interpretation supported by the authors' analysis of the abnormal microstructure observed in thin sections taken from DMNH 2818. This disease, McWhinney believed, "originated in a microbial infection in the open fractured spikes, causing an exogenous form of osteomyletis, which then progressed into a chronic state." The left spike of DMNH 2818, the authors observed, shows "either an early contiguous spread of the disease or represents a separate injury with secondary infection."

These pathologies — including an open fracture, with secondary infection — indicated to McWhinney *et al.* that both *Stegosaurus* individuals survived the initial trauma of broken spikes (possibly damaged in utilizing their tails as defensive weapons against predators; see Carpenter 1998*a*), as from about two to three

Photograph by Clifford A. Miles, courtesy North American Museum of Ancient Life.

Stegosaurus stenops skeleton (cast) showing reconstructed nuchal armor. Work by Western Paleontological Laboratories, Inc. lead to the accurate reconstruction of cervical ribs on stegosaurs.

weeks are required for the recognition of antemortem reparative changes in bone. Moreover, periods of remission and intermittent flare-ups during the chronic infectious state can span months and even years. Consequently, while the disease may not at first have been fatal, it is almost impossible to eradicate once a pyogenic infection take hold. Within time, other physiological and environmental factors, such as stress induced by drought, "might have compounded the affliction, debilitating the animals and leading to their deaths."

McWhinney *et al.*, contrary to Gilmore, who believed that the tail spikes of *Stegosaurus* primarily functioned in making the animal look larger and more formidable, suggested that their main purpose — as evidenced by trauma or infection or both sustained in the above specimens — "was to actively use them in defense and offense posturing in interspecific and intraspecific combat." Furthermore, the authors' analysis of these pathologic spikes showed that the horny sheath believed to have covered them in life must not have extended very far beyond the spike's tip; if it had, this sheath, rather than the tip of the bone spike, would have broken off. (Carpenter, McWhinney and Sanders, in preparation, will later show that this

"sheath was probably less than one cm. beyond the bone spike.")

In a brief report later published as an abstract for a poster, Sanders, Carpenter and McWhinney (2002), while interpreting the tail of *Stegosaurus* as a defensive weapon, pointed out that the mechanics for this device are not necessarily obvious. Sanders *et al.* proposed the following technical questions:

"What were the degrees of freedom for tail movement? How far could the tail swing? How fast could the tail tip move? How much momentum could be imparted to the spikes? And finally, what was the maximum striking impulse that the spikes could deliver, and to what extent could the bones as well as soft tissues of predators be penetrated?"

In an attempt to answer these questions, Sanders *et al.* examined the caudal vertebrae and tail spikes of the well-preserved skeleton (DMNH 1483) of *S. stenops* mounted at the Denver Museum of Nature and Science. The authors measured these elements, as well as maximum articulation angles for the elements. "Degrees of freedom of tail movement were established, and muscle cross sections and mass were inferred from bone sections," Sanders *et al.* developing from this data a mathematical model of tail movement.

Photograph by John Snyder, courtesy North American Museum of Ancient Life.

Preserved skin impressions from the pelvis, left side, of *Stegosaurus*. The first such impressions known from this genus, the specimen — discovered in 1994 by Ron Mjos — recovered at Bone Cabin Quarry West, Albany County, Wyoming, collected and prepared by Western Paleontological Laboratories, Inc.

The authors modeled the tail "as a set of rigid, linked rods (rod lengths being determined by dorsal plate lengths)," these rods connected by springs and muscle action represented by spring action. Information gleaned from muscle-force studies of modern animals was employed to replicate the muscle strength of *S. stenops*, and the tail's motion and functionality as a defensive device were derived.

Results of Sanders *et al.*'s study included the following: The dorsal plates constrained movement of the tail; tail movement was mostly restricted to lateral action; the maximum angle of tail movement was about 13 degrees from the body's medial line; the strike speed of a tail spike was more than eight meters per second (29 kilometers per hour); striking force was greater than 340 newtons; pressure on target tissue at a spike tip would have been greater than 10^8 pascals (1000 atmospheres), more than sufficient to penetrate and perhaps lodge within the bones of theropods like *Allosaurus fragilis*.

The authors noted that a punctured caudal vertebra of *Allosaurus fragilis* has been found, and that a broken and diseased *S. stenops* spike (DMNH 2818) may have been broken off within the body of a predator (see above).

Karbek (2002), in a potentially controversial published abstract for a poster, offered a rather novel reinterpretation of *Stegosaurus* — traditionally regarded as a somewhat slow-moving animal that walked upon all fours — as an agile, cursorial biped, this in light of a review of this dinosaur's limb proportions, general shape, the distribution of its dorsal plates, and aspects of its postulated neural development.

As observed by Karbek, a striking feature of *Stegosaurus*, as well as all other known stegosaurs, is the great length disparity between the front and hindlimbs, a greater contrast in limb lengths being known only in the habitually bipedal theropods among Dinosauria. Mapping onto a cladogram for Thyreophora the ratios of fore and hindlimbs and ratios of trunk length to hindlimb length, that author saw a convergence with agile theropods, the greatest tendency of reversion towards bipedality being seen in such derived taxa as *Kentrosaurus* and *Stegosaurus*.

According to Karbek, such features as the very small head, deep and wide caudal areas of the trunk,

Stegosaurus

Photograph by John Snyder, courtesy North American Museum of Ancient Life.

Preserved skin impressions from the pelvis, left side, of *Stegosaurus*. The first such impressions known from this genus, the specimen — discovered in 1994 by Ron Mjos — recovered at Bone Cabin Quarry West, Albany County, Wyoming, collected and prepared by Western Paleontological Laboratories, Inc.

Preserved skin impressions of *Stegosaurus* found with the *Stegosaurus* "A" skeleton from Bone Cabin Quarry West, Albany County, Wyoming. Found in 1994 by Ron Mjos, this skin is from the pelvis on the left side. At the time of its discovery, this specimen constituted the only skin impressions known for stegosaurs. Still undescribed, this material was identified by Tyler Pinegar in the fossil preparation laboratory at Western Paleontological Laboratories, Inc.

Photograph by John Snyder, courtesy North American Museum of Ancient Life.

Photograph by the author, courtesy
Museum of Western Colorado.

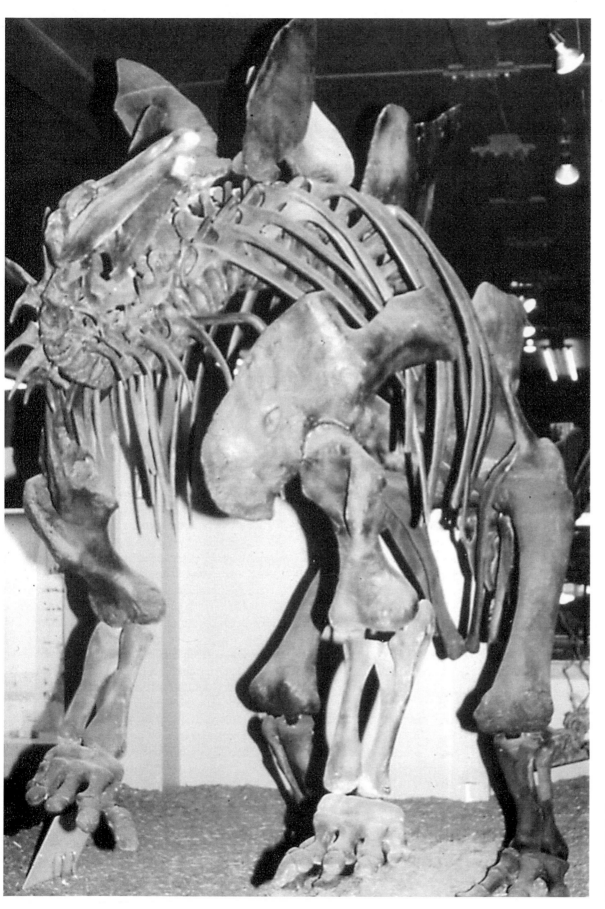

Skeleton of *Stegosaurus* mounted in a semi-bipedal posture. According to T. R. Karbeck (2002), this dinosaur was a cursorial biped rather than a slow-moving quadruped as traditionally portrayed.

Life restoration of *Stegosaurus stenops* painted by Kelly Pugh.

and deep, muscular tail suggest "that stegosaurs evolved this body shape to concentrate the body mass about the hips, and close to the longest limbs." This mass distribution resulted in the center of gravity (C.o.G.) being just cranial to the hips, greatly reducing the body's rotational inertia about both the transverse and vertical axes (low axial rotational inertia being "a hallmark of agile cursors"). In Karbek's estimation, the large dermal plates, when carried by a stegosaur in quadrupedal posture, "would have the effect of displacing the C.o.G. anteriory"; in bipedal pose, however, the center of gravity "would be displaced towards and above the hips," the latter resulting "in a dynamically unstable body enabling agility."

Finally, Karbek postulated that, with only the hindlimbs involved in locomotion, "locating the neural tissue close to the main propulsive limbs would reduce nerve impulse travel time," this constituting an important adaptation for such "less efficient, secondarily bipedal animals" such as *Stegosaurus*. Furthermore, and in a way echoing earlier notions about the brain of *Stegosaurus*, Karbek proposed that the small heads of such dinosaurs, with their resulting small brains, would require "a transfer of neural control to the sacral plexus," the most probable mechanism being "a posterior shift of motile neurons along glial tracts during embryogenesis, as occurs in the amniote brain."

Note: Carpenter (1997*b*), in an informal article, reported on two baby *Stegosaurus* partial skeletons, one specimen recovered from Dinosaur National Monument in northwestern Colorado, the other a specimen collected from the Bone Cabin Quarry site in south-central Wyoming and donated to the Denver Museum of Nature and Science by Clifford A. Miles of Western Paleontological Laboratories. The latter specimen, Carpenter noted, is especially important as "it includes a baby-sized plate, the first discovery of its kind." As no plates were found with the Dinosaur National Monument specimen, many paleontologists had previously believed that plates did not appear in this genus until maturity was attained. Composite skeletons comprising parts of both specimens were mounted at the Denver Museum and the North American Museum of Ancient Life. Each skeleton measures six feet long and two feet high. The weight of such a baby dinosaur was estimated to be approximately 200 pounds.

Key references: Carpenter (1997*b*, 1998*a*); Carpenter and Galton (2001); Galton (2001*d*); Gilmore (1914); Hopson (1979); Huene (1914); Karbek (2002); Marsh (1877*a*, 1879, 1880, 1887, 1891); McWhinney, Rothschild and Carpenter (2001); Ostrom and McIntosh (1966); Sanders, Carpenter and McWhinney (2002).

†STENOPELIX

Ornithischia: Genasauria: Cerapoda: Marginocephalia: Pachycephalosauria.

Age: Early Cretaceous (Berremian).

Comments: The classification of the type species *Stenopelix valdensis*—known only from the natural mold of a relatively small skeleton from the Wealden of north-western Germany — has, over the years, been controversial. Hermann von Meyer (1857), who named and first described this taxon, was unable to refer it to any reptilian group. Much later, Sues and Galton (1982) classified this taxon as a basal ceratopsian, this assessment based solely on the structure of the pelvis. Maryańska and Osmólska (1974), and then Sereno (1987), regarded this species as a basal pachycephalosaur. In a subsequent review of the Marginocephalia, Dodson (1990a), without giving supporting evidence, considered S. valdensis to be a basal marginocephalian and the sister taxon to Pachycephalosauria plus Ceratopsia (see D:TE).

In a more recent review of the marginocephalians of Asia, Sereno (2000) found no derived characters in the pelvis shared by Stenopelix and ceratopsians, or by ceratopsians alone. As noted by Sereno (2000), "The downwardly curved preacetabular process of the ilium in Stenopelix occurs in several ornithischian subgroups (e.g., pachycephalosaurs), and the short prepubic process figured by Sues and Galton (1982, fig. 1A) for Stenopelix is half the length of the process as preserved in the natural mould (Schmidt, 1969, fig. 1)."

In a reanalysis of the Pachycephalosauria, Sereno (2000) found Stenopelix to be a basal pachycephalosaur based upon the following synapomorphies found in its type specimen: 1. elongate caudal sacral ribs (fourth to sixth); 2. straplike distal end of scapular blade (not yet described in Stenopelix, similar to that in Stegoceras [see Sereno 1987]) and also in some basal neoceratopsians [see Brown and Schlaikjer 1940]; and 3. distal expansion of preacetabular process of ilium (similar to the condition in several pachycephalosaurs).

Key references: Brown and Schlaikjer (1940); Dodson (1990a); Maryańska and Osmólska (1974); Meyer (1857); Schmidt (1969); Sereno (1987, 2000); Sues and Galton (1982).

†STOKESOSAURUS

Saurischia: Eusaurischia: Theropoda: Neotheropoda: Tetanurae: Avetheropoda: Coelurosauria: Maniraptoriformes: Arctometatarsalia: Maniraptoriformes: Arctometatarsalia: Tyrannosauroidea: Tyrannosauridae *incertae sedis*.

Comments: In 1974, James H. Madsen, Jr. described a new theropod, *Stokesosaurus clevelandi*, founded upon a left ilium (UUVP 2938/UMNH 7434) — distinguished by a vertical median ridge that ascends from the supra-acetabular hood to the dorsal margin of the blade — recovered from the Cleveland-Lloyd Dinosaur Quarry in the Morrison Formation (Upper Jurassic) of Emery County, Utah. At the same time, Madsen referred to the type species *Stokesosaurus clevelandi* a right ilium (UUVP 2320) and a right premaxilla (UUVP 2999) (see D:TE).

Over a decade later, Britt (1991) referred three distal caudal vertebrae (BYUVP 5073, 5203, and 8908) from the Dry Mesa Dinosaur Quarry in western Colorado to *Stokesosaurus*, although Curtice and Wilhite (1996) found this referral not to be justified (see D:TE). More recently, Chure and Madsen (1998) tentatively referred to *S. clevelandi* a basicranium (UUVP 2455) from the Cleveland-Lloyd Dinosaur Quarry (see SI). Nevertheless, as noted by Foster and Chure (2000), *Stokesosaurus* remains one of the rarest theropods in the Morrison Formation" and "is among the rarest and most poorly known theropods from the Late Jurassic of North America."

In 2000, Foster and Chure described a small theropod ilium, belonging to a juvenile individual, collected from the Upper Jurassic (Kimmeridgian, as indicated by ostracods and charophytes just below quarry level; see Schudack, Turner and Petersen 1998) Wonderland Quarry (discovered by G. Szigeti 1979) in the Morrison Formation, north of Meade County, South Dakota, situated about five meters above the top of the eolian Unkpapa Sandstone Member (see Foster 1996). The site was excavated in 1980 by crews from the South Dakota School of Mines and Technology, who also recovered a partial skeleton (SDSM 25210; mainly caudal vertebrae, but also two dorsals, a partial ilium, a pubis, ischium, and partial scapula) of the sauropod *Barosaurus lentus*, teeth of the sauropod *Camarasaurus*, a metatarsal, caudal vertebra, and teeth belonging to *Allosaurus*, shell fragments of the chelonian *Glyptos*, and teeth of crocodilians.

The right ilium referred to *S. clevelandi* was discovered by John R. Foster in 1991 during preparation of a block containing the above mentioned *Barosaurus* dorsal vertebra and ilium and was mentioned by Foster in 1996. Although the specimen was lost before cataloguing, both Foster and Chure were able to examine and photograph it.

As described by Foster and Chure, the ilium measures about 8 centimeters in length as preserved. Based upon the holotype left ilium, the authors estimated the total length of the South Dakota specimen to have been about 12 centimeters.

Foster and Chure referred this specimen to *Stokesosaurus* as that is the only Morrison theropod known to have a vertical ridge on the lateral surface of the ilium, although the ridge of the South Dakota specimen is less massive, more vertically oriented, and flares more at its dorsal and ventral edges. The postacetabular blade of this specimen has a rounded caudal border as in *Stokesosaurus*, as opposed to the squared off margin found in the Morrison theropods *Allosaurus*

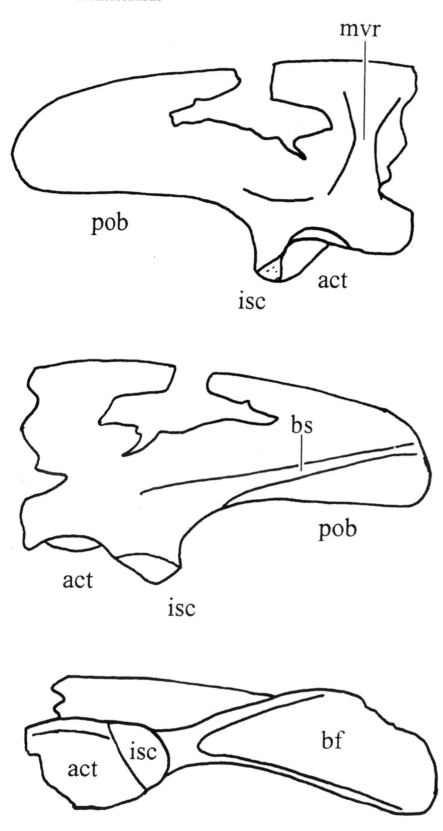

Stokesosaurus clevelandi, referred right ilium from a juvenile individual, in (top) lateral, (middle) medial, and (bottom) ventral views, collected from the Wonderland Quarry in South Dakota. (After Foster and Chure 2000.)

and *Marshosaurus*. Also, the postacetabular portion of the blade is not deflected ventrally and the dorsal margin is not as strongly convex as in the Morrison theropods *Ceratosaurus* and *Torvosaurus*; nor is the medial wall of the brevis fossa visible in side view as in *Ceratosaurus*, *Torvosaurus*, and *Marshosaurus*.

Foster and Chure further noted that the South Dakota ilium is comparable in size to the holotype incomplete ilium (BMNH R83) of *Iliosuchus incognitus* (see *D:TE*), a theropod possessing a ridged ilium from the Middle Jurassic of England. The ridge is more caudally inclined in BMNH R83; however, it is more vertically oriented in OUM J29871, the larger (and presumably ontogenetically later), incomplete, and only other specimen of *I. incognitus*. This suggested to the authors that, if this reorientation of the ridge is ontogenetic in origin, the pattern in the British theropod is opposite to that in *Stokesosaurus*.

Stokesosaurus and *I. incognitus*, Foster and Chure observed, also differ in other ways: OUM J29871 possesses additional ridges that are cranial and caudal to the main ridge; additionally, this specimen has a foramen on the ridge and another cranial to the ridge. Also, the brevis shelf in the South Dakota specimen is proportionately wider than in *I. incognitus*, with a squared-off caudal border. Foster and Chure noted that all of these differences further support the generic separation of *Stokesosaurus* and *Iliosuchus* (Galton and Jensen 1979*b*, *contra* Galton 1976*b*; see *D:TE* for details).

Until the discovery of the South Dakota specimen, *Stokesosaurus* had only been unequivocally known from the Cleveland-Lloyd Dinosaur Quarry. According to Foster and Chure, this specimen extends significantly the geographic range of the genus north and east, indicating "that *Stokesosaurus*, though relatively rare, was not geographically restricted within the Morrison ecosystem."

Ford and Chure (2001*b*), in an abstract, reported small, D-shaped theropod teeth from the Morrison Formation possibly referable to *Stokesosaurus* (supporting Madsen's previous appraisal of this genus as possibly the earliest known tyrannosaurid; see *D:TE*), and mentioned similar teeth from the Guimarota complex of Europe. As D-shaped premaxillary teeth constitute a synapomorphy of Tyrannosauridae, this new information "calls into question previous suggestions that the early evolution of the Tyrannosauridae took place in Asia," suggesting also that this lineage extends back at least to Late Jurassic times.

Furthermore, the authors suggested that the tyrannosaurid lineages seems to have been more geographically widespread in its early than later history. By the Early Cretaceous, tyrannosaurids are present in Asia, with material including the characteristic D-shaped premaxillary teeth now also known from the Early Cretaceous Sao Khu Formation of Thailand, the Middle Cretaceous Cedar Mountain Formation of North America, and the Middle Cretaceous Tetori Group of Japan, while Ford and Chure (2001*a*) also recently reported the occurrence of tyrannosaurids in the El Gallo Formation of Baja California (also reported by Molnar 1974; see also see *Aublysodon* entry).

Key references: Britt (1991); Chure and Madsen (1998); Curtice and Wilhite (1996); Ford and Chure (2001*a*, 2001*b*); Foster (1996); Foster and Chure (2000); Galton (1976*b*); Galton and Jensen (1979*b*); Madsen (1974); Molnar (1974); Szigeti (1979).

†STREPTOSPONDYLUS Meyer 1832

Saurischia: Eusaurischia: Theropoda: Neotheropoda: Tetanurae: Spinosauroidea: Megalosauridae: Megalosaurinae.

Name derivation: Greek *streptos* = "reversed" [*i.e.* "opisthocoelous" or "reversed procoelous"] + Greek *spondylos* = "vertebrae."

Type species: *S. altdorfensis* Meyer 1832.

Other species: [None.]

Occurrence: Callovo-Oxfordian, Normandy, France.

Age: Middle to Late Jurassic (Bathonian to upper Callovian or lower Oxfordian).

Known material: Various postcranial specimens, mostly vertebral elements.

Lectotypes: MNHN 8787, last cervical vertebrae, first two dorsal vertebrae; MNHN 8794, last dorsal vertebra, first two sacral vertebrae; MNHN 8788, last sacral vertebra, first caudal vertebra; MNHN 8907, series of three dorsal vertebrae; MNHN 8789, dorsal vertebra, cranial (pectoral) dorsal vertebra; MNHN 8793, cranial (pectoral) dorsal vertebra; MNHN 8605, distal end of left pubis; MNHN 8606, distal end of right femur; MNHN 8607, distal end of right tibia; MNHN 8608, right astragalus; MNHN 8609, right calcaneum.

Diagnosis of genus (as for type species): Medium sized theropod; cranial dorsal vertebrae with two hypapophyses; centrum of cranial dorsal vertebrae strongly opisthocoelous, ventrally flat, caudal dorsal vertebrae platycoelous; centra of middle and caudal dorsal vertebrae elongate; astragalus with lateral extension of "cushioning" bone overhanging dorsomedial edge, due to ascending process not extending to middle part of distal end of tibia; large depression at base of ascending process of astragalus, astragalus without posteromedial process (Allain 2001).

Comments: The history of the genus now known as *Streptospondylus* and recognized as a theropod has been a long and complex one, chronicled in greater detail by other authors (*e.g.*, Walker 1964; Allain 2001), to which I direct the reader.

Briefly, in the year 1700, the Abbé Bachelet found a "quantity of bones" in Callovo-Oxfordian-age rocks at Vaches Noires, in the region of Honfleur, in Normandy, France. The discovery was reported and the fossils figured a century later by Baron Georges Cuvier (1800*a*). This material included the following, regarded by Allain as the lectotypes (now in the collection of the Muséum d'Histoire Naturelle de Normandie): (MNHN 8787–8789, 8793–8794, 8907, and 8605–8609), mostly consisting of vertebral elements. Referred to the type species, which would later be named *Streptospondylus altdorfensis* (see below), was the distal end of a right femur (HMNH 9645).

Cuvier (1800*b*) believed that these specimens were the remains of some new species of crocodile and, in his classic *Recherchessur les ossemens fossiles*, published in 1824, identified them as the remains of gavials. In 1825, Geoffroy Saint-Hilaire, accepting that the Honfleur fossils to belong to gavials, erected for them the crocodilian type species *Steneosaurus rostro-major* (type specimen MNHN 8900), at the same time establishing a second species, *S. rostro-minor* (type specimen HMNH 8902). Later, Meyer (1830) introduced the names *Streptospondylus* and *Metriorhynchus* as *nomina nuda*, apparently with the intention (see Meyer 1832) of raising *S. rostro-major* and *S. rostro-minor* to generic status, renaming the former taxon *Streptospondylus* (type species *Streptospondylus altdorfensis*) and the other *Metriorhynchus*. As Walker explained, "Since the name *Steneosaurus* cannot be

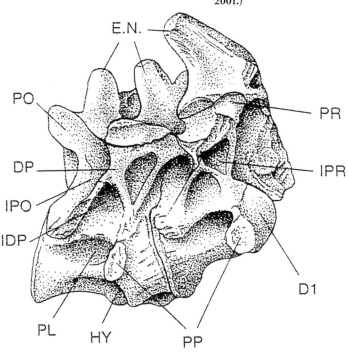

Streptospondylus altdorfensis, MNHN 8787, lectotype last cervical vertebra and first and second dorsal vertebrae, right lateral view. Scale = 9 cm. (After Allain 2001.)

Streptospondylus

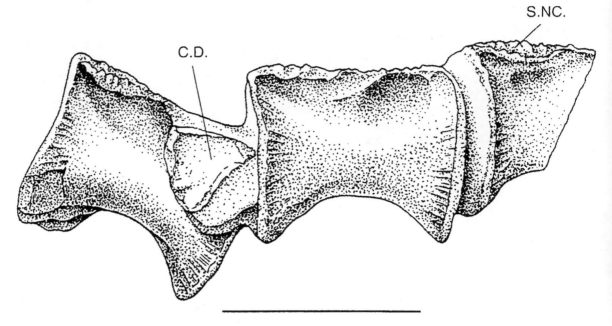

C.D.

S.NC.

eliminated in such a procedure, and *S. rostromajor* [hyphens subsequently eliminated] Geoffroy is evidently the type species of *Steneosaurus, Streptospondylus* von Meyer is thus an objective junior synonym of *Steneosaurus* Geoffroy 1825, now recognized as a genus of Crocodilia. Furthermore, *Streptospondylus altdorfensis* von Meyer (1832, p. 106), the only species of the genus named by Von Meyer, and therefore presumably the type species of *Streptospondylus*, is actually equated with *Steneosaurus rostromajor* Geoffroy in this work, the same bibliographic references serving for both, so that the former species is also an objective junior synonym of the latter."

However, a recent study of the original material and the entangled nomenclature pertaining to it was published by Ronan Allain in 2001. *Contra* Walker,

Allain pointed out that Meyer's (1832) references do not serve for the two species and that *Steneosaurus rostromajor* and *Streptospondylus altdorfensis* were not based on the same fossil material. Consequently, the name *Streptospondylus* is the valid name for the theropod specimens from Honfleur.

As demonstrated by Allain, the theropod specimens from Honfleur show a number of synapomorphies of the Tetanurae, these including the following: Cervical and cranial dorsal vertebrae strongly opisthocoelous; extensive depression on anterodistal portion of femur; distal end of tibia extended to support calcaneum; horizontal depression on condyles of astragalus; condyles of astragalus oriented anteroventrally; ascending process of astragalus reduced mediolaterally.

According to Allain, some features of *Streptospondylus* are similar to those of spinosauroids (*e.g.*, the morphology of the pubis). Furthermore, several vertebral features (*e.g.*, hypapophyses less developed than in allosauroids) suggest close relationships between *Streptospondylus* and the spinosauroid *Eustreptospondylus* (see *D:TE, S2*), indicating that both genera belong in the Spinosauroidea.

Allain referred to *S. altdorfensis* various other materials, including some of the specimens described by Owen (1842) as *Streptospondylus rostro-major* and the new species *S. cuvieri*, the latter founded on the cranial half of a cranial dorsal vertebra, a tooth, and various bone fragments, from the vicinity of the Chipping Norton Limestone, at the base of the Great Oolite Series (Middle Jurassic: early Bathonian); *Laelaps gallicus* Cope 1842 [*nomen dubium*], based on vertebrae, a pubis, the distal end of a tibia with astragalus, a calcaneum, and various fragments, from the Upper

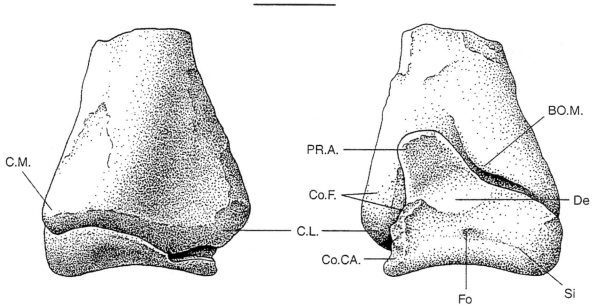

Streptospondylus altdorfensis, MNHN 8607, lectotype distal end of right tibia and astragalus, in A. caudal and B. cranial views. Scale = 5 cm. (After Allain 2001.)

Jurassic of Normandy, this material having been first figured by Cuvier (1812); and, referred by Walker "As a matter of convenience" to *Eustreptospondylus divesensis*, postcranial remains (the cranium is the holotype of the new genus and species *Pivetausaurus divesensis* Taquet and Welles 1977; see *D:TE*) from the Oxfordian of Vaches Noires, near Dives, previously regarded as belonging to *S. cuvieri* (*e.g.*, Cuvier 1836).

Note: The species *Streptospondylus lyciensis* Costa 1864 is crocodylian (E. Buffetaut, personal communication to G. Olshevsky). *S. major* Owen 1842 was referred by Lydekker (1888) to the ornithopod *Iguanodon bernissartensis*. Both *S. geoffroyi* Meyer 18?? [*nomen nudum*] and *S. juriensis* ?Gray 18?? [*nomen nudum*] are nondinosaurian (see Chure and McIntosh 1989).

Key references: Allain (2001); Cope (1842); Cuvier (1800*a*, 1800*b*, 1812, 1824, 1836); Geoffroy Saint-Hilaire (1825); Meyer (1830, 1832); Owen (1842); Taquet and Welles (1977); Walker (1964); Welles and Long (1974).

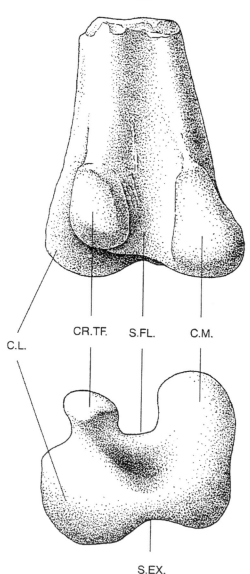

Streptospondylus altdorfensis, MNHN 9645, referred distal end of left femur, in A. caudal and B. distal views. Scale = 5 cm. (After Allain 2001.)

†STRUTHIOSAURUS—(=*Craetomus*, *Danubiosaurus*, *Pleuropeltus*, *Rhadinosaurus*; =?*Leipsanosaurus*, ?*Rhodanosaurus*)

Ornithischia: Genasaura: Thyreophora: Eurypoda: Ankylosauromorpha: Ankylosauria: Nodosauridae.

Occurrence: Gosau Formation, Muthmannsdorf, Wiener Neustadt, Austria, Siedenbergen, Hungary; Sinpetru beds, Szentpeterfalva region, Transylvania; ?Frankenhof, Germany.

Known material: Numerous specimens including at least three partial skeletons comprising over a hundred bones, immature to adult.

Diagnosis of genus (as for type species): Small-sized nodosaurid (total adult length approximately 3 meters); occiput relatively high, narrow (compared with that of more derived nodosaurids, e.g., *Edmontonia* and *Panoplosaurus*); basisphenoid projecting ventrally; distal articular condyle of quadrate nearly oval, almost symmetrical; cervical vertebrae elongated, centra longer than wide; hook-shaped acromion process centrally on scapula; lesser (cranial) trochanter forming ridge; three cervical half-rings from fusion of spines, small ossicles, and oval scutes; at least pair of hornlike spikes on trunk; tail plates tall, hollow-based, triangular (Pereda Suberbiola and Galton 2001).

Comments: *Struthiosaurus austriacus*, a rather small armored dinosaur from the Upper Cretaceous (Campanian), continental coal-bearing Gosau Formation of Muthmannsdorf, Lower Australia — beds that have yielded a wealthy assemblage including such vertebrates as dinosaurs, pterosaurs, crocodilians, turtles, lizards, and champsosaurids, but dominated by ankylosaurs — was reappraised by Pereda Suberbiola and Galton (2001; see *D:TE*, *S2*).

A systematic revision by Pereda Suberbiola and Galton of the ankylosaurian remains from this locality, most of it recovered during the nineteenth century, suggested to the authors that it all pertains to a taxon (the type species, *S. austriacus*) displaying a considerable range of size and variation, the bone discrepancies seen in these specimens interpreted as the result of ontogenetic changes and individual differences. Regarded by Pereda Suberbiola and Galton as junior synonyms of *S. austracus* were the *nomen dubia* taxa *Craetomus lepidophorus*, *C. pawlowitschii*, *Danubiosaurus anceps*, *Pleuropeltus suessii*, and [in part] *Rhadinosaurus alcimus* (see *D:TE*).

Pereda Suberbiola and Galton redescribed and offered an emended diagnosis for the type species, *Struthiosaurus austriacus*, based upon the following material: PIUW 2349/6 (holotype), a fragmentary cranium from the Grünbach Basin, Muthmannsdorf, Wiener Neustadt area, south of Vienna, Lower Austria; PIUW 2349/17 and uncatalogued, two ?orbital fragments, skull roof with associated armor; PIUW 2349/uncatalogued, right dentary; PIUW 2349/uncatalogued, rostral ends of both mandibles; PIUW/7–9, 39, 105a,b, and uncatalogued, about 18 isolated teeth; PIUW 2349/uncatalogued, two cervical vertebrae; PIUW 2349/uncatalogued, cervical rib; PIUW 2349/24, 37, 100, and uncatalogued, seven dorsal vertebrae; PIUW 2349/10 and uncatalogued, approximately 20 dorsal ribs; PIUW 2349/25 and uncatalogued, about 22 caudal vertebrae with hemal arches; PIUW 2349/1, right scapula; PIUW 2349/uncatalogued, left scapulocoracoid and right scapula; PIUW 2349/18, 19, left and right humeri; PIUW 2349/11 and uncatalogued, both radii; PIUW 2349/uncatalogued, ?ulna; PIUW 2349/uncatalogued, ilia; PIUW 2349/41, left ?ischium; PIUW 2349/31, 32, small femora; PIUW 2349/29 and uncatalogued, femora; PIUW 2349/30, left ?tibia; PIUW 2349/34 and uncatalogued, fibulae; PIUW 2349/uncatalogued, metapodial and ungual phalanx; PIUW 2349/13, 14, and uncatalogued, parts of three cervical half-rings; PIUW 2349/15 and uncatalogued, two hornlike spikes; PIUW 2349/uncatalogued, eight caudal plates, about 20 low-keeled scutes and ossicles; and PIUW 2349/20, indeterminate bone.

Additional material tentatively referred by Pereda Suberbiola and Galton to *S. austriacus* includes PIUW 2349/uncatalogued, the holotype of *Hoplosaurus ischyrus* Seeley 1881, consisting of a set of fragmentary bones (including parts of vertebrae, ribs, limb bones, and scutes), remains imbedded in a calcareous clay from an imprecise locality near Wiener Neustadt; and NHM 1861.146, the holotype of *Leipsanosaurus noricus* Nopcsa 1918, a tooth from Frankenhof, near Piesting (referred to *S. austriacus* by Nopcsa 1923*b*; see *D:TE*).

Pereda Suberbiola and Galton referred *Struthiosaurus* to the Ankylosauria based upon the following synapomorphies: Cranium low, rear of skull wider than high; supratemporal fenestra closed; pterygoid closing passage between space above palate and that below braincase; postocular shelf enclosing orbital cavity; dermal ossifications of dorsal skull roof fused; atlar neural arches joined dorsally; ilium rotated into horizontal plane; acetabulum closed; extensive armor comprising several kinds of dermal plates.

The authors identified *Struthiosaurus* as belonging to the Nodosauridae based upon the following synapomorphies: Hemispherical occipital condyle separated from ventral braincase by constricted neck; paroccipital processes posteroventrally directed, visible in dorsal aspect; basipterygoid processes comprising pair of rounded, rugose stubs; scapular spine displaced ventrally toward glenoid; three transverse rows of cervical armor; tall conical spikes; keeled plates just slightly excavated ventrally.

According to Pereda Suberbiola and Galton, *S. austriacus* seems to differ from the referred species *S. transylvanicus* in the following features: Basisphenoid less ventrally projected; cervical vertebrae less elongated; and dorsal vertebrae having lower neural arch, pedicles, and neural canal. Although these differences may suggest the validity of two species, the available material was not adequate enough for the authors to resolve this question (see *D:TE*, *S1*). These differences might also, Pereda Suberbiola and Galton noted, reflect other sources of variation, such as individual differences, ontogenetic changes, or sexual dimorphism.

The following features, observed in the holotype of *S. austriacus*, indicated to Pereda Suberbiola and Galton that the specimen represents an immature, possibly subadult animal: Skull slightly smaller than that of *S. transyvanicus*; lack of fusion of paroccipital process, dorsal end of quadrate and squamosal, open suture of quadrate-quadrojugal, and weak posterodorsal development of armor of skull roof (see also Pereda Suberbiola and Galton 1992, 1994); possibly also (see Pereda-Suberbiola, Astibia and Buffetaut 1995) absence of splenial, lack of fusion of dermal ossifications to lower jaw; possibly (Coombs 1986, regarding ankylosaurs; and Galton 1982, for stegosaurs) suture between vertebral centrum and neural arch (obliterated in adults), ungual phalanx widest at about one third down length (proximally in adults), surface of large bones having neither deep rugosities nor strong muscular insertions (contrary to adults).

Pereda Suberbiola and Galton found *Struthiosaurus*, while more derived than other known European ankylosaurs, to be a relatively conservative member of the Nodosauridae, retaining such primitive nodosaurid characters as the following: Occiput comparatively narrow and high; infratemporal fenestra relatively elongate; tooth row extending near symphysis; atlas and axis separate; and lesser (cranial) trochanter of femur not entirely obliterated by fusion.

Additionally, Pereda Suberbiola and Galton suggested that the primitive phylogenetic position and small size of this dinosaur could, as believed by previous authors, be related to the insular endemic evolution of European ankylosaurs during the Late Cretaceous, *Struthiosaurus* interpreted by them "as a pedomorphic dwarf" form.

Note: For a relatively recent biographical and historical report about Baron Franz Nopcsa, an early paleontologist who published a substantial amount of work on *Struthiosaurus*, see Pereda Suberbiola (1996).

Key references: Coombs (1986); Galton (1982*b*); Nopcsa (1918, 1923*b*); Pereda Suberbiola (1996); Pereda-Suberbiola, Astibia and Buffetaut (1995); Pereda Suberbiola and Galton (1992, 1994, 2001); Seeley (1881).

†**STYGIVENATOR**—(See *Tyrannosaurus*.)

†**SUCHOMIMUS**—(See *Baryonyx*.)

†**SUPERSAURUS**—(=*Dystylosaurus*, *Ultrasauros*; =?*Barosaurus*)
Saurischia: Eusaurischia: Sauropodomorpha: Sauropoda: Eusauropoda: Neosauropoda: Diplodocoidea: Diplodocidae.

Comments: In 1985, James A. Jensen, known popularly as "Dinosaur Jim" Jensen, described what he believed to be a new genus and species of gigantic sauropod, which he named *Dystylosaurus edwini*. This taxon was founded upon a single, almost complete cranial dorsal vertebra (BYU 4503; originally given by Jensen incorrectly as BYU 5750 see *D:TE* for photographs), collected in 1972 by Jensen and Kenneth L. Stadtman from the Dry Mesa Dinosaur Quarry (Upper Jurassic) near Delta, Colorado (see *D:TE* for information and photographs of the type specimen). It was discovered between the holotype scapula and holotype dorsal vertebrae of two other gigantic sauropod type species named that year by Jensen, *Supersaurus vivianae* and *Ultrasauros macintoshi*, respectively (the latter now regarded as a junior synonym of *S. vivianae*; see *SI*).

Jensen had distinguished *Dystylosaurus* from other sauropod taxa by the presence of dual infraprezygapophysial laminae, which that author regarded as a unique character. Other perceived distinguishing characters included the prominent opisthocoely of the specimen, the strong ventral keel, and the lack of a bifurcate neural spine.

As the morphology of this specimen seemed to preclude its referral to any known sauropod family, Jensen classified it as "family incertae sedis." Later, McIntosh (1990) interpreted BYU 4503 as "clearly brachiosaurid," based upon its overall appearance, noting also that the neural spine precludes its assignment to the genus *Brachiosaurus*.

While subsequent referrals to *D. edwini* in the paleontological literature have been basically limited to faunal lists providing no new information, Curtice and Stadtman more recently questioned the validity of this taxon, while fully redescribing the type specimen.

Comparing BYU 4503 to other Morrison Formation sauropods, Curtice and Stadtman saw numerous differences: A pair of *Brachiosaurus* vertebrae (BYU 13023) recovered from the same quarry and position (based on parapophysial location) as *Dystylosaurus*, possess straight, upwardly angled transverse processes, while the transverse process of the latter genus has a medial kink and a sub-horizontal inclination. In *Brachiosaurus*, the lateral borders of the neural spine are created by dual supradiapophysial laminae (a unique condition among known sauropods), while the lateral border of the neural spine of *Dystylosaurus* is made up exclusively of suprapostzygapophysial laminae. Unlike the *Dystylosaurus* vertebra, the vertebrae of *Brachiosaurus* are highly apneumatic and lack exquisite sculpting and complexity. In comparing *Dystylosaurus* with *Camarasaurus*, Curtice and Stadtman observed that the "u-shaped" bifurcation and neural spine

Photograph by Mark Philbrick, courtesy North American Museum of Ancient Life.

Kenneth L. Stadtman and Brian Versey working on the *Supersaurus viviane* sacrum from the Dry Mesa Quarry in Colorado.

construction of *Camarasaurus* contrast markedly with the general build of *Dystylosaurus*, while comparison with *Haplocanthosaurus* reveals similar differences.

As Curtice and Stadtman observed, the characters of the opisthocoely and ventral keel of BYU 4503 have been exaggerated by diagenetic distortion. Furthermore, close examination of the neural spine suggests that the latter may actually have been bifurcated. Indeed, the size and morphology of this specimen parallel the known vertebrae in *Supersaurus*.

Curtice and Stadtman noted that the holotype of *D. edwini* can be referred to the Diplodocidae based upon characters including the following: Delicate suprapre- and suprapostzygapophysial laminar construction of the neural spine (both continuing to the incomplete apex); supradiapophyseal laminae poorly

developed; neural spine cranio-caudally thin, showing no evidence of clublike apex; centrum highly pneumatized; overall similarity to the diplodocid *Barosaurus*. Curtice and Stadtman noted that what Jensen had perceived to be a diagnostic feature of BYU 4503, namely the supposedly unique character of dual infraprezygapophysial laminae, is also found on dorsal vertebrae of *Diplodocus carnegii* (CM 84) and *Barosaurus lentus* (YPM 429), thereby constituting "a diplodocid level character illustrating the latermost borders of pneumatic cavities."

According to Curtice and Stadtman, given the close resemblance of BYU 4503 to dorsal vertebrae of *Barosaurus* and the similar size of, morphology, and quarry location close to all other elements of *Supersaurus vivianae*, the holotype of *Dystylosaurus edwini*

(Left to right) Rod Horrocks, Clifford A. Miles, Kenneth L. Stadtman, and Brian Versey excavating the bones of *Supersaurus viviane* at the Dry Mesa Quarry in Colorado.

Photograph by Mark Philbrick, courtesy North American Museum of Ancient Life.

Supersaurus

Photograph by Clifford A. Miles, courtesy North American Museum of Ancient Life.

In situ sacrum with four vertebrae and pelvis (BYU collection) of *Supersaurus viviane*, the largest dinosaurian bone complex yet recovered. The specimen was discovered in August 1988, by Brian Versey in the Dry Mesa Quarry, Colorado. It was collected by Clifford A. Miles, Kenneth Lee Stadtman and assistants that same month.

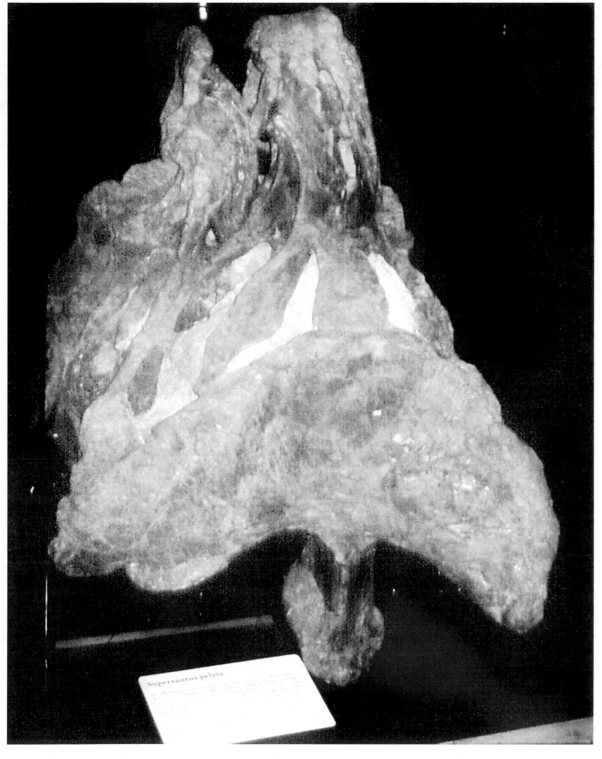

may be referred to *S. vivianae*. Furthermore, these authors opined that, based upon nonduplication of giant diplodocid elements, there seems "to be only one supergiant diplodocid in the [Dry Mesa Dinosaur] Quarry and all oversized diplodocid elements should be referred to the same individual *Supersaurus vivianae*."

Supersaurus, Curtice and Stadtman observed, resembles most closely, both axially and appendicularly, the slightly smaller *Barosaurus*, these genera regarded by the authors as sister taxa. Consequently, it would not be expected that *Supersaurus* possesses deeply bifurcate dorsal neural spines in the shoulder region, for in *Barosaurus*, by the fourth dorsal vertebra, the neural spine bifurcation is not as pronounced as that of *Diplodocus* and *Apatosaurus*. However, examination

Reconstructed skeleton (cast of DINOLAB) of the gigantic sauropod *Supersaurus viviane*, measuring 120 feet in length, mounted at the North American Museum of Ancient Life.

of the preserved spine of *Dystylosaurus* reveals thin laminae that may have continued, producing a gentle cleft. Perhaps then, Curtice and Stadtman speculated, *Supersaurus* could lose its bifurcation further forward than any other known Morrison Formation diplodocid, this condition thereby serving "as a useful generic level character for differentiating *Supersaurus* from *Barosaurus*."

In a later published abstract, Curtice (2003) also questioned the validity of *Supersaurus* itself, noting that the recent synonymies of "*Dystylosaurus*" and "*Ul-*

trasauros" with *Supersaurus* have both reduced the number of genera and also, by realizing that these three taxa actually represent a single diplodocid taxon, have allowed for a more accurate size portrayal and phylogenetic assessment of the genus *Supersaurus*. Consequently, the question of whether *Supersaurus* is a valid genus or really a junior synonym of *Barosaurus* can now be tested.

As Curtice pointed out, the dorsal vertebra of "*Dystylosaurus*" offers an autapomorphy for *Supersaurus—i.e.*, a strongly reduced bifid neural spine on

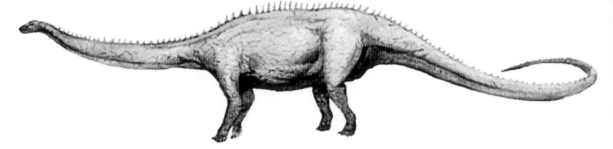

Life restoration of the gigantic sauropod dinosaur *Supersaurus viviane* by artist Kelly Pugh.

the fourth dorsal. This feature is significant, that author stated, as in all other known diplodocids the neural spine of dorsal four is deeply bifurcated. Of all known diplodocids, "Only *Barosaurus* has a reduction in cleft depth that far forward in the dorsal column." In *Supersaurus*, Curtice observed, this cleft has been all but lost, the condition "more closely resembling the sixth dorsal vertebra of *Barosaurus* than the fourth.

Key references: Curtice (2003); Curtice and Stadtman (2001); Jensen (1985); McIntosh (1990).

†**SYNTARSUS**—(See *Megapnosaurus*; =?*Coelophysis*)

†**TARBOSAURUS** Maleev 1955—(=*Jenghizkhan*, *Maleevosaurus*; =?*Shanshanosaurus*)

Saurischia: Eusaurischia: Theropoda: Neotheropoda: Tetanurae: Avetheropoda: Coelurosauria: Maniraptoriformes: Arctometatarsalia: Tyrannosauroidea: Tyrannosauridae: Tyrannosaurinae.

Name derivation: Greek *tarbo* = "terrible" + Greek *sauros* = "lizard."

Type species: *T. bataar* (Maleev 1955).

Other species: ?*T. luanchuanensis* Dong 1979 [*nomen dubium*], ?*Tarbosaurus periculosus* Riabinin 1930 [*nomen dubium*], ?*T. turpanensis* Zhai, Zheng and Tong 1978 [*nomen nudum*].

Occurrence: Nemegt Formation, Omnogov, Nemegtskaya Svita, White Beds of Khermeen Tsav, Bayankhongor, Mongolian People's Republic; Quiba Formation, Henan, Subashi Formation, Xangjiang Uygur Zizhiqu, ?unnamed formation, Heilongjiang, China.

Age: Late Cretaceous (?late Campanian or early Maastrichtian).

Known material: At least five skulls and associated skeletons, representing approximately 30 individuals, juvenile to adult.

Holotype: PIN 551-1, almost complete skull and skeleton.

Tarbosaurus bataar skeleton (cast) on exhibit at the Mesa Southwest Museum. The actual specimen was originally part of "The Great Russian Dinosaurs Exhibition," that first showed at this museum in 1996.

Courtesy Mesa Southwest Museum.

Tarbosaurus bataar skeleton (cast), detail of skull.

Diagnosis of genus (as for type species): [Modern diagnosis not yet published.]

Comments: *Tarbosaurus*, a genus now regarded as valid, has had a long, tangled, and controversial taxonomic history.

In 1955, Russian paleontologist Maleev, Evgeny [Eugene] Alexandrovich Maleev described in a brief report what he considered to be a new species of *Tyrannosaurus*, founded upon an incomplete skeleton (PIN 551-1; see *D:TE* for a photograph of the skull) lacking the right forelimb, recovered in 1955 by the Palaeontological Institute of the Academy of Sciences, [then] Union of Soviet Socialist Republics, from the Nemegt Formation, Nemegt, Omnogon, Mongolian People's Republic. Maleev (1955*a*) named this new species *Tyrannosaurus bataar*. Maleev differentiated *Tyrannosaurus bataar* from the North American type species *Tyrannosaurus rex* as being a smaller animal, having a more elongate and massive skull, and comparatively shorter forelimbs.

In that same paper, Maleev also described two other Mongolian tyrannosaurid taxa — the new genus and species, *Tarbosaurus efremovi*, based on a skull and postcranial remains (PIN AN SSR 551-3) from Tsagan Ula, and the new species *Gorgosaurus lancinator*, based on a specimen including a skull from Altran Ula, referred by him to the North American tyrannosaurid genus. Maleev (1955*b*), in a subsequent report, briefly described (but did not diagnose) another Mongolian tyrannosaurid, *Gorgosaurus novojilovi*, founded on the partial skull with associated nearly complete postcrania (PIN 552-2) of a relatively small tyrannosaurid individual from the Nemegt Formation at Tsagan Ula; while in yet another short report, Maleev (1955*c*) referred *T. bataar* to his genus *Tarbosaurus* as the new species *Tarbosaurus bataar*.

More than a decade later, another Russian paleontologist, Anatoly Konstantinovich Rozhdestvensky (1965), interpreting all of Maleev's Mongolian

Photograph by the author, courtesy Natural History Museum of Los Angeles County.

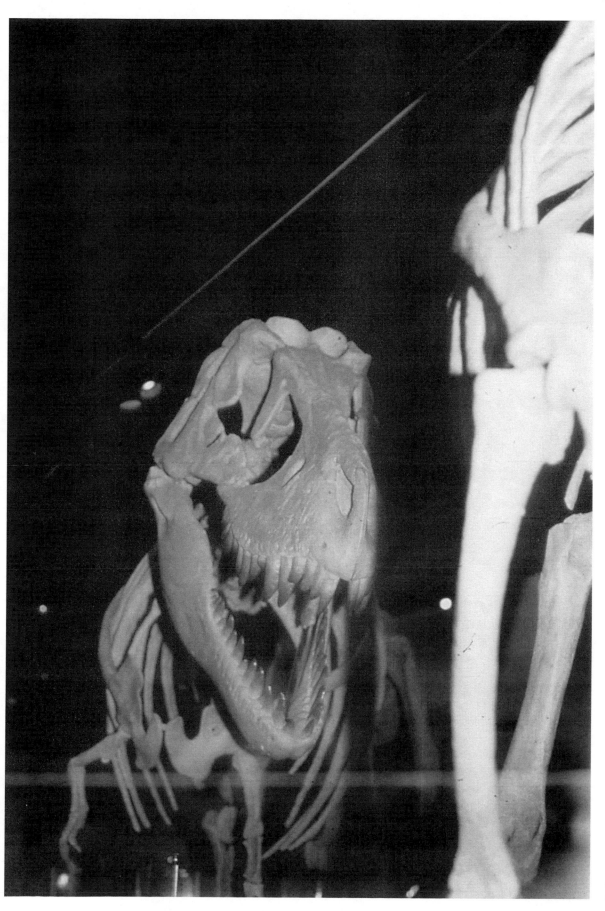

Tarbosaurus bataar skeleton (cast) displayed in the traveling "Great Russian Dinosaur Exhibition."

A pair of *Tarbosaurus bataar* confronts a group of the unusual theropod *Therizinosaurus cheloniformis* in this illustration by Gregory S. Paul.

tyrannosaurids to represent different ontogenetic stages of a single species intermediate between the North American *Albertosaurus* and *Tyrannosaurus*, referred all of those taxa to *Tarbosaurus bataar*. However, by referring these taxa to a referred rather than the type species, Rozhestvensky inadvertently, it seems, officially left the species then called *Tarbosaurus bataar* without a generic name (see below), although that binomial was generally accepted by vertebrate paleontologists and adopted into the literature as valid.

In the decades following the discovery of the above-mentioned material, numerous specimens referred to *Tarbosaurus*, representing various ontogenetic stages, have been collected (see *D:TE, S1*, and *S2* for photographs of some of these). Also, over the years, a number of paleontologists have questioned whether *Tarbosaurus* is a valid genus or an Asian junior synonym or even a subgenus of *Tyrannosaurus* (*e.g.*, see Paul 1988*b*). Later, Carpenter (1992), after reassessing

Maleev's (1955*a*, 1955*b*) figures of the Mongolian tyrannosaurids and also Rozhdestvensky's analysis and photographs of the material, concluded that *T. bataar* was a species of *Tyrannosaurus*; at the same time, Carpenter referred the species *Gorgosaurus novojilovi* to the new genus *Maleevosaurus*, describing it as a small tyrannosaurid (see *D:TE* for details).

Subsequent to Carpenter's referral of *Tarbosaurus bataar* back to its original name, *Tyrannosaurus bataar*, a number of other workers specializing in theropods (*e.g.*, Holtz 1994*a*, 2001; Carr 1996, who also referred Carpenter's *Maleevosaurus* to *Tarbosaurus* as a juvenile of that genus; see *S2*) accepted Carpenter's synonymy of these two genera. Holtz (2001), noting that numerous synapomorphies unite *T. bataar* and *T. rex*, retained the name *Tyrannosaurus bataar*, but added that using name *Tarbosaurus bataar* (as, for example, in Russell 1970) "would be no less appropriate phylogentically." As Holtz (2001) noted, "*T. bataar* is characterized by the most reduced forelimbs known within Tyrannosauridae," the general theropod reduction in digital and metacarpal elements from digits V toward I (see Wagner and Gauthier 1999) being developed more in this species than in any other known tyrannosaurid.

Various others workers, however, did not accept the synonymy of *Tarbosaurus* with *Tyrannosaurus*, noting that these taxa have been found on different continents, remains of *Tarbosaurus* predate *Tyrannosaurus* in the fossil record, most specimens of adult *Tarbosaurus* are somewhat smaller than the North American genus, and the Asian taxon has relatively shorter forelimbs. Olshevsky (*see in* Olshevsky, Ford and Yamamoto 1995*a*, 1995*b*), for example, not only regarded the Mongolian taxon as a genus distinct from *Tyrannosaurus*, but also, noting the problem Rozhdestvensky had created with his incorrect referral (see above), proposed the new name genus *Jenghizkhan* to embrace the *Tarbosaurus bataar* materials (see S2). Olshevsky's proposed name was not yet, however, generally adopted.

Among the paleontologists to continue using the name *Tarbosaurus* has been theropod authority Philip J. Currie (2000*c*), as in his recent survey paper on theropods from the Cretaceous of Mongolia. In fact, Currie has maintained the generic separation of *Tarbosaurus* and *Tyrannosaurus* even when co-authored with Carpenter (see Currie and Carpenter 2000; also Currie and Dong 2001, and *Shanshanosaurus* entry). No detailed study had yet been published demonstrating that *Tarbosaurus* is not distinct from *Tyrannosaurus*. In a recent abstract, Ryan, Russell and Currie (2002) stated that "the large Asian theropod *Tarbosaurus* has been suggested to be congeneric with the North American *Tyrannosaurus*, however detailed analyses indicate that it is a valid genus." Evidence establishing the validity of *Tarbosaurus* is to be published in a joint paper by Hurum, Sabath and Currie (in preparation; P. J. Currie, personal communication 2002).

Regarding other taxa that may pertain to *Tarbosaurus*, ?*Abertosaurus periculosus* Riabinin 1930, a *nomen dubium*, was based on a tooth crown recovered from the Amur River locality in Manchuria. Molnar (1990) tentatively referred this species to *Tarbosaurus*, although, somewhat earlier, this taxon had been regarded by Gilmore (1930) as a *nomen nudum*, having neither specific nor generic distinction. The tentative species ?*T. turpanensis*, a *nomen nudum*, was mentioned by Zhai, Zheng and Tong (1978) in a survey report on the stratigraphy of the mammal-bearing Tertiary of the Turfan Basin, Sinkiang. *Tyrannosaurus luanchuanensis* Dong 1979, based on a tooth and some postcranial remains (NIGP V4733) from the Quiba

Formation of Songping Valley, Luanchuan County, Henan Province, Inner Mongolia, China, is generally considered referrable to *Tarbosaurus*.

Hurum (2001*a*), in a brief report published as an abstract, compared the skulls of *Tarbosaurus bataar* with those of *Tyrannosaurus rex* and *Gorgosaurus* sp., following an "inside and outside" study of a skull of the Asian species, "taken apart bone by bone to reveal many new structures," this study yielding new information concerning the structure and movement of the tyrannosaurid intramandibular jaw joint. As Hurum pointed out, earlier studies have suggested that this joint had a wide range of movement that permitted the expansion of the gullet and the adjustment of the pitch and position of the mandibular teeth in relationship to the upper teeth. This mobility suggested a feeding behavior with a weak bite, as in lizards. Contrarily, other features—*e.g.*, shortening and elevation of the skull for insertion of powerful jaw muscles, increased robustness of teeth, bite marks suggesting bone fragmentation, estimation of bite force from tooth-marked bone, and bone fragments found in coprolites—point towards a high bite force in tyrannosaurids.

According to Hurum, the newly studied material reveals "fusion of the coronoid and supradentary, elongation of the medial process of the surangular, and the presence of high interlocking ridges and deep grooves on the angular and prearticular," all of these, that author noted, constituting secondary adaptations to a rigid lower jaw designed for crushing. Newly revealed details of the skull structure and lower jaw, presumably to be described fully at a later date by Hurum, "also show adaptation towards a crushing bite in North American tyrannosaurids and *T. bataar*."

Notes: Currie, in abstracts dated September 2000 and 2001, announced the recent discoveries, over the last three field trips by Nomadic Expeditions, Inc. (1999, 2000, and 2001) to Mongolia, of numerous dinosaurian specimens, at least two of *Tarbosaurus* numbering among them, including the following:

1. A *Tarbosaurus bataar* frontal from the Nemegt Formation, Western Sayr of the Nemegt Locality, this specimen found and collected by Currie (Currie 2001).

2. A *T. bataar* metatarsal IV from the Nemegt Formation, Western Sayr, found by Eva Koppelhus, collected by Albert Miniaci (Currie 2001).

3. A nearly complete *Tarbosaurus* skeleton (PJC.2000.9) of a small individual from the Nemegt Formation, Nemegt Locality, found by Ed Horton on September 10, 2000 (Currie 2001). The tail and most of the hips had been eroded away. Horton collected the pedal phalanges on September 11, Nomadic Expedition participants recovered the rest of the specimen

that same month. Three hadrosaur footprints, presumably made by the same individual, were found next to the skeleton. Likely another hadrosaur stepped on the skull after the *Tarbosaurus* died and was buried, not damaging it, but separating some of the facial bones and pushing them deep into the mud. This *Tarbosaurus* specimen has been turned over to Khishigjaw Tsogtbaatar, director of the Paleontological Institution in Ulaan Bataar (2002).

4. A heavily worn *T. bataar* premaxillary tooth, found by Demchig Badamgarav and collected by Currie, from the *Elmisaurus* quarry, Nemegt Formation, Western Sayr (Currie 2001).

5. *T. bataar* frontals plus skin impressions (from "one of the skeletons apparently destroyed by locals looking for material to sell on the black market"), collected by Currie, Badamgarav and Mona Marsovsky from the Nemegt Formation, Bugin Tsav (Currie 2001).

6. *T. bataar* frontals plus occipital condyle, from another intended "black market" specimen, collected by Currie and Badamgarav, Nemegt Formation, Bugin Tsav (Currie 2001).

7. The glenoid region of a scapula (PJC.2001.14) referred to cf. *Tarbosaurus*, from the Nemegt Formation, Nemegt Locality, found and collected by Clive Coy on September 15, 2001 (Currie 2002).

Key references: Carpenter (1992); Carr (1996); Currie (2000c, 2001, 2002); Currie and Dong (20001; Dong (1979); Gilmore (1930); Holtz (1994a, 2001); Hurum (2001a); Maleev (1955a, 1955b, 1955c); Molnar (1990); Olshevsky (1995a, 1995b); Paul (1988b); Riabinin (1930); Rozhdestvensky (1965); Russell (1970); Ryan, Russell and Currie (2002); Wagner and Gauthier (1986); Zhai, Zheng and Tong (1978).

†THECOCOELURUS

Saurischia: Eusaurischia: Theropoda: Neotheropoda: Tetanurae: Avetheropoda: Coelurosauria: Maniraptoriformes: Arctometatarsalia ?Metornithes: ?Oviraptorosauria: ?Caenagnathdae.

Occurrence: ?Wessex Formation, Isle of Wight, England.

Age: Early Cretaceous (Barrimian).

Comments: In 1923, Friedrich von Huene erected the new name of *Thecocoelurus daviesi* for a small, incomplete (lacking its caudal half) cranial cervical vertebra (BMNH R181), collected probably from the Lower Cretaceous (Barremian) Wessex Formation on the Isle of Wight, this specimen originally having been referred by Seeley (1885) to *Thecospondylus* as a new species of that dubious genus (see *D:TE*). This type species has been generally regarded as a theropod of uncertain affinities.

More recently, Naish and Martill (2002) reappraised the holotype of *T. daviesi* and, while acknowledging that the taxon is a *nomen dubium* exhibiting no diagnostic characters, found it to offer various informative features. Avoiding the observations of Seeley, Naish and Martill described the vertebra in detail, pointing out other characters and features "that have either not previously been described, or are of importance in determining the phylogenetic position of this specimen."

The specimen has been sectioned and polished, the authors noted, revealing the internal structure of the pleurocoels, their presence on the centra and the relatively elongate centrum identifying BMNH R181 as belonging to the Saurischia.

Comparing BMNH R181 with other theropod cervical vertebrae, Naish and Martill determined that Seeley's original reconstruction of the specimen, estimated by him to have been approximately 90 millimeters in length of complete, is too long, a more reasonable length being about 70 millimeters, with a total length for the animal estimated to be about 5 meters (about 17 feet). Based upon simple morphological comparison, the authors found BMNH R181 to resemble most closely the caudal cervical vertebra

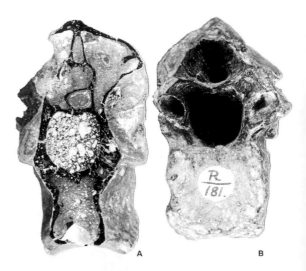

Thecocoelurus daviesi, BMNH R181, holotype incomplete cervical vertebra of *Thecospondylus daviesi*, in (left) caudal, (right) cranial, and (bottom) ventral views. (After Naish, Hutt and Martill 1999.)

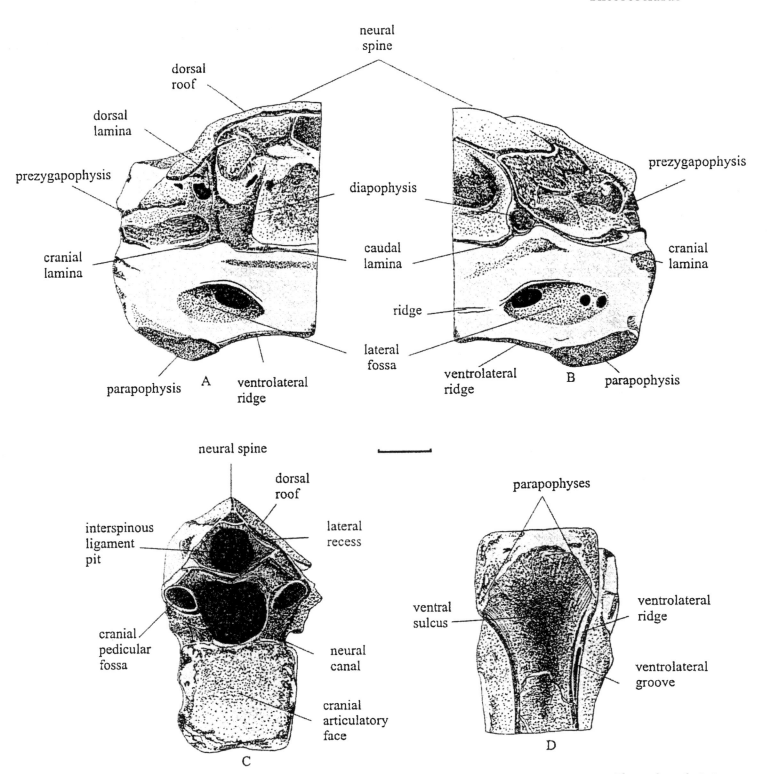

neural spine

dorsal roof

dorsal lamina

prezygapophysis

cranial lamina

parapophysis   A   ventrolateral ridge

diapophysis

caudal lamina

ridge

lateral fossa

prezygapophysis

cranial lamina

ventrolateral ridge   B   parapophysis

neural spine

interspinous ligament pit

cranial pedicular fossa

dorsal roof

lateral recess

neural canal

cranial articulatory face

C

parapophyses

ventral sulcus

ventrolateral ridge

ventrolateral groove

D

Thecocoelurus daviesi, BMNH R181, holotype cervical vertebra in A. left lateral, B. right lateral, C. cranial, and D. ventral views. Scale = 10 mm. (After Naish and Martill 2002.)

of the Late Cretaceous Canadian caenagnathid *Chirostenotes pergracilis*. Also, the ventral hourglass shape of BMNH R181, with its shallow and broad sulcus and raised lateral margins joining the parapophyses, are autapomorphic features for the clade of Oviptorosauria-Therizinosauroidea. Therizinosauroid cervical vertebrae have slit-shaped central pneumatic foramina and more robust neural spines than in oviraptorosaurs (see Makovicky 1995), while BMNH R181 has more rounded pneumatic foramina and its neural spine is not robust. Therefore, Naish and Martill regarded the Isle of White specimen as probably belonging to an oviraptorosaur.

Performing a phylogenetic analysis (following

the list of characters utilized by Frankfurt and Chiappe 1999, while adding one character proposed by Britt 1993, presence of apneumatic, camerate or camellate interior to centrum), Naish and Martill found BMNH R181 to lie within the oviraptorosaur-therizinosauroid clade, most closely resembling caenagnathid oviraptorosaurs.

Recognizing *Thecocoelurus* as an oviraptorosaur, the authors noted, extends the geographical range for the Oviraptorosauria into Europe. Furthermore, the Barremian age for this genus distinguishes *Thecocoelurus* as one of the earliest known members of that clade.

Key references: Britt (1993); Frankfurt and Chiappe (1999); Huene (1923); Makovicky (1995); Naish (2002*b*); Naish and Martill (2002); Seeley (1888).

†THECODONTOSAURUS

Saurischia: Eusaurischia: Sauropodomorpha: Prosauropoda: Thecodontosauridae.

Occurrence of new species: South Wales, United Kingdom.

Known material/holotype: Partial skeleton, juvenile.

Comments: Yates (2001), in an abstract, briefly discussed a partial skeleton of a juvenile, primitive sauropodomorph from South Wales, originally referred by Kermack (1984) to *Thecodontosaurus* sp. (see *S2*), a referral supported by the single synapomorphy of overhanging, planar cervical epipophyses. As pointed out by Yates, however, this specimen lacks certain autapomorphies of the type species *Thecodontosaurus antiquus* (*e.g.*, short, dorso-ventrally deep preacetabular blade of ilium). Also, the South Wales specimen possesses unique fossae, possibly of pneumatic origin, on the sixth, seventh, and eighth cervical vertebrae, these diagnosing this specimen as representing a new species (to be named at a later date).

According to Yates in his preliminary report, this new species exhibits a combination of character states including some that were previously regarded as diagnosing Prosauropoda, while other states indicate that the species is basal to *Plateosaurus* plus Sauropoda.

Incorporating the above new data regarding *Thecodontosaurus* into a parsimony analysis of early sauropodomorph relationships, considering Herrerasauridae, Neotheropoda, 15 "prosauropod" taxa, *Vulcanodon*, and Eusauropoda, and utilizing 164 osteological characters, Yates concluded the following: *Saturnalia* and *Thecodontosaurus* basal to all other sauropodomorphs; typical "prosauropods" forming a paraphyletic array on the stem of the Sauropoda, *Sellosaurus* being the most distal, *Blikanasaurus* the closest to Sauropoda; and excluding *Saturnalia*, *The-*

codontosaurus, and "melanorosaurids" (*Euskelosaurus*, *Melanorosaurus*, and *Blikanasaurus*) results in recovering a monophyletic Prosauropoda (inclusion of any of those taxa resulting in its fragmentation).

Results of this study indicated to Yates the importance of *Thecodontosaurus* as a key taxon in phylogenetic analyses, and also "that several proposed prosauropod synapomorphies are more likely to be sauropodomorph symplesiomorphies that were lost in Sauropoda, probably due to the extreme transformation these organisms underwent as they evolved from their 'prosauropod' ancestors." The details of Yates' new phylogeny are still to be published.

Cherry (2003), in a published abstract, briefly reported on her histological study of *Thecodontosaurus* bones collected from the Tytherington quarry, near Bristol, in southwest England, currently housed at the Bristol City Museum, University of Bristol. The surface of one sectioned bone, the author noted, is marked by a juxtacortical lesion.

Briefly, Cherry described a minimum of 10 *Thecodontosaurus* bone sections, these samplings representing a variety of skeletal elements.

As that author noted, *Thecodontosaurus* is, to date, the most primitive dinosaur upon which this kind of work has been performed. By comparing the results of Cherry's study with those of more derived dinosaurian taxa, new insights may be gleaned concerning the evolution of growth rates and patterns amongst this and other early dinosaurs. "Recent work has shown a significant difference in canalicular orientation between theropods and ornithischians," Cherry stated, "and our work sample will help map out the distribution of this interesting character."

Also accessing the Bristol City Museum collection, Lee (2003) briefly reported on morphometric analyses of various disassociated *Thecodontosaurus* bones, the aim of her study being "firstly, to investigate whether there is any evidence of dimorphism in the population, possibly sexual, as is the case with early theropod dinosaurs, and secondly to attempt to discover the long bone proportions of an individual *Thecodontosaurus*."

Lee's study involved matching on frequency histograms the distribution peaks in size classes for humeri, femora, tibeae, and ulnae. Hindlimb proportions for *Thecodontosaurus* were included by Lee in an analysis of hindlimb proportions relating to other sauropodomorphs, these proportions then plotted to determine if the inferred proportions of *Thecodontosaurus* were congruent with those of other sauroporomorphs. However, Lee did not, in this short report, state the results of this study.

Note: In a 2002 personal communication to George Olshevsky, Terry Michitsch pointed out that the referred species *Plateosaurus elizae* Huene 1907–08, erected in a short report by Sauvage (189? or ?1907) as a new species of *Thecodontosaurus* (*T. elizae*), was originally spelled by that author as *T. elisae* (in honor of Elisa Thiery, who found the fossil). *T. elisae* is therefore the correct spelling, although this taxon, based on carnivorous teeth, is referrable neither to *Thecodontosaurus* nor *Plateosaurus* (see *D:TE*).

Key references: Cherry (2003); Huene (1907–08); Kermack (1984); Lee (2003); Sauvage (189? or ?1907); Yates (2001).

†THESCELOSAURUS

Comments: In a 2000 issue of the journal *Science*, Paul E. Fisher, Dale A. Russell, Michael K. Stoskopf, Reese E. Barrick, Michael Hammer, and Andrew A. Kuzmitz, utilizing computerized tomography (CT) scanning, reported a spheroidal object which they identified as a fossilized four-chamber heart possessing a single systemic aorta, found within the chest area of a skeleton (NCSM 15728) identified as *Thescelosaurus neglectus*. This specimen of the small, Late Cretaceous ornithopod was collected from the Hell Creek Formation (a fluvial setting rarely preserving soft tissues) of northwestern South Dakota. The authors explained the preservation of the putative heat by suggesting that it had been saponified (or turned to soap) in anaerobic burial conditions, then permineralized by the brown mineral goethite as iron-bound oxygen in the muscular walls made contact with water from the ground during early diagenesis (see *S2*).

If the interpretation by Fisher *et al.* that this object represented a heart, it would indeed constitute one of the most important and spectacular dinosaur discoveries of recent years.

However, subsequent to the publication of Fisher *et al.*'s paper, this interpretation was challenged by Rowe, McBride and Sereno (2001), again in the pages of *Science* (see also Stokstad 2001*a*). Following examination of both the specimen and the CT imagery by Timothy Rowe, these authors reached the quite different conclusion that the object was not a heart but

Mounted skeletons (casts) of *Thescelosaurus neglectus*. The identification of a spheroid object as a heart in one recently described specimen of this dinosaur (see *S2*) has been challenged.

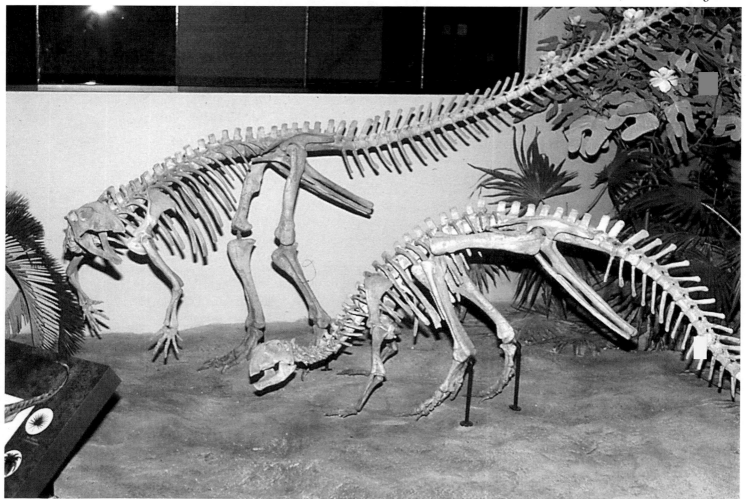

Photograph by the author, courtesy North American Museum of Ancient Life.

Thescelosaurus

Courtesy North American Museum of
Ancient Life.

**Life restoration of
Thescelosaurus neglectus
painted by Kelly Pugh. The
"comb" and dorsal "frill"
are conjectural.**

an ironstone concretion, such concretions, often found in association with dinosaur bones, being common in Upper Cretaceous fluvial sediments of the North American western interior.

As pointed out by Rowe *et al.*, soft tissues are rapidly degraded by bacteria in the oxygenated waters of river channels; therefore, permineralized soft organs is virtually unknown in sedimentary environments such as that represented by the Hell Creek Formation. Sphere-shaped goethite concretions are never primary, forming instead by near-surface oxidation of siderite concretions in sandstone and shale. As millions of years are seemingly required to produce, by diffusive processes, a concretion the size of the supposed dinosaur heart, it is unlikely that the putative organ could have been fossilized in fluvial sediments before its consumption by bacteria. Even more unlikely, it could have been permineralized directly by goethite.

While agreeing that CT imagery of the hypoth-

esized organ reveals internal cavities resembling the venticular chambers of a four-chambered heart, Rowe *et al.* noted the following: The object otherwise shows none of the other anatomical structures of a heart. The object's supposed venticular portion lies partly outside the thoracic cavity, engulfing the 11th rib. The right cavity identified by Fisher *et al.* as a ventrical is nearly closed, only its "interventricular" wall penetrated (by complex fractures containing lower density materials). The supposed aorta lies within the thoracic cavity, its lumen entirely enclosed by the same concretionary mass enclosing the interpreted ventricles. The lumen of the supposed aorta is irregularly shaped, narrows toward the supposed left ventrical (unlike a true aorta), and has none of the expected arteries emerging from it.

Finally, Rowe *et al.* pointed out the following: The lumen of both the hypothesized aorta and ventricles is completely encapsulated, yet supposedly full of iron-free quartz silt. Its walls, as revealed in cross section, comprise concentric layers marked by different densities and fracture patterns. Also, a second concretion preserving remnants of the original bedding planes exists behind the right femur. "All of these features," the authors noted, "are consistent with the identification of the structure as a spheroidal concretion." In their opinion, therefore, the object identified by Fisher *et al.* as a heart "fails both geological and anatomical tests of its unprecedented identification."

In the same issue of *Science*, directly following the criticism of Rowe *et al.*, Russell, Fisher, Barrick and Stoskopf (2001) responded to their new assessment, holding to the original interpretation that the object represents a fossilized dinosaur heart.

As countered by Russell *et al.*, and *contra* Rowe *et al.*, the object is a sandstone and not an ironstone concretion. Although poorly delimited ironstone concretions containing plant debris are found at a horizon several levels of the one that yielded the *Thescelosaurus* skeleton, no such concretions occur in strata adjacent to the skeleton, while the studied object "is intimately associated with the skeleton, in a manner unlike that of any other concretion in the vicinity of the site or reported from Upper Cretaceous strata elsewhere in the western interior of North America. Dinosaurian soft tissues have indeed been reported from the Hell Creek Formation (*e.g.*, Fisher *et al.*; Morris 1970; Horner 1984*b*; Happ and Morrow 2000; Osborn 1912*b*). As concretions often form around an organic residue, it is logical to surmise that organic residues derived from the decomposing animal constituted the nucleus of the object in question, the configuration of the rib embedded in the object suggesting that the residues were displaced toward the lower part of the skeleton. CT imaging has revealed structures embedded within the chest cavity "consistent with the shape, volume, position, and orientation of the more muscular portions of a heart (ventricles and aortic arch)," these structures conceivably forming the nucleus for the surrounding concretion. Finally, time scales of from just months to tens of years are common for many types of concretions (see Aslan and Autin 1998).

In conclusion, Russell *et al.* pointed out that, before the discovery of NCSM 15728, "No tubular structure associated with two contiguous ovoid structures has ever been reported within a concretion in such intimate association with a dinosaur skeleton"; nor need the identification of the object as a fossil dinosaur heart show a "structural identity with a crocodile heart or the preservation of relatively thin-walled structures." Investigations of the fossil, the authors stated, will continue.

Key references: Aslan and Autin (1998); Fisher, Russell, Stoskopf, Barrick, Hammer and Kuzmitz (2000); Happ and Morrow (2000); Horner (1984*b*); Morris (1970); Osborn (1912*b*); Rowe, McBride and Sereno (2001); Russell, Fisher, Barrick and Stoskopf (2001); Stokstad (2001*a*).

†TITANOSAURUS

Saurischia: Eusaurischia: Sauropodomorpha: Sauropoda: Eusauropoda: Neosauropoda: Macronaria: Camarasauromorpha: Titanosauriformes: Somphospondyli: Titanosauria: Eutitanosauria: Saltasauridae.

Comments: The genus *Titanosaurus* (the name retained here tentatively; see below) has been a problematic and controversial taxon since it was first erected in 1877 by Richard Lydekker (see *D:TE*). As briefly recounted by sauropod systematist Jeffrey A. Wilson (2002) in a published abstract, the validity of this genus has remained a central issue in the systematics of titanosaurian sauropods, the genus having subsequently "become a namesake for several higher-level taxa (*e.g.*, Titanosauria, Titanosauroidea, Titanosauridae). The type species *Titanosaurus indicus* was based on a partial femur and two incomplete caudal vertebrae, the latter distinguished from other known dinosaurs by having procoelous articular faces (see below).

Recently, prior to Wilson's report, Mohabey (2001), in a review of dinosaur eggs known from India, presumably accepted *Titanosaurus* as a valid genus. Indeed, Mohabey also rediagnosed four species referred to *Titanosaurus—T. indicus*, *T. madagascariensis* [as the incorrectly named *Laplatasaurus madagascariensis*; see below], *T. blandfordi*, and *T. colberti*.

Mohaby diagnosed *T. indicus* as follows: Caudal vertebrae markedly procoelous, basically flat, lateral sides compressed; proximal articular surface of centrum forming very deep cup, longer diameter placed vertically; longer diameter of corresponding cone (distal surface) of opposite vertebrae placed vertically, not quite reaching lower border, but contacting upper border; coalescing of neural arch with centrum in proximal half; inferior surface roughly oblong, expanded at both ends; no portion of lateral surface visible in ventral aspect; lateral and horizontal surfaces nearly at right angles; inferior surface forming deep, broad furrow, slightly constricted at middle; both pairs of articular facets for haemapophysis wide apart, projecting considerably.

Mohabey diagnosed *T. blandfordi* as follows: Caudal vertebrae procoelous, laterally compressed; centrum almost cylindrical, showing no signs of lateral compression; transverse diameter of each articular surface of centrum longer than vertical diameter;

centrum exhibiting almost entire lateral surface in ventral aspect; no hard boundary between lateral and horizontal surfaces; articular facets for chevrons lying at either extremity, not at summit of distinct ridges.

Mohaby diagnosed *T. colbertii* as follows: Caudal vertebrae strongly procoelous; cervical and dorsal vertebrae strongly opisthocoelous, having well-marked pleurocoels; centra of cervical vertebrae small, transverse processes of cervicals wide, laterally directed, robust in shoulder region; neural spines of medium height, not bifid, more caudally directed in dorsal vertebrae, transverse processes of dorsal vertebrae robust, laterally and slightly upwardly projected, sacrum having six vertebrae coosified with ribs; chevron facets on cranial rim of midcaudal vertebrae located on raised prominent ridges, on low, faint ridges on distal rims; middle part of caudal centra ventrally flat, lacking ridge; chevron facets on very low ridges in distal caudal vertebrae.

Mohaby diagnosed *T. madagascariensis* as follows: Caudal vertebrae procoelous, rims of their cups and balls having almost square outlines, possibly becoming broadly rectangular in distalmost caudals; lateral faces of centra not diverging upwards from below; very slight constriction at middle of centra; differing from *T. indicus* and *T. blandfordi* in having extremely broad neural canal, centra with noticeably longer proximally than distally (Mohabey 2001).

In 1896, Charles Depéret had erected another new species of *Titanosaurus—Titanosaurus madagascariensis—*based upon the syntype specimen comprising two procoelous caudal vertebrae, a partial humeral diapophysis, and a large osteoderm collected from Upper Cretaceous strata of Madagascar (see *D:TE*). Recently, Curry Rogers and Forster (2001), in a paper describing the new titanosaur *Rapetosaurus* (see entry), pointed out that two titanosaur taxa are currently recognized in the Upper Cretaceous Maevarano Formation in Madagascar (see Ravoavy 1991; Curry Rogers and Forster 1999*a*, 1999*b*), both distinguished in part by their caudal vertebrae. As the syntype of *T. madagascariensis* includes both caudal morphologies, this species was regarded by Curry Rogers and Forster as a *nomen dubium*.

In that same paper, Curry Rogers and Forster regarded the genus *Titanosaurus* as a "saltasaurine" (=saltasaurid of Wilson, Martinez and Alcober 1999), but gave no reasons to support this assessment.

Wilson, however, questioned the validity of *Titanosaurus* as a genus. As that author pointed out, the distribution of procoelous caudal vertebrae has, since the original description of this genus, expanded to include most titanosaurian sauropods, including a total of 13 species that, over the years, have been referred to *Titanosaurus*. If all of these species are considered

to be valid, Wilson noted, then "these species distribute the genus across Argentina, Europe, Madagascar, India, and Laos, and throughout 60 million years of the Cretaceous."

Reevaluating all of the species that have been referred to *Titanosaurus*, Wilson found only two to be diagnostic, *T. colberti* and *T. araukanicus*. All remaining species, according to that author, including the type species *T. indicus* and the genus are invalid, this also rendering invalid coordinated suprafamilial, familial, and subfamilial ranked taxa. This also implies, consequently, that a new genus name should be proposed to embrace the valid species *T. colberti* and *T. araukanicus*.

However, Wilson noted, based upon recent cladistic analyses Titanosauria remains valid, this clade and its constituent outgroups defined phylogenetically "to provide a stable taxonomic base for further investigations within the group." According to Wilson, the interpretation of the Titanosauria as a Gondwanan clade, in light of these systematic revisions, must now be reconsidered.

Key references: Depéret (1869); Ravoavy (1991); Curry Rogers and Forster (1999*a*, 1999*b*, 2001); Mohabey (2001); Lydekker (1877); Wilson (2002*b*); Wilson, Martinez and Alcober (1999).

†TOROSAURUS

Ornithischia: Genasauria: Cerapoda: Marginocephalia: Ceratopsia: Neoceratopsia: Coronosauria: Ceratopsoidea: Ceratopsidae: Chasmosaurinae.

Comments: Marshall and Barreto (2001), in a short report published as an abstract, briefly commented on a healed cranial injury in the skull of an adult specimen (MPM VP8149) of *Torosaurus latus* on display at the Milwaukee Public Museum. As noted by Marshall and Barreto, this pathology consists of an irregular, oblate perforation located in the rostral portion of the left squamosal.

The authors briefly described the pathology as follows: Measures about 10 centimeters by 13 centimeters; raised rim of thicker bone surrounding perforation, showing evidence of callus formation and bone remodeling; ridge of rough, thickened bone, compatible with callus of a healing/healed fracture, extending from dorsal ridge of perforation to left parietal-squamosal suture; left squamosal short than "normal" right.

As deduced by Marshall and Barreto, this *Torosaurus* individual must have suffered this injury before attaining full maturity and growth of the frill was complete. Furthermore, the right squamosal foramen is open while this opening has been filled in the injured bone, "presumably as a compensatory response to strengthen the damaged bone."

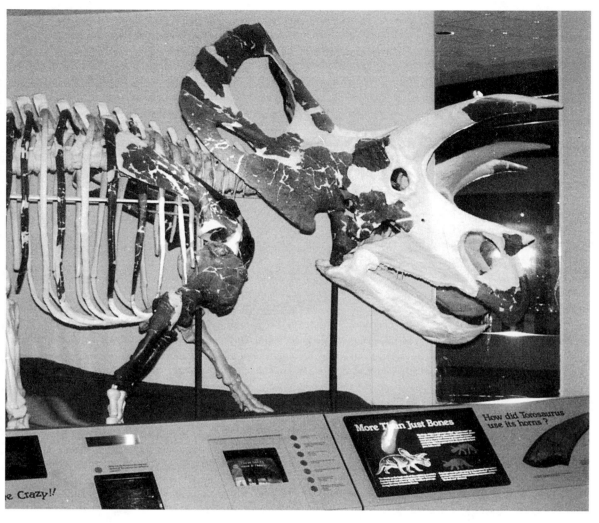

Photograph by Karl Debus, courtesy Allen A. Debus and Milwaukee Public Museum.

Reconstructed partial skeleton (MPM VP8149) of *Torosaurus latus* mounted at the Milwaukee Public Museum. A pathology of the skull of this specimen was were examined by Cynthia L. Marshall and Claudia Barreto (2001).

Marshall and Barreto pointed out that the location of this wound "enables evaluation of the pattern of forces applied to the frill by muscles of mastication," while the "cellular and morphological healing processes of a dinosaurian dermal bone" can be compared with extant taxa.

Horner and Marshall (2002), in an abstract, noted that the frills, horns, and also other areas of the skulls of ceratopsians "are indented with meandering grooves (most prominent in genera such as *Torosaurus* and *Triceratops*) that have been previously interpreted as channels that carried blood vessels," the latter, with this vasculature, suggesting a large supply of blood feeding the epidermal layer. Comparison by Horner and Marshall of these structures with Paleocene and Recent mammals and birds revealed a consistency with bony surfaces found beneath keratinous sheaths, identical vascular grooves being observed on the lateral surfaces of the unguals of the ground sloth *Megalonyx,* and on the beaks of all extant birds. According to Horner and Marshall, a keratinous sheath seems to have covered almost the entire skull (including the ventral surface of the frill) in *Torosaurus* and *Triceratops.*

Farke (2002*a*), in a published abstract for a poster, reviewed the various specimens that have been referred to *Torosaurus,* pointing out that, in the past, this genus has been reported from as far north as Saskatchewan to as far south as Texas, that some specimens have been used to confirm a late Maastrichtian age for some formations, and that this genus has been regarded as a distinctive component of the late Maastrichtian fauna of southwestern North America. However, Farke noted, many of the southwestern occurrences are founded upon incomplete or fragmentary specimens rendering dubious their assignment to this genus. In fact, reexamination by that author of eight specimens referred to *Torosaurus* housed at the Texas Memorial Museum and the New Mexico Museum of Natural History and Science showed four of these to be generically indeterminate.

According to Farke, of two specimens (TMM 41480-1 and TMM 41835-1, respectively) previously referred to *Torosaurus utahensis,* only the former, a partial parietal, can be referred with confidence to *Torosaurus* sp. The latter specimen, an isolated horn core, could only be referred to an indeterminate chasmosaurine. Of various specimens from the Naashoibito Member (possible age ranging from late Campanian to late Maastrichtian; see Sullivan, Lucas and Braman 2002) of the Kirtland Formation of New Mexico, Farke transferred a partial postorbital (NMMNH P32615) and some squamosal fragments (NMMNH P29006 and NMMNH P21100) from *Torosaurus* to Chasmosaurinae indet., referred a partial parietal (NMMNH P25074) to *Torosaurus* sp., and tentatively retained in the genus a partial parietal and squamosal (NMMNH P22884) as *Torosaurus* cf. *T. utahensis*. Farke also referred to *Torosaurus* sp. a partial skull and skeleton (NMMNH, unnumbered specimen) from the McRae Formation of New Mexico.

Farke further noted the following: Isolated brow horn cores are not generically diagnostic, although both the distinctive shape of the squamosal and the wide, thin, and fenestrated parietal are unique to the genus *Torosaurus*; confirming the validity of the species *T. utahensis* necessitates further study; and, due to its limited and fragmentary material referred, this genus is not a useful biostratigraphic indicator,

and its exact contribution to late Maastrichtian Southwestern paleoecology cannot presently be determined.

In another abstract, Farkes (2002*b*) briefly reported on two *Torosaurus* skulls (MOR 981 and 1122) recently collected by the Museum of the Rockies from the Hell Creek Formation of eastern Montana, these specimens offering a better characterization of the cranial anatomy and individual variation within this taxon. Crushed, partial skull MOR 981 measures 3.2 meters in maximum length; uncrushed, well-preserved MOR 1122 measures about 2.8 meters in greatest length. MOR 1122 displays several unusual skull features (*e.g.*, keeled epoccipitals, prominent double sulcation on postorbital horns).

Key references: Farke (2002*a*, 2002*b*); Horner and Marshall (2002); Marshall and Barreto (2001).

†TRICERATOPS

Ornithischia: Genasauria: Cerapoda: Marginocephalia: Ceratopsia: Neoceratopsia: Coronosauria: Ceratopsoidea: Ceratopsidae: Chasmosaurinae.

Skeleton (cast) of *Triceratops horridus* prepared by Triebold Paleontology, Inc.

Photograph by the author, courtesy North American Museum of Ancient Life.

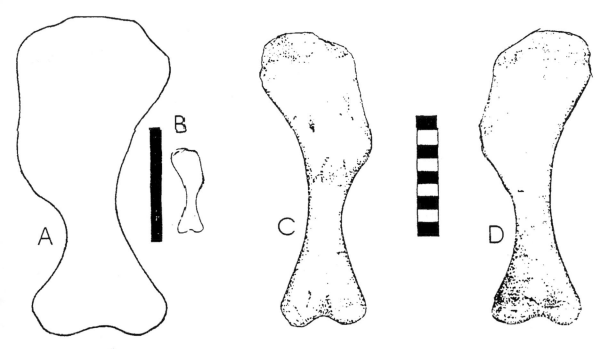

Humeri of *Triceratops*: A. and B., outline drawings of the humerus (SMNH P1163.9) of an adult *T. horridus* and a juvenile humerus (SMNH P2691.1) referred to *Triceratops* sp., respectively, scale = 29 cm.; C. and D., dorsal and ventral views of SMNH (2692.1), respectively, scale divisions = 1 cm. (After Tokaryk 2002.)

Comments: Until recently, the known record of juvenile and subadult chasmosaurine ceratopsians has been poor, as pointed out by Goodwin and Horner (2001) in an abstract, consequently limiting previous assessments of the ontogeny of the giant horned dinosaur *Triceratops*. As these authors reported, the recent recovery of skull and cranial elements from the Hell Creek Formation of Montana has offered new information regarding the ontogeny of cranial morphology, including display structures, in this genus.

Goodwin and Horner observed the following in this new material:

Regarding the nasal horn of *Triceratops*, the paired nasal bones contact along a broad, flat, and often unfused midline surface, rostrally forming a rugose sutural "boss" that makes a surface for a distinct and separate nasal horn (*e.g.*, UCMP 137263). In juveniles, a short, blunt, triangual epispinal (*e.g.*, UCMP 136306) is present. During ontogeny, the nasal horn widens, becoming curved, pointy, and slightly compressed laterally (*e.g.*, UCMP 144297). In adults, the base of this horn can extend over the nasals, obscuring sutural contacts. The midline sutural region of the nasals in the adult specimen UCMP 174838 is overgrown by a greatly expanded nasal horn, remaining visible in ventral aspect. This specimen confirmed the presence of a separate epispinal, which had previously been difficult to discern in other specimens.

The postorbital horns in *Triceratops* were found by Goodwin and Horner to develop early, growing into the well-known massive structures that dominate the skull. In the smallest collected *Triceratops* skull (UCMP 154452), these horns are transformed from tiny, slightly forwardly directed outgrowths of bone to thicker, caudally curved horns in juvenile individuals (*e.g.*, UCMP 539). In subadults (*e.g.*, UCMP 136306 and 137263), the caudally oriented postorbital horns enlarge increasingly, expanding ventrally and recurving forward during advanced ontogeny (*e.g.*, UCMP 113697, among the largest and also surprisingly unfused adult *Triceratops* skulls).

As Goodwin and Horner summarized, both nasal and postorbital horns "undergo a distinct ontogenetic sequence, and remain highly variable in size and shape in adult *Triceratops*."

Tokaryk (2002) described a small, uncrushed right humerus (SMNH P2691.1) of a juvenile *Triceratops* individual, referred to *Triceratops* sp., collected from the *Tyrannosaurus rex* quarry in the Frenchman Formation (late Maastrichtian), Chambery Coulee, Saskatchewan, Canada, a site that has also yielded the remains of *T. rex*, small theropods, ceratopsians, hadrosaurs, champsosaurs, fish, chelonians, mammals, and about 24 kinds of fossil plants.

The author referred this specimen to *Triceratops* based on the preponderance of *Triceratops* material within the ceratopsian fauna of the Frenchman Formation, and on the following features: 1. Triangular shape and dorsal location of proximal articular surface; 2. proportionally large size of deltopectoral crest; and 3. insertion for latissimus dorsal muscle, distal to proximal articular surface (a chasmosaurine feature; see Lehman 1989).

Ontogeny, Tokaryk pointed out, while well documented among centrosaurine ceratopsians, is not well known among chasmosaurines. As that author preserved, the size difference between this juvenile

Skeleton (cast) of *Triceratops horridus* mounted at the Mesa Southwest Museum.

specimens and adults (*e.g.*, SMNH P1163.9) is striking, the length of the humerus measuring 204 millimeters and 810 millimeters, respectively. Excepting the periosteal aging Tokaryk observed in SMNH P2691.1, both juvenile and adult humerus specimens are very similar in all defining features.

Performing new analyses on forelimb functional anatomy of neoceratopsian dinosaurs, Christiansen and Paul (2001) again confronted the ongoing controversy of forelimb orientation — sometimes envisioned as sprawling, straight, or somewhere in between (see *D:TE*, *S1*, *S2*) — in these animals. From calculations of strength indicator values, Christiansen and Paul achieved results consistent with their "suggestions based on limb bone scaling and limb proportions that the medium-sized ceratopsid species were anatomically comparable to extant rhinos," these also suggesting to the authors that the locomotor capabilities of such dinosaurs were also generally similar.

Christiansen and Paul recognized ceratopsids as probably having "forelimbs that operated in the near parasagittal plane, albeit with the elbows slightly more everted than in most large animals" (*e.g.*, Paul and

Christiansen 2000), this interpretation demonstrating somewhat "close similarities in bone strength with mediportal and low-intermediate grade subcursorial mammals" (*e.g.*, bison and rhinoceros). According to Christiansen and Paul's calculations, *Triceratops*, although possibly slightly less athletic than smaller neoceratopsian taxa, seems to have been "built to withstand long bone stresses exceeding those of extant elephants." Taking into consideration the functional morphology of the limbs of *Triceratops* (see Paul and Christiansen), the authors deduced that the locomotory potential of this dinosaur may have been intermediate between those of "extant rhinos and hippos, although the great length of its limbs could potentially have provided it with considerably greater absolute speed."

The findings of Christiansen and Paul, regarding forelimb posture in *Triceratops*, were somewhat reflected in another recent study, this one using computer imagery rather than mathematical calculations. Chapman, Snyder, Jabo and Andersen (2001) reported in an abstract on the complete remounting of the skeleton (USNM 4842; see *D:TE* for photograph of original mount, *S2* for casts; see Chapman, Johnson and Stevens 2001 for more details on the production of the "virtual" bones; also see Chapman, Matthews, Schweitzer and Horner 2002 for photographs of the new skeletal reconstruction, with the skull's size increased by 15 percent to accommodate postcranial remains representing more than 10 larger individuals) of *Triceratops horridus* at the National Museum of Natural History (see also Andersen, Chapman, Dickman and Hand 2001; see *S2* for more details). As noted by these authors, the new mount — accomplished utilizing rapid prototyping technology — may have answered the much-debated question regarding the forelimb posture of this giant horned dinosaur.

Via a computer-created miniaturization of the bones and an animation of the completed skeleton, Chapman *et al.* found that the forelimbs of this dinosaur "exhibit very complex patterns of articulation that probably reflect the need not only to move the animal in standard modes of locomotion, but also provide a rigid front during times of defense." Results of this study indicated an intermediate posture having less sprawl than earlier reconstructions, yet more sprawl than suggested by current graviportal or very vertical reconstructions.

The National Museum's new exhibit includes "an understandable cladogram showing the relationships of the Marginocephalia" (the ornithischian group to which *Triceratops* and all other ceratopsian dinosaurs belong) (see Deck 2001). Included in the exhibit is a flesh-out life restoration, based upon the new look and posture of the skeletal mount, as reported on in an abstract by Walters, Chapman and Snyder (2001). Building virtually upon a wide variety of computer-generated views of the skeleton, primary musculature was added, followed by skin and other components. As Walters *et al.* noted, "This is the first dinosaur reconstruction done this way and points to the great potential for making far more accurate fleshed-out reconstructions of dinosaurs by starting with the basic

skeletons that are reconstructed in a form that can be manipulated easily for use by the artist." The computer-created model, the authors further pointed out, made possible viewing in great detail and from all angles the potential muscle attachments, and allowed all noninvolved elements to be hidden so that focus could be placed on the attachments of interest, and then revealed to ensure they do not obstruct the inferred muscle path (see Walters *et al.* for more details).

Note: Over the years, the crests of ceratopsian dinosaurs have been interpreted as serving a variety of functions, these including structures utilized in defense, sites for sexual and territorial displays, and devises used for thermoregulation (see *D:TE* and *S2* for discussions and references).

In a paper to date of this writing not yet published, Anton (in preparation), interpreting ceratopsian crests as having more than a single function, proposed a new theory based on the inter-action between the ceratopsian crest and sound. Anton's hypothesis was that "Acoustic reflection by crests would theoretically increase the amount of energy translated to the ears, thereby enhancing hearing sensitivity." Anton tested this hypothesis by measuring the sound reflected from a urethane skull cast (ANSP collection; original specimen, BHIGR-214, house at Okayama, Japan, as part of the Hayashibara Cultural Project) of *Triceratops* collected by the Black Hills Institute of Geological Research. As noted by Anton, the ears in ceratopsians were placed rostro-ventrally to the proximal margin of the squamosal area of the crest. As ceratopsian skulls seem to have been pitched forward in an almost vertical orientation (see Brown 1914; Tait and Brown 1928), a greater portion of the crest would have been exposed to approaching sound. This position, according to Anton, would not only have increased "the surface area available for acoustic reflection and amplification," but also exposed "the ears directly to sound originating in front of the ceratopsian

Life restoration of *Triceratops horridus* painted by Kelly Pugh.

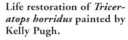

Courtesy North American Museum of Ancient Life.

as it places the epijugal more vertically than in many reconstructions."

Placing a unidirectional microphone and recorder within the right "ear" (caudodorsally to the upper portion of the quadrate) of the *Triceratops* cranial cast, and also using an electronic sound synthesizer and computer, Anton achieved results supporting the prediction that the *Triceratops* crest could have functioned as a biased sound amplifier relative to a control. Anton found that "the *Triceratops* crest amplified low frequencies (36 Hz) at least 119% relative to a control," while no sound amplification was "detected for higher frequencies (1,174 Hz)." The results are congruent with a rudimentary acoustic principle which states that low frequencies tend to reflect better than higher frequencies.

As Anton pointed out, sensitive hearing in *Triceratops* would be useful in the detection of approaching predators. Also, inter-aural effects would have allowed for a keener sense of directionality of the origin of sounds, as in assessing the direction of a predator's approach, and also long-range communication between the ceratopsian individuals. Furthermore, Anton stated that impending research "will assess the effect of frill morphology and physiology on acoustic amplification among ceratopsians." (J. A. Anton, personal communication 2002).

Key references: Andersen, Chapman, Dickman and Hand (2001); Anton (in preparation); Brown (1914); Chapman, Matthews, Schweitzer and Horner (2002); Chapman, Snyder, Jabo and Andersen (2001); Christiansen and Paul (2001); Deck (2001); Goodwin and Horner (2001); Lehman (1989); Paul and Christiansen (2000); Tait and Brown (1928); Tokaryk (2002); Walters, Chapman and Snyder (2001).

†TRIMUCRODON

Ornithischia: Genasaura: Cerapoda: ?Heterodontosauridae.

Comments: In 1973, Richard A. Thulborn named and described the genus *Trimucrodon* (see *D:TE*), known only from teeth from the Upper Jurassic of the Província do Estremadura, Portugal. Thulborn referred this genus to the Hypsilophodontidae as a form closely related to *Echinodon*.

Since that original referral, various other authors have had a number of different assessments of *Trimucrodon*. Among these, Galton (1978) found this genus to be less similar to *Echinodon* and more allied with the Fabrosauridae. Weishampel and Witmer (1990*a*), in their review of basal ornithischians, considered *Trimucrodon* to be a *nomen dubium*. Sereno (1991), in a study on *Lesothosaurus*, fabrosaurids and the early evolution of the Ornithischia, regarded *Alocodon* as Ornithischia

incertae sedis (see *D:TE*, *S2*), at the same time considering *Echinodon* to be a possible member of the Heterodontosauridae. Galton (1996) later compared *Trimucrodon* with *Taveirosaurus* (earlier considered by Weishampel and Witmer to be a *nomen dubium*), interpreting both genera as fabrosaurids. Antunes and Sigogneau-Russell (1996) reassessed *Taverirosaurus* to be a valid genus belonging to the ankylosaurian family Nodosauridae, and Pereda-Suberbiola (1999) regarded that genus as an indeterminate nodosaurid.

In a more recent study, Ruiz-Omeñaca (2001) reassessed the teeth referred to the type species, *Trimucrodon cuneatus*, finding the two most favorable hypotheses to be that *Trimucrodon* is more similar to either *Taveirosaurus* or *Echinodon*. Noting that the teeth of *Trimucrodon* most closely resemble those of *Echinodon*, Ruiz-Omeñaca found it most reasonable to regard the former, at least for the present, as an indeterminate possible heterodontosaurid.

Key references: Antunes and Sigogneau-Russell (1996); Galton (1978, 1996); Pereda-Suberbiola (1999); Ruiz-Omeñaca (2001); Sereno (1991); Thulborn (1973); Weishampel and Witmer (1990*a*).

†TROODON

Saurischia: Eusaurischia: Theropoda: Neotheropoda: Tetanurae: Avetheropoda: Coelurosauria: Maniraptoriformes: Maniraptora: Metornithes: Paraves: Deinonychosauria: Troodontidae.

Comments: Varricchio (2001*b*), in an abstract, reported on the ontogeny and osteology in *Troodon formosus*, his study based upon several specimens of this type species, ranging from embryos to adults, from the Upper Cretaceous Two Medicine Formation of Montana.

Varricchio observed the following: Embryonic specimens display several synapomorphies of the Troodontidae and two characteristics (large basal tubera; broadly rounded rostral border of maxillary fenestra) of *T. formosus*. Although hindlimb proportions exhibit a decrease during ontogeny in distal segments, humerus and femur ratios seem to remain almost constant (proportions not given in this brief report). Growth of elements is generally associated with development and increased definition of muscle attachments and articular surfaces, "mature" features, the acquisition of which varies among individuals (*e.g.*, humeri of intermediate lengths appearing either mature or immature, the latter possibly representing individuals maintaining higher juvenile growth rates longer and maturing at larger body sizes).

As Varricchio pointed out, Troodontidae exhibit several features (*e.g.*, little expansion of scapular blade, acromion extending ventral to glenoid, femur with caudal trochanter) suggesting close relationships to Dromaeosauridae and Aves, and others (*e.g.*, acromion without cranial projection, no contact between fibula and calcaneum) found only in Troodontidae and Aves. These features, the author noted, and also others (*e.g.*, outwardly rotated glenoid fossa, distal condyles on cranial aspect of humerus, possibly slightly reverted pubis), are found in Aves and *T. formosus* but not in more primitive theropods, this suggesting "widespread parallel evolution of features among birds and nonavian theropod lineages."

The genus *Troodon* has generally been portrayed as a predatory animal, this view supported by the dinosaur's relatively large brain, grasping hands, and possible stereoscopic vision.

New information regarding the possible predation habits of *Troodon* was published by Ryan, Currie, Gardner, Vickaryous and Lavigne (2000), based upon a new microvertebrate site in the Horseshoe Canyon Formation (Upper Cretaceous; early Maastrichtian) in south-central Alberta, Canada.

A total of 338 fossil vertebrate elements were recovered from this site, almost 88 percent of these belonging to indeterminate hadrosaurids. As 40 of the hadrosaurid specimens belong to baby individuals (this find constituting the first occurrence of baby dinosaurs in this formation and the geologically youngest occurrence of such fossils in Canada), Ryan *et al.* determined that a hadrosaurid nesting site of unknown size was located nearby.

The second most common fossils found at this site belong to *Troodon*, represented by a large number of teeth. These teeth are either broken below the crown or lack the root, suggesting to Ryan *et al.* that they were lost in life. In most of these specimens, the denticles are relatively unworn, indicating that these teeth were not old when lost, but rather functional and lost during feeding. Usually rare in southern Alberta at Upper Cretaceous sites, the large number of *Troodon* specimens at this site, to the near exclusion of elements relating to other dinosaurian taxa, suggested to the authors "a nonrandom association with the baby hadrosaurid elements [that] is potentially indicative of predation." Ryan *et al.* speculated that the baby hadrosaurids, being small and relatively defenseless, and their eggs, would have been ideal prey items for these theropods.

(Other, less common dinosaurian remains recovered from this site include 45 teeth or tooth fragments representing at least four other theropod taxa, ankylosaurid and ceratopsid elements, and also remains of turtles, pterosaurs, birds, and mammals.)

Another interpretation of *Troodon* was published by Holtz, Brinkman and Chandler (2000), based upon a study based upon measurements of 600 teeth belonging to this genus and also to those of therizinosauroids. Holtz *et al.* found the serrations of the troodontid and therizinosauroid teeth to be much larger per tooth width than in most other theropods of the same tooth size, but similar to those of iguanid lizards, sauropodomorphs, and many ornithischians, all of which are generally regarded as herbivorous.

According to Holtz *et al.*, these larger denticles could represent a reversal to some primitive dental condition, that the larger denticles in troodontids represent compensation of some kind for the relatively smaller tooth size in these animals (troodontids having among the smallest teeth in Theropoda), or that were used in processing food other than vertebrate muscle tissue (*e.g.*, eggs and invertebrates). However, Holtz *et al.* found it more likely that, given the similarities between the teeth of troodontids and those of confirmed or believed herbivores, that dinosaurs like *Troodon* were omnivorous. (The authors noted that this hypothesis has already been suggested for therizinosauroids; *e.g.*, see Paul 1984; Barsbold and Maryańska 1990; Russell and Dong 1993.)

Considering the possibility that troodontids were strictly herbivorous, Holtz *et al.* cited the following arguments countering that hypothesis: 1. The lower jaws in troodontids resemble those in some advanced, highly predacious theropods and squamates, having relatively loose mandibular symphyses and movable intramandibular joints (although therizinosauroids also retain these features [see Clark, Perle and Norell 1994], possibly synapomorphies of basal Theropoda [Sereno 1997; Holtz 2000]); 2. their raptorial second pedal digits are similar to those of highly predacious dromaeosaurids (Carpenter 2000) and omnivorous cariamid birds (Gauthier 1986); 3. the curvature of their manual digits conforms to that and the narrow cross section seen in dromaeosaurids, interpreted as a prey-acquisition morphology (Ostrom 1969); 4. shed teeth are sometimes found in close association with skeletal remains and eggs of ornithopods (Horner 1994); and 5. the pubes (unlike those in therizinosauroids) are not opisthopubic, the abdominal cavity therefore not enlarged relative to those of presumed hypercarnivorous theropods (found in typical amniotes having a diet exclusively based upon vegetation; see Hotton, Olson and Beerbower 1997).

Varricchio, Horner and Jackson (2002) described in detail a number of elongate and asymmetric fossil eggs (specimens including MOR 246, 247, 299, 393, 675, 676, 750, 963, and 1139) belonging to the egg taxon *Prismatoolithus levis* (see "Appendix") from the Upper Cretaceous Two Medicine Formation, Egg Island locality, in Teton County, Montana. These eggs had previously been referred by Horner and Weishampel (1988) to the ornithischian *Orodromeus makelai*, but were subsequently correctly identified as those of *Troodon formosus* (see *Troodon* entry, *S1*, for details and additional references), based on the typical association with these eggs of *T. formosus* adult and juvenile remains.

Reexamination by Varrichio *et al.* of embryos associated with these eggs revealed them as showing at least the following 24 apomorphies of the Dinosauria and that clade's various subgroups: (Dinosauria) deltopectoral crest 35 percent length of humerus; tibia with cnemial crest; (Saurischia) epipophyses on mid- and caudal cervical vertebrae; (Theropoda) cervical epipophyses prong-shaped processes; length of scapular blade more than three times distal width; (Neotheropoda) pleurocoels (cranial) on cervical vertebrae (postatlantal); proximal end of tibia having fibular crest; prominent cnemial crest; craniocaudal width of fibular midshaft 10 to 25 percent of craniocaudal width of proximal end; (Tetanurae) craniocaudal width of iliac-ischial articulation much smaller than iliac-pubic articulation; obturator process of ischium with notch (or foramen); femoral cranial trochanter blade-shaped; ("Neotetanurae") maxillary fenestra; (Coelurosauria) fourth trochanter of femur low crest or rugosity; fibular fossa occupying all of medial aspect of proximal end; ("Tyrannoraptora") femoral cranial trochanter height as tall as greater trochanter; junction of cranial and greater trochanters at distal end of cranial trochanter; (Maniraptora) acromion height (distance from axis of blade) 40 percent or less of distance from central axis of blade to acromion; half-crescent-shaped iliac postacetabular process; fourth trochanter of femur low crest or rugosity; (Paraves) acromion cranial to glenoid fossa (central axis of scapular blade horizontally oriented); scapular blade, distal expansion 130 percent or less of minimum width of blade (proximal neck); ischium, form of midshaft midsection subplanar; femur with caudal trochanter.

Also, the authors observed that the embryos show the following possibly troodontid features: Pneumatic quadrate, closely placed basal tubera, high tooth count (as suggested by the observable portion of the maxillary tooth row), metatarsal II much narrower than IV, and strongly constricted metatarsal III. Referral by the authors to *T. formosus* was based on the presence of the following: Large basal tubera and broadly rounded rostral border of maxillary fenestra.

As Varrichio *et al.* observed, most of the embryonic bones seem to be ossified. Comparison of this degree of ossification to that seen in bird embryos led the authors to surmise that this *Troodon* clutch died in the eggs at a time close to hatching.

Limb proportions of the embryos, the authors noted, differ notably from those of adults, the hatch-

lings and juveniles having long distal segments and very different limb proportions. Furthermore, the remains of *Orodromeus* and other small vertebrates found associated with *Troodon* egg horizons could "represent prey of the adults during egg-laying and brooding."

Varricchio *et al.* also noted that these eggs reveal several aspects either shared or convergent with some extant birds, including the following: Asymmetric form of egg; nonbranching angusticanaliculate (having small leaf-shaped canals) pores; distinct structural differentiation of mammillary and overlying prismatic layer; barrel-shaped mammillary cones with blocky calcite; and prismatic structure visible throughout second structural layer. These similarities, the authors pointed out, "further demonstrate the close relationship of Troodontidae and Aves."

Note: Pryor, Tanke, Currie, Spencer and Humber (2002), in an abstract reporting on the latest work in accurately mapping the Late Cretaceous vertebrate localities in Dinosaur Provincial Park, Alberta, using the Global Positioning System, reported the discovery of a new partial skeleton of *Troodon* (not yet collected on the date the report was written) and a set of almost complete *"Caenagnathus"* [=*Chirostenotes*] lower jaws (RTMO 2001.12.12), the latter significant as only the second found since 1936 (see *Caenagnathus* entry, *D:TE*). (Pryor *et al.* reported that, since 1999, they and their respective organizations have pooled computer and Global Positioning System knowledge, mapping hardware, technological resources, and technical expertise to relocate and replot almost every known Dinosaur Provincial Park and area quarries worked from 1912 to the present, but not previously adequately documented.)

Key references: Barsbold and Maryańska (1990); Carpenter (2000); Clark, Perle and Norell (1994); Gauthier (1986); Holtz (1998); Holtz, Brinkman and Chandler (2000); Horner (1994); Horner and Weishampel (1988); Hotton, Olson and Beerbower (1997); Ostrom (1969); Paul (1984); Pryor, Tanke, Currie, Spencer and Humber (2002); Russell and Dong (1993); Ryan, Currie, Gardner, Vickaryous and Lavigne (2000); Sereno (1997); Varricchio (2001*b*); Varricchio, Horner and Jackson (2002).

†**TYRANNOSAURUS**—(=*Dinotyrannus, Dynamosaurus, Manospondylus, Nanotyrannus, Stygivenator;* =?*Aublysodon*)

Saurischia: Eusaurischia: Theropoda: Neotheropoda: Tetanurae: Avetheropoda: Coelurosauria: Maniraptoriformes: Arctometatarsalia: Tyrannosauroidea: Tyrannosauridae: Tyrannosaurinae.

Type species: *T. rex* Osborn 1905.

Other species: ?*T. zhuchengensis* Hu, Cheng, Pang and Fang 2001.

Occurrence: Hell Creek South Formation, Livingston Formation, Montana, Hell Creek Formation, South Dakota, Lance Formation, Wyoming, Laramie Formation, Colorado, Javelina Formation, Texas, McRae Formation, New Mexico, North Horn Formation, Utah, United States; Scollard Formation, Willow Creek Formation, Alberta, Frenchman Formation, Saskatchewan, Canada; ?Xingezhuang Formation, Wangshi Group, Shandong Province, China.

Age: Late Cretaceous (late Maastrichtian).

Known material: Approximately 30 specimens, including partial to nearly complete skeletons, juvenile to adult.

Comments: Research continues concerning the type species *Tyrannosaurus rex*, the largest and most famous of all known North American theropods.

In 2003, Christopher A. Brochu published as a monograph the first major detailed osteological description of *Tyrannosaurus rex*, primarily based upon FMNH PR2081, popularly known as "Sue" (see also *D:TE*, *S1*, *S2*), the most complete, well-preserved, and most celebrated specimen of this taxon yet collected, while including observations of other recovered specimens.

In describing *T. rex*, Brochu noted the following:

The skull morphology of FMNH PR2081 is mostly consistent with previously published descriptions. However, the palatal morphology differs slightly from the latter in various features (*e.g.*, internal choanae slightly larger relative to skull size; elongate rostral expansion of fused vomers; caudally, vomers passing medially for almost entire length of pterygoids). CT analysis of the skull of FMNH PR2081 revealed a number of previously unrealized details (*e.g.*, exoccipital recess perforated by small foramen on caudodorsal surface of paroccipital process, possibly communicating with pneumatic chambers in atlas-axis complex; maxillary antra bound medially by thin bony wall, traces of the latter in earlier CT studies perhaps incorrectly suggesting the presence of bony maxillonasal turbinates [*e.g.*, Bakker 1992]. A digitally generated endocast also yielded new details (*e.g.*, large, presumably pneumatic sinus in prootic adjacent to pathway for maxillary-mandibular branches of trigeminal nerve).

The postcranium also mostly conforms to earlier descriptions, although "Unusual structures," previously believed to be absent in tyrannosaurids, were observed, these tentatively identified by Brochu "as a proatlas arch and a rib on the last presacral vertebrae." Discovery of a "missing chevron" between the first and second caudal vertebrae — the absence of which had been responsible, in part, for past claims that the

Photograph by the author, courtesy Natural History Museum of Los Angeles County.

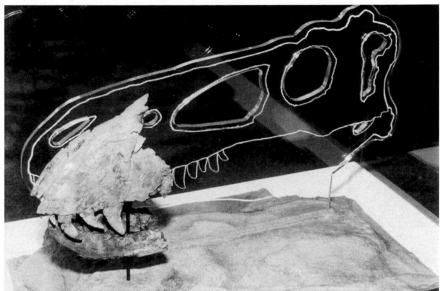

"Sue" specimen represents a female (see Larson and Frey 1992) — suggested to Brochu that FMNH PR2081 could just as likely be male. The gastralia are extensively fused cranially, the morphology of the craniomost segments resembling closely the only published description of what Lambe (1917) identified as a tyrannosaurid sternum (for the genus *Gorgosaurus*), this raising such possibilities as the absence of a bony sternum in Tyrannosauridae.

As Brochu noted, this *T. rex* specimen has been "the subject of extensive speculation from the moment of its discovery," some of this having been expressed in the popular media before the specimen was thoroughly studied. Much of this speculation focused upon the specimen's various pathologies. Addressing various abnormalities in FMNH PR2081 that have

Cast of the skull (LACM 28471) of a juvenile *Tyrannosaurus rex* as displayed again in 2001 at the Natural History Museum of Los Angeles County. In the past this specimen, originally dubbed the "Jordan theropod," has been referred both to *Aublysodon* (see *D:TE*) and to a new genus, *Stygivenator* (see *S2*).

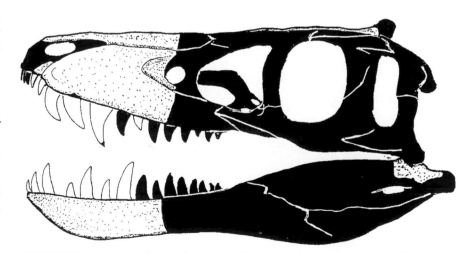

LACM 28471, reconstructed skull of a juvenile *Tyrannosaurus rex*, as reinterpreted by Tracy L. Ford and Daniel J. Chure. Scale = 10 cm. (After Ford and Chure 2001.)

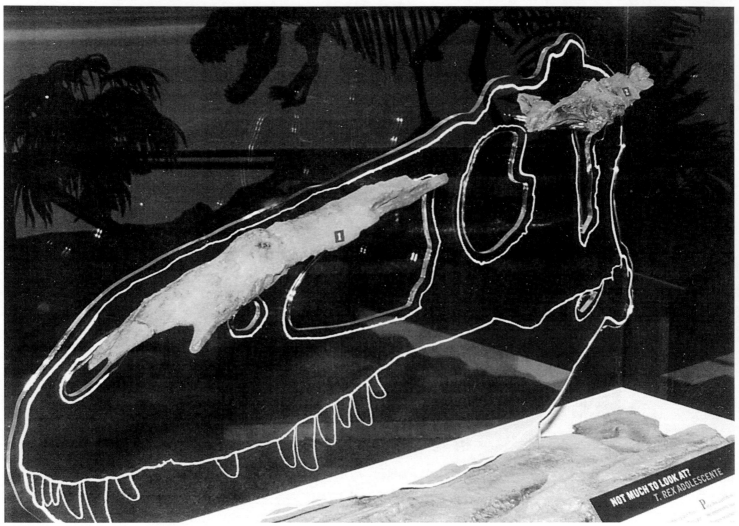

Fragmentary skull elements (LACM 23845) as displayed in 2001 at the Natural History Museum of Los Angeles County. Although this specimen was referred by George Olshevsky to the new genus and species *Dinotyrannus megagracilis*, recent work by Thomas David Carr and Thomas E. Williamson (2001) have shown this to be a juvenile *Tyrannosaurus rex*.

attracted media attention, Brochu noted the following:

Although damage on the left side of the skull has been interpreted as evidence for a bite wound from another large theropod (see, for example, *S1*, Larson 2002), Brochu found "no conclusive evidence in support of this idea"; furthermore, shallow, circular depressions on the left squamosal "are not regularly spaced and do not immediately suggest bite marks."

The rib cage offers evidence for healed fractures. "Lesions on the right scapulocoracoid and humerus coincide with fractured ribs on the right cervical-dorsal transition," this possibly indicating a trauma to the right side of the body. Although the left fibula is pathological, it may not have been fractured and its condition probably did not cripple this dinosaur in life. Consequently, this animal's "last days may have been much more prosaic than previously thought."

Brochu noted that two caudal vertebrae, numbers 26 and 27, are fused together and to their mutual hemal arch. The reason for this fusion is not known. However, the presence of long proximodistal grooves on the exostotic bone between the vertebrae, these possibly representing natural molds of the tail musculature.

More specimens of *T. rex* continue to be found, this including the first known specimen to be discovered in Utah. In an abstract reporting on the upland dinosaur fauna of the Late Cretaceous (Maastrichtian) North Horn Formation of central Utah, emphasizing recent excavations by the Utah Museum of Natural History, Loewen, Sampson, Getty and Difley (2001) announced the recovery of a large specimen within the size range of FMNH PR2081 and MOR 555, the latter being the so-called Wankel *Tyrannosaurus*, one of the most complete ever recovered (see Schweitzer and Schmitt 2002 for a recent report, published as an abstract for a poster, on the mechanism of preservation, facilitated by fungi and cyanobacteria, of endogeneous molecular components—*e.g.*, heme compounds, blood cell-like structures, collagan fragments, and DNA not attributable to any definitive source—

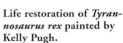

Life restoration of *Tyrannosaurus rex* painted by Kelly Pugh.

in the latter specimen; also, see Schmitt and Schweitzer 2002, an abstract for a poster). Approximately 16 percent complete, the associated skeleton (UMNH 11000) includes a postorbital, squamosal, vertebrae, a partial ilium, a tibia, fibula, and astragalus.

According to Loewen *et al.*, "stratigraphic and sedimentologic evidence from the North Horn Formation support the notion of a physiographic basin characterized by fluvio-lacustrine sedimentation," this depositional setting and its fauna, therefore, differing from more northerly and easterly contemporaneous formations indicative of coastal environments. Thus, identification of the North Horn *T. rex* "further documents this taxon as a major predator from coastal to intermontane settings." (Also known from the North Horn Formation are the "titanosaurid" sauropod *Alamosaurus* and, including newly collected skull and postcranial remains, the ceratopsid *Torosaurus*, the above-mentioned discovery, therefore, constituting "the first well-documented co-occurrence of *Tyrannosaurus rex* and a sauropod.)"

Another type species — one that was erected only recently and which has had a history spanning almost four decades — has been synonymized with *Tyrannosaurus rex*. In 1978, Ralph E. Molnar described a fragmentary, juvenile tyrannosaurid skull (LACM 28471) from the Hell Creek Formation of Montana. Molnar then referred to this specimen only as the "Jordan theropod," although it was exhibited for a while at the Natural History Museum of Los Angeles County as a juvenile *Tyrannosaurus*.

Paul (1988*b*) later referred this specimen to the genus *Aublysodon* on the basis of its unserrated teeth, as the new species *Aublysodon molnaris*, after which Molnar and Carpenter (1989) referred it to *Aublysodon* cf. *A. mirandus* (see *D:TE* and *S2* for details). Subsequently, Olshevsky, Ford and Yamamoto 1995*a*, 1995*b*

referred this specimen to a new genus and species which they named *Stygivenator molnari* (see *S2*). This presented a questionable situation — two giant theropods belonging to the same family, existing in the same time and place, one of which was known from numerous skeletons, the other from but a single fragmentary and juvenile specimen.

More recently, Carr and Williamson (2001), in an abstract, briefly reported on the "Jordan theropod." As noted by these authors, based "upon shared derived characters and a quantitative reconstruction of the growth series of *Tyrannosaurus rex*, the Jordan Theropod is a juvenile *T. rex*." Furthermore, Carr and Williams posited that, despite previous reports to the contrary, "the claimed premaxillary tooth found with LACM 28471 is actually the first maxillary tooth and still lies within its alveolus." (According to R. E. Molnar, personal communication 2002, this assessment is not correct, and "the claimed premaxillary tooth was found adherent to the outer surface of the snout and clearly not in any alveolus." In Molnar's estimation, these authors "may have found another tooth of this form, but I am seriously skeptical of their work here.")

Agreeing with Carr and Williamson's interpretation that LACM 28471 represents a juvenile *T. rex*, Ford and Chure (2001*a*) addressed Molnar's (1978) positing that the premaxillary tooth is displaced and situated near the first maxillary tooth, both premaxillary tooth first maxillary tooth having been displaced (lingual side missing inner wall of alveoli of last premaxillary tooth and first maxillary tooth position). Upon examining LACM 28471, one of these authors (Tracy L. Ford) "found a small square portion of the premaxilla that was mistaken for the tip of the maxilla. The nasals were broken off and incorrectly glued back with a down turned tip." According to Ford and Chure, the nasals of this specimen would consequently have been straight, thus "giving the premaxilla a squared edge (in lateral view) like an adult *Tyrannosaurus rex*, as in tyrannosaurids in general." Furthermore, the mandibular symphysis in LACM 28471 is V-shaped in ventral view as in *T. rex* (see Ford 1997), rather than U-shaped; also, the "dip" on the mandible of this specimen is preparation damage, the other side, which lacks this "dip," having a straight edge. Ford and Chure offered a new interpretation of this specimen, reconstructed to resemble more closely the skull of *T. rex*.

According to Carr and Williamson, the nondenticulate condition of the teeth seems to be an ontogenetically variable feature in tyrannosauroids. Therefore, the authors concluded, *T. rex* is the only tyrannosaurid species in Western North America during late Maastrichtian times. In 2001, before the publication of Carr and Williamson's abstract, the "Jordan theropod" specimen went back on exhibit at the Natural History Museum of Los Angeles County, once again identified as a juvenile *Tyrannosaurus rex*.

In a subsequent abstract, Carr and Williamson

(2002*a*) reported briefly on tyrannosauroid remains, including isolated cranial and postcranial elements and isolated teeth, recently collected from the Naashoibito Member (possible age ranging from late Campanian to late Maastrichtian; see Sullivan, Lucas and Braman 2002) of the Kirtland Formation, San Juan Basin, northwestern New Mexico, tentatively referred by those authors to *Tyrannosaurus rex*. Positively referred by them to *T. rex* was a partial adult skeleton from the Hall Lake Member, McRae Formation, at Elephant Butte Reservoir, in south-central New Mexico. As Carr and Williamson (2002) noted, "The occurrence of a single tyrannosauroid in the Late Maastrichtian of New Mexico is congruent with the rest of western North America, in which *T. rex* is the only giant top predator."

Molnar (2000), in a detailed (although preliminary) report, presented the first published mechanical analyses (the kind used in mechanical engineering) of the architecture of the skull and jaws of *Tyrannosaurus rex*. The results of these analyses were subsequently used as bases for speculation on the

The *Tyrannosaurus rex* specimen (FMNH PR2081) known as "Sue" on display at The Field Museum. The original skull, too heavy to be included on the mounted skeleton, is displayed separately (see next page).

Photograph by John Weinstein, courtesy The Field Museum (negative #GN89714_2RDc).

Original skull of the *Tyrannosaurus rex* specimen (FMNH PR2081) nicknamed "Sue," exhibited in its own display case.

function of the cranial skeleton, mostly relating to feeding.

Plane frame analysis by Molnar (2000) of the snout of *T. rex* proved to be consistent with the interpretation that its lateral compression related to the application of strong, vertically directed forces on the teeth (see also Busbey 1995; Erickson, Van Kirk, Su, Levenston, Caler and Carter 1996).

Analyzed in frame space, the skull of *T. rex* was found to have been stable under a plausible regime of forces imposed in both supporting the head and during feeding. However, Molnar (2000) found that the postorbital region required reinforcement provided by the widening of the postorbital bar and deepening of the caudal ramus of the jugal. Quadrate orientation was found to be "consistent with a role in resisting the modelled dorsoanteriorly-directed reaction at the craniomandibular joint."

Molnar (2000) found that the quadrate bar and the dorsal bones of the skull, the premaxillae, maxillae, frontals, nasals, parietals, and the braincase-occipital complex are apparently regions of the skull that are subjected to greater stresses, both in supporting the

weight of the head and in feeding. Trajectory analysis suggested that major openings in the skull (*e.g.*, orbits, fenestrae) and sinuses are located in regions away from the concentrations of major stress (*i.e.*, the maxilla-nasal-frontal-parietal line).

Probably correlated with supporting the head is the prominent supraoccipital crest, offering a large caudal surface for the attachment of supporting epaxial muscles.

Molnar (2000) explained, in part, the lingual bar of the dentary "as an adaptation to reduce the maximum torque on the anterior portions of the mandibles," the comparatively great depth of the dentary regarded "as an adaptation to reducing the maximum bending strain in this portion of the mandible." The caudal "thinning" of the dentary may be an example of the reduction of unnecessary bone, the more or less parallel force exerted by the jaw adductors to the plane of the surangular requiring reinforcement only along its dorsal edge.

Molnar (2000) differentiated these teeth into three classes of form, which grade one into the other — premaxillary form (seemingly associated with

Tyrannosaurus

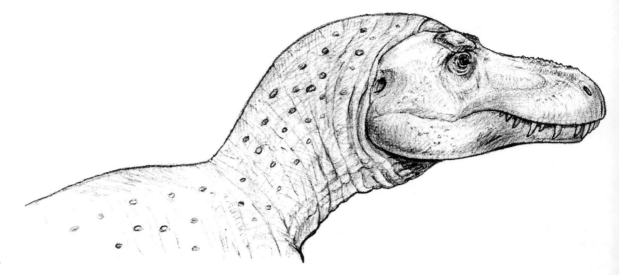

Life restoration of the *Tyrannosaurus rex* known as "Sue" by Berislav Krciz.

a grasping function), mesial maxillary form, and distal maxillary form (the latter two apparently having a more shearing function, but some grasping as well; see Alber 1992). Teeth seem to have been worn or broken primarily during their contact with food, this implying forceful contact with the bones of prey animals. The author noted that the curvature of these teeth more or less "matches the circular arcs of radius equal to the distance from the tooth tip to the craniomandibular joint."

A *T. rex* could, according to Molnar (2000), open its jaws widely enough to clamp down upon the neck of most contemporaneous hadrosaurs, cutting off the blood supply to the head, closing the trachea, and even breaking the spinal column. Different methods of attack would be employed against ankylosaurs and ceratopsians. No evidence arose from Molnar's (2000) study indicating that *T. rex* could not have been an active predator.

In an abstract, Starkov (2001) briefly discussed specialization in the teeth of *Tyrannosaurus rex*, pointing out that the teeth in this taxon are not typical of those of other tyrannosaurids. In *T. rex*, that author noted, the rear part of the skull is more extensive than in other members of Tyrannosauridae, the snout is relatively shorter, and the nuchal crest is rostrally expanded (some of these features having been observed by Starkov in only one other tyrannosaurid specimen from the late Campanian San Juan Formation), these features collectively aiding in maintaining a strong bite on captured prey and also the processing in the mouth of soft tissues and bones.

As Starkov noted, the location of the teeth in *T. rex* suggests that the most suitable prey for this theropod were moderately long-necked animals (*e.g.*, sauropods), large hadrosaurs, and ceratopsians. The largest teeth in *T. rex* are located at the more rostral region of the snout (these teeth positioned at the cen-

tral part of the snout in the tyrannosaurids *Albertosaurus*, *Daspletosaurus*, and *Tarbosaurus*. Starkov speculated that *T. rex* might have been able to bite necks and other parts of the body of prey animals that were devoid of ossicles, scutes, and shells. Indeed, using this hunting mode against armored dinosaurs such as ankylosaurs and "titanosaurids" would be "fraught with different kinds of trauma for a predator." The author further noted that, in *Daspletosaurus* and *Tarbosaurus*, the largest teeth are found in a less rostral area of the mouth, this placement apparently allowing the tyrannosaurids to overcome more effectively opposition such hard structures.

Isolated theropod teeth, occurring frequently in Mesozoic rocks, have often been neglected, their taxonomic use being elusive and their dental characters rarely entering into systematic discussions. This neglect, as noted by Smith (2002) in an abstract, "is based on an impression that it is difficult or impossible to discriminate these elements." However, according to that author, although "theropod teeth *are* simple structures possessing few homologous landmarks from which measurements concordant with modern morphometrics can be made, theropod dental anatomy is still largely unexplored and opinions regarding theropod teeth usefulness are premature."

Smith's detailed examination of the teeth of *T. rex* was "conducted to serve as the beginning of a standard against which to compare isolated teeth." Smith then attempted to devise a methodology by which teeth referred to tyrannosaurid theropods could be assigned with confidence to or discriminated from the standard. Dental variation in *T. rex* was quantified utilizing various revised common measurements (*e.g.*, total crown length, base length and width, denticle size) and also new variables describing base shape, squatness, and apex location. Also, crown curvature was described incorporating X,Y coordinate information from digital images of the mesial and distal lateral profiles of the teeth (see Smith for additional details on the methodology used in this study). Smith found it possible, by using the methods employed in this study, "to decipher both tooth positions for known *T. rex* teeth with statistical confidence and discriminately morphologically similar teeth (*e.g., Daspletosaurus*) from the *T. rex* standard. This suggested to that author that expansion of this standard should facilitate the identification of teeth pertaining to other kinds of theropods (see also Smith 2002*b*).

In another abstract, Snively (2002) pointed out that, in the past, the role the tyrannosaurid neck played in feeding has been largely neglected by researchers. Based on the idea that tyrannosaurid cervical muscles are inferable by bracketed phylogenetic comparisons with extant archosaurs, then the presence of such muscles in birds and crocodilians suggests their probable occurrence also in these dinosaurs.

Noting via dissection the toplogy of neck muscles in birds and crocodilians, and testing via examination of tyrannosaurid muscle scars interpretations based on phylogenetic inference, Snively reconstructed the cervical and cranio-cervical muscles of *T. rex*, resulting in the following notable patterns: 1. Although differences between birds and crocodilians lead to ambiguity about several neck muscles in *T. rex*, some muscles (*e.g.,* the rectus capitis group) can be reconstructed with confidence; 2. lever arms indicate the capacity for powerful, lateral head motions and high torque for dorsiflexion of the neck; and 3. extraordinary rugose scarring on some *T. rex* specimens indicates large muscles (*e.g.,* Mm. spinalis capitis, complexus, or splenius) for cranial dorsiflexion.

Snively's comparisons suggested that *T. rex* possessed more powerful neck muscles than would be expected for a tyrannosaurid of its size, this not necessarily indicating increased relative performance for eating meat, but rather that the cervical musculature could have compensated for the decreased cutting performance of the animal's large teeth. "As the animal pulled its head up and back," that author deduced, "large neck muscles may have been necessary to overcome resistance of flesh and bone against the long and laterally expanded tooth crowns." Alternatively, these muscles may have been only large enough to support the animal's proportionally heavy head.

Carrano and Hutchinson (2002) published a new reconstruction of the pelvic and hindlimb muscles of *T. rex*, one having relevance to understanding the evolutionary sequence of the specialized avian hindlimb. The authors based their study primarily on the almost complete skeleton (FMNH PR 2081), a specimen ("Sue") so large and well preserved, they noted, that its attachment sites for muscles have been

rendered exceptionally clear. Consequently, it was possible for the authors to examine the arrangement of the hindlimb muscles in this dinosaur with much greater phylogenetic and osteologic support than was previously possible.

In addition to studying FMNH PR 2081, Carrano and Hutchinson studied the following *T. rex* specimens: MOR 009 and 555; AMNH 5027; CM 9380 [the holotype]; UCMP 136517; and BHI 3033; RTMP 81.12.1. Also, the authors directly and extensively examined specimens of extant archosaurs (two crocodilians, three paleognathous birds, and 16 neognathous birds) and other reptiles (seven lizards, two turtles, and *Sphenodon*), also myriad extinct archosaurs (several hundred nonavian dinosaurs, 15 birds, 10 crocodilians, plus 30 other taxa). The extant taxa were used to establish homology arguments for the archosaurian pelvic and hindlimb muscles. These arguments were then "placed in a phylogenetic context through the compilation of a data matrix and the mapping of character states onto a 'consensus' phylogenetic framework," the distribution of osteological character states revealing "the most parsimonious (*i.e.,* least speculative) reconstruction of the soft tissues of *Tyrannosaurus rex*." Thus, the authors were able to avoid reconstructing muscles having ambiguous homologies or correlates.

Carrano and Hutchinson pointed out that their new construction covered territory visited many times earlier by other archosaur workers (*e.g.,* Romer 1923*a*, 1923*b*, 1923*c*); Russell 1982; Walker 1977; Tarsitano 1981, 1983), particularly in regards the musculature of the proximal hindlimb. However, Romer's (1923*c*) reconstruction of the hindlimb musculature in *T. rex*, the standard for more than three quarters of a century, as well as those of Walker and Tarsitano, tended to "map" crocodilian musculature onto the saurischian skeleton, eschewing the use of avian data (see Carrano and Hutchinson for comments on and criticisms of these earlier reconstructions).

As noted by Carrano and Hutchinson, *Tyrannosaurus* inherited its bipedalism from the primitive dinosaurian condition, but this received considerable modification in various subsequent ingroups. These modifications often developed in parallel, presumably constituting mechanical effects related to locomotion (Carrano 2000; Farlow, Gatesy, Holtz, Hutchinson and Robinson 2000); Hutchinson and Gatesy 2000).

Carrano and Hutchinson pointed out that some of these modifications are exemplified in *Tyrannosaurus*. The ilium is much expanded cranially and caudally over the condition observed in *Eoraptor, Herrerasaurus,* and *Staurikosaurus,* these portions of the ilium, as reconstructed by the authors, presenting the origins of various muscles—Mm. iliotibales 1–3, M.

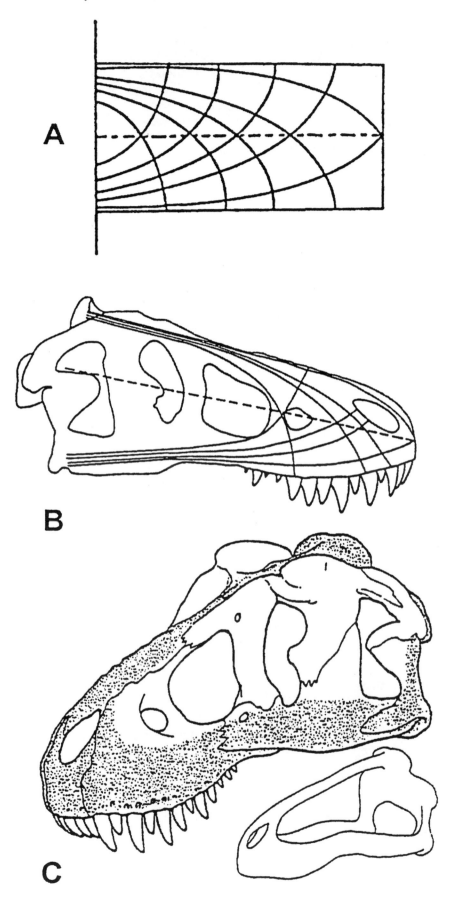

A. Cantilever beam with stress trajectories represented by two sets of roughly parabolic curves, grounded in the base, tensile trajectories above and compressive below; B. proposed approximation of the forms of the trajectories in the *Tyrannosaurus rex* skull; and C. regions of the *T. rex* skull that would resist the tensile and compressive stresses (stipple), and abstracted from the rest of the skull (small image). (After Molnar 2000.)

ambiens, M. iliofemoralis externus, M. iliotrochantericus caudalis, M. iliotrochantericus medius plus cranialis/M. puboischiofemoralis internus, M. caudofemoralis brevis, M. iliofibularis, and M. flexor tibialis externus — "that could flex, extend, or mediolaterally rotate the hip and knee joints." The enhanced capacity of these muscles to flex and extend the knee joint, the authors pointed out, could indicate an increase in the lower limb flexion's role during locomotion, a trend continuing into higher coelurosaurian phylogenetic levels (see Gatesy 1995; Carrano 1998*a*, 1998*b*). Furthermore, the expansion of these muscles would "increase their moment arms for hip expansion, reflecting a greater capability to generate muscle moments about the hip in order to control hip flexion or retract the femur during locomotion."

Furthermore, Carrano and Hutchinson observed examples in which the lower leg musculature of *Tyrannosaurus* seems more derived and closer to the avian condition than the inferred ancestral condition for Archosauria, a feature in which this genus significantly resembles many other theropods as well as nontheropod dinosaurs (see Carrano 2000; Hutchinson 2001*a*, 2001*b*). Consequently, the authors stated, although their reconstruction has focused on one specific kind of dinosaur, it should not be inferred that *Tyrannosaurus* was the only or even the first taxon to evolve such drived features. The derived conditions in this genus include increases in the sizes and moment arms of muscles acting about the ankle and pedal joints. Reduction of the planter aponeurosis and expansion of the flexor tubercles and extensor attachments on the pes could relate to the evolution of digitigrady, bipedalism, an erect posture, and possibly lower limb mechanics; reduction of the fibula correlates with the increased consolidation of the lower limb (see Farlow *et al.*). Such changes, according to Carrano and Hutchinson, "probably signal a restriction of non parasagittal motion of joints within the lower limb, such as movement of the fibula relative to the tibia or complex intratarsal motion."

Carrano and Hutchinson noted that the dominance of knee flexion/extension over hip flexion/extension in avian locomotion (*e.g.*, Gatesy 1990, 1995; Carrano 1998*a*, 1998*b*) has the potential to be related to the enlargement of the knee flexor muscles, this apparently associated with caudal iliac expansion and thereby "apparently well underway before the evolution of *Tyrannosaurus*." However, even though the presence of significant femoral protractors and retractors suggests that knee flexion/extension was well developed in this genus, this development was not at the cost of hip flexion/extension. Knee-extensor enlargement apparently evolved parallel to an increase in hip flexion capacity. Reduction in hip flexion/extension seems to have occurred subsequently in coelurosaurs even more derived than *Tyrannosaurus* (see Gatesy 1990, 1995; Carrano 1998*a*, 1998*b*).

Carrano and Hutchinson's research concluded that *Tyrannosaurus* "exemplifies numerous dinosaur modifications of the primitive archosaurian pelvic and hindlimb musculature," these seemingly "related to the evolution of parasagital limb posture in dinosauromorphs" (see Novas 1992*b*, 1996; Carrano 2000; Hutchinson and Gatesy 2000). While not entirely "avian," bipedalism in this genus exhibits "a combination of characters and character states befitting its phylogenetic position between crocodilians and neornithine birds." Thus, clarification of the musculature in *Tyrannosaurus* and its unique suite of characters "helps to partition the major changes that occurred during the evolution of birds into distinct regions of the phylogeny."

Debated for many years have been controversial topics relating to behavior in *Tyrannosaurus*, such as the top locomotion this dinosaur was capable of achieving. Hutchinson and Garcia (2002) discussed locomotion speeds in this genus, which have been estimated as ranging from simply walking to high-speed running (see *D:TE, S1, S2*). (See also Hutchinson's 2001*c* related abstract for a preliminary assessment of such speeds in *Tyrannosaurus* and other large theropods, wherein biomechanical models of various large and small theropods—including *Tyrannosaurus*, a small and probably juvenile tyrannosaur, and *Coelophysis*—and the birds *Gallus* and *Eudromia* were compared with *Homo*, *Iguana*, and *Alligator*. Comparing *Tyrannosaurus* with extant elephants, Hutchinson noted that, although "elephants are capable of some surprising locomotor activities, their extreme body size limits their range of performance, presumably as in *Tyrannosarus* and other giant theropods." The results of Hutchinson's study were in line with those of Hutchinson and Garcia, below.)

Hutchinson and Garcia addressed this topic incorporating "a method of gauging running ability by estimating the minimum mass of extensor (supportive) muscle needed for fast running." In applying this method to extant animals, Hutchinson and Garcia achieved results that matched reality. Clearly, Chickens are adept runners while alligators are not. Dissections of *Gallus* and *Alligator* corroborated this observable fact, revealing that the former possesses nearly twice the extensor muscle necessary for fast bipedal running, while the latter possesses less than half that required.

Applying this method to models of small theropod dinosaurs, which had lower mass per leg than giant forms such as *Tyrannosaurus*, Hutchinson and Garcia achieved results corroborating earlier studies, including many based upon the interpretation of fossil footprints, that they were capable of rapid locomotion. However, models for an adult *Tyrannosaurus* indicated the requirement of "an unreasonably large mass of extensor muscle" in order for the animal to be a rapid runner. According to Hutchinson and Garcia's calculations, even with their input parameter values generously weighted towards a low minimum extensor muscle mass per leg, a fast-running *Tyrannosaurus* would have needed approximately 43 percent of its body mass as extensor muscle for each leg, or 86 percent for both. Furthermore, the authors noted, according to scaling data, an adult *Tyrannosaurus* seems to have possessed only from seven to 10 percent body mass as extensor muscle per leg, allowing very limited, if any, running ability. This suggested that, if *Tyrannosaurus* was a competent runner, it should have had numerous musculoskeletal specializations not suggested by the available data.

Hutchinson and Garcia finalized their study with an isometrically scaled-up model of a chicken with a 6,000-kilogram mass, incorporating the same limb orientation as an extant form, thereby simulating a chicken the size of a *Tyrannosaurus*. A typical chicken, the authors noted, need only 4.7 percent body mass as extensor muscle per leg. However, the model indicated that this hypothetical giant chicken would require about 99 percent body mass as extensor muscle for each leg, which is obviously impossible.

The above conclusions, therefore, led Hutchinson and Garcia to find it "doubtful that *Tyrannosaurus* and other huge dinosaur (~6,000 kg) were capable runners or could reach high speed." As the authors further speculated, their conclusions may also apply to other larger dinosaurs, thereby contradicting arguments that theropods like *Tyrannosaurus* were too slow to prey upon such herbivorous contemporaries as *Triceratops* (although this study did not include quadrupedal dinosaurs; R. E. Molnar, personal communication 2002).

Hutchinson and Garcia further suggested that other theropod lineages may have independently reduced their running ability as they evolved to enormous sizes, while reduction of body size and relative increase of extensor muscle sizes most likely contributed to increasing running ability in maniraptorans (especially birds).

Hutchinson and Garcia's conclusions were sub-

Tyrannosaurus

Skeletons of *Tyrannosaurus rex* (LACM 7244/23844, most of postcrania cast from RTMP 81.6.1, specimen nicknamed "Black Beauty") and *Triceratops horridus* (LACM 7207/118118, skull cast of LACM 7207/59049), the "Dueling Dinosaurs" exhibit (see *S1*).

thor noted, the power per gram of leg muscle required to achieve high absolute speeds is too high for them to do so, while both bipedal and quadrupedal flexed-limbed giants can run with quite low mass specific power output. As an example, Leahy pointed out that ostriches, with no relative increase in leg extensor mass and similar limb flexion, run much faster than small chickens. Also, rhinoceroses weighing two metric tonnes can fast gallop despite their bulk and short, lightly muscled, but flexed limbs.

Leahy posited that tyrannosaurs of similar mass should have been at least as fast as running rhinoceroses, because the theropods' "small bellies, air-filled bodies and reduced arms allowed a high portion of total mass to be dedicated to very large leg muscles anchored on large pelves and prominent cnemial crests, and their flexed legs were very long." Leahy cited for comparison elephants, massive herbivores that cannot run, not due to their size, but because of their small leg extensors, inflexible ankles, and abbreviated feet. Contrarily, an adult *Tyrannosaurus* possessed various adaptations for reducing body weight, oversized leg muscles, and birdlike flexed leg muscles.

Leahy concluded that the remaining question is not whether *Tyrannosaurus* "could achieve an energy efficient run, but how much faster it was than elephants, which are far from maximum mechanical limits since they are an order of magnitude smaller than super sauropods."

Another often hotly debated topic was addressed by Carpenter and Smith (2001)—the purpose of the diminutive though robustly constructed forelimbs of *Tyrannosaurus*, the authors noting that hypotheses have ranged from an aid during mating (Osborn 1906), helping the animal arise from a prone position (Newman 1970), vestigial organs (Paul), and an organ the function of which lessened with maturity (Mattison and Griffin 1989) (see *D:TE*). The authors began their confrontation of this issue by, for the first time, describing in detail the entire forelimb of *T. rex*, including parts of the following specimens: Scapula and humerus of holotype CMNH 9380; right humerus, ulna, radius, metacarpals I and II, phalanges II-1 and 2, unguals I-2 and II-3 of DMNH 30665 (casts of FMNH PR2081); and parts or most of left scapula, coracoid, humerus, ulna, radius, metacarpals I and II, carpals, phalanges I-1, II-1 and 2, of MOR 555. In describing this material, Carpenter and Smith showed that the forelimb of *T. rex*, though short, "was stoutly built and well muscled."

Following their description, Carpenter and Smith examined the *T. rex* forelimb biomechanically, this analysis performed "by first determining which of two mechanical systems the forelimb represents, and then determining the power of the forelimb based on

sequently criticized by Leahy (2002) in a published abstract for a poster. According to that author, Hutchinson and Garcia, while limiting *Tyrannosaurus* to an energy expensive walk, "overestimate the leg extensors needed for a juvenile tyrannosaur to run fast by a factor of over two (42% of total mass compared to under 20% observed in similar sized ostriches), and their methodology is even less reliable when extended to giants."

According to Leahy, "Both muscle power delivery and power needed to move at a given speed scales to mass to the ⅔s power, and is similar regardless of limb number or posture." In small animals, that au-

that system" (see below). The authors compared the forelimb of *T. rex* (MOR 555) with those of the long-forelimbed theropod *Deinonychus antirrhopus* (YPM 5236, coracoid; YPM 5220, unla and radius; YPM 5236, manus; AMNH 3015, scapula and humerus), the intermediate forelimbed theropod *Allosaurus fragilis* (DINOLAB, uncatalogued, forelimb); and the forelimb of *Homo sapiens* (MOR, uncatalogued).

As Carpenter and Smith explained, the forelimb is a third-class lever, the motive force (*i.e.*, the pull of a muscle on a bone) of which is located between the resistive force (*i.e.*, the resistance of that bone to being moved) and the axis of rotation, when the forelimb is under load. The motion of the forelimb can be seen as one of two mechanical systems — 1. velocity based, as typified by cursorial mammals (insertion of limb muscles near the axis, thereby allowing more rapid movement of the limb), or 2. force based, as typified by fossorial mammals (inserting limb muscles farther from the axis, giving more power to the limb). The ratio of the resistive force to the motive force determines which of these systems is in operation. The authors accepted Kreighbaum and Barthels' (1985) recognition "that force (mass times acceleration) has four properties: (1) magnitude of force, (2) direction force is applied, (3) line of action (follows the direction of force), and (4) point of application (the attachment of the force that is being applied to the bone)."

Calculations by Carpenter and Smith established the forearm of *T. rex* to be a forced-based system. Further calculations determined that, when compared with a human, the M. biceps in *T. rex* was three and one half times stronger per newton of force in both the normal and maximum working ranges (other flexors, *e.g.*, M. brachialis, not being considered in their study, yet would have increased further the strength of the arm). Such high strengths suggested to the authors that the arms of *T. rex* "were not atrophied structures nor useless appendages, but rather had a definite function that we believe was to clutch struggling prey." This interpretation, Carpenter and Smith acknowledged, conflicts with the interpretation of this dinosaur as a huge scavenger because of the size of its arms (*e.g.*, see Horner and Lessem 1993; Horner 1994).

In support of their hypothesis that the forelimbs were employed in grasping prey, Carpenter and Smith noted the that the range of motion for the forelimb, from maximum extension to maximum flexion, varies among the taxa used in their study. The greatest range of motion is the long arms of *Homo* (relatively low mechanical advantage for the long lever arms, apparently a compromise between a velocity- and force-based system); the second greatest range is *Deinonychus* (the

long cursorial running legs and long forelimb with a high mechanical advantage, indicating pursuit and grasping of prey); the third is *Allosaurus* (proportionally shorter arms relative to *Homo* and *Deinonychus*, mechanical advantage of lever arms very low, indicating that clutching is more important than reaching out to grasp prey); and the least is *T. rex* (short arms and very low mechanical advantage). As determined by Carpenter and Smith, the limited range of motion and short lever arm of the forelimb of *T. rex* "provided a very stable platform for the very powerful M. biceps," this indicating that the forelimbs were utilized in securing struggling prey. Further supporting their hypothesis, the authors cited a pathology along the medial side of the humerus of FMNH PR2081, noting that the location of damage corresponds to the medial head of the M. triceps humeralis, the muscles that serves to adduct and extend the lower arm. This kind of pathology, the authors pointed out, is characteristic of partial avulsion caused by atypically high stress loads, as when clutching a large struggling animal such as a hadrosaur (Carpenter, in press).

In conclusion, Carpenter and Smith envisioned "that *T. rex* stalked or ambushed prey, mostly subadult or young adult hadrosaurs (see Carpenter 2000)," using first its mouth to grasp the prey, then bringing in the short yet powerful forearms "to grasp or clutch the prey against the body to prevent its escape while the teeth were disengaged and repeated bites made to kill the prey."

In an abstract, Rega (2001) reported on pathologies found throughout the mature FMNH PR2081, including healed infection (?osteomyelitis) of the left fibula, healed fractures of right and left ribs, possible well-healed infection of the proximal portion of the right humerus, infection of vertebrae, and multiple bilaterally present lesions mostly on the post-dentary elements of the mandible. Rega (as did Brochu; see above) saw no evidence of pre- or peri-mortem bite marks on this specimen.

As Rega observed, bilateral (but not bilaterally symmetrical) lesions on the jaws, rather common in large tyrannosaurid specimens, could be neoplastic or fungal in origin. The maturity of this individual coupled with the evidence of healing indicate that, despite the number of these pathologies in this single individual, "Sue" was a robust animal who died after surviving numerous insults. Rega saw the injured ribs as suggesting two traumatic events to the trunk, one of them also impacting the right pectoral complex. Evidence of nonunion (pseudoarthrosis) in two of a series of adjacent heal fractures in the right thoracic ribs further suggested to that author "the potential of not-inconsiderable movement in the rib cage during healing," this possibly implying thoracic breathing"

Tyrannosaurus

Maximum range of motion of the forelimb of *Tyrannosaurus rex* in A. lateral and B. cranial views, drawing also slowing maximum extension and flexion of the manus, dots and dashed lines showing motion path of the claw tips; C. manus in maximum extension (light lines) and flexion (dark lines). (After Carpenter and Smith 2001.)

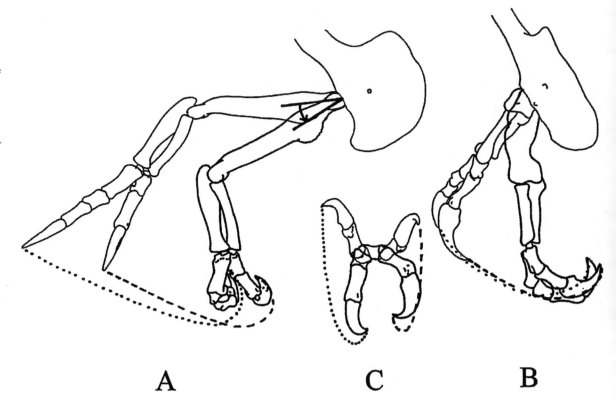

A   C   B

(for related reports, see also Rega and Brochu 2001*a*, 2001*b*).

On the same topic, Larson (2001) stated that pathologies in the skeleton of *T. rex* offer salient information regarding disease, physiology, metabolism, and behavior: This dinosaur is known to have suffered a variety of afflictions (*e.g.*, gout, bacterial infections). Major breakages healed by rapid bone growth suggest a high rate of metabolism. "Overload" injuries to caudal vertebrae are attributed to accidents during copulation, strengthening the idea that females were more robust than males. Other pathologies (*e.g.*, healed cranial puncture wounds, broken ribs, fused cervical vertebrae, injured humeri, broken fibula) indicated to Larson "that *T. rex* was actively involved in intraspecific and interspecific conduct typical of an active predator," with major healed, incapacitating injuries, as in the neck and leg, possibly indicating also "complex social behavior such as spousal care."

McIver (2002) pointed out that, despite the popularity of *Tyrannosaurus rex*, little has been written regarding the paleoenvironments in which this huge theropod lived. Recently, that author noted, excavations have continued of an at least 65 percent complete *T. rex* skeleton, nicknamed "Scotty" by local residents, from sediments in sandy facies of the Frenchman Formation (latest Maastrichtian), at Chambery Coulee, southeast of the town of Eastend, in southwestern Saskatchewan, Canada (see Tokaryk 1997, 2001). As McIver stressed, this discovery is es-

pecially important as the dinosaur's bones "were preserved in intimate association with numerous identifiable leaves, seeds, fruits, and other plant remains," a rare and improbable event, as the depositional environments necessary for preserving bones are generally not the same as those required for plants (Retallack 1997). Furthermore, that author noted, until this discovery little has been known regarding the fossil flora of the Frenchman Formation of Saskatchewan.

By analyzing both the plant fossils and sediments of this locality, McIver envisioned this dinosaur's environment of 65.5 to 65 million years ago. According to the author, the studied evidence suggests that the animal "roamed through early successional communities of stream sides and thrived in a mesothermal climate without significant winter frost, but with seasonal precipitation." Summer vegetation seems to have comprised a mixture of trees, including broad-leaved and coniferous species. Deciduousness of these forests, which supported prey (*e.g.*, hadrosaurs, *Triceratops*, and other herbivores) however, may have been scarce. Interpreted as a response to low winter light levels at high latitude, the deciduous nature of the Saskatchewan paleovegetation sharply contrasts with the contemporaneous vegetation of just a few latitudinal degrees farther south. This brings up "questions about how a dinosaur fauna survived in a region where the bulk of the vegetation entered an extended period of dormancy," and speculations regarding the possibility

that both herbivores and carnivores may have migrated southward during the winter.

As chronicled in detail by Tokaryk (2001), the above mentioned Saskatchewan *T. rex* skeleton was discovered in August, 1991 by school teacher Robert Gebhardt during a field trip for the Royal Saskatchewan Museum. The skeleton was disarticulated and also trapped hundreds of recognizable fossil plants. Excavation of the *T. rex* began in 1994, continuing through 2001 as Tokaryk's report was being written. The length of time involved in digging out this specimen was due to the position and layout of the skeleton (none of the elements articulated, with sizable gaps between some of them and with sometimes two to four bones stacked atop each other in very dense bone concentration) and also because of the difficulty in extracting the bones from the matrix (sediments comprising sandstone but mostly ironstone).

As Tokaryk noted that, included among the *T. rex* remains are fossils belonging to smaller vertebrates and some invertebrates. This associated evidence, combined with the numerous floral elements (including seeds, cones, leaves, "branches," and "trunks"), "will provide a reasonable snapshot of the biota at the time of burial."

In 2001, Hu, Cheng, Pang and Fang reported tyrannosaurid remains including some isolated teeth and a right metatarsal IV, the latter measuring 531 millimeters in length, from the same quarry that yielded the type material of the hadrosaurid *Shantungosaurus giganteus*, in the "lower part of the Upper Cretaceous" Xingezhuang Formation, Lower Member of the Wangshi (Wanngshih) Group, near Xingezhuang Village, in Zhucheng County, Shandong Province, China. Because of the metatarsal's close resemblance to that of *T. rex*, Hu (1973) originally referred the specimen to *Tyrannosaurus* cf. *rex*. After more recent studies, however, Hu *et al.* found the specimen distinct enough from *T. rex* to it to a new species, *Tyrannosaurus zhuchengensis*. It should be noted, however, that this species is geologically older than *T. rex*, and that all previously Asian species referred to *Tyrannosaurus* have subsequently been assigned to the geologically older *Tarbosaurus* (see entry and "Note" below).

Three-dimensional scanning of large fossils has generally been an expensive process not affordable by many researchers. A cost effective alternative to this process, yielding impressive results, was presented in an abstract by Andersen, Wilcox and Larson (2002). The specimen scanned was the complete skull of a *T. rex* specimen (popularly referred to as "Stan") housed in the Black Hills Institute of Geological Research. As the authors noted, this skull is mostly disarticulated, with all elements preserved with minimal distortion, and many

of the bones are extremely dense. Endeavoring to extract the maximum of morphological data with the least amount of effort, significantly reduce the overall costs, and eliminate risks to the skull, Andersen *et al.* scanned polyurethane casts of the original bones.

This led to the quick creation of "very accurate 3-D virtual models." Subsequently, these models were reduced in scale, rapidly leading to the production of an accurate one-sixth scale replica of either the individual elements or the complete, assembled skull. Finally, accurate digital files were created, offering a permanent archive of the bones in high resolution. These fossils, the authors noted, can then be tapped for making precise measurements, immediately calculating volumes of selected bones, and making digital comparisons with other specimens. Also, such virtual models can have a use in biomechanical modeling. (See also Bimber, Gatesy and Witmer 2002 for a related report, including that of a cast skull of *Deinonychus* augmented with three-dimensional models of missing bones and reconstructed soft tissues.)

Note: The species *Tyrannosaurus bataar* and ?*T. luanchuansis* have been referred to the genus *Tarbosaurus* (see entry), the latter tentatively.

Key references: Alber (1992); Andersen, Wilcox and Larson; Bakker (1992); Brochu (2003); Busbey (1995); Carpenter (2000, in press); Carpenter and Smith (2001); Carr and Williamson (2001, 2002*a*); Carrano (1998*a*, 1998*b*, 2000); Carrano and Hutchinson (2002); Erickson, Van Kirk, Su, Levenston, Caler and Carter (1996); Farlow, Gatesy, Holtz, Hutchinson and Robinson (2000); Ford (1997); Ford and Chure (2001*a*); Gatesy (1990, 1995); Horner (1994); Horner and Lessem (1993); Hu (1973); Hu, Cheng, Pang and Fang (2001); Hutchinson (2001*a*, 2001*b*, 2001*c*); Hutchinson and Garcia (2002); Hutchinson and Gatesy (2000); Kreighbaum and Barthels (1985); Lambe (1917); Larson (2001, 2002); Larson and Frey (1992); Leahy (2002); Loewen, Sampson, Getty and Difley (2001); Mattison and Griffin (1989); McIver (2002); Molnar (1978, 2000); Molnar and Carpenter (1989); Newman (1970); Novas (1992*b*, 1996); Olshevsky, Ford and Yamamoto (1995*a*, 1995*b*); Osborn (1905, 1906); Paul (1988*b*); Rega (2001); Rega and Brochu (2001*a*, 2001*b*); Retallack (1997); Romer (1923*a*, 1923*b*, 1923*c*); Russell (1972); Schmitt and Schweitzer (2002); Schweitzer and Schmitt (2002); Smith (2002*a*, 2002*b*); Snively (2002); Starkov (2001); Tarsitano (1981, 1983); Tokaryk (1997, 2001); Walker (1977).

†UTAHRAPTOR

Saurischia: Eusaurischia: Theropoda: Neotheropoda:
    Tetanurae: Avetheropoda: Coelurosauria: Mani-

Utahraptor

Photograph by the author, courtesy North American Museum of Ancient Life.

Reconstructed skeleton of *Utahraptor ostrommaysi* including cast of holotype CEUM 184v.294 material.

Life restoration of *Utahraptor ostrommaysi* painted by Kelly Pugh.

raptoriformes: Maniraptora: Metornithes: Paraves: Deinonychosauria: Dromaeosauridae: ?Dromaeosaurinae.

Age: Early to Middle Cretaceous (Barremian to Albian–Cenomanian).

Known material: Remains representing at least 10 individuals, juvenile to adult.

Comments: In an abstract, Britt, Chure, Stadtman, Madsen, Scheetz and Burge (2001) briefly reported on more than 190 disarticulated elements belonging to the giant dromaeosaurid *Utahraptor ostrommaysi* (see *D:TE, SI*), representing at least nine individuals, recently collected from the Middle Cretaceous Dalton Wells Quarry and Yellow Cat Quarry in the Cedar Mountain Formation of Utah. These remains, the authors noted, range from juvenile (length of femur 310 millimeters, indicating an animal as large as an adult *Deinonychus*) to adult (length of femur 565 millimeters, indicating an animal much larger than *Achillobator*.

As Britt *et al.* noted, this material reveals new data regarding *Utahraptor*, including the following: Premaxillary teeth semi-"D"-shaped; premaxilla differing from other known dromaeosaurs in having elongate nasal process; quadrate process of quadratojugal half as long as jugal process; quadratojugal primitive in lacking triradiate shape of *Deinonychus* and *Velociraptor*; pneumatic presacral centra camellate, only cranial dorsal centra pneumatic, arch pneumatization primarily external (underived); ilium of dromaeosaurid form with broad shelf for M. cuppedicus, form of pubic peduncle indicating retroverted pubis; ischium primitive in bearing proximally located

Hindlimb with foot of *Utahraptor ostrommaysi*, one of the specimens under recent study by Brooks B. Britt, Daniel J. Chure, Kenneth L. Stadtman, James H. Madsen, Jr., R. D. Scheetz, and Donald L. Burge.

Photograph by the author, courtesy Earth Science Museum, Brigham Young University.

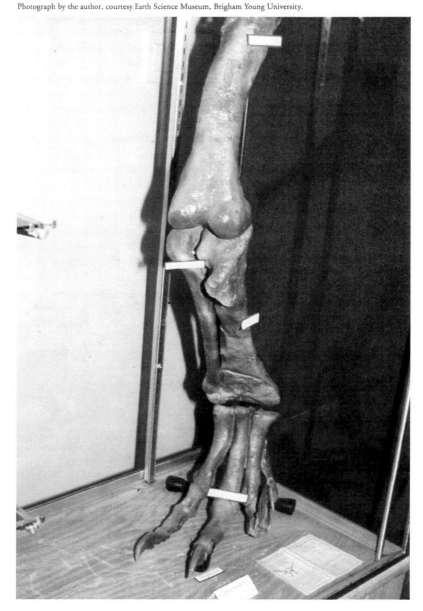

V

obturator process and slender, caudally directed shaft; femur with digitiform lesser trochanter separated by notch from greater trochanter; ascending process of astragalus short, laterally broad.

The authors pointed out that, in the original description of this genus, "a digit II pedal ungual was misidentified as manual, the surangular is a long bone fragment, and the lacrimal is a postorbital of *Gastonia*" (see Kirkland, Gaston and Burge 1993; see also *D:TE*).

In general, Britt *et al.* found *Utahraptor* to be less derived that the velociraptorine *Deinonychus* and apparently more closely related to the ?dromaeosaurine *Achillobator*.

Note: White and Lockley (2002), in an abstract for a poster, reported a new dinosaur track locality in the Cedar Mountain Formation, Arches National Park, Utah, which has thus far yielded a diverse assemblage of theropod, sauropod, ornithopod, and ?ankylosaurid tracks from two stratigraphic levels.

The upper bed has yielded two deep theropod tracks, preserved as didactyl impressions with just a trace of the proximal part of a third toe (believed to be digit II). In the opinion of White and Lockley, if this interpretation is correct, these tracks were probably made by a dromaeosaur. The length of each footprint is from 30 to 37 centimeters, the right size, the authors pointed out, "to match the foot of *Utahraptor.*

Key references: Britt, Chure, Stadtman, Madsen, Scheetz and Burge (2001); Kirkland, Gaston and Burge (1993); White and Lockley (2002).

VENENOSAURUS   Tidwell, Carpenter and Meyer 2001

Saurischia: Eusaurischia: Sauropodomorpha: Sauropoda: Eusauropoda: Neosauropoda: Macronaria: Camarasauromorpha: Titanosauriformes *incertae sedis.*

Name derivation: Latin *venenos* = "poison [Poison Strip Member, Cedar Mountain Formation]" + Greek *sauros* = "lizard."

Type species: *V. dicrocei* Tidwell, Carpenter and Meyer 2001.

Other species: [None.]

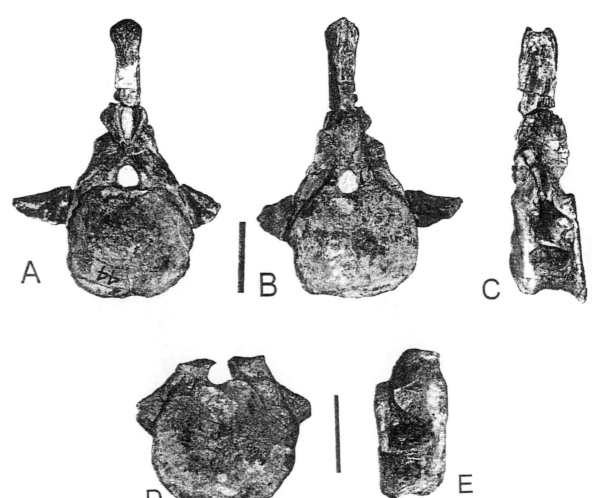

Venenosaurus dicrocei, DMNH 40932, holotype proximal caudal vertebra in A. distal, B. cranial, and C. left lateral views; proximal centrum in D. cranial and E. right lateral views. Scale = 10 cm. (After Tidwell, Carpenter and Meyer 2001.)

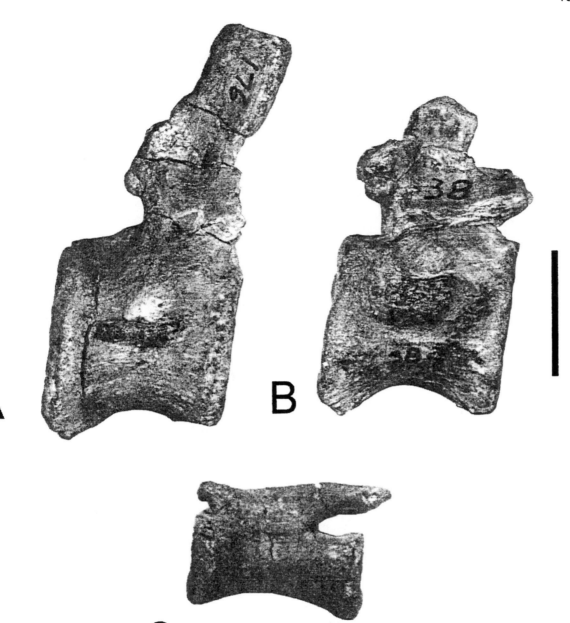

Occurrence: Cedar Mountain Formation, Utah, United States.

Age: Early Cretaceous (?Barremian).

Known material: Two postcranial specimens, adult and juvenile.

Holotype: DMNH 40932, nine articulated dorsal vertebrae, left scapula, right radius, left ulna, five metacarpals, four manual phalanges, right pubis, ischia, three metacarpals, astragalus, chevrons, ribs.

Diagnosis of genus (as for type species): Centrum of proximal caudal vertebra having convex cranial surface, flat caudal surface; neural spines of middle caudals inclining cranially (similar to *Cedarosaurus* and *Aeolosaurus*); centra amphyplatyan (as in *Bra-*

chiosaurus); cranial and middle caudal vertebrae having deep lateral fossae (shallow in *Brachiosaurus*, *Cedarosaurus*, and *Saltasaurus*); radius more slender than in other taxa (except *Cedarosaurus*); ulna with expanded medial wall, well-developed medial process (contrasting with *Camarasaurus* and *Brachiosaurus*, similar to *Cedarosaurus* and most titanosaurs); olecranon process moderately developed, ulna craniomedial process slightly concave (in contrast to *Camarasaurus* and *Brachiosaurus*, similar to titanosaurs); proximal end of metacarpal I more slender craniocaudally than other sauropods; pubis longer than ischium; pubic articulation of ischium restricted to proximal half of bone (occupying much of total length

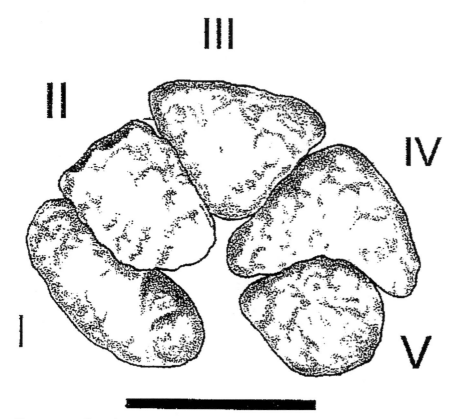

Venenosaurus dicrocei, DMNH 40932, holotype right metacarpals in dorsal view. Scale = 10 cm. (After Tidwell, Carpenter and Meyre 2001.)

in *Andesaurus* and *Saltasaurus*) (Tidwell, Carpenter and Meyer 2001).

Comments: A relatively small sauropod, *Venenosaurus* was founded on a partial adult postcranial skeleton (DMNH 40932) discovered by Tony Di-Croce, a volunteer at the Denver Museum of Natural History and Science, in medium- to coarse-grained sandstones and lenses of green mudstone, in the Poison Strip Sandstone Member of the Cedar Mountain Formation (?Barremian; Kirkland, Cifelli, Britt, Burge, DeCourten, Eaton and Parrish 1997; or more generalized ?"Neocomian"; B. B. Britt, personal communication to Tidwell, Carpenter and Meyer), near Arches National Park, in Grand County, in east-central Utah. A juvenile specimen (catalog number not given), referred to the type species *Venenosaurus dicrocei*, was also collected from this quarry. Associated dinosaurian remains from the same quarry include an unidentified ornithopod, the new ornithopod *Planicoxa venenica* (DiCroce and Carpenter 2001; see entry), and a theropod (possibly *Utahraptor ostrommaysorum*) (Tidwell, Carpenter and Meyer 2001).

In describing *V. dicrocei*, Tidwell *et al.* observed that, based upon the complete fusion of the neural arch and caudal ribs to the centra, this taxon appears to be a small (scapula measuring 1,200 millimeters in length) adult. However, a coracoid was not found fused to the scapula and the pubic foramen is not

closed, these features perhaps reflecting immaturity or taphonomic processes.

Comparing *Veneosaurus* with other sauropods, Tidwell *et al.* observed that this genus exhibits an unusual combination of plesiomorphic and derived characteristics (see below), some indicating kinship with the more primitive Brachiosauridae (*e.g.*, midcaudal vertebrae with proximally inclining neural spines), and others suggesting a more advanced relationship (slightly convex proximal surface of caudal vertebrae). Genera closely resembling *Veneosaurus* include the titanosauriformes *Brachiosaurus, Chubutisaurus, Pleurocoelus nanus*, Texas "*Pleurocoelus*" SMU 61732 (see *Cedarosaurus, S2*), *Andesaurus*, and mostly *Cedarosaurus*.

Veneosaurus and *Cedarosaurus* share a number of features (*e.g.*, relatively gracile radii); however, a number of significant autapomorphies distinguish the former genus — *e.g.*, proximalmost caudal vertebra showing deeper lateral fossa; centra with deeply concave proximal surfaces; middle caudal neural spines vertical to distally inclined; single, poorly defined radial shaft and unlar rugosity; ulna more robust; pubis more constricted below ischial articulation, lacking foramen located near caudal, medial border (seen in *Cedarosaurus*); shorter metatarsal I; posteromedial process of distal medial condyle more prominent; metatarsal II more robust.

As Tidwell *et al.* pointed out, the morphology of the proximal caudal vertebrae of *Venenosaurus*, mixing both primitive and advanced features, had not previously been reported in any other sauropod. The slightly convex proximal surface of the centra, suggesting an incipient biconvex state, is suggestive of derived titanosaurs; this feature is, however, coupled with a flat distal surface, a primitive feature that is probably a precursor to the completely derived biconvex condition. The middle caudal vertebrae display a similar mixture, combining a forward-leaning neural spine (an atypical condition also found in *Brachiosaurus, Cedarosaurus, Aeolosaurus*, "*Gondwanatitan*" [=*Aeolosaurus*], and *Lirainosaurus*) with amphiplatyan (rather than concave) centra. These two features, the authors determined, set *Venenosaurus* apart from *Cedarosaurus* as a valid genus. Tidwell *et al.* further noted that "the combination of brachiosaur and titanosaur characters found in the proximal caudal, middle caudals, and pelvic elements reinforce the close relationships of these groups.

Note: Citing the variety of recent sauropod discoveries and the growing variety of articulations of caudal vertebrae (*e.g.*, *Venenosaurus* and *Cedarosaurus*), Tidwell *et al.* stressed both the inadequacies of traditional terms used to describe these articulations (*e.g.*, amphicoelous and procoelous), and also the need for

more precise identifications (*e.g.*, procoelous/distoplatyan for the centrum articulations of *Cedarosaurus*; see *S2*) of articular face morphology.

Key references: Kirkland, Cifelli, Britt, Burge, DeCourten, Eaton and Parrish (1997); Tidwell, Carpenter and Meyer (2001).

†XENOTARSOSAURUS

Saurischia: Eusaurischia: Theropoda: Neotheropoda:
  Neoceratosauria: Abelisauroidea: Abelisauridae.

Comment: In a paper describing the new abelisaur *Ilokelesia aguadagranensis* (see *Ilokelesia* entry), Coria and Salgado (2000) addressed the type species *Xenotarsosaurus bonapartei*, a medium-sized theropod based upon a single very partial postcranial remains from the Bajo Barreal Formation (Lower Santonian) of Chubut, Argentina (see *D:TE*). Martínez, Gimènez, Rodríguez and Bochatey (1986), who named and described this new taxon, referred it to the family Abelisauridae. This referral was based mainly upon the presence of a concave articular surface in the centra of the dorsal vertebra, a condition interpreted by Martínez *et al.* as an autapomorphy of *Xenotarsosaurus*.

As pointed out by Coria and Salgado, however, the caudal dorsal vertebra of *Ilokelesia* exhibits a similar condition, which could be interpreted as a synapomorphy of both genera. Furthermore, the authors proposed that the deep pre- and postspinal depressions in the only known neural arches of *Xenotarsosaurus* could be synapomorphic for Neoceratosauria.

Because there was presently no available materials for comparing *Xenotarsosaurus* with *Ilokelesia*, Coria and Salgado found their mutual affinities to be unclear, the phylogenetic position of the former genus among Neoceratosauria problematic.

More recently, Carrano, Sampson and Forster (1002), in performing their own cladistic analysis of various theropod groups, referred *Xenotarsosaurus* to the Abelisauridae (see "Systematics" chapter).

Key references: Carrano, Sampson and Forster (2002); Coria and Salgado (2000); Martínez, Gimènez, Rodríguez and Bochatey (1986).

†YANGCHUANOSAURUS

Saurischia: Eusaurischia: Theropoda: Neotheropoda:
  Tetanurae: Avetheropoda: Carnosauria: Allosauroidea: Sinraptoridae.

Diagnosis of genus: Medium to large size (7 to 20 meters in length); skull large, moderately high; upper part of skull narrow, ratio of width to length of skull less than 1.3; skull with six pairs of external openings and one to two maxillary fossa; parietal process developed, frontal coossified with parietal; dorsal keel of supraoccipital developed; upper process of quadratojugal slender, long; large external mandibular foramen; premaxillary teeth rounded in cross section, maxillary and dentary teeth lenticular; four premaxillary, 13 to 15 maxillary, and 14 to 16 dentary teeth; nine to 10 opithocoelous cervical vertebrae, caudal cervicals having ventral keel; 13 to 14 opisthocoelous, amphiplatyan dorsal vertebrae; neural spines of dorsal vertebrae high, platelike; five sacral

Yangchuanosaurus hepingensis, ZDM0024, holotype skull in left lateral view. (After Gao 1999.)

Yangchuanosaurus

Yangchuanosaurus hepingensis, reconstructed skeleton based on holotype ZDM0024. (After Gao 1999.)

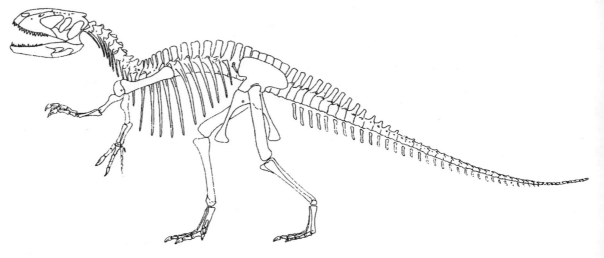

vertebrae, having firmly coossified centra; four sacral neural spines fused; proximal caudal vertebrae with high, platelike neural spines; distal caudal vertebrae having elongate prezygapophyses; moderately wide scapular shaft; pelvic girdle firm, shafts of pubes and ischia coossified; pubes with small, distal "boot"; ischia expanded distally; ascending process of astragalus low (Gao 1999).

Diagnosis of *Y. hepingensis*: Relatively large, more than 8 meters in length; skull large, moderately high, 1,040 millimeters long, 595 millimeters high, ratio of length to height (including lower jaw) about 1.75; upper part of skull narrow, ratio of width to length of skull about 28 percent; two antorbital fenestrae, first craniocaudally elongate, isosceles triangular in out-line, second small, quadrilateral in outline; maxillary fossa elliptical in outline, base of ascending process perforated by second antorbital fenestra; parietal high, well-developed winglike plates of parietal; supraoc-cipital small, narrow, dorsal keel well developed; frontal and prefrontal not contributing to upper bor-der of orbit; palatine long, narrow, upper process of quadratojugal long, slender; dentary thick, external mandibular foramen large; teeth round in cross sec-tion, maxillary teeth relatively thin, dentary teeth large; four premaxillary, 13 to 14 maxillary, and 16 dentary teeth; nine opisthocoelous cervical vertebrae; pleurocoel and epipophysis developed, caudal cervi-cal vertebra having ventral keel; 14 opisthocoelous, amphiplatyan dorsal vertebrae, relatively short, dorsal

Life restoration of the sin-raptorid theropod *Yang-chuanosaurus hepingensis*. (After Gao 1999.)

neural spines high, platelike; five sacral vertebrae having firmly coossified centra; four fused caudal sacral neural spines; more than 35 caudal vertebrae, distal caudals having elongate prezygapophyses; wide scapular shaft; ilium relatively high, pubis with short, wide distal "boot"; ischium expanded distally (Gao 1999, slightly revised after Gao 1992).

Comments: In 1999, Gao Yuhui described in detail the almost complete (forelimbs not preserved) holotype skeleton with skull (ZDM0024) belonging to the referred species *Yangchuanosaurus hepingensis* (see Gao 1992; see also *D:TE*) collected from the Middle Jurassic Upper Shaximiao Formation at Heiping, Zigong, Sichuan Province, China.

Yangchanosaurus has mostly been regarded as a sinraptorid allosauroid, the latter belonging to the more encompassing clade Carnosauria. Gao (1999), however, referred this genus to the Megalosauridae, a family now largely considered to belong to the Spinosauroidea rather than Carnosauria. It should be noted also that, in attempting to classify *Yangchuanosaurus*, Gao (1999) harkened back to the now almost universally abandoned interpretation of Carnosauria as a group including both the Late Jurassic *Allosaurus* and Late Cretaceous *Tyrannosaurus*, the latter genus no longer regarded as a carnosaur but, instead, a giant member of the Coelurosauria (see also Longrich 2002, below).

In describing ZDM0024, Gao (1999) noted the craniomandibular joint with a helical groove in the quadrate, this closely fitting a corresponding ridge in the articular glenoid, a condition resembling that seen in the crocodilian *Alligator sinensis* (also found in *Allosaurus* and *Tyrannosaurus*; R. E. Molnar, personal communication 2002). During opening and closing of the mouth, the maxillary teeth remained outside of the margins of the jaws, the dentary teeth inside, Gao (1999) suggested, cutting the animal's food in the fashion of scissors. The relatively large orbit, that author pointed out, indicates a relatively developed optic nerve; the orbits are not forwardly directed to allow for three-dimensional vision. A stapes preserved in ZDM0024 suggests a reptilian mode of hearing and the large olfactory nerve opening indicates a relatively well-developed sense of smell. The tail, Gao (1999) speculated, may have been used as an attack weapon.

In a more recent report published as an abstract, Longrich (2002) proposed the new taxon Yangchuanosauria (to include the genera *Yangchuanosaurus* and *Sinraptor*, thereby essentially equaling the existing Sinraptoridae). Yangchuanosauria, that author noted, is more primitive than the Avetheropoda, its members "possessing 4 metacarpals, a fenestrate pubis, and a robust astragalar ascending process."

Key references: Gao (1992, 1999); Longrich (2002).

†ZIGONGOSAURUS—(See *Mamenchisaurus*.)

†ZUNICERATOPS

Ornithischia: Genasauria: Cerapoda: Marginocephalia: Ceratopsia: Neoceratopsia: Coronosauria: Ceratopsoidea.

Comments: Wolfe, Beekman, McGuiness and Robira (2001), in an abstract, offered a preliminary statistical characterization of a *Zuniceratops christopherid* bonebed in the Moreno Hill Formation (Middle Cretaceous: Turonian) of New Mexico. At least five specimens of this primitive ceratopsian dinosaurs are known within this bonebed, as well as a new large theropod, these taxa represented by several hundred, mostly disarticulated bones and bone fragments associated with fossil leaves and carbonized logs. The authors found the presence of separated but associated skeletal elements, specimens with teeth and delicate processes preserved, and partially articulated specimens to indicate that "the carcasses were likely reduced to skeletons prior to burial and that transport of these elements was relatively local."

As reported by Wolfe *et al.*, *Zuniceratops* cranial and axial or appendicular elements are not equally present in these specimens identified to date. Skull elements are well represented, including five left dentaries and four left brown horns, distal appendicular elements apparently being comparatively uncommon, the latter including phalanges but no unguals. Contrarily, the theropod is more evenly represented by bones from throughout the skeleton.

According to the authors, "The generally fine sediment grain size and presence of abundant coal deposits within the Moreno Hill Formation strata is an indication of submerged, relatively stagnant floodplain depositional conditions (swamp)." The nature of the fossils in this bonebed—including the apparent "stacking" of bones and logs, the well-preserved fossil leaves, and the serendipitous preservation and orientation of some of these specimens—"indicate rapid deposition in a setting subject to intervals of high energy such as a flood or debris flow." At least seasonally emergent conditions nearby are indicated by the presence of fossil wood and charcoal. Seasonal variations in precipitation are suggested by fossil angiosperm exhibiting growth rings.

Wolfe *et al.* deduced that the *Zuniceratops* skeletons first accumulated during seasonal or extreme drought at the ground surface, after which they were transported locally during flooding induced by precipitation. A possible explanation for the under-representation of right-side or appendicular elements was a "Secondary mobilization and selective winnowing of a group of *Zuniceratops* skeletons stranded together

Zuniceratops

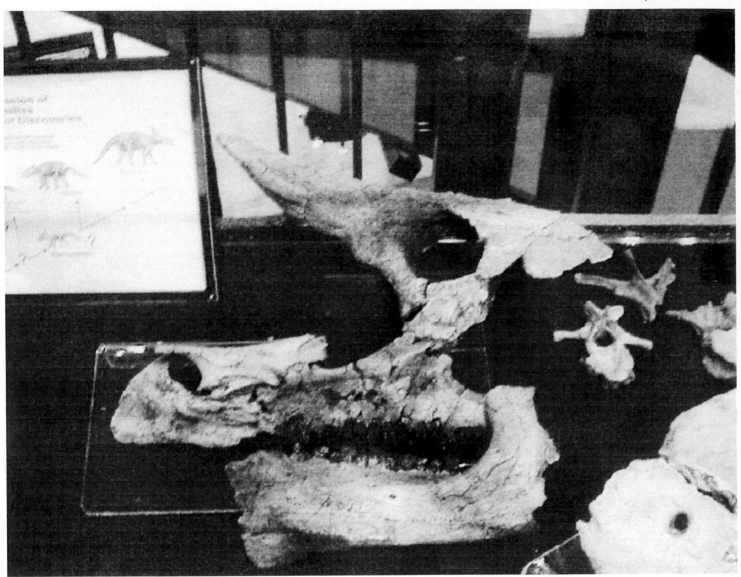

Skull, reconstructed from collected elements (both cast and real fossil bone), of *Zuniceratops christopheri* on display at the Mesa Southwest Museum.

(foundered in mud, partly buried by flood, or accumulated due to drought)," the foundered and partly buried elements lagging behind the exposed skull and other elements subsequently preserved at this site.

In another abstract, Wolfe and Kirkland (2001) briefly reported on comparable elements from five *Zuniceratops* individuals recovered from the above-mentioned bonebed, plus the holotype (MSM P2101), all representing different sizes and ages. Based upon these specimens, Wolfe and Kirkland observed the following:

Oldest and largest individuals express morphological characters (*e.g.*, resorption of roots in largest teeth resulting in slight bifurcation/sulcus to accommodate underlying replacement teeth, this morphology being intermediate between single- and double-rooted teeth) interpreted as incipient characteristics of the Ceratopsidae. In larger specimens, the number of teeth and the length-to-height ratio of the rectangular dentary increases. In younger/smaller specimens, the coronoid process, lacking the rostral-dorsal projection typical of ceratopsids, shows a thickening along its dorsal margin, this becoming more prominent and slightly projecting in the largest specimens. During ontogeny, brow horns increase greatly in size. The laterally expanded paroccipital process and occipital process, as revealed by a well-preserved braincase, resemble more those in ceratopsids than in basal neoceratopsians. The frill, as suggested by several well-preserved partial squamosals, seems have been fenestrated, nonemarginated, and lacking epoccipital processes. Nares are simple and the snout apparently lacked a horn, as evidenced by well-preserved nasal and premaxillary elements. While the recurved ischium and robust scapula seem to be relatively derived, other appendicular elements appear less so.

Photograph by Wendy Taylor, courtesy Paul C. Sereno and University of Chicago.

Reconstructed skull of a new theropod dinosaur from India, *Rajasaurus narmadensis*, discovered by Paul C. Sereno.

As stressed by Wolfe and Kirkland, *Zuniceratops*, although exhibiting individual characters in common with centrosaurs or chasmosaurs, is precluded from inclusion in Ceratopsidae by its lack of double-rooted teeth. Moreover, the taxon Ceratopsomorpha (see Wolfe and Kirkland 1998) attempts "to recocile crown- versus node-based definitions of the relation of *Zuniceratops* to the Ceratopsidae."

Key references: Wolfe, Beekman, McGuiness and Robira (2001); Wolfe and Kirkland (1998, 2001).

FINAL NOTE

As already stated elsewhere in the text, much time can pass between a book's completion and going "to press" and its actual publication. In the case of this volume, in which the editorial work is immense, over a year has elapsed since the point of "no more changes" and the actual release of the book. (My official cut-off date was March 31, 2003.) Consequently, a number of new genera and species were named and described in the paleontological literature too late for inclusion. These include the following (although there may be more):

Bainoceratops efremovi (protoceratopsid ceratopsian)

Colepiocephale lambei (pachycephalosaurine pachycephalosaurid)

Dromaeosauroides bornholmensis (dromaeosaurid theropod)

Efraasia minor (reinstated genus, new type species, plateosaurid prosauropod)

Fukuisaurus tetoriensis (iguanodontian ornithopod)

Hanssuessia sternbergi (pachycephalosaurine pachycephalosaurid)

Hongshanosaurus houi (psittacosaurid ceratopsian)

Lusotitan atalaiensis (brachiosaurid sauropod)

Mendozosaurus neguyelap (titanosaurian sauropod)

Plateosaurus gracilis (new species, formerly the type species *Sellosaurus gracilis*; platyosaurid prosauropod)

Prenocephale goodwini (new species, formerly the type species *Sphaerotholus goodwini* (pachycephalosaurine pachycephalosaur)

Rajasaurus narmadensis (abelisaurid theropod)

Struthiosaurus languedocensis (new species, nodosaurid ankylosaur)

Zupaysaurus rougieri (tetanuran theropod)

IV. Nomina Nuda

A *nomen nudum* constitutes a usually doubtful taxon that has appeared (printed in italics) in the paleontological literature (*e.g.*, in faunal lists, notes on taxa yet to be described, in popular and technical books, popular articles and reports, *etc.*), but without proper description following the rules for establishing a new genus and species (*e.g.*, without designating a type specimen). Such a taxon is, therefore, considered to be a *nomen nudum* or "naked name" (plural, *nomina nuda*). A *nomen nudum* can, however, be formally described at some future date, sometimes with the same name, with the name altered in some way, or changed altogether.

ARANCANTHUS Langston 1947 [*nomen nudum*]
Saurischia: Eusaurischia: Theropoda: Neotheropoda: Tetanurae: Avetheropoda: Carnosauria: Allosauroidea: Allosauridae.

Early name for the genus later formally to be named *Acrocanthosaurus*, introduced by Wann Langston, Jr. in his 1947 master's thesis.

CROSBYSAURUS Heckert 2002 [*nomen nudum*]
Ornithischia *incertae sedis*.
Name derivation: "Crosby" [name of person] + Greek *sauros* = "lizard."
Type species: *C. harrisae* Heckert 2002.
Occurrence: Chinle Group, Texas, Arizona, New Mexico, United States.
Age: Late Triassic (late Carnian).
Known material: Teeth, fragments.
Holotype: NMMNH P-34200, tooth crown.
    Very primitive.

GAVINOSAURUS Kelly 1998 [*nomen nudum*]—
    (See *Eotyrannus*.)
Name derivation: "Gavin [Leng]" + Greek *sauros* = "lizard."

HANWULOSAURUS [*nomen nudum*]
Ornithischia: Genasaura: Thyreophora: Thyreophoroidea: Ankylosauria *incertae sedis*.
Occurrence: Alxa Left Banner, Inner Mongolia Autonomous Region, northern China.
Known material/holotype: Skeleton including complete skull, vertebrae, ribs, scapula, ulna, femora, fibulae, armor.
Most complete ankylosaurian specimen yet found in China, head large and flat, body covered in armor, animal approximately nine meters long, two meters

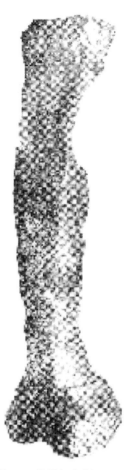

Femur of *Chinshakiangosaurus zhongheensis* [*nomen nudum*], an undescribed sauropod of uncertain affinities from the Jurassic of China (see *D:TE*). (After Zhao 1986.)

Left: Incomplete skeleton (*in situ*) of *Dachungosaurus yunnanensis* [*nomen nudum*], an undescribed sauropodomorph of uncertain affinities from the Jurassic of China (see *D:TE*). (After Zhao 1986.) *Right:* Incomplete skeleton (*in situ*) of *Damalasaurus laticostalis* [*nomen nudum*], an undescribed sauropod of uncertain affinities from the Jurassic of China (see *D:TE*). (After Zhao 1986.)

Partial articulated skeleton of *Kunmingosaurus utingensis* [*nomen nudum*], an undescribed shunosaurine sauropod from the Jurassic of China (see *D:TE*). (After Zhao 1986.)

Reconstructed skeleton (cast) of a new theropod to be named *"Tanycolagreus."*

high. Mentioned in various Xinhua News Service articles.

HEILONJIANGOSAURUS   Li and Jin 2001 [*nomen nudum*]

Ornithischia: Genasauria: Cerapoda: Ornithopoda: Iguanodontia: Euiguanodontia: Dryomorpha: Ankylopollexia: Hadrosauroidea: Hadrosauridae: Euhadrosauria *incertae sedis*.

Name derivation: "Heilongiang [Province in China]" + Greek *sauros* = "lizard."

Type species: *H. jiayinensis* Li and Jin 2001.

Occurrence: People's Republic of China.

Age: Late Cretaceous (Maastrichtian).

Apparently a new name for *Mandschurosaurus jiainensis*, but possibly an unpublished manuscript name for *Charonosaurus jiayinensis* (see *Charonosaurus* entry, *S2*).

HUAXIASAURUS   Rey 2002 [*nomen nudum*]

Saurischia: Eusaurischia: Theropoda *incertae sedis*.

Name derivation: "Hua Xi" + Greek *sauros* = "lizard."

Occurrence: Liaong, China.

An undescribed theropod, mentioned in the English translation of an article by artist Luis Rey on the 2001 meeting of the Society of Vertebrate Pale-

ontology, in the sixth issue of the Japanese *Dino Press* magazine.

ICHABODCRANIOSAURUS   Novacek   1996   [*nomen nudum*]

Saurischia: Eusaurischia: Theropoda: Neotheropoda: Tetanurae: Avetheropoda: Coelurosauria: Maniraptoriformes: Maniraptora: Metornithes: Paraves: Deinonychosauria: Dromaeosauridae: Velociraptorinae.

Name derivation: "Ichobod Crane [character from the Washington Irving story "The Legend of Sleepy Hollow"]" + Greek *sauros* = "lizard."

Occurrence: Mongolia.

Age: Late Cretaceous.

Known material/holotype: Postcranial skeleton.

Mentioned in the book Michael J. Novacek's *Dinosaurs of the Flaming Cliffs*, based on a headless skeleton; the skull later referred to this specimen could belong to another individual, perhaps a different velociraptorine taxon (M. Novacek, personal communication to G. Olshevsky 2002).

KITTYSAURUS [*nomen nudum*]—(See *Eotyrannus*.]

Name derivation: "Kitty" + Greek *sauros* = "lizard."

Photograph by the author, courtesy North American Museum of Ancient Life.

Life-sized sculptures of the new theropod to be named *"Tanycolagreus"* and the ornithischian *Othnielia rex.*

LENGOSAURUS Kelly 1998 [*nomen nudum*]— (See *Eotyrannus*.)
Name derivation: "[Gavin] Leng" + Greek *sauros* = "lizard."

LUANPINGOSAURUS Cheng *see in* Chen 1996 [*nomen nudum*]—(=?*Psittacosaurus*)
Ornithischia: Genusauria: Cerapoda: Marginocephalia: Ceratopsia: Psittacosauridae.
Name derivation: "Luanping [County]" + Greek *sauros* = "lizard."
Type species: *L. jingshanensis* Cheng *see in* Chen 1996 [*nomen nudum*].
Other species: [None.]
Occurrence: Huajiying Formation, northern Hevei Province, People's Republic of China.
Age: Late Jurassic.

Described as a synonym of *Psittacosaurus*, although it occurs in Upper Jurassic rocks.

PROTECOVASAURUS Heckert 2002 [*nomen nudum*]

Ornithischia *incertae sedis*.
Name derivation: Greek *pro* = "before" + "Tecovas [Formation] + Greek *sauros* = "lizard."
Type species: *P. lucasi* Heckert 2002
Occurrence: Chinle Group, Tecovas Formation, Texas, United States.
Age: Late Triassic (late Carnian).
Known material: Tooth crowns.
Holotype: NMMNH P-34196, tooth crown.
Very primitive.

SILESAURUS Dzik and Majer *see in* Mokoluszko 2002 [*nomen nudum*]
?Ornithischia *incertae sedis*.
Occurrence: Silesia, Poland.
Age: Late Triassic (Carnian).
Known material: Remains of at least 12 individuals including partial skeleton (holotype).

Basal ornithischian or possibly primitive Prosauropoda; presumably to be described formally in the *Journal of Vertebrate Paleontology*.

Holotype incomplete tooth of *Tyrannosaurus lanpingi* [*nomen nudum*]. From the Late Jurassic or Early Cretaceous (Tithonian–Neocomian) Redbeds of Yunnan Province, China, this tooth is too old to be referrable to *Tyrannosaurus*, but has not yet been referred to any other genus (see *Tyrannosaurus* entry, "Notes," *D:TE*). (After Yeh 1975.)

TANYCOLAGREUS [Anonymous] 2001 [*nomen nudum*]

Saurischia: Eusaurischia: Theropoda: Neotheropoda: Tetanurae: Avetheropoda: Coelurosauria *incertae sedis*:

Occurrence: Morrison Formation, Wyoming, United States.

Age: Late Jurassic (Kimmeridgian–Tithonian).

Name published in two guidebooks (see Anonymous [2001*a*, 2001*b*]) of the North American Museum of Ancient Life; "coelurid" from Bone Cabin Quarry West, Albany County, Utah, apparently collected in 1999, to be named and described formally by Kenneth Carpenter and Clifford A. Miles.

V. Excluded Genera

Previous volumes in this encyclopedic series included lists of genera that were, at one time or more, classified as dinosaurs, but are, at present, generally regarded as belonging to other nondinosaurian groups. The following list supplements those lists.

AZENDOHSAURUS

Nondinosaurian ornithodiran.

Comment: Originally described as ornithischian and later as prosauropod (see *D:TE*) and considered one of the earliest dinosaurs (Late Triassic: Carnian); according to Jalil and Knoll (2002) in an abstract, new disarticulated postcranial material (*e.g.*, presacral vertebrae, pectoral- and pelvic-girdle elements, fore- and hindlimb elements)—from the Arana Basin of Morocco, the type location of the holotype of type species *Azendohsaurus laaroussii*—show no dinosaurian synapomorphies, a suite of plesiomorphic character states (*e.g.*, imperforate acetabulum, absence of brevis fossa on ilium, femur with very proximally located fourth trochanter, head of femur not distinctly offset from shaft) suggesting a phylogenetic position outside of Dinosauria.

EUROLIMNORNIS   Kessler and Jurcsak 1986 —
(See *Paleocursornis*.)

JEHOLORNIS   Zhou and Zhang 2002 (=?*Shezouraptor*)
Avian.

Note: "Long-tailed, seed-eating Late Cretaceous bird; listed by Olshevsky (2002) on his computer list of dinosaurian taxa as probably dinosaurian as the genus has 'a long, dromaeosaurid-like tail with elongated zygapophyses,' the description very "close to that of a flying dromaeosaurid."

LIKHOELESAURUS   Ellenberger 1970 [*nomen nudum*]
Rausisuchian.

LIMNORNIS   Gould 1839 —(See *Paleocursornis*.)

PALAEOCURSORNIS   Kessler and Jurcsak 1986 (=*Eurolimnornis, Limnornis, Paleolimnornis*)
Probably avian.

Note: Currently classified as a bird; possibly nonavian dinosaurian, as suggested by Benton, Cook, Grigorescu, Popa, and Tallodi (1997).

PALEOLIMNORNIS   Kessler and Jurcsak 1985 [*nomen nudum*]—(See *Paleocursornis*.)

PATRICOSAURUS   Seeley 1887 [*nomen dubium*]
Chimera of lepidosaur or lacertilian and archosaur remains.

SALTOPUS   Huene 1910 [*nomen dubium*]
?Dinosauriformes.

Note: Previously only tentatively regarded as a dinosaur (see *D:TE*), this genus was recently reassessed by Rauhut and Hungerbühler (2000). As noted by these authors, the holotype BMNH R3915) and only specimen of the type species *Saltopus elginensis* "represents a small bipedal animal with elongated hindlimbs." Other features, however (*e.g.*, shortness of ilium, low number of sacral vertebrae [most likely two, not the four argued by Huene 1910], and subequal width of lower limb bones) make the specimen's referral to the Theropoda unlikely. Although a short ilium and only two sacral vertebrae are known in *Herrerasaurus* (see Novas 1993), the sacral ribs are much more massive in *Herrerasaurus* than seemingly in *Saltopus*. Also, some characters (*e.g.*, elongated hindlimbs, bipediality, and probable cursorial habits) are also known in primitive dinosauriformes such as *Marasuchus* (Sereno and Arcucci 1994). Consequently, Rauhut and Hungerbühler regarded *Saltopus* as a probable dinosauriform.

SHENZOURAPTOR   Ji, Ji, You, Zhang, Yuan, Ji, Li and Li 2000 (=?*Jeholornis*)
Avian.

Note: Described by Ji, Ji, You, Zhang, Ji, Li and Li as an Early Cretaceous bird from the Jiufotang Formation in Yixian County, western Liaoning Province, China (an assessment accepted by various other theropod workers, *e.g.*, R. E Molnar, personal communication 2002); characterized by lack of teeth, forelimbs longer than hindlimbs, long tail comprising over 20 caudal vertebrae, I-shaped wishbone, and remiges longer than total length of ulna and manus; interpreted as capable of flight and "representing a missing link between theropod dinosaurs and birds"; however, Olshevsky, in his 2002 computer listing of dinosaurian taxa, regarded this genus as a probable nonavian theropod.

SPONDYLOSOMA   Huene 1942
?Rauisuchid rauisuchian.

Note: In *D:TE*, *Spondylosoma* was considered to

be an indeterminate dinosaurian. Recently, however, Galton (2001) pointed out that *Spondylosoma* "is clearly not a dinosaur," lacking as it does various key characters that are synapomorphic for Dinosauriformes–Dinosauria, these including "a sigmoid curve and epipophyses in the neck and a distally placed deltopectoral crest on the humerus." Synapomorphic dinosaurian characters (*e.g.*, clongate pubis, at least three sacral vertebrae, dorsal vertebrae having accessory hyposphene-hypantrua articulations) seen in this genus are also found in rauisuchians. Galton also noted that certain features of the sacrum of *Spondylosoma* indicate that this genus could belong to the family Rauisuchidae (see paper for details).

Erratum: In *D:TE*, the name of this genus was incorrectly spelled "*Spondlyosoma*."

A List of Abbreviations

The following abbreviations, which are used in this book, refer to museums and other institutions in which fossil specimens are housed:

AK — Alaska Museum, Fairbanks, Alaska, United States

AMNH — American Museum of Natural History, New York, New York, United States

AUP — Aberdeen University Palaeontology Collection, University of Aberdeen, Scotland

BPM — Beipiao Paleontological Museum, Beipiao, Liaoning Province, China

BRSMG — Bristol City Museum and Art Galleries, Bristol, England.

BUCCM — Buckinghamshire County Museum, Aylesbury, England

BYU [also BYUVP] — Brigham Young University Vertebrate Paleontology, Provo, Utah, United States

CAGS — China Academy of Geological Sciences, Beijing, People's Republic of China

CAMSM — Sedgwick Museum, Cambridge University, Cambridge, England

CEUM — College of Eastern Utah Prehistoric Museum (also known as Prehistoric Museum), Price, Utah, United States

CGM — Egyptian Geological Museum, Cairo, Egypt

CM — Carnegie Museum of Natural History, Philadelphia, Pennsylvania, United States

CMN — Canadian Museum of Nature (formerly National Museum of Canada [NMC]), Ottawa, Canada

CMNH — Cleveland Museum of Natural History, Cleveland, Ohio, United States

CUP — Catholic University of Peking, Beijing, China

CUST — Museum of Natural History, Jilin University, Changchun, China

CV — Chongqing Natural History Museum, Beipei, Congqing, People's Republic of China

DGM — Divisao de Geologia y Minerologia, Direccion Nacional of Producao Minerologia, Rio de Janeiro, Brazil

DINO — Dinosaur National Monument, Utah, United States

DMNH — Denver Museum of Nature and Science (formerly Denver Museum of Natural History), Denver, Colorado, United States

DORCM — Dorset County Museum, Dorchester, Dorset, England

FIP — Florida Institute of Paleontology, Dania Beach, Florida, United States

FMNH — The Field Museum, Chicago, Illinois, United States

FPDM — Fukui Prefectural Dinosaur Museum (Vertebrate Collection), Katsuyama, Japan

GIN — Mongolian Geological Institute (formerly Geological Institute Section of Palaeontology and Stratigraphy), Ulan-Bataar, Mongolian People's Republic

GMH — Geological Museum of Heilongjang, Heilongjiang Province, China

GMNH — Gunma Museum of Natural History, Tomioka, Gunma, Japan

GPIT — Geological Museum, Universität Tübingen, Tübingen, Germany

HMN — Museum für Naturkunde der Humboldt-Univerität zu Berlin, Berlin, Germany

HMNH — Hayashibara Museum of Natural History, Okayama, Japan

HORSM — Horsham Museum, West Sussex, England

IGM [also GI] — Mongolian Museum of Natural History (formerly Geological Institute Section of Palaeontology and Stratigraphy), The Academy of Sciences of the Mongolian People's Republic Geological Institute, Ulan Bataar

[also] — Instituto de Geologia, University of Mexico, Mexico

IMNH — Idaho Museum of Natural History, Pocatello, Idaho, United States

IMM — Inner Mongolia Museum, Hohhot, Inner Mongolia, China

IPFUB — Institut für Paläontologie, Freie Universität Berlin, SGP, Servicos Geológicos de Portugal, Portugal

IPS — Institut de Paleontologia "M. Crusafont," Sabadell, Spain

IRScNB — Royal Institute of Natural Sciences of Belgium, Brussels, Belgium

IVP [also IVPP] — Institute of Vertebrate Paleontology and Paleoanthropology, Academia Sinica, Beijing, People's Republic of China

KS — Kyeongnam Science High School Museum, Kyeongnam, Korea

LCM — Leicester City Museums, Leicester, England

LH — [Las Hoyas] Museo de las Ciencias de Castilla-La Mancha, Cuenca, Spain

LH — Long Hao Geologic Paleontological Research Center, Nei Mongol, Hohhot, China

LPM — Liaoning Paleontological Museum, Beipiao, Liaoning Province, China

LSUMG — Louisiana State University Museum of Geoscience (a division of the Louisiana State University Museum of Natural Science), Baton Rouge, Louisiana, United States

MB — Museum für Naturkunde, Berlin, Germany

MCA — Museo "Carlos Ameghino," Cipolletti, Cipolletti, Patagonia, Argentina

A List of Abbreviations

MCF   Museo Municipal Carmen Funes, Paleontología de Vertebrados, Plaza Huincul, Argentina

MCT   Museu de Ciências da Terra, Departmento Nacional da Producão Mineral, Rio de Janeiro, Brazil

MCZ   Museum of Comparative Zoology, Harvard University, Cambridge Massachusetts, United States

MGI   Mongolian Geological Institute (formerly Geological Institute Section of Palaeontology and Stratigraphy), Ulan-Bataar, Mongolian People's Republic

MIWG   Museum of Isle of Wight Geology, Sandown, Isle of Wight, England

ML   Museum of Lourinhã, Lourinhã, Portugal

MLP   Museo de La Plata, La Plata, Argentina

MN   Museu Nacional, Universidade Federal do Rio de Janeiro, Brazil

MNA   Museum of Northern Arizona, Flagstaff, Arizona, United States

MNHN   Muséum National d'Histoire Naturelle, Paris, France

MOR   Museum of the Rockies, Bozeman, Montana, United States

MPCA   Museo de Ciencias Naturales, Universidad Nacional del Comahue, Buenos Aires, Neuquén, Argentina (see also MUCP)

MPD   Mongolian Paleontological Center, Ulaanbataar, Mongolia

MPEF   Museo Paleontologico Egidio Feruglio, Chubut Province, Argentina

MPM   Milwaukee Public Museum, Milwaukee, Wisconsin, United States

MPZ   Museo Paleontológico, Universidad de Zaragoza, Spain

MSM   Mesa Southwest Museum, Mesa, Arizona, United States

MTCO   Muzeul Tarii Crisurilor, Oradea, Romania

MUCP   Museo de Ciencias, Naturales de la Universidad Nacional del Comahue, Neuquén, Argentina

NCSM   North Carolina State Museum of Natural Sciences, North Carolina State University, Raleigh, North Carolina, United States

NGMC   National Geological Museum of China, Xisi, Beijing, People's Republic of China

NHMM   Natuurhistorisch Museum Maastricht, The Netherlands

NIGP   Nanjing Institute of Geology and Palaeontology, Nanjing, China

NM   National Museum, Bloemfontein, South Africa

NMB   Naturhistorisches Museum, Basel, Switzerland

NMC   see CMN

OTM   Old Trails Museum, Choteau, Montana, United States

OUM   Oxford University Museum, Oxford, England

PAL   Institute of Paleobiology, Warsaw, Poland

PC   Paleontological Center of the Mongolian Academy of Sciences, Ulaan Bator, Mongolia

PCM   Philips County Museum, Malta, Montana, United States

PIN   Paleontological Institute Nauk, Academy of Science, Moscow, Russia

PIU   Paläontoligisches Institut der Universität Vienna, Vienna, Austria

PKNU   Pukyong National University, Department of Environmental Geoscience, Pusan, Korea

PM TGU   Paleontological Museum, Tomsk State University, Tomsk, Russia

PMU   Paleontological Institute, Uppsala University, Sweden

POL   Musée de Poligny [specimens now housed in the Musée Archaeologique de Lons-le-Saunier, Jura, France]

PS   Museo de Salas de los Infantes, Burgos, Spain

PVPH   Paleontologia de Vertebrados, Museo "Carmen Funes" de Plaza Huincul, Neduquén, Argentina

PVL   Paleontología de Vertebrados, Instituto Lillo, Tucamán, Argentina

QM   Queensland Museum, Queensland

RTMP [also TMP]   Royal Tyrrell Museum of Palaeontology, Drumheller, Alberta, Canada

SBEI   Museum of the Shiramine Board of Education, Shiramine, Japan

SDNHM   San Diego Natural History Museum, San Diego, California, United States

SDSM   Museum of Geology, South Dakota School of Mines and Technology, Rapid City, South Dakota, United States

SGM   Ministère de l'Energie et des Mines, Rabat, Morocco

SGU   Research Institute of Geology, Saratov State University, Saratov, Russia

SIY   Geological Survey of India, Bandlaguda, Hyderabad, India

SM   Staffin Museum, Ellishadder, Isle of Skye, Scotland

SMC   The Sedgwick Museum, University of Cambridge, England

SMNH   Royal Saskatchewan Museum, Saskatchewan, Canada

SMNS   Staatliches Museum für Naturkunde, Stuttgart, Germany

SMP   State Museum of Pennsylvania, Harrisburg, Pennsylvania, United States

SQU   Sultan Qaboos University, Department of Earth Sciences, College of Science, Al-Khod, Sultanate of Oman

SUNY   State University of New York, Stony Brook, New York, United States

T   Chongqing Natural History Museum, Congqing, China

TMM   Texas Memorial Museum, The University of Texas, Austin, Texas, United States

TNP   Tianjin Museum of Natural History, Tianjin, China

TPII   Thanksgiving Point Institute, Inc., Lehi, Utah, United States

TTU   Texas Tech University, Lubbock, Texas, United States

UA   University of Alberta, Edmonton, Canada

UA   Université d'Antananarivo, Antananrivo, Madagascar

UAM   University of Alaska Museum, University of Alaska, Fairbanks, Alaska, United States

UC   University of Chicago, Chicago, Illinois, United States

UCB   Université Claude Bernard, Lyon, France

UCL   University College, London, England

UCMP   University of California Museum of Paleontology, Berkeley, California, United States

UE   Universität Erlangen, Institut für Geologie und Mineralogie, Erlangen, Germany

UGM   Urumqi Geological Museum, Urumqi, Xinjiong, People's Republic of China

UMNH   Utah Museum of Natural History, University of Utah, Salt Lake City, Utah, United States

UNM   University of New Mexico, Albuquerque, United States (collection now at NMMNH)

UNPSJB   Universidad Nacional de la Patagonia, "San Juan Bosco," Argentina

USNM   National Museum of Natural History (formerly United States National Museum), Smithsonian Institution, Washington, D.C., United States

UUVP   University of Utah, Vertebrate Paleontology Collection, Salt Lake City, Utah, United States

UW   Geological Museum, University of Wyoming, Laramie, Wyoming, United States; also, Univerität Tübingen, Institut und Museum für Geologie, Tübingen, Germany

VMNH   Virginia Museum of Natural History, Martinsville, Virginia, United States

ZDM [also ZG]   Zigong Dinosaur Museum, Zigong, China

ZIN   Zoological Institute, Russian Academy of Sciences, Saint Petersburg, Russia

ZNM   Natural History Museum of Zhejiang (also Zhejiang Natural Museum), Zhejiang, China

ZPAL   Instytut Paleobiologii (also known as Institute of Paleobiology), Polish Academy of Sciences, Warsaw, Poland

Appendix:
Dinosaur Tracks and Eggs

Fossils that do not represent the actual remains (*e.g.*, bones) of an organism, but rather reflect the presence or activity of an organism, are referred to as "trace fossils." The study of such fossils is called paleoichnology. Trace fossils (also known as ichnofossils or ichnites) include footprints, trails, bite marks, dung (coprolites), or structures in sediments such as tubes, burrows, gnawings, borings and allied features. In addition to giving indications of the existence and diversity of extinct life forms, trace fossils also offer valuable information regarding paleoenvironments, sedimentation, and the ecology and behavior of their makers.

Dinosaur Tracks

In an overview of the study of fossil vertebrate footprints, ichnite specialist William A. S. Serjeant (1986) suspected that such traces must have been noticed intermittently throughout history and could very well, along with the discovery of fossil bones, have fueled the belief in dragons and other fantastic monsters. However, the first scientific study of dinosaur tracks was made by Reverend Edward Hitchcock (1836), a Congregational minister turned geologist and teacher at Amherst College, Massachusetts. Hitchcock described numerous tracks from the Late Triassic to Early Jurassic of the Connecticut Valley. As these

Theropod tracks from the Sousa Formation (Lower Cretaceous) on the Piau farm, Municipality of Sousa, Rio do Peixe Basin, State of Paraiba, Brazil.

Photograph courtesy Giuseppe Leonardi.

Photograph by Giuseppe Leonardi.

Various ornithopod and theropod fossil tracks enhanced with charcoal and accompanied by fiberglass replicas of the kind of dinosaurs that probably made them, preserved at the Estreito farm, in the Lower Cretaceous Antenor Navarro Formation, Group Rio do Peixe, in the "Vale dos dinossauros" natural park, Municipality of Sousa, Paraiba, Brazil.

tracks constituted the impressions of three-toed feet, that author interpreted the majority of them to have been made by ancient birds. Hence, Hitchcock coined the term "ornithichnites" for these footprints and "ornithichnology" for the study of them.

Much can be learned from the study of dinosaur footprints and trackways, including the approximate size and weight of the trackmakers. They are also valuable in providing other kinds of data; for example, as shown by Alexander (1976), the relative speeds of dinosaurs can be calculated by means of a simple formula involving the size and spacing of individual prints within a trackway.

Fossil tracks are also useful in sedimentology. Hitchcock, as well as a number of more recent authors (e.g., Ostrom 1972), observed that dinosaur tracks are usually found along the edges of bodies of water near the strand line. Dinosaur footprint specialist Martin G. Lockley (1986) noted that such prints can be used to reconstruct the precise location of a marine or lacustrine shoreline by measuring the depth of tracks and direction of travel. Individual footprints within one trackway sometimes vary in depth. This variability is related to the water content of the sediment, with shallow prints apparently indicating dry land and deep prints apparently showing where the animal was wading through shallow water. As Lockley pointed out, dinosaur tracks have also been utilized to impart such sedimentological information as the depth of the water bodies in which tracks were made, estimating the power and direction of ancient water currents, and determining the amount of slope of the land when the tracks were imprinted.

Until relatively recently, dinosaur tracks did not constitute a major area of study among vertebrate paleontologists, but, as Lockley (1987b) pointed out, was "often regarded as a fringe subdiscipline outside the scientific mainstream." As that author further noted, a new "renaissance" in dinosaurian ichnology commenced with the First International Symposium on Dinosaur Tracks and Traces held in Albuquerque, New Mexico, from May 22 to 24, 1986, organized by paleontologist David D. Gillette in association with the New Mexico Museum of Natural History.

Caution must be exercised when dealing with fossil footprints. Unlike the bones by which most (dead) dinosaurs are known, tracks constitute a record of a *living* animal's activity. As such, ichnites must be considered supplementary evidence pertaining to an extinct animal. Although many generic and specific names (see below) have been assigned to various fossil tracks for more than a century, they do *not name dinosaurs*; nor, in the vast majority of cases, can these traces be linked with absolute or near certainty to any particular dinosaurian genus known from body fossil remains.

It must be further emphasized that tracks can be deceptive. Some fossil footprints lend themselves to misin-

terpretation due to problems and quirks of preservation. Some tracks may exhibit seeming morphological differences because of variables such as the speed at which the trackmaker was walking or the consistency of the material in which the tracks were laid down. As Sarjeant stated at the first Dinosaur Systematics Symposium held in 1986 at the Royal Tyrrell Museum of Palaeontology, in many instances it is not the footprints themselves that have been preserved, but rather a sometimes distorted reflection of them in higher or lower sediments than those in which the trackmaker walked. Furthermore, many tracks, particularly those made by theropods, are morphologically indistinguishable from one another, despite their source or age (J. O. Farlow, personal communication 2001).

Not all dinosaur tracks have been assigned generic or specific names. Only those that have and which have been published in the paleontological literature are herein addressed. However, unlike taxa based upon skeletal fossils, various ichnologists have brought conflicting philosophies to the recognition and naming of trace fossils. Some ichnologists (e.g., Donald Baird) have only recognized taxa for which a skeletal reconstruction of the foot can be made. Others workers (e.g., Sarjeant) have emphasized that footprints are sedimentary structures having no systematic meaning than other "form taxa." Regarding the later outlook, Sarjeant considered it proper to apply different names to different traces made by the same organism under different circumstances, as is often done with invertebrate traces. In other words, the impression of the same animal could have a different name if that creature were walking or sitting.

Following is a list of dinosaurian ichnogenera founded upon dinosaur tracks and trackways. Unless otherwise stated, these tracks pertain to the hind feet. For more detailed information, including diagnoses, more inclusive locality and stratigraphy data, datings of formations and sites, specimen numbers, referrals to families (e.g., Grallatoridae), explanations of subgeneric designations, listings of specimens referred to unspecified species, synonymies, histories of discoveries, commentaries and opinions of authors based upon their original research, ichnotaxa once described as dinosaurian but now regarded as nondinosaurian, and so forth, the author suggests that the reader consult the original literature (as listed in such sources as *A Bibliography of the Dinosauria (Exclusive of the Aves) 1677–1986* [Chure and McIntosh 1989]), Lockley (2000), and also such comprehensive studies as those appearing in the following more recent books: *Dinosaur Tracks and Traces* (Gillette and Lockley 1989), *Dinosaur Tracks* (Thulborn 1990), *Dinosaur Tracks and Other Fossil Footprints of the Western United States* (Lockley and Hunt 1995), and *Dinosaur Tracks and Other Fossil Footprints of Europe* (Lockley and Meyer 2000).

Note: See *D:TE, S1,* and *S2* for additional photographs and information on dinosaur tracks and eggs.

Appendix

AETHYOPUS   Hitchcock 1848 — (See *Sauropus*.)
Name derivation: Greek *aethes* = "unaccustomed" + Greek *pous* = "foot."
Type species: *A. lyellianus* (Hitchcock 1843).

AETONYCHOPUS   Ellenberger 1974
Name derivation: Latin *Aetatis* = "old" + Greek *onyx* = "claw" + Greek *pous* = "foot."
Type species: *A. rapidus* Ellenberger 1974.
Other species: *A. digitigradus* Ellenberger 1974.
Occurrence: Upper Elliot Formation, Mokanametsong, South Africa.
Age: Early Jurassic (Hettangian–Pliensbachian).
　　Tridactyl, theropod or prosauropod.

AGIALOPUS   Branson and Mehl 1932 — (=?*Grallator*)
Name derivation: Latin *agilis* = "nimble" + Greek *pous* = "foot."
Type species: *A. wyomingensis* Branson and Mehl 1932.
Occurrence: Popo Agie/Chinle Formation, Vernal area and Cliff Creek, Utah, Chugwater Formation, Wyoming, Moffat County, Colorado, United States.
Age: Late Triassic (?Carnian).
　　Small, tridactyl, ?theropod, track similar to *Grallator*.

AGRESTIPUS   Smith 1982
Name derivation: Latin *agrestis* = "clumsy" + Greek *pous* = "foot."
Type species: *A. hottoni* Smith 1982.
Occurrence: Bull Run Formation, Virginia, United States.
Age: Late Triassic (?Norian).
　　Bipedal, pes tetradactyl, possibly resembling a small sauropod.

AMBLONYX   Hitchcock 1858 — (See *Sauropus*.)
Name derivation: Greek *amblys* = "dull" + Greek *onyx* = "claw."
Type species: *A. giganteus* (Hitchcock 1843).

AMBLYDACTYLUS   Sternberg 1932
Name derivation: Greek *amblys* = "dull" + Greek *daktylos* = "finger."
Type species: *A. gethingi* Sternberg 1932.
Other species: *A. kortmeyer* Currie and Sarjeant 1979.
Occurrence: Gething member of Bullhead Mountain Formation, British Columbia, ?Tantalus Formation, Yukon Territory, Canada.
Age: Early Cretaceous (Aptian).
　　Pes tridactyl, some manus prints preserved; apparently made by a large ornithopod such as *Iguanodon*.

ANATOPUS   Lapparent and Montenant 1967
Name derivation: Latin *anatos* = "duck" + Greek *pous* = "foot."
Type species: *A. palmatus* Lapparent and Montenant 1967.
Occurrence: Infralias, Le Veillon region, France.
Age: Early Jurassic.
　　Bipedal, tridactyl, similar to *Grallator* (Lockley and Meyer 2002).

ANATRISAUROPUS   Ellenberger 1970
Name derivation: Latin *anatos* = "duck" + Greek *tri* = "three" + Greek *sauros* = "lizard" + Greek *pous* = "foot."
Type species: *A. ginsburgi* Ellenberger 1970 (type).
Other species: *A. hereroensis* Ellenberger 1970.
Occurrence: Lower Stormberg Series, Lesotho, South Africa; Keuper d'Anduze, France.
Age: Late Triassic (Carnian or Norian).
　　Bipedal, tridactyl, ?theropod or indeterminate.

ANCHISAURIPUS   Lull 1904 — (See *Grallator*.)
Name derivation: *Anchisaurus* + Greek *pous* = "foot."
Type species: *A. sillimani* (Hitchcock 1843).

ANOMOEPUS   Hitchcock 1848 — (=*Apatichnus*, *Deanea*, *Hitchcockia*, *Kainomoyenisauropus*, *Masitisauropezus*, *Moyenisauropus*; =*Brontozoum*, in part; =?*Plesiornis*, ?*Tarsodactylus*)
Name derivation: Greek *anomoios* = "different" + Greek *pous* = "foot."
Type species: *A. scambus* Hitchcock 1848.
Occurrence: Newark Supergroup, Massachusetts, lower Passaic Formation, New Jersey, Connecticut, Massachusetts, Pennsylvania, Glen Canyon, Arizona, United States; Europe; Upper Elliot Formation, Quthing, Lesotho.
Age: Late Triassic–Early Jurassic (Norian; Hettangian–Pliensbachian).
　　Bipedal, small, pes functionally tridactyl, sometimes showing forefeet and rump or belly impressions, small ornithischian similar to *Fabrosaurus*.

ANTICHEIROPUS   Hitchcock 1865
Name derivation: Greek *anti* = "against" + Greek *cheir* = "hand" + Greek *pous* = "foot."
Type species: *A. hamatus* Hitchcock 1865 (type)
Other species: *A. pilulatus* Hitchcock 1865.
Occurrence: Newark Supergroup, Massachusetts, United States; Etjo Sandstein (?Stormberg Series), Africa.
Age: Early Jurassic.
　　Bipedal, tridactyl, giant ?saurischian dinosaur.

APATICHNUS Hitchcock 1858 — (See *Anomoepus*; =?*Kayentapus*.)
Name derivation: Greek *apatelos* = "deceptive" + Greek *ichnos* = "track."
Type species: *A. circumagens* Hitchcock 1858 (type).

ARGOIDES Hitchcock 1845 — (=*Argozoum*; =*Plesiornis*, in part)
Name derivation: Greek *argos* = "idle" + Greek *oides* = "shape."
Type species: *A. minimus* (Hitchcock 1845).
Other species: *A. isodactyletus* Hitchcock 1845, *A. macrodactylus* (Hitchcock 1845) (type), *A. redfieldii* (Hitchcock 1845), *A. robustus* (Hitchcock 1845).
Occurrence: Portland Arkose, Massachusetts, Connecticut, United States; Aganane Formation, Morocco.
Age: Early Jurassic (Hettangian–Pliensbachian).
  Small, bipedal, tridactyl, ?theropod.

ARGOZOUM Hitchcock 1848 — (See *Argoides*.)
Name derivation: Greek *argos* = "idle" + Greek *zoon* = "animal."
Type species: *A. paridigitum* Hitchcock 1848.

ARTIODACTYLUS Abel 1926
Name derivation: "Artiodactyl [one of a group of even-toed ungulate mammals]."
Type species: *A. sinclairi* Abel 1926.
Occurrence: Passaic Formation, Princeton, New Jersey, United States.
Age: Late Triassic.
  Tetradactyl, toes small, ornithischian.

ATREIPUS Olsen and Baird 1986 — (See *Grallator*.)
Name derivation: "Atreus [Wanner, who uncovered numerous fossil tracks including *Atreipus*]" + Greek *pous* = "foot."
Type species: *A. milfordensis* Olsen and Baird 1986.

BANISTEROBATES Fraser and Olsen 1996
Type species: *B. boisseaui* Fraser and Olsen 1996.
Occurrence: Culpeper Stone Quarry, Pittsylvania County, Virginia, United States.
Age: Late Triassic.
  Small, ?Ornithischian.

BELLONA Reichenbach 1852 — (See *Grallator*.)
Name derivation: "Bellona [Roman goddess of war]."
Type species: *B. giganteus* (Hitchcock 1841).

BERNINASAUROPUS Ellenberger 1970
Name derivation: "[P.] Bernier [ichnologist]" + Greek *sauros* = "lizard" + Greek *pous* = "foot."
Type species: *B. sanariensis* Ellenberger 1970.
Occurrence: Upper Triassic of France.
Age: Late Triassic.
  Theropod.

BOSIUTRISAUROPUS Ellenberger 1970
Name derivation: "[Thaba-]Bosiu [mountain and historical site in Lesotho]" + Greek *tri* = "three" + Greek *sauros* = "lizard" + Greek *pous* = "foot."
Type species: *B. phuthiatsani* (varieties *major*, *minor*) Ellenberger 1970.
Occurrence: Lower Elliot Formation, Molteno, Lesotho.
Age: Late Triassic (Carnian or Norian).
  Bipedal, tridactyl, ?theropod or inderminate.

BREVIPAROPUS Dutuit and Quazzou 1980
Name derivation: Latin *brevi* = "short" + Latin *para* = "part" + Greek *pous* = "foot."
Type species: *B. taghbaloutensis* Dutuit and Quazzou 1980.
Occurrence: Haute-Atlas, Demnat, Taghbalout, Morocco.
Age: Early Cretaceous.
  Manus and pes impressions, giant, apparently massive sauropod.

BRONTOPODUS Farlow, Pittman and Hawthorne 1989 — (=*Chuxiongpus*)
Name derivation: Greek *bronte* = "thunder" + Greek *pous* = "foot."
Type species: *B. birdi* Farlow, Pittman and Hawthorne 1989.
Other species: *B. changlingensis* (Yang and Yang 1987).
Occurrence: Dinosaur Valley State Park (lower Glen Rose limestone), other localities, Texas; also Arkansas, United States; Upper Jurassic of Blaziny, Poland; ?Hekou Formation, Gansu, Upper Cretaceous Series, Changling, Chuxiong Prefecture, Jiang Di He Formation, near Kunming, Yunnan Province, Jing Chuan Formation, near Otog Qi, Inner Mongolia, China.
Age: Early to Middle Cretaceous (Barremian–Coniacian).
  Quadrupedal, slightly wide gauge, sauropod trackway, manus large, possibly made by *Pleurocoelus* (see *D:TE*); reveals apparent gregarious behavior.

BRONTOZOUM Hitchcock 1847 — (See *Anomoepus*, *Eubrontes*, *Grallator*.)
Name derivation: Greek *bronte* = "thunder" + Greek *zoon* = "animal."
Type species: *B. giganteum* Hitchcock 1847.

Fossil tracks named *Brontopodus birdi* preserved *in situ* at Dinosaur State Park, Glen Rose, Texas.

BÜCKEBURGICHNUS   Kuhn 1958 — (=? *Tyrannosauripus*)

Name derivation: Bückeburg [locality] + Greek *ichnos* = "track."

Type species: *B. maximus* Kuhn 1958.

Occurrence: Harrlebei Bückeburg, Germany.

Age: Late Cretaceous.

Bipedal, functionally tridactyl, large theropod.

CALOPUS   Hitchcock 1845 — (See *Platypterna*.)

Name derivations: Latin *Calor* = "heat" + Greek *pous* = "foot."

Type species: *C. delicatulus* Hitchcock 1845.

CAMPTOSAURICHNUS   Casamiquela and Fasola 1968

Name derivation: *Camptosaurus* + Greek *ichnos* = "track."

Type species: *C. fasolae* Casamiquela and Fasola 1968.

Occurrence: ?Basal part of Banos del Flaco Formation, Colchagua, Chile.

Age: Late Jurassic.

Both manus and pes impressions of a medium-sized "noniguanodontid," iguanodontoid ornithopod, both bipedal and quadrupedal locomotion.

CARIRICHNIUM   Leonardi 1984

Name derivation: "Cariri [region near Riodo Peixe]" + Greek *ichnos* = "track."

Type species: *C. magnificum* Leonardi 1984.

Other species: *C. leonardi* Lockley 1987.

Occurrence: Antenor Navarro Formation, Paraiba, Brazil; Dakota Group, Colorado, Anapra Sandstone, New Mexico, North America.

Age: Early Cretaceous.

Quadrupedal, small front feet and large hind feet, ?iguanodontoid.

CARMELOPODUS   Lockley, Hunt, Paquette, Bilbey and Hamblin 1998

Name derivation: "Carmel [Formation]" + Greek *pous* = "foot."

Type species: *C. untermannorum* Lockley, Hunt, Paquette, Bilbey and Hamblin 1998.

Occurrence: Carmel Formation, northeastern Utah, United States.

Age: Middle Jurassic (Bajocian–Bathonian).

Medium-sized theropod having an atypical sub-symmetrical foot, phalanx IV-1 elevated above the substrate.

CERATOPSIPES   Lockley and Hunt 1995

Name derivation: Greek *ceratops* = "horned face or head (alluding to ceratopsian dinosaurs)" + Latin *pes* = "foot."

Type species: *C. goldenensis* Lockley and Hunt 1995.

Occurrence: Laramie Formation, Colorado, United States.

Age: Late Cretaceous (Maastrichtian).

Large ceratopsian, similar to *Tetrapodosaurus*, trackmaker possibly *Triceratops*.

CHANGPEIPUS   Yang [Young] 1960

Name derivation: "Changpei [city in China, named for linquist Professor Luo Changpei]" + Greek *pous* = "foot."

Type species: *C. carbonicus* Yang [Young] 1960.

Other species: *C. bartholomaii* Haubold 1971, *C. luanpingeris* Yang [Young] 1979.

Occurrence: Lower Fusin Coal Measures, Fusin, Liaoning, Sunshangang Coal Mine, Jilin [Kirin] Province, Shaanxi Province, China; Walloon Group, Westvale Collery, Queensland.

Age: Early or Middle to Late Jurassic.

Manus and pes, pes tridactyl, ?large quadrupedal theropod.

CHIMAERA   Hitchcock 1858 — (Preoccupied; see *Sauropus*.)

Name derivation: Latin *chimaera* = "chimera [monster comprising parts of various animals]."

Type species: *C. barrattii* Hitchcock 1858.

CHIMAERICHNUS   Hitchcock 1871 — (See *Sauropus*.)

Name derivation: Latin *chimaera* = "chimera [monster comprising parts of various animals]."

Type species: *C. barrattii* (Hitchcock 1858).

CHONGLONGPUS   Yang and Yang 1987 — (=? *Eubrontes*, ?*Grallator*)

Name derivation: "[Wu] Chonglong [Chinese geologist]" + Greek *pous* = "foot."

Type species: *C. hei* Yang and Yang 1987.

Occurrence: Wu Ma Cun, Xin Tian Gou Formation, Sichuan, China.

Age: ?Early to ?Middle Jurassic.

Large, bipedal, tetradactyl, theropod, reveals crouching behavior.

CHONGQINGPUS   Yang and Yang 1987 — (= *Grallator*).

Name derivation: "Chongqin [Province]" + Greek *pous* = "foot."

Type species: *C. microiscus* Yang and Yang 1987.

Photograph by Giuseppe Leonardi.

Caririchnium magnificum (ornithopod) holotype trackway, attributed to a quadrupedal iguanodontoid, from the Lower Cretaceous Antenor Navarro Formation, Group Rio do Peixe, Esteito farm, Serrote do Pimenta, preserved in the "Vale dos dinosauros" natural park, Municipality of Sousa, Paraiba, Brazil.

CHUANNCHENGPUS   Yang and Yang 1987 — (See *Grallator*.)
Name derivation: ? + Greek *pous* = "foot."
Type species: *C. wuhuangensis* Yang and Yang 1987.

CHUXIONGPUS   Chen and Huang 1993 — (See *Brontopodus*)
Name derivation: "Chuxiong [Prefecture]" + Greek *pous* = "foot."
Type species: *C. changlingensis* Chen and Huang 1993.

COELUROSAURICHNUS   Huene 1941
Name derivation: "Coelurosaur" + Greek *ichnos* = "track."
Type species: *C. toscanus* Huene 1941.
Other species: *C. grancieri* Courel and Demathieu, *C. kehli* Beurlen 1950, *C. kronbergeri* Rehnelt 1959, *C. largentierensis* Gand 1986, *C. metzneri* Heller 1952, *C. moeni* Beurlen 1950, *C. palissyi* Gand 1976, *C. perriaux* Gand 1986, *C. sabiniensis* Gand 1976, *C. sassendorfensis* Kuhn 1958, *C. schlauersbachensis* Heller 1952, *C. schlehenbergensis* Kuhn 1958, *C. thomasi* Kuhn 1963, *C. ziegelangerensis* Kuhn 1958.
Occurrence: Upper Triassic of Verrucao, Toscana, Italy; Upper Triassic of Payzac, Ardèche, Massif Central, France; Middle Keuper, Semionotensandstein, Ansbacher Sandstein, Benkersandstein and Rätolias, Franken, ?Muschelkalk Formation (upper Middle Triassic), Germany, Dockum Formation, New Mexico, Texas, also Pennsylvania, New Jersey, United States.
Age: ?Middle Triassic to Early Jurassic.
    Bipedal, small to medium-sized theropod.

COLUMBOSAURIPUS   Sternberg 1932 — (=?*Gypsichnites*)
Name derivation: "[British] Columbia" + Greek *sauros* = "lizard" + Greek *pous* = "foot."
Type species: *C. ungulatus* Sternberg 1932.
Other species: ?*C. amouraenensis* Haubold 1971.
Occurrence: Gething member of Bullhead Mountain Formation, British Columbia, Canada; ?Middle Cretaceous (Cenomanian) of Djebel Bou Khahil, Algeria.
Age: Early Cretaceous, ?Middle Cretaceous (Cenomanian).
    Small, bipedal, functionally tridactyl, theropod, ?ornithomimid.

CORVIPES   Hitchcock 1858
Name derivation: Latin *corvinus* = "raven" + Latin *pes* = "foot."
Type species: *C. lacertoideus* Hitchcock 1858.
Occurrence: Early Jurassic (Hettangian–Pliensbachian).

Age: Newark Supergroup, Massachusetts, Connecticut, United States.
    Quadrupedal, tridactyl, indeterminate.

DAKOTASAURUS   Branson and Mehl 1932
Name derivation: "Dakota [Formation]" + Greek *sauros* = "lizard."
Type species: *D. browni* Branson and Mehl 1932.
Occurrence: Dakota Formation, Wyoming, United States.
Age: Late Cretaceous (Maastrichtian).
    ?Manus and pes impressions, small, hindfoot tridactyl, ?ornithischian or nondinosaurian.

DEANA   Reichenbach 1852 — (See *Anomoepus*.)
Name derivation: "[J.] Deane [early ichnologist]."
Type species: *D. fulicoides* (Hitchcock 1843).

DELATORRHINCHUS   Casamiquela 1964
Name derivation: "Delator [ancient Roman prosecutor]" + Greek *rhinos* = "nose" + Greek *ichnos* = "track."
Type species: *D. goyenechei* Casamiquela 1964.
Occurrence: Middle "Complejo Porfirico," Santa Cruz, Argentina.
Age: Middle to Late Jurassic (Callovian–Oxfordian).
    Small, quadrupedal, pes functionally tridactyl, apparently a small theropod.

DELTAPODUS   Whyte and Romano 1994
Name derivation: Greek *delta* = "delta" + Greek *pous* = "foot."
Type species: *D. brodericki* Whyte and Romano 1994.
Occurrence: Saltwick Formation, Yorkshire, England, Europe.
Age: Middle Jurassic.
    Pes prints symmetrical, probably thyreophoran (stegosaurian or, more likely, ankylosaurian).

DEUTEROTRISAUROPUS   Ellenberger 1970 — (See *Grallator*.)
Name derivation: Greek *deuteros* = "second" + Greek *tri* = "three" + Greek *sauros* = "lizard" + Greek *pous* = "foot."
Type species: *D. socialis* Ellenberger 1970.

DILOPHOSAURIPUS   Welles 1971 — (=?*Grallator*)
Name derivation: *Dilophosaurus* + Greek *pous* = "foot."
Type species: *D. williamsi* Welles 1971.
Occurrence: Kayenta Formation (Glen Canyon Group), Arizona, United States.
Age: Early Jurassic.

Life-sized model of the Early Jurassic neoceratosaurian *Dilophosaurus wetherilli* made by Richard Rush Studios based upon a scale model sculpted by Gregory S. Paul. Footprints named *Diliphosauripus* were probably made by dinosaurs such as this.

Tridactyl, possibly a medium-sized theropod such as *Dilophosaurus* (skeletons of which have been found in the Kayenta flats approximately 45 feet above the level of the tracks).

DINEHICHNUS Lockley, Santos, Meyer and Hunt 1998

Name derivation: Greek *deinos* = "fearfully great" + Greek *ichnos* = "track."

Type species: *D. socialis* Lockley, Santos, Meyer and Hunt 1998.

Occurrence: Connecticut Valley, United States; Europe.

Age: Late Triassic to Early Jurassic.

Ornithopod, possibly referrable to *Dryosaurus* or *Hypsilophodon*.

DINOSAURICHNIUM Rehnelt 1950—(See *Parachirotherium*.)

Name derivation: "Dinosaur" + Greek *ichnos* = "track."

Type species: *D. postchirotheroides* Renhelt 1950.

Note: *Dinosauripus* Rehnelt 1950, for which no species name has been published, may be an error for *Dinosaurichnium*.

DINOSAUROPODES Strevell 1932 [*nomen nudum*]

Name derivation: "Dinosaur" + Greek *pous* = "foot."

Species: *D. bransfordii* Strevell 1932 [*nomen nudum*], *D. crawfordii* Strevell 1932 [*omen nudum*], *D. lamphii* Strevell 1932 [*nomen nudum*], *D. magrawi* Strevell 1932 [*nomen nudum*], *D. nettletoni* Strevell 1932 [*nomen nudum*], *D. osborni* Strevell 1932 [*nomen nudum*], *D. pulveri* Strevell 1932 [*nomen nudum*], *D. sweeti* Strevell 1932 [*nomen nudum*], *D. wilsoni* Strevell 1932 [*nomen nudum*] (no type species designated).

Occurrence: Mesaverde Group, Utah, also Colorado, Wyoming, United States.

Age: Late Cretaceous.

Tridactyl and tetradactyl tracks made by giant theropods, ornithopods, and ceratopsians.

Note: Coined by Earl Douglass, the term *Dinosauropodes* has no scientific validity, representing diverse taxa, with Strevell's original descriptions not conforming to accepted systematic procedure (see Lockley and Jennings 1987).

ELEPHANTOPOIDES Kaever and Lapparent 1974
Name derivation: Greek *elephas* = "elephant" + Greek *pous* = "foot" + Greek *oeides* = "like."
Type species: *E. barkhausensis* Kaever and Lapparent 1974.
Occurrence: Malm, Lower Saxony, Germany.
Age: Late Jurassic (early Kimmeridgian).
    Quadrupedal, sauropod.

EUBRONTES Hitchcock 1845 — (=*Brontozoun* [in part], *Jinlijingpus, Tuojianpus*; = ?*Chonglongpus*, ?*Grallator*, ?*Weiyaunpus*)
Name derivation: Greek *eu* = "good" + Greek *brontos* = "thunder."
Type species: *E. giganteus* Hitchcock 1845.
Other species: *E. approximatus* (Hay 1902), *E. bessieri* Ellenberger 1972, *E. divaricatus* (Lull 1904), *E. euskelosauroides* (Haubold 1971), *E. expansum* (Hitchcock 1845), *E. giganteus* (Hitchcock 1845), *E. gracillimus* (Hitchcock 1845), *E. platypus* (Lull 1904), *E. thianschianicum* (Efremov and Vjushkov 1955), *E. thomasi* (Haubold 1971), *E. titanopelobatidus* (Shuler 1917) [*nomen dubium*], *E. tuberatus* (Lull 1904), *E. tuberosus* (Lull 1904), *E. veillonensis* (Lapparent and Montenant 1967); cf. *Eubrontes* sp. (Yang and Yang 1987).
Occurrence: Newark Supergroup, Brunswick Formation, Massachusetts, Newark Supergroup, Virginia, Dinosaur State Park, Connecticut, United States; France; ?Lufeng Formation, Yunnan Province, Xin Tian Gou Formation, Sichuan Province, China.
Age: Late Triassic (Carnian or Norian) to Early Jurassic.
    Tridactyl, bipedal, relatively large and ?robust theropods.

EUTYNICHNIUM Nopcsa 1923
Name derivation: Greek *euthyno* = "go straight" + Greek *ichnos* = "track."
Type species: *E. lusitanicum* Nopcsa 1923.
Other species: *E. pombali* Haubold 1971.
Occurrence: Upper Jurassic ("Lusitanian") of Cabo (or Cap) Mondego, Portugal.
Age: Late Jurassic (Oxfordian).
    Medium-sized, tetradactyl, functionally tridactyl theropod, with small and slender antero-medially directed hallux, smaller than *Megalosauripus*.

EXALLOPUS Harris, Johnson, Hicks and Tauxe 1996 — (See *Saurexallopus*.)
Name derivation: Latin *ex* = "without" Greek *allos* = "other" + Greek *pous* = "foot."
Type species: *E. lovei* Harris, Johnson, Hicks & Tauxe 1996.

FULICOPUS Hitchcock 1845 — (See *Sauropus*.)
Name derivation: *Fulica* [generic name for the American coot] + Greek *pous* = "foot."
Type species: *F. lycellianus* (Hitchcock 1843).

GIGANDIPUS Hitchcock 1855 — (=*Gigantotherium*)
Name derivation: Latin *gigas* = "giant" + Latin *pes* = "foot."
Type species: *G. caudatus* Hitchcock 1855.
Occurrence: Newark Supergroup, Massachusetts, East Berlin Formation, Portland Arkose, Connecticut, Massachusetts, United States.
Age: Early Jurassic (Hettangian–Pliensbachian).
    Large, bipedal, functionally tridactyl, theropod.

GIGANTOSAUROPUS Mensink and Mertmann 1984
Name derivation: Latin *gigas* = "giant" + Greek *sauros* = "lizard" + Greek *pous* = "foot."
Type species: *G. asturiensis* Mensink and Mertmann 1984.
Occurrence: "Terenes Marl," Asturias, Provincia de La Rioja, Spain.
Age: Late Jurassic (Kimmeridgian).
    Giant, sauropod.

GIGANTOTHERIUM Hitchcock 1858 — (See *Gigandipus*.)
Name derivation: Latin *gigas* = "giant" + Greek *therion* = "beast."
Type species: *G. caudatum* Hitchcock 1858.

GOSEONGOSAURIPUS Kim 1986
Name derivation: "Goseong-gun [area in South Gyeongsang Province, Korea]" + Greek *sauros* = "lizard" + Greek *pous* = "foot."
Type species: *G. kimi* Kim 1986.
Occurrence: Hayang Group, Nagdon Series, Kyungsang System, Goseong-gun, Republic of Korea.
Age: Early to Middle Cretaceous (Aptian–Albian).
    Bipedal, iguanodont.
    Note: This may not be a valid ichnotaxon.

GRALLATOR Hitchcock 1858 — (=*Anchisauripus, Atreipus, Bellona, Brontozoum* [in part], *Chongqingpus,*

Appendix

Photograph by Giuseppe Leonardi.

Grallator tracks preserved with associated Indian ingraving in fan-sandstone on the Estrela farm, in the Lower Cretaceous Antenor Navarro Formation, Group Rio do Peixe, in the "Vale dos dinossauros" natural park, Municipality of Sousa, Paraiba, Brazil.

Chuannchengpus, Deuterotrisauropus, Kainotrisauropus, Neotrisauropus, Prototrisauropus, Qemtrisauropus; =?*Agialopus*, ?*Dilophosauripus*, ?*Eubrontes*, ?*Jeholosauripus*, ?*Stenonyx*)

Name derivation: "Grallae [group of extant birds including herons and storks, named after the Greek *grallator* = 'stilt-walker']" + [suffix] "tor" = "having a similar shape."

Type species: *G. (G.) cursorius* Hitchcock 1858.

Other species: *G. (A.) australis* (Lull 1942), *G. (G.) bibractensis* (Demathieu 1961), *G. (G.) cuneateus* Hitchcock 1858, *G. (G.) damanei* Ellenberger 1970, *G. (A.) dananus* (Hitchcock 1845), *G. (G.) dananus* (Lull 1904), *G. emeiensis* Zhen, Han and Kim 1993, *G. (A.) exertus* (Lull 1904), *G. (G.) formosus* Hitchcock 1858, *G. (G.) giganteus* Olsen 1981, *G. (G.) gracilis* (Hitchcock 1865), *G. (A.) gwyneddesis* (Bock 1952), *G. (A.) hitchcocki* (Lull 1904), *G. (G.) limnosus* Zhen, Li, Rao and Hu 1986, *G. (G.) matsiengensis* Ellenberger 1970, *G. (G.) maximus* Lapparent and Montenant 1967, *G (A.) minor* (Kuhn 1963), *G. (A.) minusculus* (Lull 1904), *G. (G.) molapoi* Ellenberger 1970, *G. (G.) oloensis* Lapparent and Montenant 1967, *G. (A.) parallelus* (Lull 1904), *G. (A.) poolei* (Baird 1957), *G. (A.) sillimani* (Hitchcock 1843), *G. (G.) sillimani* Olsen 1981, *G. (G.) sulcatus* Baird 1957, *G. (G.) tenuis* Hitchcock 1858, *G. (A.) tuberosus* (Hitchcock 1845), *G (A.) validus* (Lull 1953), *G (G.) variabilis* Lapparent and Montenant 1967; *Grallator* sp. (Yang and Yang 1987).

Occurrence: Newark Supergroup, Brunswick Formation, Massachusetts, Newark Supergroup, Virginia, Dinosaur State Park, Connecticut, New Jersey, also Colorado, Dockum Group, New Mexico, Chinle Formation, Redonda Formation, New Mexico, Paluxy River at Glen Rose, Texas, Church Rock Member at Hite Bed, Utah, United States; France; lower Elliot Formation, Lesotho, Upper Elliot Formation, Karoo Basin, South Africa, Aganane Formation, Moroccan High Atlas, Morocco, also Niger; lower Fengjiahe Formation, ?Lufeng Formation, Yunnan Province, ?Hekou Formation, Gansu, Xin Tian Gou Formation, Sichuan Province, China; Blackstone Formation, Queensland; Ørsted Dal Member, uppermost Fleming Fjord Formation, Jameson Land, East Greenland; Upper Triassic of Massif Central, France; also Brazil, Russia.

Age: Late Triassic (Carnian or Norian) to Early Jurassic (Hettangian–Pliensbachian).

Tridactyl, small, representing coelurosaurs probably ancestral to birds; Greenland tracks (Gatesy, Middleton, Jenkins and Shuban 1999; Jenkins, Shuban, Amaral, Gatesy, Schaff, Clemmenssen, Downs, Davidson, Bonde and Osbaeck 1994) preserving skin impressions as records of foot movement (see Gatesy 2001).

GREGARIPUS   Smith 1982
Name derivation: Latin *gregarius* = "sociable" + Latin *pes* = "foot."

Type species: *G. bairdi* Smith 1982.

Occurrence: Bull Run Formation, Virginia, North America.

Age: Late Triassic (?Norian).

Small, tridactyl, primitive ornithischian probably similar to *Heterodontosaurus tucki*.

GYPSICHNITES   Sternberg 1932
Name derivation: Greek *gypsos* = "chalk" + Greek *ichnos* = "track."

Type species: *G. pacensis* Sternberg 1932.

Occurrence: Goething member of Bullhead Mountain Formation, British Columbia, Tantalus Formation, Yukon Territory, Canada, Morrison Formation, Colorado, United States.

Age: Early to Middle Cretaceous (upper Albian–upper Aptian).

Bipedal, tridactyl, digits II and IV acute and laterally directed, large iguanodontoid.

GYROTRISAUROPUS   Ellenberger 1970
Name derivation: Greek *guro* = "circle" + Greek *tri* = "three" + Greek *sauros* = "lizard" + Greek *pous* = "foot."

Type species: *G. planus* Ellenberger 1970.

Occurrence: Upper Elliot Formation, Kolo, Lesotho.

Age: Early Jurassic (Hettangian–Pliensbachian).

Bipedal, tridactyl, ?theropod or indeterminate.

HADROSAURICHNUS   Alonso 1980—(=*Kuwajimasauropus*)
Name derivation: "Hadrosaur" + Greek *ichnos* = "track."

Type species: *H. australis* Alonso 1980.

Occurrence: Salta Group, Salta, Argentina; Teton Group, Japan.

Age: Early to Late Cretaceous (Berriasian–Barremian; Maastrichtian).

Bipedal, tridactyl, digits relatively more pronounced, with heel impression, ornithopod.

HAMANOSAURIPUS   Kim 1986 [*nomen dubium*]
Name derivation: "Haman [track site in Haman Formation]" + Greek *sauros* = "lizard" + Greek *pous* = "foot."

Type species: *H. ovalis* Kim 1993.

Other species: *H. ungulatus* Kim 1986 [*nomen dubium*].

Occurrence: Haman Formation, Hayang Group, Nagdong Series, Kyungsang System, Kyungsang Province, Republic of Korea.

Age: Early to Middle Cretaceous (Aptian–Albian).

Sauropod.

Note: This may not be a valid ichnotaxon. Kim erected *Hamanosauripus* as a new genus both in 1986 and 1993. In the latter paper he formally diagnosed the ichnogenus and designated *H. ovalis* as the type species.

HISPANOSAUROPUS   Mensink and Mertmann 1984 — (=?*Megalosauripus*)
Name derivation: Latin *Hispana* = "Spain" + Greek *sauros* = "lizard" + Greek *pous* = "foot."

Occurrence: "Terenes Marl," Asturias, Provincia de La Rioja, Spain.

Age: Late Jurassic (Kimmeridgian).

Type species: *H. hauboldi* Mensink and Mertmann 1984.

Medium-sized, bipedal, tridactyl, theropod, ?megalosaurid.

HITCHCOCKIA   Reichenback 1852 — (See *Anomoepus*.)
Name derivation: "[Edward] Hitchcock."

Type species: *H. gracillima* Reichenback 1852.

HOPIICHNUS   Welles 1971
Name derivation: "Hopi [Native American Indian tribe]" + Greek *ichnos* = "track."

Type species: *H. shingi* Welles 1971.

Occurrence: Kayenta Formation, Arizona, United States.

Age: Early Jurassic.

Tridactyl, ornithomimid theropod.

HUANGLONGPUS   Yang and Yang 1987
Name derivation: "Huanglong [National Park in Sichuan]" + Greek *pous* = "foot."

Type species: *H. shengouensis* Yang and Yang 1987.

Occurrence: Middle Jurassic of Sichuan Province, China.

Age: Middle Jurassic (Bathonian–Callovian).

Ornithischian.

Appendix

HUNANPUS Zeng 1982
Name derivation: "Hunan [province of China]" + Greek *pous* = "foot."
Type species: *H. jiuquwanensis* Zeng 1982.
Occurrence: Upper Cretaceous of Hunan, China.
Age: Late Cretaceous.

HYPHEPUS Hitchcock 1858 — (=?*Grallator*)
Name derivation: Greek *hyphe* = "web" + Greek *pous* = "foot."
Type species: *H. fieldi* Hitchcock 1878.
Occurrence: Newark Supergroup, Portland Arkose, Massachusetts, Lower Jurassic at Lily Pond, Massachusetts, United States.
Age: Early Jurassic.
　　Bipedal, tetradactyl, theropod very similar or identical to *Grallator*.

ICHNITES Huene 1932
Name derivation: Greek *ichnos* = "track."
Type species: *I. euskelosauroides* Huene 1932.
Occurrence: Upper Triassic, Cave Sandstone, Lesotho.
Age: Late Triassic (upper Carnian or lower Norian).
　　Bipedal, tridactyl, suggested trackmaker has been the plateosaurid prosauropod *Euskelosaurus*.

IGUANODON Tagert 1846
Name derivation: "Iguana [lizard]" + Greek *odous* = "tooth."
Type species: [None designated.]
Occurrence: Wealden, Sussex, England, Belgium, Purbeck Beds, Dorset, England; sands of Hastings, Germany; Festingen, Helvetiafjelet Formation, Heer Land, Spitzbergen, Norway; Lower Cretaceous of Lagosteiros, Portugal.
Age: Late Jurassic to Early Cretaceous.
　　Large ornithopod tracks.
　　Note: This is the only instance in which fossil tracks have been given a generic name also referring to a taxon based upon skeletal remains.

IGUANODONICHNUS Casamiquela and Fasola 1968
Name derivation: *Iguanodon* + Greek *ichnos* = "track."
Type species: *I. frenkii* Casamiquela and Fasola 1968.
Occurrence: Basal part of Banos del Flaco Formation, Colchagua, Chile.
Age: Early Cretaceous.
Other species: *I. teste* Leonardi 1981.
　　Large, bipedal, at least three functional toes, "non-iguanodontid," iguanodontoid ornithopod.

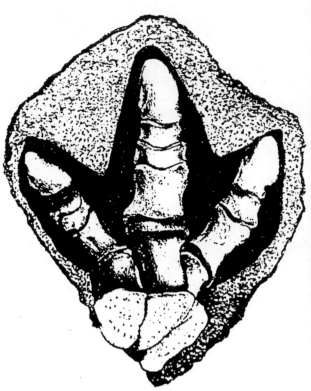

Bones of the right pes of *Iguanodon bernissartensis* set upon an ichnite of *Iguanodontipus burreyi*. (After Sarjeant, Delair and Lockley 1998, modified after Dollo 1905.)

IGUANODONTIPUS Sarjent, Delair and Lockley 1998
Name derivation: "Iguanodont" + Greek *pous* = "foot."
Type species: *I. burreyi* Sargeant, Delair and Lockley 1998.
Occurrence: Wealden, Isle of Wight, England.
Age: Early Cretaceous (Berriasian).
　　Tridactyl, attributed to an iguanodont ornithopod, possibly *Iguanodon*.

IRANOSAURIPUS Lapparent and Sadat 1975
Name derivation: "Iran" + Greek *sauros* = "lizard" + Greek *pous* = "foot."
Type species: *I. zerzbensis* Lapparent and Sadat 1975.
Occurrence: Shemshak Formation, Kerman, Iran.
Age: Middle Triassic.
　　Bipedal, tridactyl, small theropod.

IRENESAURIPUS Sternberg 1932
Name derivation: Greek *ierene* = "peace [for Peace River locality]" + Greek *sauros* = "lizard" + Greek *pous* = "foot."
Occurrence: Upper Cretaceous of British Columbia, Gates Formation, Grand Cache, Alberta, Canada; Glen Rose Formation, Comanchean Series, Wise County, Texas, United States.
Age: Early to Late Cretaceous (upper Albian–Campanian).
Type species: *I. mcleanni* Sternberg 1932.

Other species: *I. acutus* Sternberg 1932, *I. glenrosensis* Langston 1974, *I. gracilis* Currie 1983, *I. occidentalis* Sternberg 1932,

Large, functionally tridactyl, theropod the size of an average *Allosaurus*; tridactyl manus impression (Gates Formation; see McCrae, Currie and Pemberton 2002).

Note: These tracks might also pertain to some other theropod ichnotaxon, *e.g., Eubrontes* (J. O. Farlow, personal communication 2002).

IRENICHNITES Sternberg 1932 — (=?*Ornithomimipus*)
Name derivation: Greek *ierene* = "peace [for Peace River locality]" + Greek *ichnos* = "track."
Type species: *I. gracilis* Sternberg 1932.
Other species: *I. acutus* Haubold 1984, *I. mcclearni* Haubold 1984, *I. occidentalis* Haubold 1984.
Occurrence: Gething member of Bullhead Mountain Formation, British Columbia, Canada.
Age: Early Cretaceous.
Small, functionally bipedal, very birdlike, medium-sized theropod or ornithopod.

JEHOLOSAURIPUS Yabe, Inai and Shikama — (=?*Grallator*, ?*Shiraminesauropus*)
Name derivation: "Jehol [former name for Chengteh, city in northeastern China]" + Greek *sauros* = "lizard" + Greek *pous* = "foot."
Type species: *J. s-satori* Yabe, Inai and Shikama 1940.
Occurrence: Upper Triassic to Lower Jurassic of Yangshan and Liaoning (Chengteh), Manchuria.
Age: ?Cretaceous.
Tridactyl, plantigrade, digit III relatively long, slender, digit IV more acute.

JIALINGPUS Zhen, Li and Zhen 1983
Name derivation: "Jialing [river that flows through Sichuan]" + Greek *pous* = "foot."
Type species: *J. yuechiensis* Zhen, Li and Zhen 1983.
Occurrence: Pengliazhen Formation, Huanglong, Sichuan, China.
Age: Late Jurassic.
Bipedal, semiplantigrade, ornithopod.

JINLIJINGPUS Yang and Yang 1987 — (=*Eubrontes*.)
Name derivation: "Jinlijing [Chinese word]" + Greek *pous* = "foot."
Type species: *J. nianpanshanensis* Yang and Yang 1987.

KAINOMOYENSISAUROPUS Ellenberger 1970 — (see *Anomoepus*.)
Name derivation: Greek *kainos* = "recent" + French *moyen*

= "middle or average" + Greek *sauros* = "lizard" + Greek *pous* = "foot."
Type species: *K. ranivorus* Ellenberger 1970.

KAINOTRISAUROPUS Ellenberger 1970 — (See *Grallator*.)
Name derivation: Greek *kainos* = "recent" + Greek *tri* + Greek *sauros* = "lizard" + Greek *pous* = "foot."
Type species: *K. morijiensis* Ellenberger 1970.

KALASAUROPUS Ellenberger 1970 — (See *Otozoum*.)
Name derivation: "Kalo [city in Lesotho]" + Greek *sauros* = "lizard" + Greek *pous* = "foot."
Type species: *K. masitisii* Ellenberger 1970.

KAYENTAPUS Welles 1971 — (=*Megaichnites*; =?*Apatichnus*)
Name derivation: "Kayenta [Formation]" + Greek *pous* = "foot."
Type species: *K. hopii* Welles 1971.
Other species: cf. *Kayentapus* sp. (Yang and Yang 1987).
Occurrence: Kayenta Formation, Arizona, Utah, United States; Xin Tian Gou Formation, Sichuan Province, China.
Age: Early Jurassic.
Tridactyl, theropod, similar to *Grallator* (*Anchisauripus*) and (*Grallator*) (*Eubrontes*).

KLEITOTRISAUROPUS Ellenberger 1972
Name derivation: "Kleito [daughter of Uenur, mythical father of the Berbers]" + Greek *tri* = "three" + Greek *sauros* = "lizard" + Greek *pous* = "foot."
Type species: *K. moshoeshoei* (varieties *decoratus, ingens, profundus*) Ellenberger 1972.
Occurrence: Uppermost Stormberg Series, Lesotho.
Age: Late Jurassic (Hettangian–Pliensbachian).
Tridactyl, large theropod.

KOMLOSAURUS Kordos 1983 [*nomen dubium*]
Name derivation: "Komló [town in southern Hungary]" + Greek *sauros* = "lizard."
Type species: *K. carbonis* Kordos 1983 [*nomen dubium*].
Occurrence: Meesek coal formation, Komló, Hungary.
Age: Early Jurassic (Hettangian).
Bipedal, tridactyl, small ornithischian.

KOREANOSAUROPUS Kim 1986
Name derivation: "Korean" + Greek *sauros* = "lizard" + Greek *pous* = "foot."

Type species: *K. cheongi* Kim 1986.

Occurrence: Hayang Group, Nagdong Series, Kyungsang System, Kyungsang Province, Republic of Korea.

Age: Early to Middle Cretaceous (Aptian–Albian).
Sauropod.

KOSEONGOSAURIPUS   Kim 1993

Name derivation: "Koseong [district in Kangwondo Province, Korea]" + Greek *sauros* = "lizard" + Greek *pous* = "foot."

Type species: *K. onychion* Kim 1993.

Occurrence: Kyeongsang System, Republic of Korea.

Age: Early Cretaceous.
Iguanodontoid ornithopod.

KUWAJIMASAUROPUS   Azuma and Takeyama 1991—(See *Hadrosaurichnus*.)

Name derivation: "Kuwajima ['Stage']" + Greek *sauros* = "lizard" + Greek *pous* = "foot."

Type species: *K. shiraminensis* Azuma and Takeyama 1991.

LAPPARENTICHNUS   Haubold 1971

Name derivation: "Albert F. de] Lapparent [ichnologist]" + Greek *ichnos* = "track."

Type species: *L. oleronensis* Haubold 1971.

Occurrence: Upper Jurassic of Ile d'Oleror, France.

Age: Late Jurassic.
Bipedal, tridactyl and slender, small ?theropod.

LEPTONYX   Hitchcock 1865 — (Preoccupied; see *Stenonyx*.)

Name derivation: Greek *leptos* = "slender" + Greek *onyx* = "claw."

Type species: *L. lateralis* Hitchcock 1865.

LIGABUEICHNIUM   Leonardi 1984

Name derivation: "[Giancarlo] Ligabue" + Greek *ichnos* = "track."

Type species: *L. bolivianum* Leonardi 1984.

Occurrence: El Molino Formation, Toro Toro, Department of Potosi, Bolivia.

Age: Late Cretaceous (Campanian).
Large, quadrupedal, with prints superimposed upon each other to give appearance of biped, front feet probably smaller than hind feet, ornithischian, possibly made by an unusually large ankylosaur or by a ceratopsian.

MACROPODOSAURUS   Zakharov 1964

Name derivation: Greek *makros* = "large" + Greek *pous* = "foot" + Greek *sauros* = "lizard."

Type species: *M. gravis* Zakharov 1964.

Occurrence: Shirabad Suite, Schirkent Tal, Tadzhikistan, Russia.

Age: Late Cretaceous (Cenomanian).
Large, tetradactyl, ?ankylosaurian, similar to *Metatetropus valdensis*.

MAFATRISAUROPUS   Ellenberger 1970

Name derivation: "Mafa [group of people in Lesotho]" + Greek *tri* = "three" + Greek *sauros* = "lizard" + Greek *pous* = "foot."

Type species: *M. errans* Ellenberger 1970.

Occurrence: Lower Stormberg Series, Maphustang-Majakeneng, Subeng, Lesotho; France; Argentina.

Age: Late Triassic (Carnian or Norian).
Bipedal, tridactyl, trackmaker possibly rather small and robust with relatively large pelvic girdle, large theropod.

MAGNOAVIPES   Lee 1997

Name derivation: Latin *magnus* = "large" + Latin *avis* = "bird" + Latin *pes* = "foot."

Type species: *M. lowei* Lee 1997.

Other species: *M. caneeri* Lockley, Wright and Matsukawa 2001.

Occurrence: Woodbine Formation, Texas, Dinosaur Ridge, upper part of South Platte Formation, Dakota Group, near Morrison, Colorado, United States.

Age: Middle Cretaceous (Cenomanian).
Slender, very birdlike, narrow-toed, widespread, bipedal, theropod, possibly ornithomimid.

Note: For a collection of articles covering a variety of topics about Dinosaur Ridge, see *The Mountain Geologist*, July, 2001, Volume 38, Number 3.

MALUTITRISAUROPUS   Ellenberger 1970

Name derivation: "Maluti [mountain in South Africa]" + Greek *tri* + Greek *sauros* = "lizard" + Greek *pous* = "foot."

Type species: *M. sp.* Ellenberger 1970.

Occurrence: Stormberg Volcanic, basal Drakensberg Lavas, South Africa.

Age: Late Triassic.
?Dinosaurian.

MASITISAUROPEZUS   Ellenberger 1974—(See *Anomoepus*.)

Photograph by Giuseppe Leonardi.

Theropod footprints from the Sousa Formation (Lower Cretaceous) on the Piau farm, Municipality of Sousa, State of Paraiba, Brazil.

Name derivation: "Masiti [city in Lesotho]" + Greek *sauros* = "lizard" + Greek *pous* = "foot."

Type species: *M. perdiciform* Ellenberger 1974.

MASITISAUROPODISCUS   Ellenberger 1974

Name derivation: "Masiti [city in Lesotho]" + Greek *sauros* = "lizard" + Greek *pous* = "foot" + [suffix] "iscus" = "like."

Type species: *M. fringilla* Ellenberger 1974.

Other species: *M. perdiciforma* Ellenberger 1974, *M. turdus* Ellenberger 1974.

Occurrence: Upper Elliot Formation, Lesotho.

Age: Early Jurassic (Hettangian–Pliensbachian).

Tridactyl, ?theropod.

MASITISISAUROPODISCUS   Ellenberger 1974

Name derivation: "Masitisi [South African native tribe]" + + Greek *sauros* = "lizard" + Greek *pous* = "foot" + [suffix] "iscus" = "like."

Type species: *M. turdus* Ellenberger 1974.

Other species: *M. fringilla* Ellenberger 1974, *M. perficiforma* (variety *plumosus*) Ellenberger 1974.

Occurrence: Upper Elliot Formation, Mokanametsong, Lesotho.

Age: Early Jurassic (Hettangian–Pliensbachian).

Tridactyl, resembles *Trisauropodiscus*, small, very birdlike theropod.

MASITISISAUROPUS   Ellenberger 1974

Name derivation: "Masitisi [South African native tribe]" + Greek *sauros* = "lizard" + Greek *pous* = "foot."

Type species: *M. palmipes* (varieties *palmatus, planus, plumiger, pugnax, volatilis*) Ellenberger 1974.

Other species: *M. angustus* (varieties *cursor, procedans*) Ellenberger 1974, *M. exiguus* (varieties *curos, digitigradus, palmatus, ruber*) Ellenberger 1974, *M. levicauda* Ellenberger 1974.

Occurrence: Upper Elliot Formation, Mokanametesong, Lesotho.

Age: Early Jurassic (Hettangian–Pliensbachian).

Bipedal, manus and pes, manus with ?feather impressions, pes tridactyl, small ?birdlike theropod or inderminate.

MEGAICHNITES   Yang and Yang 1987 — (see *Kayentapus*)

Name derivation: Greek *megas* = "large" + "icnhite."

Type species: *M. jizhaoshiensis* Yang and Yang 1987.

MEGALOSAURIPUS   Lockley, Meyer and Santos 2000 — (=?*Hispanosauripus*)

Name derivation: *Megalosaurus* + Greek *pous* = "foot."

Type species: *M. uzsbekistanicus* (Gabuniya and Kurbatov 1982).

Other species: *M. barkhausensis* Lockley, Meyer and Santos 2000.

Occurrence: Mergandava Creek, Yakkabag Mountains, near Tashkurgan, Kodja Pil Ata, Turkmenistan, Uzbekistan; Barkhausen, Germany; Upper Jurassic of Blaziny, Poland; Upper Jurassic of Cabo (or Cap) Mondego, Portugal; Upper Summerville Formation, Northwest Carrizo Mountains, Arizona, United States.

Age: Late Jurassic (upper Oxfordian–lower Kimmeridgian).

Medium to large megalosaurid theropod, elongate tridactyl prints lacking hallux impressions, the largest known Jurassic tracks.

Notes: Originally, Lessertisseur (1955) named *Megalosauripus* (no specific name given) for bipedal, functionally tridactyl tracks from Upper Jurassic of Demnat, France, made by a large theropod presumed to be similar to *Megalosaurus*. As that name is a *nomen nudum*, Lockley, Meyer and Santos reused it "for the purposes of maintaining historical stability, and because it also appears probable that the tracks were made by megalosaurid dinosaurs." Lockley *et al.* transferred to this taxon tracks previously referred to *Megalosauropus* from Germany by Kaever and Lapparent (1974) and from Uzbekistan by Gabunia and Kurbatov (1982).

(See "Note" under *Megalosauropus*.)

MEGALOSAUROPUS   Colbert and Merriless 1967

Name derivation: *Megalosaurus* + Greek *pous* = "foot."

Type species: *M. broomensis* Colbert and Merriless 1967.

Other species: *M. brionensis* Haubold 1971, *M. titanopelobatidus* Haubold 1971.

Occurrence: Broome Sandstone, Broome, Western Australia; Trinity Group, ?Glen Rose Formation, Texas, United States; Germany; Portugal; Yugoslavia.

Age: Early Cretaceous (?Necomanian).

Bipedal, tridactyl, large theropod.

Note: Kaever and Lapparent (1974) erected their own ichnogenus *Megalosauropus* founded on tridactyl tracks made by a large theropod from the Late Jurassic (lower Kimmeridgian–Portlandian) to ?Early Cretaceous (Hauterivian) Malm, Lower Saxony, Germany. The authors named the type species *M. teutonicus*. Later, Antunes (1976) named a new species, *M. gomesi*, based on tracks from the Upper Jurassic or Lower Cretaceous Lagosteiros, Portugal. Recently, Lockley, Meyer and Santos (2000) referred this material to *Megalosauripus* (see entry).

MEHLIELLA Strand 1932 —(=*Waltheria*)
Name derivation: "[M. G.] Mehl [ichnologist]."
Type species: *M. jeffersoniensis* Strand 1932.
Occurrence: Cretaceous of Jefferson County, Colorado, United States.
Age: Cretaceous.
  Quadrupedal, plantigrade, pentadactyl, indeterminate.

METATETRAPOUS Haubold 1971
Name derivation: Greek *meta* = "after" + Greek *tetras* = "four" + Greek *pous* = "foot."
Type species: *M. valdensis* Haubold 1971.
Occurrence: Wealden Beds, Niedersachsen, Germany.
Age: Early Cretaceous (Berriasian).
  Quadrupedal, manus digitigrade, tetradactyl, pes plantigrade, tetradactyl, larger than manus, ankylosaurian, similar to *Tetrapodosaurus borealis*.

MICRICHNUS Abel 1926
Name derivation: Greek *mikros* = "small"+ Greek *ichnos* = "track."

Type species: *M. scotti* Abel 1926.
Occurrence: Upper Triassic of Princeton, New Jersey, United States.
Age: Late Triassic.
  Very small, almost completely bipedal, also tail impression, indeterminate.

MINISAURIPUS Zhen, Han and Kim 1993
Name derivation: Latin *minimus* = "least" + Greek *sauros* = "lizard" + Greek *pous* = "foot."
Type species: *M. chuanzhuensis* Zhen, Han and Kim 1993.
Occurrence: Lower Cretaceous of Emei County, Sichuan Province, China.
Age: Early Cretaceous.
  Iguanodontoid ornithopod.

MORAESICHNIUM Leonardi 1979
Name derivation: "[L. J. de] Moraes [ichnologist who registered similar Brazillian tracks]"+ Greek *ichnos* = "track."

Left: Moraesichnium barberenae (theropod) trackway crossing *Sousaichium pricei* (ornithopod) trackway at the Ilha farm, Passagem das Pedras, in the Early Cretaceous Sousa Formation, Group Rio do Peixe, in the "Vale dos dinossauros" natural park, Municipality of Sousa, Paraiba, Brazil. Photographs by Giuseppe Leonardi.

Appendix

Ichnologist Giuseppe Leonardi with two *Moraesichnium barberenae* (theropod) trackways crossing *Souaichnium pricei* (ornithopod) trackway, from the Ilha farm, Passagem das Pedras, in the Early Cretaceous Sousa Formation, Group Rio do Peixe, in the "Vale dos dinossauros" natural park, Municipality of Sousa, Paraiba, Brazil.

Type species: *M. barbernae* Leonardi 1979.
Occurrence: Sousa Formation, District of Sousa, Brazil.
Age: Early Cretaceous.
    ?Hypsilophodontid.

MOYENISAUROPEZUS   Ellenberger 1972
Name derivation: "Moyeni [city in South Africa]" + Greek *sauros* = "lizard" + Greek *pous* = "foot."
Type species: *M. perdiciforma* Ellenberger 1972.
Occurrence: Upper Elliot Formation, South Africa.
Age: Early Jurassic (Hettangian–Pliensbachian).
    Bipedal, theropod.

MOYENISAUROPODISCUS   Ellenberger 1970
Name derivation: "Moyeni [city in South Africa]" + + Greek *sauros* = "lizard" + Greek *pous* = "foot" + [suffix] "iscus" = "like."
Type species: *M. perdiciforma* Ellenberger 1970.
Occurrence: Upper Elliot Formation, Lesotho.
Age: Early Jurassic (Hettangian–Pliensbachian).
    Bipedal, ?ornithopod or indeterminate.

MOYENISAUROPUS   Ellenberger 1970—(See *Anomoepus*.)
Name derivation: "Moyeni [city in South Africa]" + + Greek *sauros* = "lizard" + Greek *pous* = "foot."

NAVAHOPUS   Baird 1980
Name derivation: Spanish *Navajo* = "Navajo [Sandstone]" and "Navajo [Indian Reservation]" + Greek *pous* = "foot."
Type species: *N. falcipollex* Baird 1980.
Occurrence: Upper Navajo Sandstone, Glen Canyon Group, Arizona, United States.
Age: Early Jurassic (Sinemurian to Pliensbachian).
    Quadrupedal, pes tetradactyl, ?plateosaurid prosauropod, or possibly nondinosaurian trilophodont (*e.g.*, see Lockley and Hunt 1995).

NEOSAUROPUS   Antunes 1976
Name derivation: Greek *neos* = "new" + Greek *sauros* = "lizard" + Greek *pous* = "foot."
Type species: *N. lagosteirensis* Antunes 1976.
Occurrence: Wealden, coast of de Lagosteiros near Espichel Cape, Portugal.
Age: Early Cretaceous (Hauterivian).
    Giant, bipedal, ornithopod.

NEOTRIPODISCUS   Ellenberger 1970
Name derivation: Greek *neos* = "new" + Greek *tripous* = "three-footed" + [suffic] "iscus" = "like."

Type species: *N. makoetiani* Ellenberger 1970.
Occurrence: Upper Elliot Formation, Maphutseng, Lesotho.
Age: Early Jurassic (Hettangian–Pliensbachian).
    Tridactyl, ?theropod or indeterminate.

NEOTRISAUROPUS   Ellenberger 1970—(See *Grallator*.)
Name derivation: Greek *neos* = "new" + Greek *sauros* = "lizard" + Greek *pous* = "foot."
Type species: *N. deambulator* Ellenberger 1970.

ORCAUICHNITES   Llompart, Casanovas and Santafé 1984
Name derivation: "Orcau [region in Spain having Upper Cretaceous rocks]" + Greek *ichnos* = "track."
Type species: *O. garumniensis* Llompart, Casanovas and Santafé 1984.
Occurrence: Tremp basin, northern Spain.
Age: Late Cretaceous (Maastrichtian).
    Small, digits relatively long and slender, rounded distally, ?ornithopod.

ORNITHICHNITES   Hitchcock 1836—(See *Sillimanius*.)
Name derivation: Greek *ornis* = "bird" + Greek *ichnos* = "track."
Type species: *O. tetradactylus* Hitchcock 1836.

ORNITHOIDICHNITES   Hitchcock 1943—(See *Sauropus*.)
Name derivation: Greek *ornis* = "bird" + Greek *oeides* = "shape" + Greek *ichnos* = "track."
Type species: *O. lyelli* Hitchcock 1843.

ORNITHOMIMIPUS   Sternberg 1926—(=?*Irenichnites*)
Name derivation: "Ornithomimid" + Greek *pous* = "foot."
Type species: *O. angustus* Sternberg 1926.
Other species: *O. gracilis* (Sternberg 1932).
Occurrence: Horseshoe Canyon Formation, Alberta, Gething Member of Bullhead Mountain Formation, British Columbia, Tantalus Formation, Yukon Territory, Canada.
Age: Late Cretaceous (Maastrichtian).
    Bipedal, digitigrade, tridactyl, indeterminate.

ORNITHOPODICHNITES   Llompart, Casanovas and Santafe-Llopis 1984
Name derivation: Greek *ornis* = "bird" + Greek *pous* = "foot" + Greek *ichnos* = "track."

Type species: *O. magna* Llompart, Casanovas and Santafé 1986.

Occurrence: Upper Cretaceous of Tremp basin, northern Spain.

Age: Late Cretaceous (Maastrichtian).

Digit III larger than lateral digits, distally inflated, rounded, prominent heel impression, ?large ornithopod.

ORNITHOPUS   Hitchcock 1848 — (See *Sillimanius.*)

Name derivation: Greek *ornis* = "bird" + Greek *pous* = "foot."

Type species: *O. gallinaceus* Hitchcock 1848.

OTOZOUM   Hitchcock 1847 — (=*Kalasauropus*)

Name derivation: Greek *ous* = "ear" + Greek *zoon* = "animal."

Type species: *O. moodi* Hitchcock 1847.

Other species: *O. caudatum* Hitchcock 1871, *O. lineatus* Bock 1952, *O. minus* Lull 1915, *O. parvum* Hitchcock 1889, *O. swinnertoni* Sarjeant 1970.

Occurrence: Massachusetts, Connecticut Valley, New Jersey, Connecticut, Portland Formation, United States; Yorkshire, England; Upper Triassic of Massif Central, France.

Age: Late Triassic to Early Jurassic (late Carnian–early Hettangian).

Relatively large tracks, manus tetradactyl (digit I held off the ground), pes small, tetradactyl, occasional tail drag. ?Prosauropod, ?"thecodontian," ?crocodilian.

PARABRONTOPODUS   Lockley, Farlow and Meyer 1994

Name derivation: Greek *para* = "beside" + Greek *bronte* = "thunder" + Greek *pous* = "foot."

Type species: *P. mcintoshi* Lockley, Farlow and Meyer 1994.

Other species: *P. distercii* Fuentes, Vidarte and Calvo 1999.

Occurrence: Lower Cretaceous of the Cameros Basin, Valdemurillo, Weald (Soria), Iberian Peninsula, Spain.

Age: Early Cretaceous (early to middle Berriasian).

"Narrow" sauropod trackway, similar to "broad" *Brontopodus*.

PARACHIROTHERIUM   Kuhn 1958 — (=*Dinosaurichnium*)

Name derivation: Greek *para* = "beside" + *Chirotherium*.

Type species: *P. postcheirotheroides* (Rehnalt 1950).

Occurrence: Lower Gipskeuper of Beyreuth, Franken, Germany.

Age: Late Triassic (Carnian to Norian).

Pes digitigrade, pentadactyl.

PARACOELUROSAURICHNUS   Zhen, Li, Rao and Hu 1986

Name derivation: Greek *para* = "beside" + "coelurosaur" + Greek *ichnos* = "track."

Type species: *P. monax* Zhen, Li, Rao and Hu 1986.

Occurrence: Lower Fengjiah Formation, Jinning, ?Lufeng Formation, Yunnan Province, China.

Age: Early Jurassic.

Bipedal, tridactyl, theropod.

PARAGRALLATOR   Ellenberger 1972

Name derivation: Greek *para* = "beside" + *Grallator*.

Type species: *P. matsiengensis* Ellenberger 1972.

Occurrence: Elliot Formation, Matsieng, Lesotho.

Age: Early Jurassic (Hettangian–Pliensbachian).

Small theropod.

PARASAUROPODOPUS   Ellenberger 1982

Name derivation: Greek *para* = "beside" + Greek *sauros* = "lizard" + Greek *pous* = "foot" + Greek *pous* = "foot."

Type species: *P. corbesiensis* Ellenberger 1972.

Occurrence: Keuper d'Anduze, France.

Age: Late Triassic.

?Ornithischian.

PARATETRASAUROPUS   Ellenberger 1970

Name derivation: Greek *para* = "beside" + Greek *tetras* = "four" + Greek *sauros* = "lizard" + Greek *pous* = "foot."

Type species: *P. seakensis* Ellenberger 1970.

Occurrence: Lower Elliot Formation, Seaka, Lesotho.

Age: Late Triassic (Carnian or Norian).

Manus and pes of similar form and with curved nails, prosauropod.

PARATRISAUROPUS   Ellenberger 1970

Name derivation: Greek *para* = "beside" + Greek *tri* = "three" + Greek *sauros* = "lizard" + Greek *pous* = "foot."

Type species: *P. mendrezi* Ellenberger 1970.

Other species: *P. equester* Ellenberger 1970, *E. lifofanensis* Ellenberger 1970.

Occurrence: Lower Elliot Formation, Seaka-Falatsa, Maseru (Race Course), Lesotho.

Age: Late Triassic (Carnian or Norian).

Bipedal, tridactyl, digitigrade, ?ornithopod, ?ornithischian, ?indeterminate.

PELARGANAX   Reichenbach 1852 — (See *Sillimanius.*)

Name derivation: Greek *pelargos* = "stork" + Greek *anax* = "master, ruler, king."

Type species: *P.* [species?].

PELARGIDES   Reichenback 1852 — (See *Steropoides*.)
Name derivation: Greek *pelargos* = "stork" + Greek *oides* = "having a similar shape."
Type species: *P. danae* Reichenback 1852.

PENGXIANPUS   Yang and Yang 1987
Name derivation: "Pengxian [County]" + Greek *pous* = "foot."
Type species: *P. cifengensis* Yang and Yang 1987.
Occurrence: Xujiahe Formation, Sichuan Province, China.
Age: Late Triassic.
  Prosauropod.

PLASTISAUROPUS   Ellenberger 1974
Name derivation: Greek *plastos* = "formed" + Greek *sauros* = "lizard" + Greek *pous* = "foot."
Type species: *P. ingens* Ellenberger 1974.
Occurrence: Upper Elliot Formation, Moyeni, South Africa.
Age: Early Jurassic (Hettangian–Pliensbachian).
  Bipedal, functionally tridactyl, small theropod.

PLATYPTERNA   Hitchcock 1845 — (=*Calopus*; =*Harpedactylus*, *Ornithoidichnites*, in part)
Name derivation: Greek *platy* = "flat" + Greek *pteron* = "wing."
Type species: *P. deanii* Hitchcock 1845.
Other species: *P. concatmerata* Hithcock 1841, *P. delicatula* (Hitchcock 1841), *P. digitigrada* Hitchcock 1858, *P. recta* (Hitchcock 1848), *P. tenuis* Hitchcock 1841.
Occurrence: Newark Supergroup, Alle Portland Arkose, Connecticut, Massachusetts, Lockatong Formation, Pennsylvania, United States.
Age: Early Jurassic (Hettangian–Pliensbachian).
  Bipedal, tridactyl, platigrade or digitigrade, small theropod or "thecodontian."

PLATYSAUROPUS   Ellenberger 1970
Name derivation: Greek *plata* = "flat" + Greek *sauros* = "lizard" + Greek *pous* = "foot."
Type species: *P. ingens* Ellenberger 1970.
Occurrence: Upper Elliot Formation, Phahamengo, Lesotho.
Age: Early Jurassic (Hettangian–Pliensbachian).
  Bipedal, tridactyl, ?theropod, ?saurischian, ?indeterminate.

PLATYTRISAUROPUS   Ellenberger 1972
Name derivation: Greek *plata* = "flat" + Greek *tri* = "three" + Greek *sauros* = "lizard" + Greek *pous* = "foot."

Type species: *P. lacunensps* Ellenberger 1972.
Occurrence: Upper Elliot Formation, Leribe, Lesotho.
Age: Early Jurassic (Hettangian–Pliensbachian).
  Theropod.

PLESIORNIS   Hitchcock 1858 — (=*Argoides*, in part; =?*Anomoepus*)
Name derivation: Greek *plesios* = "near" + Greek *ornis* = "bird."
Type species: *P. pilulatus* Hitchcock 1858.
Other species: *P. aequalipes* Hitchcock 1858, *P. giganteus* Hitchcock 1889, *P. mirabilis* Hitchcock 1865, *P. quadrupes* Hitchcock 1858.
Occurrence: Newark Supergroup, Massachusetts, United States.
Age: Early Jurassic (Hettangian–Pliensbachian).

PLESIOTHORNIPOS   Harkness 1850
Name derivation: Greek *plesios* = "near" + Middle and Old English *thorn* = "thorn" + Greek *pous* = "foot."
Type species: *P.* [species?].
Occurrence: Bunter Sandstone, Cheshire, England.
Age: Late Triassic.
  Presumably dinosaurian (type specimen lost).

PROTOTRISAUROPODISCUS   Ellenberger 1970
Name derivation: Greek *proto* = "first" + Greek *tri* = "three" + Greek *sauros* = "lizard" + [suffix] "iscus" = "like."
Type species: *P. minimus* Ellenberger 1970.
Occurrence: Lower Elliot Formation, Seaka-Falatsa-Sud, Lesotho.
Age: Late Triassic (Carnian or Norian).
  Tridactyl, pes straight resembling that of larger "*Prototrisauropus*" [=*Grallator*], small ?theropod or indeterminate.

PROTOTRISAUROPUS   Ellenberger 1970 — (See *Grallator*.)
Name derivation: Greek *protos* = "first" + Greek *tri* = "three" + Greek *sauros* = "lizard" + Greek *pous* = "foot."
Type species: *P. crassidigitus* Ellenberger 1970.

PSEUDOTETRASAUROPUS   Ellenberger 1970
Name derivation: Greek *pseudos* = "false" + Greek *tetras* = "four" + Greek *sauros* = "lizard" + Greek *pous* = "foot."
Type species: *P. mekalingensis* Ellenberger 1970.
Occurrence: Lower Stormberg Series, Molteno Formation, Lesotho, South Africa; Redondo Formation (Chinle Group), east-central New Mexico, North America; also Wales; France.
Age: Late Triassic (Carnian–?"Rhaetian").
  Tetradactyl, prosauropod, similar to *Otozoum*.

PSEUDOTRISAUROPUS   Ellenberger 1970
Name derivation: Greek *pseudo* = "false" + Greek *tri* = "three" + Greek *sauros* = "lizard" + Greek *pous* = "foot."
Type species: *P. humilis* Ellenberger 1970
Other species: *P. dieterleni* Ellenberger 1970, *P. maserui* Ellenberg 1970, *P. minusculus* Ellenberger 1970, *P. molekoi* Ellenberger 1970, *P. subengensis* Ellenberger 1970.
Occurrence: Lower Elliot Formation, Thabana-Boroko, Maphustang, Subeng, Leribe and Maseru (Race Course), Lesotho.
Age: Late Triassic (Carnian or Norian).
    Bipedal, functionally tridactyl, digit III remarkably elongated, primitive ?theropod or indeterminate.

PSILOTRISAUROPUS   Ellenberger 1970
Name derivation: Greek *psilos* = "without trees" + Greek *tri* = "three" + Greek *sauros* = "lizard" + Greek *pous* = "foot."
Type species: *P. equester* Ellenberger 1970.
Occurrence: Lower Elliot Formation, Subeng, Lesotho.
Age: Late Triassic (Carnian or Norian).
    Tridactyl, toes parallel to one another, ornithischian.

QEMETRISAUROPUS   Ellenberger 1970—(See *Grallator*.)
Name derivation: "Qeme [plateau in Lesotho]" + Greek *tri* = "three" + Greek *sauros* = "lizard" + Greek *pous* = "foot."
Type species: *Q. princeps* Ellenberger 1970.

QOMOQOMOSAUROPUS   Ellenberger 1970
Name derivation: "Qomoqomong [city in Lesotho]" + Greek *sauros* = "lizard" + Greek *pous* = "foot."
Type species: *Q. acutus* Ellenberger 1970.
Occurrence: Upper Elliot Formation, Qomoqomong, Lesotho.
Age: Early Jurassic (Hettangian–Pliensbachian).
    ?sauropod, ?large theropod, ?indeterminate.

RALIKHOMPUS   Ellenberger 1972 [*nomen nudum*]
Type species: *R. aviator* Ellenberger 1972 [*nomen nudum*].
Occurrence: Elliot Formation, South Africa.
Age: Late Triassic.
    Birdlike tracks with feather-like impressions.

ROTUNDICHNUS   Hendricks 1981
Name derivation: Latin *rotundus* = "round" + Greek *ichnos* = "tracks."
Type species: *R. münchenhagensis* Hendricks 1981.
Occurrence: Haupstanstein of the Bückeberg Formation, Berrias, Germany.

Age: Late Jurassic to Early Cretaceous.
    Almost circular footprints, ?sauropod.

SALTOPOIDES   Lapparent and Montenant 1967
Name derivation: Latin *saltus* = "leaping" + Greek *pous* = "foot."
Type species: *S. ingalensis* Lapparent and Montenant 1967.
Occurrence: Lower Jurassic of Veillon, France.
Age: Early Jurassic.
    Bipedal, tridactyl, theropod similar to *Grallator*.

SARMIENTICHNUS   Casamiquela 1964
Name derivation: "Sarmiento [city in the province of Chubut, Argentina]" + Greek *ichnos* = "track."
Type species: *S. scagliali* Casamiquela 1964.
Occurrence: "Complejo Porfirico," Santa Cruz, Argentina.
Age: Middle Jurassic.
    Bipedal, functionally "monodactyl" with two toes closely appressed, digitigrade, small theropod.

SATAPLIASAURUS   Gabouniya [Gabunia] 1951
Name derivation: "Sataplia [National Park in Georgia, Russia, featuring dinosaur footprints]" + Greek *sauros* = "lizard."
Type species: *S. tschaboukianii* Gabouniya [Gabunia] 1951.
Occurrence: Neokom-Sataplia, Georgia, Russia; Lower Cretaceous of England.
Age: Early Cretaceous.
    Small, tridactyl, tail impression, sauropod or ornithopod.

SAUREXALLOPUS   Harris 1997 (=*Exallopus*)
Name derivation: Greek *sauros* = "lizard" + Latin *ex* = "without" Greek *allos* = "other" + Greek *pous* = "foot."
Type species: *S. lovei* (Harris, Johnson, Hicks and Tauxe 1996).
Occurrence: Harebell Formation, Lance Formation, Wyoming, United States.
Age: Late Cretaceous.
    Theropod, track with very slender digits and large hallux impression.
    Note: This taxon was originally named *Exallopus lovei* by Harris, Johnson, Hicks and Tauxe 1996.

SAURICHNIUM   Gurich 1926
Name derivation: Greek *sauros* = "lizard" + Greek *ichnos* = "track."
Type species: [None designated.]
Species: *P. anserinum* Gurich 1926, *P. damarense* Gurich 1926, *P. parallelum* Gurich 1926, *P. tetractis* Gurich 1926.

Occurrence: Elliot Formation, Etjo-Sandstein, South Africa.
Age: Late Triassic.
    ?Dinosaurian.

SAUROIDICHNITES   Hitchcock 1837 — (See *Sauropus*.)
Name derivation: Greek *sauros* = "lizard" + Greek *oides* = "shape" + Greek *ichnos* = "track."
Type species: *S. barrattii* Hitchcock 1837.

SAUROPODICHNUS   Calvo 1991
Name derivation: "Sauropod" + Greek *ichnos* = "track."
Type species: *S. giganteus* Calvo 1991.
Occurrence: Candeleros Member of the Río Limay Formation, Province of Nequen, Patagonia, Argentina.
Age: Middle Cretaceous (Albian–Cenomanian).
    Non-titanosaurian, possibly diplodocoid, medium-sized sauropod.

SAUROPUS   Hitchcock 1845 — (=*Aethyopus, Amblonyx, Chimaerichnus, Fullicopus, Ornithoidichnites, Sauroidichnites*)
Name derivation: Greek *sauros* = "lizard" + Greek *pous* = "foot."
Type species: *S. barrattii* Hitchcock 1845.
Occurrence: Newark Supergroup, Massachusetts, United States.
Age: Early Jurassic (Hettangian–Pliensbachian).
    Manus and pes, ?ornithischian similar to *Hypsilophodon* or *Camptosaurus*, ?theropod, ?indeterminate.

SCHIZOGRALLATOR   Zhen, Li, Rao and Hu 1986
Name derivation: Greek *skhizo* = "to split" + *Grallator*.
Type species: *S. xiaohebaensis* Zhen, Li, Rao and Hu 1986.
Occurrence: Lower Fengiahe Formation, Jinning, ?Lufeng Formation, Yunnan Province, China.
Age: Early Jurassic.
    Bipedal, tridactyl, digitigrade with claws, theropod.

SEAKATRISAUROPUS   Ellenberger 1970
Name derivation: "Seaka [town and bridge in Lesotho]" + Greek *tri* = "three" + Greek *sauros* = "lizard" + Greek *pous* = "foot."
Type species: *S. unguiferus* Ellenberger 1970.
Other species: *S. divergens* Ellenberger 1970.
Occurrence: Lower Elliot Formation, Seaka, Lesotho.
Age: Late Triassic (Carnian or Norian).
    Bipedal, tridactyl, ?theropod or indeterminate.

SELENICHNUS   Hitchcock 1858
Name derivation: Greek *selene* = "moon" + Greek *ichnos* = "track."
Type species: *S. falcatus* Hitchcock 1858.
Other species: *S. breviusculus* Hitchcock 1858.
Occurrence: Newark Supergroup, Massachusetts, United States.
Age: Early Jurassic (Hettangian–Pliensbachian).
    Bipedal, tridactyl, small or possibly baby ?theropod, possibly crocodilian (M. G. Lockley, personal communication, 2002).

SENQUITRISAUROPUS   Ellenberger 1970
Name derivation: "Senqu [ancient name of the valley of Fleuve, Orange Free State, Lesotho]" + Greek *tri* = "three" + Greek *sauros* = "lizard" + Greek *pous* = "foot."
Type species: *S. priscus* Ellenberger 1970.
Occurrence: Lower Elliot Formation, Morobong, Lesotho.
Age: Late Triassic (Carnian or Norian).
    Pes small, tridactyl, digits slender, tapering, and with claws, large ?theropod or indeterminate.

SHENSIPUS   Yang [Young] 1966
Name derivation: "Shensi [Province of China]" + Greek *pous* = "foot."
Type species: *S. tungchuanensis* Yang [Young] 1966.
Occurrence: Jiaopig coal mine, Tongchuan County, Shanxi Province, China.
Age: Middle Jurassic.
    Bipedal, tridactyl, ?small theropod, ?bird.

SHIRAMINESAUROPUS   Azuma and Takeyama 1991 — (=?*Jeholosauripus*)
Name derivation: "Shiramin [city in Japan]" + Greek *sauros* = "lizard" + Greek *pous* = "foot."
Type species: *S. reini* Azuma and Takeyama 1991.
Other species: *S. hayashidamiensis* Azuma and Takeyama 1991.
Occurrence: Tetori Group, Japan.
Age: Early Cretaceous (Berresian–Barremian).
    Tridactyl, digit III relatively long, slender, digit IV more acute.

SILLIMANIUS   Hitchcock 1845 — (=*Ornithichnites, Ornithopus, Pelarganax*)
Name derivation: "[Benjamin] Silliman."
Type species: *S. tetradactylus* (Hitchcock 1836).
Other species: *S. adamanus* Hitchcock 1845, *S. gracilior* (Hitchcock 1836).
Occurrence: Newark Supergroup, Connecticut, Massachusetts, United States.

Age: Early Jurassic (Hettangian–Pliensbachian).
 Bipedal, tetradactyl, small theropod.

SINOICHNITES   Kuhn 1958
Name derivation: Greek *Sinai* = "China" + Greek *ichnos* = "track."
Type species: *S. youngi* Kuhn 1958.
Occurrence: Upper Jurassic of Shanxi, North Shanxi Province, China.
Age: Late Jurassic.
 Bipedal, tridactyl, toes broad with claws, iguanodontoid ornithopod.

SKARTOPUS   Thulborn and Wade 1984
Name derivation: Greek *skartes* = "nimble" + Greek *pous* = "foot."
Type species: *S. australis* Thulborn and Wade 1984.
Occurrence: Middle Winton Formation, Lark Quarry, Queensland.
Age: Middle Cretaceous (Cenomanian).
 Bipedal, digitigrade, small theropod.

SOUSAICHNIUM   Leonardi 1979
Name derivation: "Sousa [Formation and municipal district in Brazil]" + Greek *ichnos* = "track."
Type species: *S. pricei* Leonardi 1979.
Occurrence: Sousa Formation, Sousa, Paraiba State, Brazil.
Age: ?Early Cretaceous.
 Bipedal to semibipedal, iguanodontoid ornithopod.

STAURICHNIUM   Leonardi 1979
Name derivation: Greek *staurikos* = "of a cross" + Greek *ichnos* = "track."
Type species: *S. diogenis* Leonardi 1979.
Occurrence: Sousa Formation, Sousa, Paraiba State, Brazil.
Age: Early Cretaceous.
 Indeterminate ornithopod.

STENONYX   Lull 1904 —(=*Leptonyx*; =?*Grallator*)
Name derivation: Greek *steonos* = "narrow" + Greek *onyx* = "claw."
Type species: *S. lateralis* (Hitchcock 1865).
Occurrence: Newark Supergroup, Massachusetts, United States.
Age: Early Jurassic (Hettangian–Pliensbachian).
 Very small, bipedal, tridactyl or tetradactyl, theropod possibly having the relative proportions of *Coelophysis* or *Compsognathus*.

STEROPEZOUM   Hitchcock 1848 —(See *Steropoides*.)

Name derivation: Greek *stereos* = "solid" + Greek *pous* = "foot" + Greek *zoon* = "animal."
Type species: *S. elegans* Hitchcock 1848.

STEROPOIDES   Hitchcock 1845
Name derivation: Greek *stereos* = "solid" + Greek *pous* = "foot."
Type species: *S. diversus* (Hitchcock 1836).
Other species: *S. divaricatus* (Hitchcock 1841), *S. infelix* Hay 1902, *S. ingens* (Hitchcock 1836), *S. uncus* (Hitchcock 1958).
Occurrence: Newark Supergroup, Massachusetts, Connecticut, lower Passaic Formation, New Jersey, United States.
Age: Late Triassic (Norian) to Early Jurassic (Hettangian–Pliensbachian).
 Bipedal, tetradactyl, subdigitigrade to plantigrade, ?theropod or indeterminate.

STRUTHOPUS   Ballerstedt 1922
Name derivation: Greek *strouthion* = "ostrich" + Greek *pous* = "foot."
Type species: *S. schaumburgensis* Ballerstedt 1922.
Occurrence: Wealdensandstein, Bückeburg, Germany.
Age: Early Cretaceous.
 Bipedal, tridactyl, ?iguanodontoid ornithopod.

SWINNERTONICHNUS   Sarjeant 1967
Name derivation: "[H. H.] Swinnerton" + Greek *ichnos* = "track."
Type species: *S. mapperleyensis* Sarjeant 1967.
Occurrence: Waterstones, Nottinghamshire, England.
Age: Middle Triassic.
 Bipedal, tridactyl, platigrade, ?dinosaurian.

TALMONTOPUS   Lapparent and Montenat 1967
Name derivation: "Talmont [village in France]" + Greek *pous* = "foot."
Type species: *T. tersi* Lapparent and Montenat 1967.
Occurrence: Infralias-Veillon, department of Vendée, France.
Age: Early Jurassic.
 Tridactyl, plantigrade, theropod.

TAUPEZIA   Delair 1963
Name derivation: Greek *tau* = [letter equivalent of] "T" + Greek *pous* = "foot."
Type species: *T. landeri* Delair 1963.
Occurrence: Upper Jurassic of Worth Matravers, Dorset, England.

Left: "*Sousaichnium magnificum*" (iguanodontoid) holotype semi-bipedal trackway, preserved in cracked mud and rippled rocky pavement. *Right:* Ichnologist Giuseppe Leonardi with "*Sousaichnium magnificum*" (iguanodontoid) holotype trackway. Both photographs taken in the Early Cretaceous Sousa Formation, Group Rio do Peixe, at Ilha farm, "Vale dos dinossauros" natural park, Municipality of Sousa, Paraiba, Brazil.

Age: Late Jurassic (lower–middle Oxfordian).

Bipedal, tridactyl, third digit forming a "T" with second and fourth, trackmaker a ?theropod similar to *Coelurus* or *Ornitholestes*, ?dinosaurian.

TETRAPODIUM   Gurich 1926
Name derivation: Greek *tetras* = "four" + Greek *pous* = "foot."
Type species: *T. elmenhorsti* Gurich 1926.
Occurrence: Etjo Sandstein, South-West Africa.
Age: Triassic.

?Dinosaurian, indeterminate.

TETRAPODOSAURUS   Sternberg 1932
Name derivation: Greek *tetras* = "four" + Greek *pous* = "foot" + Greek *sauros* = "lizard."
Type species: *T. borealis* Sternberg 1932.

Occurrence: Gething Formation, Peace River Valley, British Columbia, Gates Formation, Grande Cache, Alberta, Canada.
Age: Early to Middle Cretaceous (Aptian–lower Albian).

Quadrupedal, manus short, pentadactyl, digitigrade, pes tetradactyl, semiplantigrade, ankylosaur.

TETRASAUROPUS   Ellenberger 1972
Name derivation: Greek *tetras* = "four" + Greek *sauros* = "lizard" + Greek *pous* = "foot."
Type species: *T. unguiferus* Ellenberger 1972.
Occurrence: Lesotho.
Age: Late Triassic.

?Sauropodomorph, ?prosauropod walking bipedally.

THECODONTICHNUS   Huene 1941
Name derivation: "Thecodont" + Greek *ichnos* = "track."

Appendix

Shallow sauropod (probably "titanosaurid") trackways, representing at least 15 individuals, crossing a gully, from the Estreito farm, in the Lower Cretaceous Antenor Navarro Formation, Group Rio do Peixe, in the "Vale dos dinossauros" natural park, Muncipality of Sousa, Paraiba, Brazil.

Photographs by Giuseppe Leonardi.

Left: Semi-pedal sauropod trackway representing a "climber" vulcanodontid, from the Lower Jurassic (Hettangian-Sinemurian crossing) Calcari Grigi Formation, on the Lavini di Marco rockslide in the valley of the river Adige at Roverto, province of Trento, Italy. This locality, preserving hundreds of dinosaur tracks, is under study by G. Leonardi and P. Mietto (2000). *Right:* Bipedal trackway, dubiously attributed to large, graviportal early ornithischians, from the Lower Jurassic (Hettangian-Sinemurian crossing) Calcari Grigi Formation, on the Lavini di Marco rockslide in the valley of the river Adige at Roverto, province of Trento, Italy.

Type species: *T. verrucae* Huene 1941.
Other species: *T. fucinii* Huene 1941.
Occurrence: Upper Triassic of Verrucano, Toscana, Italy.
Age: Late Triassic.
 Quadrupedal, wide, ?prosauropod, ?dinosaurian.

THERANGOSPODUS   Lockley, Meyer and Moratalla 2000
Name derivation: "Ther[opod]" + Latin *angustus* = "narrow" + Greek *pous* = "foot."
Type species: *T. pandemicus* Lockley, Meyer and Moratalla 2000.
Occurrence: Moab Megatracksite, eastern Utah, United States; Oncala Group, Cameros Basin, Spain; Khodja Pil Ata site, Turkmenistan, Uzbekistan, Tadjikistan, Central Asia.

Age: ?Middle to Late Jurassic.
 Medium-sized to large theropod.
 Note: These tracks were previously named *T. oncalensis* by Moratalla (1993) in an unpublished doctoral thesis.

TRIDENTIPES   Hitchcock 1858 —(See *Steropoides.*)
Name derivation: Latin *tridens* = "three-toothed" + Latin *pes* = "foot."
Type species: *T. elegans* Hitchcock 1858.

TRIHAMUS   Hitchcock 1865]
Name derivation: Greek *tri* = "three" + Latin *hamus* = "hook."
Type species: *T. elegans* Hitchcock 1865.

Other species: *T. magnus* Hitchcock 1889.

Occurrence: Newark Supergroup, Portland Arkose, Massachusetts, Connecticut, United States.

Age: Early Jurassic.

Bipedal, tridactyl, plantigrade, small theropod.

TRISAUROPODACTYLUS   Ellenberger 1974

Name derivation: Greek *tri* = "three" + Greek *sauros* = "lizard" + Greek *pous* = "foot" + Greek *dactylos* = "finger."

Type species: *T. superviges* Ellenberger 1974.

Occurrence: Upper Elliot Formation, Matsepe, Lesotho.

Age: Early Jurassic (Hettangian–Pliensbachian).

Bipedal, tridactyl, very birdlike, large though relatively gracile theropod, ornithischian, or indeterminate.

TRISAUROPODISCUS   Ellenberger 1970

Name derivation: Greek *tri* = "three" + Greek *sauros* = "lizard" + Greek *pous* = "foot" + [suffix] "iscus" = "like."

Type species: *T. superaviforma* Ellenberger 1970.

Other species: *T. aviforma* (varieties *columba*, *turtur*, *merula*, *passer*, *vanellus*) Ellenberger 1970, *T. galliforma* Ellenberger 1970, *T. levis* Ellenberger 1970, *T. phasianiforma* Ellenberger 1970, *T. popompoi* Ellenberger 1970.

Occurrence: Lower Elliot Formation, Maphutseng-Majakeneng, Upper Elliot Formation, Lesotho; Hettangian of Sanary-sur-Mer, France.

Age: Late Triassic (Carnian or Norian) to Early Jurassic (Pliensbachian).

Bipedal, tridactyl, toes small and threadlike, terminating in rounded points, small, birdlike ?theropods or indeterminate.

TRITOTRISAUROPUS   Ellenberger 1970

Name derivation: Greek *tritos* = "third" + Greek *tri* = "three" + Greek *sauros* = "lizard" + Greek *pous* = "foot."

Type species: *T. medius* Ellenberger 1970.

Occurrence: Lower Elliot Formation, Maphutseng, Lesotho.

Age: Late Triassic (Carnian or Norian).

Tridactyl, ?anchisaurid prosauropod, ?saurischian, ?indeterminate.

TUOJIANGPUS   Yang and Yang 1987 — (See *Eubrontes*.)

Name derivation: "Tuojiang [River]" + Greek *pous* = "foot."

Type species: *T. shuinanensis* Yang and Yang 1987.

TYRANNOSAURIPUS   Lockley and Hunt 1994

Name derivation: Name derivation: *Tyrannosaurus* + Greek *pous* = "foot."

Type species: *T. pillmorei* Lockley and Hunt 1994.

Occurrence: Raton Formation, near and north of Cimmaron, New Mexico, United States.

Age: Late Cretaceous (Maastrichtian).

Largest dinosaur track known, tridactyl, resembling *Büeckeburgichnus*, presumably made by the giant theropod *Tyrannosaurus*.

Notes: Lessertisseur (1955) previously gave the name *Tyrannosauripus* to very large-theropod tracks from the Upper Cretaceous of Utah, Colorado. He did not assign them a specific name. Lessertisseur's taxon — which may be synonymous with *Bückeburgichnus*— is, therefore, a *nomen nudum*.

In most instances, ichnotaxa cannot be unequivocally associated with taxa based upon skeletal fossils. However, *Tyrannosaurus* is the only late Maastrichtian theropod known from this region large enough to have made a track of this size (maximum length and width 86 and 64 centimeters, respectively).

TYRANNOSAUROPUS   Haubold 1971

Name derivation: *Tyrannosaurus* + Greek *pous* = "foot."

Type species: *T. petersoni* Haubold 1971.

Occurrence: Mesaverde Formation, Colorado, Utah, United States; ?Winton Formation, Lark Quarry, Queensland.

Age: Late Cretaceous (?Cenomanian–Maastrichtian).

Bipedal, tridactyl, very large theropod.

ULTRASAURIPUS   Kim 1993

Name derivation: *Ultrasaurus* + Greek *pous* = "foot."

Type species: *U. ungulatus* 1993.

Occurrence: Hayang Group, Gyeongsang System, Gyeongsang Province, Republic of Korea.

Age: Early to Middle Cretaceous (Aptian–Albian).

Sauropod.

VELOCIRAPTORICHNUS   Zhen, Han and Kim 1993

Name derivation: *Velociraptor* + Greek *ichnos* = "track."

Type species: *V. sichuanensis* Zhen, Han and Kim 1993.

Occurrence: Lower Cretaceous of Emei County, Sichuan Province, People's Republic of Chia.

Age: Early Cretaceous.

Dromaeosaurid theropod.

WALTHERIA   Mehl 1931—(Preoccupied; see *Mehliella*.)

Name derivation: "[J.] Walther [ichnologist]."

Type species: *W. jeffersonensis* Mehl 1931.

WEALDENICHNITES   Kuhn 1958

Name derivation: "Wealden" + Greek *ichnos* = "track."

Type species: *W. iguanodontoides* Kuhn 1958.

Photograph courtesy Martin G. Lockley.

Ichnologist Martin G. Lockley with a cast of *Tyrannosauripus pillmorei*, a giant theropod footprint ascribed to *Tyrannosaurus rex*.

Occurrence: Wealden, Niedersachsen, Germany.

Age: Early Cretaceous (Berriasian).

Bipedal, tridactyl, mostly subdigitigrade, toes ending in blunt ends, iguanodontoid ornithopod, trackmaker ?*Iguanodon*.

WILDEICHNUS Casamiquela 1964

Name derivation: "Wilde [city in Argentina]" + Greek *ichnos* = "track."

Type species: *W. navesi* Casamiquela 1964.

Occurrence: "Complejo Portifico," Santa Cruz, Argentina; Rät, Sanary-sur-Mer, Toulon, Var, Lias of Lotharinguen, Severac-le-Château, Aveyron, Hettangian of Lodéve, Herault and Saint-de-Trêves, France.

Age: Early to Middle Jurassic.

Bipedal, functionally tridactyl, digitigrade, small ?theropod.

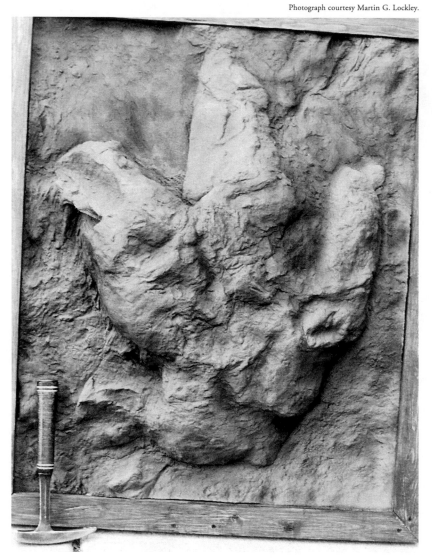

Photograph courtesy Martin G. Lockley.

Cast of the ichnotaxon *Tyrannosauripus pillmorei*, a footprint believed to have been made by the giant theropod dinosaur *Tyrannosaurus rex.*

WINTONOPUS Thulborn and Wade 1984
Name derivation: "Winton [Formation]" + Greek *pous* = "foot."
Type species: *W. latomorum* Thulborn and Wade 1984.
Occurrence: Middle Winton Formation, Lark Quarry, Queensland.
Age: Middle Cretaceous (Cenomanian).
    Bipedal, digitigrade, narrow trackway, digits broad with rounded or bluntly angular tips, small ornithischian.

XIANGXIPUS Zeng 1982
Name derivation: "Xiangi [town and prefecture in China]" + Greek *pous* = "foot."
Type species: *X. chenxiensis* Zeng 1982.
Other species: *X. youngi* Zeng 1982.
Occurrence: Jinjiang Formation (middle Upper Cretaceous), Hunan Province, China.

Age: Late Cretaceous.
    Theropod.

YANGTZEPUS Yang [Young] 1960
Name derivation: "Yangtz [Kiang, river in China]" + Greek *pous* = "foot."
Type species: *Y. yipingensis* Yang [Young] 1960.
Occurrence: Lower Chiating Series, Sichuan, China.
Age: Late Jurassic.
    Quadrupedal, tridactyl, toes thick, ?ornithischian.

YOUNGICHNUS Zhen, Li, Rao and Hu 1986
Name derivation: "Young [Chung-Chien, earlier incorrectly published spelling of Yang Zhungjian]" + Greek *ichnos* = "track."
Type species: *Y. xiyangensis* Zhen, Li, Rao and Hu 1986.
Occurrence: Lower Fengjiahe Formation, Xiyang, ?Lufeng Formation, Yunnan Province, China.
Age: Early Jurassic.
    Bipedal, tridactyl, digitigrade, large theropod.

YUNNANPUS Chen and Huang 1993
Name derivation: "Yunnan [Province]" + Greek *pous* = "foot."
Type species: *Y. huangcaoensis* Chen and Huang 1993.
Other species: *C. zheni* Chen and Huang 1993.
Occurrence: Late Cretaceous.
Age: Upper Cretaceous Series, Changling, Chuxiong Prefecture, Yunnan Province, China.
    Sauropod.

ZHENGICHNUS Zhen, Li, Rao and Hu 1986
Name derivation: "Zeng [Xiangyuan]" + Greek *ichnos* = "track."
Type species: *Z. jinningensis* Zhen, Li, Rao and Hu 1986.
Occurrence: Lower Fengjiahe Formation, Jinning, ?Lufeng Formation, Yunnan Province, China.
Age: Early Jurassic.
    Tridactyl, digitigrade, theropod.

ZIZHONGPUS Yang and Yang 1987 —(See *Kayentapus.*)
Name derivation: "Zizhong" + Greek *pous* = "foot."
Type species: *Z. wumaensis* Yang and Yang 1987.

Dinosaur Eggs

In the past, fossilized dinosaurian eggs and eggshell pieces, were also regarded as trace fossils. In more recent years, however, that designation no longer applies to these fossils "because they are biocrystalline structures produced by the organism and convey taxa-specific information through their microstructure and histostructure (unlike footprints and burrows that are sedimentary structures creatd by the interaction of an organism and the substrate)" (E. S. Bray, personal communication 2002).

The remains of dinosaur eggshells have been known since the middle nineteenth century. In 1869, M. Philippe Matheron, in describing *Hypselosaurus priscus*, a new sauropod genus and species from the Aix Basin in southern France, also reported on pieces of fossil eggshell found at the same locality. Although these eggs are now regarded as sauropod, at the time Matheron cautiously speculated that these eggs might be associated either with this dinosaur or with some unknown extinct giant bird (see *D:TE*, *Hypselosaurus* entry, for more information and photograph of a reconstructed egg; see also "*Megaloolithus*" entry, below). Eggs were not unequivocally associated with dinosaurs until the 1920s, when fossilized egg specimens were found in proximity with skeletal specimens of the primitive horned dinosaur *Protoceratops* (see *D:TE*, *Protoceratops* entry for details; see also Zelenitsky 2000 for a history of collecting dinosaur eggs in Asia and North America up to the present).

Like dinosaur footprints, eggshells have been described, sometimes given generic and specific names, and also referred to their own higher families (*i.e.*, Elongatoolidae). As with tracks, some eggs have been interpreted or named on the basis of what dinosaurian genera were assumed to have laid them, sometimes via the direct association of adult skeletal evidence (*e.g.*, Dong and Currie 1996; see *SI*, *Oviraptor* entry) or even the identification of embryonic remains (*e.g.*, Horner and Makela 1979; see *D:TE*, *Maiasaura* entry); others have been grouped together and named on the basis of their shapes or microstructure (*e.g.*, Mikhailov 1991; Sabath 1991)

The following list comprises only dinosaurian egg specimens and types for which generic and specific names have been erected. As with the preceding list of footprints, the reader is advised and encouraged to consult the paleontological literature for more detailed information regarding dinosaur eggs, and also the books *Dinosaur Eggs and Babies* (Carpenter, Hirsch and Horner 1994) and *Walking on Eggs* (Chiappe and Dingus 2001).

APHELOOLITHUS (?author, ?date)
Name derivation: Greek *apo* = "away" + Greek *helios* = "sun" + Greek *oon* = "egg" + Greek *lithos* = "stone."
Type species: *A. shuinanensis* (?author, ?date).
Occurrence: Nanxiong Basin, China.
Note: This may not be a valid ootaxon.
Age: Late Cretaceous (Maastrichtian).

CAIRANOOLITHUS Vianey-Liaud, Mallan, Buscail and Montegelard 1994
Name derivation: "[La] Cairanne" [locality] + Greek *oon* = "egg" + Greek *lithos* = "stone."
Type species: *C. dughii* Vianey-Liaud, Mallan, Buscail and Montegelard 1994.
Other species: *C. roussetensi* Viany-Liaud, Mallan, Buscail and Montegelard 1994.
Occurrence: La Cairanne, Roquchautes-Grand Creux, Villeveyrac Basin, and Rousset-Village localities, France.
Age: Late Cretaceous (Maastrichtian).

CONTINUOOLITHUS Zelenitsky, Hills and Currie 1996
Name derivation: Latin *continuus* = "continuous" + Greek *oon* = "egg" + Greek *lithos* = "stone."
Type species: *C. canadensis* Zelenitskty, Hills and Currie 1996.
Occurrence: Oldman Formation, southern Alberta, Canada; Two Medicine Formation, Montana, United States.
Age: Late Cretaceous (Middle to Late Campanian–Maastrichtian).
      Theropod.
Note: Although not assigned to an oogenus, this type of eggshell has also been found in the Upper Jurassic (late Kimmeridgian) Brushy Basin Member of the Morrison Formation of New Mexico (see Bray and Lucas 1997).

DENDROOLITHUS Zhao 1988
Name derivation: Greek *dendron* = "tree" + Greek *oon* = "egg" + Greek *lithos* = "stone."
Type species: *D. wangdianensis* Zhao and Li 1988.
Other species: ?*D. dentriticus* (?author, ?date), ?*D. furcatus* (?author, ?date), *D. microporosus* Mikhailov 1994, ?*D. sanlimiaoensis* (?author, ?date), *D. verrucarius* Mikhailov 1994, *D. xichuanensis* Zhao 1998, ?*D. zhaoyin-gensis* (?author, ?date).
Occurrence: ?Lower Cretaceous of China; Upper Cretaceous of Anlu County, Hubei Province, China; Upper Cretaceous of Mongolian People's Republic; Lower Cretaceous of South Korea.
Age: Early to Late Cretaceous.
      ?Therizinosauroid theropod.

DICTYOOLITHUS Zhao 1994
Name derivation: Greek *diktyon* = "net" + Greek *oon* = "egg" + Greek *lithos* = "stone."
Type species: *D. hongpoensis* Zhao 1994.
Other species: *D. neixiangensis* Zhao 1994.
Occurrence: Xixia Basin locality, Hongpo, Chishuigou, Shibangou, Chimei, Henan Province, China.
Age: Early Cretaceous.

Dinosaur eggs (FMNH P12991) collected in 1926 during the Third Central Asiatic Expedition of the American Museum of Natural History (co-sponsored by the formerly named Field Museum of Natural History) to Mongolia. These eggs have not yet been thoroughly studied, nor have they been positively assigned to any dinosaurian group.

DUGHIOOLITHUS   Vianey-Liaud, Mallan, Buscail and Montegelard 1994 — (See *Cairanoolithus*.)
Name derivation: "[R.] Dughi" + Greek *oon* = "egg" + Greek *lithos* = "stone."
Type species: *D. roussetensis* Vianey-Liaud, Mallan, Buscail and Montegelard 1994.
Occurrence: Upper Cretaceous of France.
Age: Late Cretaceous.

ELLIPSOOLITHUS   Mohabey 1998
Name derivation: Greek *elleipsis* = "falling short [meaning ellipsoidal shape]" + Greek *lithos* = "stone."
Type species: *E. khedaensis* Mohabey 1998.
Occurrence: Lameta Formation, Upper Sandy Carbonate, Rahioli, district Kheda, Gujarat, India.
Age: Late Cretaceous (middle Maastrichtian).
    ?Abelisaurid theropod.

ELONGATOOLITHUS   Zhao 1975
Name derivation: "Elongate [Latin *ex* = 'out' + Latin *longus* = 'long']" + Greek *oon* = "egg" + Greek *lithos* = "stone."
Type species: *E. elongatus* Yang [Young] 1954.
Other species: *E. andrewsi* Zhao 1975, *E. excellens* Mikhailov 1994, *E. frustrabilis* Mikhailov 1994, *E. magnus* Zeng and Zhang 1979, *E. sigillarius* Mikhailov 1994, *E. subtitectorius* Mikhailov 1994.
Occurrence: Yuanpu Formation, Pingling Formation, upper part of Wangshih Series, China; Upper Cretaceous of Mongolian People's Republic; Upper Cretaceous of Kirghizia; Upper Cretaceous of Zaisan Basin, Kazakhstan; Upper Cretaceous of France; Two Medicine Formation, Montana, United States.
Age: Late Cretaceous (Maastrichtian).
    Oviraptorosaurid theropod.

FAVEOOLITHUS   Zhao and Ding 1976
Name derivation: Latin *favus* = "honeycomb" + Greek *oon* = "egg" + Greek *lithos* = "stone."
Type species: *F. ningxiaensis* Zhao and Ding 1976.
Occurrence: Upper Cretaceous of China; Upper Cretaceous of Mongolian People's Republic.
Age: ?Early to Late Cretaceous.
    ?Sauropod.

MACROOLITHUS   Zhao 1975
Name derivation: Greek *makros* = "large" + Greek *oon* = "egg" + Greek *lithos* = "stone."
Type species: *M. yaotunensis* Zhao 1975.
Other species: *M. mutabilis* Zhao 1975, *M. rugustus* Yang [Young] 1965.
Occurrence: Pingling Formation, China; Upper Cretaceous of Mongolian People's Republic; Upper Cretaceous eastern Kazakhstan.
Age: Late Cretaceous (Maastrichtian).
    Oviraptorosaurid theropod.

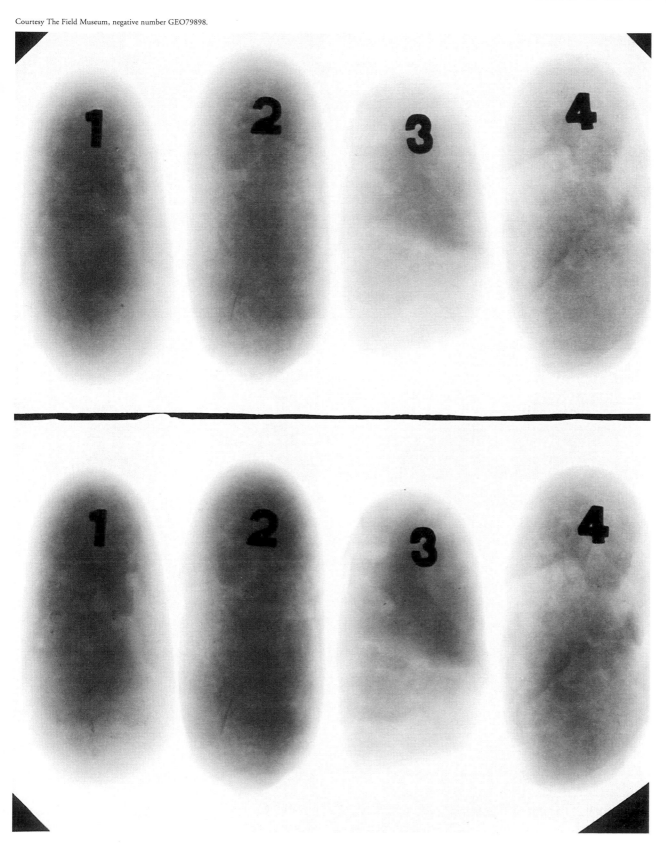

X-ray photographs of dinosaur eggs (FMNH 12991) from Mongolia revealing no embryos inside.

MACROELONGATOOLITHUS Li, Yin and Liu 1995

Name derivation: + Greek *lithos* = "stone."
Type species: *M. xixiaensis* Li, Yin and Liu 1995.
Occurrence: Xixia, China.
Age: Cretaceous.

MEGALOOLITHUS Vianey-Liaud, Mallan, Buscail and Montegelard 1994

Name derivation: Greek *megalo* = "big" + Greek *oon* = "egg" + Greek *lithos* = "stone."
Type species: *M. mammilare* Vianey-Liaud, Mallan, Buscail and Montegelard 1994.
Other species: *M. aureliensis* Vianey-Liaud, Mallan, Buscail and Montegelard 1994, *M. balasinorensis* Mohabey 1998, *M. dhoridungriensis* Mohabey 1998, *M. khempurensis* Mohabey 1998, *M. matleyi* Mohabey 1998, *M. megadermus* Mohabey 1998, *M. microtuberculata* Garcia and Vianey-Liaud 2001, *M. petralta* Vianey-Liaud, Mallan, Buscail and Montegelard 1994, *M. phensaniensis* Mohabey 1998, *M. rahioliensis* Mohabey 1998, *M. trempii* Moratella 1993.
Occurrence: Gujaret, Maharashtra, Madhya Pradesh, India; Aix-en-Provence Basin, Languedoc, France; Aren Formation, Tremp Formation, Gosol locality, Catalonia, Spain.
Age: Late Cretaceous (Maastrichtian).
     ?"Titanosaurid" sauropod.
     Note: Although not assigned to an oogenus, this type of eggshell has also been found in the Upper Jurassic (late Kimmeridgian) of the Morrison Formation of Utah and Colorado (see Bray and Hirsch 1998).

NANSHIUNGOOLITHUS Zhao 1975

Name derivation: "Nanshiung [Province in China]" + Greek *oon* = "egg" + Greek *lithos* = "stone."
Type species: *N. chuetiensis* Zhao 1975.
Occurrence: Yuanpu Formation, Pingling Formation, China.
Age: Late Cretaceous (Maastrichtian).
     ?Oviraptorosaurian theropod.

OVALOOLITHUS Zhao 1979

Name derivation: Latin *ovalis* = "oval" + Greek *oon* = "egg" + Greek *lithos* = "stone."
Type species: *O. chinkangkouensis* Zhao and Jiang 1974.
Other species: *O. dinornithoides* Mikhailov 1994, *O. laminadermus* Zhao and Jiang 1974, *O. mixtistriatus* Zhao 1979, *O. monostriatus* Zhao 1979, ?*O. sangpingensis* (?author, ?date), *O. tristriatus* Zhao 1979.
Occurrence: Yuanpu Formation, Pingling Formation, upper part of Wangshih Series, China; Upper Creta-

ceous of Mongolian People's Republic; North Horn Formation, United States.
Age: Late Cretaceous (Maastrichtian).

PARASPHEROOLITHUS Zhao and Jiang 1974

Name derivation: Greek *para* = "beside" + Greek *oon* = "egg" + Greek *lithos* = "stone."
Type species: *P. irenensis* Zhao and Jiang 1974.
Occurrence: Upper part of Wangshih Series, Donting Basin, Hunan Province, China.
Age: Late Cretaceous (Maastrichtian).

PHACELOOLITHUS Zeng and Zhang 1979

Name derivation: Greek *phakelos* = "bundle of sticks" + Greek *oon* = "egg" + Greek *lithos* = "stone."
Type species: *P. hunanensis* Zeng and Zhang 1979.
Occurrence: Upper Cretaceous of Donting Basin, Hunan Province, China.
Age: Late Cretaceous.

PLACOOLITHUS Zhao 1979

Name derivation: Greek *plax* = "plate" + Greek *oon* = "egg" + Greek *lithos* = "stone."
Species: *P. taohensis* Zhao 1979.
Occurrence: Upper Cretaceous of China.
Age: Late Cretaceous.

PREPRISMATOOLITHUS Hirsch 1994.

Name derivation: Latin *prae* = "before" + *Prismatoolithus*.
Type species: *P. coloradensis* Hirsch 1994.
Occurrence: Morrison Formation, Utah, Colorado, United States; Upper Jurassic of Lourinha, Portugal.
Age: Late Jurassic (Kimmeridgian–Tithonian).
     ?Allosauroid theropod.
     Note: Although not assigned to an oogenus, this type of eggshell has also been found in the Upper Jurassic (late Kimmeridgian) Morrison Formation of Utah and Colorado (see Bray and Hirsch 1998).

PRISMATOOLITHUS Zhao 1993

Name derivation: Latin *prisma* = "prism" + Greek *oon* = "egg" + Greek *lithos* = "stone."
Type species: *P. gebiensis* Hirsch 1994.
Other species: *P. hukouensis* Zhao 2000, *P. jenseni* Bray 1999, *P. levis* Zelenitsky and Hills 1996, *P. tenuis* Vianey-Liaud and Crochet 1993.
Occurrence: Upper Cretaceous of Xixia Basin, Henan Province, Djadokhta Formation, Bayan Manduhu, Inner Mongolia, Nanxiong Basin, Guangdong Province, China; Oldman Formation, southern Alberta, Canada;

Two Medicine Formation, Montana, North Horn Formation, Utah, United States.

Age: Late Cretaceous (Middle to Late Campanian–Maastrichtian).

Troodontid theropod, *Troodon* cf. *T. formosus*; Asian eggs apparently hypsilophodontid ornithopods.

Note: Although not assigned to an oogenus, this type of eggshell has also been found in the Upper Jurassic (late Kimmeridgian) of the Morrison Formation of Utah and Colorado (see Bray and Hirsch 1998).

PROTOCERATOPSIDOVUM   Mikhailov 1994

Name derivation: "Protoceratopsid" + Latin *ovum* = "egg."

Type species: *P. sincerum* Mikhailov 1994.

Other species: *P. minumum* Mikhailov 1994.

Occurrence: Upper Cretaceous of Mongolian People's Republic.

Age: Late Cretaceous.

Protoceratopsid ceratopsian.

SHIXINGOOLITHUS   Zhao, Jie, Huamei, Zhenhua and Zheng 1991

Name derivation: "Shixing [County]" + Greek *oon* = "egg" + Greek *lithos* = "stone."

Type species: *S. erbeni* Zhao, Jie, Huamei, Zhenhua and Zheng 1991.

Occurrence: Pingling Formation, China.

Age: Late Cretaceous (Maastrichtian).

SPHAEROVUM   Mones 1980

Name derivation: Greek *sphaira* = "globe" + Latin *ovum* = "egg."

Type species: *S. erbeni* Mones 1980.

Occurrence: Soriano Site, Mercedes Formation, Uruguay.

Age: Late Cretaceous (Cenomanian).

Titanosaurid sauropod.

SPHEROOLITHUS   Zhao 1979

Name derivation: Greek *sphaira* = "globe" + Greek *oon* = "egg" + Greek *lithos* = "stone."

Type species: *S. chianchengensis* Zhao 1979.

Other species: *S. albertensis* Zelenitsky and Hills 1996, *S. chiangchiungtingensis* Zhao and Jiang 1974, *S. maiasauroides* Mikhailov 1994, *S. megadermus* (Yang [Young] 1959), *S. tenuicorticus* Mikhailov 1994.

Occurrence: Oldman Formation, southern Alberta, Canada; ?upper part of Wangshih Series, China; Upper Cretaceous of Mongolian People's Republic; Upper Cretaceous of Kirghizia; Two Medicine Formation, Montana, Lower Cretaceous, Utah, United States.

Age: Early to Late Cretaceous.

Hadrosaurid ornithopod.

Note: This type of eggshell, almost identical to *S. albertensis* from the Two Medicine Formation, is also found in the Upper Jurassic (late Kimmeridgian) Morrison Formation of Southeastern Utah (see Hirsch, Bray, Demko, Currie and Ekart 1996).

SPHERUPRISMATOOLITHUS   Bray 1999

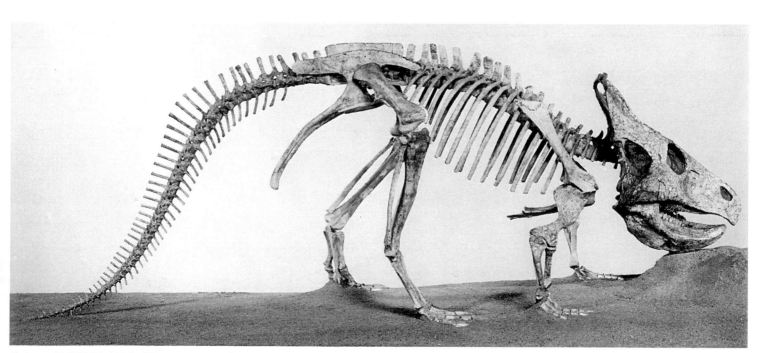

Skeleton (FMNH PR12991) of *Protoceratops andrewsi*, a protoceratopsid dinosaur from Mongolia. Fossil eggs given the generic name *Protoceratopsidovum* have been associated with protoceratopsids.

Photograph by the author, North American Museum of Ancient Life.

Detail of an undescribed skeleton of the protoceratopsid ceratopsian *Protoceratops andrewsi* collected in Mongolia. Protoceratopsids are among the dinosaurian groups for which fossil eggs are known.

Name derivation: "Spherulitic [structural morphotype]" + Latin *prisma* = "prism" + Greek *oon* = "egg" + Greek *lithos* = "stone."
Type species: *S. condensus* Bray 1999.
Occurrence: North Horn Formation, Utah, Two Medicine Formation, Montana, Judith River Formation, Montana, United States.
Age: Late Cretaceous (Campanian–Maastrichtian).

STROMATOOLITHUS Zhao, Ye, Li, Zhao and Yan 1991
Name derivation: Greek *stroma* = "bedding" + Greek *oon* = "egg" + Greek *lithos* = "stone."
Type species: *S. pinglingensis* Zhao, Ye, Li, Zhao and Yan 1991.
Occurrence: Pingling Formation, China.
Age: Late Cretaceous (Maastrichtian).

SUBTILIOLITHUS Khosla and Sahni 1995

Name derivation: Latin *subtilis* = "subtle" + Greek *oon* = "egg" + Greek *lithos* = "stone."
Type species: *S. kachhchensis* Khosla and Sahni 1995.
Occurrence: Anjar Intertrappean bed, Lameta Formation, India.
Age: Late Cretaceous (Maastrichtian).
Of questionable validity.

TACUMAREMBOVUM Mones 1980
Name derivation: "Tacumarembo [city in Uruguay]" + Latin *ovum* = "egg."
Type species: *T. oblongum* Mones 1980.
Occurrence: Algorta Site, Mercedes Formation, Uruguay.
Age: Late Cretaceous (Cenomanian).
?Ornithischian.

TRACHOOLITHUS Mikhailov, Sabath and Kurzanov 1994
Name derivation: Greek *trachys* = "rough" + Greek *oon* = "egg" + Greek *lithos* = "stone."

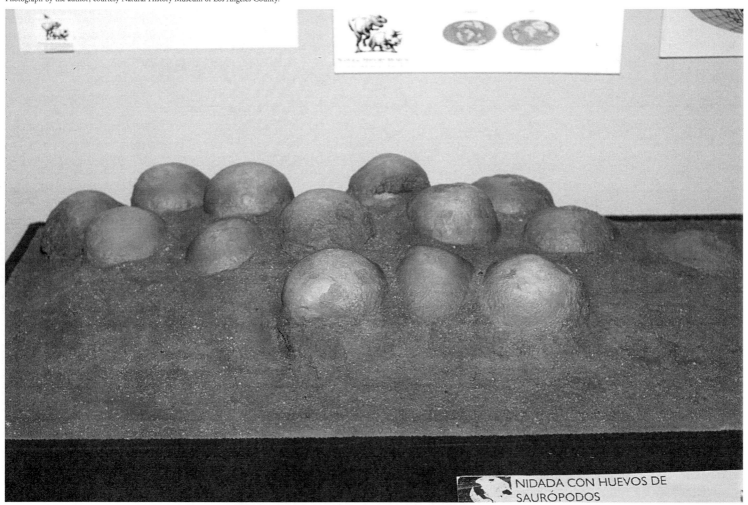

Sauropod eggs from the Upper Cretaceous (Campanian) Barun Goyot Group, Gobi Desert, southern People's Republic of Mongolia, displayed in 1999 at "The Great Russian Dinosaurs Exhibition," here presented at the Natural History Museum of Los Angeles County.

Type species: *T. faticanus* Mikhailov, Sabath and Kurzanov 1994.

Occurrence: Upper Cretaceous of Mongolian People's Republic.

Age: Late Cretaceous.

?Oviraptorosaurian theropod.

WEIAUNPUS [author and date?]— (=?*Eubrontes*.)

Name derivation: + Greek *pous* = "foot."

Type species: ?

Occurrence: Zhenzhuchong Formation, Sichuan Province, China.

Age: Early Jurassic.

Tridactyl, theropod, very similar to *Eubrontes*.

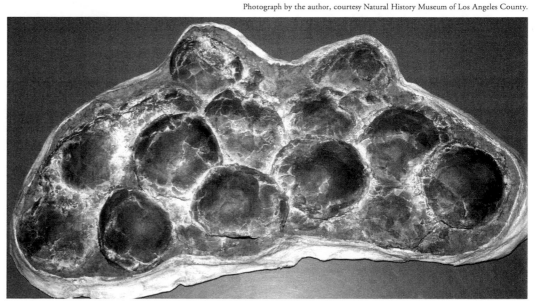

Titanosaur eggs (cast) from the Auca Mahuevo site in Patagonia (see "Introduction," section under sauropods).

Restoration of a titanosaur nest, with eggs and hatchlings, from the Auca Mahuevo site in Patagonia (see "Introduction," section under sauropods), part of the traveling exhibit "The Tiniest Giants: Discovering Dinosaur Eggs" debuting in 2001 at the Natural History Museum of Los Angeles County.

YOUNGOOLITHUS Zhao 1979
Name derivation: "Young [Chung-Chien, earlier incorrectly published spelling of Yang Zhungjian]" + Greek *oon* = "egg" + Greek *lithos* = "stone."
Type species: *Y. xiaguanensis* Zhao 1979.

Other species: ?*Y. xipingensis* (?author, ?date)
Occurrence: Lower to Upper Cretaceous of China.
Age: Early Cretaceous.
    ?Sauropod.

Glossary

Included herein are technical and some nontechnical terms that appear in this volume, but which are generally not defined anywhere else in the text. Definitions of terms were based in part upon those published in a number of earlier sources, these including various dictionaries of the English language, and also the following texts: A Dictionary of Scientific Terms *(Kenneth and Henderson 1960),* The Penguin Dictionary of Geology *(Whitten and Brooks 1972),* The Illustrated Encyclopedia of Dinosaurs *(Norman 1985),* The Dinosauria *(Weishampel, Dodson and Osmólska 1990),* Encyclopedia of Dinosaurs *(Currie and Padian 1997),* The Complete Dinosaur *(Farlow and Brett-Surman 1998), and "Ceratosaurus (Dinosauria, Theropoda), a Revised Osteology" (Madsen and Welles 2000).*

A PRIORI   Conclusion reached about a specific instance based upon something generally known.

ABDUCTION   Movement of part of the body away from the midline axis of the body (opposite of adduction).

ABDUCTOR   Muscle that brings one boney part away from another.

ABERRANT   Out of the ordinary; outside the normal range of variation.

ABRADED   Worn.

ABSTRACT   Relatively brief, concise summary of information that is presented (or is intended for presentation) in detail in a formal paper.

ACAMERATE   Vertebrae in which pneumatic characters are restricted to fossae, fossae not significantly invading the centrum.

ACCTRAN   Character states present at a node under accelerated transformation.

ACETABULUM   Cup-shaped socket in the pelvic girdle for the head of the femur.

ACOELOUS   Vertebrae having flattened centra.

ACROMIAL   Artery, process, or ligament pertaining to the acromion.

ACROMION   Ventral prolongation of the scapular spine.

ACUMINATE   Tapering to a point.

ADAPTATION   Ability of a species or population of organisms to undergo change in response to its environment.

ADIPOSE TISSUE   Animal fat.

ADDUCTION   Movement of part of a body toward the midline of the axis of the body (opposite of abduction).

ADDUCTOR   Muscle that brings one bony part towards another.

AEROBIC   Thriving only in the presence of free oxygen.

AKINETIC   Incapable of movement.

ALA   Winglike projection or structure.

ALIFORM   Wing-shaped.

ALLOMETRY   Study of relative growth; change of proportions relating to growth.

ALEATORY   Dependent on chance or some other uncertain outcome.

ALTRICIAL BEHAVIOR   Behavior in which a parent or parents care for the newly born.

ALVEOLI   Pits or sockets on the surface of an organ or a bone.

AMBIENS   Thigh muscle.

AMMONITE   Any of various invertebrate organisms of the Mesozoic, belonging to the Cephalopoda, having a flat, coiled, chambered shell.

AMNIOTE   Animal characterized by possession of amnion (membrane of reptiles, birds, and mammals) during fetal life.

AMPHIBIAN   Tetrapod adapted to live on both land and in water.

AMPHIBIOUS   Adapted to live on both land and in water, depending on their ontogenetic stage of development.

AMPHICOELOUS   Concave on both surfaces of a vertebral centra.

AMPHYPLATYAN   Flat on both ends of vertebral centra.

ANALAGOUS   Describing structures in different kinds of organisms which serve the same function, without being derived from the same ancestral structure.

ANASTOMOSING   Connecting in a branchlike manner.

ANGIOSPERM   Seed plant in which its seed is enveloped by a seed vessel fruit; the flowering plants.

ANGULAR   In most vertebrates, a dermal bone in the lower jaw, upon which rest the dentary and splenial bones.

ANLAGE   First structure or cell group showing development of part of an organ.

ANOXIC   Lacking oxygen.

ANTEBRACHIUM   Forearm or corresponding portion of a forelimb.

ANTERIOR   Toward the front end, also referred to as "cranial."

ANTHOPHILOUS   Attracted or feeding on to flowers.

ANTITROCHANTER   Articular surface of the ilium of birds, against which the trochanter of the femur plays.

ANTORBITAL   In front of the orbits of a skull, sometimes referred to as "preorbital."

ANTORBITAL FENESTRA   Opening in the skull, behind the external nares and in front of the orbit.

ANTORBITAL FOSSA   Depression surrounding the antorbital fenestra.

ANTRUM   Sinus or cavity.

APICAL   At the summit or tip.

APOPHYSIS   Process from a bone, usually serving as a place for muscle attachment.

APOMORPHIC   In cladistics, the derived state occurring only within members of an ingroup, when a character exhibits two states within that ingroup.

APOMORPHY   In cladistics, a derived character.

APONEUROSIS   Flattened tendon for insertion of, or investing of membrane, muscles.

APPENDICULAR SKELETON   That part of the skeleton including the pectoral girdles, forelimbs, pelvic girdles and hindlimbs.

Glossary

ARBOREAL Living mostly or exclusively in trees, bushes, or shrubs.

AQUATIC Living in the water.

ARCADE In anatomy, a bony bridge.

ARCHOSAURIA Diapsid group of reptiles (archosaurs) including dinosaurs, pterosaurs, "thecodontians," and crocodiles, defined primarily by the possession of an antorbital fenestra.

ARCTOMETATARSALIAN CONDITION Central metatarsal (III) pinched proximally, therefore obscured from view cranially, reduced or excluded from contact with the tibiotarsus.

ARMOR Bony scutes, plates, shields, horns, spikes and clubs possessed by some dinosaurs.

ARTICULAR In dinosaurs, the bone toward the rear of the mandible by which the lower jaw articulates with the quadrate bone.

ARTICULATED Jointed or joined together.

ASPIRATION Act of expelling breath.

ASSEMBLAGE Large group of fossils and other items found at the same location, considered to originate from the same time period.

ASTRAGALOCALCANEUM The astragalus fused to the calcaneum.

ASTRAGALUS Larger tarsal bone which mostly articulates with the tibia dorsally and metatarsus ventrally.

ATLANTAL Pertaining to the atlas bone.

ATLAS First cervical vertebra.

ATTRITIONAL Bone accumulations resulting from recurring "normal" death events of numerous individual animals over a long span of time (as opposed to a catastrophic, short-term mass mortality event).

AUTAPOMORPHY In cladistics, a character state unique to one taxon.

AVIAN Pertaining to birds.

AXIAL SKELETON That part of the skeleton including the vertebral column and ribs.

AXIS Second cervical vertebra.

BADLANDS Area of barren land heavily roughly eroded by water and wind into ridges, mesas, and peaks.

BARB Delicate threadlike structure that extends obliquely from a feather rachis, forming the vane.

BARBULE Small hooked process fringing the barbs of a feather.

BASAL Placed at or near the base; in cladistics, placed at or neat the base or "trunk" or a phylogenetic tree; a group outside a more derived clade; the earliest form of a lineage.

BASI- Prefix meaning "basis."

BASICRANIUM Base of the skull.

BASIOCCIPITAL Median bone in the occipital region of the skull, forming at least part of the occipital condyle.

BASIPTERYGOID Process of the basisphenoid contacting the pterygoid.

BASISPHENOID Cranial bone between the basioccipital and presphenoid.

BATTERY Distinctive tooth pattern wherein a number of small, slender teeth are tightly wedged together along the length of the jaw, with multiple teeth stacked in a single tooth position (as in hadrosaurs), forming a grinding or cutting surface.

BAUPLAN General body plan for a group of organisms; literally, a German word meaning an architect's or a building plan.

BED In geology, distinct layers of sedimentary rock.

BERINGIA Northerly land ridge connecting Asia and North America during the Cretaceous period.

BICONCAVE Concave on both ends.

BIFURCATED Forked; having two prongs or branches.

BINOMIAL Traditional system of nomenclature using two scientific names (for genus and species) in the formal scientific name of a species.

BIOCHRONOLOGIAL Pertaining to biochronology (the study of a short interval of geologic time defined on the basis of fossil evidence).

BIOGEOGRAPHIC Relating to biogeography, the study of the location and distribution of life on Earth.

BIOHERM Combining of two or more organisms into a single larger mass.

BIOLOGY Science of life.

BIOMASS Total estimated body mass or weight of all the animals of a population combined; also, the total mass or weight of a single individual.

BIOME Major community of living organisms.

BIOMECHANICS Study of the motion of a body of a given organism in the context of mechanical laws and principles.

BIOSTRATIGRAPHY Study of the distribution of fossils in distinct strata.

BIOTA Flora and fauna of a region.

BIOTURBATION Turning around of parts of a plant or animal during fossilization.

BIPED Animal that habitually walks on two feet.

BIPEDAL Habitually walking on two feet.

BIPEDALITY State of habitually walking on two feet.

BIVALVE Invertebrate organism consisting of two valves or plates, such as a mussel shell.

BIVARIATE Variable condition occurring simultaneously with another variable.

BODY FOSSIL Fossil consisting of an actual part of the organism.

BONEBED (also **BONE BED**) Sedimentary layer having a large concentration of fossil remains.

BOSS Raised ridge or rounded body part, such as the bony mass on the snout of some ceratopsians; in polacanthid ankylosaurs, an elongate or rounded keeled element incorporated into a pelvic shield.

BRAINCASE Part of the skull enclosing the brain.

BREVIS SHELF Median shelf on the postacetabular section of the ilium for the origin of some of the caudifumoralis brevis muscle.

BROWSER Animal that feeds on high foliage (*e.g.*, bushes, not grasses).

BUCCAL Pertaining to the cheek; the surface of a tooth toward the cheek or lip.

BUTTRESS Bony structure for reinforcement.

CALCANEUM Smaller tarsal bone, lateral to the astragalus and distal to the fibula.

CALCAREOUS Composed of, containing, or characteristic of calceum carbonate, calcium, or limestone.

CALLUS Bone growth.

CAMELLAE Pneumatic cavities in vertebrae.

CAMELLATE Vertebrae in which the internal structure is composed entirely of camellae, the neural arch laminae is not reduced, and with large external fossae also possibly present.

CAMERATE Vertebrae having large and enclosed camerae having a regular branching pattern, cameral generations usually being at least three, and with more branches at each generation.

CANALICULATE Possessing canals.

CANCELLOUS Made up of lamillae and slender fibres, joining to form a network-like structure.

CANINIFORM Teeth of "canine" form.

CAPITULAR Knoblike swelling at the end of a bone.

CARAPACE Hard outer covering to the body, like the shell of a turtle.

CARCASS Dead body of an animal.

CARINA On some bones and teeth, a keel-like ridge or edge.

CARNIVORE Flesh-eater.

CARNOSAUR In the original (and

abandoned) usage, an informal term generally referring to any large theropod; in the modern sense, a member of the Carnosauria, a restricted group of large theropods.

CARPAL   Pertaining to the wrist; also, a bone of the wrist.

CARTILAGE   Translucent firm and elastic tissue usually found in connection with bones and on the articular ends of limb bones.

CAT SCAN   (See CT scan.)

CATASTROPHIC   Pertaining to theories and beliefs that mass extinctions were the result of cataclysmic events.

CAUDAL   Pertaining to the tail; toward the tail; more recently, used in place of "posterior."

CENTRUM   Main body of the vertebra (ventral to the neural chord) from which rise the neural and hemal arches.

CERVICAL   Pertaining to the neck.

CERVICAL RING   (See RING.)

CHARACTER   Distinctive feature or trait of an organism, or any difference among organisms, that can be used in classification or in estimating phylogeny.

CHARACTER STATE   Range of expressions or conditions of a character.

CHELONIAN   Member of the Chelonia, a reptilian group including turtles and tortoises.

CHEVRON   Bone that hangs below a caudal vertebra.

CHIASMA   Crossing in an "X" shape of fibers.

CHOANA   Funnel-shaped internal nasal opening.

CHONDRIN   Gelatinous substance obtained from cartilage.

CHORISTODERE   Primitive, crocodile-like lepidosaur.

CINGULUM   Girdle-like structure on teeth.

CLADE   Monophyletic taxon as diagnosed by synapomorphies.

CLADISTICS   Scientific approach in taxonomy to classify groups of organisms in terms of the recency of their last common ancestor.

CLADOGRAM   Diagram representing the distribution of shared-derived characters for groupings of organisms.

CLASSIFICATION   Process of organizing clades into groups related by common descent.

CLAST   Made up of fragments.

CLAVICLE   Collar-bone forming the cranial portion of the shoulder-girdle.

CNEMIAL CREST   Crest along the cranial dorsal margin of the tibia.

COCHLEAR   Pertaining to the cochlea (part of the labyrinth of the ear).

COLD-BLOODED   Informal term for "ectothermic."

COEL   A hollow or excavation in a bone.

COELUROSAUR   In the original (and abandoned) usage, an informal term generally referring to all small theropods; in the modern sense, a large group of theropods including both small and gigantic forms.

COEVAL   Originating or living during the same time period.

COLLAGEN   Gelatinous protein present in all multicellular organisms, particularly in connective tissue.

COMMON ANCESTOR   In cladistics, a taxon exhibiting all synapomorphies of that taxon but neither autapomorphies nor the synapomorphies at higher levels within that taxon.

COMMUNITY   Ecological relationships between a local environment and all its fauna and flora.

COMPETITION   Simultaneous use of a limited resource by more than one species, resulting in conflicting efforts by them for continued survival.

CONDYLE   Process on a bone utilized in articulation.

CONE   (See Mammilla.)

CONGENERIC   Belonging to the same genus.

CONIFER   One of a group of gymnosperms including pines, spruces, larches, firs, and related plants.

CONSERVATIVE   Tending to remain unchanged, as in being similar to an ancestral group.

CONSPECIFIC   Belonging to the same species.

CONTINENTAL DRIFT   Continents moving on the Earth.

CONVERGENCE (also **CONVERGENT EVOLUTION**)   Organisms evolving similar appearances due to responses to similar lifestyle demands, though not sharing direct common ancestors.

COOSSIFIED   Bones fused together.

COPROLITE   Fossilized dung.

CORACOID   Bone between the scapula and the sternum, participates in the shoulder joint.

CORONOID PROCESS   In reptiles, prong-shaped bony process on the lower jaw for the attachment of jaw-closing muscles.

CORONUS (plural: **CORONUCES**) In ankylosaurids, usually conelike or hornlike bones, extending laterally from the caudal margins of the skull.

CORTICAL BONE   Bone tissue on the outer surface.

COSMOPOLITAN   Having a very wide or worldwide distribution.

COSTAL   Involving the ribs.

COTYLE   Cuplike cavity in a bone.

COTYPE   Additional type specimen, usually collected at the same time and from the same locality as the holotype, or a specimen, along with others, from which the type is defined.

CRANIA (also **CRANIAL SKELETON**)   Bones of the skull, excluding those of the lower jaws.

CRANIAL   Toward the head; more recently, used in place of "anterior."

CRANIUM   Skull, particularly the braincase, but excluding bones of the lower jaw.

CREST   Ridge or rounded area of bone; in hadrosaurids, a rounded area of bone on the upper part of the skull, sometimes containing hollow passages.

CRETACEOUS PERIOD   Third and latest division of the Mesozoic Era, 141 to 65 million years ago.

CRISTA   Crest or ridge.

CROCODILIAN   Member of the Crocodilia, a successful group of Mesozoic and extant archosaurs related to dinosaurs.

CROWN   Exposed part of the tooth.

CROWN GROUP   All descendants of the closest common ancestor of living forms.

CRUS   Shank.

CRUSTACEAN   A member of the Crustacea, a group of mostly aquatic invertebrates having segmented bodies, chitinous skeletons, and paired, jointed limbs.

CT SCAN (also **CAT SCAN**)   Process by which a computer is used to process data from a tomograph in order to display a reconstructed cross section of an organism's body without physically cutting into it.

CUIRASS   Protective covering of bony plates or scales.

CULTRIFORM   Sharp-edged and pointed.

CURSORIAL   Running.

CYCAD   Flowering gymnosperm prevalent from the Triassic to Early Cretaceous.

DECIDUOUS   Foliage that is shed or lost at the end of a growing season.

DELTOID   Thick, triangular muscle covering the shoulder joint.

DELTOPECTORAL CREST   Bony flange of the humerus for attachment of the deltoid and pectoralis muscles.

DELTRAN   Character states present at a node under delayed transformation.

DENTARY   Largest bone of the lower jaw, usually bearing teeth.

DENTICLE   Small bumplike processes along the edges of teeth.

DENTICULATE   Having denticles.

DENTIGEROUS   Tooth-bearing.

DENTITION   Teeth.

DEPOSIT   Accumulation of a substance (*e.g.*, sediment, bones).

DERIVED CHARACTER   More specialized character evolved from a simpler, more primitive condition.

DERM or **DERMAL**   Pertaining to the skin.

DERMAL ARMOR   Platelets or small plates of bone that grew in the flesh but were not connected to the skeleton.

DERMAL PLATE   (See Plate.)

DERMATOCRANIUM   Parts of the skull apparently having become externally embossed with continuous, amorphous, or rugose bone, or a combination of these.

DESCRIPTION   In paleontology, a detailed verbal representation of material.

DIAGENESIS   Processes affecting a sediment while it is at or near the Earth's surface.

DIAGNOSIS   Concise statement enumerating the distinctive characters of a particular organism.

DIAPOPHYSIS   Lateral or transverse process of the neural arch.

DIAPSID   Reptiles with a skull having a pair of openings behind the orbit, belonging to the group Diapsida.

DIASTEMA   Toothless space in a jaw, generally between two different kinds of teeth (such as the canine and post-canines in mammals).

DICOT   Plant having two seed-leaves.

DIDACTYL   Having two digits.

DIGIT   Toe or finger.

DIGITIGRADE   Walking with only the digits touching ground.

DIMORPHISM   State of having two different forms, usually according to sex.

DINOSAUR   One of a diverse group (Dinosauria) of terrestrial archosaurian reptiles that flourished from the Late Triassic through the Late Cretaceous periods of the Mesozoic Era, with an erect gait, closely related to other archosaurian groups such as crocodilians and pterosaurs, one lineage (maniraptoran theropods) seemingly the direct ancestors of birds.

DINOSAUROMORPHA   Ornithodiran clade including "lagosuchids," dinosaurs, and birds.

DINOSAUROMORPH   Member of the clade Dinosauromorpha.

DISARTICULATED   Pulled apart.

DISPERSAL   In biogeography, spreading out.

DISTAL   End of any structure farthest from the midline of an organism, or from the point of attachment; away from the mass of the body; segments of a limb or of elements within a limb; the edge of a tooth away from the symphysis along the tooth row.

DIVERGENCE   In evolution, moving away from a central group or changing in form.

DIVERTICULA   Sacs or tubes, "blind" at the distal end, that branch off from a cavity or canal.

DORSAL   Relating to the back; toward the back.

DORSI- (also **DORSO**)   Prefix meaning "back."

DORSUM   Back or upper surface.

DURA MATER   Tough membrane that lines the entire cerebro-spinal canal of the brain.

ECOSYSTEM   Ecological system formed by interaction of organisms and their environment.

ECOLOGY   Biological study of the relationship between organisms and their environment.

ECTEPICONDYLE   Lateral projection of the distal end of the humerus.

ECTETHMOID   In birds, lateral ethmoid bone ["ethmoids" being bones that form much of the walls of the nasal cavity].

ECTO   Prefix meaning "outer" or "outside."

ECTOCONDYLAR   Relating to the outer condyle of a bone.

ECTOPTERYGOID   Ventral membrane bone behind the palatine, extending to the quadrate.

ECTOTHERMIC   Relying on external sources of heat to maintain body temperature; popularly, "cold-blooded."

EDENTULOUS   Toothless.

EMBAYMENT   A baylike shape or depression in a bone.

EMBRYO   Young organism in pre-birth stages of development.

EMBRYOGENESIS   Origin of an embryo.

ENAMEL   Form of calceum phosphate forming the hard outer covering on teeth.

ENANTIOTHORNES   Group of Mesozoic birds.

ENDEMIC   Relating to an indigenous species or population occurring in a specific geographic range.

ENDO   Suffix meaning "within."

ENDOCAST   Fill-in of the brain cavity by sediment, revealing the shape of the brain.

ENDOGENOUS   Originating in an organism.

ENDOTHERMIC   Able to generate body heat internally by means of chemical reactions; popularly, "warm-blooded."

ENTAXONI   Within a group.

ENTEPICONDYLE   Lower end of the humerus.

ENVIRONMENT   Surroundings in which organisms live.

EOLIAN (also spelled **AEOLIAN**)   Caused by the wind.

EPAXIAL   Above the axis; dorsal.

EPICONDYLE   Medial/inner projection at the distal end of the humerus and femur.

EPICONTINENTAL SEAS   Large bodies of water that invade large land masses.

EPIDERMIS   Outer, nonvascular, and protective layer of the skin.

EPIGENIC   Pertaining to the development or growth on a surface.

EPIJUGAL   Hornlike projection off the jugal in ceratopsians.

EPIPHYSEAL   Pertaining to the part or process of a bone formed from a separate center of ossification, later fusing with the bone.

EPIPHYSIS   Part or process of a bone formed from a separate center of ossification, later fusing with the bone.

EPITHELIUM   Cellular tissue covering a free surface or lining a cavity or tube.

EPOCH   Lesser division of geologic time, part of a period.

EPOCCIPITAL   Small bone located on the edge of the ceratopsian frill.

ERA   Largest division of geologic time.

EROSION   Result of weathering on exposed rocks.

EUTHERIAN   Member of a large group of placental mammals.

EVOLUTION   Change in the characteristics of a population of organisms, caused by natural selection over time.

EXOCCIPITAL   Bone of the skull on each side of the foramen magnum.

EXOGENOUS   Originating outside an organism.

EXOSTIC BONE   Bone that has grown as a result of partial parietal detachment.

EXPIRATION   Act of emitting air from the lungs.

EXPOSURE   In geology, where rock is exposed due to weathering.

EXTENSOR   Muscle that extends a limb or part of a limb; also used to designate surfaces of a limb, manus, or pes.

EXTINCTION   Termination of a species.

FACIES   In geology, one of different types of contemporaneous deposits in a lateral series of deposits; also, the paleontological and lithological makeup of a sedimentary deposit.

FACULTATIVE   Having the ability to live and adapt to certain conditions, while not being restricted to those conditions.

FAMILY In Linnaean classification, a grouping of similar genera.

FAUNA All the animals of a particular place and time.

FEMUR Thigh-bone.

FENESTRA Opening in a bone or between bones.

FIBRO-LAMELLAR [also FIBRO-LAMELLAR] BONE Somewhat open hard tissue, filled with blood vessels, indicative of fast-growing bone.

FIBULA Smaller, outer shin bone.

FLEXOR Muscle which bends a joint; also used to designate surfaces of a limb, manus, or pes.

FLOAT Fossil material collected on the surface, rather than being excavated.

FLORA All the plants of a particular place and time.

FLUVIO- Pertaining to a river, stream, or sea.

FONTANELLE Opening on the frill in some ceratopsians.

FORAMEN Opening through a bone or membraneous structure.

FORAMEN MAGNUM Opening in the occipital area of the skull through which the spinal cord passes.

FORMATION In geology, a formally defined and mappable unit of sedimentary rock.

FOSSA Pit or trenchlike depression.

FOSSIL Preserved remains of an animal or plant at least 10,000 years old, usually formed through burial and possibly involving a chemical change; evidence of life in the geologic past.

FOSSILIZED Having become a fossil.

FOSSORIAL Animals adapted for digging.

FRACTURE Break in a bone.

FRONTAL Bone of the skull roof in front of the parietal.

FRONTOPARIETAL Frontal and parietal bones, usually referring to suture or fusion of both bones.

FUNCTIONAL MORPHOLOGY Study of the movements and patterns of locomotion of an organism, mostly relative to its form or structure.

FUSION In anatomy, the firm joining together of bones, either naturally or abnormally.

FUSED Firmly jointed together, usually when bones grow together; coossified.

GASTRALIA Belly ribs that help to support the viscera in some dinosaurs.

GASTROLITH Small "stomach" stone or "gizzard" stone that is swallowed for ballast or to grind up already consumed food.

GASTROPOD Mollusc belonging to the class Gastropoda.

GENESIS Suffix meaning "descent" or "formation."

GENUS Group of closely related species.

GEOLOGIC TIME Period of time spanning the formation of the Earth to the beginning of recorded history.

GEOLOGY Science of the study of the Earth.

GHOST LINEAGE Missing sections of a clade, unknown from the fossil record, but implied by phylogeny; theorized geological extension of the range of a taxon before its earliest known occurrence.

GINGLYMOID Hinge joint, or constructed like one.

GIRDLE Curved or circular structure, particularly one that encircles another.

GIZZARD Muscular portion of the stomach utilized in grinding up food.

GIZZARD STONE (See Gastrolith).

GLENOID Socket in the pectoral girdle to which the head of the humerus attaches.

GLIAL Having to do with glia, a supporting (neuroglia) cell of nervous tissue.

GLOSSOPHARYNGEAL NERVE Ninth cranial nerve.

GONDWANA Southern continent including South America, Africa, India, Madagascar, Australia, and Antarctica.

GRACILE Having a graceful or slim build of form.

GRADE In cladistics, a paraphyletic taxon as diagnosed by the absence and presence of synapomorphies, delineated based upon morphologic distance; also, in a series of bones, the gradual changing of shape of those bones.

GRAVIPORTAL Slow-moving or lumbering.

GREGARIOUS Animals of the same species living in groups rather than in isolation.

GYMNOSPERM Seed plant in which the seed is not enveloped by a fruit, including cycadophytes, seed ferns, conifers, and related plants.

HABITAT Place in which an organism or population of organisms normally lives or occurs.

HAEMAL (See HEMAL.)

HAEMAPOPHYSIS Platelike or spinelike process of the latero- ventral surfaces of a vertebral centrum.

HALF-RING In ankylosaurs, the unification of the first and second transverse rows of keeled plates to form a pair of yokes around the neck.

HALLUX First digit of the pes.

HALOPHYTIC PLANTS Plants capable of growing on salt-impregnated soils (*e.g.*, shores).

HATCHLING Organism newly hatched from an egg.

HAVERSIAN BONE Kind of secondary bone that replaces primary bone, forming a series of vascular canals called "Haversian canals."

HEAD-BUTTING Behavior in which two (usually male) individuals of the same species compete for dominance of their group by repeatedly colliding head to head.

HEMAL (or HAEMAL) Pertaining to blood or blood vessels.

HERBIVORE Plant-eater.

HERD Large group of (usually herbivorous) animals of the same species.

HETERO- Prefix meaning "other" or "different."

HETEROCHRONY Condition of having a different beginning and ending of growth, or a different growth rate for a different feature, relative to the beginning and end, or the rate of development, of the same feature in an ancestor; a kind of evolutionary mechanism.

HETEROGAMETIC Having an unequal pair of sex chromosomes.

HISTO Pertaining to tissue.

HISTOGENESIS Tissue-producing.

HISTOLOGY Study of the fine structure of body tissues.

HOLOTYPE Single specimen chosen to designate a new species.

HOMEOTHERMY Maintaining a fairly constant body temperature regardless of environmental temperature changes.

HOMEOTIC Having to do with the assumption of one part of likeness to another (*e.g.*, modification of a dorsal vertebra into a sacral vertebra).

HOMO- Prefix meaning "same" or "alike."

HOMODONTY Condition of having similar teeth throughout.

HOMOLOGOUS Similar because of common ancestry; similarity.

HOMOPLASY In cladistics, a shared similarity between taxa explained by character reversal, convergence, or chance, and not a result of common ancestry.

HORIZON Soil layer formed at a definite time and characterized by definite fossil species.

HUMERUS Upper arm bone.

HYOID Pertaining to a bone or series of bones lying at the base of the tongue.

HYPANTRUM In some reptiles, a notch on a vertebra for articulation with the hyposphene.

HYPAPOPHYSIS Ventral process on a vertebral centrum.

Glossary

HYPAXIAL Below the vertebral column; ventral.

HYPER- Prefix meaning "more than," "greater than," *etc.*

HYPEREXTENSION Atypical extension of a body part.

HYPERTROPHY Atypical enlargement or expansion of a body part.

HYPOCLEIDEUM Interclavicle bone.

HYPOGLOSSAL Relating to a cranial nerve distributed to the base of the tongue.

HYPOSPHENE In some reptiles, a wedge-shaped process on the neural arch of a vertebra, fitting into the hypantrum.

IBERIAN PENINSULA Region of southwestern Europe, consisting of Spain and Portugal, separated from France by the Pyrenees mountains.

ICHNITE Fossil footprint.

ICHNO- Prefix meaning "track" or "footprint."

ICHNOGENUS Genus name for a trackmaker.

ILIO-FEMORALIS Muscle attached to the ilium and femur.

ILIUM Dorsal bone of the pelvic arch; hipbone.

IMBRICATE Having edges that overlap in a regular arrangement.

IN OVO Referring to specimens preserved within fossil eggs.

IN SITU Referring to specimens in place in the ground where they are discovered.

INCISIFORM Incisor-shaped.

INCISOR Teeth at the very front of the mouth.

INCRASSATE Thickened or becoming thicker.

INDETERMINATE Incapable of being defined or classified.

INDEX FOSSIL Fossil restricted to a particular span of geologic time which can, therefore, be reliably utilized to date rocks in which other fossils are found.

INDEX TAXA Taxons known from abundant fossils that are restricted to a particular span of geologic time, and which can, therefore, reliably be used to date the rocks in which its fossils are found.

INFRA- Prefix meaning "below."

INFRAORDER In Linnaean classification, category between family and suborder.

INFRAPREZYGAPOPHYSAL Below the prezygapophysis.

INGROUP In cladistics, a monophyletic grouping of taxa.

INSECTIVOROUS Insect-eating.

INSPIRATION Act of drawing air into the lungs.

INTEGUMENT Outer covering, usually pertaining to skin.

INTERCENTRUM Second central ring in a vertebra having two vertical rings in each centrum.

INTERMONTANE Between mountains.

INTERORBITAL Between the orbits.

INTRA- Prefix meaning "within."

INTRASPECIFIC Within the same species.

INVERTEBRATE Animal without a backbone.

ISCHIUM Ventral and posterior bone of each half of the pelvic girdle.

ISOGNATHOUS Having both jaws alike.

ISOLATED Set apart from similar items.

ISOMETRICALLY Exhibiting equality in measurements or dimensions.

ISOTOPE Atom that differs in atomic weight from another atom of the same element.

JUGAL Skull bone between the maxilla and quadrate.

JUNIOR SYNONYM Taxon suppressed because another name, pertaining to the same fossil materials, was published previously.

JURASSIC PERIOD Second and middle division of the Mesozoic Era, 196.6 to 141 million years ago.

JUVENILE Young or immature animal.

JUXTACORTICAL Concerning surface lesions of extracortical origin.

KERATIN Matter composed of fibrous protein, the main constituent in vertebrates of such epidermal structures as hair, nails, and horn.

KINETIC In zoology, bones joined together but capable of movement.

K-T BOUNDARY (also **KT** and **K/T BOUNDARY**) In geologic time, the transition from the end of the Cretaceous (K) period to the beginning of the Tertiary (T), approximately 65 million years ago.

K-T EXTINCTION (also **KT EXTINCTION**) The termination of numerous (but not all) groups of animals and plants at the end of the Cretaceous period.

LABIAL Near the lip.

LACERTILIAN Member of the Lacertilia, a reptilian suborder comprising lizards.

LACRIMAL (also **LACRIMAL BONE**, **LACHRIMAL**) Skull bone contributing to the rostral border of the orbit.

LACUNAE Cavities in bones; also, spaces between cells.

LACUSTRINE Living in or beside a lake.

LAGS (See Lines of Arrested Growth.)

LAMELLA Thin scale- or platelike structure.

LAMELLAR Referring to a thin, scale- or platelike tissue structure.

LAMINA Thin sheet or layer.

LANDMARK (Morphologically) certain homologous features that are recognizable between animals (*e.g.*, orbit, teeth, *etc.*).

LATERAL At the side externally; away from the midline.

LATEROSPHENOID One of the bones of the braincase.

LAURASIA Hypothetical northern super-continent including North America, Europe, and parts of Asia.

LECTOTYPE Specimen chosen from syntypes to redesignate the type of a species.

LEPIDOSAUR Reptilians including lizards, snakes and their close relatives.

LIGAMENT Strong fibrous band of tissue that support joints between bones and joins muscles to bones.

LIGNACEOUS Pertaining to wood.

LINEAGE Continuous line of descent, over an evolutionary span of time, from a particular ancestor.

LINEAR In a line.

LINES OF ARRESTED GROWTH (also **LAGs**) Pattern of development wherein there are pauses in the deposition of bone and a related slower growth rate.

LINGUAL Pertaining to the tongue; the surface of a tooth toward the tongue.

LOCALITY In geology, a named place where specimens have been found.

LOCOMOTION An organism's ability to move from place to place; also, the manner in which an organism moves.

LONG BONE Limb bone.

LUMEN Cavity of an organ.

LUNATE Crescent-shaped.

M. Abbreviation identifying a muscle, preceding the formal name for that muscle.

MAMMILLA (also **MAMILLA**) Nipple-shaped structure; lower part of an eggshell unit, with a characteristic shape, also called the "cone."

MANDIBLE Lower jaw.

MANDIBULAR Relating to the mandible.

MANUS Part of the forelimb corresponding to the hand, comprising metacarpals and phalanges.

MARINE Pertaining to the sea.

MARL Muddy limestone.

MASS EXTINCTION Death of all members of a number of diverse animal groups apparently due to a common cause.

MATRIX Fossil-embedded rock.

MAXILLA Usually tooth-bearing principal bone in the upper jaw.

MAXILLARY Relating to the maxilla.

MEDIAL From the inside or inner; toward the midline.

MEDULLARY Pertaining to the medulla (posterior portion of the brain, continuous with the spinal cord).

MEGA- Prefix meaning "large."

MESIAL In a middle longitudinal or vertical plane; the edge of a tooth toward the symphysis or premaxillary midline; more recently, used in place of "anterior" in regards teeth.

MESIC Conditioned by moist, temperate climate.

MESODERM Embryonic layer lying between the ectoderm and endoderm.

MESOZOIC ERA Geologic time span during which nonavian dinosaurs flourished, 248 to 65 million years ago.

METABOLISM Constructive and destructive chemical changes in the body for maintenance, growth, and repair of an organism.

METACARPAL Relating to the metacarpus; also, a bone of the metacarpus, generally one per digit.

METACARPUS Bones of the manus between the wrist and fingers.

METAPHYSEAL Having to do with growing bone (see Metaphysis).

METAPODIAL In tetrapods, a bone of the metacarpus and metatarsus.

METAPODIUM In tetrapods, the metacarpus and metatarsus.

METATARSAL Relating to the metatarsus; also, a bone of the metatarsus, generally one per digit.

METATARSUS Part of the foot between the tarsus and toes.

MICRO- Prefix meaning "very small."

MIDLINE Imaginary line extending dorsally along the length of an animal.

MIGRATION Behavior pattern whereby a group of animals of the same species move from one location to another on a regular or recurring basis.

MINERALIZED Formerly organic matter that has been transformed into mineral matter, "petrified."

MODERN Living now or recently.

MOLLUSC (also MOLLUSK) Member of the Mollusca, a group of bilaterally symmetrical invertebrates, such as snails, clams, cephalopods, and other forms.

MONIMOSTYLIC Having quadrate united to squamosal and sometimes to other bones; exhibiting "monimostyly."

MONOPHYLETIC Group of taxa including a common ancestor and all of its descendants; derived from a single origin; having the condition of "monophyly."

MONOTREME A member of Monotremata, an order of mammals possessing jaws with horny sheaths.

MORPH Shape; also used as a suffix to denote a general shape, as for a group of organisms, in "archosauromorph" or "dinosauromorph."

MORPHOGENESIS Development of shape.

MORPHOLOGY Science of form.

MORPHOMETRIC Regarding the analysis or measurement of an organism's shape or form.

MORPHOMETRICS Quantitative analysis of shape.

MORPHOTYPE Type specimen of one form of a polymorphic species.

MOSASAURS Large Cretaceous marine lizards related to the modern monitor (not dinosaurs).

MULTI- Prefix meaning "many."

MULTITUBERCULATE Member of the Multituberculata, a successful group of early mammals that may have been the first herbivorous members of the Mammalia.

MUMMIFIED A state in which parts of a dead animal (e.g., soft tissues), which would normally not be preserved over time, are preserved.

MUMMY A dead body having some of its soft tissues preserved.

MUSCULATURE Arrangement of muscles.

MUZZLE Anterior part of the head containing the nostrils and jaws.

MYLOHYOID In the area of the hyoid bone and the posterior part of the mandible.

MYOLOGY Study of muscles.

NARIAL Pertaining to the nostrils.

NARIS Nostril opening.

NASAL Bone near the front of the skull, between the premaxilla and the frontal; also, that which pertains to the nostrils or nose.

NEO- Prefix meaning "new."

NEOCOMIAN Old term used to designate a subdivision of the Early Cretaceous period, equivalent to Hauterivian.

NEOGNATHOUS More advanced palate of modern birds (excluding ratites).

NEONATE Newly born organism.

NEONTOLOGICAL Pertaining to neontology (the study of newly born organisms).

NEOPANGAEA (also NEOPANGEA) Giant land mass comprising all major land masses apart from Central Asia.

NEOPLASIA Process of providing new or added tissue, generally involving pathology.

NEORNITHES Avian crown group including modern birds.

NEOTENOUS (also NEOTENY, NEOTENIC) State of being sexually mature while having retained some juvenile characteristic.

NEURAL Closely connected with nerves or nervous tissues.

NEURAL ARCH Bony bridge over the passage of the spinal cord.

NEURAL CANAL Canal formed by the neural arch and centrum.

NEURAL SPINE Spine rising up from the neural arch.

NEUROCENTRAL Having to do with a neurocentrum, a type of centrum in primitive vertebrates.

NEUROCENTRUM Type of centrum in primitive vertebrates.

NEUROCRANIUM Bony or cartilaginous case containing the brain and capsules of specials sense organs.

NICHE Unique place occupied by a particular species within a larger ecological community.

NODE (In cladistic classification) point on a cladogram where two or more lines meet, this constituting a taxon including all descendant taxa that will meet at that point; (morphologically) a knob or swelling.

NODE-BASED Defining a taxonomic group as the descendants of the most recent common ancestor of two other groups and all descendants of that ancestor.

NOMEN DUBIUM Taxon founded upon material of questionable diagnostic value; plural, *nomina dubia.*

NOMEN NUDUM Taxon improperly founded without published material, diagnosis, type designation, and figure; plural, *nomina nuda.*

NOMEN OBLATIM Taxon obsolete from disuse.

NOMENCLATURE Official naming or system of naming of taxa.

NONAVIAN (also NON-AVIAN) Pertaining to dinosaurs other than birds; also, not pertaining to birds in general.

NOTOCHORD Dorsal supporting axis of lowest vertebrates.

NUCHAL Pertaining to the neck.

OBLIGATE Limited or restricted to a particular mode of behavior or environmental condition.

OBTURATOR Pertaining to any structure in the area of the obturator foramen.

OBTURATOR FORAMEN Oval foramen within the ischium for the passage of the obturator nerve/vessels.

Glossary

OCCIPUT Back part of the skull.

OCCIPITAL CONDYLE Condyle with which the skull moves on the atlas and axis.

OCCLUSAL Where surfaces of upper and lower teeth touch when the jaws are closed.

OCCLUSION Surfaces of the upper and lower teeth making contact with each other when the jaws are closed in a bite.

ODONTOID Toothlike process.

OLECRANON Process for insertion of the triceps muscle at the proximal end of the ulna.

OLFACTORY Pertaining to the sense of smell.

OMNIVORE Animal that eats both plant and animal food.

ONTOGENY Growth and development of an individual.

OOID Oval.

OOSPECIES Specific name given to a genus of fossil egg.

OPISTHOCOELOUS Having the centrum concave posteriorly.

OPISTHOPUBIC Pubis that is directed rearward.

OPISTHOTIC Inferior caudal bony element of the otic capsule.

OPTIC Pertaining to vision.

ORBIT Bony cavity in which the eye is housed.

ORBITOSPHENOID Paired elements in the skull located between the presphenoid and frontal.

ORDER In Linnaean classification, a category including related families within a class.

ORGANIC Relating to things alive.

ORGANISM Any individual living being.

ORNAMENTATION Visible external body feature (*e.g.*, horn, frill, *etc.*) that primarily functions in social behavior.

ORNITH- Prefix meaning "bird" or "birdlike."

ORNITHODIRAN Member of Ornithodira (clade including, among other taxa, pterosaurs and dinosauromorphs).

ORNITHOLOGY Study of birds.

ORNITHURAE Group of modern birds.

ORTHAL Jaw movement that is straight up and down.

OSSEOUS Resembling or composed of bone.

OSSICLE Bony platelets set under the skin, serving as secondary armor, often round, oval, or subtriangular.

OSSIFICATION The process by which bone forms.

OSSIFIED TENDONS In ornithischians, strandlike calcified tissues that connect and strengthen the vertebrae.

OSSIFY To change into bone.

OSTEO- Prefix meaning "bone" or "relating to bones."

OSTEOCYTE Bone cell.

OSTEODERM Bony plates or scutes in the skin.

OSTEOGENESIS Formation of bone.

OSTEOLOGY Part of zoology dealing with the structure and development of bones.

OSTEON Haversian bone growth.

OSTRACOD Microscopic crustacean consisting of a hinged, bivalved shell.

OUTGROUP In cladistics, the character state occurring in the nearest relatives of an ingroup.

PALATE Roof of the mouth.

PALATINE One of the bones of the palate, located near the front of the skull and to the side of the vomer; also, pertaining to the palate.

PALEO- (also **PALAEO-**) Prefix meaning "ancient" or "past," pertaining to something very old or prehistoric.

PALEOBIOLOGY Study of ancient extinct organisms.

PALEOECOLOGICAL Pertaining to paleoecology (the study of the relationships between extinct organisms and their paleoenvironments).

PALEOECOLOGY Study of the relationships between extinct organisms and their paleo-environments.

PALEOENVIRONMENT Environmental conditions in the geologic past.

PALEOGEOGRAPHIC Pertaining to paleogeography (the study of the geographic distribution of life forms in the geologic past).

PALEOGNATHOUS BIRDS Primitive birds (including ratites).

PALEONTOLOGY Scientific study of past life, based on the study of fossil and fossil traces.

PALEOSOL Ancient soil that has become fossilized.

PALMER Surface of the manus in contact with the ground.

PALPEBRAL Small bone located on the rim of the eye socket, often forming a bony eyelid.

PALYNOLOGICAL Pertaining to palynology (the study of fossil pollen grains and spores).

PALYNOMORPH Spores, pollen, and cysts of certain algae.

PANGAEA (also **PANGEA**) Deduced huge super-continent formed by the collision of all Earth's continents during the Permian period.

PAPILLATED Having papillae (conical dermal structures constituting the beginning of feathers).

PARA- Prefix meaning "beside."

PARALIC Referring to tidal wave environments.

PARALLELISM (See Convergence.)

PARAPHYLETIC In cladistics, relating to a taxonomic group including a hypothetical common ancestor and only some of that ancestor's descendants.

PARASAGITTAL Parallel to the midline of an animal.

PARASPHENOID Membrane bone forming the floor of the braincase.

PARATYPE Specimen used along with the holotype in defining a new species.

PARIETAL Bone of the skull roof behind the frontal.

PAROCCIPITAL PROCESS Bony process at the back of the skull.

PARSIMONY In cladistic analysis, a subjective criterion for selecting taxa, usually that which proposes the least number of homoplasies.

PATHOGEN Disease-producing micro-organism.

PATHOLOGY The study of disease.

PATHOLOGIC Diseased.

PECTORAL Pertaining to the chest area of the skeleton.

PECTORAL GIRDLE Bones of the shoulder, including scapula, corocoid, sternum, and clavicle.

PEDAL Pertaining to the foot.

PEDICLE Backward-projecting vertebral process.

PEDOGENESIS Formation of soil.

PEDUNCLE Stalk- or stemlike process of a bone.

PELVIC GIRDLE Hip area of the skeleton, composed of the ilium, ischium, and pubis.

PELYCOSAUR One of a group of mammal-like reptiles of the Carboniferous and Permian periods, some having dorsal "sails" supported by elongated neural spines (not dinosaurs).

PENNACEOUS STRUCTURE Feather having a visible plumage (as opposed to down).

PENTADACTYL Having five digits.

PERAMORPHOSIS Evolutionary change wherein juveniles of a descendant species exhibit some adult characteristics of the ancestral species.

PERINATAL Close to the time of hatching or birth.

PERIOD Division of geologic time, a subdivision of an Era.

PERIOSTEAL BONE Bone formed by the periosteum.

PERIOSTEUM Tissue that forms bone at the periphory or outermost region of a growing bone.

PERMINERALIZED Having gone through the fossil forming process, wherein additional mineral materials are deposited in pore spaces of the originally hard parts of animals.

PES Foot.

PHALANGEAL FORMULA Formula giving the number of phalanges in the digits of the manus and pes.

PHALANX Segment of the digits, a bone of the fingers or toes.

PHYLOGENETIC Concerning the evolutionary relationships within and among groups of organisms.

PHYLOGENY Evolutionary treelike diagram or "tree" showing the relationships between ancestors and descendants.

PHYSIOLOGY Biological study dealing with the functions and activities of organisms.

PHYTOSAUR crocodile-like, semi-aquatic "thecodontians" of the Triassic (not dinosaurs).

PISCIVOROUS Fish-eating.

PLANTAR Pertaining to the sole of the foot.

PLANTIGRADE Walking with the entire sole of the foot touching the ground.

PLATE (also **DERMAL PLATE**) In paleobiology, a piece of bone embedded in the skin; in thyreophorans, a dermal bone consisting of a tall dorsal keel with rounded or sharp points.

PLATE TECTONICS Study of the plates making up the Earth's crust.

PLATIFORM Flattened shape.

PLATYCOELOUS Condition in which the posterior articular end of a vertebral centrum is flat.

PLESIOMORPHIC In cladistics, the more primitive character state of two that are exhibited within members of an ingroup while also occurring in the nearest outgroup; a primitive feature.

PLESIOSAUR General term for a member of a group of Mesozoic marine reptiles, some with smaller heads and longer necks, others with longer heads and shorter necks (not dinosaurs).

PLEUROCOEL Cavity in the side of a vertebral centrum.

PLEUROKINESIS Adaptation of skull bones to move to the side.

PLUMULACEOUS Downy feathers.

PNEUMATIC Bones penetrated by canals and air spaces.

PNEUMATOPORE Minute air cavity.

POLLEX In the manus, the thumb or innermost digit of the normal five.

POLYCAMERATE Vertebrae with large and enclosed camerae having a regular branching pattern, cameral generations usually numbering at least three, with more branches at each generation.

POLYPHYLETIC Associated groups that do not share a single common ancestor.

POLYTOMY In cladistics, more than two branchings of a tree.

POPLITEAL Region behind and above the knee-joint.

PORE Minute opening.

POST- Prefix meaning "after"; in anatomy, meaning "closer to the rear."

POSTACETABULAR PROCESS Portion of the ilium posterior to the acetabulum.

POSTCOTYLOID PROCESS Portion of jugal posterior to cup-shaped acetabular cavity.

POSTCRANIA (or **POSTCRANIAL SKELETON**) Skeleton excluding the skull.

POSTER Presentation of data at a technical gathering (*e.g.*, a symposium or annual meeting of the Society of Vertebrate Paleontology) in the form of a poster, generally including drawings, photographs, charts, cladograms, graphs, *etc.*

POSTERIOR Toward or at the rear end, more recently generally referred to as "caudal."

POSTMORTEM Following the death of an organism.

POSTURE Walking or standing position.

POSTZYGAPOPHYSIS Process on the posterior face of the neural arch, for articulation with the vertebra behind it.

POSTURE Walking or standing position.

PRE- Prefix meaning "before."

PREACETABULAR PROCESS Portion of the ilium cranial to the acetabulum.

PREARTICULAR Bone in the lower jaw of primitive tetrapods.

PRECOCIAL Species in which the young are relatively advanced upon hatching.

PROCUMBENT Forwardly directed.

PRECURSOR Earlier form of life from which a later form is descended.

PREDATOR Organism that hunts and eats other organisms.

PREDENTARY In ornithischians, a small crescent-shaped bone located at the tip of the lower jaw.

PREMAXILLA A usually paired bone at the front of the upper jaw.

PREOCCUPIED In zoological nomenclature, a taxonomic name identical to one published previously by another author.

PREORBITAL Anterior to the orbit, sometimes referred to as "antorbital."

PREPARATION One or more procedures applied to a fossil specimen so that the specimen can be strength-ened, handled, preserved, studied, displayed, *etc.*

PREPARATOR Person who prepares fossils for study or display.

PRESERVATION General condition of a fossil specimen, referring to its quality and completeness.

PREY Creature hunted and caught for food.

PREZYGAPOPHYSIS Process on the cranial face of the neural arch, for articulation with the vertebra in front of it.

PRIMARY BONE Bone that is formed as an organism grows.

PRIMITIVE Characters or features found in the common ancestor of a taxonomic group, which are also found in all members of that group, also referred to as "plesiomorphic"; also (more generally), less developed, earlier.

PRIORITY Rule in scientific nomenclature stating that, in the case of different taxonomic names given to the same form or groupings of forms, the name published first is valid.

PRO- Prefix meaning "for."

PROCAMERATE Vertebrae in which deep fossae penetrate the median septum, are not enclosed by ostial margins.

PROCESS Outgrowth or projection of bone.

PROCOELOUS Condition in which the cranial articular end of a vertebral centrum is concave and the caudal end strongly convex.

PROGENESIS Evolutionary change wherein sexual maturity takes place earlier in the descendant species than in the ancestor.

PROKINESIS Primitive avian kind of cranial kinesis derived from either akinetic or mesokinetic archosaurian skulls.

PROOTIC Anterior bone of the otic capsule.

PROPALINY Back and forward movement of the jaws.

PROTO- Prefix signifying "first" or "earliest."

PROTOFEATHER Incipient feather including branching barbs, but lacking the aerodynamic quality of the true avian feather.

PROVENANCE Place of origin.

PROVENTRICULUS Second stomach; in birds, the glandular stomach cranial to the gizzard.

PROXIMAL Nearest to the center of the body; toward the mass of the body; segment of a limb or of elements within a limb.

PTEROSAUR One of a group of flying reptile of the Mesozoic, related to (but not) dinosaurs, with batlike wings consisting of membrane stretched from an elongated finger to the area of the hips, one group generally having teeth and long tails, the other toothless and possessing short tails.

PTERYGOID Winglike posterior bone of the palate.

PUBIC Relating to the pubis.

PUBIS Antero-ventral bone of the pelvic girdle.

PUBOISCHIAL Place where the pubis and ischium meet.

PYGOSTYLE In birds and some theropods, a structure at the tail end of the vertebral column consisting of fused vertebrae.

PYOGENIC Pus-forming material, involving bacteria.

QUADRATE In birds, reptiles and amphibians, the bone with which the lower jaw articulates.

QUADRATOJUGAL Bone bone connecting or overlying the quadrate and jugal.

QUADRUPED Animal that walks on all four feet.

QUADRUPEDALITY Habitually walking on four legs.

RACHIS (also spelled **RHACHIS**) Shaft of a feather.

RADIALE Carpal bone aligned with the radius.

RADIATION Process by which a group of species diverge from a common ancestor, thereby producing an increased biological diversity, usually over a relatively short span of time.

RADIOMETRIC DATA Information gleaned via the measurement of decay, as in radiometric age dating.

RADIOMETRIC AGE DATING Dating method involving the measurement of decay, at a constant known rate, in various naturally occurring radioactive isotopes.

RADIUS Smaller forelimb bone between the humerus and carpals, lying next to the ulna.

RAMUS Branchlike structure.

RANK In classification, the position of a given level relative to levels above and below it.

RAPTOR One of various modern birds of prey, including falcons and hawks; also, a suffix used in the names of a number of sometimes rather diverse theropods; more recently, a popular term inaccurately used to designate any dromaeosaur.

RAPTORIAL Subsisting by or adapted for the seizure of prey.

RATITE One of a group of flightless birds having an unkeeled sternum; also, an eggshell morphotype in which the shell structure is discrete only in the inner one-sixth to one half of the shell thickness (mammillary layer); most of the eggshell formed of a single, continuous layer.

RECONSTRUCTION Drawn or modeled skeleton or partial skeleton, based upon the original fossil remains, often incorporating extrapolation or knowledge of the more complete remains of other taxa (sometimes used to mean "restoration").

RECTRICES Stiff tail feathers of a bird or some non-avian theropods, used in steering.

RECTUS CAPITUS A neck muscle.

RECURVED Curved backward.

RED BEDS Sedimentary beds that are reddish in color.

RELICT Not functional, although originally adaptive.

REMEX (plural: **REMIGES**) Large feather or quill on a bird's wing, consisting of primaries and secondaries.

REMODELING Resorption and reprecipitation of bone for the purpose of maintaining its physiological and mechanical competence.

RENAL Pertaining to the kidneys.

RESONATOR Device that causes sound to be produced through sympathetic vibrations at specific frequencies.

RESPIRATION Breathing process, accomplished by an exchange of gases between an organism and its surrounding atmosphere.

RESPIRATORY TURBINATE (also **RT**) Thin, complex structure consisting of cartilage or bone in the nasal airway.

RESTORATION In paleontology, a drawn, sculpted, or other representation of a fossil organism as it may have appeared in life (sometimes used as synonymous with "reconstruction").

RETICULAR Bone possessing networklike interstices.

REVERSAL (In cladistic classification) transformation of a character in an advanced lineage back to its ancestral state.

"REVUELETIAN" Infrequently used term, often employed by authors in the New Mexico area, referring to the early to middle Norian stage of the Late Triassic period.

"RHAETIAN" Mostly obsolete term referring to a stage of the Upper Triassic of England.

"RHAETIC" Basically lithostratigraphic obsolete term referring to a sequence representing a part of "Rhaetian" time, the lower part of the Westbury Formation.

RHAMPHOTHECA Horny sheath of a bird's beak.

RHYNCHOSAUR A member of the Rhynchosauria, a group of large, squat, beaked, archosaur-like reptiles of the Triassic.

RIB Elongate and sometimes curved bone of the trunk articulating with vertebrae.

RIGOR MORTIS Temporary muscular stiffening after death.

RIMO- Prefix meaning "with a cleft."

RING (also **CERVICAL RING**) In ankylosaurs, curved group of from two to six elements surrounding the dorsal and lateral areas of the neck.

RIPARIAN Living on, growing on, or frequenting the banks of rivers or streams.

ROBUST Strongly formed or built; also, a method of study or analysis, verified by past results, which will probably result in a correct inference.

ROSTRAL (also **ROSTRUM**) In ceratopsians, median unpaired bone located at the tip of the upper jaw; also, toward the rostrum or tip of the head (term replacing "anterior").

RUGOSE Possessing a rough surface (or "rugosity").

SACRAL Pertaining to the sacrum.

SACRAL RIB Rib that connects the sacral vertebrae to the pelvis.

SACRUM Structure formed by the sacral vertebrae and pelvic girdle.

SAGITTAL Pertaining to the midline on the dorsal aspect of the cranium.

SAUROPOD HIATUS Expanse of time (from the Cenomanian to the Maastrichtian) during which sauropods seem to have been absent from the North American continent.

SAUROPSID All reptiles excluding synapsids.

SCANSORIAL Adapted to climbing.

SCAPULA Shoulder blade.

SCAVENGER Animal that feeds on dead animal flesh or other decomposing organic matter.

SCLEROTIC RING Ring of a series of overlapping bones around the outside of the eyeball.

SCUTE Low ridged, keeled, oval-shaped, horny or bony element embedded in the skin.

SECONDARY BONE Bone formed during internal reconstruction following the dissolution and reconstitution of preexisting bone.

SEDIMENT Deposit of inorganic or organic particles.

SEDIMENTARY ROCKS (also **SEDIMENTS**) Rocks formed from sediment.

SELECTION Principle that organisms having a certain hereditary characteristic will have a tendency to reproduce at a more successful rate than those of the same population not having this characteristic, consequently increasing their numbers in later generations.

SELLA   Depression.

SEMICAMELLATE   Vertebrae having limited camellae, with possible presence of large camerae also.

SEMILUNATE   Having the approximate shape of a half-crescent.

SENIOR SYNONYM   Taxon having priority over another identically named taxon and regarded as the valid name, because of the former's earlier publication.

SEPTUM   Partition separating spaces.

SERRATED   Having a notched cutting edge.

SEXUAL DIMORPHISM   Marked differences in shape, shape, color, structure, *etc*. between the male and female of the same species.

SHIELD   In polacanthid ankylosaurs, a flat, broad layer of bone that covers the pelvis and sacrum (including the presacral rod).

SIGMOID   S-shaped.

SILICICLASTIC   Relating to clastic, noncarbonate rocks that are almost exclusively silicon-bearing, as forms of quartz or as silicates.

SINUS   Space within a body.

SINUSOIDALLY   Having a small space for blood.

SISTER GROUP (or SISTER TAXON, SISTER CLADE)   Group of organisms descended from the same common ancestor as its closest group.

SOCIAL BEHAVIOR   Association of two or more individuals of a single species over a period of time other than the usual interaction of males and females for the purpose of reproduction.

SOMPHOSPONDYLUS   Vertebrae in which internal structure is made up entirely of camellae, the neural arch laminae are reduced, and the neural spine has an inflated appearance.

SPATULATE   Spatula-shaped.

SPECIALIZATION   Modification in a particular way.

SPECIALIZED   Modified in a particular way in response to certain environmental conditions.

SPECIES   In paleontology, a group of animals with a unique shared morphology; in zoology, a group of naturally interbreeding organisms that do not naturally interbreed with another such group.

SPECIMEN   Sample for study.

SPHENETHMOID   A principal bone of the ethmoid [regarding bones forming a considerable part of the walls of the nasal cavity] region of the skull.

SPHENOID   Large, wedge-shaped bone at the base of the skull.

SPINE   In thyreophorans, a tall, pointed element having a solid, rounded base, its diameter less than the total height.

SPINAL   Having to do with the backbone or tail.

SPINAL COLUMN   Backbone and tail, comprising articulated vertebrae.

SPINAL CORD   Nervous tissue contained in the vertebral or spinal canal.

SPLATE   In thyreophorans, a plate with a spinelike cranial leading edge bearing a point taller than the upper margin of the plate, tending to incline posteriorly.

SPLENIAL   Dermal bone in the lower jaw, covering much of Meckel's groove.

SQUAMOSAL   In the vertebrate skull, a bone that forms part of the posterior side wall.

STEM-BASED   Pertaining to a taxonomic group defined as all those entities that share a more recent common ancestor with one group than with another.

STEREOSCOPIC   Pertaining to the ability to see in three dimensions.

STERNAL   Pertaining to the breastbone or chest.

STERNUM   Breastbone.

STRATIGRAPHY   Study of the pattern of deposition.

STRATUM   Layer of sediment.

STREPTOSTYLY   Adaptation of the skull in which the quadrate is in movable articulation with the squamosal.

SUB-   Prefix meaning "under."

SUBFAMILY   In Linnaean classification, a category smaller than a family, including genus one or more.

SUBGENUS   Subtle classification between a genus and a species; a group of related species within a genus.

SUBORDER   In Linnaean classification, a category smaller than an order, larger than an infraorder, including one or more families.

SUITE   Group of characters associated with a particular organism or species.

SULCATION   Fluting; formation of furrows and ridges in a bone.

SULCUS   Groove in a bone.

SUPER-   Prefix meaning "greater" or "above."

SUPRA-   Prefix meaning "above" or "over."

SUPRAORBITAL   Small bone along the upper rim of the orbit of the skull; in ceratopsians, a horn above the eye or brow.

SUPRATEMPORAL FENESTRA   Opening in the top of the skull, posterior to the orbit.

SURANGULAR   Bone of the upper rear area of the lower jaw, contacting (and posterior to) the dentary, the angular, and the articular.

SUTURE   Line where bones contact each other.

SYMPHYSIS   Line of junction of two pieces of bone.

SYMPLESIOMORPY   In cladistics, a character state shared by a member of one higher-level taxon with a member of a more primitive higher-level taxon.

SYN-   Prefix meaning both "together" and "with"; also "united" or "fused."

SYNAPOMORPHY   Shared/derived feature defining a monophyletic group; unique character shared by two or more taxa.

SYNAPSID   Member of the Synapsida, a group of tetrapods having a skull with one opening behind the eye socket, including pelycosaurs, therapsids, and mammals.

SYNCLINE   In bedrock, a low, troughlike area in which rocks incline together from opposite sides.

SYNONYM   Different names for the same taxon.

SYNSACRUM   Single-unit structure formed by the fusion of several vertebrae.

SYNTYPE   When a holotype and paratypes have not been selected, one of a series of specimens used to designate a species.

SYSTEMATICS   Scientific study that involves the classification and naming of organisms according to specific principles.

TABLE   In a vertebra, a bony platform lateral to the base of a neural spine; also, the top of the skull.

TACHYMETABOLIC   Having a rapid metabolic rate.

TAPHONOMY   Study of the processes of burial and fossilization of organisms.

TARSAL   Ankle bone.

TARSOMETATARSUS   In birds and some dinosaurs, a bone formed by the fusion of the distal row of tarsals with the second to fourth metatarsals.

TARSUS   Region where the leg and foot join; ankle bones.

TAXON   Definite unite in the classification of animals and plants.

TAXONOMY   Science of naming and classifying biological organisms.

TECTUM SYNOTICUM   Cartilaginous arch between otic capsules representing cartilaginous roof in higher vertebrates, tegmen or roof of cranium in lower vertebrates.

TEMPORAL   Bone on either side of

the skull that forms part of its lateral surface; also, pertaining to that area of the skull.

TERRESTRIAL   Land-dwelling.

TERRITORIAL   Displaying a pattern of behavior whereby an organism or group of organisms of one species inhabit a particular area, and defend that area against intrusion by other individuals of that species.

TETHYS OCEAN (also TETHYSIAN SEAWAY)   Seaway that existed between Laurasia and Gondwana during the early Cretaceous.

TETRADACTYL   Having four digits.

TETRAPOD   Vertebrate with four limbs.

TEXTURE   Concerning fossil eggs, a sequence of horizontal ultrastructural zones of an eggshell, also called "eggshell unit macrostructure."

THECODONT   Teeth set in sockets.

"THECODONTIAN" (also, formerly "THECODONT")   One of an obsolete and artificial "order" (Thecodontia) of early archosaurian reptiles of the Late Permian and Early Triassic, some of which may have been ancestral to dinosaurs, pterosaurs, and crocodiles.

THERIAN   Group of more advanced mammals, including marsupials and placentals.

THERMOREGULATION   One of various processes by which the body of an organism maintains internal temperature.

THORACIC   Pertaining to the thorax; in the chest region.

THORAX   Part of the body between the neck and abdomen.

TIBIA   Shin bone.

TIBIOTARSUS   In birds and some dinosaurs, the tibial bone to which are fused the proximal tarsals.

TOMOGRAPHY   Recording internal images in a body via X-rays; a CT (or CAT) scan.

TOOTH BATTERY   (See Battery.)

TOPOLOGICAL   Pertaining to the specific areas of a skeleton or body.

TRABECULAE   Small sheets of bone.

TRACE FOSSIL   Not the actual remains of an extinct organism, but rather the fossilized record of something left behind by that organism (*e.g.*, a footprint); the fossil record of a living animal.

TRACKSITE   Location of fossil footprints.

TRACKWAY   Series of at least three successive footprints made by a moving animal.

TRANSGRESSION   In geology, in the intrusion of a body of water onto a land mass.

TRANSVERSE PROCESS   Laterally directed process of the vertebral centrum, for attachment of intervertebral muscles.

TRI-   Prefix meaning "three."

TRIASSIC PERIOD   First and earliest division of the Mesozoic Era, 248 to 196.6 million years ago.

TRIDACTYL   Having three digits.

TRIGEMINAL   Consisting of or pertaining to three structures.

TRIGEMINAL NERVE   Fifth cranial nerve.

TRIPODAL   Upright stance incorporating the hind feet and tail.

TROCHANTER   Prominence or process on the femur to which muscles are attached.

TROCHLEAR   Pulley-shaped.

TROPHIC   Pertaining to food or the feeding process.

TROPICAL   Hot and humid area with lush vegetation.

TUBER (plural TUBERA)   Rounded protuberance; a cranial projection of the tibia.

TUBERCLE   Small, rounded protuberance; in polacanthid ankylosaurs, a raised knob of bone, groups of which are clustered and packed between the bosses of the sacral shields.

TUBERCULATE   Having or resembling tubercles.

TUBULE   Small, hollow, cylindrical structure.

TUFFACEOUS   Rock comprising compacted volcanic ash that varies in size from fine sane to coarse gravel.

TYMPANIC   Pertaining to the ear or eardrum.

TYPE LOCALITY   Geographic site at which a type specimen or type species was found and collected.

TYPE SPECIMEN   Specimen used to diagnose a new species.

ULNA   In the forearm, the larger long bone on the medial side, parallel with the radius.

ULNARE   In the proximal row of carpals, the bone at the distal end of the ulna.

UNCINATE PROCESS   In birds and some reptiles, a process on the ribs which overlaps other ribs.

UNGUAL   Phalanx bearing a nail or claw.

UNGULIGRADE   Walking on hoofs.

VACUITY   Open space.

VAGUS   Tenth cranial nerve.

VARIATION   Range of appearance within a group of organisms.

VARIETY   In biology, a taxonomic category below the species level, comprising naturally occurring or selectively bred individuals having varying characteristics.

VASCULAR   Of or pertaining to the circulatory system.

VASCULARIZED   Possessing blood vessels.

VASCULARIZATION   Formation or development of blood vessels.

VENTER   Smooth concave surface; also, abdomen, or a lower abdominal surface.

VENTRAL   From beneath, relating to the belly or venter [abdomen or lower abdominal surface]; toward the belly.

VENTRI- (also VENTRO)   Prefix meaning "belly."

VERTEBRA   Bony segment of the backbone.

VERTEBRATE   Animal with a backbone.

VERTEBRATE PALEONTOLOGY   Scientific study of fossil animals having backbones.

VICARIANCE   Branching pattern of faunal distribution.

VISCERA   Internal organs of the body, particularly those of the digestive tract.

VOLANT   Flying or capable of flying.

VOLCANISM   Volcanic activity or force.

VOMER   Bone at the front of the palate.

ZOOLOGICAL   Pertaining to zoology (the science dealing with the structure, behavior, functions, classification, evolution and distribution of animals).

ZOOPHILOUS   Plants that are assisted in their propagation by animals.

ZYGAPOPHYSIS   Bony, usually peg-like process on the neural arch of a vertebra, by which it articulates with other vertebrae.

ZYGOMATIC   Bony arch of the cheek.

Bibliography

[Anonymous], 1865. See Owen 1865.

[Anonymous], 1995, *Polacanthus* found in museum: *Geology Today*, March-April, p. 45.

[Anonymous, 2001], The big ones are here! (foldout guidebook to the North American Museum of Ancient Life, Lehi, Utah, 8 pages.

[Anonymous, 2001], Field guide foldout guidebook to the North American Museum of Ancient Life, Lehi, Utah, 12 pages.

Abel, Othenio, 1926, *Amerikafahrt, Eindrücke, Beobachtungen und Studien eines Naturforschers auf eine Reise nach Nordamerika und Westindien.* Jena: Gustav Fischer, x, 462 pages.

Abler, William, 2001, A kerf-and-drill model of tyrannosaur tooth serrations, *in*: Darren Tanke and Kenneth Carpenter, editors, *Mesozoic Vertebrate Life: New Research Inspired by the Paleontology of Philip J. Currie.* Bloomington and Indianapolis, Indiana: Indiana University Press, pp. 84–89.

Ackerman, Jennifer, 1998, Dinosaurs taking wing: *National Geographic*, 194 (1), pp. 74–99.

Adams, Jason, and Chris Organ, 2001, Descriptive histology of ossified tendons from an articulated specimen of *Brachylophosaurus canadensis*: *Journal of Vertebrate Paleontology*, 21 (Supplement to Number 3), Abstracts of Papers, Sixty-first Annual Meeting, p. 27A.

Alber, W. L., 1992, The serrated teeth of tyrannosaurid dinosaurs and biting structures in other animals: *Paleobiology*, 18, pp. 161–183.

Alexander, R. McN., 1976, Estimates of speeds of dinosaurs: *Nature*, 261, pp. 129–130.

_____, 1985, Mechanics of posture and gait of some large dinosaurs: *Zoological Journal of the Linnean Society*, 83, pp. 1–25.

_____, 1996, *Tyrannosaurus* on the run: *Nature*, 379, p. 121.

_____, 1998, All-time giants: the largest animals and their problems: *Palaeontology*, 31, pp. 1231–1245.

Alexander, R. McN., G. M. O. Maloiy, R. Njau, and A. S. Jayes, 1979, Mechanics of running of the ostrich (*Struthio camelus*): *Journal of Zoology, London*, 187, pp. 169–178.

Alif'anov, Vladimir R. Averianov, A.O. in press, *Ferganasaurus verzilini* gen. & sp. n., a new sauropod (Dinosauria, Saurischia, Sauropoda) from the Middle Jurassic of Fergana Valley, Kirghizia: *Journal of Vertebrate Paleontology*, 23 (2), pp. 358–372.

Alif'anov, Vladimir R., Mikhail B. Ef'imov, I. V. Novikov, and Michael Morales, 1999, [A new psittacosaur complex of tetrapods from the Lower Cretaceous Shestakova locality (southern Siberia)]: *Doklady Akademii Nauk*, 369, pp. 491–493.

Allain, Ronan, 2001, Redescription de *Streptospondylus altdorfensis*, le dinosaure théropode de Cuvier, du Jurassique de Normandie: *Geodiversitas*, 23 (3), pp. 349–367.

_____, 2002a, Discovery of megalosaur (Dinosauria, Theropoda) in the Middle Bathonian of Normandy (France) and its implications for the phylogeny of basal Tetanurae: *Journal of Vertebrate Paleontology*, 23 (3), pp. 548–563.

_____, 2002b, The phylogenetic relationships of Megalosauridae within basal tetanurine theropods (Dinosauria): *Journal of Vertebrate Paleontology*, 23 (Supplement to Number 3), Abstracts of Papers, Sixty-second Annual Meeting, p. 31A.

_____, 2002c, Les Megalosauridae (Dinosaur, Theropoda). Nouvelle découverte et révision systématique: implications phylogénetiques et paléobiogéographiques. PhD thesis, Muséum National d'Histoire Naturelle, Paris, 322 pages (unpublished).

Allain, Ronan, and Daniel J. Chure, 2002, *Poekilopleuron bucklandii*, the theropod dinosaur from the Middle Jurassic (Bathonian) of Normandy): *Palaeontology*, 45 (6), pp. 1107–1121.

Alonso, R. N., 1980, Icnitas de dinosaurios (Ornithopoda, Hadrosauridae) en el Cretácico superior del norte Argentina: *Acta Geológica Lilloana*, 15 (2), pp. 55–63.

Ambrose, D., 1991, A tentative history of Lesotho palaeontology: *National University of Lesotho Journal of Research, Occasional Publication*, 1, pp. 1–38.

Amédro, F., F. Magniez-Jannin, C. Colleté, and C. Fricot, 1995, L'Albien-type de l'Aube, France: une revision nécessaire: *Geologie de la France*, 2, pp. 25–42.

Andersen, Arthur F., Ralph E. Chapman, Jason Dickman, and Kelly Hand, 2001, Using rapid prototyping technology in vertebrate paleontology: *Journal of Vertebrate Paleontology*, 21 (Supplement to Number 3), Abstracts of Papers, Sixty-first Annual Meeting, p. 28A.

Andersen, Arthur F., Brian Wilcox, and Peter Larson, 2002, 3-D scan of *Tyrannosaurus rex* skull: *Journal of Vertebrate Paleontology*, 23 (Supplement to Number 3), Abstracts of Papers, Sixty-second Annual Meeting, p. 32A.

Anderson, J. F., A. Hall-Martin, and Dale A. Russell, 1985, Long-bone circumferences and weight in mammals, birds and dinosaurs: *Journal of the Zoological Society of London*, 207, pp. 53–61.

Anderson, J. M., and H. M. Anderson, 1984, The fossil content of the Upper Triassic Molteno Formation, South Africa: *Palaeontologia Africana*, 25, pp. 39–59.

Anton, John A., 2001, Thermo-powered ceratopsians? A thermodynamic model proposing another role for gastroliths: *Journal of Vertebrate Paleontology*, 21 (Supplement to Number 3), Abstracts of Papers, Sixty-first Annual Meeting, pp. 28A–29A.

_____, in preparation, Acoustic amplification by the crest of *Triceratops*.

Antunes, Miguel Telles, 1976, *Dinossáurios Eocretácicos de Lagosteiros.* Lisban: Universidade Nova de Lisboa, Ciencias de Terra, 35 pages.

Antunes, Miguel Telles, and Denise Sigogneau-Russell, 1996, Le Crétacé terminal portugais et son apport au problèm de l'extinction des dinosaures: *Bulletin du Muséum National d'Histoire Naturelle, Paris*, série 4C, 18 (4), pp. 595–606.

Apesteguía, Sebastian, and Olga Gimènez, 2001a, The Late Jurassic–Early Cretaceous worldwide record of basal titanosauriforms and the origin of titanosaurians (Sauropoda): new evidence from the Aptian (Lower Cretaceous) of Chubut Province, Argentina: *Journal of Vertebrate Paleontology*, 21 (Supplement to Number 3), Abstracts of Papers, Sixty-first Annual Meeting, p. 29A.

_____, 2001b, A titanosaur (Sauropoda) from the Gorro Frigio Formation (Aptian, Lower Cretaceous), Chubut Province, Argentina: *Ameghiniana*, XVII Jornadas Argentinas de Paleontologia de Vertebrados, Resúmes, Esquel, 16–18 de mayo de 2001, p. 4R.

Archer, Brad, and John P. Babiarz, 1992, Another tyrannosaurid dinosaur from the Cretaceous of northwest New Mexico: *Journal of Paleontology*, 66, pp. 690–691.

Archibald, J. David, Hans-Dieter Sues, Alexander O. Averianov, I. Danilov, A. Rezvyi, D. Ward, C. King, and N. Morris, 1999, New paleontologic, biostratigraphic, and sedimentologic results at Dzharakuduk (U. Cret.) Kyzylkum Desert, Uzbekistan: *Journal of Vertebrate Paleontology*, 19 (Supplement to Number 3), Abstracts of Papers, Fifty-ninth Annual Meeting, pp. 29A–30A.

Archangelsky, M. S., and A. O. Averianov, 2003, On the find of a primitive hadrosauroid dinosaur (Ornithischia, Hadrosauroidea) in the Cretaceous of the Belgorod Region: *Paleontological Journal*, 37 (1), pp. 58–61 (translated from *Paleontologicheskii Zhurnal*, 2003, pp. 60–63).

Aslan, A., and W. J. Autin, 1998, Holocene flood-plain soil formation in the southern

Bibliography

lower Mississippi Valley: implications for interpreting alluvial paleosols: *Geological Society of America Bulletin*, 110, pp. 433–449.

Attridge, John, and Alan J. Charig, 1967, Crisis in evolution: the Stormberg series: *Science Journal*, 3 (July), pp. 48–54.

Auffenberg, Walter, 1981, *The Behavioral Ecology of the Komodo Monitor*. Gainesville: University of Florida Press, 406 pages.

Averianov, Alexander O., 2002, An ankylosaurid (Ornithischia: Ankylosauria) braincase from the Upper Cretaceous Bissekty Formation of Uzbekistan: *Bulletin de l'Institut Royal des Sciences Naturelles de Belgique, Sciences de la Terre (Bulletin van het koninklijk Belgisch Instituut voor Naturwetenschappen, Aardwetenschappen)*, 72, Bruxelles (Brussels), pp. 97–110.

Averianov, Alexander O., Alexei V. Voronkevich, Evgeny N. Maschenko, Sergei V. Leshchinskiy, and Alexei V. Faungertz, 2002, A sauropod foot from the Early Cretaceous of Western Siberia: *Acta Palaeontologica Polonica*, 47 (1), pp. 117–124.

Azuma, Yoichi, and Ken-chi Takeyama, 1991, Dinosaur footprints from the Teton Group, central Japan-Research of dinosaurs from the Teton Group (4): *Bulletin of the Fukui Prefectural Museum*, 4, pp. 33–51.

Bachman, G. H., G. Beutler, H. Hagdorn, and N. Hauschke, 1999, Stratigraphie der Germanischen Trias, *in*: N. Hauschke and V. Wilde, editors, *Trias. Eine ganz andere Welt. Mitteleuropa im frühen Erdmittelalter*. München: Pfeil, pp. 81–104.

Badeer, H. S., and J. W. Hicks, 1996, Circulation to the head of *Barosaurus* revised: theoretical considerations: *Comparative Biochemistry & Physiology*, A1114, pp. 197–203.

Bailey, Jack Bowman, 1997, Neural spine elongation in dinosaurs: sailbacks or buffalo-backs: *Journal of Paleontology*, 7 (6), pp. 1124–1126.

Baird, Donald, 1957, Triassic reptile footprint faunules from Milford, New Jersey: *Bulletin of the Museum of Comparative Zoology*, 117 (5), pp. 449–520.

———, 1980, A prosauropod trackway from the Navajo Sandstone (Lower Jurassic) of Arizona, *in*: Louis L. Jacobs, editor, *Aspects of Vertebrate History: Essays in Honor of Edwin Harris Colbert*. Flagstaff: Museum of Northern Arizona Press, pp. 219–230.

Bajpai, S., and G. V. R. Prasad, 2000, Cretaceous age for ir-rich Deccan intertrappean deposits: palaeontological evidence from Anjar, western India: *Journal of the Geological Society, London*, 157, pp. 257–260.

Bakker, Robert T., 1986, *The Dinosaur Heresies: New Theories Unlocking the Mystery of the Dinosaurs and Their Extinction*. New York: William Morrow and Company, 481 pages.

———, 1992, Inside the head of a tiny *T. rex*: *Discover*, 13, pp. 58–69.

———, 2000, Brontosaur killers: Late Jurassic allosaurids as sabre-tooth cat analogues: *in* B. P. Pérez-Moreno, Thomas R. Holtz, Jr., José Luis Sanz, and José J. Moratalla, editors, Aspects of theropod paleobiology: *Gaia*, 15 (cover dated December 1998), pp. 145–158.

———, 2002, Speed in tyrannosaurs: *Journal of Vertebrate Paleontology*, 23 (Supplement to Number 3), Abstracts of Papers, Sixty-second Annual Meeting, p. 34A.

Bakker, Robert T., and Peter M. Galton, 1985, The cranial anatomy of the prosauropod dinosaur "*Efraasia diagnostica*," a juvenile individual of *Sellosaurus gracilis* from the Upper Triassic of Nordwürttemberg, West Germany: *Stuttgarter Beiträge zur Naturkunde*, (B), 117, pp. 1–15, Stuttgart.

Bakker, Robert T., Michael Williams, and Philip J. Currie, 1988, *Nanotyrannus*, a new genus of pygmy tyrannosaur, from the Latest Cretaceous of Montana: *Hunteria*, 1 (5), pp. 1–30.

Ballerstedt, M., 1922, Zwei grosse, zweichige Fährten hochbeiniger Bipeden aus dem Wealdensandstein bei Bückeburg: *Zeitschrift der Deuthschen Geologischen Gesellschaft, Briefliche Mitteilungen*, 73, pp. 76–91.

Bandtopadhyay, Saswati, Tapan K. Roy-Chowdhury, and Dhurjati P. Sengupta, 2002, Taphonomy of some Gondwana vertebrate assemblages of India: *Sedimentary Geology*, 147, pp. 219–245.

Barale, G., M. Philippe, B. Tayech-Mannai, and M. Zarbout, 1997, Découverte d'une flore à ptéridophytes et gymnospermes dans le Crétacé inférieur de la région de Tatouine (Sud tunesien): *Comtes Rendu des Séances de l'Académie des Sciences, Paris*, 2 (325), pp. 221–224.

Barco, J. L., 1999, Proximal cervical vertebra of a new big sauropod (Saurischia) from the Tithonian–Berriasian (Jurassic–Cretaceous transition) from Galve (Teruel, Spain): *IV European workshop on Vertebrate Paleontology*, Albarracín, p. 20.

Barreto, Claudia, Cynthia Marshall, and John R. Horner, 2001, Differential and determinate growth in dinosaurs and other reptiles: *Journal of Vertebrate Paleontology*, 21 (Supplement to Number 3), Abstracts of Papers, Sixty-first Annual Meeting, pp. 31A–32A.

Barrett, Paul M., 1996, Feeding mechanisms and diet in the sauropodomorph dinosaurs: a functional and palaeoecological approach, *in*: J. E. Repekski, editor, *Sixth North American Paleontological Convention: Abstracts of Papers*, Special Publication, Paleontological Society, 8, p. 25.

———, 2000, Paradigms, prosauropods and iguanas: speculation on the diets of extinct reptiles, *in*: Hans-Dieter Sues, editor, *Evolution of Terrestrial Herbivory, Perspectives from the Fossil Record*. New York: Cambridge University Press, pp. 48–72.

———, 2001, Tooth wear and possible jaw action of *Scelidosaurus harrisonii* Owen and a review of feeding mechanisms in other thyreophoran dinosaurs, *in*: Kenneth Carpenter, editor, *The Armored Dinosaurs*. Bloomington and Indianapolis: Indiana University Press, pp. 25–52.

———, 2003, Diet of the ostrich dinosaurs (Ornithomimosauria), *in*: David B. Norman and Paul Upchurch, editors, *SVPCA 50, Cambridge 2002, 11–13 September, Abstract Volume*, unpaginated.

Barrett, Paul M., Jane B. Clarke, David B.

Brinkman, S. D. Chapman, and P. C. Ensom, 2002, Morphology, histology and identification of the "granicones" from the Purbeck Limestone Formation (Lower Cretaceous: Berriasian) of Dorset, southern England: *Cretaceous Research*, 23, pp. 279–295.

Barrett, Paul M., Yoshikazu Hasegawa, Makoto Manabe, Shinji Isaji, and Hiroshige Matsuoka, 2002, Sauropod dinosaurs from the Lower Cretaceous of eastern Asia: taxonomic and biogeographical implications: *Palaeontology*, 45 (6), pp. 1197–1217.

Barrett, Paul M., and Paul Upchurch, 1994, Feeding mechanisms of *Diplodocus*: *Gaia: Revista de Geociencias, Museuo Nacional de Historia Natural*, University of Lisbon, 10, pp. 195–203.

———, 2001, Feeding mechanisms and changes in sauropod palaeoecology through time: *Journal of Vertebrate Paleontology*, 21 (Supplement to Number 3), Abstracts of Papers, Sixty-first Annual Meeting, p. 32A.

Barrett, Paul M., and Katherine J. Willis, 2001, Did dinosaurs invent flowers? Dinosaur-angiosperm coevolution revisited: *Biology Review*, 76, pp. 411–447.

Barrick, Reese E., and Dale A. Russell, 2001, Physiologic implications of ontogenetic variability in oxygen isotope distribution in sauropods: *Journal of Vertebrate Paleontology*, 21 (Supplement to Number 3), Abstracts of Papers, Sixty-first Annual Meeting, p. 32A.

Barsbold, Rinchen, 1976, [New information on *Therizinosaurus* (Therizinosauridae, Theropoda]: [*Soviet-Mongolian Palaeontological Expedition, Transactions*], 19, pp. 5–117.

———, 1981, Predatory toothless dinosaurs from Mongolia: *Trudy Somestnaya Sovetsko-Mongol'skaya Paleontologischeskaya Ekspeditsiya*, 15. pp. 28–39.

———, 1983, Carnivorous dinosaurs from the Cretaceous of Mongolia: *Trudy, Sovmestnaâ Sovetsko-Mongolskaâ Paleontologiceskaâ Ekspediciâya* [*The Joint Soviet-Mongolian Palaeontological Expedition: Transactions*], 19, 117 pages.

———, 1986, Raubdinosaurier Oviraptoren, *in*: E. I. Vorobyeva, editor, *Herpetologische Untersuchungen in der Mongolischen Volksrepublik*. Moscow: Akademia Nauk SSSR Institut Evolyucionnoy Morfologii i Ekologii Zhivotnikhim, A.M. Severtsova, pp. 210–223.

———, 1997, Oviraptorosauria, *in*: Philip J. Currie and Kevin Padian, editors, *Encyclopedia of Dinosaurs*. San Diego: Academic Press, pp. 505–509.

Barsbold, Rinchen, Teresa Maryańska, and Halszka Osmólska, 1990, Oviraptorosauria, *in*: David B. Weishampel, Peter Dodson, and Osmólska, editors, *The Dinosauria*. Berkeley and Los Angeles: University of California Press, pp. 249–258.

Barsbold, Rinchen, and Halszka Osmólska, 1990, Ornithomimosauria, *in*: David B. Weishampel, Peter Dodson, and Halszka Osmólska, editors, *The Dinosauria*. Berkeley and Los Angeles: University of California Press, pp. 225–244.

Barsbold, Rinchen, and Altangerel Perle, 1980, Segnosauria, a new infraorder of carnivorous dinosaurs: *Acta Palaeontologica Polonica*, 25 (2), pp. 185–195.

Baszio, Sven, 1997*a*, Investigations on Canadian dinosaurs: palaeoecology of dinosaur assemblages throughout the Late Cretaceous of south Alberta, Canada: *Courier Forschungsinstitut Senkenberg*, 196, pp. 1–31.

_____, 1997*b*, Investigations on Canadia dinosaurs: systematic palaeontology of isolated dinosaur teeth from the Latest Cretaceous of south Alberta, Canada: *Ibid.*, 196, pp. 33–77.

Bell, C. J., 1980, The scaling inertia in lizards: *Journal of Experimental Biology*, 86, pp. 79–85.

Benton, Michael J., 1990, Origin and Interrelationships of Dinosaurs, *in*: David B. Weishampel, Peter Dodson, and Halszka Osmólska, editors, *The Dinosauria*. Berkeley and Los Angeles: University of California Press, pp. 11–30.

Benton, Michael J., Elizabeth Cook, Dan Grigorescu, E. Popa, and E. Tallodi, 1997, Dinosaurs and other tetrapods in an Early Cretaceous bauxite-filled fissure, northwestern Romania: *Palaeogeography, Palaeoclimatology, Palaeoecology*, 130, pp. 275–292.

Benton, Michael J., and P. S. Spencer, 1995, *Fossil Reptiles of Great Britain*. London: Chapman and Hall, 386 pages.

Berner, R. A., 1968, Calcium carbonate conretions formed by the decomposition of organic matter: *Science*, 159, pp. 195–197.

Bertini, Reinaldo J., and Aldirene C. Franco-Rosas, 2001, Scanning electronic microscopic analysis on Maniraptoriformes teeth from the Upper Cretaceous of southeastern Brazil: *Journal of Vertebrate Paleontology*, 21 (Supplement to Number 3), Abstracts of Papers, Sixty-first Annual Meeting, p. 33A.

Beurlen, K., 1950, Neue Fährtenfunde aus der Frankischen Trias: *Neus Jahrbuch für Geologie und Paläontologie, Monatshefte*, B., pp. 308–320.

Beutler, G., 1999*a*, Intraplate tectonics in the Let Cretaceous of Central Europe: *Hallesches Jb. Geowiss.*, (B) Beih, 5, pp. 13–14, Halle (Salle).

_____, 1999*b*, The Keuper of Germany: an overview. Results of the German Keuper Working Group: *Ibid.*, (B) Beih, 5, pp. 15–16, Halle (Salle).

Bhandari, A., P. N. Shukla, Z. G. Ghevariya, and S. M. Sundaram 1995, Impact did not trigger Deccan volcanism: evidence from Anjar K/T boundary intertrappean sediments: *Geophysical Research Letters*, 22, pp. 433–436.

Bidar, Alain, Louis Demay, and Gérard Thomel, 1972, *Compsognathus corralestris*, nouvelle espèce de Dinosaurien Théropode du Portlandien de Canjuers (Sud-Est de la France): *Annales du Muséum d'Historie Naturelle de Nice*, 1 (1), pp. 1–34.

Bigot, A., 1945, La destruction des collections et des bibliothèques scientifiques de Caen: *Bulletin de la Société Linnéenne de Normandie, Volume Supplémentaire*, pp. 1–75.

Bilbey, Sue Ann, and J. E. Hall, 1999, Marsh

and "*Megalosaurus*" — Utah's first theropod dinosaur, *in*: David D. Gillette, editor, *Vertebrate Paleontology in Utah*, Utah Geological Survey, Miscellaneous Publication, 99-1, pp. 67–69.

Bimber, Oliver, Stephen M. Gatesy, and Lawrence M. Witmer, 2002, Augmented paleontology: merging fossil specimens with computer generated information for analysis and education: *Journal of Vertebrate Paleontology*, 23 (Supplement to Number 3), Abstracts of Papers, Sixty-second Annual Meeting, p. 36A.

Bir, Gary, Becky Morton, and Robert T. Bakker, 2002, Dinosaur social life: evidence from shed-tooth demography: *Journal of Vertebrate Paleontology*, 23 (Supplement to Number 3), Abstracts of Papers, Sixty-second Annual Meeting, p. 37A.

Bird, John H., Donald Burge, and Maria Ciccontetti, 2002, An analysis of disarticulated juvenile *Eolambia* bones in the Cedar Mountain Formation of eastern Utah: *Journal of Vertebrate Paleontology*, 23 (Supplement to Number 3), Abstracts of Papers, Sixty-second Annual Meeting, p. 37A.

Blaine, Mike, 2002, The Dino-trekker: interview with Larry D. Martin, Part 3, conclusion: *Prehistoric Times*, 52, pp. 50–53.

Blanco, R. Ernesto, and Gerardo V. Mazzetta, 2001, A new approach to evaluate the cursorial ability of the giant theropod *Giganotosaurus carolinii*: *Acta Palaeontologica Polonica*, 46 (2), pp. 193–202.

Blows, William T., 1983, William Fox, a neglected dinosaur collector of the Isle of Wight: *Archives of Natural History*, 11, pp. 299–313.

_____, 1987, The armoured dinosaur *Polacanthus foxii* from the Lower Cretaceous of the Isle of Wight: *Palaeontology*, 30, pp. 557–580.

_____, 1995, The Early Cretaceous brachiosaurid dinosaurs *Ornithopsis* and *Eucamerotus* from the Isle of Wight, England: *Ibid.*, 38 (1), pp. 187–197.

_____, 1996. A new species of *Polacanthus* (Ornithischia: Ankylosauria) from the Lower Cretaceous of Sussex, England: *Geological Magazine*, 133 (6), pp. 671–682.

_____, 2001*a*, Possible stegosaur dermal armor from the Lower Cretaceous of southern England, *in*: Kenneth Carpenter, editor, *The Armored Dinosaurs*. Bloomington and Indianapolis: Indiana University Press, pp. 130–140.

_____, 2001*b*, Dermal armor of the polacanthine dinosaurs, *in*: Kenneth Carpenter, editor, *The Armored dinosaurs*. Bloomington and Indianapolis: Indiana University Press, pp. 363–385.

Bock, W.J., 1952, Triassic reptilian tracks and trends of locomotor evolution: *Journal of Paleontology*, 26, pp. 395–433.

_____, 1986, The arboreal origin of avian flight: *Memoirs of the California Academy of Sciences*, 8, pp. 57–72.

Bohlin, Birger, 1953, Fossil reptiles from Mongolia and Kansu: *The Sino-Swedish Expedition Publication*, 37 (6), pp. 1–105.

Bonaparte, José F., 1982, Faunal replacement in

the Triassic of South America: *Journal of Vertebrate Paleontology*, 2 (3), pp. 362–371.

_____, 1991, Los vertebrados fosiles de la Formacion Rio Colorado, de la ciudad de neuquen y cercanias, Cretacico Superior, Argentina: *Revista del Museo Argentino de Ciencias Naturales (Bernardino Rivadavia), el Instituto Nacional de Investigacion de las Ciencias Naturales*, 4 (3), pp. 68–101.

Bonaparte, José F., Wolf-Dieter Heinrich, and Rupert Wild, 2000, Review of *Janenschia* Wild, with the description of a new sauropod from the Tendaguru beds of Tanzania and a discussion on the systematic value of procoelous caudal vertebrae in sauropods: *Palaeontographica*, Abt. A, 256 (1–3), pp. 25–76, Stuttgart.

Bonaparte, José F., Fernando E. Novas, and Rodolfo A. Coria, 1990, *Carnotaurus sastrei* Bonaparte, the horned, lightly built carnosaur from the Middle Cretaceous of Patagonia: *Natural History Museum of Los Angeles County Contributions in Science*, 416, pp. 1–42.

Bonaparte, José F., and Jaime E. Powell, 1980, A continental assemblage of tetrapods from the Upper Cretaceous beds of El Brete, northwestern Argentina (Sauropoda-Coelurosauria-Carnosauria-Aves): *Memoires de la Société Géologique de France, Nouvelle Serie*, pp. 19–28.

Bonaparte, José F., and J. A. Pumares, 1995, Notas sobre el primer cráneo de *Riojasaurus incertus* (Dinosauria, Prosauropoda, Melanorosauridae) del Triásico superior de La Rioja, Argentina: *Ameghiniana*, 32, pp. 341–349.

Bonaparte, José F., and M. Vince, 1979, El hallazgo del primer nido de Dinosaurios triásicos (Saurischia, Prosauropoda), Triásico Superior de Patagonia, Argentina: *Ameghiniana*, 16, pp. 173–182.

Bonnan, Matthew F., 2001, Separating size from shape: using thin-plate splines to evaluate humerus functional morphology in *Apatosaurus*, *Diplodocus*, and *Camarasaurus*: *Journal of Vertebrate Paleontology*, 21 (Supplement to Number 3), Abstracts of Papers, Sixty-first Annual Meeting, pp. 34A–35A.

_____, 2002, Pes anatomy in sauropod dinosaurs: implications for functional morphology, evolution, and phylogeny: *Ibid.*, 22 (Supplement to 3), Abstracts of Papers, Sixty-second Annual Meeting, p. 38A.

Boscarolli, D., M. Laprocina, M. Tentor, G. Tunis, and S. Venturini, 1993, Prima segnalazione di resti di dinosauro nei calcari hauteriviani di plattaforma dell' Istria meridionale (Croatia): *Natura Nascosta*, 7, pp. 1–20.

Boyd, Clint, and Christopher J. Ott, 2002, Probable lambeosaurine (Ornithischia, Hadrosauridae) specimen from the Late Cretaceous Hell Creek Formation of Montana: *Journal of Vertebrate Paleontology*, 23 (Supplement to Number 3), Abstracts of Papers, Sixty-second Annual Meeting, p. 38A.

Branson, E. B., and M. G. Mehl, 1932, Foot-

Bibliography

print records from the Paleozoic and Mesozoic of Missouri, Kansas and Wyoming: *Bulletin of the Geological Society of America*, 43, p. 151.

Bray, Emily S., 1999, Eggs and eggshell from the Upper Cretaceous North Horn Formation, Central Utah: *Utah Geological Survey Miscellaneous Publication*, 99 (1), pp. 360–375.

Bray, Emily S., and Karl F. Hirsch, 1998, Eggshell from the Upper Jurassic Morrison Formation: *Modern Geology*, 23, pp. 219–240.

Bray, Emily S., and Spencer G. Lucas, 1997, Theropod eggshell from the Upper Jurassic of New Mexico: *New Mexico Museum of Natural History and Science Bulletin*, 11, pp. 41–43.

Brett-Surman, Michael K. [Keith], 1975, The appendicular anatomy of hadrosaurian dinosaurs: M.A. thesis, University of California (Berkeley), 70 pages (unpublished).

_____, 1979, Phylogeny and palaeobiography of hadrosaurian dinosaurs: *Nature*, 277, pp. 560–562.

Brill, Kathleen, and Kenneth Carpenter, 2001, A baby ornithopod from the Morrison Formation of Garden Park, Colorado, *in*: Darren Tanke and Kenneth Carpenter, editors, *Mesozoic Vertebrate Life: New Research Inspired by the Paleontology of Philip J. Currie*. Bloomington and Indianapolis, Indiana: Indiana University Press, pp. 197–205.

Brinkman, David B., David A. Eberth, Michael J. Ryan, and Pei-Jin Chen, 2001, The occurrence of *Psittacosaurus xinjiangensis* Sereno and Chow, 1988 in the Urho area, Junggar Basin, Xinjiang, People's Republic of China: *Canadian Journal of Earth Sciences*, 38 (12), pp. 1781–1786.

Britt, Brooks B., 1991, The theropods of Dry Mesa Quarry (Morrison Formation, Late Jurassic), Colorado: with an emphasis on the osteology of *Torvosaurus tanneri*: *Brigham Young University Geology Studies*, 37, pp. 1–72.

_____, 1993, Pneumatic postcranial bones in dinosaurs and other archosaurs, Ph.D dissertation, University of Calvary (unpublished).

_____, 1997, Postcranial pneumaticity, *in*: Philip J. Currie and Kevin Padian, editors, *Encyclopedia of Dinosaurs*. San Diego: Academic Press, pp. 590–593.

Britt, Brooks B., Daniel J. Chure, Kenneth L. Stadtman, James H. Madsen, Jr., R. D. Scheetz, and Donald L. Burge, 2001, New osteological data and the affinities of *Utahraptor* from the Cedar Mountain Fm. (Early Cretaceous) of Utah: *Journal of Vertebrate Paleontology*, 21 (Supplement to Number 3), Abstracts of Papers, Sixty-first Annual Meeting, p. 36A.

Brochu, Christopher A., 2001, Tyrannosaurid systematics and the phylogenetic position of Tyrannosauridae within Therpoda: *The Paleobiology and Phylogenetics of Large Theropods*, A. Watson Armour III Symposium, The Field Museum, 12 May 2001, unpaginated.

_____, 2003, Osteology of *Tyrannosaurus rex*:

insights from a nearly complete skeleton and high-resolution computed tomographic analysis of the skull: *Society of Vertebrate Paleontology Memoir*, 7, *Journal of Vertebrate Paleontology*, Volume 22, Supplement to Number 4, 138 pages.

Broom, Robert, 1915, Catalogue of the type and figured specimens of fossil vertebrates in the American Museum of Natural History. III. Permian, Triassic and Jurassic reptiles of South Africa: *Bulletin of the American Museum of Natural History*, 25, pp. 105–164.

Brown, Barnum, 1908, The Ankylosauridae, a new family of armored dinosaurs from the Upper Cretaceous: *Bulletin of the American Museum of Natural History*, 24, pp. 187–201.

_____, 1914, *Anchiceratops*, a new genus of horned dinosaur from the Edmonton Cretaceous of Alberta. With discussion of the origin of the ceratopsian crest and the brain casts of *Anchiceratops* and *Trachodon*: *Ibid.*, 33, pp. 539–548.

Brown, Barnum, and Erich Maren Schlaikjer, 1940, The structure and relationships of *Protoceratops*: *New York Academy of Sciences, Annals*, 40, pp. 133–66.

_____, 1943, A study of the troödont dinosaurs with the description of a new genus and four new species: *Bulletin of the American Museum of Natural History*, 82, pp. 1–149.

Bryan, K., 1931, Wind-worn stones or ventifacts: a discussion and bibliography, *in*: *Natural Resources Council Report on Sedimentation 1929–1930*. Washington, D.C.: National Academy of Sciences, pp. 28–50.

Buchholz, Peter W., 2002, Phylogeny and biogeography of basal Ornithischia: *Tate 2002: Wyoming in the Age of Dinosaurs — Creatures, Environments and Extinctions*, p. 11.

Buckland, William, 1824, Notice on the *Megalosaurus* or great fossil lizard of Stonesfield: *Transactions of the Geological Society of London*, 2, pp. 390–396.

Buckley, Lisa Glynis, 2002, New material of *Elmisaurus* (Theropoda, Elmisauridae) from the Late Cretaceous Hell Creek Formation of southeastern Montana: *Journal of Vertebrate Paleontology*, 23 (Supplement to Number 3), Abstracts of Papers, Sixty-second Annual Meeting, p. 39A.

Buckman, J., 1859, On some fossil reptilian eggs from the Great Oolite of Ciren Cester: *Quarterly Journal of the Geological Society of London*, 16, pp. 107–110.

Buffetaut, Éric, 1999, Mantell, Cuvier, Buckland and the identification of *Iguanodon*: a contribution based on unpublished annotations by Mantell: *Oryctos*, 2, pp. 101–109.

_____, 2000, Mantell, Cuvier, Buckland and the identification of *Iguanodon*: a correction: *Ibid.*, 3, pp. 95–97.

Buffetaut, Éric, and Mohamed Ouaja, 2002, A new specimen of *Spinosaurus* (Dinosauria, Theropoda) from the Lower Cretaceous of Tunesia, with remarks on the evolutionary history of the Spinosauridae: *Bulletin of the Geological Society of France*, 173 (5), pp. 415–421.

Buffetaut, Éric, and Varavudh Suteethorn, 1998a, The biogeographical significance of the Mesozoic vertebrates from Thailand, *in*: R. Hall and J. D. Holloway, editors, *Biogeography and Geological Evolution of SE Asia*. Leiden, Netherlands: Backhuys, pp. 83–90.

_____, 1998b, Early Cretaceous dinosaurs from Thailand and their bearing on the early evolution and biogeographical history of some groups of Cretaceous dinosaurs, *in*: Spencer G. Lucas, James I. Kirkland, and John W. Estep, editors, *Lower and Middle Cretaceous Terrestrial Ecosystems*. Albuquerque: New Mexico Museum of Natural History and Science, Bulletin No. 14, pp. 205–210.

_____, 1999, A short review of the dinosaurs of Thailand: *Actas de las I Journadas Internacionales Sobre Paleontología de Dinosaurios y su Entorno (Proceedings of the 1st International Symposium about Paleontology of Dinosaurs and their Environment*, Salas de los Infantes (Burgos, España), Septiembre de 1999, pp. 19–24.

_____, 2003, *Phuwiangosaurus* and the relationsips of the nemegtosaurid sauropods: *in*: David B. Norman and Paul Upchurch, editors, *SVPCA 50, Cambridge 2002, 11–13 September, Abstract Volume*, unpaginated.

Buffetaut, Éric, and Rucha Ingavat, 1986, Unusual theropod dinosaur teeth from the Upper Jurassic of Phu Wiang, northeastern Thailand: *Revue de Paléobiologie*, 5 (2), pp. 217–220.

Buffetaut, Éric, Varavudh Suteethorn, Gilles Cuny, Haiyan Tong, Jean Le Loeuff, Sasidhorn Khansubha, and Sutee Jongautchariyakul, 2000, The earliest known sauropod dinosaur: *Nature*, 407 (7), pp. 72–74.

Buffetaut, Éric, Varavudh Suteethorn, Jean Le Loeuff, Gilles Cuny, Haiyan Tong, and Sasidhorn Khansubha, 2002a, The first giant dinosaurs: a large sauropod from the Late Triassic of Thailand: *C. R. Palevol*, 1, pp. 103–109.

_____, 2002b, A review of the sauropod dinosaurs of Thailand: *The Symposium on Geology of Thailand, 26–31, August 2002, Bangkok. Thailand*, pp. 95–101.

Buffetaut, Éric, Varavudh Suteethorn, and Haiyan Tong, 1996, The earliest known tyrannosaur from the Lower Cretaceous of Thailand: *Nature*, 381, pp. 689–691.

_____, 2001, The first thyreophoran dinosaur from Southeast Asia: a stegosaur vertebra from the Late Jurassic Phu Kradung Formation of Thailand: *Neus Jahrbuch für Geologie und Paläontologie, Monatshefte*, 2001 (2), pp. 95–102.

Bultnck, P., 1992, An assessment of posture and gait in *Iguanodon bernissartensis* Boulenger, 1881: *Bulletin de l'Institut Royal des Sciences Naturelles de Belgique/Bulletin van het Koninklijk Belgisch Instituut voor Natuurwetenschappen, Aardwetenschappen*, 63, pp. 5–11.

Bulynnikova, A. A., and L. Ya. Trushkova [Truśkova], 1967, [Continental Cretaceous deposits of eastern and central parts of the Western Siberian lowland], *in*: G.

G. Martinson, editor, *Stratigrafiâ i paleontologia mezozojskih i paleogenneogenovyh kontinental'nyh otozenij aziatskoj casti SSSR.* Leningrad: Nauka, pp. 40–46.

Bunzel, Emanuel, 1871, Die Reptilfauna der Gosauformation in der neuen Welt bei Wiener-Neustadt: *Abh. Geol. Reichsant. Vienna,* 5, pp. 1–18.

Burge, Donald L., John H. Bird, Brian K. McClelland, and Maria A. Ciconnetti, 1999, Comparison of four armored dinosaurs from the Cedar Mountain Formation of eastern Utah: *Journal of Vertebrate Paleontology,* 19 (Supplement to Number 3), Abstracts of Papers, Fifty-ninth Annual Meeting, p. 34A.

Burnham, David A., Philip J. Currie, Robert T. Bakker, Zhonghe Zhou, and John H. Ostrom, 2000, Remarkable new birdlike dinosaur (Theropoda: Maniraptora) from the Upper Cretaceous of Montana: *The University of Kansas Paleontological Contributions,* New Series, 13, pp. 1–14.

Burnham, David A., and Larry Martin, 2002, Why small dinosaurs have big brains: *Journal of Vertebrate Paleontology,* 23 (Supplement to Number 3), Abstracts of Papers, Sixty-second Annual Meeting, p. 40A.

Busbey, A. B., 1995, The structural consequences of skull flattening in crocodilians, *in:* J. Thomason, editor, *Functional Morphology in Vertebrate Paleontology.* Cambridge: University of Cambridge Press, pp. 173–192.

Bybee, Paul, 1997, Histological bone structure differences in various sized elements from the Late Jurassic dinosaur, *Allosaurus fragilis,* of central Utah. Ph.D dissertation, Brigham Young University, Provo, Utah, 99 pages.

Calder, W. A., III, 1984, *Size, Function, and Life History.* Cambridge, Massachusetts: Harvard University Press.

Callison, George, and Helen M. Quimby, 1987, Tiny dinosaurs: are they fully grown?: *Journal of Vertebrate Paleontology,* 3 (4), pp. 200–209.

Calvo, Jorge O. [Orlando], 1989, Un gigantesco theropodo del Miembro Candeleros (Albiano–Cenomaniano) de la Formación Río Limay, Provincia del Neuquén, Patagonia, Argentina. VII Journadas Argentinas de Paleontologia de Vertebrados, Buenos Aires, 1990: *Ameghiniana,* 26 (3–4), p. 241.

_____, 1991, Huellas de dinosaurios en la Formación Río Limay (Albiano–Cenomaniano?), Picún Leufú, Provincia del Nequen, República Argentina (Ornithischia–Saurischia: Sauropoda–Theropoda): *Ibid.,* 28, pp. 241–258.

_____, 1994a, Feeding mechanisms in sauropod dinosaurs: M.S. thesis, University of Illinois at Chicago (unpublished).

_____, 1994b, Jaw mechanics in sauropod dinosaurs: *GAIA,* 10, 183–193.

_____, 1996, Phylogenetic relationships of *Asiatosaurus* (Sauropoda): *Ameghina,* 33, p. 461.

_____, 2002, Un gigantesco Titanosauridae (Cretácico Superior) del norte de la provincia de Neuquen: *Ibid.,* 39 (4), Supplemento, p. 7R.

Calvo, Jorge O., and José F. Bonaparte, 1991, *Andesaurus delgadoi* gen. et sp. nov. (Saurischia–Sauropoda), dinosaurio Titanosauridae de la Formación Rio Limay (Albiano–Cenomaniano), Nequén, Argentina: *Ameghiana,* 28 (3–4), pp. 303–310.

Calvo, Jorge Orlando, and Rodolfo A. Coria, 2000, New specimen of *Giganotosaurus carolinii* (Coria and Salgado, 1995), supports it as the largest theropod ever found, *in* B. P. Pérez-Moreno, Thomas R. Holtz, Jr., José Luis Sanz, and José J. Moratalla, editors, Aspects of theropod paleobiology: *Gaia,* 15 (cover dated December 1998), pp. 117–122.

Calvo, Jorge Orlando, Juan Porfiri, and Federico Poblete, 2001, A giant titanosaurid sauropod from the Upper Cretaceous of Neuquén, Patagonia, Argentina: *Ameghiniana,* XVII Jornadas Argentinas de Paleontologia de Vertebrados, Resúmes, Esquel, 16–18 de mayo de 2001, p. 5R.

Calvo, Jorge Orlando, Juan Porfiri, Claudio Veralli, and Federico Poblete, 2001, One of the largest titanosaurid sauropods ever found, Upper Cretaceous, Neuquén, Patagonia, Argentina: *Journal of Vertebrate Paleontology,* 21 (Supplement to Number 3), Abstracts of Papers, Sixty-first Annual Meeting, p. 37A.

Calvo, Jorge Orlando, D. Rubilar, and K. Moerno, in press, Report on a new theropod dinosaur from Northwest Patagonia: *Ameghiniana,* XVII Jornadas Argentinas de Paleontologia de Vertebrados, Resúmes.

Camp, Charles L., 1936, A new type of small bipedal dinosaur from the Navajo Sandstone of Arizona: *University of California Publications, Bulletin, Department of Geology and Science,* 24, pp. 39–56.

Campbell, Kenneth E., 2002, Theropod vs avian hindlimb locomotion: *Journal of Vertebrate Paleontology,* 23 (Supplement to Number 3), Abstracts of Papers, Sixty-second Annual Meeting, p. 41A.

Campos, Diogenes de A., and Alexander W. A. Kellner, 1999, On sauropod (Titanosauridae) pelves from the continental Cretaceous of Brazil, *in:* Yukimitsu Tomida, Thomas R. Rich, and Patricia Vickers-Rich, editors, *Second Symposium Gondwana Dinosaur, 12–13 July, 1998, National Science Museum, Tokyo, Abstracts with Program,* pp. 143–166.

Canudo, José Ignacio, J. L. Barco, R. Royo-Torres, and J. I. Ruiz-Omeñaca, 2001, Los saurópodos (Dinosauria) del Tithónico (Jurásico Superior) y del Cretácico de Aragón: *Actas de las i jornadas internacionales sobre paleontología de dinosaurios y su entrorno,* pp. 309–318.

Canudo, José Ignacio, Gloria Cuenca-Bescós, Luis Ardévol, and N. Lopez-Martinez, 1999, The youngest sauropod of western Europe: *IV European workshop on Vertebrate Paleontology,* Albarracín, pp. 30–31.

Canudo, José Ignacio, Nieves Lopez Martínez, and J. I. Ruiz-Omeñaca, 2001, Los dinosaurios del Maastrichtiense superior (Cretácico Superior) del Pirineo de Huesca (España): *Actas de las i jornadas internacionales sobre paleontología de dinosaurios y su entrorno,* pp. 319–328.

Canudo, José Ignacio, José Ignacio Ruiz-Omeñaca, José Luis Barco, and Rafael Royo Torres, 2002, ¿Saurópodos asiáticos en el Barremiense inferior (Cretácico Inferior) de España?: *Ameghianana.*

Cao You-Shu, and You Hai-Lu, 2000, The jaw of *Datousaurus bashanensis* Dong and Tang, 1984: *Acta Palaeontologica Sinica,* 39 (3), pp. 391–395.

Carpenter, Kenneth, 1982, Baby dinosaurs from the Late Cretaceous Lance and Hell Creek formations and a description of a new species of theropod: *Contributions to Geology,* 20 (2), pp. 123–134.

_____, 1984, Skeletal reconstruction and life restoration of *Sauropelta* (Ankylosauria: Nodosauridae) from the Cretaceous of North America: *Canadian Journal of Earth Sciences,* 21, pp. 1491–1498.

_____, 1987, Paleoecological significance of droughts during the Late Cretaceous of the Western Inerior, *in:* Philip J. Currie and E. Koster, editors, Fourth Symposium on Mesozoic Terrestrial Ecosystems, Short Papers: *Occasional Papers, Tyrrell Museum of Palaeontology,* 3, pp. 42–47.

_____, 1992, Tyrannosaurids (Dinosauria) of Asia and North America, *in:* Niall J. Mateer and Chen Pei-Ji, editors: *International Symposium on Non-marine Cretaceous Correlation.* Beijing: China Ocean Press, pp. 250–268.

_____, 1997a, Ankylosauria, *in:* Philip J. Currie and Kevin Padian, editors, *Encyclopedia of Dinosaurs.* San Diego: Academic Press, pp. 16–20.

_____, 1997b, It's a baby!: *MQ,* 6 (2), p. 16.

_____, 1998a, Armor of *Stegosaurus stenops,* and the taphonomic history of a new specimen from Garden Park, Colorado, *in:* Kenneth Carpenter, Daniel J. Chure, and James I. Kirkland, editors, *The Upper Jurassic Morrison Formation: An Interdisciplinary Study, Modern Geology (Special Issue),* 23, pp. 127–144.

_____, 1998b, Vertebrate biostratigraphy of the Morrison Formation near Cañon City, Colorado: *Modern Geology,* 23, pp. 407–426.

_____, 1998c, Ankylosaur odds and ends: *Ibid.,* p. 31A.

_____, 2000, Evidence of predatory behavior by carnivorous dinosaurs, *in* B. P. Pérez-Moreno, Thomas R. Holtz, Jr., José Luis Sanz, and José J. Moratalla, editors, Aspects of theropod paleobiology: *Gaia,* 15 (cover dated December 1998), pp. 135–144.

_____, editor, 2001a, *The Armored Dinosaurs.* Bloomington and Indiana: Indiana University Press, xvi, 483 pages.

_____, 2001b, Skull of the polacanthid ankylosaur *Hylaeosaurus armatus* Mantell, 1833, from the Lower Cretaceous of England, *in:* Kenneth Carpenter, editor, *The Armored Dinosaurs.* Bloomington and Indianapolis: Indiana University Press, pp. 169–172.

_____, 2001c, Phylogenetic analysis of the Ankylosauria, *in:* Kenneth Carpenter, editor, *The Armored Dinosaurs.* Bloomington and Indianapolis: Indiana University Press, pp. 455–483.

_____, 2002, Forelimb biomechanics of nonavian theropod dinosaurs in predation: *Senckenbergiana lethaea*, 82 (1), pp. 59–76.

Carpenter, Kenneth, and Peter M. Galton, 2001, Othniel Charles Marsh and the myth of the eight-spiked *Stegosaurus*, *in*: Kenneth Carpenter, editor, *The Armored Dinosaurs*. Bloomington and Indianapolis: Indiana University Press, pp. 76–102.

Carpenter, Kenneth, Karl F. Hirsch, and John R. Horner, editors, 1994, *Dinosaur Eggs and Babies*. Cambridge: Cambridge University Press, 372 pages.

Carpenter, Kenneth, and James I. Kirkland, 1998, Review of Lower and Middle Cretaceous ankylosaurs from North America, *in*: Spencer G. Lucas, Kirkland, and J. W. Estep, editors, *Lower and Middle Cretaceous Terrestrial Ecosystems*. Albuquerque: New Mexico Museum of Natural History and Science, Bulletin No. 14, pp. 249–270.

Carpenter, Kenneth, James I. Kirkland, Donald Burge, D., and John H. Bird, J., 1999, Ankylosaurs (Dinosauria: Ornithischia) of the Cedar Mountain Formation, Utah. *Utah Geological Survey, Miscellaneous Publication*, 99, pp. 243–251.

_____, 2001, Disarticulated skull of a new primitive ankylosaurid from the Lower Cretaceous of Eastern Utah, *in*: Kenneth Carpenter, editor, *The Armored Dinosaurs*. Bloomington and Indiana: Indiana University Press, pp. 211–238.

Carpenter, Kenneth, James I. Kirkland, Clifford A. Miles, Karen C. Cloward, and Donald L. Burge, 1996, Evolutionary significance of new ankylosaurs (Dinosauria) from the Upper Jurassic and Lower Cretaceous, Western interior: *Journal of Vertebrate Paleontology*, 16 (Supplement to Number 3), Abstracts of Papers, Fifty-sixth Annual Meeting, p. 25A.

Carpenter, Kenneth, and Clifford A. Miles, 1997, New, primitive stegosaur (Ornithischia) from the Upper Jurassic: *Journal of Vertebrate Paleontology*, 17 (Supplement to Number 3), Abstracts of Papers, Fifty-seventh Annual Meeting, p. 35A.

Carpenter, Kenneth, Clifford A. Miles, and Karen Cloward, 2001, New primitive stegosaur from the Morrison Formation, Wyoming: *in*: Kenneth Carpenter, editor, *The Armored Dinosaurs*. Bloomington and Indianapolis: Indiana University Press, pp. 55–75.

Carpenter, Kenneth, and Matt B. Smith, 2001, Forelimb osteology and biomechanics of *Tyrannosaurus rex*, *in*: Darren Tanke and Kenneth Carpenter, editors, *Mesozoic Vertebrate Life: New Research Inspired by the Paleontology of Philip J. Currie*. Bloomington and Indianapolis, Indiana: Indiana University Press, pp. 90–116.

Carr, Thomas D. [David], 1996, Craniofacial ontogeny in tyrannosaurids: taxonomic implications: *Journal of Vertebrate Paleontology*, 16 (Supplement to Number 3), Abstracts of Papers, Fifty-sixth Annual Meeting, p. 25A.

_____, 1999, Craniofacial ontogeny in Tyrannosauridae (Dinosauria: Coelurosauria): *Ibid.*, 19 (3), pp. 497–520.

Carr, Thomas David, and Thomas E. Williamson, 1991, A new tyrannosaurid (Theropoda: Coelurosauria) from the San Juan Basin of New Mexico: *Journal of Vertebrate Paleontology*, 19 (Supplement to Number 3), Abstracts of Papers, Fifty-ninth Annual Meeting, p. 36A.

_____, 2001, Resolving tyrannosaurid diversity: skeletal remains referred to *Aublysodon* belong to *Tyrannosaurus rex* and *Daspletosaurus*: *Ibid.*, 21 (Supplement to Number 3), Abstracts of Papers, Sixty-first Annual Meeting, p. 38A.

Carrano, Matthew T., 1998a, Locomotion in non-avian dinosaurs: integrating data from hindlimb kinematics, in vivo strains, and bone morphology: *Paleobiology*, 24, pp. 450–469.

_____, 1998b, The evolution of dinosaur locomotion: functional morphology, biomechanics, and modern analogs: Ph.D. dissertation, University of Chicago.

_____, 2000, Homoplasy and the evolution of dinosaur locomotion: *Paleobiology*, 26 (3), pp. 489–512.

_____, 2001a, Implications of limb bone scaling, curvature and eccentricity in mammals and non-avian dinosaurs: *Journal of the Zoological Society of London*, 254, pp. 41–55.

_____, 2001b, Size and scaling in large theropod dinosaurs: *The Paleobiology and Phylogenetics of Large Theropods*, A. Watson Armour III Symposium, The Field Museum, 12 May 2001, unpaginated.

_____, 2001c, The evolution of sauropod locomotion: morphological diversity of a secondarily quadrupedal radiation: *Journal of Vertebrate Paleontology*, 21 (Supplement to Number 3), Abstracts of Papers, Sixty-first Annual Meeting, p. 38A.

_____, 2001d, The evolution of dinosaur locomotion: *International Congress of Vertebrate Morphology, Abstracts*, p. 214.

Carrano, Matthew T., and John R. Hutchinson, 2002, Pelvic and hindlimb musculature of *Tyrannosaurus rex* (Dinosauria: Theropoda): *Journal of Morphology*, 253 (3), pp. 207–228.

Carrano, Matthew T., and Scott D. Sampson, 2002, Ceratosaurs: a global perspective: *Journal of Vertebrate Paleontology*, 23 (Supplement to Number 3), Abstracts of Papers, Sixty-second Annual Meeting, p. 41A.

Carrano, Matthew T., Scott D. Sampson, and Catherine R. Forster, 2002, The osteology of *Masiakasaurus knopfleri*, a small abelisauroid (Dinosauria: Theropoda) from the Late Cretaceous of Madagascar: *Journal of Vertebrate Paleontology*, 22 (3), pp. 510–534.

Carrano, Matthew T., and Jeffrey A. Wilson, 2001, Taxon distribution and the tetrapod track record: *Paleobiology*, 27 (3), pp. 564–582.

Carrier, David R., Rebecca M. Walter, and David V. Lee, 2001, Influence of rotational inertia on turning performance of theropod dinosaurs: clues from humans with increased rotational inertia: *The Journal of Experimental Biology*, 204, pp. 3917–3926.

Carvalho, Ismar de Souza, and Leonardo Avilla, 2002, A new sauropod from the Aptian–Albian of Brazil and its phylogenetic relationships: *Journal of Vertebrate Paleontology*, 23 (Supplement to Number 3), Abstracts of Papers, Sixty-second Annual Meeting, p. 42A.

Carvalho, Ismar de Souza, and Elizabete Pedrão, 2000, Brazilian theropods from the equatorial Atlantic Margin: behavior and environmental setting: *in* B. P. Pérez-Moreno, Thomas R. Holtz, Jr., José Luis Sanz, and José J. Moratalla, editors, Aspects of theropod paleobiology: *Gaia*, 15 (cover dated December 1998), pp. 369–378.

Casamiquela, Rodolfo M., 1964, *Estudios Ichnológicos. Problemas y métodos de la Icnologia con aplicación al estudio de pisadas Mesozóicas (Reptilia, Mammalia) de la Patagonia*. Buenos Aires: Colegio Industrial Pio X, 229 pages.

_____, 1980, La presencia del genero *Plateosaurus* (Prosauropoda) en el Triásico superior de la Formación, Patagonia: *Actas II, Congreso Argentino de Paleontología y Biostratigrafía y 1ero Congreso Latinoamericano de Paleontología, Buenos Aires, 1978*, 1, pp. 143–159.

Casamiquela, Rodolfo M., and Armando Fasola, 1968, Sobre pisadas de dinosaurios del Cretácico Inferior de Colchagua (Chile): *Publicaciones, Facultad de Ciencias Físcas y Matemáticas, Departmento de Geología, Universidad de Chile*, 30, pp. 5–24.

Casanovas [see also Casanovas-Cladellas], M. Lourdes, Santafé, José-Vte Santafé-Llopis, and José Luis Sanz, 2001. *Losillasaurus giganteus*, un nuevo sauropodo del transito Jurasico-Cretacico de la cuenca de "Los Serranos" (Valencia, Espaqa): *Paleontologia i Evolucio*, 32–33, pp. 99–122.

Casanovas, M. Lourdes, José-Vte Santafé-Llopis and A. Isidoro-Llorens, 1993, *Pararhabdodon isonense*, n. gen. n. sp. (Dinosauria) Estudio morfológico, radio-tomográfico y consideraciones biomecánicas: *Paleontologia y Evolució*, 26–27, pp. 121–131.

Casanovas, M. Lourdes, Xabier Pereda Suberbiola, Jose Vincente Santafé, and David B. Weishampel, 1999a, A primitive euhadrosaurian dinosaur from the uppermost Cretaceous of the Ager syncline (southern Pyrenees, Catalonia): *Geologie en Mijnbouw*, 78, pp. 345–356.

_____, 1999b, First lambeosaurine hadrosaurid from Europe: palaeobiogeographical implications: *Geological Magazine*, 136, pp. 205–211.

Casanovas-Cladellas, M. Lourdes, and José-Vte Santafé-Llopis, 1986, Dinosaur footprints in Spain with special reference to Lower Cretaceous from "Sierra de los Cameros" (La Rioja, Spain), *in*: David D. Gillette, editor, *First International Symposium on Dinosaur Tracks and Traces*, *Abstracts of Program, New Mexico Museum of Natural History, Albuquerque, N.M. 22–24 May 1986*, p. 12.

Case, T. J., 1978a, On the evolution and adaptive significance of postnatal growth rates in the terrestrial vertebrates: *Quartely Review of Biology*, 53, pp. 243–282.

_____, 1978b, Speculations on the growth rate

and reproduction of some dinosaurs: *Paleobiology*, 4, pp. 320–328.

Case, Judd A., James E. Martin, Dan S. Chaney, Marcelo Reguero, and Micael O. Woodburne, 1998, The first hadrosaur from Antarctica: *Journal of Vertebrate Paleontology*, 18 (Supplement to Number 3), Abstracts of Papers, Fifty-eighth Annual Meeting, p. 32A.

Case, Judd A., James E. Martin, Dan S. Chaney, Marcelo Reguero, Sergio A. Marenssi, Sergio M. Santillana, and Michael O. Woodburne, 2000, The first duck-billed dinosaur (family Hadrosauridae) from Antarctica: *Journal of Vertebrate Paleontology*, 20 (3), pp. 612–614.

Casier, Edgard, 1960, *Les Iguanodons de Bernissart*. Brussels: Editions du Patrimoine, Institute Royal des Sciences Naturelles de Belgique, 134 pages.

Castanet, J., K. Curry Rogers, J. Cubo, and J. J. Boisard, 2000, Quantification of periosteal osteogenesis in ostrich and emu: implications for assessing growth in dinosaurs: *Comtes Rendu des Séances de l'Académie des Sciences, Paris, de la Terre et des Planètes*, III (323), pp. 543–550.

Chapman, Ralph E., Rolf Johnson, and Kent Stevens, 2001, The posture of *Triceratops*: insight from three-dimensional modeling, scanning, and prototyping: *International Congress of Vertebrate Morphology, Abstracts*, p. 215.

Chapman, Ralph E., Neffra A. Matthews, Mary H. Schweitzer, and Celeste C. Horner, 2002, Applying 21st Century technology to very old animals, *in*: Judith G. Scotchmoor, Dale A. Springer, Brent H. Breithaupt, and Anthony R. Fiorillo, 2002, editors, *Dinosaurs: The Science Behind the Stories*. Northbrook, IL, Lawrence KS, and Alexandria, VA: Society of Vertebrate Paleontology, The Paleontological Society, and American Geological Institute, pp. 137–144.

Chapman, Ralph E., Rebecca A. Snyder, Steve Jabo, and Arthur Andersen, 2001, On a new posture for the horned dinosaur *Triceratops*: *Journal of Vertebrate Paleontology*, 21 (Supplement to Number 3), Abstracts of Papers, Sixty-first Annual Meeting, pp. 39A–40A.

Chapman, Ralph E., Peter M. Galton, J. John Sepkoski, and William P. Wall, 1981, A morphometric study of the pachyocephalosaurid dinosaur *Stegoceras*: *Journal of Paleontology*, 55 (3), pp. 608–618.

Charig, Alan G., 1989, The Cretaceous–Tertiary boundary and the last of the dinosaurs: *Philosophical Transactions of the Royal Society of London*, B325, pp. 387–400.

Charig, Alan G., John Attridge, and A. W. Crompton, 1965, On the origin of the sauropods and the classification of the Saurischia: *Proceedings of the Linnean Society of London*, 176 (2), pp. 197–221, London.

Charig, Alan J., and Angela C. Milner, 1990, The systematic position of *Baryonyx walkeri*, in the light of Gauthier's reclassification of the Teropoda, *in*: Kenneth Carpenter and Philip J. Currie, editors, *Dinosaur Systematics: Approaches and Per-*

spectives. Cambridge, New York and Melbourne: Cambridge University Press, pp. 127–140.

———, 1997, *Baryonyx walkeri*, a fish-eating dinosaur from the Wealden of Surrey: *Bulletin of The Natural History Museum, London*, (Geology) 53 (1), pp. 11–70.

Charig, Alan J., and Barney H. Newman, 1962, Footprints in the Purbeck: *New Scientist*, 14, pp. 234–235.

Chatterjee, Sankar, 1978, *Indosuchus* and *Indosaurus*, Cretaceous carnosaurs from India: *Journal of Paleontology*, 52 (3), pp. 570–580.

———, 1993, *Shuvosaurus*, a new theropod: *Natural Geographic Research Exploration*, 9 (3), pp. 274–285.

———, 1997, *The Rise of Birds*. Baltimore: Johns Hopkins University Press, 312 pages.

Chatterjee, Sankar, and D. K. Rudra, 1996, KT events in India: impact, rifting, volcanism and dinosaur extinction: *Proceedings of the Gondwanan Dinosaur Symposium: Memoirs of the Queensland Museum*, 39 (part 3), pp. 489–532.

Chatterjee, Sankar, and Zhong Zheng, 2002, Cranial anatomy of *Shunosaurus*, a basal sauropod dinosaur from the Middle Jurassic of China: *in*: David B. Norman and David J. Gower, editors, *Archosaurian Anatomy and Palaeontology. Essays in Memory of Alick D. Walker. Zoological Journal of the Linnean Society*, 136, pp. 145–169.

Chen Pei-Ji, 1996, Nonmarine Jurassic strata of Arizona, *in*: Michael Morales, editor, *Museum of Northern Arizona Bulletin*, 60, pp. 395–412.

Chen, Pei-Ji, Zhi-ming Dong, and Shuo-nan Zhen, 1998, An exceptionally well-preserved theropod dinosaur from the Yixian Formation of China: *Nature*, 391, pp. 147–152.

Chen Shuyun, and Huang Xiaozhong, 1993, Preliminary study of dinosaur tracks in Cangling, Chuxiong Prefecture: *Journal of Yunnan Geology*, 12 (3), pp. 267–276.

Cheng-Ming Chuong, 2001, The making of integumentary appendages: dinosaur feathers and chicken teeth?: *International Congress of Vertebrate Morphology, Abstracts*, p. 217.

Cherry, Collette, 2003, Bone histology of the primitive dinosaur *Thecodontosaurus antiquus*: *in*: David B. Norman and Paul Upchurch, editors, *SVPCA 50, Cambridge 2002, 11–13 September, Abstract Volume*, unpaginated.

Chiappe, Luis M., 1996, Late Cretaceous birds of Southern South America: anatomy and systematics of Enanithornithes and *Patagopteryx deferralist*: *Münchner Geowissenschaftliche Abhandlung*, Abh (A), 30, pp. 203–244.

———, 2002, Basal bird phylogeny: problems and solutions, *in*: Luis M. Chiappe and Lawrence W. Witmer, editors, 2002, *Mesozoic Birds: Above the Heads of Dinosaurs*. Berkeley: University of California Press, pp. 448–472.

Chiappe, Luis M., Rodolfo A. Coria, and Lowell Dingus, 2001, Sauropod reproductive behavior: evidence from the Auca Ma-

huevo nesting site (Upper Cretaceous, Patagonia, Argentina): *International Congress of Vertebrate Morphology, Abstracts*, p. 216.

Chiappe, Luis M., Rodolfo A. Coria, Lowell Dingus, Frankie Jackson, Anusuya Chinsamy, and Marilyn Fox, 1998, Sauropod dinosaur embryos from the Late Cretaceous of Patagonia: *Nature*, 396, pp. 258–261.

Chiappe, Luis M., Rodolfo A. Coria, Lowell Dingus, Leonardo Salgado, and F. Jackson, 2001, Titanosaur eggs and embryos from Auca Mahuevo (Patagonia, Argentina): implications for sauropod reproductive behavior: *Journal of Vertebrate Paleontology*, 21 (Supplement to Number 3), Abstracts of Papers, Sixty-first Annual Meeting, p. 40A.

Chiappe, Luis M., and Lowell Dingus, 2000, *Walking on Eggs: The Astonishing Discovery of Dinosaur Eggs in the Badlands of Patagonia*. New York: Scribner, 219 pages.

Chiappe, Luis M., S. A. Ji, Q. Ji, and Mark A. Norell, 1999, Anatomy and systematics of the Confuscionithidae (Theropoda: Aves) from the Late Mesozoic of northeastern China: *Bulletin of the American Museum of Natural History*, 242, pp. 1–89.

Chiappe, Luis M., Mark A. Norell, and James M. Clark, 1996, Phylogenetic position of *Mononykus* (Aves: Alvarezsauridae) from the Late Cretaceous of the Gobi Desert, *in*: Fernando S. Novas and Ralph E. Molnar, editors, *Proceedings of the Gondwanan Dinosaur Symposium: Memoirs of the Queensland Museum*, 39 (part 3), pp. 557–582.

———, 1998, The skull of a relative of the stem-group bird *Mononykus*: *Nature*, 392, pp. 275–278.

———, 2002, The Cretaceous, short-armed Alvarezsauridae: *Mononykus* and its kin, *in*: Luis M. Chiappe and Lawrence W. Witmer, editors, *Mesozoic Birds: Above the Heads of Dinosaurs*. Berkeley: University of California Press.

Chin, Karen, Tim T. Tokaryk, G. M. Erickson, and L. C. Calk, 1998, A king-sized theropod coprolite: *Nature*, 393, pp. 680–682.

Chinnery, Brenda J., 2002, Morphometric analysis of evolution and growth in the ceratopsian postcranial skeleton: *Journal of Vertebrate Paleontology*, 23 (Supplement to Number 3), Abstracts of Papers, Sixty-second Annual Meeting, pp. 43A–44A.

Chinnery, Brenda J., and David B. Weishampel, 1998, *Montanoceratops cerorhynchus* (Dinosauria: Ceratopsia) and relationships among basal neoceratopsians: *Journal of Vertebrate Paleontology*, 18 (3), pp. 569–585.

Chinsamy, Anusuya, 1990, Physiological implications of the bone histology of *yntarsus rhodesiensis* (Saurischia: Theropoda): *Palaeontologia Africana*, 27, pp. 7–82.

———, 1993, Bone histology and growth trajectory of the prosauropod dinosaur *Massospondylus carinatus*: *Modern Geology*, 18, pp. 319–329.

———, 2001, Growth patterns in dinosaurs: *International Congress of Vertebrate Morphology, Abstracts*, p. 216.

Bibliography

Chopard, S., 1883, La géologie du Jura. Considérations préliminaires sur les environs de Poligny. Rapport de la commission de géologie et de paléontologie sur une excursion entre Poligny et Saint-Lothian, faite le 23 juin 1862: *Bull. Soc. Agric. Sci. Arts Poligny*, pp. 1–22, Poligny.

Chow, M., 1954, [Additional notes on the microstructure of the supposed dinosaur egg shells from Laiyang, Shantung]: *Acta Palaeontologica Sineca*, 2 (14), pp. 389–394.

Chow, M., and Anatoly Konstantinovich Rozhdestvensky, 1961, Exploration of Inner Mongolia: a preliminary account of the 1959 field work of the Sino-Soviet paleontological expedition (SSPE): *Vertebrata Palasiatica*, 4 (1), pp. 1–10.

Christian, Andreas, 2002, Neck posture and overall body design in sauropods: *Mitteilungen Museum für Naturkunde der Humboldt-Universität zu Berlin, Geowissenschaftliche Reihe*, 5, pp. 271–281.

Christian, Andreas, and Wolf-Dieter Heinrich, 1998, The neck posture of *Brachiosaurus brancai*: *Mitteilungen Museum für Naturkunde der Humboldt-Universität zu Berlin, Geowissenschaftliche Reihe*, 1, pp. 73–80.

Christian, Andreas, and Holger Preushoft, 1996, Deducing the body posture of extinct large vertebrates from the shape of the vertebral column: *Palaeontology*, 39 (4), pp. 801–812.

Christiansen, Per, 1996, The evidence for and implications of gastroliths in sauropods (Dinosauria: Sauropoda): *Gaia*, 12, pp. 1–7.

_____, 1997, Locomotion in sauropod dinosaurs: *Ibid.*, 14, pp. 45–75.

_____, 1999, Feeding mechanics in some sauropod dinosaurs: *Historical Biology*, 14, pp. 137–152.

_____, 2000a, Feeding mechanisms of the sauropod dinosaurs *Brachiosaurus, Camarasaurus, Diplodocus*, and *Dicraeosaurus*: *Historical Biology*, 14, pp. 137–152.

_____, 2000b, On the head size of sauropodomorph dinosaurs: implications for ecology and physiology: *Ibid.*, pp. 269–297.

_____, 2000c, Strength indicator values of theropod long bones, with comments on limb proportions and cursorial potential: *in* B. P. Pérez-Moreno, Thomas R. Holtz, Jr., José Luis Sanz, and José J. Moratalla, editors, Aspects of theropod paleobiology: *Gaia*, 15 (cover dated December 1998), pp. 241–255.

Christiansen, Per, and Gregory S. Paul, 2001, Limb bone scaling, limb proportions, and bone strength in neoceratopsian dinosaurs: *Gaia*, 16, pp. 13–29.

Chure, Daniel J., 2000a, Observations on the morphology and pathology of the gastral basket of *Allosaurus*, based on a new specimen from Dinosaur National Monument: *Oryctos*, 3, pp. 29–37.

_____, 2000b, Utah's first *Allosaurus* — Marsh's "*Megalosaurus*" specimen rediscovered: *Brigham Young University Geology Studies*, 45, pp. 1–4.

_____, 2001a, On the type and referred material of *Laelaps trihedrodon* Cope 1877 (Dinosauria: Theropoda), *in*: Darren Tanke and Kenneth Carpenter, editors, 2001, *Mesozoic Vertebrate Life: New Research Inspired by the Paleontology of Philip J. Currie*. Bloomington and Indianapolis, Indiana: Indiana University Press, pp. 10–18.

_____, 2001b, A new sauropod with a well preserved skull from the Cedar Mountain Fm. (Cretaceous) of Dinosaur National Monument, Utah: *Journal of Vertebrate Paleontology*, 21 (Supplement to Number 3), Abstracts of Papers, Sixty-first Annual Meeting, p. 40A.

_____, 2001c, The second record of the African theropod *Elaphrosaurus* (Dinosauria, Ceratosauria) from the Western Hemisphere: *Neus Jahrbuch für Geologie und Paläontologie, Monatshefte*, 9, pp. 565–576.

Chure, Daniel J., Anthony R. Fiorillo, and Aase Jacobsen, 2000, Prey bone utilization by predatory dinosaurs in the Late Jurassic of North America, with comments on prey bone use by dinosaurs throughout the Mesozoic: *in* B. P. Pérez-Moreno, Thomas R. Holtz, Jr., José Luis Sanz, and José J. Moratalla, editors, Aspects of theropod paleobiology: *Gaia*, 15 (December 1998), pp. 227–240.

Chure, Daniel J., and James H. Madsen, Jr., 1996, On the presence of furculae in some non-maniraptoran Theropoda: *Journal of Vertebrate Paleontology*, 16 (3), pp. 573–577.

_____, 1998, An unusual braincase (?*Stokesosaurus clevelandi*) from the Cleveland-Lloyd Dinosaur Quarry, Utah (Morrison Formation: Late Jurassic): *Ibid.*, 18 (1), pp. 115–125.

Chure, Daniel J., and John S. McIntosh, 1989, *A Bibliography of the Dinosauria (Exclusive of the Aves), 1677–1986*. Grand Junction, Colorado: Museum of Western Colorado, Paleontology Series 1, 226 pages.

Chure, Daniel J., David K. Smith, Art Anderson, James H. Madsen, Jr., and Peter M. Galton, 2002, The medial pharyngeal pneumatic system (MPPS) in *Allosaurus fragilis*: morphology and phylogenetic significance: *Journal of Vertebrate Paleontology*, 23 (Supplement to Number 3), Abstracts of Papers, Sixty-second Annual Meeting, p. 44A.

Cifelli, Richard, James I. Kirkland, Anne Weil, A. L. Deino, and B. J. Kowallis, 1997, High-precision ^{40}Ar/^{39} geochronology and the advent of North America's Late Cretaceous terrestrial fauna: *Proceedings of the National Academy of Sciences, USA*, 94, pp. 11,163–11,167.

Cifelli, Richard L., Randall L. Nydam, James D. Gardner, Anne Weil, Jeffrey G. Eaton, James I. Kirkland, and Scott K. Madsen, 1999, Medial Cretaceous vertebrates from the Cedar Mountain Formation, Emory County, Utah: the Mussentuchit local fauna, *in*: David D. Gillette, editor, *Vertebrate Paleontology in Utah*, Utah Geological Survey Miscellaneous Publication 99-1, pp. 219–242.

Clark, James M., Catherine A. Forster, Yuan Wang, and Brian Andres, 2002, New small dinosaurs from the Upper Jurassic Shishugou Formation at Wucaiwan, Xinjiang, China: *Journal of Vertebrate Paleontology*, 23 (Supplement to Number 3), Abstracts of Papers, Sixty-second Annual Meeting, p. 44A.

Clark, James M., Mark A. Norell, and Luis M. Chiappe, 1999, An oviraptorid skeleton from the Late Cretaceous of Ukhaa Tolgod, Mongolia, preserved in an avian-like brooding position over an oviraptorid nest: *American Museum Novitates*, 3265, pp. 1–36.

Clark, James M., Mark A. Norell, and Timothy Rowe, 2002, Cranial anatomy of *Citipati osmolskae* (Theropoda, Oviraptorosauria), and a reinterpretation of the holotype of *Oviraptor philoceratops*: *American Museum Novitates*, 3364, 24 pages.

Claessens, Leon, 2001, The function of the gastralia in theropod lung ventilation: *The Paleobiology and Phylogenetics of Large Theropods*, A. Watson Armour III Symposium, The Field Museum, 12 May 2001, unpaginated.

Clark, James M., 1995, The egg thief exonerated: *Natural History*, 6 (95), p. 56.

Clark, James M., Mark A. Norell, and Rinchen Barsbold, 2001, Two new oviraptorids (Theropoda: Oviraptorosauria), Upper Cretaceous Djadokhta Formation, Ukhaa Tolgod, Mongolia: *Journal of Vertebrate Paleontology*, 21 (2), pp. 209–213.

Clark, James M., Altangerel Perle, and Mark A. Norell, 1994, The skull of *Erlikosaurus andrewsi*, a Late Cretaceous "segnosaur" (Theropoda: Therizinosauridae) from Mongolia: *American Museum Novitates*, 3115, pp. 1–39.

Clark, N. D. L., 2001, A thyreophoran dinosaur from the early Bajocian (Middle Jurassic) of the Isle of Skye, Scotland: *Scottish Journal of Geology*, 37 (1), pp. 19–26.

Clements, R. G., 1999, Type-section of the Purbeck Limestone Group, Durlston Bay, Swanage, Dorset: *Proceedings of the Dorset Natural History and Archaeological Society*, 114, pp. 52–90.

Clemmensen, L. B., D. V. Kent, and Farrish A. Jenkins, Jr., 1998, A Late Triassic lake system in East Greenland: facies, depositional cycles and palaeolatitude: *Palaeogeography, Palaeoclimatology, Palaeoecology*, 140, pp. 135–159.

Cohen, S., A. R. I. Cruickshank, K. A. Josey, T. W. Manning, and P. Upchurch 1995, *The Dinosaur Egg and Embryo Project, Exhibition Guide*. Leicester: Rock Art, 16 pages.

Colbert, Edwin H. [Harris], 1965, *The Age of Reptiles*. New York: W. Norton and Company, 228 pages.

_____, 1989, The Triassic dinosaur *Coelophysis*: *Museum of Northern Arizona Bulletin*, 57, xv, 160 pages.

_____, 1993, Feeding strategies and metabolism in elephants and sauropod dinosaurs: *American Journal of Science*, 293A, pp. 1–19.

Colbert, Edwin H., and Duncan Merriless, 1967, Cretaceous dinosaur footprints from Western Australia: *Journal of the Royal Society of Western Australia*, 50, pp. 21–25.

Company, J., A. Galobart, and R. Gaete, 1998, First data on the hadrosaurid dinosaurs (Ornithischia, Dinosauria) from the Upper Cretaecous of Valencia Spain: *Oryctos*, 1, pp. 87–104.

Connely, Melissa V., 2002, Paleoecology of the Morrison Formation, Como Bluff, Wyoming: *Tate 2002: Wyoming in the Age of Dinosaurs: Creatures, Environments and Extinctions*, p. 13.

Coombs, Walter P., Jr., 1971, The Ankylosauria, Ph.D. thesis, Ann Arbor (Michigan) Microfilms Intern., Columbia University, New York, 487 pages (unpublished).

_____, 1978a, The families of the ornithischian dinosaur order Ankylosauria: *Paleontology*, 21, part 1, pp. 143–170.

_____, 1978b, Theoretical aspects of cursorial adaptations in dinosaurs: *Revisions in Biology*, 53 (4), pp. 393–410.

_____, 1982, Juvenile specimens of the ornithischian dinosaur *Psittacosaurus*: *Palaeontology*, 25, part 1, pp. 89–107.

_____, 1986, A juvenile dinosaur referable to the genus *Euoplocephalus* (Reptilia, Ornithischia): *Journal of Vertebrate Paleontology*, 6, pp. 162–173.

_____, 1995, Ankylosaurian tail clubs of middle Campanian to early Maastrichtian age from western North America, with descriptions of a tiny tail club from Alberta and discussion of tail orientation and tail club function: *Canadian Journal of Earth Sciences*, 32, pp. 902–912.

Coombs, Walter P., Jr., and Thomas A. Demere, 1996, A Late Cretaceous nodosaurid ankylosaur (Dinosauria: Ornithischia) from marine sediments of coastal California: *Journal of Paleontology*, 70, pp. 311–326.

Coombs, Walter P., Jr., and Teresa Maryańska, 1990, Ankylosauria, *in*: David B. Weishampel, Peter Dodson, and Halszka Osmólska, editors, *The Dinosauria*. Berkeley and Los Angeles: University of California Press, pp. 456–483.

Coombs, Walter P., Jr., and Ralph E. Molnar, 1981, Sauropoda (Reptilia, Saurischia) from the Cretaceous of Queensland: *Memoirs of the Queensland Museum*, 20, pp. 351–373.

Cope, Edward Drinker, 1867, Remarks on extinct reptiles which approach birds: *Proceedings of the Academy of Natural Sciences of Philadelphia*, 9, pp. 234–235.

_____, 1877a, On some extinct reptiles and Batrachia from the Judith River and the Fox Hills beds of Montana: *Ibid.*, 28, pp. 340–349.

_____, 1877b, On a gigantic saurian from the Dakota epoch of Colorado: *Paleontology Bulletin*, 27, pp. 5–10.

Coria, Rodolfo A. [Anibal], 1999, Ornithopod dinosaurs from the Neuquén Group, Patagonia, Argentina: Phylogeny and Biostratigraphy: *in*: Yukimitsu Tomida, Rich, and Vickers-Rich, editors, *Proceedings of the Second Gondwanan Dinosaur Symposium*, National Science Museum Monographs, 15, Tokyo, pp. 47–60.

_____, 2001, New theropod from the Late Cretaceous of Patagonia, *in*: Darren Tanke and Kenneth Carpenter, editors, *Mesozoic Vertebrate Life: New Research Inspired by the Paleontology of Philip J. Currie*. Bloomington and Indianapolis, Indiana: Indiana University Press, pp. 3–9.

_____, 2002, Un gran terópod celurosaurio en el Cretácico Superior de Neuquén: *Ameghiana*, 39 (4), Supplemento, p. 9R.

Coria, Rodolfo A., and Jore O. Calvo, 1996, Analisis filogenético preliminar del primer dinosaurio Iguanodontia registrado en la Formacion Río Limay: *XII Jornadas Argentinas de Paleontología de Vertebrados, Ameghiniana*, 33, p. 462.

_____, 2002, A new iguanodontian ornithopod from Neuquen Basin, Patagonia, Argentina: *Journal of Vertebrate Paleontology*, 22 (3), pp. 503–509.

Coria, Rodolfo A., and Luis M. Chiappe, 2001, Tooth replacement in a sauropod premaxilla from the Upper Cretaceous of Patagonia, Argentina: *Ameghiniana*, 38 (4), pp. 463–466.

Coria, Rodolfo A., Luis M. Chiappe, and Lowell Dingus, 2002, A new close relative of *Carnotaurus sastrei* Bonaparte 1985 (Theropoda: Abelisauridae) from the Late Cretaceous of Patagonia: *Journal of Vertebrate Paleontology*, 22 (2), pp. 460–465.

Coria, Rodolfo A., Luis M. Chiappe, and Giuliana Negro, 2001, Sauropod embryonic integument from Auca Mahuevo (Late Cretaceous), Argentina: *Journal of Vertebrate Paleontology*, 21 (Supplement to Number 3), Abstracts of Papers, Sixty-first Annual Meeting, p. 42A.

Coria, Rodolfo A., and Philip J. Currie, 1997, A new theropod from the Río Limay Formation: *Journal of Vertebrate Paleontology*, 17 (Supplement to Number 3), Abstracts of Papers, Fifty-seventh Annual Meeting, p. 40A.

_____, 2003, The braincase of *Giganotosaurus carolini*, (Dinosauria: Theropoda) from the Upper Cretaceous of Argentina: *Journal of Vertebrate Paleontology*, 22 (4), pp. 802–811.

Coria, Rodolfo A., and Leonardo Salgado, 1995, A new giant carnivorous dinosaur from the Cretaceous of Patagonia: *Nature*, 377, pp. 224–226.

_____, 1996, A basal iguanodontian (Ornithischia: Ornithopoda) from the Late Cretaceous of South America: *Journal of Vertebrate Paleontology*, 16 (3), pp. 445–457.

_____, 2000, A basal Abelisauria Novas 1992 (Theropoda–Ceratosauria) from the Cretaceous of Patagonia, Argentina, *in* B. P. Pérez-Moreno, Thomas R. Holtz, Jr., José Luis Sanz, and José J. Moratalla, editors, Aspects of theropod paleobiology: *Gaia*, 15 (cover dated December 1998), pp. 89–102.

_____, 2001, South American ankylosaurs, *in*: Kenneth Carpenter, editor, 2001, *The Armored Dinosaurs*. Bloomington and Indiana: Indiana University Press, pp. 159–168.

Coria, Rodolfo A., Leonardo Salgado, and Jorge O. Calvo, 1991, Premeros restos de dinosaurios Theropoda del Miembro Huincul, Formación Río Limay (Cretácico Tardío Presenoniano), Neuquén, Argentina: *Ameghiniana*, 28, pp. 405–406.

Courel, Louis, and Georges R. Demathieu, 2000, Une nouvelle ichnospèce *Coelurosaurichnus grancieri* du Trias supérieur de l'Ardèche, France: *Geodiversitas*, 22 (1), pp. 35–46.

Courtillot, V., J. J. Jaeger, Z. Yang, G. Feraud, and C. Hofmann, 1996, The influence of continental flood basalts on mass extinctions: where do we stand?, *in*: G. Ryder, D. Fastovsky, and S. Gartner, editors, *The Cretaceous–Tertiary Event and Other Catastrophes in Earth History*. Geological Society of America Special Papers, 307, pp. 513–525.

Cracraft, Joel, 1971, Caenagnathiformes, Cretaceous birds convergent in jaw mechanism of dicynodont reptiles: *Journal of Paleontology*, 45 (5), pp. 805–809.

Cranwell, Gregory P., 2001, A preliminary report of new fossils from the Shellenberger Canyon Formation (upper Lower Cretaceous) of southern Arizona, USA: *Western Association of Vertebrate Paleontologists with Mesa Southwest Museum and Southwest Paleontological Society, Mesa Arizona, First Meeting of the New Millenium* [sic], *February 17, 2001*, abstracts, not paginated.

_____, 2003, New evidence of dinosaurs from the Shellenberger Canyon Formation (Lower Cretaceous) of southeastern Arizona, USA: *Southwest Paleontological Symposium 2003, Guide to Presentations*, Mesa Southwest Museum, January 25, 2003, unpaginated.

Crompton, A. W., and John Attridge, 1986, Masticatory apparatus of the larger herbivores during Late Triassic and Early Jurassic times, *in*, Kevin Padian, editor, *The Beginning of the Age of Dinosaurs*. New York: Cambridge University Press, pp. 223–236.

Cuenca Bescós, G., J. I. Canudo, and J. I. Ruiz-Omeñaca, 1997, Dinosaurios del tránsito Jurásico-Cretácico en Aragón, *in*: J. A. Gámez and E. Liñan, editors, *V Jornadas Aragonesas de Paleontología "Vida y ambientes del Jurásico."* Zaragoza, Spain: Institucion Fernando el Católico, pp. 193–221.

Cuny, Gilles, and Peter M. Galton, 1993, Revision of the Airel theropod dinosaur from the Triassic–Jurassic boundary (Normandy, France): *Neus Jahrbuch für Geologie und Paläontologie, Abhandlungen*, 187 (3), pp. 261–288.

Currie, Philip J., 1983, Hadrosaur trackways from the Lower Cretaceous of Canada: *Acta Palaeontologica Polonica*, 28 (1/2), pp. 63–73.

_____, 1988, The discovery of dinosaur eggs at Devil's Coulee: *Alberta* 1 (1), pp. 3–10.

_____, 1987, Birdlike characteristics of the jaws and teeth of troodontid theropods (Dinosauria: Saurischia): *Journal of Vertebrate Paleontology*, 7, pp. 72–81.

_____, 1995, New information on the anatomy and relationships of *Dromaeosaurus albertensis* (Dinosauria: Theropoda): *Ibid.*, 15 (3), pp. 237–249.

_____, 1997, Sino-Soviet Expeditions, *in*: Philip J. Currie and Kevin Padian, editors, *Encyclopedia of Dinosaurs*. San Diego: Academic Press, pp. 661–662.

_____, 2000a, On a pack of theropods from Argentina: *DinoPress*, 1, pp. 79–89 (in Japanese; "English Text," pp. 17–23).

_____, 2000b, Possible evidence of gregarious behavior in tyrannosaurids: *in* B. P. Pérez-

Bibliography

Moreno, Thomas R. Holtz, Jr., José Luis Sanz, and José J. Moratalla, editors, Aspects of theropod paleobiology: *Gaia*, 15 (cover dated December 1998), pp. 271–277.

_____, 2000c, Theropods from the Cretaceous of Mongolia: *in*: M. J. Benton, M. A. Shishkin, D. M. Unwin and E. N. Kurochkin, editors, *The Age of Dinosaurs in Russia and Mongolia*. Cambridge: Cambridge University Press, pp. 434–455.

_____, 2001, Nomadic Expeditions, Inc., report of fieldwork in Mongolia, September 2000: *Alberta Palaeontological Society, Fifth Annual Symposium, Abstract Volume*, January 20, 2001, Mount Royal College, Calgary, Alberta, pp. 12–16.

_____, 2002, Report on fieldwork in Mongolia, September 2001: *Alberta Palaeontological Society, Sixth Annual Symposium, "Fossils 2002," Abstract Volume*, January 26–27, 2002, Mount Royal College, Calgary, Alberta, pp. 8–12.

Currie, Philip J., and Kenneth Carpenter, 2000, A new specimen of *Acrocanthosaurus atokensis* (Theropoda, Dinosauria) from the Lower Cretaceous Antlers Formation (Lower Cretaceous, Aptian) of Oklahoma, USA: *Geodiversitas*, 22 (2), pp. 207–246.

_____, in press, A new specimen of *Acrocanthosaurus atokensis* from the Lower Cretaceous Antlers Formation (Lower Cretaceous, Aptian) of Oklahoma, USA: *Bulletin du Muséum National d'Historie Naturelle* (Paris).

Currie, Philip J., and Pei-ji Chen, 2001, Anatomy of *Sinosauropteryx prima* from Liaoning, northeastern China: *Canadian Journal of Earth Sciences*, 38 (12), pp. 1705–1727.

Currie, Philip J., and Peter Dodson, 1984, Mass death of a herd of ceratopsian dinosaurs, *in*: W. E. Reif and F. Westphal, editors, *Third Symposium on Mesozoic Terrestrial Ecosystems, Short Papers*. Tübingen, Germany: Attempto Verlag, pp. 61–66.

Currie, Philip J., and David A. Eberth, 1993, Palaeontology, sedimentology and palaeoecology of the Iren Dabasu Formation (Upper Cretaceous), Inner Mongolia, People's Republic of China: *Cretaceous Research*, 14, pp. 127–144.

Currie, Philip J., and Dale A. Russell, 1988, Osteology and relationships of *Chirostenotes pergracilis* (Saurischia, Theropoda) from the Judith River (Oldman) Formation of Alberta, Canada: *Canadian Journal of Earth Sciences*, 25, pp. 972–986.

Currie, Philip J., and Dong Zhiming, 2001a, New information on *Shanshanosaurus huoyanshanensis*, a juvenile tyrannosaurid (Theropoda, Dinosauria) from the Late Cretaceous of China: *Canadian Journal of Earth Sciences*, 38 (12), pp. 1729–1737.

_____, 2001b, New information on Cretaceous troodontids (Dinosauria, Theropoda) from the People's Republic of China: *Ibid.*, pp. 1753–1766.

Currie, Philip J., G. C. Nadon, and Martin G. Lockley, 1991, Dinosaur footprints with skin impressions from the Cretaceous of Alberta and Colorado: *Canadian Journal of Earth Sciences*, 28, pp. 102–115.

Currie, Philip J., J. Keith Rigby, Jr., and Robert E. Sloan, 1990, Theropod teeth from the Judith River Formation of southern Alberta, Canada, *in*: Kenneth Carpenter and Currie, editors, *Dinosaur Systematics: Approaches and Perspectives*. Cambridge, New York and Melbourne: Cambridge University Press, pp. 107–125.

Currie, Philip J., and William A. S. Sarjeant, 1979, Lower Cretaceous dinosaur footprints from the Peace River Canyon, British Columbia, Canada: *Palaeogeography, Palaeoclimatology, Palaeoecology*, 28, pp. 103–115.

Currie, Philip J., and Xi-Jin Zhao, 1993, A new carnosaur (Dinosauria, Theropoda) from the Jurassic of Xinjiang, People's Republic of China: *Canadian Journal of Earth Sciences*, 30 (10–11), pp. 2037–2081.

Curry [Rogers], Kristina A., 1999, Ontogenetic histology of *Apatosaurus* (Dinosauria: Sauropoda): new insights on growth rates and longevity: *Journal of Vertebrate Paleontology*, 19 (4), pp. 654–665.

_____, 2001a, A new sauropod from Madagascar: implications for titanosaur lower-level phylogeny: *Journal of Vertebrate Paleontology*, 21 (Supplement to Number 3), Abstracts of Papers, Sixty-first Annual Meeting, p. 43A.

_____, 2001b, The anatomy and phylogeny of a new titanosaurid from Madagascar (Upper Cretaceous Maevarano Formation): *Ameghiniana*, XVII Jornadas Argentinas de Paleontologia de Vertebrados, Resúmes, Esquel, 16–18 de mayo de 2001, p. 18R.

Curry Rogers, Kristina, and Catherine A. Forster, 1999a, *in*: *VII International Symposium on Mesozoic Terrestrial Ecosystems*, (Museo de Ciencas Naturales, Buenos Aires), pp. 20–21.

_____, 1999b, New sauropods from Madagascar: a glimpse into titanosaur cranial morphology and evolution: *Journal of Vertebrate Paleontology*, 19 (Supplement to Number 3), Abstracts of Papers, Fifty-ninth Annual Meeting, p. 41A.

_____, 2001, The last of the dinosaur titans: a new sauropod from Madagascar: *Nature*, 412, pp. 530–534.

Curtice, Brian D., 2003, Two genera down, one to go? The potential synonymy [sic] of *Supersaurus* with *Barosaurus*: *Southwest Paleontological Symposium 2003, Guide to Presentations*, Mesa Southwest Museum, January 25, 2003, unpaginated.

Curtice, Brian D., and Kenneth L. Stadtman, 2001, The demise of *Dystylosaurus edwini* and a revision of *Supersaurus vivianae*: *Western Association of Vertebrate Paleontologists and Mesa Southwest Museum and Southwest Paleontological Symposium, Bulletin*, 8, pp. 33–40.

Curtice, Brian D., and D. R. Wilhite, 1996, A re-evaluation of the Dry Mesa Dinosaur Quarry sauropod fauna with a description of juvenile sauropod elements, *in*: A. C. Huffman, W. R. Lund, and L. H. Godwin, editors, *Geology and Resource of the Paradox Basin*, Utah Geological Association Guidebook, 25, pp. 325–338.

Cuvier, Georges, 1800a, A quantity of bones found in the rocks in the environs of Honfleur, by the late Abbé Bachelet: *Philosophical Magazine*, 8, p. 290.

_____, 1800b, Sue une nouvelle espèce de crocodile fossile: *Bulletin de la Société philomatique de Paris*, 2, p. 159.

_____, 1812, *Recherches sur les ossemens fossiles*. Paris.

_____, 1824, *Ibid.*, 2nd edition, 5 (2). Paris and Amsterdam: Dufour and D'Ocagne.

_____, 1825, *Discours sur les révolutions de la surface du globe*, 3rd edition. Paris and Amsterdam: Dufour and D'Ocagne.

_____, 1836, *Recherches sur les ossemens fossiles*, 4th edition, Paris.

Czerkas, Stephen A., and Chongxi Yuan, An arboreal maniraptoran from northeast China, *in*: Sylvia J. Czerkas, editor, 2002, *Feathered Dinosaurs*. Blanding, Utah: The Dinosaur Museum, pp. 63–95.

Czerkas, Stephen A., Dianshuang Zhang, Jinglu Li, and Yinxian Li, 2002, Flying dromaeosaurs, *in*: Sylvia J. Czerkas, editor, 2002, *Feathered Dinosaurs*. Blanding, Utah: The Dinosaur Museum, pp. 97–126.

Czerkas, Sylvia J., editor, 2002, *Feathered Dinosaurs*. Blanding, Utah: The Dinosaur Museum, vi, 136 pages.

Czerkas, Sylvia J., and Stephen A. Czerkas, 1991, *Dinosaurs: A Global View*. New York: Mallard Press, 247 pages.

Daffner, R. H., 1978, Stress fractures: current concepts: *Skeletal Radiology*, 2, pp. 221–229.

Dahn, R. D., and J. F. Fallon, 2000, Interdigital regulation of digit identity and homeotic transformation by modulated BMP signaling: *Science*, 289, pp. 438–441.

Dalla Vecchia, Fabio Marco, 1998, Remains of Sauropoda (Reptilia, Saurischia) in the Lower Cretaceous (Upper Hauterivian/Lower Barremian) Limestone of SW Istria (Croatia): *Geologia Croatia*, 51 (2), pp. 105–134.

_____, 2000, Macrovegetali terrestri nel Mesozoico italiano: un'ulteriore evidenza di frequenti empersioni: *Natura Nascosta*, 20, pp. 18–35.

_____, 2001a. A new theropod dinosaur from the Lower Jurassic of Italy: *Dino Press*, 3, pp. 81–87.

_____, 2001b, A vertebra of a large sauropod dinosaur from the Lower Cretaceous of Istria (Croatia): *Natura Nascosta*, 22, pp. 14–33.

_____, 2001c, An odd dinosaur bone from the Lower Cretaceous of Istria (Croatia): *Ibid.*, pp. 34–35.

_____, 2001d, Terrestrial ecosystems on the Mesozoic peri-Adratic carbonate platforms: the vertebrate evidence: *Asociación Paleontológica Argentina*, Publicación Especial 7, VII International Symposium on Mesozoic Terrestrial Ecosystems, Buenos Aires, 30-6-2001, pp. 77–83.

Dalton, Rex, 2000, Feathers fly in Beijing: *Nature*, 405, p. 992.

Dames, W., 1884, Vorlegung eines Zahnes von *Megalosaurus* aus dem Wealden des Deisters: *Sitzungsberichte der Gesellschaft Naturforschender Freunde zu Berlin*, pp. 186–188.

Dashveg, Demberelynin, Michael J. Novacek, Mark A. Norell, James M. Clark, Luis M. Chiappe, Amy Davidson, Malcolm C. McKenna, Lowell Dingus, C. C. Swisher, III, and Altangerel Perle, 1995, Unusual preservation in a new vertebrate assemblage from the Late Cretaceous of Mongolia: *Nature*, 374, pp. 446–449.

Day, Julia J., Paul Upchurch, David B. Norman, Andrew S. Gale, and H. Philip Powell, 2002, Sauropod trackways, evolution, and behavior: *Science*, 296, p. 1659.

De Valais, F. E. Novas, and S. Apesteguia, 2002, Morfologia del pie de los terópodos abelisaurios: neuvas evidencias del Cretácico de Patagonia: *Ameghiana*, 39 (4), Supplemento, pp. 9R–10R.

Debus, Allen A., and Dian E. Debus, 2002, *Paleoimagery: The Evolution of Dinosaurs in Art*. Jefferson, North Carolina: McFarland & Company, vii, 285 pages.

Deck, Linda T. 2001, Using cladograms successfully in an exhibit: *Triceratops* at the Smithsonian: *Journal of Vertebrate Paleontology*, 21 (Supplement to Number 3), Abstracts of Papers, Sixty-first Annual Meeting, p. 44A.

Delair, Justin B., 1963, Notes on Purbeck fossil footprints, with descriptions of two hitherto unknown forms from Dorset: *Proceedings of the Dorset Natural History and Archaeological Society*, 87, pp. 67–66.

_____, 1993, Reptilia of the Portland Stone (Upper Jurassic) of England: a preliminary survey of the material and literature: *Modern Geology*, 18, pp. 331–348.

Delair, Justin B., and William A. S. Sarjeant, 1975, The earliest discoveries of dinosaurs: *Isis*, 66, pp. 5–25.

_____, 2002, The earliest discoveries of dinosaurs: the records re-examined: *Proceedings of the Geologists' Association*, 113, pp. 185–197.

Demathieu, Georges, 1966, *Rhynchosauroides petri* et *Sphingopus ferox*, nouvelle empreintes des Reptiles des gres triassiques de la bordure Nord-Est du Massif Central: *Comptes Rendus des Séances de l'Academie des Sciences, Paris*, sèrie D, 263, pp. 483–486.

Demere, Thomas A., 1988, An armored dinosaur from Carlsbad: *Environment Southwest*, 523, pp. 12–15.

Depéret, Charles, 1869, Note sur les dinosauriens sauropodes et théropodes du Crétacé de Madagascar: *Bulletin, Société Géologique de France*, Series 3, 24, pp. 176–194.

Dial, Kenneth P., 2003, Wing-assisted incline running and the evolution of flight: *Science*, 299, pp. 402–404.

DiCroce, Tony, and Kenneth Carpenter, 2001, New ornithopod from the Cedar Mountain Formation (Lower Cretaceous) of Eastern Utah, *in*: Darren Tanke and Kenneth Carpenter, editors, 2001, *Mesozoic Vertebrate Life: New Research Inspired by the Paleontology of Philip J. Currie*. Bloomington and Indianapolis, Indiana: Indiana University Press, pp. 183–196.

Dilkes, David W., 2001, An ontogenetic perspective on locomotion in the Late Cretaceous dinosaur *Maiasaura peeblesorum* (Ornithischia: Hadrosauridae): *Canadian Journal of Earth Sciences*, 38, pp. 1205–1227.

Dingus, Lowell, Julia Clarke, G. R. Scott, C. Swisher, Luis M. Coria, and Rodolfo A. Coria, 2000, Stratigraphy and magnetostratigraphy/faunal constraints for the age of sauropod embryo-bearing rocks in the Neuquén Group (Late Cretaceous, Neuquén Province, Argentina): *American Museum Novitates*, 3290, pp. 1–11.

Dingus, Lowell, 1996, Eugene S. Gaffney, Mark A. Norell, and Scott D. Sampson, 1996, *The Halls of Dinosaurs: A Guide to Saurischians and Ornithischians*. New York: American Museum of Natural History, 100 pages.

Dodson, Peter, 1976, Quantitative aspects of relative growth and sexual dimorphism in *Protoceratops*: *Journal of Paleontology*, 50 (5), pp. 929–940.

_____, 1990a, Marginocephalia, *in*: David B. Weishampel, Peter Dodson, and Halszka Osmólska, editors, *The Dinosauria*. Berkeley and Los Angeles: University of California Press, pp. 402–407, 562–563.

_____, 1990b, Neoceratopsia, *Ibid.*, pp. 593–618.

_____, 2000, Origin of birds: the final solution?: *American Zoologist*, 40 (4), pp. 504–512.

Dodson, Peter, Anna K. Behrensmeyer, Robert T. Bakker, and John S. McIntosh, 1980, Taphonomy and paleoecology of the dinosaur beds of the Jurassic Morrison Formation: *Paleobiology*, 6, pp. 208–232.

Dodson, Peter, and Jerald D. Harris, 2001, Necks of sauropod dinosaurs: support for a nuchal ligament?: *International Congress of Vertebrate Morphology, Abstracts*, p. 224.

Dodson, Peter, and Allison Tumarkin, 1998, Problematic ceratopsids: don't throw baby out with the bathwater, *in*: Donald L. Wolberg, K. Gittis, S. Miller, and A. Raynor, editors, *The Dinofest Symposium* [abstracts], Presented by The Academy of Natural Sciences of Philadelphia, Pennsylvania, pp. 12–13.

Doh, S. J., C. S. Hwang, and K. H. Kim, 1994, A paleomagnetic study of sedimentary rocks from Kyeongsang Supergroup in Milyang Subbasin: *Journal of the Geological Society of Korea*, 30, pp. 211–228.

Dollo, Louis, 1883, Note sur les restes de dinosauriens rencontrés dans le Crétacé Supérieur de la Belgique: *Bulletin du Musée Royale d'Histoire Naturelle de Belgique*, 2, pp. 205–221.

_____, 1905, Les dinosauriens binèdes retournés a l'ètat quadrupède: *Ibid.*, 19.

Dong Zhiming [also Zhi-Ming], 1973, Cretaceous stratigraphy of Wuerho district, Dsunger Basin. Reports of Paleontological Expedition to Sinkiang (II). Pterosaurian Fauna from Wuerho, Sinkiang: *Memoirs of the Institute of Vertebrate Paleontology and Paleoanthropology*, 11, pp. 1–7.

_____, 1977, On the dinosaurian remains from Turpan, Xinjiang: *Vertebrata PalAsiatica*, 15 (1), pp. 59–66.

_____, 1978, [A new genus of pachycephalosaur from Laiyang, Shantung]: *Ibid.*, 16 (4), pp. 225–228.

_____, 1979, [Cretaceous dinosaurs of Huanan (south China)], *in*: *Mesozoic and Cenozoic Redbeds in Southern China*. Beijing: Science Press, pp. 342–350.

_____, 1997, Introduction, *in*: Dong Zhiming, editor, *Sino-Japanese Silk Road Dinosaur Expedition*. Beijing: China Ocean Press, pp. 1–2.

_____, 2001a, Primitive armored dinosaur from the Lufeng Basin, China, *in*: Darren Tanke and Kenneth Carpenter, editors, 2001, *Mesozoic Vertebrate Life: New Research Inspired by the Paleontology of Philip J. Currie*. Bloomington and Indianapolis, Indiana: Indiana University Press, pp. 237–242.

_____, 2001b, A forefoot of sauropod from the Tuchengzi Formation of Chaoyang Area in Liaoning, China: *in*: Deng Tao and Wang Yuan, editors, *Proceedings of the Eighth Annual Meeting of the Chinese Society of Vertebrate Paleontology*. Beijing: China Ocean Press, pp. 29–33.

_____, 2002: A new armored dinosaur (Ankylosauria) from Beipiao Basin, Liaoning Province, northeastern China: *Vertebrata PalAsiatica* 40 (3), pp. 276b–283.

Dong Zhi-Ming [formerly Zhiming], and Yoichi Azuma, 1997, On a primitive neoceratopsian from the Early Cretaceous of China, *in*: Dong Zhi-Ming, editor, *Sino-Japanese Silk Road Dinosaur Expedition*. Beijing: China Ocean Press, pp. 68–89.

Dong Zhi-Ming [formerly Zhiming], and Philip J. Currie, 1993, Protoceratopsian embryos from Inner Mongolia, Peoplés Republic of China: *Canadian Joural of Earth Sciences*, 30 (10–11), pp. 2248–2254.

_____, 1996, On the discovery of an oviraptorid skeleton on a nest of eggs at Bayan Mandahu, Inner Mongolia, Peoplés Republic of China: *Canadian Journal of Earth Sciences*, 33, pp. 631–636.

Dong Zhiming, Paik In Sung, and Kim Hyun Joo, 2001, A preliminary report on a sauropod from the Hasandong Formation (Lower Cretaceous), Korea, *in*:, Deng Tao and Wang Yuan, editors, *Proceedings of the Eighth Annual Meeting of the Chinese Society of Vertebrate Paleontology*. Beijing: China Ocean Press, pp. 41–53.

Dong Zhi-Ming [formerly Zhiming] and Tang Zilu, 1984, Note on a new mid–Jurassic Sauropod (*Datousaurus bashanensis*) gen. et. sp. nov.) from Sichuan Basin, China: *Vertebrata PalAsiatica*, 22 (1), pp. 69–75.

Dragastan, O., M. Coman, and E. Stiuca, 1988, Bauxite-bearing formations and facies in the Padurea Craiului and Bihor Mountains (Northern Apuseni): *Revue Roumaine de Géologie, Géophysique et Géographie*, 32, pp. 67–81.

Drushel, R. F., and A. I. Caplan, 1991, Three-dimensional reconstruction and cross-sectional anatomy of the thigh musculature of the developing chick embryo (*Gallus gallus*): *Journal of Morphology*, 208, pp. 2913–309.

Bibliography

Dufeau, David, 2002, The cranial morphology of *Shuvuuia deserti* (Theropoda: Alvarezsauridae): *Journal of Vertebrate Paleontology*, 23 (Supplement to Number 3), Abstracts of Papers, Sixty-second Annual Meeting, p. 50A.

Durand, J. F., 1996, First vertebrate fossil discovery in the Kruger National Park: *South African Journal of Science*, 92, p. 302.

_____, 2001, The oldest juvenile dinosaur from Africa: *Journal of African Earth Sciences*, 33 (3–4), pp. 597–603.

Dutuit, J.-M., and A. Quazzou 1980, Découverte d'une piste de dinosaures sauropodes sur le site d'empreintes de Demnate (Haut-Atlas marocain): *Memoires de la Société Géologique de France* (N.S.), 59 (139), pp. 95–102.

Ebel, Klaus, 2000, Biomechanics of the vertebral column and implications for the lifestyle of dinosaurs and certain pelycosaurs: *Freiberger Forschungshefte*, 490, pp. 27–50.

Eberth, David A., 1997*a*, Edmonton Group, *in*: Philip J. Currie and Kevin Padian, editors, *Encyclopedia of Dinosaurs*. San Diego: Academic Press, pp. 199–204.

_____, 1997*b*, Judith River wedge, *Ibid.*, pp. 379–388.

Eberth, David A., and A. P. Hamblin, 1993, Tectonic, stratigraphic, and sedimentologic significance of a regional discontinuity in the Upper Judith River group (Belly River wedge) of southern Alberta, Saskatchewan, and northern Montana: *Canadian Journal of Earth Sciences*, 30, pp. 174–200.

Eberth, David A., and Richard T. McCrea, 2001, Were large theropods gregarious?: *Journal of Vertebrate Paleontology*, 21 (Supplement to Number 3), Abstracts of Papers, Sixty-first Annual Meeting, pp. 46A–47A.

_____, 2002, Were large theropods normally gregarious?: *Alberta Palaeontological Society, Sixth Annual Symposium, "Fossils 2002," Abstract Volume*, January 26–27, 2002, Mount Royal College, Calgary, Alberta, pp. 13–15.

Economos, A. C., 1981, The largest land mammal: *Journal of Theoretical Biology*, 89, pp. 211–215.

Efremov, Ivan A., and Vjuschkov, 1955, [Catalog of Permian and Triassic land vertebrates in the territory of the USSR]: *Trudy Paleozoologicheskogo Instituta, Akademiya Nauk USSR*, 46, 185 pages.

Egi, Naoko, 2002, Morphometric analyses of humeral shapes in hadrosaurids (Ornithopoda, Dinosauria): *Senckenbergiana lethaea*, 82 (1), pp. 43–58.

Ellenberger, Paul, 1970, Les niveaux paléontologiques de prémière apparition des mammiferes primordiaux en Afrique du Sud at leur ichnologie: *Proceedings and Papers of the Second Gondwana Symposium, South Africa, 1970*, pp. 343–370.

_____, 1972, Contribution à la classification des pistes de vertébrés du Trias: les types du Stormberg d'Afrique du Sud (III): *Palaeovertebrata, Mémoire Éxtraordinaire*, Laboratoire de Paléontologie des Vertébrés, Montepellier, pp. 1–152.

_____, 1974, *Ibid.*, pp. 1–148.

Elźanowski, Andrzej, 1981, Embryonic bird skeletons from the late Cretaceous of Mongolia: *Palaeontologica Polonica*, 42, pp. 147–179.

_____, 1999, A comparison of the jaw skeleton in theropods and birds, with a description of the palate in the Oviraptoridae: *Smithsonian Contributions to Paleobiology*, 89, pp. 311–323.

_____, 2001, The life style of *Archaeopteryx* (Aves): *Asociaćion Paleontológical Argentina*, Publicatión Especial 7, VII International Symposium on Mesozoic Terrestrial Ecosystems, Buenos Aires, 30-6-2001, pp. 91–99.

Elźanowski, Andrzej, and Peter Wellnhofer, 1996, Cranial morphology of *Archaeopteryx*: evidence from the seventh skeleton: *Journal of Vertebrate Paleontology*, 16 (1), pp. 81–94.

Erickson, Bruce R., and H. Douglas Hanks, 2001, A puzzling young diplodocid: *Journal of Vertebrate Paleontology*, 21 (Supplement to Number 3), Abstracts of Papers, Sixty-first Annual Meeting, p. 47A.

Erickson, Gregory M., 2001, The bite of *Allosaurus*: *Nature*, 409, pp. 987–988.

Erickson, Gregory M., Kristina Curry Rogers, and Scott A. Yerby, 2001, Dinosaurian growth patterns and rapid avian growth rates: *Nature*, 412, pp. 429–433.

Erickson, Gregory M., S. D. Van Kirk, J. Su, M. E. Levenston, W. E. Caler, and D. R. Carter, 1996, Bite-force estimation for *Tyrannosaurus rex* from tooth-marked bones: *Nature*, 382, pp. 706–708.

Estes, Richard D., 1964, Fossil vertebrates from the Lower Cretaceous Lance Formation, eastern Wyoming: *University of California, Publications in Geological Sciences*, 49, pp. 1–42.

Eudes-Deslongchamps, J. A., 1838, Mémoire sur le *Poekilopleuron bucklandii*, grand saurien fossile, intermédiaire entre les crocodiles et lézards: *Mémoire de la Société Linnéenne de Normandie*, 5, pp. 37–146.

Evans, David C., 2001, Hadrosaurs of DPP: *Canadian Paleobiology/Paléobiologie Canadienne*, 6, pp. 5–9.

_____, 2002*a*, Notes on the cranial ontogeny of *Corythosaurus casuarius*: *Alberta Palaeontological Society, Sixth Annual Symposium, "Fossils 2002," Abstract Volume*, January 26–27, 2002, Mount Royal College, Calgary, Alberta, p. 16.

_____, 2002*b*, A detailed description of the lambeosaurine presphenoid: implications for olfactory system anatomy and hadrosaurid phylogeny: *Journal of Vertebrate Paleontology*, 23 (Supplement to Number 3), Abstracts of Papers, Sixty-second Annual Meeting, pp. 51A–52A.

Farke, Andrew Allen, 2002*a*, A review of *Torosaurus* (Dinosauria: Ceratopsidae) specimens from Texas and New Mexico: *Journal of Vertebrate Paleontology*, 23 (Supplement to Number 3), Abstracts of Papers, Sixty-second Annual Meeting, p. 52A.

_____, 2002*b*, New specimens of the horned dinosaur *Torosaurus* (Dinosauria, Ceratopsia) from the Late Cretaceous Hell Creek Formation of Montana: *GSA Abstracts with Programs*, p. 430.

Farlow, James O., 1981, Estimates of dinosaurs speeds from a new trackway site in Texas: *Nature*, 294, pp. 747–748.

_____, 1987, Speculations about the diet and digestive physiology of herbivorous dinosaurs: *Paleobiology*, 13 (1), pp. 60–72.

_____, 2001, *Acrocanthosaurus* and the maker of Commanchean large-theropod footprints: *in*: Darren Tanke and Kenneth Carpenter, editors, *Mesozoic Vertebrate Life: New Research Inspired by the Paleontology of Philip J. Currie*. Bloomington and Indianapolis, Indiana: Indiana University Press, pp. 408–427.

Farlow, James O., David L. Brinkman, William L. Abler, and Philip J. Currie, 1991, Size, shape and serration density of theropod dinosaur lateral teeth: *Modern Geology*, 16, pp. 161–197.

Farlow, James O., Stephen M. Gatesy, and Thomas R. Holtz, Jr., John R. Hutchinson, and John M. Robinson, 2000, Theropod locomotion: *American Zoologist*, 40, pp. 640–663.

Farlow, James O., Jeffrey G. Pittman, and J. Michael Hawthorne, 1989, *Brontopodus birdi*, Lower Cretaceous sauropod footprints from the U.S. Gulf Coastal Plain, *in*: David D. Gillette and Martin G. Lockley, editors, *Dinosaur Tracks and Traces*. Cambridge, New York, and Melbourne: Cambridge University Press, pp. 371–394.

Farlow, James O., Matt B. Smith, and John M. Robinson, 1995, Body mass, bone "strength indicator," and cursorial potential of *Tyrannosaurus rex*: *Journal of Vertebrate Paleontology*, 15 (4), pp. 713–725.

Fassett, James E., 1982, Dinosaurs of the San Juan Basin, New Mexico, may have survived the event that resulted in creation of an iridium-enriched zone near the Cretaceous-Tertiary boundary: *Geological Society of America, Special Paper*, 190, pp. 435–447.

Feduccia, Alan, 1974, Endothermy, dinosaurs and *Archaeopteryx*: *Evolution*, 28 (3), pp. 503–504.

_____, 1996, *The Origin and Evolution of Birds*. New Haven, Connecticut: Yale University Press, 420 pages.

_____, 1999*a*, 1,2,3 = 2,3,4: accommodating the cladogram: *Proceedings of the National Academy of Sciences*, 96, pp. 4740–4742.

_____, 1999*b*, *The Origin and Evolution of Birds*, second edition. New Haven, Connecticut: Yale University Press, 466 pages.

_____, 2002, Birds are dinosaurs: simple answer to a complex problem: *The Auk*, 119 (4), pp. 1187–1201.

Feng, T., X. Jin, X. Kang, and G. Zhang, G., 2001. *Omeisaurus maoianus*: a complete Sauropoda from Jingyan, Sichuan: *Research Works of the Natural Museum of Zhejiang*. Beijing: China Ocean Press, 128 pp.

Fiorillo, Anthony R., 1987, Significance of juvenile dinosaurs from Careless Creek Quarry (Judith River Formation), Wheatland County, Montana, *in*: P. J. Currie and E. H. Koster, editors, *Fourth Sympo-*

sium on Mesozoic Terrestrial Ecosystems: Short Papers, Tyrrell Museum of Palaeontology, Occasional Paper 3, pp. 89–95.

_____, 1989, The vertebrate fauna of the Judith River Formation (Late Cretaceous) of Wheatland and Golden Valley Counties, Montana: *Mosasaur*, 4, pp. 127–142.

_____, 1991, Taphonomy and depositional setting of Careless Creek Quarry (Judith River Formation), Wheatland County, Montana, U.S.A.: *Palaeogeography, Palaeoclimatology, Palaeoecology*, 81, pp. 281–311.

_____, 1998, Microwear on the teeth of theropod dinosaurs (Judith River Formation) of south-central Montana: inferences on diet: *Journal of Vertebrate Paleontology*, 18 (Supplement to Number 3), Abstracts of Papers, Fifty-eighth Annual Meeting, p. 41A.

Fiorillo, Anthony R., and Philip J. Currie, 1994, Theropod teeth from the Judith River Formation (Upper Cretaceous) of south-central Montana: *Journal of Vertebrate Paleontology*, 14 (1), pp. 74–80.

Fiorillo, Anthony R., and Roland A. Gangloff, 2001, Theropod teeth from the Prince Creek Formation (Cretaceous) of Northern Alaska, with speculations on Arctic dinosaur paleoecology: *Journal of Vertebrate Paleontology*, 20 (4), pp. 675–682.

Fiorillo, Anthony R., and H. Montgomery, 2001, Depositional setting and paleoecological significance of a new sauropod bonebed in the Javelina Formation (Cretaceous) of Big Bend National Park, Texas: *Journal of Vertebrate Paleontology*, 21 (Supplement to Number 3), Abstracts of Papers, Sixty-first Annual Meeting, p. 49A.

Fisher, Paul E., Dale A. Russell, Michael K. Stoskopf, Reese E. Barrick, Michael Hammer, and Andrew A. Kuzmitz, 2000, Cardiovascular evidence for an intermediate or higher metabolic rate in an ornithischian dinosaur: *Science*, 288, pp. 503–505.

Flynn, John J., J. Michael Parrish, Berthe Rakotosamimanana, William F. Simpson, Robin L. Whatley, and André R. Wyss, 1999, A Triassic fauna from Madagascar, including early dinosaurs: *Science*, 286, pp. 763–765.

Ford, Tracy L., 1997, Did theropods have lizard lips?: *Southwest Paleontological Symposium—Proceedings*, 5, pp. 65–78.

_____, 2001, The armor of sauropods: *Journal of Vertebrate Paleontology*, 21 (Supplement to Number 3), Abstracts of Papers, Sixty-first Annual Meeting, p. 50A.

_____, 2002, A new look at the armor of *Ankylosaurus*—just how did it look?: *Tate 2002: Wyoming in the Age of Dinosaurs: Creatures, Environments and Extinctions*, p. 15.

Ford, Tracy L., and Daniel J. Chure, 2001a, "*Aublysodon*" teeth from the El Gallo Formation (Late Campanian) of Baja California: the southernmost record of tyrannosaurid theropods: *Western Association of Vertebrate Paleontologists with Mesa Southwest Museum and Southwest Paleontological Symposium, Proceedings 2001, Mesa Southwest Museum Bulletin*, 8, pp. 75–89.

_____, 2001b, Ghost lineages and the paleogeographic and temporal distribution of tyrannosaurids: *Journal of Vertebrate Paleontology*, 21 (Supplement to Number 3), Abstracts of Papers, Sixty-first Annual Meeting, pp. 50A–51A.

Ford, Tracy L., and James I. Kirkland, 2001, Carlsbad Ankylosaur (Ornithischia, Ankylosauria): An ankylosaurid and not a nodosaurid, in: Kenneth Carpenter, editor, *The Armored Dinosaurs*. Bloomington and Indiana: Indiana University Press., 2001: pp. 239–260.

Forster, Catherine A., 1997a, Phylogeny of the Iguanodontia and Hadrosauridae: *Journal of Vertebrate Paleontology*, 17 (Supplement to Number 3), Abstracts of Papers, Fifty-seventh Annual Meeting, p. 47A.

_____, 1997b, Hadrosauridae, in: Philip J. Currie and Kevin Padian, editors, *Encyclopedia of Dinosaurs*. San Diego: Academic Press, pp. 293–299.

Forster, Catherine A., Andrea Beatriz Arcucci, C. A. Marsicano, F. Abdata, and C. L. May, 1995, New vertebrate material from the Los Rastros Formation (Middle Triassic), La Rioja province, northwestern Argentina: *Journal of Vertebrate Paleontology*, 15 (Supplement to Number 3), Abstracts of Papers, Fifty-fifth Annual Meeting, p. 29A.

Forster, Catherine A., and Scott D. Sampson, 2002, Phylogeny of the horned dinosaurs (Ornithischia, Ceratopsidae): *Journal of Vertebrate Paleontology*, 23 (Supplement to Number 3), Abstracts of Papers, Sixty-second Annual Meeting, p. 54A.

Forster, Catherine A., Scott D. Sampson, Luis M. Chiappe, and David W. Krause, 1998, The theropod ancestry of birds: new evidence from the Late Cretaceous of Madagascar: *Science*, 279, pp. 1915–1919.

Foster, John R., 1996, Fossil vertebrate localities in the Morrison Formation (Upper Jurassic) of western South Dakota, in: Michael Morales, editor, *The Continental Jurassic*, Museum of Northern Arizona Bulletin, 60, pp. 255–263.

_____, 2001, Relative abundances of the Sauropoda (Dinosauria, Saurischia) of the Morrison Formation and implications for Late Jurassic paleoecology of North America: *Western Association of Vertebrate Paleontologists and Southwest Paleontological Symposium, Proceedings, 2001, Mesa Southwest Museum Bulletin*, 8, pp. 47–60.

Foster, John R., and Daniel J. Chure, 1998, Patterns of theropod diversity and distribution in the Late Jurassic Morrison Formation, western USA: *Abstracts and Program for the Fifth International Symposium on the Jurassic System, International Union of Geological Sciences, Subcommisson on Jurassic Stratigraphy*, Vancouver, British Columbia, Canada, pp. 30–31.

_____, 2000, An ilium of a juvenile *Stokesosaurus* (Dinosauria, Theropoda) from the Morrison Formation (Upper Jurassic: Kimmeridgian), Meade County, South Dakota: *Brigham Young University Geology Studies*, 45, pp. 5–9.

Foster, John R., Thomas R. Holtz, Jr., and Daniel J. Chure, 2001, Contrasting pat-

terns of diversity and community structure in the theropod faunas of the Late Jurassic and Late Cretaceous of Western North America: *Journal of Vertebrate Paleontology*, 21 (Supplement to Number 3), Abstracts of Papers, Sixty-first Annual Meeting, p. 51A.

Fouch, T. D., T. F. Lawton, D. J. Nichols, W. B. Cashion, and W. A. Cobban, 1983, Patterns and timing of synorogenic sedimentation in Upper Cretaceous rocks of central and northeast Utah, in: M. Reynolds, E. Dolly, and D. R. Spearing, editors, *Mesozoic Paleography of West-central United States*. Society of Economic Paleontologists and Mineralogists, Rocky Mountain Section, Symposium, volume 2, pp. 305–334.

Fox, William [anonymous], 1866, Another new Wealden reptile: *The Athenaeum*, 2014, p. 740. (Reprinted in: *Geological Magazine*, 3, p. 383.)

Fraas, Eberhard, 1896, Die Schwäbischen Trias-Saurier nach dem Material der Kgl. Naturalien-Sammlung in Stuttgart zusammengestellt: *Mitt. königl. Naturalien-Cabinett Stuttgart*, 5, pp. 1–18, Stuttgart.

_____, 1913, Die neuesten Dinosaurierfunde in der Schwäbischen Trias: *Naturwissenschaften*, 45, pp. 1097–1100, Stuttgart.

Frankfurt, Nicholas G., and Luis M. Chiappe, 1999, A possible oviraptorosaur from the Late Cretaceous of northwestern Argentina: *Journal of Vertebrate Paleontology*, 19 (1), pp. 101–105.

Franzosa, Jonathan W., 2001, Constructing digital endocasts of theropods using a high-resolution X-ray computed tomography scanner: *Journal of Vertebrate Paleontology*, 21 (Supplement to Number 3), Abstracts of Papers, Sixty-first Annual Meeting, p. 51A.

_____, 2002, A description of the anatomy of a digitally constructed *Acrocanthosaurus atokensis* (Theropoda: Allosauroidea) endocast, and its uses: *Journal of Vertebrate Paleontology*, 23 (Supplement to Number 3), Abstracts of Papers, Sixty-second Annual Meeting, p. 55A.

Fraser, Nicholas C., and Paul E. Olsen, 1996, A new dinosauromorph from the Triassic of Virginia: *Jeffersonia*, 7, pp. 1–17.

Fraser, Nicholas C., Kevin Padian, G. M. Walkden, and A. L. M. Davis, 2002, Basal dinosauriform remains from Britain and the diagnosis of the Dinosauria: *Palaeontology* 45, pp. 79–95.

Frazzetta, T. H., and Kenneth V. Kardong, 2002, Prey attack by a large theropod dinosaur: *Nature*, 416, pp. 387–388.

Freeman, E. F., 1979, A Middle Jurassic mammal bed from Oxfordshire: *Palaeontology*, 22, pp. 135–166.

Fuentes, F. Meijide, C. Fuentes Vidarte, and M. Meijide Calvo, 1999, Primeras huellas de sauropodo en el Weald de Soria (España), *Parabrontopodus distercii*, nov. ichnoesp.: *Actas de las I Journadas Internacionales Sobre Paleontología de Dinosaurios y su Entorno (Proceedings of the 1st International Symposium about Paleontology of Dinosaurs and their Environment*, Salas de

Bibliography

los Infantes (Burgos, España), Septiembre de 1999, pp. 407–415.

Gabouniya [also spelled Gabunia and Gabuniya], L. K., 1951, O sledakh dinozavrov iz nizhnemelovykh otlozhenii Zapadnof Gruzii [On the tracks of dinosaurs from the Lower Cretaceous of western Georgia]: *Doklady Akademiya Nauk SSSR*, 81 (5), pp. 917–919.

Gabuniya, L. K., and V. Kurbatov, 1982, Jurassic dinosaur tracks of Tashkurgan (Uzbekistan SSR): Abstracts Sci. Session, Tbilisi, pp. 20–22.

Gallina, P. A., S. Apesteguia, and F. E. Novas, 2002, ¿Un elefante bajo la alfombra? Los Rebbachisauridae (Sauropoda, Diplodocimorpha) del Cretácico de Gondwana. Neuvas evidencias en "La Buitrera" (Formación Candeleros), provincia de Rio Negro): *Ameghiana*, 39 (4), Supplemento, pp. 10R–11R.

Galton, Peter M., 1969, The pelvic musculature of the dinosaur *Hypsilophodon* (Reptilia, Ornithischia): *Postilla*, 131, pp. 1–64.

_____, 1970, The posture of hadrosaurian dinosaurs: *Journal of Paleontology*, 44 (3), pp. 464–473.

_____, 1973, A femur of a small theropod dinosaur from the Lower Cretaceous of England: *Ibid.*, 47 (5), pp. 996–997.

_____, 1974, The ornithischian dinosaur *Hypsilophodon* from the Wealden of the Isle of Wight: *Bulletin of the British Museum (Natural History)*, 25 (1), 152 pages.

_____, 1976a, Prosauropod dinosaurs (Reptilia: Saurischia) of North America: *Postilla*, 169, pp. 1–98.

_____, 1976b, *Iliosuchus*, a Jurassic dinosaur from Oxfordshire and Utah: *Palaeontology*, 19 (3), pp. 587–589.

_____, 1978, Fabrosauridae, the basal family of ornithischian dinosaurs (Reptilia: Ornithischia): *Paläontographica Zeitschrift*, 52 (1/2), pp. 138–159.

_____, 1981, *Dryosaurus*, a hypsilophodontid from the Upper Jurassic of North America and Africa. Postcranial skeleton: *Paläontologische Zeitschrift*, 55, pp. 271–312.

_____, 1982a, *Elaphrosaurus*, an ornithomimid dinosaur from the Upper Jurassic of North America and Africa: *Ibid.*, 56 (3/4), pp. 265–275.

_____, 1982b, Juveniles of the stegosaurian dinosaur *Stegosaurus* from the Upper Jurassic of North America: *Journal of Vertebrate Paleontology*, 2 (1), pp. 47–62.

_____, 1983, The cranial anatomy of *Dryosaurus*, a hypsilophodontid dinosaur from the Upper Jurassic of North America and East Africa with a review of hypsilophodonts from the Upper Jurassic of North America: *Geologica et Palaeontologica*, 17, pp. 207–243.

_____, 1984a, Cranial anatomy of the prosauropod dinosaur *Plateosaurus*, from the Knollenmergel (Middle Keuper, Upper Triassic) of Germany. 1. Two complete skulls from Trossingen/Württ with comments on the diet: *Ibid.*, 18, pp. 139–171.

_____, 1984b, An early prosauropod from the Upper Triassic of Nordwürttemberg, West Germany: *Stuttgarter Beiträge zur Naturkunde*, (B), 196, pp. 1–25, Stuttgart.

_____, 1985a, the poposaurid thecodontian *Teratosaurus suevicus* v. Meyer, plus referred specimens mostly based on prosauropod dinosaurs, from the Middle Stubensandstein (Upper Triassic of Nordwürttemberg: *Ibid.*, Serie B (Geologie und Paläontologie), 116, pp. 105–123, Oslo.

_____, 1985b, Cranial anatomy of the prosauropod dinosaur *Sellosaurus gracilis* from the Middle Stubensandstein (Upper Triassic) of Nordwürttemberg: *Ibid.*, (B), 118, pp. 1–39, Stuttgart.

_____, 1985c, Cranial anatomy of the prosauropod dinosaur *Plateosaurus* from the Knollenmergel (Middle Keuper) of Germany, II. all the cranial material and details of soft-part anatomy: *Geologica et Palaeontologica*, 19, pp. 119–159.

_____, 1985d, Notes on the Melanorosauridae, a family of large prosauropod dinosaurs (Saurischia: Sauropodomorpha): *Geobios*, 18 (5), pp. 671–676, Lyon.

_____, 1986a, Prosauropod dinosaur *Plateosaurus* (=*Gresslyosaurus*) (Saurischia: Sauropodomorpha) from the Upper Triassic of Switzerland: *Geologica et Palaeontologica*, 20, pp. 167–183.

_____, 1986b, Herbivorous adaptations of Late Triassic and Early Jurassic dinosaurs, in, Kevin Padian, editor, *The Beginning of the Age of Dinosaurs*. New York: Cambridge University Press, pp. 203–221.

_____, 1990a, Basal Sauropodomorpha—Prosauropoda, in: David B. Weishampel, Peter Dodson and Halszka Osmólska, editors, *The Dinosauria*. Berkeley and Los Angeles: University of California Press, pp. 320–344.

_____, 1990b, Stegosauria, in: David B. Weishampel, Peter Dodson, and Halszka Osmólska, editors, *The Dinosauria*. Berkeley and Los Angeles: University of California Press, pp. 435–455.

_____, 1992, Basal Sauropodomorpha—Prosauropoda, in: David B. Weishampel, Peter Dodson, and Halszka Osmólska, editor, *The Dinosauria*, paperback edition. Berkeley: University of California Press, pp. 320–344.

_____, 1996, Notes on Dinosauria from the Upper Cretaceous of Portugal: *Neus Jahrbuch für Geologie und Paläontologie, Monatshefte*, 2, pp. 83–90.

_____, 1998, The prosauropod dinosaur *Plateosaurus* (*Dimodosaurus*) *poligniensis* (Pidancet & Chopard, 1861) (Upper Triassic, Poligny, France): *Neus Jahrbuch für Geologie und Paläontologie, Abhandlungen*, 207 (2), pp. 255–288.

_____, 1999, Sex, sacra and *Sellosaurus gracilis* (Saurischia, Sauropodomorpha, Upper Triassic, Germany)—or why the character "two sacral vertebrae" is plesiomorphic for Dinosauria: *Ibid.*, 213 (1), pp. 19–55.

_____, 2000, The prosauropod dinosaur *Plateosaurus* Meyer 1837 (Saurischia: Sauropodomorpha). 1. the syntypes of *P. engelhardti* Meyer 1837 (Upper Triassic, Germany), with notes on other European prosauropods with "distally straight" femora: *Revue Paléobiologie, Genève*, 216 (2), pp. 233–275.

_____, 2001a, Are *Spondylosoma* and *Stau-*

rikosaurus (Santa Maria Formation, Middle-Upper Triassic, Brazil) the oldest saurischian dinosaurs?: *Paläontologische Zeitschrift*, 74 (3), pp. 393–423.

_____, 2001b, Prosauropod dinosaurs from the Upper Triassic of Germany, in: Colectivo Arqueologico-Paleontologico de Salas, C.A.S., editors, *Actas de las I Jornadas Internacionales sobre Paleontologia de Dinosaurios y su Entorno (Proceedings of the 1st International Symposium on Paleontology of Dinosaurs and their Environment)*. Burgos, Spain, pp. 25–92.

_____, 2001c, Valid species or prosauropod dinosaurs from the Upper Triassic of Germany: *Journal of Vertebrate Paleontology*, 21 (Supplement to Number 3), Abstracts of Papers, Sixty-first Annual Meeting, p. 52A.

_____, 2001d, Endocranial casts of the plated dinosaur *Stegosaurus* (Upper Jurassic, Western USA): a complete undistorted cast and the original specimens of Othniel Charles Marsh, in: Kenneth Carpenter, editor, *The Armored Dinosaurs*. Bloomington and Indianapolis: Indiana University Press, pp. 103–129.

_____, 2001e, The prosauropod dinosaur *Plateosaurus* Meyer, 1837 (Saurischia: Upper Triassic). II. Notes on the referred species: *Revue de Paleobiologie*, 20 (2), Geneve, pp. 435–502.

_____, 2002, New material of ornithischian (?heterodontosaurid) dinosaur *Echinodon* (Early Cretaceous, southern England) from the Late Jurassic of Fruita near Grand Junction, Colorado: *Journal of Vertebrate Paleontology*, 23 (Supplement to Number 3), Abstracts of Papers, Sixty-second Annual Meeting, pp. 55A–56A.

_____, in press, Prosauropod dinosaur *Sellosaurus gracilis* (Upper Triassic, Germany): third sacral vertebra as either a dorsosacral or a caudosacral: *Neus Jahrbuch für Geologie und Paläontologie, Mh.*, Stuttgart.

_____, in preparation, Postcranial anatomy of the prosauropod dinosaur *Sellosaurus gracilis* from the Lower and Middle Stubensandstein (Upper Triassic) of Nordwürttemberg, Germany: *Stuttgarter Beiträge zur Naturkunde*, (B), Stuttgart.

Galton, Peter M., and James A. Jensen, 1979a, Remains of ornithopod dinosaurs from the Lower Cretaceous of North America: *Brigham Young University Studies in Geology*, 25 (3), pp. 1–10.

_____, 1979b, A new large theropod from the Upper Jurassic of Colorado: *Ibid.*, 26 (2), pp. 1–12.

Galton, Peter M., and Jacques van Heerden, 1998, Anatomy of the prosauropod dinosaur *Blikanasaurus cromptoni* (Upper Triassic, South Africa), with notes on the other tetrapods from the lower Elliot Formation: *Paläontologische Zeitschrift*, 72 (1/2), pp. 163–177, Stuttgart.

Galton, Peter M., and H. Phillip Powell, 1980, The ornithischian dinosaur *Camptosaurus prestwichii* from the Upper Jurassic of England: *Paleontology*, 23, pp. 411–443.

Galton, Peter M., and Philippe Taquet, 1982, *Valdosaurus*, a hypsilophodontid dinosaur from the Lower Cretaceous of Europe and Africa: *Geobios*, 15, pp. 147–159.

Galton, Peter M., and Paul Upchurch, in press, Basal Sauropodomorpha — Prosauropoda, *in*: David B. Weishampel, Peter Dodson, and Halszka Osmólska, editor, *The Dinosauria*, second edition. Berkeley: University of California Press.

Gand, G., 1976a, *Coelurosaurichnus palissyi*: *Bulletin of the Society of Natural History of Autun, N.S.*, 79, pp. 11–14.

_____, 1976b, *Coelurosaurichnus sabriensis*: *Ibid.*, pp. 16–22.

Gangloff, Roland A., *Edmontonia* sp., the first record of an ankylosaur from Alaska: *Journal of Vertebrate Paleontology*, 15 (1), pp. 195–200.

_____, 1986, Interprétations paléontologique et paléoécologique de quatre niveaux à traces de vertébrés observés dans l'Autunien du Lodévois (Hérault): *Géologie de la France*, 2, pp. 155–176.

Gao, Yuhui, 1992, *Yangchuanosaurus hepingensis* — a new species of carnosaur from Zigong, Sichuan: *Vertebrata PalAsiatica*, 30, pp. 313–324.

_____, 1999, A complete carnosaur skeleton from Zigong, Sichuan: 80 pages.

Garcia, Géraldine, Sylvain Duffaud, Monique Feist, Bernard Marandat, Yvette Tambareau, Juliette Villate, and Bernard Sigé, 2000, La neuve, gisement à plantes, invertébrés et vertébrés du Bégudien (Sénonian supérieur continental) du bassin d'Aix-en-Provence: *Geodiversitas*, 22 (3), pp. 325–348.

Garcia, Géraldine, and Monique Vianey-Liaud, 2001a, Dinosaur eggshells as biochronological markers in Upper Cretaceous continental deposits: *Palaeogeography, Palaeoclimatology, Palaeoecology*, 169, pp. 153–164.

_____, 2001b, Nouvelles données sur les coquilles d'oeufs de dinosaures Megaloolithidae du Sud de la France: systématique et variabilité entraspéfique: *Comptes Rendus des Séances de l'Academie des Sciences, Paris, Sciences de la Terre et des planètes*, 332, pp. 185–191.

Garcia, R. A., L. Salgado, and R. A. Coria, 2002, Primeros restos de un saurópodo en el Jurasico Superior de la Cuenca Neuquina: *Ameghiana*, 39 (4), Supplemento, p. 11R.

Garland, T., Jr., 1983, Scaling the ecological cost of transport to body mass in terrestrial mammals: *American Naturalist*, 121, pp. 571–587.

Garrido, Alberto C., 2000, Estudio estratigrafico y reconstrucción paleoambiental de las secuencias fosilíferas continentales del Cretácico Superior en las inmediaciones de Plaza Huincul, Provincia del Neuquén: Trabajo Final de grado Carrera de Geología, Universidad Nacional de Córdoba, Córdoba, Argentina, 78 pages.

Garrido, Alberto C., Luis M. Chiappe, F. Jackson, J. Schmitt, and Lowell Dingus, 2001, First sauropod nest structures: *Journal of Vertebrate Paleontology*, 21 (Supplement to Number 3), Abstracts of Papers, Sixty-first Annual Meeting, pp. 52A–53A.

Gasparini, Zulma, Eduardo B. Olivero, R. Scasso, and C. Rinaldi, 1987, Un ankylosaurio (Reptilia, Ornithischia) campaniano en el continente antártico: *Anais do 10th Congreso Brasileiro de Paleontologia*, Rio de Janeiro 1987, 1, pp. 131–141.

Gasparini, Zulma, Xabier Pereda Suberbolia, and Ralph E. Molnar, 1996, New data on the ankylosaurian dinosaur from the Late Cretaceous of the Antarctic Peninsula: *Memoirs of the Queensland Museum*, 39, pp. 583–594.

Gaston, Robert W., Jennifer Schellenbach, and James I. Kirkland, 2001, Mounted skeleton of the polacanthine ankylosaur *Gastonia burgei*, *in*: Kenneth Carpenter, editor, *The Armored Dinosaurs*. Bloomington and Indianapolis: Indiana University Press, pp. 386–398.

Gates, Terry A., 2002, Murder in Jurassic Park: the Cleveland-Lloyd Dinosaur Quarry as a drought-induced assemblage: *Journal of Vertebrate Paleontology*, 23 (Supplement to Number 3), Abstracts of Papers, Sixty-second Annual Meeting, pp. 56A–57A.

Gates, Terry A. [Bucky], Scott D. Sampson, and James H. Madsen, Jr., 2001, Taphonomic reanalysis of the Cleveland-Lloyd Dinosaur Quarry: *Journal of Vertebrate Paleontology*, 21 (Supplement to Number 3), Abstracts of Papers, Sixty-first Annual Meeting, p. 53A.

Gatesy, Stephen M., 1990, Caudofemoral musculature and the evolution of theropod locomotion: *Paleobiology*, 16 (2), pp. 170–186.

_____, 1991, Hindlimb scaling in birds and other theropods: implications for terrestrial locomotion: *Journal of Morphology*, 209 (1), pp. 83–96.

_____, 1995, Functional evolution of the hindlimb and tail from basal theropods to birds, *in*: J. J. Thomason, editor. *Functional Morphology in Vertebrate Paleontology*. Cambridge, United Kingdom: Cambridge University Press, pp. 219–234.

_____, 2001, Skin impressions of Triassic theropods as records of foot movement, *in*: Farish A. Jenkins, Jr., Michael D. Shapiro, and TomaszOwerkowicz, editors, "Studies in Organismic and Evolutionary Biology in honor of A. W. Crompton": *Bulletin of the Museum of Comparative Zoology*, 156 (1), pp. 137–149.

Gatesy, Stephen M., and K. P. Dial, 1996, Locomotor modules and the evolution of avian flight: *Evolution*, 50, pp. 331–340.

Gatesy, Stephen M., K. M. Middleton, Farish A. Jenkins, and N. H. Shuban, 1999, Three-dimensional preservation of foot movements in Triassic theropod dinosaurs: *Nature*, 399, pp. 141–144.

Gaudry, A., 1890, *Les enchainements du monde animal dans les temps géologiques: Fossiles secondaires*. Paris: Masson, 323 pages.

Gauthier, Jacques A., 1986, Saurischian monophyly and the origin of birds, *in*: Kevin Padian, editor, The Origin of Birds and the Evolution of Flight. *Memoirs of the California Academy of Sciences*, 8, pp. 1–55.

Gauthier, Jacques A., and Kevin Padian, 1985, Phylogenetic, functional, and aerody-namic analyses of the origin of birds and their flight, *in*: Max K. Hecht, John H. Ostrom, G. Viohl and Peter Wellnhoffer, editors, *The Beginnings of Birds*. Eichstätt: Freunde des Jura-Museums, pp. 185–197.

Gay, Robert, 2001a, Evidence for sexual dimorphism in the Early Jurassic theropod dinosaur *Dilophosaurus* and a comparison with other related forms: *Journal of Vertebrate Paleontology*, 21 (Supplement to Number 3), Abstracts of Papers, Sixty-first Annual Meeting, p. 53A.

_____, 2001b, New specimens of *Dilophosaurus wetherilli* (Dinosauria: Theropoda) from the Early Jurassic Kayenta Formation of Northern Arizona: *Western Association of Vertebrate Paleontologists and Southwest Paleontological Symposium, Proceedings, 2001, Mesa Southwest Museum Bulletin*, 8, pp. 19–23.

_____, 2002, The myth of cannibalism in *Coelophysis bauri*: *Journal of Vertebrate Paleontology*, 23 (Supplement to Number 3), Abstracts of Papers, Sixty-second Annual Meeting, p. 57A.

Geist, Nicholas R., and Alan Feduccia, 2000, Gravity-defying behaviors: identifying models for protoaves: *American Zoologist*, 40 (4), pp. 664–675.

Geist, Nicholas R., and Terry D. Jones, 1996, Juvenile skeletal structure and the reproductive habits of dinosaurs: *Science*, 272, pp. 712–714.

Geist, Nicholas R., Terry D. Jones, and John A. Ruben, 1997, Implications of soft tissue preservation in the compsognathid dinosaur, *Sinosauropteryx*: *Journal of Vertebrate Paleontology*, 17 (Supplement to Number 3), Abstracts of Papers, Fifty-seventh Annual Meeting, p. 48A.

Geoffroy Saint-Hilaire, E., 1825, Recherches sur l'organisation des gavials, etc.: *Memoires de la Muséum National d'Histoire Naturelle, Paris*, 12, p. 97.

Gibbons, A., 1997, Plucking the feathered dinosaur: *Science*, 278, pp. 1229–1230.

Giffin, Emily B., 1989, Notes on pachycephalosaur (Ornithischia): *Journal of Paleontology*, 63 (4), pp. 525–529.

Gillette, David D., 1991, *Seismosaurus halli*, gen. et sp. nov., a new sauropod dinosaur from the Morrison Formation (Upper Jurassic/Lower Cretaceous) of New Mexico, USA: *Journal of Vertebrate Paleontology*, 11 (4), pp. 417–433.

_____, 1994, Seismosaurus, *The Earth Shaker*. New York: Columbia University Press, 205 pages.

_____, 1995, True grit: *Natural History*, 104 (6), pp. 41–43.

Gillette, David D., L. Barry Albright, Alan L. Titus, and Merle Graffam, 2001, Discovery and paleogepgraphic implications of a therizinosaurid dinosaur from the Turonian (Late Cretaceous) of southern Utah: *Journal of Vertebrate Paleontology*, 21 (Supplement to Number 3), Abstracts of Papers, Sixty-first Annual Meeting, p. 54A.

Gillette, David D., and Martin G. Lockley, 1989, editors, *Dinosaur Tracks and Traces*. Cambridge, New York, and Melbourne: Cambridge University Press, 454 pages.

Gilmore, Charles Whitney, 1909, Osteology of

Bibliography

the Jurassic reptile *Camptosaurs*, with a revision of the species of the genus and a description of two new species: *Proceedings of the United States National Museum*, 36, pp. 197–332.

———, 1914, Osteology of the armored Dinosauria in the United States National Museum, with special reference to the genus *Stegosaurus*: *Memoirs of the United States National Museum*, 89, pp. 1–316.

———, 1920, Osteology of the carnivorous dinosauria in the United States National Museum, with special reference to the genera *Antrodemus* (*Allosaurus*) and *Ceratosaurus*: *Bulletin of the United States National Museum*, 110, pp. 1–154.

———, 1922, A new sauropod dinosaur from the Ojo Alamo Formation of New Mexico: *Smithsonian Miscellaneous Collections*, 72 (2), pp. 1–9.

———, 1924, A new coelurid dinosaur from the Belly River Cretaceous of Alberta: *Geogocical Survey of Canada, Bulletin*, 38, Geological Series 43, pp. 1–12.

———, 1930, On dinosaurian reptiles from the Two Medicine Formation of Montana: *United States National Museum Proceedings*, 77, pp. 1–39.

———, 1933, Two new dinosaurian reptiles from Mongolia with notes on some fragmentary specimens: *American Museum Novitates*, 679, pp. 1–20.

———, 1936, Osteology of *Apatosaurus*, with special reference of specimens in the Carnegie Museum: *Memoirs of the Carnegie Museum*, 11, pp. 175–300.

———, 1946, Reptilian fauna of the North Horn Formation of Central Utah: *United States Geological Survey Professional Paper*, 210-C, pp. 29–53.

Gilpin, David, Kenneth Carpenter, and Tony Dicroce, 2002, New ornithopod with hadrosaur-like features from the Lower Cretaceous of Utah: *Journal of Vertebrate Paleontology*, 23 (Supplement to Number 3), Abstracts of Papers, Sixty-second Annual Meeting, pp. 58A–59A.

Gimènez, Olga del, 2001, Materiales craneanos de dinosaurios en el Cretácico Superior de la provincia del Chubut: *Ameghiniana*, XVII Jornadas Argentinas de Paleontologia de Vertebrados, Resúmes, Esquel, 16–18 de mayo de 2001, p. 9R.

Gimènez, Olga del, and Sebastian Apesteguia, 2001, The Late Jurassic–Early Cretaceous worldwide record of basal titanosauriforms and the origin of titanosaurians (Sauropoda): new evidence from the Aptian (Lower Cretaceous) of Chubut Province, Argentina: *Journal of Vertebrate Paleontology*, 21 (Supplement to Number 3), Abstracts of Papers, Sixty-first Annual Meeting, p. 54A.

Gishlick, A. D., 2001*a*, Evidence for muscular control of avian style automatic extension and flexion of the manus in the forearm of maniraptors: *Journal of Vertebrate Paleontology*, 21 (Supplement to Number 3), Abstracts of Papers, Sixty-first Annual Meeting, pp. 54A–55A.

———, 2001*b*, The functional morphology of the manus and forelimb of *Deinonychus*

antirrhopus and its importance for the origin of avian flight, *in*: Jacques A. Gauthier, editor, *Perspectives on the Origin and Evolution of Birds*. New Haven: Yale University press in press.

Glasby, G. P., and H. Kunzendorf, 1996, Multiple factors in the origin of the Cretaceous/Tertiary boundary: the role of environmental stress and Deccan Trap volcanism: *Geologische Rundschau*, 85, pp. 191–210.

Glut, Donald F., 1997, *Dinosaurs: The Encyclopedia*. Jefferson, North Carolina: McFarland & Company, xi, 1076 pages.

———, 1999, *Dinosaurs: The Encyclopedia, Supplement 1*. Jefferson, North Carolina: McFarland & Company, xiii, 442 pages.

———, 2002, *Dinosaurs: The Encyclopedia, Supplement 2*. Jefferson, North Carolina: McFarland & Company.

Godefroit, Pascal, and Yuri Bolotsky, 2001, The Maastrichtian hadrosaurid fauna from the Amur region (China and Russia): *Journal of Vertebrate Paleontology*, 21 (Supplement to Number 3), Abstracts of Papers, Sixty-first Annual Meeting, p. 55A.

Godefroit, Pascal, Dong Zhi-Ming, Pierre Bultynck, Li Hong, and Feng Lu ["with the collaboration in the field of Shang Chang-Yong, Guo Dian-Yong, Dong Yu-Long, Sun Yan, Zhang Zhe-Min, Hugo De Potter, Georges Lenglet, Thierry Smith, and Eric Dermience"], 1998, Sino-Belgian Cooperation Program, "Cretaceous dinosaurs and mammals from Inner Mongolia," Part 1: New *Bactrosaurus* (Dinosauria: Euhadrosauria) material from Iren Dabasu (Inner Mongolia, P. R. China): *The Sino-Belgian Dinosaur Expedition in Inner Mongolia, Bulletin, Institut Royal des Sciences Naturelle de Belgique*, Suppl. 68, pp. 1–70.

Godefroit, Pascal, Shuqin Zan, and Liyong Jin, 2000, *Charonosaurus jiayiensis*, n.g., n.sp., a lambeosaurine dinosaur from the Late Maastrichtian of northeastern China: *Comptes rendus de l'Académie des Sciences de Paris, Sciences de la Terre et des Planètes*, 330, pp. 875–882.

———, 2001, The Maastrichtian (Late Cretaceous) lambeosaurine dinosaur *Charonosaurus jiayinensis* from north-eastern China: *Bulletin de l'Institut Royal des Sciences Naturelle de Belgique, Sciences de la Terre*, 71, pp. 119–168.

González, J. A., 2002, Prodedimineto de reconstructioń del aspecto externo de la cabeza de *Carnotaurus sastrei*: *Ameghiana*, 39 (4), Supplemento, p. 12B.

González, Riga, Cricyt Ianigla, and Jorge O. Calvo, 2001, A new genus and species of titanosaurid sauropod from the Upper Cretaceous on Rincón de los Sauces, Neuquén, Argentina: *Journal of Vertebrate Paleontology*, 21 (Supplement to Number 3), Abstracts of Papers, Sixty-first Annual Meeting, pp. 55A–56A.

Goodwin, Mark B., 1990, Morphometric landmarks of pachycephalosaurid cranial material from the Judith River Formation of northcentral Montana, *in*: Kenneth Carpenter and Philip J. Currie, editors, *Dinosaur Systematics: Approaches and Per-*

spectives. Cambridge and New York: Cambridge University Press, pp. 189–201.

———, 2002, Stable isotopes and dinosaur endothermy: effects of the burial environment on hadrosaur biogeochemistry: *Journal of Vertebrate Paleontology*, 23 (Supplement to Number 3), Abstracts of Papers, Sixty-second Annual Meeting, p. 59A.

Goodwin, Mark B., Emily A. Buchholtz, and Rolfe E. Johnson, 1998, Cranial anatomy and diagnosis of *Stygimoloch spinifer* (Ornithischia: Pachycephalosauria) with comments on cranial display structures in agonistic behavior: *Journal of Vertebrate Paleontology*, 18 (2), pp. 363–375.

Goodwin, Mark B., and John R. Horner, 2001, How *Triceratops* got its horns: new information from a growth series on cranial morphology and ontogeny: *Journal of Vertebrate Paleontology*, 21 (Supplement to Number 3), Abstracts of Papers, Sixty-first Annual Meeting, p. 56A.

Gow, Christopher E., 1981, Taxonomy of the Fabrosauridae (Reptilia, Ornithischia) and the *Lesothosaurus* myth: *South African Journal of Science*, 77, p. 43.

Gow, Christopher, and E. M. Latimer, 1999, Preliminary report of dinosaur tracks in Qwa Qwa, South Africa: *Palaeontologia Africana*, 35, pp. 41–43.

Gower, David J., 2001, Possible postcranial pneumaticity in the last common ancestor of birds and crocodilians: evidence from *Erythrosuchus* and other Mesozoic archosaurs: *Naturwissenschaften*, 88, pp. 119–122.

Granger, Walter, and William King Gregory, 1923, *Protoceratops andrewsi*, a preceratopsian dinosaur from the lower Cretaceous of Mongolia: *American Museum Novitates*, 72, pp. 1–6.

Gregory, William King, and Charles C. Mook, 1925, On *Protoceratops*, a primitive ceratopsian dinosaur from the Lower Cretaceous of Mongolia: *American Museum Novitates*, 156, pp. 1–9.

Griffiths, Peter J., 1993, The question of *Compsognathus* eggs: *Revue de Paléobiologie*, 7, pp. 85–94, Geneva.

———, 1996, The isolated *Archaeopteryx* feather: *Archaeopteryx*, 14, pp. 101–106.

———, 2000*a*, The evolution of feathers from dinosaur hair: *in* B. P. Pérez-Moreno, Thomas R. Holtz, Jr., José Luis Sanz, and José J. Moratalla, editors, Aspects of theropod paleobiology: *Gaia*, 15 (cover dated December 1998), pp. 399–403.

———, 2000*b*, Compsognathus eggs revisited: *First International Symposium on Dinosaur Eggs and Babies/Extended Abstracts/2000*, pp. 77–83.

———, 2003, The agility of theropod dinosaurs when turning: evidence from trackways from Crayssac, France: *in*: David B. Norman and Paul Upchurch, editors, *SVPCA 50, Cambridge 2002*, 11–13 September, Abstract Volume, unpaginated.

Grolier, M. J., and W. C. Overstreet, 1978, *Geologic Map of the Yemen Arab Republic (San'na)*. Washington, D.C.: United States Geological Survey Miscellaneous Investigations Series, Government Printer.

Gunther, R. T., 1945, *Early Science in Oxford: Life and Letters of Edward Lhuyd*, volume 14. Oxford: the Author.

Gunga, Hanns-Christian, Karl Kirsch, Jörn Rittweger, Lothar Röcker, Andrew Clarke, Jörg Albertz, Albert Wiedermann, Sascha Mokry, Tim Suthau, Aloys Wehr, Wolf-Dieter Heirich, and Hans-Peter Schultze, 1999, Body size and body volume distribution in two sauropods from the Upper Jurassic of Tendaguru (Tanzania): *Mitteilungen Museum für Naturkunde der Humboldt-Universität zu Berlin, Geowissenschaftliche Reihe*, 2, pp. 91–102.

Gunga, Hanns-Christian, Karl Kirsch, Jörn Rittweger, Andrew Clarke, Jörg Albertz, Albert Wiedermann, Aloys Wehr, Wolf-Dieter Heirich, and Hans-Peter Schultze, 2002, Dimensions of *Brachiosaurus brancai*, *Dicraeosaurus hansaemanni* and *Diplodocus carnegii* and their implications for gravitational physiology, *in*: J. Moravec, N. Takeda, and P. K. Singal, editors, *Adaptation Biology and Medicine*, volume 3. New Delhi: Narosa Publishing House, pp. 156–169.

Günther, Bruno, Enrique Morgado, Karl Kirsch, and Hans-Christian Gunga, 2002, Gravitational tolerance and size of *Brachiosaurus brancai*: *Mitteilungen Museum für Naturkunde der Humboldt-Universität zu Berlin, Geowissenschaftliche Reihe*, 5, pp. 265–269.

Gunther, R. T., 1945, *Early Science in Oxford: Life and Letters of Edward Lhuyd*, volume 14. Oxford: Author.

Gurich, G., 1926, Über Saurier-Fährten aus dem Etjo-Sandstein von Südwestafrika: *Paläontographica Zeitschrift*, 8, pp. 112–120.

Haas, George, 1969, On the muscles of ankylosaurs: *American Museum Novitates*, 2399, pp. 1–11.

Halstead, L. Beverly, 1970, *Scrotum humanum* Brookes 1763 — the first named dinosaur: *Journal of Insignificant Research, Chicago, Illinois*, 5, pp. 14–15.

Halstead, L. Beverly, and William A. S. Sarjeant, 1993, *Scrotum humanum* Brookes — the earliest name for a dinosaur?: *Modern Geology (Halstead Memorial Volume)*, 18, pp. 221–224.

Hamm, Shawn A., and Michael J. Everhart, 2001, Notes on the occurrence of nodosaurs (Ankylosauridae) in the Smoky Hill Chalk (Upper Cretaceous) of western Kansas: *Journal of Vertebrate Paleontology*, 21 (Supplement to Number 3), Abstracts of Papers, Sixty-first Annual Meeting, p. 58A.

Hancox, P. J., 2000, The continental Triassic of South Africa: *Zbl. Geol. Palaont.*, Teil 1, 1998, pp. 1285–1324.

Hanna, Rebecca R., 2002, Multiple injury and infection in a sub-adult theropod dinosaur *Allosaurus fragilis* with comparisons to allosaur pathology in the Cleveland-Lloyd Dinosaur Quarry Collection: *Journal of Vertebrate Paleontology*, 22 (1), pp. 76–90.

Happ, John W., and Christopher M. Morrow, 2000, Evidence of soft tissue associated with nasal and supraorbital horn cores, rostral and exoccipital of *Triceratops*: *Jour-*

nal of Vertebrate Paleontology, 20 (Supplement to Number 3), Abstracts of Papers, Sixtieth Annual Meeting, p. 47A.

Harkness, R., 1850, Notice of a tridactylous footmark from the Bunter Sandstone of Weston Point, Cheshire: *Annals and Magazine of Natural History*, 2 (6), pp. 440–442.

Harris, Jerald Davic, 1998, A reanalysis of *Acrocanthosaurus atokensis*, its phylogenetic status, and paleobiogeographic implications, based on a new specimen from Texas: *New Mexico Museum of Natural History and Science, Bulletin 13*, 75 pages.

Harris, Jerald D., K. R. Johnson, J. Hicks, and L. Tauxe, 1996, Four-toed theropod footprints and a paleomagnetic age from the Whetstone Falls Member of the Harebell Formation (upper Cretaceous: Maastrichtian), northwestern Wyoming: a correction: *Cretaceous Research*, 17, pp. 381–401.

Hartman, Scott, 2002, Nuchal-ligament depth in Hadrosauridae: paleoecological evidence for niche partitioning amongst the duckbills?: *Tate 2002: Wyoming in the Age of Dinosaurs: Creatures, Environments and Extinctions*, p. 17.

Harwell, Amy, Devon Van Leer, John Ruben, and Terry Jones, 2002, New evidence for diaphram breathing in the theropod dinosaurs: *Journal of Vertebrate Paleontology*, 23 (Supplement to Number 3), Abstracts of Papers, Sixty-second Annual Meeting, p. 63A.

Hatcher, John Bell, 1901, *Diplodocus* (Marsh): its osteology, taxonomy, and probable habits, with a restoration of the skeleton: *Memoirs of the Carnegie Museum*, 1 (1), pp. 1–61.

Haughton, Sidney H., 1924, The fauna and stratigraphy of the Stormberg Series: *Annals of the South African Museum*, 12 (8), pp. 323–497, Cape Town.

Hay, Oliver P., 1902, *Bibliography and Catalogue of the Fossil Vertebrates of North America*, Bulletin USGS 179, 868 pages.

Haubold, Hartmut, 1971, Ichnia Amphibiorum et Reptiliorum Fossilium, *in*: Oskar Kuhn, editor, *Handbuch der Palaeoherpetologie, Pt. 18*. Stuttgart: Gustav Fischer Verlag, 124 pages.

_____, 1974, Die Fossilen Saurierfährten: *N. Brehm-Büch*, 479, 168 pages, A. Ziemsen, Wittenberg Lutherstadt.

_____, 1984, *Saurierfährten* (2nd edition). Wittenberg Lutherstadt: A. Ziemsen, Verlag, 231 pages.

He Xinlu, Li Kui, and Cai Kaiji, 1988, *The Middle Jurassic Dinosaurian Fauna from Dashanpu, Zigong, Sichuan, volume IV, The Sauropod Dinosaurs (II)*. Chengdu: Sichuan Publishing House of Science and Technology, pp. 114–135.

He Xinlu, Wang Changsheng, Liu Shangzhong, Zhou Fengyun, Liu Tuqiang, Cai Kaiji, and Dai Bing, 1998, A new sauropod dinosaur from the Early Jurassic in Gongxian County, South Sichuan: *Acta Geologica Sichuan*, 18 (1), pp. 1–6 (reprinted and translated by Will Downs, Bilby Research Center, Northern Arizona University, 1999).

Head, Jason J., 1999, Reassessment of the systematic position of *Eolambia caroljonesa* (Dinosauria, Iguanodontia) and the North American iguanodontian record: *Journal of Vertebrate Paleontology*, 19 (Supplement to Number 3), Abstracts of Papers, Fifty-ninth Annual Meeting, p. 50A.

_____, 2001, A reanalysis of the phylogenetic position of *Eolambia caroljonesa* (Dinosauria, Iguanodontia): *Journal of Vertebrate Paleontology*, 21 (2), pp. 392–396.

Head, Jason J., and Yoshitsugu Kobayashi, 2001, Biogeographic histories and chronologies of derived iguanodontians: *Asociacíon Paleontológical Argentina*, Publicatíon Especial 7, VII International Symposium on Mesozoic Terrestrial Ecosystems, Buenos Aires, 30-6-2001, pp. 107–111.

Headden, Jaime A., 2001, Jaw function in Oviraptoridae (Dinosauria: Theropoda): *Journal of Vertebrate Paleontology*, 21 (Supplement to Number 3), Abstracts of Papers, Sixty-first Annual Meeting, p. 59A.

Heckert, Andrew B., 2002a, Taxonomy and biostratigraphic significance of the ornithischian dinosaur *Revueltosaurus* from the Chinle Group (Upper Triassic), Arizona and New Mexico: *New Mexico Geology*, 24 (2), pp. 65–66.

_____, 2002b, The microvertebrate record of the Upper Triassic lower Chinle Group (Carnian), southwestern United States, and the early evolution of dinosaurs: University of New Mexico 2001 Ph.D. dissertation, 465 pages (unpublished).

_____, 2002c, The microvertebrate record of the Upper Triassic lower Chinle Group (Carnian), southwestern U.S.A. and the early evolution of dinosaurs: *New Mexico Geology*, 24 (3), p. 102 [abstracts].

_____, 2002d, The microvertebrate record of the Upper Triassic Lower Chinle Group (Carnian), southwestern U.S.A. and the early evolution of dinosaurs. Ph.D. dissertation abstract, Department of Earth and Planetary Sciences, University of New Mexico, Albuquerque, NM 87131, 465 pp., published in *New Mexico Geology*, 24 (3), 102 pages.

Heckert, Andrew B., and Spencer G. Lucas, 2000, Global correlation of the Triassic theropod record, *in* B. P. Pérez-Moreno, Thomas R. Holtz, Jr., José Luis Sanz, and José J. Moratalla, editors, Aspects of theropod paleobiology: *Gaia*, 15 (December 1998), pp. 63–74.

_____, 2001, North America's oldest herbivorous dinosaurs: *Paleontology, Stratigraphy, and Sedimentology: GSA Rocky Mountain Section and South-Central Section Meeting*, abstracts, p. A-21.

_____, 2002, Origin and early evolution of dinosaurs: new ecosystems, not the same old "extinctions": *GSA Abstracts with Programs*, p. 360.

Heerden, Jacques van, 1979, The morphology and taxonomy of *Euskelosaurus* (Reptilia: Saurischia; Late Triassic) from South Africa: *Navors-Res. Nasl. Mus. Bloemfontein*, 4 (2), pp. 21–84, Bloemfontein.

Heilmann, Gerhard, 1926, *The Origin of Birds*. London: H.F.G. Witherby, 208 pages.

Bibliography

Heinrich, Wolf-Dieter, Robert Bussert, Martin Aberhan, Oliver Hampe, Saidi Kapilima, Eckart Schrank, Stephan Schultka, Gerhard Maier, Emma Masky, Benjamin Sames, and Remigius Chami, 2001, The German-Tanzanian Tendaguru Expedition 2000: *Mitteilungen Museum für Naturkunde der Humboldt-Universität zu Berlin, Geowissenschaftliche Reihe*, 4, pp. 223–237.

Heller, K., 1952, Reptilifährten-Funde aus dem Ansbacher Sandstein des Mittleren Keupers von Franken: *Geologische Blätter für Nordost-Bayern und angrezende Gebiete*, 8, pp. 146–152.

Helmbach, F.-F., 1971, Stratigraphy and ostracod-fauna from the coalmine Guimarota (Upper Jurassic): *Memória dos Servicos Geológicos de Portugal, Neuva Series*, 17, pp. 41–88.

Henderson, Donald M., 2000, Show some backbone! Axial body mass distribution and differing support strategies in theropod and ornithopod dinosaurs: *48th Symposium of Vertebrate Palaeontology and Comparative Anatomy, Portsmouth, 2000*, University of Portsmouth, abstracts, unpaginated.

––––––, 2001, Tension, tendons and trellises: a predictive model for the orientation of ossified tendons and vertebral structure in iguanodontian dinosaurs: *Journal of Vertebrate Paleontology*, 21 (Supplement to Number 3), Abstracts of Papers, Sixty-first Annual Meeting, p. 60A.

––––––, 2002, Wide- and narrow-guage sauropod trackways as a consequence of body mass distribution and the requirements for stability: *Journal of Vertebrate Paleontology*, 23 (Supplement to Number 3), Abstracts of Papers, Sixty-second Annual Meeting, p. 64A.

––––––, 2003, The eyes have it: the sizes, shapes and orientations of theropod orbits as indicators of skull strength and bite force: *Journal of Vertebrate Paleontology*, 22 (4), pp. 677–778.

Henderson, Donald M., and David B. Weishampel, 2002, Convergent evolution of the maxilla-dental-complex among carnovorous archosaurs: *Senckenbergiana lethaea*, 82 (1), pp. 77–92.

Hendricks, Alfred, 1981, Die Saurierfährte von München bei Rehburg-Loccum (NW-Deutschland). *Abhandlungen aus dem Landesmuseum für Naturkunde zu Münster in Westfalen*, 43 (2), pp. 1–22.

Hengst, Richard A., 2002, Upper Jurassic dinosaur assemblage in Yunnan Province, PRC: *GSA Abstracts with Programs*, p. 430.

Henriques, Deise D. R., Alexander W. A. Kellner, Sergio A. K. Azevedo, Domenica D. Santos, and Maureen M. T. Craik, 2002, On a sauropod dinosaur (Titanosauridae) from the Adamantina Formation (Late Cretaceous): *Journal of Vertebrate Paleontology*, 23 (Supplement to Number 3), Abstracts of Papers, Sixty-second Annual Meeting, p. 63A.

Hieronymous, Tobin L., 2001, Sharpey's fiber pits on the periosteal surface of a pachycephalosaurid dome: *Journal of Vertebrate Paleontology*, 21 (Supplement to Number 3), Abstracts of Papers, Sixty-first Annual Meeting, p. 61A.

Hill, Robert V., Diego Pol, Guillermo Rougier, Paula Muzzopappa, and Pablo Puerta, 2002, New dinosaur fossils from the Late Cretaceous La Colonia Formation, Chubut Province, Argentina: *Journal of Vertebrate Paleontology*, 23 (Supplement to Number 3), Abstracts of Papers, Sixty-second Annual Meeting, p. 65A.

Hill, Robert V., Lawrence W. Witmer, and Mark A. Norell, 2001, A new juvenile specimen of *Pinacosaurus grangeri*: ontogeny and phylogeny of ankylosaurs: *Journal of Vertebrate Paleontology*, 21 (Supplement to Number 3), Abstracts of Papers, Sixty-first Annual Meeting, p. 61A.

Hinic, Sanja, 2002, The cranial anatomy of *Massospondylus carinatus* Owen, 1854 and its implications for prosauropod phylogeny: *Journal of Vertebrate Paleontology*, 23 (Supplement to Number 3), Abstracts of Papers, Sixty-second Annual Meeting, p. 65A.

Hirsch, Karl F., 1994, Jurassic eggshell from the Western Interior, *in*: Kenneth Carpenter, Karl F. Hirsch, and John R. Horner, editors, *Dinosaur Eggs and Babies*. Cambridge: Cambridge University Press, pp. 137–150.

Hirsch, Karl F., Emily S. Bray, T. M. Demko, B. Currie, and D. Ekart, 1996, Dinosaur eggshell from the uppermost part of the Upper Jurassic Morrison Formation, Southeastern Utah: *Geological Survey of America Abstracts*, p. A-296.

Hitchcock, Charles H., 1871, (account and complete list of the Ichnozoa of the Connecticut Valley): *Walling and Gray's Official Topographical Atlas of Massachusetts*, xx–xxi.

––––––, 1889, Recent progress in ichnology: *Proceedings of the Boston Society of Natural History*, 24, pp. 117–127.

Hitchcock, Edward, 1836, Ornithichnology. Description of the footmarks of birds (Ornithoidichnites) on New Red Sandstone in Massachusetts: *American Journal of Science*, 29 (2), pp. 307–340.

––––––, 1841, Final report on the geology of Massachusetts, 2, Northampton, Massachusetts, 1841, pp. 301–831.

––––––, 1843, Description of five new species of fossil footmarks, from the red sandstone of the valley of the Connecticut River: *Transactions of the Association of American Geologists and Naturalists*, pp. 254–264.

––––––, 1845, An attempt to name, classify, and describe the animals that made the fossil footmarks of New England: *6th Annual Meeting of the Association of American Geology and Nature*, pp. 23–25.

––––––, 1847, Description of two new species of fossil footprints found in Massachusetts and Connecticut or, of the animals that made them: *American Journal of Science* [2], 4 (10), pp. 46–57.

––––––, 1848, An attempt to discriminate and describe the animals that made the fossil footmarks of the United States, and especially of New England: *Memoirs of the American Academy of Arts and Sciences*, series 2 (3), pp. 129–256.

––––––, 1855, Shark remains from the Coal formation of Illinois, and bones and tracks from the Connecticut River sandstone: *American Journal of Science*, [2], 20, pp. 416–417.

––––––, 1858, *Ichnology of New England. A Report on the Sandstone of the Connecticut Valley, Especially its Fossil Footmarks*. Boston: W. White, 220 pages (reprinted by Arno Press, 1974).

––––––, 1865, Supplement to the ichnology of New England. A report to the government of Massachusetts in 1863, Boston, 1865, x, 96 pages.

Hokkanen, H., 1986, The size of the largest land animals: *Journal of Theoretical Biology*, 118, pp. 491–499.

Holmes, Robert B., Catherine A. Forster, Michael J. Ryan, and Kieran M. Shepherd, 2001, A new species of *Chasmosaurus* (Dinosauria: Ceratopsia) from the Dinosaur Park Formation of southern Alberta: *Canadian Journal of Earth Sciences*, 38, pp. 1423–1438.

Holmes, Robert, Kieren Shepherd, and Catherine A. Forster, 1999, An unusual chasmosaurine ceratopsid from Alberta: *Journal of Vertebrate Paleontology*, 19 (Supplement to Number 3), Abstracts of Papers, Fifty-ninth Annual Meeting, p. 52A.

Holtz, Thomas R., Jr., 1994a, The phylogenetic position of the Tyrannosauridae: implications for theropod systematics: *Journal of Paleontology*, 68 (5). pp. 1100–1117.

––––––, 1994b, The arctometatarsalian pes, an unusual structure of the metatarsus of Cretaceous Theropoda (Dinosauria: Saurischia): *Journal of Vertebrate Paleontology*, 14 (4), pp. 480–519.

––––––, 1996, Phylogenetic taxonomy of the Coelurosauria (Dinosauria: Theropoda): *Ibid.*, 70, pp. 536–538.

––––––, 2000, A new phylogeny of the carnivorous dinosaurs, *in* B. P. Pérez-Moreno, Thomas R. Holtz, Jr., José Luis Sanz, and José J. Moratalla, editors, Aspects of theropod paleobiology: *Gaia*, 15 (cover dated December 1998), pp. 5–61.

––––––, 2001, The phylogeny and taxonomy of the Tyrannosauridae, *in*: Darren Tanke and Kenneth Carpenter, editors, *Mesozoic Vertebrate Life: New Research Inspired by the Paleontology of Philip J. Currie*. Bloomington and Indianapolis, Indiana: Indiana University Press, pp. 64–83.

Holtz, Thomas R., Jr., Daniel Brinkman, and Christine L. Chandler, 2000, Denticle morphometrics and a possibly omnivorous feeding habit for the theropod dinosaur *Troodon*: *in* B. P. Pérez-Moreno, Thomas R. Holtz, Jr., José Luis Sanz, and José J. Moratalla, editors, Aspects of theropod paleobiology: *Gaia*, 15 (December 1998), pp. 159–166.

Holtz, Thomas R., Jr., and Kevin Padian, 1995, Definition and diagnosis of Theropoda and related taxa: *Journal of Vertebrate Paleontology*, 15 (Supplement to Number 3), Abstracts of Papers, Fifty-fifth Annual Meeting, p. 35A.

Hopp, Thomas P., and Mark J. Orsen, 2001, Dinosaur brooding and the origin of avian flight: *Journal of Vertebrate Paleontology*, 21 (Supplement to Number 3), Abstracts of Papers, Sixty-first Annual Meeting, p. 63A.

Hopson, James A., 1979, Paleoneurology, *in*: C. Gans, R. G. Northcutt, and P. Ulinski, editors, *Biology of the Reptilia*, Vol. 9. New York: Academic Press, pp. 39–146.

Hopson, James A., and Luis M. Chiappe, 1998, Pedal proportions of living and fossil birds indicate arboreal or terrestrial specialization: *Journal of Vertebrate Paleontology*, 18 (Supplement to Number 3), Abstracts of Papers, Fifty-eighth first Annual Meeting, p. 52A.

Horner, Celeste C., John R. Horner, and David B. Weishampel, 2001, Comparative internal cranial morphology of some hadrosaurian dinosaurs using computerized tomographic X-ray analysis and rapid prototyping: *Journal of Vertebrate Paleontology*, 21 (Supplement to Number 3), Abstracts of Papers, Sixty-first Annual Meeting, p. 64A.

Horner, John R., 1982, The nesting behavior of dinosaurs and "site fidelity" among ornithischian dinosaurs: *Nature*, 297, pp. 675–575.

_____, 1984a, The nesting behavior of dinosaurs: *Scientific American*, 250 (4), pp. 130–137.

_____, 1984b, A "segmented" epidermal tail frill in a species of hadrosaurian dinosaur: *Journal of Paleontology*, 58 (1), pp. 270–271.

_____, 1988, A new hadrosaur (Reptilia, Ornithischia) from the Upper Cretaceous Judith River Formation of Texas: *Journal of Vertebrate Paleontology*, 8 (3), pp. 314–321.

_____, 1990, Evidence of diphlyetic origination of the hadrosaurian (Reptilia: Ornithischia) dinosaurs, *in*: Kenneth Carpenter and Philip J. Currie, editors, *Dinosaur Systematics: Approaches and Perspectives.* Cambridge and New York: Cambridge University Press, pp. 179–182.

_____, 1994a, Comparative taphonomy of some dinosaur and extant bird colonial nesting grounds, *in*: Kenneth Carpenter, Karl F. Hirsch, and John R. Horner, editors, *Dinosaur Eggs and Babies.* Cambridge: Cambridge University Press, pp. 116–123.

_____, 1994b, Steak knives, beady eyes, and tiny arms (a portrait of *T. rex* as a scavenger), *in*: Gary D. Rosenberg and Donald L. Wolberg, editors, *DinoFest: Paleontological Society Special Papers*, 7, pp. 157–164.

Horner, John R., and Philip J. Currie, 1994, Embryonic and neonatal morphology and ontogeny of a new species of *Hypacrosaurus* (Ornithischia: Lambeosauridae) from Montana and Alberta, *in*: Kenneth Carpenter, Karl F. Hirsch, and John R. Horner, editors, *Dinosaur Eggs and Babies.* New York: Cambridge University Press, pp. 312–336.

Horner, John R., and Don Lessem, 1993, *The Complete* T. rex. New York: Simon and Schuster, 239 pages.

Horner, John R., and Robert Makela, 1979,

Nest of juveniles provides evidence of family structure among dinosaurs: *Nature*, 282 (5736), pp. 296–298.

Horner, John R., and Cynthia Marshall, 2002, Keratinous dinosaur skulls: *Journal of Vertebrate Paleontology*, 23 (Supplement to Number 3), Abstracts of Papers, Sixty-second Annual Meeting, p. 67A.

Horner, John R., Kevin Padian, and Armand de Ricqlès, 2001, Comparative osteohistology of some embryonic and perinatal archosaurs: developmental and behavioral implications for dinosaurs: *Paleobiology*, 27 (1), pp. 39–58.

Horner, John R., Armand de Ricqlès, and Kevin Padian, 2000, Long bone histology of the hadrosaurid dinosaur *Maiasaura peeblesorum*: growth dynamics and physiology based on an ontogenetic series of skeletal elements: *Journal of Vertebrate Paleontology*, 20 (1), pp. 115–129.

Horner, John R., and David B. Weishampel, 1988, A embryological study of two ornithischian dinosaurs: *Nature*, 332, pp. 256–257.

Hotton, Nicholas, III, Everet C. Olson, and R. Beerbower, 1997, Amniote origins and the discovery of herbivory, *in*: S. S. Sumida and K. L. M. Martin, editors, *Amniote Origins: Completing the Transition to Land.* San Diego: Academic Press, pp. 207–264.

Hou Lian-hai [Lianhai], 1977, [A new primitive Pachycephalosauria from Anhui, China]: *Vertebrata PalAsiatica*, 15 (3), pp. 198–202.

_____, 2001, Chinese Mesozoic birds and early evolution of birds: *International Congress of Vertebrate Morphology, Abstracts*, p. 243.

Hou Lian-haim Yeh H. K., and Chou Minchen, 1975, Fossil reptiles from Fusui, Kwangshi: *Vertebrata PalAsiatica*, 13 (1), pp. 23–33.

Hu Cheng-Chin, 1973, Shantung Chuchcheng geesing yadze long hwashih [A new hadrosaur from the Cretaceous of Chucheng, Shantung]: *Acta Geologica Sinica*, 2, pp. 179–206.

Hu Chengzhi [formerly Cheng-Chin], Cheng Zhengwu, Pang Qiping, and Fang Xiaosi, 2001, *Shantungosaurjus giganteus*, pp. 123–135.

Hu Show-yung, 1964, Carnosaurian remains from Alashan, Inner Mongolia: *Vertebrata PalAsiatica*, 8 (1), pp. 42–63.

Hubert, J. F., and Daniel J. Chure, 1992, Taphonomy on an *Allosaurus* quarry in the deposits of a Late Jurassic braided river with a gravel-sand bedload, Salt Wash Member, Dinosaur National Monument, Utah, *in*: J. R. Wilson, editor, *Field Guide to Geologic Excursions in Utah and Adjacent Areas of Nevada, Idaho, and Wyoming.* Utah Geological Survey, Miscellaneous Publication, 92-3, pp. 375–381.

Huene, Friderich von, 1901, Der vermutliche Hautpanzer des *Compsognathus longipes* Wagner: *Neus Jarbuch für Mineralogie, Geologie, und Paläontologie*, 1901, 1 (1), pp. 157–160.

_____, 1905, Über die Nomenklatur von *Zanclodon*: *Ibid.*, 1905, pp. 10–12, Stuttgart.

_____, 1907–08, Die Dinosaurier der eu-

ropäischen Triasformation mit Berucksichtigung der europaischen Vorkommisse: *Geologische und Palaeontologische Abhandlungen*, Supplement 1, 419 pages.

_____, 1910, Ein primitiver Dinosaurier aus Elgin: *Ibid.*, N. F., 8 (6), pp. 25–30.

_____, 1914, Über die Zweistammigkeit der Dinosaurier, mit Beitragen zur Kenntnis einiger Schädel: *Neus Jahrbuch für Mineralogie, Geologie und Paläeontologie (Bell.-Bd.)*, 37, pp. 577–589.

_____, 1915, Beiträge zur Kenntnis einiger Saurischier der schwäbischen Trias: *Centralblatt fur Mineralogie, Geologie und Palaontologie, Stuttgart, Abhandlungen*, 1915, pp. 1–27, Stuttgart.

_____, 1921, Coelurosaurier-Reste aus dem obersten Keuper von Halberstadt: *Ibid.*, 1921, 10, pp. 315–320.

_____, 1923, Carnivorous Saurischia in Europe since the Triassic: *Bulletin of the Geological Society of America*, 34, pp. 449–458.

_____, 1926, Volstaph"ndige Osteologie eines Plateosauriden aus der schwäbischen Trias: *Neus Jahrbuch Fuer Geologie und Paläontologie Abhandlungen*, 15, pp. 129–179, Berlin.

_____, 1928, Lebensbild des Saurischiervorkommens im obersten Keuper von Trössingen: *Palaeobiologica*, 1, pp. 103–116, Wien.

_____, 1932, Die fossile Reptil-Ordnung Saurischia, ihre Entwicklung und Geschichte: *Monographien zur Geologie und Palaeontologie*, series 1, 4, 361 pages.

_____, 1934, Ein neuer Coelurosaurier in der thüringischen Trias: *Paläeontologische Zeitschrift*, 1935, 16, pp. 10–170.

_____, 1941, Die Tetrapoden-Fährten im toskanischen Verrucano und ihre Bedeutung: *Neus Jarbuch für Mineralogie, Geologie, und Paläontologie*, Abt. B, 1941, pp. 1–34.

_____, 1942, *Die fossilen Reptilien des süamerikanischen. Ergebnissen der Sauriergrabungen in Südbrasilien 1928/29.* Munich: Beck'sche Verlagbuchhandlung, viii, 332 pages.

_____, 1961 [not 1959, despite printed date], *Paläontologie und Phylogenie der Niederen Tetrapoden. Nachträge und Ergänzungen.* Jena: Fischer, pp. 1–58.

Huene, Friedrich von, and Charles Alfred Matley, 1933, The Cretaceous Saurischia and Ornithischia of the Central Provinces of India: *Paleontologica Indica*, 21 (1), pp. 1–74.

Huh, Min, and Darla K. Zelenitsky, 2002, Rich dinosaur nesting site from the Cretaceous of Bosung County, Chullanamdo Province, South Korea: *Journal of Vertebrate Paleontology*, 22 (3), pp. 716–718.

Hulke, James W., 1872, Appendix to a "Note on a new and undescribed Wealden vertebra," read 9th February 1870, and published in the Quartely Journal for August in the same year: *Quarterly Journal of the Geological Society of London*, 28, pp. 36–37.

_____, 1887, Notes on some dinosaurian remains in the collection of A. Leeds, Esq., of Eyebury, Northhamptonshire. Part 1. *Ornithopsis leedsii. Ibid.*, 42, pp. 435–436.

Bibliography

Hunt, Adrian P., 1989, A new ?ornithischian dinosaur from the Bull Canyon Formation (Upper Triassic) of east-central New Mexico, *in*: Spencer G. Lucas and Adrian P. Hunt, editors, *The Dawn of the Age of Dinosaurs in the American Southwest*. Albuquerque: New Mexico Museum of Natural History, pp. 355–358.

_____, 1996, A new clade of herrerasaur-like theropods from the Late Triassic of western North America: *Journal of Vertebrate Paleontology*, 16 (Supplement to Number 3), Abstracts of Papers, Fifty-sixth Annual Meeting, p. 43A.

_____, 1994, Vertebrate paleontology and biostratigraphy of the Bull Canyon Formation (Chinle Group, Norian), east-central New Mexico with revisions of the families Metoposauridae (Amphibia: Temnospondyli) and Parasuchidae (Reptilia: Archosauria), Ph.D. dissertation, University of New Mexico, Albuquerque, 403 pages (unpublished).

Hunt, Adrian P., and Spencer G. Lucas, 1994, Ornithischian dinosaurs from the Upper Triassic of the United States, *in*: Nicholas C. Fraser and Hans-Dieter Sues, editors, *In the Shadow of the Dinosaurs: Early Mesozoic Tetrapods*. Cambridge: University of Cambridge Press, pp. 225–241.

Hunt, ReBecca K., 2002, An Early Cretaceous theropod foot from southwestern Arkansas as a possible track maker in central Texas and southwestern Utah: *Journal of Vertebrate Paleontology*, 23 (Supplement to Number 3), Abstracts of Papers, Sixty-second Annual Meeting, p. 68A.

Hurum, Jørn H., 2001a, *Tarbosaurus* vs. *Tyrannosaurus*: *International Congress of Vertebrate Morphology, Abstracts*, pp. 243–244.

_____, 2001b, Lower jaws of *Gallimimus bullatus*: *in*: Darren Tanke and Kenneth Carpenter, editors, *Mesozoic Vertebrate Life: New Research Inspired by the Paleontology of Philip J. Currie*. Bloomington and Indianapolis, Indiana: Indiana University Press, pp. 34–41.

Hurum, Jørn H., and Philip J. Currie, in press, The crushing bite of tyrannosaurids: *Journal of Vertebrate Paleontology*.

Hutchinson, John R., 2001a, The evolution of pelvic osteology and soft tissues on the line to extant birds (Neornithes): *Zoological Journal of the Linnean Society of London*, 131, pp. 123–168.

_____, 2001b, The evolution of femoral osteology and soft tissues on the line to extant birds (Neornithes): *Ibid.*, 131, pp. 169–197.

_____, 2001c, The evolutionary biomechanics of locomotion and body size in theropod dinosaurs: *The Paleobiology and Phylogenetics of Large Theropods*, A. Watson Armour III Symposium, The Field Museum, 12 May 2001, unpaginated.

Hutchinson, John R., and Mariano Garcia, 2002, *Tyrannosaurus* was not a fast runner: *Nature*, 415, pp. 1018–1021.

Hutchinson, John R., and Stephen M. Gatesy, 2000, Adductors, abductors, and the evolution of archosaur locomotion: *Paleobiology*, 26 (4), pp. 734–751.

Hutt, Steve [Stephen], 2002, Mr. Leng's dinosaur: *The Geological Society of the Isle of Wight Newsletter*, 2 (6).

Hutt, Stephen, Darren Naish, David M. Martill, Michael J. Barker, and Penny Newbery, 2001. A preliminary account of a new tyrannosauroid theropod from the Wessex Formation (Early Cretaceous) of southern England: *Cretaceous Research*, 22 (2), pp. 227–242.

Hwang, Sunny H., Mark A. Norell, and Keqin Gao, 2002, A large primitive coelurosaur from the Yixian Formation of northeastern China: *Journal of Vertebrate Paleontology*, 23 (Supplement to Number 3), Abstracts of Papers, Sixty-second Annual Meeting, p. 69A.

Hwang, Sunny H., Mark A. Norell, and Ji Qiang, 2001, New information on Jehol theropods: *Journal of Vertebrate Paleontology*, 21 (Supplement to Number 3), Abstracts of Papers, Sixty-first Annual Meeting, p. 64A.

Hwang, Sunny H., Mark A. Norell, Ji Qiang, and Gao Kelin, 2002, New specimens of *Microraptor zhaoianus* (Theropoda: Dromaeosauridae) from northeastern China: *American Museum Novitates*, 3381, 44 pages.

International Code of Zoological Nomenclature, 1999, fourth edition, International Trust for Zoological Nomenclature, London, pp. 1–306.

Irby, Grace V., 1996, Paleoichnological evidence for running dinosaurs worldwide, *in*: Michael Morales, editor, *The Continental Jurassic*, Museum of Northern Arizona Bulletin, 60, Flagstaff, pp. 109–112.

Irmis, Randall, 2002, The first reported ornithischian dinosaur postcrania from the Early Jurassic Lufeng Formation, China: *Journal of Vertebrate Paleontology*, 23 (Supplement to Number 3), Abstracts of Papers, Sixty-second Annual Meeting, p. 70A.

Ivie, M. A., S. A. Slipinski, and P. Wegrzynowicz, 2001, Generic homonyms in the Colydiinae (Coleoptera: Zopheridae): *Insecta Mundi*, 15, pp. 63–64.

Jackson, Frankie D., A. C. Garrido, and D. B. Loope, 2001, Sauropod egg clutches containing abnormal eggs from the Late Cretaceous of Patagonia: clues to reproductive biology: *Journal of Vertebrate Paleontology*, 21 (Supplement to Number 3), Abstracts of Papers, Sixty-first Annual Meeting, p. 65A.

Jacobs, Louis L., Phillip A. Murray, William R. Downs, and Hamed A. El-Nakhal, 1999, A dinosaur from the Republic of Yemen, *in*: Peter J. Whybrow and Andrew Hill, editors: *Fossil Vertebrates of Arabia*. New Haven and London: Yale University Press, pp. 454–459.

Jacobs, Louis L., and Dale A. Winkler, 1998, Mammals, archosaurs, and the Early to Late Cretaceous transition in North-Central Texas, *in*: Y. Tomida, I. J. Flynn, and L. L. Jacobs, editors, *Advances in Vertebrate Paleontology and Geochronology*. Tokyo: National Science Museum Monographs, 14, pp. 253–280.

Jacobs, Louis L., Dale A. Winkler, William R. Downs, and Elizabeth M. Gomani, 1993, New material of an Early Cretaceous titanosaurid sauropod dinosaur from Malawi: *Palaeontology*, 36 (3), pp. 523–534.

Jacobsen, Aase Roland, 1995, Ecological interpretations based on theropod tooth marks feeding behaviors of carnivorous dinosaurs: *Journal of Vertebrate Paleontology*, 15 (Supplement to Number 3), Abstracts of Papers, Fifty-fifth Annual Meeting, p. 37A.

_____, 1998, Feeding behavior of carnivorous dinosaurs as determined by tooth marks on dinosaur bones: *Historical Biology*, 13, pp. 17–26.

_____, 2001, Tooth-marked small theropod bone: an extremely rare trace, *in*: Darren Tanke and Kenneth Carpenter, editors, *Mesozoic Vertebrate Life: New Research Inspired by the Paleontology of Philip J. Currie*. Bloomington and Indianapolis, Indiana: Indiana University Press, pp. 58–63.

Jaekel, O., 1911, *Die Wirbeltiere. Eine Überischt über die fossilien und lebenden Formen*. Berlin: Borntraeger, pp. 1–252.

_____, 1913–14, Über die Wirbeltierfunde in der oberon Trias von Halberstadt: *Paläontologische Zeitschrift*, I, pp. 155–215, Berlin.

_____, 1929, Die Spur eines neunen Urvogels (*Protornis bavarica*) und deren Bedeutung für Urgeschchte der Vögel: *Ibid.*, 11, pp. 201–238.

Jalil, Nour-Eddine, and Fabien Knoll, 2002, Is *Azendohsaurus laaroushii* (Carnian, Morocco) a dinosaur?: *Journal of Vertebrate Paleontology*, 23 (Supplement to Number 3), Abstracts of Papers, Sixty-second Annual Meeting, p. 70A.

Janensch, Werner, 1914, Die Gliederung der Tendaguru-Schichten im Tendaguru-Gebiet und die Entstechung der Saurier-Lagerstätten: *Archiv für Biontologie*, 3 (3), pp. 227–261.

_____, 1929, Magensteine bei Sauropoden der Tendaguru Schichten: *Palaeontographica* (Supplement 7), 2, pp. 135–144.

_____, 1935–1936, Die Sch del der Sauropoden *Brachiosaurus, Barosaurus*, und *Dicraeosaurus* aus den Tendaguruschiechten Deutsch-Ostafrikas: *Ibid.*, (1), teil 2, lieferung 3, pp. 145–298.

_____, 1950, Die Skelettrekonstruktion von *Brachiosaurus brancai*: *Ibid.*, 1, teil 3, lieferung 2, pp. 95–103.

_____, 1961, Skelettrekonstruktion von *Dysalotosaurus lettow-vorbecki*: *Ibid.*, 1, teil 3, lieferung 4, pp. 237–240.

Janzen, D. H., 1976, The depression of reptile biomass by large herbivores: *The American Naturalist*, 110, pp. 371–400.

Jasinoski, Sandra Christine, 2002a, Reconstruction of the theropod shoulder apparatus using the comparative method: *Alberta Palaeontological Society, Sixth Annual Symposium, "Fossils 2002," Abstract Volume*, January 26–27, 2002, Mount Royal College, Calgary, Alberta, p. 29.

_____, 2002b, Morphological transformation of the theropod scapulocoracoid: a thin-plate spline analysis: *Journal of Vertebrate Paleontology*, 23 (Supplement to Number 3), Abstracts of Papers, Sixty-second Annual Meeting, p. 71A.

Jenkins, Farish A., Jr., N. H. Shubin, W. W. Amaral, M. Gatesy, C., R. Schaff, L. B. Clemmensen, L. B. Downs, A. R. Davidson, N. Bonde, and F. Osbraek, 1994, Late Triassic continental vertebrates and depositional environments of the Fleming Fjord Formation, Jameson Land, East Greenland: *Meddeleser om Grønland, Geoscience.*, 32, pp. 1–25.

Jennings, Debra S., 2002, Detailed sedimentary and taphonomic analysis of a dinosaur quarry, Hot Springs Ranch, Wyoming: *Journal of Vertebrate Paleontology*, 23 (Supplement to Number 3), Abstracts of Papers, Sixty-second Annual Meeting, p. 71A.

Jensen, James A., 1985, Three new sauropod dinosaurs from the Upper Jurassic of Colorado: *Great Basin Naturalist*, 45 (4), pp. 697–709.

_____, 1988, A fourth new sauropod dinosaur from the Upper Jurassic of the Colorado Plateau and sauropod bipedalism: *Ibid.*, 48 (2), pp. 121–145.

Jerison, Harry J., and Celeste C. Horner, 2001, Dinosaur forebrains: *Journal of Vertebrate Paleontology*, 21 (Supplement to Number 3), Abstracts of Papers, Sixty-first Annual Meeting, p. 65A.

Jerzykiewicz, T., Philip J. Currie, David A. Eberth, P. A. Johnson, E. H. Koster and J. J. Zheng, 1993, Djadokhta Formation correlative strata in Chinese Inner Mongolia: an overview of the stratigraphy, sedimentary geology, and paleontology and comparisons with the type locality in the pre–Altai Gobi: *Canadian Journal of Earth Sciences*, 30, pp. 2180–2195.

Jerzykiewicz, T., and Dale A. Russell, 1991, Late Mesozoic stratigraphy and vertebrates of the Gobi Basin: *Cretaceous Research*, 12, pp. 345–377.

Ji Qiang, Philip J. Currie, Mark A. Norell, and Ji Shu-An, 1998, Two feathered dinosaurs from northeastern China: *Nature*, 393, pp. 753–761.

Ji Qiang, and Ji Shúan, 1997, [Protarchaeopterygid Bird (*Protarchaeopteryx* gen. nov.) — fossil remains of Archaeopterygids from China)]: *Chinese Geology*, 238, pp. 38–41.

Ji Qiang, Ji Shúan, You Hailu, Zhang Jianping, Yuan Chongxi, Ji Xinxin, Li Jinglu, and Li Yinxian, 2002, Discovery of an avialae bird *Shenzhouraptor sinensis* gen. et sp. nov.— from China: *Geological Bulletin of China*, 21 (7), pp. 363–369.

Ji Qiang, Mark A. Norell, Ke-Qin Gao, Shu-An Ji, and Dong Ren, 2001, The distribution of integumentary structures in a feathered dinosaur: *Nature*, 410, pp. 1084–1088.

Jiang Fu-Xing, Chen Jin-Hua, Cao Mei-Zhen, and Toshifumi Komatsu, 2000, A discussion of the age of the feathered dinosaurs-bearing beds of Liaoning, China: *Acta Palaeontologica Sinica*, 39 (3), pp. 310–311.

Jones, M. D., 1970, *Cetiosaurus oxoniensis*, Phillips J., a Middle Jurassic sauropod from Rutland, England: *Transactions of the Leicester Literary and Philosophical Society*, 64, pp. 144–150.

Jones, Terry D., John A. Ruben, Ronald W.

Havner, and Nicholas R. Geist, 2002, SEM analysis of fossilized integument from Liaoning ornithodirans: *Journal of Vertebrate Paleontology*, 23 (Supplement to Number 3), Abstracts of Papers, Sixty-second Annual Meeting, p. 72A.

Jones, Terry D., John A. Ruben, Larry D. Martin, Evgeny N. Kurochkin, Alan Feduccia, Paul F. A. Maderson, William J. Hillenius, Nicholas R. Geist, and Vladimir Alif'anov, 2000, Nonavian feathers in a Late Triassic archosaur: *Science*, 288, pp. 2202–2205.

Jurcsák, Tiberiu, 1982, Occurrences nouvelles des sauriens mesozoiques de Roumania: *Vertebrata Hungarica*, 21, pp. 175–184.

Jurcsák, Tiberiu, and Elisabeto Popa, 1983, Le fauna de dinosauriens du Bihor (Romanie), *in*: E. Buffetaut, J.-M. Mazin, and E. Salmon, editors, *Actes du Symposium Paleontologique G. Cuvier, Montbeliard*. Ville de Montbeliard, pp. 323–335.

Jurcsák, Tiberiu, and E. Kessler, 1991, Evolutsia avifaunei pe territorul Roumaniei. II Morfologia speciilor fosile: *Nymphaea*, 17, pp. 583–609.

Kaever, Mathias, and Albert F. de Lapparent, 1974, Les traces de pas de Dinosaures du Jurassique de Barkhausen (Basse Saxe, Allemagne): *Bulletin de la Société Géologique de France*, série 7, 16 (5), pp. 516–525.

Karbek, T. R., 2002, The case for *Stegosaurus* as an agile, cursorial biped: *Journal of Vertebrate Paleontology*, 23 (Supplement to Number 3), Abstracts of Papers, Sixty-second Annual Meeting, p. 73A.

Kardong, Kenneth V., 1998, *Vertebrates: Comparative Anatomy, Function, Evolution*. Boston: McGraw-Hill, 747 pages.

Karhu, A. A., and A. S. Rautian, 1995, A new family of Maniraptora (Dinosauria: Saurischia) from the Late Cretaceous of Mongolia: *Paleontological Journal*, 30 (5), pp. 583–592.

Kellner, Alexander W. A., 1996, Remarks on Brazillian dinosaurs, *in*: Fernando S. Novas and Ralph E. Molnar, editors, *Proceedings of the Gondwanan Dinosaur Symposium: Memoirs of the Queensland Museum*, 39 (part 3), pp. 611–626.

_____, 1999, Short note on a new dinosaur (Theropoda, Coelurosauria) from the Santana Formation (Romualdo Member, Albian), northeastern Brazil: *Boletim do Museu Nacional*, Nova Série, 49, pp. 1–8, Rio de Janeiro.

_____, 2001, New information on the theropod dinosaurs from the Santana Formation (Aptian–Albian), Araripe Basin, northeastern Brazil: *Journal of Vertebrate Paleontology*, 21 (Supplement to Number 3), Abstracts of Papers, Sixty-first Annual Meeting, p. 67A.

_____, 2002, Methological parameters for the identification and taxonomic classification of isolated theropodomorph teeth: *Anais da Academia Brasileira de Ciencias*, 74 (2), Summary of Communications, p. 367.

Kellner, Alexander W. A., Sergio A. K. de Azevedo, Atila A. S. Rosa, Ruben A. Boelter, and Luciano A. Leal, 1999, The occurrence of Prosauropoda in the terres-

trial Late Triassic Santa Maria Formation, southern Brazil: *Journal of Vertebrate Paleontology*, 19 (Supplement to Number 3), Abstracts of Papers, Fifty-ninth Annual Meeting, p. 57A.

Kermack, D., 1984, New prosauropod material from South Wales: *Zoological Journal of the Linnean Society*, 82, pp. 101–117.

Kessler, E., and Tiberiu Jurcsák, 1986, New contributions to the knowledge of the Lower Cretaceous bird remains from Cornet (Romania): *Trav. Mus. d'Histoire natur. Grigore Antipa*, 25, pp. 393–401.

Kielan-Jaworowska, Zofia, and Rinchen Barsbold, 1972, Narrative of the Polish-Mongolian Palaeontological Expeditions 1967–1971: *Acta Palaeontologica Polonica*, 42, pp. 201–242.

Kielan-Jaworowska, Zofia, and N. Dovchin, 1968/1969, Narrative of the Polish-Mongolian Palaeontological Expeditions 1963–1965, *in*: Kielan-Jaworowska, Zofia, editor, Results of the Polish-Mongolian Palaeontological Expeditons: *Palaeontologica Polonica*, 19, pp. 7–30.

Kim, Haang Mook, 1983, Cretaceous dinosaurs from Korea: *The Journal of the Geological Society of Korea*, 19 (3), pp. 115–126.

_____, 1986, New early Cretaceous dinosaur tracks from Republic of Korea, *in*: David D. Gillette, editor, *First International Symposium on Dinosaur Tracks and Traces, Abstracts of Program, New Mexico Museum of Natural History, Albuquerque, N.M. 22–24 May 1986*, p. 17.

_____, 1993, Taphonomy of the Cretaceous dinosaur bones from Korea: *Journal of Natural History and Environments*, 1 (1), pp. 39–64.

Kirkland, James I. [Ian], 1998, A new hadrosaurid from the Upper Cedar Mountain Formation (Albian–Cenomanian: Cretaceous) of eastern Utah — the oldest known hadrosaurid (lambeosaurine?), *Lower and Middle Cretaceous Terrestrial Ecosystems*. Albuquerque: New Mexico Museum of Natural History and Science, Bulletin 14, pp. 283–296.

Kirkland, James I., Brooks B. Britt, Donald L. Burge, Kenneth Carpenter, Richard L. Cifelli, Frank L. DeCourten, Jeffrey G. Eaton, Stephen Hasiotis, and Tim F. Lawton, 1997, Lower to Middle Cretaceous dinosaur faunas of the central Colorado Plateau: A Key to understanding 35 million years of tectonics, sedimentology, evolution, and biogeography: *Brigham Young University Geology Studies*, 42, part II, pp. 69–103.

Kirkland, James I., Donald Burge, and Robert Gaston, 1993, A large dromaeosaur (Theropod) from the Lower Cretaceous of eastern Utah: *Hunteria*, 2, pp. 2–16.

Kirkland, James Ian, and Kenneth Carpenter, 1994, North Americás first pre-Cretaceous ankylosaur (Dinosauria) from the Upper Jurassic Morrison Formation of Western Colorado: *BYU Geology Studies 1994*, 40, pp. 25–42.

Kirkland, James I., Richard L. Cifelli, Brooks B. Britt, Donald L. Burge, Frank L. DeCourten, Jeffrey G. Eaton, and J. Michael

Bibliography

Parrish, 1999, Distribution of vertebrate faunas in the Cedar Mountain Formation, east-central Utah, *in*: David D. Gillette, editor, *Vertebrate Paleontology in Utah*, Utah Geological Survey, Miscellaneous Publication, 99-1, pp. 201–217.

Kirkland, James I., Donald Deblieux, Joshua Smith, and Scott D. Sampson, 2002, New ceratopsid cranial remains from the lower Campanian Wahweap Formation, Grand Staircase-Escalante National Monument, Utah: *Journal of Vertebrate Paleontology*, 23 (Supplement to Number 3), Abstracts of Papers, Sixty-second Annual Meeting, p. 74A.

Kirkland, James I., Robert Gaston, and Donald Burge, 1993, A large dromaeosaur (Theropoda) from the Lower Cretaceous of eastern Utah: *Hunteria*, 2 (10), pp. 1–16.

Kirkland, James I., Spencer G. Lucas, and John W. Estep, 1998, Cretaceous dinosaurs of the Colorado Plateau, *in*: Spencer G. Lucas, James I. Kirkland, and John W. Estep, editors, *Lower and Middle Cretaceous Terrestrial Ecosystems*. Albuquerque: New Mexico Museum of Natural History and Science, Bulletin 14, pages 67–89.

Kirkland, James I., and Douglas G. Wolfe, 2001, A therizinosaurid (Dinosauria: Theropoda) braincase from the middle Turonian (Cretaceous) of North America: *Journal of Vertebrate Paleontology*, 21 (Supplement to Number 3), Abstracts of Papers, Sixty-first Annual Meeting, p. 68A.

Klimov, A. F., 1950, *Anatomiya domashnikh zhivotnykh*. Moscow: Gos. Sel'khoz. Lit., 1950, vol. 1.

Knoll, Fabien, 2002*a*, Nearly complete skull of *Lesothosaurus* (Dinosauria: Ornithischia) from the Upper Elliot Formation (Lower Jurassic: Hettangian) of Lesotho: *Journal of Vertebrate Paleontology*, 22 (2), pp. 238–243.

———, 2002*b*, New skull of *Lesothosaurus* (Dinosauria: Ornithischia) from the Upper Elliot Formation (Lower Jurassic) of southern Africa: *Geobios*, 35, pp. 595–603.

Knoll, Fabien, Claude Colleté, Bruno Dubus, and Jean-Louis Petit, 2000, On the presence of a sauropod dinosaur (Saurischia) in the Albian of Aube (France): *Geodiversitas*, 22 (3), pp. 389–394.

———, 2002, Nearly complete skull of *Lesothosaurus* (Dinosauria: Ornithischia) from the Upper Elliot Formation (Lower Jurassic: Hettangian) of Lesotho: *Journal of Vertebrate Paleontology*, 22 (2), pp. 238–243.

Kobayashi, Yoshitsugu, and Yoichi Azuma, 1999, Cranial material of a new iguanodontian dinosaur from the Early Cretaceous Kitadani Formation of Japan: *Journal of Vertebrate Paleontology*, 19 (Supplement to Number 3), Abstracts of Papers, Fifty-ninth Annual Meeting, p. 57A.

Kobayashi, Yoshitsugu, Yoichi Azuma, Zhiming Dong, and Richchen Barsbold, 2001, Bonebed of a new gastrolith-bearing ornithomimid dinosaur from the Upper Cretaceous Ulansuhai Formation of Nei Mongol Autonomous Region, China:

Journal of Vertebrate Paleontology, 21 (Supplement to Number 3), Abstracts of Papers, Sixty-first Annual Meeting, pp. 68A–69A.

Koken, E., 1900, [Review of E. Fraas: Triassaurier]: *Neus Jarbuch für Mineralogie, Geologie, und Paläontologie*, 1900, 1, pp. 302–303, Stuttgart.

Kordos, Laszló, 1983, Fontosabb szórványleletek a máfi Gerinces-Gyüjteményében (8 közlemény) [Major finds of scattered fossils in the paleovertebrate collection of the Hungarian Institute (Communication 8): *A Maygar Állami Földtani Intézet évi Jelentése Az* 1981, Évröl, pp. 503–511.

Khosla, Ashu, and Ashok Sahni, 1995, Parataxonomic classification of Late Cretaceous dinosaur eggshells from India: *Journal of the Paleontological Society of India*, 40, pp. 87–102.

Kowalevsky, Vladimir Onufrievich, 1873, Monographie der Gattung *Anthracotherium* CUVIER und Versuch einer naturlichen Classification der fossilen Hufthiere: *Paleontographica*, 22, pp. 131–210.

Kozisek, Jacqueline M., 2002, A comparison of the pelvic girdle from a new juvenile hypsilophodontid found in the Morrison Formation of northeastern Wyoming to decribed specimens: *Journal of Vertebrate Paleontology*, 23 (Supplement to Number 3), Abstracts of Papers, Sixty-second Annual Meeting, pp. 75A–76A.

Krause, David W., Raymond Robert Rogers, Catherine A. Forster, Joseph H. Hartman, G. A. Buckley, and Scott D. Sampson, 1999, The Late Cretaceous vertebrate fauna of Madagascar: implications for Gondwanan paleobiogeography: *GSA Today*, 9 (8), pp. 1–7.

Krauss, David A., 2001, An analysis of the feeding habits of herbivorous dinosaurs through the examination of phytoliths trapped on tooth grinding surfaces: *Journal of Vertebrate Paleontology*, 21 (Supplement to Number 3), Abstracts of Papers, Sixty-first Annual Meeting, p. 69A.

Krebs, Bernard, 1991, Das Skelett von *Henkelotherium guimarotae* gen. et sp. nov. (Eupantotherium, Mammalia) aus dem Oberen Jura von Portugal. *Berliner geowissenschaftliche Abhandlungen (A)*, 133, p. 110.

Kreighbaum, Ellen, and Katherine M. Barthels, 1985, *A Qualitative Approach for Studying Human Movement*. Minneapolis: Burgess Publishing, 768 pages. Kuhn, Oskar, 1958, *Die Fährten der vorzeitlichen Amphibien und Reptilien*, Bamberg, 64 pages.

———, 1959, Ein neuer Microsaurier aus dem deutschen Rotliegenden: *Neus Jahrbuch für Geologie und Paläontologie, Monatshefte, 1959*, pp. 424–426.

———, 1963, *Fossilium Catalogus I (Animalia) Pars 101: Ichnia tetrapodorum*. Junk: s'Gravenhage, 176 pages.

———, 1966, *Die Reptilien. System und Stammesgeschichte*. Krailling b. Munchen, Oeben, 154 pages.

Kummer, B., 1959, Bauprinzipien des Säugerskeletes von *Brachiosaurus brancai*: *Palaeontographica, Supplement VII*, 1. Reihe, Teil 3, Lieferung 2, pp. 95–103.

Kundrát, Martin, Arthur R. I. Cruickshank, Terry W. Manning, and Kenneth A. Joysey, 2001, Structure of the embryonic parabasisphenoid in a therizinosaurid dinosaur: *International Congress of Vertebrate Morphology, Abstracts*, pp. 251–252.

Kundrát, Martin, and Philip J. Currie, 2001, On the embryonic neural endocranium of lambeosaurid hadrosaurs: *International Congress of Vertebrate Morphology, Abstracts*, p. 252.

Kurzanov, Sergei Mikhailovich, 1976, A new Late Cretaceous carnosaur from Nogon-Tsav, Mongolia: *Soviet-Mongolian Paleontological Expedition, Transactions*, 20, pp. 93–104.

———, 1990, Novy rod protoceratopsid iz pozdnego mela Mongolii: *Palaeontoloicheski Zhurnal*, 4, pp. 91–91 (Translation: A new Late Cretaceous protoceratopsid from Mongolia: *Paleontological Journal*, 24 [4], pp. 85–91).

Kurzanov, Sergei Mikhailovich, Mikhail B. Ef'imov, and Yuri M. Gubin, 2001, Jurassic dinosaurs of Yakuta: *Journal of Vertebrate Paleontology*, 21 (Supplement to Number 3), Abstracts of Papers, Sixty-first Annual Meeting, p. 70A.

———, 2003, New archosaurs from the Jurassic of Siberia and Mongolia: *Paleontological Journal*, 37 (1), pp. 53–57 (translated from *Paleontologicheskii Zhurnal*, 1, 2003, pp. 55–59).

Kurzanov, Sergei Mikhailovich, and Tat'yana A. Tumanova, 1978, [On the structure of endocranium in some ankylosaurs of Mongolia]: *Paleontologicheskii Zhurnal*, 1978, 3, pp. 90–95 (translated in: *Palaeontological Journal*, 12 [3], pp. 369–374).

Kusmer, K. D., 1990, Taphonomy of owl pellet deposition: *Journal of Paleontology*, 64, pp. 829–637.

Lacovara, Kenneth J., Matthew C. Lamanna, Joshua B. Smith, Barbara Grandstaff, and Jennifer R. Smith, 2002, Concentration and preservation potential of vertebrate fossils within coastal lithosomes: examples from the Upper Cretaceous Bahariya Formation of Egypt: *Journal of Vertebrate Paleontology*, 23 (Supplement to Number 3), Abstracts of Papers, Sixty-second Annual Meeting, p. 77A.

Lacovara, Kenneth J., Joshua B. Smith, Jennifer R. Smith, Matthew C. Lamanna, Kirk R. Johnson, Peter Dodson and Douglas J. Nichola, (2001), Coastal environments of Cretaceous dinosaurs: examples from North Africa and western North America: *Journal of Vertebrate Paleontology*, 21 (Supplement to Number 3), Abstracts of Papers, Sixty-first Annual Meeting, p. 70A.

Lamanna, Matthew C., Rubén D. Martinez, Marcelo Luna, Gabriel Casal, Peter Dodson, and Peter Smith, 2001, Sauropod faunal transition through the Cretaceous Chubut Group of Central Patagonia: *Journal of Vertebrate Paleontology*, 21 (Supplement to Number 3), Abstracts of Papers, Sixty-first Annual Meeting, p. 70A.

Lamanna, Matthew C., Rubén D. Martinez,

and Joshua B. Smith, 2002, A definitive abelisaurid theropod dinosaur from the early Late Cretaceous of Patagonia: *Journal of Vertebrate Paleontology*, 22 (1), pp. 58–69.

Lambe, Lawrence M., 1902, On vertebra of the Mid-Cretaceous of the North West Territory. 2. New genera and species from the Belly River Series (Mid-Cretaceous): *Geological Survey of Canada, Contributions to Canadian Paleontology*, 3, part 2, pp. 23–81.

_____, 1904, On the squamoso-parietal crest of two species of horned dinosaurs from the Cretaceous of Alberta: *Ottawa Naturalist*, 17, pp. 133–139.

_____, 1917, The Cretaceous theropodous dinosaur *Gorgosaurus*: *Canada Department of Mines, Geological Survey Memoir 100*, pp. 1–84.

_____, 1918, The Cretaceous genus *Stegoceras* typifying a new family provisionally referred to the Stegosauria: *Transactions of the Royal Society of Canada*, 12, pp. 23–36.

Lambert, Olivier, Pascal Godefroit, Hong Li, Chang-Young Shang, and Zhi-Ming Dong, 2001, A new species of *Protoceratops* (Dinosauria, Neoceratopsia) from the Late Cretaceous of Inner Mongolia (P. R. China): *Bulletin de l'Institut Royal des Sciences Naturelles de Belgique/Bulletin van het Koninklijk Belgisch Instituut voor Natuurwetenschappen*, 71, supp. 5–28, pp. 5–21.

Lander, Bruce, 1998, Oreodontoidea, *in*: C. M. Janis, K. M. Scott, and L. L. Jacobs, editors, *Evolution of Tertiary Mammals of North America, Volume 1: Terrestrial Carnivores, Ungulates, and Ungulatelike Mammals*. Cambridge: Cambridge University Press, pp. 402–420.

Langer, Max C. [Cardoso], 2000, Postcranial anatomy and the diagnosis of Dinosauria: *48th Symposium of Vertebrate Palaeontology and Comparative Anatomy, Portsmouth, 2000*, University of Portsmouth, abstracts, unpaginated.

_____, 2001, Early dinosaur phylogeny: are any of the hypotheses better supported?: *Journal of Vertebrate Paleontology*, 21 (Supplement to Number 3), Abstracts of Papers, Sixty-first Annual Meeting, p. 71A.

Langston, Wann, Jr., 1974, Non-mammalian Comanchean tetrapods: *Geoscience and Man*, 8, pp. 77–102.

Lapparent, Albert F. de, and C. Montenant, 1967, Les empreintes de pas de reptiles de l'Infralias de Veillon (Vendée): *Memoires de la Société Géologique de France*, 107, pp. 1–41.

Lapparent, Albert F. de, and Nowgol Sadat, M.A.A., 1975, Une trace de pas de Dinosaure dans le Lias de l'Elboura, en Iran: *Comptes Rendus des Séances de l'Academie des Sciences, Paris*, série D, 280, pp. 161–163.

Larson, Neal L., 2001, The North American Museum of Ancient Life: *DinoPress*, 6, pp. 4–13.

Larson, Peter L., 2000, The theropod reproductive system: *in* B. P. Pérez-Moreno, Thomas R. Holtz, Jr., José Luis Sanz, and José J. Moratalla, editors, Aspects of

theropod paleobiology: *Gaia*, 15 (cover dated December 1998), pp. 389–397.

_____, 2001, Pathologies in *Tyrannosaurus rex*: snapshots of a killer's life: *Journal of Vertebrate Paleontology*, 21 (Supplement to Number 3), Abstracts of Papers, Sixty-first Annual Meeting, pp. 71A–72A.

_____, 2002, *Rex Appeal: The Amazing Story of Sue, the Dinosaur that Changed Science, the Law, and My Life*. Montpelier, Vermont: Invisible Cities Press, 384 pages.

Larson, Peter L., and Eberhard Frey, 1992, Sexual dimorphism in the abundant Upper Cretaceous theropod *Tyrannosaurus rex*: *Journal of Vertebrate Paleontology*, 12 (Supplement to Number 3), Abstracts of Papers, Fifty-third Annual Meeting, p. 38A.

Larsson, Hans C. E., 2001a, Evolution and development of theropod hand reduction: *The Paleobiology and Phylogenetics of Large Theropods*, A. Watson Armour III Symposium, The Field Museum, 12 May 2001, unpaginated.

_____, 2001b, Endocranial anatomy of *Carcharodontosaurus saharicus*, *in*: Darren Tanke and Kenneth Carpenter, editors, *Mesozoic Vertebrate Life: New Research Inspired by the Paleontology of Philip J. Currie*. Bloomington and Indianapolis, Indiana: Indiana University Press, pp. 19–33.

Larsson, Hans C. E., and Gunter Wagner, 2002, New evidence of the evolution and development of bird wing digits: *Journal of Vertebrate Paleontology*, 23 (Supplement to Number 3), Abstracts of Papers, Sixty-second Annual Meeting, pp. 77A–78A.

Lauder, George V., 1995, On the inference of function from structure, *in*: J. J. Thomason, editor. *Functional Morphology in Vertebrate Paleontology*. Cambridge, United Kingdom: Cambridge University Press, pp. 1–18.

Laurent, Yves, Jean Le Loeuff, M. Bilotte, Éric Buffetaut, and Gilles S. Odin, 2001, Campanian–Maastrichtian continental-marine connection at the Aquitaine-Pyrenees-Provence area (S France), *in*: Giles S. Odin, editor, *The Campanian-Maastrichtian Stage Boundary*, volume 36 of the International Union of Geological Sciences Special Publications (monograph) Series. Amsterdam: Elsevier, pp. 657–674.

Laurent, Yves, Jean Le Loeuff, and Éric Buffetaut, 1997, Les Hadrosauridae (Dinosauria, Ornithopoda) du Maastrichtien superieur des Corbiéres orientales (Aude, France): *Revue de Paléobiologie, Genève*, 16 (2), pp. 411–423.

Le Loeuff, Jean, 1998, Evolution palébiogéographique des faunes de vertébrés continentaux du Jurassique supérieur à la fin du Crétacé. Mémoire d'habitation à dirger des recherches. Université Paul Sabatier, Toulouse, Tome 1, pp. 1–68.

Leahy, Guy D., 2002, Speed potential of tyrannosaurs great and small: *Journal of Vertebrate Paleontology*, 23 (Supplement to Number 3), Abstracts of Papers, Sixty-second Annual Meeting, p. 78A.

Leahy, Guy D., and Gregory S. Paul, 2001, Metabolic implications of growth rates in dinosaurs: *Journal of Vertebrate Paleontology*, 21 (Supplement to Number 3), Ab-

stracts of Papers, Sixty-first Annual Meeting, p. 72A.

Leal, Lucuiano A., Alexander W. A. Kellner, Sergio A. K. Azevedo, and Tila A. S. da Rosa, 2001, Taphonomic aspects of a prosauropod dinosaur from the Caturrita Formation, Late Triassic, southern Brazil: *Journal of Vertebrate Paleontology*, 21 (Supplement to Number 3), Abstracts of Papers, Sixty-first Annual Meeting, p. 72A.

Leanza, Héctor, and Carlos A. Hugo, 1997, Hoja Geológica 3969-III — Picún Leufú, provincias del Neuquén y Río Negro: *Instituto de Geologia y Recuros Naturales. SEGEMAR* (Buenos Aires), 218, pp. 1–135.

_____, 2001, Cretaceous red beds from southern Neuquén Basin (Argentina): age, distribution and stratigraphic discontinuities: *Asociacíon Paleontológical Argentina, Publicatión Especial* 7, VII International Symposium on Mesozoic Terrestrial Ecosystems, Buenos Aires, 30-6-2001, pp. 117–122.

Leckey, Erin, 2002, Cretaceous distribution patterns of herbivorous dinosaurs and vascular plants: using map sequences to examine evolutionary patterns: *2002 California Paleontology Conference, Abstracts*, Department of Geological Sciences, University of California, Santa Barbara, California, April 12–13, 2002, p. 7.

Lee, Suzanne, 2003, A morphometric analysis of *Thecodontosaurus*: *in*: David B. Norman and Paul Upchurch, editors, *SVPCA 50, Cambridge 2002, 11–13 September, Abstract Volume*, unpaginated.

Lee, Yuong-Nam, 1997, Bird and dinosaur footprints in the Woodbine Formation (Cenomanian), Texas: *Cretaceous Research*, 18, pp. 849–864.

Lee, Yuong-Nam, Kang-Min Yu, and Craig B. Wood, 2001, A review of vertebrate faunas from the Gyeongsang Supergroup (Cretaceous) in South Korea: *Palaeogeography, Palaeoclimatology, Palaeoecology*, 165, pp. 357–373.

Legarreta, L., and C. A. Gulisano, 1989, Análisis estratigráfico secuencial de la Cuenca Neuquina (Triásico Superior-Terciario Inferior), *in*: G. Chebli and R. Spaletti, editors, *X Congreso Geológico Argentino; Cuencas Sedimentarias Argentinas, Serie Correlacion Geológica 6, Buenos Aires*, pp. 221–243.

Lehman, Thomas M., 1989, *Chasmosaurus mariscalensis*, sp. nov., a new ceratopsian dinosaur from Texas: *Journal of Vertebrate Paleontology*, 9 (2), pp. 137–162.

_____, 2002, The enigma of endothermic infant herbivorous dinosaurs: *Journal of Vertebrate Paleontology*, 23 (Supplement to Number 3), Abstracts of Papers, Sixty-second Annual Meeting, p. 78.

Lehman, Thomas M., and Kenneth Carpenter, 1990, A partial skeleton of the tyrannosaurid dinosaur *Aublysodon* from the Upper Cretaceous of New Mexico: *Journal of Paleontology*, 64, pp. 1026–1032.

Lehman, Thomas M., and Alan B. Coulson, 2002, A juvenile specimen of the sauropod dinosaur *Alamosaurus sanjuanensis* from the upper Cretaceous of Big Bend

Bibliography

Park, Texas: *Journal of Paleontology*, 76 (1), pp. 156–172.

Leonardi, Giuseppe, 1979, Note préliminar sobre seis pistas de dinosauro ornithischia da Bacio do Rio de Peixe em Sousa, Paraiba, Brasil: *Anais da Academia Brasileira de Ciencias*, 51 (3), pp. 501–516.

———, 1981, As Localidades com rastros Fossels de Tetrapodes na America Latina: *An. II Congr. Latinoamer. Pal., Porto Allegre*, 2, pp. 929–940.

———, 1984, Le impronte di Dinosauri, *in*: José F. Bonaparte, Edwin H. Colbert, Philip J. Currie, Armand de Ricqlès, Zofia Kielan-Jaworowska, Giuseppe Leonardi, N. Morello, and Phillipe Taquet, editors, *Sulla Orme dei Dinosauri*. Venice: Erizzo Editrice, pp. 165–168.

Leonardi, Giuseppe, and P. Mietto, editors, 2000, *Dinosauri in Italia. Le orme giurassiche dei Lavini di Marco (Trentino) e gli altri resti fossili italiani*. Pisa-Rome: Accademia Editoriale, 497 pages.

Leshchinsky [Leśinskij], Sergei V., Alexei V. Fayngertz, Alexi V. Voronkevich [Voronkevic], Evgeny N. Maschenko [Maśenko], and Alexander O. Averianov [Avereânov], 2000, [Preliminary results of the investigation of the Shestakovo localities of Early Cretaceous vertebrates], *in*: A. V. Komarov, editor, *Materialy regional'noj konferencii geologov Sibiri, Dal'nego Vostoka i Severo-Vostoka Rossii*, Tom III. Tomsk: GalaPress, pp. 363–366.

Lessertisseur, Jacques, 1955, Traces fossiles d'activite animale et leur signification paleobiologique: *Memoires de la Société Géologique de France* (N.S.), 74, 150 pages.

Lhuyd, Edward, 1699, *Lithophylacii Britannici Ichnographia, sive lapidium aliorumque fossilium Britannicorum singulari figura insignium*. London: Gleditsch and Weidmann.

Li Kui, Zhang Yuguang, and Cai Kaiji, 1999, The characteristics of composition of trace elements in Jurassic dinosaur bones in Sichuan Basin, *in*: Wang Yuanqing and Deng Tao, editors, *Proceedings of the Seventh Annual Meeting of the Chinese Society of Vertebrate Paleontology*. Beijing: China Ocean Press, pp. 89–95.

Li Weirong, and Jin Jidong, 2001, On the Upper Cretaceous Jiayin Group of Heilongjiang Province, China, *in*: Deng and Wang, editors, pp. 65–74.

Li, Y., Z. Yin, and Liu Y., 1995, The discovery of a new genus of dinosaur egg from Xixia, Henan, China: *Journal of Wuhan Institute of Chemical Technology*, 17, pp. 38–41.

Lim, Jong-Deock, Larry D. Martin, and K.-S. Baek, 2001, The first discovery of a brachiosaurid from the Asian continent: *Naturwissenschaften*, 88, pp. 82–84.

Lipkin, Christine, and Paul C. Sereno, 2002, A spinosaurid furcula: a tetanuran invention: *Journal of Vertebrate Paleontology*, 23 (Supplement to Number 3), Abstracts of Papers, Sixty-second Annual Meeting, p. 79A.

Llompart, C., M. L. Casnovas, and J. V. Santafé, 1984, Un nuevo yacimiento de icnitas de dinosaurios en las facies garumniensis de la Conca de Trempe (Lleido,

Espania): *Acta Geológica Hispanica*, 19, pp. 143–147.

Lockley, Martin G., 1986, The paleobiological and paleoenvironmental importance of dinosaur footprints: *Palaios*, 1, pp. 37–47.

———, 1987*a*, Dinosaur footprints from the Dakota Group of Eastern Colorado: *The Mountain Geologist*, 24 (4), pp. 107–122.

———, 1987*b*, Dinosaur tracks symposium signals a renaissance in vertebrate ichnology: *Paliobiology*, 13 (2), pp. 246–252.

———, 1995, *Dinosaur Tracks and Other Fossil Footprints of the Western United States*. New York: Columbia University Press, 338 pages.

———, 2000, Philosophical perspectives on theropod track morphology: blending qualities and quantities in the science of ichnology: *in* B. P. Pérez-Moreno, Thomas R. Holtz, Jr., José Luis Sanz, and José J. Moratalla, editors, Aspects of theropod paleobiology: *Gaia*, 15 (cover dated December 1998), pp. 279–300.

Lockley, Martin G., James O. Farlow, and Christian Meyer, 1994, *Brontopodus* and *Parabrontopodus* ichnogen. nov. and the significance of wide- and narrow-guage sauropod trackways: *Gaia*, 10, 135–145.

Lockley, Martin G., and Adrian P. Hunt, 1994, A track of the giant theropod dinosaur *Tyrannosaurus* from close to the Cretaceous/Tertiary boundary, Northern New Mexico: *Ichnos*, 3, pp. 213–218.

———, 1995, Ceratopsid tracks and associated ichnofauna from the Laramie Formation (Upper Cretaceous: Maastrichtian) of Colorado: *Journal of Vertebrate Paleontology*, 15 (3), pp. 592–614.

Lockley, Martin G., Adrian P. Hunt, Marc Paquette, Sue-Ann Bilbey, and Alden Hamblin, 1998, Dinosaur tracks from the Carmel Formation, northeastern Utah: implications for Middle Jurassic Paleoecology: *Ichnos*, 5, pp. 255–267.

Lockley, Martin G., and C. Jennings, 1987, Dinosaur tracksites of western Colorado and eastern Utah, *in*: W. R. Averett, editor, *Paleontology and Geology of the Dinosaur Triangle*. Grand Junction Colorado: Museum of Western Colorado, pp. 85–90.

Lockley, Martin G., and Christian Meyer, 2000, *Dinosaur Tracks and Other Fossil Footprints of Europe*. New York: Columbia University Press, 323 pages.

Lockley, Martin G., Christian Meyer, and José J. Moratalla, 1998, *Therangospodus*: trackway evidence for the widespread distribution of a Late Jurassic theropod with well-padded feet: *in* B. P. Pérez-Moreno, Thomas R. Holtz, Jr., José Luis Sanz, and José J. Moratalla, editors, Aspects of theropod paleobiology: *Gaia*, 15 (cover dated December 1998), pp. 339–353.

Lockley, Martin G., Christian A. Meyer, and Vanda Faria dos Santos, 1998, *Megalosauripus* and the problematic concept of megalosaur footprints: *in* B. P. Pérez-Moreno, Thomas R. Holtz, Jr., José Luis Sanz, and José J. Moratalla, editors, Aspects of theropod paleobiology: *Gaia*, 15 (cover dated December 1998), pp. 313–337.

Lockley, Martin G., Vanda Faria dos Santos,

Christian A. Meyer, and Adrian P. Hunt, 1998, A new dinosaur tracksite in the Morrison Formation, Boundary Butte, Southeastern Utah, *in*: Kenneth Carpenter, Daniel J. Chure, and James I. Kirkland, editors, The Upper Jurassic Morrison Formation: An interdisciplinary study, *Modern Geology*, 23, pp. 317–330.

Lockley, Martin G., Joanna L. Wright, and Masaki Matsukawa, 2001, A new look at *Magnoavipes* and so-called "big bird" tracks from Dinosaur Ridge (Cretaceous, Colorado): *The Mountain Geologist*, 38 (3), pp. 137–146.

Lockley, Martin G., Joanna L. Wright, D. White, Masaki Matsukawa, Li Jianjun, Feng Lu, and Li Hong, 2002, The first sauropod trackways from China: *Cretaceous Research*, 23, pp. 363–381.

Loewen, Mark A., Matthew T. Carrano, and Scott D. Sampson, 2002, Ontogenetic changes in hindlimb musculature and function in the Late Jurassic theropod *Allosaurus*: *Journal of Vertebrate Paleontology*, 23 (Supplement to Number 3), Abstracts of Papers, Sixty-second Annual Meeting, p. 80A.

Loewen, Mark A., Scott D. Sampson, Mike A. Getty, and Rose L. Difley, 2001, The upland dinosaur fauna of the Late Cretaceous (Maastrichtian) North Horn Formation: *Journal of Vertebrate Paleontology*, 21 (Supplement to Number 3), Abstracts of Papers, Sixty-first Annual Meeting, p. 74A.

Long, Robert A., and Phillip A. Murry, 1995, Late Triassic (Carnian and Norian) tetrapods from the southwestern United States: *New Mexico Museum of Natural History and Science Bulletin*, 4, 254 pages.

Longman, Heber A., 1933, A new dinosaur from the Queensland Cretaceous: *Memoirs of the Queensland Museum*, 10, pp. 131–141.

Longrich, Nicholas R., 2001, Secondarily flightless maniraptoran theropods?: *Journal of Vertebrate Paleontology*, 21 (Supplement to Number 3), Abstracts of Papers, Sixty-first Annual Meeting, p. 74A.

———, 2002, Systematics of *Sinosauropteryx*: *Journal of Vertebrate Paleontology*, 23 (Supplement to Number 3), Abstracts of Papers, Sixty-second Annual Meeting, p. 80A.

López-Martinez, Nieves, José Ignacio Canudo, Luis Ardèvol, Xabier Pereda-Suberbiola, Xabier Orue-Etxebarria, Gloria Cuenca-Bescós, José Ignacio Ruiz-Omeñaca, Xabier Murelaga, and Monique Feist, 2001, New dinosaur site correlated with Upper Maastrichtian pelagic deposits in the Spanish Pyrenees: implications for the dinosaur extinction pattern in Europe: *Cretaceous Research*, 22, pp. 41–61.

López-Martinez, Nieves, José Ignacio Canudo, and Gloria Cuenca, 1999, Latest Cretaceous eggshells from Arén (Southern Pyrenees, Spain): *First International Symposium on Dinosaur Eggs and Babies/Extended Abstracts/2000*, pp. 35–36.

Loyal, Raminder S., Dhananjay M. Mohabey, Ashu Khosla, and Ashok Sahni, 2000, Status and palaeobiology of the Late Cretaceous Indian theropods with description of a new theropod eggshell oogenus and oospecies, *Ellipsoolithus khedaensis*, from the Lameta Formation, District Kheda, Gujarat, western India: *in* B. P. Pérez-Moreno, Thomas R. Holtz, Jr., José Luis Sanz, and José J. Moratalla, editors, Aspects of theropod paleobiology: *Gaia*, 15 (cover dated December 1998), pp. 379–387.

Lü, Junchang, 2003, A new oviraptorosaurid (Theropoda: Oviraptorosauria) from the Late Cretaceous of southern China: *Journal of Vertebrate Paleontology*, 22 (4), pp. 871–875.

Lü, Junchang, Zhiming Dong, Yoichi Azuma, Rinchen Barsbold, and Yukimitsu Tomida, 2002, Oviraptorosaurs compared to birds, *in*: Zhonghe Zhou and Fucheng Zhang, editors, *Proceedings of the 5th Symposium of the Society of Avian Paleontology and Evolution*. Beijing: Science Press, pp. 175–189.

Lü, Jun-Chang, Yoshitsugu Kobayashi, Yoichi Azuma, Dong Huang, and Li-Cheng Qiu, 2002, The pectoral girdle and forelimb of a new oviraptorosaur: *Journal of Vertebrate Paleontology*, 23 (Supplement to Number 3), Abstracts of Papers, Sixty-second Annual Meeting, p. 81A.

Lucas, A. M., and P. R. Stettenheim, 1972, *Avian Anatomy—Integument*. Washington, D.C.: United States Department of Agriculture Handbook.

Lucas, Spencer G., and Andrew B. Heckert, 2001, Theropod dinosaurs and the Early Jurassic age of the Moenave Formation, Arizona-Utah, USA: *Neus Jahrbuch für Geologie und Paläontologie, Monatshefte*, 7, pp. 435–488.

Lucas, Spencer G., and Adrian P. Hunt, 1989, *Alamosaurus* and the sauropod hiatus in the Cretaceous of North American Western Interior, *in*: James O. Farlow, editor, *Paleobiology of the Dinosaurs*, Geological Society of America Special Paper 238, Boulder, Colorado, pp. 75–85.

Lucas, Spencer G., and Robert M. Sullivan, 2000, Stratigraphy and vertebrate biostratigraphy across the Cretaceous–Tertiary boundary, Betonnie Tsosie Wash, San Juan Basin, New Mexico, *in*: Spencer G. Lucas and Andrew B. Heckert, editors, *Dinosaurs of New Mexico*. Albuquerque: New Mexico Museum of Natural History and Science, Bulletin 17, pp. 95–103.

Lull, Richard Swann, 1904, Fossil footprints of the Jura-Trias of North America: *Memoirs of the Boston Society of Natural History*, 5 (11), pp. 461–557.

_____, 1915a, Triassic life of the Connecticut Valley: *Bulletin of the Connecticut State Geological and Natural History Survey*, 24, pp. 1–285.

_____, 1915b, Sauropods and Stegosauria of the Morrison of North America compared with those of Europe and eastern Africa: *Bulletin of the Geological Society of America*, 26, pp. 323–334.

_____, 1942, Triassic footprints from Argentina: *American Journal of Science*, 240, pp. 421–425.

_____, 1953, Triassic life in the Connecticut Valley: *Bulletin of the Connecticut State*

Geological and Natural History Survey, 81, pp. 1–333 (revised edition).

Lull, Richard Swann, and Nelda E. Wright, 1942, The hadrosaurian dinosaurs of North America: *Geological Society of America Special Paper* 40, xii, 242 pages.

Luo Yaonan, and Wang Changsheng, 2000, A new sauropod, *Gongxianosaurus*, from the Lower Jurassic of Sichuan, China: *Acta Geologica Sinica*, 74 (2), pp. 132–136.

Luo, Z., and X.-C. Wu, 1994, The small tetrapods of the Lower Lufeng Formation, Yunnan, China, *in*: Nicholas C. Fraser and Hans-Dieter Sues, editors, *In the Shadow of the Dinosaurs: Early Mesozoic Tetrapods*. Cambridge: University of Cambridge Press, pp. 251–270.

Luttrell, P., 1987, Basin analysis of the Kayenta Formation (lower Jurassic), central portion, Colorado Plateau. Northern Arizona University, masters thesis, 217 pages (unpublished).

Lydekker, Richard, 1877, Notices of new and other Vertebrata from Indian Tertiary and Secondary rocks: *Records of the Geological Society of India*, 10, pp. 30–43.

_____, 1888, *Catalogue of Fossil Reptilia and Amphibia in the British Museum (Natural History), Part 1, Containing the orders Ornithosauria, Crocodilia, Dinosauria, Squamata, Rhynchocephalia, and Proterosauria*. London: British Museum (Natural History), 309 pages.

Lyman, R. L., 1994, *Vertebrate Taphonomy*. Cambridge: Cambridge University Press, 524 pages.

Maderson, P. F. A., 1972, On how an archosaurian scale may have given rise to an avian feather: *American Naturalist*, 106 (949), pp. 424–428.

Madsen, James J., Jr., 1974, A new theropod dinosaur from the Upper Jurassic of Utah: *Journal of Paleontology*, 48 (1), pp. 27–31.

_____, 1976, *Allosaurus fragilis*: a revised Osteology: *Utah Geological and Mineral Survey, a division of the Utah Department of Natural Resources*, Bulletin 109, xii, 163 pages.

Madsen, James H., and Samuel P. Welles, 2000, *Ceratosaurus* (Dinosauria, Theropoda, a revised osteology: *Miscellaneous Publication*, 00-2, Utah Geological Survey, Utah Department of Resources, 80 pages.

Main, Derek J., Gregory Gordon, Jill S. Shipman, and Erik Brandlen, 2001, New techniques in paleontology: the application of GPR as a surveying technique at vertebrate fossil (Dinosauria: Sauropoda) excavations: *Journal of Vertebrate Paleontology*, 21 (Supplement to Number 3), Abstracts of Papers, Sixty-first Annual Meeting, p. 76A.

Maisey, John G., 2000, Continental break up and the distribution of fishes of Western Gondwana during the Early Cretaceous: *Cretaceous Research*, 21, pp. 281–314.

Makovicky, Peter J., 1995, Phylogenetic aspects of the vertebral morphology of Coelurosauria (Dinosauria: Theropoda). MSc thesis, University of Cambridge.

_____, 2001, A *Montanoceratops cerorhynchus* (Dinosauria: Ceratopsia) braincase from the Horseshoe Canyon Formation of Al-

berta: *in*: Darren Tanke and Kenneth Carpenter, editors, *Mesozoic Vertebrate Life: New Research Inspired by the Paleontology of Philip J. Currie*. Bloomington and Indianapolis, Indiana: Indiana University Press, pp. 243–262.

Makovicky, Peter J., and Gerald Grellet-Tinner, 2000, Association between theropod eggshell and a specimen of *Deinonychus antirrhopus*: *First International Symposium on Dinosaur Eggs and Babies/Extended Abstracts/2000*, pp. 123–128.

Makovicky, Peter J., and Hans-Dieter Sues, 1998, Anatomy and phyologenic relationships of the theropod dinosaur *Microvenator celer* from the Lower Cretaceous of Montana: *American Museum Novitates*, 3240, pp. 1–26.

Maleev, Evgeny [Eugene] Alexandrovich, 1955a, Gigantskiye Khishchnye Dinosavri Mongoll [Giant carnivorous dinosaurs from the Upper Cretaceous of Mongolia]: *Dokladi Akademii Nauk S.S.S.R.*, 104 (4), 104 (4), pp. 779–782.

_____, 1955b, [New carnivorous dinosaurs from the Upper Cretaceous of Mongolia: *Ibid.*, 104 (5), pp. 779–782.

_____, 1955c, [Carnivorous dinosaurs Mongolia]: *Piroda*, June, pp. 112–115.

_____, 1974, [Gigantic carnosaurs of the family Tyrannosauridae]: *Trudy Somestnaya Sovetsko-Mongol'skaya Paleontologicheskaya Ekspeditsiya [Transactions of the Joint Soviet-Mongolian Paleontological Expedition]*, 1: pp. 32–191.

Malkani, M. S., J. A. Wilson, and P. D. Gingerich, 2001, First dinosaurs from Pakistan: *Journal of Vertebrate Paleontology*, 21 (Supplement to Number 3), Abstracts of Papers, Sixty-first Annual Meeting, p. 77A.

Maltese, Anthony, 2002, Discovery of a divided initial chevron in *Camarasaurus* (Dinosauria, Sauropoda): *Journal of Vertebrate Paleontology*, 23 (Supplement to Number 3), Abstracts of Papers, Sixty-second Annual Meeting, p. 83A.

Manning, Terry W., Kenneth A. Josey, and Arthur R. I. Cruickshank, 1997, Observations of microstructures within dinosaur eggs from Henan Province, Peoplés Republic of China, *in*: Donald L. Wolberg, Edmund Stump, and Gary Rosenberg, editors. *Dinofest International: Proceedings of a Symposium Held at Arizona State University*. Philadelphia: Academy of Natural Sciences, pp. 287–290.

_____, 2000, *In ovo* tooth replacement in a therizinosaurid dinosaur: *First International Symposium on Dinosaur Eggs and Babies/Extended Abstracts/2000*, pp. 129–134.

Mantell, Gideon Algernon, 1825, Notice on the *Iguanodon*, a newly discovered fossil reptile, from the sandstone of Tilgate Forest, in Sussex: *Philosophical Transactions of the Royal Society*, 115 (1), pp. 179–186.

_____, 1833, *The Geology of the South-East of England*. London: Longman, xix, 415 pages.

Marsh, Othniel Charles, 1871, On the geology of the eastern Uintah Mountains: *American Journal of Science*, Series 3, 1, pp. 191–198.

Bibliography

_____, 1877a, A new order of extinct Reptilia (Stegosauria) from the Jurassic of the Rocky Mountains: *Ibid.*, Series 3, 14, pp. 513–514.

_____, 1877b, Notice on new dinosaurian reptiles from the Jurassic formations: *Ibid.*, Series 3, 14 (53), pp. 514–516.

_____, 1879, Notice of new Jurassic reptiles: *Ibid.*, Series 3, 18, pp. 501–505.

_____, 1880, Principle characters of American Jurassic dinosaurs, Part III: *Ibid.*, Series 3, 119, pp. 253–259.

_____, 1887, Principle characters of American Jurassic dinosaurs, Part 9. The skull and dermal armor of *Stegosaurus*: *Ibid.*, 34, pp. 413–417.

_____, 1891, Restoration of *Stegosaurus*: *Ibid.*, Series 3, 42, pp. 179–181.

_____, 1896, The Dinosaurs of North America: *Sixteenth Annual Report of the U. S. Geological Survey*, 1, pp. 133–415.

Marshall, Cynthia L., and Claudia Barreto, 2001, A healed *Torosaurus* skull injury and the implication for developmental morphology of the ceratopsian frill: *International Congress of Vertebrate Morphology, Abstracts*, p. 259.

Marshall, Cynthia L., and Christopher L. Organ, 2001, Re-examination of ossified tendons in ornithischians: *Journal of Vertebrate Paleontology*, 21 (Supplement to Number 3), Abstracts of Papers, Sixty-first Annual Meeting, p. 77A.

Martill, David M., A. R. I. Cruickshank, Eberhard Frey, P. G. Small, and M. Clarke, 1996, A new crested maniraptoran dinosaur from the Santana Formation (Lower Cretaceous) of Brazil: *Journal of the Geological Society, London*, 153, pp. 5–8.

Martill, David M., Eberhard Frey, Hans-Dieter Sues, and Arthur R. I. Cruickshank, 2000, Skeletal remains of a small theropod dinosaur with associated soft structures from the Lower Cretaceous Santana Formation of northeastern Brazil: *Canadian Journal of Earth Sciences*, 37, pp. 891–900.

Martill, David M., and Steve Hutt, 1996, Possible baryonychid teeth from the Wessex Formation (Lower Cretaceous, Barremian) of the Isle of Wight, England: *Proceedings of the Geologists' Association*, 107, pp. 81–84.

Martin, Larry D., David Burnham, and Jong-Deock Lim, 2002, The new and improved sauropod: *Journal of Vertebrate Paleontology*, 23 (Supplement to Number 3), Abstracts of Papers, Sixty-second Annual Meeting, p. 83A.

Martin, Larry D., David Burnham, T. Swearingen, Anthony Maltese, and Jong-Deock Lim, 2001, Mounting a *Camarasaurus* skeleton in compact space: *Journal of Vertebrate Paleontology*, 21 (Supplement to Number 3), Abstracts of Papers, Sixty-first Annual Meeting, p. 77A.

Martin, Larry D., and Stephen A. Czerkas, 2000, The fossil record of feather evolution in the Mesozoic: *American Zoologist*, 40 (4), pp. 687–694.

Martin, Larry D., Zhonghe Zhou, Lian-Hai Hou, and Alan Feduccia, 1998, *Confuciusornis sanctus* compared to *Archaeopteryx*

lithographica: *Naturwissenschaften*, 85, pp. 286–289.

Martin-Rolland, Valérie, 1999, Les sauropodes chinois: *Revue Paléobiologie, Genève*, 18 (1), pp. 287–315.

Matrtinez, Ricardo N., 2002, The monophyly and interrelationships of Prosauropoda: *Journal of Vertebrate Paleontology*, 23 (Supplement to Number 3), Abstracts of Papers, Sixty-second Annual Meeting, p. 84A.

Martínez, Rubén, Olga del Gimènez, Jorge Rodríguez and Graciela Bochatey, 1986, *Xenotarsosaurus bonapartei* nov. gen et nov. sp. (Carnosauria, Abelisauridae), un nuevo therópoda de la Formación Bajo Barreal Chubut, Argentina: *IV Congreso Argentino de Paleontoliga y Biostratigrafica, Actas*, 2, pp. 23–31.

Martínez, Rubén, A. Maure, M. Oliva, and M. Luna, 1993, Un maxilar de Theropoda (Abelisauria) de la Formacion Bajo Barreal, Cretacico Tardio, Chubut, Argentina: *Ameghiniana*, 30, pp. 109–110.

Maryańska, Teresa, 1977, Ankylosauridae (Dinosauria) from Mongolia: *Palaeontologica Polonica*, 37, pp. 85–151.

_____, 1990, Pachycephalosauria, *in*: Philip J. Currie and Kevin Padian, editors, *Encyclopedia of Dinosaurs*. San Diego: Academic Press, pp. 564–577.

_____, 1997, Segnosaurs (Therizinosaurs), *in*: James O. Farlow and Michael K. Brett-Surman, editors, *The Complete Dinosaur*. Bloomington and Indianapolis, Indiana University Press, pp. 234–241.

Maryańska, Teresa, and Halszka Osmólska, 1974, Results of the Polish-Mongolian Palaeontological Expedition. Part V. Pachycephalosauria, a new suborder of ornithischian dinosaurs: *Acta Palaeontologia Polonica*, 30, pp. 45–102.

_____, 1975, Results of the Polish-Mongolian Palaeontological Expedition. Part VI. Protoceratopsidae (Dinosauria) of Asia: *Ibid.*, 33, pp. 133–182.

_____, 1979, Aspects of hadrosaurian cranial anatomy: *Lethaia*, 12, pp. 265–273.

_____, 1981, Cranial anatomy of *Saurolophus angustirostris* with comments on the Asian Hadrosauridae (Dinosauria): *Acta Palaeontologia Polonica*, 42, pp. 5–24.

Maryańska, Teresa, Halszka Osmólska, and Mieczyslaw Wolson, 2002, Avialan status for Oviraptorosauria: *Acta Palaeontologica Polonica*, 47 (1), pp. 97–116.

Mateus, Octavio, and Miguel Telles Antunes, 2001, *Draconyx loureiroi*, a new Camptosauridae (Dinosauria, Ornithopoda) from the Late Jurassic of Lourinha, Portugal: *Annales de Paléontologie*, 87 (1), pp. 67–73.

Matheron, Philippe, 1869, Notice sur les reptiles fossiles des dépôts fluvio-lacustres crétacés du bassin à lignite de Fuveau: *Mémoires de l'Académie des sciences, belles-lettres et arts de Marseille*, pp. 345–379.

Matthew, William Diller, and Barnum Brown, 1922, The family Deinodontidae, with notice of a new genus from the Cretaceous of Alberta: *Bulletin of the American Museum of Natural History*, 46, pp. 367–385.

Mattison, Rebecca G., and E. Griffin, 1989,

Limb use and disuse in ratites and tyrannosaurids: *Journal of Vertebrate Paleontology*, 9, (Supplement to Number 3), Abstracts of Papers, Forty-ninth Annual Meeting, p. 32A.

Mäuser, M., 1983, Neue Gedanken über *Compsognathus longipes* (Wagner) und dessen Fundlort: Erwin Rutte-Festchrift, Weltenburger Akademie, 3, Abb., pp. 157–162.

Maxwell, W. Desmond, and Richard L. Cifelli, 2000, Last evidence of sauropod diosaurs (Saurischia: Sauropodomorpha) in the North American Mid-Cretaceous: *Brigham Young University Geology Studies*, 45, pp. 19–24.

_____, 2002, Reanalysis of the ornithischian dinosaur *Eolambia*: *Journal of Vertebrate Paleontology*, 23 (Supplement to Number 3), Abstracts of Papers, Sixty-second Annual Meeting, p. 85A.

Mayr, E., 1960, The emergence of evolutionary novelties, *in*: S. Tax, editor, *The Evolution of Life*. Chicago: University of Chicago Press, pp. 349–380.

Mazzetta, Gerardo V., 2000, Some functional aspects of the skull of the South American horned theropod *Carnotaurus sastrei* (Saurischia: Theropoda): *48th Symposium of Vertebrate Palaeontology and Comparative Anatomy, Portsmouth, 2000*, University of Portsmouth, abstracts, unpaginated.

Mazzetta, Gerardo V., and R. Ernesto Blanco, 2001, Speeds of dinosaurs from the Albian–Cenomanian of Patagonia and sauropod stance and gait: *Acta Palaeontologica Polonica*, 46 (2), pp. 235–246.

Mazzetta, Gerardo V., Richard A. Fariña, and Sergio F. Vizcaíno, 2000, On the palaeobiology of the South American horned theropod *Carnotaurus sastrei* Bonaparte: *in* B. P. Pérez-Moreno, Thomas R. Holtz, Jr., José Luis Sanz, and José J. Moratalla, editors, Aspects of theropod paleobiology: *Gaia*, 15 (cover dated December 1998), pp. 185–192.

McCarville, Katherine, and Gale A. Bishop, 2002, To pee or not to pee: evidence for liquid urination in sauropod dinosaurs: *Journal of Vertebrate Paleontology*, 23 (Supplement to Number 3), Abstracts of Papers, Sixty-second Annual Meeting, p. 85A.

McCrea, Richard T., Philip J. Currie, and George S. Pemberton, 2002, Forelimb impressions associated with a large theropod trackway from the Gates Formation (Lower Cretaceous, Albian) of Western Canada: *Journal of Vertebrate Paleontology*, 23 (Supplement to Number 3), Abstracts of Papers, Sixty-second Annual Meeting, p. 86A.

McIntosh, John S., 1990, Sauropoda, *in*: David B. Weishampel, Peter Dodson, and Halszka Osmólska, editors, *The Dinosauria*. Berkeley and Los Angeles: University of California Press, pp. 345–401.

_____, 1995, Remarks on the North American sauropod *Apatosaurus* Marsh, *in*: A. Sun and Y. Wang, editors, *Sixth Symposium on Mesozoic Terrestrial Ecosystems and Biota, Short Papers*. Beijing: China Ocean Press, pp. 119–123.

_____, 1998, New information about the Cope

collection of sauropod from Garden Park, Colorado, *in*: Kenneth Carpenter, Daniel J. Chure, and James I. Kirkland, editors, The Upper Jurassic Morrison Formation: An interdisciplinary study, *Modern Geology*, 23, pp. 465–480.

McIntosh, John S., Clifford A. Miles, Karen C. Cloward, and Jeffrie R. Parker, 1996, A new nearly complete skeleton of *Camarasaurus*: *Bulletin of Gunma Museum of Natural History*, 1, 87 pages. McIver, Elisabeth E., 2002, The paleoenvironment of *Tyrannosaurus rex* from southwestern Saskatchewan, Canada: *Canadian Journal of Earth Sciences*, 39, pp. 207–221.

McKenzie, D. B., 1972, Tidal and flat deposits in Lower Cretaceous, Dakota Group near Denver, Colorado: *Mountain Geology*, 9, pp. 269–277.

McWhinney, Lorrie A., Kenneth Carpenter, and Bruce M. Rothschild, 2001, Dinosaurian humeral periostitis: a case of a juxtacortical lesion in the fossil record, *in*: Darren Tanke and Kenneth Carpenter, editors, *Mesozoic Vertebrate Life: New Research Inspired by the Paleontology of Philip J. Currie*. Bloomington and Indianapolis, Indiana: Indiana University Press, pp. 364–377.

McWhinney, Lorrie A., Bruce M. Rothschild, and Kenneth Carpenter, 2001, Posttraumatic chronic osteomyelitis in *Stegosaurus* dermal spikes, *in*: Kenneth Carpenter, editor, *The Armored Dinosaurs*. Bloomington and Indianapolis: Indiana University Press, pp. 141–156.

Meese, M. A., and W. J. Sevastianelli, 1996, Periostitis of the upper extremity: *Clinical Orthopaedics and Related Research*, 324, pp. 222–226.

Mensink, Hans, and Dorothee Mertmann, 1984, Dinosaurier-Fährten (*Gigantosauropus asturiensis* n.g.n.sp.; *Hispanosauropus hauboldi* n.g.n.sp.) im Jura Asturiens bei La Griega und Ribadsella (Spanien): *Neus Jahrbuch für Geologie und Paläontologie, Monatshefte*, 1984, 7, pp. 405–415.

Meyer, Hermann von, 1830, Abbildungen von Resten thieroscher Organismen: *Isis*, 23 (5), p. 518.

———, 1832, *Paleologica zur Geischichte der Erde*. Frankfurt am Main, 560 pages.

———, 1837, Mitteilung an Prof. Bronn (*Plateosaurus engelhardti*): *Neus Jarbuch für Mineralogie, Geologie, und Paläontologie*, 1837, p. 817, Stuttgart.

———, 1857, *Stenopelix valdensis* aus der Wealden-Formation Deutschland's: *Paläontologie*, 7, pp. 25–34.

———, 1861, Vogul-Federn und *Palpipes priscus* von Solnhofen: *Neus Jarbuch für Mineralogie, Geologie, und Paläontologie*, 1861, p. 561.

Mikhailov, Konstantin E., 1991, Classification of fossil eggshells of amniotic vertebrates: *Palaeontologica*, 36 (2), pp. 193–238.

———, 1994a, Eggs of sauropod and ornithopod dinosaurs from the Cretaceous deposits of Mongolia: *Paleontological Journal*, 28, pp. 141–159.

———, 1994b, Theropod and protoceratopsian dinosaur eggs from the Cretaceous of Mongolia and Kazakhstan: *Ibid.*, 28, pp. 101–120.

Mikhailov, Konstantin E., K. Sabath, and Sergei Mikhailovich Kurzanov, 1994, Eggs and nests from Cretaceous of Mongolia, *in*: Kenneth Carpenter and Philip J. Currie, editors, *Dinosaur Systematics: Approaches and Perspectives*. Cambridge, New York and Melbourne: Cambridge University Press, pp. 88–115.

Milner, Angela C., 2002, Theropod dinosaurs of the Purbeck Limestone Group, southern England: *Special Papers in Paleontology*, 68, pp. 191–201.

Milner, Angela G., R. C. Hall, A. M. Milan, R. J. Waddington, and M. Langely, 2003, Identification of proteinaceous material in the bone of the dinosaur *Iguanodon*: *in*: David B. Norman and Paul Upchurch, editors, *SVPCA 50, Cambridge 2002, 11–13 September, Abstract Volume*, unpaginated.

Mohabey, David M., 1998, Search for dinosaur nests, track-sites and associated skeletal remains from the Late Cretaceous sediments of Chandrapur, Wardha and Nagpur Districts, Maharashtra Ree: *Geological Survey of India*, 132 (6), pp. 141–142.

———, 2001, Indian dinosaur eggs: a review: *Journal Geological Society of India*, 58, pp. 479–508.

Mohr, B. A. R., 1987, Mikrofloren aus Vertebraten-fürenden Unterkreide-Schichten bei Galve und Uña (Ostspanien): *Berliner Geowissenschaftliche Abhandlungen (A)*, 86, pp. 69–85.

Mokolouszko, 2002. *Gazeta Wyborcza* (October issue).

Molnar, Ralph E., 1974, A distinctive theropod dinosaur from the Upper Cretaceous of Baja California (Mexico): *Journal of Paleontology*, 48 (5), pp. 1009–1017.

———, 1978, A new theropod dinosaur from the Upper Cretaceous of central Montana: *Journal of Paleontology*, 52 (1), pp. 73–82.

———, 1980, An ankylosaur (Ornithischia: Reptilia) from the Lower Cretaceous of southern Queensland: *Memoirs of the Queensland Museum*, 20 (1), pp. 77–87.

———, 1990, Problematic Theropoda, "carnosaurs," *in*: David B. Weishampel, Peter Dodson, and Osmólska, editors, *The Dinosauria*. Berkeley and Los Angeles: University of California Press, pp. 306–317.

———, 1991, The cranial morphology of *Tyrannosaurus rex*: *Paleontographica*, 217, pp. 137–176, Stuttgart.

———, 1996, Preliminary report on a new ankylosaur from the Early Cretaceous of Queensland, Australia: *Proceedings of the Gondwanan Dinosaur Symposium. Memoirs of the Queensland Museum*, 39, pp. 653–668.

———, 2000, Mechanical factors in the design of the skull of *Tyrannosaurus rex* (Osborn, 1905): *in* B. P. Pérez-Moreno, Thomas R. Holtz, Jr., José Luis Sanz, and José J. Moratalla, editors, Aspects of theropod paleobiology: *Gaia*, 15 (cover dated December 1998), pp. 193–218.

———, 2001a, Theropod paleopathology: a literature survey, *in*: Darren Tanke and Kenneth Carpenter, editors, *Mesozoic Vertebrate Life: New Research Inspired by the Paleontology of Philip J. Currie*. Bloom-

ington and Indianapolis, Indiana: Indiana University Press, pp. 337–363.

———, 2001b, A reassessment of the phylogenetic position of Cretaceous sauropod dinosaurs from Queensland, Australia: *Asociación Paleontológical Argentina*, Publicatión Especial 7, VII International Symposium on Mesozoic Terrestrial Ecosystems, Buenos Aires, 30-6-2001, pp. 139–144.

———, 2001c, Armor of the small ankylosaur *Minmi*, *in*: Kenneth Carpenter, editor, *The Armored Dinosaurs*. Bloomington and Indianapolis: Indiana University Press, pp. 341–362.

Molnar, Ralph E., A. L. Angriman, and Zulma Gasparini, 1996, An Antarctic theropod: *Memoirs of the Queensland Museum*, 39, pp. 669–674.

Molnar, Ralph E., and Kenneth Carpenter, 1989, The Jordan theropod (Maastrichtian, Montana, U.S.A.) referred to the genus *Aublysodon*: *Geobios*, 22 (4), pp. 445–454.

Molnar, Ralph E., and H. Trevor Clifford, 2000, Gut contents of a small ankylosaur: *Journal of Vertebrate Paleontology*, 20 (1), pp. 194–196.

———, 2001, An ankylosaurian cololite from the Lower Cretaceous of Queensland, Australia, *in*: Kenneth Carpenter, editor, *The Armored Dinosaurs*. Bloomington and Indianapolis: Indiana University Press, pp. 399–412.

Molnar, Ralph E., Seriozha M. Kurzanov, and Dong Zhi-Ming [Zhiming], 1990, Carnosauria, *in*: David B. Weishampel, Peter Dodson, and Halszka Osmölska, editors, *The Dinosauria*. Berkeley and Los Angeles: University of California Press, pp. 169–209.

Mones, A., 1980, Nuevos elementos de la paleoherpetofauna del Uruguay (Crocodylia y Dinosauria): *Actas 2 Congress Argentina Paleontológica y Biostratigrafica y 1 Congress Latinoamerica Paleontológica, (Buenos Aires)*, 1, pp. 265–277 (1978).

Morales, Michael, 1993, Tetrapod biostratigraphy of the Lower-Middle Triassic Moenkopi Formation, *in*: Spencer G. Lucas and Michael Morales, editors, *The Nonmarine Triassic, New Mexico Museum of Natural History and Science Bulletin*, 3, p. 335.

———, 1994, First dinosaur body fossils from the Lower Jurassic Dinosaur Canyon Member, Moenave Formation of northeastern Arizona: *Journal of Vertebrate Paleontology*, 14 (Supplement to Number 3), Abstracts of Papers, Fifty-fourth Annual Meeting, p. 39A.

Moratalla, José J., 1993, Restos indirectos de dinosaurios del registro español: paleoichnologica de la Cuenca de Cameros (Jurasico Superior-Cretacico Inferior) y Paleoologia del Cretacico Superior: Thesis doctoral, Faculdad de Ciencias Universidad Autonoma, Madrid, 729 pages, unpublished.

Moratalla, José J., Joaquin García-Mondéjar, Vanda Faria dos Santos, Martin G. Lockley, José L. Sanz, and Santiago Jiménez, 1994, Sauropod trackways from the Lower Cretaceous of Spain: *Galia*, 10, pp. 75–83.

Bibliography

Morris, William J., 1970, Hadrosaurian dinosaur bills — morphology and function: *Natural History Museum of Los Angeles County Contributions in Science*, 193, pp. 1–14.

_____, 1976, Mesozoic and Tertiary vertebrates of Baja, California: *National Geographic Geological Society Research Reports*, 1968 project, pp. 305–316.

Murphy, Nate I., David Trexler, and Mark Thompson, 2002, Exceptional soft-tissue preservation in a mummified ornithopod dinosaur from the Campanian lower Judith River Formation: *Journal of Vertebrate Paleontology*, 23 (Supplement to Number 3), Abstracts of Papers, Sixty-second Annual Meeting, p. 91A.

Murry, Philip A., and Robert A. Long, 1997, Dockum Group, in: Philip J. Currie and Kevin Padian, editors, *Encyclopedia of Dinosaurs*. San Diego: Academic Press, pp. 191–193.

Myhrvold, Nathan P., and Philip J. Currie, 1997, Supersonic sauropods? Tail dynamics in the diplodocids: *Paleobiology*, 23 (4), pp. 393–409.

Naish, Darren, 1998, Birds of a feather: *Fortean Times*, 108, pp. 35–37.

_____, 1999*a*, Fox, Owen and the small Wealden theropods *Calamospondylus* and *Aristosuchus*: *Journal of Vertebrate Paleontology*, 19 (Supplement to Number 3), Abstracts of Papers, Fifty-ninth Annual Meeting, p. 66A.

_____, 1999*b*, New insights into *Baryonyx* and its relatives: *Dinonews*, 13, pp. 5–6.

_____, 2000*a*, Theropod dinosaurs in the trees: a historical review of arboreal habits amongst nonavian theropods: *Archaeopteryx*, 18, pp. 35–41, Eichstätt.

_____, 2000*b*, 130 years of tree-climbing dinosaurs: *Archaeopteryx*, "arbrosaurs" and the origin of avian flight: *The Quarterly Journal of the Dinosaur Society*, 4 (3), not paginated.

_____, 2001, *Eotyrannus lengi*, a new coelurosaur from the Isle of Wight: *Dino Press*, 5, pp. 82–91 (translation from the Japanese, pp. 23–27).

_____, 2002*a*, The historical taxonomy of the Lower Cretaceous theropods (Dinosauria) *Calamospondylus* and *Aristosuchus* from the Isle of Wight: *Proceedings of the Geologists' Association*, 113, pp. 153–163.

_____, 2002*b*, Thecocoelurians, calamosaurs and Europe's largest sauropod: the latest on the Isle of Wight's dinosaurs: *Dino Press*, 7, pp. 85–95 (translation pp. 21–25).

_____, 2003, Palaeopathologies in *Neovenator*, Europe's largest sauropod and more late news from the Isle of Wight: in: David B. Norman and Paul Upchurch, editors, *SVPCA 50, Cambridge 2002, 11–13 September, Abstract Volume*, unpaginated.

Naish, Darren, Stephen Hutt, and David M. Martill, 1999, Saurischian dinosaurs 2: theropods, in, David M. Martill and Darren Naish, editors, *Dinosaurs of the Isle of Wight*. London: The Palaeontological Association, pp. 242–309.

Naish, Darren, and David M. Martill, 2002, A reappraisal of *Thecocoelurus daviesi* (Di-nosauria: Theropoda) from the Early Cretaceous of the Isle of Wight: *Proceedings of the Geologists' Association*, 113, pp. 23–30.

Nath, T. T., P. Yadagiri, and A. K. Moitra, 2002, First record of armoured dinosaur from the Lower Jurassic Kota Formation, Pranhita Valley, Andhra Pradesh: *Journal of the Geological Society of India*, Short Communications, 59, pp. 575–577.

Negro, Giuliana, 2001*a*, A phylogenetic study of hadrosaurian dinosaur skin: *PaleoBios*, 21, supplement to No. 1, 2001 California Paleontology Conference, Abstracts, p. 7.

_____, 2001*b*, Phylogenetic interpretation of hadrosaurian dinosaur skin: *Journal of Vertebrate Paleontology*, 21 (Supplement to Number 3), Abstracts of Papers, Sixty-first Annual Meeting, p. 83A.

_____, 2003, On the value of hadrosaurian dinosaur skin in phylogenetic analysis: in: David B. Norman and Paul Upchurch, editors, *SVPCA 50, Cambridge 2002, 11–13 September, Abstract Volume*, unpaginated.

Nesbitt, Sterling, 2001, An update on fossil reptile material from the upper Moenkopi Formation, Holbrook Member (Middle Triassic), Northern Arizona: *Western Association of Vertebrate Paleontologists and Southwest Paleontological Symposium, Proceedings, 2001, Mesa Southwest Museum Bulletin*, 8, pp. 3–7.

Nessov, Lev A., 1995, [Dinosaurs of Northern Eurasia: new data about assemblages, ecology and paleobiogeography]: *Izdatelstvo Sankt-Petersburgskogo universiteta*, St. Petersburg, 156 pages.

Nessov, Lev A., and L. F. Kaznyshkina, 1989, Dinozavry-tseratopsii i krokodily mezozoya Sredney Asii, in: T. N. Bogdanova and L. I. Khozatskiy, editors, *Teoreticheskiye i prikladnyye aspekty sovremennoy paleontologii; trudy XXXIII sessii Vsesoyuznogo, Lenningrad*, pp. 144–154.

Newton, Edwin Tully, 1899, On a megalosauroid jaw from Rhaetic beds near Bridgend (Glamorganshire): *Quarterly Journal of the Geological Society of London*, 55, pp. 89–96.

Newman, Barney, 1970, Stance and gait in the flesh-eating dinosaur *Tyrannosaurus*: *Biological Journal of the Linnean Society*, 2, pp. 119–123.

Nopcsa, Baron Franz [also Ferencz, Francis] (von Felsö-Szilvás), 1900, Dinosaurierreste aus Siebenbürgen. I. Schädel von *Limnosaurus transsylvanicus* nov. gen. et spec.—*Denkschriften der Akademie der Wissenschaften*, 68, pp. 555–591.

_____, 1918, *Leipsanosaurus* n. gen. in neur Thyreophore aus der Gosau: *Födtani Közlöny*, 48, pp. 100–116.

_____, 1923*a*, Die Familien der Reptilien: *Fortschr. Geol. Pal.*, 2, 210 pages.

_____, 1923*b*, On the geological importance of the primitive reptilian fauna in the uppermost Cretaceous of Hungary; with a description of a new tortoise (*Kallokibotion*). *Quarterly Journal of the Geological Society of London*, 79, pp. 100–116.

Norell, Mark A., and James M. Clark, 1997, Birds are dinosaurs: *Science Spectrum*, 8, pp. 28–34.

Norell, Mark A., James M. Clark, and Luis M. Chiappe, 2001, An embryonic oviraptorid (Dinosauria: Theropoda) from the Upper Cretaceous of Mongolia: *American Museum Novitates*, 3315, pp. 1–17.

Norell, Mark A., James M. Clark, Luis M. Chiappe, and Demberelynin Dashveg, 1995, A nesting dinosaur: *Science*, 378, pp. 774–776.

Norell, Mark A., James M. Clark, Demberelynin Dashveg, Rinchen Barsbold, Luis M. Chiappe, Amy R. Davidson, Malcolm C. McKenna, Altangerel Perle, and Michael J. Novacek, 1994, A theropod dinosaur embryo and the affinities of the Flaming Cliffs dinosaur eggs: *Science*, 266, pp. 779–882.

Norell, Mark A., and Peter J. Makovicky, 1997, Important features of the dromaeosaur skeleton: information from a new specimen: *American Museum Novitates*, 3215, 28 pages.

Norell, Mark A., Peter J. Makovicky, and Philip J. Currie, 2001*a*, Three cases of soft-tissue preservation in theropod dinosaurs: changing our perception of theropod appearance: *Journal of Vertebrate Paleontology*, 21 (Supplement to Number 3), Abstracts of Papers, Sixty-first Annual Meeting, p. 83A–84A.

_____, 2001*b*, The beaks of ostrich dinosaurs: *Nature*, 412, pp. 873–874.

Norell, Mark A., Qiang Ji, Keqin Gao, Chongxi Yuan, Yibin Zhao, and Lixia Wang, 2002, "Modern" feathers on a non-avian dinosaur: *Nature*, 416, pp. 36–37.

Norman, David B. [Bruce], 1977, On the anatomy of the ornithischian dinosaur *Iguanodon*. PhD dissertation, King's College London, 630 pages (unpublished).

_____, 1980, On the ornithischian dinosaur *Iguanodon bernissartensis* from Belgium: *Mémoires de l'Institut Royal des Sciences Naturelles de Belgique*, 178, pp. 1–105.

_____, 1984, On the cranial morphology and evolution of ornithopod dinosaurs: *Symposium of the Zoological Society of London*, 1984, pp. 521–547.

_____, 1985, *The Illustrated Encyclopedia of Dinosaurs: An Original and Compelling Insight into Life in the Dinosaur Kingdom*. New York: Crescent Books (Crown Publishing, Inc.), 208 pages.

_____, 1986, On the anatomy of *Iguanodon atherfieldensis* (Ornithischia: Ornithopoda): *Bulletin de l'Institut Royal d'Histoire Naturelle de Belgique*, 56, pp. 281–372.

_____, 1987, Wealden dinosaur biostratigraphy, in: Philip J. Currie and E. Koster, editors, Fourth Symposium on Mesozoic Terrestrial Ecosystems, Short Papers: *Occasional Papers, Tyrrell Museum of Palaeontology*, 3, pp. 165–70.

_____, in preparation, On Asian ornithopods (Dinosauria: Ornithischia). 5. New hadrosaurids from Bainshin Tsav.

_____, 1998, On Asian ornithopods (Dinosauria: Ornithischia). 3. A new species of iguanodontid dinosaur: *Zoological Journal of the Linnean Society*, 122, pp. 291–348.

_____, 1999, A perspective on ornithopod dinosaurs: 1825–1999, *Actas de las I Jornadas Internacionales Sobre Paleontología de Dinosaurios y su Entorno (Proceedings of the 1st International Symposium about Paleontology of Dinosaurs and their Environment*, Salas de los Infantes (Burgos, España), Septiembre de 1999, pp. 93–145.

_____, 2000, A new dinosaur from Transylvania: *48th Symposium of Vertebrate Palaeontology and Comparative Anatomy, Portsmouth, 2000*, University of Portsmouth, abstracts, unpaginated.

_____, 2001a, The anatomy and systematic position of *Scelidosaurus harrisonii* Owen 1861: *Journal of Vertebrate Paleontology*, 21 (Supplement to Number 3), Abstracts of Papers, Sixty-first Annual Meeting, p. 86A.

_____, 2001b, *Scelidosaurus*, the earliest complete dinosaur: *in*: Kenneth Carpenter, editor, *The Armored Dinosaurs*. Bloomington and Indianapolis: Indiana University Press, pp. 3–24.

_____, 2002, On Asian ornithopods (Dinosauria: Ornithischia). 4. *Probactrosaurus* Rozhdestvensky, 1966, *in*: David B. Norman and David J. Gower, editors, *Archosaurian Anatomy and Palaeontology. Essays in Memory of Alick D. Walker*. *Zoological Journal of the Linnean Society*, 136, pp. 113–144.

Norman, David B., and Paul M. Barrett, 2002, Ornithischian dinosaurs from the Lower Cretaceous (Berriasian) of England: *Special Papers in Palaeontology*, 68, pp. 161–189.

Norman, David B., and Hans-Dieter Sues, 2000, Ornithopods from Kazakhstan, Mongolia and Siberia, *in*: M. J. Benton, M. A. Shishkin, D. M. Unwin and E. N. Kurochkin, editors, *The Age of Dinosaurs in Russia and Mongolia*. Cambridge: Cambridge University Press, pp. 462–479.

Norman, David B., and David B. Weishampel, 1985, Ornithopod feeding mechanisms: their bearing on the evolution of herbivory: *American Naturalist*, 126, pp. 151–164.

_____, in press, Iguanodontian ornithopods, *in*: David B. Weishampel, Peter Dodson, and Halszka Osmólska, editors, *The Dinosauria*. Berkeley: University of California Press.

Norton, James M., 2001, Ventilatory performance of a theropod rib cage model: *Journal of Vertebrate Paleontology*, 21 (Supplement to Number 3), Abstracts of Papers, Sixty-first Annual Meeting, p. 84A.

Nothdurft, William, with Josh Smith, Matt Lamanna, Ken Lacovara, Jason Poole, and Jen Smith, 2002, *The Lost Dinosaurs of Egypt*. New York: Random House, vii, 242 pages.

Noto, Christopher, P. McAlister Rees, Alfred M. Ziegler, and David B. Weishampel, 2002, Rocks, bones and plants: a pattern of latitudinal dependence demonstrated by the distribution of Jurassic dinosaurs: *Journal of Vertebrate Paleontology*, 23 (Supplement to Number 3), Abstracts of Papers, Sixty-second Annual Meeting, pp. 92A–93A.

Novacek, Michael J., 1996, *Dinosaurs of the Flaming Cliffs*. New York: Doubleday and Company.

Novacek, Michael J., Mark A. Norell, and Malcolm C. McKenna, and James M. Clark, 1994, Fossils of the Flaming Cliffs: *Scientific American*, 12 (94), pp. 60–69.

Novas, Fernando E., 1991, Relaciones filogeneticas de los dinosaurios tetropodos ceratosaurios: *Ameghiniana*, 28, p. 410.

_____, 1992a, Phylogenetic relationships of the basal dinosaurs, the Herrerasauridae: *Palaeontology*, 35, pp. 51–62, London.

_____, 1992b, La evolución de los dinosaurios carnívoros, *in*: José Luis Sanz and Ang'gelà D. Buscalioni, editors, *Los Dinosaurios y su Entorno Biótico. Actas II Curso de Paleontologica en Cuenca*. Spain: Instituto "Juan de Valdés," Ayuntamiento de Cuenca, pp. 123–163.

_____, 1993, New information on the systematics and postcranial skeleton of *Herrerasaurus ischigualastensis* (Theropoda: Herrerasauridae) from the Ischigualasto Formation (Upper Triassic) of Argentina: *Journal of Vertebrate Paleontology*, 13 (4), pp. 400–423.

_____, 1996a, Dinosaur monophyly: *Ibid.*, 16 (4), pp. 723–741.

_____, 1996b, Alvarezsauridae, Cretaceous basal birds from Patagonia and Mongolia, *in*: Fernando S. Novas and Ralph E. Molnar, editors, *Proceedings of the Gondwanan Dinosaur Symposium: Memoirs of the Queensland Museum*, 39 (part 3), pp. 675–702.

_____, 1997, New evidence concerning avian origins from the Late Cretaceous of Patagonia: *Nature*, 387, pp. 390–392.

Novas, Fernando E., and Saswati Bandyopadhyay, 1999, New approaches on the Cretaeous theropods from India: *7th International Symposium on Mesozoic Terrestrial Ecosystems (Buenos Aires), Abstract*, pp. 46–47.

_____, 2001, Abelisaurid pedal unguals from the Late Cretaceous of India: *Asociacíon Paleontológical Argentina*, Publicatión Especial 7, VII International Symposium on Mesozoic Terrestrial Ecosystems, Buenos Aires, 30-6-2001, pp. 145–149.

Novas, Fernando E., and Pablo F. Puerta, 1997, New evidence concerning avian origins from the Late Cretaceous of Patagonia: *Nature*, 387, pp. 390–92.

Novas, Fernando E., and S. de Valais, 2001, Preliminary study of possible carcharodontosaurids (Dinosauria, Theropoda) from the Cerro Barcino Formation, Chubut Province: *Ameghiniana*, XVII Jornadas Argentinas de Paleontologia de Vertebrados, Resúmes, Esquel, 16–18 de mayo de 2001, pp. 14R–15R.

O'Connor, M. P., and Peter Dodson, 1999, Biophysical constraints on the thermal ecology of dinosaurs: *Paleobiology*, 25, pp. 341–368.

Olivero, Eduardo B., Zulma Gasparini, C. A. Rinaldi, and R. Scasso, 1991, First record of dinosaurs in Antarctica (Upper Cretaceous, James Ross Island): palaeogeographical implications, *in*: M. R. A. Thomson, J. A. Crame, and J. W. Thomson, editors, *Geological Evolution of An-* tarctica. Cambridge: Cambridge University Press, pp. 617–622.

Olsen, Paul E., 1981, Comment on "Eolian dune field of Late Triassic age, Fundy Basin, Nova Scotia": *Geology*, 9 (12), pp. 557–559.

Olsen, Paul E., and Donald Baird, 1986, The ichnogenus *Atreipus* and its significance for Triassic biostratigraphy, *in*: Kevin Padian, editor, *The Beginning of the Age of Dinosaurs*. Cambridge: Cambridge University Press, pp. 61–87.

Olsen, Paul E., and A. Johannson, 1994, Field guide to Late Jurassic tetrapod sites in Virginia and North Carolina, *in*: Nicholas C. Fraser and Hans-Dieter Sues, editors, *In the Shadow of the Dinosaurs. Early Mesozoic Tetrapods*. New York: University of Cambridge Press, pp. 408–430.

Olsen, Paul E., D. V. Kent, H.-D. Sues, C. Koeberl, H. Huber, A. Montanari, E. C. Rainforth, S. J. Fowell, M. J. Szajna, and B. W. Hartline, 2002, Ascent of dinosaurs linked to an iridium anomaly at the Triassic–Jurassic Boundary: *Science*, 296, pp. 1305–296.

Olshevsky, George, 1991, *A Revision of the Parainfraclass Archosauria Cope 1869, Excluding the Advanced Crocodylia: Mesozoic Meandering*, 1, iv, 196 pages.

_____, 1992, *A Revision of the Parainfraclass Archosauria Cope 1869, Excluding the Advanced Crocodylia: Ibid.*, 2, iv, 196 pages.

_____, 2000, An annotated checklist of dinosaur species by continent: *Mesozoic Meanderings*, 3, 157 pages.

Olshevsky, George, Tracy L. Ford, and S. Yamamoto, 1995a, [The origin and evolution of the tyrannosaurids, (part 1): *Kyoryugaku Saizensen* [*Dino-Frontline*], 9, pp. 92–119.

_____, 1995b, _____, (part 2): *Ibid.*, 10, pp. 75–99.

Olson, Storrs L., 1973, Evolution of the rails in the south Atlantic islands (Aves: Ralliedae): *Smithsonian Contributions to Zoology*, 152, pp. 1–53.

Osborn, Henry Fairfield, 1905, *Tyrannosaurus* and other Cretaceous carnivorous dinosaurs: *Bulletin of the American Museum of Natural History*, 21, pp. 259–265.

_____, 1906, *Tyrannosaurus*, Upper Cretaceous carnivorous dinosaur: *Ibid.*, 22, pp. 281–296.

_____, 1912a, Crania of *Tyrannosaurus* and *Allosaurus*: *American Museum of Natural History Memoirs* (new series), 1, pp. 1–30.

_____, 1912b, Integument of the iguanodont dinosaur *Trachodon*: *Ibid.* (new series), 1, pp. 33–54.

_____, 1917, Skeletal adaptations of *Ornitholestes, Struthiomimus, Tyrannosaurus*: *Bulletin of the American Museum of Natural History*, 35, pp. 733–771.

_____, 1923, Two Lower Cretaceous dinosaurs of Mongolia: *American Museum Novitates*, 95, 10 pages.

_____, 1924a, *Psittacosaurus* and *Protiguanodon*: two Lower Cretaceous iguanodonts from Mongolia: *Ibid.*, 127, pp. 1–16.

_____, 1924b, Three new Theropoda, *Protoceratops* zone, central Mongolia: *Ibid.*, 144, pp. 1–12.

Bibliography

_____, 1931, *Cope: Master Naturalist*. Princeton, New Jersey: Princeton University Press, xvi, 740 pages (reprinted by Arno Press, 1980).

Osmólska, Halszka, 1976, New light on skull anatomy and systematic position of *Oviraptor. Nature*, 262, pp. 683–684.

Osmólska, Halszka, Ewa Roniewicz, and Rinchen Barsbold, 1972, A new dinosaur, *Gallimimus bullatus* n. gen., n. sp. (Ornithomimidae) from the Upper Cretaceous of Mongolia: *Paleontologica Polonica*, 27, pp. 103–143.

Ostrom, John H., 1964, A reconstruction of the paleoecology of hadrosaurian dinosaurs: *American Journal of Science*, 262, pp. 975–997.

_____, 1966, Functional morphology and evolution of the ceratopsian dinosaurs: *Evolution*, 20, pp. 290–308.

_____, 1969, A new theropod dinosaur from the Lower Cretaceous of Montana: *Postilla, Peabody Museum of Natural History*, 128, pp. 1–17.

_____, 1970, Stratigraphy and paleontology of the Cloverly Formation (Lower Cretaceous) of the Bighorn Basin area, Wyoming and Montana: *Peabody Museum of Natural History, Yale University*, 35, 234 pages.

_____, 1976, Startling finds prompt … a new look at dinosaurs: *National Geographic*, 154 (2), pp. 152–185.

_____, 1978, The osteology of *Compsognathus longipes: Zitteliana Abhandlungen der Bayerischen taatssammlung für Paläontologie und historische Geologie (München)*, 4, pp. 73–118.

_____, 1987, Romancing the dinosaurs. Review of *The Dinosaur Heresies* by R. T. Bakker: *The Sciences*, 27 (3), pp. 56–63.

_____, 1990, The Dromaeosauria, *in*: David B. Weishampel, Peter Dodson, and Osmólska, editors, *The Dinosauria*. Berkeley and Los Angeles: University of California Press, pp. 269–279.

_____, 1997, How bird flight might have come about, *in*: Donald L. Wolberg, Edmund Stump, and Gary Rosenberg, editors. *Dinofest International: Proceedings of a Symposium Held at Arizona State University*. Philadelphia: Academy of Natural Sciences, pp. 301–310.

Ostrom, John H., and John S. McIntosh, 1966, *Marsh's Dinosaurs. The Collections from Como Bluff*. New Haven, Connecticut: Yale University Press, 338 pages.

_____, 1999, *Ibid*. New Haven, Connecticut: Yale University Press. Revised edition "With a new foreword by Peter Dodson and a historical update by Clifford A. Miles and David W. Hamblin."

Ott, Christopher J., and Lisa Buckley, 2001, First report of protoceratopsidae from the Hell Creek Formation: *Journal of Vertebrate Paleontology*, 21 (Supplement to Number 3), Abstracts of Papers, Sixty-first Annual Meeting, p. 86A.

Ouyang, H., and Ye Y., 2002, The first mamenchisaurian skeleton with complete skull, *Mamenchisaurus youngi*, pp. 1–111.

Owen, Richard, 1842, Report on British fossil reptiles. Part II. *Report of the British Association for the Advancement of Science 1842 (1841)*, pp. 60–204.

_____, 1854, On some fossil reptilian and mammalian remains from the Purbecks: *Quarterly Journal of the Geological Society*, 10, pp. 420–433.

_____, 1861, A monograph of the fossil Reptilia of the Liassic formations. Part I. *Scelidosaurus harissonii: Monographs of the Palaeontological Society*, 13, pp. 1–14.

_____ [anonymous], 1865, A new Wealden dragon. Order Sauria, family Dinosaurian; genus, *Polacanthus*; species, *foxii: Illustrated London News*, 47, p. 270.

_____, 1874, A monograph of the fossil Reptilia of the Wealden and Purbeck formations. Supplement V. Dinosauria (*Iguanodon*): *Monographs of the Palaeontological Society*, 27, pp. 1–18.

_____, 1876, Monograph of the fossil Reptilia of the Wealden and Purbeck Formations. Supplement 7. Crocodilia (*Poikilopleuron*), Dinosauria (*Chondrosteosaurus*): *Ibid.*, 30 (Supplement 7), pp. 1–7.

_____, 1878, On the fossils called "granicones": being a contribution to the histology of the exo-skeleton in "Reptilia": *Journal of the Royal Microsopical Society*, 1, pp. 232–236.

_____, 1879, Monograph of the fossil Reptilia of the Wealden and Purbeck formations. Supplement IX. Crocodilia (*Goniopholis, Brachydectes, Nannosuchus, Theropsuchus, and Nuthetes*), *Monographs of the Palaeontological Society*, 33, pp. 1–19.

Padian, Kevin, 1985, The origins and aerodynamics of flight in extinct vertebrates: *Palaeontology*, 28, pp. 423–433.

_____, 2001, Cross-testing adaptive hypotheses: phylogenetic analysis and the origin of bird flight: *American Zoologist*, 41, pp. 598–607.

Padian, Kevin, John R. Horner, and Armand J. de Ricqlès, 2002, How dinosaurs grew: growth rates and strategies: *GSA Abstracts with Programs*, 268.

Padian, Kevin, John R. Hutchinson, and Thomas R. Holtz, Jr., 1997, Phylogenetic definitions and nomenclature of the major taxonomic categories of the theropod dinosaurs: *Journal of Vertebrate Paleontology*, 18 (Supplement to Number 3), Abstracts of Papers, Fifty-eighth Annual Meeting, p. 68A.

_____, 1999, Phylogenetic definitions and nomenclature of the major taxonomic categories of the carnivorous Dinosauria (Theropoda): *Journal of Vertebrate Paleontology*, 19 (1), pp. 69–80.

Padian, Kevin, Ji Qiang, and Ji Shu-An, 2001, Feathered dinosaurs and the origin of flight, *in*: Darren Tanke and Kenneth Carpenter, editors, *Mesozoic Vertebrate Life: New Research Inspired by the Paleontology of Philip J. Currie*. Bloomington and Indianapolis, Indiana: Indiana University Press, pp. 117–135.

Padian, Kevin, and Paul E. Olsen, 1984, Ratite footprints and the stance and gait of Mesozoic theropods, *in*: David D. Gillette and Martin G. Lockley, editors, *Dinosaur Tracks and Traces*. Cambridge: Cambridge University Press, pp. 231–241.

Pagnac, Darrin C., 2000, Variation within the pectoral region and its implications concerning species level taxonomy of the North American sauropod, *Camarasaurus: PaleoBios, 2000 California Conference Abstracts*, p. 7.

Paik, In Sung, Hyun Joo Kim, Kye Hun Park, Yong Sun Song, Yong Il Lee, Jin Yeon Hwang, and Min Huh, 2001, Palaeoenvironments and taphonomic preservation of dinosaur bone-bearing deposits in the Lower Cretaceous Hasandong Formation, Korea: *Cretaceous Research*, 22, pp. 627–642.

Paladino, Frank V., James R. Spotila, and Peter Dodson, 1997, A blueprint for giants: modeling the physiology of large dinosaurs, *in*: James O. Farlow and Michael K. Brett-Surman, editors, *The Complete Dinosaur*. Bloomington and Indianapolis, Indiana University Press, pp. 491–504.

Pal'fy, J., P. L. Smith, and J. K. Mortensen, 2000, A U-Pb and $^{40/30}$Ar time scale for the Jurassic: *Canadian Journal of Earth Sciences*, 37, pp. 923–944.

Parks, William A., 1920, The osteology of the trachodont dinosaur *Kritosaurus incurvimanus: University of Toronto Geological Studies*, Series 11, pp. 1–74.

Parkes, K. C., 1966, Speculations on the origin of feathers: *Living Bird*, 5, pp. 77–86.

Parras, A., and B. J. González Riga, 2001, Primer registro de dinosaurios saurópodos, procedentes de la Formación Río Colorado (Santoniano–Campaniano temprano), en la provincia de La Pampa, Argentina: *Ameghiniana*, XVII Jornadas Argentinas de Paleontología de Vertebrados, Resúmes, Esquel, 16–18 de mayo de 2001, pp. 38R–39R.

Parvish, J. Michael, 1997, Evolution of the archosaurs, *in*: James O. Farlow and Michael K. Brett-Surman, editors, *The Complete Dinosaur*. Bloomington and Indianapolis: Indiana University Press, pp. 191–203.

Parrish, H. Michael, and Kent A. Stevens, 2001, Neck mobility in long-necked vertebrae: from modern mammals to sauropods: *International Congress of Vertebrate Morphology, Abstracts*, p. 270.

_____, 2002, Rib angulation, scapular position, and body profiles in sauropod dinosaurs: *Journal of Vertebrate Paleontology*, 23 (Supplement to Number 3), Abstracts of Papers, Sixty-second Annual Meeting, p. 95A.

Parrish, J. Michael, 1997, Evolution of the archosaurs, *in*: James O. Farlow and Michael K. Brett-Surman, editors, *The Complete Dinosaur*. Bloomington and Indianapolis, Indiana University Press, pp. 191–203.

Parsons, William L., and Kristen M. Parsons, 2001, Description of a new skull of *Sauropelta* cf. *S. edwardsi* Ostrom, 1970 (Ornithischia: Ankylosauria): *Journal of Vertebrate Paleontology*, 21 (Supplement to Number 3), Abstracts of Papers, Sixty-first Annual Meeting, p. 87A.

Pasch, Anne D., and Kevin C. May, 1995, The significance of a new hadrosaur (Hadrosauridae) from the Matanuska Formation (Cretaceous) in south central Alaska:

Journal of Vertebrate Paleontology, 15 (Supplement to Number 3), Abstracts of Papers, Fifty-fourth Annual Meeting, p. 48A.

_____, 1997, First occurrence of a hadrosaur (Dinosauria) from the Matanuska Formation (Turonian) in the Talkeetna Mountains of south-central Alaska: *Short Notes on Alaska Geology*, Professional Report 118, pp. 99–109.

_____, 2001, Taphonomy and paleoenvironment of a hadrosaur (Dinosauria) from the Matanuska Formation (Turonian) in south-central Alaska, *in*: Darren Tanke and Kenneth Carpenter, editors, *Mesozoic Vertebrate Life: New Research Inspired by the Paleontology of Philip J. Currie*. Bloomington and Indianapolis, Indiana: Indiana University Press, pp. 219–236.

Patchus, Robert, and Kraig Derstler, 2002, A hadrosaurine dinosaur mummy from the Lance Formation (upper Maastrichtian), Niobrara, Wyoming: *Journal of Vertebrate Paleontology*, 23 (Supplement to Number 3), Abstracts of Papers, Sixty-second Annual Meeting, p. 95A.

Patchus, Robert, William Straight, Reese Barrick, William Showers, and Bernie Genna, 2001, Biologic and ecologic information from oxygen and carbon isotope records in hadrosaur tooth enamel: *Journal of Vertebrate Paleontology*, 21 (Supplement to Number 3), Abstracts of Papers, Sixty-first Annual Meeting, pp. 87A–88A.

Paul, Gregory S., 1984, The segnosaurian dinosaurs: relics of the prosauropod-ornithischian transition?: *Journal of Vertebrate Paleontology*, 4 (4), pp. 507–515.

_____, 1987*a*, Predation in the meat-eating dinosaurs [revised edition]: *Tyrrell Museum of Palaeontology, Occasional Paper*, 3, pp. 171–176.

_____, 1987*b*, The science and art of restoring the life appearance of dinosaurs and their relatives, *in*: Sylvia J. Czerkas and Everett C. Olson, *Dinosaurs Past and Present*, Volume II. Los Angeles: Natural History Museum of Los Angeles County, pp. 5–49.

_____, 1988*a*, The brachiosaur giants of the Morrison and Tendaguru with a description of a new subgenus, *Giraffatitan*, and a comparison of the world's largest dinosaurs: *Hunteria*, 3 (3), pp. 1–14.

_____, 1988*b*, *Predatory Dinosaurs of the World: A Complete Illustrated Guide*. New York: Simon and Schuster, 403 pages.

_____, 1988*c*, The small predatory dinosaurs of the mid–Mesozoic: the horned theropods of the Morrison and Great Oolite — *Ornitholestes* and *Proceratosaurus* — and the sickle-claw theropods of the Cloverly, Djadokhta and Judith River — *Deinonychus*, *Velociraptor* and *Saurornitholestes*: *Hunteria*, 2 (4), pp. 1–9.

_____, 2000, Limb design, function and running performance in ostrich-mimics and tyrannosaurs: *in* B. P. Pérez-Moreno, Thomas R. Holtz, Jr., José Luis Sanz, and José J. Moratalla, editors, Aspects of theropod paleobiology: *Gaia*, 15 (December 1998), pp. 257–270.

_____, 2001, Increasing evidence for an arboreal origin of dinosaur-avian flight, and for losses of flight in post-ürvogel di-nosaurs: *Journal of Vertebrate Paleontology*, 21 (Supplement to Number 3), Abstracts of Papers, Sixty-first Annual Meeting, p. 88A.

_____, 2002*a*, *Dinosaur of the Air: The Evolution and Loss of Flight in Dinosaurs and Birds*. Baltimore and London: The Johns Hopkins University Press, 460 pages.

_____, 2002*b*, Problems with sauropod neck posture: *Journal of Vertebrate Paleontology*, 23 (Supplement to Number 3), Abstracts of Papers, Sixty-second Annual Meeting, p. 95A.

Paul, Gregory S., and Per Christiansen, 2000, Forelimb posture in neoceratopsian dinosaurs: implications for gait and locomotion: *Paleobiology*, 26 (3), pp. 450–465.

Pearson, Dean A., Terry Schaefer, Kirk R. Johnson, Douglas J. Nichols, and John P. Hunter, 2002, Vertebrate biostratigraphy of the Hell Creek Formation in southwestern North Dakota and northwestern South Dakota: *Geological Society of America, Special Paper*, 361, pp. 145–167.

Peng, J.-H., 1997*a*, Palaeoecology of vertebrate assemblages from the upper Cretaceous Judith River Group (Campanian) of southern Alberta, Canada. Unpublished Ph.D. dissertation, University of Calgary, 312 pages.

_____, 1997*b*, Fabrosauridae, *in*: Philip J. Currie and Kevin Padian, editors, *Encyclopedia of Dinosaurs*. San Diego: Academic Press, pp. 237–240.

Penkalski, Paul, 2001, Variation in specimens referred to *Euoplocephalus tutus*, *in*: Kenneth Carpenter, editor, *The Armored Dinosaurs*. Bloomington and Indianapolis: Indiana University Press, pp. 261–298.

Pereda-Suberbiola, Xabier [Javier, Xavier], 1994, *Polacanthus* (Ornithischia, Ankylosauria), a Transatlantic armoured dinosaur from the Early Cretaceous of Europe and North America: *Palaeontographica, A*, 323, pp. 133–159.

Pereda-Suberbiola [Pereda Suberbiola], Xabier [Javier, Xavier], 1993, Les dinosaures ankylosauriens d'Europe: systematique et évolution: *Mémoires des Sciences de la Terra, Université Pierre et Marie Curie, Paris*, 9320, 302 pages.

_____, 1996, La contribucion del Baron Nopcsa al estudio de las faunas de vertebrados continentales del Cretacico Final de Europa: *Gaia*, 13, pp. 43–66.

_____, 1999, Ankylosaurian dinosaur remains from the Upper Cretaceous of Laño (Iberian Peninsula): *Estudios del Museo de Ciencias Naturales de Álava*, 14 (1), 273–288.

Pereda Suberbiola, Xabier, and Peter M. Galton, 1992, On the taxonomic status of the dinosaur *Struthiosaurus austriacus* from the Late Cretaceous of Austria: *Comptes Rendus de l'Académie des Sciences Paris*, 314, pp. 1275–1280.

_____, 1994, A revision of the cranial features of the dinosaur *Struthiosaurus austriacus* Bunzel (Ornithischia: Ankylosauria) from the Late Cretaceous of Europe: *Neus Jahrbuch für Geologie und Paläontologie, Abhandlungen*, 191, pp. 173–200.

_____, 1999, Thyreophoran ornithischian di-nosaurs from the Iberian Peninsula: *Actas de las I Journadas Internacionales Sobre Paleontología de Dinosaurios y su Entorno (Proceedings of the 1st International Symposium about Paleontology of Dinosaurs and their Environment*, Salas de los Infantes (Burgos, España), Septiembre de 1999, pp. 147–161.

_____, 2001, Reappraisel of the nodosaurid ankylosaur *Struthiosaurus austriacus* Bunzel from the Upper Cretaceous Gosau Beds of Austria, *in*: Kenneth Carpenter, editor, *The Armored Dinosaurs*. Bloomington and Indianapolis: Indiana University Press, pp. 173–210.

Pereda-Suberbiola, Xabier, M. Meijide, F. Torcida, J. Welle, C. Fuentes, L. A. Izquierdo, D. Montero, G. Pérez, and y V. Urién, 1999, Espinas dermicas del dinosaurio anquilosaurio *Polacanthus* en la facies Weald de Salas de los Infantes (Burgos, Spain): *Estudios Geologicos*, 55, pp. 267–272.

Pérez-Moreno, Bernardino P., Daniel J. Chure, C. Pires, C. Marques da Silva, V. Dos Santos, P. Dantas, L. Póvoas, M. Cachão, José Luis Sanz, and A. M. Galopim de Carvalho (1999), 1999, On the presence of *Allosaurus fragilis* (Theropoda: Carnosauria) in the Upper Jurassic of Portugal: first evidence of an intercontinental dinosaur species: *Quarterly Journal of the Geological Society of London*, 156, pp. 449–452.

Pérez-Oñate, J., G. Cuenca-Bescós, and J. L. Sanz, 1994, Un neuvo saurópodo del Jurásico Superior de Galve (Teruel): *Comunicaciones d las X Jornadas de Paleontologia, Madrid*, pp. 159–162.

Pérez-Moreno, B. P., José Luis Sanz, J. Sudre, and B. Sigé, 1993, A theropod dinosaur from the Lower Cretaceous of southern France: *Revue de Paléobiologie*, vol. spéc. 7, pp. 173–188.

Perle, Altangerel, 1979, [Segnosauridae a new family of theropods from the Late Cretaceous of Mongolia]: [*Soviet-Mongolian Palaeontological Expedition, Transactions*], 8, pp. 45–55.

Perle, Altangerel, Luis M. Chiappe, Rinchen Barsbold, James M. Clark, and Mark A. Norell, 1994, Skeletal morphology of *Mononykus olecrans* (Theropoda: Aviale) from the Late Cretaceous of Mongolia: *American Musuem Novitates*, 3105, pp. 1–29.

Perle, Altangerel, Teresa Maryańska, and Halszka Osmólska, 1982, *Goyocephale latimorie* gen. et sp. n., a new flat-headed pachycephalosaur (Ornithischia, Dinosauria) from the Upper Cretaceous of Mongolia: *Acta Palaeontologica Polonica*, 27, pp. 115–127.

Pérez-Moreno, B. P., Thomas R. Holtz, Jr., José Luis Sanz, and José J. Moratalla, 2000, editors, Aspects of theropod paleobiology: *Gaia*, 15 (cover dated December 1998), 403 pages.

Peters, Dieter Stefan, 1984, Konstruktionmorphologischen Geischtspunkte zur Entstehung der Vögel: *Natur und Museum*, 114 (17), pp. 199–210.

_____, 1985, Functional and constructive limitations in the early evolution of birds, *in*:

Bibliography

Max K. Hecht, John H. Ostrom, G. Viohl and Peter Wellnhoffer, editors, *The Beginnings of Birds*. Eichstätt: Freunde des Jura-Museums, pp. 243–249.

_____, 2002, Anagenesis of early birds reconsidered: *Senckenbergiana lethaea*, 82 (1), pp. 347–354.

Peters, Robert Henry, 1983, *The Ecological Implications of Body Size*. Cambridge: Cambridge University Press 329 pages.

Phillips, John, 1871, *Geology of Oxford and the Valley of the Thames*. Oxford, England: Clarendon Press, xxiv, 523 pages.

Pi, Ouyang and Ye, 1996, A new species of a sauropod from Zigong, Sichuan: *Papers on Geosciences*, 50, pp. 87–91.

Pidancet, J., and S. Chopard, 1862, Note sur un saurien gigantesque aux Marnes irisées: *Comptes Rendus des Séances de l'Academie des Sciences, Paris*, 54, pp. 1259–1262, Paris.

Pierce, Stephanie E., 2002, Two juvenile *Prosaurolophus* (Hadrosaurinae) specimens from marine sediments: unique taphonomy or paleobiology?: *Journal of Vertebrate Paleontology*, 23 (Supplement to Number 3), Abstracts of Papers, Sixty-second Annual Meeting, pp. 96A–97A.

Pincemaille, M., 1997, *Un ornithopode du Crétacé Supérieur de Vitrolles (Bouches du Rhône)*, Rhabdodon priscus. Diplôme d'Études Approfondies, Université Montpellier II, 44 pages (unpublished).

_____, 1999, Discovery of a skeleton of *Rhabdodon priscus* (Ornithopoda, Dinosauria) in the Upper Cretaceous of Vitrolles (Bouches du Rhône, France): *IV European Workshop on Vertebrate Palaeontology*, Albarracín, 76.

Pisani, Davide, Adam M. Yates, and Max C. Langer, 2001, The first supertree for the Dinosauria: *Journal of Vertebrate Paleontology*, 21 (Supplement to Number 3), Abstracts of Papers, Sixty-first Annual Meeting, p. 89A.

Platt, Philip R., 2001, The pectoral girdle of *Apatosaurus*: *Western Association of Vertebrate Paleontologists and Mesa Southwest Museum and Southwest Paleontological Symposium, Bulletin*, 8, pp. 41–46.

Plieninger, T., 1846a, Über ein neues Sauriergenus und die Einreihung der Saurier mit flachen, schneidenden Zähnen in Eine Familie: *Jh. Ver. vaterl. Naturkde. Württemberg*, 2, pp. 148–154, Stuttgart.

_____, 1846b, Nachträgliche Bemerkungen zu dem Vortage (S. 148 disses Heftes) über ein neues Sauriergenus und die Einreihung der Saurier mit flachen, schneidenden Zahnen in Eine Familie: *Ibid.*, 2, pp. 247–254, Stuttgart.

_____, 1857, *Belodon plieningeri* H. v. Meyer. Ein Saurier der Keuperformation: *Ibid.*, 8 (Suppl.), pp. 389–524, Stuttgart.

Pope, Kevin O., 2002, Impact dust not the cause of the Cretaceous–Tertiary mass extinction: *Geology*, 30 (2), pp. 99–102.

Posmosanu, Erika, and Elizabeth Cook, 2000, Vertebrate taphonomy and dinosaur palaeopathology from a Lower Cretaceous bauxite lens, North West Romania: *Oryctos*, 3, pp. 39–51.

Powell, Jaime Eduardo, 1979, Sobre una aso-ciación de dinosauros y ostras evidencias de vertebrados del Cretácico Superior de la región de La Candelaria, Prov. de Salta, Argentina: *Ameghiniana*, 16 (1–2), pp. 191–204.

_____, 1986, Revisión de los Titanosauridos de América del Sur. Tésis Doctoral inédita Fac. de Ciencias Exactas y Naturales, Universidad Nacional de Tucumán, Argentina, 472 pages (unpublished).

_____, 1987a, Morfologia del esqueleto axial de los dinosaurios titanosáuridos (Saurischia–Sauropoda) del Estado de Minas Gerais, Brasil: *Anain X Congreso Brasileiro de Paleontologia*, pp. 155–171, Rio de Janeiro.

_____, 1987b, Hallazgo de un dinosaurio hadrosaurido (Ornithischia, Ornithopoda) en la Formación Allen (Cretacico Superior) de Salitral Moreno, Provincia de Río Negro, Argentina: *Décimo Congreso Geologico Argentino, Actas*, 3, pp. 149–152.

Preuschoft, Holger, 1976, Funktionelle Anpassung evoluierender Systeme: *Aufsätze und Reden der Senckenbergischen Naturforscheden Gesellschaft*, 28, pp. 98–117.

Prieto-Márquez, Albert, 2001, Osteology and variation of *Brachylophosaurus canadensis* (Dinosauria, Hadrosauridae) from the Upper Cretaceous Judith River Formation of Montana: *Journal of Vertebrate Paleontology*, 21 (Supplement to Number 3), Abstracts of Papers, Sixty-first Annual Meeting, p. 90A.

Prieto-Márquez, Albert, Rodrigo Gaete, Angel Galobart, and Lluis Ardèvol, 2000, A *Richardoestesia*-like theropod tooth from the Late Cretaceous foredeep, south-central Pyrenees, Spain: *Ecologae geolicae Helvetiae*, 93, pp. 497–501.

Prum, Richard O., 2002, Perspectives in ornithology: why ornithologists should care about the theropod origin of birds: *The Auk*, 119 (1), pp. 1–17.

Pruss, S. B., 2002, Anachronistic facies in the Early Triassic: implications for a prolonged recovery from the end Permian extinction event: *2002 California Paleontology Conference, Abstracts*, Department of Geological Sciences, University of California, Santa Barbara, California, April 12–13, 2002, p. 7.

Pryor, R., Darren Tanke, Philip J. Currie, B. Spencer, and J. Humber, 2002, Mapping of Late Cretaceous vertebrate localities in Dinosaur Provincial Park, Alberta using the Global Positioning System — an update: *Alberta Palaeontological Society, Sixth Annual Symposium, "Fossils 2002," Abstract Volume*, January 26–27, 2002, Mount Royal College, Calgary, Alberta, pp. 39–41.

Qiu Licheng, and Huang Dong, 2001, Dinosaur fossils from the Heyuan Basin in Guangdong Province, China, *in*: Deng Tao and Wang Yuan, editors, *Proceedings of the Eighth Annual Meeting of the Chinese Society of Vertebrate Paleontology*. Beijing: China Ocean Press, pp. 59–63.

Quenstedt, F. A., 1967–68, *Handbuch der Petrefactenkunde*, 2nd edition. Tübingen: Laupp, pp. 1–982 [reprinted by Arno Press, 1980].

Raath, Michael R., 1969, A new coelurosaurian dinosaur from the Forest Sandstone of Rhodesia: *Arnoldia (Rhodesia)*, 4 (28), pp. 1–25.

_____, 1977, The anatomy of the Triassic theropod *Syntarsus rhodesiensis* (Saurischia: Podokesauridae) and a consideration of its biology, Ph.D thesis, Rhodes University, Grahamstown (unpublished).

Rauhut, Oliver W. M., 1997, Zur Schädelanatomie von *Shuvosaurus inexpectatus* (Dinosauria; Theropoda), *in*: S. Sachs, O. W. M. Rauhut, and A. Weigert, editors, *Treffen der deutschsprachigen Palaeoherpetologen, Düsseldorf*, extended abstracts, pp. 21–23 (On the cranial anatomy of *Shuvosaurus inexpectatus* [Dinosauria: Theropoda], translated by Rauhut).

_____, 1998, *Elaphrosaurus bambergi* and the early evolution of theropod dinosaurs: *Journal of Vertebrate Paleontology*, 18 (Supplement to Number 3), Abstracts of Papers, Fifty-eighth Annual Meeting, p. 71A.

_____, 2000a, The dinosaur fauna from the Guimarota Mine, *in*: T. Martin and B. Krebs, editors, *Guimarota: A Jurassic Ecosystem*. Munchen: Verlag Dr. Friedrich Pfeil, pp. 75–82.

_____, 2000b, The interrelationships and evolution of basal theropods (Dinosauria, Saurischia). Ph.D. dissertation, University of Bristol, Bristol, 583 pages.

_____, 2001a, Morphology and mechanics of the jaws of spinosaurid theropods (Dinosauria): implications for predation: *Ameghiniana*, XVII Jornadas Argentinas de Paleontologia de Vertebrados, Resúmes, Esquel, 16–18 de mayo de 2001, p. 16R.

_____, 2001b, Herbivorous dinosaurs from the Late Jurassic (Kimmeridgian) of Guimarota, Portugal: *Proceedings of the Geologists' Association*, 112, pp. 275–283.

_____, 2002, Dinosaur teeth from the Berremian of Uña, Province of Cuenca, Spain: *Cretaceous Research*, 23, pp. 255–263.

Rauhut, Oliver W. M., and Axel Hungerbüler, 2000, A review of European Triassic theropods, *in* B. P. Pérez-Moreno, Thomas R. Holtz, Jr., José Luis Sanz, and José J. Moratalla, editors, Aspects of theropod paleobiology: *Gaia*, 15 (cover dated December 1998), pp. 75–88.

Rauhut, Oliver W. M., and C. Werner, 1995, First record of the family Dromaeosauridae (Dinosauria: Theropoda) in the Cretaceous of Gondwana (Wadi Milk Formation, northern Sudan): *Paläontologische Zeitschrift*, 69, pp. 475–489.

Rauhut, Oliver W. M., and J. Zinke, 1995, A description of the Barremian dinosaur fauna from Uña with a comparison to that of Las Hoyas, *in*: *II International Symposium on Lithographic Limestones, Lleida-Cuenca (Spain), 9th–16th July, Extended Abstracts*, (Universidad Autónoma de Madrid, Madrid), pp. 123–126.

Ravoavy, Florent, 1991, Identification et mise en catalogue des vertebras fossils récoltes dans le Crétace supérieur continental de la region de Berivotra (Majunga) fouille

1987: *Univ. d'Antananarivo Mem. Rech*, II, pp. 55–104. Rayfield, Emily J., 2001, Functional morphology of the skull of *Allosaurus fragilis*: a study using the finite element method: *International Congress of Vertebrate Morphology, Abstracts*, p. 274.

Rayfield, Emily J., David B. Norman, Celeste C. Horner, John R. Horner, Paula May Smith, Jeffrey J. Thomason, and Paul Upchurch, 2001, Cranial design and function in a large theropod dinosaur: *Nature*, 409, pp. 1033–1037.

Rayfield, Emily J., David B. Norman, and Paul Upchurch, 2002, response to Frazzetta and Kardong, 2002, p. 388.

Rayner, J. M. V., 1985a, Mechanical and ecological constraints of flight evolution, *in*: Max K. Hecht, John H. Ostrom, G. Viohl and Peter Wellnhoffer, editors, *The Beginnings of Birds*. Eichstätt, Germany: Freunde des Jura-Museums, pp. 279–288.

_____, 1985b, Cursorial gliding in protobirds: *Ibid.*, pp. 289–292.

Reese, A., 1915, *The Alligator and Its Allies*. New York: Knickerbocker, 358 pages.

Rega, Elizabeth A., 2001, Paleopathology of a mature *Tyrannosaurus rex* skeleton: *The Paleobiology and Phylogenetics of Large Theropods*, A. Watson Armour III Symposium, The Field Museum, 12 May 2001, unpaginated.

Rega, Elizabeth A., and Christopher A. Brochu, 2001a, Paleopathology of a mature *Tyrannosaurus rex* skeleton: *Journal of Vertebrate Paleontology*, 21 (Supplement to Number 3), Abstracts of Papers, Sixty-first Annual Meeting, p. 92A.

_____, 2001b, Evidence of thoracic breathing in *Tyrannosaurus rex*, based upon recent anatomical and pathological evidence from "Sue": *International Congress of Vertebrate Morphology, Abstracts*, p. 274.

Rehnelt, K., 1950, Ein Beitrag über Fährterspuren im unteren Gipskeuper von Bayreuth: *Beircht Naturwissenschaftlichen Gesellschaft, Bayreuth 1950*, pp. 27–36.

Reichenbach, L., 1852, *Avium System Naturale*. 36 pages.

Reid, Robin E. H., 1997, Dinosaurian physiology: the case for "intermediate" dinosaurs: *in*: Farlow and Brett-Surman, editors, *The Complete Dinosaur*. Bloomington and Indianapolis: Indiana University Press, pp. 449–473.

Rensberger, John M., David Bowdle, Ryan Daugherty, Rachel Desler, Robert Gilmore, and James Henderson, 2002, Exceptional osteocyte sizes in *Triceratops* and *Tyrannosaurus*: *Journal of Vertebrate Paleontology*, 23 (Supplement to Number 3), Abstracts of Papers, Sixty-second Annual Meeting, p. 99A.

Rensberger, John M., and H. B. Krentz, 1988, Microscopic effects of predator digestion on the surfaces of bones and teeth: *Scanning Microscopy*, 2, pp. 1541–1551.

Resnick, D., and G. Niwayama, 1988, editors, *Diagnosis of Bone and Joint Disorders*. Philadelphia: Saunders, 1040 pages.

Retallack, G. J., 1997, Dinosaurs and dirt, *in*: Donald L. Wolberg, Edmund Stump, and Gary Rosenberg, editors. *Dinofest International: Proceedings of a Symposium Held at Arizona State University*. Philadelphia: Academy of Natural Sciences, pp. 345–359.

Riabinin, Anatoly Nikolaenvice N., 1925, [A mounted skeleton of the gigantic reptile *Trachodon amurense*, nov sp.]: *Invest. Geol. Kom. [Museum of the Geological Committee]*, 44 (1), pp. 1–12.

_____, 1930, [*Mandschurosaurus amurensis*, nov. gen., nov. sp., a hadrosaurian dinosaur from the Upper Cretaceous of Amur River]: *Memoir II, Société Paléontologique de Russie*, Obschest, 2, pp. 1–36.

Rich, Thomas H., Patricia Vickers-Rich, Fernando E. Novas, Rubén Cuneo, Pablo Puerta, and Raul Vacca, 2000, Theropods from the "Middle" Cretaceous Chubut Group of the San Jorge Sedimentary Basin, Central Patagonia, a preliminary note, *in* B. P. Pérez-Moreno, Thomas R. Holtz, Jr., José Luis Sanz, and José J. Moratalla, editors, Aspects of theropod paleobiology: *Gaia*, 15 (cover dated December 1998), pp. 111–115.

Richardson, P. R. K., P. J. Mundy, and I. Plug, 1986, Bone crushing carnivores and their significance to osteodystrophy in griffon vulture chicks: *Journal of the Zoological Society of London* (Series A), 210, pp. 23–43.

Ricqlès, Armand de, John R. Horner, and Kevin Padian, 2001, The bone histology of basal birds in phylogenetic and ontogenetic perspectives, *in*: Jacques A. Gauthier, editor, *Perspectives on the Origin and Evolution of Birds*. New Haven: Yale University Press.

Ricqlès, Armand de, F. J. Meunier, J. Castanet, and H. Francillon-Viellot, 1991, *in*: B. K. Hall, editor, *Bone*. Boca Raton, Florida: CRC, pp. 1–78.

Ricqlès, Armand de, Octávio Mateus, Miguel Telles Antunes, and Philippe Taquet, 2001, Histomorphogenesis of embryos of Upper Jurassic theropods from Lourinhã (Portugal): *Comtes Rendu des Séances de l'Académie des Sciences, Paris, de la Terre et des Planètes*, 332, pp. 647–656.

Ricqlès, Armand de, Xabier Pereda-Suberbiola, Zulma Gasparini, and Eduardo B. Olivero, 2001, Histology of dermal ossifications in an ankylosaurian dinosaur from the Late Cretaceous of Antarctica: *Asociacíon Paleontológical Argentina*, Publicatión Especial 7, VII International Symposium on Mesozoic Terrestrial Ecosystems, Buenos Aires, 30-6-2001, pp. 171–174.

Rigby, J. Keith, Jr., L. W. Sneel, D. M. Unruh, S. S. Harlan, J. Guan, F. Li, J. Keith Rigby, and B. J. Kowalis, 1993, ^{40}Ar/^{39} and U-Pb dates for dinosaur extinction, Nanxiong Basin, Guangdong Province, Peoplés Republic of China: *Geological Society of America Conference, Boston, Abstract Program*, 25, p. A296.

Rinehart, L. F., Spencer G. Lucas, and Andrew B. Heckert, 2001a, Preliminary quantification of the robust and gracile forms of the Triassic dinosaur *Coelophysis* using probability plots: *Paleontology, Stratigraphy, and Sedimentology: GSA Rocky Mountain Section and South-Central Section Meeting*, abstracts, p. A-55.

_____, 2001b, Preliminary statistical analysis defining the juvenile, robust and gracile forms of the Triassic dinosaur *Coelophysis*: *Journal of Vertebrate Paleontology*, 21 (Supplement to Number 3), Abstracts of Papers, Sixty-first Annual Meeting, p. 93A.

Rogers, Raymond Robert, and Joshua Miller, 2002, Paleoenvironmental and taphonomic perspectives on the Late Cretaceous world of the abelisaurid theropod *Majungatholus atopus*: *Journal of Vertebrate Paleontology*, 23 (Supplement to Number 3), Abstracts of Papers, Sixty-second Annual Meeting, p. 100A.

Romer, Alfred S. [Sherwood], 1923a, Crocodilian pelvic muscle and their avian and reptilian homologies: *Bulletin of the American Museum of Natural History*, 28, pp. 533–552.

_____, 1923b, The ilium in dinosaurs and birds: *Ibid.*, 48, pp. 141–145.

_____, 1923c, The pelvic musculature of saurischian dinosaurs: *Ibid.*, 48, pp. 605–617.

_____, 1927, The pelvic musculature of ornithischian dinosaurs: *Acta Zoologica*, 8, pp. 226–275.

Romer, R. L., 2000, Implication of diagenetic mobility of U and Pb on the U-Pb dating of fossils: *Berichte der Deutschen Mineralogischen Gesellschaft*, 2000 (1), 170 pages.

_____, 2001, Isotopiclly heterogenous initial Pb and continuous ^{222}Rn-loss in fossils: the U-Pb systematics of *Brachiosaurus brancai*: *Geochimica et cosmochimica acta*.

Ross, C. T. F., 1990, *Finite Element Methods in Engineering Science*. London: Ellis Horwood, 519 pages.

Rothschild, Bruce M., 1997, Dinosaurian paleopathology, *in*: James O. Farlow and Michael K. Brett-Surman, editors, *The Complete Dinosaur*. Bloomington and Indianapolis, Indiana University Press, pp. 426–448.

_____, 2002, Anatomy of data-based diagnosis: bone surface disruption and disease origins: *Journal of Vertebrate Paleontology*, 23 (Supplement to Number 3), Abstracts of Papers, Sixty-second Annual Meeting, pp. 100A–101A.

Rothschild, Bruce M., Darren H. Tanke, and Tracy L. Ford, 2001, Theropod stress fractures and tendon avulsions as a clue to activity, *in*: Darren Tanke and Kenneth Carpenter, editors, *Mesozoic Vertebrate Life: New Research Inspired by the Paleontology of Philip J. Currie*. Bloomington and Indianapolis, Indiana: Indiana University Press, pp. 331–336.

Rowe, Timothy, 1989, A new species of theropod dinosaur *Syntarsus* from the Early Jurassic Kayenta Formation of Arizona: *Journal of Vertebrate Paleontology*, 9 (2), pp. 125–136.

Rowe, Timothy, Richard L. Cifelli, Thomas M. Lehman, and Anne Weil, 1992, The Campanian Terlingua local fauna, with a summary of other vertebrates from the Aguja Formation, Trans-Pecos Texas: *Journal of Vertebrate Paleontology*, 12 (4), pp. 472–493.

Rowe, Timothy, and Jacques A. Gauthier,

Bibliography

1990, Ceratosauria, *in*: David B. Weishampel, Peter Dodson, and Halszka Osmólska, editors, *The Dinosauria*. Berkeley and Los Angeles: University of California Press, pp. 151–168.

Rowe, Timothy, Earle F. McBride, and Paul C. Sereno, 2001, Dinosaur with a heart of stone: *Science*, 291 (5505), pp. 783–785.

Royo-Torres, R., and José Ignacio Canudo, 1999, El dinosaurio saurópodo (Aptiense, Cretacico Ingferior) de Peñarroya de Tastavins (Teruel): *Actas de las I Journadas Internacionales Sobre Paleontología de Dinosaurios y su Entorno (Proceedings of the 1st International Symposium about Paleontology of Dinosaurs and their Environment*, Salas de los Infantes (Burgos, España), Septiembre de 1999, pp. 417–425.

Royo-Torres, R., José Ignacio Canudo, and J. I. Ruiz-Omeñaca, 1999, Neuva descripción del pubis de *Aragosaurus ischiaticus* Sanz, Buscalioni, Casanovas y Santafé 1987 (Dinosuria, Sauropoda) del Hauteriviense superior (Cretácico inferior) en Galve (Teruel): *Actas XV Jornadas de Paleontología*, 1, pp. 325–330.

Rozhdestvensky, Anatoly Konstantinovich, 1965, Growth changes in Asian dinosaurs and some problems of their taxonomy: *Palaeontologicheskii Zhurnal*, 3, pp. 95–109.

———, 1966, Novye iguanodonty iz Tsentral'nol Azii. Filogeneticheskie i taksonomicheskie vzaimootnosheniya poznik Iguanodontidae i rannikh Hadrosauridae: *Ibid.*, 3, pp. 103–116. (New iguanodonts from Central Asia. Phylogenetic and taxonomic relationships of late Iguanodontidae and early Hadrosauridae: *Palaeontological Journal*, 3, pp. 103–116.)

———, 1968, The finding of a giant dinosaur: *Prioda*, 2, pp. 115–116.

———, 1969, *In Search for Dinosaurs to the Gobi*, 3rd edition, Moscow: Nauko, 293 pages.

Ruben, John A., Christiano Dal Sasso, Nicholas R. Geist, William J. Hillenius, Terry D. Jones, and Marco Signore, 1999, Pulmonary function and metabolic physiology of theropod dinosaurs: *Science (Washington, D.C.)*, 283, pp. 514–516.

Ruben, John A., and Terry Jones, 2000, Selective factors associated with the origin of fur and feathers: *American Zoologist*, 40, pp. 585–596.

———, 2001, Feathered dinosaurs and other myths: a cold, hard look at reality: *International Congress of Vertebrate Morphology, Abstracts*, p. 278.

Rudra, D. K., and P. K. Maulik, 1994, Lower Jurassic Kota limestone of India, *in*: E. Gierlowski-Kordesch and K. Kelts, editors, *Global Geological Record of Lake Basins*. Cambridge: Cambridge University Press, pp. 185–191.

Rüle von Lilienstern, Hugo, 1935a, Die Entstehung der beichen Gleichberge und ihr geologischer Aufbau: *Mitteil. Gemeinde Steinsburgfreunde*, 2 (3), pp. 6–11 (also *Fränkische Heimat*, 7 [1938], pp. 24–27).

———, 1935b, Die Riesenechsenvom Grossen Gleichberg: *Ibid.*, pp. 11–17 (*Ibid.*, pp. 24–27).

———, 1936, Weitere Saurierfunde vom Gr. Gleichberg: *Ibid.*, 3 (H1), pp. 19–20.

Rühle von Lilienstern, Hugo, M. Lang, and Friedrich von Huene, 1952, Die Saurier Thüringens. Jena: Fischer, pp. 1–42.

Ruiz-Omeñaca, J. I., 2001, Dinosaurios hipsilofodontidos (Ornithischia: Ornithopoda) en la Península Ibérica: *Actas de las I Jornadas Internacionales sobre Paleontologia de Dinosaurios y su Entorno (Proceedings of the 1st International Symposium on Paleontology of Dinosaurs and their Environment)*. Burgos, Spain, pp. 175–249.

Ruiz-Omeñaca, J. I., J. I. Canudo, and G. Cuenca-Bescós, 1998, Primera evidencia de un área de alimentación de dinosaurios herbívoros en el Cretácico Inferior de España (Teruel): *Monografías de la Academia de Ciencias de Zaragoza*, 10, 48 pages.

Ruiz-Omeñaca, J. I., J. I. Canudo, G. Cuenca-Bescós, and R. Royo-Torres, 1998, Restos vertebrales de dinosaurios (Ornithischia, Saurischia) en el Barremiense Superior (Cretácico Inferior) de "Vallipón 2" (Castellote, Truel): *Mas dee las Matas*, 17, pp. 251–269.

Russell, Dale A., 1970, Tyrannosaurs from the Late Cretaceous of western Canada: *National Museum of Natural Sciences, Publications in Paleontology*, 1, viii, 34 pages.

———, 1972, Ostrich dinosaurs from the Late Cretaceous of western Canada: *Canadian Journal of Earth Sciences*, 9, pp. 375–402.

———, 1993, The role of Central Asia in dinosaurian biogeography: *Ibid.*, 20, pp. 2002–2012.

Russell, Dale A., and Dong Zhi-Ming, 1993a, The affinities of a new theropod from the Alxa Desert, Inner Mongolia, Peoplés Republic of China: *Canadian Journal of Earth Sciences*, 30 (10–11), pp. 2107–2127.

———, 1993b, A nearly complete skeleton of a troodontid dinosaur from the Early Cretaceous of the Ordos Basin, Inner Mongolia, China: *Ibid.*, pp. 2163–2173.

———, 1996, The meaning of the extinction of the dinosaurs, *in*: G. Ryder, *et al.*, editors, *The Cretaceous–Tertiary Event and Other Catastrophes of Earth History, Geological Society of America, Special Paper*, 307, pp. 381–388.

Russell, Dale A., Paul E. Fischer, Reese E. Barrick, and Michael K. Stoskopf, 2001, response to Rowe, McBride, and Sereno, 2001, pp. 785–787.

Russell, Dale A., and Makoto Manabe, 2002, Synopsis of the Hell Creek (uppermost Cretaceous) dinosaur assemblage: *Geological Society of America, Special Paper*, 361, pp. 169–176.

Russell, Dale A., and Zhao Xijin, 1996, New psittacosaur occurrences in Inner Mongolia: *Canadian Journal of Earth Sciences*, 33, pp. 637–648.

Russell, Dale A., and Zhong Zheng, 1993, A large mamenchisaurid from the Junggar Basin, Xinjiang, Peoplés Republic of China: *Canadian Journal of Earth Sciences*, 30 (10–11), pp. 2082–2095.

Russell, Loris L., 1935, Fauna of the Upper Milk River beds, southern Alberta: *Royal Society of Canada, Transactions* (series 3, section 4), 29, pp. 115–127.

———, 1940, *Edmontonia rugosidens* (Gilmore), an armoured dinosaur from the Belly River Series of Alberta: *University of Toronto Studies, Geological Series*, 43, pp. 3–27.

Rütimeyer, Ludwig, 1856, Reptiles fossiles du Jura: *Archives des Sciences Physiques et Naturalles*, 33, p. 53.

Ruxton, Graeme D., 2001, Heat loss from giant extinct reptiles: *Proceedings of the Royal Society of London*, series B, v. 268, pp. 1921–1924.

Ryan, Michael J., and Philip J. Currie, 1998, First report of protoceratopsians (Neoceratopsia) from the Late Cretaceous Judith River Group, Alberta, Canada: *Canadian Journal of Earth Sciences*, 35, pp. 820–826.

Ryan, Michael J., Philip J. Currie, James D. Gardner, Matthew K. Vickaryous, and Jason M. Lavigne, 2000, *in* B. P. Pérez-Moreno, Thomas R. Holtz, Jr., José Luis Sanz, and José J. Moratalla, editors, Aspects of theropod paleobiology: *Gaia*, 15 (cover dated December 1998), pp. 123–133.

Ryan, Michael J., Philip J. Currie, and Anthonly P. Russell, 2001, New material of *Avimimus portentosus* (Theropoda) from the Iren Dabasu Formation (Upper Cretaceous) of the Erenhot Region of Inner Mongolia: *Journal of Vertebrate Paleontology*, 21 (Supplement to Number 3), Abstracts of Papers, Sixty-first Annual Meeting, p. 95A.

Ryan, Michael J., and Anthony P. Russell, 2001, Dinosaur of Alberta (exclusive of Aves), *in*: Darren Tanke and Kenneth Carpenter, editors, *Mesozoic Vertebrate Life: New Research Inspired by the Paleontology of Philip J. Currie*. Bloomington and Indianapolis, Indiana: Indiana University Press, pp. 279–297.

Ryan, Michael J., Anthony P. Russell, and Philip J. Currie, 2002, Asian small theropods in North America: evidence from Avimidae: *Alberta Palaeontological Society, Sixth Annual Symposium, "Fossils 2002," Abstract Volume*, January 26–27, 2002, Mount Royal College, Calgary, Alberta, p. 44.

Ryan, Michael J., Anthony P. Russell, David A. Eberth, and Philip J. Currie, 2001, The taphonomy of a *Centrosaurus* (Ornithischia: Ceratopsidae) bone bed from the Dinosaur Park Formation (upper Campanian), Alberta, Canada, with comments on cranial ontogeny: *Palaios*, 16, pp. 482–506.

Rybczynski, Natalia, and Matthew K. Vickaryous, 2001, Evidence of complex jaw movement in the Late Cretaceous ankylosaurid *Euoplocephalus tutus* (Dinosauria: Thyreophora), *in*: Kenneth Carpenter, editor, *The Armored Dinosaurs*. Bloomington and Indianapolis: Indiana University Press, pp. 299–317.

Sabath, K., 1991, Upper Cretaceous amniotic eggs from the Gobi Desert: *Paleontological Polonica*, 36, pp. 151–192.

Sahni, A., S. K. Tandon, A. Jolly, S. Baipai, A. Sood, and S. Srinivasan, 1994, Upper Cretaceous dinosaur eggs and nesting sites from the Deccan volcano-sedimentary province of peninsular India, *in*: Carpenter, Kenneth, Karl F. Hirsch, and John R. Horner, editors, *Dinosaur Eggs and Babies*. Cambridge: Cambridge University Press, pp. 204–226.

Salgado, Leonardo, and Jorge Orlando Calvo, 1997, Evolution of titanosaurid sauropods. II. The cranial evidence: *Ameghiniana*, 34 (1), pp. 33–48.

Salgado, Leonardo, and Rodolfo A. Coria, 1993, Un nuevo titanosaurino (Sauropoda–Titanosauridae) de la Fm. Allen (Campaniano–Maastrichtiano) de la Provincio de Río Negro, Argentina: *Ameghiniana*, 33, pp. 367–371.

Salgado, Leonardo, Rodolfo Aníbal Coria, and Jorge Orlando Calvo, 1997, Evolution of titanosaurid sauropods. I: Phylogenetic analysis based on the postcranial evidence: *Ameghiniana*, 34 (1), pp. 3–32.

Salgado, Leonardo, Rodolfo Aníbal Coria, and Luis M. Chiappe, 2001, Cráneos de embriones de titanosaurios (Sauropoda) del Cretácico Superior de Patagonia (Auca Mahuevo, Neuquén, Argentina): *Ameghiniana*, XVII Jornadas Argentinas de Paleontologia de Vertebrados, Resúmes, Esquel, 16–18 de mayo de 2001, p. 19R.

Samman, Tanya, G. Larry Powell, Philip J. Currie, and Len V. Hills, 2002a, Determining tooth replacement in the jaw of tyrannosaurid dinosaurs — biting off more than you can chew?: *Alberta Palaeontological Society, Sixth Annual Symposium, "Fossils 2002," Abstract Volume*, January 26–27, 2002, Mount Royal College, Calgary, Alberta, pp. 45–46.

_____, 2002b, *Journal of Vertebrate Paleontology*, 23 (Supplement to Number 3), Abstracts of Papers, Sixty-second Annual Meeting, pp. 101A–102A.

Sampson, Scott D., 2001, Speculations on the socioecology of ceratopsid dinosaurs (Ornithischia: Neoceratopsia), *in*: Darren Tanke and Kenneth Carpenter, editors, *Mesozoic Vertebrate Life: New Research Inspired by the Paleontology of Philip J. Currie*. Bloomington and Indianapolis, Indiana: Indiana University Press, pp. 263–276.

Sampson, Scott D., Matthew T. Carrano, and Catherine A. Forster, 2001, A bizarre predatory dinosaur from the Late Cretaceous of Madagascar: *Nature*, 409, pp. 504–506.

Sampson, Scott D., and Catherine A. Forster, 2001, Parallel evolution in hadrosaurid and ceratopsid dinosaurs: *Journal of Vertebrate Paleontology*, 21 (Supplement to Number 3), Abstracts of Papers, Sixty-first Annual Meeting, p. 96A.

Sampson, Scott D., Michal J. Ryan, and Darren H. Tanke, 1997, Craniofacial ontogeny in centrosaurine dinosaurs (Ornithischia: Ceratopsidae): taphonomic and behavioral phylogenetic implications: *Zoological Journal of the Linnean Society*, 121, pp. 293–337.

Sampson, Scott D., Lawrence M. Witmer, Catherine A. Forster, David W. Krause, M. P. O'Connor, Peter Dodson, and Florent Ravoavy, 1998, Predatory dinosaur remains from Madagascar: implications for the Cretaceous biogeography of Gondwana: *Science*, 280, pp. 1048–1051.

Sandberger, F., 1894, *Zanclodon* im obersten Keuper Unterfrankens: *Neus Jarbuch für Mineralogie, Geologie, und Paläontologie*, 1894, 1, pp. 203–204, Stuttgart.

Sander, P. Martin, and Nicole F. Klein, 2001a, Life history studies on sauropodomorph dinosaurs facilitated by controlled paleohistologic sampling of growth series: *Journal of Vertebrate Paleontology*, 21 (Supplement to Number 3), Abstracts of Papers, Sixty-first Annual Meeting, p. 96A.

_____, 2001b, Heterochrony in sauropodomorph dinosaur evolution as deduced from bone histology: *International Congress of Vertebrate Morphology, Abstracts*, p. 279.

Sanders, Frank, Kenneth Carpenter, and Lorrie McWhinney, 2002, Mechanics of stegosaur tails as weapons: a mathematical analysis: *Journal of Vertebrate Paleontology*, 23 (Supplement to Number 3), Abstracts of Papers, Sixty-second Annual Meeting, p. 102A.

Sanders, Frank, Kim Manley, and Kenneth Carpenter, 2001, Gastroliths from the Lower Cretaceous sauropod *Cedarosaurus weiskopfae, in*: Darren Tanke and Kenneth Carpenter, editors, *Mesozoic Vertebrate Life: New Research Inspired by the Paleontology of Philip J. Currie*. Bloomington and Indianapolis: Indiana University Press, pp. 166–180.

Sanders, H. L., 1968, Marine benthic diversity: A comparative study: *American Naturalist*, 102, pp. 243–282.

Sankey, Julia T., 2001a, Late Campanian southern dinosaurs, Aguja Formation, Big Bend, Texas: *Journal of Paleontology*, 75 (1), pp. 208–215.

_____, 2001b, Late Cretaceous theropod dinosaurs from new microvertebrate sites, Big Bend National Park, Texas: *Journal of Vertebrate Paleontology*, 21 (Supplement to Number 3), Abstracts of Papers, Sixty-first Annual Meeting, p. 96A.

_____, 2002, Theropod diversity in the latest Cretaceous (Maastrichtian) of North America: *Journal of Vertebrate Paleontology*, 23 (Supplement to Number 3), Abstracts of Papers, Sixty-second Annual Meeting, p. 103A.

Sankey, Julia T., Donald B. Brinkman, Merrilee Guenther, and Philip J. Currie, 2002, Small theropod and bird teeth from the Late Cretaceous (late Campanian) Judith River Group, Alberta: *Journal of Paleontology*, 76 (4), pp. 751–763.

Santa Luca, Albert P., 1980, The postcranial skeleton of *Heterodontosaurus tucki* (Reptilia, Ornithischia) from the Stormberg of South Africa: *Annals of the South African Museum*, 79 (7), pp. 159–211.

Santafé, José-Vte Llopis, M. Lourdes Casanovas, José Luis Sanz, and S. Calzada, 1982, *Geologia y Paleontologia (Dinosaurios) de las Capas rojas de Morella (Castellón, España)*. Diputación Provincial de Castellon y Diputación de Barcelona, 169 pages.

Santucci, Rodrigo Miloni, and Rinaldo Bertini, 2001a New titanosaurids from the Bauru Group, Continental Upper Cretaceous of southeastern Brazil: *Journal of Vertebrate Paleontology*, 21 (Supplement to Number 3), Abstracts of Papers, Sixty-first Annual Meeting, p. 96A.

_____, 2001b, Presence of probable basal Titanosauria, with pleurocoels in the caudal vertebrae, in the Bauru Basin, southeastern Brazil: *Ameghiniana*, XVII Jornadas Argentinas de Paleontologia de Vertebrados, Resúmes, Esquel, 16–18 de mayo de 2001, p. 19R.

Sanz, José Luis, 1983, A nodosaurid ankylosaur from the Lower Cretaceous of Salas de los Infantes (Province of Burgo, Spain): *Geobios*, 16, pp. 615–621.

Sanz, José Luis, A. D. Buscalion, M.-L. Casanovas, and J.-L. Santafe, 1987, Dinosaurios del Cretácico Inferior de Galve (Teruel, España): *Estudios geológicos, vol. extr. Galve-Tremp.* pp. 45–64.

Sanz, José Luis, A. D. Buscalion, B. Pérez Moreno, J. Moratalla, and S. Jiménez, 1990, Los dinosaurios de Castilla y León, *in*: E. Jiménez Fuentes, editor, *Vertebrados fósiles de Castilla y León*. Museo de Salamanca, pp. 47–57.

Sanz, José Luis, Luis M. Chiappe, Yolanda Fernández-Jalvo, Francisco Ortega, Begoña Sánchez-Chillón, Francisco J. Poyato-Ariza, and Bernardino P. Pérez-Moreno, 2001, An Early Cretaceous pellet: *Nature*, 409, pp. 998–999.

Sanz, José Luis, Jaime E. Powell, Hean Le Loeuff, Rubén Martinez, and Xabier Suberbiola, 1999, Sauropod remains from the Upper Cretaceous of Laño (northcentral Spain), Titanosaur phylogenetic relationships: *Est. Museo de Ciencias Naturales de Alava*, 14 (1), pp. 235–255.

Sarjeant, William A. S., 1967, Fossil footprints from the Middle Triassic of Nottinghamshire and Derbyshire: *Mercian Geologist*, 2 (3), pp. 327–341.

_____, 1970, Fossil footprints from the Middle Triassic of Nottinghamshire and the Middle Jurassic of Yorkshire: *Mercian Geology*, 3 (3), pp. 269–282.

_____, 1986, Footprints before the flood: incidents in the study of vertebrate footprints in 19th-century Britain, *in*: David D. Gillette, editor, *First International Symposium on Dinosaur Tracks and Traces, Abstracts of Program, New Mexico Museum of Natural History, Albuquerque, N.M.* 22–24 May 1986, p. 24.

Sarjeant, William A. S., Justin B. Delair, and Martin G. Lockley, 1998, The footprints of *Iguanodon*: a history and taxonomic study: *Ichnos*, 6, pp. 183–202.

Sauvage, H. E., 1907, Note sur l'Infralias Provenchérches-sur-Meuse: *Chaumont*, 3 (3), pp. 14–15.

Scheele, William E., 1954, *Prehistoric Animals: A Pictorial History of the First Five Hundred Million Years of Life*. Cleveland and New York: The World Publishing Company, 125 pages.

Scheetz, Rodney D., Brooks B. Britt, Donald L. Burge, Kenneth L. Stadtman, and James H. Madsen, Jr., 2001, New iguanodontian-grade ornithopod taxa from the Cedar Mountain Formation (Early Cretaceous) of Utah: *Journal of Vertebrate Paleontology*, 21 (Supplement to Number 3),

Bibliography

Abstracts of Papers, Sixty-first Annual Meeting, p. 97A.

Schmidt, H., 1969, *Stenopelix valdensis* H. v. Meyer, der kleine Dinosaurier des norddeutschen Wealden: *Paläontologische Zeitschrift*, 43 (3/4), pp. 194–198.

Schmitt, James G., and Mary E. Moran, 1982, Stratigraphy of the Cretaceous Wayan Formation, Caribou Mountains, southeastern Idaho thrust belt: *University of Wyoming Contributions to Geology*, 21, pp. 55–71.

Schmitt, Jim, and Mary H. Scweitzer, 2002, Paleoenvironmental controls on modes of extraordinary vertebrate fossil preservation, Upper Cretaceous Hell Creek Formation, northeast Montana: *Journal of Vertebrate Paleontology*, 23 (Supplement to Number 3), Abstracts of Papers, Sixty-second Annual Meeting, p. 104A.

Schudack, Michael E., 1989, Charophytenfloren aus dem unterkretazischen Vertebraten-Fundschichten bei Galve und Uña (Ostspanien): *Berliner geowissenschaftliche Abhandlungen (A)*, 106, pp. 409–443.

_____, 1993, Charophyten aus dem Kimmeridgium der Kohlengrube Guimarota (Portugal). Mit einer eingehenden Diskussion zur Datierung der Fundstelle: *Ibid.*, (E), 9, pp. 211–231.

_____, 2000, Geological setting and dating of the Guimarota beds, *in*: Thomas Martin and Bernard Krebs, editors, *Guimarota. A Jurassic Ecosystem*. Munich: Verlag Dr. Friedrich Pfeil, pp. 21–26.

Schudack, Michael E., C. E. Turner, and F. Petersen, 1998, Biostratigraphy, paleoecology and biogeography of charophytes and ostracodes from the Upper Jurassic Morrison Formation, Western Interior, USA, *in*: Kenneth Carpenter, Daniel J. Chure, and James I. Kirkland, editors, *The Upper Jurassic Morrison Formation: An Interdisciplinary Study, Modern Geology (Special Issue)*, 22 (1–2), pp. 379–414.

Schulp, Anne S., Samir S. Hanna, Axel F. Hartman, and John W. M. Jagt, 2000, A Late Cretaceous theropod caudal vertebra from the Sultanate of Oman: *Cretaceous Research*, 21, pp. 851–856.

Schwartz, Hilde I., and David D. Gillette, 1994, Geology and taphonomy of the *Coelophysis* Quarry, Upper Triassic Chinle Formation, Ghost Ranch, New Mexico: *Journal of Paleontology*, 68 (5), pp. 1118–1130.

Schweitzer, Mary Higby, J. A. Watt, R. Avci, L. Knapp, Luis M. Chiappe, Mark A. Norell, and M. Marshall, 1999, Beta-ketarin specific immunological reactivity in feather-like structures of the Cretaceous alvarezsaurid, *Shuvuuia deserti*: *Journal of Experimental Zoology (Molecular and Developmental Evolution)*, 285, pp. 146–157.

Schweitzer, Mary Higby, and Jim Schmitt, 2002, Mechanism of preservation of endogeneous molecular components in a *Tyrannosaurus rex* skeleton: *Journal of Vertebrate Paleontology*, 23 (Supplement to Number 3), Abstracts of Papers, Sixty-second Annual Meeting, p. 104A.

Scotese, C. R., and J. Golokna, 1993, Paleogeographic atlas: *PALEOMAP Report 90-0497*. Arlington, Texas: University of Texas at Arlington, Department of Geology.

Seebacher, Frank, 2001, A new method to calculate allometric length-mass relationships of dinosaurs: *Journal of Vertebrate Paleontology*, 21 (1), pp. 51–60.

_____, 2003, Dinosaur body temperatures: the occurrence of endothermy and ectothermy: *Paleobiology*, 29 (1), pp. 105–122.

Seebacher, Frank, G. C. Grigg, and L. A. Beard, 1999, Crocodiles as Dinosaurs: behavioural thermoregulation in very large ectotherms leads to high and stable body temperatures: *Journal of Experimental Biology*, 202, pp. 77–86.

_____, 2003, Dinosaur body temperatures: the occurrence of endothermy and ectothermy: *Paleobiology*, pp. 105–122.

Seeley, Harry Govier, 1881, On the reptile fauna of the Gosau Formation preserved in the Geological Museum on the University of Vienna: *Quarterly Journal of the Geological Society of London*, 37, pp. 619–707.

_____, 1887, On *Aristosuchus pusillus* (Owen), being further notes on the fossils descried by Sir R. Owen as *Poikilopleuron pusillus*, Owen: *Ibid.*, 43, pp. 221–228.

_____, 1888, On *Thecospondylus daviesi* (Seeley), with some remarks on the classification of the Dinosauria: *Ibid.*, 44, pp. 79–86.

Senter, Philip J., and John R. Hutchinson, 2001, New information on the skeleton of the theropod *Segisaurus halli*: *Journal of Vertebrate Paleontology*, 21 (Supplement to Number 3), Abstracts of Papers, Sixty-first Annual Meeting, p. 100A.

Seo, S. J., 1985, Lower Cretaceous geology and paleontology (Charophyta) of central Gyeongsang Basin, South Korea, Ph.D thesis, Kyungbuk National University, 177 pages (unpublished).

Sereno, Paul C., 1986, Phylogeny of the bird-hipped dinosaurs (order Ornithischia): *National Geographic Research*, 2, pp. 234–256.

_____, 1987, The ornithischian dinosaur Psittacosaurus *from the Lower Cretaceous of Asia and the relationships of the Ceratopsia*, Ph.D. dissertation, Columbia University, 554 pages.

_____, 1990a, Clades and grades in dinosaur systematics, *in*: Kenneth Carpenter and Currie, editors, *Dinosaur Systematics: Approaches and Perspectives*. Cambridge, New York and Melbourne: Cambridge University Press, pp. 203–210.

_____, 1990b, Psittacosauridae, *in*: David B. Weishampel, Peter Dodson, and Osmólska, editors, *The Dinosauria*. Berkeley and Los Angeles: University of California Press, pp. 579–592.

_____, 1991, *Lesothosaurus*, "fabrosaurids," and the early evolution of Ornithischia: *Journal of Vertebrate Paleontology*, 11 (2), pp. 168–197.

_____, 1993, The pectoral girdle and forelimb of the basal theropod *Herrerasaurus ischigualastensis*: *Journal of Vertebrate Paleontology* 13 (4), pp. 425–450.

_____, 1997, The origin and evolution of dinosaurs: *Annual Review of Earth and Planetary Sciences*, 25, pp. 435–490.

_____, 1998, A rationale for phylogenetic definitions, with application to the higher-level taxonomy of Dinosauria: *Neus Jahrbuch für Geologie und Paläontologie, Abhandlungen*, 1998 (189).

_____, 1999a, Alvarezsaurids (Dinosauria, Coelurosauria), birds or ornithomimosaurs?: *Journal of Vertebrate Paleontology*, 19 (Supplement to Number 3), Abstracts of Papers, Fifty-ninth Annual Meeting, p. 75A.

_____, 1999b, The evolution of dinosaurs: *Science*, 284, pp. 2137–2147.

_____, 2000, The fossil record, systematics and evolution of pachycephalosaurs and ceratopsians from Asia, *in*: M. J. Benton, M. A. Shishkin, D. M. Unwin and E. N. Kurochkin, editors, *The Age of Dinosaurs in Russia and Mongolia*. Cambridge: Cambridge University Press, pp. 480–516.

_____, 2001, Alvarezsauridae: birds or ornithomimisaurs?, *in*: Jacques Gauthier and I. F. Gall, editors, *New Prospectives on the origin and early evolution of birds: proceedings of the International Symposium in Honor of John H. Ostrom*. New Haven, Connecticut: Peabody Museum of Natural History, pp. 69–98.

Sereno, Paul C., and Andrea Beatriz Arcucci, 1994, Dinosaurian precursors from the Middle Triassic of Argentina: *Marasuchus lilloensis*, gen. nov.: *Journal of Vertebrate Paleontology*, 14, pp. 53–73.

Sereno, Paul C., Allison L. Beck, Didier B. Dutheil, Boubacar Gado, Hans C. E. Larsson, Gabrielle H. Lyon, Jonathan D. Marcot, Oliver W. M. Rauhut, Rudyard W. Sadleir, Christian A. Sidor, David D. Varricchio, Gregory P. Wilson, and Jeffrey A. Wilson, 1998, A long-snouted predatory dinosaur from Africa and the evolution of spinosaurids: *Science*, 282 (5392), pp. 1298–1302.

Sereno, Paul C., Allison L. Beck, Didier B. Dutheil, M. Iarochene, Hans C. E. Larsson, Gabrielle H. Lyon, Paul M. Magwene, Christian A. Sidor, David J. Varracchio, and Jeffrey A. Wilson, 1996, Predatory dinosaurs from the Sahara and Late Cretaceous faunal differentiation: *Science*, 272, pp. 996–990.

Sereno, Paul C., and Chao Shichin [Zhao Xijin], 1988, *Psittacosaurus xinjiangensis* (Ornithischia: Ceratopsia), a new psittacosaur from the Lower Cretaceous of Northwestern China: *Journal of Vertebrate Paleontology*, 8 (4), pp. 353–356.

Sereno, Paul C., Chao Shichin [Zhao Xijin], and Rao Chenggang, 1988, *Psittacosaurus meileyingensis* (Ornithischia: Ceratopsia), a new psittacosaur from the Lower Cretaceous of Northeastern China: *Journal of Vertebrate Paleontology*, 8 (4), pp. 366–377.

Sereno, Paul C., Jack Conrad, and Jeffrey A. Wilson, 2002, Abelisaurid theropods from Africa: phylogenetic and biogeographic implications: *Journal of Vertebrate Paleontology*, 23 (Supplement to Number 3), Abstracts of Papers, Sixty-second Annual Meeting, p. 106A.

Sereno, Paul C., Hans C. E. Larsson, Christain A. Sidor, and Boubé Gado, 2001, The giant crocodyliform *Sarcosuchus* from the Cretaceous of Africa: *Science*, 294, pp. 1516–1519.

Sereno, Paul C., and Fernando E. Novas, 1992, The complete skull and skeleton of an early dinosaur: *Science*, 258, pp. 1137–1140.

———, 1994, The skull and neck of the basal theropod *Herrerasaurus ischigualastensis*: *Joural of Vertebrate Paleontology*, 13 (4), pp. 451–476.

Sereno, Paul C., and Rupert Wild, 1992, *Procompsognathus*: theropod, "thecodont" or both?: *Journal of Vertebrate Paleontology*, 12 (4), pp. 435–458.

Sereno, Paul C., and Jeffrey A. Wilson, 2001, A sauropod tooth battery: structure and evolution: *Journal of Vertebrate Paleontology*, 21 (Supplement to Number 3), Abstracts of Papers, Sixty-first Annual Meeting, pp. 100A–101A.

Sereno, Paul C., Jeffrey A. Wilson, Hans C. E. Larsson, Didier B. Dutheil, and Hans-Dieter Sues, 1994, Early Cretaceous dinosaurs from the Sahara: *Science*, 266, pp. 267–271.

Sharov, A. G., 1970, Svoyeobraznaya reptilia iz nizhnego triasa Fergany: *Palaeontoloicheeski Zhurnal*, 1, pp. 127–130 (translation: An unusual reptile from the Lower Triassic of Fergana: *Paleontological Journal*, 1, pp. 112–116).

Shimada, K., 1997, Paleoecological relationships of the Late Cretaceous lamniform shark, *Cretoxyrhina mantelli* (Agassiz): *Journal of Paleontology*, 71, pp. 926–933.

Shubin, Neil H., Paul E. Olsen, and Hans-Dieter Sues, 1994, Early Jurassic small tetrapods from the McCoy Brook Formation of Nova Scotia, Canada, *in*: Nicholas C. Fraser and Hans-Dieter Sues, editors, *In the Shadow of the Dinosaurs. Early Mesozoic Tetrapods*. New York: University of Cambridge Press, pp. 244–250.

Shuler, E. W., 1917, Dinosaur tracks in the Glen Rose limestone, near Glen Rose, Texas: *American Journal of Science*, 4 (44), pp. 294–298.

Sigeti, G., 1979, Sedimentology and paleontology of the Upper Jurassic Unkpapa Sandstone and Morrison Formation, east flank of Black Hills, South Dakota. Master's Thesis, South Dakota School of Mines and Technology, Rapid City, South Dakota, 77 pages.

Signore, Marco, 2001*a*, Mantids and dinosaurs: learning to fly: *Journal of Vertebrate Paleontology*, 21 (Supplement to Number 3), Abstracts of Papers, Sixty-first Annual Meeting, p. 101A.

———, 2001*b*, Predatory strike in maniraptoran dinosaurs: *International Congress of Vertebrate Morphology, Abstracts*, p. 285.

———, 2003, Mantids and dinosaurs: learing to fly: *in*: David B. Norman and Paul Upchurch, editors, *SVPCA 50, Cambridge 2002, 11–13 September, Abstract Volume*, unpaginated.

Simmons, Lewis M., 2000, *Archaeoraptor* fossil trail: *National Geographic*, October, pp. 128–132.

Simon, E., and Jorge O. Calvo, 2002, Un primitivo titanosaurio (Sauropoda) del Chocón, Formación Candeleros (Cenomanian Temprano), Neuquén, Argentina: *Ameghiana*, 39 (4), Supplemento, p. 17R.

Simón, M. E., 2001, A giant sauropod from the Upper Cretaceous of El Chocón, Newquén, Argentina: *Ameghiniana*, XVII Jornadas Argentinas de Paleontologia de Vertebrados, Resúmes, Esquel, 16–18 de mayo de 2001, pp. 19R–20R.

Skoczykas, R., 1978, Physiology of the digestive tract, *in*: C. Gans and K. A. Gans, editors, *Biology of the Reptilia*, Volume 8: Chicago: University of Chicago Press, pp. 589–717.

Sloan, Christopher P., 2003, Just a salad, thanks: *National Geographic*, January, p. unpaginated.

Smith, David K., 1993, The type specimen of *Oviraptor philoceratops*, a theropod dinosaur from the Upper Cretaceous of Mongolia: *Neus Jahrbuch für Geologie und Paläontologie, Abhandlungen*, 186 (3), pp. 365–388.

Smith, Jennifer R., 1982, Dinosaurs in Virginia: evidence of two new genera?: *Lapidary Journal*, 36 (6), pp. 1110–1111.

Smith, Joshua B., 2002*a*, Dental morphology and variation in *Tyrannosaurus rex*: implications for taxonomy, systematics, and the identification of shed teeth: *Journal of Vertebrate Paleontology*, 23 (Supplement to Number 3), Abstracts of Papers, Sixty-second Annual Meeting, p. 109A.

———, 2002*b*, Dental morphology and variation in theropods: implications for the identification of shed teeth: *GSA Abstracts with Programs*, pp. 33–34.

Smith, Joshua B., Jerald D. Harris, Gomaa I. Omar, Peter Dodson, and You Hailu, 2001, Biostratigraphy and avian origins in northeastern China, *in*: J. Gauthier and L. F. Gall, editors, *New Perspectives on the Origin and Early Evolution of Birds: Proceedings of the International Symposium in Honor of John H. Ostrom*. New Haven: Peabody Museum of Natural History, Yale University, pp. 549–589.

Smith, Joshua B., Matthew C. Lamanna, Peter Dodson, Yousry Attia, and Kenneth J. Lacovara, 2001, Evidence of a new theropod from the Late Cretaceous of Egypt: *Journal of Vertebrate Paleontology*, 21 (Supplement to Number 3), Abstracts of Papers, Sixty-first Annual Meeting, p. 102A.

Smith, Joshua B. Matthew C. Lamanna, Kenneth J. Lacovara, Peter Dodson, Jennifer R. Smith, Jason C. Poole, Robert Giegengack and Yousry Attia, 2001, A giant sauropod dinosaur from an Upper Cretaceous Mangrove deposit in Egypt. *Science*, 292 (5522), pp. 1704–1706.

Snively, Eric, 2002, Neck musculature of *Tyrannosaurus rex*: *Alberta Palaeontological Society, Sixth Annual Symposium, "Fossils 2002," Abstract Volume*, January 26–27, 2002, Mount Royal College, Calgary, Alberta, p. 54.

Snively, Eric, and Anthony P. Russell, 2002*a*, The tyrannosaurid metatarsus: bone strain and inferred ligament function: *Senckenbergiana lethaea*, 82 (1), pp. 35–42.

———, 2002*b*, Kinematic model of tyran-nosaurid (Dinosauria: Theropoda) arctometatarsus function: *Journal of Morphology*, 255, pp. 215–227.

Southwell, Elizabeth H., Brent Breithaupt, Thomas Adams, Sam Drucker, and Mike Whitmore, 2002, Bone Cabin Quarry: myths, fables and untold tales: *Journal of Vertebrate Paleontology*, 23 (Supplement to Number 3), Abstracts of Papers, Sixty-second Annual Meeting, p. 110A.

Spencer, Matthew, 2002, Description and preliminary taphonomy of the partial skeletal remains of a juvenile diplodocid sauropod from the Jurassic Morrison Formation of Utah: *1001 GSA Southeastern and North-Central Section Meetings*, abstracts, p. A-96.

Spinar, Zdenek V., Philip J. Currie, and Jan Sovak, 1994, *The Great Dinosaurs: A Story of the Giant's Evolution*. New York: Longmeadow Press, 176 pages.

Starck, J. Matthias, and Anusuya Chinsamy, 2002, Bone Microstructure and developmental plasticity in birds and other dinosaurs: *Journal of Morphology*, 254, pp. 232–246.

Starkov, Alexei I., 2001, Specialization of teeth of *Tyrannosaurus rex* to the limited number of prey hunting: *Journal of Vertebrate Paleontology*, 21 (Supplement to Number 3), Abstracts of Papers, Sixty-first Annual Meeting, p. 104A.

Steel, Rodney, 1970, Saurischia, *in*, Oskar Kuhn, editor, *Handbuch der Palaeoherpetologie*, part 16. Stuttgart: Gustav Fischer Verlag, 87 pages.

Steeman, Mette Eistrup, 2001, The stance of *Iguanodon bernissartensis* comments on the forelimb: *Gaia*, 16, pp. 97–100.

Sternberg, Charles M., 1926, Dinosaur tracks from the Edmonton Formation of Alberta: *Canadian Field-Naturalist*, 44, Geological Series, 46, pp. 85–87.

———, 1932, Dinosaur tracks from Peace River, British Columbia: *Bulletin of the National Museum of Canada*, 68 (for 1930), pp. 59–85.

———, 1938, *Monoclonius* from southeastern Alberta compared with *Centrosaurus*: *Journal of Paleontology*, 12 (3), pp. 284–286.

———, 1953, A new hadrosaur from the Oldman Formation of Alberta, discussion of nomenclature: *Ibid.*, 128, pp. 275–286.

———, 1955, A juvenile hadrosaur from the Oldman formation of Alberta: *National Museum of Canada, Bulletin*, 136, pp. 120–122.

Stets, J., A. R. Ashraf, H. K. Erben, U. Hambach, K. Krumsiek, J. Thein, and P. Wurster, 1996, The Cretaceous–Tertiary boundary in the Nanxiong Basin (continental facies, southeast China), *in*: N. MacLeod and G. Keller, editors, *Cretaceous–Tertiary Extinctions: Biotic and Environmental Changes*. New York and London: W. W. Norton & Company, pp. 349–371.

Stevens, Kent A., 2002, DinoMorph: parametric modeling of skeletal structures: *Senckenbergiana lethaea*, 82 (1), pp. 23–34.

Stevens, Kent A., and J. Michael Parrish, 1999, Neck posture and feeding of two Jurassic sauropod dinosaurs: *Science*, 284, pp. 798–800.

_____, 2001, Biological implications of digital reconstructions of the whole body of sauropod dinosaurs: *Journal of Vertebrate Paleontology*, 21 (Supplement to Number 3), Abstracts of Papers, Sixty-first Annual Meeting, p. 104A.

_____, 2002, Mass-based biomechanical computations on sauropod dinosaurs: *Journal of Vertebrate Paleontology*, 23 (Supplement to Number 3), Abstracts of Papers, Sixty-second Annual Meeting, p. 111A.

Stevens, Kent A., and Eric D. Wells, 2001, Gracile versus robust cervical vertebral designs in sauropods: *Journal of Vertebrate Paleontology*, 21 (Supplement to Number 3), Abstracts of Papers, Sixty-first Annual Meeting, p. 104A.

Stidham, Thomas, 2002, Evolutionary and developmental origin of the extant bird tarsometatarsus from its theropod dinosaur ancestry: *Journal of Vertebrate Paleontology*, 23 (Supplement to Number 3), Abstracts of Papers, Sixty-second Annual Meeting, p. 111A.

Stokosa, Kathleen M., 2001, Enamel variation within the Theropoda and its biomechanical implications: *Journal of Vertebrate Paleontology*, 21 (Supplement to Number 3), Abstracts of Papers, Sixty-first Annual Meeting, p. 105A.

Stokstad, Erik, 2001*a*, Doubts raised about dinosaur heart: *Science*, 291, p. 811.

_____, 2001*b*, New dig at old trove yields giant sauropod: *Ibid.*, 292, pp. 1623–1625.

_____, 2001*c*, Dinosaur nostrils get a hole new look: *Ibid.*, 293, p. 779.

Storrs, Glenn W., and William J. Garcia, 2001, Preliminary analysis of a monospecific sauropod locality from Carbon County, Montana: *Journal of Vertebrate Paleontology*, 21 (Supplement to Number 3), Abstracts of Papers, Sixty-first Annual Meeting, p. 105A.

Straight, William H., Reese E. Barrick, W. Showers, and B. Genna, 2001, Late Cretaceous continental seasonality derived from Oxygen isotopes from *Albertosaurus* tooth enamel: *Journal of Vertebrate Paleontology*, 21 (Supplement to Number 3), Abstracts of Papers, Sixty-first Annual Meeting, p. 105A.

Strevell, C. N., 1932, *Dinosauropodes*. Salt Lake City, Utah, 16 pages.

Stromer, Ernst, 1915, Ergebnisse der Forschungsreisen Prof. E. Stromers in den Wüsten Ägyptens. II. Wirbeltierreste der Baharîje-Stufe (unterstes Cenoman). III. Das Original des Theropoden *Spinosaurus aegyptiacus* n. g. n. sp.: *Abhandlungen der Bayerischen Akademie der Wissenschaften*, 18 (3), pp. 1–32.

_____, 1932, Wirbeltier-Reste der Baharîje-Stufe, II: Sauropoda: *Ibid.*, 10, pp. 1–20.

Sues, Hans-Dieter, 1997, On *Chirostenotes*, a Late Cretaceous oviraptorosaur (Dinosauria: Theropoda) from Western North America: *Journal of Vertebrate Paleontology*, 17 (4), pp. 698–716.

Sues, Hans-Dieter, Eberhard Frey, David M. Martill, and Diane M. Scott, 2002, *Irri-*

tator challengeri, a spinosaurid (Dinosauria: Theropoda) from the Lower Cretaceous of Brazil: *Journal of Vertebrate Paleontology*, 22 (3), pp. 535–547.

Sues, Hans-Dieter, and Peter M. Galton, 1982, The systematic position of *Stenopelix valdensis* (Reptilia: Ornithischia) from the Wealden of north-western Germany: *Palaeontographica*, Abteilung A 178, pp. 183–190.

_____, 1987, Anatomy and classification of the North American Pachycephalosauria (Dinosauria: Ornithischia): *Ibid.*, Abteilung A 198, pp. 1–40.

Sues, Hans-Dieter, and David B. Norman, 1990, Hypsilophodontidae, *Tenontosaurus*, Dryosauridae, *in*: David B. Weishampel, Peter Dodson and Halszka Osmólska, editors, *The Dinosauria*. Berkeley and Los Angeles: University of California Press, pp. 498–509.

Sullivan, Robert M., 2000*a*, *Prenocephale edmontonensis* (Brown and Schlaikjer) new comb. and *P. brevis* new comb. (Dinosauria: Ornithischia: Pachycephalosauria) from the Upper Cretaceous of North America, *in*: Spencer G. Lucas and Andrew B. Heckert, editors, *Dinosaurs of New Mexico*. Albuquerque: New Mexico Museum of Natural History and Science, Bulletin 17, pp. 177–190.

_____, 2000*b*, *Stegoceras* revisited: *Journal of Vertebrate Paleontology*, 20 (Supplement to Number 3), Abstracts of Papers, Sixtieth Annual Meeting, p. 72A.

Sullivan, Robert M., Spencer G. Lucas, and Dennis Braman, 2002, Paleocene dinosaurs? A critique of the ages assigned to the upper Kirtland Formation, San Juan Basin, New Mexico: *Journal of Vertebrate Paleontology*, 23 (Supplement to Number 3), Abstracts of Papers, Sixty-second Annual Meeting, p. 112A.

Sun, A. L., and G. Cui, 1986, A brief introduction to the Lower Lufeng saurischian fauna (Lower Jurassic: Lufeng, Yunnan, P. R. China), *in*: Kevin Padian, editor, *The Beginning of the Age of Dinosaurs*. New York: Cambridge University Press, pp. 275–278.

Sundell, Craig, 2002, The real Jurassic Park: *Tate 2002: Wyoming in the Age of Dinosaurs: Creatures, Environments and Extinctions*, p. 25.

Sussman, M., 1964, *Growth and Development*. Upper Saddle River, New Jersey: Prentice-Hall.

Suzuki, Shigeru, Luis M. Chiappe, Gareth J. Dyke, Mahito Watabe, Rinchen Barsbold, and Khisigjaw Tsogtbaatar, 2002, A new specimen of *Shuvuuia deserti* Chiappe et al., 1998 from the Mongolian Late Cretaceous with a discussion of the relationships of Alvarezsaurids to other theropod dinosaurs: *Contributions to Science*, 494, pp. 1–8.

Swain, T., 1976, Angiosperm-reptile coevolution, *in*: A. d'A Bellairs and C. B. Cox, editors, *Morphology and Biology of Reptiles*. London: Academic Press, pp. 107–122.

Sweet, A. R., 2001, Plants, a yardstick for measuring the environmental consequences of

the Cretaceous–Tertiary boundary event: *Geoscience Canada*, 28 (3), pp. 127–138.

Swisher, C. C., III, Wang Xiaolin, Zhou Zhonghe, Wang Yuanqing, Jin Fan, Zhang Jiangyong, Xu Xing, Zhang Fucheng, and Wang Yuan, 2002, Further support for a Cretaceous age for the feathered-dinosaur beds of Liaoning, China: New $^{40}Ar/^{39}$ Ar dating of the Yixoan and Tuchengzi Formation: *Chinese Science Bulletin*, 47 (2), pp. 135–138.

Tagert, E., 1846, On markings in the Hastings sands near Hastings, supposed to be the footprints of birds: *Quarterly Journal of the Geological Society of London*, 2, p. 267.

Tait, J., and Barnum Brown, 1928, How the Ceratopsia carried and used their head: *Royal Society of Canada, Canada*, 22 (5), pp. 13–23.

Tallodi-Posmosanu, Erika, and E. Popa, 1997, Notes on Camptosaurid dinosaurs from the Lower Cretaceous bauxite, Cornet, Romania: *Nymphaea*, 23–25, pp. 35–44.

Tang Feng, Jin Xinsheng, Kang Ximin, and Zhang Guojun, 2001, *Omeisaurus maoianus*, a complete Sauropoda from Jingyan, Sichuan. Beijing: China Ocean Press, Research Works on Natural History of Zhejiang, 128 pages.

Tang Feng, Kang Xi-Min, Jin Xing-Sheng, Wei Feng, and Wu Wei-Tang, 2001, A new sauropod dinosaur of Cretaceous from Jiangshan, Zhejiang Province: *Vertebrata PalAsiatica*, 39 (4), pp. 272–281.

Tang, Feng, Z.-X. Lou, Luo, Z.-H. Zhou, H.-L. You, A. Georgi, Z.-L. Tang, and X.-Z. Wang, 2001, Biostratigraphy and palaeoenvironment of the dinosaur-bearing sediments in Lower Cretaceous of Mazongshan area, Gansu Province, China: *Cretaceous Research*, 22, pp. 115–129.

Tanimoto, Masahiro, 1999, The Early Cretaceous vertebrate fossils of Toba City, Mie Prefecture, southwest Japan, *in*: Wang Yuanqing and Deng Tao, editors, *Proceedings of the Seventh Annual Meeting of the Chinese Society of Vertebrate Paleontology*. Beijing: China Ocean Press, pp. 45–48.

Tanke, Darren H., and Michael K. Brett-Surman, 2001, Evidence of hatchling-and-nestling size hadrosaurs (Reptilia: Ornithischia) from Dinosaur Provincial Park (Dinosaur Park Formation: Campanian), Alberta, *in*: Darren Tanke and Kenneth Carpenter, editors, *Mesozoic Vertebrate Life: New Research Inspired by the Paleontology of Philip J. Currie*. Bloomington and Indianapolis, Indiana: Indiana University Press, pp. 206–218.

Tanke, Darren H., and Kenneth Carpenter, editors, 2001, *Mesozoic Vertebrate Life: New Research Inspired by the Paleontology of Philip J. Currie*. Bloomington and Indianapolis, Indiana: Indiana University Press, xviii, 542 pages.

Tanke, Darren H., and Philip J. Currie, 2000, Head-biting behavior in theropod dinosaurs: paleopathological evidence: *in* B. P. Pérez-Moreno, Thomas R. Holtz, Jr., José Luis Sanz, and José J. Moratalla, editors, Aspects of theropod paleobiology: *Gaia*, 15 (cover dated December 1998), pp. 167–184.

Tanke, Darren H., and Andrew Farke, 2002, Bone resorption, bone lesions, and extra fenestrae in ceratopsid dinosaurs: *Journal of Vertebrate Paleontology*, 23 (Supplement to Number 3), Abstracts of Papers, Sixty-second Annual Meeting, p. 133A.

Taquet, Philippe, 1976, Géologie et Paléontologie du Gisement de Gadoufaoua (Aptien du Niger): Cahiers de Paléontologie. Paris: *Editions du Centre National de la Recherche Scientifique*, pp. 1–191.

_____, 1984, Une curieuse spécialisation du crâne de certainss dinosauriens carnivores du Crétacé le meseau long et étroit des Spinosauridés: *Comptes Rendus des Séances de l'Academie des Sciences*, 299 II (5), pp. 217–222. Taquet, Philippe, and Dale A. Russell, 1998, New data on spinosaurid dinosaurs from the Early Cretaceous of the Sahara: *Comptes Rendus des Séances de l'Académie des Sciences*, 327, pp. 347–353.

Taquet, Philippe, and Samuel Paul Welles, 1977, Redescription du cráne de dinosaure theropode de Dives (Normandie): *Annales de Paléontologie (Vertébrés)*, 63 (2), pp. 191–206.

Tarsitano, S., 1981, Pelvic and hindlimb musculature of archosaurian reptiles. Ph.D. dissertation, City University of New York.

_____, 1983, Stance and gait in theropod dinosaurs: *Acta Palaeontologica Polonica*, 28, pp. 251–264.

Tereschenko, V. S., 2001, Sexual dimorphism in the postcranial skeleton of protoceratopsids (Neoceratopsia, Protoceratopsidae) from Mongolia: *Paleontological Journal*, 35 (4), pp. 415–425.

Therrien, Francois, and David E. Fastovsky, 2001, Paleoenvironments of early theropods, Chinle Formation (Late Triassic), Petrified Forest National Park, Arizona: *Palaios*, 15, pp. 194–211.

Thulborn, Richard A., 1973, Teeth of ornithischian dinosaurs from the Upper Jurassic of Portugal with description of the hypsilophodontid (*Phyllodon henkeli* gen. et sp. nov) from the Guimarota Lignite: *Memoria Servicos Geologicos de Portugal (new series)*, 22, pp. 89–134.

_____, 1981, Estimated speed of a giant bipedal dinosaur: *Nature*, 292, p. 273.

_____, 1982, Speeds and gaits of dinosaurs: *Palaeogeography, Palaeoclimatology, Palaeoecology*, 38, pp. 227–256.

_____, 1984, Preferred gaits of bipedal dinosaurs: *Alcheringa*, 8, pp. 243–252.

_____, 1990, *Dinosaur Tracks*. London and New York: Chapman and Hall, xvii, 410 pages.

_____, 1992, Taxonomic characters of *Fabrosaurus australis*, an ornithischian dinosaur from the Lower Jurassic of Southern Africa: *Geobios*, 25, pp. 283–292.

Thulborn, Richard A., and Mary Wade, 1984, Dinosaur trackways in the Winton Formation (mid–Cretaceous) of Queensland: *Memoirs of the Queensland Museum*, 21 (2a), pp. 413–517.

Tidwell, Virginia, Preliminary report on the megafossil flora of the Upper Jurassic Morrison Formation: *Hunteria*, 2 (8), pp. 1–11.

Tidwell, Virginia, and Kenneth Carpenter, 2002, Bridging the Atlantic: new correlations of Early Cretaceous Titanosauriformes (Sauropoda) from England and North America: *Journal of Vertebrate Paleontology*, 23 (Supplement to Number 3), Abstracts of Papers, Sixty-second Annual Meeting, p. 114A.

Tidwell, Virginia, Kenneth Carpenter, and William Brooks, 1999, New sauropod from the Lower Cretaceous of Utah, USA: *Oryctos*, 2, pp. 21–37.

Tidwell, Virginia, Kenneth Carpenter, and Susanne Meyer, 2001, New titanosauriform (Sauropoda) from the Poison Strip Member of the Cedar Mountain Formation (Lower Cretaceous), Utah, *in*; Darren Tanke and Kenneth Carpenter, editors, 2001, *Mesozoic Vertebrate Life: New Research Inspired by the Paleontology of Philip J. Currie*. Bloomington and Indianapolis, Indiana: Indiana University Press, pp. 139–165.

Tischer, G., 1966, El delta wealdico de las montañas ibericas occidentales y sus enlaces tectónicos: *Notasy Communicaciones*, 81, pp. 57–78.

Titus, Alan L., David D. Gillette, and Barry L. Albright, 2001, Significance of an articulated lambeosaurine hadrosaur from the Kaiparowits Formation (Upper Cretaceous), southern Utah: *Journal of Vertebrate Paleontology*, 21 (Supplement to Number 3), Abstracts of Papers, Sixty-first Annual Meeting, p. 108A.

Tokaryk, Tim T., 1997, A rex with a new home: *Geology Today*, September-October, pp. 190–193.

_____, 2001, Progress report: Saskatchewan *T. rex* skeleton: *Canadian Paleobiology*, Fall, 2001, pp. 13–16.

_____, 2002, A humerus from a juvenile *Triceratops* sp. (Ornithischia; Ceratopsidae) from the Frenchman Formation (Late Maastrichtian), Saskatchewan: *Summery of Investigations 2002, Saskatchewan Geological Survey, Saskatchewan Industry and Resources, Miscellaneous Reports 2002-4.1*, 1, pp. 151–154.

Tomida, Yukimitsu, Yoshihiro Katsura, and Yoshihiro Tsumura, 2001, A new titanosauroid sauropod the Early Cretaceous of Japan: *Journal of Vertebrate Paleontology*, 21 (Supplement to Number 3), Abstracts of Papers, Sixty-first Annual Meeting, p. 108A.

Torres, Sandra R., Leonardo S. Avilla, Érika A. L. Abrantes, and Lílian P. Bergqvist, 2002, Dinosaur osteoderms from the Adamantina Formation, Upper Cretaceous of São Paulo State, Brazil: *Anais da Academia Brasileira de Ciencias*, 74 (2), Summary of Communications, pp. 366–367.

Trotta, Marcelo F. F., 2002, Morphological variation among the appendicular bones of the Titanosauridae (Dinosauria: Sauropoda) from the Bauru Basin (Upper Cretaceous) of Periópolis (MG), Brazil: *Anais da Academia Brasileira de Ciencias*, 74 (2), Summary of Communications, p. 366.

Tsuihiji, Takanobu, 2001, Hologies of cervical axial muscles in diapsids as a basis for muscular reconstruction of the neck in extinct dinosaurs: *Journal of Vertebrate Paleontology*, 21 (Supplement to Number 3), Abstracts of Papers, Sixty-first Annual Meeting, p. 109A.

_____, 2002, A preliminary assessment of the evolution of the cervical musculature in Diapsida with an emphasis on Dinosauria: *Ibid.*, 23 (Supplement to Number 3), Abstracts of Papers, Sixty-second Annual Meeting, pp. 115A–116A.

Tumanova, Tat'yana A., 1981, [On the morphological peculiarity of ankylosaurs]: *Paleontologicheskii Zhurnal*, 1977-3, pp. 92–100.

_____, 1983, The first ankylosaurs from the Lower Cretaceous of Mongolia: *Transactions of the Joint Soviet-Mongolian Palaeontological Expedition*, 24, pp. 110–118.

_____, 1985, Cranial morphology of the ankylosaur *Shamosaurus scutatus* from the Lower Cretaceous of Mongolia, *in*: *Actes du Colloque "Les Dinosaures de la Chine á la France."* Muséum d'Histoire Naturelle, Tolouse, 2–6, pp. 73–79.

_____, 1987, [The armoured dinosaurs of Mongolia]: *Trudy Sovmetsko-Mongol'skoi Paleontologicheskoi Ekspeditsii*, 32, pp. 1–80.

_____, 2000, Armoured dinosaurs from the Cretaceous of Mongolia, *in*: M. J. Benton, M. A. Shishkin, D. M. Unwin and E. N. Kurochkin, editors, *The Age of Dinosaurs in Russia and Mongolia*. Cambridge: Cambridge University Press, pp. 317–332.

Turner, C. E., and F. Peterson, 1999, Biostratigraphy of dinosaurs in the Upper Jurassic Morrison Formation of the Western Interior, U.S.A., *in*: David D. Gillette, editor, *Vertebrate Paleontology in Utah*, Utah Geological Survey, Miscellaneous Publication, 99-1, pp. 76–114.

Turner, J. S., 1987, The cardiovascular control of heat exchange: consequences for body size: *American Zoologist*, 27, pp. 69–79.

Tykoski, Ronald S., 1998, The osteology of *Syntarsus kayentakatae* and its implications for ceratosaurid phylogeny, M.S. thesis, University of Texas, Austin.

Upchurch, Paul, 1994, Sauropod phylogeny and palaeoecology: *Gaia: Revista de Geociencias, Museuo Nacional de Historia Natural*, University of Lisbon, 10, pp. 249–260.

_____, 1995, The evolutionary history of sauropod dinosaurs: *Philosophical Transactions of the Royal Society of London*, Series B 349, pp. 365–390.

_____, 1998, The phylogenetic relationships of sauropod dinosaurs: *Zoological Journal of the Linnean Society of London*, 124, pp. 43–103.

_____, 1999, The phylogenetic relationships of the Nemegtosauridae (Saurischia, Sauropoda): *Journal of Vertebrate Paleontology*, 19 (1), pp. 106–125.

Upchurch, Paul, and Paul M. Barrett, 2001, A phylogenetic perspective on sauropod diversity: *Journal of Vertebrate Paleontology*, 21 (Supplement to Number 3), Abstracts of Papers, Sixty-first Annual Meeting, p. 100A.

Upchurch, Paul, and Craig A. Hunn, 2003, An analysis of dinosaur biogeography: *in*:

Bibliography

David B. Norman and Paul Upchurch, editors, *SVPCA 50, Cambridge 2002, 11–13 September, Abstract Volume*, unpaginated.

Upchurch, Paul, Craig A. Hunn, and David B. Norman, 2001, An analysis of dinosaurian biogeography: evidence for the existence of vicariance and dispersal patterns caused by geological events: *Proceedings of the Royal Society of London*, 269, pp. 613–621.

Upchurch, Paul, and John Martin, 2002, The Rutland *Cetiosaurus*: the anatomy and relationships of the Middle Jurassic British sauropod dinosaur: *Palaeontology*, 45 (6), pp. 1049–1074.

_____, in press, The anatomy and taxonomy of *Cetiosaurus* (Saurischia, Sauropoda) from the Middle Jurassic of England: *Journal of Vertebrate Paleontology*.

Valais, S. de, and Sebastian Apesteguía, 2001, Dientes asignables a *Giganotosaurus* (Carcharodontosauria, Theropoda) provenientens de "La Buitera," Formación Candeleros, provincia de Río Negro: *Ameghiniana*, XVII Jornadas Argentinas de Paleontologia de Vertebrados, Resúmes, Esquel, 16–18 de mayo de 2001, pp. 6R–7R.

Van Itterbeeck, Jimmy, Pierre Bultynck, Guo Wen Li, and Noel Vandenberghe, 2001, Stratigraphy, sedimentology and palaeoecology of the dinosaur-bearing Cretaceous strata at Dashuiguo (Inner Mongolia, Peoplés Republic China): *Bulletin de l'Institut Royal des Sciences Naturelle des Belgique, Sciences de la Terre*, 71, supp., pp. 51–70.

Van Leer, Amy Harwell, John Rubin, and Terry Jones, 2002, Abdominal Visceral anatomy in theropod dinosaurs: *Journal of Vertebrate Paleontology*, 23 (Supplement to Number 3), Abstracts of Papers, Sixty-second Annual Meeting, p. 116A.

Van Valkenburgh, Blaire, and Ralph E. Molnar, 2002, Dinosaurian and mammalian predators compared: *Paleobiology*, 28 (4), pp. 527–543.

Vargas, A., 2002, La extrema reduccion del radio y ulna en la evolución de *Carnotaurus sastrei*: posible pérdida de función de los genes Hoxall y Hoxdll: *Ameghiana*, 39 (4), Supplemento, p. 17R.

Varrichio, David J., 1997, Growth and embryology, *in*: Philip J. Currie and Kevin Padian, editors, *Encyclopedia of Dinosaurs*. San Diego: Academic Press, pp. 282–288.

_____, 2001*a*, Gut contents from a Cretaceous tyrannosaurid: implications for theropod dinosaur digestive tracts: *Journal of Paleontology*, 75 (2), pp. 401–406.

_____, 2001*b*, "Beautiful wounding tooth": ontogeny and osteology in the theropod *Troodon formosus*: *Journal of Vertebrate Paleontology*, 21 (Supplement to Number 3), Abstracts of Papers, Sixty-first Annual Meeting, p. 110A.

_____, 2001*c*, Late Cretaceous oviraptorosaur (Theropoda) dinosaurs from Montana: *in*: Darren Tanke and Kenneth Carpenter, editors, *Mesozoic Vertebrate Life: New Research Inspired by the Paleontology of Philip J. Currie*. Bloomington and Indianapolis, Indiana: Indiana University Press, pp. 42–57.

Varricchio, David J., and John R. Horner, 1993, Hadrosaurid and lambeosaurid bone beds from the Upper Cretaceous Two Medicine Formation of Montana: taphonomic and biologic implications: *Canadian Journal of Earth Sciences*, 30, pp. 997–1006.

Varricchio, David J., John R. Horner, and Frankie D. Jackson, 2002, Embryos and eggs for the Cretaceous theropod dinosaur *Troodon formosus*: *Journal of Vertebrate Paleontology*, 22 (3), pp. 564–576.

Varricchio, David J., Frankie Jackson, J. J. Borkowski, and John R. Horner, 1997, Nest and egg clutches of the dinosaur *Troodon formosus* and the evolution of avian reproductive traits: *Nature*, 385, pp. 247–250.

Vezina, A. F., 1985, Empirical relationships between predator and prey size among terrestrial vertebrate predators: *Oecologia*, 67, pp. 555–565.

Vianey-Liaud, M., and J. Y. Crochet, 1993, Dinosaur eggshells from the Late Cretaceous of Languedoc (southern France): *Revue de Paleobiologie, Geneve*, 7, pp. 237–249.

Vianey-Liaud, M., Karl Hirsch, Ashok Sahni, and Bernard Sige, 1997, Late Cretaceous Peruvian Eggshells and their relationships with Laurasian and eastern Gondwanian material: *Geobios*, 30 (1), pp. 75–90.

Vickaryous, Matthew K., and Allan P. Russell, 2001, The osseous secondary palate of ankylosaurs: variation in configurations of the nasal pathways: *International Congress of Vertebrate Morphology, Abstracts*, p. 295.

_____, 2003, A redescription of the skull of *Euoplocephalus tutus* (Archosauria: Ornithischia): a foundation for comparative and systematic studies of ankylosaurian dinosaurs: *Zoological Journal of the Linnean Society*, 137, pp. 157–186.

Vickaryous, Matthew K., Allan P. Russell, and Philip J. Currie, 2001, Cranial ornamentation of ankylosaurs (Ornithischia: Thyreophora): reappraisal of developmental hypotheses, *in*: Kenneth Carpenter, editor, *The Armored Dinosaurs*. Bloomington and Indianapolis: Indiana University Press, pp. 318–340.

Vickaryous, Matthew K., Allan P. Russell, Philip J. Currie, and Zhao Xin Jin, 2001, A new ankylosaurid (Dinosauria: Ankylosauria) from the Lower Cretaceous of China, with comments on ankylosaurian relationships: *Canadian Journal of Earth Sciences*, 38 (12), pp. 1767–1780.

Vickers-Rich, Patricia, Thomas H. Rich, D. R. Lanus, L. S. V. Rich, and R. Vacca, 1999, "Big Tooth" from the Early Cretaceous of Chubut Province, Patagonia — a possible carcharodontosaurid: *National Science Museum Monographs*, 15, pp. 85–88.

Vidarte, Fuentes C., and Meijide M. Calvo, 1999, Presencia de un grupo de juveniles de *Hypsilophodon* cf. *foxii* (Dinosauria, Ornithopoda) en el Weald de Salas de los Infantes (Burgos, España): *Actas de las I Journadas Internacionales Sobre Paleontología de Dinosaurios y su Entorno (Proceedings of the 1st International Symposium about Paleontology of Dinosaurs and their Environment*, Salas de los Infantes (Bur-

gos, España), Septiembre de 1999, pp. 339–348.

Vidarte, Fuentes C., Meijide M. Calvo, L. A. Izquiderdo, D. Montero, G. Pérez, F. Torcida, V. Urién, F. Meijide Fuentes, and M. Meijide Fuentes, 1999, Restos fosiles de *Baryonyx* (Dinosauria, Theropoda) en el Cretácico Inferior de Salas de Los Infantes (Burgos, España): *Actas de las I Journadas Internacionales Sobre Paleontología de Dinosaurios y su Entorno (Proceedings of the 1st International Symposium about Paleontology of Dinosaurs and their Environment*, Salas de los Infantes (Burgos, España), Septiembre de 1999, pp. 349–359.

Wagner, Günter P., and Jacques A. Gauthier, 1999, 1,2,3 = 2,3,4: a solution to the problem of the homology of the digits of the avian hand: *Proceedings of the National Academy of Sciences*, 96, pp. 5111–5116.

Wagner, Jonathan R., and Thomas M. Lehman, 2001, A new species of *Kritosaurus* from the Cretaceous of Big Bend National Park, Brewster County, Texas: *Journal of Vertebrate Paleontology*, 21 (Supplement to Number 3), Abstracts of Papers, Sixty-first Annual Meeting, pp. 110A–111A.

Walkden, G. M., and N. C. Fraser, 1993, Late Triassic fissure sediment and vertebrate faunas: environmental change and faunal succession at the Cromhall SSSI, southwest Britain locality. PhD thesis, University College London, 385 pages.

Walker, Alick D., 1964, Triassic reptiles from the Elgin areas: *Ornithosuchus* and the origin of carnosaurs: *Philosophical Transactions of the Royal Society of London*, 248, pp. 53–134.

_____, 1977, Evolution of the pelvis in birds and dinosaurs, *in*: S. M. Andrews, R. S. Miles, and Walker, editors, *Problem in Vertebrate Evolution*. New York: Acedemic Press, pp. 319–357.

_____, 1985, The braincase of *Archaeopteryx*, *in*: Max K. Hecht, John H. Ostrom, G. Viohl and Peter Wellnhoffer, editors, *The Beginnings of Birds*. Eichstätt, Germany: Freunde des Jura-Museums, pp. 91–97.

Walker, W. F., Jr., and K. F. Liem, 1994, *Functional Anatomy of the Vertebrates: An Evolutionary Perspective*. Fort Worth: Saunders Colleges Publishing, 788 pages.

Wall, William P., and Peter M. Galton, 1979, Notes on pachycephalosaurian dinosaurs (Reptilia: Ornithischia) from North America, with comments on their status as ornithopods: *Canadian Journal of Earth Sciences*, 16, pp. 1176–1186.

Walters, Robert, Ralph E. Chapman, and Rebecca A. Snyder, 2001, Fleshing-out *Tricertops*: adding muscle and skin to the virtual *Triceratops*: *Journal of Vertebrate Paleontology*, 21 (Supplement to Number 3), Abstracts of Papers, Sixty-first Annual Meeting, p. 111A.

Wang Xiaohong, Pang Qiqing, Yin Chungu, Wang Yimin, Cheng Zhengwu, and Zhang Yun, 1999, The chemical element characteristics of dinosaur bones from the Late Cretaceous of Tianzhen, Shanxi Province, *in*: Wang Yuanqing and Deng Tao, editors, *Proceedings of the Seventh An-*

nual Meeting of the Chinese Society of Vertebrate Paleontology. Beijing: China Ocean Press, pp. 97–103.

Wang et al., 2000: Vertebrata PalAsiatica, 38, p. 92.

Wang Ying, 2002, Fossil supports dinosaur-into-bird theory: Geological Bulletin of China.

Wang Xiaolin, and Xu Xing, 2001a, A new genus and species of iguanodont from the Yixian Formation in Liaoxi: Yang's Jinzhou dragon [Jinzhousaurus yangi]: Chinese Science Bulletin 46 (5), pp. 419–423.

———, 2001b, A new iguanodontid (Jinzhousaurus yangi gen. et sp. nov.) from the Yixian Formation of western Liaoning, China: Ibid., 46 (19), pp. 1669–1672.

Warrener, P. 1983, An archosaurian fauna from a Welsh locality, Ph.D. Thesis, Department of Zoology, University College London, 226 pages (unpublished).

Watabe, Mahito, David B. Weishampel, Rinchen Barsbold, Khisigjaw Tsogtbataar, and S. Suzuki, 2000, New nearly complete skeleton of the bird-like theropod, Avimimus, from the Upper Cretaceous of the Gobi Desert, Mongolia: Journal of Vertebrate Paleontology, 20 (Supplement to Number 3), Abstracts of Papers, Sixtieth Annual Meeting, p. 77A.

Watson, Doug, 2002–03, Reconstructing the skull of a new species of chasmosaur: Prehistoric Times, 57, pp. 50–51.

Weaver, J. C., 1983, The improbable endotherm: the energies of the sauropod dinosaur Brachiosaurus: Paleobiology, 9, pp. 173–182.

Webster, Donovan, 1996, Dinosaurs of the Gobi: National Geographic, 190, pp. 70–89.

Wedel, Mathew J., 2001, The evolution of vertebral pneumaticity in the Sauropoda: Journal of Vertebrate Paleontology, 21 (Supplement to Number 3), Abstracts of Papers, Sixty-first Annual Meeting, p. 111A.

———, 2002, An unusually large cervical rib of Apatosaurus from the Morrison Formation of Oklahoma, with comments on the cervical musculature of sauropods: 2002 California Paleontology Conference, Abstracts, Department of Geological Sciences, University of California, Santa Barbara, California, April 12–13, 2002, p. 8.

Wedel, Mathew J., Matthew F. Bonnan, and R. K. Sanders, 2002, Two previously unreported sauropod dinosaurs from the Upper Jurassic Morrison Formation of Oklahoma: Journal of Vertebrate Paleontology, 23 (Supplement to Number 3), Abstracts of Papers, Sixty-second Annual Meeting, p. 118A.

Wedel, Mathew J., Richard L. Cifelli, and R. Kent Sanders, 2000a, Sauroposeiden proteles, a new sauropod from the early Cretaceous of Oklahoma: Journal of Vertebrate Paleontology, 20 (1), pp. 109–114.

———, 2000b, Osteology, paleobiology, and relationships of the sauropod dinosaur Sauroposeiden: Acta Palaeontologica Polonica, 45 (4), pp. 343–388.

Wedel, Mathew J., and R. Kent Sanders, 2002, Osteological correlates of cervical muscu-

lature in Aves and Sauropoda (Dinosauria: Saurischia), with comments on the cervical ribs of Apatosaurus: PaleoBios, 22 (3), pp. 1–6.

Wei Mingrui, Hu Shusheng, and Zhang Yan, 2001, The diet of prosauropods and sauropods from Lufeng, Yunnan Province, China: in: Deng Tao and Wang Yuan, editors, Proceedings of the Eighth Annual Meeting of the Chinese Society of Vertebrate Paleontology. Beijing: China Ocean Press, pp. 21–27.

Weishampel, David B., 1984, Evolution of jaw mechanisms in ornithopod dinosaurs: Advances in Anatomy, Embryology, and Cell Biology, 87, pp. 1–110.

———, 1990, Dinosaurian distribution, in: David B. Weishampel, Peter Dodson and Halszka Osmólska, editors, The Dinosauria. Berkeley and Los Angeles: University of California Press, pp. 63–139.

Weishampel, David B., and R. E. Heinrich, 1992, Systematics of Hypsilophodontidae and basal Iguanodontia (Dinosauria: Ornithopoda), Historical Biology, 6, pp. 159–184.

Weishampel, David B., and John R. Horner, 1990, Hadrosauridae, in: David B. Weishampel, Peter Dodson, and Halszka Osmólska, editors, The Dinosauria. Berkeley and Los Angeles: University of California Press, pp. 534–561.

Weishampel, David B., Mason B. Meers, William A. Akersten, and Allen D. McCrady, 2002, New Early Cretaceous dinosaur remains, including possible ceratopsians, from the Wayan Formation of eastern Idaho, in: W. A. Akersten, M. E. Thompson, D. J. Meldrum, R. A. Rapp, and H. G. McDonald, editors, And Whereas … Papers on the Vertebrate Paleontology Honoring John A. White, Volume 2. Idaho Museum of Natural History Occasional Paper, 37, pp. 5–17.

Weishampel, David B., David B. Norman, and Dan Grigorescu, 1993, Telmatosaurus transsylvanicus from the Late Cretaceous of Romania: the most basal hadrosaurid dinosaur: Palaeontology, 36, pp. 361–385.

Weishampel, David B., and Lawrence M. Witmer, 1990a, Lesothosaurus, Pisanosaurus, and Technosaurus, in: Weishampel, Peter Dodson, and Halszka Osmólska, editors, The Dinosauria. Berkeley and Los Angeles: University of California Press, pp. 416–426.

———, 1990b, Heterodontosauridae, Ibid., pp. 486–497.

Welles, Samuel P., 1971, Dinosaur footprints from the Kayenta Formation of northern Arizona: Plateau, 44 (1), pp. 27–38.

———, 1984, Dilophosaurus wetherilli (Dinosauria, Theropoda)—osteology and comparisons: Palaeontographica, Abteilung A, 185, pp. 88–180.

Wellnhofer, Peter, 1992, A new specimen of Archaeopteryx from the Solnhofen Limestone, in: Kenneth E. Campbell, editor, Papers in Avian Paleontology. Los Angeles: Natural History Museum of Los Angeles County, pp. 3–23.

———, 1993, Prosauropod dinosaurs from the Feuerletten (Middle Norian) of Ellingen near Weissenburg in Bavaria: Revisions in

Paleobiology, special volume 7, pp. 263–271, Geneva.

Westgate, James, R. B. Brown, Diane Cope, and Jeffrey Pittman, 2002, Discovery of dinosaur remains in coastal deposits near Ojinaga, Mexico: Journal of Vertebrate Paleontology, 23 (Supplement to Number 3), Abstracts of Papers, Sixty-second Annual Meeting, pp. 118A–119A.

Westgate, James, Jeffrey Pittman, R. B. Brown, and Dana Cope, 2002, Continued excavation on the first dinosaur community from Chihuana, Mexico: Journal of Vertebrate Paleontology, 23 (Supplement to Number 3), Abstracts of Papers, Sixty-second Annual Meeting, p. 118A.

Wharton, Deborah S., The evolution of the avian brain: Journal of Vertebrate Paleontology, 21 (Supplement to Number 3), Abstracts of Papers, Sixty-first Annual Meeting, p. 113A.

White, Diane, and Martin G. Lockley, 2002, Probable dromaeosaur tracks and other dinosaur footprints from the Cedar Mountain Formation (Lower Cretaceous) Utah: Journal of Vertebrate Paleontology, 23 (Supplement to Number 3), Abstracts of Papers, Sixty-second Annual Meeting, p. 119A.

Whyte, M. A., and Romano, M. 1994, Probable sauropod footprints from the Middle Jurassic of Yorkshire, England: Gaia: Revista de Geociencias, Museu Nacional de Historia Natural, 10, pp. 15–26.

Wieland, G. R., 1911, Notes on the armored Dinosauria: American Journal of Science 4, pp. 112–124.

Wilhite, Ray, 2002, The tales that tails can tell: chevron function in North American diplodocid sauropods: Tate 2002, Wyoming in the Age of Dinosaurs: Creatures, Environments and Extinctions, p. 29. Williamson, Thomas E., and Thomas D. Carr, 2001, Dispersal of pachycephalosaurs and tyrannosauroids between Asia and North America: Journal of Vertebrate Paleontology, 21 (Supplement to Number 3), Abstracts of Papers, Sixty-first Annual Meeting, p. 114A.

———, 2002, A juvenile pachycephalosaur (Dinosauria: Pachycephalosauridae) from the Fruitland Formation, New Mexico: New Mexico Geology, 24 (2), pp. 67–68.

———, 2003, A new genus of derived pachycephalosaurian from western North America: Journal of Vertebrate Paleontology, 22 (4), pp. 799–801.

Wilson, Jeffrey A., 1997, A reevaluation of Mongolian sauropods: implications for sauropod biogeography: Journal of Vertebrate Paleontology, 17 (Supplement to Number 3), Abstracts of Papers, Fifty-seventh Annual Meeting, pp. 84A–85A.

———, 1999a, master's thesis, University of Chicago, (unpublished).

———, 1999b, A nomenclature for vertebral laminae in sauropods and other saurischian dinosaurs: Journal of Vertebrate Paleontology, 19 (4), pp. 639–653.

———, 2001, Anatomy of Jobaria tiguidensis and the relationsips of Neosauropoda: Journal of Vertebrate Paleontology, 21 (Supplement to Number 3), Abstracts of Papers, Sixty-first Annual Meeting, p. 115A.

Bibliography

_____, 2002a, Evolution of herbivory, neck elongation, and locomotion in sauropod dinosaurs: *1001 GSA Southeastern and North-Central Section Meetings*, abstracts, p. A-13.

_____, 2002b, A revision of the genus *Titanosaurus* (Dinosauria: Sauropoda) and its implications for titanosaur systematics: *Journal of Vertebrate Paleontology*, 23 (Supplement to Number 3), Abstracts of Papers, Sixty-second Annual Meeting, p. 120A.

_____, 2003, Evolution of neck elongation in sauropod dinosaurs: *in*: David B. Norman and Paul Upchurch, editors, *SVPCA 50, Cambridge 2002, 11–13 September, Abstract Volume*, unpaginated.

Wilson, Jeffrey A., Ricardo N. Martinez, and Oscar Alcober, 1999, Distal tail segment of a titanosaur (Dinosauria: Sauropoda) from the Upper Cretaceous of Mendoza, Argentina: *Journal of Vertebrate Paleontology*, 19 (3), pp. 591–594.

Wilson, Jeffrey A., and Paul C. Sereno, 1998, Early evolution and higher-level phylogeny of sauropod dinosaurs: *Journal of Vertebrate Paleontology*, 15 (Supplement to Number 2), Society of Vertebrate Paleontology Memoir 5, 68 pages.

Wilson, Michael Clayton, and Philip J. Currie, 1985, *Stenonychosaurus inequalis* (Saurischia, Theropoda) from the Judith River (Oldman) Formation of Alberta: new findings on metatarsal structure: *Canadian Journal of Earth Sciences*, 22 (12), pp. 1813–1817.

Wiman, Carl, 1929, Die Kreide-Dinosaurier aus Shantung: *Palaeontologia Sinica*, Series C, 6 (1), pp. 1–67.

Witmer, Lawrence M., 1997, The evolution of the antorbital cavity of archosaurs: a study in soft-tissue reconstruction in the fossil record with an analysis of the function of pneumaticity: *Memoirs of the Society of Vertebrate Paleontology*, 3, pp. 1–73.

_____, 2001, Nostril position in dinosaurs and other vertebrates and its significance for nasal function: *Science*, 293, pp. 850–853.

Wolfe, Douglas G., Steve Beekman, Dan McGuiness, and Thomas Robira, 2001, Preliminary statistical characterization of a *Zuniceratops* bone bed from the Middle Cretaceous (Turonian) Moreno Hill Formation: *Western Association of Vertebrate Paleontologists with Mesa Southwest Museum and Southwest Paleontological Society, Mesa Arizona, First Meeting of the New Millenium* [*sic*], *February 17, 2001*, abstracts, not paginated.

Wolfe, Douglas G., and James I. Kirkland, 1998, *Zuniceratops christopheri* n. gen. & n. sp., a ceratopsian dinosaur from the Moreno Hill Formation (Cretaceous, Turonian) of west-central New Mexico, *in*: Spencer G. Lucas, James I. Kirkland, and John W. Estep, editors, *Lower and Middle Cretaceous Terrestrial Ecosystems*. Albuquerque: New Mexico Museum of Natural History and Science, Bulletin 14, pages 303–318.

_____, 2001, Variation in multiple specimens of *Zuniceratops*: *Journal of Vertebrate Paleontology*, 21 (Supplement to Number 3),

Abstracts of Papers, Sixty-first Annual Meeting, pp. 115A–116A.

Xing, Y. L., T. X. Yu, and H. M. Dong, 1994, [The dinosaur fossil locality in Jiayin County of Heilongjiang Province and its research history]: *Heilongjang Geology*, 5, pp. 17–26.

Xu Xing, 1997, A new psittacosaur (*Psittacosaurus mazonghanensis* sp. nov.) from Mazongshan Area, Gansu Province, China, *in*: Dong Zhiming, editor, *Sino-Japanese Silk Road Dinosaur Expedition*. Beijing: China Ocean Press, pp. 48–67.

Xu Xing, Yen-Nien Cheng, Xio-Lin Wang, Chun-Hsiang Chang, 2002, An unusual oviraptorosaurian dinosaur from China: *Nature*, 419, pp. 291–293.

Xu Xing, Peter J. Makovicky, Xiao-lin Wang, Mark A. Norell, and Hai-lu You, 2002, A ceratopsian dinosaur from China and the early evolution of Ceratopsia: *Nature*, 416, pp. 314–317.

Xu, Xing, Mark A. Norell, X.-L. Wang, Peter J. Makovicky, and X.-C. Wu, 2002, A basal troodontid from the Early Cretaceous of China: *Nature*, 415, pp. 780–784.

Xu Xing, Zhi-lu Tang, and Xiao-lin Wang, 1999, A therizinosauroid dinosaur with integumentary structures from China: *Nature*, 399, pp. 350–354.

Xu, Xing, Xiao-Lin Wang, and Xiao-Chun Wu, 1999, A dromaeosaurid dinosaur with a filamentous integument from the Yixian Formation of China: *Nature*, 401 (16), pp. 262–265.

Xu, Xing, Xiao-Lin Wang, and Hai-Lu You, 2001, a juvenile ankylosaur from China: *Naturwissenschaften*, 88, pp. 297–300.

Xu, Xing, and Xiao-Chun Wu, 2001, Cranial morphology of *Sinornithosaurus millenii* Xu et al. 1999 (Dinosauria: Theropoda: Dromaeosauridae) from the Yixian Formation of Liaoning, China: *Canadian Journal of Earth Sciences*, 38 (12), pp. 1739–1752.

Xu Xing, Zhang Xiao-hong, Paul C. Sereno, Zhao Xi-jin, Kuang Xue-wen, Han Jun and Tan Lin, 2002, A new Therizinosauroid (Dinosauria, Theropoda) from the Upper Cretaceous Iren Dabasu Formation of Nei Mongol: *Vertebrata Palasiatica*, 40 (3), pp. 228–240.

Xu Xing and Zhao Xijin, 1999, Psittacosaur fossils and their stratigraphical implication, *in*: Wang Yuanqing and Deng Tao, editors, *Proceedings of the Seventh Annual Meeting of the Chinese Society of Vertebrate Paleontology*. Beijing: China Ocean Press, pp. 75–80.

Xu, Xing, Xijin Zhao, and James M. Clark, 2001, A new therizinosaur from the Lower Jurassic (Lufeng Foration) of Yunnan, China: *Journal of Vertebrate Paleontology*, 21 (3), pp. 477–483.

Xu, Xing, Zhong-he Zhou, and Richard O. Prum, 2001, Branched integumental structures in *Sinornithosaurus* and the origin of feathers: *Nature*, 410, pp. 200–204.

Xu, Xing, Zhonghe Zhou, and Xiaolin Wang, 2000, The smallest known non-avian theropod dinosaur: *Nature*, 408, pp. 705–708.

Xu, Xing, Zhonghe Zhou, Xiaolin Wang, Xuewen Kuwang, Fucheng Zhang, and Xiangke Du, 2003, Four-winged dinosaurs from China: *Nature*, 421, pp. 335–340.

Yabe, H., Y. Inai, and T. Shikama, 1940, The discovery of dinosaurian footprints from the Cretaceous (?) of Yangshan, Chinchou. Preliminary note: *Proceedings of the Imperial Academy of Tokyo*, 16 (10), pp. 560–563.

Yadagiri, P., 2001, A new sauropod *Kotasaurus yamanpalliensis* from Lower Jurassic Kota Formation of India: *Records of the Geological Survey of India*, 11, pp. 102–127.

_____, The osteology of *Kotasaurus yamanpalliensis*, a sauropod from the Early Jurassic Kota Formation of India: *Journal of Vertebrate Paleontology*, 21 (2), pp. 242–252.

Yalden, D. W., 1985, Forelimb function in *Archaeopteryx*, *in*: Max K. Hecht, John H. Ostrom, G. Viohl and Peter Wellnhoffer, editors, *The Beginnings of Birds*. Eichstätt, Germany: Freunde des Jura-Museums, pp. 91–98.

_____, 1997, Climbing *Archaeopteryx*: *Archaeopteryx*, 15, pp. 107–108.

Yang, Dashan, and Zhengyi Wei, 1986, Preliminary note on some hadrosaurs from the Cretaceous of Jiayin County, Heilongjiang Province (Manchuria), in: Peter J. Whybrow and Andrew Hill, editors, *Fossil Vertebrates of Arabia*. New Haven and London: Yale University Press, pp. 1–10 (translated by Will Downs, Department of Geology, Northern Arizona University).

Yang, Zhungjian [formerly Young Chung-Chien], 1943, Note on some fossil footprints in China: *Bulletin of the Geological Society of China*, 23, pp. 151–154, Nanking.

_____, 1948, On two new saurischians from Lufeng, Yunnan: *Ibid.*, 28, pp. 73–90, Nanking.

_____, 1954, Fossil reptilian eggs from Laiyang, Shantung, China: *Scientia Sinica*, 3, pp. 505–522.

_____, 1958, [The dinosaurian remains of Laiyang, Shantung]: *Palaeontologica Sinica*, series C, 16, whole number 142, pp. 1–138.

_____, 1960, Fossil footprints in China: *Vertebrata PalAsiatica*, 4 (2), pp. 53–66.

_____, 1965, Fossil eggs from Nansiung (Kwantung Province) and Kanchou (Changsi): *Ibid.*, 9 (2), pp. 141–170.

_____, 1966, Two footprints from the Jiaoping coal mine of Tungchuan, Shensi: *Ibid.*, 10 (1), pp. 64–67.

_____, 1979, Footprints from Launping, Hebei: *Ibid.*, 17, pp. 116–117.

Yang, Xing Long, and Yang Dai Huan, 1987, *Dinosaur footprints from Mesozoic of Sichuan Basin*. Sichuan, China: Science and Technology Publications, 30 pages.

Yao Jin-Xian, Zhang Yun, and Tang Zhi-Lu, 2002, Histological study on the Late Cretaceous ornithomimid and hadrosaurid: *Acta Palaeontologica Sinica*, 41 (2), pp. 241–250.

Yates, Adam M., 2001, A new look at *Thecodontosaurus* and the origin of sauropod dinosaurs: *Journal of Vertebrate Paleontology*, 21 (Supplement to Number 3), Abstracts of Papers, Sixty-first Annual Meeting, p. 116A.

_____, 2003, The species taxonomy of the sauropodomorph dinosaurs from the Löenstein Formation (Norian, Late Triassic) of Germany: *in*: David B. Norman and Paul Upchurch, editors, *SVPCA 50, Cambridge 2002, 11–13 September, Abstract Volume*, unpaginated.

Ye Yong, Ouyang Hui, and Fu Qian-Ming, 2001, New material of *Mamenchisaurus hochuanensis* from Zigong, Sichuan: *Vertebrata PalAsiatica*, 39 (4), pp. 266–271.

Yeh H. K., 1975, *Mesozoic Redbeds of Yunnan*. Beijing: Academia Sinica.

You Hai-lu, 2002, Mazongshan dinosaur assemblage from late Early Cretaceous of northwest China, Ph.D. dissertation, University of Pennsylvania, 164 pages.

Zakharov, S. A., 1964, [On a Cenomanian dinosaur, whose tracks were found in the Shirkent River Valley], *in*: V. M. Reinman, editor, [*Palaeontology of Tadzhikistan*]. Dushanbe, Russia: Akademiya Nauk Tadzhikskoi SSR, pp. 31–35.

Zelenitsky, Darla K., 2000, Dinosaur eggs from Asia and North America: *Paleontological Society of Korea Special Publication*, 4, pp. 13–26.

Zelenitsky, Darla K., and L. V. Hills, 1996, An egg clutch of *Prismatoolithus* oosp. nov. from the Oldman Formation (Upper Cretaceous), Devil's Coulee, southern Alberta: *Canadian Journal of Earth Sciences*, 33, pp. 1127–1131.

Zelenitsky, Darla K., L. V. Hills, and Philip J. Currie, 1996, Parataxonomic classification of ornithoid eggshell fragments from the Oldman Formation (Judith River Group; Upper Cretaceous), southern Alberta: *Canadian Journal of Earth Sciences*, 33, pp. 1655–1667.

Zeng Xiangyuan, 1982, [Fossil footprints], *in*: [*Paleontological Handbook of Hunan Province*]. Beijing: Geological Press, pp. 485–489.

Zeng Xiangyuan, and Zhang J. J., 1979, Fossil dinosaur eggs from the western part of the Dongting Basin, Hunan Province: *Vertebrata PalAsiatica*, 17 (2), pp. 131–136.

Zhai R., Zheng J., and Tong J., 1978, The stratigraphy of the mammal-bearing Tertiary of the Turfan Basin, Sinkiang: *Memoirs of Institute of Vertebrate Paleontology and Paleoanthropology, Academia Sinica*, 13, pp. 68–81.

Zhang Fucheng, Zhonghe Zhou, Xing Xu, and Xiaolin Wang, 2002, A juvenile coelurosaurian theropod from China indicates arboreal habits: *Naturwissenschaften*, 89, pp. 394–398.

Zhang Yihong, 1988, *Shunosaurus*, sauropod dinosaurs (1): The Middle Jurassic dinosaur fauna from Dashanpu, Zigong, Sichuan: *Journal of the Chengdu College of Geology*, 2 (supplement), pp. 1–12.

Zhang Yihong, and Chen Wei, 1996, Preliminary research on the classification of sauropods from Sichuan Basin, China, *in*:

Michael Morales, editor, *Museum of Northern Arizona Bulletin*, 60, pp. 97–108.

Zhang Yuguang and Li Jianjun, 2001, A study of new materials of *Mamenchisaurus jingyanensis*, *in*: Deng Tao and Wang Yuan, editors, *Proceedings of the Eighth Annual Meeting of the Chinese Society of Vertebrate Paleontology*. Beijing: China Ocean Press, pp. 35–39.

Zhang Xiao-Hong, Xu Xing, Zhao Xi-Jin, Paul C. Sereno, Kuang Xue-Wen, and Tan Lin, 2001, A long-necked therizinosauroid dinosaur from the Upper Cretaceous Iren Dabasu Formation of Nei Mongol, Peoplés Republic of China: *Vertebrata PalAsiatica*, 39 (4), pp. 282–290.

Zhao, H., 1998, Dinosaur eggs from Xichuan Basin, Henan Province: *Vertebrata PalAsiatica*, 36 (4), pp. 282–296.

Zhao, Xin Jim [formerly Xijin], 1978, A preliminary investigation on the thinning of the dinosaurian eggshells of the Late Cretaceous and some related problems: *Vertebrata PalAsiatica*, 16, pp. 213–221.

_____, 1986, The Jurassic Reptilia: *Stratigraphy of China*, II (The Jurassic System of China), pp. 286–347.

_____, 1994, The dinosaur eggs in China: on the structure and evolution of eggshells, *in*: Kenneth Carpenter, Karl F. Hirsch, and John R. Horner, editors, *Dinosaur Eggs and Babies*. Cambridge: Cambridge University Press, pp. 184–203.

Zhao, Xin Jin [formerly Xijin], and Xu Xing, 1998, The oldest coelurosaurian: *Nature*, 394, pp. 234–235.

Zhao, Zi-Kui, 1975, [The microstructure of the dinosaurian eggshells of Nanshiung, Kwangtung]: *Vertebrata PalAsiatica*, 13 (2), pp. 105–117.

_____, 1979, Development of studies on Chinese dinosaur eggs, *in*: Mesozoic and Cenozoic Redbeds of Hunnan, pp. 330–340.

_____, 1988, A new structural type of the dinosaur eggs from Anly county, Hubei Province: *Vertebrata PalAsiatica*, 26 (2), pp. 107–115.

_____, 1993, Structure, formation and evolutionary trends of dinosaur eggshells, *in*: I. Kobayashi, H. Mutvei, and A. sahni, editors, *Structure, Formation and Evolution of Fossil Hard Tissues*. Tokyo: Tokai University Press, pp. 195–212.

_____, 1994, Dinosaur eggs in China: on the structure and evolution of eggshells: *in*: Kenneth Carpenter, Karl F. Hirsch, and John R. Horner, editors, *Dinosaur Eggs and Babies*. Cambridge: Cambridge University Press, pp. 184–203.

_____, 2000, Nesting behavior of dinosaurs as interpreted from the Chinese Cretaceous dinosaur eggs: *Paleontological Society of Korea Special Publication*, 4, pp. 115–126.

Zhao, Zi-Kui, and Philip J. Currie, 1993, A large crested theropod from the Jurassic of Xinjiang, People's Republic of China: *Canadian Journal of Earth Sciences*, 30 (10–11), pp. 2027–2036.

Zhao, Zhi-Kui, and Ding S. R., 1976, Discov-

ery of the dinosaurian eggshells from Alxa Zuoqi, Ningxia (Alashanzuoqi) and its stratigraphical meaning: *Vertebrata PalAsiatica*, 14, pp. 42–45.

Zhao [Chao], Zi-Kui, and Jiang [Chiang] Y. K., 1974, Microscopic studies on the dinosaurian eggshells from Liayang, Shandong Province: *Scientia Sinica*, 17, pp. 73–83.

Zhao, Zi-Kui, L. Jie, Z. Huamei, Z. Zhenhua, and Y. Zheng, 1991, Extinction of the dinosaurs across the Cretaceous–Tertiary boundry in the Nanxiong Basin, Guangdong Province: *Vertebrata PalAsiatica*, 29, pp. 13–20.

Zhao, Zi-Kui, and Li Z., 1988, A new structural type of the dinosaur eggs from Anlu County, Hubei Province: *Vertebrata PalAsiatica*, 26, pp. 107–15.

Zhao, Zi-Kui, Xue-ying Mao, Zhi-fang Chai, Gao-chuang Yang, Ping Kong, Mitsuru Ebihara, and Zhen-hua Zhao, 2002, A possible causal relationship between extinction of dinosaurs and K/T iridium enrichment in the Nanxiong Basin, South China: evidence from dinosaur eggshells: *Palaeogeography, Palaeoclimatology, Palaeoecology*, 178, pp. 1–17.

Zhao, Zi-Kui, Ye J., Li H.-M., Zhao Z. H., and Yan Z., 1991, Extinction of the dinosaurs across the Cretaceous–Tertiary boundary in Nanxiong basin, Guangdong Province: *Vertebrata PalAsiatica*, 29, pp. 1–20.

Zhen, Shuonan, Jianjun Li, and Haang Mook Kim, 1993, Comparative studies of dinosaur remains in China and Korea: *Journal of Natural History and Environments*, 1 (1), pp. 1–21.

Zhen, Shuo-nan, Jianjun Li, Chenggang Rao, and S. Hu, 1986, Dinosaur footprints of Jinning, Yunnan: *Memoirs of the Beijing Natural History Museum*, 33, pp. 1–19.

Zhen, Shuo-nan, Jianjun Li, and B. Zhen 1983, Dinosaur footprints of Yuechi, Sichuan: *Memoirs of the Beijing Natural History Museum*, 25, pp. 1–19.

Zhou Zhong-He and Wang Xiao-Lin, 2000, A new species of *Caudipteryx* from the Yixian Formation of Liaoning, northeast China: *Vertebrata PalAsiatica*, 38 (2), pp. 111–127.

Zhou Zong-He, Wang Xiao-Lin, Zhang Fucheng, and Xu Xing, 2000, Important features of *Caudipteryx*— evidence from two nearly complete new specimens: *Vertebrata PalAsiatica*, 38 (4), pp. 241–254.

Zhou Zhonghe, and Zhang Fucheng, 2002, A long-tailed, seed-eating bird from the Early Cretaceous of China: *Nature*, 418, pp.

Zienkiewicz, O. C., 1971, *in*: *The Finite Element Method in Engineering Science*. London: Mc-Graw Hill, 521 pages.

Zils, W., C. Werner, A. Moritz, and G. Saanane, 1995, Tendaguru, the most famous dinosaur locality of Africa. Review, survey and future prospects: *Documenta naturae*, 97, pp. 1–41.

Index

Abel, Othenio 617, 631
Abelisaurus 34, 38, 148, 178–179, 276; *A. comahuensis* 276
L'Abeller site 477
Abler, William L. 217–218, 423–424
Abrictosaurus 153, 207, 207; *A. consors* 207
Abrosaurus 151, 207–208; *A. dongpoensis* see *Abrosaurus dongpoi*; *A. dongpoi* 207; *A. gigantorhinus* see *Abrosaurus dongpoi*
Academia Sinica v, 526
The Academy of Natural Sciences of Philadelphia 200, 404
Academy of Science 30
Acanthopholis 152
Achelousaurus 154, 291
Achillobator 138, 150, 177, 589–590
Ackerman, Jennifer 135
Acrocanthosaurus 37, 41, 148, 164, 174, 180, 207–209, 232, 445, 601; *A. atokensis* 37, 41, 174, 208, 232, 445
Adamantina Formation 47, 49, 82, 85–86, 88
Adams, Jason 259–260
Adasaurus 138, 150
Aegyptosaurus 151, 230
Aeolosaurus 71, 82, 86, 151, 591–592
Aepisaurus 150
Aethyopus see *Sauropus*; *A. lyellianus* see *Sauropus*
Aetonychopus 616; *A. digitigradus* 616; *A. rapidus* 616
aetosaurs 33
Afrovenator 148, 157, 180, 180–181; *A. abakensis* 180
Aganane Formation 617, 624
Agathaumas 154
Agialopus 616, 624; *A. wyomingensis* 616
Agilisaurus 152, 190
Agnostiphys 147, 155, 207, 209, 209–210, 210; *A. cromhallensis* 209, 209–210, 210
Agrestipus 616; *A. hottoni* 616
Agrosaurus see *Thecodontosaurus*; *A. macgillivrayi* see *Thecodontosaurus antiquus*
Aguja Formation 47, 211, 380, 474, 476–478

Agustinia 80, 150; *A. ligabuei* 80
Ain el Guettar Formation 528
air sacs 61, 482, 482, 484–485, 493
Aitken, Colin 92
Al-Khod Formation 42
Alamosaurus 151, 207, 211, 211–212, 212–213, 213–214, 215, 216, 374, 577; *A. sanjuanensis* 211–212, 212, 213–214, 216
Alashansaurus 347
Alber, W. L. 580, 587
Albertosaurus 40, 43, 51, 149, 172, 207, 214, 215–217, 217–218, 218, 229, 302, 326, 350–351, 558, 580; *A. libratus* see *Gorgosaurus libratus*; *A. periculosus* see *Tarbosaurus periculosus*; *A. sarcophahus* 172, 214, 215, 351
Alcobaca Formation 432
Alectoris chukar 120
Alectrosaurus 149, 172; *A. olseni* 172
Aletopelta 207, 218–219, 219–220, 220–221; *A. coombsi* 218–219, 219–220
Alexander, R. McN. 115, 345–347, 484–485, 615
Algorta Site 652
Alioramus 149, 171–172, 497, 500; *A. remotus* 172
Alifanov, Vladimir R. 87, 124, 124, 338–339
Aliwalia 147
Allain, Ronan 162, 179–181, 390, 404, 406, 419, 444, 444–445, 445–446, 446, 545, 545–546, 546–547, 547
Allaru Formation 412
Allaru Mudstone 249, 412
Alle Portland Arkose 635
Allen Formation 468–470
Alligator 117, 225, 583, 595; *A. missippiensis* 225; *A. sinensis* 595
allometry see ontogeny
Allosaurus 4, 17, 20, 27, 30, 31, 34, 37, 40–42, 51, 53–55, 55, 56, 78, 120–121, 124, 147–148, 159–160, 164, 174–175, 180, 180, 207, 209, 221–222, 222–225, 225–226, 226–228, 228–229, 229, 230–233, 243, 255, 268–269, 273, 276, 311, 318, 373, 390, 404, 419, 423–424, 445, 539,

543, 585, 595; *A. fragilis* 4, 37, 53, 159–160, 174–175, 180, 222, 223, 224–225, 225, 226–229, 230, 232, 318, 339, 351, 419, 445, 539, 585, 627; "A. jim-madseni" 233; *A. maximus* 318; *Allosaurus* sp. 20, 30, 31, 41
Alocodon 151, 189, 207, 233, 572; *A. kuehnei* 233
Alonso, R. N. 625
Alte Akademie 529
Altirhinus 153, 155, 193, 196, 207, 234, 322, 451–452
Altispinax 148
altriciality see parental care
Alvarezsaurus 138, 150, 172, 176–177; *A. calvoi* 172, 176–177
Alwalkeria 147, 530
Alxasaurus 136, 149, 167, 330–332, 421, 421–422; *A. elesitaiensis* 167
Amargasaurus 20, 61, 150; *A. cazaui* 61
Amblonyx see *Sauropus*; *A. giganteus* see *Sauropus*
Amblydactylus 616; *A. gethingi* 616; *A. kortmeyeri* 616
Ambrose, D. 384
Amédro, F. 75
Ameghino, Florentino 478
American Association of Museum xi
American Museum of Natural History 28, 77, 197, 203, 215, 266, 280, 293, 304, 316, 340, 413, 456, 485, 508, 646
The American Ornithologists' Union 132
Amherst College 613
ammonites 422
Ammosaurus 150, 443–444, 495
Ampelosaurus 81, 151; *A. atacis* 81
amphibians 17, 56, 74, 126, 392, 461, 477, 489, 491
Amphicoelias 76, 150
Amtosaurus 95, 152, 207, 234, 234–235, 235–236 *A. archibaldi* 234, 234–235, 235; *A. magnus* 234–235
Amur River locality 559
Amurosaurus 102, 153, 286; *A. riabinini* 102, 286

Amygdalodon 150
Ana clypeata 341
Anabisetia 152, 207, 236, 236–237, 237–238, 238, 239; *A. saldiviai* 236, 236–237, 237, 238, 239
Anacleto Foration 82
Anapra Sandstone 619
Anas platyrhynchos 54
Anatopus 616; *A. palmatus* 616
Anatotitan 153, 362, 380; *A. copei* 362, 380
Anatriasauropus 616; *A. ginsburgi* 616; *A. hereoensis* 616
Anchiceratops 154
Anchisauripus see *Grallator*; *A. sillimani* see *Grallator* (*A.*) *sillimani*
Anchisaurus 114, 150, 181, 443, 505; *A. polyzelus* 114
Andersen, Arthur F. 570–572, 587
Anderson, J. F. 208–209
Anderson, J. M. 530
Andesaurus 74, 82, 151, 250, 592
Angaturama see *Irritator*; *A. limai* see *Irritator challengeri*
Animantarx 152, 347, 360; *A. ramaljonesi* 347
Ankylosaur Flats 292
Ankylosaurus 5, 108, 140, 152, 187, 207, 239, 332, 334; *A. magniventris* 108, 187, 332
Anodontosaurus lambei see *Euoplocephalus tutus*
Anomoepus 616–617, 621, 625, 627, 629–630, 633, 635; *A. scambus* 616
Anoplosaurus 152
Ansbacher Sandstein 621
Anser anser 54
Anserimimus 149
Antarctosaurus 69, 151, 183–184, 472; *A. septentrionalis* see *Jainosaurus septentrionalis*
Antenor Navarro Formation 614, 619, 620, 624, 640
Anticheiropus 616; *A. hamatus* 616; *A. pilulatus* 616
Antlers Formation 73, 482–483
Anton, John A. v, 463, 465, 570–571
"Antonio" 97, 98
Antrodemus 148, 406

Index

Antunes, Miguel Telles 310, *310–311*, 311–312, *312*, 572, 630, 633

Apatichnus see *Anomoepus*; *A. circumagens* see *Anomoepus*

Apatosaurus 17, 24, 62–64, 66, 76–77, *77*, 114, 151, 207, 239, *240*, 241–242, 353, *484*, 553; *A. ajax* 241; *A. excelsus* 24, *77*, *240*, 241; *A. louisae* 114, 241; *A. yahnapin* 241, 353

Apesteguia, Sebastian 33–34, 61, 74

Apheloolithus 142, 645; *A. shuinanensis* 142, 645

aquatic dinosaurs 17, *19*, 19–20, 28, 390, 392, 454, 534, 615

Aragosaurus 67, *68*, 151; *A. ischiaticus* 67, *68*

Aralosaurus 153

Arancanthus see *Acrocanthosaurus*

arboreality 119, 124–125, 130–134, 138, 412, 489–491

Archaeoceratops 126, 153, 201–202, 385; *A. lithographica* 126

Archaeopteryx 117, 119, 123, 128–131, 133, 136–138, 174, 177, 300, 340, 369, 410–411, 488–491, 512–516, 524–525; *A. lithographica* 136, 174

Archaeornithoides 147

Archaeornithomimus 27, 51, 149, 175; *A. asiaticus* 175

Archer, Brad 526, 528

Arches National Park 436, 590, 592

Archibald, J. David 235, 251, 414, 485

Arctosaurus 150

Arcucci, Andrea Beatriz 607

Ardley Quarry 71–72

Arén Formation 101

Arén Sandstone 139

Aren Sandstone Formation *475*, 477

Argentinosaurus 24, *25–26*, 151, 230; *A. huenculensis* 25–26

Argoides 617, 635; *A. isodactyleus* 617; *A. macrodactylus* 617; *A. minumus* 617; *A. redfieldii* 617; *A. robustus* 617

Argozoum see *Argoides*; *A. argos* see *Argoides*

Argyrosaurus 151

Aristosuchus 148, 207, 242–243, *243*, 244, 519; *A. pusillus* 243, *243*; *Aristosuchus* sp. 243

Arizona Republic 422

Arkhangelsky, M. S. 96, *97*

Arrhinoceratops 152

Arstanosaurus 103, 153

Artiodactylus 617; *A. sinclairi* 617

Ashmonian Museum 406

Asiaceratops 153, 203, 207, 244, 385; *A. salsopaludalis* 203, 244

Asiamerica 147

Asiatosaurus 150, 244, *244*, 291; *A. kwangshiensis* 244, *244*; *A. mongoliensis* 244, 291

Aslan, A. 565

asteroids 30

Astrodon 70, 72, 151, 154, 406

Atlantosaurus 150

Atlasaurus 151

Atlascoposaurus 152

Atreipus see *Grallator*; *A. milfordensis* see *Grallator*

Atreus, Wanner 617

Attia, Yousry 428–429, *429*, 430

Attridge, John 383–384

Aublysodon 6, 149, 171–172, 207, 545, 574, *575*, 577; *A. mirandus* 577; *A. molnaris* see *Tyrannosaurus rex*; cf. *Aublysodon mirandus* see *Tyrannosaurus rex*

Auca Mahuevo site 82–83, *83*, 84, *85*, 245–246, *651–652*

Aucasaurus 148, 169–170, 178, 207, 245–246, *246–248*, 249; *A. garridoi* 170, 245–246, *246–248*, 248

Audubon 132

Auffenberg, Walter 208, 228, 233, 316–317

Augustina ligabuei see *Agustina ligabuei*

The Auk 132

Austrosaurus 151, 207, *249*, 249–250; *A. mckillopi* 249, 249–250

Avaceratops 114, 154, *200*; *A. limmersi* 200

Averianov [also Averánov], Alexander O. *86–87*, 87, 96, *97*, 234, *234–235*, 235, 251, 338–339, 414, 485

avian theropods see birds

Avimimus 121, 130, 136, 149, 155, 207, 250–251; *A. portentosus* 250–251

Avisaurus 149

Azendohsaurus 607; *A. laaroussii* 607

Azevedo, Sergio Alex Kugland, de 58, 82, 530

Azuma, Yoichi 44–45, 137, 193, 369, *369–370*, 370, 408, 628

B. M. Birla Science Center 379

Bachelet, Abbé 545

Bachman, G. H. 387, 438, 440, 481, 495

Bachman, G. H. 387, 438, 440, 481, 495

bacteria 317, 421, 564, 576, 586

Bactrosaurus 96, 151, 193–194, 197, 322

Badamgarav, Demchig 560

Badeer, H. S. 65

Baerecke quarry 465

Bagaceratops 108, *110–112*, 153, 200–201, 203, 207, 251, 260, 352, 455, 459; *B. rozhdestvenskkyi* 459; *Bagaceratops* sp. *110–112*

Bagaraatan 148, 158, 165

Bahariasaurus 46, 148

Bahariya Formation 46, 428–429

Bailey, Jack Bowman 19

Bainoceratops efremovi 597

Bainshire Formation 234

Baird, Donald 13, 615, 617, 624, 633

Bajo Barreal Formation 38, 69–70, 593

Bajpai, S. 141–142

Bakirov, A. 339

Bakker, Robert T. vii, 24, 36–37, 44, 65, 221–222, *222–223*, 228, 233, 324, 328, 339, 341, 346–347, 352, 467, 484–485, *495*, 514, 517, 575, 587

Balabansai Formation 338–339

Balaenoptera musculus 24

Ballerstedt, M. 638

Bambiraptor 138, 150, *178–179*, 513–515; *B. feinbergi* 178–179

Bandyopadhyay, Saswati 33–34, 34, 251–252, 402–403

Banisterobates 617; *B. boisseaui* 617

Banos del Flaco Formation 619, 626

Barale, G. 528

Barapasaurus 150, 207, 251–252, 379–380

Barco, J. L. 67, *68*, *73*, 80

Barosaurus 63, 76, 151, 265, 268, 389, 543, 549–550, 553–555; *B. lentus* 543, 550

Barreto, Claudia 123, 566–567, *567*, 568

Barrett, Paul M. 29, 45, 60, 66–67, 74–76, 244, *244*, 269, *270*, 271–272, 291, *291*, 312–313, *313*, 314–315, 335, 337, 404, 413, 423–424, 443–444, 492–493

Barrick, Reese E. 103, 115, 217–218, 563–565

Barsbold, Rinchen 44–45, 137, 155, 172–177, 292–295, 325, 328, 369, *369–370*, 370, 378, 422–423, 428, 506, *507*, 507–508, 574

Barsboldia 153, 207, 252, 286; *B. sickinskii* 252, 286

Barungoiot [also Barun Goyot] Formation *110*, *112*, 468, *651*

Baryonyx 6, 16, 37, 39, 148, 207, 252, *253–254*, 254–255, 299, *372*, 372–373, 529, 549; *B. tenerensis* 16, 37, 252, *253–254*, 254–255, 372; *B. walkeri* 252, *253*, 254–255, 529; *Baryonyx* sp. 252

Baszio, Sven 475–476, 478, 486

Bauru Group 47, 49, 82, 85–86

Bavarian State Collection of Paleontology and Historical Geology *529*

Bavariasaurus macrodactylus 296–297

Bayan Mandahu Formation 454–456, 458–459

Bearpaw Formation 259, 454

Bearreraid Sandstone Formation 92

Beckles, Samuel H. 93, 312

Becklespinax 148

Beijing (Peking) Museum of Natural History 500

Beipiaosaurus 7, 131, 136, 149, 300, 330–332, 414–415, 422, 521, 523–524

Bell, C. J. 115

Bellona see *Grallator*; *B. giganteus* see *Grallator*

Bellusaurus 151

Belly River Formation see Oldman Formation

Belodon plieningeri 442

Benkersandstein 621

Benton, Michael J. 190, 243–244, 271–272, 404, 406, 607

Benz, Georg 441, 444

Berner, R. A. 98

Bernier, P. 617

Berninasauropus 617; *B. sanariensis* 617

Berosia, Aldo *468–469*

"Bertha" 352

Bertini, Reinaldo J. 47, 85–86

Betasuchus 147, 178

Beurlen, K. 621

Beutler, G. 387, 438, 440, 481, 495

Bhandari, A. 142

A Bibliography of the Dinosauria (Exclusive of Aves) 1677–1986 615

Bidar, Alain 519, 523

Bien, M. N. 255

Bienosaurus 91, 152, 207, 255–256, *256*, 492; *B. lufengensis* 255, *256*

"Big Al" 232–233

Big Bend National Park 211, 380, 474, 476

Bigot, A. 444, 446

Bihariosaurus 153

Bilbey, Sue Ann 231, 233, 278, 619

"Bilbeyhallorum" see *Cedarpelta*

Bimber, Oliver 587

Bir, Morton 36–37

Bird, John H. 185, 278–279, *279*, 280, 323, 347–348

birds vii, 6–7, 11, 20–25, *25*, 27, 29, 36–37, 40–41, 45, 54, *56*, 56–57, 60–62, 64, 74, 76, 83, 85, 116–124, *124*, 125–126, 128–138, 140, 142, 147, 155, 157–158, 169, 171–174, 177, 180, 184, 209, 239, 241, 250–251, 259–260, 271, 273–274, 276, 287, 294, 299–301, *304*, 315–316, 332, 338–339, 341, 345–346, 360–361, 368–370, 390, 408, 410–413, 420, 437, 461, 463, 476–477, *482*, 484–485, 489–491, 493, 507–508, 512–517, 519–521, 524–526, 567, 573–574, 581–584, 607, 615, 624–625, 627–628, 630, 633–634, 636, 642, 645

Bissekty Formation 234–235

Bisti/De-ne-zin Wilderness Area 107, 526, 528

biting, bite forces, and bite marks 16, 51 *51–52*, 52, 76, 98, 221–222, 225, *225–226*, 226, 228–229, 231–232, 262–263, 267, 271, 276, 316–317, 328, 420, 486, 492–493, 559, 576, 580–581, 585, 595, 613

bivalves 82, 301, 307, 423

"Black Beauty" *484*

Black Hills Institute of Geological Research v, *x*, *18*, *198*, 571, 587

Black Peaks Formation 213

Blackstone Formation 624

Blaine, Mike 133

Blanco, R. Ernesto 344–347

Blesa Formation 364

Blikanasaurus 150, 530, 562

blood see circulation

Blows, William T. 93, 185–186, 292, 337, 447, *447–448*, 448–449, *449*

Bock, W. J. 131, 624, 634

Bogorovia 101

Bohlin, Birger 291, *291*, 408

Bonaparte, José F. *25*, 157, 246, 249–250, 338–339, 341, 443, 530

Bone Cabin Quarry *92*, 266, 542

Bone Cabin Quarry West *186*, *272*, *536*, *539–540*, 604

bone histologies 24–25, 94, 107, 125, 259, 263, 390, 426, 505, 562

bone resorption 112

Bonebed 43 280

bonebeds 17, 40, 46, 90, 211–213, 215–217, 259, 284, 301, 323, 337, 441, 528, 590, 595–596

Bonnan, Matthew F. 61–62, 241–242

Borogovia 101, 138, 149
Boscarolli, D. 80
Bosiutrisauropus 617; *B. phuthiat-sani* 617
Bothriospondylus 151
Boyd, Clint 362
Brachiosaurus 17, 22, 62, 64–66, 70, *71*, 72–77, 87, 114, 151, 181, 207, 242, 244, 256, *257–258*, 258, 309–310, 318–319, 482–485, 549, 591–592; *B. altithorax* 70, *71*, *258*; *B. brancai* 22, 64–65, 70, 73–75, 114, 257, 258, 309, 319, 482; *Brachiosaurus* sp. 74
Brachyceratops 114, 154, 207, 258, 282
Brachylophosaurus 104, 153, 207, 258–260; *B. canadensis* 104, 258–260; *B. goodwini* 259
Brachypodosaurus 152
Bradycneme 148
brains and endocasts 36, 41, 66, 106, 114, 123–124, 208–209, 230, 259, *273*, 273–274, 315–316, 398, 413, 502, *504*, 506, 535, 537, 542, 575
Branson, E. B. 616, 621
Bray, Emily S. v, 645, 648–651
breathing *see* respiration
Breithaupt, Brent H. v, 266, 353
Brett-Surman, Michael K. [Keith] v, *191*, 195, 285, 287–288, 391, 398–399, 653
Breviceratops see *Bracyceratops*; *B. kozlowskii* see *Bagaceratops*
Brevicolporties colpella 143
Breviparopus 617; *B. taghbaloutensis* 617
Brigham Young University v, *4–6*, 9–10, *266*, *269*, 343, *589*
Brill, Kathleen 426–428
Brinkman, Daniel L. 423–424, 461–462, *462–464*, 465, 485, 573–574
Brinkman, Donald B. 477–478, 486
Bristol City Museum 562
Britt, Brooks B. 61, 72, 96, 279–280, 436–437, 543, 545, 562, *589*, 589–590, 592–593
Brochu, Christopher A. 172, 575–576, 585–587
Brontopodus 309, 617, *618*, 621, 634; *B. birdi* 309, 617, *618*; *B. changlingensis* 617
Brontozoum see *Anomoepus, Eubrontes, Grallator*
brooding 57, 83, 120, 122, 126, 129, 574
Brookes, Richard 406
Broom, Robert 443–444
Broome Sandstone 630
Brown, Barnum 171, 215, *217*, 239, 304, 316, 385–386, 459, 526, 528, 531–532, 543, 571–572
Bruhathkayosaurus 148
Brunswick Formation 623–624
Bryan Small *Stegosaurus* Quarry 263, 317
Bubo virginianus 260
Buchholtz, Peter W. 189–191, 530, 532
Buck, Landis 266
Bückeberg Formation 636
Bückeburgichnus 619, 642; *B. maximus* 619

Buckland, William 404, 406
Buckley, Lisa Glynis 320, 381
Buffetaut, Éric 13, *59*, 59–60, 81, *91*, 91–92, 172, 255, 363–365, 431, 508, *528*, 528–529, 547, 549
Bugenasaura 152
"La Buitrera" locality 61, 343
Bull Canyon Formation 474
Bull Run Formation 616, 625
Bullhead Mountain Formation 616, 621, 625, 627, 633
Bultnck, P. 194, 364
Bulynnikova, A. A. 87
Bunter Sandstone 635
Bunzel, Emanuel 301, 364–365
Burge, Donald L. 72, 96, 185, 278–279, *279*, 280, 323, 347–348, 436–437, 514, 517, 590, 592–593
Burian, Zdenek *21*
Burnham, David A. 36, 265, 268, 514, 517
Busbey, A. B. 579, 587
Bybee, Paul 232–233
Byers Bed 46
Byronosaurus 138, 149, 173–174, *175*; *B. jaffei* 173–174, *175*

Cactus Park bonebed 9–10
Caen University 388
Caenagnathasia 136, 149
Caenagnathus see *Chirostenotes*; *C. collinsi* see *Chirostenotes pergracilis*; *C. sternbergi* see *?Chirostenotes elegans*
Cai Kaiju 143, 349–350, 424, 426
Caiman sp. 54, 120
Cairanoolithus 143, 645–646; *C. dughi* 143, 645; *C. roussetensi* 143, 645
Cairirichnium 619, *620*; *C. leonardi* 619; *C. magnificum* 619, *620*
Calamosaurus 147
Calamospondylus 147, 207, 243–244, 260–261; *C. oweni* 261; *C. foxii* see *Calamosaurus foxii*
Calcaire de Caen Formation 444, 446, *641*
Calder, W. A., III 25
California Academy of Sciences *160*
Callison, George 314
Callovosaurus 152, 311; *C. leedsi* 311
Calopus see *Platypternus*; *C. delicatulus* see *Platypternus delicatula*
Calvo, Jorge O. 69–70, 75–76, 82, 84–85, 88, 236, *236–237*, 237–238, *238*, 239, 244, 250, 291, 343, *345*, 347, 362, *362*, 418–419, 473–474, 634, 637
Camarasaurus 19, 19–20, 30, *31*, 59, 62–64, 70, 73, 75–76, 114, 151, 181, *182*, 207, 232, 242, 244, 261–262, *262–263*, 263, *264–265*, 265–266, *266–267*, 267–268, 393–394, 543, 549–550, 591; *C. grandis* 19, 261–263, *263–265*, 267; *C. lentus* see *Camarasaurus supremus*; *C. lewisi* 261–262, *266*, 267; *C. supremus* 114, *182*, 261–262, *262*, 265
Cambridge University 406, 478
Cambridge University Press 478
Camelotia 58, 150, 443; *C. boralis* 58, 443

Camelus sp. 64
camouflage 122, 519, 521
Camp, Charles L. 493–494
Campbell, Kenneth E. 134
Campos, Diogenese de A. 215
Camposaur site 390
Camposaurus 147
Camptosaurichnus 619; *C. fasolae* 619
Camptosaurus 4, 96, 101, 152, 195, 207, 238, *240*, 268–269, *269–271*, 271–272, *272*, 310–311, 322, 365, 376, 451, 637; *C. amplus* see *Allosaurus*; "*C.*" *depressus* 271; *C. dispar* 4, *240*, 268–269, *269*, *272*, 311; *C. hoggii* 268–269, *270*; *C. prestwichii* 271, 311; *Camptosaurus* sp. see *Draconyx loureiroi*; *Camptosaurus* "A" *271*; *Camptosaurus* "C" *272*
Campylodoniscus 151
Canadian Museum of Nature 104, *288–290*, 289–290, *302*, 347
Candeleros Formation 61, 82
cannibalism 52, 296, 392
Canning, L. 404
Canon de Santa Elena National Area of Protection 380
La Cantalera, locality 364
Canudo, José Ignacio 67, *68*, 72, *72–73*, 80, 138–139, *139*, 252, 255
Cao You-Shu 303, *303–304*
Carcharodon megalodon 194
Carcharodontosaurus 37, 42, 46, 148, 164, 180, 207–209, 273, *274*, 273–274, 344, *345*, 529; *C. saharicus* 37, 273, *273*, *345*
Cardiodon 150, 283; *C. rugolosus* 283
"Carlin Giant" 353
Carmel Formation 619
Carmelopodus 619; *C. untermannorum* 619
Carnegie Museum of Natural History 77, 241
carnivory (in prosauropods) 443
Carnotaurus 34, 37–38, 148, 169, *169*, 178–179, 207, 245–246, 249, 274, *274–275*, 276, 340, 519; *C. sastrei* 37, 169, *169*, 245–246, 274, *274–275*, 276
Carpenter, Kenneth v, *32*, 51, 53–55, *55*, 56, 56, 72, 94, 96–97, *159*, *167*, 185–187, *187*, 189, 208–209, 256, 263, 268, 276–277, *277–278*, 278–279, *279*, 280, 301–302, *316*, 316–317, 319, 326, 328, *334*, 337, *342*, 347–348, 353, 355, 355, 358, *359*, 360, 386, 412–413, 426–428, 435, *435–436*, 437, 476, 478, *492*, 492–493, 532–533, *533–534*, 534, *536*, 537, 538–539, 542, 558–560, 573–574, 577, 584–585, *586*, 587, 590, *590–592*, 592–593, 604, 645
Carr, Thomas D. [David] 107, 170–171, 301–302, 312, 498, 500, 526–527, *527*, 528, 530–532, 558, 560, *576*, 577–578, 587
Carrano, Matthew T. 12–13, 28–29, 39, 67, 155, 177–179, 230–231, 233, 399–400, *400–401*, 401–403, 581–583, 587, 593

Carrier, David R. 229–230, 233
Carvalho, Ismar de Souza 42, 61
Casamiquela, Rodolfo M. 443–444, 619, 621, 626, 636, 643
Casanovas, M. Lourdes 67, *68*, 102, *102*, 388–389, *389*, 430–431, 449, 633–634; *see also* Casanovas-Cladellas
Casanovas-Cladellas, M. Lourdes *see* Casanovas
Case, T. J. 24–25, 195
Caseosaurus 147
Casier, Edgard 365
Castanet, J. 24
Castellar Formation 67
Catalogue of Casts of Fossils from the Principal Museums of Europe and America with Short Descriptions and Illustrations 194
catastrophies 44, 66, 252, 268
Cathayornis 132
Cathetosaurus see *Camarasaurus*; *C. lewisi* see *Camarasaurus lewisi*
Catholic University of Peking 91
Caturrita Formation 58
Caudipteryx 6–7, 118, 120, 122–123, 126, 129–131, 133–137, 149, 155, 343, 300, 410–411, 489, 514, 524
Cave Sandstone 626
Cedar Mountain Formation 70, 72, 96–97, 276–278, 322–323, 341, *342*, 435–436, 545, 589–592
Cedarosaurus 87, 151, 207, 276–277, *277*, 278, 591–592; *C. weiskopfae* 276, *277*
Cedarpelta 185, 207, 278, *278–279*, 279–280; *C. bilbeyhallorum* 278, *278–279*, 279
Central Geological Museum 398
Centrosaurus 21, 112, 153, 204, 207, 258, 280, *281*, 282; *C. apertus* 21, 280, *281*
Ceratops 154
Ceratopsipes 619; *C. goldenensis* 619
Ceratosaurus 6, 17, 30, 37, 148, 177–179, 181, 230, 232, 268, 276, 318, 340, 404, 469, 519, 544, 653; *C. dentisulcatus* 318; *C. magnicornis* 318; *C. nasicornis* 6, 37, 318
Cerro Barcino Formation 50
Cerro Los Candeleros locality 343
Cetiosauriscus 150
Cetiosaurus 150, 207, 282–283, *283–284*, 284; *C. brachyurus* 282–283; "*C.*" *brevis* see *Pelorosaurus conybeari*; *C. conybeari* see *Pelorosaurus conybeari*; *C. epioolithicus* 283; *C. giganteus* 283; "*C.*" *glymptonensis* 283; "*C.*" *humerocristatus* 283; *C. hypoolithicus* 283; *C. leedsi* 282–283; *C. longus* 282–283; *C. medius* 282–284; *C. oxoniensis* 282–283, *283–284*, 284; *C. rugolosus* see *Cardiodon rugolosus*
champsosaurs 548, 569
Chandler, Christine L. 231, 485, 573–574
Chang, Meeman 526
Changchengornis 516; *C. hengdaoziensis* 516
Changchun Geological College *see* Changchun University of Sciences and Technology

Index

Changchun University of Sciences and Technology 285
Changdusaurus 152
Changhengornis 131
Changpei, Luo 619
Changpeipus 619; *C. bartholomaii* 619; *C. carbonicus* 619; *C. luanpingeris* 619
Chao Shichin *see* Zhao Xijin
Chaoyangsaurus 153, 199, 201, 385
Chapman, Ralph E. 106, 570–572
Chapman, S. D. 423–424
Charig, Alan G. 142, 154, 252, 254–255, 324, 328, 364–365, 371, 373, 383–384
Charonosaurus 153, 207, 284–285, 285–286, 286–287, 287–288, 288, 398–399, 602; *C. jiayinensis* 285, 285–286, 286–287, 287–288, 602
charophytes 543
Chasmosaurus 154, 207, 288, 288–289, 289–290, 290, 291, 380–381; *C. belli* 289–291; *C. irvinensis* 288, 288–289, 289–290, 290; *C. mariscalensis* 290, 380–381; *C. russelli see Chasmosaurus belli*
Chatterjee, Sankar 34, 412, 502, 502–503, 503–504, 504, 505–506, 506, 524, 526
Chauna chavaria 41
Chayoyangia 132
chelonians 20, 42–43, 45, 60, 70, 74, 82, 85, 94, 125, 139, 265, 314, 323, 341, 364, 381, 392, 398–399, 423, 534, 543, 548, 573, 581
Chen Pei-Ji 135, 208, 296–297, 461–462, 462–464, 464, 465, 517, 517–518, 518–520, 520, 521–522, 522, 523, 603
Chen Shuyun 621, 645
Chenini Sandstones 528
Cherry, Collette 562–563
Cherty Freshwater Beds 313–314
Chialingosaurus 152
Chiappe, Luis M. v, vii, 57, 69, 69–70, 82–84, 118–119, 125–126, 132, 134, 138, 169–170, 172–177, 245–246, 246–247, 249, 292–293, 295, 369–370, 507, 507–508, 515, 562, 645
Chiayüsaurus 151, 207, 291, 291; *C. asianensis* 291; *C. lacustris* 291, 291
Chicago Children's Museum 253
Chicago Natural History Museum *see* The Field Museum
Chicxulub crater 140–141
Chilantaisaurus 148, 347, 422; *C. maortuensis see* "Alashansaurus"; *C. zheziangensis* 422
Chimaera see Sauropus; *C. barrattii see Sauropus*
Chimaerichnus see Sauropus; *C. barrattii see Sauropus*
Chin, Karen 301–302
Chindesaurus 147
Chinese Academy of Geological Sciences 410
Chinese Academy of Sciences *see* Academia Sinica
Chingkankousaurus 149
Chinle Formation 32, 616, 624
Chinle Group 17, 89, 474, 530, 601, 603, 635

Chinnery, Brenda J. 113–114, 201, 258
Chinsamy, Anusuya 24, 27, 246, 249
Chinshakiangosaurus 150, 601; *C. zhongheensis* 601
Chipping Norton Limestone 546
Chirostenotes 136, 140, 149, 174, 207, 291, 292, 476, 560, 574; *C. pergracilis* 174, 560; *?C. elegans* 291–292, 292
Chondrosteosaurus 151, 207, 278, 292
Chonglongpus 619, 623
Chongqing Natural History Museum 303
Chongqingpus see Grallator; *C. microiscus see Grallator* sp.; *C. nananensis see Grallator* sp.; *C. yemiaoxiensis see Grallator* sp.
Chopard, S. 441, 444
Chos Malal locality 60
Choung, Cheng-Ming 129
Chow M. 450, 452
Christian, Andreas 64–65
Christiansen, Per 53, 57, 64, 67, 71, 75–76, 78, 81, 114–115, 570, 572
Chritonsaurus 152
Chuandongocoelurus 147
Chuanjiesaurus 150
Chuannchengpus see Grallator; *C. wuhuangensis see Grallator* sp.
Chubut Group 38, 70
Chubutisaurus 74, 151, 592
Chungkingosaurus 92
Chure, Daniel J. 40, 70, 78, 172, 221, 228–229, 230–233, 262–263, 268, 317–318, 318–319, 319, 404, 406, 444, 444–445, 445–446, 446, 543–544, 544, 545, 547, 575, 577–578, 587, 589, 589–590, 615
Chuxiongpus see Brontopodus; *C. changlingensis see Brontopodus changlingensis*; *C. zheni see Brontopodus changlingensis*
Cifelli, Richard L. 47, 72–73, 278–280, 322–323, 422–423, 436–437, 481, 481–482, 482–485, 592–593
Cionodon 153
circulation 20, 27, 65–66, 230, 316, 567, 576, 580
Citipati 136, 149, 207, 292–293, 293–294, 294–295, 378, 428; *C. osmolskae* 292, 293–294, 295, 428
Cladocyclus 371
Claessens, Leon 115–116
Claorhynchus 153
Claosaurus 151, 194, 196
Clark, James M. 42, 125–126, 173, 176, 292–293, 293–294, 294–295, 331–332, 332, 369–370, 378, 422–423, 428, 507–508, 573–574
Clark, N. D. L. 92, 93
Clasmodosaurus 150
Clements, R. G. 423–424
Clemmensen, L. B. 443–444
Cleveland-Lloyd Dinosaur Quarry 40, 230, 232–233, 262, 268, 543–544
Cleveland Museum of Natural History v, 77
Clevosaurus 444

climate 17, 29, 66, 82, 115–117, 128, 141–142, 217, 268, 319, 392, 452, 586
climbing *see* scansoriality
Clioscaphites 420; *C. vermiformis* 420; *C. choteauensis* 420
Cloverly Formation 73, 278, 304–305, 481
Cloward, Karen v, 32, 96, 266–268, 353, 355, 358
Coelophysis 32–33, 37, 40, 54–55, 55, 56, 121, 136, 147, 179, 181, 207, 230, 295–296, 307, 453, 555, 583, 638; *C. bauri* 37, 54, 136, 295, 307
Coeluroides 147
Coelurosaurichnus 621; *C. grancieri* 621; *C. kehli* 621; *C. kronbergei* 621; *C. largentierensis* 621; *C. metzneri* 621; *C. moeni* 621; *C. palissyi* 621; *C. perriauxi* 621; *C. sabienensis* 621; *C. sassendorfensis* 621; *C. schlauersbachensis* 621; *C. schlehenbergensis* 621; *C. thomasai* 621; *C. toscanus* 621; *C. ziegelangerensis* 621
Coelurus 54–55, 55, 56, 148, 157, 165, 231, 523, 638; *C. agilis* 157; cf. *Coelurus* sp. 54
Cohen, S. 45
Colbert, Edwin H. [Harris] v, 114, 295–296, 316–17, 630
cold bloodedness *see* ectothermy
Colepiocephale lambei 597
Collado Formation 388–389
College of Eastern Utah 77, 322–323, 341
College of Eastern Utah Prehistoric Museum 77, 322, 343
Collignoniceras woollgari Zone 421
cololites 412–413
La Colonia Formation 17
Coloradisaurus 150, 183
Columbian Museum 77, 194
Columbosauripus 621; *C. amouraensis* 621; *?C. ungulatus* 621
Colville Group 46
Comanchean Series 627
comets 140
Como Bluff 37, 535, 537
Company, J. 102
"Complejo Porfirico" 621, 636, 643
Compsognathus 27, 37, 148, 175, 207, 243, 296–297, 297, 514, 517–519, 523, 638; *C. longipes* 37, 175, 296, 297
Compsosuchus 148
computer imagery and tomography (CT) 37, 41–42, 53, 61–64, 76, 90, 94, 104, 116, 143, 208, 223, 226, 230, 233, 256, 258–259, 263, 273–274, 295, 305, 309, 318, 350, 410, 485, 537, 563–564, 570–571, 574–575, 587
Conchoraptor 136–137, 149, 292, 294–295, 378
Confuciusornis 131, 133, 136–138, 177, 369, 515–516, 521; *C. sanctus* 136, 369, 516
Connely, Melissa V. 535
continental drift *see* plate tectonics
Continuoolithus 646; *C. canadensis* 646
Coombs, Walter P., Jr. 53, 178, 184, 219, 220–221, 235, 249–250, 334–337, 348, 385–387, 447, 449, 493, 549

Cooper, David 75
Cope, Edward Drinker 231, 233, 546–547
coprolites 297, 301, 364, 559, 613
Coran, R. 423
Coria, Rodolfo A. [Anibal] 25–26, 43, 60, 69, 69–70, 82–84, 169–170, 208–209, 236, 236–237, 237–238, 238, 239, 245–246, 246–247, 249–250, 339, 341, 343–344, 344–346, 347, 365–366, 366–367, 367, 468, 468–469, 469–470, 473–474, 593
Corvipes 621; *C. lacertoideus* 621
Corythosaurus 104, 153, 207, 297–298, 322; *C. casuarius* 104; *Corythosaurus* sp. 104
Coturnix japonica 27
Council for Geoscience of South Africa 337
Coupled Plasma-Atomic Emission Spectometry (ICP-MS) 143
Courel, Louis 621
Courtillot, V. 141
Coy, Clive 341, 560
Cracraft, Joel 291
Craetomus see Struthiosaurus; *C. lepidophorous see Struthiosaurus austriacus*; *C. pawlowitschi see Struthiosaurus austracus*
Cranwell, Gregory P. 70, 209
Craspedodon 152
Craterosaurus 93, 152; *C. pottonensis* 93
Creisler, Ben 526
Creosaurus see Allosaurus
Crerar Library 180
Cretoxyrhina mantelli 420
Crichton, Michael 298
Crichtonsaurus 151, 207, 298, 298–299, 299; *C. bohlini* 298, 298–299
Cristatusaurus see Baryonyx; *C. laparenti see Baryonyx* sp.
crocodilians and crocodyliforms 15, 16–17, 20–21, 23, 25, 27, 37, 43, 54, 56–57, 60–61, 70, 82–83, 85, 94, 115–117, 120, 121–123, 125, 139, 209, 243, 265–266, 273, 293, 301, 308, 323, 338, 345, 352, 361, 364, 381, 392, 408, 437, 463, 474, 493, 501, 529, 543, 545–548, 565, 581, 583, 595, 634, 637
Crocodylus porosus 25
Crosbysaurus 151, 474, 601; *C. harrisae* 474, 601
Cruickshank, Arthur R. I. 45, 46–47, 371, 373, 493
crustaceans 371
Cryolophosaurus 148
Cryptodraco 151
Cryptovolans 138, 150, 207, 299–301, 490; *C. pauli* 299
Cuenca-Bescós, Gloria [also Cuenca Bescós] 67, 101–102, 102, 138–139, 252, 255, 363, 364–365
Culpepper Stone Quarry 617
Cuny, Gilles 13, 59–60, 387–388
Currie, Philip J. 40, 43–44, 47, 49–50, 51, 51–52, 52, 126, 127–128, 129, 136, 157, 171, 208–209, 215–216, 217, 218, 235, 250–251, 258, 280, 282, 300–301, 308, 310, 320, 324, 328, 336–

337, 339–341, 343–344, *344,* *346,* 347–348, *348,* 350, 360–362, 390–391, 408, 413–414, 423–424, 455, 458–459, 469–470, 517, *517–518,* 518–520, *520,* 521–522, *522,* 523; 474–478, 485–486, *496–497,* 497–498, *498–499,* 500, 506, 508–509, *509–511,* 511, 514–515, 517, *517–518,* 518–520, *520,* 521–522, *522,* 523, 559–560, 573–574, 616, 627, 646, 650, 653

Curry Rogers, Kristina A. [also Curry, Kristina A.] 24, *25,* 418–419, 468, 470, *470–471,* 471–472, *472–473,* 473–474, 566

cursoriality 39, 44, 53, *54,* 117–119, 130–131, 133, 216, 237, 276, 328, 344–346, 412, 490, 439, 539, *541,* 542, 583, 585, 607

Curtice, Brian D. 543, 545, 549–550, 553–555

Cuvier, Baron Georges 363–365, 404, 406, 545, 547

cynodonts 58

Czerkas, Stephan A. v, *130,* 132, 134–135, 138, *156,* 241–242, 275, 299–301, *304,* 486–487, *487,* 488–491, 515, 517

Czerkas, Sylvia J. v, 138, 488, 491

Dacentrurus 91–92, 152, 355, 358, 389, 449; *D. armatus* 389

Dachungosaurus 150, *601; D. yunnanensis* 601

Daffner, R. H. 51

Dahn, R. D. 132

The Daily Mail 328

Dakota Formation 621

Dakota Group 619, 628

Dakotasaurus 621; *D. browni* 621

Dalangshan Formation 137, 358–359

Dalla Vecchia, Fabio Marco 40, 79, *79–80,* 80, 97, *98,* 99, 101, *101*

Dalton, Rex 515, 517

Dalton Wells Quarry 343, 589

Damalasaurus 150, *601; D. laticostalis* 601

Dames, W. 423–424

Dandakosaurus 147

Danubiosaurus see Struthiosaurus; D. anceps see Struthiosaurus austriacus

Daohugou locality 491

Dark Red Beds 255

Darwin, Charles 119

Dashanpu quarry 303, 502

Dashveg, Demberelynin 125–126, 292, 295

Daspletosaurus 37, 44, 51–52, 149, 172, 174, 207, 216, 301–302, *302,* 350, 497, 528, 580–581; *D. torosus* 37, 51, 172, 174, *302; Daspletosaurus sp.* 301, *302*

Datousaurus 151, 207, 303, *303–304; D. bashanensis* 303, *303–304*

Daubentonia 489

Davis, P. G. 297

Dawangzhansi site 487

Day, Julia J. 71

Dean, J. 621

Deana see Anomoepus; D. fulicoides see Anomoepus

Debus, Allen A. v, *3, 41,* 63, *535, 567, 579, 622*

Debus, Diane E. v, 63, *376–377*

Debus, Karl *567*

Deccan Traps 141–142

Deck, Lina T. 571

Degex, Jean-Michel 81

Deinocheirus 147, 341

Deinodon 149

Deinonychus 20, 40, 46, 54–55, *55,* 56, 108, 116, 119, 123, *130,* 138, 150, 174, 207, 300, *304,* 304–305, 423, 513, 585, 587, 589–590; *D. antirrhopus* 54, 108, *130,* 174, *304,* 304–305, 585

Delair, Justin B. 269, 314–315, 404, 406, 626, *626,* 638

Delanshan locality 463

Deltadromeus 148, 178

Deltapodus 621; *D. brockericki* 621

Deltorrischnus 621; *D. goyenechei* 621

Demathieu, Georges R. 621, 624

Demere, Thomas A. *219,* 220–221, 337

de Moraes, L. J. 631

Dendroolithus 645; *?D. dentriticus* 645; *?D. furcatus* 645; *?D. microporosus* 645; *?D. sanlimiaoensis* 645; *D. verrucarius* 645; *D. wangdianensis* 645; *?D. xichuanensis* 645; *?D. zhaoyin-gensis* 645

Denver Museum of Nature and Science v, 77, *159, 186, 277, 278,* 316, *316,* 426, 436, 538, 542, 592

Denver Natural History Museum *see* Denver Museum of Nature and Science

Department of Land and Resources, Hohhot 414

Department of Mineral Resources, Bangkok 91, *91*

Departamento Nacional de Produão Mineral 88

De Pauw, L. F. 364

Depéret, Charles 566

De Queen Limestone 36

Deuterotrisauropus see Grallator

De Valais, S. 33–34, 343–344, 347

Devil's Coulee locality 391

Dial, Kenneth P. 120

Dianchungosaurus 91, 153

Diceratops 154, *204; D. hatchery* 204

Diclonius 153

Dicraeosaurus 62, 64–66, 75–76, 114, 150, 244, 318, 389, 416; *D. hansemanni* 64–65, 114

DiCroce, Tony 96–97, 435, *435–436,* 437, 592

Dictyoolithus 645; *D. hongpoensis* 645; *D. neixiangensis* 645

dicynodonts 17, 45, 530

diet 3, 6, *14,* 16–17, *18,* 20, 29, 32–33, 35, 44–47, 53, 57, 57, 59, 66–68, *71,* 76, 78, 78–79, *81,* 89–90, 97–98, 114–116, 135, 139–140, 155, 180, 208, 215–216, *218,* 221–222, 229, 231, 259–260, 265, 268, 273–274, 291, 297, 301, 303, 307, 335, 338, 341, 345, 364, 368, 373, 392, 398, 401, 403, 412, 432, 439, 443–444, 474, 476, 483–486, 502, 573, 581, 583–584, 586–587, 607

Dilkes, David W. 390–391, *391*

Dilophosauripus 621–622, *622; D. williamsi* 621

Dilophosaurus 19, 30, 121, 147, 207, 305, *305–306,* 306–307, 310, 340, 366–367, 388, 465, 622, *622; D. wetherilli* 305–306, 306–307, 310, 340, 388, 622

Dimodosaurus poligniensis see Plateosaurus longiceps

Dinehichnus 622; *D. socialis* 622

Dingus, Lowell 82–84, 169–170, 245–246, *246–247,* 249, 292, 295, 378, 645

Dinheirosaurus 151

Dinodontosaurus 17

Dinofest *78, 81, 130, 198, 304,* *376–377, 343*

DINOLAB v, *4, 159–160, 182*

DinoPress 40, 75, 324, 419

"The Dinosaur Egg and Embryo Project" 45

Dinosaur Eggs and Babies 645

Dinosaur Hill 32

Dinosaur Hollow 32

"Dinosaur Jim" *see* James A. Jensen

Dinosaur Museum v, *419*

Dinosaur National Monument 70, 77, 115, 231–232, 398, 542

Dinosaur Park Formation 51, 90, 126, 280, 288–290, 297–298, 302, 335, 381, 474, 476–477, 486

"Dinosaur Project" 347

Dinosaur Provincial Park 48, 51–52, 112, *113,* 297, 391, 574

"Dinosaur Renaissance" vii

Dinosaur Ridge 628

Dinosaur State Park *618, 622,* 623–624

Dinosaur Systematics: Approaches and Perspectives 478

Dinosaur Systematics Symposium 615

Dinosaur Tracks 615

Dinosaur Tracks and Other Fossil Footprints of Europe 615

Dinosaur Tracks and Other Fossil Footprints of the Western United States 615

Dinosaur Tracks and Traces 615

Dinosaur Valley State Park 617

Dinosaur Wash 32

"Dinosaur World Tour" *see* "Dinosaur Project"

The Dinosauria 413, 653

Dinosauria International, Ltd. *81*

Dinosaurichnium see Parachirotherium; D. postchirotheroides see Parachirotherium postchirotheroides

Dinosauripus see Dinosaurichnium

Dinosauropodes 622–623; *D. bransfordii; D. crawfordii* 622; *D. lamphii* 621; *D. magrawi* 622; *D. nettletoni* 622; *D. osborni* 622; *D. pulveri* 622; *D. sweeti* 622; *D. wilsoni* 622

Dinosaurs of the Flaming Cliffs 602

Dinotyrannus megagracilis see Tyrannosaurus rex

Diplodocus 62–66, 70, 75–76, *78, 81,* 114, 151, 181, *184,* 207, 307–308, *308–309,* 309–310, 318, 389, 416, 50, 553; *D. carnegii*

64–65, *78,* 114, *184,* 309, 550; *D. hayi* 184

Diplotomodon 148

Diprotodon 249

Dire Straits 400

Dirt Bed 313

Discours sur les révolutions de la surface du globe 364

disease 51, 112, 232–233, 260, 263, 265, 267, 316–317, 537–539, 586

Djadokhta Formation 250, 292, 378, 455, 485, 508, 649

DNA 576

Dockum Formation 506, 621

Dockum Group 624

Dr. Lee's Pit 269

Dodson, Peter v, 38, 46, 64, 70–71, 115, 118–119, 216, 218, 280, 282, 375–376, 384, 386–387, 408, 413, 428–429, *429,* 430, 456, 458–459, 467, 484–485, 515, 517, 523, 526, 543, 653

Doh, S. J. 465,

Dolichosuchus 147, 207, 310; *D. cristatus* 310

Dollo, Louis 364–365, *626*

Dong Zhi-Ming [formerly Zhiming] 44–45, 73–74, *74,* 126, 194, 201, 251, 255–256, *256,* 296–298, *298–299,* 299, 303, 332, 369, *369–370,* 370, 381, 399, 404, 406, 408, 421–423, 450, 452, 454, *454–455,* 455–456, *456–457,* 458–459, 465–466, *466–467,* 467–468, 485, 492–493, *496–497,* 497–498, *498–499,* 500, 508–509, *509–511,* 511, 516–517, 521, 523, 555, 559–560, 573–574, 645

Douglass, Earl 623

Downs, William R. 60, 250, 398

Draconyx 152, 207, 310, *310–311,* 311–312, *312; D. loureiroi* 310, *310–312,* 312

Dracopelta 152, 449

Drinker 152, 433–434

Dromaeosauroides bornholmensis 597

Dromaeosaurus 37, *38,* 46–47, *48,* 49, 138–140, 150, 174, *176,* 325, 477–478, 486, 515; *D. albertensis* 37, *38,* 46–47, *48,* 49, 139, 174, *176,* 486; *Dromaeosaurus* morphotype A 477

Dromiceiomimus 149, 340; *D. brevetertius* 340

drought 40, 217, 268, 317, 538, 595

Drushel, R. A. 437

Dry Mesa Dinosaur Quarry 9–10, 74, 230, 543, 549, *550–552,* 553

Dryosaurus 27, 152, 190, 195, 237–239, 318, *622; D. altus* 190; *D. lettowvorbecki* 27

Dryptosauroides 148

Dryptosaurus 147–148, 157, 170–171, 207, 312

Dubreuil, A. 446

"Dueling Dinosaurs" *174,* 584

Dufeau, David 508

Dughi, R. 646

Dughioolithus see Cairanoolithus; D. roussetensis see Cairanoolithus dughii

Durand, J. F. 337–338, *338*

Dutuit, J.-M. 617

Index

dwarfism 72, 271, 549
Dynamosaurus see *Tyrannosaurus*
Dyoplosaurus acutosquameus see
 Euoplocephalus tutus
Dysganus 154
Dyslocosaurus 76, 150
Dystrophaeus 76, 150
Dystylosaurus see *Supersaurus*; *D.
 edwini* see *Supersaurus viviane*
Dzhadokhtskaya Formation *110–
 111*

"E. Feruglio" museum 74
Earth Science Museum v, *4–6*, 9–
 11, 77, *266, 269*, 341, *589*
East Berlin Formation 623
East *Camarasaurus* Quarry *19,
 263*, 266
Eaton, Jeffrey G. 72, 279–280,
 322–323, 436–437, 592–593
Ebel, Klaus 17, *19*, 19–20
Eberth, David A. v, 40, *41*, 215,
 216–218, 235, 258, 280, 282,
 289, 291, 413–414, 455, 459,
 461–462, *462–464*, 465
Echinodon 153, 207, 312–313, *313*,
 314–315, 572; *E. becklesii* 312,
 313, 314; *Echinodon* sp. 314
Echkar Formation 37
Economos, A. C. 256, 258
ectothermy 64, 114–117, 121, 208,
 225
Edmarka 148, 180; *E. rex* 180
Edmonton Formation *112*
Edmontonia 93–94, 152, 185–187,
 189, 348, 548; *E. rugosidens* 93
Edmontosaurus x, 17, *18*, 98–99,
 104, 153, 195, *195–196*, 207,
 259, 315, *315–316*, 316–317, *317*,
 362, 381, 500–501; *E. annectens*
 196, 316, *316*, 362; *E. regalis* x,
 18, 104, *195, 315, 317*, 500–501
Efraasia see *Sellosaurus*; *see also*
 597; *E. minor* see *Sellosaurus
 minor*; *see also* 597
Efremov, Ivan A. 623
Egg Island 573
eggs, eggshells, and egg beds v,
 45–46, *46–47*, 56, 82–83, *83*,
 102, 110, 120, 122, 129, 137, 142–
 143, *218*, 249, 292–294, 296–
 297, 301, 305, 338, 341, 364,
 370, 373, 391, 427, 469, 565,
 573–574, 615, 645–646, *646–
 647*, 648–649, *649–650*, 650–
 651, *651–652*, 652
Egi, Naoko 104–105
Einiosaurus 154, *202*, 291; *E. pro-
 curvicornis 202*
Ejinhoro Formation 485, 508
El Molino Formation 628
Elaphrosaurus 46, 147–148, 178–
 179, 207, 317–318, *318–319*, 319,
 404; *E. bambergi* 317–318, *318*,
 319
Elephant Butte Reservoir 578
Elephantopoides 623; *E. barkhause-
 nensis* 623
Ellenberger, F. 381
Ellenberger, Paul 381, 384, 607,
 616–617, 621, 623–625, 627–
 628, 630, 633–637, 639, 642
Elliot Formation 207, 337, *338*,
 383, 443, 530, 616–617, 624–
 625, 630, 633–637, 642
Ellipsoolithus 646; *E. khedaensis* 646

Ellison, Mick *340*
Elmisaurus 121, 136, 149, 207, 291,
 319–320, *320–321*, 341, 560; *E.
 elegans* 319–320, *320–321*
Elmisaurus quarry 560
Elongatoolithus 142, 647–648; *E.
 andrewsi* 647; *E. elongatus* 647;
 E. excellens 647; *E. frustrabilis*
 647; *E. magnus* 647; *E. sigillarius* 647; *E. subtitectorius* 647
Elopteryx 149
Elrhaz Formation 252
Elżanowski, Andrzej 131, 136–137,
 293, 295, 339, 341, 369–370,
 428, 513–515, 517
Emausaurus 152, 493
Embasaurus 147
embryos 24, 40, 45–46, *46–47*,
 57, 82–84, 119, 125–126, 292–
 293, 294, 305, 361–362, 389–
 390, 458, 572, 574, 645, *647*
endocasts *see* brains and endocasts
endothermy 57, 64, *78, 81*, 114–
 117, 121, 123, 126, 128, 208, 225,
 259–260, 519
Enigmosaurus 136, 149
Eobrontosaurus 151
Eoenantiornis 131, 516; *E. buhler*
 516
Eolambia 96, 152, 193–194, 196,
 207, 234, 320, 322–323; *E. caroljonesa* 322
Eoraptor 6, *13–14*, 147, 154–155,
 157–158, 210, 255, 530, 581; *E.
 lunensis 13–14*
Eotyrannus 149, 207, 323–324,
 324–325, 325–326, *326–327*,
 327–328, *328*, 601–603; *E.
 lengi* 323–324, *324–328*
Epachthosaurus 70, 151
Epanterias see *Allosaurus*
Epidendrosaurus see *Scansoriopteryx*; *E. ningchengensis* see
 Scansoriopteryx heilmanni
Equijubus 151, 207, 328–329; *E.
 normani* 329
Erectopus 46, 148, 181, 334; *E. su-
 perbus* 445
Erickson, Bruce R. 301–302, 308,
 310
Erickson, Gregory M. 24, *25*,
 225, 233, 579, 587
Erliansaurus 149, 207, 329, *329–
 330*, 330–331; *E. bellamanus*
 329, *329–330*, 330–331
Erlikosaurus 45, 149, 330, 340,
 422; *E. andrewsi* 422
Erythrosuchus africanus 61
Eshanosaurus 136, 149, 207, 331–
 332, *332*, 422; *E. deguchiianus*
 331, *332*
Estancia "Ocho Hermanos" 38
Estes, Richard D. 476, 478
Estreito farm *614, 620, 624, 640*
Estuarine Series 283
Etjo Sandstein 616, 638
Eubrontes 30, 40, 617, 623–624,
 626, 642, 652; *E. approximatus*
 623; *E. bessieri* 623; *E. divaricatus* 623; *E. euskelosauroides* 623;
 E. expansum 623; *E. giganteus*
 30, 623; *E. gracillimus* 623; *E.
 platypus* 623; *E. thianschianicum*
 623; *E. thomasi* 623; *E. tuberatus* 623; *E. veillonensis* 623; *Eubrontes* sp. 623
Eudromia 583

Eucamerotus see *Chondrosteosaurus*; *E. foxii* see *Chondrosteosaurus*
Eucoelophysis 147
eucynodonts 59
Eudes-Deslongchamps, J. A. 444–
 446
Euhelopus 64, *73*, 75, 80, 87, 114,
 151, *211–212*, 291, 465, 467; *E.
 zdanskyi 73*, 114, *211–212*
Euoplocepalus 93–95, 152, 185,
 187, 189, 207, 332–333, *333–
 334*, 334–337, 447; *E. tutus* 94,
 333, *333–334*, 334–336
Eurolimnornis see *Paleocursornis*
Euronychodon 102, 138, *139*, 149,
 474; cf. *Euronychodon* sp. 138,
 139
Euskelosaurus 150, 337–338, *338*,
 495, 530, 562, 626; *E. browni*
 337; cf. *Euskelosaurus* sp. indet.
 see *Plateosaurus stormbergensis*
Eustreptospondylus 148, 180–181,
 546–547; *E. divesensis* see *Pivetausaurus divesensis*
Eutynichnium 623; *E. lusitanicum*
 623; *E. pombali* 623
Evans, David C. *105*, 105–106,
 297–298
evolution vii, 16–17, 25, 27–29,
 39–40, 42, 62, 66–71, 76, 78,
 84, 89–90, 93, 95–96, 106, 113–
 115, 117–124, 126, 128–137, 154,
 157–158, 177–178, 180, 194, 197,
 204, 209, 221–222, 233, 255,
 258, 273–274, 276, 298, 300,
 302–303, 315–316, 327, 350,
 368, 374–375, 385–387, 396,
 411–412, 420, 474, 482, 484–
 485, 489–491, 506, 515–516,
 519–521, 531, 542, 544, 549,
 562, 572, 581–583
"Evolutionary Origin of Feathers"
 symposium 118–119, 133–134
Exallopus see *Saurexallopus*; *E.
 lovei* see *Saurexallopus lovei*
extinction 12, 15, 17, 22, 28, 30,
 41, 57, 60, 72, 111, 125, 138–141,
 141, 142–143, 180, 223, *226*,
 301, 336, 484, 613, 615, 645
eyesight *see* vision

Fabre, J. 381
Fabrosaurus 152, 616
Fallon, J. F. 132
Fanzhangzi quarry 516
Farke, Andrew Allen 111–112, *113*,
 567
Farlow, James O. v, 53, 118, 208–
 209, 277–278, 345–347, 423–
 424, 515, 517, 581–582, 587,
 615, 617, *618*, 627, 634, 653
Fassett, James R. 143
Fastovsky, David E. 32–33
faunal exchange 15, 20, 72, 86,
 178, 180, 194–195, 201, 203,
 279, 312, 318, 323, 344, 381,
 403, 473, 587
Faveoloolithus 646; *F. ningxiaensis*
 646
*Feathered Dinosaurs and the Origin
 of Flight* 138, 488
feathers and feather impressions
 6–7, 57, 115, 117–118, 120, 122,
 124, *124*, 126, 128–129, *130–131*,
 131–135, 137–138, 251, 299–

300, *304*, 369, 408, 410–411,
 411, 412, 486, 488, 512, *514*,
 515–521, 524, 607, 636
Feduccia, Alan 124, *124*, 126, 132–
 135, 369–370, 515, 517, 519,
 523
Feist, Monique 101–102, *102*
Felch, Marshal P. 534–535
Fengiahe Formation 624, 634,
 637, 644–645
Ferganasaurus 150, 207, 338–339;
 F. verzilini 338–339
The Field Museum [formerly
 Chicago Natural History Mu-
 seum and Field Museum of
 Natural History] v, *3*, 8, *41, 71,
 77*, 77, *105, 109, 156, 173, 194,
 225, 257, 457, 537, 578, 579,
 646–647, 649*
Figgins, J. 317
Filla, James 353
Fiorillo, Anthony R. *46–47, 48*,
 51, 76, 211–213, 215, 231–233,
 262–263, 268, 391
First International Symposium on
 Dinosaur Tracks and Traces 615
Fisher, Paul E. 563–565
fishes 6, 9, 42, 56, 60, 74, 85,
 139, *194*, 265, 297, 371–373,
 381, 392, *405*, 406, 408, 420,
 476–477, 489, 516, 529
Fleming Fjord Formation 443,
 624
flight 118–124, 126, 128–131, 133–
 136, 138, 299–301, 411–412,
 489–491, 501, 516–517, 519, 521,
 607
floods and flooding 40, 66, 84,
 141, 213, 217, 222, 252, 268,
 280, 307, 324, 337–338, 392,
 476, 595–596
Florida Symposium on Dino-
 saur/Bird Evolution 489
Flynn, John J. 530
"Fontllonga" hadrosaurid 102, 153
footprints v, 12–13, 30, 36, 40, 42,
 44, 49, 60, 62, 67, 71–72, 74,
 89, 98, 118, 208, 213, 297, 309,
 312, 341, 343, 346, 364, 390,
 408, 560, 583, 590, 613, *613–
 614*, 614–617, *618*, 619, *620*,
 621–622, *622*, 623–624, *624*,
 625–626, *626*, 627–628, *629*,
 630–631, *631–632*, 633–639,
 639–641, 641–643, *643–644*,
 644–645
Ford, Tracy L. v, 51, 89, 172, 218–
 219, *219–220*, 220–221, 239,
 545, 559–560, *575*, 577–578,
 587
Forest Marble 314
Forster, Catherine A. 38, 42, 90,
 134, 155, 173, 178–179, 183–184,
 194, 204, 286, 288–291, 399–
 400, *400–401*, 401–403, 413,
 418–419, 431, 468, 470–471,
 471–472, 472–474, 566, 593
Fort Union Formation 140
Foster, John R. 40, 76–79, 221,
 231, 233, 543–544, *544*, 545
Fouch, T. D. 465
Fowler, Denver 254
Fox, William 93
Fraas, Eberhard 437, 440, 444
Frankfurt, Nicholas G. 562
Franzosa, Jonathan W. 41–42,
 208–209

Fraser, Nicholas C. v, 155–157, 209, *209–210*, 210, 617
Frazzetta, T. H. 228–229, 233
Fredericks, Mike v
Freeman, E. F. 314–315
Frenchman Formation 476, 569, 575, 586
Friday, Robert 36
"Fruita fabrosaurid" 314
Fruitland Formation 107
Fuente Espudia locality 449
Fuentes, Federico Meijide 252, 255, 634
"Fukui iguanodontian" 193
Fukuiraptor 148
Fukuisaurus tetoriensis 597
Fulengia 150
Fulgurotherium 152
Fulicopus see *Sauropus*; *F. lycellianus* see *Sauropus*
"Fusinanus" see *Eoraptor*

Gabounia [also Gabunia, Gabuniya], L. K. 630, 636
Gallimimus 37, 126, 149, 174–176, 207, *340*, 340–341; *G. bullatus* 37, 126, 174–176, *340*, 340–341; cf. *Gallimimus* 341
Gallina, P. A. 61
Gallo Formation, El 545
Gallus 54, 583; *G. gallus* 54
Galton, Peter M. v, 57–58, 76, 91, 96, 106, 190, 197, 230–231, 233, 239, *243*, 272, 287–288, 310, 312, 314–315, 318–319, 322–323, 335, 337–338, 364, 384, 387–388, 427–428, 437–438, *438–439*, 439–440, *440*, 441–444, 449, 478, *479–480*, 480–481, 494–495, *495*, 496, 504–505, 529–530, 531–532, 532–533, *533–534*, 534, 537, 542–545, 548–549, 572, 608
Galtonia 89, 151
Gand, G. 621
Gangloff, Roland A. 46, *48*, 99
Gangxianosaurus 149
Gansu yumenensis 131
Gao, Yuhui 133, 138, 516–517, 523, *593–594*, 594–595
Garcia, Géraldine *19*, 143, 648
Garcia, R. A. 60
Gargoyleosaurus 7–8, 11, 152, 185, *186–197*, 360, 386; *G. parkpini* see *Gargoyleosaurus parkpinorum*; *G. parkpinorum* 7, 11, 185, *186–187*
Garland, T., Jr. 208
Garrido, Alberto C. 83–84, 236, 239, 245
Garudimimus 149, 174; *G. brevipes* 174
Gasosaurus 148, 157; *G. constructus* 157
Gasparini, Zulma 94, 445–446
Gasparinisaura 152, 190, 237, 239
Gaston, Robert 341, *342*, 343, 514, 517, 590
Gaston Quarry 343
Gastonia 152, 185–187, 189, 207, 235, 341, *342–343*, 343, 590; *G. burgei* 185, 235, 341, *342–343*
gastroliths 45, 57, 76, 126, 165, 276–277, 297, 301, 307, 341, 412–413, 444, 463

gastropods 301
Gates, Terry 268
Gates Formation 627, 639
Gatesy, Stephen M. 118, 122, 215, 218, 345, 347, 581–583, 587, 624
Gaudry, A. 441, 444
Gauthier, Jacques A. 53, 56, 118, 132, 154, 156, 177, 306–307, 324, 328, 388, 407–408, 420, 423, 453–454, 465, 469–470, 489, 481, 494, 504–506, 514, 517, 559–560, 573–574
Gavinosaurus see *Eotyrannus*
Gay, Robert J. 296, 305–306
Gebhardt, Robert 587
Geist, Nicholas R. 124, *124*, 125–126, 133–135, 493, 520–523
Genusaurus 148, 178–179
Genyodectes 148, 178
Geoffroy Saint-Hilaire, E. 545–547
Geological Museum (University of Wyoming) v, 353
Geological Museum of Heilongjang 285
Geological Society of America 11
Geranosaurus 153
German-Tanzanian Tendaguru Expedition 2000 318
Gething Formation 639
ghost lineages 13, 170, 314, 332
Ghost Ranch quarry 33
Gibbons, A. 515, 517
Giffin [Buchholtz], Emily A. 526, 528
Gigandipus 623; *G. caudatus* 623
Giganotosaurus 50, 148, 164, 180, 207–208, 274, 343–344, *344–345*, 345–346, *346–347*, 347, 469–470; *G. carolinii* 50, 343, *344–347*
Gigantosauropus 623; *G. asturiensis* 623
Gigantosaurus 151
Gigantotherium see *Gigandipus*; *G. asturiensis* see *Gigandipus*
Gillette, David D. 33, 76, 301–302, 422–423, 431, 615
Gilmore, Charles Whitney 215, *229*, 232–233, 241–242, 244, 271–272, 337, 374, 475, 478, 532, 535, 537–538, 542, 559–560
Gilmoreosaurus 151, 193–194, 322
Gilpin, David 96–97
Gimènez, Olga del 60, 74, 469–470, 593
Ginsburg, L. 381, 384
Giraffa camelopardalis 64
Gishlick, A. D. 119, 123
Glasby, G. P. 141
Glen Canyon Group 407, 621, 633
Glen Rose Formation 36, 627, 630
Glen Rose limestone 617
Glenrock Paleontological Museum 353
Global Positioning System 574
Glyptodontopelta 152
Glyptos 543
Gobisaurus 152, 207, 347–348, *348*; *G. domuculus* 347, *348*
Gobititan 151, 207, 349; *G. shenzouensis* 349
Godefroit, Pascal 102, 194, 200,

284–285, *285–286*, 286–287, *287–288*, 288, 381, 398–399, 454, *454–455*, 455–456, *456–457*, 458–459
Gojirasaurus 147
Gondwana 15, 29, 34, 38–39, 61, 87, 178, 180, 190, 208, 249–251, 403, 566
Gondwanatitan see *Aeolosaurus*
Gongbusaurus 43, 152
Gongxianosaurus 150, 207, *349*, 349–350; *G. shibeiensis* 349, *349*
González, Riga 88, 276
Goodwin, Mark B. 198, 259–260, 530–532, 569, 572
Gorgosaurus 3, 37, 44, 51, *52*, 149, 172, 174, 207, 280, 350–351, *351*, 575; *G. lancinator* see *Tarbosaurus bataar*; *G. libratus* 37, 51, *52*, 172, 174, 280, 350–351, *351*; *Gorgosaurus* sp. 559
Gorro Frigio Formation 74
Gosau Formation 547–548
Goseongosauripus 623; *G. kimi* 623
Gow, Christopher E. 383–384
Gower, David J. 61
Goyocephale 153, 190, 197–198; *G. lattimorei* 190
Graciliceratops 153, 200, 207, 351–352, *352*, 408; *G. mongoliensis* 352, *352*
Gracilisuchus 17
Grallator 30, 616–617, 619, 621, 623–624, *624*, 625–627, 633–637; *G. (A.) australis* 624; *G. (G.) bibractensis* 624; *G. (G.) cuneateus* 624; *G. (G.) cursorius* 624; *G. (G.) damanei* 624; *G. (G.) emeiensis* 624; *G. (G.) exertus* 624; *G. (G.) formosus* 624; *G. (G.) giganteus* 624; *G. (G.) gracilis* 624; *G. (A.) gwyneddesis* 624; *G. (A.) hitchcocki* 624; *G. (G.) limnosus* 624; *G. (G.) matsiengensis* 624; *G. (G.) maximus* 624; *G. (A.) minor* 624; *G. (A.) minusculus* 624; *G. (G.) molapoi* 624; *G. (G.) oloensis* 624; *G. (A.) parallelus* 624; *G. (A.) poolei* 624; *G. (A.) sillimani* 624; *G. (G.) sillimani* 624; *G. (G.) sulcatus* 624; *G. (G.) tenuis* 624; *G. (E.) tuberosus* 624; *G. (A.) validus* 624; *G. (G.) variabilis* 624; *Grallator* sp. 624
Grand Staircase–Escalante National Monument 111, 431
Granger, Walter 455, 459
Granger's Hill locality 378
"granicones" 314, 423
Graves Museum of Archaeology and Natural History 489
Gravitholus see *Stegoceras*; *G. albertae* see *Stegoceras* sp.; *G. sternbergi* see *Stegoceras* sp.
"The Great Russian Dinosaurs Exhibition" *458*, *555*, *557*, *651*
"Greatest Show Unearthed" see "Dinosaur Project"
gregariousness 40, *41*, 42, 52, 72, 83, 90, 112–113, 216, 280, 307, 337, *351*, 617, *640*
Gregaripus 625; *G. bairdi* 625
Gregory, William King 108, 339, 455, 459
Gresham College 406

Gresslyosaurus see *Plateosaurus*; "*Gresslyosaurus* cf. *plieningeri*" see *Plateosaurus engelhardti*; *G. ingens* see *Plateosaurus ingens*; *G. robustus* see *Plateosaurus robustus*
Griffiths, Peter J. 126, 128–129, *130*, 296–297
Grigorescu, Dan 97, *101*, 102, 196–197, 243–244, 271–272, 322–323, 607
Grolier, M. J. 60
Ground Penetrating Radar (GPR) 212
Group Rio do Peixe *620*, *624*, *631–632*, *639–640*
growth see ontogeny
growth rings 27
Gryposaurus 104, 153, 259; *Gryposaurus* sp. 104
Guabisaurus 147, 154, 530
Guimarota locality 432–433, 544
Günga, Hanns-Christian 65–66, 256, 258
Gunma Museum of Natural History *265*, 267
Günther, Bruno 256, 258
Gunther, R. T. 406
Gurich, G. 636, 639
gut contents 301, *302*
Gyeongsang Supergroup 305, 465
Gyeongsang System 642
Gyposaurus sinensis see *Lufengosaurus hueni*
Gypsichnites 621, 625; *G. pacensis* 625
Gyrotrisauropus 625; *G. planus* 625

Haas, George 335, 337
Hadrosaurichnus 625, 628; *H. australis* 626
Hadrosaurus 153, 194; *H. foulkii* 194
hair (in dinosaurs, birds, and pterosaurs) 128, *130*, 135, 491, 515, 519
Hall, Evan 278
Hallett, Mark v, *470*, *473*
Halstead, L. Beverly 406
Halticosaurus 147, 207, 310, 352–353; *H. longotarsus* 353, *353*; *H. orbitoangulatus* 353
Haman Formation 625
Hamanosauripus 625; *H. ovalis* 625; *H. ungulatus* 625
Hamblin, David 266
Hamm, Shawn A. 420
Hammer, Michael 563–565
Hancox, P. J. 381, 443, 530
Hanna, Rebecca R. 232–233
Hanssuessia sternbergi 597
Hancock, P. J. 381, 443, 530
Hanwulosaurus 152, 601–602
Haplocanthosaurus 60, 76, 151, 207, 239, 284, 353, 550
Happ, John W. 565
Harbicht, Darwin 316
Harebell Formation 636
Hargreaves, Richard 328
Harkness, R. 635
Harpymimus 149
Harris, Jerald Davic 64, 118, 208–209, 232, 233, 375–376, 384, 386–387, 512, 517, 523, 526, 623, 636
Hartman, Axel F. 42, *42*
Hartman, Scott 298

Index

Harvard University 383
Harwell, Amy 116–117, 493
Hasadong Formation 465–466, 468
Hatcher, John Bell 79, 114
hatchlings 27, 37, 120, 122, 125–126, 129, 158, 198, 297, 338, 428, *458*, 489, *652*
Haubold, Hartmut 13, 619, 521, 623, 627–628, 630–631, 642
Haupstandstein 535
Haversian bone 259
Hawkins, Benjamin Waterhouse *194*
Hay, Oliver P. 623
Hayang Group 623, 625, 642
Hayashibara Cultural Project 571
Hayashibara Museum of Natural Sciences 507
Haystack Butte locality 421
He Xinlu 349–350, 424, 426
Head, Jason J. 193–197, 322–323, 430–431
Headden, Jaime A. 45
hearing 571–572, 595
"heart" (*Thescelosaurus* specimen) *563*, 563–565
Heckert, Andrew B. 17, 89, 295–296, *407*, 407–408, 474, 530, 601, 603
Heerden, Jacques van 443–444, 530
Heilmann, Gerhard 132, 411–412
Heilongjiang Provincial Geologic Survey 398
Heilongjiang Provincial Museum 285, 398–399
Heilongjiangosaurus 151, 602; *H. jiayinensis* 602
Heinrich, Wolf-Dieter 256, 258, 318–319, 440, 481
Hekou Formation 617, 624
Hell Creek Creations v
Hell Creek Formation x, 40–41, 47, *106*, 139–140, 316–317, 319–320, 362, 381, 474, 476, 526, 528, 563–565, 568–569, 575, 577
Hell Creek South Formation 575
Heller, F. 621
Helmdach, F.-F. 432
Helochelydra 314, 423; *H. anglica* 314, 423; *H. bakewelli* 314, 423
Helvetiafjelet Formation 626
heme compounds 576–577
Henderson, Donald M. v, 16–17, *18*, 27–28, *28*, 37, 90, 308–310, 515, 517
Hendricks, Alfred 636
Hengst, Richard A. 398
Henriques, Deise D. R. 8
herbivory (in theropods) 45, 368, 403, 485
herds and herding 42, 78, 112–113, 252, 280, 337, *351, 397, 640*
Herrerasaurus 6, 13, *13–14*, 16–17, 27, 37, 136, 147, 155–156, *156*, 182, 210, 230, 255, 530, 581, 607; *H. ischigualastensis 13–14*, 37, 136, *156*
Hesperosaurus 11, 152, 207, 353, *354–355*, 355, *356–358, 358*, *359*; *H. mjosi* 11, 353, *354–358*, 358, *359*
heterochrony 59
Heterodontosaurus 153, 190–191, *191*, 315, 625; *H. tucki* 190, *191*, 625

Heyuan Museum 358–359
Heyuannia 149, 207, 358–360, *360*; *H. huangi* 358–360, *360*
Hieronymous, Tobin L. 106–107
Hierosaurus 152, 420; *H. sternbergii* 420
Hill, Robert V. 17, 434
Hillenius, William J. 124, *124*, 493, 515, 517, 520, 522–523
Hinic, Sanja 181, 183, 403–404
Hirsch, Carl F. 645, 648–650
Hispanosauropus 625, 630; *H. hauboldi* 625
Histriasaurus 150
Hitchcock, Charles H. 619
Hitchcock, Edward 613, 615–617, 619, 621, 623–626, 628, 633–635, 637–638, 641
Hitchcockia see *Anomoepus*
Hobbs, Bill 341
Hokkanen, H. 256, 258
Holmes, Robert B. *288*, 288–291
Holtz, Thomas R., Jr. v, 23, 40, 53, 118, 134, 136, 147, 155–173, 215, 218, 254, 324, 326–328, 350–351, 445–446, 485, 490–491, 500, 506–507, 517, 523, 558, 560, 573–574, 581–582, 587
Homalocephale 153, 197–198
homeothermy 115, 117, 225
Homo see humans
Hongshanosaurus houi 597
Hopiichnus 625; *H. shingi* 625
Hoplitosaurus 152, 185, 448; *H. marshi* 185, 448
Hoplosaurus ischyrus see *Struthiosaurus austriacus*
Hopp, Thomas P. 120, 129
Hopson, James A. 119, 535, 542
Horner, Celeste C. 223, *224*, 225–226, *226*, 228–229, 233, 259–260, 315–317, 585, 587, 645
Horner, John R. 24, 99, 102, 121, 123, 125 126, 192–194, 196, 216, 218, 223, *224*, 225–226, *226*, 228–229, 233, 259–260, 301–302, 381, 398–399, 565, 567–568, 569, 571–574
Horricks, Rod 551
Horseshoe Canyon Formation 40, 215–217, *217*, 335, 362, 413–414, 474, 476, 531, 573, 633
Horsham Museum 448
Horton, Ed 559
Hot [Warm] Springs Ranch 34
Hotton, Nicholas, III 573–574
Hou Lian-hai [also Lianhai] 131–132, 197, 244, *244*, 369–370
Houston Museum of Science *184*
Hu Chengzhi [formerly Cheng-Chin] 500, *500–501*, 501, 575, 587
Hu Show-yung 347–348
Huabeisaurus 150
Huajiying Formation 603
Huanglongpus 625–626
Huaxiasaurus 147, 602
Huayangosaurus 91–92, 152, 355, 493; *H. taibaii* 355
Hudiesaurus 151
Huene, Friedrich von 34, 296–297, 310, 339, 341, 352, *352*, 387–388, 437, *438*, 439–444, 465, *465*, 480, 494, *495*, 496, 519, 523, 535, 542, 560, 562, 607, 621, 626, 639–640

Huincul Formation 40
Hulke, James W. 282, 284, 292
Hulsanpes 138, 150
humans 54, 229–230, 346, 406, 583, 585
Hunanpus 626; *H. jiuquwanensis* 626
Hunicul Formation 33
Hunt, Adrian P. 474, 484–485, 530, 615, 619, 622, 633
Hunt, ReBecca K. 36
Huntarian Museum 92
Hurum, Jørn H. 339–341, 559–560
Hutchinson, John R. 118, 122, 490–491, 493–494, 581–584, 587
Hutt, Stephen [Steve] *243*, 252, 255, 323–324, *324*, 325–326, *327*, 328, 419, *560*
Hwang, Sunny H. 47, 408–409, *409*, 410, 412, 523
Hylaeosaurus 93, 152, 207, 360, 447
Hypacrosaurus 102, 104, 153, 207, 259, 360–361, *361*, 362; *H. altispinus* 102, 104, *361*; *H. stebingeri* 259, 361
Hyperodapedon 530
Hyphepus 626; *H. fieldi* 626
Hypselosaurus 151, 645; *H. priscus* 645
Hypsibema 153
Hypsilophodon 96, 117, 152, 189–191, *192*, 207, 237, 287, 328, 362, *362*, 437, *622*, 637; *H. cf. Foxii* 362, *362*; *H. foxii* 96, *192*, 362

Iberomesornis 137
Ichabodcraniosaurus 138, 150, 602
ichnites *see* footprints
Ichnites 626; *I. Euskelosauroides* 626
Ichthyornis 136
ICZN *see* International Commission for Zoological Nomenclature
Iguana 194, 583
Iguanodon 17, 90, 96, 153, 155, 193, 195–196, 207, 234, 238, 269, *270*, 271, 286–287, 322, *363*, 363–365, 375, 419, 451, *451*, 616, 626, *626*, 643; *I. atherfieldensis* 96, 271, 419, 451, *451*; *I. bernissartensis* 90, 96, 234, 286–287, 364, *626*; *I. Fittoni* 271; *I. hoggii* see *Camptosaurus hogii*; *I. Lakotaensis* 96; *I. suessi* 364; *Iguanodon* sp. 364, *363*
Iguanodonichnus 626; *I. Frenkii* 626; *I. Teste* 626
Iguanodontipus 626, *626*; *I. burryei* 626, *626*
Ilek Formation 86–87
Ilha do Cajual locality 42
Ilha do Medo locality 42
Ilha farm *631–632, 639*
Iliosuchus 148, 544; *Iliosuchus incognitus* 544
The Illustrated London News 448
Ilokelesia 148, 178–179, 207, 245, 365, *365–366*, 366–367, *367*, 593; *I. Aguadagranensis* 365, *365–367*

impacts 140–143
In Search for Dinosaurs to the Gobi 339
Incisivosaurus 3, 137, 149, 207, 367–368, *368*, 369; *I. Gauthieri* 367–368, *368*, 369
index fossils 38, 90, 143, 474, 567–568
Indian Statistical Institute 251
Indiana-Purdue University v
indicator fossils *see* index fossils
Indosaurus 148, 178
Indosuchus 34, 38, 148, 178
Inductive Coupled Plasma-Mass Spectrometry (ICP-MS) 143
Ingenia 136–137, 149, 207, 292, 294–295, 341, 369, *369–370*, 370, 378; *I. Yanshini* 370; *Ingenia* sp. 137, 369, *369–370*
Inosaurus 147
insects and insectivory 29, 52, 54, 56, 123, 403, 407, 468, 476, 491
Institute of Geology 30
Institute of Vertebrate Paleontology and Paleoanthropology v, 347, 410, 502, 526
Instrumental Neutron Activation Analysis (INAA) 143
integument 7, *10–11*, 83–84, 103, *104*, 118, 120, 122, *125*, 126, 128–129, *131*, 132, 134–135, 260, 265, 276, 300, 341, *394*, 396, 411–412, 454, 486, 488, 512, *514*, 515–516, 519, 521, *522*, 524, *539–540*, 560, 571, 625
International Code on Zoological Nomenclature 406, 442
International Commission for Zoological Nomenclature (ICZN) 284, 406, 478
intraspecific display, rivalry, recognition, and combat x, 36, 51, *51–52*, 52, 112, 122, 204, 233, 276, 336, 411, 419, 519, 521, 538, 571, 586
invertebrates 12, 29, 52, 54, 56, 75, 78, 82, 85, 98, 123, 142, 221, 271, 301, 307, 318, 341, 364, 371, 375, 384, 386, 391, 403, 407, 422, 432, 468, 474, 476, 491, 523, 543, 573, 587, 615
Iranosauripus 626; *I. zerabensis* 626
Iren Dabasu Formation 25, 250–251, 329, 414, 485
Irenesauripus 626–627; *I. Acutus* 627; *I. Glenrosensis* 627; *I. gracilis* 627; *I. mcleani* 627; *I. occidentalis* 627
Irenichnites 627, 633; *I. Acutus* 627; *I. gracilis* 627; *I. mcclearni* 627; *I. occidentalis* 627
iridium 30, 140–142
Irmis, Randall 90–91
Iron and Steel Corporation of South Africa 337
Irritator 148, 207, 254, 370–371, *371–372*, 372–373, 528; *I. challengeri* 254, 370–371, *371–372*, 372–373
Irving, Washington 602
Isanosaurus 13, 59, 150; *I. attavipachi* 59
Ischigualasto Formation 530
Ischyrosaurus 151
Itapecuru Formation 61

Itemirus 147, 158; *I. Medullaris* 158
Itoshiro Subgroup 74
Iucitosaurus 151
Ivie, M. A. 407–408

Jackson, Frankie D. 82–84, 126, 246, 249, 573–574
Jacobs, Louis L. 60, 193, 250
Jacobsen, Aase Roland 51, 231–233, 262–263, 268, 486
Jaekel, O. 437, *439*, 440, 444
Jainosaurus 151, 207, 373; *J. septentrionalis* 373
Jalil, Nour-Eddine 607
Janensch, Werner 76, 244, 318–319, 483
Janenschia 59, 151, 318
Janzen, D. H. 78
Jasinoski, Sandra Christine 120–121
Javelina Formation 211, 213, 575
jaw action and mechanics 29, 36, 39, 45, 66–67, 75–76, *78*, 114, 221–222, *222–223*, *226*, 228–229, 334–335, 492–493, 503, 559, 578–580, 595
Jaxartosaurus 153, 286; *J. aralensis* 286
Jehol Group 47, 376, 410, 523
Jeholornis 607
Jeholosauripus 624, 627; *J. s-satori* 627
Jeholosaurus 152, 523
Jenghiskhan see *Tarbosaurus*
Jenkins, Farrish A., Jr. 443–444, 625
Jennings, Debra S. 34–35
Jensen, James A. 3, *4*, 9–10, 74, 269, 322–323, 544–545, 549–550, 555
Jerison, Harry J. 315–317
Jerzykiewicz, T. 455, 458, 467
Ji Qiang 47, 118, 122, *131*, 133–134, 138, 300–301, 369–370, 515–517, 520–521, 523, 607
Jialingpus 627; *J. yuechiensis* 627
Jiang Di He Formation 617
Jiang Fu-Xing 375–376, 384, 386–387, 523
Jiangshanosaurus 151, 207, 373, *373–374*, 374; *J. lixianensis* 373, *373–374*, 374
Jiao coal mine 637
Jin Xingsheng [also Xing Sheng] 373, *373–374*, 374, 424, *424–425*, 425–426, 505
Jing Chuan Formation 617
Jingshanosaurus 150, 495
Jinhua Formation 274
Jinjiang Formation 644
Jinju Formation 73
Jinlijingpus see *Eubrontes*; *J. nianpanshanensis* see *Eubrontes*
Jinzhousaurus 153, 207, 374–375, *375*, 376; *J. yangi* 374–375, *375*, 376
Jiufotang Formation 299, 408, 410, 607
Jobaria 37, 60, *78*, 150, 207, 339, 376, *376–377*, 376; *J. tiguidensis 78*, 376, *376–377*
Johns Hopkins University v
Jones, M. D. 282–283
Jones, Terry D. 116–117, 124, *124*, 125–126, 132, 135, 493, 515, 517, 520–523

Jones Ranch Sauropod Quarry 212
"Jordan theropod" *see Tyrannosaurus rex*
Journal of Vertebrate Paleontology 603
Jubbulpuria 147
"La Juanita" site 50
Judith River Formation 47, 259–260, 651
Judith River Group 40–41, 139, 250–251, 291, 477, 486, 530–531
Jurassic Park vii
Jurcsák, Tiberiu 243–244, 271–272, 607
juveniles and subadults 6, *6–7*, 11, *16*, 17, 27, *28*, 30, 37, 40–41, 44, 47, 51–52, *52*, 57–59, 87, *92*, 96–98, 103, *103–104*, 104–105, 107, 109, 113–116, 118, 120–121, 125–126, 172, *195*, *197*, 212–213, *214*, 215, 217–218, 221, 230–232, 244, 246, 251, 254–255, 258–260, 265–266, 268–269, 271, 280, 284, 295–296, 297, 301–302, 306–308, *308*, 317, 322–324, 335–338, *338*, *340*, 340–341, *342*, 352, *352*, *361*, 362, 381, 382, 383–385, *385–386*, 386–387, *387*, 390–392, 413, 420, 423, 426–427, 433–434, 437, 443, 454–456, *457*, 458–459, 462, 471, *472*, 485–487, *487–488*, 490–492, 494–495, *496*, 497–498, 500, 502, 507–508–509, *509–511*, 516, 517, *517–518*, *520*, 528, 530–532, 537, 542–543, *544*, 547, 549, 555, 558, 562, 566, *569*, 569–570, 572–575, *575–576*, 577–578, 584, 589, 591–592, 596

Kaever, Mathias 623, 630
Kaijiangosaurus 148
Kainomoyenisauropus see *Anomoepus*; *K. ranivorus* see *Anomoepus*
Kainotrisauropus see *Grallator*; *K. morijiensis* see *Grallator*
Kaiparowits Formation 431
Kaisen, Peter 215
Kakuru 148
Kalasauropus see *Otozoum*; *K. masitisii* see *Otozoum*
Kalosauropus see *Otozoum*
Kang Xi-Min [also Ximin] 373, *373–374*, 374, 424, *424–425*, 425–426, 505
Kangnasaurus 152
Karbek, T. R. 539, *540*, 542
Kardong, Kenneth V. 301–302
Kayenta Formation 306–307, 621–622, 625, 627
Kayentapus 527, 630, 644; *K. hopii* 627; cf. *Kayentapus* sp. 627
Kellner, Alexander W. A. 39, 49, 58, 82, 215, 371, 373, 530
Kelly, J. 328, 601, 603
Kelmayisaurus 148
Kennedy, Clayton 290
Kentrosaurus 92, 152, 307, 318, 355, 537, 539
Kermack, D. 562–563
Kessler, E. 607
Keuper d'Anduze 634
Khaan 136, 149, 207, 292, 294–

295, 378; *K. mckennai* 292, 294, 378
Khermin-Tsav locality *112*
Khodja Pil Ata site 641
Khok Hin Poeng site 59
Khosla, Ashu 651–652
Kielan-Jaworowska, Zofia 339, 341
Kikak-Tegoseak bonebed 46
Kim, Haang Mook 305, 623–625, 631, 642
kineticism 123, 191, 197, 201–202, 221–222, 229, 276, 335, 345–346, 428
Kirkland, James I. [Ian] 72, 96, 111, 185, 193, 196, 218–219, *219–220*, 220–221, 278–279, *279*, 280, 314, 322–323, 331, 341, *342*, 343, 347–348, 420–421, *421*, 422–423, 436–437, 513, 517, 590, 592–593, 596–597
Kirtland Formation 143, 526, 528, 531, 568, 578
Kittysaurus see *Eotyrannus*
Klamelisaurus 151
Kleitotrisauropus 627; *K. moshoeshoei* 627
Klimov, A. F. 110
Knoll, Fabien 75, *75*, 381, *382–383*, 383–384, 607
Knollenmergel 387, 440–442, 465, 480
Knopfler, Mark 400
Knollenmergel 387, 440–442, 465, 480
Kobayashi, Yoshitsugu 44–45, 137, 193–195, 323
Koken, E. 442, 444
Komlosaurus 627–628; *K. carbonis* 627
Koparian 138, 149
Koppelhus, Eva 559
Kordos, Laszló 627
Koreanosaurus 138, 150
Koseongosauripus 627; *K. onychion* 627
Kota Formation 94–95, *95*, 251–252, 379
Kotasaurus 150, 207, 378–379, *379–380*, 380; *K. yamanpalliensis* 379, *379–380*
Kowalevsky, Vladimir Onufrievich 221–222
Kozisek, Jacqueline M. 96
Krause, David W. 38, 134, 173, 473–474
Krauss, David A. 89–90
Krebs, Bernard 432, 434
Kreighbaum, Ellen 585, 587
Kritosaurus 153, 207, 380–381, 501; "*Kritosaurus*" incurvimanus *101*, 104; *Kritosaurus* sp. 380–381
Kronosaurus 249
Kruger National Park 337–338
Krzic, Berislav v, *131*, *175*, 193, *202, 204, 309, 402–403, 516*, 580
Kuhn, Oskar 189, 442, 444, 619, 621, 624, 634, 638, 643
Kulceratops 153
Kummer, B. 64
Kunmingosaurus 151, *601*; *K. utingensis 601*
Kundrát, Martin 360–361
Kunmingosaurus 151, *601*; *K. utingensis 601*
Kurzanov, Sergei M. [Mikhailovich] 20, 30, *31*, *32*, 234–235, 251, 404, 406, 497, 500, 652
Kusmer, K. D. 301–302
Kuwajima Formation 74

Kuwajimasauropus see *Hadrosaurichnus*; *Kuwajimasauropus shiraminensis* see *Hadrosaurichnus*
Kuzmitz, Andrew A. 563–565
Kyungsang System 73, 623, 625, 628

Labocania 148, 158; *L. anomala* 158
Laboratório de Macrofósseis/IGEO/UFRJ 88
"*Labrosaurus*" 30; "*L. sulcatus* 30; "*L.*" stechowi 30
lacertilians 21–23, 57, 74, 78, 85, 115, 156–157, *194*, 208, 228, 287, 296–297, 341, 413, 423, 443–444, 493, 548, 559, 573, 581, 607
Lacovara, Kenneth [Ken] J. 428–429, *429*, 430, *529*
Laelaps gallicus see *Streptospondylus altdorfensis*
Laelaps trihedrodon see *Allosaurus*
Laevisuchus 148, 178–179, 401–402
Lagerpeton 155–156
LAGs *see* lines of arrested growth
Lakes, Arthur 534–535
Lakota Sandstone Formation 271
Lamanna, Matthew [Matt] C. v, *35*, 38–39, 46, 70–71, 331, 422, 428–429, *429*, 430, *529*
Lambe, Lawrence 280, 282, 336–337, 500, 530, 532, 575, 587
Lambeosaurus 28, 90, 104, *105*, 153, *197*, 322; *L. lambei* 28, 90, 104, *105*, *197*
Lambert, Olivier 200, 381, 454, *454–455*, 455–456, *456–457*, 458–459
Lameta Formation *33*, 34
Lametasaurus 152, 178
Lamm, Ellen-Therese 203
Lanasaurus 153
Lancanjiangosaurus 150
Lance Formation 44, 139, 260, 381, 474, 476, 575, 636
Lander, Bruce 125
Langer, Max C. [Cardoso] v, 154–155
Langston, Wann, Jr. *184*, 289, 601, 627
Laosaurus 152
Lapparent, Albert F. de 616, 623–624, 626, 630, 636, 638
Lapparentichnus 628; *L. oleronensis* 628
Lapparentosaurus 151
Laramie Formation 575, 619
Lark Quarry 642–643
Larson, Neal L. v, 10
Larson, Peter L. 56–57, 575–576, 586–587
Larsson, Hans C. E. 15, 39–40, 252, 254–255, *273*, 273–274, 529
Larus 340
Lauder, George V. 177
Laurasia 75, 190, 195, 470
Laurent, Yves 81, 189, 430–431
Leaellynsaura 152
Leahy, Guy D. 116, 584, 587
Leal, Lucuiano A. 58, 530
Leanza, Héctor A. 34, 40, 82, 343, 347, 366–367

Index

Leckey, Erin 29
Lee, Suzanne 562–563
Lee, Yuong-Nam 305, 628
Legarreta, L. 236, 239
Lehman, Thomas M. 47, 116, 211, 211–213, 213, 214, 215, 301–302, 326, 328, 380–381, 569
Leicester City Museums 282
Leipsanosaurus 152, 154, 547–548
Le Loeuff, Jean 13, 59–60, 81, 430–431
Leng, Gavin 75, 324, 601, 603
Lengosaurus see *Eotyrannus*
Leningrad State University 339
Leonardi, Giuseppe v, 613–614, 619, 620, 624, 626, 628, 629, 631, 631–632, 632, 638, 639–641
"Leonardo" 260
lepidosaurs 21–23, 74, 78, 85, 115, 229, 607
Leptoceratops 107–108, 153, 199–200, 202–203, 207, 381, 413; *L. gracilis* 107–108, 202–203, 413; *Leptoceratops* (cf. *gracilis*) 381
Leptonyx see *Stenonyx*; *L. lateralis* see *Stenonyx lateralis*
Leshchinsky [also Leśinskij], Sergei V. 87
Lesothosaurus 27, 91, 107, 152, 207, 233, 335, 381, 382–383, 383–384, 572; *L. diagnosticus* 107, 381, 383–384; *Lesothosaurus* sp. 383, 384; *Lesothosaurus* sp. indet. 381, 382
Lessem, Don 216, 218, 585, 587
Lessemsaurus 150
Lessertisseur, Jacques 630, 642
Lexovisaurus 91, 152
Lhuyd, Edward 405, 406
Li, Y. 142
Li Kui 143, 424, 426
Li Weirong 602
Liaoxiornis 131
Liaoceratops 153, 202, 207, 384–385, 385–386, 386; *L. yanzigounsis* 384–385, 385–386
Liaoning Fossil Protection Bureau 300
Liaoningornis 131
Liaoningosaurus 152, 207, 386–387, 387; *L. paradoxus* 386, 387
Ligabueichnium 628; *L. bolivianum* 628
Ligabueino 148
ligaments see muscles, musculature, and ligaments
Likhoelesaurus 607
Lilienstern, Hugo Rühle von 478, 479, 480–481
Liliensternus 147, 179, 207, 310, 340, 387–388, 465; ?*L. airelensis* 387–388; *L. liliensterni* 310, 387–388
Lim, Jong-Deock 73, 73, 265, 268
Limestone Formation 71
Limnornis see *Paleocursornis*
Lindoe, Luke 289
lines of arrested growth (LAGs) 27, 116, 259
Lipkin, Christine 255
Lirainosaurus 81, 151, 592; *L. astibiai* 81
Lisandro Formation 236, 239
Liscomb, Robert L. 46
Liscomb bonebed 46

"Little Tooth" 43
lizards see lacertilians
"Lizzie" 98, 99–100
Llompart, C. 633–634
Lockatong Formation 635
Lockley, Martin G. v, 390–391, 590, 615–616, 619, 622–623, 626, 626, 628, 630, 633–634, 637, 634–641, 643–644
locomotion 17, 19, 28, 36, 39, 53, 62, 66–67, 105, 110, 118–119, 121–122, 124, 126, 131, 134, 216, 224, 229–230, 241–242, 258, 260, 263, 276, 286–287, 288, 309, 317, 328, 345–346, 347, 364, 390–391, 484, 539, 542, 570–571, 581–584, 615, 619
Loewen, Mark A. 230–231, 233, 576, 587
Loncosaurus 152
Long, Robert A. v, 506
Longisquama 124, 124–125, 132, 135; *L. insignis* 124–125
Longman, Heber A. 249–250
Longrich, Nicholas 122, 129–130, 158, 180, 519, 523, 595
López-Martinez, Nieves 67, 101–102, 138–139, 139
Lophorhothon 152
Loricosaurus 151
Losillasaurus 150, 207, 388–389, 389; *L. giganteus* 388–389, 389
The Lost Dinosaurs of Egypt 529
Lourinhanosaurus 148, 181, 207, 389–390
Lourinhasaurus 151
Louw, Adriaan 337
Lovell's Quarry 314
Löwenstein Formation 496
Lower Bauxite Formation 271
Lower Elliot Formation 337, 338, 443, 530, 617, 634–637, 642
Lower Fusin Coal Measures 619
Lower Lufeng Formation 57, 255, 331
Lower Saurian Bed 318
Lower Shaximiao Formation 424
Lower Stormberg Series 616, 628, 635
Lower Stubensandstein 494–495
Lü, JunChang 137, 359–360, 360, 369, 369–370, 370
Luanpingosaurus 153, 460, 463, 465, 602; *L. jingshanensis* 463, 602
Lucas, A. M. 515, 517
Lucas, O. W. 231
Lucas, Spencer G. 89, 142–143, 295–296, 407, 407–408, 484–485, 530, 568, 578, 645
Lucianosaurus 151
Lufeng Formation 57, 91, 398, 623–624, 634, 637, 644–645
Lufengosaurus 114, 150, 181, 183, 495; *L. hueni* 114, 495
Lukousaurus 147
Lull, Richard Swann 318–319, 322–323, 616, 623–624, 638
Lulworth Formation 423
Luo, Z. 331
Lurdusaurus 152, 234
Lusitanosaurus 152
Lusotitan ataloniensis 597
Luttrell, P. 307
Lycoptera 516
Lycorhinus 153, 207; *L. angustidens* 207

Lydekker, Richard 243–244, 565–566
Lyman, R. L. 301–302

Mabdi Formation 60
Macrodontophion 147
Macroelongatoolithus 648; *M. xixianensis* 648
Macroolithus 142, 646; *M. mutabilis* 646; *M. rugustus* 646; *M. yaotunensis* 142, 646
Macropodosaurus 628; *M. gravis* 628
Macrurosaurus 150
Maderson, P. F. A. 124, 124, 126
Madsen, James H., Jr. v, 54, 96, 230, 233, 268, 322–323, 326, 328, 339, 341, 543–545, 589, 589–590, 653
Maevarano Formation 392, 399–400, 403, 470–471, 566
Mafatrisauropus 628; *M. errans* 628
Magnoavipes 628; *M. caneeri* 628; *M. lowei* 628
Magnosaurus 148
Magyarosaurus 151
Maiasaura 24, 125, 153, 207, 259, 291, 390–391, 391, 645; *M. peeblesorum* 24, 259, 390, 391
Main, Derek J. 211, 215
Maisey, John G. 372
Majungatholus 6, 34, 38, 42, 148, 178–179, 207, 276, 391–392; *M. atopus* 392
Makela, Robert 125, 645
Makovicky, Peter J. v, 59, 126, 127, 129, 177, 201–204, 251, 300–301, 304–305, 330–332, 340, 340–341, 381, 384–385, 385–386, 386, 408, 410, 412–414, 523–524, 524–525, 525–526, 561–562
Makuya Nature Reserve 337
"Malagasy Taxon A" see *Rapetosaurus*
"Malagasy Taxon B" 392
Malawisaurus 151, 183–184, 211–212, 250, 418, 472; *M. dixeyi* 211–212
Maleev, Evgeny [Eugene] Alexandrovich 497, 500, 555–556, 558, 560
Maleevosaurus novojilovi see *Tarbosaurus bataar*
Maleevus 95, 235; *M. disparoserratus* 235
Maleri Formation 530
Malkani, M. S. 87
Maltese, Anthony 265–266, 268
Malutitrisauropus 628; *Malutitrisauropus* sp. 628
Mamenchisaurus 61, 151, 183, 207, 392, 392–393, 393–394, 394–395, 395–396, 396–397, 397–398, 424, 457, 483, 595; *M. anyuensis* 396; *M. constructus* 396; *M. hochuanensis* 394, 395, 396, 397; *M. jingyanensis* 395, 395–396, 396; *M. sinocanadorum* 396; *M. youngi* 183, 392–393, 393–394, 394, 396, 398; *Mamenchisaurus* sp. indet. 396
Mammal Bed 314, 423–424
mammals 3, 9, 17, 19–20, 22, 24, 27–30, 35–36, 39, 44, 53–54,

57, 62–67, 76, 78, 94, 107, 110, 112, 114–117, 123–125, 128, 130, 194, 208, 221–222, 222, 225–226, 229–230, 232, 241, 249, 256, 274, 276, 298, 314, 316, 328, 341, 345–364, 368, 396, 402, 406, 412, 423–424, 429, 434, 461, 474, 484, 519–520, 523, 533, 590, 567, 569–570, 573, 583–585, 617
Mandschurosaurus 153, 207, 284–285, 398–399, 501, 602; *M. amurensis* 285; "*Mandschurosaurus magnus* see *Charonosaurus jiayinensis*
Manning, T. W. 45, 46–47
Manospondylus see *Tyrannosaurus*
Mantell, Gideon Algernon 360, 363–365
Marambio Group 94
Marasuchus 155–156, 607
Marchant Ranch 195, 315
Marilia Formation 47, 49, 86
Marjanovic, David 526
Mark's Second Egg locality 378
Marsh, Othniel Charles 70, 231, 233, 532–535, 537, 542
Marshall, Cynthia L. 123, 260, 566–567, 567, 568
Marshosaurus 148, 231, 404, 544
Marsovsky, Mona 560
Martill, David M. 243, 252, 254–255, 323–324, 324, 325–326, 327, 328, 370–371, 371–372, 372–373, 493, 560, 560–561, 561–562
Martin, Larry D. 36, 73, 73, 124, 124, 134–135, 265, 268, 369–370, 515, 517
Martin, T. 339
Martin-Rolland, Valérie 155
Martinez, Ricardo Néstor 81, 181, 183, 469–470, 566
Martínez, Rubén D. 38–39, 70–71, 593
Maryan'ska, Teresa 45, 136–137, 178, 184, 190, 198, 235–236, 251, 285, 288, 295, 298, 335–337, 348, 352, 369–370, 386–387, 398–399, 408, 459–460, 543, 573–574
Maschenko, Evgeny N. 86
Masiakasaurus 3, 33, 148, 178–179, 207, 392, 399–400, 401, 402, 402–403, 403; *M. knopfleri* 392, 399–400, 400–401, 401, 402–403
Masitisauropezus see *Anomoepus*; *M. perdiciform* see *Anomoepus*
Masitisauropodiscus 630; *M. fringilla* 630; *M. perdiciforma* 630
Masitisisauropus 630; *M. angustus* 630; *M. exiguus* 630; *M. levicauda* 630; *M. palmipes* 630
Massospondylus 24, 150, 181, 183, 207, 403–404, 495, 530; *M. carinatus* 404
Matanuska Formation 97
Matasiete Formation 70–71
Mateus, Octávio 310, 310–311, 311–312, 312, 389–390
Matheron, M. Philippe 645
mating see sex and mating
Matley, Charles Alfred 34
Matsuo Group 80, 84
Matthew, William Diller 171

Mattison, Rebecca G. 584, 587
Maxwell, W. Desmond 72, 323
May, Kevin C. 97–99, 99–100, 194
May, Lizzie 98
May, Virginia 97
Mayr, E. 519, 523
Mayr, Helmut 529
Mazzetta, Gerardo V. 274, 276
McCarville, Katherine 89
McCrea, Richard T. 40, 41, 215, 216–218, 627
McDonald, Lucy 266
McIntosh, John S. v, 10, 79, 231, 233, 241–242, 244, 250, 266–268, 284, 291, 416, 419, 467–468, 504–505, 537, 542, 547, 549, 555, 615
McIver, Elisabeth E. 586–587
McRae Formation 568, 575, 578
McWhinney, Lorrie A. 263, 268, 537, 537–539, 542
medial pharyngeal pneumatic system (MPPS) 230
Meesak coal formation 627
Meese, M. A. 263
Megacervixosaurus 151
Megaichnites see Kayentapus; M. jizhaoshiensis see Kayentapus sp.
Megalancosaurus 134
Megaloceros 194
Megalonyx 567
Megaloolithus 143, 645, 648; M. aureliensis 143, 648; M. balasinorensis 648; M. dhoridungrensis 648; M. khempurensis 648; M. mammilare 648; M. matleyi 648; M. megadermus 648; M. microtuberculata 648; M. petralta 648; M. phensaniensis 648; M. rahioliensis 648; M. trempii 648
Megalosauripus 623, 625, 630; M. barkhausensis 630; M. usbekistanicus 630
Megalosauropus 630; M. brionensis 630; M. broomensis 630; M. gomesi see Megalosauripus; M. teutonicus see Megalosauripus; M. titanopelobatidus 630
Megalosaurus 27, 148, 157, 207, 231, 385, 404, 404–405, 406, 423, 445–446, 630; M. bucklandii 404, 404–405, 406, 423, 445; ?M. cambrensis 385
Megapnosaurus 3, 24, 27, 40, 121, 147, 179, 207, 295, 307, 340, 407, 407–408, 453, 465, 555; M. kayentakatae 407; M. rhodesiensis 24, 307, 340, 407; ?Megapnosaurus sp. 407, 407, 453, 453
Megaraptor 43, 148
Mehl, M. G. 631
Mehliella 631, 642; M. jeffersoniensis 631
Meilyn Quarry 10–11
Melanorosaurus 150, 443, 495, 530, 562
Meleagris gallopavo 54
Mendozasaurus neguyelap 597
Mendrez, C. 381
Mensink, Hans 623, 625
Mercedes Formation 650, 652
Mesa Southwest Museum v, 43, 262, 458, 555–556, 570, 596
Mesaverde Formation 642
Mesaverde Group 622

Mesozoic Meanderings 478
metabolism 51, 66, 114–115, 128, 484, 586
Metatetrapous 628, 631; M. valdensis 628, 631
Metriacanthosaurus 148, 181
Metriorhynchus 545
Meyer, Hermann von 406, 437, 438, 444, 543, 545–547
Michitsch, Terry 562
Micrichnus 631; M. scotti 631
Microceratops 153, 203, 207, 352, 408; M. gobiensis 203, 352, 408; M. sulsidens 408
Microdontosaurus 150
Microhadrosaurus 153
Micropachycephalosaurus 153, 207, 408; M. hongtuyanensis 408
Microraptor 7, 24, 47, 119, 121, 130–131, 138, 150, 207, 300, 408–409, 409–410, 410–411, 411, 412, 516, 525; M. gui 408, 410, 410–411, 411–423; M. zhaoianus 24, 47, 408–409, 409, 410–411; Microraptor sp. 411
Microvenator 136, 149, 157, 167–168; M. celer 136
Middle Purbeck Beds see Cherty Freshwater Beds
Middle Saurian Bed 318
Middle Stubensandstein 388, 453, 494–495
migration see faunal exchange
"Mike's Baby" 426
Mikhailov, Konstantin 645–650, 652
Miles, Clark J. v
Miles, Clifford A. v, 8, 10–11, 16, 32, 48, 96, 113, 141, 186, 222, 263, 264, 265, 266–268, 271, 272, 279–280, 308, 315, 353, 354–355, 355, 356–358, 358, 359, 536, 538, 542, 551–552, 604
Milk River Formation 474–476
Miller, Wade E. 10
Milner, Angela C. 154, 252, 254–255, 324, 328, 364–365, 371, 373, 423–424
Milwaukee Public Museum 566, 567
Miniaci, Albert 341
Minisauripus 631; M. chuanzhuensis 631
Minmi 152, 185–186, 207, 347, 378, 412–413; M. paravertebra; Minmi sp. 347, 412
Mjos, Ron 267, 354, 539–540
Moab Megatracksite 641
Mochlodon robustus 364
Moenave Formation 36, 407, 407–408
Moenkopi Formation 32
Mohabey, David M. 373, 565–566, 646, 648
Mohr, B. A. R. 477
mollusks 98, 221, 341
Molnar, Ralph E. v, 35–36, 94, 164, 177, 208–209, 225, 249, 249–250, 254, 295, 312, 326, 328, 335, 337, 347–348, 404, 406, 412–413, 445–446, 489, 491, 515, 517, 545, 559–560, 577–580, 582, 583, 587, 595, 607
Molteno Formation 530, 635
Momipites tenuipolis 143

Mones, A. 650, 652
Mongol Highland International Dinosaur Project 44, 369
Mongolian Academy of Sciences 293, 508
Mongolian Paleontological Center 507
Mongolosaurus 150, 207, 413; M. haplodon 413
Monkonosaurus 152
Monoclonius 154, 207, 282, 413
Monolophosaurus 37, 148; M. jiangi 37
Mononykus 6, 138, 150, 175–176, 507–508; M. olecranus 175–176, 507–508
Montanoceratops 107–108, 112, 153, 200–202, 207, 381, 413–414; M. cerorhynchus 107–108, 112, 201–202, 413
Mook, Charles C. 108
Moraesichnium 631, 631–632, 633; M. barbernae 631–632, 633
Morales, Michael 32, 87, 407–408
Moratalla, José J. 449, 640–641, 648
Moreno Formation 259
Moreno Hill Formation 421, 595
Morinosaurus 151
Morris, William J. 565
Morrison Formation 4, 9, 11, 30, 34, 40–41, 76–78, 89, 96, 115, 181, 221, 231–232, 241, 263, 265, 268, 307–308, 312, 314, 317–318, 353, 355, 426–427, 467, 535, 543–544, 549, 554, 604, 625, 646, 648–650
Morrison Museum of Natural History 532
mosasaurs 98, 259
Moscow Paleontological Institute 339
Moser, M. 437, 440, 442
Mother's Day Site 307
The Mountain Geologist 628
Moyenisauropezus 633; M. perdiciforma 633
Moyenisauropodiscus 633; M. percidiforma 633
Moyenisauropus see Anomoepus
mummies 260
Municipality of Valle/Bale 79–80
Murelaga, Xabier 101–102, 102
Murphy, Nate I. 260
Murry, Philip A. 60, 506
Muschelkalk Formation 621
muscles, musculature, and ligaments 8, 16, 23–24, 28–29, 37, 39, 45, 51–55, 62, 64–67, 71, 75, 90, 95, 104–105, 107, 110, 114–118, 120–123, 130, 134, 137–138, 157–158, 161–166, 168–169, 171, 221–222, 223, 225–226, 226, 228–231, 239, 241, 256, 258–260, 263, 274, 276, 278, 287, 298, 301, 307–308, 317, 324, 330, 334, 345, 350–351, 363, 369, 373, 390–391, 391, 392, 402, 437, 456, 482, 498, 522–523, 538–539, 542, 549, 563, 566–567, 569, 571–573, 576, 579, 581–585, 589
Musée de la Faculté des Sciences de Caen 444
Musée Royal d'Histoire Naturelle 364, 384
Museo Argentino de Ciencias Nat-

urales "Bernardo Rivadavia" 274, 274,
Museo Arqueológico de Salas de los Infantes 252
Museo Civico di Storia Naturale of Trieste 97
Museo de la Universidad Nacional del Comahue 82
Museo Municipal Carmen Funes (Museum "Carmen Funes") 84, 236, 245
Museo Municipal Ernesto Bachmann 86
Museo Paleontologico Cittadino of Monfalcone 79
Museum für Naturkunde der Humboldt-Universität zu Berlin 65, 256, 483
Muséum National d'Histoire Naturelle 81, 445–446, 545
Museum of Comparative Zoology 77, 383
Museum of Geology v
Museum of Isle of Wight Geology 324
Museum of Northern Arizona v, 306
Museum of the Rockies 232, 568
Museum of Western Colorado 77, 227, 541
Mussaurus 114, 150, 337–338, 443; M. patagonicus 114, 443
Muttaburrasaurus 152, 189, 234
Mymoorapelta 93, 152, 185, 343; M. maysi 185
Myhrvold, Nathan P. 308, 310

Nagdong Series 623, 625
Naish, Darren v, 75, 124–125, 133, 136, 243, 243–244, 252, 254–255, 323–324, 324–325, 325–326, 326–327, 327–328, 328, 419, 420, 485, 519, 523, 560, 560–561, 561–562
Nam Phong Formation 59
Nanchao Formation 45, 46
Nanjiung Institute of Geology and Paleontology 521
Nanosaurus 152
Nanotyrannus see Tyrannosaurus
Nanshiungoolithus 142, 648; N. chuetiensis 142, 648
Nanshiungosaurus 149, 330, 416, 422
Nath, T. T. 94–95, 95
National Geographic 132, 368
National Geological Museum of China 47, 500
National Museum (Bloemfontein) 383
National Museum of Natural History (USA) v, 77, 104, 216, 232, 571; (Japan) 536
National Museum of Natural Sciences see Canadian Museum of Nature
National Science Museum 334
Natural History Museum 132
The Natural History Museum, London 383, 492, 514
Natural History Museum of Los Angeles County v, vii, 15, 23, 25–26, 83, 84, 85, 104, 170, 174, 192, 245, 247–248, 249, 275, 306, 557, 575–576, 577–578, 584, 651–652

Index

Natural History of Oxfordshire 406
Nature 132
Naturwissenschaften 490
Navahopus 633; *N. falcipollex* 633
Navajo Sandstone 493, 633
Nedcolbertia 148
Negro, Giuliana 83–84, 103, *104*
Neimongosaurus 207, 329–331, 414, *414–415*, 415–416, *416*; *N. yangi* 329–331, 414, *414–416*
Nemegt Formation 126, 341, 369, 416, 428, 473, 555–556, 559–560
Nemegt locality 560
Nemegtosaurus 151, 184, 207, 215, 341, 416–417, *417–418*, 418–419, 431, 468, 472; *N. mongoliensis* 416, *417–418*, 468
Neosauropus 633; *N. lagosteirensis* 633
Neotripodiscus 633; *N. makoetlani* 633
Neotrisauropus see *Grallator*; *N. deambulator* see *Grallator*
Neovenator 27, 148, 164, 181, 207, 324, 419, *419–420*, 445; *N. salerii* 419, *419–420*
Nequensaurus 215; *N. australis* 215
Nerinea Bed 318
Nesbitt, Sterling 32
Nessov, Lev A. 96, 234, 236, 244, 339
nests and nestlings 52, 57, 82–83, *83*, 84, 120, 122, 125–126, *218*, 292–293, 338, 370, 390–391, 462, 477, 573
Neuquén Group 84, 87, 366
Neuquensaurus 151
New Mexico Museum of Natural History and Science [formerly New Mexico Museum of Natural History] 77, *182*, 567, 615
New York Times 422
Newark Supergroup 30, 89, 616, 621, 623–624, 626, 635, 637–638, 641
Newman, Barney 364–365, 584, 587
The News 328
Newton, Edwin Tully 388
Ngexisaurus 148
"*Nicrosaurus*" sp. 388
Nigersaurus 82, 151, 207, 419–420; *N. taqueti* 420
"1999 Geologic Time Scale" 11
Niniluk site 46
Niobrara Chalk 420
Niobrarasaurus 152, 207, 221; *N. coleii* 420
Nipponosaurus 153
Noasaurus 33, 148, 178–179, 401
nocturnality 124
Nodocephalosaurus 152, 235; *N. kirtlandensis* 235
Nodosaurus 152, 221, 343
Nomadic Expeditions, Inc. 341, 559
Nomingia 136–137, 149, 294, 378
Nopcsa, Franz 364–365, 548–549, 623
Norell, Mark A. 47, 118, 125–126, *127*, *129*, *131*, 132–133, 138, 173, 176–177, 202–203, 292–293, *293–294*, 294–295, 300–301, 305, 340–341, 369–370, 378, 384–385, *385–386*, 386, 408–409, *409*, 410, 412, 428, 434, 507–508, 515–517, 523, 573–574

Norman, David B. 15, 29, 71, 97, *99*, *101*, 102, 103, *103*, 189, 191–197, 223, *224*, 225–226, *226*, 228–229, 233–234, 252, 269, *270*, 271–272, 287–288, 312–313, *313*, 314–315, 322–323, 363–365, 398–399, 430–431, 448–449, 450, *450–451*, 451–452, *452*, 491–493, 523–524, *524*, 525–526, 653
Normand, Ch. 81
North American Museum of Ancient Life v, *x*, *6–10*, 10–11, *11*, *13–14*, *18–19*, *32*, *38*, *48*, *54*, *92*, *106*, *168*, *178*, *181*, *183*, *186*, *195*, *199*, *222*, *254*, *258*, *263*, *263*, *267*, *271–272*, *290*, *297*, *308*, *315*, *317*, *343*, *354–359*, *370*, *427*, *459*, *461*, *464*, *536*, *538–540*, *542*, *542*, *550–554*, *563–564*, *568*, *571*, *577*, *588–589*, *602–603*, 604, *650*
North Horn Formation 575–577, 649, 651
Northern Arizona University 398
Norton, James M. 116
Nothdurft, William *529*
Nothronychus 3, 136, 149, 207, 330–331, 420–421, *421*, 422–423; *N. mckinleyi* 421, *421*
Noto, Christopher 29
Notoceratops 151
Notohypsilophodon 152
Novacek, Michael J. 293, 295, 602
Novas, Fernando E. *33*, 33–34, *34*, 49, *49–50*, 50–51, 56, *56*, 61, 154–157, 176, 246–249, *274*, 339, 341, 366–367, 402–403, 407–408, 443, 453–454, 495–496, 529–530, 583, 587, 607
Nowiński, Alecksander 416, 419
Nqwebasaurus 27, 148
Nurosaurus 151, 154
Nuthetes 3, 138, 150, 207, 423–424; *N. destructor* 423
Nyasaurus 147

O'Connor, M. P. 38, 115
Oehler, Father E. 91
Office National des Mines, Tunis 528, *528*
Ogden Eccles Dinosaur Park *271*
Ohmdenosaurus 150
Old Bone Beach 46
Oldman Formation *104*, 474, 476, 531, 645, 649–650
olfaction 20–21, 36, *105*, 105–106, 209, 259, 595
Olivero, Eduardo B. 94
Olsen, Paul E. 13, 30, 345, 347, 444, 617 624
Olshevsky, George v, 190–191, 207, 476, 478, 489–491, 526, 547, 559–560, 562, *576*, 577, 587, 602, 607
Olson, Everet C. 573–574
Olson, Kate 267
Olson, Storrs L. 489, 491
Omeisaurus 151, 155, 207, 303, 308, 380, 396–398, 424, *424–425*, 425–426, 505; *O. junghsiensis* 424–425; *O. maoianus* 424, *424–425*, 425, 505; *O. tianfuensis* 303, 424–425
omnivery (in theropods) 339, 403, 573; (in prosauropods) 443–444

Oncala Group 641
ontogeny 21–5, *25*, 27, 30, 36, 42, 58, 61, 65–66, 84, 105, 107–110, 112–117, 120–123, 125, 171, 198–199, 204, 217, 230–232, 235, 254–256, 258–259, 273–274, 280, 282, 295, 298, 301, 307–308, 322–323, 335–338, 361–362, 384–385, 387, 389–391, 419, 434, 456, 458–459, 462, 497–498, 508, 516, 528, 532, 544, 548, 558, 562, 569–570, 572, 577–578, 596
Onychosaurus 150
Opisthocoelicaudia 81, 151, *212*; *O. skarzynskii* 81, *212*
Oplosaurus 151
Orcauichnites 633; *O. garumniensis* 633
Oriain, Bearnard 337
Orlov's Paleontological Museum 339
Ornatotholus see *Stegoceras*; *O. browni* see *Stegoceras validum*
Ornithichnites see *Sillimanius O. tetradactylus* see *Sillimanius tetradactylus*
Ornithodesmus 138, 149
Ornithoidichnites see *Sauropus*; *O. lylelli* see *Sauropus*
Ornitholestes 36, 149, 157, 165, 523, 638
Ornithomimipus 627, 633; *O. angustus* 633; *O. gracilis* 633
Ornithomimoides 148
Ornithomimus 51, 126, *127–128*, 149, 174, 166–77, 330, 341, 416; *O. edmontonensis* 126, *127–128*, 174; ?*O. sedens* 177
Ornithopodichnites 633–634; *O. magna* 634
Ornithopus see *Sillimanius*; *O. gallinaceus* see *Sillimanius*
Ornithotarsus 153
Orodromeus 125–126, 152, 291, 573–574; *O. makelai* 573
Orthogoniosaurus 148
Orthomerus 153
Orue-Etxebarria, Xabier 101–102, *102*, 477
Osborn, Henry Fairfield 230–231, 233, 326, 328, 339, 342, 390–391, 428, *460*, 462, 465, 565, 574, 584, 587
Oshanosaurus 153
Osmólska, Halszka 136–137, 190, 198, 251, 285, 288, 295, 298, 325, 328, 352, 369–370, 398–399, 408, 422–423, 428, 459–460, 506, 543, 653
ossified tendons 28, *28*, 90, 97–98, 132, 185, 189, 259–260, 305, 353, 431, 447, 454, 460, 515
ostracods 341, 432, 543
Ostrom, John H. vii, 10, 29, 73, 114, 119, 243, 296–297, 390–391, 514, 516–517, 519, 523, 535, 542, 573–574, 615
Othnielia 96, 152, 207, 237, 426–427, *427*, 428, *603*; *O. rex* 96, 427, *427*, *603*
Otozoum 627, 634–635; *O. caudatum* 634; *O. lineatus* 634; *O. minus* 634; *O. moodi* 634; *O. parvum* 634; *O. swinnertoni* 634
Ott, Christopher J. 362, 381

Ouranosaurus 19, 153, 155, 193, 196, 234, 322, 376, 451
Ouyang, H. 183, 208, *392–393*, 393–394, *394–395*, 396–398
Ovaloolithus 142, 648; *O.* cf. *O. laminadermus* 142; *O. chinkangkouensis* 648; *O. dinornithoides* 648; *O. laminadermus* 648; *O. mixtistriatus* 648; *O. monostriatus* 648; ?*O. sangpingensis* 648; *O. tristriatus* 648
Oviraptor 6, 57, 120, 126, 129, 136–137, 149, 207, 292, 294–295, 330, 369, 378, 416, 428, 645; "*O.*" *mongoliensis* 294, 428; *O. philoceratops* 136, 292, 294–295, 369, 428
Owen, Richard 156, 243–244, 268–269, *270*, 272, 282, 284, 314–315, 404, 406, 423–424, 447–449, 491–493, 521, 546–547
Oxford University 406
oxygen isotope analyses 103, 115, 217, 260
Ozraptor 147

Pab Formation 87
Pachycephalosaurus 106, *106*, 140, 153, 197–198, *198–199*, 199, 528, 531; *P. wyomingensis* 106, *198–199*
Pachyrhinosaurus 112, 154
Pachysauriscus see *Plateosaurus ajax*
Pachysaurops see *Plateosaurus*
Pachysaurus see *Plateosaurus*; *P. giganteus* see *Plateosaurus giganteus*; *P. magnus* see *Plateosaurus magnus*
packs and pack-hunting 40, 52, 216
Padian, Kevin v, 24, 53, 56, 119–122, 125–126, 134, 155–157, 209, *209–210*, 210, 345, 347, 490–491, 520–521, 523
Pagnac, Darrin C. 261–262, 268
Paladino, Frank V. 484–485
Palaeontological Institute of the Academy of Sciences 556
Palaeoscincus 152, 333; *P. asper* 333
Paläontologische Museum, Bayerisch Staatssammlung für Paläontologie und Geologie *529*
Paläontologisches Heimatmuseum Bedheim *479*
Paleocene dinosaurs 142–143
Paleocursornis 607
Paleolimnornis see *Paleocursornis*
Paleontological Institute (Ulaan Bataar) 560
Paleontological Institute Nauk 30, 103, 108, 347, 450, *450*
Paleontological Institution 341
Paleorhinus 530
Pal'fy, J. 12
Palmer, A. R. 11
Pangaea 13, 15, 17, 178, 180, 332
Panoplosaurus 152, 348, 447, 548
Pant-y-ffunnon locality 453
Parabrontopodus 634; *P. disterichii* 634; *P. mcintoshi* 634
Parachirotherium 622, 634; *P. postcheirotheroides* 634
Paracoelurosaurichnus 634; *P. monax* 634

Paragrallator 634; *P. matsiengensis* 634

Paralititan 3, 70, 151, 207, 428–429, *429*, 430; *P. stromeri* 428–429, *429*, 430

Paranthodon 152

Pararhabdodon 102, 153, 207, 430–431; *P. isonensis* 430

Parasaurolophus 104, 153, 207, 286–287, 431; *P. walkeri* 104

Parasauropodus 634; *P. corbesiensis* 634

parasites 52

Paraspheroolithus 648; *P. irenensis* 648

Paratetrasauropus 634; *P. seakensis* 634

Paratrisauropus 634; *P. equester* 634; *P. lifofanensis* 634; *P. mendrezi* 634

parental care 24–25, *25*, 37, 52, 83, 125–126, 294

Parker, Jeffrie 266–268

Parkes, K. C. 519, 523

Parksosaurus 152, 190

Parks, William A. *101*

Paronychodon see *Richardoestesia isosceles*; *P. lacustris* see *Richardoestesia*

Parras, A. 87

Parrish, J. Michael 62–65, 72, *77*, 117, 436–437, 530, 592–593

Parsons, William L. 481

Parvicursor 138, 150, 507; *P. remotus* 507

Pasch, Anne D. v, 97–99, *99–100*, 194

Passaic Formation 616–617, 638

Passer domesticus 136

PAST (Prehistoric Animal Structures, Inc.) *15*, 253, *257*

Patagonykus 138, 150, 172, 175–177; *P. puertai* 172, 175–177

Patagopteryx 121, *137*

Patagosaurus 75, 150

Patchus, Robert 103, 260

pathology *51*, 51–52, 112, 142, 164, 208, *229*, 232–233, 259–260, 263, 265, 267–268, *316*, 316–317, 350–351, *358*, 419, 537–539, 566–567, 575–576, 585–586

Patricosaurus 607

Pattersoncypris 371

Paul, Gregory S. v, 53, *54*, 56, 65–66, 116, 130, 136–137, *218*, 258, 265, 300–301, 346–347, *351*, *397*, 446, 483, 489–491, 497, 500, 514, 517, 558, *558*, 560, 570, 572–574, 577, 584, 587, *622*

Pawpawsaurus 152, 185, 221, 235; *P. campbelli* 185, 235

Peabody Museum of Natural History 77, 231, *240*, 280, 445, 533–534, *534*, *535*

Pearson, Dean A. 139–140

Peishansaurus 152

Pekinosaurus 89; *P. olseni* 89

Pelarganax see *Sillimanius*

Pelargides see *Steropoides*; *P. danae* see *Steropoides*

Pelecanimimus 128, 135, 149, 174; *P. polydodon* 174

Pellegrinisaurus 151

pellets 57

Pelorosaurus 151, 278, 283, 292; *P. conybeari* 283

pelycosaurs 19

Peng, J.-H. 384, 476, 478

Pengliazhen Formation 627

Pengxianpus 635; *P. cifengensis* 635

Penkalski, Paul *333–334*, 335–337

Pennystone, Sir Thomas 406

Pentaceratops 154, 290

Pereda-Suberbiola [also Pereda Suberbiola, Suberbiola], Xabier 81, 94, 101–102, *102*, 233, 430–431, 447–449, 548–549, 572

Pérez-Moreno, B. P. 171, 318–319, 449

Pérez-Oñate, J. 67

Perle, Altangerel 45, 190, 198, 292, 295, 421–423, 508, 573–574

"Perspectives in Ornithology: Why Ornithologists Should Care About the Theropod Origins of Birds" 132

Peters, Dieter Stefan 117–118, 134–136

Peters, Robert Henry 208–209

Peterson, O. A. 535

Petit, Jean-Louis 75, *75*

Petrified Forest National Park 33

Phaceloolithus 648–649; *P. hunanensis* 648–649

Phaedrolosaurus 138, 150

Philbrick, Mark *550–551*

Phillips, John 282, 284

Phillips County Museum 260

Phu Kradung Formation 91

Phu Phan Formation 60

Phuwiangosaurus 80, 151, 207, 431; *P. strindhornae* 431

Phyllodon 152, 207, 431–432, *432–433*, 433–434; *P. henkeli* 431–432, *432–433*, 433

phytosaurs 33, 442, 530

Piatnitzkysaurus 148, 162, 180, 276, 445, 470; *P. floresi* 180, 445

Piau farm *613*, *629*

Pidancet, J. 441, 444

Pierce, Stephanie E. 454

Pinacosaurus 152, 207, 221, 235, 334, 336, 341, 434, *434*; *P. grangeri* 235, 334, 336, 434, *434*; *P. mephistocephalus* 434; *P. mirus* see *Pinacosaurus grangeri*

Pincemaille, M. 189

Pinegar, Stan 266

Pinegar, Tyler 266, *540*

Pingling Formation 142, 647, 648, 650–651

Pinilla de los Moros Formation 252

Pinuspollenites 57

Pioneer Trails Museum 139

Pisani, Davide 154–155

Pisanosaurus 91, 154

Piveteausaurus 148, 547; *P. divesensis* 547

Placerias quarry 474

Placoolithus 649; *P. taohensis* 649

Planicoxa 153, 207, 435, *435–436*, 436–437, 592; *P. venenica* 435, *435–436*, 592

plants 17, 29–30, 33, 36, 52, 57, 59, 65–67, 70, *71*, 74, 76, 79, 82, 89–90, 103, 114, 124–125, 129, 131, 142–143, *218*, 251–252, 260, 265, 303, 318, 323–324, 335, 338, 341, 364, 381, 398,

403, 408, 412–413, 420, 429–430, 452, 465, 474, 477, 483–485, 491, 502, 565, 569, 573, 576, 585–587, 595, 607

Plastisauropus 635; *P. ingens* 635

plate tectonics 13, 15–16, 29, 38–39

Plateosaurus 13, 58, 114, 150, 181, 183, 207, 437–438, *438–439*, 439–440, *440*, 441–444, *479*, 494–496, 562, 597; *P. ajax* 437, 442; *P. bavaricus* 437, 439–440; *P. cullingworthi* see *Euskelosaurus browni*; *P. engelhardti* 13, 58, 114, 437, *438*, 440–443, 494, 496; *P. erlenbergiensis* 58, 437, 439, *440*, 441; *P. fraasianus* see *Plateosaurus longiceps*; *P. giganteus* 437, 443; *P. gracilis* 597; *P. ingens* see *Plateosaurus longiceps*; *P. intiger* see *Plateosaurus longiceps*; *P. longiceps* 58, 437, *438–440*, 440, *479*; *P. magnus* 437, 442; *P. plieningeri* 437, 439, *439*, 441–442, *479*, 480; "*P.*" *plieningeri* see *Zanclodon plieningeri*; *P. poligniensis* see *Plateosaurus ingens*; *P. quenstedti* 437, 439, 442, *479*; *P. reinigeri* 437, 442; *P. robustus* 437, 442; *P. stormbergensis* 443; *P. torgeri* 442; *P. trossingensis* see *Plateosaurus longiceps*; *P. wetzelianus* 437, *438*, 442–443; *Plateosaurus* sp. *479*; *see also Mussaurus patagonicus*

Platt, Philip R. 241–242, *242*

Platypterna 635; *P. concatmerata* 635; *P. deanii* 635; *P. delicatula* 635; *P. digitigrada* 635; *P. recta* 635; *P. tenuis* 635

Platysauropus 635; *P. ingens* 635

Platytrisauropus 635; *P. lacunensps* 635

Plesiornis see *Argoides*; *P. aequalipes* 635; *P. giganteus* 635; *P. mirabilis* 635; *P. pilulatus* 635; *P. quadrupes* 635

plesiosaurs 17, 249, 259

Plesiothornipos 635

Pleurocoelus 70, 75, 87, 151, 154, 310, 592, 616; *P. nanus* 592

Pleuropeltus see *Struthiosaurus*; *P. suessii* see *Struthiosaurus austriacus*

Plieninger, T. *439*, 441–442, 444

pliosaurs 249

Plot, Robert 406

pneumaticity 60, 162–165, 177, 180, 230, 295, 343, 359–360, 374, 378, 401, 410, 421–422, 469, *481–482*, 482–483, 485, 507, 550, 561–562, 574–575, 589

Pneumatoarthrus 153

Podokesaurus 147

Poekilopleuron 148, 179–181, 207, 243, 404, 444, *444–445*, 445–446, *446*; *P. bucklandii* 444, *444–445*, 445–446, *446*; *P. pusillus* see *Aristochus pusillus*; *P.? valesdunensis* 181, 444, 446, *446*

Point Loma Formation 218–219

Poison Creek Quarry 308

poisoning 142–143

Polacanthus 152, 185, 207, 360,

447, *447–448*, 448–449, *449*; *P. foxii* 185, 447–449, *449*; *P. rudgwickensis* 447, *447–448*, 448, *449*; *Polacanthus* 449; cf. *Polacanthus* sp. 235

Polish-Mongolian Palaeontological Expeditions 340, 352

Polyonax 154

Ponta da Guia locality 42

Ponta do Farol locality 42

Pope, Kevin O. 140–141

Popo Agie beds 616

Popov, E. V. 96

Portezuelo Formation 82

Portland Arkose 617, 623, 626, 641

Portland Formation 634

Portland Stone 314

Posmosanu, Erika 271–272

posture *4*, 17, 19–20, 23–25, 27–28, 53, 57, 62, 64–68, 78–79, 105, 113–114, 117–119, 121, 124, 134, *160*, 229, 241, 265, 269, 286–287, 289, 293, 297, 300, 307–308, 339, 345–346, 364, 390–391, *391*, 443, 455, 462–463, *464*, 483, 502–503, 529, 539, *541*, 542, 570–571, 581–584, 607, 616–617, 619, *620*, 621, 623, 625–628, 630–631, 633–639, *639*, *641*, 641–644

Powell, H. Phillip 272, 404

Powell, Jaime Eduardo 70–71, 81, 183, 215, 468–470

Praia de Baronesa locality 42

Praia do Boqyeirão locality 42

Prata site 82

precociality 24–25, 120, 125–126

predation 16–17, 33–37, 39–41, 46, *48*, 51–55, 57, 78, 112–113, 120, 123, 130, 136, 171, 208, 221–222, *224*, 226, 228–229, 232–233, 260, 263, 268, 276, 302, *316*, 316–317, 323, 327–328, 338, 341, *351*, 373, 392, *397*, 400, 419, 443, 463, 485–486, 491, 538–539, 572–573, 577–578, 580, 583, 585–586

Predatory Dinosaurs of the World: A Complete Illustrated Guide 136, *397*

prehension 403

Prehistoric Animals 63

Prehistoric Times v, 133, 290

Prenocephale 107, 153, 199, 526–528, 530–531; *P. brevis* see *Stegoceras breve*; *P. edmontonensis* see cf. *Sphaerotholus* sp.; *P. goodwini* 597

Preprismatoolithus 648; *P. coloradensis* 648

Price, L. I. 88

Prieto-Márquez, Albert 259–260, *475*, 477–478

Prince Creek Formation 46

Princeton University 390

Priodontognathus 152, 493

Prismatoolithus 142, 573, 648; *P. gebiensis* 648; *P. hukouensis* 648; *P. jenseni* 648; *P. levis* 573; *P. tenuis* 648

Probactrosaurus 153, 193–196, 207, 322–323, 376, 450, *450–451*, 451–452, *452*; *P. alashanicus* see *Probactrosaurus gobiensis*; *P. gobiensis* 450, *450–451*, 451–452, *452*; "*P.*" *mazongshanensis* 450

Proceratosaurus 148, 157, 165; *P. bradleyi* 157
Procheneosaurus praeceps see *Lambeosaurus lambei*
Procompsognathus 147, 207, 310, 452–453, *453*, 454, 465; *P. triassicus* 454–455
Proctor Lake ornithopod 96
Prodeinodon 147
Prosaurolophus 104, 153, 207, 259, 454; *P. maximus* 104; *Prosaurolophus* cf. *Maximus* 454
Protarchaeopteryx 6–7, 118, 120, 122, 130, 134–136, 149, 489, 524
Proteacidites 143; *P. retusus* 143; *P. thalmanni* 143
Protecovasaurus 151, 474, 603; *P. lucasi* 603
proteins 364
Protiguanodon see *Psittacosaurus*
Protoavis 147
Protoceratops 107–108, *109–110*, 111, *112*, 153, 200–201, 203, 207, 244, 251, 316, 352, 381, 385, 454, *454–455*, 455–456, *456–458*, 458–459, *459*, 460, 462, 645, *649*; *P. andrewsi* 107–108, *109–110*, *111–112*, 251, 455–456, *457–458*, 458, *459*, 459, *649*; *P. hellenikorhinus* 201, 381, 454, *454–455*, 455–456, *456–457*, 459; *?Protoceratops kozlowskii* see *Bagaceratops*; *Protoceratops* sp. 458
Protoceratopsidovum 649, *649*; *P. minimum* 649; *P. sincerum* 649
"protofeathers" 6, 7, 122, 126, 133–135, 515–516, 519–521, *522*
Protognathosaurus 150, 303; *P. oxyodon* 303
Protohadros 152–153, *193*, 193–194, 196, 234, 323; *P. byrdi* 193
Protosuchus 408
Prototrisauropodiscus 635; *P. minimus* 635
Prototrisauropus see *Grallator*; *P. crassidigitus* 635
Prum, Richard O. 132, 300–302, *512*, 515, 517
Pruss, S. B. 12
Pryor, R. 574
Pseudolagosuchus 155
pseudosuchians 489
Pseudotetrasauropus 635–636; *P. mekalingensis* 635
Pseudotrisauropus 636; *P. dieterleni* 636; *P. humilis* 636; *P. maserui* 636; *P. minusculus* 636; *P. molekoi* 636; *P. subengensis* 636
Psilotrisauropus 636; *P. equester* 636
Psittacosaurus 24, 107, 113, 191, *199*, 207, 385, 460, *460–461*, 461–462, *462–463*, 463–464, *464*, 465, 523, 603; *P. mazongshanensis* 460; *P. meileyingensis* 460; *P. mongoliensis* 24, 460, *460*, 462; *P. neimongoliensis* 460; *P. ordosensis* 460; *P. sinensis* 460; *P. xinjiangensis* 460–462, *462–463–464*
Pteranodon 420
pterosaurs 43, 57, 61, 74, 124, 130, 271, 339, 371, *397*, 420, 146, 491, 548, 573
Pterospondylus 147, 207, 310, 465, *465*; *P. trielbae* 465, *465*

pygostyle 7, 135, 137, 341
Pyroraptor 138, 150
Pugh, Kelly *8–9, 14, 38, 54, 168, 179, 181, 183, 199, 254, 258, 267, 272, 290, 297, 317, 343, 359, 370, 427, 459, 464, 542, 554, 564, 571, 577, 589*
Pukyong National University 465–466
Pukyongosaurus 151, 207, 465–466, *466–467*, 467–468; *P. millenniumi* 465–466, *466–467*, 467
Purbeck Beds 269, 313, 389, 626
"Purbeck facies" 389
Purbeck Limestone Formation 268–269, 314
Purbeck Limestone Group 423
Purgatoire Tracksite 89

Qantassaurus 152
Qemetrisauropus see *Grallator*; *Q. princeps* see *Grallator*
Qinlingosaurus 150
Qiu Licheng 370
Qomoqomosauropus 636; *Q. acutus* 636
Quaesitosaurus 151, 184, 207, 418–419, 431, 468; *Q. orientalis* 468
Queensland Museum v, 249, 412
Quenstedt, F. A. 442, 444
Quiba Formation 555, 559
Quilmesaurus 148, 207, 468, *468–469*, 469–470; *Q. curriei* 468, *468–469*

Raath, Michael R. 339, 341, 407–408, 453–454, 465
Rahonavis 134, 410
Rajasaurus narmadensis 597
Ralikhompus 636; *R. aviator* 636
Rapator 147
Rapetosaurus 151, 183–184, 207, 392, 418–419, 468, 470, *470–471*, 471–472, *472–473*, 473–475, *566*; *R. krausei* 470, *470–471*, 471, *473*
Raton Formation 642
Rauhut, Oliver W. M. 39, 179, 243–244, 252, 254–255, 310, 326, 328, 352, *352*, 387–388, 423–424, 432, *432–433*, 433–434, 452–453, *453*, 454, 465, *465*, 476, 476–478, 506, *506*, 529, 607
rauisuchians 16–17, 506, 607–608
Ravoavy, Florent 38, 566
Rayfield, Emily J. 223, *224*, 225–226, *226*, 228–229, 233
Raymond M. Alf Museum *281*
Rayner, J. M. V. 119
Rayosaurus 61, 71, 150; *R. tessonei* 61, 71
Razumovskaya, E. B. 96
Rebbachisaurus 150
Recherches sur les ossemens fossiles 364, 545
Red Beds of Sichuan Basin 143
Red Beds of Yunnan *604*
Redonda Formation 624
Redondo Formation 635
Reed, William H. (Bill) 231, 534
Reed's Quarry R 231
Reese, A. 293, 295
Rega, Elizabeth A. 585–587
Regnosaurus 93, 152; *R. northamp-*

toni 93
Rehnelt, K. 621–622, 634
Reichenbach, L. 617, 625, 635
Reid, Robin E. H. 24, 115
Reiniger, Albert 442
Reisz, Robert 124
Rensberger, John M. 30, 301–302
Repenomamus 524
reproduction see sex and mating
Research Institute of Geology 96
Resnick, D. 51
respiration 20–21, 63, 66, 110, 116–117, 287, 484, 586
respiratory turbinates (RTs) 105, 259
Retallack, G. J. 586–587
Revueltosaurus 151, 207, 474; *R. callenderi* 474; "*R. hunti*" 474
Rey, Luis 602
Rezvyi, A. S. 339
Rhabdodon 17, 152, 189, 364; *Rhabdodon* aff. *robustus* 17, *18*
Rhadinosaurus see *Struthiosaurus*; *R. alcimus* see *Struthiosaurus australis*
Rhaz Formation, El 15
Rhodanosaurus 152, 547
Rhoetosaurus 150
rhynchosaurs 17, 530
Riabinin, Anatoly Nikolaenvice N. 398–399, 555, 559–560
Ricardoestesia see *Richardoestesia*
Rich, Thomas H. 49, *49–50*, 50
Richard Rush Studios *622*
Richardoestesia 17, *19*, 43–44, 47, 136, 139, 149, 207, 431, 474, *474–475*, 475–476, *476*, 477–478, 486; *R. gilmorei* 47, 486; *R. isosceles* 139, *474*, 474–477, 486; *R. isosceles* Morph 1; *Richardoestesia* sp. 17, 139, 476; *see also Richardoestesia isosceles*; cf. *Richardoestesia* sp. 477
Richardson, P. R. K. 301–302
Ricqlès, Armand J. de vii, 24, 94, 121, 125–126, 389–390
Rigby, J. Keith, Jr. 49–50, 142, 171, 474–478, 485
"*Rinchenia*" 428
Rinehart, L. F. 295–296
Río Colorado Formation 87–88, 245–246
Río Limay Formation 34, *34*, 86, 236, 343, 365–366, 367
Río Limay Group 236
Río Limay Subgroup 239
Rio Neuquén Formation 84
Riojasaurus 150, 181, 443, 495, 530
Robinet, Jean-Baptiste 406
Rocasaurus 151
Rock Head Quadrangle 306
Rodovia quarry 88
Rogers, Raymond Robert 183–184, 392
Romer, Alfred S. [Sherwood] 189, 437, 581, 587
Romeral, D. A. Diaz 57
"Rondon" 82
Ross, C. T. F. 223, 233
Rothschild, Bruce M. 51–52, 263, 265, 268, 537–538, 542
Rotundichnus 636; *R. münchenhagensis* 636
Rowe, Timothy 47, 157, 292, *293–294*, 295, 306–307, 388, 407–408, 428, 453–454, 465,

469–470, 494, 514, 517, 563–565
Royal Ontario Museum 104
Royal Tyrrell Museum of Palaeontology v, *14*, 78, 98, 139, *167*, *176*, *187–188*, 190, 214, 280, *305*, 347, 477–478, 486, 615
Royal Veterinary and Agricultural University 114
Roy-Chowdhury, Tapan K. 251–252
Royo-Torres, R. 67, *68*, 72, *72–73*, 80
Rozhdestvensky, Anatoly Konstantinovich 339, 450–452, 556, 558–560
RTs see respiratory turbinates
Ruben, John A. 116–117, 124, *124*, 132, 135, 493, 515, 517, 520, 521–523
Rudgewick Brickworks Company quarry 448
Rudra, D. K. 34, 252
Ruehleia 58, 150, 207, 441, 478, *479–480*, 480–481; *R. bedheimensis* 58, 478, *479–480*, 480–481
Ruiz-Omeñaca, José Ignacio 67, *68*, *73*, 80, 101–102, *102*, 138–139, *139*, 189, 233, 252, 255, *363*, 364–365, 572
Russell, Allan P. 93–94, 333–334, 336–337, 347–348, *348*, 413
Russell, Anthony P. 40, 250–251, 258, 279–280, 282, 332, 350–351, 559–560, 573–574
Russell, Dale A. 73, 115, 118, 140, 208–209, 215, 218, 254–255, 289, 320, 350–351, 371, 373, 421–423, 467, 504–505, 509, 511, 558, 560, 563–565, 581, 587
Russell, Loris S. 335, 337, 476, 478
Russian Academy of Sciences 103, 108
Rutellum implicatum 405, 406
Rütimeyer, Ludwig 441, 444
Ruxton, Graeme D. 115
Ryan, Michael J. 40, 112, 250–251, 258, 280, 282, 288–291, 413–414, 458, 460, 461–462, *462–464*, 465, 485, 559–560, 573–574
Rybczynski, Natalia 335, 337

S. B. Smith Ranch 355
Sabalites sp. 381
Sabath, K. 559, 645, 652
Sacrison, Stan x
Saev, V. I. 86
Sahni, Ashok 467, 651–652
Saichania 95, 152, 221, 235; *S. chulsanensis* 235
St. Mary River Formation 414
Saldivia, Roberto 236
Salgado, Leonardo 60, 70, 82, 250, 343, 347, 365–366, *366–367*, 367, 418–419, 468–470, 473–474, 593
Salitral Ojo de Agua locality 468
Salta Group 625
Saltaposuchus 352
Saltasaurus 69, 151, 183, *183*, *211–212*, 215, 472, 591–592; *S. loricatus* *183*, *211–212*, 215
Saltopoides 636; *S. ingalensis* 636

Saltopus 607; *S. elginensis* 607
"Saltriosaurus" 40
Saltwick Formation 621
Sam Noble Oklahoma Museum of Natural History v, 322–323
Samman, Tanya 44
Sampson, Scott D. 38, 90, 111–113, 134, 155, 173, 177–179, 204, 230–231, 233, 258, 268, 280, 282, 378, 399–400, *400–401*, 401–403, 413, 458, 460, 462, 465, 473–474, 576, 587, 593
San Carlos Formation 381
San Diego Natural History Museum 220
San Juan Formation 580
Sandberger, F. 437, 440, 444
Sander, P. Martin 58
Sanders, Frank 140, 276–278, *537*, 538–539, 542
"Sandy Quarry" 106
Sankey, Julia T. v, 139, *474*, 474–478, 486
Sanpasaurus 147
Santa Luca, Albert P. 190–191
Santa Maria Formation 58, 94, 529–530
Santafé, José-Vte Llopis (Santafé-Llopis) 67, *68*, 102, 388–389, *389*, 430–431, 449, 633–634
Santana Formation 38, 370–372
Santanaraptor 39, 148
Santucci, Rodrigo Miloni 85–86
Sanz, José Luis 57, 67, *68*, 81, 171, 388–389, *389*, 449
Sao Khu Formation 508, 545
Saratov State University 96
Sarcolestes 152
Sarcosaurus 147
Sarcosuchus imperator 15
Sarjeant, William A. S. 404, 406, 613, 615–616, 626, *626*, 634, 638
Sarmientichnus 636; *S. scagliai* 636
Satapliasaurus 636; *S. tschaboukianii* 636
Saturnalia 150, 154–155, 495, 530, 562
Sauers, Laverne 107
Saurexallopus 636; *S. lovei* 636
Saurichnium 636–637; *S. anserinu* 636; *S. damarense* 636; *S. parallelum* 636; *S. tetractis* 636
Sauroidichnites see *Sauropus*; *S. barrattii* see *Sauropus barrattii*
Saurolophus 153, 341, 362
Sauropelta 152, 207, 209, 221, 343, 447, 481; *S. edwardsi* 481; *Sauropelta* cf. *S. edwardsi* 481
Sauroplites 152
"sauropod hiatus" 484
Sauropodichnus 637; *S. giganteus* 637
Sauroposeidon 3, 75, 151, 207, 481, *481–482*, 482–483, *483–484*, 484–485; *S. proteles* 75, *481–482*, 482, *483–484*
Sauropus 616, 619, 623, 637; *S. barratii* 637
Saurornithoides 138, 150, 173, 207, 423, 485; *S. mongoliensis* 173, 485
Saurornitholestes 46–47, 120–121, 138–139, 150, 207, 301, 477–478, 485–486, 509; *S. langstoni* 46–47, 139, 486; *Saurornitholestes* sp. 139
Saurosuchus 17

Sauvage, H. E. 563
scansoriality 29, 119, 124–125, 131, 320, 489–491
Scansoriopteryx 138, 149, 207, 300, 328, 486–487, *487–488*, 488–491; *S. heilmanni* 486, *487–488*, 488, 490–491
Scaphonyx 17
scavengers and scavenging 35, 52, 58, 78, 98, *100*, 216, 232, 267–268, 280, 317, 392, 420, 430, 443–444, 467–468, 486, 585
Scelidosaurus 91, 152, 185–186, 207, 256, 307, 412, 491–492, *492*, 493; *S. harrisonii* 491, *492*
Scheele, William E. v, 63
Scheetz, Rodney D. 96, *589*, 589–590
Schellenbach, Jennifer 342, *342*, 343
Schizograllator 637; *S. xiaohebaensis* 637
Schlaikjer, Erich Maren 385–386, 459, 526, 528, 531–532, 543
Schloss Bedheim *479*
Schmidt, H. 543
Schmitt, James G. 107, 576–577, 587
Schudack, Michael E. 432, 543
Schulp, Anne S. 42, *42*
Schwartz, Hilde I. 33
Schweitzer, Mary Higby 132, 571–572, 576–577, 587
Science 132, 563, 565
Science Museum of Minnesota 77
Scientific American 132
Scipionyx 8, 148, 157–158, 165, 207, 493, 522; *S. samniticus* 8, 148, 157, 158
Scollard Formation 381, 476, 575
Scolosaurus cutleri see *Euoplocephalus tutus*
Scotese, C. R. 38
"Scotty" 586
Scrotum humanum 406; *see also* *Megalosaurus*
Scutellosaurus 91, 152, 493; *S. lawleri* 91
Seakatrisauropus 637; *S. divergens* 637; *S. unguiferus* 637
Sealey, Paul 528
Secernosaurus 151, 196
Sedgwick Museum 406
Seebacher, Frank 21–23, 115, 117
Seeley, Harry Govier 242–244, 298, 444, 474, 560, 562, 607
Segisaurus 147, 207, 493–494; *S. halli* 493
Segnosaurus 136, 149, *168*, 330–331, 339, 416, 421–422; *S. hallorum* 168
Seismosaurus 3, 76, *81*, 151; *S. hallorum* 81
Selenichnus 637; *S. breviusculus* 637; *S. falcatus* 637
Sellosaurus 58, 114, 150, 181, 183, 207, 494–495, *495*, 496, 530, 562; *S. diagnosticus* see *Sellosaurus gracilis* 494–495, *495*; *S. fraasi* 494; *S. gracilis* 58, 114, 494–495, *495*, 496, 530; *S. hermannianus* see *Sellosaurus gracilis*; *S. minor* 494, 496; *S. trossingensis* 494
Semionotensandstein 621
Senqutrisauropus 637; *S. priscus* 637
Senter, Philip J. 493–494

Sereno, Paul C. 13, *15*, 37–38, 69–70, 79, 106, 134, 154–157, 169, 171–173, 175–177, *180*, 185, 191, 193, 195, 197–201, 203, 215, 233, 235–236, 244, 250–252, *253*, 254–255, *273*, 273–274, 284, 291, 312, 314–315, 329, *329–330*, 330–331, 335, 337, 339–341, 352, *352*, 371–373, 379–381, 383–386, 408, 414, *414–415*, 415–416, *416*, 419–420, 437, 453–545, 460, 465, 473–474, 495–496, 504–505, *505*, 508, 514, 517, 526, 528–530, 532, 543, 563–565, 572–574, 607
Serjeant, William A. S. 613
Serra da Galga quarry 88
sex and mating 21, 52, 56–57, 83, 90, 110, 112–113, 116, 130, 260, 282, 337, 584, 586
sexual dimorphism 106, 108–109, *109–110*, 110–111, *111–112*, 112–113, 171, 254, 259, *263*, 267, 295, 298, 307–308, 314, 335, 336–337, 402, 455–456, 458–459, 495–496, 519, 530, 548, 562, 575, 586
Shamosaurus 95, 235, 278–280, 347–348; *S. scutatus* 235, 348
Shang-Sha-Xi-Miao (also Shang-shaximiao) Formation 396, 424
Shanghu Formation 142
Shanshanosaurus 149, 207, 496, *496–497*, 497–498, *498–499*, 500, 555, 559; *S. huoyanshanensis* 496, *496–497*, 497, *498–499*
Shantungosaurus 27, 153, 207, 500, *500–501*, 587; *S. giganteus* 500, *500–501*, 587
Shanxia 152, 235; *S. tianzhensis* 235
Sharov, A. G. *124–125*
Sharpey's fiber pits 107
Shayangosaurus 149
Shell Oil Company 46
Shellenberger Canyon Formation 70, 209
Shemshak Formation 626
Shensipus 637; *S. tungchuanensis* 637
Shenzhouraptor 207, 501, 607; *S. sinensis* 501
Sheridan College 76
Shestakovo locality 86, *86–87*, 87
Shimada, K. 301–302
Shirabad Suite 628
Shiraminesauropus 637 *S. hayashidamiensis* 637; *S. reini* 637
Shishugou Formation 42
Shixingoolithus 142, 649–650; *S. erbeni* 142, 650
Shubin, Neil H. 443–444
Shuler, E. W. 623
Shuler Museum of Paleontology 60
Shunosaurus 114, 151, 155, 207, 303, 308, 380, 426, 501–502, *502–503*, 503–504, *504–505*, 505; *S. lii* 114, 303, 502, *502–503*, 504, *504–505*, 505
Shuvosaurus 207, 506, *506*; *S. inexpectatus* 506, *506*
Shuvuuia 24, 132, 138, 150, 172–176, 207, *507*, 507–508; *S. deserti* 24, 172–176, *507*, 507–508
Siamosaurus 147, 255; *S. sute-*

ethorni 255
Siamotyrannus 148, 158, 172, 207, 508; *S. isanensis* 158, 508
Sierra Sculpture *174*
Sigé, Bernard 17, *19*, 171
Signore, Marco 54, 123, 493, 520, 522–523
Silesaurus 151, 603
Sillimanius 633–634, 637; *S. adamanus* 637; *S. gracilior* 637; *S. tetradactylus* 637
Siluosaurus 152
Silvisaurus 152, 235; *S. condrayi* 235
Simon, E. 82, 86
Simmons, Louis M. 118
Simpson, Martin 254
Simpson, William F. 530
Sindong Group 465
Sino-Belgian Expeditions 455
Sino-Canadian Dinosaur Project 251, 347, 458, 485, 508
Sino-Soviet Expeditions 251, 347, 450
Sinocoelurus 147
Sinoichnites 638; *S. youngi* 638
Sinornis 132
Sinornithoides 138, 150, 207, 485, 508–509, *509–511*, 511, 513; *S. youngi* 485, 508, *508–511*
Sinornithosaurus 130–131, *131*, 132–133, 135, 138, 150, 207, 300, 411, 511–512, *512–513*, 513–514, *514*, 515–516, *516*, 517, 524–525; *S. milleni* 512, *512–516*
Sinosauropteryx 6, 117, 122, 129, 132, 134–135, 148, 158, 207, 296, 515, 517, *517–518*, 518–520, *520*, 521–522, *522*, 523–524; *S. prima* 517, *517–518*, 520, 521, *522*
Sinosaurus 147, *438*, 495
Sinovenator 138, 150, 177, 207, 410–411, 523–524, *524–525*, 525–526; *S. changiae* 523, *524–525*, 526
Sinpetru beds 547
Sinraptor 34, 37, *51*, 51–52, 148, 174, 180, 340, 344, 469, 595; *S. dongi* 37, 51, *51*, 174
Sisson, Brock A. *10–11*
Skartopus 638; *S. australis* 638
skin impressions *see* integument
Skoczulas, R. 301–302
Skrepnick, Michael W. *51–52, 129*
Sling Point site 46
Sloan, Christopher O. 368–369
Sloan, Portia 369
Sloan, Robert E. 49–50, 171, 474–478, 485
Small, Bryan *263*, 371–372, 537
smell *see* olfaction
Smilodon laevis see *Zanclodon plieningeri*
Smith, David K. 230, 233, 428
Smith, Jennifer [Jen] R. 428–429, *429*, 430, 529, 616, 625
Smith, Joshua [Josh] B. 38–39, 46, 111, 118, 375–376, 384, 386–387, 428–429, *429*, 430, 512, 517, 523, 526, *529*, 580–581, 587
Smith, Matt B. 51, 53, 55, 208–209, 345, 347, 584–585, *586*, 587
Smith, P. L. 12
Smithsonian Institution v

Index

Smokejack's Pit 364
snakes *see* lepidosaurs
Snively, Eric 350–351, 581, 587
Snyder, John x, *539–540*
Society for Integrative and Comparative Biology 119
Society of Vertebrate Paleontology (SVP) v, xi, 521, 602
Solnhofen lithographic limestone 296–297
Sonorasaurus 151
Soriano Site 650
sound 571–572
Sousa Formation 613, 629, 631–632, 633, 638, *639*
Sousaichnium 631–632, 638, *639*; "*S. magnificum*" *639*; *S. pricei 631–632*, 638
South African Society for Amateur Palaeontologists 337
South Dakota School of Mines and Technology v, 77, 543
South Platte Formation 628
Southern Methodist University 60
Southwell, Elizabeth H. 266
Soviet-Mongolian Palaeontological Expeditions 103
Spencer, Matthew 307, 310
Sphaerotholus 153, 207, 526–527, *527*, 528, 530; *S. buchholtzae* 526–528; *S. goodwini* 526, *526*; cf. *Sphaerotholus goodwini* 526; *Sphaerotholus* sp. 528; cf. *Sphaerotholus* sp. 527
Sphaerovum 650; *S. erbeni* 650
Sphenodon 581
sphenodontians and sphenodontids 78, 444
sphenosuchians 352
Spheroolithus 650; *S. albertensis* 650; *S. chiangchiungtingensis* 650; *S. chuanchengensis* 650; *S. maiasauroides* 650; *S. megadermus* 650; *S. tenuicorticus* 650
Spheruprismatoolithus 649–650; *S. condensus* 650
Spinar, Zdenek V. 347–348
Spinosaurus 19, 42, 46, 148, 207, 370, 372, 528, *528–529*, 529; *Spinosaurus aegyptiacus* 372, 529, *529*; *Spinosaurus* cf. *Aegyptiacus* *528*, 529
Spondylosoma 147, 607–608
Springer Verlag 490
Staatliches Museum für Naturkunde Stuttgart 388
Stadtman, Kenneth L. [Lee] v, *4–6*, 10, 96, 269, 549–550, *550–552*, 553–555, *589*, 589–590
"Stan" x, *18*, 587
Stanley, John 422
Starck, J. Matthias 27
Starkov, Alexei I. 580, 587
State Museum of Pennsylvania v
Staurichnium 638; *S. diogenis* 638
Staurikosaurus 32, 147, 207, 529–530, 581; *S. pricei* 529
Steel, Rodney 284
Steeman, Mette Eistrup 364
Stego 99 Quarry *308*
Stegoceras 106–107, 153, 197–199, 207, 352, 526–528, 530–532, 543; *S. breve* 530; *S. edmontonense* see cf. *Sphaerotholus* sp.; *S. sternbergi* see *Stegoceras* sp.; *S. validum* 530–532
Stegopelta 220–221

Stegosaurides 152
Stegosaurus 5, 14, 20, 30, 91–92, *92*, 93, 151, *159*, 185, *188*, 207, 268, 279, 317, 353, 355, *356*, 358, 532–533, *533–534*, 534–535, *535–536*, 537, *537–538*, 538–539, *539–542*, 542; ?*S. affinis* 532; *S. armatus 14*, *188*, 532, *533–534*, 535; *S. longispinus* 532; *S. stenops* 92, *159*, 353, 355, 532, 535, *536*, 537, *538*, 539, *542*; *S. ungulatus* 92, 355, 532–535, *535*, 537; *Stegosaurus* sp. 20, 30, 535
Steneosaurus 545–546; *S. rostromajor* 545–546; *S. rostrominor* 545–546
Stenonyx 624, 628, 638; *S. lateralis* 638
Stenopelix 153, 197, 207, 542–543; *Stenopelix valdensis* 542–543
Stepanov, N. P. 398
Sternberg, Charles H. 280
Sternberg, Charles M. 258, 260, 282, 391, 616, 621, 625, 626–627, 633, 639
Sternberg, Levi 104
Steropezoum see *Steropoides*; *S. elegans* see *Steropoides*
Steropoides 635, 638, 641; *S. divaricatus* 638; *S. diversus* 638; *S. infelix* 638; *S. ingens* 638; *S. uncus* 638
Stevens, Kent A. 62–65, *77*, 571–572
Stidham, Thomas 121–122
Stokesosaurus 148, 158, 171, 207, 231, 326, 404, 543–544, *544*, 545; *S. clevelandi* 158, 543, *544*
Stokosa, Kathleen M. 43–44, 307, 310
Stokstad, Erik 20, 429–430, 563, 565
Stollo quarry 96
Stonesfield Slate 406
Stormberg Series 384, 616, 627–628, 635
Stormberg Volcanic 628
Storrs, Glenn W. 307, 310
Stoskopf, Michael K. 563–565
Stoval, J. W. 241
Stovall's Quarry 1 241
Straight, William H. 103, 217–218
straining behavior (in ornithomimids) 126, *129*, 341
Streptospondylus 3, 148, 180–181, 207, 545, *545–546*, 546–547, *547*; *S. altdorfensis* 180, 545, *545–546*, 546, *547*; *S. cuvieri* see *Streptospondylus altdorfensis*; "*S.*" *geoffroyi* 547; "*S.*" *juriensis* 547; "*S.*" *lyciensis* 547; *S. major* see *Iguanodon bernissartensis*; *S. rostro-major* see *Streptospondylus altdorfensis*
Strevell, C. N. 622–623
Stromatoolithus 651; *S. pinglingensis* 651
Stromer, Ernst 372–373, 429–430, *529*
Struthio camelus 25, *482*
Struthiomimus x, *54*, 101, 149, 173, 175, 320, 340; *S. altus* x, *54*, 173, 175
Struthiosaurus 152, 207, 235, 298, 301, 444, 474, 547–549, 597; *S. austriacus* 235, 547–549; *S.*

languedocensis 597; *S. transylvanicus* 548–549
Struthopus 638; *S. schaumburgensis* 638
Stubensandstein 310, 352
Stygimoloch 153, 199, 528, 531; *S. molnari* see *Tyrannosaurus rex*
Stygivenator see *Tyrannosaurus*
Styracosaurus 112, *113*, 154, *351*; *S. albertensis 113, 351*
subadults *see* jveniles and subadults
Subashi Formation 497, 555
Suberbiola, Xabier see Xavier Pereda-Suberbiola
Subtiliolithus 651–652; *S. kachhchensis* 652
Suchomimus see *Baryonyx*; *S. tenerensis* see *Baryonyx tenerensis*
"Sue" *3*, 8, 40, *41*, 51, 172, *173*, 575, *578–580*, 581, 585
Sues, Hans-Dieter 30, 102, *103*, 124, 157, 177, 189, 191–193, 197, 234–235, 251–252, 254–255, 330–332, 363–365, 370–371, *371–372*, 372–373, 398–399, 414, 422–423, 444, 478, 485, 493, 543
Sullivan, Robert M. v, 142–143, *417–418*, *434*, 526, 528, 530–532, 568, 578
Sun, A. L. 331
Sundell, Craig 265, 268
Sunjiawin Formation 298
"Super Croc" 15
Supersaurus 11, 76, 151, 207, 549–550, *550–553*, 553–554, *554*, 555; *S. viviane* 11, 549–550, *550–553*, 553, *554*
Sussman, M. 24
Suteethorn, Varavudh 13, *59*, 59–60, *91*, 91–92, 172, 431, 508
Suzuki, Shigeru 155, 172–177, *507*, 507–508
SVP see Society of Vertebrate Paleontology
Swain, T. 29
Sweet, A. R. 140
Swinnerton, H. H. 638
Swinnertonichnus 638; *S. mapperleyensis* 638
Swisher, C. C., III 118, 246, 292, 295, 375–376, 384, 386, 523
Syntarsus see *Megapnosaurus*; *S. kayentakatae* see *Megapnosaurus kayentakatae*; *S. rhodesiensis* see *Megapnosaurus rhodesiensis*; *Syntarsus* sp. see *Megapnosaurus* sp.
"*Szechuanoraptor dongi*" 233
Szechuanosaurus 148
Szigeti, G. 543

Tacumarembovum 650; *T. oblongum* 650
Tagert, E. 626
Talarurus 152, 235; *T. plicatospineus* 235
Tallodi-Posmosanu, Erika [Tallodi] 243–244, 271–272, 607
Talmontopus 638; *T. tersi* 638
Tang Feng 373, *373–374*, 374, 415–416, 424, *424–425*, 425–426, 505
Tangvayosaurus 151
Tanimoto, Masahiro 80
Tanius 151, 194, 501; *T. sinensis*

501; *T. chinkankouensis* see *Tanius sinensis*
Tanke, Darren H. 51, *51–52*, 52, 111–112, *113*, 258, 267, 280, 282, 391, 413, 458, 460, 462, 465, 574
Tantalus Formation 616, 625, 633
Tanycolagreus 9, 11, 148, *602–603*, 604
Tanystrophaeus 388; *T. postumous* see "*Nicrosaurus*" sp.
taphonomy 29, 34, 40, 45, 58, 78, 83, *92*, 98, 140, 213, 217, 220–221, 251–252, 259, 265, 268, 271, 280, 296, 307, 324, 334, 380–381, 392, 422, 430–431, 454, 467–468, 482, 521–522, 550, 560, 563–565, 576, 592, 595–596
Taquet, Philippe 254–255, 272, 322–323, 371, 373, 389–390, 547
Tarascosaurus 147, 178
Tarbosaurus 3, 30, 149, 172, 207, 218, 312, 341, 373, 392, *496*, 496–497, 555, *555–556*, 556, *557–558*, 558–560, 580, 587; *T. bataar* 172, *496*, 497, 555, *555–556*, 556, *556–558*, 558–560, 587; *T. efremovi* see *Tarbosaurus bataar*; ?*T. luanchuanensis* 555, 559; ?*T. periculosus* 218, 255, 559; ?*T. turpanensis* 555, 559; cf. *Tarbosaurus* 560
Tarchia 95, 152, 235; *T. gigantea* 235; *T. kielanae* 235; cf. *Tarchia* 341
Tarsitano, S. 581, 587
Tarsodactylus 616
Tate Museum 77
Tatisaurus 91, 152
Taupezia 638–639; *T. landeri* 638
Taveirosaurus 151, 449, 572
Tawasaurus 150
Technosaurus 152
Tecovas Formation 603
Tecovasaurus 89, 151; *T. murryi* 89
Teete locality 20, 30, *31*, 32
Tegama Group 252, 254
Tehuelchesaurus 151
Teinurosaurus 147
Telmatosaurus* 97, *101*, 101–102, 151, 193–196; *T. transsylvanicus 101*, 101–102
Tendaguria 151, 318
Tendaguru Beds 318
Tendaguru Formation 30, 32, 318
Tenontosaurus 152, 189, 239, 304–305, 483; *T. tilletti* 304–305
"Terenes Marl" 634, 625
Tereshchenko, V. S. 108–109, *109–110*, 110, *111*
Terrestrisuchus 117
Tethys Ocean 271
Teton Group 625
Tetori Group 74, 545
Tetrapodium 639; *T. elmenhorsti* 639
Tetrapodosaurus 343, 619, 631, 639; *T. borealis* 343, 631, 639
Tetrasauropus 639; *T. unguiferus* 639
Teyuwasu 147
Texas Memorial Museum 567
Texas Tech University 502
Texasetes 152
Thecocoelurus 149, 207, 560, *560–*

561, 561–562; *T. daviesi* 560, 560–561; "*T.*" *elisae* 563
"thecodontians" 132, 134, 338, 634–635
Thecodontichnus 639–640; *T. fucinii* 640; *T. verrucae* 640
Thecodontosaurus 114, 150, 207, 441, 495, 562–563; *T. antiquus* 114; *Thecodontosaurus* sp. 562
Thecospondylus 147, 560; *T. daviesi* see *Thecocoelurus daviesi* 147
Therangospodus 641; *T. pandemicus* 641; *T. oncalensis* see *Therangospodus pandemicus*
Therizinosaurus 45, 136, 149, 330, 416, *558*; *T. cheloniformis* 558
thermoregulation 115, 117, 120, 122, 128, 185, 463, 571
Therrien, Francois 32–33
Thescelosaurus 152, 207, 563, *563–564*, 564–565; *T. neglectus* 563, *563–564*
Thespesius 153
Third Central Asiatic Expedition of the American Museum of Natural History *109*, 251, 485, 646
Thotobolosaurus 150
Thulborn, Richard A. 118, 233, 346–347, 364, 383–384, 432, 434, 572, 615, 638, 644
Thybony site 407
Tianchungosaurus 153
Tibeinia 131
Tichosteus 147
Tidwell, Virginia 79, 263, 267, 278, 436–437, 590, *590–592*, 592–593
Timimus 27, 149
"The Tiniest Giants: Discovering Dinosaur Eggs" *25–26, 84, 85, 652*
Tiouraren Formation 37
Titanosaurus 86, 151, 183, 207, *211–212*, 215, 373, 472, 565–566; *T. blandfordi* 565; *T. colberti 211–212*, 215, 472, 565–566; *T. indicus* 373, 565–566; *T. madagascariensis* 565–566
Titus, Alan L. 422–423, 431
Tochisaurus 138, 150
Tögrögiin Shiree locality 507
Tokaryk, Tim T. 301–302, *569*, 569–570, 572, 586–587
Tomida, Yukimitsu 84, 137, 369, *369–370*, 370
Tomsk State University 86
Tong, Haiyan 508
Tony's Bone Bed 437
tooth replacement 44–45, 68–70, 76, 82, 192, 196, 271, 420, 451, 486, 502–503, *505*, 596
Torosaurus 112, 140, 154, *203*, 207, 566–567, *567*, 568, 577; *T. latus* 566; *T. utahensis* 566–568; *Torosaurus* cf. *T. utahensis* 568; *Torosaurus* sp. 567–568
Torres, Sandra R. 88
tortoises *see* chelonians
Torvosaurus 5, 148, 180, *181*, 232, 318, 404, 519, 544; *T. tanneri* 5, *181*, 318
trace fossils *see* coprolites, footprints, nests
Trachodon 153, 398; *T. amurense* see *Mandschurosaurus amurensis*
Trachoolithus 650–651; *T. faticanus*

651
tracks and trackways *see* footprints
Tranquilo Formation, El 337, 443
Tremp Formation 101, 139
"*Tretosternon*" *bakewelli* see *Helochelydra bakewelli*
Triceratops x, *16*, 17, *23*, 30, 112, 140, *141*, 154–155, *174*, 197, 199–200, 203, *203*, 204, 207, 381, 567, 568, *568–569*, 569–570, *570–571*, 571–572, 583, *584*, 586, 619; *T. horridus* x, *16*, *23*, *141*, *174*, 203, *203*, 568, 571, *584*; *Triceratops* sp. 568, *568*
Tricolpites microreticulatus 143
Tridentius see *Steropoides*; *T. elegans* see *Steropoides*
Triebold Paleontology, Inc. *x, 106*, 568
Trigonia schwarzi Bed 318
Trigonia smeei Bed 318
Trihamus 641–642; *T. elegans* 641; *T. magnus* 641
Trimucrodon 153, 189, 207, 572; *T. cuneatus* 572
Trinity Group 36, 630
Trisauropodactylus 642; *T. superviges* 642
Trisauropodiscus 630; *T. aviforma* 642; *T. galliforma* 642; *T. levis* 642; *T. phasianiforma* 642; *T. popompoi* 642; *T. superaviforma* 642
Tritotrisauropus 642; *T. medius* 642
tritylodonts 43
Troodon 27, 43–44, 46–47, 50, 57, 124, 126, 138–139, 150, 207, 274, 477–478, 509, 526, 572–574, 649; *T. edmontonensis* see cf. *Sphaerotholus* sp.; *T. formosus* 46–47, 50, 572–574; *Troodon* cf. *T. formosus* 649; *Troodon* sp. 139, 477
Tropic Shale 422
Trossingen Formation 442, 478, 480
Trotta, Marcelo N. F. 88
Tsagantegia 95, 152, 235, 333; *T. longicrainialis* 235, 333
Tsaruk, Oleg 235
Tsintaosaurus 153
Tsogtbaatar, Khishigjaw 103, 155, 172–177, 341, *507*, 507–508, 560
Tsuihiji, Takanobu 23–24, 157
Tuchengzi Formation 73, *74*, 375, 384–386, 523
Tugrikiin-Shire locality *110–112*
Tugulu Group 461
Tugulusaurus 147
Tumanova, Tat'yana A. 24, 95–96, 184–186, 234–236, 348
Tuojiangosaurus 91, 152
Tuojiangpus see *Eubrontes*; *T. shuinanensis* see *Eubrontes* sp.
Turanoceratops 154, 200, 204
Turner, C. E. 115, 317, 319, 543
turtles *see* chelonians
Twin Mountains Formation 96, 212
Two Medicine Formation 291, 301, 335, 337, 381, 390, 572–573, 645, 647, 649–651
Tykoski, Ronald S. 407–408
Tylocephale 107, 153, 199, 527–528, 531

Tylosaurus 98
Tyrannosauripus 619, 642, *643–644*; *T. pillorei* 642, *643–644*
Tyrannosauropus 642; *T. petersoni* 642
Tyrannosaurus 3, 6, 8, 16–17, *18*, *22*, 23, 27, 30, 37, 40–41, *41*, 43–44, 51, 54–55, *55*, 133, 140, 149, 171–172, *173–174*, 174, 225–226, 228–230, 274, 276, 302, 312, 317, 326, 343, 345, *345*, 350–351, 373, 497, 501, 515, 549, 556, 558–559, 569, 574–575, *575–576*, 576–577, *577–578*, 578–579, *579–580*, 580–582, 582, 583–584, *584*, 585–586, *586*, 587, 595, *604*, 642, *643–644*; *T. bataar* see *Tarbosaurus bataar*; ?*T. lanpingi* 604; ?*T. luanchuanis* see ?*Tarbosaurus luanchuanis*; *T. rex* x, *3*, 8, 16, *18, 22*, 37, 40–41, *41*, 43, 51, 54, 147, 107, 172, *173–174*, 174, 225–226, 228, 230, 302, 317, 343, *345*, 351, 497, 515, 556, 558–559, 569, 574–575, *575–576*, 576–577, *577–578*, 578–579, *579–580*, 580–581, *582*, 584, *584*, 585–586, *586*, 587, 642, *643–644*; ?*T. zhuchengensis* 501, 575; *Tyrannosaurus* cf. *rex* see ?*Tyrannosaurus zhuchengensis*
Tyrannosaurus rex quarry 569
Tytherington quarry 562

Uberaba Formation 85–86
Udanoceratops 108, *111*, 114, 153, 199, 202–203, 381, 413; *U. tschizhovi 111*, 202–203, 413
Uintatherium 194
Ukhaa Tolgod locality 434
Ulanhushao (Suhongtu) Formation 347
Ulansuhai Formation 44
Ultrasauripus 642; *U. ungulatus* 642
Ultrasauros see *Supersaurus*
Ultrasaurus 150
Uña Formation 477
uncinate processes 137
Unenlagia 54, 56, *56*; *U. comahuensis* 54, 56, *56*
Universidad Nacional de Tucumán 468
University Microfilms International 17, 233, 474
University Natural History Museum 265
University of Alaska v, 46, 98
University of Alaska Museum 98, *99*
University of Bridgeport v
University of Bristol v
University of California Museum of Paleontology v, 32, 139, 306
University of Chicago 180, *273*
University of Colorado v, 77
University of Kansas 96, 132, 265
University of Maryland v
University of New Mexico 17, 474
University of Oklahoma v
University of Pennsylvania v
University of Portsmouth v
University of Utah 232, 400
University of Wyoming 77

Unquillosaurus 148
Upchurch, Paul 15–16, 45, 60, 66–67, 71, 76, 223, *224*, 225–226, *226*, 228–229, 233, 244, 250, 282–283, *283–284*, 284, 291, 418–419, 437–438, 441, 473–474, 481, 485, 494, 504–505
Upper Cretaceous Series 645
Upper Elliot Formation 207, 381, 383, 616, 624–625, 630, 633, 635–636, 642
Upper Keuper 440
Upper Lufeng Formation 57
Upper Nemegt Beds 340
Upper Saurian Bed 318–319
Upper Shaximiao Formation 595
Upper Stubensandstein 443
Upper Summerville Formation 630
Upper "*Zanclodon*" Knollenmergel 441
Urho locality 461–463
urination (in sauropods) 89
Utah Museum of Natural History 77, 233, 576
Utahraptor 11, 138, 150, 207, 437, 587, *588–589*, 589–590, 592; *U. ostrommaysi* 11, 437, *588–589*, 589, 592
Uzbek-Russian-British-American-Canadian project (URBAC-98) 235

Valais, S. de 50–51
Valdoraptor 148
Valdosaurus 152, 272, 324, *324*, 328; cf. *Valdosaurus* sp. 324, *324*
"Vale dos dinossauros" *614, 620, 624, 631–632, 639–640*
Van Howd, Douglas *174*
Van Itterbeeck, Jimmy 452
Van Leer, Devon 116–117, 493
Van Valkenburgh, Blaire 35–36
Varanus komodoensis 228
Vargas, A. 276
Variraptor 138, 150
Varricchio, David J. 24, 126, 252, 254–255, 273–274, 291, *292*, 301–302, 329–320, *320–321*, 371–373, 486, 529, 572, 574
Vectis Formation 278
Velocipes 147
Velociraptor 123, *131*, 138, 150, 229, 300, 305, 316, 330, 341, 416, 513, 515, 589; *V. mongoliensis 131*, 305
Velociraptorichnus 642; *V. sichuanensis* 642
Velocisaurus 148, 178
Venenosaurus 151, 207, 278, 437, 590, *590–591*, 591–592, *592*, 593; *V. dicrocei* 590–592, *592*
Versey, Brian *550–552*
Verzilin, Nikita N. 339
Vezina, A. F. 16
Vianey-Liaud, M. 143, 645–646, 648–649
Vickaryous, Matthew K. 93–94, 333–337, 347–348, *348*, 485, 573–574
Vickers-Rich, Patricia 49, *49–50*, 50
Vidarte, Fuentes C. 252, 254–255, 362, *362*, 634
Virginia Museum of Natural His-

Index

tory v
vision 36, 47, 209, 276, 398, 595
volcanoes and volcanism 12, 141–143, 323, 468
Volkeimeria 151
Von Sholly Pete v, *529*
Vulcanodon 150, 562

Wade, Mary 638, 644
Wagner, Günter P. 132, 559–560
Wagner, Jonathan R. 380–381
Wahweap Formation 111
Wakinosaurus 148
Walgettosuchus 148
Walkden, G. M. 155–157, 209, *209–210*, 210
Walker, Alick D. 515, 517, 545–547, 581, 587
Walker, W. F., Jr. 287
Walking on Eggs: The Astonishing Discovery of Dinosaur Eggs in the Badlands of Patagonia 82, 249, 645
Wall, William P. 531–532
Walloon Group 619
Walters, Robert 571–572
Walther, J. 642
Waltheria see *Mehliella*; *W. jeffersoniensis* see *Mehliella jeffersoniensis*
Wang Xiaolin [also Xiaohong] 374–375, *375*, 376, 384–385, *385–386*, 386–387, *387*, 408–410, *410–411*, 411–412, 421, 423, 465, *488*, 490–491, 512, 515–517, 523
Wang Ying 501
Wangshi (Wanngshih) Group 500, 575, 587
Wangshi Series 646, 648, 650
Wannanosaurus 153, 197–198
Ward, Henry A. *194*
Ward, Jim 341
Ward Terrace 407
warm bloodedness *see* endothermy
Warrener, P. 453–454
Watabe, Mahito 155, 172–177, *507*, 507–508
Watinoceras coloradoense-lower *Mammites nodosaiodes* biozone 422
Watson, Doug v, *288–290*, 290–291
Wayan Formation 107–108, *108*
Weald (Soria) 634
"Weald facies" 389, 449
Wealden Group 93, 96, 271, 278, 324, 448, 543, 626, 631, 633, 643
Wealden Marls 292, 447
Wealdenichnites 642–643; *W. iguanodontoids* 642–643
Wealdensandstein 638
Weaver, J. C. 114, 484–485
Webster, Donovan 378
Wedel, Mathew J. v, 60–61, 73, 239, 241–242, 481, *481–482*, 482–483, *483–484*, 484–485
Wei Feng 373, *373–374*, 374
Wei Mingrui 57
Weiaunpus 651
Weichselia reticulata 429
Weinstein, John *156, 173, 578*
Weishampel, David B. 16–17, *18*,

29, 97, 99, *101*, 102, 104–105, 107–108, *108*, 125, 155, 189, 191–197, 201, 237–239, 259–260, 322–323, 335, 337, 339, 398–399, 430–431, 443, 450, 452, 472, 573–574, 653
Weisser Steinbruch quarry 494
Weiyaunpus 623
Welles, Samuel P. [Paul] 32, 306–307, 339, 341, 387–388, 547, 621, 625, 627, 653
Wellnhofer, Peter 296, 339, 341, 442–444, 513–515, 517
Welman, J. 383
Werneburg, R. *479*
Wesleyan University v
Wessex Formation 243, *243*, 252, 278, 292, 323–324, 419, 485, 560
Western Interior Seaway 170, 193, 280, 312, 423, 467
Western Paleontological Laboratories, Inc. v, *9–10*, 10–11, *11, 16, 92, 141, 186, 222, 264*, 266–267, *271–272, 308, 354, 536*, *538–540*, 542
Westfield College 269
Westgate, James 380–381
Wharton, Deborah S. 123–124
White, Diane 590
White Beds of Khermeen Tsav 555
Whyte, M. A. 621
Wieland, G. R. 186
Wild, Rupert 453–454
Wildeichnus 643; *W. navesi* 643
Wilhite, Ray 307–308, 310, 543, 545
Williams, Michael 324, 328, 339, 341
Williams, Mike 426
Williamson, Thomas E. 107, 170–171, 301–302, 312, 526–527, *527*, 528, 530–532, *576*, 577–578, 587
Willow Creek Formation 575
Wilson, Jeffrey A. 12–13, 37–38, 67–70, 79, 87, 157, 183, 215, 239, 242, 244, 250, 252, 254–255, 273–274, 284, 291, 339, 371–373, 376, 378–380, 418–420, 468, 473–474, 504–505, *505*, 529, 565–566
Wilson, Michael Clayton 485
Wiman, Carl *73*
Winkler, David 193, 250
Winton Formation 249, 638, 643–644
Wintonopus 644; *W. latomorum* 644
Witmer, Lawrence M. 20–21, *21–23*, 38, 157, 191, 434, 472, 474, *472*, 587
Wolberg, Donald L. 118
Wolfe, Douglas G. *43*, 331, 420–421, *421*, 422–423, 595–596, *596*, 497
Wonderland Quarry 543, *544*
Woodbine Formation 628
Woodward, John 406
Woodwardian Collection 406
Wright, Nelda E. 322–323
Wu Wei-Tang 373, *373–374*, 374
Wuerhosaurus 152, 463
Wyleia 147
Wyoming Dinosaur Center 34, 77

Xang Xiaohong [Xiaolin] 132, 137–138, 143, 177, 202–203, 243–244, 328, 331
Xenotarsosaurus 38, 148, 178–179, 207, 469, 593; *X. bonapartei* 38, 593
Xiangxipus 644; *X. chenxiensis* 644; *X. youngi* 644
Xiaosaurus 151
Xin Tian Gou Formation 619, 623–624, 627
Xing, Y. L. 285, 288
Xingezhuang Formation 500, 575, 587
Xinminbao Group 329, 349
X-raying 20, 54, 263, 508, *647*
Xu Xing 118, 132, 137–138, 177, 202–203, 300–301, 328, 329, *329–330*, 330–332, *332*, 367–368, *368*, 369, 374–375, *375*, 376, 384–385, *385–386*, 386–387, *387*, 408–410, *410–411*, 411–412, 414, *414–415*, 415–416, *416*, 421–423, 460–461, 465, *488*, 490–491, 512, *512–513*, 513–514, *514*, 515–517, 523–524, *524*, 525–526
Xuanhanosaurus 148
Xujiahe Formation 349, 635

Yabe, H. 627
Yadagiri, P. 94–95, *95*, 378–379, *379–380*, 380
Yalden, D. W. 119
Yale University 231, *240*, 445, 534, *535*
Yandusaurus 152
Yang, Dashan 285, 288, 398–399
Yang, Zhungjian [formerly Young Chung-Chien] 398–399, *438*, 460, 465, 619, 637, 644, 648, 650
Yang Xing Long 617, 619, 621, 623–627, 630, 635, 642, 645
Yangchuanosaurus 148, 180, 207, *397*, 519, 593, *593–594*, 594–595; *Y. hepingensis* 593–594, 594–595; *Y. shangyouensis* 397
Yangtzepus 644; *Y. yipingensis* 644
Yao Jin-Xian 25, 27
Yates, Adam M. 154–155, 496, 562–563
Yaverlandia 106, 153, 198
Ye Yong 183, *392–393*, 393–394, *394–395*, 395–398
Yeh H. K. 244, *244, 604*
Yellow Cat Quarry 589
Yimenosaurus 150
Yingshanosaurus 152
Yixian Formation 118, 126, 367, 374–375, 384–386, 486–487, 512, 516, 521, 523–524
You Hai-lu [also Hailu] 118, 202–203, 303, *303–304*, 328–329, 349, 375–376, 384–385, *385–386*, 386–387, *387*, 512, 517, 523, 526
Young Chung-Chien *see* Yang, Zhungjian
Youngichnus 644; *Y. xiyangensis* 644
Youngoolithus 652; *Y. xiaguanensis* 652; *?Y. xipingensis* 652
Yu Young *392–393*

Yuanpu Formation 647, 648
Yuliangze Formation 284
Yunnanosaurus 114, 150, 495; *Y. huangi* 114
Yunnanpus 645; *Y. huangcaoensis* 645; *Y. zheni* 645

Zakharov, S. A. 628
Zanclodon 388, 441–442; *Z. cambrensis* see *?Megalosaurus cambrensis*; *Z. laevis* see *Zanclodon plieningeri*
Zatomus 147
Zelenitsky, Darla K. 645, 649–650
Zeng Xiangyuan 626, 644, 646, 648–649
Zephyrosaurus 152
Zhai, J. 555, 559–560
Zhang Fucheng v, 118, 138, 328, 375–376, 384, 386, 408–410, *410–411*, 411–412, *488*, 490–491, 523, 607
Zhang Guojun 424, *424–425*, 425–426, 505
Zhang Xiao-Hong 329, *329–330*, 330–331, 414, *414–415*, 415–416, *416*
Zhang Yihong 208, 424, 502, 504–505
Zhao, Xin Jin [also Xijin, Chao Shichin] 329, *329–330*, 330–332, *332*, 347–348, *348*, 399, 414, *414–415*, 415–416, *416*, 422–423, 460–461, 465, 468–470, *601–602*, 646–652
Zhao, Zi-Kui 142, 339, 341
Zhejiang Natural Museum *373–374*, 374, 424, 502
Zhen, Shuo-nan [also Shuonan] 135, 296–297, 521, 523, 624, 627, 631, 634, 637, 642, 644–645
Zheng, Zhong 73, 502, *502–503*, 503–504, *504*, 505
Zhengichnus 644; *Z. jinningensis* 644
Zhenzhuchong Formation 652
Zhizhongpus see *Gigandipus*
Zhou Zhonghe [also Zhong-He] 118, 132, 138, 243–244, 300–301, 328, 369–370, 375–376, 384, 386, 408–410, *410–411*, 411–412, *488*, 490–491, *514*, 515, 517, 523, 607
Zienkiewicz, O. C. 223, 233
Zigong Dinosaur Museum *394*, 502
Zigongosaurus see *Mamenchisaurus*; *Z. fuxiensis* see *Mamenchisaurus* sp. indet.
Ziliujing Formation 349
Zils, W. 319
Zizhongosaurus 151
Zizhongpus see *Kayentapus*; *Z. wumaensis* see cf. *Kayentapus* sp.
Zoological Museum 114
Zuniceratops 3, 154, 203–204, 207, 421–422, 595–596, *596*, 597; *Z. christopheri* 421–422, 595, *596*
Zupaysaurus rougieri 597